DATE DUE

BRODART, CO.   Cat. No. 23-221-003

WITHDRAWN

WORLD WORDS

WORLD WORDS

Recommended Pronunciations

W. CABELL GREET
Professor of English in Barnard College, Columbia University
Speech Consultant, Columbia Broadcasting System

SECOND EDITION
REVISED AND ENLARGED

19 48

COLUMBIA UNIVERSITY PRESS, NEW YORK
By arrangement with the Columbia Broadcasting System

COPYRIGHT 1944, 1948
COLUMBIA UNIVERSITY PRESS, NEW YORK

*First Edition (published for the Columbia
Broadcasting System), 1944*

Second Edition, 1948

MANUFACTURED IN THE UNITED STATES OF AMERICA

To the Memory of

GEORGE PHILIP KRAPP
LATE PROFESSOR OF ENGLISH, COLUMBIA UNIVERSITY
IN THE CITY OF NEW YORK

and

ARTHUR LLOYD JAMES
LATE PROFESSOR OF PHONETICS, UNIVERSITY OF LONDON

"Speak the speech, I pray you, as I pronounced it to you,
trippingly on the tongue . . ." HAMLET, III. 2

PREFACE TO THE FIRST EDITION

SINCE the publication of *War Words* a year ago, the relentless battle fronts have brought more strange names into communiqués and press dispatches. Names long alien have now become hallowed in the English language as the places where American soldiers fought and died—*Tarawa, Arawe, Salerno, Garigliano, Carroceto*. The list is daily lengthening.

In this book of *World Words*, about twelve thousand names and words are pronounced. They include the battlefields and air force objectives of the past two years, the likely places of attack during the coming months, names that will figure in the peace and appear on the air routes, names of important persons, and words that are difficult for broadcasters. Pronunciations for two thirds or three quarters of these cannot be found in any other volume of easy access.

Whatever the defects of this book, it shows the need of pronunciations as well as of accurate spellings in all reference works, and particularly in gazetteers and map indexes. The construction of pronunciations is a fascinating business; it combines the interest of making crossword puzzles with the excitement of betting on an election. Nevertheless, every branch of lexicography is better pursued at leisure. This book has been prepared in great haste. To be readily understood and, in radio parlance, to be on the nose, were its prime requirements. It is desirable that the United States Board on Geographical Names and the Permanent Committee on Geographical Names for British Official Use be granted the necessary funds to give reasonable pronunciations for all names that are spelled on maps. Or in the absence of government support, perhaps the National Geographic Society and the boards of the Encyclopedia Britannica Atlas and similar organizations will undertake to complete their indexes by supplying pronunciations. In this radio-minded world, pronunciations are quite as important as spelling.

To anyone who works with pronunciation and the other parts of rhetoric, the nicest fable for critics is in Holofernes' speech, beginning "He draweth out the thread of his verbosity finer than the staple of his argument" (*Love's Labor's Lost*, Act V, scene 1); Holofernes in lambasting Don Adriano's rhetoric shows himself just as fantastic, and pedantic to boot. For effective radio (or so we believe at CBS), pronunciation is not an opportunity to be elegant but an everyday problem of what to do with difficult names and debatable words. This book is an effort to find reasonable solutions, fanciful as some of the respellings may at first seem.

[vii]

The pleasures of working with learned experts are great and long remembered. A hundred or more busy professors, consular agents, and foreign correspondents have directly contributed to these judgments on pronunciation. Professor L. Carrington Goodrich and Professor Cyrus H. Peake of Columbia University and Dr. Lin Lin of the Chinese Ministry of Information showed the patience of the East before hundreds of queries. Dr. J. van Beusekom of the Netherlands Information Bureau and Mr. Chris O'Sullivan and Mr. Alwyn Lee of the Australian News and Information Bureau gave in their pronunciations a sense of nearness to the life of the South Pacific. Professor Einar Haugen of the University of Wisconsin, Dr. F. G. Nelson of the University of Minnesota, and Mr. Oka Fen of the Royal Norwegian Information Service provided authority for many Scandinavian pronunciations and evidence of a great variety of usage. Mr. A. E. Gilliat of the Burma Civil Service, Mr. T. A. Raman, head of the Indian Information Service, Washington, Mr. Paul A. Eakin of the Presbyterian Mission, Bangkok, and Mr. and Mrs. J. J. Van Hine of the Christian and Missionary Alliance, Tonkin, had much more to say of east Asia than could be set down in phonetics. Mr. Jonas Budrys, Consul General of Lithuania, Mr. Ernst Jaakson of the Estonian Consulate General, Mr. Harry W. Lielnors, Mr. Otto G. Lindberg, and Dr. Thomas A. Sebeok of Indiana University, interpreted the names of the Baltic languages and Hungarian. Dr. Fred Householder was ever the admirable consultant on Greek. Professor Clarence A. Manning and Professor Arthur P. Coleman of the Department of East European Languages, Columbia University, Mr. Vladimir Alexieff, and members of the American Association of Teachers of Slavonic and East European Languages made an indispensable contribution to the difficult problems of comparative Slavonic pronunciations. Dr. J. A. W. Bennett of Queens College, Oxford, and the British Library of Information, Dr. Charles E. Funk of the Funk & Wagnalls Company, and Mr. Edward Artin and Dr. John P. Bethel of G. & C. Merriam Co. contributed good cheer when the burdens were heavy. Mr. Ambrose Lansing and Mr. C. K. Wilkinson of the Metropolitan Museum of Art were delightful instructors in the ways of Arabic and Persian. Professor Oswaldo Serpa of Rio de Janeiro sent a phonograph recording of his own pronunciation of important Brazilian names. Prof. Leon Feraru, Long Island University, chanted the Rumanian list like a medieval epic. Mr. Solomon V. Arnaldo of the Philippine Bureau of Information checked the pronunciation of many Philippine names; Mr. Raif Erisken of the Turkish Consulate General passed on the Turkish. Professor Harry Morgan Ayres, Professor Adriaan J. Barnouw, Professor Carl F. Bayerschmidt, Professor Dino Bigongiari, Dr. William Bridgwater, Professor

Elliott V. K. Dobbie, Professor Robert Herndon Fife, Mr. Philip Hayden, Professor Frederick W. Heuser, Professor Frédéric Hoffherr, Mr. Roger Howson, Mr. André Mesnard, Professor Tomás Navarro, and Professor Henry H. L. Schulze—to these and to other colleagues and masters at Columbia University the debt is deeper than probably they realize. Professor Ayres, Mr. Alexieff, Professor Bigongiari, Professor Dobbie, Professor Haugen, Dr. Householder, Mr. Mesnard, and Dr. Sebeok—bless them—read the proofs.

When such men are the consultants for a little dictionary, it is obvious that any merits of the work are their due. Blame for faults is the due of the editor, but he will pass it on to Mr. Roy Langham and Mr. James Seward of the Columbia Broadcasting System, for they have abetted the work since its small beginnings two years ago as a mimeographed bulletin.

So many languages are represented on these pages, it will do no harm to add Old English of the time when the Danes were invading England. To all who labor at meritorious works that cannot be perfected even in a life time, the words of King Alfred, brilliant leader and noble scholar, bring comfort, as he wrote in his preface to the Anglo-Saxon Translation of Boethius' *Consolation of Philosophy*: "King Alfred was the translator of this book, and he turned it from Latin into English, as it now is done. Sometimes he translated word for word, sometimes meaning for meaning, just as he could tell it most clearly and distinctly, despite the various and manifold worldly ills which troubled him either in mind or in body. Our troubles are difficult to count that in his days came upon the kingdom he had undertaken. Nevertheless he studied this book and translated it from Latin to English speech and published it again for the nation, just as it is now done. He asks and, in God's name, he entreats each man who is pleased to read the book that he pray for him and not blame him if he understands it more correctly than Alfred could; for each man must, according to the measure of his understanding and according to his leisure, speak what he speaks, and do what he does."

Ælfred Kuning wæs wealhstod thisse bec, and hie of boc-lædene on englisc wende, swa hio nu is gedon. Hwilum he sette word be worde, hwilum andgit of andgite, swa swa he hit tha sweotolost and andgitfullicast gereccan mihte for tham mistlicum and manigfealdum weoruldbisgum the hine oft ægther on mode ge on lichoman bisgodan. Tha bisgu us sint swithe earfoth-rime the on his dagum on tha ricu becoman the he underfangen hæfde, and theah tha thas boc hæfde geleornode and of lædene to engliscum spelle gewende, and geworhte hi eft to leothe, swa swa heo nu gedon is; and bit and for Godes naman he halsath ælcne thara the thas boc rædan lyste, thæt he for hine gebidde, and him ne wite gif he hit rihtlicor ongite thonne he mihte; forthamthe ælc mon sceal be his andgites mæthe and be his æmettan sprecan thæt he sprecth, and don thæt thæt he deth.

At the end of a section in his Anglo-Saxon Reader, George Philip Krapp put this passage. It serves as a requiescat for him, for Lloyd James, and for all good workers.

W. CABELL GREET

Columbia University
February, 1944

PREFACE TO THE REVISED EDITION

THE CONTINUAL FLOW of new names in the news made the first edition of *World Words* inadequate, and on the promise of a new edition it was allowed to go out of print. There is a difference of opinion as to whether the publisher begged the author to bring the work up to date, or whether the author entreated the publisher to contract for the revision. There is no doubt, however, that the Columbia Broadcasting System made the book possible. And at last it appears, late by a year and a day. There are some 25,000 entries, twice as many as in the first edition. They represent the pronunciation files of CBS and the gleanings of a motor trip to the west coast in the summer of 1947. I wish I could say that the list will be adequate to all broadcasting needs, but every person, every crossroads has a name. A plane crashes at the crossroads, Everyman attends the meetings of the United Nations, and we must perforce speak the names of both. Still the book will be of use, for there are here many crossroads and many people whose names may be difficult to pronounce. In these years after the war, a period sometimes called the enduration, the names in the news are more difficult to predict than when interest was focused on "theaters of operations."

The pleasantest moments in preparing the book were those spent with kind gentlemen who enlightened the darkness and bore witness to the *correct* pronunciations—may heaven help us poor mortals still searching for the correct and infallible in this too fallible world. To the consultants named in the first preface, I again express my obligation and gratitude. For new material I am indebted also to Dean James K. Finch, Professor Harold G. Henderson, Professor Andrés Iduarte, Professor Giuseppe Prezzolini, and Mr. Ryusaku Tsunoda, of Columbia University; Mr. Z. M. Peixoto, Consul of Brazil; Mr. B. Landheer and Mr. J. W. F. Stoppelman of the Netherlands Information Bureau; Doctor Alexander Hertz of the Polish Consulate; Mr. Olaf Kaijser, Consul of Sweden; Doctor N. Chandler Foot of the Cornell Medical School; Doctor Frederick Hard, President of Scripps College; Mr. Bernard L. Koten of the American-Russian Institute; Miss Marion C. Orr, Librarian, of Idaho Falls; Mr. Storrs Henry Seeley; Mr. Ichiro Shirato; Mr. John J. Wheeler of the Bonneville Power Administration; Mr. Clifford B. Wrightman, Librarian, Lancaster, Pennsylvania; and my CBS colleagues Ted W. Cooke, KOYN, Portland, Oregon; Bill Corcoran, KIRO, Seattle; Rex H. Hudson, KDAL, Duluth; and Wayne Kearl, KSL, Salt Lake City.

Only one important change in practice has been made. Badgered by Don Mosely of KQW, San Francisco, I have marked stresses in the transcriptions of Japanese. The long vowels are indicated in the spelling. I hope the stresses will please Mr. Mosely, but I doubt that they will. English and Japanese differ in essential characteristics. "How an essential of one, nonessential to the other, is to be interpreted by an essential of the other, nonessential to one, who shall say?" said Tweedledum to Tweedledee. The room for difference of opinion and of practice is so great that agreement in detail would be miraculous. However, many men agree in principle that it is rather silly for speakers of English to continue to pronounce Japanese as if it were an uncertain Spanish. Perhaps the marking of long vowels and the gratuitous stresses will move professional lexicographers to study the problem and to give more satisfactory answers than they have given hitherto. You have entered the debate yourself if you have an opinion on the pronunciation of *Hiroshima*.

I am especially grateful to three friends for their critical comments on the first edition. My oldest friend in New York, Professor Ernest Hunter Wright, said I was not to worry at attempting so many languages; the little dictionary was obviously an *ad hoc* job and answered its purpose. Paul Hollister, who has the right word for everything—a poet born, an executive made—wrote recently of these *plausible* pronunciations of un-English names. John Bethel of the G. and C. Merriam Co. took me to lunch and allowed that around his shop they thought me a pretty good *amateur lexicographer*. Praise from Sir Hubert . . . (I wouldn't have believed him if I had taken him to lunch.) Perhaps I ought to dedicate this revision to Wright, Hollister, and Bethel, for they are as kind as truth allows, or kinder, and as truthful as kindness permits. But on second thought the dedication to Krapp and Lloyd James shall stand (if a dictionary has any business with a dedication), for they were *amateur lexicographers* who removed the blinders from the eyes of professionals, they were so *plausible* that their works have permanent value, their *ad hoc* was a true understanding of English, reconciling practice and preachment.

W. C. G.

New York
October, 1947

[xii]

INTRODUCTION

ENGLISH PRONUNCIATION

Correct English

This pronouncing dictionary is designed to assist speakers of the Columbia Broadcasting System. They have the problems of correct usage that every American has, with this difference—that as radio speakers they meet their problems in public while millions are listening in. Naturally no group has greater desire to be right.

The recurring question "Which is correct?" is best met by the doctrine of "levels of usage." Ask not only which is *correct*, but *correct for what purpose*. To the styles appropriate for the pulpit, the Supreme Court, after-dinner speaking, conversation, familiar speech, and so on, we must add the styles appropriate to radio. Radio is peculiar: though the subject matter may be serious and formal, the radio audience hears it in the familiar surroundings of home. The platform and pulpit styles become incongruous; the listeners wish the broadcaster to be natural and friendly, but well spoken and easily understood. Agreeable pronunciation is one part of an agreeable oral style. It is probably not the most important part, but it is the most easily questioned and often the most difficult to maintain before a wide audience in a nation where there are regional types of speech.

Included here with the names that the War has made prominent are certain common English words whose alternative pronunciations cause domestic conflict of a different order. The debates as to which pronunciation is "correct" can be settled only by future generations, for in 1944 these words actually have two or more pronunciations and each of them is held by millions of Americans to be "correct." It is not the province of CBS to regulate the English language, but it is desirable to avoid the awkwardness that conflicting pronunciations on one program may cause. A choice therefore has been made in the light, we hope, of common sense, guided by the fact that CBS is a national American network. Without seeking to impair any citizen's right to be his own professor of English, we look for what is national, contemporary, and reputable.

The English Pronunciation of Foreign Names

Just as the names of the older countries and the principal regions of Europe have English variants—as Germany, Italy, and Spain for

Deutschland, Italia, and España—many European cities, provinces, and rivers have, during the centuries, acquired English pronunciations and even English spellings, which are commonly preferred in English contexts. But of course for the most formal occasions and for musical programs, and also in the case of foreign speakers, the nuance of foreign pronunciations may be desirable. Broadcasters, particularly announcers, should know both.

Although the English forms are stable, there is here, as in all other aspects of language, the possibility of change. Nowadays the "French" pronunciations of *Marseille* and *Lyon* are probably better American usage than the Anglicized *Marseilles* and *Lyons*. We now pronounce *Prague* in the French style, ignoring the time-honored English variant, as well as the Czech and the German. One sign of the falling off of classical studies is a general ignorance of the English pronunciation of Greek place names. The press reports usually give English spellings which don't quite make sense if they are pronounced as modern Greek, as, for example, *Piraeus* and *Athens*. If the classical traditions grow even weaker, such forms may be displaced. *Piraeus*, especially, gives trouble now.

When faced with the necessity of choosing between English and foreign pronunciations, broadcasters should of course use the pronunciations commonly employed in the comfortable English of educated people acquainted with the place and the subject. Names that are not Anglicized in English dictionaries probably have no English pronunciation, and they should be pronounced in foreign style. We cannot be so conservative (or so radical?) as the English family who, according to Ned Calmer, spoke of happy holidays in Brittany and pronounced *Saint Michel* as if it were English *Saint Mitchell*.

Why Don't We Anglicize All Foreign Names?

The language of a strong and confident people usually has the power to take over and "domesticate" foreign names. Why cannot we say *Saint Mitchell* or *Michael* for French *Saint Michel?* In the past English borrowed and domesticated thousands of foreign names. It was as easy for English to absorb them as for French to Gallicize names today. But the present generations of English speakers are remarkably curious about the native pronunciations of foreign places. In the case of names that are not already Anglicized they are inclined to prefer the foreign pronunciations, especially on formal and semiformal occasions. English and especially American reference books and maps give native pronunciations and spellings much more often than do similar French works. Our public speakers and editors are rebuked by audiences if they freely Anglicize foreign names. For one reason or another there is a new and somewhat foreign standard of correctness or appropriateness of pronunciation.

[xiv]

There are several plausible explanations but none without opposition. Today we are perhaps more aware of foreign cultures, but familiarity alone has never preserved foreign names in English or in any European language. There is a higher degree of literacy and education among speakers of English than ever before. Yet educated Frenchmen do not hesitate to pronounce all foreign names as French. Professor H. M. Ayres suggests that when the schools gave up the "English" pronunciation of Latin and adopted the so-called "Roman" pronunciation, English speakers lost their model and the necessary precedents for Anglicizing foreign names. Our spelling of English words is eccentric and there are many exceptions to the rules. Perhaps because we simply don't know what to do with foreign names we ask the "correct" or foreign pronunciation. Uncertainty as to whether *Cracow* should be pronounced krā'-kō, krăk'-ou (*ou* as in *house*), or krăk'-ō, has not yet driven us to *Kraków*, krä'-kŏŏf, but it may! On a higher plane it is argued that with two world wars to preserve democracy, a belief in the linguistic rights of small nations has become generally accepted in this age of rapid travel and almost instant communication (when the three great powers are willing). But my grumpy neighbor says, "Stuff! Radio commentators have imposed these absurd foreignisms upon a suffering public that cannot object."

Of all these explanations, I am most impressed by Professor Ayres': the dilemma of *Cracow*, the impossibility of *Przemyśl!* Mr. Grump's wish to blame the world's babel on the broadcasters who have to pronounce foreign names is unjust. Radio provides a wonderful means for popularizing new names and new pronunciations, but the public objects and ignores when it wishes. Radio has implemented but it did not inaugurate nor does it alone sustain the present vogue. Radio usage is a symptom of the taste of the times, as are for instance the "foreign" spellings of the National Geographic Society which American news services employ so far as is possible within their typographical limitations.

Whatever the causes, there is established today a learned standard of handling newly arrived foreign names. We may well call it a new kind of Anglicizing: the rule, or the aspiration, is to adopt the foreign pronunciation insofar as it can be rendered by customary English sounds in the phrasing and rhythm of an English sentence. It is not good taste to introduce sounds that are foreign to English. Often, as with strange Chinese names, we succeed only in giving what seems to us a "foreign" flavor that means nothing whatever to a Chinese. Nevertheless the tendency is commendable as the opposite of a smug, indifferent attitude. It may well lead to a growth of understanding and sympathy. So far as radio is concerned, the tendency has to be taken as a fact, with such disturbing inconsistencies as the occasional preservation of native stress in *Táráwá* and an Englishing of *Truk*, "truck."

I have learned to respect the new rule for Anglicizing because of a bad guess I made as to what the public would do with foreign names as they became familiar. For centuries Russian *kh* as in *Kharkov* has been Anglicized as *k*. In *War Words* I therefore transcribed Russian *kh* as *k*. To my surprise when *Kharkov* became a daily headline, there was a strong drift to "Harkof." Russian *kh* is neither English *k* nor English *h*, but when Anglicized one would expect *k* as in the past on the analogy of the spelling, *h* on the analogy of the sound. We are evidently an ear-minded generation. Because *Kharkov* is an old name in English, I am still inclined to prefer *k*, but I have found great difficulty in defending any recommended pronunciation of a foreign name that is not as close as may be convenient to the native. Our bright people seem to be more interested in the present international world than in the traditions of English pronunciation.

But a word of caution must be added. Absurd foreignisms will be labeled pretentious and asinine, fine as the line is between what seems absurd and what seems "correct." The pronunciations must conform to the customs of idiomatic English. The "Parisian" *r*, for instance, is not welcomed. As Fowler cogently put it: "To say a French word in the middle of an English sentence exactly as it would be said by a Frenchman in a French sentence is a feat demanding an acrobatic mouth; the muscles have to be suddenly adjusted to a performance of a different nature, and after it as suddenly recalled to the normal state; it is a feat that should not be attempted; the greater its success as a *tour de force*, the greater its failure as a step in the conversational progress; for your collocutor, aware that he could not have done it himself, has his attention distracted, whether he admires or is humiliated."[1] To this Lloyd James added: "A technique that obtrudes, in speech as in most other forms of human activity, is offensive; it should be the aim of those who have to handle the spoken word to evoke neither admiration nor humiliation."[2]

FOREIGN LANGUAGES

The principal element in our idea of a foreign pronunciation is that the vowels a, e, i, o, u, are pronounced ah, eh, ee, oh, $\overline{oo}$. In the following notes on foreign languages this is taken for granted and comment is made on the vowels when they do not follow this expectation. Only the unusual consonants are treated, and they are equated with the nearest English sounds. In most foreign languages *r* is a trill or rolled

[1] H. W. Fowler, *A Dictionary of Modern English Usage*, p. 194.
[2] A. Lloyd James, *Broadcast English VI* (BBC, 1937), p. 16.

sound made with the tip of the tongue; occurence of uvular or "Parisian" *r* is mentioned. These notes are intended to inform the user of the book of the premises underlying the pronunciations given in the list and to enable him in some languages to construct pronunciations of names that, unfortunately, will have been omitted. The notes are not designed for consultants who know the languages. They are so simplified that they may irritate the learned.

Sometimes, as in the case of German *ch* and the "Parisian" *r*, an effort is made to describe the sounds, completely foreign to English, because they serve as touchstones in phonetics. As they are famous because we cannot pronounce them and the similar sounds, the descriptions are awkward and probably fruitless. "Go and hear them" is the best advice for any one who is interested in foreign languages. Foreign broadcasts and recordings, such as the Linguaphone Persian records, can tell more of sounds than volumes of printed words.

On a world scale the problem of whether a foreign vowel is close or open, tense or slack, is nigh insoluble. When you first use the lists of the British Permanent Committee on Geographical Names, you may complain that vowel values are not indicated in the International Phonetic Alphabet or by English ā and ĕ, ō and ô, ē and ĭ, and so on. When you try to solve the problem yourself, you may decide that the PCGN chose the wise course in setting down merely *e* and *o* and *i*. Professor Bigongiari remarked, when I grumbled at the uncertainty of vowel-quality in lesser-known Italian names, "Why should Americans complain if the Italians are satisfied?" And he might have added—"particularly when Americans tolerate several varieties of English and seldom speak foreign languages well." I tried to use colorless symbols, but after hearing in one evening six instances of *Stalin* pronounced stä-leen' (on other networks of course) I felt obliged to bring back ĭ for the unstressed *i* in Slavic names such as *Stalin* and *Mihailovich*. The pronunciations -lēn and -vēch cannot be recommended as acceptable English. The object of this book is to assist American speakers about to go before a microphone—speakers moreover who are used to the symbols in old-fashioned reference books. An effort has been made, however, to improve the English pronunciation of foreign *e* and *o* by avoiding when possible the symbols ā and ō. See the discussion of Italian and the note on page xlvii.

ALBANIAN

Albanian names have two forms, the indefinite and the definite; e.g., *Tiranë* and *Tirana*. The indefinite forms seem better suited to the habits of English speech. Unfortunately our atlases are inconsistent. If Albanian names crowd the news, our best chance of avoiding confusion is to follow the PCGN and adopt as standard the indefinite forms of the Geg dialect.

Pronunciation

In words of more than one syllable the accent is usually on the next to the last syllable.

Albanian	*Explanation*
c	*ts* as in *rats*.
ç	*ch* as in *church*.
dh	*th* as in *this*. (Cf. *th*)
ë	ə (schwa) or *uh*.
gj	*gy*, like the *g* of *legume* or of "gyarden" (for *garden*).
j	*y* as in *yet*.
l	the "bright *l*" of *lit*.
ll	the "dark *l*" of *wall*.
nj	*ny* as in Spanish *cañón*. (French *gn*). Cf. English *canyon*.
q	*ky*, like the k-sound of *cue* or of "kyard" (for *card*).
th	"*th*" as in *thin*. (Cf. *dh*.)
x	*dz* as in *adze*.
xh	*j* as in *joy*.
y	*ü* as in French *lune* and German *über*.
zh	*zh*, the medial consonant of *leisure* and *pleasure*.

ARABIC

The pronunciation of names on the African front was determined after consultation with Mr. Ambrose Lansing of the Metropolitan Museum of Art and Mr. Amin A. Dahab, Vice-Consul of Egypt, New York City. It necessarily represents a compromise between various dialects of Arabic, Italian, French, and the resources of American English. The diphthong *ei* is subject to various renderings; the best general rule is to pronounce it ā (as in *Beirut*).

BULGARIAN. See *Slavic Languages*

BURMAN

The principal advisor on Burmese names was Mr. A. E. Gilliat of the British Embassy, Washington, for many years Financial Commissioner at Rangoon. All or almost all the pronunciations recommended will pass current among English speakers in Burma. It seemed wise at this time and for the purposes of this list to attempt nothing more, but here is an interesting field for investigation.

The Burman stress is often on the last syllable. As in other eastern languages "short *a*" lies between schwa [ə] (the *a* of *about*) and the ä of *father* and the ă of *rat*. Any one of these symbols seems to be misleading. In transcribing Burman names, I have employed the symbol that seemed to recreate the most vivid pronunciation that I heard—not to correct other pronunciations but to present at least one acceptable pronunciation. See also the note on the names of India.

> *th* is pronounced as in English *thin* or *this*, contrary to the Indian usage, q.v.
>
> *gy* is pronounced practically *j* as in *jill*.
>
> *ky* is pronounced *ch* as in *chill*.
>
> See also the note on Indian names.

CHINESE

The phonetics of Chinese are so different from English phonetics that we should gratefully accept the English pronunciation of all names that have acquired an English pronunciation. Fantastic as some of these pronunciations are, they are no stranger to the Chinese than some of our unlearned attempts to give a "Chinese" pronunciation of their familiar names. The modern ideal that in English the "correct" pronunciation of a place name is that current in the place itself is never more severely tested than in the case of China; here it is sometimes absurd.

English-speaking traders and travelers have given English pronunciations to seaports and river ports, to provinces and many large cities, and radio speakers may wisely adopt them, just as we use English pronunciations or names of Paris, Rome, Florence, and Munich. The old capital Peiping is an exception, for we pronounce it in Chinese fashion bā-pǐng (bay-ping), probably because as a new name of political importance it was described in the news a few years ago. These English pronunciations are, or were, current in Chinese railroad and steamship offices, and we may expect to hear them from our correspondents in the East. However, the wide choice of pronunciation that a Chinese name affords—even in China, because of the variety of dialects—makes a forecast uncertain.

As the most reasonable course under the circumstances the following list gives English pronunciations wherever they are acceptable. The Chinese names that have not acquired English pronunciations are transcribed in the conventional Mandarin style of Western dictionaries. English speakers should try to pronounce Chinese names with level stress, giving to each syllable a full share of force and time. The list has been prepared in consultation with Professor L. Carrington Goodrich, head of the Department of Chinese and Japanese, Columbia University.

Unfortunately our periodicals and popular books omit the diacritical marks necessary for the interpretation of the Roman spelling of Chinese. The reader therefore cannot distinguish sounds almost as different as *p* and *b*, *t* and *d*, and so on. The value of a scholarly work like Herrmann's *Atlas of China* (Harvard University Press, 1936) is that the accents are marked and the place names located on maps. The index of the Atlas can serve fairly well as a pronouncing dictionary of Chinese place names, if the following rules are observed.

Rules for the Pronunciation of Non-Anglicized Chinese Names

When Chinese is spelled in our alphabet, with appropriate accents, the symbols have approximately these values:

VOWELS

Chinese	Explanation
a	ä as in *father*.
ao	ou as in *out*.
e	ĕ as in *let*.
ê	ŭ as in *cut*.
eh	ĕ (as in *let*) in some syllables; ŭ (as in *cut*) in others.
ho, ko *or* he, ke	hŭ, kŭ (with the vowel of *cut*).
i	ē as in *machine*.
ih	û as in *urn*.
o	ô as in *more*; but see *ho, ko*.
ou, ow	ō as in *go*.
u	ōō as in *mood*.
ü	like Ger. *ü* or Fr. *u*.
ŭ	ə (schwa) or ŭ as in *cut*.

CONSONANTS

Aspirated		Unaspirated	
ch'	*ch* as in *chin*.	ch	*j* as in *jin*.
k'	*k* as in *koko*.	k	*g* as in *go*.
p'	*p* as in *pay*.	p	*b* as in *bay*.
t'	*t* as in *too*.	t	*d* as in *do*.
ts', tz'	*ts* as in *rats*.	ts, tz	*dz* as in *adz*.

j is a uvular sound like the "Parisian *r*" and the *j* of Spanish. English *r* is a poor rendering but almost inevitable with English speakers.
hs is properly pronounced *hsh*, but for ease it is equated to *sh*.
sh and the other consonants are pronounced much as in English.

STRESS

The syllables may be pronounced with level stress. Without special training we cannot attempt the Chinese tones.

The CBS Program Department has a limited number of copies of "A Practical Romanized List of Words and Syllable Sounds for Aid in the Pronunciation of Chinese" by Harry S. Aldrich, U.S.A. It will be useful to anyone who has access to publications in which the accents are marked, and it will be sent to any station that requests it.

CROAT. See *Slavic Languages*

CZECH. See *Slavic Languages*

DANISH. See *Scandinavian Languages*

DUTCH AND FLEMISH

The accent is usually on the first syllable. When common nouns serve as names of places or persons, the accent is often moved to the last syllable; e.g. *Breda*, brä-dä'. As suffixes the elements -dam, -deel, -dijk, -hoek, -meer, -zijl are usually accented.

aa and *ae* are pronounced long ä as in English *father*.

au and *ou* are pronounced much like the *ou* of *house* and *out*.

ch is pronounced as in Scottish *loch* and German *ach*.

d when final is pronounced *t*.

ee, and stressed *e* when not followed by a consonant in the same syllable, are pronounced ā as in English *made*. Stressed *e* when followed by a consonant in the same syllable is pronounced ĕ as in *bet*.

e unstressed is pronounced ə [uh].

eeuw is pronounced, when final, ā͞o; when followed by a vowel, ā + *w*.

ei and *ij* are transcribed ī [ai] rather than ĕĭ, which seemed beyond our resources, or ā [ay], which proved misleading.

eu is pronounced û as in *urn*. But *euw* is a variant of *eeuw* (see above).

g, voiced or voiceless, is similar to the *ch* of Scottish *loch* and German *ach*. It is here transcribed *k(h)*. It may be Anglicized to *g* (voiced) or *k* (voiceless).

ie is pronounced ē as in English *beet*.

ieuw is pronounced, when final, ēo͞o; when followed by a vowel, ē + *w*.

ij is a common variant of *ei* (see above).

j is pronounced *y* as in *yes*.

n when final in word or syllable is often lost.

oe is pronounced o͞o as in *boom*. With lack of stress it tends to become the o͝o of *book*.

oo has the sound of English ō as in *go*.

ou and *au* are pronounced like the *ou* of *house* and *out*.

sch is *sk(h)* or, when final, *s*. Du. *Schelde*, sk(h)ĕl'-də; *Bosch*, bôs'.

uu, and stressed *u* when not followed by a consonant in the same syllable, are pronounced ü (like French *u* and German *ü*). Stressed *u* when followed by a consonant in the same syllable is pronounced between the û of *urn* and the ŭ of *but*.

u in unstressed final syllables is pronounced ə [uh].

The dipthong in *huis* is here transcribed û͝ı [œi], a sound reminiscent of *oi* (as in *oil*) pronounced by some New Yorkers. Dutch *ui* is often Anglicized to *oi*, but Professor Elliott V. K. Dobbie and Dutch friends insisted that we should try a diphthong combining the vowel of *urn* and the vowel of *hit*.

w (labial continuant) is here given the sound of English *w*, though in many dictionaries rendered *v*.

y is a common variant of *ij* (see above).

ESTONIAN

Estonian is always stressed on the first syllable.

Vowel and consonant quantity is important in Estonian. A long vowel is indicated by doubling the symbol, *aa*, *ii*, etc. Estonian, like Finnish, q.v., has a number of diphthongs without English parallel.

õ is pronounced very like û in *urn*.

ä is pronounced ă as in *hat*.

FINNISH

The Finnish accent is on the first syllable. Compound words also have secondary accents. In this list the secondary accent is marked only when it does not agree with the usual English pattern of 'x 'x, stressed, unstressed, stressed, unstressed.

Vowel and consonant quantity is important in Finnish. A long vowel and a long consonant are both indicated by doubling the symbol, *aa*, *ee*, *ii*, *pp*, *tt*, etc. Finnish has a large number of diphthongs without English parallel, such as *uo* and *ie*. In these diphthongs, the two vowels have approximately equal importance, and it seemed better to transcribe them, when stressed, ōō'-ô' and ē'-ĕ' than wô' and yĕ'.

ä or *ae* is pronounced ă as in *hat*.

j has the value of *y* as in *yet*.

The influence of Sweden is very strong in Finland and many places have Swedish as well as Finnish names, especially where Swedish is the language spoken by the majority. In a few instances the Swedish names are better known than the Finnish.

FRENCH

It is the practice of American dictionaries to indicate the accent of a

French word; but we should remember that from the point of view of
English speakers, a French word has a level stress—i.e., each vowel
(except schwa) receives practically the same time and energy. The last
syllable in a phrase is uttered with a little more force and on a higher
tone, while the final syllable in a sentence is on a lower tone. However,
in the emphatic pronunciation of a single word, the first syllable may
be stressed. When a Frenchman is asked the pronunciation of a single
name or word, he will often give this emphatic form. But neither this
nor an English heavy stress on the last syllable is so generally appropriate as a level stressing. (See Webster's [1934], Sec. 272, p. lv for an
excellent account of the French "accent".)

An accent mark placed above a vowel in French spelling indicates
quality, not stress.

VOWELS

See also *Nasalized Vowels.*

French	Explanation
â, a + s	ä as in *father.* Fr. *Châlons,* shä-lôN'.
a	a sound lying between the ä of *father* and the ă of *fat.* Fr. *Laval,* lä-väl' or lă-văl'.
ai	ĕ as in *bed.* Fr. *Calais,* kä-lĕ' or kă-lĕ'.
aĩ, aill-, -ail (final)	ī (practically) as in *ice* or ä + y as in *yes.* Fr. *Versailles,* vĕr-sī' or vĕr-sä'(y).
au	ō as in *go.* Fr. *de Gaulle,* də gōl'; *Giraud,* zhē-rō'.
e (stressed), é, ê, è	ĕ as in *bed.* Fr. *Angers,* äN-zhĕ'; *Pétain,* pĕ-tăN'; *Angoulême,* äN-gōō-lĕm'; *Sète,* sĕt'. See page xlvii.
e (unstressed)	ə (schwa) like the *e* of *moment,* mō'-mənt. Silent when final (Fr. *Curie,* kü-rē') and when, within a word, it is not needed for an easy pronunciation of the adjacent con- sonants. Fr. *Abbeville,* äb-vēl'.
eau	ō as in *go.* Fr. *Clemenceau,* klĕ-mäN-sō'. See *au.*
eill-, eil (final), ey	ĕĭ or ĕy. Fr. *Marseille,* mär-sĕĭ' or mär-sĕ'(y).
eu	û as in *urn.* Fr. *Honfleur,* ôN-flûr'.
ey	See *eill-.*
i before a consonant	ē as in *machine.* Fr. *Lille,* lēl'.
before a vowel	y as in *yet.* Fr. *St. Pierre,* săN pyĕr'.
ill-, il (final)	ē + y (as in *yes*). Fr. *Billancourt,* bē-yäN-kōōr'. Exception: Fr. *ville,* vēl'.
ô, o (final), o + s	ō as in *go.* Fr. *Bône,* bōn'; *St. Malo,* săN mä-lō'; *rose,* rōz'; *Rosny,* rō-nē'.
otherwise	ô as in *more* or ŭ as in *but.* Fr. *Somme,* sôm' or sŭm'.

œ, œu	û as in *urn*. Fr. *Sacré Cœur*, sä-krĕ′kûr′. See *eu*.
oi	wä as in *waft*. Fr. *Oise*, wäz′.
ou	ōō as in *pool*, (Fr. *Cherbourg*, shĕr-bōōr′); but before a vowel pronounced *w*. Fr. *oui*, wē′.
u	ü (ē pronounced with the lips rounded as for ōō). May be Anglicized as the front ōō of Eng. *toot*. Fr. *Debussy*, də-bü-sē′.
ue	A variant of *eu*. Fr. *Arcueil*, är-kûĭ′ or är-kû′(y).
ui	wē
y (final)	A variant of *i*, pronounced ē. Fr. *Puy*, pwē′.

NASALIZED VOWELS

The French nasalized vowels are somewhat like a nasal American pronunciation of l*o*ng, s*a*ng, and *urn* (with *r* silent as in the South). Nasalized *e, a, o* are pronounced like l*o*ng; Nasalized *i, ai, ei, y* like s*a*ng. Nasalized *ie* like *yang*, yăng; nasalized *oi* and *ui* like *wang*, wăng; nasalized *u, eu* like *urn*. The symbol N indicates that the preceding vowel is nasalized.

A single *m* and *n* not followed by a vowel, and *ng* nasalize the preceding vowel. French *vingt*, văN′; *Paimpol*, păN-pôl′; *Reims*, răNs′; *Amiens*, ä-myăN′; *un*, ûN′; *Meung*, mûN′; *Rouen*, rwäN′; *Caen*, käN′; *Clermont-Ferrand*, klĕr-môN′ fĕ-räN′. (The nasal äN is between a nasalized ä of *father* and a nasalized ô of *orb*. The nasal ôN is between a nasalized ô of *orb* and a nasalized ō of *go*.)

CONSONANTS

The consonants *c, f, l,* and *r* are pronounced when final in monosyllables. Fr. *Cher*, shĕr′. Otherwise consonants, singly or in groups, when final are usually silent. (But *l* and *r* provide exceptions.) In some family names and some place names, final -*s* is pronounced. Fr. *Noguès*, nô-gĕs′; *Aix*, ĕks′.

c before e, i, y	s as in *see*. Fr. *Cette*, sĕt′.
otherwise	k as in *koko*. Fr. *Mâcon*, mä-kôN′.
ç	s as in *see*. Fr. *Monluçon*, môN-lü-sôN′.
ch	sh as in *shall*. Fr. *Chartres*, shär′tr.
g before e, i, y	zh, the medial consonant of *pleasure* and *leisure*. Fr. *Angers*, äN-zhĕ′.
otherwise (except gn, ng)	g as in *go*. Fr. *Gounod*, gōō-nō′.
gn	ny as in Sp. *cañón*, almost Eng. *canyon*. Fr. *Avignon*, ä-vē-nyôN′.
gu before e, i, y	g as in *get*. Fr. *guerre*, gĕr′.
h	silent. Fr. *Henri*, äN-rē′.

j	*zh*, the medial consonant of *pleasure* and *leisure*. Fr. *Jean*, zhäN′.
l	*l* as in *lip*, except in *-ill-* and *-il* (which see). Often pronounced when final. Fr. *Toul*, tōol′. Pronounced in Fr. *ville*, vēl′.
m, n, ng	nasalize a preceding vowel in the same syllable. See *Nasalized Vowels*. Doubled, *mm*, *nn* are pronounced as in English. Fr. *Rennes*, rĕn′.
q, qu	*k* as in *key*. Fr. *Quimper*, kăN-pĕr′; *cinq*, săNk′.
s initial and final, and *ss*	*s* as in *see*. Fr. *Sousse*, sōos′.
between vowels	*z* as in *zebra*. Fr. *Toulouse*, tōo-lōoz′; *maison*, mĕ-zôN′.
th	*t* as in *Tom*. Fr. *Thierry*, tyĕ-rē′.
w	*v* as in *very*. Fr. *Weygand*, vĕ-gäN′.

NOTE ON "R"

For American radio it is usually desirable to use an American *r*. The "Parisian" *r* has no parallels in American English. If the *h* in *hole* is made further back so that the breath causes audible friction, or still further back so that the breath causes the uvula to vibrate, the sounds are voiceless correspondents to two types of Parisian *r* (customarily voiced). In many parts of France, *r* is a tip-of-tongue trill.

GERMAN

Names are accented upon the first syllable or, after the prefixes *be-*, *ent-* (*emp-*), *er-*, *ge-*, *ver-*, upon the second syllable.

VOWELS

Vowels are pronounced long when stressed before *h* and before one consonant, short before two or more consonants and when unstressed. However before *ch* and *ss*, a vowel may be long or short (thus leading to a recent disagreement on the pronunciation of *Bochum*—bō′-k(h)ŏom or bôk(h)′-ŏom).

German	*Explanation*
a, aa	ä as in *father*.
ä, ae	ĕ as in *bed* or ă as in *care*.
ai	ī as in *aisle* and *ride*. See *ei*.
au	ou as in *out*.
äu	oi as in *oil*. See *eu*.
e stressed	ā as in *late*, when long; ĕ as in *let*, when short.
unstressed	ə (schwa) or sometimes silent.

ei	ī as in *ride* and *aisle*. See *ai*.
eu	oi as in *oil*. See *äu*.
i	ē as in *meet*, when long; ĭ as in *sit*, when short.
ie	ē as in *eve, meet*.
ö, oe	û as in *urn* (or ā as in *may* pronounced with lips rounded).
ü, ue	ē as in *eve* pronounced with lips rounded. May be Anglicized as the front ōō of Eng. *toot*.
y	a variant of *i*, pronounced ē when long; ĭ when short.

CONSONANTS

Except for indicating the length of preceding vowels there is no distinction between doubled or single consonants.

b		when initial or followed by vowel, like Eng. *b*; otherwise tends to *p*.
c	before e, i (y), ä, ĕ	*ts* as in *rats*.
	before a, o, u, or cons.	*k* as in *koko*.
ch	after a, o, u (but not *äu, eu*)	*k(h)* as in Scot. *loch*; like Eng. *ck* as in *lock*, except that the sound continues. The back of the tongue approaches the velum but does not cut off the breath.
	otherwise	like Eng. *k* in *kit* or Virginian *kyard* (for *card*) but a continuant reminiscent of Eng. *h* in *hue* or *sh* in *shall*. The diminutive *-chen* always has this front *ch*.
		The pronounciation of *ch* varies in Germany according to dialect areas. It is Anglicized to *k*.
ck		*kk*
d		when initial or followed by vowel, like English *d*; otherwise tends to *t*.
dt		*t* as in *set*.
g	initial	*g* as in *go* and *get*.
	between vowels	as above in Austria and southern Germany; in the north pronounced like Ger. *ch*, which see, but voiced.
	final	*k* in Austria and southern Germany; in the north like Ger. *ch*, which see.
h	initial	*h* as in *hat*.
	after a vowel	silent but in stressed syllables indicates a long vowel.
j		*y* as in *yes*.
ng		*ng* as in *singer*, not as in *finger*.

qu	*kv*
r	uvular *r* (like the "Parisian" *r* of French) or a trilled or rolled *r* made with the tip of the tongue.
s before a vowel and initial	*z* as in *zone.*
otherwise (and *ss*)	*s* as in *so.*
sp, st initial in stressed syllable (or root)	*shp* and *sht*; otherwise *sp* and *st. Strasse* shträs'-ə, but *Fürsten,* für'-stən.
sch	*sh* as in *shall.*
t	as in English, except that before *i* plus vowel in Latin loan words, *t* is pronounced *ts.*
th	*t* as in *tat.*
tz	*ts* as in *rats.*
v	*f* as in *father.*
w	*v* as in *very.* Final *-ow* is ō as in *go.*
y	variant of *i.*
z	*ts* as in *rats.*

GREEK

There is no simple rule for the accenting of Greek names.

VOWELS

Greek (Romanized)	*Explanation*
a	ä as in *father.*
ai	ĕ as in *bet.*
e (epsilon)	ĕ as in *bet.*
e (eta), i, y	ē as in *beet.*
o	ô as in *on* (rounded).
ou	ōō as in *boot.*
ei, oi, yi, ui	ē as in *beet.*
av (au), ev (eu) before b, g, d, z, l, m, n, r	äv, ĕv (*v* as in *every*).
before th, k, x, p, s, t, f, h (kh), ps	äf, ĕf (*f* as in *off*).

CONSONANTS

b (v)	*v* as in *very.*
kh (ch) before vowels	*h* as in *he.*
otherwise	*k(h)* as in Scot. *loch* and Ger. *ach.*
d (dh)	*th* as in *then.* (Cf. *th.*) Anglicized as *d.*

[xxvii]

g (gh)	before ē and ĕ	y as in *yes*.
	before ä, ŏ, ōō, and all consonants	properly "gh" (voiced velar fricative), but here transcribed g as in *go*.
gi (ghi)	before vowels	y as in *yes*.
gg (ng), gk (nk)		ngg as in *stronger*.
gch (nch, nkh)		ngh as in *bring' her'*
h		When initial, h is sometimes silent.
mb, mp		mb or b
nd, nt		nd or d

Final *n* after *o*, and final *on* after a vowel are frequently not pronounced.

ph		f as in *ferry*.
ps		ps as in *leaps*.
r (rh)		r trilled with tip of tongue.
s	before b, d, g, m, n, r	z as in *maze*.
	otherwise	s as in *so* and *yes*.

In the names of islands of the Aegean, final *s* is frequently not pronounced.

| th | | "th" as in *thin*. (Cf. *d*.) |

HUNGARIAN

In Hungarian or Magyar the accent is normally on the first syllable. In compound words, the first syllable of each component after the first receives secondary stress. Note that an acute accent placed above a vowel in the spelling indicates a long vowel, not a stress.

Hungarian	*Explanation*
a	ŏ as in *odd* (with some rounding).
á	ä as in *father*.
c, cz	ts as in *rats*.
cs	ch as in *church*.
gy	d(y) or by assimilation to following voiceless consonants, t(y). Compare *duty* and *tune* pronounced dyōō'-tĭ and tyōōn'.
h	h as in *hat*, but silent after g and t.
j	y as in *yes*. Sometimes this sound occurs after a vowel. It seems odd to an English speaker but it is similar to the vowel ĭ as in *it*.
ö, ő	û as in *urn*, ö being short and ő long.
s	sh as in *shall*.
sz	s as in *sit*.
y	"liquifies" a preceding g, l, n, t. Compare the *ny* of English *canyon* with the *n* of *can*,

and the *li* of *million* with the *l* of *mill*. See
gy above. Otherwise *y* is ĭ or ē.

zh, the medial consonant of *leisure*.

In Hungarian as in English there is much assimilation of consonants,
as some of the names show. A voiceless consonant (p, t, k, s, f, *etc.*) will
cause a preceding voiced consonant (b, d, g, z, v, *etc.*) to become voiceless. Likewise a voiced consonant voices a preceding voiceless consonant.

NAMES OF INDIA

The names of India are continually more and less Anglicized. It is
often difficult to tell which is the most suitable of the various pronunciations a name has. For example, the "short *a*" is pronounced in the
neighborhood of ŭ (the vowel of *but*) or schwa (the *a* of *about* and so*fa*).
When it is Anglicized, it is pronounced like the *a* of *bat*. Thus every
name with short *a* has at least two pronunciations of that vowel, ŭ and
ă, and sometimes a third, ä. It is usually safer to take a recognized
English pronunciation than to attempt to construct a native one from
the accepted spelling, for the spelling is often an English corruption,
misleading except for an English pronunciation.

The syllables of Indian names are accented almost evenly. The plac-
ing of an accent mark, therefore, is often an effort to prevent false
stressing, and sometimes it is unfortunate. But one cannot omit the
marks, as in the case of Chinese, because many of the names have been
spelled and pronounced as if they were English, or half-English. Many
Indians in the civil services have accepted the Anglicized forms.

In India *th* is an aspirated *t*. It is not *th* as in *thin* or as in *this*. Compare
the usage of Burmaṅ.

ITALIAN

Words of more than one syllable are frequently accented on the next
to the last; there are, however, many exceptions. A mistaken accent is
made more painful by the American habit of overstressing foreign words.
It is always better to stress lightly.

As an authority on the accenting of place names, we have, on Professor Dino Bigongiari's advice, followed the *Indice Generale della Carta
d'Italia del T. C. I.* (Touring Club Italiano).

VOWELS

Italian has two or three qualities of *e* and of *o*. The American English
sounds which most closely approach all of them are ĕ as in *bed* and ô as
in *bawd*, though these vowels are more "open" than Italian "close *e*"
and "close *o*". American ā (as in *ate*) and ō (as in *go*) are diphthongal—
āĭ and ōŏ, and quite out of place in Italian words. A skilled speaker of

Italian will of course make subtle distinctions in vowels. An American, not very familiar with the language, had better stick to ä, ĕ, ē, ô, ōō. There is no other error so bad as *Enna* pronounced ā′-nä, for this pronunciation is not Italian and not English. See page xlvii.

In vowel compounds, *a*, *e*, and *o* keep their own values; *i* and *u*, unstressed, become glide sounds, *y* and *w*. It. *Gaeta*, gä-ĕ′-tä; *Leone*, lĕ-ô′-nĕ; *Scuola*, skwô′-lä; *Pistoia*, pē-stô′-yä; but note *Pavia*, pä-vē′-ä.

CONSONANTS

Italian consonants are not difficult to pronounce, but the spelling may mislead Americans. An Italian makes doubled consonants long.

Italian		*Explanation*
c, cc	before a, o, u, or cons.	*k* as in *kit*. It. *Capri*, kä′-prē; *Croce*, krô′-chĕ.
	before e, i	*ch* as in *church*. It. *Cenci*, chĕn′-chē. Followed by *a*, *o*, and *u*, the *i* is practically silent. It. *Ciano*, chä′-nô; *Boccaccio*, bôk-kät′-chô.
ch, cch		*k* as in *kit*. The *k*- sound is indicated by *c* before *o*, *a*, and *u*, and by *ch* before *i* and *e*. It. *bianco*, byän′-kô; *bianchi*, byän′-kē (or byä′-nkô, byä′-nkē); *vecchio*, vĕk′-kyô. Note also the pronunciation of *i* as a glide in *Chianti*, kyän′-tē (or kyä′-ntē); *Chiesa*, kyĕ′-zä; *Chioggia*, kyôd′-jä; *Chiusa*, kyōō′-sä.
g, gg	before a, o, u, or cons.	*g* as in *go*. It. *Gaeta*, gä-ĕ′-tä; *Grancia*, grän′-chä. See also *gh*, *gli*.
	before e, i	*j* as in *judge*. It. *Genova*, jĕ′-nô-vä. Followed by *a*, *o*, and *u*, the *i* is practically silent. It. *Giovanni*, jô-vän′-nē; *Perugia*, pĕ-rōō′-jä; *Foggia*, fôd′-jä.
gh		*g* as in *go*. This sound is indicated by *g* before *o*, *a*, and *u*, and by *gh* before *i* and *e*. It. *Ghigo*, gē′-gô. Note also the pronunciation of *i* as a glide in *Ghiaia*, gyä′-yä.
gli		*ly* as in Eng. *hellion*. It. *Ventimiglia*, vĕn-tē-mē′-lyä; *Gigli*, jē′-lyē.
gn		*ny* as in Sp. *cañón* (French *gn*), almost Eng. *canyon*. It. *Foligno*, fô-lē′-nyô.
gu		*gw* as in *Gwendolyn*. It. *Guardia*, gwär′-dyä; *Guido*, gwē′-dô. (In French and Spanish, to the contrary, *gu* before *e* and *i* is pronounced simply *g* as in *get*, the *u* being silent.)

[xxx]

i	ē, when alone and with consonants; *y* in the neighborhood of vowels. It. *Pistoia*, pē-stô′-yä; *Siena*, syĕ′-nä; *Fiume*, fyōō′-mĕ.
j	a variant spelling of *i*.
qu	*kw* as in *question*. It. *Quirinale*, kwē-rē-nä′-lĕ. (In French and Spanish, to the contrary, *qu* before *e* and *i* is pronounced simply *k* as in *kit*, the *u* being silent.)
s	*s* as in *sit*, except it becomes *z* before voiced consonants and, from Naples to the south, between vowels. It. *Sbarco*, zbär′-kô; *Cosenza*, kô-zĕn′-tsä.
sc before a, o, u, or cons.	*sk* as in *sky*. It. *Scuola*, skwô′-lä.
before e, i	*sh* as in *shall*. It. *Bisceglie*, bē-shĕ′-lyĕ. Followed by *a, o, u*, the *i* is practically silent. It. *Sciacca*, shäk′-kä.
sch	*sk* as in *sky*. The *sk-* sound is indicated by *sc* before *a, o,* and *u*, and by *sch* before *i* and *e*. It. *Scalea*, skä-lĕ′-ä; *scherzo*, skĕr′-tsô. Note also the pronunciation of *i* as a glide in *Ischia*, ē′-skyä.
z, zz	*ts* as in *rats*. It. *Spezia*, spĕ′-tsyä; *Arezzo*, ä-rĕt′-sô.
	dz, occasionally, as in *beds*. It. *mezzo*, mĕd′-zô; *Gozzano*, gôd-zä′-nô.

JAPANESE

Japanese does not employ accent in the manner of English. The stresses marked in this book will serve to prevent misstressing, if they are not overemphasized. However, it may well seem better to ignore them and to give each syllable the same stress—so far as a level accent is possible in an English sentence.

Japanese vowels are normally short—appreciably shorter than the corresponding sounds in English. The Japanese values can be suggested by a distinct but quick utterance of the half-stressed syllables in Jeho*vah* [a], du′t*y* [i], r*ou*lette′ [u], ch*a*otic, [e], ob*ey*′ [o].

The Japanese long vowels are much longer than the short vowels and the Roman spellings *aa, ii, ee* are appropriate. Unfortunately long *o* and long *u* are not often distinguished by doubling (oo, uu) or by macron (ō, ū) although, as Professor Harold Henderson opines, Mr. Ohashi ("Littlebridge") and Mr. Ōhashi ("Bigbridge") would be two quite different people. In this book long vowels are indicated by doubling or by the macron.

Short *i* and short *u* have a tendency to be reduced in value and even to disappear, especially when the neighboring consonants are voiceless (t, ch, s, sh, k, h, p, f). The vowels, technically speaking, become voiceless. Short *u* when final, especially when the preceding consonant is *s* or *k*, may suffer the same fate. Thus *Shikoku* approaches shkôk, and *Yokosuka* is almost yô-kôs-kä. Perhaps for American radio the longer forms are preferable, but for well-known names the shorter forms are here listed as variants.

The consonants of Japanese show dialectal variety, but *j* may be pronounced as in *jam*, *g* as in *go*, *ch* as in *cheap*. The combinations *ae*, *ai*, *oi*, *ui* are not true diphthongs but two separate vowels.

NOTE: In the first edition of *World Words* accents were not marked. Because of the great differences between Japanese and English, and the absence of generally accepted patterns for anglicizing Japanese names, it seemed wise to recommend simply "level stress." However, level stress is often so un-English that this recommendation gave broadcasters little help. Stresses would appear with force and variety. In this edition an attempt is made to locate the stresses where they will do the least harm. We are indebted to Mr. Ichiro I. Shirato and to the Japanese pronouncing dictionary with pitch accent indicated, which was prepared by Kaku Jimbō and Senri Tsunemi (Tōkyō: Kōseikaku, 1932).

It is noteworthy that differences of pitch pattern as well as of vowel quantity will distinguish pairs such as *Oyama*, little mountain, and *Ōyama*, big mountain. *Oyama* may be transcribed ô′-yä-mä; *Ōyama*, ô-ô′-yä′-mä′.

KOREAN

The names should be pronounced with level stress, each syllable receiving its full share of force and time.

LATVIAN

Lettish or Latvian is always stressed on the first syllable.

A long vowel is indicated by the macron, ā, ē, ī, *etc.*

Diphthongs such as *ie* are transcribed, when stressed, ē′-ĕ′ rather than yĕ, for the elements are of approximately equal importance. Compare the Finnish diphthongs.

Latvian		Explanation
c	before e, i	*ts* as in *rats*.
	otherwise	*k* as in *koko*.
j		*y* as in *yet*.

ņ		*ny* as in Sp. *cañón* (Fr. *gn*), almost Eng. *canyon*.
v	final	*f* as in *off*.
	otherwise	*v* as in *very*.
ž		*zh*, the medial consonant in *pleasure* and *leisure*.

LITHUANIAN

Lithuanian has both stress and pitch accents which can not be reduced to English rules.

In the pronunciation of the Lithuanian informants *ai* was nearer to ĕĭ than to ī, the transcription here used for convenience.

Lithuanian may employ *i* to indicate the palatal quality of a preceding consonant. It is here transcribed *y*, although one may not be conscious of its effect in listening to the speech of Lithuanians. *Šiauliai* sounds like a Virginian's shou′-lĭ *or* -lĕĭ, quite as much as shyou′-lyĭ *or* -lyĕĭ. Similarly one may hear palatal quality where the spelling does not indicate it (as before high and mid front vowels). For example *Panĕvežis*, q.v.

Lithuanian *e* indicates an open vowel, ĕ or ă, while *ė* indicates a close vowel like the first part of English ā [ay]. Both are here transcribed ĕ, except that stressed *ė*, like *ei*, is transcribed ā [ay].

j is pronounced *y*.

š and ž are pronounced, respectively, *sh* as in *shall* and *zh* like the medial consonant of *leisure* and *pleasure*.

y is a vowel pronounced ē as in English *beet*.

MALAYAN

The Indonesian or Malayan languages are spoken in Madagascar, the Malay Peninsula, the East Indies, Formosa, and the Philippines. The place names that appear in the news are spelled and usually pronounced according to the usage of European nations that controlled these territories—France, England, Holland, Portugal, China, and Spain. The Indonesian languages and the Oceanic together form the Austronesian family. See *Languages of the Pacific.*

NORWEGIAN. See *Scandinavian Languages*

LANGUAGES OF THE PACIFIC

It is important to remember that the accent usually falls on the next to the last syllable in names of the East Indies and the myriad islands of Oceania. This is the most comfortable accent for Americans, but in an effort to be correct, we frequently are overcorrect and stress the last syllable of names that are properly accented on the penult, as Bandung, Balik-Papan, Balabac, Denpasar. The vowels have the "continental" values of Spanish or Italian. The consonants we may pronounce as in English, with *g* as in *get* and *ng* as in *singer* (seldom as in *finger*). For evidence of variety of usage and opinion among scholarly travelers who know the islands, see *Betio, Tahiti, Tarawa*, and *Tulagi*.

PERSIAN or IRANIAN

"Persian orthography is by no means fixed and consistent, and especially is there uncertainty about the identity and length of many vowels." *PCGN.*

In Persian the sound of "long *a*" may suggest English ô, or, in poetry, ôu, rather than English ä, but the transcription ä is here employed as more suitable for American radio speakers.

The pronunciations were prepared in consultation with Mr. C. K. Wilkinson of the Metropolitan Museum of Art, New York.

PHILIPPINES. *See note appended to the section on Spanish*

POLISH. See *Slavic Languages*

PORTUGUESE

Words ending in vowels, except ã, or in *m* or *s*, are accented on the next to the last syllable. Words ending in consonants, except *m* or *s*, or in ã, are accented on the last syllable. Words that do not conform to these rules carry in Portuguese orthography a written accent (circumflex or acute). See the last paragraph.

Unstressed vowels tend, like unstressed vowels in English, to become "centralized." That is to say, they tend towards schwa (ə or *uh*) or short *i* (ĭ).

VOWELS

Portuguese	Explanation
a stressed	ä (ah) as in *father*. Before *l* it becomes ô as in Eng. *all*. Port. *Natal*, nä-tôl′.
unstressed, expecially if final	tends to become ə (*uh*) as in *tellable* and *sofa*. In Brazil, often remains ä.
ã	See *Nasalized Vowels and Diphthongs*.
e stressed	ĕ as in *edify*. See page xlvii.
unstressed, especially if final	ə (*uh*) in Portugal, ĭ in the islands and in Brazil. Practically silent or ĭ when initial in words like *espirito* (ĭ)spē′-rē-tŏŏ [(i)spee′-ree-tu].

ei		ā as in *aid*. However it may be reduced to ĕ in unstressed syllables. Port. *Figueiredo*, fē-gĕ-rĕʹ-dŏŏ.
o	stressed	ô as in *more*. See page xlvii.
	unstressed, especial-ly if final	ŏŏ as in *pull*.
oi		ŏĭ as in *oil*, but sometimes the *o* is "weak" and *oi* is pronounced wē. Port. *Coimbra*, kwēmʹ-brə.
ou		ō as in *go*.

NASALIZED VOWELS AND DIPHTHONGS

Vowels marked with a til, for example ã, õ, and vowels before *m* + cons., *n* + cons., or final *m* are strongly nasalized.

ã	ûN. Like a Virginian's nasal pronunciation of *long*. In Brazil, almost ĕ as in nasal *men*.
ãe, ãi	ã (as above) + ĭ. Not far from a Virginian's nasal pronunciation of *mind;* and (for Brazil) Eng. *aim* (or āng).
ão	ã (as above) + ŭ. Similar to Virginian nasal pronunciations of the diphthong in *house*.
-em (final)	ã (as above) + ĭ. Similar to nasal American *mind;* and (for Brazil) Eng. *aim* (or āng).
õe	o + ĭ. Similar to a nasal pronunciation of Eng. *poem*, pōʹ-ĭm (or -ĭng). (Port. *põem* is another story.)

CONSONANTS

c	before e, i	s as in *so*.
	otherwise	k as in *koko*.
ç		s as in *so*.
ch		sh as in *shall*.
d		d initially; otherwise th as in *gather*. Anglicized as d.
g	before e, i	zh, the medial consonant of *pleasure* and *leisure*.
	otherwise	g as in *go*.
gu	before e, i	g as in *get*. The u is silent.
gu	before a	voiced spirant g + w. Anglicized as gw.
h		silent
j (only before a, o, u)		zh, the medial consonant of *pleasure* and *leisure*.
lh		ly as in *million*. Cf. It. *gli*.
m		For -em see *Nasalized Vowels* above.

nh		*ny* as in Sp. *cañón*. Almost Eng. *canyon*.
qu	before e, i	*k* (the *u* is silent)
	otherwise	*kw*
s	initial, following a consonant, and when doubled (ss)	*s* as in *so*.
	between vowels	*z* as in *zebra*.
	before c, f, p, q, t, and when final	*sh* as in *shall*, but in Brazil usually *s* as in *so*.
	before b, d, g (as in *go*), or any voiced consonant.	*zh*, the medial consonant of *leisure* and *pleasure*, but in Brazil usually *z* as in *zebra*.

Note: The pronunciation of final *s* and *z* will be affected by the initial sound of the next word in the same phrase.

x		*sh* or *s* or *ks;* there is no dependable rule.
z	initial and between vowels	*z* as in *zebra*.
	before c, f, p, q, t, s	*sh* as in *shall*, but in Brazil usually *s*.
	before b, d, g (as in *go*) or any voiced consonant.	*zh*, the medial consonant of *leisure* and *pleasure*, but in Brazil usually *z*.

NOTE

No distinction is here made between close and open vowels. In Portuguese orthography a circumflex accent indicates a stressed close vowel. An acute accent indicates a stressed open vowel. A grave accent is placed only on an unaccented vowel to indicate that it receives special attention. For a much more detailed account of the pronunciation of Portuguese, see Joseph Dunn, *Grammar of the Portuguese Language* (New York, Hispanic Society of America; London, D. Nutt, 1930); Edwin B. Williams, *Introductory Portuguese Grammar* (New York, 1942).

RUMANIAN

There is no simple rule of accent in Rumanian.

With the following exceptions, Rumanian spelling has usual English values.

Rumanian		*Explanation*
ă	stressed	*û* as in *urn*.
	unstressed	*ə* (uh) as in *about*.
â		*û* as in *urn*.
c	before e, i	*ch* as in *church*. Compare Italian.
	otherwise	*k* as in *kit*.
ch		*k* as in *kit*. Compare Italian.

e		sometimes, esp. when initial, pronounced yĕ as in *yes*.
e	unstressed before a vowel	*y* as in *you*. After *c* (see above) and *g* (see the following), it is practically silent.
g	before e, i	*j* as in *judge*. Compare Italian.
	otherwise	*g* as in *go*.
gh		*g* as in *go*. Compare Italian.
h		*h* before vowels, otherwise *k(h)* as in Ger. *ach*.
i	unstressed before a vowel	*y* as in *yes*. After *c* and *g* (see above), it is practically silent. Compare Italian.
	final	ĭ or *y* pronounced so short that it practically disappears. Rumanian *Ploeşti*, plô-yĕsht′.
î		variant of â (see above).
j		*zh*, the medial consonant in *pleasure*.
o	unstressed before *a*	*w* as in *wash*.
ou		ō as in *both*.
ş		*sh* as in *shall*.
ţ		*ts* as in *rats*.
u	unstressed before a vowel	*w* as in *wash*. Compare Italian.
	final	o͝o (very short).

NOTE

In Rumanian the definite article is a suffix -*l*, -*ul*, -*le* (masculine) and -*a* (feminine). It may or may not be added to the names of rivers and mountains when they are referred to in the news. Compare the definite and indefinite forms of Albanian names. The suffixes -(*u*)*lui* and -*ei* are genitives with the definite article.

RUSSIAN. *See Slavic Languages*

SCANDINAVIAN LANGUAGES

Usually the first syllable bears the principal accent of the word.

VOWELS

In stressed syllables a vowel is long if it is final or followed by one consonant; otherwise, and in unstressed syllables, a vowel is short.

Spelling		Norwegian	Swedish	Danish
a	long	ä	ä or ô	ä or ă
	short	ä or ŭ	ä or ŭ	ä or ŭ
aa, å		ô or ō	ō or ô	ô
æ, ä		ĕ or ă	ĕ or ă	ĕ or ă
(long and short)				

Sometimes *e* is written for *æ*.

		Norwegian	Swedish	Danish
e	long	ā or ĭ	ā or ĭ	ā or ĭ
	short	ĕ (or ă)	ĕ	ĕ or ĭ
	unstressed	ə	ə	ə
i	long	ē	ē	ē
	short	ē	ē	ē or ĭ
o	long	ō or o͞o	o͞o	ō
	short	o͝o or o͞o	o͞o	ō

Sometimes *o* is pronounced ô, as if it were *aa* or *å*.

	Norwegian	Swedish	Danish
ö, ø, œ	û	û	û
(long and short)			

		Norwegian	Swedish	Danish
u	long	o͞o or ü	ü	o͞o
	short	o͞o or ü	o͝o or ŭ	o͞o or o͝o
y		ü	ü	ü

CONSONANTS

In Norwegian and Swedish all doubled consonants are pronounced long.

Spelling	Norwegian	Swedish	Danish
b	As in English.	As in English.	*b* or *p*
c	Before *e, i, y, æ, ä,* in all *c* is pronounced *s*; otherwise in all pronounced *k*.		
d	Silent after *l* and *n* and often when final in word or syllable.	As in English.	Initially *d* or *t*. After vowels, *th* as in *this*. Silent as in Norwegian.
f	As in English.	As in English.	As in English, but silent in the word *af*.
g	pronounced as in *go* — before *a, o, u, e æ, ø, å,* and cons.	before *a, o, u, å,* and cons.	before all vowels and consonants. May suggest *k* as in *koko*.

In all, *g* pronounced *ng* before *n* (but occasionally ĭ in Danish and Norwegian).

g	pronounced *y* as in *yet* — before *i, y, j.* Silent in *og, -ig, fugl, søndag,* etc.	before *e, i, y, ä, ö, j* and after *l, r.* Silent in *-ig, -igt, morgon, dag,* etc.	pronounced voiced *k(h)* or velar *y* after vowels and *l, r.* Sometimes silent. *k(h)* before *t. gg* is pronounced *kk.*
h	Silent before *j, v.*	Silent before *j.*	Silent before *j, v.*
j	In all, pronounced *y* as in *yet*.		

k	as in *koko*	before *a, e, o, u,* *æ, ø, å* and consonants including *n*.	before *a, o, u, å,* and consonants, including *n*.	As in English but pronounced before *n*.
		before *i, y, j,* suggests *ky* or *ch* or *h*. Before these vowels *sk* is pronounced *sh*.	before *e, i, y,* *ä, ö, j,* pronounced like the *ch* of *church*. Before these vowels *sk* is pronounced *sh*.	
r		trilled	trilled	uvular or "Parisian" *r*.
rs		sh	sh	unvoiced uvular *r* + *s*.
s	In all three, pronounced *s* as in *so* except in *rs, sj,* which see. Never pronounced *z*.			
sj		sh	sh	sh
skj		sh	sh	sk(y)-
v		Oc. silent when final.	As in English.	Oc. silent when final.
w	In all, pronounced *v*.			
x	In all, pronounced *ks*.			
z	In all, pronounced *s* as in *so*.			

NOTE ON "EI, EJ" AND "AU, AV"

The diphthong *ei, ej* is here transcribed ā (ay) though it varies in dialects from ī (ai) to ā (ay). The diphthong *au, av* is pronounced ău or, as in Oslo, ăv. The nearest English sound is the *ou* [*au*] of *house*, and it is so transcribed.

NOTE

This outline is based on materials provided by Prof. Einar Haugen. While it is too complicated to follow easily, it will explain contradictory transcriptions of Scandinavian place names. Convenient grammars in English are Einar Haugen, *Beginning Norwegian* (New York, 1937); W. G. Johnson, *Beginning Swedish* (Rock Island, 1939); Ingeborg Stemann, *A New Danish Reader* (Copenhagen, 1939); and Stefán Einarsson, *Icelandic* (Baltimore, 1945).

SERBIAN. See *Slavic Languages.*

SIAMESE. See *Thai or Siamese.*

SLAVIC LANGUAGES

There is no simple rule for the accenting of Russian and Bulgarian. Polish is accented on the syllable next to the last. Czech (Bohemian) and Slovak are accented on the first syllable. Serb-Croat values of intonation and quantity are foreign to English. However, in English contexts an accent is given, usually to the first or the second syllable. Occasionally in this list two accents are marked to prevent mispronunciation or to reconcile contradictory authorities, each of which in its way is right.

In Czech and Slovak spelling an acute accent placed above a vowel is a sign of length, not stress. An apostrophe indicates a liquid sound. The accent of Polish ó indicates quality not stress.

In the following table are explained symbols of the official roman spelling of Czechoslovakia, Poland, and Yugoslavia (which also has an official Cyrillic spelling). Added in parenthesis are comments on difficult points in the customary American transliteration of the official Cyrillic spelling of Russia and Bulgaria.

Czechosl.	Polish	Serb-Croat	Explanation
ä			ă as in *fat*.
	ą		ôN as in Fr. *bon*.
c	c	c	ts as in *rats*. In Polish c before *i* or *j* + vowel approaches ć.
	ć	ć	ch as in *cheese* (or *tsy*).
č	cz	č	ch as in *choke*.
ch *or* h	ch (Also Russian and Bulgarian *kh*.)	h	h (as in *hat*) before a vowel; otherwise *k(h)*, as in Scot. *loch*. Rus. and Bulg. *kh* is Anglicized as *k*.
	dz		dz as in *buds;* when final, *ts* as in *rats;* before *i* it is pronounced *j* as in *judge*.
dž	dż	dž	j as in *judge*.
d'	dź	đ, dj,	nearly *j* as in *jill* (or *dy*).
d + i		gj	

(Russian *ё* is pronounced yô as in English *yawl*. For example, *Orël*, ŏr-yôl´.)

	ę		ăN as in Fr. *fin*.
ě			yĕ as in *yet*.
h		h	(See *ch* above.)
j	j	j	y (consonant) as in *yes;* but when after a vowel and followed by a consonant, or final, it forms a diphthong: *ej* = ā (ay).
	i + vowel		
	ł		(Pronounce *ł* and *l*, like English *l*. See note on page xli below.)

(For Russian and Bulgarian *kh*, see *ch* above.)

l			when a vowel, pronounced as in English *cradle*.
ň	ń	nj	*ny* as in Sp. *cañón* (Fr. *gn*), almost English *canyon*.
n + i			
ou			ō as in *go*.
	ó		ŏŏ as in *pull* (or ōō as in *food*).
r	r	r	when a vowel, pronounced like Am. Eng. *err*, *ûr*. When a cons., pronounced as a trilled *r*.
ř			*rzh* (*r* + *zh* as below)
	rz		*zh*, the medial consonant of *leisure* and *pleasure*. When final in word or syllable it tends toward *sh* as in *show*.
	ś		*sh* as in *sheen* (or *sy*).
	s + i + vowel		
š	sz	š	*sh* as in *show*.
šč	szcz, ść	šč, šć	*sh* + *ch*. Compare English "ru*sh ch*icken." For convenience it may be simplified to *s* + *ch*.
(Russian and Bulgarian *shch*)			
t', t + i			nearly *ch* as in *chill* (or *ty*).
ů			ōō as in *food*.
	w		*v* as in *very*; when final *f* as in *off*.
(Russian and Bulgarian *v*)			
y, ý	y		ĭ as in *it* or ē as in *beet* or wē.
(Also Russian and Bulgarian *y*.)			
	z		*z* as in *zebra* except after *r*. See *rz*.
ž	ż	ž	*zh*, the medial consonant of *leisure* and *pleasure*. When final in word or syllable it may become *sh* as in *shall*.
	ź		*zh*, as described above (or *zy*).

Otherwise the letters have approximately the usual English values except that the voiced consonants (b, d, dz, dž, g, v, w, z, ž) tend, especially in Russian, to become the corresponding voiceless consonants (p, t, c, č, k, f, s, š) if followed by a voiceless consonant or if final. This tendency is not marked in Serb-Croat.

NOTE ON POLISH "Ł"

In English usage Polish ł and l should both be pronounced *l*, **not** *w* and *l* respectively. Polish speakers make a distinction between l and ł, something like the difference between the usual English *l*'s in *lip* and *old*. The question is whether this distinction is important enough for English speakers to use *w* for ł, as is the recommendation in many dictionaries.

Our consultants inform us that in the pronunciation of Polish cultivated by Polish radio announcers, singers, and clergymen, *l* and *ł*, though different, will be heard by English listeners as *l*. Polish friends say that *w* for *ł* sounds as odd to them as to other Americans. So *Łuck* should be simply lŏŏtsk (lutsk), which isn't too simple after all. And the learned can try to give this *ł* the quality of the *l* in *old*.

NOTE ON ENGLISH, FRENCH, AND GERMAN SPELLINGS

Because of the peculiarities of the Roman alphabets of Czechoslovak, Polish, and Serb-Croat, and in the absence of official Roman spellings of Russian and Bulgarian, the sounds of these languages may be spelled according to English, French, or German conventions. Accordingly we find *Drazha*, *Draja*, and *Drascha* for *Draža; Chetnik*, *Tchetnik*, and *Tschetnik* for *Četnik; Kiev* or *Kieff*, *Kiev* or *Kief*, and *Kijew; Lapats* and *Lapatz* for *Lapac;* and so on. *Moscow*, *Moscou*, and *Moskau* for *Moskva* (Rus. transliterated) show older variations of sound as well as of spelling.

For English speakers the English spellings are comparatively simple, though we need a better indication than *ë* for the sound yô in *Orël*. The French spellings sometimes mislead us, as for instance in *Chaliapin*, a Russian name that we should spell *Shalyapin*. Even the official British PCGN continues to use *j* with its French value in spelling *Jitomir*, which is familiar to American readers as *Zhitomir*. In our press dispatches the spelling of place names usually follows, within typographical limitations, the examples of the National Geographic Society, Webster's Dictionary, and other standard American reference works. Personal names, however, are often spelled as if they were French, because the French cultural tradition is strong in Europe and these names have not been respelled by the editors of our reference works.

NOTES ON RUSSIAN

Because of the gender of words understood but not expressed, the names of small villages may end in *a* (or *aya*), and the names of large villages in *o;* the names of cities may lack a suffix. As a community grows, it may pass through all three stages: *Gavrilova*, *Gavrilovo*, and *Gavrilov*. This and another picturesque habit—that of changing the names to honor new heroes—cause maps and sometimes dispatches to disagree. The forms preferred here are those of the recent map of the National Geographic Society.

The Russian *a*, stressed and unstressed, is here transcribed ä, though its quality may approach ŭ, the vowel of *but*, especially as pronounced by an Englishman. Whether the spelling *o* is to be rendered in phonetics ŏ, ô, ō, or ŭ is a problem that has confused makers of dictionaries. This editor has tried to follow a consistent practice, stressed *o* being usually rendered as ô, unstressed *o* as ŏ. Many phoneticians would prefer the use of ŭ for the sounds of *a* and unstressed *o*, but for the purpose of this list it seemed wise not to depart too far from present dictionary transcription and from customary spelling. Most Russian unstressed vowels in rapid speech will sound to a foreign ear like schwa.

Between a consonant and a following vowel, *y* is written to indicate a soft sign in the Russian Cyrillic spelling. If a vowel does not follow, *y* is written for the soft sign only with *l*, *m*, and *n*. A soft vowel is indicated by prefixing *y*, as in *Orel*, ŏr-yôl′. Russian *e* is "softer" to American ears than ě; hence the frequent spellings of *ie* and *ye* as in *Dniepr* for *Dnepr*; *Izvyestia* for *Izvestia*; and *Soviet*. In this list, however, *y* is not used to show this quality of *e*.

English *i* and *y* may stand for a diphthong in Russian. Here, however, it is usually transcribed ï.

SPANISH

Words ending in a vowel, or in *n* or *s*, stress the next to the last syllable. Words ending in a consonant, except *n* or *s*, stress the last syllable. Words not following these rules bear an accent mark. The *Pequeño Larousse Ilustrado*, in the second or encyclopedic half, shows the exceptional accents of almost all Spanish names that will appear in the news, e.g. *Ávila*, *Cárdenas*, *Nájera*.

Spanish		Explanation
b		See note on page xliv.
c	before e, i	*s* (Am. Sp.) as in *so*, or "th" (Castilian) as in *thin*.
	otherwise	*k* as in *koko*. Sp. *cocer*, kô-sĕr′ *or* -thĕr′; *acción*, äk-syôn′. The *k*-sound before *e* and *i* is indicated by *qu*, which see.
d	initial	very like English *d*.
	medial	*th* as in *gather*. Sp. *dedo*, dĕ′-thô. Anglicized as *d*.
	final and in *-ado*	*th* as in *gather*, or it may disappear, as is amiably illustrated in the last phrases of the song *La Paloma*. Anglicized as *d*.
g	before e, i	*h* as in *heat* (or a voiceless uvular sound similar to the voiced Parisian *r*.) Sp. *gente*, hĕn′-tĕ. For the *h*-sound before a, o, u, see *j*.
	otherwise	*g* as in *go*. Sp. *gato grande*, gä′-tô grän′-dĕ. See *gu*.
gu	before e, i	*g* as in *go*. Sp. *guerra*, gĕ′-rä. The *u* is silent.
	before a, o	voiced spirant *g* + *w*. Anglicized as *gw* or, esp. when intervocalic, *w*. Sp. *agua*, ä′-wä, *Guadalajara* (g)wä′-dä-lä-hä′-rä.
h		silent. Sp. *Chihuahua*, chē-wä′-wä.
j		*h* as in *hot* (or a voiceless uvular sound similar to the voiced Parisian *r*). Sp. *Jorge*, hôr′-hĕ.

ll	*y* (Am. Sp.) as in *yet*, or *ly* (Castilian) like *li* in Eng. *million* and like It. *gli*. In Argentina and Uruguay often *j* as in *just* or *zh*, the medial consonant of *leisure* and *pleasure*.
ñ	*ny* as in Eng. *canyon*, *ni* as in Eng. *onion*. Fr. and It. *gn*.
qu before e, i	*k* as in *kit*. Sp. *que*, kĕ′. This convention of silent *u* French shares, but not Italian. The *k*-sound before *a* and *o* is indicated by *c*, which see.
s	*s* as in *so*.
v	See note below.
x between vowels	ks. Sp. *éxito*, ĕk′-sē-tô.
before consonants	s. Sp. *extranjero*, ĕs-trän-hĕ′-rô.
for *j*	*h*, formerly *sh*. *México* or *Méjico*, mĕ′-hē-kô. *Oaxaca*, wä-hä′-kä. *Quixote* or *Quijote*, kē-hô′-tĕ, formerly kē-shô′-tĕ. *Jerez*, hĕ-rĕth′, formerly *Xeres*, shĕ′-rĕs. But *Xochimilco*, sô-chē-mēl′-kô *or* shô- *or* hô-.
y (consonant)	*y* as in *yes*. In Argentina and Uruguay often *j* as in *judge* or *zh*, the medial consonant of *leisure* and *pleasure*. Sp. *yo*, yô; Arg., Urug. jô *or* zhô.

VOWELS AND DIPHTHONGS

Weak vowels *i* (*y*) and *u* combine with strong vowels *a*, *e*, *o* and with one another to form diphthongs. In these the strong vowel takes the stress or, in the case of *iu* and *ui*, the second vowel. Sp. *Teruel*, tĕ-rwĕl′; *baile*, bī′-lĕ; *hay*, ī′; *Ruiz*, rwēs′ *or* rwēth′. Exceptions are indicated by an accent. Sp. *Pía*, pē′-ä.

Strong vowels remain distinct from one another. Spanish *creer*, crĕ-ĕr′; *faena*, fä-ĕ′-nä; *Saavedra*, sä′-ä-vĕ′-*th*rä. See also p. xlvii.

NOTE ON "B" AND "V"

b is usually a spirant sound like English *v* but made with both lips instead of the lower lip and the upper teeth. It is like *b* (*bb*) in our southern dialect pronunciation of *river*, often spelled "ribber." In Spanish, *b* and *v* are alternatives in spelling. They are usually Anglicized, however, as English *b* and English *v* respectively, according to the Spanish form most familiar in English; e.g., *Havana* rather than *Habana*.

CASTILIAN AS A STANDARD

American Spanish is related to Castilian Spanish much as American English is related to the "Received Standard" of England. In the new world, the dialects of Spanish provinces, particularly in southern Spain, and the Midland dialects of England formed the basis of the Spanish of Latin American capitals and the American English of the great cities of the United States. Thus what had been provincial speech in the homelands became metropolitan speech in America. Meanwhile in Spain the dialect of Castile and in England the dialect of London literary and political circles gained still more prestige at the expense of provincial dialects. At home the provincial accents more or less lost the battle, in the former colonies they won it. However, Castilian Spanish still has a prestige in the Spanish-speaking world that may seem curious to the proud or satisfied speakers of American English. If you ask the correct pronunciation of the Spanish name of a prominent leader, it will often be given in the Castilian form without regard to the speech of his constituents. Thus recently the female secretaries of both President Quezon and Senator Chavez gave me a detailed description of the Castilian quality of z in these names, although it is rare in the Rio Grande Valley and in the Philippines. But this phenomenon is not exactly parallel to an American's acquiring a broad a, for a remarkable number of non-Castilian speakers of Spanish regard Castilian as the standard. If you ask for a pronunciation, they wish to give you the best. Nevertheless this courtesy complicates the making of dictionaries where what is current in educated speech of the region is "standard" and "correct." For American radio the Spanish American s for c and z is certainly preferable for programs concerned with Spanish America. In pronouncing the names of famous cities and persons in Spain the circumstances of the broadcast should determine the accent.

SPANISH IN THE PHILIPPINES

The popular languages of the Philippines are Indonesian or Austronesian. Tagalog is especially important. English and Spanish are predominantly the languages of the schools, the government, and the churches. Place names and family names are Hispanicized Indonesian or Spanish. Spanish has controlled the spelling of the local languages, which, in turn, have probably influenced the pronunciation of Spanish in the Philippines.

a in unaccented syllables tends to become schwa (the a of *about* and of *sofa*).

c before e and i, and z are pronounced s rather than "th" as in *thin*. d has less tendency to become *th*.

SWEDISH. See *Scandinavian Languages*

THAI or SIAMESE

Like Chinese, Thai is a tonal language with at least five, and in some dialects, seven tones. As the tone changes, the meaning of a syllable is changed. There is no accent in the English sense, but to our ear the tone itself, especially the high-pitched tone, may give the impression of an accent. Accent marks have here been used to assist pronunciation or at least to prevent greater mispronunciation.

One characteristic that Thai shares with English is a number of seemingly useless letters in its spelling. Some of the pronunciations here set forth may arouse disbelief, but our consultant, the Rev. Paul A. Eakin of Bangkok, said them so, and he was born there. Moreover I have found no one to say him nay. Mr. Eakin writes, "Each tone is indicated in the written language by combinations of different class consonants with long and short vowels and by use of about three tonal marks placed over the syllable. There are definite rules for tones, and there are practically no exceptions. Difficulties arise mainly in connection with the 'silent' letters, which are retained in words originating in the Pali or Sanskrit to indicate the origin of the word. The alphabet is an adaptation of the Cambodian script existing in the middle of the thirteenth century. It contains some 44 consonants and as many vowel sounds. Since there are but 21 consonant sounds, this means that in many cases one sound is represented by several letters. The Thai Government is attempting to reduce the number of these consonants and so simplify the alphabet." See also Thomas A. Sebeok, "The Languages of Southeastern Asia," *The Far Eastern Quarterly*, August, 1943. There is no distinction between White Thai and Black Thai.

l, r, y, when final in a syllable, have the sound of *n.*

ch, chj, d, dt, s, st, when final in a syllable, have the sound of *t.*

b, bp, when final in a syllable, have the sound of *p.*

ph is pronounced *p.*

th is pronounced *t.*

TURKISH

Turkish has no accent in the English sense of the word. The stresses here marked will serve to prevent misstressing, if they are not over-emphasized, but they may be ignored in favor of a level pronunciation— so far as that is possible in an English sentence. The Turkish informants did not recommend a slight accent upon final syllables, but this device in English may prevent the obscuring of vowels.

The circumflex is a sign of length and in the case of â it may indicate the sound *yah.*

Turkish	Explanation
c	*j* as in *just.*
ç	*ch* as in *church.*
g	*g* as in *go.*
ğ after a, i, o, u ("hard" vowels)	silent or a voiced sound similar to *ch* in Scottish *loch* and German *ach.*

[xlvi]

ǧ after e, i, ö, ü ("soft" vowels)	forms a diphthong: eǧ = ā [ay]; öǧ = ǔĭ; üǧ = üĭ; iǧ is practically ē.
before vowels	y as in *you*.
i (with dot)	ē as in *beet* or ĭ as in *sit*.
ı (without dot)	ĭ as in *bit*. (The Turkish sound, called "hoarse," "guttural," and "retracted," has no equivalent in English. It lies between ĭ and û. It may be transcribed schwa.)
j	zh, the medial consonant of *leisure* and *pleasure*.
ş	sh as in *shall*.
y	y introducing a diphthong, as in *you*, and y (or ĭ) completing a diphthong, as in *joy, oil, day, aid*.

A NOTE ON THE TRANSCRIPTION OF "E" AND "O"

English ĕ (eh) is usually preferable to English ā (ay) to indicate the pronunciation of French *é* and the close *e* of many other non-Germanic languages. The diphthongal character of English ā (ay), and its inevitable stress and length, is more painful than a failure to distinguish close and open *e*'s, at least in the pronunciation of occasional foreign names in an English context. The use of ĕ (eh) rather than ā (ay) is a departure from the practice of *War Words* (1st edition)—made at some cost. It was necessary when one heard on the same program the French learned in America and the French learned, by Americans, in France.

The use of ĕ (eh) rather than ā (ay) may also help to change the notion that every Italian *e* should be pronounced ā. The pronunciation of *Enna* as ā'-nä (ay'-nah), was the most unfortunate episode of the Sicilian verbal campaign. Insistence upon ĕ (eh) as the value of Italian *e* will extend to *Grosseto* and *Velletri*, where the vowel certainly is close, but in a stressed open syllable the symbol ĕ, interpreted by American speakers with our usual linguistic habits, may be sounded not too far from a close *e*. In any case this must be our reliance if we are to avoid a greater error.

Likewise ĕ (eh) has been preferred to ā (ay) in the transcription of Slavic languages. In the case of Russian, ā (ay) for stressed *e* and ĕ (eh) for unstressed *e*, worked well enough, but when it was necessary to devise a system for names in all the Slavic languages, it seemed better to use one symbol for stressed and unstressed *e*. If one symbol is used, ĕ (eh) is better than ā (ay).

The sound of ō as in *go* in American English is diphthongal ōŏ́, in British English triphthongal or more. The associations of ô as it may occur in *orb, more, often, all* are nearer than ō to the sounds spelled *o* in many foreign languages.

At any time, of course, one could have adopted or devised special symbols for these foreign sounds. They would, however, have no special meaning for the users of this handbook. To the contrary, elaboration of symbols, a comfort to phoneticians, usually confuses and discourages everybody who has not a technical interest in phonetic problems. One man's meat is another man's person, as they say in New York.

USEFUL REFERENCE WORKS

The following reference books are all but indispensable for a study of American and English pronunciation:

American College Dictionary (New York, 1947).

British Broadcasting Corporation, *Broadcast English* (London, 1932-1939). Seven pamphlets prepared for the BBC by A. Lloyd James.

Canadian Broadcasting Corporation, *Handbook for Announcers* (Ottawa, 1942). For Canadian place names.

Columbia Encyclopedia, The (New York, 1935).

Fowler, H. W., *A Dictionary of Modern English Usage* (Oxford, 1926).

Funk, Charles E., *What's the Name, Please?* (New York, 1936).

Funk and Wagnalls' College Standard Dictionary (New York, 1947).

Funk and Wagnalls' New Standard Dictionary (New York, 1925).

Holt, Alfred H., *American Place Names* (New York, 1938).

Jones, Daniel, *An English Pronouncing Dictionary* (4th ed., New York, 1937).

Kenyon, J. S., *American Pronunciation* (8th ed., Ann Arbor, Mich., 1940).

Kenyon, J. S., and Knott, T. A., *A Pronouncing Dictionary of American English* (Springfield, Mass., 1944).

Krapp, G. P., *The English Language in America* (New York, 1925).

Mawson, C. O. Sylvester, *International Book of Names* (New York, 1933).

[Oxford], *The Concise Oxford Dictionary of Current English* (1934).
The Shorter Oxford English Dictionary on Historical Principles (1945).

Permanent Committee on Geographical Names for British Official Use, *Lists* (Royal Geographical Society, London).

Thorndike-Century Senior Dictionary (New York, 1941).

U. S. Board on Geographical Names, *Reports* (Washington, D. C.)

Webster's Biographical Dictionary (Springfield, Mass., 1943).

Webster's New International Dictionary (2d. ed., Springfield, Mass., 1934), as interpreted by its prefatory "Guide to Pronunciation" (pp. xxii-lxxviii). Section 277 (pp. lix *ff*) lists for about 1100 debatable words the pronunciations given in seven authoritative dictionaries.

Who's Who in America (Chicago, 1944, 1946).

Wyld, H. C. *The Universal English Dictionary* (London and New York, 1932).

Consult also the files of the journal *American Speech*.

Announcers and program directors will find useful the following abridged dictionaries of French, German and Spanish:

Cassell's New French-English and English-French Dictionary (New York, 1930).

Cassell's New German-English and English-German Dictionary (New York, 1936, 1939).

Nouveau Petit Larousse Illustré (Paris, 1943).

Pequeño Larousse Ilustrado (Paris, 1938).

The Cassell volumes have pronunciations indicated in the alphabet of the International Phonetic Association. *Petit Larousse* includes a small encyclopedia which lists many of the French names that appear in scripts, and exceptions to standard rules of French pronunciation are marked. *Pequeño Larousse* has a similar encyclopedia of Spanish.

INDEX TO ABBREVIATIONS

The symbols > and < are used for *to* and *from*. A question
mark is added where the sovereignty is still undecided.

Afghan.	Afghanistan	Flem.	Flemish
Afr.	Africa, African	for.	foreign
Ala.	Alabama	Fr.	France, French
Alb.	Albania, Albanian	Fr. Eq. Afr.	French Equatorial Africa
Alg.	Algeria		
Am.	American	Fr. Som.	French Somaliland
arch.	archipelago	Fr. W. Afr.	French West Africa
Arg.	Argentina	Ga.	Georgia
Ark.	Arkansas	Ger.	Germany, German
Austral.	Australia	gov.	government
Baluch.	Baluchistan	Gr.	Greece, Greek
Belg.	Belgium, Belgian	Guat.	Guatemala, Guatemalan
Bol.	Bolivia, Bolivian		
Br., Brit.	British	Hond.	Honduras, Honduran
Braz.	Brazilian		
Bulg.	Bulgaria, Bulgarian	Hung.	Hungary, Hungarian
Calab.	Calabria	Icel.	Iceland, Icelandic
Calif.	California	Ill.	Illinois
Can.	Canada, Canadian	Ind.	Indiana
Ch.	China	Ind. Oc.	Indian Ocean
co.	county	Indo.	Indonesian
col.	colony	Indo-Ch.	Indo-China
Col.	Colorado	Iran.	Iranian
collab.	collaborator with the Axis powers	isl., isls.	island, islands
		It.	Italy, Italian
Colom.	Colombia	Jap.	Japan, Japanese
Conn.	Connecticut	Kan.	Kansas
cons.	consonant	Kor.	Korea, Korean
Cz.	Czechoslovakia	La.	Louisiana
Del.	Delaware	L. I.	Long Island
Den.	Denmark, Danish	Liecht.	Liechtenstein
dist.	district	Lith.	Lithuania, Lithuanian
Dodec.	Dodecanese Isls.		
Dom. Rep.	Dominican Republic	Lux.	Luxemburg
Du.	Dutch	Madag.	Madagascar
Du. W. I.	Dutch West Indies	Manchu.	Manchuria
E. Afr.	East Africa	Mass.	Massachusetts
Ecuador.	Ecuadorian	Md.	Maryland
Eng.	England, English	Mex.	Mexico
Est.	Estonia, Estonian	Mich.	Michigan
Europ.	European	Minn.	Minnesota
Fil.	Filipino	Miss.	Mississippi
Fin.	Finland, Finnish	Mo.	Missouri

[1]

Mon.	Monaco	P. R.	Puerto Rico, Puerto Rican
Mont.	Montana	Pres.	President
Mor.	Morocco	protec.	protectorate
Mozam.	Mozambique	prov.	province
mt.	mountain	repub.	republic
N.	North	Rh.	Rhodes
nat. pk.	national park	riv.	river
N. B.	New Brunswick, Can.	Rum.	Rumania, Rumanian
N. C.	North Carolina	Rus.	Russia, Russian
N. D.	North Dakota	S.	South
N. E.	North East	S. A.	South America
NEI	Netherlands East Indies	S. Afr.	South Africa, South African
Neth.	Netherlands	Salv.	El Salvador, Salvadoran
Nev.	Nevada		
Newf.	Newfoundland	Sans.	Sanscrit
N. H.	New Hampshire	Sard.	Sardinia
Nicar.	Nicaragua, Nicaraguan	S. C.	South Carolina
		S.-C.	Serb-Croat
N. Ire.	Northern Ireland	S. D.	South Dakota
N. J.	New Jersey	Scot.	Scotland, Scottish
N. Mex.	New Mexico	sg.	singular
Nor.	Norway, Norwegian	Siam.	Siamese
N. Y.	New York	Som.	Somaliland
N. Z.	New Zealand	Sp.	Spain, Spanish
Oc.	Oceania	Sp. Mor.	Spanish Morocco
oc.	occasionally	str.	strait
Ont.	Ontario, Can.	Sw.	Sweden, Swedish
Ore.	Oregon	S. W. Afr.	South-West Africa
Pa.	Pennsylvania	Switz.	Switzerland
Pac.	Pacific	Tenn.	Tennessee
Pal.	Palestine, Palestinian	Tex.	Texas
Pan.	Panama, Panamanian	Tun.	Tunisia
		Turk.	Turkey, Turkish
Para.	Paraguay, Parguayan	Ukrain.	Ukrainian
		U. of S. A.	Union of South Africa
PCGN	Permanent Committee on Geographical Names for British Official Use	Urug.	Uruguay, Uruguayan
		U. S.	United States
		U. S. A.	United States Army
		U. S. N.	United States Navy
pen.	peninsula	Va.	Virginia
Per.	Persian	Ven.	Venezuela
Peru.	Peruvian	Vt.	Vermont
P. I.	Philippine Islands	W. Afr.	West Africa
pl.	plural	Wash.	Washington
Pol.	Poland, Polish	W. Asia	West Asia
polit.	political leader, political	W. I.	West Indies
		Wis.	Wisconsin
Port.	Portugal, Portuguese	Yugosl.	Yugoslavia

KEYS TO PRONUNCIATION

IN THE first column is the word to be pronounced. In the second column the pronunciation is given by a simplified Websterian alphabet, and in the third column by a phonetic respelling without special accents.

The symbols of the second column, except ə, should present no difficulty to those who are familiar with American dictionaries. The symbol ə, which is named *schwa*, is used for unstressed vowels, however spelled, which in speech are sounded "uh"—for example, *a*bout, tak*e*n, penc*i*l, lem*o*n, circ*u*s.

The spelling of the third column should be self-evident. With only two or three exceptions the letters have customary *English* values. "*Th*" (italic) is the initial sound of *then:* "th" (roman) is the initial sound of *thin*.

There is often no exact equivalent in English for the sounds of foreign languages. Therefore the symbols in the third group (Foreign Sounds) are only desperate reachings for a sign that will suggest to an American a sound not too far removed from the foreignism. See also the discussions in the Introduction.

The accent mark is placed after the syllable to be stressed. Where it is difficult to decide which syllable more often bears the principal stress of a word, both syllables have been accented. No orthographic distinction is made between primary and secondary accents. In American speech the distinction is idiomatic and will usually take care of itself. For Chinese and Korean, no accent is indicated unless the word has been Anglicized. In foreign words the stress accent should not be emphasized.

ENGLISH VOWELS

Key Word	Key 1	Key 2
*a*t, b*a*ton	ăt′, bă-tŏn′	at′, ba-ton′
*a*te	āt′	ayt′
f*a*ther	fä′-*th*ər	fah′-*th*uhr
c*a*re	kăr′	kehr′
*e*vent	ĭ-vĕnt′	i-vent′
*e*ve	ēv′	eev′
th*e*re	th*ĕ*r′	*th*ehr′
c*i*ty	sĭt′-ĭ	sit′-i
f*e*ar	fĭr′	fihr′
*i*ce	īs′	ais′
*o*dd	ŏd′	od′
g*o*	gō′	goh′

Key Word	Key 1	Key 2
awe	ô′	o′ or aw′
pull	po͝ol′	pul′
pool	po͞ol′	pool′
but	bŭt′	buht′
urn	ûrn′ or ərn′	uhrn′
use	yo͞os′	yoos′
oil	oil′	oil′
out	out′	aut′
above, sofa, further, taken, charity, convey, until	ə (*schwa*)	uh

ENGLISH CONSONANTS

	Key 1	Key 2
chat	chăt′	chat′
get	gĕt′	get′
jet	jĕt′	jet′
singer	sĭng′-ər	sing′-uhr
finger	fĭng′-gər	fing′-guhr
pleasure	plĕzh′-ər	plezh′-uhr
thin	thĭn′	thin′
this	thĭs′	this′
yet	yĕt′	yet′

The other consonant symbols have the usual English value.

FOREIGN SOUNDS

	Key 1	Key 2	Often Anglicized
Fr. sud	süd′	süd′	o͞o or ū as in *rude*
Fr. peur	pûr′	pœr′	û as in *purr*
Fr. bon	bôN′	boN′	ôn as in *wrong*
Fr. fin	făN′	faN′	ăn as in *sang*
Du. huis	hûĭs′	hœis′	oi as in *hoist*
Scot. loch	lôk(h)′	lok(h)′	k (*or* ck) as in *lock*
Sp. cañón	kä-nyôn′	kah-nyon′	ny as in *canyon*
It. gli	lyē′	lyee′	ly (*or* li) as in *million*

See the Introduction for descriptions of foreign sounds.

RECOMMENDED PRONUNCIATIONS

RECOMMENDED PRONUNCIATIONS

a   ə   uh

The indefinite article *a* should be pronounced schwa [ə], not ā, in order to give the effect of speech and not of awkward, even childish reading aloud. There is of course a place for an emphatic ā-pronunciation of even an indefinite article, but this headline style is seldom safe from abuse, and it is an awkward way of securing emphasis. Stressing the article breaks up the characteristic pattern of spoken English, and radio speakers do this at the risk of losing their audience.

aa, å

The spelling *aa* in Danish represents the sound ô. The same spelling was formerly common in Norway, but has now largely given way to the Swedish spelling å, which is pronounced more like ō. (There are many Swedish place names in Finland.) In Dutch and German *aa* is pronounced *ah* (as in *father*).

Aa (Neth., riv.)	ä′	ah′
Aabenraa (Den.)	ô′-bən-rô′	o′-buhn-ro′
Aabo (Fin.)	See *Åbo.*	
Aachen (Ger.)	ä′-k(h)ən	ah′-k(h)uhn
French *Aix la Chapelle*, ĕks lä shä-pĕl′ [eks lah shah-pel′].		
Aagtekerke (Neth.)	äk(h)′-tə-kĕr′-kə	ahk(h)′-tuh-kehr′-kuh
Aahus (Sw.)	See *Åhus.*	
Aal (Nor.)	ôl′	ol′
Aaland (Fin.)	See *Åland.*	
Aalborg (Den.)	ôl′-bôr	ol′-bor
Aalen (Ger.)	ä′-lən	ah′-luhn
Aalesund (Nor.)	ô′-lə-sŏŏn	o′-luh-sun
Aalsmeer (Neth.)	äls′-mär	ahls′-mayr
Aalst (Belg.)	älst′	ahlst′
French *Alost*, ä-lôst′ [ah-lost′].		
Aalten (Neth.)	äl′-tən	ahl′-tuhn
Aamli (Nor.)	ôm′-lē	om′-lee
Aamot (Nor.)	ô′-mŏŏt	o′-mut
Aandalsnes (Nor.)	ôn′-däls-nĕs	on′-dahls-nes
aan Zee	än zā′	ahn zay′
An element, meaning *by the sea*, in Dutch place names.		
Aar *or* Aare (Switz., riv.)	är′ *or* ä′-rə	ahr′ *or* ah′-ruh
Aarau (Switz.)	är′-ou	ahr′-au

[1]

Aardal (Nor.)	ôr'-däl	or'-dahl
Aarhus (Den.)	ôr'-hōōs	or'-hoos
Aarle (Neth.)	är'-lə	ahr'-luh
Aasgaardsstrand (Nor.)	ôs'-gôrs-strän	os'-gors-strahn
Aavasaksa (Fin.)	ä'-vä-säk-sä	ah'-vah-sahk-sah
Abadan (Iran)	*Per.* ä-bä-dän'	ah-bah-dahn'
	Eng. ăb-ă-dăn'	ab-a-dan'
Abagaituev (Rus.)	ä-bä-gī-tōō'-yĕf	ah-bah-gai-too'-yef
Abaiang (Oc., Gilberts)	ä-bī'-äng	ah-bai'-ahng
Abakan (Rus.)	ä-bä-kän'	ah-bah-kahn'
Abau (New Guinea, Papua)	ä'-bou	ah'-bau
Abava (Latvia, riv.)	ä'-bä-vä	ah'-bah-vah
Abaya (Ethiopia)	ä'-bä-yä	ah'-bah-yah
Abbadia (It.)	äb-bä-dē'-ä	ahb-bah-dee'-ah
Abbai (Ethiopia, riv.)	äb'-bī'	ahb'-bai'
In Sudan, the *Blue Nile.*		
Abbeville	*Eng.* ăb'-ĭ-vĭl	ab'-i-vil
	Fr. äb-vēl'	ahb-veel'
Abbottabad (India)	ăb'-ə-tə-băd'	ab'-uh-tuh-bad'
Abd el Krim	*Eng.* ăb' dĕl krĭm'	ab' del krim'
(Moorish polit.)	*Arabic* äb' dōōl kə-rēm'	ahb' duhl kuh-reem'
Abdoude Baambrugge	äp-kou'-də bäm'-	ahp-kau'-duh bahm'-
(Neth.)	brûk(h)-ə	brœk-uh
Abdul Ghaffar Khan	äb'-dōōl gä-fär'	ahb'-dul gah-fahr'
(Afghan polit.)	kän'	kahn'
Or k(h)ä-fär' k(h)än' [k(h)ah-fahr' k(h)ahn']		
Abdul Hosayn Aziz	äb'-dōōl hŭ-sän'	ahb'-dul huh-sayn'
(Afghan polit.)	ä-zēz'	ah-zeez'
Abdul Hussein Aziz	äb'-dōōl hōōs-sän	ahb'-dul hus-sayn'
(Afghan polit.)	ä-zēz'	ah-zeez'
Abdullah al Suleiman *or*	äb-dōōl-lä' äl	ahb-dul-lah' ahl
Sulayman	sōō-lä-män'	soo-lay-mahn'
(Saudi Arabia, leader)		
Abdullah Ibn Hussein	äb-dōōl-lä' ĭb'n	ab-dul-lah' ib'n
(King of Trans-Jordan)	hōōs-sän'	hus-sayn'
Abdul Majid	äb'-dōōl mə-jēd'	ahb'-dul muh-jeed'
(Afghan polit.)		
Abdul Rahman Azzam	äb'-dōōl rä-män'	ahb'-dul rah-mahn'
Pasha (Arab polit.)	ä-zäm' pä'-shä	ah-zahm' pah'-shah
Abe, Isoo (Jap. polit.)	ä-bĕ', ē-sô'-ô'	ah-beh', ee-so'-o'
Abe, Yoshishige	ä-bĕ', yô-shē'-shē-gĕ	ah-beh', yo-shee'-
(Jap. educator)		shee-geh
Abemama (Oc., Gilberts)	ä-bĕ-mä'-mä	ah-beh-mah'-mah

Abernethy, Thomas G.   ăb′-ər-nĕth-ĭ   ab′-uhr-neth-i
  (U.S. representative)
Aberystwith (Wales)   *Eng.* ăb′-ə-rĭst′-wĭth   ab′-uh-rist′-with
     Welsh ä-bər-ŭst′-wĭth   ah-buhr-uhst′-with
Abganerovo (Rus.)   äb-gä-nĕ′-rŏ-vŏ   ahb-gah-neh′-ro-vo
  Also called *Abganerova.*
Abi Addi (Ethiopia)   ä′-byäd′-dē   ah′-byahd′-dee
Abimolong (P.I., riv.)   ä-bē-mô-lông′   ah-bee-mo-long′
Abkhazia (Rus., repub.)   *Eng.* ăb-kăz′-ĭ-ə   ab-kaz′-i-uh
     Rus. äb-hä′-zĭ-yä   ahb-hah′-zi-yah
Abkoude (Neth.)   äp-kou′-də   ahp-kau′-duh
Abkoude Proosdij (Neth.)   äp-kou′-də prōs′-dī   ahp-kau′-duh prohs′-
     dai
Ablis (Fr.)   ä-blē′   ah-blee′
Åbo (Fin.)   *Sw.* ō′-bōō   oh′-boo
  Finnish *Turku,* q.v.
Aboul *or* Abul (Arab   ä-bōōl′   ah-bool′
  name)
Abra de Ílog (P.I.)   ä′-brä dĕ ē′-lôg   ah′-brah deh ee′-log
Abreschwiller (Fr.)   äb-rĕsh-vē-lĕr′   ahb-resh-vee-lehr′
Abrud (Rum.)   ä-brōōd′   ah-brud′
  Hungarian *Abrudbánya,* ŏb′-rōōd-bä′-nyŏ [ob′-rud-bah′-nyo].
absorb, -ing   ăb-sŏrb′, -ĭng   ab-sorb′, -ing
  The *s* should not be pronounced *z.*
abu   ə-bōō *or* ä′-bōō   uh-boo′ *or* ah′-boo
  An element, meaning *father,* in Arabic personal names. Western
  Arabic *bou,* bōō′.
Abu Hashaifa (Egypt)   ä′-bōō hä-shī′-fä   ah′-boo hah-shai′-fah
Abukir (Egypt)   ä-bōō-kēr′   ah-bu-keer′
Abul Mo-iz Abdul Satar   ä-bōōl′ mō-ĭz′   ah-bool′ moh-iz′
  (Arab leader)   äb′-dŏŏl sə-tär′   ahb′-dul suh-tahr′
Abúyog (P.I.)   ä-bōō′-yôg   ah-boo′-yog
Abyssinia (Afr.)   ăb′-ĭ-sĭn′-ĭ-ə   ab′-i-sin′-i-uh
  Official English *Ethiopia,* q.v.
Acapulco (Mex.)   ä-kä-pōōl′-kô   ah-kah-pool′-ko
Acciarello (It.)   ät-chä-rĕl′-lô   aht-chah-rel′-lo
Accra (Gold Coast)   ə-krä′ *or* ăk′-rə   uh-krah′ *or* ak′-ruh
Achaia and Elis   *Eng.* ə-kā′-yə *and*   uh-kay′-yuh *and*
  (Gr.)   ē′-lĭs   ee′-lis
  Also called in English *Achaea,* ə-kē′-ə [uh-kee′-uh]. Greek *Achaia kai*
  Elis, ä-hī′-ä kĕ ē′-lēs [ah-hai′-ah keh ee′-lees].
Achaia kai Elis (Gr.)   ä-hī′-ä kĕ ē′-lēs   ah-hai′-ah keh ee′-lees
  Also called in English *Achaea,* ə-kē′-ə [uh-kee′-uh].
Achain (Fr.)   ä-shăN′   ah-shaN′

Acheloos (Gr., riv.)   ä-hĕ-lô′-ôs   ah-heh-lo′-os

Acheux (Fr.)   ä-shû′   ah-shœ′

Achinsk (Rus.)   ä′-chĭnsk   ah′-chinsk

Achkel (Tun., lake)   äsh′-kĕl   ahsh′-kel
  Also called *Garaet Achkel*, q.v.

Achtkarspelen (Neth.)   äk(h)t′-kär′-spǝ-lǝn   ahk(h)t′-kahr′-spuh-
                    luhn

Achuev (Rus.)   ä-cho͞o′-yĕf   ah-choo′-yef

Achzib (Pal.) See *Ez Zib*.

Acireale (Sicily)   ä′-chē-rĕ-ä′-lĕ   ah′-chee-reh-ah′-leh

Acker, Achille Van (Belg. polit.) See *Van Acker, Achille*.

Acoma (N.M.)   *Eng.* ăk′-ǝ-mǝ   ak′-uh-muh
              Sp. ä′-kô-mä   ah′-ko-mah
  The erroneous pronunciation ă-kō′-mǝ [a-koh′-muh] is occasionally
heard even in New Mexico.

Acquapendente (It.)   äk-kwä-pĕn-dĕn′-tĕ   ahk-kwah-pen-den′-
                    teh

Acre (Brazil)   ä′-krĭ   ah′-kri

Acre (Pal.)   ā′-kǝr *or* ä′-kǝr   ay′-kuhr *or* ah′-kuhr

Acroceraunia (Alb., pen.)   *Eng.* ăk′-rô-sĭ-rô′-nĭ-ǝ ak′-ro-si-ro′-ni-uh
  Albanian *Karaburun*, q.v.   See also Cape *Glossa*.

acronym   ăk′-rǝ-nĭm   ak′-ruh-nim

Ada (Yugosl.)   ä′-dä   ah′-dah

Adak (Alaska, isl.)   ā′-dăk   ay′-dak

Adalia (Turk.)   ǝ-däl′-ĭ-ǝ   uh-dahl′-i-uh
  Also called *Antalya*, q.v.

Adamawa (Nigeria)   ä-dä-mä′-wä   ah-dah-mah′-wah

Adanà (It., riv.)   ä-dä-nä′   ah-dah-nah′

Adana (Turk.)   ä′-dä-nä   ah′-dah-nah

Adapazarı (Turk.)   ä-dä-pä-zä′-rĭ   ah-dah-pah-zah′-ri

Addes, George F.   ăd′-ĭs   ad′-is
  (Am. labor leader)

Addis Ababa (Ethiopia)   *Eng.* ăd′-ĭs ăb′-ǝ-bǝ   ad′-is ab′-uh-buh
              native äd-dēs ä-bǝ-bä   ahd-dees ah-buh-bah

Addis Alem (Ethiopia)   *Eng.* ăd′-ĭs ăl′-ǝm   ad′-ĭs al′-uhm
              native äd-dēs ä-lǝm   ahd-dees ah-luhm

Adelup (Oc., Guam)   ä-dĕ-lo͞op′   ah-deh-loop′

Adem, el (Libya)   ă′-dĕm, ĕl   a′-dem, el

Aden (Arabia)   ā′-dǝn *or* ä′-dǝn   ay′-duhn *or* ah′-duhn

Adernò (Sicily)   ä-dĕr-nô′   ah-dehr-no′

Adige (It., riv.)   ä′-dē-jĕ   ah′-dee-jeh

Adigrat (Ethiopia)   *Eng.* ăd-ĭ-grät′   ad-i-grat′
              native ä-dē-grät   ah-dee-graht

ad infinitum   ăd′ ĭn′-fǝ-nĭ′-tǝm   ad′ in′-fuh-nai′-tuhm
           or äd′ ēn-fē-nē′-   ahd′ een-fee-nee′-

      to͞om   toom

Adjidarmo (Indo. polit.)	ä-jē-där′-mô	ah-jee-dahr′-mo
Adler (Rus.)	äd′-lər	ahd′-luhr
Adone (It., mt.)	ä-dô′-nĕ	ah-do′-neh
Adour (Fr., riv.)	ä-dōor′	ah-door′
Adowa (Ethiopia) See *Aduwa.*		
Adrano (Sicily)	ä-drä′-nô	ah-drah′-no
Adrianople (Turk.)	*Eng.* ā′-drĭ-ə-nō′-pəl	ay′-dri-uh-noh′-puhl
Turkish *Edirne*, q.v.		
Aduard (Neth.)	ä′-dü-ärt	ah′-dü-ahrt
Aduwa (Ethiopia)	ä′-dōō-wä	ah′-du-wah
advertisement	ăd′-vər-tīz′-mənt	ad′-vuhr-taiz′-muhnt
	or ăd-vûr′-tĭs-mənt	ad-vuhr′-tis-muhnt

The first is the pronunciation of most educated Americans and is therefore preferable for network usage. It is placed first by the *Thorndike-Century Senior Dictionary* (1941), and by Kenyon and Knott (1944).

Adžibegovac, Stari (Yugosl.)	ä′-jĭ-bĕ′-gô-väts	ah′-ji-beh′-go-vahts
Æbeltoft (Den.)	ĕ′-bəl-tôft	eh′-buhl-toft
Aegadian Isles (It.)	*Eng.* ĭ-gā′-dĭ-ən	i-gay′-di-uhn
Italian *Egadi*, q.v.		
Aegean Sea	ĭ-jē′-ən	i-jee′-uhn
Aegina (Gr.)	*Eng.* ĭ-jī′-nə	i-jai′-nuh
Greek *Aigina*, ā′-yē-nä [ay′-yee-nah].		
aelurophobe, -phile	ĭ-lōō′-rō-fōb′, -fīl′	i-loo′-roh-fohb′, -fail′
Cat-hater, -lover. Also spelled ailuro-.		
aerial	ăr′-ĭ-əl	ehr′-i-uhl

The old learned pronunciation ā-ē′-rĭ-əl has been displaced as the word has become popular. The first syllable of ăr′-ĭ-əl, the common pronunciation today, is to be pronounced like the word *air*. It should not be pronounced ăr.

Æroe *or* Ærö (Den., isl.)	ĕr′-û	ehr′-œ
aeroplane	ăr′-ə-plān′	ehr′-uh-playn′

The spelling *aeroplane* and its pronunciations have been displaced generally by the dissyllable *airplane*, ăr′-plān [ehr′-playn]. Sometimes the old-fashioned spelling *aeroplane* is given the pronunciation of *airplane*.

Aerschot (Belg.)	är′-sk(h)ôt	ahr′-sk(h)ot
Aetolia and Acarnania (Gr.)	*Eng.* ē-tō′-lĭ-ə *and* ăk′-ər-nā′-nĭ-ə	ee-toh′-li-uh *and* ak′-uhr-nay′-ni-uh
Greek *Aitolia kai Akarnania*, ĕ-tô-lē′-ä kĕ ä-kär-nä-nē′-ä [eh-to-lee′-ah keh ah-kahr-nah-nee′-ah].		
Aetos (Gr.)	ä-ĕ-tôs′	ah-eh-tos′
Affile (It.)	äf-fē′-lĕ	ahf-fee′-leh
‘Affule (Pal.)	äf-fōō′-lĕ	ahf-foo′-leh

Afghanistan (W. Asia)	ăf-găn'-ĭ-stăn	af-gan'-i-stan
	or ăf-gän'-ĭ-stän'	af-gahn'-i-stahn'
Afifi (Egypt. polit.) See *Hafez Afifi Pasha.*		
Aftonbladet	äf'-tōōn-blah'-dĕt	ahf'-toon-blah'-det
(Sw. newspaper)		
Afyon Karahisar (Turk.)	äf-yōōn' kä-rä-hĭ-	ahf-yoon' kah-rah-hi -
	sär'	sahr'
Also called *Karahisar*, q.v.		
Aga (Rus.)	ä-gä'	ah-gah'
Agadir (Mor.)	ä-gä-dēr'	ah-gah-deer'
Aga Khan (Indian polit.)	ä'-gə k(h)än'	ah'-guh k(h)ahn'
Agaña (Guam)	ä-gä'-nyä	ah-gah'-nyah
Agar, Herbert S.	ā'-gär	ay'-gahr
(Am. editor)		
Agareb (Tun.)	ä'-gä-rĕb	ah'-gah-reb
Agat (Oc., Guam)	ä'-gät	ah'-gaht
Agattu (Alaska)	ăg-ă-tōō'	ag-a-too'
Agay (Fr.)	ä-gĕ'	ah-geh'
Agde (Fr.)	ägd'	ahgd'
Agdenes (Nor.)	äg'-də-nĕs	ahg'-duh-nes
Agedabia (Libya)	ä-jĕ-dä'-byä	ah-jeh-dah'-byah
Agelat, el (Libya)	ä-gĕ-lăt', ĕl	ah-geh-lat', el
Agen (Fr.)	ä-zhäN'	ah-zhahN'
Agheila, el (Libya)	ä-gā'-lä, ĕl	ah-gay'-lah, el
Agiguan (Oc., Marianas)	ä-gē-gwän'	ah-gee-gwahn'
Agilla (Ger.)	ä'-gĭl-ä	ah'-gil-ah
Agingan (Oc., Saipan)	ä-gēn-gän'	ah-geen-gahn'
Aginsk (Rus.)	ä-gēnsk'	ah-geensk'
Aginskoe (Rus.)	ä-gēn'-skŏ-yĕ	ah-geen'-sko-yeh
Agioi Saranta (Alb.) See *Saranta* and *Saranda.*		
agios, agioi (Gr.)	ĭ'-yôs, ĭ'-yē	ai'-yos, ai'-yee

An element, meaning *saint(s)*, in Greek place names. Look up the other part of the name. *Agios* is an alternative spelling of *hagios*, q.v. Similarly *Agia.*

Agira (Sicily)	ä-jē'-rä	ah-jee'-rah
Agnena (It.)	ä-nyĕ'-nä	ah-nyeh'-nah
Agnides Tanassis *or*	äg-nə'-dēs, tä-nä'-sēs	ahg-nee'-dees, tah-
Athanasios (Gr. polit.)	*or* ä-thä-nä'-syôs	nah'-sees *or* ah-
		thah-nah'-syos
Agno (P.I., riv.)	äg'-nô	ahg'-no
Ago (P.I., riv.)	ä'-gô	ah'-go
Agoó (P.I.)	ä-gô-ô'	ah-go-o'
Agosta (Sicily)	ä-gôs'-tä	ah-gos'-tah

Also called *Augusta*, q. v.

Agoulinitsa (Gr.)	ä-gōō-lē-nē'-tsä	ah-goo-lee-nee'-tsah
Agra (India)	ăg'-rə *or* ä'-grə	ag'-ruh *or* ah'-gruh
Agria (Crete, pen.)	ä'-grē-ä	ah'-gree-ah
Agricola (It.)	ä-grē'-kô-lä	ah-gree'-ko-lah
Agrigento (Sicily)	ä-grē-jĕn'-tô	ah-gree-jen'-to

Also called *Girgenti*, jēr-jĕn'-tē [jeer-jen'-tee].

Agrihan (Oc., Marianas)	ä-grē-hän'	ah-gree-hahn'
Agrinion (Gr.)	ä-grē'-nē-ô(n)	ah-gree'-nee-o(n)

Also called *Vrakhori*, vrä-hô'-rē [vrah-ho'-ree].

Agropoli (It.)	ä-grô'-pô-lē	ah-gro'-po-lee
Agua Caliente (Mex.)	ä'-(g)wä kä-lyĕn'-tĕ	ah'-(g)wah kah-lyehn'-teh
Aguacate (Cuba)	ä-(g)wä-kä'-tĕ	ah-(g)wah-kah'-teh
Aguada de Pasajeros (Cuba)	ä-(g)wä'-dä dĕ pä-sä-hĕ'-rôs	ah-(g)wah'-dah deh pah-sah-heh'-ros
Agua Prieta (Mex.)	ä'-(g)wä pryĕ'-tä	ah'(g)wah pryeh'-tah
Aguascalientes (Mex.)	ä'-(g)wäs-kä-lyĕn'-tĕs	ah'-(g)wahs-kah-lyehn'-tes

Border English ou'-wəs- [au'-wuhs-].

Aguijan (Oc., Marianas)	ä-gē-hän'	ah-gee-hahn'
Âguila (Mex.)	ä'-gē-lä	ah'-gee-lah
Âguila (Sp., *eagle*)	ä'-guē-lä	ah'-guee-lah
Aguilar (P.I)	ä-gē-lär'	ah-gee-lahr'
Aguinaldo, Emilio (Fil. polit.)	ä-gē-näl'-dô, ĕ-mē'-lyô	ah-gee-nahl'-do, eh-mee'-lyo
Agulhas (S. Afr., cape)	*Eng.* ə-gŭl'-əs	uh-gul'-uhs
	Port. ä-gōō'-lyəsh	ah-goo'-lyuhsh
Agumdir (Ethiopia)	*Eng.* ə-goum'-dĭr	uh-gaum'-dir
	native ä-gŭm-dûr	ah-gum-dur
Agyia (Gr.)	ī-yä'	ai-yah'
Ahe (Oc., Tuamotu)	ä'-hĕ	ah'-heh
Ahmedabad (India)	ăm'-ə-də-băd'	am'-uh-duh-bad'
Ahmedi, Ahmad (Iran. polit.)	ä-mĕ-dē', ä'-mäd	ah-meh-dee', ah'-mahd
Ahmed Lotfi el Seyed Pasha (Egypt. polit.)	ä'-mĕd lŭt'-fē ĕs sä-'yĕd pä'-shä	ah'-med lut'-fee es say'-yed pah'-shah
Ahmednagar (India)	ăm'-əd-nŭg'-ər	am'-uhd-nuhg'-uhr
Ahmed Qavam Sultaneh (Iran. polit.)	ä'-mĕd kə-väm' səl-tä-nĕ'	ah'-med kuh-vahm' suhl-tah-neh'

Also spelled in English *Ghavam, Kavam, Kawam*, etc., and pronounced gə-väm' [guh-vahm'], k(h)ə-väm' [k(h)uh-vabm'], kä-wäm' [kah-wahm'], etc.

Ahmed Shukairy	ä'-mĕd shōŏk'-rē	ah'-med shuk'-ree

(Arab polit.) Also spelled *Shukri*.

Ahr (Ger., riv.)	är′	ahr′
Ahrdorf (Ger.)	är′-dôrf	ahr′-dorf
Ahrweiler (Ger.)	är′-vī-lər	ahr′-vai-luhr
Ahuachapán (Sal.)	ä-wä-chä-pän′	ah-wah-chah-pahn′
Åhus (Sw.)	ō′-hüs	oh′-hüs
Ahvenanmaa (Fin., isls.)	ä′-vĕ-nän-mä′	ah′-veh-nahn-mah′

Also called *Åland*, q.v.

Ahwaz (Iran)	ä-wäz′	ah-wahz′
Aiano (It.)	ä-yä′-nô	ah-yah′-no
Aichi (Jap.)	ä′-ē′-chē	ah′-ee′-chee
Aielli *or* Ajelli (It.)	ä-yĕl′-lē	ah-yel′-lee
Aigila (Gr., isl.)	ā′-yē-lä	ay′-yee-lah

Also called *Antikythera*, q.v., and *Tserigoto*, tsĕ-rē-gô′-tô [tseh-ree-go′-to], and *Lious*, lē-ōōs′ [lee-oos′].

Aigina (Gr.)   See *Aegina*.

Aigion (Gr.)	ā′-yôn	ay′-yon

English *Aegion*, ē′-jĭ-ŏn [ee′-ji-on].

Aigoudista (Gr.)	ĕ-gōō′-dē-stä	eh-goo′-dee-stah
Aigrefeuille (Fr.)	ĕ-grə-fü′(y)	eh-gruh-fœ′(y)
Aiguesmortes (Fr.)	ĕg-môrt′	eg-mort′
Aigun (Manchu.)	ī-gōōn	ai-gun

Also called *Aihun*, ī-hōōn [ai-hun].

Aikaterine (Gr.)   See *Katerine*.

Aikawa, Yoshisuke (Jap. executive)	ä′-ē′-kä-wä, yô-shē′-sōō-kĕ	ah′-ee′-kah-wah, yo-shee′-soo-keh
Ailinginae (Oc., Marshalls)	ä-ē′-lĭng-ē-nä′-ĕ	ah-ee′-ling-ee-nah′-eh
Ailinglapalap (Oc., Marshalls)	ä-ē′-lĭng-lä′-pä-läp	ah-ee′-ling-lah′-pah-lahp
Aillant (Fr.)	ä-yäN′	ah-yahN′
Ailuk (Oc., Marshalls)	ī′-lōōk	ai′-look

ailurophobe See *aelurophobe*.

Ain (Fr.)	ăN′	aN′

'ain See *'ein*.

Ainaži (Latvia)	ī′-nä-zhē	ai′-nah-zhee

Russian *Gainasch*, q.v.

Ain Beida (Alg.)	än bä′-dä	ayn bay′-dah
Ain Draham (Tun.)	än drä′-häm	ayn drah′-hahm
Ain Mestour (Tun.)	än mĕs-tōōr′	ayn mes-toor′

Ainos (Turk.)   See *Enez*.

Ain Rhelal (Tun.)	än rə-lăl′	ayn ruh-lal′
Aio (Oc., Solomons)	ī-ô′	ai-o′
Aire (Fr., riv.)	ăr′	ehr′
Aisch (Ger., riv.)	īsh′	aish′

Aisne (Fr., riv.)   *Eng.* ān'   ayn'
                          Fr. ĕn'   en'

Aïstrates (Gr., isl.)   See *Evstratios, Agios.*

Aitape (N.E. New Guinea) ĭ-tä-pĕ'   ai-tah-peh'

Aitolia (Gr.)   See *Aetolia and Acarnania.*

Aitos (Bulg.)   ĭ'-tŏs   ai'-tos

Aitutake (Oc., Cook isl.) ĭ-tōo-tä'-kĕ   ai-too-tah'-keh

Aiud (Rum.)   ä'-yŏōd   ah'-yud

Aix (Fr.)   *Eng.* āks'   ayks'
                          Fr. ĕks'   eks'

Aix la Chapelle   *Eng.* āks' lə shə-pĕl'   ayks' luh shuh-pel'
   (Ger.)   *Fr.* ĕks lä shä-pĕl'   eks lah shah-pel'
   German *Aachen,* ä'-k(h)ən [ah'-k(h)uhn].

Aizpute (Latvia)   ĭz'-pŏō-tĕ   aiz'-pu-teh
   Russian *Gasenpot,* q.v. German *Hasenpoth,* q.v.

Aizu (Jap.)   ä-ē'-zōō'   ah-ee'-zoo'

Ajaccio (Corsica)   ä-yät'-chô   ah-yaht'-cho

Ajayan (Oc., Guam)   ä-hä-yän'   ah-hah-yahn'

Ajelli (It.) See *Aielli.*

Ajlun (Trans-Jordan) See *Gilead.*

Ajmer (India)   ăj-mēr'   aj-meer'

Ajoe *or* Ayu (NEI)   ä'-yōō   ah'-yoo

Ajud (Rum.)   ä-zhŏŏd'   ah-zhud'

Ak.   The abbreviation of Greek *akroterion,* q.v.

Akarit, el (Tun.)   ä-kä-rēt', ĕl   ah-kah-reet', el

Akarnania (Gr.)   See *Aetolia and Acarnania.*

Akasaka (Jap.)   ä-kä'-sä-kä   ah-kah'-sah-kah

Akashi (Jap.)   ä'-kä-shē   ah'-kah-shee

Akcaguayan (P.I., bay)   äk'-kä-gwä'-yän   ahk'-kah-gwah'-
                                              yahn

Akçehisar (Alb.)   See *Krujë.*

Akershus (Nor.)   ä'-kərs-hōōs   ah'-kuhrs-hoos

Akersloot (Neth.)   ä'-kər-slōt   ah'-kuhr-sloht

Akhmatova, Anna   ak(h)-mä'-tŏ-vä,   ak(h)-mah'-to-vah,
   (Rus. poet)   än'-nä   ahn'-nah

Akhtopol (Bulg.)   äk(h)'-tŏ-pŏl(y)   ahk(h)'-to-pol(y)

Akhtyrka (Rus.)   äk-tĭr'-kä   ahk-tihr'-kah

Akhtyrskaya (Rus.)   äk-tĭr'-skä-yä   ahk-tihr'-skah-yah

Akhziv (Pal.) See *Ez Zib.*

Akihito, Tsugu no Miya   ä-kē'-hē-tô, tsōō-gōō'   ah-kee'-hee-to,
   (Jap. crown prince)   nô mē-yä   tsoo-goo' no mee-
                                             yah

   Akihito may approach ä-kēsh'-tô [ah-keesh'-to].

Akita (Jap.)   ä'-kē-tä   ah'-kee-tah

[9]

Akiyama (Jap.)   ä-kē'-yä-mä   ah-kee'-yah-mah
Akkerman (Rum. > Rus.)   äk'-ər-män   ahk'-uhr-mahn
    Rumanian *Cetatea Albă*, q.v.
Ak Mechet (Rus.)   äk mĕ-chĕt'   ahk meh-chet'
Akmolinsk (Rus.)   äk-mŏ-lēnsk'   ahk-mo-leensk'
Akouda (Tun.)   ä-kōō'-dä   ah-koo'-dah
Akritas (Gr., cape)   ä-krē'-täs   ah-kree'-tahs
    Also called *Gallo*, gä'-lô [gah'-lo].
Akrokeraunia (Alb.)   See *Acroceraunia*.
akroterion   ä-krô-tē'-rē-ô(n)   ah-kro-tee'-ree-o(n)
    An element, meaning *cape* or *point*, in Greek place names. Look up
    the other part of the name.
Aksel *or* Axel (Neth.)   äk'-səl   ahk'-suhl
Aksha (Rus.)   äk'-shä   ahk'-shah
Ak Sheikh (Rus.)   äk' shāk'   ahk' shayk'
Aksu (Ch., Sinkiang)   äk-sōō   ahk-soo
Akte (Crete, point)   ä-ktē'   ah-ktee'
Aktyubinsk (Rus.)   äk-tyōō'-bĭnsk   ahk-tyoo'-binsk
Akutagawa, Ryūnosuke   ä-kōō-tä'-gä-wä,   ah-koo-tah'-gah-wah,
  (Jap. writer)   ryōō'-nô-sōō-kĕ   ryoo'-no-soo-keh
Akutan (Alaska, isl.)   ä-kōō-tăn'   ah-koo-tan'
Akyab (Burma)   ăk-yăb' *or* äk-yäb'   ak-yab' *or* ahk-yahb'
al *or* el   äl, ĕl   ahl, el
    The Arabic article complicates alphabetical listing. It may or may not
    be omitted; it may be spelled with *e* or *a*; the consonant *l* may be as-
    similated to that of the following word. Thus *El Kerak* and *Kerak*
    both occur. *El Djem* is pronounced and may be written *Ed Djem* or
    Edjem. *Alhambra* is from Arabic *al hamra'*; *Suez* from Arabic *Es
    Suweis*. The consultant may have to look for several forms or for the
    second element of the name.
Alabama (U.S.)   ăl'-ə-băm'-ə   al'-uh-bam'-uh
    The pronunciation äl'-ə-bäm'-ə [ahl'-uh-bahm'-uh] is cordially dis-
    liked by most Alabamians.
Alabang (P.I.)   ä-lä'-bäng   ah-lah'-bahng
Alagir (Rus.)   ä-lä-gēr'   ah-lah-geer'
Alagoas (Brazil)   ä-lə-gô'-əs   ah-luh-go'-uhs
Alais (Fr.) See *Alès*.
Alamagan (Oc., Marianas)   ä-lä-mä-gän'   ah-lah-mah-gahn'
Alameda (Calif.)   *Eng.* ăl'-ə-mē'-də   al'-uh-mee'-duh
             Sp. ä'-lä-mĕ'-dä   ah'-lah-meh'-dah
Alamein, el (Egypt)   ä-lä-mān', ĕl   ah-lah-mayn', el
Alaminos (P.I.)   ä-lä-mē'-nôs   ah-lah-mee'-nos
Alamogordo (N.M.)   *Eng.* ăl'-ə-mə-gôr'-də   al'-uh-muh-gor'-duh
             Sp. ä'-lä-mô-gôr'-dô   ah'-lah-mo-gor'-do

Åland (Fin., isls.) ō'-län oh'-lahn
The Swedish name for islands which the Finns call *Ahvenanmaa*, q.v.

Alanya (Turk.) ä-län-yä' ah-lahn-yah'
Also called *Alaiye*.

Alas, Antonio de las ä'-läs, än-tô'-nyô ah'-lahs, ahn-to'-nyo
  (Fil. polit.) dĕ läs deh lahs

Alassio (It.) ä-läs'-syô ah-lahs'-syo

Alatri (It.) ä-lä'-trē ah-lah'-tree

Alatyr (Rus.) ä-lä-tĭr' ah-lah-tihr'

Ālava (Sp., prov.) ä'-lä-vä ah'-lah-vah

Alazán (Tex., creek) *Eng.* ăl'-ə-zăn' al'-uh-zan'
  Sp. ä-lä-sän' ah-lah-sahn'

Alba (It.) *Eng.* ăl'-bə al'-buh
  Alban, Eng. adj, ôl'-bən [awl'-buhn] *or* ăl'-bən [al'-buhn]. It. *Albano*.

Albacete (Sp.) äl-bä-thĕ'-tĕ ahl-bah-theh'-teh
  or -sĕ'- *or* -seh'-

Albacore ăl'-bə-kôr' al'-buh-kor'
British naval carrier-plane.

Alba Julia (Rum.) ăl'-bä yŏŏ'-lyä ahl'-bah yu'-lyah
Inevitably English ăl'-bə jŏŏl'-yə [al'-buh jool'-yuh]. Hungarian
Gyulafehérvár, dyŏŏ'-lŏ-fĕ'-här-vär [dyu'-lo-feh'-hayr-vahr].

Albani, Monti *or* Colli (It.) äl-bä'-nē, môn'-tē ahl-bah'-nee, mon'-
  or kôl'-lē tee *or* kol'-lee
English *Alban Hills*, ôl'-bən [awl'-buhn] *or* ăl'-bən [al'-buhn].

Albania *Eng.* ăl-bān'-yə al-bayn'-yuh
The pronunciation ôl-bān'-yə [awl-bayn'-yuh] is not recommended.
The Albanians call their country *Shqipni*, q.v., or a variant thereof.

Albanian ăl-bā'-nyən al-bay'-nyuhn
  or ôl-bā'-nyən awl-bay'-nyuhn
The first is preferable for natives of Albania, the second for citizens
of Albany, N. Y.

Albano (It.) äl-bä'-nô ahl-bah'-no
In Sicily *Albano* is stressed on the first syllable.

Albano Laziale (It.) äl-bä'-nô ahl-bah'-no
  lä-tsyä'-lĕ lah-tsyah'-leh

Albay (P.I.) äl-bī' ahl-bai'

Albegna (It.) äl-bĕ'-nyä ahl-beh'-nyah

Albemarle (N.C., Va.) ăl'-bə-märl' al'-buh-mahrl'

Alberta (Can.) ăl-bûr'-tə al-bur'-tuh
The *Elberta* peach is sometimes incorrectly called *Alberta*.

Alberti Irsa (Hung.) ăl'-bĕr-tĭ ĭr'-shŏ ahl'-behr-ti ihr'-sho

Alberto, João äl-bĕr'-tŏŏ, ahl-behr'-tu,
  (Braz. polit.) zhô-ouN' zho-auN'

Albes (Fr., riv.) älb' ahlb'

Alblasserdam (Neth.)	äl'-bläs-ər-däm'	ahl'-blahs-uhr-dahm'
Albuera (P.I.)	äl-bwĕ'-rä	ahl-bweh'-rah
Albuquerque (N.Mex.)	ăl'-bə-kûr'-kĭ	al'-buh-kuhr'-ki
Alburquerque (Sp.)	äl-bōōr-kĕr'-kĕ	ahl-boor-kehr'-keh
Alcalá (Sp.)	äl-kä-lä'	ahl-kah-lah'
Alcamo (Sicily)	äl'-kä-mô	ahl'-kah-mo
Alcántara (Sp.)	äl-kän'-tä-rä	ahl-kahn'-tah-rah
Alcázar (Sp.)	*Sp.* äl-kä'-thär	ahl-kah'-thahr
	or -sär	or -sahr
	Eng. ăl-kăz'-ər	al-kaz'-uhr
Aldea (P.I.)	äl-dĕ'-ä	ahl-deh'-ah
Aldeno (It.)	äl-dĕ'-nô	ahl-deh'-no
Aleichem, Sholem *or*	ä-lā'-k(h)ĕm, shō-lĕm	ah-lay'-k(h)ehm,
Shalom (Yiddish author)	*or* shä-lōm'	shoh'-lehm *or* shah-lohm'
Aleksandriya (Rus.)	ä-lĕk-sän-drē'-yä	ah-lek-sahn-dree'-yah
Aleksandrovac (Yugosl.)	ä'-lĕk-sän'-drô-väts	ah'-lek-sahn'-dro-vahts
Aleksandrovsk (Rus.)	ä-lĕk-sän'-drŏfsk	ah-lek-sahn'-drofsk
Aleksandrów (Pol.)	ä-lĕk-sän'-drōŏf	ah-lek-sahn'-druf
Alekseev, Kirill	ä-lĕ-ksĕ'-yĕf,	ah-leh-kseh'-yehf,
(former Rus. official)	kĭ-rēl'	ki-reel'
Alekseev, Peter I.	ä-lĕ-ksĕ'-yĕf	ah-leh-kseh'-yehf
(Rus. polit.)		
Aleksikovo (Rus.)	ä-lĕk'-sĭ-kŏ-vŏ	ah-lek'-si-ko-vo
Aleksin (Rus.)	ä-lyŭk'-sĭn	ah-lyuhk'-sin
Aleksinac (Yugosl.)	ä'-lĕk'-sĭ-näts	ah'-lek'-si-nahts
Alemán, Fernando Casas (Mex. diplomat) See *Casas Alemán.*		
Alemán, Miguel	ä-lĕ-män', mē-gĕl'	ah-leh-mahn',
(Mex. polit.)		mee-gel'
Alemtejo (Port.)	ä-lĕm-tĕ'-zhŏŏ	ah-lem-teh'-zhu
	or ä-līN-tĕ'-zhŏŏ	ah-laiN-teh'-zhu
Alençon (Fr.)	ä-läN-sôN'	ah-lahN-soN'
Aléria (Corsica)	*Eng.* ə-lē'-rĭ-ə	uh-lee'-ri-uh
	It. ä-lĕ'-ryä	ah-leh'-ryah
Alès (Fr.)	ä-lĕs'	ah-les'
Also called *Alais,* ä-lĕ' [ah-leh'].		
Alessandria (It.)	ä-lĕs-sän'-dryä	ah-les-sahn'-dryah
Alessandri Palma, Arturo	ä-lĕs-sän'-drē	ah-lehs-sahn'-dree
(Chilean polit.)	päl'-mä, är-tōō'-rô	pahl'-mah, ahr-too'-ro
Alessio (Alb.)	*It.* ä-lĕs'-syô	ah-les'-syo
Albanian *Lesh,* q.v.		
Ålesund (Nor.) See *Aalesund.*		

Aleut	ăl'-ĭ-o͞ot *or* ăl'-yo͞ot	al'-i-oot *or* al'-yoot
Aleutian Isls. (Alaska)	ə-lyo͞o'-shən	uh-lyoo'-shuhn
Alexandretta (Syria)	*Eng.* ăl'-ĕg-zăn-drĕt'-ə	al'-eg-zan-dret'-uh

French Alexandrette, ä-lĕk-säN-drĕt' [ah-lek-sahN-dret'].
Turkish *Iskenderun*, q.v.

Alexandria (Egypt)	ăl'-ĕg-zăn'-drĭ-ə	al'-eg-zan'-dri-uh

Arabic *El Iskandariya*, ĕl ēs-kän-dä-rē'-yä [el ees-kahn-dah-ree'-yah].
French *Alexandrie*, ä-lĕk-säN-drē' [ah-lek-sahN-dree'].

Alexandroupolis (Gr.)	ä-lĕk-sän-dro͞o'-pô-lē(s)	ah-lek-sahn-droo'-po-lee(s)

Formerly *Dede Agach*, dĕ-dĕ' ä-gäch' [deh-deh' ah-gahch'].

Alexeev, Peter I. (Rus. polit.)	See *Alekseev*.	
Alexishafen (N. E. New Guinea)	ä-lĕk'-sĭs-hä'-fən	ah-lek'-sis-hah'-fuhn
Alfedena (It.)	äl-fĕ-dĕ'-nä	ahl-feh-deh'-nah
Alfen (Neth.)	äl'-fən	ahl'-fuhn
Algarve (Port., prov.)	äl-gär'-və	ahl-gahr'-vuh
Algeciras (Sp.)	*Eng.* ăl'-jə-sĭr'-əs	al'-juh-sihr'-uhs
	Sp. äl-hĕ-thē'-räs	ahl-heh-thee'-rahs
	or äl-hĕ-sē'-räs	ahl-heh-see'-rahs
Algeria (Afr., Fr.)	ăl-jĭr'-ĭ-ə	al-jir'-i-uh
Alghero (Sard.)	äl-gĕ'-rô	ahl-geh'-ro
Algiers (Afr., Fr. col.)	ăl-jĭrz'	al-jihrz'

French *Alger*, äl-zhĕ' [ahl-zheh']. Arabic *Al Jezair*, äl jə-zīr' [ahl juh-zair'].

Algonquian, Algonkian	ăl-gŏn'-kĭ-ən	al-gon'-ki-uhn
Al Hammam (Egypt)	äl häm-măm'	ahl hahm-mam'
Alhucemas (Mex.)	ä-lo͞o-sĕ'-mäs	ah-loo-seh'-mahs
Alia (Sicily)	ä-lē'-ä	ah-lee'-ah
Alia, el (Tun.)	ä'-lĭ-ä, ĕl	ah'-li-ah, el
Aliaga (P.I.)	ä-lyä'-gä	ah-lyah'-gah
Aliakmon (Gr., riv.)	ä-lē-äk'-môn	ah-lee-ahk'-mon
Alibunar (Yugosl.)	ä'-lē-bo͞o-när'	ah'-lee-boo-nahr'
Alicante (Sp.)	ä-lē-kän'-tĕ	ah-lee-kahn'-teh
Alice (It., Calab.)	ä-lē'-chĕ	ah-lee'-cheh

Elsewhere in Italy *Alice* is customarily stressed on the first syllable.

Alice Springs (Austral.)	ăl'-ĭs	al'-is
Alicudi (It., isl.)	ä-lē-ko͞o'-dē	ah-lee-koo'-dee
Alifan (Guam, mt.)	ä-lē-fän'	ah-lee-fahn'
Alife (It.)	ä-lē'-fĕ	ah-lee'-feh
Aligarh (India)	ăl-ē-gär'	ae-ee-gahr'
	or ə-lē-gûr'	uh-lee-guhr'
Alika (Gr.)	ä'-lē-kä	ah'-lee-kah

Ali Khan, Liaquat (Indian polit.) See *Liaquat Ali Khan.*

Alikyanou (Crete)	ä-lē-kyä-nōō'	ah-lee-kyah-noo'
Alim (Oc., Bismarck arch.)	ä'-lĭm	ah'-lim
Alince (Yugosl.)	ä'-lĭn-tsĕ	ah'-lin-tseh
Ali Soheily (Iran. polit.)	ä-lē' sô-hä'-lē	ah-lee' so-hay'-lee
Alkemade (Neth.)	äl'-kə-mä'-də	ahl'-kuh-mah'-duh
Alkmaar (Neth.)	älk'-mär	ahlk'-mahr
Al Kuweit (Arabia)	äl kŏŏ-wät'	ahl ku-wayt'
	or kŏŏ-wīt'	ku-wait'

Also spelled *Al Kuwait.*

Allanmyo (Burma)	ă'-lən-myō'	a'-luhn-myoh'
Allegheny (U.S., mts.)	ăl'-ə-gā'-nĭ	al'-uh-gay'-ni

This name is also spelled *Alleghany* in North Carolina and Virginia, and *Allegany* in Maryland and New York.

Allekakat (Alaska)	ăl'-ə-kăk'-ət	al'-uh-kak'-uht
Allenkul (Est.)	*Rus.* äl'-lĕn-kūl(y)	ahl'-len-kyool(y)

Estonian *Türi*, q.v. German *Allenkühl*, äl'-ən-kül [ahl'-uhn-kül].

Allenstein (Ger.>Pol.)	äl'-ən-shtīn	ahl'-uhn-shtain

Polish *Olsztyn*, q. v.

Aller (Ger., riv.)	äl'-ər	ahl'-uhr
Allis-Chalmers Co.	ăl'-ĭs chäl'-mərz	al'-is chahl'-muhrz
(West Allis, Wis.)		

Allxhinë (Alb.) See *Llixhë.*

Alma Ata (Rus.)	äl'-mä ä'-tä	ahl'-mah ah'-tah
Almaza (Egypt, Cairo,	äl-mä'-zə	ahl-mah'-zuh
airport)		
Almeloo (Neth.)	äl'-mə-lō	ahl'-muh-loh
Almería (Sp.)	äl-mĕ-rē'-ä	ahl-meh-ree'-ah
Almyron (Crete, gulf)	äl-mē-rô(n)'	ahl-mee-ro(n)'
	or är-mē-rô(n)'	ahr-mee-ro(n)'

Also called *Amphimallikos*, äm-fē-mä-lē-kôs' [ahm-fee-mah-lee-kos'].

Almyros (Crete)   See *Georgioupolis.*

Alonesos (Gr., isl.)	ä-lô'-nē-sôs	ah-lo'-nee-sos

Also called *Khiliodromia*, hē-lē-ô-drô'-mē-ä [hee-lee-o-dro'-mee-ah] or *Liadromia*, lē-ä-drô'-mē-ä [lee-ah-dro'-mee-ah].

Alor Star (Malaya)	ä'-lôr stär'	ah'-lor stahr'

Alost (Belg.)   See *Aalst.*

Alpujarras (Sp.)	äl-pōō-hä'-räs	ahl-poo-hah'-rahs
Als (Den., isl.)	äls'	ahls'

German *Alsen*, äl'-zən [ahl'-zuhn].

Alsdorf (Ger.)	äls'-dôrf	ahls'-dorf
Alsónémedi (Hung.)	ŏl'-shô-nā'-mĕ-dĭ	ol'-sho-nay'-meh-di
Alta (Nor.)	äl'-tä	ahl'-tah
Altagnana (It.)	äl-tä-nyä'-nä	ahl-tah-nyah'-nah

[14]

Altai (Rus., mts.)   ăl-tī' *or* äl-   al-tai' *or* ahl-

Altanski (Rus.)   äl-tän'-skĭ   ahl-tahn'-ski

Altdamm (Ger. > Pol.)   ält'-däm   ahlt'-dahm
Polish *Dąb*, q.v.

Alten (Nor., fjord)   äl'-tən   ahl'-tuhn

Altena (Ger.)   äl'-tə-nä   ahl'-tuh-nah

Althing (Icelandic   äl'-thĭng   ahl'-thing
parliament)

In Icelandic usage the definite article is usually added as a suffix, *Althingi*, äl'-thĭnk-yĭ [ahl'-think-yi], the (old) parliament.

Altieri (It.)   äl-tyĕ'-rē   ahl-tyeh'-ree

altimeter   ăl-tĭm'-ə-tər   al-tim'-uh-tuhr
    or ăl'-tĭ-mē'-tər   al'-ti-mee'-tuhr

Arthur Godfrey prefers ăl'-tĭ-mē'-tər and opines that ăl-tĭm'-ĭ-tər is a pronunciation for "hot rocks." The dictionaries are, by this token, hot rocks. They ignore the pronunciation ăl-tĭ-mē'-tər, although it is widely used by engineers and mechanics and all the brethren whose lives may depend upon a quick reading of *meters*. Cp. *kilometer*.

Altkirch (Fr.)   ält'-kĭrk(h)   ahlt'-kihrk(h)

Altona (Ger.)   äl'-tô-nä   ahl'-to-nah

Altoona (Pa.)   ăl-tōō'-nə   al-too'-nuh

Altruppin (Ger.)   ält-rŏŏp-pēn'   ahlt-rup-peen'

Alu (Oc., Solomons)   ä'-lōō   ah'-loo

Alūksne (Latvia)   ä'-lōōks-nĕ   ah'-looks-neh
Russian and German *Marienburg*, q.v.

Alupka (Rus.)   ä-lŏŏp'-kä   ah-lup'-kah

Alushta (Rus.)   ä-lōōsh'-tä   ah-loosh'-tah

Álvarez (Sp. name)   *Am. Sp.* äl'-vä-rĕs   ahl'-vah-rehs
    Sp.   äl'-vä-rĕth   ahl'-vah-rehth

Álvaro (Sp. name)   äl'-vä-rô   ahl'-vah-ro

Alvito (It.)   äl-vē'-tô   ahl-vee'-to

Alytus (Lith.)   ä-lē'-tōōs   ah-lee'-toos
Russian *Olita*, q.v.

Alzey (Ger.)   äl'-tsī   ahl'-tsai

Amadeo (It., Sp. name)   ä-mä-dĕ'-ô   ah-mah-deh'-o

Amadeus (name)   *Eng.* ăm'-ə-dē'-əs   am'-uh-dee'-uhs
    Ger. ä-mä-dā'-ŏŏs   ah-mah-day'-us

Amadeus (Austral., lake)   ə-măd'-ĭ-əs   uh-mad'-i-uhs

Amadis (name)   *Eng.* ăm'-ə-dĭs   am'-uh-dis
    Fr. ä-mä-dēs'   ah-mah-dees'

Amador Guerrero, Manuel   ä-mä-dôr'   ah-mah-dor' gehr-
(Pan. polit.)   gĕr-rĕ'-rô, mä-nwĕl'   reh'-ro, mah-nwel'

Amagasaki (Jap.)   ä-mä-gä-sä'-kē   ah-mah-gah-sah'-kee

Amalfi (It.)   ä-mäl'-fē   ah-mahl'-fee

[15]

Amalias (Gr.)	ä-mäl-yäs′	ah-mahl-yahs′
Amalienborg (Den.)	ä-mä′-lĭ-ən-bôr	ah-mah′-li-uhn-bor
Amami (Jap.)	ä-mä′-mē′	ah-mah′-mee′
A Manhã (Braz. news- paper)	ä mə-nyäN′	ah muh-nyahN′
Amantea (It.)	ä-män-tĕ′-ä	ah-mahn-teh′-ah
Amaral Peixoto (Braz. polit.)	ä-mə-räl′ pā-shô′-tōō	ah-muh-rahl′ pay- sho′-tu
Amarillo (Tex.)	ăm′-ə-rĭl′-ə	am′-uh-ril′-uh
Amaseno (It.)	ä-mä-sĕ′-nô	ah-mah-seh′-no
Amay (Belg.)	ä-mĕ′	ah-meh′
Amazon (S.A., riv.)	ăm′-ə-zən *or* -zŏn	am′-uh-zuhn *or* -zon
Portuguese *Amazonas*, q.v.		
Amazonas (Brazil, riv., prov.)	äm-mä-zô′-näs	ahm-mah-zo′-nahs

Peninsular Portuguese ä-mə-zô′-nəsh [ah-muh-zo′-nuhsh].

Ambala (India)	əm-bä′-lä	uhm-bah′-lah
Ambedkar, Bhimrao Ramji (Indian polit.)	äm-bĕd′-kär, bēm′- rou räm′-jē	ahm-bed′-kahr, beem′- rau rahm′-jee
Amberg (Ger.)	äm′-bĕrk(h)	ahm′-behrk(h)
Ambil (P.I.)	äm-bēl′	ahm-beel′
Also called *Amul*, ä-mōōl′ [ah-mool′].		
Ambitle (Oc., Bismarck arch.	äm-bēt-lĕ′	ahm-beet-leh′
Ambleteuse (Fr.)	ämbl-tûz′	ahmbl-tœz′
Amboina (NEI)	*Eng.* ăm-boi′-nə	am-boi′-nuh
Malay *Ambon*, q.v.		
Ambolón (P.I.)	äm-bô-lôn′	ahm-bo-lon′
Ambon (NEI, Moluccas) English *Amboina*, q.v.	*Malay* äm-bôn′(y)	ahm-bon′(y)
Ambos Camarines (P.I.)	äm′-bôs kä-mä-rē′- nĕs	ahm′-bos kah-mah- ree′-nes
Ambrières (Fr.)	äN-bryĕr′	ahN-bryehr′
Ambrogio (It.)	äm-brô′-jô	ahm-bro′-jo
Ambrosi (It.)	äm-brô′-sē	ahm-bro′-see
Ambunti (New Guinea)	äm-bōōn′-tē	ahm-boon′-tee
Amchitka (Alaska, isl.)	ăm-chĭt′-kə	am-chit′-kuh
Ameland (Neth., isl.)	ä′-mə-länt	ah′-muh-lahnt
Ameln (Ger.)	ä′-məln	ah′-muhln
amen	ä′-mĕn′	ah′-men′
	or ā′-mĕn′	ay′-men′

The first is expected in song and usually in liturgical use. The latter is the old-fashioned English pronunciation, and it persists in some Protestant groups and often in everyday speech.

Ameri (Per. name)   ä-mə-rē'   ah-muh-ree'
America   ə-mĕr'-ə-kə   uh-mehr'-uh-kuh

A British pronunciation with a "single-tap *r*" (similar to *d*) was once cultivated by American singers and announcers; it was as obvious as a sore thumb, if not indecent. The equally painful "Uh-muhrr'-ruh-kuh" is avoided by announcers.

Amerika (Neth.)   *Eng.* ə-mĕr'-ə-kə   uh-mehr'-uh-kuh
     Du. ä-mā'-rĭ-kä   ah-may'-ri-kah
Amerongen (Neth.)   ä'-mə-rông'-ən   ah'-muh-rong'-uhn
Amersfoort (Neth.)   ä'-mərs-fōrt   ah'-muhrs-fohrt
Amery, Sir John (Br. polit.)   ā'-mə-rĭ   ay'-muh-rih
Amezaga, Juan José (Urug. polit.)   ä-mĕ-sä'-gä, hwän' hô-sĕ'   ah-meh-sah'-gah, hwahn' ho-seh'
Amgun (Rus., riv.)   äm-gōōn'   ahm-goon'
Amhara (Ethiopia)   äm'-hä-rä   ahm'-hah-rah
Amherst (Mass.)   ăm'-ərst   am'-uhrst
Amiens (Fr.)   *Fr.* ä-myăN'   ah-myaN'
     Eng. ăm'-ĭ-ĕnz   am'-i-enz

The French pronunciation is probably the more common even in English contexts.

Amine, Sidi Mohammed el (Arab polit.) See *El Amine.*
amir, ameer (title or honorific) See *emir.*
Åmli (Nor.) See *Aamli.*

Amman (Trans-Jordan)   äm'-män   ahm'-mahn
Ancient *Philadelphia.*
Ammersooien (Neth.)   äm'-ər-sō'-yən   ahm'-uhr-soh'-yuhn
Ammokhostos (Cyprus)   ä-mô'-hô-stôs   ah-mo'-ho-stos
Amorgos (Gr., isl.)   *Eng.* ə-môr'-gəs   uh-mor'-guhs
     Gr. ä-môr-gô(s)'   ah-mor-go(s)'
Amory (Miss.)   ā'-mə-rĭ   ay'-muh-ri
Amoy (Ch., Fukien)   ə-moi'   uh-moi'
Chinese *Szê-ming,* sŭ-mĭng [suh-ming].
Ampelakia (Gr.)   äm-bĕ-lä'-kyä   ahm-beh-lah'-kyah
Amphilokhia (Gr.)   äm-fē-lô-hē'-ä   ahm-fee-lo-hee'-ah
Also called *Karvasaras,* kär-vä-sä-räs' [kahr-vah-sah-rahs'].
Amphimallikos (Crete, gulf) See *Almyron.*
Amphissa (Gr.)   äm'-fē-sä   ahm'-fee-sah
Also called *Salona,* sä'-lô-nä [sah'-lo-nah].
Amritsar (India)   əm-rĭt'-sər   uhm-rit'-suhr
Amselfeld (Yugosl.)   *Ger.* äm'-səl-fĕlt   ahm'-suhl-felt
Serb-Croat *Kosovo Polje,* q.v.
Amsterdam (Neth.)   *Eng.* ăm'-stər-dăm   am'-stuhr-dam
     Du. äm'-stər-däm'   ahm'-stuhr-dahm'

Amstetten (Austria)	äm'-stĕt-ən	ahm'-stet-uhn
Amul (P.I.) See *Ambil*.		
Amundsen, Roald (Nor. explorer)	ä'-mŏŏn-sən, rō'-äl	ah'-mun-suhn, roh'-ahl
Amur (Ch. and Rus., riv.) Cf. *Heilungkiang*.	ä-mōōr'	ah-moor'
Anagni (It.)	ä-nä'-nyē	ah-nah'-nyee
Anahao (P.I.)	ä-nä'-hou	ah-nah'-hau
Anam (Indo-Ch.) See *Annam*.		
Anambas (NEI)	ä-näm'-bäs	ah-nahm'-bahs
Ananda Mahidol (late King of Siam)	ə-nän' mä-hē-dōn'	uh-nahn' mah-hee-dohn'
Ananev (Rus.)	ä-nän'-yĕf	ah-nahn'-yef
Anao (P.I.)	ä-ɲou'	ah-nau'
Anapa (Rus.)	ä-nä'-pä	ah-nah'-pah
Anaphe (Gr., isl.)	ä-nä'-fē	ah-nah'-fee
Anastasievskaya (Rus.)	ä-näs-täs'-yĕf-skä-yä	ah-nahs-tahs'-yef-skah-yah
Anatahan (Oc., Marianas)	ä-nä-tä-hän'	ah-nah-tah-hahn'
Ancash (Peru)	än-käsh'	ahn-kahsh'
An-chi (Ch., Chekiang)	än-jē	ahn-jee
An-ch'ing (Ch., Anhwei) Also called *An-k'ing*, q. v.	än-chĭng	ahn-ching
Ancón (Peru)	än-kôn'	ahn-kon'
Ancona (It.)	än-kô'-nä	ahn-ko'-nah
Åndalsnes (Nor.) See *Aandalsnes*.		
Andalusia (Sp.) Spanish *Andalucía*, än-dä-lōō-thē'-ä [ahn-dah-loo-thee'-ah].	*Eng.* ăn'-də-lōō'-zhə	an'-duh-loo'-zhuh
Andaman (India, isls.)	ăn'-də-măn	an'-duh-man
Andamsk (Rus.)	än-dämsk'	ahn-dahmsk'
Andelle (Fr., riv.)	äN-dĕl'	ahN-del'
Andelys, les (Fr.)	äNd-lē' *or* lĕ zäNd-lē'	ahNd-lee' *or* leh zahNd-lee'
Anderlecht (Belg.)	än'-dər-lĕk(h)t	ahn'-duhr-lek(h)t
Andernach (Ger.)	än'-dər-näk(h)	ahn'-duhr-nahk(h)
Anders, Władisław (Pol. general)	än'-dĕrs, vlä-dĭ'-släf	ahn'-dehrs, vlah-di'-slahf
Andersen, H. Carl (U.S. representative)	ăn'-dər-sən	an'-duhr-suhn
Andijk (Neth.)	än-dīk'	ahn-daik'
Andimiskh (Iran)	än-dĭm'-ĭsk(h)	ahn-dim'-isk(h)
Andino, Tiburcio Carías (Hond. polit.) See *Carías Andino*.		
Andizhan (Rus.)	än-dĭ-zhän'	ahn-di-zhahn'

Andō (Jap.)	än'-dô	ahn'-do
Andoey *or* Andöy	än'-ûĭ	ahn'-œi
(Nor., isl.)		
Andorra (Sp.)	än-dô'-rä	ahn-do'-rah
Andrássy, Count Gyula	ŏn'-drä-shĭ, dyŏŏ'-lŏ	on'-drah-shi, dyu'-lo
(Hung. statesman)		
Andravida (Gr.)	än-drä-vē'-dä	ahn-drah-vee'-dah
Andrea (It.)	än-drĕ'-ä	ahn-dreh'-ah
Andreanof (Alaska, isls.)	än-drĕ-ä'-nŏf	ahn-dreh-ah'-nof
Andreas, Agios (Cyprus,	än-drĕ'-äs, ĭ'-yôs	ahn-dreh'-ahs,
cape)		ai'-yos
Andreev (Pol.) See *Jędrzejów.*		
Andreevka (Rus.)	än-drĕ'-yĕf-kä	ahn-dreh'-yef-kah
Andresen, August H.	än-drē'-sən	ahn-dree'-suhn
(U.S. representative)		
Andreyev, Andrei A.	än-drĕ'-yĕf,	ahn-dreh'-yef,
(Rus. polit.)	än-drā'	ahn-dray'
Andria (It.)	än'-dryä	ahn'-dryah
Andrijevica (Yugosl.)	än'-drē'-yĕ-vĭ-tsä	ahn'-dree'-yeh-vi·tsah
Andros (Bahamas)	ăn'-drŏs *or* -drəs	an'-dros *or* -druhs
Andros (Gr., isl.)	*Eng.* ăn'-drŏs	an'-dros
	Gr. än'-drô(s)	ahn'-dro(s)
Andrychów (Pol.)	än-drĭ'-hŏŏf	ahn-dri'-huf
Anet (Fr.)	ä-nĕ'	ah-neh'
Aneta (Du. News Agency)	ä-nā'-tä	ah-nay'-tah
Aneurin (Welsh name)	ä'-nĕ-ŏŏ-rĭn	ah'-neh-u-rin

Aneurin is sometimes pronounced like its variant *Aneiren,* ä'-nī-rĭn [ah'-nai-rin]. See *Bevan, Aneurin.*

An-fu (Ch., Kiangsi)	än-fŏŏ	ahn-foo
Angara (Rus., riv.)	än-gä-rä'	ahn-gah-rah'

Angarita, Isaías Medina (Ven. polit.) See *Medina Angarita.*

Angat (P.I.)	än-gät'	ahn-gaht'
Angaur (Oc., Carolines)	äng-our'	ahng-aur'

Angel, Eduardo Zuleta (Colom. diplomat) See *Zuleta Angel.*

Angeleno, -s	ăn'-jə-lē'-nō, -nōz	an'-juh-lee'-noh,
		-nohz

Nickname of citizens of Los Angeles.

Ángeles (P.I.)	*Eng.* ăn'-jə-ləs	an'-juh-luhs
	Sp. än'-hĕ-lĕs	ahn'-heh-les
Angelo (It.)	än'-jĕ-lô	ahn'-jeh-lo
Angerburg (Ger. >Pol.)	äng'-ər-bŏŏrk(h)	ahng' -uhr-burk(h)
Polish *Węgobork,* q.v.		
Angerloo (Neth.)	äng'-ər-lō	ahng'-uhr-loh
Angers (Fr.)	*Eng.* ăn'-jĭrz'	an'-jihrz'
	Fr. äN-zhĕ'	ahN-zheh'

Anghiari (It.)	än-gyä'-rē	ahn-gyah'-ree
Angitola (It.)	än-jē'-tô-lä	ahn-jee'-to-lah
Angkor Thom (Indo-Ch.)	ăng'-kōr tôm'	ang'-kohr tawm'
Angkor Wat (Indo-Ch.)	ăng'-kōr wät'	ang'-kohr waht'
Angola (Afr.)	ăng-gō'-lə	ang-goh'-luh

Also called *Portuguese West Africa.*

Angono (P.I.)	än-gô'-nô	ahn-go'-no

Also called *Angona,* än-gô'-nä [ahn-go'-nah].

Angoulême (Fr.)	äN-gōō-lĕm'	ahN-goo-lem'
Angra do Heroismo	äN'-grə dōō	ahN'-gruh du
(Azores)	ĕ-rōō-ēzh'-mōō	eh-ru-eezh'-mu
Anguillara (It.)	än-gwēl-lä'-rä	ahn-gweel-lah'-rah
Angvik (Nor.)	äng'-vēk	ahng'-veek
Anholt (Den., isl.)	än'-hôlt	ahn'-holt
Anholt (Ger.)	än'-hôlt	ahn'-holt
An-hsi (Ch.) See *Ansi.*		
An-hsiang (Ch., Hunan)	än-shyäng	ahn-shyahng
An-hua (Ch., Hunan)	än-whä	ahn-whah
An-hwei (Ch., prov.)	än-whā	ahn-whah
An-i (Ch., Chekiang,	än-ē	ahn-ee
Kiangsi, Shansi)		
Aniche (Fr.)	ä-nēsh'	ah-neesh'
Aniene (It., riv.)	ä-nyĕ'-nĕ	ah-nyeh'-neh
Anina (Rum.)	ä-nē'-nä	ah-nee'-nah
Anir (Oc., Bismarck arch.)	ä-nēr'	ah-neer'
Also called *Feni,* q.v.		
Anjou (Fr.)	*Eng.* ăn'-jōō	an'-joo
	Fr. äN-zhōō'	ahN-zhoo'
Ankara (Turk.)	äng'-kä-rä	ahng'-kah-rah

Another form of the word, with different accent, *Angora,* ăng-gō'-rə [ang-goh'-ruh], is a familiar attributive.

An-k'ing (Ch., Anhwei)	än-kĭng	ahn-king
Anklam (Ger.)	än'-kläm	ahn'-klahm
Ankober (Ethiopia)	än'-kô-bər	ahn'-ko-buhr
Anloo (Neth.)	än'-lō	ahn'-loh
Annam (Indo-Ch.)	ăn-năm' *or* ə-năm	an-nam' *or* uh-nam
	or än-näm'	*or* ahn-nahm'
Annamese (Indo-Ch.)	ăn'-ə-mēz' *or* -mēs'	an'-uh-meez' *or* -mees'
Annamite (Indo-Ch.)	ăn'-ə-mīt	an'-uh-mait
Anna-Paulowna (Neth.)	än'-ä pō-lō'-nä	ahn'-ah poh-loh'-nah
Anne Boleyn	bŏŏl'-ĭn	bul'-in
(Henry's queen)	*or* bŏŏl'-lĭn'	bul'-lin'
Annebault (Fr.)	än-bō'	ahn-boh'
Annecy (Fr.)	än-sē'	ahn-see'

Annemasse (Fr.)	än-mäs′	ahn-mahs′
An-ning (Ch., Yünnan)	än-nĭng	ahn-ning
Annonay (Fr.)	ä-nô-nĕ′	ah-no-neh′
Annovka (Rus.)	än′-nŏf-kä	ahn′-nof-kah
Annunziata (It.)	än-nōōn-tsyä′-tä	ahn-noon-tsyah′-tah
Annunziatella (It.)	än-nōōn-tsyä-tĕl′-lä	ahn-noon-tsyah-tel′-lah
Annunzio (It.)	än-nōōn′-tsyô	ahn-noon′-tsyo
Anogia (Crete)	ä-noi′-yä	ah-noi′-yah
A Noite (Braz. newspaper)	ä noi′-tĭ	ah noi′-ti
Anomaur (New Guinea)	ä-nô-mour′	ah-no-maur′
Anosova (Rus.)	ä-nô′-sŏ-vä	ah-no′-so-vah
Anouilh, André	ä-nōō′(y),	ah-noo′(y),
(Fr. playwright)	äN-drĕ′	ahN-dreh′
Anschluss	än′-shlōōs	ahn′-shlus

"Union" of Germany and Austria.

An-shan (Manchu.)	än-shän	ahn-shahn
An-shu (Korea)	än-shū	ahn-shyoo
An-si or An-hsi (Ch., Kansu)	än-sē or än-shē	ahn-see or ahn-shee
Anska (Yugosl.)	än′-skä	ahn′-skah
Ansoedoe or Ansudu (NEI,	än′-sōō-dōō′	ahn′-soo-doo′
New Guinea)		
Antalaha (Madag.)	än′-tə-lä′-hə	ahn′-tuh-lah′-huh
Antalya (Turk.)	än-täl-yä′	ahn-tahl-yah′
Also called Adalia, q.v.		
Antananarivo (Madag.)	ăn′-tə-nä′-nə-rē′-vō	an′-tuh-nah′-nuh-ree′ -voh
Officially Tananarive, q.v.		
antarctic	ănt-ärk′-tĭk	ant-ahrk′-tik
See arctic.		
Anterion (Gr., cape)	än-dē′-rē(-ôn)	ahn-dee′-ree(-on)
Antheil, George	ăn′-tīl	an′-tail
(Am. musician)		
anti-	ăn′-tĭ-	an′-ti-

In compounds, such as anti-aircraft, the i of anti- should be short, not long. The long i (as in tie) is overemphatic and characteristic of reading aloud rather than of speaking. It should be avoided on the radio.

Antibes (Fr.)	äN-tēb′	ahN-teeb′
Anticoli (It.)	än-tē′-kô-lē	ahn-tee′-ko-lee
Antietam (Md.)	ăn-tē′-təm	an-tee′-tuhm
Antifer (Fr., cape)	äN-tē-fĕr′	ahN-tee-fehr′
Antigonish (Can.)	ăn′-tĭ-gō-nĭsh′	an′-ti-goh-nish′
Antigua (Guat.)	Eng. ăn-tē′-gwə	an-tee′-gwuh
Antikythera (Gr., isl.)	än-dē-kē′-thē-rä	ahn-dee-kee′-thee-rah
Also called Aigila, q.v.		

Antimakhia (Dodec., Cos)	än-dē-mä′-hē-ä	ahn-dee-mah′-hee-ah
Antipolo (P.I.)	än-tē-pô′-lô	ahn-tee-po′-lo
Antique (P.I.)	än-tē′-kĕ	ahn-tee′-keh
Antiskari (Crete)	än-dē-skä′-rē	ahn-dee-skah′-ree
Antivari (Yugosl.)	*It.* än-tē′-vä-rē	ahn-tee′-vah-ree
Serb-Croat *Bar*, q.v.		
Antofagasta (Chile)	*Eng.* ăn′-tə-fə-găs′-tə	an′-tuh-fuh-gas′-tuh
	Sp. än-tô-fä-gäs′-tä	ahn-to-fah-gahs′-tah
Antonescu, Ion (Rum.	än-tô-nĕ′-skŏŏ, yôn′	ahn-to-neh′-sku, yon′
polit.)		
Antrain (Fr.)	äN-trăN′	ahN-traN′
Antrim (No. Ire.)	ăn′-trĭm	an′-trim
Antrodoco (It.)	än-trô-dô′-kô	ahn-tro-do′-ko
Antsirabe (Madag.)	än′-tsĭ-rä′-bĕ	ahn′-tsi-rah′-beh
Antsirane (Madag.)	än′-tsĭ-rä′-nĕ	ahn′-tsi-rah′-neh
An-tung (Manchu.)	*Eng.* ăn-tŏŏng	an-tung
	Ch. än-dŏŏng	ahn-dung
Antwerp (Belg.)	*Eng.* ănt′-wərp	ant′-wuhrp

Flemish *Antwerpen*, änt′-vĕr-pən [ahnt′-vehr-puhn]. French *Anvers*,
äN-vĕr′ [ahN-vehr′].

An-yi (Ch.) See *An-i*.		
Anyox (Canada)	ăn′-ĭ-ŏks	an′-i-oks
An-yüan (Ch., Kiangsi)	än-yüän	ahn-yü-ahn
Anzio (It.)	än′-tsyô	ahn′-tsyo
Aola (Oc., Guadalcanal)	ä-ô′-lä	ah-o′-lah
Aomon (Oc., Eniwetok)	ä-ô′-môn	ah-o′-mon
Aomori (Jap.)	ä-ô′-mô-rē	ah-o′-mo-ree
Aoos (Balkan riv.)	*Gr.* ä-ô′-ôs	ah-o′-os
Albanian *Vijosë*, q.v.		
Aosta (It.)	ä-ô′-stä	ah-o′-stah
Aouana, el (Tun.)	ä-wă′-nä, ĕl	ah-wa′-nah, el
Aouaria, el (Tun.)	ä-wä-rē′-yä, ĕl	ah-wah-ree′-yah, el
Apache (Am. Indian)	ə-păch′-ĭ	uh-pach′-i

In the sense of hoodlum, pronounced as French, ä-päsb′ [ah-pahsh′],
or English, ə-păsh′ [uh-pash′].

Apálit (P.I.)	ä-pä′-lĭt	ah-pah′-lit
Apanasenko, J. R.	ä-pä-nä′-sĕn-kŏ	ah-pah-nah′-sen-ko
(Rus. general)		
Aparri (P.I.)	ä-pär′-rē	ah-pahr′-ree
Apatin (Hung.)	ŏ′-pŏ-tĭn	o′-po-tin
Apatin (Yugosl.)	ä′-pä-tĭn	ah′-pah-tin
Apayaos (P.I.)	ä-pä-yä′-ôs	ah-pah-yah′-os
Apeldoorn (Neth.)	äp′-əl-dōrn	ahp′-uhl-dohrn

Apennines (It., mts.) ăp'-ə-nīnz ap'-uh-nainz
Italian *Appennino*, äp-pĕn-nē'-nô [ahp-pen-nee'-no].
Apia (Oc., Samoa) ä'-pē'-ä ah'-pee'-ah
Apo (P.I.) ä'-pô ah'-po
Apolda (Ger.) ä-pôl'-dä ah-pol'-dah
Apollonia (Alb.) *Eng.* ăp'-ə-lōn'-yə ap'-uh-lohn'-yuh
Albanian *Pojan*, q.v.
Appalachian (U.S., mts.) ăp'-ə-lā'-chən ap'-uh-lay'-chuhn
  or ăp'-ə-lăch'-ən ap'-uh-lach'-uhn
Appelscha (Neth.) äp'-əl-sk(h)ä ahp'-uhl-sk(h)ah
Appian Way (It., road) ăp'-ĭ-ən ap'-i-uhn
Appingedam (Neth.) äp'-ĭng-ə-däm' ahp'-ing-uh-dahm'
Apra (Guam) ä'-prä ah'-prah
Also called *San Luis d'Apra*, sän lōō-ēs' dä'-prä [sahn lu-ees' dah'-prah].
apricot ā'-prĭ-kŏt ay'-pri-kot *or* ap'-ri-kot
  or ăp'-rĭ-kŏt
Seven out of eight authoritative dictionaries list first the pronunciation with ā-. See *economic(s)* and the note thereon.
Aprilia (It.) ä-prē'-lyä ah-pree'-lyah
Apsos (Alb., riv.) *Gr.* äp'-sôs ahp'-sos
Albanian *Berat*, q.v., and *Seman*, q.v.
Apt (Fr.) äpt' ahpt'
Apulia (It.) *Eng.* ə-pyōō'-lyə uh-pyoo'-lyuh
Italian *Puglia*, pōō'-lyä [poo'-lyah].
Apurauan (P.I.) ä-pōō-rou'-än ah-poo-rau'-ahn
Aqqaba (Pal.) äk-kä'-bĕ ahk-kah'-beh
Aquila (It.) ä'-kwē-lä ah'-kwee-lah
Aquileja *or* Aquileia ä-kwē-lä'-yä ah-kwee-lay'-yah
  (It.)
Aquino (It.) ä-kwē'-nô ah-kwee'-no
Arabatskaya Strelka (Rus.) ä-rä-bät'-skä-yä ah-rah-baht'-skah-
  strĕl'-kä yah strel'-kah
Aracajú (Brazil) ä-rə-kä-zhōō' ah-ruh-kah-zhoo'
Arad (Rum.) *Rum.* ä-räd' ah-rahd'
  Hung. ŏ'-rŏd o'-rod
Arafura Sea (Austral.) ä-rə-fōō'-rə ah-ruh-foo'-ruh
Aragnes (Fr., riv.) ä-rän'(y) ah-rəhn'(y)
Aragón (Sp.) ä-rä-gôn' ah-rah-gon'
Aragona (Sicily) ä-rä-gô'-nä ah-rah-go'-nah
Arakan (Burma) ä'-rə-kăn' a'-ruh-kan'
Araks *or* Aras (W. Asia, ä-räks' *or* ä-räs' ah-rahks' *or* ah-rahs'
  riv.)
English *Araxes*, q.v.

Aral (Rus., lake)	ăr′-əl or ä′-räl′	ehr′-uhl ah′-rahl′
Russian *Aralskoe More,* ä-räl′(y)-skŏ-yĕ mô′-rĕ [ah-rahl′(y)-sko-yeh mo′-reh].		
Arambeĭ (Gr., mt.)	ä-rä-bā′	ah-rah-bay′
Aranci (Sard.)	ä-rän′-chē	ah-rahn′-chee
Aranđelovac (Yugosl.)	ä′-rän′-dyĕ-lô-väts	ah′-rahn′-dyeh-lo-vahts
Aranha, Oswaldo (Braz. polit.)	ä-rä′-nyə, ŏz-väl′-dŏŏ	ah-rah′-nyuh, oz-vahl′-du
Aranha may approach ə-rĕ′-nyə [uh-reh′-nyuh].		
Aranjuez (Sp.)	ä-rän-hwĕth′ or -hwĕs′	ah-rahn-hweth′ or -hwes′
Aranyaprathet (Siam)	ä-rŭn′-yə prä-tāt′	ah-ruhn′-uh prah-tayt′
Also spelled *Aranya Prades.*		
Aras (W. Asia) See *Araks.*		
ʻArava (Pal.) See ʻ*Arrabe.*		
Arawe (Oc.)	ä-rä′-wĕ	ah-rah′-weh
Araxes (W. Asia, riv.)	ä-răk′-sĭs	ah-rak′-sis
Also called *Aras* and *Araks.*		
Araxos (Gr.)	ä′-rä-ksôs	ah′-rah-ksos
Aráyat (P.I.)	ä-rä′-yät	ah-rah′-yaht
Arbatax (Sard.)	är-bä′-täks	ahr-bah′-tahks
Arbe (Yugosl.)	*It.* är′-bĕ	ahr′-beh
Serb-Croat *Rab,* q.v.		
Arc (Fr., riv.)	ärk′	ahrk′
Arca, Rt (Yugosl.)	är′-tsä, ərt′	ahr′-tsah, uhrt′
Arcachon (Fr.)	är-kä-shôN′	ahr-kah-shoN′
Arçay (Fr.)	är-sĕ′	ahr-seh′
Arc de Triomphe (Fr., Paris)	ärk də trē-ôNf′	ahrk duh tree-oNf′
Arce (It.)	är′-chĕ	ahr′-cheh
Arce, José (Arg. diplomat)	är′-sĕ, hô-sĕ′	ahr′-seh, ho-seh′
arch-	ärch-	ahrch-
Exceptions, *archangel,* ärk′-ān′-jəl [ahrk′-ayn′-juhl], and derivatives. See also *archetype* and *archi-.*		
Archangel (Rus.)	*Eng.* ärk-ān′-jəl	ahrk-ayn′-juhl
Russian *Arkhangelsk,* är-hän′-gĕlsk [ahr-hahn′-gelsk].		
Arche (It.)	är′-kĕ	ahr′-keh
archetype	är′-kĭ-tīp	ahr′-ki-taip
archi-	är′-kĭ-	ahr′-ki-
As in *archipelago, architect, architectonic.*		
archipelago	är′-kĭ-pĕl′-ə-gō	ahr′-ki-pel′-uh-goh
This word trips many good men.		

archive	är'-kīv	ahr'-kaiv
archivist	är'-kĭ-vĭst	ahr'-ki-vist
Arcis sür Aube (Fr.)	är-sēs sür ōb'	ahr-sees sür ohb'
Arciszewski, Tomasz (Pol. polit.)	är-chĭ-shĕf'-skĭ, tô'-mäsh	ahr-chih-shef'-ski, to'-mahsh
Arcot (India)	är'-kŏt	ahr'-kot
Arcs, les (Fr.)	ärk', lĕz	ahrk', lez
arctic, antarctic	ärk'-tĭk, ănt-ärk'-tĭk	ahrk'-tik, ant-ahrk'-tik

The common "erroneous" pronunciations är'-tĭk [ahr'-tik] and ănt-är'-tĭk [ant-ahr'-tick] are not original American sins, but a continuation of the usual medieval pronunciations of English, French, and Latin. The etymological spelling of the Renaissance restored the "correct" c (Greek k), and it has bothered speakers of English ever since. The learned form became fixed in French too, but not in Italian where the comfortable vernacular *artico* and *antartico* are standard. Though there is thus a good scholarly defense for English är'-tĭk and ănt-är'-tĭk, the school-marms have long since won the fight for a polite ärk'-tĭk and ănt-ärk'-tĭk. Announcers had better conform to their rule despite the contrary examples of Chaucer, Burton, and some worthy geographers to 1777. For these see the *Oxford English Dictionary on Historical Principles*.

Arda (Balkan riv.)	är'-dä	ahr'-dah
Ardahan (Turkey)	är-dä-hän'	ahr-dah-hahn'
Russian *Ardagan*, är-dä-gän' [ahr-dah-gahn'].		
Årdal (Nor.) See *Aardal*.		
Ardatov (Rus.)	är-dä'-tŏf	ahr-dah'-tof
Ardea (It.)	är'-dĕ-ä	ahr'-deh-ah
Ardeatine Caves (It.)	*Eng.* är'-dĭ-ə-tīn'	ahr'-di-uh-tain'
Ardèche (Fr.)	är-dĕsh'	ahr-desh'
Ardres (Fr.)	är'dr	ahr'dr
Arendal (Nor.)	ä'-rən-däl	ah'-ruhn-dahl
Arends, Leslie C. (U.S. representative)	ăr'-əndz	ehr'-uhndz
Arenfels (Ger.)	ä'-rən-fĕls	ah'-ruhn-fels
Arensburg (Est.) Estonian *Kuresaari*, q.v.	*Ger.* ä'-rĕns-bōŏrk(h)	ah'-rens-burk(h)
Arents Eilanden (NEI)	ä'-rĕnts ī'-län-dən	ah'-rents ai'-lahn-duhn
Areopolis (Gr.)	ä-rĕ-ô'-pô-lē(s)	ah-reh-o'-po-lee(s)
Arequipa (Peru)	ä-rĕ-kē'-pä	ah-reh-kee'-pah
Arévalo, Juan José (Guat. polit.)	ä-rĕ'-vä-lô, hwän' hô-sĕ'	ah-reh'-vah-lo, hwahn' ho-seh'
Arezzo (It.)	ä-rĕt'-sô	ah-ret'-so

Argao (P.I.)	är-gou′	ahr-gau′
Argences (Fr.)	är-zhäNs′	ahr-zhahNs′

Argenlieu, Georges Thierry d′ (Fr. admiral) See *d′ Argenlieu.*

Argens (Fr., riv.)	är-zhäNs′	ahr-zhahNs′
Argenta (It.)	är-jĕn′-tä	ahr-jen′-tah
Argentan (Fr.)	är-zhäN-täN′	ahr-zhahN-tahN′
Argenteuil (Fr.)	är-zhäN-tû′(y)	ahr-zhahN-tœ′(y)
Argentia (Newf.)	är-jĕn′-shə *or* -shĭ-ə	ahr-jen′-shuh *or* -shi-uh
Argentiera (It.)	är-jĕn-tyĕ′-rä	ahr-jen-tyeh′-rah
Argentina	*Eng.* är′-gən-tē′-nə	ahr′-juhn-tee′-nuh
	Sp. är-hĕn-tē′-nä	ahr-hen-tee′-nah

Argentina as a zoological term is pronounced är′-jən-tī-nə [ahr′-juhn-tai′-nuh]

Argentine	*Eng.* är′-jən-tēn′	ahr′-juhn-teen′
	or -tīn′	*or* -tain′

Many speakers who normally prefer -tēn′, [-teen′] will pronounce -tīn [-tain′] in the phrase *The Argentine.* The word *argentine* (meaning silver) is pronounced är′-jən-tĭn [ahr′-juhn-tin] *or* -tīn [-tain].

Argenton sur Creuse	är-zhäN-tôN	ahr-zhahN-toN
(Fr.)	sür krûz′	sür krœz′
Argentré du Plessis (Fr.)	är-zhäN-trĕ dü	ahr-zhahN-treh dü
	plĕ-sē′	pleh-see′
Arges (Rum., riv.)	är′-jĕsh	ahr′-jesh
Argine (It.)	är′-jē-nĕ	ahr′-jee-neh
Argolis (Gr.)	*Eng.* är′-gō-lĭs	ahr′-goh-lis
	Gr. är-gô-lēs′	ahr-go-lees′
Argos (Gr.)	är′-gô(s)	ahr′-go(s)
Argüelles, Agustín	är-gwĕ′-lyĕs,	ahr-gweh′-lyes,
(Sp. statesman)	ä-gōōs-tēn′	ah-goos-teen′
Arguello (Sp. name)	*Am. Sp.* är-gĕ′-yô	ahr-geh′-yo
	Sp. är-gĕ′-lyô	ahr-geh′-lyo
Arguello, Leonardo	är-gĕ′-yô,	ahr-geh′-yo,
(Nicar. polit)	lĕ-ô-när′-dô	leh-o-nahr′-do
Argustolion (Gr.)	är-gôs-tô′-lē(-ôn)	ahr-gos-to′-lee(-on)
Argyle (Austral.)	är′-gīl′	ahr′-gail′
Argyn (Rus., riv.)	är-gōōn′	ahr-goon′
Argyrokastron (Alb.)	*Gr.* är-yē-rô′-käs-trô(n)	ahr-yee-ro′-kahs-tro(n)

Albanian *Gjinokastër,* q.v.

Ariana (Tun.)	ä-rĭ-ä′-nä	ah-ri-a′-nah
Ariano (It.)	ä-ryä′-nô	ah-ryah′-no
Arica (Chile)	ä-rē′-kä	ah-ree′-kah
Ariccia (It.)	ä-rēt′-chä	ah-reet′-chah

Arielli (It.)	ä-ryĕl'-lē	ah-ryel'-lee
Arilje (Yugosl.)	ä'-rĭ-lyĕ	ah'-ri-lyeh
Arima, el (Tun.)	ä-rē'-mä, ĕl	ah-ree'-mah, el
Arimo (Idaho)	är'-ĭ-mō	ehr'-i-moh
Aríngay (P.I., riv.)	ä-rēng'-ī	ah-reeng'-ai
Ariniccia (It.)	ä-rē-nēt'-chä	ah-ree-neet'-chah
Aris (N.E. New Guinea)	ä'-rēs	ah'-rees
Also called *Botsa*, q.v		
Arish, el (Egypt)	ä-rēsh', ĕl	ah-reesh', el
Aristazabal (Canada)	ă'-rĭ-stăz-ə-bäl'	a'-ri-staz-uh-bahl'
Arkansan	är-kăn'-zən	ahr-kan'-zuhn
Arkansas (U.S., state)	är'-kən-sô	ahr'-kuhn-saw

As the name of the state of *Arkansas* this pronunciation was established by resolution of the State Legislature in 1881. The resolution, however, was without effect in the State of Kansas, where *Arkansas City* and the Kansas portion of the *Arkansas River* are pronounced är-kăn'-zəs [ahr-kan'-zhus].

Arkansas City (Kansas)	är-kăn'-zəs	ahr-kan'-zuhs
Arkansawyer	är'-kən-sô'-yər	ahr'-kuhn-saw'-yuhr

A colloquial or comical synonym of *Arkansan*, q.v.

Arkhanes (Crete)	är-hä'-nĕs	ahr-hah'-nes
Arkhara (Rus.)	är-hä'-rä	ahr-hah'-rah
Arles (Fr.)	*Eng.* ärlz'	ahrlz'
	Fr. ärl'	ahrl'
Arlon (Belg.)	är-lôN'	ahr-loN'
armada	*Eng.* är-mä'-də	ahr-mah'-duh
	or är-mā'-də	ahr-may'-duh
	Sp. är-mä'-dä	ahr-mah'-dah
Armagh (No. Ire.)	är-mä'	ahr-mah'
Armavir (Rus.)	är-mä-vēr'	ahr-mah-veer'
Armeni (Crete)	är-mĕ'-nē	ahr-meh'-nee
Armentières (Fr.)	*Eng.* är'-mən-tĭrz'	ahr'-muhn-tihrz'
	Fr. är-mäN-tyĕr'	ahr-mahN-tyehr'
Armorica (Fr.)	är-môr'-ĭ-kə	ahr-mor'-i-kuh

French *Armorique*, är-mô-rēk' [ahr-mo-reek'].

Armyansk (Rus.)	är-myänsk'	ahr-myahnsk'
Arnall, Ellis (Ga. polit.)	är'-nəl	ahr'-nuhl
Arnara (It.)	är-nä'-rä	ahr-nah'-rah
Arnavon (Oc.)	är-nä'-vôn	ahr-nah'-von
Arnemuiden (Neth.)	är'-nə-mûĭ'-dən	ahr'-nuh-mœi'-duhn
Arnhem (Austral.)	ärn'-əm	ahrn'-uhm
Arnhem (Neth.)	ärn'-hĕm	ahrn'-hem
Arno (It., riv.)	är'-nô	ahr'-no
Arno (Oc., Marshalls)	är'-nô	ahr'-no

[27]

Arnswalde (Ger. > Pol.) Polish *Choszczno*, q.v.	ärns'-väl-də	ahrns'-vahl-duh
Aroe *or* Aru (NEI)	ä'-rōō	ah'-roo
Aroostook (Me.)	ə-rōōs'-tŏŏk	uh-roos'-tuk
Arorae (Oc., Gilberts)	ä-rô'-rä-ĕ *or* -rī	ah-ro'-rah-eh *or* -rai
Aroussa, el (Tun.)	ä-rōō'-sä, ĕl	ah-roo'-sah, el
Arpajon (Fr.)	är-pä-zhôN'	ahr-pah-zhoN'
Arpino (It.)	är-pē'-nô	ahr-pee'-no
'Arrabe (Pal.) Hebrew *'Arava*.	är-rä'-bĕ	ahr-rah'-beh
Arras (Fr.)	*Eng.* ăr'-əs *Fr.* ä-räs'	ehr'-uhs ah-rahs'
Arrau, Claudio (Chilean pianist)	är-rou', klou'-dyô	ahr-rau', klau'-dyo
Arromanches (Fr.)	ä-rô-mäNsh'	ah-ro-mahNsh'
arroyo	*Eng.* ə-rô'-yə *Sp.* är-rô'-yô	uh-raw'-yuh ahr-ro'-yo
Arsoli (It.)	är'-sô-lē	ahr'-so-lee
Arta (Alb., lake) Albanian *Knetë e Nartës*.	*Eng.* är'-tä	ahr'-tah
Arta (Gr., riv.)	är'-tä	ahr'-tah
Artëm (Rus.)	är-tyôm'	ahr-tyom'
Artëmov (Rus.)	är-tyô'-môf	ahr-tyo'-mof
Artëmovsk (Rus.)	är-tyô'-môfsk	ahr-tyo'-mofsk
Artena (It.)	är-tĕ'-nä	ahr-teh'-nah
Artenay (Fr.)	är-tə-nĕ'	ahr-tuh-neh'
Artigas (Urug.)	är-tē'-gäs	ahr-tee'-gahs
Artois (Fr.)	*Eng.* är'-toiz *Fr.* är-twä'	ahr'-toiz ahr-twah'
Aru (NEI) See *Aroe*.		
Aruba (Du. W.I.)	ä-rōō'-bä	ah-roo'-bah
Aruba (Sp.)	ä-rōō'-bä	ah-roo'-bah
Arundel	*U.S.* ə-rŭn'-dəl *Eng.* ăr'-ən-dəl	uh-ruhn'-duhl ehr'-uhn-duhl
Also ə-rŭn'-əl [uh-ruhn'-uhl] and ärn'-dəl [ahrn'-duhl].		
Arz (Fr., riv.)	ärz'	ahrz'
Arzamas (Rus.)	är-zä-mäs'	ahr-zah-mahs'
Arzen (Alb., riv.) See *Erzen*.		
Arzeu (Alg.)	är-zĕ-ōō'	ahr-zeh-oo'
Arzfeld (Ger.)	ärts'-fĕlt	ahrts'-felt
Arzgir (Rus.)	ärz'-gēr'	ahrz'-geer'
Arzila (Sp. Mor.) Arabic *Asila*.	är-sē'-lä	ahr-see'-lah

Asab (Eritreia). See *Assab.*

Asahi (Jap., Tokyo,   ä'-sä-hē   ah'-sah-hee
  newspaper)
  Also called *Asahi Shimbun,* ä-sä'-hē' shēm'-bōōn [ah-sah'-hee' sheem'-
  boon].

Asano (Jap., zaibatsu)   ä-sä'-nô'   ah-sah'-no'
Asbach (Ger.)   äs'-bäk(h)   ahs'-bahk(h)
Asch (Ger.)   äsh'   ahsh'
Aschaffenburg (Ger.)   ä-shäf'-ən-bōōrk(h)   ah-shahf'-uhn-
                                        burk(h)
Aschersleben (Ger.)   äsh'-ərs-lā'-bən   ahsh'-uhrs-lay'-buhn
Ascoli (It.)   ä'-skô-lē   ah'-sko-lee
Asénsio Cabanillas, Carlos ä-sĕn'-syô   ah-sen'-syo
  (Sp. polit.)   kä-bä-nē'-lyäs   kah-bah-nee'-lyahs
                 (*or* -yäs), kär'-lôs (*or* -yahs), kahr'-los
Aseri (Est.)   ä'-sĕ-rĭ   ah'-seh-ri
Åsgårdsstrand (Nor.) See *Aasgaardsstrand.*

Ashby de la Launde (Eng.) ăsh'-bĭ də lä lônd'   ash'-bi duh lah lawnd'
Ashby de la Zouch (Eng.) ăsh'-bĭ də lä zōōsh' ash'-bi duh lah zoosh'
  "I suppose that in quick casual pronunciation lä often becomes lə,
  but the above is what the railway announcer would say."—J.A.W.B.

Ashida, Hitoshi   ä-shē'-dä', hē-tô'-   ah-shee'-dah', hee-
  (Jap. polit.)   shē'   to'-shee'
Ashishina (Tun.)   ä-shē-shē'-nä   ah-shee-shee'-nah
Ashkhabad (Rus.)   äsh-kä-bäd'   ahsh-kah-bahd'
Ashtabula (Ohio)   ăsh'-tə-byōō'-lə   ash'-tuh-byoo'-luh
Asinara (Sard., isl.)   ä-sē-nä'-rä   ah-see-nah'-rah
Asine (Gr.) See *Korone.*
Asinello (It. > Yugosl. isl.) ä-sē-nĕl'-lô   ah-see-nel'-lo
  Serb-Croat *Sveti Petar.*

Asingan (P.I.)   ä-sĭng'-än   ah-sing'-ahn
Asker (Nor.)   äs'-kər   ahs'-kuhr
Asmara (Eritrea)   äs-mä'-rä   ahs-mah'-rah
Asnelles (Fr.)   äs-nĕl'   ahs-nel'
Asnières (Fr.)   ä-nyĕr'   ah-nyehr'
Asprano (It.)   ä-sprä'-nô   ah-sprah'-no
Assab (Eritrea)   ä'-säb   ah'-sahb
assail, assailant   ə-sāl', ə-sāl'-ənt   uh-sayl', uh-sayl'-
  Avoid ə-sī'-lənt [uh-sai'-luhnt].   uhnt
Assam (India)   ăs-săm'   as-sam'
Asse (Fr., riv.)   äs'   ahs'
Assebrouck (Belg.)   äs'-ə-brōōk   ahs'-uh-bruk
Assen (Neth.)   äs'-ən   ahs'-uhn
Assendelft (Neth.)   äs-ən-dĕlft'   ahs-uhn-delft'

Assenede (Belg.)	*Flem.* ä-sĕn'-ə-də	ah-sehn'-uh-duh
	Fr. ä-sə-nĕd'	ah-suh-ned'
Assisi (It.)	äs-sē'-zē	ahs-see'- zee
Assling (Yugosl.)	*Ger.* äs'-lĭng	ahs'-ling
Serb-Croat *Jesenica*, q.v.		
association	ə-sō'-sĭ-ā'-shən	uh-soh'-si-ay'-shuhn
	or ə-sō'-shĭ-ā'-shən	uh-soh'-shi-ay'-shuhn

By the principle of dissimilation, *associate* is pronounced ə-sō'-shĭ-ĭt *or* -āt' [uh-soh'-shih-it *or* -ayt']. In the case of *association*, however, there are two current pronunciations of the syllable *-ci-*. The *s*-sound preceding and the *sh*-sound following confuse the forces of dissimilation and assimilation.

Astakos (Gr.)	ä-stä-kôs'	ah-stah-kos'
Asten (Neth.)	äs'-tən	ahs'-tuhn
Asterabad *or* Astrabad (Iran) See *Gurgan*.		
Astheim (Ger.)	äst'-hīm	ahst'-haim
Astier de la Vigerie	äs-tyĕ' də lä	ahs-tyeh' duh lah
(Fr. polit.)	vē-zhĕ-rē'	vee-zheh-ree'
Astrakhan (Rus.)	*Eng.* ăs'-trə-kăn'	as'-truh-kan'
	Rus. ä'-strä-hän(y)	ah'-strah-hahn(y)
Astrid	*Eng.* ăs'-trĭd	as'-trid
(Nor. princess)	*Nor.* äs'-trē	ahs'-tree
Astritsi (Crete)	ä-strē'-tsē	ah-stree'-tsee
Astrolabe (N.E. New	ăs'-trō-lāb	as'-troh-layb
Guinea, bay)		
Astropalea (Dodec.) See *Astypalea* and *Stampalia*.		
Astura (It., riv.)	ä-stōō'-rä	ah-stoo'-rah
Asturias (Sp., prov.)	*Eng.* ăs-tyōō'-rĭ-əs	as-tyoo'-ri-uhs
	Sp. äs-tōōr'-yäs	ahs-toor'-yahs
Astypalea (Dodec.)	ä-stē-pä-lĕ'-ä	ah-stee-pah-leh'-ah

Also called *Astropalea*, ä-strô-pä-lyä' [ah-stro-pah-lyah']. Italian *Stampalia*, q.v.

Asunciön (Sp; Oc., Mari-	ä-sōōn-syôn'	ah-soon-syon'
anas)	*or* -thyôn'	*or* -thyon'
Aswân (Egypt)	äs-wän'	ahs-wahn'
Asyut (Egypt, prov.)	ä-syōōt'	ah-syoot'
Aszód (Hung.)	ä'-sôd	ah'-sod
atabrine	ăt'-ə-brēn'	at'-uh-breen'
Atafu (Oc., Tokelau)	ä-tä-fōō'	ah-tah-foo'
Atalante (Gr.)	*Gr.* ä-tä-län'-dē	ah-tah-lahn'-dee
	Eng. ăt-ə-lăn'-tĭ	at-uh-lan'-ti
Ataliklikun (Oc., New		
Britain)	ä-tä-lēk'-lē-kōōn	ah-tah-leek'-lee-koon

ataman   *Eng.* ăt'-ə-măn   at'-uh-man
                    Rus. ä-tä-män'   ah-tah-mahn'
A Cossack title, disregarded in alphabetical listing.

Atatürk, Kemal (Turk. polit.) See *Kemal Atatürk.*

Ataúro (Port. Timor, isl.)   ä-tä-ōō'-rô   ah-tah-oo'-ro

Atavyri (Dodec., Rh., mt.)   ä-tä-vē'-rē   ah-tah-vee'-ree
    Italian *Attairo,* ät-tī'-rô [aht-tai'-ro].

Atbara (Sudan, riv.)   ät'-bə-rə   aht'-buh-ruh

Atet (Burma)   ə-tĕt'   uh-tet'
    An element in place names meaning *lower.*

Ath (Belg.)   ät'   aht'

Athanasios, Tanassis (Gr. polit.) See *Agnides, Tanassis.*

Athenai (Gr.)   See *Athens.*

Athens (Gr.)   *Eng.* ăth'-ĭnz   ath'-inz
    Greek *Athenai,* ä-thē'-nĕ [ah-thee'-neh]—often *Athena,* ä-thē'-nä
    [ah-thee'-nah].

Athis (Fr.)   ä-tēs'   ah-tees'

'Athlit (Pal.)   ät-lēt'   aht-leet'

Athlone (Eire)   ăth-lōn'   ath-lohn'
    Gaelic *Áth Luain,* ä lōō'-ĭn [ah loo'-in].

Athos (Gr., pen., mt.)   *Eng.* ăth'-ŏs   ath'-os
                   or ā'-thŏs   ay'-thos
                   Gr. ä'-thôs   ah'-thos
    Also called *Agion Oros,* ī'-yôn ô'-rôs [ai'-yon o'-ros].

Atiles, J. A. Bonilla (Dom. polit.) See *Bonilla Atiles.*

Atilio Bramuglia,   ä-tē'-lyô   ah-tee'-lyo brah-
   Juan (Arg. polit.)   brä-mōō'-lyä, hwän'   moo'-lyah, hwahn'

Atina (It.)   ä-tē'-nä   ah-tee'-nah

Atiu (Oc., Cook)   ä-tē-ōō'   ah-tee-oo'

Atka (Alaska, isl.)   ăt'-kə   at'-kuh

Atkarsk (Rus.)   ät-kärsk'   aht-kahrsk'

Atna (Nor.)   ät'-nä   aht'-nah

atoll   ăt'-ŏl *or* ə-tŏl'   at'-ol *or* uh-tol'

Atsugi (Jap., airfield)   ä-tsōō'-gē'   ah-tsoo'-gee'

Attairo (Dodec., Rh., mt.)   See *Atavyri.*

Attlee, Clement Richard   ăt'-lĭ   at'-li
   (Br. polit.)

Attu (Alaska, isl.)   ăt'-tōō'   at'-too'

Aubagne (Fr.)   ō-bän'(y)   oh-bahn'(y)

Aubenas (Fr.)   ōb-näs'   ohb-nahs'

Aubervilliers (Fr.)   ō-bĕr-vē-yĕ'   oh-behr-vee-yeh'

Aubigny (Fr.)   ō-bē-nyē'   oh-bee-nyee'

Aubrac, Raymond   ō-bräk' rĕ-môN'   oh-brahk', reh-moN'
   (Fr. polit.)

Aubusson (Fr.)	ō-bü-sôN′	oh-bü-soN′
Auby (Fr.)	ō-bē′	oh-bee′
Auch (Fr.)	ōsh′	ohsh′
Auchel (Fr.)	ō-shĕl′	oh-shel′
Auchincloss, James C.	ô′-kĭn-klŏs	aw′-kin-klos

(U.S. representative)

| Auchinleck (Scot.) | ô′-kĭn-lĕk | o′-kin-lek |

The old pronunciation ă-flĕk′ is associated with James Boswell.

Auckland (N.Z.)	ôk′-lənd	awk′-luhnd
Aude (Fr., riv.)	ōd′	ohd′
Audemer, Pont (Fr.)	ōd-mĕr′ *or*	ohd-mehr′ *or*
	pôN tōd-mĕr′	poN tohd-mehr′
Audruicq (Fr.)	ō-drwēk′	oh-drweek′
Aue (Ger., riv.)	ou′-ə	au′-uh
Auegia (Libya)	ä-wā′-jä	ah-way′-jah

Also called *Marsa* (q.v.) *el Auegia.*

| Auer, Paul | ou′-ər | au′-uhr |

(Hung. diplomat)

Auge (Fr.)	ōzh′	ohzh′
Augsburg (Ger.)	*Eng.* ôgz′-bûrg	ogz′-buhrg
	Ger. ouk(h)s′-boŏrk(h)	auk(h)s′-burk(h)
Augusta (Sicily)	*Eng.* ə-gŭs′-tə	uh-guhs′-tuh
	It. ou-goō′-stä	au-goo′-stah
Augustów (Pol.)	ou-goō′-stôof	au-goo′-stuf

Russian *Avgustov,* äv-goō′-stôf [ahv-goo′-stof].

| Augustowski, Kanał (Pol.) | ou-goō-stôf′-skĭ, | au-gu-stof′-ski, |
| | kä′-näl | kah′-nahl |

Russian *Avgustovski Kanal,* äv-goō-stôf′-skĭ kä-näl′ [ahv-goo-stof′-ski kah-nahl′].

Auki (Oc., Solomons)	ou′-kē	au′-kee
Auletta (It.)	ou-lĕt′-tä	au-let′-tah
Aulnay sous Bois (Fr.)	ō-nĕ soō bwä′	oh-neh soo bwah′
Ault (Fr.)	ō′	oh′
Aumetz (Luxem.)	*Fr.* ō-mĕs′	oh-mes′
	Ger. ou′-mĕts	au′-mets
Aunay (Fr.)	ō-nĕ′	oh-neh′
Aung San (Burman polit.)	oung′ sän′	aung′ sahn′
Aunis (Fr.)	ō-nēs′	oh-nees′
Aunus (Fin., isthmus)	ou′-noŏs	au′-nus

Russian *Olonets,* q.v.

Aups (Fr.)	ōps′	ohps′
Aur (Oc., Marshalls)	our′	aur′
Aurangabad (India)	ô-rŭng′-gə-băd′	o-ruhng′-guh-bad′
	or ou-rŭng-gä-bäd′	au-ruhng-gah-bahd′

Auray (Fr.)	ō-rĕ′	oh-reh′
Aure (Fr.)	ōr′	ohr′
Aurès (Alg., mts.)	ō-rĕs′	oh-rehs′
Aurich (Ger.)	ou′-rĭk(h)	au′-rik(h)
Aurignac (Fr.)	ō-rē-nyäk′	oh-ree-nyahk′
Aurillac (Fr.)	ō-rē-yäk′	oh-ree-yahk′
Auriol, Vincent	ô-ryôl′, văN-säN′	o-ryol′, vaN-sahN′
(Fr. polit.)		
Aurland (Nor.)	our′-län	aur′-lahn
Aurskog (Nor.)	our′-skōg	aur′-skohg
	or oush′-kōg	aush′-kohg

Formerly spelled *Oerskog* or *Örskog* and pronounced ûr′-skōg [œr′-skohg] or ûsh′-kōg [œsh′-kohg].

Aurunci (It., mt.)	ou-rōōn′-chē	au-roon′-chee
Ausa (It., riv.)	ou′-sä	au′-sah
Au Sable (Mich., riv.)	ô sä′-bəl	aw say′-buhl
Ausable (N. Y., riv.)	ô-sä′-bəl	aw-say′-buhl
Auschwitz (Pol.) See *Oświęcim*.		
Ausente (It., riv.)	ou-sĕn′-tĕ	au-sen′-teh
Ausonia (It.)	ou-sô′-nyä	au-so′-nyah
auspices	ôs′-pĭ-sĭz	os′-pi-siz

The plural ôs′-pĭ-sēz [os′-pi-seez] is incorrect. The singular is *auspice*; the plural therefore should be formed, not on the analogy of *basis*, *bases* (bā′-sĭs, -sēz), but of *base*, *bases* (bās, bā′-sĭz).

Aust Agder (Nor.)	oust′ äg′-dər	aust′ ahg′-duhr
Austerlitz (Cz.)	*Eng.* ôs′-tər-lĭts	os′-tuhr-lits
	Ger. ous′-tər-lĭts	aus′-tuhr-lits

Czech *Slavkov*, släf′-kôf [slahf′-kof].

Austraat (Nor.)	ou′-strôt	au′-strot
Auteuil (Fr.)	ō-tû′ï	oh-tœ′i
Authie (Fr., riv.)	ō-tē′	oh-tee′
Authion (Fr., riv.)	ō-tyôN′	oh-tyoN′
Authon du Perche (Fr.)	ō-tôN′ dü pĕrsh′	oh-toN′ dü pehrsh′
autogyro	ô′-tō-jī′-rō	aw′-toh-jai′-roh
autopsy	ô′-tŏp-sĭ	aw′-top-si
	or ô′-təp-sĭ	aw′-tuhp-si
Autrie (Fr., riv.)	ō-trē′	oh-tree′
Autun (Fr.)	ō-tûN′	oh-tœN′
Auvergne (Fr.)	ō-vĕrn′(y)	oh-vehrn′(y)
Aux Cayes (Haiti)	ō kĕ′	oh keh′
Auxerre (Fr.)	ō-sĕr′	oh-sehr′
Auxonne (Fr.)	ō-sôn′	oh-son′
Avala (Yugosl.)	ä′-vä-lä	ah′-vah-lah
Avallon (Fr.)	ä-vä-lôN′	ah-vah-loN′

Ávalos (Sp. name)	ä'-vä-lôs	ah'-vah-los
Avdeevka (Rus.)	äv-dĕ'-yĕf-kä	ahv-deh'-yef-kah
Aveiro (Port.)	ä-vä'-rŏŏ	ah-vay'-ru
Avellaneda (Arg.)	ä-vĕ-lyä-nĕ'-dä	ah-veh-lyah-neh'-dah
Aventine (It., Rome)	*Eng.* ăv'-ən-tīn	av'-uhn-tain
Italian *Aventino*, ä-vĕn-tē'-nô [ah-ven-tee'-no].		
Aversa (It.)	ä-vĕr'-sä	ah-vehr'-sah
Avesnes (Fr.)	ä-vĕn'	ah-ven'
Aveyron (Fr.)	ä-vĕ-rôN'	ah-veh-roN'
Avezzano (It.)	ä-vĕt-sä'-nô	ah-vet-sah'-no
Avgustov (Pol.) See *Augustów*.		
Aviazione (It.)	ä-vyä-tsyô'-nĕ	ah-vyah-tsyo'-neh
Avignon (Fr.)	ä-vē-nyôN'	ah-vee-nyoN'
Ávila (Sp.)	ä'-vē-lä	ah'-vee-lah
Ávila Camacho, Manuel	ä'-vē-lä kä-mä'-chô,	ah'-vee-la kah-mah'-
(Mex. polit.)	mä-nwĕl'	cho, mah-nwel'
Avisio (It., riv.)	ä-vē'-syô	ah-vee'-syo
Avlon (Alb.) See *Vlonë*.		
Avola (Sicily)	ä'-vô-lä	ah'-vo-lah
Avon (Conn.)	ā'-vŏn	ay'-vŏn
Avon (Eng., riv.)	ā'-vən	ay'-vuhn
Avord (Fr.)	ä-vôr'	ah-vor'
Avranches (Fr.)	ä-vräNsh'	ah-vrahNsh'
Awaji (Jap., isl.)	ä-wä'-jē	ah-wah'-jee
Also called *Awaji Jima*.		
Awash (Ethiopia)	ä-wäsh	ah-wahsh
Aweleng (Oc., New Britain)	ä-wĕ-lĕng'	ah-weh-leng'
Axel (Neth.) See *Aksel*.		
Axios (Balkan riv.)	*Gr.* ä-ksē-ôs'	ah-ksee-os'
Also called *Vardar*, q.v.		
Axos (Crete)	ä-ksôs'	ah-ksos'
Axtell, Enos (Am. polit.)	ăks'-tĕl, ē'-nəs	aks'-tel, ee'-nuhs
Ay (Fr., riv.)	ĕ'	eh'
Ayala (P.I.)	ä-yä'-lä	ah-yah'-lah
Ayan (Rus.)	ä-yän'	ah-yahn'
Aydelotte, Frank	äd'-ə-lŏt	ayd'-uh-lot
(Am. educator)		
Aydin (Turk.)	ī-dēn'	ai-deen'
Aylsham (Eng.)	āl'-shəm	ayl'-shuhm
Ayot St. Lawrence (Eng.)	ā'-yət	ay'-yuht
Ayr (Austral.)	ăr'	ehr'
Ayu (NEI) See *Ajoe*.		
Ayutthaya (Siam)	ä-yōō'-tē-ä	ah-yoo'-tee-ah
Also spelled *Ayudhya*, *Ayuthya*, and *Ayuthia*.		

Azad, Abdul Kalam   ä-zäd′, äb′-dŏŏl   ah-zahd′, ahb′-dul
   (Indian polit.)   kə-läm′   kuh-lahm′
Azad, Maulana Abul   ä-zäd′, mou-lä′-nə   ah-zahd′, mau-lah′-
   Kalam (Indian polit.)   ə-bŏŏl′ kə-läm′   nuh uh-bul′ kuh-
                                                   lahm′
Azali (Crete)   ä-zä′-lē   ah-zah′-lee
Azanja (Yugosl.)   ä′-zä′-nyä   ah′-zah′-nyah
Azay (Fr.)   ä-zĕ′   ah-zeh′
Azbukovica (Yugosl.)   äz′-bŏŏ-kô-vĭ-tsä   ahz′-boo-ko-vi-tsah
Azeis (Libya)   ä-zäs′   ah-zays′
Azerbaijan (Iran, Rus.)   ä-zər-bĭ-jän′   ah-zuhr-bai-jahn′
Azib, el (Tun.)   ä′-zĭb, ĕl   ah′-zib, el
Azimgarh (India)   ä-zĭm-gär′ *or* -gûr′   ah-zim-gahr′ *or* -gur′
Azizia, el (Libya)   ă-zĭ-zē′-ä, ĕl   a-zi-zee′-ah, el
Azores (Port., isls.)   *Eng.* ə-zōrz′   uh-zohrz′
   Portuguese *Açores*, ä-sô′-rĭsh [ah-so′-rish], and ə-sô′-rĕzh [uh-so′-rezh].
Azov *or* Azof (Rus.)   ä-zôf′   ah-zof′
   The sea of Azov is called in Russian *Azovskoe More*, ä-zôf′-skŏ-yĕ mô′-
   rĕ [ah-zof′-sko-yeh mo′-reh].
Azuero (Pan., pen.)   ä-swĕ′-rô   ah-sweh′-ro
Azzam Pasha (Arab polit.) See *Abdul Rahman Azzam*.
Azzolini, Vincenzo   ät-sô-lē′-nē,   aht-so-lee′-nee,
   (It. polit.)   vēn-chĕn′-tsô   veen-chen′-tso

b, *bh*, and *v* are interchangeable in Greek; *b* and *v* in Spanish and other
languages. It may be necessary to look up all these spellings.
Baafjellmoen (Nor.)   bô-fyĕl-mŏŏ′-ən   bo-fyel-mu′-uhn
Baambrugge (Neth.)   bäm-brûk(h)′-ə   bahm-brœk(h)′-uh
Baarderadeel (Neth.)   bär′-də-rä-dāl′   bahr′-duh-rah-dayl′
Baarle-Nassau (Neth.)   bär′-lə näs′-ou   bahr′-luh nahs′-au
Baarlo(o)   bär′-lō   bahr′-loh
Baarn (Neth.)   bärn′   bahrn′
Baba (Yugosl., mts.)   bä′-bä   bah′-bah
Babadag (Rum.)   bä-bä-däg′   bah-bah-dahg′
Babaevo (Rus.)   bä-bä′-yĕ-vŏ   bah-bah′-yeh-vo
Babase (Oc., New Ireland)   bä′-bä-sĕ   bah′-bah-seh
Babatungon (P.I.)   bä-bä-tōōng′-ôn   bah-bah-toong′-on
Bab el Mandeb (str.,   bäb′ ĕl män′-dĕb   bahb′ el mahn′-deb
   Red Sea, Indian Ocean)   *or* băb′ ĕl măn′-dĕb   bab′ el man′-deb
Babelthuap (Oc., Carolines)   bä-bĕl-tōō′-äp   bah-bel-too′-ahp
   Also called *Babeldoab*, bä-bĕl-dô-äb′ [bah-bel-do-ahb′].
Babička Gora (Yugosl.)   bä′-bĭch-kä gô′-rä   bah′-bich-kah go′-rah
Babo (NEI, New Guinea)   bä′-bô   bah′-bo

[35]

Babol (Iran)   bä-bôl'   bah-bawl'
   Also called *Babul*, bä-bōōl' [bah-bul'] and *Barfrush*, q.v.
Babol Sar (Iran)   bä-bôl' sär'   bah-bawl' sahr'
   Also called *Babul Sar*, bä-bōōl' sär' [bah-bul' sahr'].
Babuán (P.I.)   bä-bwän'   bah-bwahn'
Babuna (Yugosl., riv.   bä'-bōō-nä   bah'-boo-nah
   and mts.)
Babušnica (Yugosl.)   bä'-bōōsh'-nĭ-tsä   bah'-boosh'-ni-tsah
Babuyán (P.I.)   bä-bōō-yän'   bah-boo-yahn'
Bacarra (P.I.)   bä-kär'-rä   bah-kahr'-rah
Bacău (Rum.)   bä-kû'-ŏŏ   bah-kuh'-u
Baccano (It.)   bäk-kä'-nô   bahk-kah'-no
Baccarat (Fr.)   bä-kä-rä'   bah-kah-rah'
Bache, Jules   bāch', jōōlz'   baych', joolz'
   (Am. banker, art collector)
Bacher Gebirge (Yugosl.)   *Ger.* bä'-k(h)ər   bah'-k(h)uhr
   Serb-Croat *Pohorje*, q.v.   gə-bēr'-gə   guh-beer'-guh
Bacher, Robert Fox   bā'-chər   bay'-chuhr
   (Am. scientist)
Bačina (Yugosl.)   bä'-chĭ-nä   bah'-chi-nah
Bačka (Yugosl.)   bäch'-kä   bahch'-kah
Backhouse (Eng. name)   băk'-əs *or* băk'-hous'   bak'-uhs *or* bak'-haus'
Bačko Gradište (Yugosl.)   bäch'-kô   bahch'-ko
                 grä'-dĭ-shtĕ   grah'-di-shteh
Baclieu (Indo-Ch.)   bäk-lyû'   bahk-lyœ'
Bacninh (Indo-Ch.)   bäk-nĭn'   bahk-nin'
Bacó (P.I.)   bä-kô'   bah-ko'
Bacolod (P.I.)   bä-kô'-lôd   bah-ko'-lod
Bacolor (P.I.)   bä-kô-lôr'   bah-ko-lor'
Bacoor (P.I.)   bä-kô-ôr'   bah-ko-or'
Bacqueville (Fr.)   bäk-vēl'   bahk-veel'
Bacuit (P.I.)   bä-kwēt'   bah-kweet'
Bad   *Eng.* băd'   bad'
         Ger. bät   baht
   An element, meaning *bath*, *spring* or *watering place*, in German place
   names. It may be necessary to look up the other part of the name.
Badajos (Sp., prov.)   bä-dä'-hôs   bah-dah'-hos
Badawi Pasha   bä'-dä-wē pä'-shä   bah'-dah-wee
   (Egypt. polit.)   pah'-shah
Bad Ems (Ger.) See *Ems*.
Baden (Austria, Ger.,   bä'-dən   bah'-duhn
   Pa., Switz.)
Baden Baden (Ger.)   bä'-dən bä'-dən   bah'-duhn bah'-duhn

Baden Powell (Eng. family)	bā'-dən pō'-əl	bay'-duhn poh'-uhl
Bad Freienwalde (Ger.)	bät' frī'-ən-väl'-də	baht' frai'-uhn-vahl'-duh
Badgastein (Austria)	bät'-gä'-stĭn	baht'-gah'-stain
Badino (It.)	bä-dē̅'-nô	bah-dee'-no
Bad Ischl (Austria)	bät' ĭsh'l	baht' ish'l
Bad Kissingen (Ger.)	*Eng.* băd kĭs'-ĭng-gən	bad kis'-ing-guhn
	Ger. bät kĭs'-ĭng-ən	baht kis'-ing-uhn
Badnjevac (Yugosl.)	bäd'-nyĕ-väts	bahd'-nyeh-vahts
Badoc (P.I.)	bä-dôk'	bah-dok'
Badoglio, Pietro (It. general)	bä-dô'-lyô, pyĕ'-trô	bah-do'-lyo, pyeh'-tro
Badolo (It.)	bä'-dô-lô	bah'-do-lo
Badovinci (Yugosl.)	bä'-dô'-vĭn-tsĭ	bah'-do'-vin-tsi
Badrinath (India, mt.)	bŭd-rē̅-nät'	bud-ree-naht'
Badwein (It. Som.)	bäd'-wān'	bahd'-wayn'
Baekeland, Leo H. (Am., Du. chemist)	bāk'-lănd	bayk'-land
Baerendorf (Fr.)	bĕr'-ən-dôrf'	behr'-uhn-dorf'
Baerwalde (Ger.)	bĕr'-väl-də	behr'-vahl-duh
Bafloo (Neth.)	bäf'-lō	bahf'-loh
Baga (Oc., Solomons)	bä'-gä	bah'-gah
Bagabag (N.E. New Guinea)	bä-gä-bäg'	bah-gah-bahg'
Bagac (P.I.)	bä-gäk'	bah-gahk'
Bagacay (P.I.)	bä-gä'-kī	bah-gah'-kai
Baganga (P.I.)	bä-gäng'-gä	bah-gahng'-gah
Bagdad *or* Baghdad (Iraq)	*Eng.* băg'-dăd	bag'-dad
	Arabic bäg-däd'	bahg-dahd'
Bagehot, Walter (Br. author)	băj'-ət	baj'-uht

The name *Bagehot* is often pronounced băg'-ət [bag'-uht] in England, but the eminent economist and journalist *Walter Bagehot* preferred băj'-ət [baj'-uht].

Bagemdir (Ethiopia)	bə-gām'-dûr	buh-gaym'-dœr
Bagheria (Sicily)	bä-gĕ-rē̅'-ä	bah-geh-ree'-ah
Bagnacavallo (It.)	bä'-nyä-kä-väl'-lô	bah'-nyah-kah-vahl'-lo
Bagnara (It.)	bä-nyä'-rä	bah-nyah'-rah
Bagnara Calabra (It.)	bä-nyä'-rä kä'-lä-brä	bah-nyah'-rah kah'-lah-brah
Bagnoles de l'Orne (Fr.)	bä-nyôl də lôrn'	bah-nyol duh lorn'
Bagnols sur Cèze (Fr.)	bä-nyôl sür sĕz'	bah-nyol sür sez'

| Bagramian, Ivan K. (Rus. general) | bä-grä-myän′, ĭ-vän′ | bah-grah-myahn′, i-vahn′ |
| Bagrationovsk (Ger. >Rus.) | bä-grä-tĭ-ô′-nôfsk | bah-grah-ti-o′-nofsk |

German *Preussisch Eylau*, q.v.

Bagrdan (Yugosl.)	bä′-gər′-dän	bah′-guhr′-dahn
Bagrianov, Ivan (Bulg. polit.)	bä-gryä′-nŏf′, ĭ-vän′	bah-gryah′-nof′, i-vahn′
Baguió (P.I)	*Eng.* băg′-ĭ-ō′	bag′-i-oh′
	Sp. bä′-gē-ô′	bah′-gee-o′

The pronunciation bŭg′-ē-ō′ [buhg′-ee-oh′] is also heard.

| bahadur | bə-hä′-dŏŏr | buh-hah′-dur |

A title or honorific in India. It is disregarded in alphabetical listing.

| Bahamas (Isls.) | bə-hā′-məz | buh-hay′-muhz |
| | *or* bə-hä′-məz | buh-hah′-muhz |

The latter is the pronunciation in the islands themselves.

Bahan (Burma)	bə-hän′	buh-hahn′
Bahawalpur (India)	bə-hä′-wəl-pŏŏr′	buh-hah′-wuhl-pur′
	or bä′-wəl-pŏŏr′	bah′-wuhl-pur′
bahía	bä-ē′-ä	bah-ee′-ah

A Spanish word meaning *bay*.

Bahia (Brazil) *See Baía.*

Bahrami (Iran. polit.)	bä-rä-mē′	bah-rah-mee′
Bahrdar Giyorgis (Ethiopia)	bä′-hər-där gĭ-yôr′-gĭs	bah′-huhr-dahr gi-yor′-gis
Bahrein (isls., Persian gulf)	*Eng.* bä′-rān′	bah′-rayn′
	Persian bäk(h)-rān′	bahk(h)-rayn′
Baía *or* Bahia (Brazil)	bä-ē′-ə *or* bə-ē′-ə	bah-ee′-uh *or* buh-ee′-uh

Officially called *São Salvador*, q.v.

| Baia Mare (Rum.) | bä′-yä mä′-rĕ | bah′-yah mah′-reh |

Hungarian *Nagybánya*, nŏd′(y)-bä-nyŏ [nod′(y)-bah-nyo].

Baie de Chaleur (Can., bay)	*Eng.* bā′ (də) shə-lŏŏr′	bay′ (duh) shuh-loor′
	Fr. bĕ də shä-lûr′	beh duh shah-lœr′
Baikal (Rus.)	bī-käl′	bai-kahl′
Baile Átha Cliath (Eire)	blô′ klē′-ĕ	blaw′ klee′-eh
	or bwäl′ ä klē′-ə	bwahl′ ah klee′-uh

English *Dublin*, q.v.

Bailén (P.I.)	bī-lĕn′	bai-len′
Băileşti (Rum.)	bə-ē-lĕsht′	buh-ee-lesht′
Bailleau (Fr.)	bä-yō′	bah-yoh′
Bailleul (Fr.)	bä-yûl′	bah-yœl′

Baillieu, Clive (Br. industrialist)	bāl'-yōō, klīv'	bayl'-yoo, klaiv'
Bain (Fr.)	băN'	baN'
Bairiki (Oc., Tarawa)	bĭ-rē'-kē	bai-ree'-kee
Bais (Fr.)	bĕ'	beh'
Baisan (Pal.) See *Beisan*.		
Baja (Hung.)	bŏ'-yŏ	bo'-yo
Baja California (Mex.) English *Lower California*.	bä'-hä kä-lē-fôr'-nyä	bah'-hah kah-lee-for'-nyah
Bajina Bašta (Yugosl.)	bä'-yĭ-nä bäsh'-tä	bah'-yi-nah bahsh'-tah
Bajmok (Yugosl.)	bĭ'-môk	bai'-mok
Bakar (Yugosl.) Italian *Buccari*, q.v.	bä'-kär	bah'-kahr
Bakarač (Yugosl.) Italian *Buccarizza*, q.v.	bä'-kä-räch	bah'-kah-rahch
Bakel (Neth.)	bä'-kəl	bah'-kuhl
Baker, Philip Noel (Br. polit.) See *Noel Baker*.		
Bakhatere (Oc., New Ireland)	bä-k(h)ä'-tĕ-rĕ	bah-k(h)ah'-teh-reh
Bakhchisarai (Rus.)	bäk(h)'-chĭ-sä-rī'	bahk(h)'-chi-sah-rai'
Bakhireva (Rus.)	bä-hē'-rĕ-vä	bah-hee'-reh-vah
Bakhmach (Rus.)	bäk(h)-mäch'	bahk(h)-mahch'
Bakhtiari (Iran. tribe)	băk(h)-tē-är-ē'	bak(h)-tee-ahr-ee'
Bakony (Hung., forest)	bŏ'-kôn(y)	bo'-kon(y)
Baku (Rus.)	bä-kōō'	bah-koo'
Balábac (P.I., str.)	bä-lä'-bäk	bah-lah'-bahk
Balakiás (P.I., bay)	bä-lä-kē-äs'	bah-lah-kee-ahs'
Balaklava (Rus.)	*Eng.* băl'-ə-klä'-və *Rus.* bä-lä-klä'-vä	bal'-uh-klah'-vuh bah-lah-klah'-vah
Balakleya (Rus.)	bä-lä-klĕ'-yä	bah-lah-kleh'-yah
Balanga (P.I.)	bä-läng'-gä	bah-lahng'-gah
Balangiga (P.I.)	bä-län-hē'-gä	bah-lahn-hee'-gah
Balanguingui (P.I.)	bä-län-gēn'-gē	bah-lahn-geen'-gee
Balaruc les Bains (Fr.)	bä-lä-rōōk lĕ băN'	bah-lah-rook leh baN'
Balashov (Rus.)	bä-lä-shôf'	bah-lah-shof'
Balasore (India)	băl'-ə-sōr'	bal'-uh-sohr'
Balassagyarmat (Hung.)	bŏ'-lŏ-shŏ-dyŏr'-mŏt	bo'-lo-sho-dyor'-mot
Balateros (P.I., bays)	bä-lä-tĕ'-rôs	bah-lah-teh'-ros
Chico, chē'-kô [chee'-ko], and *Grande*, grän'-dĕ [grahn'-deh].		
Balaton (Hung., lake)	bŏ'-lŏ-tôn	bo'-lo-ton
Balaton Berény (Hung.)	bŏ'-lŏ-tôn bĕ'-rān(y)	bo'-lo-ton beh'-rayn(y)

Balatonboglár (Hung.)	bŏ'-lŏ-tôn-bôg'-lär	bo'-lo-ton-bog'-lahr
Balatonfüred (Hung.)	bŏ'-lŏ-tôn-fü'-rĕd	bo'-lo-ton-fü'-red
Balayán (P.I.)	bä-lä-yän'	bah-lah-yahn'
Balboa (Canal Zone)	*Eng.* băl-bō'-ə	bal-boh'-uh
	Sp. bäl-bô'-ä	bahl-bo'-ah
Balbuena (Mexico City, airport)	bäl-bwĕ'-nä	bahl-bweh'-nah
Balchi (Ethiopia)	băl-chē'	bal-chee'
Balcic (Rum.)	bäl'-chēk'	bahl'-cheek'
Bâle *or* Basle (Switz.)	bäl'	bahl'
Officially *Basel*, bä'-zəl [bah'-zuhl].		
Balearic Isls. (Sp.)	*Eng.* băl'-ĭ-ă'-rĭk	bal'-i-a'-rik
Spanish *Baleares*, bä-lĕ-ä'-rĕs [bah-leh-ah'-res].		
Baler (P.I.)	bä-lĕr'	bah-lehr'
Balestrand (Nor.)	bäl'-ə-strän	bahl'-uh-strahn
Balete (P.I.)	bä-lĕ'-tĕ	bah-leh'-teh
Balgai (New Ireland)	bäl-gī'	bahl-gai'
Bali (NEI)	bä'-lē	bah'-lee
Balıkesir (Turk.)	bä-lĭ-kĕ-sēr'	bah-li-keh-seer'
Balikpapan (NEI, Borneo)	*Eng.* bä'-lēk-pä'-pän	bah'-leek-pah'-pahn
	Du. bä'-lē-pä'-pän	bah'-lee-pah'-pahn
Balimbing (P.I.)	bä-lĭm-bĭng'	bah-lim-bing'
Balincaguin (P.I., riv.)	bä-lēn-kä'-gēn	bah-leen-kah'-geen
Balintang (P.I.)	bä-lĭn-täng'	bah-lin-tahng'
Balíuag (P.I.)	bä-lē'-wäg	bah-lee'-wahg
Balkhash, Ozero (Rus.)	bäl-häsh', ô'-zĕ-rŏ	bahl-hahsh', o'-zeh-ro
Balki (Rus.)	bäl'-kĭ	bahl'-ki
Ballale (Oc., Solomons)	bäl-lä'-lĕ	bahl-lah'-leh
Balleroy (Fr.)	bä-lə-rwä'	bah-luh-rwah'
Ballia (India)	băl'-ĭ-ə	bal'-i-uh
Ballon (Fr.)	bä-lôN'	bah-loN'
Balmoral (No. Ire., Scot.)	băl-mŏr'-əl	bal-mor'-uhl
Balogh, István *or* Stephen (Hung. polit.)	bŏl'-ôg, ĭsht'-vän	bol'-og, isht'-vahn
Balogo (P.I.)	bä-lô'-gô	bah-lo'-go
Baloy (P.I., riv.)	bä-loi'	bah-loi'
Balsfjord (Nor.)	bäls'-fyōr	bahls'-fyohr
Balsorano (It.)	bäl-sô-rä'-nô	bahl-so-rah'-no
Balstad (Nor.)	bäl'-stä	bahl'-stah
Balta (Rus.)	bäl'-tä	bahl'-tah
Bălti (Rum. >Rus.)	bûlts'	buhlts'
Russian *Beltsi*, bĕl'(y)-tsĭ [bel'(y)-tsi].		
Baltiisk (Ger. >Rus.)	bäl-tēsk'	bahl-teesk'
German *Pillau*, q.v.		

[40]

Baltiski Port (Est.) Estonian *Paltiski*, q.v.	*Rus.* bäl-tē'-skĭ pôrt'	bahl-tee'-ski port'
Baluan (Oc., Admiralties)	bä'-lōō-än	bah'-loo-ahn
Baluchistan (India)	bə-lōō'-chĭ-stän'	buh-loo'-chi-stahn'
Balut (P.I.)	bä-lōōt'	bah-loot'
Bamako (Fr. W. Afr.)	bä-mä-kô'	bah-mah-ko'
Bambán (P.I.)	bäm-bän'	bahm-bahn'
Bambatana (Oc., Solomons)	bäm-bä-tä'-nä	bahm-bah-tah'-nah
Bambini (Gr.)	bäm-bē'-nē	bahm-bee'-nee
Banaczyk, Władysław (Pol. polit.)	bä-nä'-chĭk, vlä-dĭ'-släf	bah-nah'-chik, vlah-di'-slahf
Banat (Rum., Yugosl.)	*Rum.* bä-nät' *S.-C.* bä'-nät'	bah-naht' bah'-naht'
Banda (India; Oc., sea)	băn'-də *or* bän'-dä	ban'-duh *or* bahn'-dah
bandar	băn'-dər *or* bŭn'-dər	ban'-duhr *or* buhn'-duhr

An element, meaning *port*, in Persian and Indian place names.

Bandar Abbas (Iran)	băn'-dər ăb-bäs'	ban'-duhr ab-bahs'
Bandar Pahlavi (Iran)	băn'-dər pä-lä-vē'	ban'-duhr pah-lah-vee'
Bandar Shah (Iran)	băn'-dər shä'	ban'-duhr shah'
Bandar Shapur (Iran)	băn'-dər shă-pōōr'	ban'-duhr sha-poor'
Bandırma (Turk.) Also called *Panderma*, q.v.	bän-dĭr-mä'	bahn-dihr-mah'
Banditella (It.)	bän-dē-tĕl'-lä	bahn-dee-tel'-lah
Bandjermasin (NEI, Borneo)	băn'-jər-mä'-sĭn	bahn'-juhr-mah'-sin
Bandoeng *or* Bandung (NEI, Java)	bän'-dōōng	bahn'-doong
Ban Don (Siam)	bän' dôn	bahn' dawn
Bandouvas, Christos (Gr. polit.)	bä(n)-dōō'-väs, hrē'-stôs	bah(n)-doo'-vahs, hree'-stos
Bandouvas, Manolis (Cretan polit.)	bä(n)-dōō'-väs, mä-nô'-lēs	bah(n)-doo'-vahs, mah-no'-lees
Bandung (NEI) See *Bandoeng*.		
Baneh (Iran)	bä'-nĕ	bah'-neh
Bangalore (India)	băng-gə-lôr'	bang-guh-lor'
Bangao (P.I.)	bäng-ou'	bahng-au'
Bangatang (Oc., New Ireland)	bäng'-ä-täng	bahng'-ah-tahng
Bangka (NEI)	*Eng.* băng'-kə *Du.* bäng'-kä	bang'-kuh bahng'-kah
Bangkok (Siam)	băng'-kŏk'	bang'-kok'

Siamese *Krung Thep* or *Krungdheb*, krōōng-täp' [krung-tayp'].

Bangor (Me., Wales)	băng'-gôr *or* -gər	bang'-gor *or* -guhr
Bangor (Pa.)	băng'-gər	bang'-guhr
Bangued (P.I.)	bäng-gĕd'	bahng-ged'
Bangui (P.I.)	bäng'-gē	bahng'-gee
Baniata (Oc., Solomons)	bä-nē-ä'-tä	bah-nee-ah'-tah
Banika (Oc., Solomons)	bä-nē'-kä	bah-nee'-kah
Banjak *or* Banyak (NEI)	bän'-yäk	bahn'-yahk
Banjaluka (Yugosl.)	bä'-nyä-lōō'-kä	bah'-nyah-loo'-kah
Banjani (Yugosl.)	bä'-nyä-nĭ	bah'-nyah-ni
Banjoewangi *or* Banyu- wangi (NEI, Java)	bän-yōō-wäng'-ē	bahn-yoo-wahng'-ee
Banná	bä-nä'	bah-nah'
Banog (P.I.) See *Ulugan*.		
Banogboc (P.I.)	bä-nôg-bôk'	bah-nog-bok'
Baños, Los (P.I.) See *Los Baños*.		
banská (Cz.)	bän'-skä	bahn'-skah

A common element, meaning *springs* or *baths*, in Czech place names.
It may be necessary to look up the other part of the name.

Banská Bystrica (Cz.)	bän'-skä bĭ'-strĭ-tsä	bahn'-skah bi'-stri- tsah
Banská Štiavnica (Cz.)	bän'-skä shtyäv'-nĭ-tsä	bahn'-skah shtyahv'-ni-tsah
Bansko (Bulg.)	bän'-skŏ	bahn'-sko
Bantam (NEI)	*Eng.* băn'-təm	ban'-tuhm
	Du. bän-täm'	bahn-tahm'

Most Americans have an affection for the derivatives *bantam, bantie,*
meaning small, slight.

Banyak (NEI)   See *Banjak*.
Banyuwangi (NEI)   See *Banjoewangi*.

Bao Dai (King of Annam)	bou dī'	bau dai'
Baoe-baoe (NEI, Boetoeng)	bä'-ōō bä'-ōō	bah'-oo bah'-oo
Bapaume (Fr.)	bä-pōm'	bah-pohm'
Bar (Rus.)	bär'	bahr'
Bar (Yugosl.)	bär'	bahr'

Italian *Antivari*, q.v.

Baracoa (Cuba)	bä-rä-kô'-ä	bah-rah-ko'-ah

Baragwanath, Neysa McMein (Am. illustrator) See *McMein, Neysa*.

Barahun (Oc., New Ireland)	bä-rä-hōōn'	bah-rah-hoon'
Barajas (Madrid, airport)	bä-rä'-häs	bah-rah'-hahs
Baram (Borneo, riv.)	bä'-räm	bah'-rahm
Baranof (Alaska, isl.)	*Eng.* băr'-ə-nŏf	behr'-uh-nof
	Rus. bä-rä'-nŏf	bah-rah'-nof
Baranovichi (Pol. > Rus.)	bä-rä-nô'-vĭ-chĭ	bah-rah-no'-vi-chi

Polish *Baranowicze*, bä-rä-nô-vē'-chĕ [bah-rah-no-vee'-cheh].

Baranya (Hung., Yugosl.)	*Hung.* bŏ'-rŏ-nyŏ	bo'-ro-nyo
	S.-C. bä'-rä-nyä	bah'-rah-nyah
Barás (P.I.)	bä-räs'	bah-rahs'
Barasoáin (P.I.)	bä-rä-swĭn'	bah-rah-swain'
Barbados (Br. W. I.)	bär-bä'-dōz *or* -dŏs	bahr-bay'-dohz *or* -dos
Barbarevo (Yugosl.)	bär'-bä'-rĕ-vô	bahr'-bah'-reh-vo
Barberini (It.)	bär-bĕ-rē'-nē	bahr-beh-ree'-nee
Barca (Libya)	bär'-kä	bahr'-kah
Barcelona (Sp.)	*Eng.* bär'-sə-lō'-nə	bahr-suh-loh'-nuh
	Sp. bär-thĕ-lô'-nä	bahr-theh-lo'-nah
Bardejov (Cz.)	bär'-dĕ-yôf	bahr'-deh-yof

German *Bartfeld*, bärt'-fĕlt [bahrt'-felt].

Barden, Graham A.	bär'-dən	bahr'-duhn
(U.S. representative)		
Bardia (Libya)	bär-dē'-ä *or* bär'-dĭ-ä	bahr-dee'-ah *or* bahr'-di-ah
Bardo (Tun.)	bär'-dō	bahr'-doh

Also called *Le Bardo*, q.v.

Bardufoss (Nor.)	bär'-dŏŏ-fôs	bahr'-du-fos
Bareilly (India)	bə-rä'-lē	buh-ray'-lee
Barendrecht (Neth.)	bä'-rən-drĕk(h)t	bah'-ruhn-drek(h)t
Barenton (Fr.)	bä-räN-tôN'	bah-rahN-toN'
Barents Sea	*Eng.* bär'-ĕnts	behr'-ents
	Rus. bä-rĕnts'	bah-rents'
Bareveld (Neth.)	bä'-rə-vĕlt	bah'-ruh-velt
Barfleur (Fr., point)	bär-flûr'	bahr-flœr'
Barfrush (Iran)	bär-frōōsh'	bahr-froosh'

Officially *Babol*, q.v.

Barga (It.)	bär'-gä	bahr'-gah
Bârgău (Rum., mts.)	bûr-gû'-ŏŏ	buhr-guh'-u
Barguzin (Rus.)	bär-gōō-zēn'	bahr-goo-zeen'
Bari (It.)	bä'-rē	bah'-ree
Barič (Yugosl.)	bä'-rĭch	bah'-rĭch
Barili (P.I.)	bä-rē'-lē	bah-ree'-lee
Barisal (India)	bə-rĭ-säl'	buh-ri-sahl'
Barjols (Fr.)	bär-zhôl'	bahr-zhol'
Barka (Libya)	bär'-kä	bahr'-kah

Also spelled *Barca*, q.v.

| Barköl (Ch., Sinkiang) | bär-kûl | bahr-kuhl |

Also called *Chen-hsi*, q.v.

Bârlad (Rum.)	bûr-läd'	buhr-lahd'
Bar le Duc (Fr.)	bär lə dük'	bahr luh dük'
Barlee (Austral.)	bär'-lē'	bahr'-lee'

Barletta (It.)	bär-lĕt′-tä	bahr-let′-tah
Barnard College (N.Y.)	bär′-nərd kŏl′-ĭj	bahr′-nuhrd kol′-ij
Barnaul (Rus.)	bär-nä-ōōl′	bahr-nah-ool′
Barnegat (N.J., bay)	bär′-nĭ-găt′	bahr′-ni-gat′
Barneveld (Neth.)	bär′-nə-vĕlt	bahr′-nuh-velt
Barneville (Fr.)	bär-nə-vēl′	bahr-nuh-veel′
Bar Nicobar (India, isl.)	bär′ nĭk-ō-bär′	bahr′ nik-oh-bahr′
Baroda (Ethiopia)	bä-rō′-dä	bah-roh′-dah
Baroda (India)	bə-rō′-də	buh-roh′-duh
Barola (Oc., Solomons)	bä-rô′-lä	bah-ro′-lah
Baron (Fr.)	bä-rôN′	bah-roN′
Barradeel (Neth.)	bä-rä-dāl′	bah-rah-dayl′
Barrafranca (Sicily)	bär-rä-frän′-kä	bahr-rah-frahn′-kah
barrage	bə-räzh′ or bə-räj′	buh-rahzh′ or buh-rahj′

Also British băr′-äzh [behr′-ahzh].

Barranquilla (Colom.)	bär-rän-kē′-yä	bahr-rahn-kee′-yah
Barre (Mass., Vt.)	băr′-ĭ	behr′-i
Barreiro (Port.)	bä-rā′-rŏŏ	bah-ray′-ru
Barrême (Fr.)	bä-rĕm′	bah-rem′
Barrett, William A.	băr-′ĭt	behr′-it
(U.S. representative)		

Barrio, Diego Martínez (Sp. polit.) See *Martínez Barrio*.

Barros, João Alberto Lins de (Braz. polit.) See *Lins de Barros*.

Bârsa (Rum., riv.)	bûr′-sä	buhr′-sah

Barszcz (Ger.) See *Forst*.

Bartenstein (Ger. >Pol.)	bär′-tən-shtīn	bahr′-tuhn-shtain
Polish *Bartoszyce*, q.v.		

Bartfeld (Cz.) See *Bardejov*.

Bartica (Br. Guiana)	bär-tē′-kä	bahr-tee′-kah
Bartók, Béla	bŏr′-tôk, bā′-lŏ	bor′-tok, bay′-lo
(Hung. musician)		
Bartoszyce (Ger. >Pol.)	bär-tô-shĭ′-tsĕ	bahr-to-shi′-tseh
German *Bartenstein*, q.v.		

Bartsch (Pol., riv.) See *Barycz*.

Baruch, Bernard	bär′-ōōk or bə-rōōk′,	bahr′-ook or buh-
Mannes (Am. leader)	bûr′-närd′ măn′-əs	rook′, buhr′-nahrd′ man′-uhs
Barugh (Eng.)	bärk′	bahrk′
Barugo (P.I.)	bä-rōō′-gô	bah-roo′-go
Barvenkova (Rus.)	bär-vĕn′-kŏ-vä	bahr-ven′-ko-vah
Bärwalde (Ger.)	bĕr′-väl-də	behr′-vahl-duh
Barwon (Austral.)	bär′-wən	bahr′-wuhn

Barycz (Pol., riv.)   bä′-rĭch   bah′-rich
   German *Bartsch*, bärtsh′ [bahrtsh′].
Barzas (Rus.)   bär-zäs′   bahr-zahs′
Basbás (P.I.)   bäs-bäs′   bahs-bahs′
Basdevant, Jules   bäd-väN′, zhül′   bahd-vahN′, zhül′
   (Fr. polit.)
Basel (Switz.)   bä′-zəl   bah′-zuhl
   French *Basle* or *Bâle*, bäl′ [bahl′].
bases (pl. of *base*)   bā′-sĭz   bay′-siz
   This word is often confused with the next entry.
bases (pl. of *basis*)   bā′-sēz   bay′-seez
Basey (P.I.)   bä-sā′   bah-say′
Bashanta (Rus.)   bä-shän′-tä   bah-shahn′-tah
bashaw   bə-shô′   buh-shaw′
   A variant of *pasha* q.v.
bashi   bä-shē   bah-shee
   An element, meaning *bridge*, in Japanese place names. See *hashi*.
Bashi (P.I., channel)   bä′-shē   bah′-shee
Bashkir (Rus., repub.)   bäsh-kēr′   bahsh-keer′
   Also called *Bashkiria*, bäsh-kĭr′-ĭ-ə [bahsh-kir′-i-uh].
basil   băz′-əl *or* băs′-əl   baz′-uhl *or* bas′-uhl
   The personal name *Basil* may be pronounced bā′-zəl [bay′-zuhl].
Basilan (P.I.)   bä-sē′-län   bah-see′-lahn
Baška (Yugosl.)   bä′-shkä   bah′-shkah
   Italian *Bescanuova*, q.v.
Basle (Switz.) See *Basel* and *Bâle*.
Basov, Nicolai   bä′-sŏf, nĭ-kŏ-lī′   bah′-sof, ni-ko-lai′
   D. (Rus. diplomat)
Basque (Eur. people)   băsk′   bask′
Basra (Iraq)   băz′-rə *or* bŭs′-rə   baz′-ruh *or* buhs′-ruh
Bassac (Indo-Ch.)   bäs-säk′   bahs-sahk′
Bassano (It.)   bäs-sä′-nô   bahs-sah′-no
Bassein (Burma)   băs-sēn′   bas-seen′
   Burman *Pathein*.
Bassens (Fr.)   bä-säN′   bah-sahN′
Basses Alpes (Fr.)   bäs zälp′   bahs zahlp′
Bassiano (It.)   bäs-syä′-nô   bahs-syah′-no
Bastia (Corsica)   bä-stē′-ä   bah-stee′-ah
   See *Terranova* and *Terravecchia*. Also English bäs′-chə [bahs′-chuh].
Bastogne (Belg.)   bäs-tôn′(y)   bahs-ton′(y)
Basutoland (Afr., Br. col.)   bə-sōō′-tō-lănd   buh-soo′-toh-land
                      or -zōō′-   *or* -zoo′-
Bat'a, Tomáš   bä′-tyä, tô′-mäsh   bah′-tyah, to′-mahsh
   (Cz. manufacturer)

Bataán (P.I.)	*Eng.* bă-tăn′	ba-tan′
	local bä-tä-än′	bah-tah-ahn′
Bátac (P.I.)	bä′-täk	bah′-tahk
Bataisk (Rus.)	bä-tīsk′	bah-taisk′
Batalha (Port.)	bə-tä′-lyə	buh-tah′-lyah
Batam (NEI, Riouw)	bä′-täm	bah′-tahm
Batán (P.I.)	bä-tän′	bah-tahn′

Also called *Batanes*, bä-tä′-nĕs [bah-tah′-nes], and *Bashi*, bä′-shē [bah′-shee]. *Batán* should be distinguished from *Bataán*, q.v.

Batang (Ch., Sikang)	bä-täng	bah-tahng
Batangas (P.I.)	bä-täng′-gäs	bah-tahng′-gahs
Batanja, Nova (Yugosl.)	bä′-tä-nyä, nô′-vä	bah′-tah-nyah, no′-vah
Batao (P.I.)	bä-tä′-ô	bah-tah′-o
Batavia (NEI, Java)	*Eng.* bə-tä′-vyə	buh-tay′-vyuh
	Du. bä-tä′-vĭ-ä	bah-tah′-vi-ah
Bates Isl. (Oc., Solomons)	bāts′	bayts′
Batetsk (Rus.)	bä′-tĕtsk	bah′-tetsk
Bathurst (English name)	băth′-ûrst	bath′-uhrst
Batina (Yugosl.)	bä′-tĭ-nä	bah′-ti-nah
Batjan (NEI)	bä-chän′	bah-chahn′
Batna (Alg.)	bät′-nä	baht′-nah
Batnfjordsoera *or*	bät′n-fyôrs-û′-rä	baht′n-fyohrs-œ′-rah
Batnfjordsöra (Nor.)		
Bató (P.I)	bä-tô′	bah-to′
Batočina (Yugosl.)	bä′-tô′-chĭ-nä	bah′-to′-chi-nah
Batoe *or* Batu (NEI)	bä′-tōō	bah′-too
Batoe Kilat (NEI)	bä′-tōō kē′-lät	bah′-too kee′-laht
Batraki (Rus.)	bä-trä-kē′	bah-trah-kee′
Batschka (Yugosl.)	*Ger.* bäch′-kä	bahch′-kah
Serb-Croat *Bačka*, q.v.		
Battaglia (It.)	bät-tä′-lyä	baht-tah′-lyah
Battambang (Indo-Ch.)	bät′-əm-bäng	baht′-uhm-bahng

Siamese *Phratabong*, prät′-ə-bông′ [praht-uh-bong′].

Battenheim (Fr.)	*Fr.* bä-tə-nīm′	bah-tuh-naim′
	Ger. bät′-ən-hīm	baht′-uhn-haim
Batticaloa (Ceylon)	bät-tē-kä-lō′-ə	baht-tee-kah-loh′-uh
Battipaglia (It.)	bät-tē-pä′-lyä	baht-tee-pah′-lyah
Batu (NEI) See *Batoe*.		
Batum (Rus.)	bä-tōōm′	bah-tum′
Batz (Fr., isl.)	bä′	bah′
Bauan (P.I.)	bä′-wän	bah′-wahn
Baudouin (Fr. name)	bō-dwăN′	boh-dwaN′
Baudreville (Fr.)	bō-drə-vēl′	boh-druh-veel′

Baugé (Fr.)	bō-zhĕ′	boh-zheh′
Baume (Fr.)	bōm′	bohm′
Baume les Dames (Fr.)	bōm lĕ däm′	bohm leh dahm′
Baupte (Fr.)	bōt′	boht′
Bauscheim (Ger.)	bou′-shīm	bau′-shaim
Bauska (Latvia)	bous′-kä	baus′-kah
German *Bausk*, bousk′ [bausk′].		
Bautista (P.I.)	bou-tēs′-tä	bau-tees′-tah
Bautzen (Ger.)	bout′-sən	baut′-suhn
Baux, les (Fr.)	bō′, lĕ	boh′, leh
Bavanište (Yugosl.)	bä′-vä-nĭ-shtĕ	bah′-vah-ni-shteh
Bavaria (Ger.)	*Eng.* bə-vĕr′-ĭ-ə	buh-vehr′-i-uh
German *Bayern*, q.v.		
Bawean (NEI)	bä′-vĕ-än	bah′-veh-ahn
Bay, Laguna de (P.I.)	bī′ *or* bä′-ē′	bai′ *or* bah′-ee′,
	lä-gōō′-nä dĕ	lah-goo′-nah deh
Bayambán (P.I.)	bä-yäm-bän′	bah-yahm-bahn′
Bayambang (P.I.)	bä-yäm-bäng′	bah-yahm-bahng′
Bayamo (Cuba)	bä-yä′-mô	bah-yah′-mo
Bayar, Jelâl (Turk. polit.)	bä-yär′, zhĕ-läl′	bah-yahr′, zheh-lahl′
Bayard, Fort (Ch.,	*Eng.* bī′-ərd	bai′-uhrd
Kwangtung, Fr. colony)	*Fr.* bä-yär′	bah-yahr′
Bayat, Morteza Qoli	bä-yät′, môr′-tĕ-zə	bah-yaht′, mor′-teh-
(Iran. polit.)	kōō-lē′	zuh koo-lee′
Qoli is also spelled *Koli* and *Kuli*.		
Baybay(P. I.)	bī′-bī′	bai′-bai′
Baydary (Rus.)	bī-dä′-rĭ	bai-dah′-ri
Baydur, Hüseyin Ragıp	bī-dŏŏr′, hü-sä-yĭn′	bai-dur′, hü-say-yin′
(Turk. diplomat)	rä-gĭp′	rah-gip′
Bayern (Ger.)	bī′-ərn	bai′-uhrn
English *Bavaria*, q.v.		
Bayeux (Fr.)	bä-yû′	bah-yœ′
Bayon (Fr.)	bä-yôN′	bah-yoN′
Bayonne (Fr.)	bä-yôn′	bah-yon′
Bayonne (N.J.)	bā′-yōn′	bay′-yohn′
Bayreuth (Ger.)	bī′-roit′	bai′-roit′
This name should be distinguished in pronunciation and spelling from		
Beirut or *Beyrouth* (Syria).		
Bayuyungán (P.I.)	bä-yōō-yōōng-gän′	bah-yoo-yoong-gahn′
Bazargic (Rum.)	bä′-zär′-jēk′	bah-zahr′-jeek′
Also called *Dobrici*, q.v.		
Beall, J. Glenn	bĕl′	bel′
(U.S. representative)		

Beals, Ralph A.	bēlz′	beelz′
(Am. librarian)		
Beaucaire (Fr.)	bō-kăr′	boh-kehr′
Beaufort (except in South	bō′-fərt	boh′-fuhrt
Carolina)		
Beaufort (S.C.)	byōō′-fərt	byoo′-fuhrt
Beaufort bomber	bō′-fərt	boh′-fuhrt
Beaugency (Fr.)	bō-zhäN-sē′	boh-zhahN-see′
Beaumont le Roger (Fr.)	bō-môN lə rô-zhĕ′	boh-moN luh ro-zheh′
Beaune (Fr.)	bōn′	bohn′
Beausset, le (Fr.)	bō-sĕ′, lə	boh-seh′, luh
Beauvais (Fr.)	*Eng.* bō-vā′	boh-vay′
	Fr. bō-vĕ′	boh-veh′
Bebler, Aleš	bĕ′-blĕr,	beh′-blehr,
(Yugosl. diplomat)	ä′-lĕsh	ah′-lesh

because

We have received a letter from Fresno (frĕz′-nō) asking, "Why do announcers say 'be-cuz' for *because?*" The answer is probably— because most Americans do. However, dictionaries allow -kôz or -kŏz, and it is well not to give the vowel an emphatic ŭ value. Our correspondent would not like New York bĭ-kôs′ [bi-kaws′] or Texas bĭ-kŭ′ŭz [bi-kuh′uhz].

Bečej, Novi (Yugosl.)	bĕ′-chā, nô′-vĭ	beh′-chay, no′-vi
Bechara el Khoury,	bə-shä′-rä ĕl	buh-shah′-rah el
Sheik (Lebanese polit.)	k(h)ōō′-rē	k(h)oo′-ree
Bechateur (Tun.)	bĕ-shä-tûr′	beh-shah-tœr′
Bécherel (Fr.)	bĕsh-rĕl′	besh-rel′
Bechuanaland	bĕch′-ŏŏ-ä′-nə-lănd	bech′-u-ah′-nuh-land
(Afr., Br.)		
Bečkerek, Veliki (Yugosl.)	bĕch′-kĕ′-rĕk,	bech′-keh′-rek,
	vĕ′-lĭ-kĭ	veh′-li-ki

Hungarian *Nagybecskerek,* nŏd′(y)-bĕch′-kĕ-rĕk [nod′(y)-bech′-keh-rek].

Beckum (Ger.)	bĕk′-ŏŏm	bek′-um
Beco (NEI)	bĕ′-kô	beh′-ko
Bédarieux (Fr.)	bĕ-dä-ryû′	beh-dah-ryœ′
Bedburg (Ger.)	bĕt′-bŏŏrk(h)	bet′-burk(h)
Bednyakov (Rus. name)	bĕd-nyä-kôf′	bed-nyah-kof′
Bedum (Neth.)	bā′-dəm	bay′-duhm
Będzin (Pol.)	băN′-jĭn	baN′-jin

Russian *Bendin,* bĕn′-dĭn [ben′-din]. German *Bendzin,* bĕn′-dzĭn [ben′-dzin].

Beeck (Ger.)	bāk′	bayk′

Beek (Neth.)	bāk'	bayk'
Beekbergen (Neth.)	bāk'-bĕr-k(h)ən	bayk'-behr-k(h)uhn
Beelitz (Ger.)	bā'-lĭts	bay'-lits
Beemster (Neth.)	bām'-stər	baym'-stuhr
Beerbohm, Max (Br. author)	bĭr'-bōm	bir'-bohm
Beersheba (Pal.)	bĭr-shē'-bə or bĭr'-shĭ-bə	bir-shee'-buh bir'-shi-buh

Modern *Bir es Seba*, bēr' ĕs sĕb'-ä [beer' es seb'-ah], or *Saba*, säb'-ə [sahb'-uh].

Beerte (Neth.)	bār'-tə	bayr'-tuh
Beesd (Neth.)	bāst'	bayst'
Beeskow (Ger.)	bās'-kō	bays'-koh
beg *or* bey	bĕg', bā'	beg', bay'

A title or honorific in the Middle East and Africa, usually following the name. It is disregarded in alphabetical listing.

Begaljica (Yugosl.)	bĕ'-gä'-lyĭ-tsä	beh'-gah'-lyi-tsah
Begej (Yugosl., riv.)	bĕ'-gā	beh'-gay
Beggendorf (Ger.)	bĕg'-ən-dôrf	beg'-uhn-dorf
begum (Indian heiress)	*Eng.* bē'-gəm	bee'-guhm

A feminine form of *beg*, q.v.

Behncke, David (Am. labor leader)	bĕng'-kĭ	beng'-ki
Bei el Chebir (Libya)	bā ĕl kə-bēr'	bay el kuh-beer'
Beilen (Neth.)	bī'-lən	bai'-luhn
Beira (Port., Mozambique)	bā'-rə	bay'-ruh
Beira Alta (Port.)	bā'-rə äl'-tə	bay'-ruh ahl'-tuh
Beira Baixa (Port.)	bā'-rə bī'-shə	bay'-ruh bai'-shuh
Beirne, Joseph (Am. labor leader)	bûrn'	buhrn'
Beirut (Syria)	bā'-rōōt'	bay'-root'

Also spelled *Beyrouth*. This name should be distinguished in pronunciation and spelling from *Bayreuth* (Ger.).

Beisan (Pal.)	bā-sän'	bay-sahn'

Also called *Baisan*.

beit *or* beet	bāt'	bayt'

English *beth*, bĕth. An element, meaning *house*, in Hebrew and Arabic place names.

Beit Dejan (Pal.)	bāt dĕj'-än	bayt dej'-ahn

Beit Haarava (Pal.) See *Beth Haarava*.

Beiuş (Rum.)	bā-yōōsh'	bay-yush'

Hungarian *Belényes*, bĕ'-lā-nyĕsh [beh'-lay-nyesh].

Beja (Port.)	bĕ'-zhə	beh'-zhuh
Beja (Tun.)	bĕ-zhä'	beh-zhah'

[49]

Béjar (Sp.)	bĕ'-här	beh'-hahr
Bejraburi (Siam) See *Phet Buri*.		
Békés (Hung.)	bā'-kāsh	bay'-kaysh
Békéscsaba (Hung.)	bā'-kāsh-chŏ-bŏ	bay'-kaysh-cho-bo
Bekkaria (Alg.)	bĕk-kə-rē'-ä	bek-kuh-ree'-ah
Bela (India)	bā'-lə	bay'-luh
Bela Crkva (Yugosl.)	bĕ'-lä tsər'-kvä	beh'-lah tsuhr'-kvah
German *Weisskirchen*.		
Belanovica (Yugosl.)	bĕ'-lä-nô'-vĭ-tsä	beh'-lah-no'-vi-tsah
Bela Palanka (Yugosl.)	bĕ'-lä pä'-län-kä	beh'-lah pah'-lahn-kah
Belasica planina	bĕ'-lä'-sĭ-tsä	beh'-lah'-si-tsah
(Balkan mts.)	plä'-nē'-nä	plah'-nee'-nah
Greek *Kerkine*, q.v.		
Belaya Glina (Rus.)	bĕ'-lä-yä glē'-nä	beh'-lah-yah glee'-nah
Also called *Byeloglina*, q.v.		
Belaya Tserkov (Rus.)	bĕ'-lä-yä tsĕr'-kŏf	beh'-lah-yah tsehr'-kof
Belbek (Rus.)	bĕl-bĕk'	bel-bek'
Bełchatów (Pol.)	bĕl-hä'-tŏŏf	bel-hah'-tuf
Russian *Belkhatov*, bĕl-hä'-tŏf [bel-hah'-tof].		
Belém (Port., Brazil)	bĕ-lĕN'	beh-leN'
Belém, Brazil, is also called *Pará*, q.v.		
Belényes (Rum.) See *Beiuş*.		
Belestinon (Gr.)	vĕ-lĕ-stē'-nô(n)	veh-leh-stee'-no(n)
Also called *Pherai*, q.v.		
Belev (Rus.)	bĕ'-lĕf	beh'-lef
Belfort (Fr.)	bĕl-fôr'	bel-for'
Belgard (Ger. >Pol)	bĕl'-gärt	bel'-gahrt
Polish *Białogard*, q.v.		
Belgaum (India)	bĕl-goum'	bel-gaum'
Belgorod (Rus.)	*Eng.* bĕl'-gŏ-rŏd	bel'-go-rod
	Rus. bĕl'-gŏ-rŏt	bel'-go-rot
Belgrade (Yugosl.)	*Eng.* bĕl'-grād'	bel'-grayd'
Serb-Croat *Beograd*, q.v.		
Belica (Yugosl.)	bĕ'-lĭ-tsä	beh'-li-tsah
Beli Drim (Balkan riv.)	*S.-C.* bĕ'-lĭ drēm'	beh'-li dreem'
Albanian *Drin i Bardhë*, q.v.		
Beli Krest (Rus.)	bĕ'-lĭ krĕst'	beh'-li krest'
Belisha, Hore- (Br. polit.)	bə-lē'-shə, hōr	buh-lee'-shuh, hohr
The pronunciation to rhyme with *Elisha* is incorrect.		
Belitong (NEI)	bĕ-lē'-tŏng	beh-lee'-tong
Also called *Billiton*, q.v.		
Belize (Br. Hond.)	bĕ-lēz'	beh-leez'

Beljak (Austria)   See *Villach*.

Beljanica (Yugosl., mts.)	bĕ'-lyä'-nĭ-tsä	beh'-lyah'-ni-tsah
Bellary (India)	bĕ-lä'-rē	beh-lah'-ree
Belle Fourche (U.S., riv.)	bĕl' fŏōrsh'	bel' fursh'
Belle Garde (Fr.)	bĕl gärd'	bel gahrd'
Bellème (Fr.)	bĕ-lĕm'	beh-lem'
Bellingwolde (Neth.)	bĕl'-ĭng-wôl'-də	bel'-ing-wol'-duh
Belloc, Hilary *or pen name*	bĕl'-ŏk, hĭl'-ə-rĭ	bel'-ok, hil'-uh-ri
Hilaire (Br. author)	*or* hĭ-lăr'	*or* hi-lehr'
Bellona (Oc., Solomons)	bĕl-lō'-nä	bel-loh'-nah
Belluno (It.)	bĕl-lōō'-nô	bel-loo'-no
Beloe (Rus., lake)	bĕ'-lŏ-yĕ	beh'-lo-yeh
Belo Horizonte (Brazil)	bĕ'-lô-rē-zôn'-tĭ	beh'-lo-ree-zon'-ti
Belopole (Rus.)	bĕ-lŏ-pô'-lyĕ	beh-lo-po'-lyeh
Beloretsk (Rus.)	bĕ-lŏ-rĕtsk'	beh-lo-retsk'
Belorussia (Rus., repub.)	bĕ'-lô-rōō'-sĭ-yä	beh'-lo-roo'-si-yah

White Russian Soviet Republic. It should not be confused with the "White Russian" army that fought against the "Red Russians" in 1919-1920.

Beloshitsi (Rus.)	bĕ-lô'-shĭ-tsĭ	beh-lo'-shi-tsi
Belotince (Yugosl.)	bĕ'-lô'-tĭn-tsĕ	beh'-lo'-tin-tseh
Belozersk (Rus.)	bĕl-ŏ-zĕrsk'	bel-o-zehrsk'
Belsen (Ger.)	bĕl'-zən	bel'-zuhn
Beltramí, Raúl Morales	bĕl-trä-mē',	bel-trah-mee',
(Chilean polit.)	rä-ōōl' mô-rä'-lĕs	rah-ool' mo-rah'-les
Beltsy (Rum. > Rus.)	bĕl'(y)-tsĭ	bel'(y)-tsi
Rumanian *Bălţi*, q.v.		
Belušić (Yugosl.)	bĕ'-lōō'-shĭch	beh'-loo'-shich
Belyi (Rus.)	bĕ'-lĭ	beh'-li
Bełz (Pol.)	bĕls'	bels'
Bemmel (Neth.)	bĕm'-əl	bem'-uhl
ben	bĕn'	ben'

An element, meaning *son*, in Hebrew personal names.
Arabic *ibn*, q.v.

Bena Bena (N.E. New	bĕ'-nä bĕ'-nä	beh'-nah beh'-nah
Guinea)		
Benares (India)	bə-nä'-rĭz	buh-nah'-riz
	native bə-nä'-rəs	buh-nah'-ruhs
Bénat (Fr., cape)	bĕ-nä'	beh-nah'

bender.   An alternative spelling of *bandar*, q.v.

Bender (Rum. > Rus.)	bĕn'-dər	ben'-duhr
Rumanian *Tighina*, q.v.		
Bendigo (Austral.)	bĕn'-dĭ-gō	ben'-di-goh

Bendin, Bendzin (Pol.)   See *Będzin*.

Benediktsson, Bjarni   bĕ'-nĕ-dĭk(h)ts'-sôn,   beh'-neh-dik(h)ts'-
  (Icel. diplomat)   byäd'-nĭ   son, byahd'-ni
Beneš, Eduard (Cz. polit.) bĕ'-nĕsh   beh'-nesh
Benešov (Cz.)   bĕ'-nĕ-shôf   beh'-neh-shof
Benét, Stephen Vincent   bĕ-nā'   beh-nay'
  and William Rose (Am. authors)
Benevento (It.)   bĕ-nĕ-vĕn'-tô   beh-neh-ven'-to
Bengal (India)   bĕng'-gôl'   beng'-gol'
Bengal (NEI)   *Du.* bĕn'-gäl'   ben'-gahl'
                         native bə-ngäl'   buh-ngahl'
Ben Gardane (Tun.)   bĕn gär-dăn'   ben gahr-dan'
Bengasi *or* Benghazi   bĕn-gä'-zē   ben-gah'-zee
  (Libya)
Bengkalis (NEI)   bĕng-kä'-lēs   beng-kah'-lees
Bengodi (It.)   bĕn-gô'-dē   ben-go'-dee
Benguela (Angola)   bĕn-gĕl'-ə   ben-gel'-uh
Benguet (P.I.)   bĕng-gĕt'   beng-get'
Ben Gurion, David   bĕn gōōr'-ĭ-ôn   ben goor'-i-on
  (Zionist leader)
Benha (Egypt)   bĕn'-hä   ben'-hah
Beni (Bol., riv.)   bĕ'-nē   beh'-nee
Benicio Silva, Valentim (Braz. polit.) See *Silva, Valentim Benicio.*
Benin (Nigeria)   bĕ-nēn'   beh-neen'
Beni Suef (Egypt)   bĕ'-nē swāf'   beh'-nee swayf'
Benítez Vera, Victoriano bĕ-nē'-tĕs vĕ'-rä,   beh-nee'-tes veh'-rah,
  (Para. polit.)   vēk-tô-ryä'-nô   veek-to-ryah'-no
Beni Ulid (Libya)   bĕ'-nē ōō'-lĭd   beh'-nee oo'-lid
Benkoelen *or* Benkulen bĕn-kōō'-lĕn   ben-koo'-len
  (NEI, Sumatra)
Benkovac (Yugosl.)   bĕn'-kô-väts   ben'-ko-vahts
Bennebroek (Neth.)   bĕn'-ə-brōōk   ben'-uh-brook
Benrath (Ger.)   bĕn'-rät   ben'-raht
Benthuizen (Neth.)   bĕnt'-hûĭ-zən   bent'-hœi-zuhn
Bentinck, V. F. W. Cavendish (Br. diplomat) See *Cavendish Bentinck.*
Bény Bocage (Fr.)   bĕ-nē bô-käzh'   beh-nee bo-kahzh'
Beograd (Yugosl.)   bĕ'-ô'-gräd   beh'-o'-grahd
  The English form, probably more suitable for American radio, is
  Belgrade, bĕl'-grād' [bel'-grayd'].
Beogradska (Yugosl.)   bĕ'-ô'-gräd-skä   beh'-o'-grahd-skah
Beppu (Jap.)   bĕp-pōō'   bep-poo'
Berane (Yugosl.)   bĕ'-rä-nĕ   beh'-rah-neh
Berat (Alb., town, riv.) bĕ'-rät   beh'-raht
  The town is also called *Berati* and *Beligrad.* The river is part of the
  Seman, q.v., and is the ancient *Apsos,* q.v.

Berber (N. Afr. race)	bûr′-bər	bur′-buhr
Berbera (Br. Som.)	bĕr′-bĕ-rä	behr′-beh-rah
	or bûr′-bə-rə	bur′-buh-ruh
Berchem (Belg.)	bĕr′-k(h)əm	behr′-k(h)uhm
Berchtesgaden (Ger.)	bĕrk(h)′-təs-gä′-dən	behrk(h)′-tuhs-gah′-
		duhn
Berck (Fr.)	bĕrk′	behrk′
Berck sur Mer (Fr.)	bĕrk sür mĕr′	behrk sür mehr′
Berdichev (Rus.)	bĕr-dē′-chĕf	behr-dee′-chef
Berdyansk (Rus.)	bĕr-dyänsk′	behr-dyahnsk′
Berehovo (Cz.)	bĕ′-rĕ-hô-vô	beh′-reh-ho-vo

Hungarian *Beregszász*, bĕ′-rĕk-säs [beh′-rek-sahs].

Berendsen, Sir Carl	bĕr′-ənd-sən	behr′-uhnd-suhn
(New Zealand diplomat)		
Berësovka (Rus.)	bĕ-ryô′-sôf-kä	beh-ryo′-sof-kah
Berettyó (Hung., riv.)	bĕ′-rĕt-tyô	beh′-ret-tyo
Bereza Kartuska (Pol.)	bĕ-rĕ′-zä	beh-reh′-zah
	kär-tōō′-skä	kahr-too′-skah

Russian *Kartuzskaya Bereza*, kär-tōōz′-skä-yä bĕ-ryô′-zä [kahr-tooz′-skah-yah beh-ryo′-zah].

Berezina (Pol. > Rus., riv.)	bĕ-rĕ-zē-nä′	beh-reh-zee-nah′

Polish *Berezyna*, bĕ-rĕ-zĭ′-nä [beh-reh-zi′-nah].

-berg	*Eng.* bûrg	buhrg
	Du., Ger. bĕrk(h)	behrk(h)

An element, meaning *mountain*, in Germanic place names. See *-burg*.

Bergambacht (Neth.)	bĕrk(h)-äm′-bäk(h)t	behrk(h)-ahm′-
		bahk(h)t
Bergamo (It.)	bĕr′-gä-mô	behr′-gah-mo
Bergeik (Neth.)	bĕrk(h)-īk′	behrk(h)-aik′
Bergen (Nor.)	*Eng.* bûr′-gən	buhr′-guhn
	Nor. bĕr′-gən	behr′-guhn
Bergen op Zoom (Neth.)	bĕr′-k(h)ən ôp zōm′	behr′-k(h)uhn op
		zohm′
Berggrav, Eivind	bĕrg′-gräv, ā′-vĭn	behrg′-grahv, ay′-vin
(Bishop of Oslo, Nor.)		
Bergheim (Ger.)	bĕrk(h)′-hīm	behrk(h)′-haim
Bergisch Gladbach (Ger.)	bĕr′-gĭsh	behr′-gish
	glät′-bäk(h)	glabt′-bahk(h)
Bergolo (It.)	bĕr′-gô-lô	behr′-go-lo
Bergschenhoek (Neth.)	bĕrk(h)′-sən-hōōk′	behrk(h)′-suhn-hook′
Bergues (Fr.)	bĕrg′	behrg′
Berhampore (India)	bûr′-əm-pôr′	buhr′-uhm-por′
Beria, Lavrentii P.	bĕ′-rĭ-yä,	beh′-ri-yah,
(Rus. polit.)	lä-vrĕn′-tĭ	lah-vren′-ti
Bering Sea	bĕr′-ĭng *or* bĭr′-ĭng	behr′-ing *or* bihr′-ing

Berislav (Rus.)	bĕ-rĭ-släf′	beh-ri-slahf′
Berkaak (Nor.)	bĕrk′-ôk	behrk′-ok
Berkel (Ger., Neth., riv.)	bĕr′-kəl	behr′-kuhl
Berkhout (Neth.)	bĕrk′-hout	behrk′-haut
Berkovitsa (Bulg.)	bĕr′-kŏ-vĭ-tsä	behr′-ko-vi-tsah
Berle, Adolph Augustus (Am. lawyer)	bûr′-lĭ	buhr′-li
Berlevaag (Nor.)	bĕr′-lə-vôg	behr′-luh-vog
Berlikum (Neth.)	bĕr′-lĭ-kəm	behr′-li-kuhm
Berlin (Ger.)	Eng. bər-lĭn′	buhr-lin′
	Ger. bĕr-lēn′	behr-leen′
Berlioz, Louis Hector (Fr. composer)	bĕr-lyōz′	behr-lyohz′
Bermeo (Sp.)	bĕr-mĕ′-ô	behr-meh′-o
Bern or Berne (Switz.)	Eng. bûrn′	buhrn′
	Fr. bĕrn′	behrn′
Bernadotte, Folke (Sw. count)	bĕr-nä-dôt′, fôl′-kə	behr-nah-dot′, fol′-kuh
Bernau (Ger.)	bĕr′-nou	behr′-nau
Bernay (Fr.)	bĕr-nĕ′	behr-neh′
Bernburg (Ger.)	Eng. bĕrn′-bûrg	behrn′-buhrg
	Ger. bĕrn′-bo͞ork(h)	behrn′-burk(h)
Berncastel-Cues (Ger.)	bĕrn′-käs-təl ko͞os′	behrn′-kahs-tuhl koos′
Berneval (Fr.)	bĕr-nə-väl′	behr-nuh-vahl′
Bernières (Fr.)	bĕr-nyĕr′	behr-nyehr′
Bernina (Switz., pass)	bĕr-nē′-nä	behr-nee′-nah
Beroun (Cz.)	bĕ′-rōn	beh′-rohn
Berovo (Yugosl.)	bĕ′-rô-vô	beh′-ro-vo
Berre (Fr.)	bĕr′	behr′
Berre, Étang de (Fr.)	bĕr′, ĕ-täN′ də	behr′, eh-tahN′ duh
Besançon (Fr.)	bə-zäN-sôN′	buh-zahN-soN′
Bescanuova (Yugosl.) Serb-Croat Baška, q.v.	It. bĕ-skä-nwô′-vä	beh-skah-nwo′-vah
Besch (Ger.)	bĕsh′	besh′
Bështriq (Balkan mt.) More correctly called Pushtrik, q.v.	Alb. bəsh′-trēk(y)	buhsh′-treek(y)
Beskid Mountains (Pol., Cz.)	bĕ′-skĭd or bĕs-kēd′	beh′-skid bes-keed′
Bessarabia (Rum. > Rus.)	Eng. bĕs′-ə-rā′-byə	bes′-uh-ray′-byuh
	Rus. bĕ-sä-rä′-bĭ-yä	beh-sah-rah′-bi-yah
Rumanian Basarabea, bä-sä-rä′-byä [bah-sah-rah′-byah].		
Besse (Fr.)	bĕs′	bes′
Bessheim (Nor.)	bĕs′-hām	bes′-haym
Bessin (Fr.)	bĕ-säN′	beh-saN′

[54]

| Best (Neth.) | bĕst′ | best′ |

Beszterce (Rum.) See *Bistriţa*.

Betaf (NEI)	bā′-täf′	bay′-tahf′
Betancourt, Rómulo	bĕ-täN-kōōr′,	beh-tahN-koor′,
(Ven. polit.)	rô′-mōō-lô	ro′-moo-lo
Bethany (Pal.)	bĕth′-ə-nĭ	beth′-uh-ni

Modern *El Azaria*, ĕl ä-zä-rē′-yĕ [ah-zah-ree′-yeh].

Bethe, Hans A.	bā′-tə	bay′-tuh
(Ger. Am. scientist)		
Bethesda (Md.)	bə-thĕz′-də	buh-thez′-duh
Beth Haarava (Pal.)	bĕth′ hä-ä-rä-vä′	beth′ hah-ah-rah-
Also spelled *Beit Haarava*.		vah′
Bethlehem (Pal.)	bĕth′-lĭ-əm *or* -hĕm	beth′-li-uhm *or* -hem
Arabic *Beit Lahm*.		
Bethsaida (Pal.)	bĕth-sā′-ə-də	beth-say′-uh-duh
Béthune (Fr.)	bĕ-tün′	beh-tün′
Betio (Oc., Tarawa)	*native* bĕ′-shĭ-ô	beh′-shi-o
	Eng. bā′-shĭ-ō	bay′-shi-oh

The latter is the pronunciation preferred by Mr. Robert Sherrod, author of *Tarawa, the Story of a Battle*, and by Miss J. D. Baldwin of Orange N. J., a retired missionary. Both rhyme *Betio* with the English word *ratio*. Two other missionaries, Miss J. R. Hoppin, Ashland, Wis., and Mrs. I. M. Channon, Rochester, N. Y., agree on the "soft character" of the Gilbertese "ti," but transcribe it "chĭ" rather than "shĭ." Mr. V. Fox-Strangways, then Resident Commissioner of the Gilbert and Ellice Islands, wrote from Tarawa October 27, 1945: "Most of my elders, and those whom I should trust in such a matter, plump for the pronunciation (1) bay′-tsi-oh or (2) bay′-tsee-oh with a marked accent on first syllable, second and third syllables shorter. (Actually the *bay* part is like French *bé*, a softer sound than the crude *ā* or *ay*.) Nowadays, however (and this is particularly noticeable on certain islands of the Gilberts), we get the softer (3) bay′-tshi-oh or even (4) bay′-shi-oh (as Miss Baldwin says, very like the English word *ratio*). To my mind, (1), (2), (3), and (4), in that order, are the best representations of our most common local pronunciations: but as I say, islands differ."

Betis (P.I.)	bĕ′-tĭs	beh′-tis
Betoeng (NEI)	bĕ-tŏōng′	beh-tung′
Betong (Sarawak)	bĕ-tông′	beh-tong′
Betżyce (Pol.)	bĕt-zhĭ′-tsĕ	bet-zhi′-tseh
Beuel (Ger.)	boi′-əl	boi′-uhl
Also called *Vilich*, fē′-lĭk(h) [fee′-lik(h)].		
Beugen (Neth.)	bû′-k(h)ən	bœ′-k(h)uhn
Beuningen (Neth.)	bû′-nĭng-ən	bœ′-ning-uhn

| Beuthen | boi′-tən | boi′-tuhn |

(Ger. Silesia > Pol.) Near Katowice. Polish *Bytom*, q.v.

| Beuthen (Ger. >? Pol.) | boi′-tən | boi′-tuhn |

Near Neusalz and Glogau. Polish *Białobrzezie*, q.v.

Beuvron (Fr., riv.)	bû-vrôN′	bœ-vroN′
Beuxes (Fr.)	bûks′	bœks′
Beuzeville (Fr.)	bûz-vēl′	bœz-veel′
Bevan, Aneurin	bĕv′-ən,	bev′-uhn
(Br. Minister of Health)	ä′-nĭ-rĭn	ah′-nai-rin
Beveland (Neth.)	bā′-və-länt	bay′-vuh-lahnt
Beverwijk (Neth.)	bā′-vər-wĭk	bay′-vuhr-waik
Bevin, Ernest	bĕv′-ĭn	bev′-in
(Br. Foreign Secretary)		
Bexar (Tex.)	băr′	behr′

Spanish *Béjar* or *Béxar*, bĕ′-här [beh′-hahr].

| bey *or* beg | bā′, bĕg′ | bay′, beg′ |

A title or honorific in the Middle East and Africa, usually following
the name. It is disregarded in alphabetical listing.

| Beyersdorf (Ger.) | bĭ′-ərs-dôrf | bai′-uhrs-dorf |

Beyrouth (Syria)   See *Beirut*.

Bezdan (Yugosl.)	bĕz′-dän	bez′-dahn
Bezel (Neth.)	bā′-zəl	bay′-zuhl
Bezhetsk (Rus.)	bĕ′-zhĕtsk	beh′-zhetsk
Béziers (Fr.)	bĕ-zyĕ′	beh-zyeh′
Bezwada (India)	bĕz-wä′-də	bez-wah′-duh

Bhadhalung (Siam) See *Phatthalung*.

Bhagalpur (India)	bä′-gəl-pŏŏr′	bah′-guhl-pur′
Bhamo (Burma)	bä′-mō	bah′-moh
Burman *Bamaw*.		

Bhangnga (Siam) See *Phangnga*.

| Bhaunagar (India) | bou-nŭg′-ər | bau-nuhg′-uhr |

Bhejburi (Siam) See *Phet Buri*.

Bhisanulok (Siam) See *Phitsanulok*.

Bhopal (India)	bō′-päl′	boh′-pahl′
Bhusaval (India)	bōō-sä′-vəl	boo-sah′-vuhl
Bhutan (India)	bōō′-tän′	boo′-tahn′
Biafra, Bight of (Afr.)	bĭ-ä′-frə	bi-ah′-fruh
Biagio (It.)	byä′-jô	byah′-jo
Biak (NEI, Schouten isls.)	*Eng.* bē′-ăk *or* bĭ′-ăk	bee′-ak *or* bai′-ak
	native bē′-äk *or* bē′-ä	bee′-ahk *or* bee′-ah
Biała Podlaska (Pol.)	byä′-lä pô-dlä′-skä	byah′-lah po-dlah′-skah

Russian *Byela*, bĕ′-lä [beh′-lah].

Białobrzezie (Ger. >? Pol) byä-lô-bzhĕ'-zhĕ   byah-lo-bzheh'-zheh
    German *Beuthen*, q.v.
Białogard (Ger. >Pol.)   byä-lô'-gärt   byah-lo'-gahrt
    German *Belgard*, q.v.
Białowieża (Pol.)   byä-lô-vyĕ'-zhä   byah-lo-vyeh'-zhah
    Russian *Byelovyezh*, bĕ-lŏ-vĕzh' [beh-lo-vezh'].
Białystok (Pol.)   byä-lĭ'-stôk   byah-li'-stok
    Russian *Byelostok*, bĕ-lŏ-stôk' [beh-lo-stok'].
Biancanigo (It.)   byän-kä-nē'-gô   byahn-kah-nee'-go
Biancavilla (Sicily)   byän-kä-vēl'-lä   byahn-kah-veel'-lah
Biarritz (Fr.)   *Eng.* bĭ'-ə-rĭts   bi'-uh-rits
              Fr. byä-rēts'   byah-reets'
Bícol (P.I., riv.)   bē'-kôl   bee'-kol
Bidault, Georges   bē-dō', zhôrzh'   bee-doh', zhorzh'
    (Fr. polit.)
Bidon 5 (Alg., airport) bē-dôN sănk'   bee-doN saNk'
Biel (Switz.)   bēl'   beel'
    French *Bienne*, byĕn' [byen'].
Bielawa (Ger. >? Pol.) byĕ-lä'-vä   byeh-lah'-vah
    German *Langenbielau*, q.v.
Bielefeld (Ger.)   bē'-lə-fĕlt   bee'-luh-felt
Bielsko (Pol.)   byĕl'-skô   byel'-sko
    German *Bielitz*, bē'-lĭts [bee'-lits].
Biemiller, Andrew J.   bē'-mĭl-ər   bee'-mil-uhr
    (U.S. representative)
Bienen (Ger.)   bē'-nən   bee'-nuhn
Bienne (Switz.) See *Biel*.
Bierum (Neth.)   bē'-rəm   bee'-ruhm
Bierut, Bolestaw (Pol. byĕ'-rŏŏt, bô-lĕ'-släf byeh'-rut, bo-leh'-
    polit.)   slahf
Biervliet (Neth.)   bēr'-vlēt   beer'-vleet
Biesdorf (Ger.)   bēs'-dôrf   bees'-dorf
Biesenthal (Ger.)   bē'-zən-täl   bee'-zuhn-tahl
Biferno (It., riv.)   bē-fĕr'-nô   bee-fehr'-no
Bigaá (P.I.)   bē-gä-ä'   bee-gah-ah'
Bigej (Oc., Kwajalein) bē'-gĕj   bee'-gej
Biggerann (Oc., Kwajalein) bĭg'-gə-rän   big'-guh-rahn
Bihać (Yugosl.)   bē'-häch   bee'-hahch
Bihaćska (Yugosl.)   bē'-häch-skä   bee'-hahch-skah
Bihar (India)   bē-här'   bee-hahr'
Bihor (Rum.)   bē-hôr'   bee-hor'
    Hungarian *Bihar*, bē'-hŏr [bee'-hor].
Bihorului (Rum., mts.) bē-hô'-rŏŏ-lwē bee-ho'-ru-lwee
Bijade, la (Fr.)   bē-zhäd', lä   bee-zhahd', lah

Bijeljina (Yugosl.)	bĭ'-yĕ'-lyĭ-nä	bi'-yeh'-lyi-nah
Bijelo Polje (Yugosl.)	bĭ'-yĕ'-lô pô'-lyĕ	bi'-yeh'-lo po'-lyeh
Bikaj (Alb.)	bē'-kī	bee'-kai
Bikaner (India)	bē'-kə-nēr'	bee'-kuh-neer'
Bikar (Oc., Marshalls)	bē'-kär	bee'-kahr
Bikin (Rus.)	bē-kēn'	bee-keen'
Bikini (Oc., Marshalls)	bē-kē'-nē	bee-kee'-nee
Bilán (P.I., riv.)	bē-län'	bee-lahn'

There is also authority for *Bilan*, bē'-län [bee'-lahn].

Bilaspur (India)	bē-läs-pŏŏr'	bee-lahs-pur'
Bilatan (P.I.)	bē-lä'-tän	bee-lah'-tahn
Bilbao (Sp.)	*Eng.* bĭl-bou'	bil-bau'
	Sp. bēl-bä'-ô	beel-bah'-o
Bilbeis (Egypt)	bĭl-bās'	bil-bays'
Bilbo, Theodore G.	bĭl'-bō	bil'-boh
(U.S. senator)		
Bileća (Yugosl.)	bē'-lĕ-chä	bee'-leh-chah
Biłgoraj (Pol.)	bĭl-gô'-rī	bil-go'-rai

Russian *Byelgorai*, bĕl'-gŏ-rī [bel'-go-rai].

Bilíbid (P.I., Manila)	*Eng.* bĭl'-ə-bĭd	bil'-uh-bid
	native bē-lē'-bĭd	bee-lee'-bid
Bilin (Burma, riv.)	bē'-lĭn	bee'-lin
Biliran (P.I.)	bē-lē'-rän	bee-lee'-rahn
Bilisht (Alb.)	bē'-lēsht	bee'-leesht
Bilishti (Alb.) See *Bilisht*.		
Billancourt (Fr.)	bē-yän-kōōr'	bee-yahn-koor'
Billiton *or* Belitong (NEI)	bēl'-lē-tŏn	beel'-lee-ton
	or bĕ-lē'-tŏng	beh-lee'-tong
Billoux, François	bē-yōō', fräN-swä'	bee-yoo', frahN-
(Fr. polit.)		swah'
Biloxi (Miss.)	bĭ-lŭk'-sĭ	bi-luk'-si
Bilt, de (Neth.)	bĭlt', də	bilt', duh
Bilt, Het (Neth.)	bĭlt', hĕt	bilt', het
Bima (NEI, Soembawa)	bē'-mä	bee'-mah
Binačka Morava	bē'-näch-kä	bee'-nahch-kah
(Yugosl., riv.)	mô'-rä'-vä	mo'-rah'-vah
Binaco (P.I.) See *Santa Ignacia*.		
Binahaán (P.I., riv.)	bē-nä-hä-än'	bee-nah-hah-ahn'
Binalonan (P.I.)	bē-nä-lô'-nän	bee-nah-lo'-nahn
Biñang (P.I.)	bē-nyäng'	bee-nyahng'
Binangonan (P.I.)	bē-näng-ô'-nän	bee-nahng-o'-nahn
Binas (Fr.)	bē-nä'	bee-nah'
Binghamton (N.Y.)	bĭng'-əm-tən	bing'-uhm-tuhn
Binhdinh (Indo-Ch.)	bĭn-dĭn'	bin-din'

Binmaley (P.I.)   bĕn-mä-lä′   been-mah-lay′
The river is also called *Dagupan*, q.v.

Binnigem (Oc.)   bĭn-nē-gĕm′   bin-nee-gem′

Binondo (P.I.)   bē-nôn′-dô   bee-non′-do

Bintan (NEI, Riouw)   bĭn′-tän   bin′-tahn

Binunsalián (P.I.)   bē-nōōn-sä-lē-än′   bee-noon-sah-lee-ahn′

Bio (Oc., Solomons)   bē′-ô   bee′-o

Bioč (Yugosl., mt.)   bē′-ôch   bee′-och

Biograd (Yugosl.)   bē′-ô′-gräd   bee′-o′-grahd
Italian *Zaravecchia*, q.v.

bir *or* beer   bēr′   beer′
An element, meaning *well*, in Arabic and Hebrew place names.

Bira (Rus.)   bē′-rä   bee′-rah

Birac (P.I.)   bē-räk′   bee-rahk′

Birdum (Austral.)   bûr′-dəm   buhr′-duhm

Bir el Gobi (Libya)   bēr ĕl gō′-bē   beer el goh′-bee

Bir es Seba (Pal.) See *Beersheba*.

Bires Sof (Tun.)   bēr′-ĕs sôf′   beer′-es sof′

Bir Hacheim (Libya)   bēr hə-kä′-yĭm   beer huh-kay′-yim

Biri (NEI, riv.)   bē′-rē′   bee′-ree′

Biriukov (Rus.)   bĭ-ryōō-kôf′   bi-ryoo-kof′

Birjand (Iran)   bēr-jănd′   beer-jand′

Birkenfeld (Ger.)   bĭr′-kən-fĕlt   bihr′-kuhn-felt

Bir Mcherga (Tun.)   bēr mə-shĕr′-gä   beer muh-shehr′-gah

Bir Mrabbott
(Tun., pass)   bēr mə-räb′-bŭt   beer muh-rahb′-buht

Birnbaum (Pol.)   See *Międzychód*.

Birobidjan (Rus.)   bĭ′-rŏ-bĭ-jän′   bi′-ro-bi-jahn′

Bir Tebeul (Tun.)   bēr tə-bûl′   beer tuh-bœl′

Biryusov, Sergei E.   bĭ-ryōō-zôf′, sĕr-gä′   bi-ryoo-zof′, sehr-
(Rus. general)   gay′

Birzula (Rus.)   bēr′-zōō-lä   beer′-zu-lah

Bisayas (P.I.)   bē-sä′-yäs   bee-sah′-yahs
Also called *Visayan* (Islands), q.v.

Biscari (Sicily)   bē′-skä-rē   bee′-skah-ree

Biscaya (Sp., prov.)   bēs-kä′-yä   bees-kah′-yah
Also called *Vizcaya*, q.v. English *Biscay*, bĭs′-kā [bis′-kay].

Bisceglie (It.)   bē-shĕ′-lyĕ   bee-sheh′-lyeh

Bischwiller (Fr.)   bēsh-vē-lĕr′   beesh-vee-lehr′
German *Bischweiler*, bĭsh′-vī-lər [bish′-vai-luhr].

Bisegna (It.)   bē-sĕ′-nyä   bee-seh′-nyah

Biševo (Yugosl., isl.)   bē′-shĕ-vô   bee′-sheh-vo
Italian *Busi*, q.v.

Bishenpur (India)   bĭsh′-ĕn-pŏŏr′   bish′-en-pur′

bisht (Alb.)   bĕsht′   beesht′
An element, meaning *cape* (literally *tail*), in Albanian place names.
Look up the other part of the name.

Bisk (Rus.)   bĕsk′   beesk′
Biskra (Alg.)   bĭs′-krä   bis′-krah
Bisnulok (Siam) See *Phitsanulok.*
Bisopra (It.)   bē-sô′-prä   bee-so′-prah
Bissagos (Port. Guinea)   bĭ-sä′-gōs   bi-sah′-gohs
Portuguese *Bijagos,* bĭ-zhä′-gōŏsh [bi-zhah′-gush].
Bistra planina (Yugosl.,   bē′-strä plä′-nē′-nä   bee′-strah plah′-nee′-
    mts.)   nah
Bistrica (Yugosl., riv.)   bē′-strĭ-tsä   bee′-stri-tsah
Bistriţa (Rum.)   bē′-strē-tsä   bee′-stree-tsah
Hungarian *Beszterce,* bĕs′-tĕr-tsĕ [bes′-tehr-tseh].
Bitburg (Ger.)   bĭt′-bōŏrk(h)   bit′-burk(h)
Bitche (Fr.)   bēch′   beech′
German *Bitsch,* bĭch′ [bich′].

Bititu (Gilberts, Tarawa). None of our correspondents acquainted with
the Gilbert Islands has ever heard of *Bititu.* One suggests that it may
be "an error that crept into the British Admiralty Charts many
years ago. The Admiralty are very conservative about amending such
errors and I should not be surprised to find it still repeated half a
century hence." On the National Geographic Society's Map of the
Pacific Ocean, September, 1943, *Bititu* is given in brackets presumably
as an alternative of *Betio.*

Bitolj (Yugosl.)   bē′-tôl(y)   bee′-tol(y)
Old Turkish *Monastir,* q.v. Greek *Monastérion.* Local Macedonian
pronunciation almost bē′-toi [bee′-toi], as Rebecca West reports.
Bitoljsko Polje (Yugosl.)   bē′-tôl(y)-skô   bee′-tol(y)-sko
                               pô′-lyĕ   po′-lyeh
Bitsch (Fr.) See *Bitche.*
bituminous   bĭ-tyōō′-mə-nəs   bi-tyoo′-muh-nuhs
Bityuk (Rus., riv.)   bē-tyōōk′   bee-tyook′
Bivona (Sicily)   bē-vô′-nä   bee-vo′-nah
bivouac   bĭv′-wăk *or*   biv′-wak *or*
                             bĭv′-ŏŏ-ăk   biv′-u-ak
Biwako (Jap.)   bē-wä′-kô′   bee-wah′-ko′
Bizerta (Tun.)   bĭ-zĕr′-tä   bi-zehr′-tah
French *Bizerte,* bē-zĕrt′ [bee-zehrt′]. English bĭ-zûr′-tə [bi-zuhr′-tuh], is
in the making.
Bjelasica (Yugosl., mts.)   byĕ′-lä′-sĭ-tsä   byeh′-lah′-si-tsah
Bjelica (Yugosl., riv.)   byĕ′-lĭ-tsä   byeh′-li-tsah
Bjelostock (Pol.)   See *Białystok.*
Bjelovar (Yugosl.)   byĕ′-lô-vär   byeh′-lo-vahr

Bjoernevatn *or* Björnevatn (Nor.)	byûr′-nə-vätn	byœr′-nuh-vahtn
Bjorli (Nor.)	byōr′-lē	byohr′-lee
Björneborg (Fin.) See *Pori.*		
Blace (Yugosl.)	blä′-tsĕ	blah′-tseh
Black Sea. Also called the *Euxine,* q.v. Russian *Chërnoe More,* q.v.		
Blagnac (Fr.)	blä-nyäk′	blah-nyahk′
Blagodarnoe (Rus.)	blä-gŏ-där′-nŏ-yĕ	blah-go-dahr′-no-yeh
Blagoveshchensk (Rus.)	blä-gŏ-vĕ′-shchĕnsk	blah-go-veh′- shchensk
Blaguša planina (Yugosl., mts.)	blä′-gōō-shä plä′-nē′-nä	blah′-goo-shah plah′-nee′-nah
Blain (Fr.)	blăN′	blaN′
Blajnica (Yugosl., mts.)	blĭ′-nĭ-tsä	blai′-ni-tsah
Blâmont (Fr.)	blä-môN′	blah-moN′
Blanc (Tun., cape) See *Cap Blanc.*		
Blangy le Château (Fr.)	bläN-zhē′ lə shä-tō′	blahN-zhee′ luh shah-toh′

Blankenberghe (Belg.)	*Eng.* blăng′-kən-bûrg
	Flem. bläng′-kən-
	  bĕr-k(h)ə
		blang′-kuhn-buhrg
		blahng′-kuhn-behr-
		  k(h)uh

Blashki (Pol.) See *Błaszki.*		
Blašica (Yugosl., riv.)	blä′-shĭ-tsä	blah′-shi-tsah
Błaszki (Pol.)	bläsh′-kĭ	blahsh′-ki
Russian *Blashki,* blä′-shkĭ [blah′-shki].		
Blatec (Yugosl.)	blä′-tĕts	blah′-tets
Blatnik, John A. (U.S. representative)	blät′-nĭk	blaht′-nik
Blato (Yugosl.)	blä′-tô	blah′-to
Blatta (Yugosl.)	*It.* blät′-tä	blaht′-tah
Serb-Croat *Blato,* q.v.		
Blatzheim (Ger.)	bläts′-hīm	blahts′-haim
Blavet (Fr., riv.)	blä-vĕ′	blah-veh′
Bled (Yugosl.)	blĕd′	bled′
Bleiburg (Austria)	blĭ′-bŏŏrk(h)	blai′-burk(h)
Bleiswijk (Neth.)	blīs′-wīk	blais′-waik
Bléneau (Fr.)	blĕ-nō′	bleh-noh′
Blenheim	*Eng.* blĕn′-əm	blen′-uhm
The English (and French) variant of German *Blindheim,* blĭnt′-hīm [blint′-haim].		
Bleone (Fr., riv.)	blə-ôn′	bluh-on′
Bléquin (Fr.)	blĕ-kăN′	bleh-kaN′
Blida (Alg.)	blē′-dä	blee′-dah
Blies (Fr., Ger., riv.)	blēs′	blees′

Bliesbruck (Fr.)	blēs-brük′	blees-brük′

Blindheim (Ger.) See *Blenheim*.

Blinisht (Alb.)	blē′-nēsht	blee′-neesht

Blinishti (Alb.) See *Blinisht*.

Bloemendaal (Neth.)	blōō′-mən-däl	bloo′-muhn-dahl
Bloemfontein (S. Afr.)	blōōm′-fŏn-tān′	bloom′-fon-tayn′
Blois (Fr.)	blwä′	blwah′
Blokzijl (Neth.)	blôk-zīl′	blok-zail′
Błonie (Pol.)	blô′-nyĕ	blo′-nyeh

Russian *Blone*, blô′-nĕ [blo′-neh].

Blora (NEI, Java)	blô′-rä	blo′-rah
Bluie	blōō′-ĭ	blu′-i

U. S. Army air bases in Greenland were called *Bluie East 1, 2,* and so on, and *Bluie West, 1, 2,* and so on.

Blum, Léon (Fr. polit.)	blōōm′, lĕ-ôN′	bloom′, leh-oN′
Blumberg, Gross (Ger.)	grōs′ blōōm′-bĕrk(h)	grohs′ bloom′-behrk(h)
Blupblup (Oc.)	blōōp-blōōp′	bloop-bloop′
B'nai B'rith	*formal* bə-nā′ bə-rēth′	bun-nay′ buh-reeth′
	informal . . . brĭth′	. . . brith′
Bö (Nor.)	bû′	bœ′
Bóak (P.I.)	bô′-äk	bo′-ahk

Also called bou′-äk [bau′-ahk] and bwäk′ [bwahk′].

Bober (Ger. >? Pol., riv.)	bō′-bər	boh′-buhr

Polish *Bobr*, q.v.

Böblingen (Ger.)	bûb′-lĭng-ən	bœb′-ling-uhn
Bobol (P.I.)	bô-bôl′	bo-bol′

Also called *San Felipe de Bobol*, sän fĕ-lē′-pĕ dĕ bô-bôl′ [sahn feh-lee′-peh deh bo-bol′].

Bobón (P.I.)	bô-bôn′	bo-bon′
Bobonán (P.I.)	bô-bô-nän′	bo-bo-nahn′
Bobovište (Yugosl.)	bô′-bô-vĭ-shtĕ	bo′-bo-vi-shteh
Bobr (Ger. >? Pol., riv.)	bôb′r	bob′r

German *Bober*, q.v.

Bobrinets (Rus.)	bŏ-brĭ-nĕts′	bo-bri-nets′
Bobruisk (Rus.)	bŏ-brōō′ĭsk	boh-bru′isk
Bocage (Fr.)	bô-käzh′	bo-kahzh′
Boca Raton (Fla.)	bō′-kə rə-tŏn′	boh′-kuh ruh-ton′

Compare *Raton*, N. M., which keeps a quasi-Spanish pronunciation.

Bocaue (P.I.)	bô-kä′-wĕ	bo-kah′-weh
Bocboc (P.I.)	bôk-bôk′	bok-bok′
Bocca di Falco (Sard.)	bôk′-kä dē fäl′-kô	bok′-kah dee fahl′-ko
Boccea (It.)	bôt-chĕ′-ä	bot-cheh′-ah

Bocceola (It.)	bôt-chĕ-ô′-lä	bot-cheh-o′-lah
Bocche di Cattaro	*It.* bôk′-kĕ dē	bok′-keh dee
(Yugosl., gulf)	kät′-tä-rô	kaht′-tah-ro
Serb-Croat *Boka Kotorska*, q.v.		
Bochkarevo (Rus.)	bŏch-kä-ryô′-vŏ	boch-kah-ryo′-vo
Bochnia (Pol.)	bôk(h)′-nyä	bok(h)′-nyah
Bocholt (Ger.)	bôk(h)′-ôlt	bok(h)′-olt
Bochum (Ger.)	bō′-k(h)ŏŏm	boh′-k(h)um
	or bôk(h)′-ŏŏm	bok(h)′-um
Bodegraven (Neth.)	bō′-də-k(h)rä′-vən	boh′-duh-k(h)rah′-vuhn
Bodena (Gr.)	vô-dĕ-nä′	vo-deh-nah′
Bodenbach (Cz.) See *Podmokly.*		
Boden See (Ger., lake)	bō′-dən zä′	boh′-duhn zay′
English *Lake of Constance.*		
Bodjanegara *or* Bodjone-	bô-jŏ-nə-gŏ′-rŏ	bo-jo-nuh-go′-ro
goro (NEI, Java)		
In this neighborhood *a* is pronounced ŏ.		
Bodoe *or* Bodö (Nor.)	bō′-dû	boh′-dœ
Boe (Nor.)	bû′	bœ′
Boeblingen (Ger.)	bûb′-lĭng-ən	bœb′-ling-uhn
Boehlen (Ger.)	bû′-lən	bœ′-luhn
Boehme (Ger., riv.)	bû′-mə	bœ′-muh
Boehmer Wald (Ger., Cz.) See *Böhmer Wald.*		
Boeing, William E.	bō′-ĭng	boh′-ing
(American manufacturer of airplanes)		
Boekel (Neth.)	bōō′-kəl	boo′-kuhl
Boela (NEI)	bōō′-lä	boo′-lah
Boeloe (NEI)	bōō′-lōō	boo′-loo
Boemlafjord (Nor.)	bûm′-lä-fyōr	bœm′-lah-fyohr
Boeo (Sicily, cape)	bô-ĕ′-ô	bo-eh′-o
Also called *Lilebeo*, q.v.		
Boeroe *or* Buru (NEI)	bōō′-rōō	boo′-roo
Boersen Zeitung, Berliner	bûr′-sən tsī′-tŏŏng,	bœr′-suhn tsai′-tung
(Ger. newspaper)	bĕr-lē′-nər	behr-lee′-nuhr
Boetoeng *or* Butung (NEI)	bōō′-tŏŏng	boo′-toong
Also called *Boeton*, bōō′-tôn [boo′-ton].		
Boetong *or* Butong	bōō′-tông	boo′-tong
(NEI, Borneo)		
Boettcher (Col. family)	bĕch′-ər	bech′-uhr
Boettiger, John	bŏt′-ɪ-gər	bot′-ih-guhr
(Am. publisher)		
Boetzow (Ger.)	bû′-tsō	bœ′-tsoh
Bogadyim (N.E. New	bô-gä′-jĭm	bo-gah′-jim
Guinea)		

[63]

Bogatić (Yugosl.)	bô'-gä-tĭch	bo'-gah-tich
Boğaziçi (Turk., str.) See *Bosporus*.		
Bogdanci (Yugosl.)	bôg'-dän-tsĭ	bog'-dahn-tsi
bogey	bō'-gĭ	boh'-gi
Also familiar or childish boo͞'-gĭ [boo'-gi]. Compare *booger*, bo͞og'-ər [bug'-uhr].		
Boggeric (Oc., Kwajalein)	bôg'-gə-rĭk	bog'-guh-rik
Bogia (New Guinea)	bô-gē'-ä	bo-gee'-ah
Bogićevica (Yugosl.)	bô'-gē'-chĕ-vĭ-tsä	bo'-gee'-cheh-vi-tsah
Bogodukhov (Rus.)	bŏ-gŏ-do͞o'-hŏf	bo-go-doo'-hof
Bogojevo (Yugosl.)	bŏ'-gô'-yĕ-vô	bo'-go'-yeh-vo
Bogolyubov, Efim D. (Rus. chess player)	bŏ-gŏ-lyo͞o'-bŏf, ĕ-fēm'	bo-go-lyoo'-bof, eh-feem'
Bogomolets, Alexander (Rus. scientist)	bŏ-gŏ-mô'-lĕts	bo-go-mo'-lets
Bogomila (Yugosl.)	bô'-gô'-mĭ-lä	bo'-go'-mi-lah
Bogomolov (Rus. name)	bŏ-gŏ-mô'-lŏf	bo-go-mo'-lof
Bogon (Oc., Eniwetok)	bô'-gôn	bo'-gon
Bogoroditsk (Rus.)	bŏ-gŏ-rô'-dĭtsk	bo-go-ro'-ditsk
Bogoslof (Alaska, isl.)	bō'-gə-slôf	boh'-guh-slof
Bogotá (Colom.)	bô-gô-tä'	bo-go-tah'
Bogota (N.J.)	bə-gō'-tə	buh-goh'-tuh
Bogotu (Oc.) See *Bugotu*.		
Bogoyavlensk (Rus.)	bŏ-gŏ-yäv-lĕnsk'	bo-go-yahv-lensk'
Boguchar (Rus.)	bŏ-go͞o-chär'	bo-goo-chahr'
Bohan (Yugosl.)	bô'-hän	bo'-hahn
Bohdanów (Pol.)	bôk(h)-dä'-no͞of	bok(h)-dah'-nuf
Bohemia (Cz.) Czech *Čechy*, q.v.	*Eng.* bō-hē'-myə	boh-hee'-myuh
Bohinj (Yugosl.)	bô'-hēn'(y)	bo'-heen'(y)
Böhlen (Ger.)	bû'-lən	bœ'-luhn
Böhme (Ger., riv.)	bû'-mə	bœ'-muh
Böhmer Wald (Ger., Cz.) English *Bohemian Forest*.	bû'-mər vält'	bœ'-muhr vahlt'
Bohol (P.I.)	bô-hôl'	bo-hol'
Bohr, Niels (Dan. scientist)	bōr', nēls'	bohr', neels'
Bohrod, Aaron (Am. painter)	bō'-rŏd, ăr'-ən	boh'-rod, ehr'-uhn
Boibeis (Gr., lake)	vē-vē-ēs'	vee-vee-ees'
Also called *Karla*, kär'-lä [kahr'-lah].		
Bois de Bavent (Fr.)	bwä də bä-väN'	bwah duh bah-vahN'
Bois de Boulogne (Fr.)	bwä də bo͞o-lôn'(y)	bwah duh boo-lon'(y)
Bois de Limbourg (Fr.)	bwä də lăN-bo͞or'	bwah duh laN-boor'

Boise (Idaho)	boi'-sĭ	boi'-si
Boisson, Pierre (Fr. polit.)	bwä-sôN', pyĕr'	bwah-soN', pyehr'
Boissy St. Léger (Fr.)	bwä-sē sǎN lĕ-zhĕ'	bwah-seesaNleh-zheh'
Bojana (Balkan riv.)	S.-C. bô'-yä'-nä	bo'-yah'-nah

Albanian *Buna*, q.v.

Bojeador (P.I., cape)	bô-hĕ-ä-dôr'	bo-heh-ah-dor'
Boka Kotorska	bô'-kä kô-tôr'-skä	bo'-kah ko-tor'-skah

(Yugosl. str.) Also called *Verige*, q.v. Italian *Le Catene*, q.v.

Bokhara *or* Bukhara	*Eng.*, bō-kä'-rä	boh-kah'-rah
(Rus.)	*Rus.*, bōō-hä'-rä	bu-hah'-rah
Boknfjord (Nor.)	bōōk'n-fyōr	buk'n-fyohr
Bokovskaya (Rus.)	bŏ-kŏf-skä'-yä	bo-kof-skah'-yah

Boksmeer (Neth.) See *Boxmeer*.

Bokstel (Neth.) See *Boxtel*.

Bolbec (Fr.)	bôl-bĕk'	bol-bek'
Bolechów (Pol., Rus.)	bô-lĕ'-hōōf	bo-leh'-huf
Bolesławiec (Ger. >? Pol.)	bô-lĕ-slä'-vyĕts	bo-leh-slah'-vyets

German *Bunzlau*, q.v.

Bolgrad (Rum.>Rus.)	bôl'-gräd	bol'-grahd
Bolinao (P.I.)	bô-lē-nou'	bo-lee-nau'
Bolin Odzhal (Rus., lake)	bŏ-lēn' ŏd-zhäl'	bo-leen' od-zhahl'
Bolitho, Henry Hector	bō-lĭ'-*th*ō	boh-lai'-*th*oh

(New Zealand author)

Hector Bolitho asked that the last syllable of his name be pronounced like the word *though*. However the BBC's pamphlet, "Broadcast English, VII, Recommendations . . . regarding the Pronunciation of Some British Family Names . . ." gives for *Bolitho* only a pronunciation with "th" as in *thought*.

Bolivar (Miss., N.Y., Tex.)	bŏl'-ə-vər	bol'-uh-vuhr
Bolívar, Simón	bô-lē'-vär, sē-môn'	bo-lee'-vahr, see-mon'

South American patriot. Pronounced in English sī'-mən bôl-ə-vər [sai'-muhn bol'-uh-vuhr].

Bolivia (S.A.)	*Eng.* bə-lĭv'-ĭ-ə	buh-liv'-i-uh
	Sp. bô-lē'-vyä	bo-lee'-vyah
Boljaniéi (Yugosl.)	bô'-lyä'-nĭ-chĭ	bo'-lyah'-ni-chi
Boljevac (Yugosl.)	bô'-lyĕ-väts	bo'-lyeh-vahts
Boljeviéi (Yugosl.)	bô'-lyĕ'-vĭ-chĭ	bo'-lyeh'-vi-chi
Bolkesjoe *or*	bôl'-kə-shû	bol'-kuh-shœ
Bolkesjö (Nor.)		
Bolkhov (Rus.)	bŏl-hôf'	bol-hof'
Bollaert, Émile (Fr. polit.)	bô-lĕr', ĕ-mēl'	bo-lehr', eh-meel'
Bologna (It.)	*Eng.* bə-lōn'-yə	buh-lohn'-yuh
	It. bô-lô'-nyä	bo-lo'-nyah

There is also a popular English pronunciation, bə-lō'-nə [buh-loh'-nuh].

Bologoe (Rus.)   bŏ-lŏ-gŏ'-yĕ   bo-lo-go'-yeh
Bolong (P.I.)   bô'-lông'   bo-long'
Bolsena (It., lake)   bôl-sĕ'-nä   bol-seh'-nah
Bolshevik   bŏl'-shə-vĭk   bol'-shuh-vik
    Bolsheviki, Eng. bŏl'-shə-vē'-kĭ [bol'-shuh-vee'-ki] or bōl'- [bohl'-],
    Rus. bŏl-shĕ-vĭ-kē' [bol-sheh-vi-kee'].
Bolshoy Tokmak (Rus.)   bŏl(y)-shoi'   bol(y)-shoi'
                   tŏk-mäk'   tok-mahk'
Bolso (P.I., riv.)   bôl'-sô   bol'-so
Bolsward (Neth.)   bôls'-wärt   bols'-wahrt
Bolte, Charles G.   bōl'-tĕ   bohl'-teh
   (Am. author)
Bolzano (It.)   bôl-tsä'-nô   bol-tsah'-no
   German *Bozen*, bō'-tsən [boh'-tsuhn].
Bomba (Libya)   bôm'-bä   bom'-bah
Bombala (Austral.)   bŏm-bä'-lə   bom-bah'-luh
    Sometimes an *r* is inserted, making bŏmbär'-lə [bom-bahr'-luh].
bombardier   bŏm'-bər-dĭr'   bom'-buhr-dihr'
   It has been an English word for centuries.
Bombay (India)   bŏm'-bā'   bom'-bay'
Bömlafjord (Nor.)   bûm'-lä-fyōr   bœm'-lah-fyohr
Bon (Alg., cape)   See *Cap Bon*.
Bonchaung (Burma)   bōn'-choung'   bohn'-chaung'
Boncour, Joseph Paul (Fr. polit.) See *Paul Boncour, Joseph*.
Bondi (Austr.)   bôn'-dī   bon'-dai
Bondog (P.I., pen.)   bôn-dôg'   bon-dog'
   Also called *Bondoc*, bôn-dôk' [bon-dok'].
Bondowoso (NEI)   bôn-dô-wô'-sô   bon-do-wo'-so
Bondy (Fr.)   bôN-dē'   boN-dee'
Bône (Alg.)   bōn'   bohn'
Bone *or* Boni (NEI)   bô'-nĕ *or* bô'-nē   bo'-neh *or* bo'-nee
Bonga (P.I.)   bông'-ä   bong'-ah
Bongabon (P.I., Luzón)   bông-ä'-bôn   bong-ah'-bon
Bongabong (P.I., Mindoro) bông-ä'-bông   bong-ah'-bong
Bongao, Port   bông-ou'   bong-au'
   (NEI, Sulu arch.)
Bonhomme (Fr., pass)   bôN-ôm'   boN-om'
Bonifacio (Sard.,   bô-nē-fä'-chô   bo-nee-fah'-cho
   Corsica, str.)
Bonilla Atiles, J. A.   bô-nē'-yä ä-tē'-lĕs   bo-nee'-yah
   (Dom. polit.)   ah-tee'-les
Bonin (Rus., isl.)   bô'-nēn   bo'-neen
Bonin Isls. (Oc.)   bō'-nĭn   boh'-nin
   Japanese *Ogasawara Jima*, q.v.

Bonn (Ger.)	bôn′	bon′
Bonnebosq (Fr.)	bôn-bôsk′	bon-bosk′
Bonner (Calif., Idaho)	bŏn′-ər	bon′-uhr
Bonnet, Georges (Fr. polit.)	bô-nĕ′, zhôrzh′	bo-neh′, zhorzh′
Bonnet, Henri (Fr. polit.)	bô-nĕ′, äN-rē′	bo-neh′, ahN-ree′
Bonneval (Fr.)	bôn-väl′	bon-vahl′
Bonneville (Idaho, Ore., Utah)	bŏn′-ə-vĭl or bŏn′-ĭ-vĭl	bon′-uh-vil or bon′-i-vil

The name of a county in Idaho, a dam in Oregon, and a racecourse in Utah. Important local agencies prefer, or give only, a pronunciation of three syllables, not bŏn′ -vĭl [bon′ -vil].

Bonnières (Fr.)	bô-nyĕr′	bo-nyehr′
Bonomi, Ivanoe (It. polit.)	bô-nô′-mē, ē-vä′-nô-ĕ	bo-no′-mee, ee-vah′-no-eh
Bontoc (P.I.)	*Eng.* bŏn-tŏk′ *Sp.* bôn-tôk′	bon-tok′ bon-tok′
Boom (Belg.)	bōm′	bohm′
Boos (Fr.)	bō′	boh′
Boppard (Ger.)	bôp′-ärt	bop′-ahrt
Bor, General (Pol. polit.)	See *Komorowski, Tadeusz.*	
Bor (Rus., Yugosl.)	bôr′	bor′
Boranja (Yugosl.)	bô′-rä-nyä	bo′-rah-nyah
Bordeaux (Fr.)	bôr-dō′	bor-doh′
Bordighera (It.)	bôr-dē-gĕ′-rä	bor-dee-geh′-rah
Bordj Bou Hamra (Tun.)	bôrj′ bōo häm′-rä	borj′ boo hahm′-rah
Also called *Bou Hamran.*		
Bordj le Boeuf (Tun.)	bôrj lə bûf′	borj luh bœf′
Boren, Lyle H. (U.S. representative)	bō′-rĕn	boh′-ren
Borgå (Fin.) See *Borgo.*		
Borger (Neth.)	bôr′-k(h)ər	bor′-k(h)uhr
Borgerhout (Belg.)	bôr′-k(h)ər-hout	bor′-k(h)uhr-haut
Borghese, Stefano (It. prince)	bôr-gĕ′-sĕ, stĕ′-fä-nô	bor-geh′-seh, steh′-fah-no
Borgo (Fin.) Swedish spelling *Borgå.*	bôr′-gō	bor′-goh
Borgo Isonzo (It.)	bôr′-gô ē-sôn′-dzô	bor′-go ee-son′-dzo
Borgo Piave (It.)	bôr′-gô pyä′-vĕ	bor′-go pyah′-veh
Borgund (Nor.)	bôr′-gōon	bor′-gun
Borinage (Belg.)	bô-rē-näzh′	bo-ree-nahzh′
Borislav (Pol. >Rus.) Polish *Borysław,* q.v.	bŏ-rē′-släf	bo-ree′-slahf
Borisoglebsk (Rus.)	bŏ-rē′-sŏ-glĕpsk′	bo-ree′-so-glepsk′

Borisov (Rus.)	bŏ-rē′-sŏf	bo-ree′-sof
Borisovka (Rus.)	bŏ-rē′-sŏf-kä	bo-ree′-sof-kah
Borizzo (Sicily)	bô-rēt′-sô	bo-reet′-so
Borkeloo (Neth.)	bôr′-kə-lō	bor′-kuh-loh
Borken (Ger.)	bôr′-kən	bor′-kuhn
Borkum (Ger., isl.)	bôr′-kŏŏm	bor′-kum
Bormes (Fr.)	bôrm′	borm′
Borne (Neth.)	bôr′-nə	bor′-nuh
Borneo (Malay arch.)	bôr′-nĭ-ō	bor′-ni-oh
Bornholm (Den.)	bôrn′-hôlm	born′-holm
Borodino (Rus.)	bŏ-rŏ-dĭ-nô′	bo-ro-di-no′
Borongan (P.I.)	bô-rông′-än	bo-rong′-ahn
Borovichi (Rus.)	bŏ-rŏ-vĭ-chē′	bo-ro-vi-chee′
Borovsk (Rus.)	bŏ′-rŏfsk	bo′-rofsk
Borroloola (Austral.)	bôr′-ə-lōō′-lä	bor′-uh-loo′-lah
Borşa (Rum.)	bôr′-shä	bor′-shah
Börsen Zeitung (Ger.) See *Boersen Zeitung*.		
Boruku (NEI)	bô-rōō′-kōō	bo-roo′-koo
Boryslaw (Pol. > Rus.)	bô-rĭ′-släf	bo-ri′-slahf
Russian *Borislav*, q.v.		
Borzna (Rus.)	bôrz′-nä	borz′-nah
bos *or* bosch	bôs′	bos′

A common element, meaning *wood* or *forest*, in Dutch place names.
Bos, den (Neth.) See *Den Bos*.

| Bosa (Sard.) | bô′-sä | bo′-sah |
| Bosanska | bô-sän′-skä | bo-sahn′-skah |

An element, meaning *Bosnian*, in Serb-Croat place names. It may be necessary to look up the other part of the name.

Bosanska Dubica	bô′-sän-skä	bo′-sahn-skah
(Yugosl.)	dōō′-bĭ-tsä	doo′-bi-tsah
Bosanska Gradiška	bô′-sän-skä	bo′-sahn-skah
(Yugosl.)	grä′-dĭ-shkä	grah′-di-shkah
Bošava (Yugosl.)	bô′-shä-vä	bo′-shah-vah
Bose, Subash Chundra	bōs′, sōō-bäsh′	bohs′, soo-bahsh′
(Indian polit.)	chŭn′-drə	chuhn′-druh
Bosiljgrad (Yugosl.)	bô′-sĭl(y)-gräd	bo′-sil(y)-grahd
Boskija (Yugosl., mt.)	bô′-skĭ-yä	bo′-ski-yah
Boskoop (Neth.)	bôs′-kōp	bos′-kohp
Bosnek (NEI)	bôs′-něk	bos′-nek
Bosnia (Yugosl.)	*Eng.* bôz′-nĭ-ə	boz′-ni-uh
Serb-Croat *Bosna*, bôs′-nä [bos′-nah].		
Bosoboso (P.I.)	bô-sô-bô′-sô	bo-so-bo′-so
Bosporus (Turk., str.)	*Eng.* bŏs′-pə-rəs	bos′-puh-ruhs

Turkish *Boğaziçi*, bô-äz′-ē-chē′ [bo-ahz′-ee-chee′], or *Karadeniz Boğazı*.

Bossekopp (Nor.)	bôs'-sə-kôp	bos'-suh-kop
Bossoglina (Yugosl.) Serb-Croat *Marina*, q.v.	*It.* bôs-sô-lyē'-nä	bos-so-lyee'-nah
Botelho Moniz, Júlio (Port. polit.)	bŏŏ-tĕ'-lyŏŏ mô- nēzh', zhŏŏ'-lyŏŏ	bu-teh'-lyu mo- neezh', zhoo'-lyu
Boterhoek (Neth.)	bō'-tər-hŏŏk	boh'-tuhr-huk
Botevgrad (Bulg.)	bô'-tĕf-grät	bo'-tef-graht
Botn (Nor.)	bôt'n	bot'n
Botolan (P.I.)	bô-tô'-län	bo-to'-lahn
Botoşani (Rum.)	bô-tô-shän'	bo-to-shahn'
Botsa (N.E. New Guinea) Also called *Aris*, q.v.	bôt-sä'	bot-sah'
Bottaccia, la (It.)	bôt-tät'-chä, lä	bot-taht'-chah, lah
Bottrop (Ger.)	bôt'-rôp	bot'-rop
Bötzow (Ger.)	bû'-tsō	bœ'-tsoh
bou	bŏŏ'	boo'

An element, meaning *father*, in Western Arabic names. See *abu*.

Bou Arada (Tun.)	bŏŏ ä-rǎ'-dä	boo ah-ra'-dah
Bou Chebka (Tun.)	bŏŏ shĕb'-kä	boo sheb'-kah
Bou Chekka (Tun., Alg.)	bŏŏ shĕk'-kä	boo shek'-kah
Bouches du Rhône (Fr.)	bŏŏsh dü rōn'	boosh dü rohn'
Bou Ficha (Tun.)	bŏŏ fē'-shä	boo fee'-shah
Bougainville (Oc., Solo- mons)	*Eng.* bŏŏ'-gĕn-vĭl *or* bō'- *Fr.* bŏŏ-gǎN-vēl'	boo'-gen-vil *or* boh'- boo-gaN-veel'
Bougie (Alg.)	bŏŏ-zhē'	boo-zhee'
Bougival (Fr.)	bŏŏ-zhē-väl'	boo-zhee-vahl'
Bou Hamran (Tun.)	bŏŏ häm-rǎn'	boo hahm-ran'
Bou Krin (Tun.)	bŏŏ' krēn'	boo' kreen'
Boulay (Fr.)	bŏŏ-lĕ'	boo-leh'
Boulia (Austral.)	bŏŏl'-yə	bool'-yuh
Boulogne (Fr.)	*Eng.* bŏŏ-lōn' *or* bŏŏ-loin' *Fr.* bŏŏ-lôn'(y)	bu-lohn' bu-loin' boo-lon'(y)
Bouloire (Fr.)	bŏŏ-lwär'	boo-lwahr'
Bourbon	*Eng.* bŏŏr'-bən *Fr.* bŏŏr-bôN'	bur'-buhn boor-boN'

The Kentucky county is called bûr'-bən [buhr'-buhn]; so, often, is the corn whiskey which is its namesake.

Bourbonnais (Fr.)	bŏŏr-bô-nĕ'	boor-bo-neh'
Bourbourg (Fr.)	bŏŏr-bŏŏr'	boor-boor'
Bourdouxhe, Madeleine (Belg. author)	bŏŏr'-dŏŏks', mǎ-dlĕn'	boor'-dooks', ma-dlen'
Bourg Achard (Fr.)	bŏŏr ä-shär'	boor ah-shahr'
Bourg en Bresse (Fr.)	bŏŏr äN brĕs'	boor ahN bres'

Bourges (Fr.)	bōōrzh′	boorzh′
Bourget, le (Fr.)	bōōr-zhĕ′, lə	boor-zheh′, luh
Bourguébus (Fr.)	bōōr-gĕ-büs′	boor-geh-büs′
Bourgueil (Fr.)	bōōr-gû′(y)	boor-gœ′(y)
Bourheim (Ger.)	bōōr′-hīm	boor′-haim
Bourke White, Margaret (Am. photographer)	bûrk whīt′	buhrk whait′
Bourrasol (Fr.)	bōō-rä-sôl′	boo-rah-sol′
Bou Saada (Alg.)	bōō sä′-dä	boo sah′-dah
Bou Thadi (Tun.)	bōō tä′-dē	boo tah′-dee
Bouxwiller (Fr.)	bōōks-vē-lĕr′	books-vee-lehr′

German *Buchsweiler*, bŏŏk(h)s′-vī-lər [buk(h)s′-vai-luhr].

Bouza (Crete, cape) See *Vouxa*.

Bou Znika (Mor.)	bōō zə-nē′-kə	boo zuh-nee′-kuh
Bouzonville (Fr.)	bōō-zôN-vēl′	boo-zoN-veel′
Bou Zouita (Tun.)	bōō zōō-ē′-tä	boo zoo-ee′-tah
Bou Zoumit (Tun.)	bōō zōō′-mĭt	boo zoo′-mit
Bovenkarspel (Neth.)	bō′-vən-kär′-spəl	boh′-vuhn-kahr′-spuhl
Boville (It.)	bô-vēl′-lĕ	bo-veel′-leh
Bowdoin College	bōd′n	bohd′n
Bow Street (London)	bō′	boh′
Boxmeer *or* Boksmeer (Neth.)	bôks-mär′	boks-mayr′
Boxtel *or* Bokstel (Neth.)	bôks′-təl	boks′-tuhl
Boża Góra (Ger. >? Pol.)	bô′-zhä gōō′-rä	bo′-zhah gu′-rah

German *Gottesberg*, q.v.

Bozeman (Mont.)	bōz′-mən	bohz′-muhn

Bozen (It.) See *Bolzano*.

Boževac (Yugosl.)	bô′-zhĕ-väts	bo′-zheh-vahts
Bozhilov, Dobri (Bulg. polit.)	bô′-zhĭ-lôf, dô′-brĭ	bo′-zhi-lof, do′-bri
Božička (Yugosl.)	bô′-zhĭch-kä	bo′-zhich-kah
Brabant (Neth., Belg.)	brä′-bänt	brah′-bahnt

English brə-bănt′ [bruh-bant′], brä′-bənt [brah′-buhnt], and brăb′-ənt [brab′-uhnt].

Brač (Yugosl., isl.)	bräch′	brahch′

Italian *Brazza*, q.v.

Bracciano (It.)	brät-chä′-nô	braht-chah′-no
Braćevac (Yugosl.)	brä′-chĕ-väts	brah′-cheh-vahts
Brachelen (Ger.)	brä′-k(h)ə-lən	brah′-k(h)uh-luhn
Brad (Rum.)	bräd′	brahd′
Braden, Spruille (Am. diplomat)	brā′-dən, sprōō′-ĭl	bray′-duhn, sproo′-il

Braga (Port.)   brä′-gə   brah′-guh
Bragança (Port., Brazil)   brä-gän′-sə   brah-gahn′-suh
Brahmaputra (India, riv.)   brä-mə-pōō′-trə   brah-muh-poo′-truh
Brăila (Rum.)   brə-ē′-lä   bruh-ee′-lah
Braitenstain (Ger. >Rus.) See *Breitenstein.*
Braljina (Yugosl.)   brä′-lyĭ-nä   brah′-lyi-nah
Bramuglia, Juan Atilio (Arg. polit.) See *Atilio Bramuglia.*
Brandenburg (Ger.)   *Eng.* brăn′-dən-bûrg   bran′-duhn-buhrg
                       Ger. brän′-dən-   brahn′-duhn-burk(h)
                         bōŏrk(h)
Brandis (Ger.)   brän′-dĭs   brahn′-dis
Brandscheid (Ger.)   bränt′-shīt   brahnt′-shait
Braničevo (Yugosl.)   brä′-nē′-chĕ-vô   brah′-nee′-cheh-vo
Branjin Vrh (Yugosl.)   brä′-nyĭn vərk(h)′   brah′-nyin vuhrk(h)′
Braque, Georges   bräk′, zhôrzh′   brahk′, zhorzh′
    (Fr. painter)
Bras (NEI)   bräs′   brahs′
Braslav (Pol. >Rus.)   brä′-släf   brah′-slahf
    Polish spelling *Brasław.*
Braşov (Rum.)   brä-shôv′   brah-shov′
    Hungarian *Brassó,* brŏsh′-shô [brosh′-sho].
Brătianu, Ion   brə-tĭ-ä′-nŏŏ,   bruh-ti-ah′-nu,
    (Rum. polit.)   yôn′   yon′
Brătianu, Vintilă   brə-tĭ-ä′-nŏŏ,   bruh-ti-ah′-nu, ,
    (Rum. polit.)   vēn-tē′-lə   veen-tee′-luh
Bratislava (Cz.)   brä′-tĭ-slä-vä   brah′-ti-slah-vah
    German *Pressburg,* prĕs′-bōŏrk(h) [pres′-burk(h)]. Hungarian *Pozsony,* pô′-zhôn(y) [po′-zhon(y)].
Bratland (Nor.)   brät′-län   braht′-lahn
Braun, Eva   broun′, ā′-vä   braun′, ay′-vah
    (Hitler's consort)
Braunsberg (Ger.>Pol.)   brouns′-bĕrk(h)   brauns′-behrk(h)
    Polish *Brunsberga,* q.v.
Braunschweig (Ger.)   broun′-shvīk(h)   braun′-shvaik(h)
    English *Brunswick,* q.v.
Bray (Fr.)   brĕ′   breh′
Brazil (S.A.)   *Eng.* brə-zĭl′   bruh-zil′
               Port. brä-zēl′   brah-zeel′
Brazos (Tex.)   brăz′-əs   braz′-uhs
Brazza (Yugosl., isl.)   *It.* brät′-sä   braht′-sah
    Serb-Croat *Brač,* q.v.
Brazzaville (Afr.)   brä-zä-vēl′   brah-zah-veel′
Brčko (Yugosl.)   bərch′-kô   buhrch′-ko

Brda (Pol., riv.)	bər-dä'	buhr-dah'
German *Brada*.		
Brda (Yugosl.)	bər'-dä	buhr'-dah
Brécey (Fr.)	brĕ-sĕ'	breh-seh'
Břeclav (Cz.)	brzhĕts'-läf	brzhets'-lahf
Breda (It.)	brĕ'-dä	breh'-dah
Breda (Neth.)	brā-dä'	bray-dah'
Brega (Libya)	brā'-gä	bray'-gah
Also called *Mers el Brega*, mĕrs [mehrs].		
Bregalnica (Yugosl., riv.)	brĕ'-gäl'-nĭ-tsä	breh'-gahl'-ni-tsah
Bregenz (Austria)	brā'-gĕnts	bray'-gents
Bréhal (Fr.)	brĕ-äl'	breh-ahl'
Bréhat (Fr.)	brĕ-ä'	breh-ah'
Brehm, Walter E.	brĕm'	breem'
(U.S. representative)		
Breifonn (Nor.)	brā'-fôn	bray'-fon
Breitbach (Ger.)	brīt'-bäk(h)	brait'-bahk(h)
Breitenstein (Ger. > Rus.)	brī'-tən-shtīn'	brai'-tuhn-shtain'
Russian spelling *Braitenstain*.		
Bremen (Ger.)	*Eng.* brĕm'-ən	brem'-uhn
	Ger. brā'-mən	bray'-muhn
Bremerhaven (Ger.)	*Eng.* brĕm'-ər-hä'-vən	brem'-uhr-hay'-vuhn
	Ger. brā'-mər-hä'-fən	bray'-muhr-hah'-fuhn
Bremerton (Wash.)	brĕm'-ər-tən	brem'-uhr-tuhn
Brenner Pass	brĕn'-ər	bren'-uhr
The pronunciation brā'-nər (bray'-nuhr) is hyper-correct.		
Brento (It.)	brĕn'-tô	bren'-to
Brescia (It.)	brĕ'-shä	breh'-shah
Breskens (Neth.)	brĕs'-kəns	bres'-kuhns
Breslau (Ger. > Pol.)	*Eng.* brĕz'-lou	brez'-lau
	Ger. brĕs'-lou	bres'-lau
Polish *Wrocław*, vrôts'-läf [vrots'-lahf].		
Breslavl (Rus.)	brĕ-släv'l	breh-slahv'l
Bresle (Fr., riv.)	brĕl'	brel'
Bresles (Fr.)	brĕl'	brel'
Bressanone (It.)	brĕs-sä-nô'-nĕ	bres-sah-no'-neh
Bresse (Fr.)	brĕs'	bres'
Bressuire (Fr.)	brĕ-swĕr'	breh-sweer'
Brest (Pol.) See *Brześć Kujawski*.		
Brest Litovsk (Pol. > Rus.)	*Rus.* brĕst' lĭ-tôfsk'	brest' li-tofsk'
Polish *Brześć nad Bugiem*, q.v.		
Brestovac (Yugosl.)	brĕ'-stô-väts	breh'-sto-vahts

Bretagne (Fr.)	brə-tän′(y)	bruh-tahn′(y)
English *Brittany*, q.v.		
Breteuil (Fr.)	brə-tû′(y)	bruh-tœ′(y)
Bretteville (Fr.)	brĕt-vēl′	bret-veel′
Bretton Woods (N.H.)	brĕt′n	bret′n
Breughel (Du. name)	*Eng.* brōō′-gəl *or* brû′-	broo′-guhl *or* brœ′-
	Du. brû′-k(h)əl	brœ′-k(h)uhl
Breukelen Nijenrode (Neth.)	brû′-kə-lən nī′-ən-rō′-də	brœ′-kuh-luhn nai′-uhn-roh′-duh
brevet	brĕv′-ĭt *or* brə-vĕt′	brev′-it bruh-vet′

The first is military usage for noun and verb.

Brevik (Nor.)	brā′-vēk	bray′-veek
Bréville (Fr.)	brĕ-vēl′	breh-veel′
Brežice (Yugosl.)	brĕ′-zhĭ-tsĕ	breh′-zhi-tseh
German *Rann*.		
Brezolles (Fr.)	brə-zôl′	bruh-zol′
Briand, Aristide (Fr. polit.)	brē-äN′, ä-rēs-tēd′	bree-ahN′, ah-rees-teed′
Briatico (It.)	bryä′-tē-kô	bryah′-tee-ko
Bricquebec (Fr.)	brĕk-bĕk′	brœk-bek′
Bricy (Fr.)	brē-sē′	bree-see′
Brie (Fr.)	brē′	bree′
Brieg (Ger. > ? Pol.)	brĕk(h)′	breek(h)′
Polish *Brzeg*, q.v.		
Briel, den (Neth.)	brēl′, dən	breel′, duhn
Also called *Brielle*, q.v.		
Brielle (Neth.)	*Du.* brē′-lə *Eng.* brē-ĕl′	bree′-luh bree-el′

Also called *Den Briel*, dən brēl′ [duhn breel′]. English *The Bril*, brĭl [bril].

Brielle (N.J.)	brĭ-ĕl′	bri-el′
Briesen (Ger.)	brē′-zən	bree′-zuhn
Brieskow (Ger.)	brēs′-kō	brees′-koh
Briey (Fr.)	brē-ĕ′	bree-eh′
Brig (Switz.)	*Ger.* brĕk(h)′	breek(h)′
French *Brigue*, brēg′ [breeg′].		
Brignoles (Fr.)	brē-nyôl′	bree-nyol′
Brigue (Switz.) See *Brig*.		
Brilon (Ger.)	brē′-lôn	bree′-lon
Brindisi (It.)	brēn′-dē-zē	breen′-dee-zee
English brĭn′-dĭ-zĭ [brin′-di-zi] or brĭn-dē′-zĭ [brin-dee′-zi].		
Brinje (Yugosl.)	brē′-nyĕ	bree′-nyeh

Brinon, Fernand de	brē-nôN',	bree-noN',
(Fr. polit.)	fĕr-näN' də	fehr-nahN' duh
Briollay (Fr.)	brē-ô-lĕ'	bree-o-leh'
Brion (Fr.)	brē-ôN'	bree-oN'
Brionne (Fr.)	brē-ôn'	bree-on'
Briouze (Fr.)	brē-ōōz'	bree-ooz'
Brisbane (Austral.)	brĭz'-bən	briz'-buhn

As a family name in the U.S., pronounced brĭz'-bān [briz'-bayn].

Brise Norton (Eng.)	brīz' nôrt'n	braiz' nort'n
Brisighella (It.)	brē-sē-gĕl'-lä	bree-see-gel'-lah
British Guiana (S.A.)	gē-ä'-nə	gee-ah'-nuh
Brittany (Fr.)	brĭt'-ə-nĭ	brit'-uh-ni
French *Bretagne*, q.v.		
Brix (Fr.)	brē'	bree'
Brixham (Eng.)	brĭk'-səm	brik'-suhm
Brno (Cz.)	bər'-nô	buhr'-no
German *Brünn*, brün' [brün'].		
brochure	*Eng.* brō-shōōr'	broh-shur'
	Fr. brô-shür'	broh-shür'
Brod (Yugosl.)	brôd'	brawd'
Brodarevo (Yugosl.)	brô'-dä'-rĕ-vô	bro'-dah'-reh-vo
Brodnica (Pol.)	brôd-nē'-tsä	brod-nee'-tsah
Brody (Pol. > Rus.)	brô'-dĭ	bro'-di
Broek op Langendijk	brōōk' ôp läng'-ən-	brook' op lahng'-
(Neth.)	dīk	uhn-daik
Broennoeysund (Nor.)	brün'-nûĭ-sōŏn	brœn'-nœi-sun
Broglie (Fr.)	brô-lyē'	bro-lyee'
Brohl (Ger.)	brōl'	brohl'
Broich (Ger.)	broik(h)'	broik(h)'
Bromberg (Pol.)	*Eng.* brŏm'-bûrg	brom'-buhrg
	Ger. brôm'-bĕrk(h)	brom'-behrk(h)
Polish *Bydgoszcz*, q.v.		
Bromma (Sw., Stockholm,	brôm'-mä	brom'-mah
airport)		
Bronnitsi (Rus.)	brŏn'-nĭ-tsĭ	bron'-ni-tsi
Brönnöysund (Nor.)	brün'-nûĭ-sōŏn	brœn'-nœi-sun
Bronte (Sicily)	brŏn'-tĕ	bron'-teh
Brontë, Charlotte	brŏn'-tĭ	bron'-ti
(Eng. author)		
Brooks, Van Wyck	brōōks, văn wīk'	bruks, van waik'
(Am. author)		
Broome (Austral.)	brōōm'	broom'
Broons (Fr.)	brôN'	broN'
Broquière, la (Fr.)	brô-kyĕr', lä	bro-kyehr', lah

Brouwershaven (Neth.)   brou-wərs-hä′-vən   brau-wuhrs-hah′-vuhn

Brown, Horace Seely (U.S. representative) See *Seely Brown*.

Broz, Josip (Yugosl.   brôz′, yô′-sĭp   broz′, yo′-sip
polit.)
    Nicknamed *Marshall Tito*.

Bruay (Fr.)   brü-ĕ′   brü-eh′

Bruche (Fr., riv.)   brüsh′   brüsh′

Bruchhausen (Ger.)   bro͞ok(h)-hou′-zən   bruk(h)-hau′-zuhn

Bruchsal (Ger.)   bro͞ok(h)′-zäl   bruk(h)′-zahl

Brueghel (Du. name) See *Breughel*.

Bruehl (Ger.)   brül′   brül′

Bruenn (Cz.)   See *Brno*.

Bruex *or* Brüx (Cz.) See *Most*.

Bruges (Belg.)   *Eng.* bro͞ozh′   broozh′
    Flemish *Brugge*, q.v.

brugge   brûk(h)′-ə   brœk(h)′-uh
    A common element, meaning *bridge*, in Dutch place names.

Brugge (Belg.)   brûk(h)′-ə   brœk(h)′-uh
    English *Bruges*, q.v. French *Bruges*, brüzh′.

Brühl (Ger.)   brül′   brül′

Bruin, Albert (Fr. polit.)   brwăN′, äl-bĕr′   brwaN′, ahl-behr′

Bruinisse (Neth.)   brûĭ-nĭs′-ə   brœi-nis′-uh

Brumbaugh, D. Emmert   bro͞om′-bô   broom′-baw
    (U.S. representative)

Brummen (Neth.)   brûm′-ən   brœm′-uhn

Brunei (Br. Borneo)   *Eng.* bro͞o-nī′   bru-nai′
        Du. bro͞o′-nä′   broo′-nay′

Brünn (Cz.)   See *Brno*.

Brunsberga (Ger. >Pol.)   bro͞ons-bĕr′-gä   bruns-behr′-gah
    German *Braunsberg*, q.v.

Brunsbuettel *or*   bro͞ons′-büt-əl   bruns′-büt-uhl
    Brunsbüttel (Ger.)

Brunsum (Neth.)   brûn′-səm   brœn′-suhm

Brunswick (Ger.)   *Eng.* brŭnz′-wĭk   bruhnz′-wik
    German *Braunschweig*, q.v.

Brus (Yugosl.)   bro͞os′   broos′

Brusnik (Yugosl.)   bro͞o′-snĭk   broo′-snik

Brussels (Belg.)   *Eng.* brŭs′-əlz   bruhs′-uhlz
    Flemish *Brussel*, brûs′-əl [brœs′-uhl]. French *Bruxelles*, brük-sĕl′
    [brük-sel′] *and* brü-sĕl′ [brü-sel′].

Brüster Ort (Ger. >Rus.,   brüs′-tər ôrt′   brüs′-tuhr ort′
    point)

Brüx (Cz.)   See *Most*.

Bruyères (Fr.)	brü-yĕr′	brü-yehr′
Bruylants, Jan (Du. author)	brûĭ′-länts, yän	brœi′-lahnts, yahn
Bruz (Fr.)	brü′	brü′
Bryansk (Rus.)	*Eng.* brĭ-änsk′	bri-ahnsk′
	Rus. bryänsk′	bryahnsk′
Brynkovsk (Rus.)	brĭn′-kŏfsk	brin′-kofsk
Bryn Mawr (Pa.)	brĭn′ mär′	brin′ mahr′
	or brĭn′ môr′	brin′ mor′
Brynmawr (Wales)	brĭn-mour′	brin-maur′
Brzan (Yugosl.)	bər′-zän	buhr′-zahn
Brza Palanka (Yugosl.)	bər′-zä pä′-län-kä	buhr′-zah pah′-lahn-kah
Brzeg (Ger. >? Pol.) German *Brieg*, q.v.	brzhĕk′	brzhek′
Brześć Kujawski (Pol.> Rus.) Russian *Brest*, brĕst′ [brest′].	bzhĕshch′ kŏŏ-yäf′-skĭ	bzheshch′ ku-yahf′-ski
Brześć nad Bugiem (Pol.) Russian *Brest Litovsk*, q.v.	bzhĕshch′ näd bŏŏ′-gyĕm	bzheshch′ nahd bu′-gyem
Brzeżany (Pol.)	bzhĕ-zhä′-nĭ	bzheh-zhah′-ni
Brzezini (Pol.)	bzhĕ-zē′-nĭ	bzheh-zee′-ni
Bua (Yugosl., isl.) Serb-Croat *Čiovo*, q.v.	*It.* bŏŏ′-ä	boo′-ah
Buan (P.I.)	bwän′	bwahn′
Buayan (P.I.)	bwä′-yän	bwah′-yahn
Bübingen (Ger.)	bü′-bĭng-ən	bü′-bing-uhn
Bubuán (P.I.)	bŏŏ-bwän′	boo-bwahn′
Buccari (Yugosl.) Serb-Croat *Bakar*, q.v.	*It.* bŏŏk′-kä-rē	book′-kah-ree
Buccarizza (Yugosl.) Serb-Croat *Bakarač*, q.v.	*It.* bŏŏk-kä-rēt′-sä	book-kah-reet′-sah
Buchach (Pol. >Rus.) Polish spelling *Buczacz*.	bŏŏ′-chäch	boo′-chahch
Bucharest (Rum.) Rumanian *Bucureşti*, bŏŏ-kŏŏ-rĕsht′ [bu-ku-resht′].	*Eng.* bŏŏ′-kə-rĕst′ *or* byŏŏ′-kə-rĕst′	boo′-kuh-rest′ byoo′-kuh-rest′
Buchen (Ger., Baden)	bŏŏ′-k(h)ən	boo′-k(h)uhn
Büchen (Ger., Lauenburg)	bü′-k(h)ən	bü′-k(h)uhn
Buchenwald (Ger.)	bŏŏ′-k(h)ən-vält	boo′-k(h)uhn-vahlt
Buchholz (Ger.)	bŏŏk(h)′-hôlts	buk(h)′-holts
Buchsweiler (Fr.) See *Bouxwiller*.		
Buchy (Fr.)	bü-shē′	bü-shee′

Bückeberg (Ger.)	bük'-ə-bĕrk(h)	bük'-uh-behrk(h)
Buckow (Ger.)	bŏŏk(h)'-ō	buk(h)'-oh
Bucovina (Rum.)	bŏŏ-kô-vĕ'-nä	bu-ko-vee'-nah
Bucquoy (Fr.)	bü-kwä'	bü-kwah'
Bucureşti (Rum.) See *Bucharest*.		
Buczacz (Pol. > Rus.) See *Buchach*.		
Bud (Nor.)	bŏŏd'	bood'
Budafapuszto (Hung.)	bŏŏ'-dŏ-fŏ-pŏŏs'-tô	bu'-do-fo-pus'-to
Budaörz (Hung.)	bŏŏ'-dŏ-ûrsh'	bu'-do-uhrsh'
Budapest (Hung.)	*Eng.* bōō'-də-pĕst'	boo'-duh-pest'
	Hung. bŏŏ'-dŏ-pĕsht'	bu'-do-pesht'
Budĕjovice (Cz.)	bŏŏ'-dyĕ-yô-vĭ-tsĕ	boo'-dyeh-yo-vi-tseh
German *Budweis*, bŏŏt'-vĭs [but'-vais].		
Budel (Neth.)	bü'-dəl	bü'-duhl
Budënnovsk (Rus.)	bŏŏ-dyô'-nôfsk	boo-dyo'-nofsk
Budënny, Semyon	bŏŏ-dyô'-nĭ,	bu-dyo'-ni,
(Rus. marshal)	sĕm-yôn'	sem-yon'
There is also an English pronunciation, bōō-dĕn'-ĭ [boo-den'-i].		
Budhlada (India)	bŏŏd-lä'-də	bud-lah'-duh
Budrio (It., riv.)	bŏŏ'-dryô	boo'-dryo
Budrum (Turk.)	bŏŏd'-rŏŏm'	bud'-rum'
Budua (Yugosl.)	*It.* bōō'-dwä	boo'-dwah
Serb-Croat *Budva*, q.v.		
Budva (Yugosl.)	bŏŏd'-vä	bood'-vah
Budweis (Cz.)	*Ger.* bŏŏt'-vĭs	but'-vais
Czech *Budĕjovice*, q.v.		
Buebingen (Ger.)	bü'-bĭng-ən	bü'-bing-uhn
Buechen (Ger.)	bü'-k(h)ən	bü'-k(h)uhn
Bueckeberg (Ger.)	bük'-ə-bĕrk(h)	bük'-uh-behrk(h)
Bued (P.I., riv.)	bwĕd'	bwed'
Buehl (Ger.)	bül'	bül'
Bueil (Fr.)	bwĕ'(y)	bweh'(y)
Buelow (Ger.)	bü'-lō	bü'-loh
Bue Marino	bwĕ' mä-rē'-nô	bweh' mah-ree'-no
(Pantelleria, point)		
Buenos Aires (Arg.)	bwĕ'-nôs ĭ'-rĕs	bweh'-nos ai'-res
English bwā'-nəs ĕr'-ĭz [bway'-nuhs ehr'-iz] or the old-fashioned bō'-nəs ärz' [boh'-nuhs ehrz'].		
Buerat el Hsun (Libya)	bŏŏ-ĕ-rắt' ĕl hə-sōōn'	boo-eh-rat' el huh-soon'
Bueschdorf (Ger.)	büsh'-dôrf	büsh'-dorf
Buetelborn (Ger.)	bü'-təl-bôrn	bü'-tuhl-born
Buetow (Ger. > Pol.)	bü'-tō	bü'-toh
Polish *Bytów*, q.v.		

Bug (Pol., Rus., rivs.)	bŏŏg′ or bōōg′	bug′ or boog′
Bugaz (Rum. > Rus.)	bŏŏ-gäz′	bu-gahz′
Bugnara (It.)	bŏŏ-nyä′-rä	boo-nyah′-rah
Bugojno (Yugosl.)	bōō′-goi′-nô	boo′-goi′-no
Bugotu (Oc., Solomons)	bōō-gô′-tōō	boo-go′-too
Also spelled *Bogotu*.		
Bugsangá (P.I.)	bŏŏg-säng-ä′	boog-sahng-ah′
Bugut, Port (P.I.)	bōō-gōōt′	boo-goot′
Port Bugut is also called *Carmen*, kär′-mĕn [kahr′-men].		
Bühl (Ger.)	bül′	bül′
Buhl (Idaho)	byōōl′	byool′
Bui (Rus.)	bōō′(y) or bōō′ĭ	boo′(y) or boo′i
Buin (Oc., Solomons)	bōō′-ēn	boo′-een
Buir (Ger.)	bōō′-ĭr	boo′-ihr
Buitenpost (Neth.)	bûĭ′-tən-pôst	bœi′-tuhn-post
Buitenzorg (NEI, Java)	bûĭ′-tən-zôrk(h)	bœi′-tuhn-zork(h)
Bujanovce (Yugosl.)	bōō′-yä′-nôv-tsĕ	boo′-yah′-nov-tseh
Bujnurd (Iran)	bŏŏj-nōōrd′	buj-noord′
Bük (Hung.)	bük′	bük′
Buka (Oc., Bougainville)	bŏŏ′-kä	boo′-kah
Bukan (Iran)	bŏŏ-kän′	bu-kahn′
Bukhara (Rus.) See *Bokhara*.		
Bukorovce (Yugosl.)	bōō′-kô′-rôv-tsĕ	boo′-ko′-rov-tseh
Bukovče (Yugosl.)	bōō′-kôv-chĕ	boo′-kov-cheh
Bukovik (Yugosl., mts.)	bōō′-kô-vĭk	boo′-ko-vik
Bukovina See *Bucovina*.		
Bukulja (Yugosl., mt.)	bōō′-kōō-lyä	boo′-koo-lyah
Bulacán (P.I.)	bōō-lä-kän′	boo-lah-kahn′
Bulačane (Yugosl.)	bōō′-lä′-chä-nĕ	boo′-lah′-chah-neh
Bulalácao (P.I.)	bōō-lä-lä′-kou	boo-lah-lah′-kau
Bulganin, Nikolai A.	bŏŏl-gä′-nĭn,	bul-gah′-nin,
(Rus. general)	nĭ-kô-lī′	nih-ko-lai′
Bulgaria	bəl-gĕr′-ĭ-ə	buhl-gehr′-i-uh
The first syllable may also be pronounced bŭl′- or bŏŏl′. Bulgar *Blgariya*, bəl-gä′-rĭ-yä [buhl-gah′-ri-yah].		
Bulken (Nor.)	bŏŏl′-kən	bul′-kuhn
Bülow (Ger.)	bü′-lō	bü′-loh
Bulwinkle, Alfred L.	bŏŏl′-wĭng-kəl	bul′-wing-kuhl
(U.S. representative)		
buna (synthetic rubber)	*Eng.* byōō′-nə	byoo′-nuh
	Ger. bōō′-nä	boo′-nah
Probably in American usage the English will supplant the German pronunciation.		
Buna (Balkan riv.) See *Bunē*.		

Buna (New Guinea, Papua)	bŏō'-nä	boo'-nah
Bund	*Eng.* bŏŏnd' *or*	bund' *or* buhnd'
(Ger., "league")	bŭnd'	
	Ger. bŏŏnt'	bunt'
Bunē (Balkan riv.)	*Alb.* bŏō'-nə	boo'-nuh
Serb-Croat *Bojana*, q.v.		
Bungana (Oc., Solomons)	bŏōng'-ä-nä	boong'-ah-nah
Buninga (Oc., New Heb-	bŏō-nĭng'-ä	boo-ning'-ah
rides)		
Bunschoten (Neth.)	bŭn'-sk(h)ō-tən	bœn'-sk(h)oh-tuhn
Bunzlau (Ger. >? Pol.)	bŏŏnts'-lou	bunts'-lau
Polish *Bolesławiec*, q.v.		
Buqbuq (Egypt)	bŏŏk'-bŏŏk'	buk'-buk'
Buraku (Oc., Solomons)	bŏō-rä'-kŏō	boo-rah'-koo
Burauen (P.I.)	bŏō-rä'-wĕn	boo-rah'-wen
Burbach (Ger.)	bŏŏr'-bäk(h)	bur'-bahk(h)
Burdwan (India)	*Eng.* bûrd'-wän'	burd'-wahn'
	native bər-də-wän'	buhr-duh-wahn'
Burenj (Yugosl., mts.)	bŏō'-rĕn(y)	boo'-ren(y)
-burg(h)	*Eng.* bûrg'	buhrg'
	Scot. bŭr'-ə	buhr'-uh
	Du. bûrk(h)'	bœrk(h)'
	Ger. bŏŏrk(h)'	burk(h)'

An element, meaning *fortified house* or *town*, in Germanic place names.
See *-berg*.

Burg, den (Neth.)	bûrk(h)', dən	bœrk(h)', duhn
Burg el Arab (Egypt)	bŏŏrg ĕl är'-əb	burg el ehr'-uhb
Burgajet (Alb.)	bŏŏr-gä'-yĕt	boor-gah'-yet
Burgajeti (Alb.) See *Burgajet*.		
Burgas (Bulg.)	bŏŏr'-gäs'	bur'-gahs'
Burgin, W. O.	bûr'-gĭn	buhr'-gin
(U.S. representative)		
Burgos (Sp.)	bŏōr'-gôs	boor'-gos
Burias (P.I.)	bŏō'-ryäs	boo'-ryahs
Burji (Ethiopia)	bŏŏr'-jē	bur'-jee
Burleson, Omar	bûr'-lə-sən, ō'-mär	buhr'-luh-suhn,
(U.S. representative)		oh'-mahr
Burnie (Austral.)	bûr'-nĭ	buhr'-ni
Burrel (Alb.)	bŏōr'-rĕl	boor'-rel
Burreli (Alb.) See *Burrel*.		
Burrinjuck (Austral.)	bûr'-ĭn-jŭk	buhr'-in-juhk
Buru (NEI) See *Boeroe*.		
Burujird (Iran)	bŏō-rŏō-jērd'	bu-roo-jeerd'
Buruncan (P.I.)	bŏō-rŏōn'-kän	boo-roon'-kahn

Bury (Eng.)   bĕr'-ĭ   behr'-i

As a place name and as a personal name in England usually so pronounced. As a personal name in America, usually byŏŏr'-ĭ [byur'-i].

Büschdorf (Ger.)   büsh'-dôrf   büsh'-dorf

Bush, Vannevar   bŏŏsh', və-nē'-vər   bush', vuh-nee'-vuhr
(Am. scientist)

This pronunciation of *Vannevar* is preferable, although văn'-ə-vär' [van'-uh-vahr'] is also heard.

Bushire (Iran)   *Eng.* bŏŏ-shēr'   boo-sheer'
                 Per. bŏŏ'-shăr'   boo'-shehr'

Busi (Yugosl.)   *It.* bŏŏ'-sē   boo'-see
Serb-Croat *Biševo*, q.v.

Busko (Pol.)   bŏŏ'-skô   bu'-sko
Russian *Busk*, bŏŏsk' [boosk'].

Bussang (Fr., pass)   bü-säN'   bü-sahN'

Busse (Rus.)   bŏŏs'-sĕ   bus'-seh

Bussum (Neth.)   bûs'-əm   bœs'-uhm

Busto Arsizio (It.)   bŏŏ'-stô är-sē'-tsyô   boo'-sto ahr-see'-tsyo

Bustos (P.I.)   bŏŏs'-tôs   boos'-tos

Buštranje (Yugosl.)   bŏŏ'-shträ-nyĕ   boo'-shtrah-nyeh

Busuanga (P.I.)   bŏŏ-swäng'-ä   boo-swahng'-ah

butadiene   byŏŏ-tə-dī'-ēn   byoo'-tuh-dai'-een

Butaritari (Oc., Makin)   bŏŏ-tä-rē-tä'-rē   boo-tah-ree-tah'-ree
Properly the name of an island and its village but often applied to the whole of Makin atoll, Gilbert Islands. See *Makin*.

Bütelborn (Ger.)   bü'-təl-bôrn   bü'-tuhl-born

Butenbach (Belg.)   bü'-tən-bäk(h)   bü'-tuhn-bahk(h)

Buthidaung (Burma)   bŏŏ'-*th*ē-doung'   boo'-*thee*-daung'

Butong (NEI)   See *Boetong*.

Bütow (Ger. > Pol.) See *Buetow*.

Butrint (Alb., town, lake)   bŏŏ'-trĭnt   boo'-trint
Italian *Butrinto*, bŏŏ-trēn'-tô [boo-treen'-to].

Butrinti (Alb., town, lake)   See *Butrint*.

Butte (Mont.)   byŏŏt'   byoot'

Butte Montmartre   büt môN-mär'tr   büt moN-mahr'tr
(Fr., Paris)

Butúan (P.I.)   bŏŏ-tŏŏ'-än   boo-too'-ahn

Butung (NEI) See *Boetoeng*.

butyl   byŏŏ'-tĭl   byoo'-til

butylene   byŏŏ'-tĭ-lēn'   byoo'-ti-leen'

Butzdorf (Ger.)   bŏŏts'-dôrf   buts'-dorf

Butzweiler (Ger.)   bŏŏts'-vĭ-lər   buts'-vai-luhr

Buxar (India)   bŭk'-sər   buk'-suhr

Buxtehude (Ger.)   bŏŏks'-tə-hŏŏ'-də   buks'-tuh-hoo'-duh

Buzançais (Fr.)   bü-zäN-sĕ'   bü-zahN-seh'
Buzău (Rum.)   bŏŏ-zú'-ŏŏ   bu-zuh'-u
Buzuluk (Rus.)   bōō-zōō-lōōk'   boo-zoo-look'
Byántig (P.I., riv.) byän'-tĭg   byahn'-tig
Bydgoszcz (Pol.)   bĭd'-gôshch   bid'-goshch
  German *Bromberg*, q.v.
Byela (Pol.) See *Biała Podlaska*.
Byelgorai (Pol.) See *Biłgoraj*.
Byeloglina (Rus.)   bĕ-lŏ-glē'-nä   beh-lo-glee'-nah
  Also called *Belaya Glina*, q.v.
Byelorussia (Rus., repub.) See *Belorussia*.
Byelostok (Pol.) See *Białystok*.
Byelovyezh (Pol.) See *Białowieża*.
Byeltsi (Rum.) See *Bălţi*.
Bygdin (Nor.)   büg'-dĭn   büg'-din
Byglandsfjord (Nor.) büg'-läns-fyŏr   büg'-lahns-fyohr
Bykhov (Rus.)   bwē'-hŏf   bwee'-hof
Bystrica (Cz., riv.) bĭ'-strĭ-tsä   bi'-stri-tsah
Bytom (Ger., Silesia > Pol.) bĭ'-tôm   bi'-tom
  German *Beuthen*, q.v.,
Bytów (Ger. > Pol.) bĭ'-tŏŏf   bi'-tuf
  German *Buetow*, q.v.
Bzura (Pol., riv.)   bzŏŏ'-rä   bzu'-rah

c and *k* are interchangeable in Greek and other languages. It may be
 necessary to look up both spellings. In Greek *k* is officially preferred.
Cabalían (P.I.)   kä-bä-lē'-än   kah-bah-lee'-ahn
Caballo Isl. (P.I.)   kä-bä'-yô   kah-bah'-yo
  Also called *Puló Caballo*, pōō-lô' . . . . [poo-lo'].
Cabán (P.I., isl.)   kä-bän'   kah-bahn'
Cabañas, Gustavo Martínez (Mex. diplomat) See *Martínez Cabañas*.
Cabanatuán (P.I.)   kä-bä-nä-twän'   kah-bah-nah-twahn'
Čabar (Yugosl.)   chä'-bär   chah'-bahr
Cabarruyan (P.I.)   kä-bär-rōō'-yän   kah-bahr-roo'-yahn
Cabell, James Branch kăb'-əl   kab'-uhl
  (Am. author)
Cabiao (P.I.)   kä-byou'   kah-byau'
cabo   kä'-bô   kah'-bo
  An element, meaning *cape*, in Spanish place names. Look up the other
  part of the name.
Cabo (P.I.)   kä'-bô   kah'-bo
Cabourg (Fr.)   kä-bōōr'   kah-boor'
Cabras (Oc., Guam) kä'-bräs   kah'-brahs
Cabu (P.I.)   kä'-bōō   kah'-boo

Cabucan (P.I.)	kä-bōo′-kän	kah-boo′-kahn
Cabunganan (P.I.)	kä-bōong-ä′-nän	kah-boong-ah′-nahn
Cabungbungan (P.I., mt.)	kä-bōong-bōong′-än	kah-boong-boong′-ahn
Cabusilan (P.I., mts.)	kä-bōo-sē′-län	kah-boo-see′-lahn
Čačak (Yugosl.)	chä′-chäk	chah′-chahk
Caccia (Sard., cape)	kät′-chä	kaht′-chah
Cacciarella (It.)	kät-chä-rĕl′-lä	kaht-chah-rel′-lah
Cáceres (Sp.)	kä′-thĕ-rĕs or -sĕ-	kah′-theh-res or -seh-
Cáceres, Julián (Hond. polit.)	kä′-sĕ-rĕs, hōo-lyän′	kah′-seh-rehs, hoo-lyahn′
Cachin, Marcel (Fr. polit.)	kä-shäN′, mär-sĕl′	kah-shaN′, mahr-sel′
Cádiz (Sp.)	Eng. kā′-dĭz or kə-dĭz′	kay′-diz or kuh-diz′
	Sp. kä′-dēth or dēs	kah′-deeth or dees
Cadogan, Sir Alexander (Br. diplomat)	kə-dŭg′-ən	kuh-duhg′-uhn
Cadwgan (Welsh name)	kə-dōog′-ən	kuh-dug′-uhn
cadre	Eng. kăd′-rĭ	kad′-ri
	Fr. kä′dr	kah′dr
Cadzand (Neth.)	kät-sänt′	kaht-sahnt′
Caelian (It., Rome)	Eng. sē′-lĭ-ən	see′-lih-uhn
Italian Celio, chĕ′-lyô [cheh′-lyo].		
Caen (Fr.)	käN′	kahN′
Caernarvon (Wales)	kär-när′-vŏn	kahr-nahr′-von
Caesarea (Pal.)	sĕz′-ə-rē′-ə	sehz′-uh-ree′-uh
	or sĕs′-	sehs′-
Modern Qisarya, kĭ-sär′-yə [kih-sahr′-yuh].		
Caffery, Jefferson (Am. diplomat)	kăf′-ə-rĭ	kaf′-uh-ri
Cagayán (P.I.)	kä-gä-yän′	kah-gah-yahn′
Often Anglicized to kä-gä′-yən [kah-gah′-yuhn].		
Cagli (It.)	kä′-lyē	kah′-lyee
Cagliari (Sard.)	kä′-lyä-rē	kah′-lyah-ree
Cagul (Rum. > Rus.)	kä-gōol′	kah-gool′
Rumanian Cahul, kä-hōol′ [kah-hul′].		
Cagúrai (P.I.)	kä-gōo′-rī	kah-goo′-rai
Cahors (Fr.)	kä-ôr′	kah-or′
Caiazzo (It.)	kä-yät′-sô	kah-yaht′-so
Caibarién (Cuba)	kī-bär-yĕn′	kai-bahr-yen′
Caibiran (P.I.)	kī-bē′-rän	kai-bee′-rahn
There is also authority for stressing the last syllable.		
Caicos (Bahamas)	kī′-kōs	kai′-kohs
Caievola (It., mt.)	kä-yĕ′-vô-lä	kah-yeh′-vo-lah
Caintá (P.I.)	kä-ēn-tä′	kah-een-tah′

Cairns (Austral.)	kărnz′	kehrnz′
Cairo (Egypt)	kī′-rō	kai′-roh
Cairo (Ill.)	kā′-rō	kay′-roh
Cajagnaán *or*	kä-häg-nä-än′	kah-hahg-nah-ahn′
Cajaguaán (P.I.)	*or* kä-hä-gwä-än′	kah-hah-gwah-ahn′
Čajetina (Yugosl.)	chä′-yĕ′-tĭ-nä	chah′-yeh′-ti-nah
Čajniče (Yugosl.)	chī′-nĭ-chĕ	chai′-ni-cheh
Çakmak, Fevzi (Turk. general)	chäk-mäk′, fĕv-zē′	chahk-mahk′, fev-zee′
Čakovec (Yugosl.)	chä′-kô-vĕts	chah′-ko-vets
Calabanga (P.I.)	kä-lä-bäng′-ä	kah-lah-bahng′-ah
Calabria (It.)	*Eng.* kə-lä′-brĭ-ə	kuh-lay′-bri-uh
	It. kä-lä′-bryä	kah-lah′-bryah

The English pronunciation is preferable for American speakers, especially as the Italian kä-lä′-bryä [kah-lah′-bryah] degenerates with English speakers to kə-lăb′-rĭ-ə [kuh-lab′-ri-uh].

Calacá (P.I.)	kä-lä-kä′	kah-lah-kah′
Calafat (Rum.)	kä-lä-fät′	kah-lah-faht′
Calais	*Eng.* kăl′-ā *or* kăl′-ĭs	kal′-ay *or* kal′-is
	Fr. kä-lĕ′	kah-leh′

For the French town the French pronunciation is probably the most common among American radio speakers. *Calais*, Maine, is pronounced kăl′-ĭs [kal′-is].

Calamcá, Puló (P.I., isl.)	kä-läm-kä′, pōō-lô′	kah-lahm-kah′,poo-lo′

Also called *Dampálit*, däm-pä′-lĭt [dahm-pah′-lit].

Calamián (P.I.)	kä-lä-myän′	kah-lah-myahn′
Calamianes (P.I., isls.)	kä-lä-myä′-nĕs	kah-lah-myah′-nes
Calamotta (Yugosl., isl.)	*It.* kä-lä-môt′-tä	kah-lah-mot′-tah
Serb-Croat *Koločen*, q.v.		
Calapán (P.I.)	kä-lä-pän′	kah-lah-pahn′

Also called *Tibao*, tē-bou′ [tee-bau′].

Călăraşi (Rum.)	kə-lə-räsh′	kuh-luh-rahsh′

The name of towns in Bessarabia, Muntenia, and Transylvania. The Bessarabian town is now Russian *Kalarash*, q.v. The Transylvanian town has a Hungarian variant *Harasztos*, hŏ′-rŏs-tôsh [ho′-ros-tosh].

Calarian (P.I.)	kä-lä′-ryän	kah-lah′-ryahn
Calasiao (P.I.)	kä-lä-sē-ou′	kah-lah-see-au′
Calatagán (P.I.)	kä-lä-tä-gän′	kah-lah-tah-gahn′
Calavà (Sicily, point)	kä-lä-vä′	kah-lah-vah′
Calaveras (Calif.)	kăl′-ə-vĕr′-əs	kal′-uh-vehr′-uhs
Calbayog (P.I.)	käl-bä′-yôg	kahl-bah′-yog
Calcar (Ger.)	käl′-kär	kahl′-kahr
Calchi (Dodec.)	*It.* käl′-kē	kahl′-kee
Greek *Khalke*, q.v.		

Calcutta (India)	kăl-kŭt′-ə	kal-kuht′-uh
Caldera (P.I.)	kăl-dĕ′-rä	kahl-deh′-rah
Calessina (It.)	kä-lĕs-sē′-nä	kah-les-see′-nah
Caleta (Cuba)	kä-lĕ′-tä	kah-leh′-tah
Calgary (Can.)	kăl′-gə-rĭ	kal′-guh-ri
Caliacra (Rum.)	kä-lyä′-krä	kah-lyah′-krah
Calicut (India)	kăl′-ĭ-kŭt	kal′-i-kuht
Calimere (India, cape)	kăl-ĭ-mĭr′	kal-i-mihr′
Calino (Dodec.) See *Kalymnos*.		
Callac (Fr.)	kä-läk′	kah-lahk′
Callantsoog (Neth.)	kä′-länt-sōk(h)′	kah′-lahnt-sohk(h)′
Callao (Peru)	kä-you′	kah-yau′
calle	*Am. Sp.* kä′-yĕ	kah′-yeh
	Sp. kä′-lyĕ	kah′-lyeh
A Spanish word meaning *street*.		
Calle, la (Alg.)	käl′, lä	kahl′, lah
Calmay (P.I., riv.)	käl-mī′	kahl-mai′
Caloocan (P.I.)	kä-lô-ô′-kän	kah-lo-o′-kahn
Calore (It., riv.)	kä-lô′-rĕ	kah-lo′-reh
Caltagirone (Sicily)	käl′-tä-jē-rô′-nĕ	kahl′-tah-jee-ro′-neh
Caltanissetta (Sicily)	käl′-tä-nēs-sĕt′-tä	kahl′-tah-nees-set′-tah
Calúlut (P.I.)	kä-lōō′-lōōt	kah-loo′-loot
Calumpán (P.I.)	kä-lōōm-pän′	kah-loom-pahn′
Calumpit (P.I.)	kä-lōōm-pēt′	kah-loom-peet′
Calvados (Fr.)	käl-vä-dōs′	kahl-vah-dohs′
Calvi (It., Corsica)	käl′-vē	kahl′-vee
Camacho. See *Ávila Camacho*.		
Camagüey (Cuba)	kä-mä-gwĕ′	kah-mah-gweh′
Camajore (It.)	kä-mä-yô′-rĕ	kah-mah-yo′-reh
Camalaniugan (P.I.)	kä-mä-lä-nyōō′-gän	kah-mah-lah-nyoo′-gahn
Camao *or* Camau (Indo-Ch.)	kä-mä′-ô *or* kä-mou′	kah-mah′-o *or* kah-mau′
Camarat (Fr., cape)	kä-mä-rä′	kah-mah-rah′
Camargue (Fr., isl.)	kä-märg′	kah-mahrg′
Camas (Idaho, Wash.)	kăm′-əs	kam′-uhs
Cambay (India)	kăm-bā′	kam-bay′
Cambodia (Indo-Ch.)	*Eng.* kăm-bō′-dĭ-ə	kam-boh′-di-uh
Indonesian *Caomien*, kou′-myĕn [kau′-myen].		
Cambrai (Fr.)	*Eng.* kăm-brā′	kam-bray′
	Fr. käN-brĕ′	kahN-breh′
Cambremer (Fr.)	käN-brə-mĕr′	kahN-bruh-mehr′

Cameroons (Nigeria and   kăm'-ə-rōōnz'   kam'-uh-roonz'
Fr. Eq. Afr.)
Portuguese *Camarões*, kä-mə-roiNsh' [kah-muh-roiNsh'] meaning
prawns. French *Cameroun*, käm-rōōn' [kahm-roon']. German *Kamerun*,
kä-mə-rōōn' [kah-muh-roon'].

Camiguín (P. I.)   kä-mē-gĕn'   kah-mee-geen'
Camiling (P.I.)   kä-mē-lĭng'   kah-mee-ling'
There is also authority for *Camíling.*

Cammarano (It., riv.)   käm-mä-rä'-nô   kahm-mah-rah'-no
Camões, Luis Vaz de   kə-moinsh', lŏō-ēzh' kuh-moinsh', lu-
  (Port. poet)   väzh' dĭ   eezh' vahzh' di
Camooweal (Austral.)   kăm'-ŏŏ-wēl'   kam'-u-weel'
Camorra   kä-môr'-rä   kah-mor'-rah
Illegal Italian secret society.

Camotes (P.I., sea)   kä-mô'-tĕs   kah-mo'-tes
Campagnano (It.)   käm-pä-nyä'-nô   kahm-pah-nyah'-no
Campeche (Mex.)   *Eng.* kăm-pē'-chĭ   kam-pee'-chi
                Sp. käm-pĕ'-chĕ   kahm-peh'-cheh
Campha (Indo-Ch.)   käm-fä'   kahm-fah'
Campilli, Pietro   käm-pēl'-lē,   kahm-peel'-lee,
  (It. polit.)   pyĕ'-trô   pyeh'-tro
Câmpina (Rum.)   kûm'-pē-nä   kuhm'-pee-nah
Campobasso (It.)   käm-pô-bäs'-sô   kahm-po-bahs'-so
Campodigrano (It.)   käm-pô-dē-grä'-nô kahm-po-dee-grah'-
                                 no
Campodimele (It.)   käm-pô-dē-mĕ'-lĕ kahm-po-dee-meh'-
                                 leh
Campofelice (Sicily)   käm'-pô-fĕ-lē'-chĕ kahm'-po-feh-lee'-
                                 cheh
Campoleone (It.)   käm-pô-lĕ-ô'-nĕ   kahm-po-leh-o'-neh
Campoli (It.)   käm'-pô-lē   kahm'-po-lee
Campos, Francisco   käm'-pŏŏs,   kahm'-pus,
  (Braz. polit.)   frän-sēs'-kŏŏ   frahn-sees'-ku
Campo Selva (It.)   käm'-pô sĕl'-vä   kahm'-po sel'-vah
Câmpulung (Rum.)   kûm-pŏŏ-lŏŏng' kuhm-pu-lung'
Also called *Kimpolung*, kĭm-pô-lŏŏng' [kim-po-lung'].
Câmpulung pe Tisa   kûm-pŏŏ-lŏŏng' kuhm-pu-lung'
  (Rum.)   pĕ tē'-sä   peh tee'-sah
Camranh (Indo-Ch.,   käm'-rän'   kahm'-rahn'
  bay)   *or* käm'-răng'   kam'-rang'
Also spelled *Kamrang.* French käm-räN' [kahm-rahN']. Indonesian
käm-rän'(y) [kahm-rahn'(y)].
Cañacao (P.I.)   kä-nyä-kou'   kah-nyah-kau'
Çanakkale Boğazı (Turk., strait) See *Dardanelles.*

Canarén, Laguna de (P.I.)   kä-nä-rĕn',   kah-nah-ren',
                             lä-gōō'-nä dĕ   lah-goo'-nah deh

Canarias, Islas (Sp.) See *Canary Islands.*

Canary Islands (Sp.)   kə-nĕr'-ĭ   kuh-nehr'-i
  Spanish *Islas Canarias,* kä-nä'-ryäs [kah-nah'-ryahs].

Canberra (Austral.)   kăn'-bĕr-ə   kan'-behr-uh
  There is a story that government employees who receive more than
  £500 yearly pronounce the name of the capital kăn'-bə-rə [kan'-buh-
  ruh]; and those who receive less say kăn-bĕr'-ə [kan-behr'-uh].

Cancabató (P.I.)   kän-kä-bä-tô'   kahn-kah-bah-to'
Cancale (Fr.)   käN-käl'   kahN-kahl'
Cancello (It.)   kän-chĕl'-lô   kahn-chel'-lo
Canche (Fr., riv.)   käNsh'   kahNsh'
Candaba (P.I.)   kän-dä'-bä   kahn-dah'-bah
Candaba, Pinac de (P.I., lagoon) See *Pinac de Candaba.*
Candé (Fr.)   käN-dĕ'   kahN-deh'
Candelaria (Mex., P.I.)   kän-dĕ-lä'-ryä   kahn-deh-lah'-ryah
Candia (Crete)   *Eng.* kăn'-dĭ-ə   kan'-di-uh
  Greek *Herakleion,* q.v.

candidate   kăn'-də-dāt *or* -dĭt   kan'-duh-dayt *or* -dit
  The infantilism "canny-date" should be avoided. Cp. "canny" for
  candy.

Canea (Crete)   *Eng.* kä-nē'-ä   kah-nee'-ah
                   Gr. hän-yä'   hahn-yah'
  Also spelled *Khania,* q.v.
Canicatti (Sicily)   kä-nē-kät'-tē   kah-nee-kaht'-tee
Caniff, Milton A.   kă-nĭf' *or* kăn'-ĭf   ka-nif' *or* kan'-if
  (Am. cartoonist)
  "My family pronounces it kă-nĭf', but we used kăn'-ĭf when we came
  East. However, my personal preference is for kă-nĭf'." M. A. C.,
  April 15, 1947.

Canisius College (N.Y.) kə-nē'-shəs   kuh-nee'-shuhs
Canisteo (N.Y.)   kăn'-ə-stē'-ō   kan'-uh-stee'-oh
Canistro (It.)   kä-nē'-strô   kah-nee'-stro
Canisy (Fr.)   kä-nē-zē'   kah-nee-zee'
Cannes (Fr.)   *Eng.* kănz'   kanz'
                   Fr. kän'   kahn'
Cannosa (Yugosl.)   *It.* kän-nô'-sä   kahn-no'-sah
  Serb-Croat *Trsteno,* q.v.
Canobie (Austral.)   kă-nō'-bĭ   ka-noh'-bi
Canol   kăn'-ŏl   kan'-ol
  An abbreviation of *Canadian oil line.*
Cantábrico (Sp.)   kän-tä'-brē-kô   kahn-tah'-bree-ko
Cantal (Fr.)   käN-täl'   kahN-tahl'

Čantavir (Yugosl.) chän′-tä-vēr chahn′-tah-veer
Canterano (It.) kän-tĕ-rä′-nô kahn-teh-rah′-no
Cantiere (It.) kän-tyĕ′-rĕ kahn-tyeh′-reh
Cantigny (Fr.) käN-tē-nyē′ kahN-tee-nyee′
Cantilan (P.I.) kän-tē′-län kahn-tee′-lahn
Canton (Ch., *Eng.* kăn′-tŏn′ kan′-ton′
   Kwangtung)
Chinese *Fan-yü*, fän-yü [fahn-yü].
Canton (N.Y., Ohio, Pa.) kănt′n *or* kăn′-tən kant′n *or* kan′-tuhn
cantonment kăn′-tən-mənt kan′-tuhn-muhnt
   or kăn-tŏn′-mənt kan-ton′-muhnt
The first seems to be more common in military usage. There is also a
British pronunciation kăn-tōōn′-mənt [kan-toon′-muhnt].
Caolanh (Indo-Ch.) kou′-län′ kau′-lahn′
Capanema, Gustavo kä-pə-nĕ′-mə, kah-puh-neh′-muh,
   (Braz. polit.) gōōs-tä′-vŏŏ goos-tah′-vu
Capannacce (It.) kä-pän-nät′-chĕ kah-pahn-naht′-
      cheh
Capari (Yugosl.) tsä′-pä-rĭ tsah′-pah-ri
Capas (P.I.) kä′-päs kah′-pahs
Cap Blanc (Tun.) käp bläN′ kahp blahN′
English *Cape Blanc*, kāp′ blänk′ [kayp′ blahnk′].
Cap Bon (Tun.) käp bôN′ kahp boN′
English *Cape Bon*, kāp′ bŏn′ [kayp′ bon′].
cape kāp′ kayp′
Cape is often ignored in the alphabetical listing. It may be necessary
to look up the other part of the name.
Čapec, Karel chä′-pĕk, kä′-rĕl chah′-pek, kah′-rel
   (Cz. dramatist)
Cape Gloucester glŏs′-tər *or* glôs′- glos′-tuhr *or* glaws′-
Capehart, Homer E. kāp′-härt kayp′-hahrt
   (U.S. senator)
Capelle (Neth.) kä-pĕl′-ə kah-pel′-uh
Also spelled *Kapelle*, q.v.
Capello (It.) kä-pĕl′-lô kah-pel′-lo
Capena (It.) kä-pĕ′-nä kah-peh′-nah
Cape Verde (Port., isls.) *Eng.* vûrd′ vuhrd′
Portuguese *Cabo Verde*, kä′-bŏŏ vĕr′-dĭ [kah′-bu vehr′-di]. French
Cap Vert, käp vĕr′ [kahp vehr′].
Cape Zebib (Tun.) zə-bēb′ zuh-beeb′
Cap Gris Nez (Fr.) käp grē nĕ′ kahp gree neh′
Cap Haitien (Haiti) *Fr.* käp ä-ē-syăN′ kahp ah-ee-syaN′
English *Cape Haitian*, hā′-tĭ-ən [hay′-ti-uhn].
Capiccio (It., mt.) kä-pēt′-chô kah-peet′-cho

Capistrello (It.)   kä-pē-strĕl'-lô   kah-pee-strel'-lo
Capitoline (It., Rome)   *Eng.* kăp'-ĭ-tə-lĭn   kap'-ih-tuh-lain
   Italian *Capitolino*, kä-pē-tô-lē'-nô [kah-pee-to-lee'-no].
Cápiz (P.I.)   kä'-pēs   kah'-pees
capo (It.)   kä'-pô   kah'-po
   An element, meaning *cape*, in Italian place names. It may be necessary
   to look up the other part of the name.
Capocesto (Yugosl.)   *It.* kä-pô-chĕ'-stô   kah-po-cheh'-sto
   Serb-Croat *Primošten*, q.v.
Capocotta (It.)   kä-pô-kôt'-tä   kah-po-kot'-tah
Capo di Chino (It.,   kä'-pô dē kē'-nô   kah'-po dee kee'-no
   airfield)
   An English pronunciation, chē'-nō [chee'-noh], may or may not be
   inevitable. It would be confused with *Cappuccino*.
Capoocan (P.I.)   kä-pô-ô'-kän   kah-po-o'-kahn
Capoterra (Sard.)   kä-pô-tĕr'-rä   kah-po-tehr'-rah
Capozzoli, Louis J.   kä-pō-zō'-lĭ   kah-poh-zoh'-li
   (U.S. representative)
Cappadocia (Asia Minor) kăp'-ə-dō'-shə   kap'-uh-doh'-shuh
Cappadocia (It.)   käp-pä-dô'-chä   kahp-pah-do'-chah
Capra, Frank (director)   kăp'-rə   kap'-ruh
Capraia (It., isls.)   kä-prĭ'-ä   kah-prai'-ah
Caprara (Sard., cape)   kä-prä'-rä   kah-prah'-rah
Capranica (It.)   kä-prä'-nē-kä   kah-prah'-nee-kah
Caprarola (It.)   kä-prä-rô'-lä   kah-prah-ro'-lah
Capreo (It., mt.)   kä-prĕ'-ô   kah-preh'-o
Capri (It., isl.)   kä'-prē   kah'-pree
   The pronunciation kä'-prē [kah'-pree] is preferable to kə-prē' [kuh-pree'].
Capri (Yugosl.)   *It.* kä'-prē   kah'-pree
   Serb-Croat *Kaprije*, q.v.
Capriquet (Fr.)   kä-prē-kĕ'   kah-pree-keh'
Cap St. Jaques   käp säN zhäk'   kahp sahN zhahk'
   (Indo-Ch.)
Cap Serrat (Tun.)   käp sĕr-rä'   kahp sehr-rah'
   English *Cape Serrat*, kăp sə-răt' [kayp suh-rat'].
Capua (It.)   *Eng.* kăp'-yo͝o-ə   kap'-yu-uh
                    It. kä'-pwä   kah'-pwah
Capul (P.I.)   kä-pōōl'   kah-pool'
Capuzzo, Fort (Libya)   kä-pōōt'-tsō   kah-poot'-tsoh
Caraballos (P.I., mts.)   kä-rä-bä'-yôs   kah-rah-bah'-yos
Carabao (P.I.) See *Limbones*.
carabinieri (pl.; It. state kä-rä-bē-nyĕ'-rē   kah-rah-bee-nyeh'-
   police)   ree
   Singular, *carabiniere*, kä-rä-bē-nyĕ'-rĕ [kah-rah-bee-nyeh'-reh].

Caracal (Rum.)	kä-rä-käl′	kah-rah-kahl′
Caracas (Ven.)	kä-rä′-käs	kah-rah′-kahs
Caraga (P.I.)	kä-rä′-gä	kah-rah′-gah
Carandini, Nicolò	kä-rän-dē′-nē,	kah-rahn-dee′-nee,
(It. polit.)	nē-kô-lô′	nee-ko-lo′
Carano (It.)	kä-rä′-nô	kah-rah′-no
Caransebeş (Rum.)	kä-rän-sĕ′-bĕsh	kah-rahn-seh′-besh

Hungarian *Karansebes,* kä′-rän-shĕ-bĕsh [kah′-rahn-sheh-besh].

Carao (P.I.)	kä-rou′	kah-rau′
Carapanayotis, Byron	kä-rä-pä-nä-yô′-tēs,	kah-rah-pah-nah-
(Gr. polit.)		yo′-tees,
	Eng. bĭ′-rən,	*Eng.* bai′-ruhn,
	Gr. vē′-rôn	*Gr.* vee′-ron
Caraway, Hattie W.	kăr′-ə-wā	kehr′-uh-way
(U.S. senator)		
Carbaix (Fr.)	kär-bĕ′	kahr-beh′
Carbonara (Sard., cape)	kär-bô-nä′-rä	kahr-bo-nah′-rah
Carbone (It.)	kär-bô′-nĕ	kahr-bo′-neh
Carbonia (Sard.)	kär-bô-nē′-ä	kahr-bo-nee′-ah
carburetor	kär′-byə-rā′-tər	kahr′-byuh-ray′-tuhr

Before 1940 our dictionaries rhymed *carburetor* with *letter,* not *later,* although few Americans had ever heard this pronunciation. Similarly *carburetion* was transcribed -rĕsh′-ən [-resh′-uhn] instead of -rā′-shən [-ray′-shuhn], the usual American pronunciation.

Carcassonne (Fr.)	kär-kä-sôn′	kahr-kah-son′
Cárdenas (Cuba)	kär′-dĕ-näs	kahr′-deh-nahs
Cárdenas, Lázaro	kär′-dĕ-näs,	kahr′-deh-nahs,
(Mex. polit.)	lä′-zä-rô	lah′-zah-ro
Cardona (P.I.)	kär-dô′-nä	kahr-do′-nah
Carei (Rum.)	kä-rä′	kah-ray′

Hungarian *Nagykároly,* nät′(y)-kä-roi [naht′(y)-kah-roi].

Carentan (Fr.)	kä-räN-täN′	kah-rahN-tahN′
Carevac (Yugosl.)	tsä′-rĕ-väts	tsah′-reh-vahts
Carevo Selo (Yugosl.)	tsä′-rĕ-vô sĕ′-lô	tsah′-reh-vo seh′-lo
Carey, James B.	kăr′-ĭ	kehr′-i
(Am. labor leader)		
Carhaix (Fr.)	kä-rĕ′	kah-reh′
Cariaco (S.A., gulf)	kä-ryä′-kô	kah-ryah′-ko
Carías Andino, Tiburcio	kä-rē′-äs än-dē′-nô,	kah-ree′-ahs ahn-
(Hond. polit.)	tē-bōōr′-syô	dee′-no, tee-boor′-
		syo
Caribbean	kăr′-ĭ-bē′-ən	kehr′-i-bee′-uhn

The pronunciation kə-rĭb′-ĭ-ən [kuh-rib′-i-uhn] is a variation mysterious in origin. It has a "British" quality to American ears, and

to the British it sounds like an American invention. (*See penicillin.*)
"A competent phonetically trained observer in the Caribbean region
tells me that repeated inquiries elicit the information that Caribbéan
is almost universally recognized as the old established pronunciation
but that many informants 'have recently heard Carib'bean and sup-
posed it must be right'. I find no evidence that the neophony issues
from England but some evidence that it may have spread from New
York City. [John S. Kenyon, *Am. Sp.*, vol. 17, p. 284.]" Prof. H. M.
Ayres suggests that Carib'bean may be based on the old form Carib'-
bee and on the analogy of Európean, the popular 18th-century pronunciation of *European* [Walker, 1791, 1794, English eds.].

Caribrod (Yugosl.)	tsä'-rĭ-brôd	tsah'-ri-brod
Caridad (P.I.)	kä-rē-däd'	kah-ree-dahd'
Also called *Estanzuela*, q.v.		
Carigara (P.I.)	kä-rē-gä'-rä	kah-ree-gah'-rah
Carini (Sicily)	kä-rē'-nē	kah-ree'-nee
Carinola (It.)	kä-rē'-nô-lä	kah-ree'-no-lah
Carioca	*Eng.* kăr'-ĭ-ō'-kə	kehr'-i-oh'-kuh
	Port. kä-ryô'-kä	kah-ryo'-kah

A Portuguese word meaning anyone born or brought up in *Rio de
Janeiro.*

Cârlibaba (Rum.)	kûr-lē-bä'-bä	kuhr-lee-bah'-bah
Carloforte (Sard.)	kär-lô-fôr'-tĕ	kahr-lo-for'-teh
Carlsbad *or* Karlsbad	*Eng.* kärlz'-băd	kahrlz'-bad
(Cz.)	*Ger.* kärls'-bät	kahrls'-baht
Czech *Karlovy Vary*, kär'-lô-vĭ vä'-rĭ [kahr'-lo-vi vah'-ri].		
Carmel (Calif.)	kär-mĕl'	kahr-mel'
Carmel, Mount (Pal.)	kär'-məl	kahr'-muhl
Carmen (P.I.)	kär'-mĕn	kahr'-men
Carmen, Cebú, is also called Port *Bugut*, bōō-gōōt' [boo-goot'].		
Carmona (P.I.)	kär-mô'-nä	kahr-mo'-nah
Carmona, Antonio	kər-mô'-nə,	kuhr-mo'-nuh,
Oscar de Fragoso	än-tô'-nyōō	ahn-to'-nyu
(President of Portugal)	ōōsh-kär' də	ush-kahr' duh
	frə-gô'-zōō	fruh-go'-zu
Carnahan, A. S. J.	kär'-nə-hăn	kahr'-nuh-han
(U.S. representative)		
Carnarvon (Austral.,	kär-närr'-vən	kahr-nahr'-vuhn
U. of S. Afr.)		
Carneville (Fr.)	kär-nə-vēl'	kahr-nuh-veel'
Carolano (It., riv.)	kä-rô-lä'-nô	kah-ro-lah'-no
Carolles (Fr.)	kä-rôl'	kah-rol'
Carpathian Mts. (Europe)	*Eng.* kär-pā'-thĭ-ən	kahr-pay'-thi-uhn

Carpatho-Ruthenia	kär-pā'-thō	kahr-pay'-thoh
(Cz. > Rus.)	rōō-thē'-nyə	roo-thee'-nyuh
Carpathos (Dodec.)	kär'-pä-thô(s)	kahr'-pah-tho(s)
For variants see *Karpathos.*		
Carpentaria (Austral.,	kär-pən-tăr'-ĭ-ə	kahr-puhn-tehr'-i-uh
gulf)		
Carpentras (Fr.)	kär-päN-träs'	kahr-pahN-trahs'
Carpineto (It.)	kär-pē-nĕ'-tô	kahr-pee-neh'-to
Carpiquet (Fr.)	kär-pē-kĕ'	kahr-pee-keh'
Carranglán (P.I.)	kär-räng-glän'	kahr-rahng-glahn'
Carranza, Venustiano	*Eng.* kə-răn'-zə	kuh-ran'-zuh
(Mex. polit.)	*Sp.* kär-rän'-sä,	kahr-rahn'-sah,
	vĕ-nōōs-tyä'-nô	veh-noos-tyah'-no
Carrara (It.)	kär-rä'-rä	kahr-rah'-rah
Carrasco (Urug.)	kär-räs'-kô	kahr-rahṣ'-ko
Carriacou (W.I.)	kăr'-ĭ-ə-kōō'	kehr'-i-uh-koo'
Carroceto (It.)	kär-rô-chĕ'-tô	kahr-ro-cheh'-to
Carrouges (Fr.)	kä-rōōzh'	kah-roozh'
Carsoli (It.)	kär'-sô-lē	kahr'-so-lee
Carstensz Toppen	kär'-stənz tôp'-ən	kahr'-stuhnz top'-
(NEI, New Guinea)		uhn
Cartagena (Sp.)	*Eng.* kär'-tə-jē'-nə	kahr'-tuh-jee'-nuh
	Sp. kär-tä-hĕ'-nä	kahr-tah-heh'-nah
Cartales, Georgios (Gr. polit.) See *Kartalis, Georgios.*		
Carteret (Fr.)	*Eng.* kär'-tə-rĕt	kahr'-tuh-ret
	Fr. kär-trĕ'	kahr-treh'
Carton de Wiart, Henri (Belg. polit.) See *Wiart, Henri Carton de.*		
Carúpano (Ven.)	kä-rōō'-pä-nô	kah-roo'-pah-no
Car Vrh (Yugosl., mt.)	tsär' vərk(h)'	tsahr' vuhrk(h)'
Casablanca (Mor.)	*Eng.* kăs'-ə blănk'-ə	kas'-uh blank'-uh
	Sp. kä'-sä bläng'-kä	kah'-sah blahng'-kah
Also heard, especially in England, kăz'-ə blănk'-ə [kaz'-uh blank'-uh].		
Casaccia (It.)	kä-sät'-chä	kah-saht'-chah
Casalattico (It.)	kä-sä-lät'-tē-kô	kah-sah-laht'-tee-ko
Casale Nuovo (It.)	kä-sä'-lĕ nwô'-vô	kah-sah'-leh nwo'-vo
Casano (It.)	kä-sä'-nô	kah-sah'-no
Casape (It.)	kä-sä'-pĕ	kah-sah'-peh
Casas Alemán, Fernando	kä'-säs ä-lĕ-män',	kah'-sahs ah-leh-
(Mex. diplomat)	fĕr-nän'-dô	mahn', fehr-nahn'-
		do
Casciana (It.)	kä-shä'-nä	kah-shah'-nah
Cascina (It.)	kä-shē'-nä	kah-shee'-nah
Caserta (It.)	kä-zĕr'-tä	kah-zehr'-tah
Caso (Dodec.) See *Kasos.*		

Casola, -e, -i (It.)   kä'-sô-lä, -ĕ, -ē   kah'-so-lah, -eh, -ee

Casola Valsenio (It.)   kä'-sô-lä   kah'-so-lah
        väl-sĕ'-nyô   vahl-seh'-nyo

Casona, -e, -i (It.)   kä-sô'-nä, -ĕ, -ē   kah-so'-nah, -eh, -ee

Caspian Sea   *Eng.* kăs'-pĭ-ən   kas'-pi-uhn
    Russian *Kaspiskoe More*, kä-spē'-skô-yĕ mô'-rĕ [kah-spee'-sko-yeh
    mo'-reh].

Cassel (Ger.)   See *Kassel.*

Cassino (It.)   käs-sē'-nô   kahs-see'-no

Cassis (Fr.)   kä-sē'   kah-see'

Casson (Yugosl.)   See *Kason.*

Castaneda, Salvador   käs-tä-nĕ'-dä,   kahs-tah-neh'-dah,
   (Salv. polit.)   säl-vä-dôr'   sahl-vah-dor'

Castel Arcionè (It.)   kä-stĕl'   kah-stel'
        är-chyô-nĕ'   ahr-chyo-neh'

Castel Benito (Libya)   käs-tĕl' bĕ-nē'-tô   kahs-tel' beh-nee'-to

Castelbottaccio (It.)   kä-stĕl'-bôt-tät'-chô   kah-stel'-bot-taht'-
                     cho

Castel d'Aiano (It.)   käs-tĕl' dä-yä'-nô   kahs-tel' dah-yah'-
   Also spelled *Ajano.*   no

Castel di Guido (It.)   kä-stĕl'   kah-stel'
        dē gwē'-dô   dee gwee'-do

Castel di Jeri (It.)   kä-stĕl' dē yĕ'-rē   kah-stel' dee yeh'-ree

Castel di Stabia (It.)   kä-stĕl' dē stä'-byä   kah-stel' dee stah'-
                     byah

Castel di Velia (It.)   kä-stĕl' dē vĕ'-lyä   kah-stel' dee veh'-
                     lyah

Castelforte (It.)   kä-stĕl'-fôr'-tĕ   kah-stel'-for'-teh

Castel Gandolfo (It.)   kä-stĕl' gän-dôl'-fô   kah-stel' gahn-dol'-fo

Castel Giubileo (It.)   kä-stĕl' jōō-bē-lĕ'-ô   kah-stel' joo-bee-
                     leh'-o

Castel Giuliano (It.)   kä-stĕl' jōō-lyä'-nô   kah-stel' joo-lyah'-
                     no

Castel Guerrino (It., mt.)   käs-tĕl' gwĕr-rē'-nô   kahs-tel' gwehr-ree'-
                     no

Castellabate (It.)   käs-tĕl'-lä-bä'-tĕ   kahs-tel'-lah-bah'-teh

Castellaccio (It.)   kä-stĕl'-lät'-chô   kah-stel'-laht'-cho

Castellafiume (It.)   kä-stĕl'-lä-fyōō'-mĕ   kah-stel'-lah-fyoo'-
                     meh

Castellammare (It.)   kä-stĕl'-läm-mä'-rĕ   kah-stel'-lahm-mah'-
                     reh

Castellane (Fr.)   käs-tĕ-län'   kahs-teh-lahn'

Castelliri (It.)   kä-stĕl'-lē'-rē   kah-stel'-lee'-ree

Castellón (Sp.)   käs-tĕ-lyôn' *or* -yôn'   kahs-teh-lyon' *or* -yon'

Castellonorato (It.)	kä-stĕl'-lô-nô-rä'-tô	kah-stel'-lo-no-rah'-to
Castelluccio (It.)	kä-stĕl'-lōōt'-chô	kah-stel'-loot'-cho
Castelmadama (It.)	kä-stĕl'-mä-dä'-mä	kah-stel'-mah-dah'-mah
Castelnuovo (Yugosl.)	*It.* kä-stĕl'-nwô'-vô	kah-stel'-nwo'-vo

Serb-Croat *Ercegnovi*, q.v.

Castelo Branco (Port.)	kəsh-tĕ'-lŏŏ brän'-kŏŏ	kuhsh-teh'-lu brahn'-ku
Castelo de São Jorge (Port.)	kəsh-tĕ'-lŏŏ dĭ souN zhôr'-zhə	kuhsh-teh'-lu di sauN zhor'-zhuh
Castelrosso (Dodec.)	*It.* kä-stĕl'-rôs'-sô	kah-stel'-ros'-so

Greek *Kastelorizon*, q.v.

Castel San Pietro (It.)	kä-stĕl' sän pyĕ'-trô	kah-stel' sahn pyeh'-tro
Castel Sant' Angelo (It.)	kä-stĕl' sän tän'-jĕ-lô	kah-stel' sahn tahn'-jeh-lo
Casteltermini (Sicily)	kä-stĕl'-tĕr'-mē-nē	kah-stel'-tehr'-mee-nee
Castelvecchio (It.)	kä-stĕl'-vĕk'-kyô	kah-stel'-vek'-kyo
Castelvetrano (Sicily)	kä-stĕl'-vĕ-trä'-nô	kah-stel'-veh-trah'-no
Castiglione (It.)	kä-stē-lyô'-nĕ	kah-stee-lyo'-neh
Castilla (Sp.)	käs-tē'-lyä	kahs-tee'-lyah

English *Castile*, kăs-tēl' [kas-teel']. Old Castile, *Castilla la Vieja*, lä vyĕ'-hä [lah vyeh'-hah]. New Castile, *Castilla la Nueva*, lä nwĕ'-vä [lah nweh'-vah].

Castillejos (P.I.)	käs-tē-yĕ'-hôs	kahs-tee-yeh'-hos
Castillo, Ramón (Sp., polit.)	käs-tē'-lyô *or* -yô, rä-môn'	kahs-tee'-lyo *or* -yo, rah-mon'
Castillo Nájera, Francisco (Mex. diplomat)	käs-tē'-yô nä'-hĕ-rä, frän-sēs'-kô	kahs-tee'-yo nah'-heh-rah, frahn-sees'-ko
Castrén, Urho Jonas (Fin. polit.)	käs-trän', ŏŏr'-hô yô'-näs	kahs-trayn', ur'-ho yo'-nahs
Castres (Fr.)	käs'tr	kahs'tr
Castrocielo (It.)	kä-strô-chyĕ'-lô	kah-stro-chyeh'-lo
Castro dei Volsci (It.)	kä'-strô dā vôl'-shē	kah'-stro day vol'-shee
Castrop Rauxel (Ger.)	käs'-trôp rouk'-səl	kahs'-trop rauk'-suhl
Castroreale (Sicily)	kä'-strô-rĕ-ä'-lĕ	kah'-stro-reh-ah'-leh
Catablas (P.I.)	kä-tä'-bläs	kah-tah'-blahs
Çatalca (Turk.)	chä-täl'-jä	chah-tahl'-jah
Catalonia (Sp.)	kăt'-ə-lō'-nyə	kat'-uh-loh'-nyuh

Spanish *Cataluña*, kä-tä-lōō'-nyä [kah-tah-loo'-nyah].

Catanduanes (P.I.)	kä-tän-dwä′-nĕs	kah-tahn-dwah′-nes
Catania (Sicily)	kä-tän′-yä	kah-tahn′-yah
Catanzaro (It.)	kä-tän-dzä′-rô	kah-tahn-dzah′-ro
Catarabán (P.I., mt.)	kä-tä-rä-bän′	kah-tah-rah-bahn′
Catarmán (P.I.)	kä-tär-män′	kah-tahr-mahn′
Catbalogan (P.I.)	kät′-bä-lô′-gän	kaht′-bah-lo′-gahn
Catel Viejo (P.I.)	kä-tĕl′ vyĕ′-hô	kah-tel′ vyeh′-ho
Catene, le (Yugosl., str.)	It. kä-tĕ′-nĕ, lĕ	kah-teh′-neh, leh
Serb-Croat Verige, q.v.		

cat-hater, -lover. See aelurophobe, -phile.

Catoctin (Md.)	kə-tŏk′-tĭn	kuh-tok′-tin
Catroux, Georges	kä-trōō′,	kah-troo′,
(Fr. general)	zhôrzh	zhorzh
Cattaro (Yugosl.)	It. kät′-tä-rô	kaht′-tah-ro
Serb-Croat Kotor, q.v.		
Cattolica (It.)	kät-tô′-lē-kä	kaht-to′-lee-kah
Catúbig (P.I.)	kä-tōō′-bĭg	kah-too′-big
Cauayan (P.I.)	kä-wä′-yän	kah-wah′-yahn
Caucasian	kô-kā′-zhən	kaw-kay′-zhuhn

Other acceptable pronunciations are given in the dictionaries, but this
is the most common in good American usage.

Caudebec en Caux (Fr.)	kōd-bĕk äN kō′	kohd-bek ahN koh′
Caudebec lès Elbeuf (Fr.)	kōd-bĕk lĕ zĕl-bûf′	kohd-bek leh zel-bœf′
Caudillo, el (Sp.)	kou-dē′-lyô, ĕl	kau-dee′-lyo, el
	or kou-dē′-yô, ĕl	kau-dee′-yo, el

Spanish for the leader. Cf. il Duce and der Fuehrer.

Caudry (Fr.)	kō-drē′	koh-dree′
Cáuit (P.I.)	kä′-wĭt	kah′-wit
Caulnes (Fr.)	kōn′	kohn′
Caulonia (It.)	kou-lô′-nyä	kau-lo′-nyah
Caume (Fr., mt.)	kōm′	kohm′
Čaušli (Yugosl.)	chou′-shlĭ	chau′-shli
Cautín (Chile)	kou-tēn′	kau-teen′
Cauvery (India, riv.)	kô′-və-rĭ	ko′-vuh-ri
Cauville (Fr.)	kō-vēl′	koh-veel′

Cauwelaert, Frans Van (Belg. polit.) See Van Cauwelaert, Frans.

Caux (Fr.)	kō′	koh′
Cavaia (Alb.)	It. kä-vä′-yä	kah-vah′-yah
Albanian Kavajë, q.v.		
Cavaillon (Fr.)	kä-vä-yôN′	kah-vah-yoN′
Cavendish Bentinck,	kăv′-ən-dĭsh	kav′-uhn-dish
V.F.W. (Br. diplomat)	bĕn′-tĭnk	ben′-tink
Caviglia (It.)	kä-vē′-lyä	kah-vee′-lyah

Cavite (P.I.)	kä-vē′-tĕ	kah-vee′-teh
Cavite Viejo (P.I.)	kä-vē′-tĕ vyĕ′-hô	kah-vee′-teh vyeh′-ho
Čavka (Yugosl., mt.)	chäv′-kä	chahv′-kah
Cavtat (Yugosl.)	tsäv′-tät	tsahv′-taht
Cawnpore (India)	kôn′-pôr′	kawn′-por′

Also called *Cawnpur*, kôn′-poŏr′ [kawn′-pur′].

cay ("islet")	kē′ *or* kā′	kee′ *or* kay′

Also spelled *key*.

Cayenne (Fr. Guiana)	kī-ĕn′	kai-en′

Cayes (Haiti) See *Aux Cayes*.

Cayeux (Fr.)	kä-yû′	kah-yœ′
Caylungán (P.I.)	kī-lōōng-gän′	kai-loong-gahn′
Cayman Islands (W.I.)	kī-män′	kai-mahn′
Cayuga (N.Y.)	kā-yōō′-gə	kay-yoo′-guh
Cazenovia (N.Y.)	kăz′-ə-nō′-vĭ-ə	kaz′-uh-noh′-vi-uh
Cazin (Yugosl.)	tsä′-zĭn	tsah′-zin
Čazma (Yugosl.)	chäz′-mä	chahz′-mah
Cazza (It. > Yugosl., isl.)	kät′-sä	kaht′-sah

Serb-Croat *Sušac*, sōō′-shäts [soo′-shahts].

Ceará (Brazil)	sĕ-ä-rä′	seh-ah-rah′
Cebú (P.I.)	sĕ-bōō′	seh-boo′
Ceccano (It.)	chĕk-kä′-nô	chek-kah′-no
Cecchino (It.)	chĕ-kē′-nô	cheh-kee′-no
Čechy (Cz.)	chĕ′-hĭ	cheh′-hi

English *Bohemia*, q.v.

Cecil County (Md.)	sē′-səl	see′-suhl

According to the BBC, *Cecil*, Marquess of Exeter, is pronounced sĕs′-əl [ses′-uhl], but *Cecil*, Marquess of Salisbury, is sĭs′-əl [sis′-uhl].

Cecina (It.)	chĕ′-chē-nä	cheh′-chee-nah
Cedro (It., mt.)	chĕ′-drô	cheh′-dro
Ceduna (Austral.)	sə-dōō′-nə	suh-doo′-nuh
	or kĕ-dōō′-nə	keh-doo′-nuh
Cefalù (Sicily)	chĕ-fä-lōō′	cheh-fah-loo′
Cegléd (Hung.)	tsĕg′-lād	tseg′-layd
Cekhira (Tun.)	sə-kē′-rä	suh-kee′-rah

Also spelled *Skhirra*, q.v.

Celano (It.)	chĕ-lä′-nô	cheh-lah′-no

See *Fucino*.

Celaya (Mex.)	sĕ-lä′-yä	seh-lah′-yah
Celebes (NEI)	*Eng.* sĕl′-ə-bēz	sel′-uh-beez
	Du. sĕ-lä′-bĕs	seh-lay′-bes

Celio (It.) See *Caelian*.

Celje (Yugosl.)	tsĕ′-lyĕ	tseh′-lyeh

Celle (Ger.)	tsĕl'-ə	tsel'-uh
Celle (It.)	chĕl'-lĕ	chel'-leh
Celler, Emanuel	sĕl'-ər	sel'-uhr
(U.S. representative)		
Celles (Belg.)	sĕl'	sel'
Čemerna planina	chĕ'-mĕr-nä	cheh'-mehr-nah
(Yugosl., mts.)	plä'-nē'-nä	plah'-nee'-nah
Čemernik (Yugosl., mt.)	chĕ'-mĕr-nĭk	cheh'-mehr-nik
Cemi (Balkan riv.)	*Alb.* tsĕ'-mē	tseh'-mee
Serb-Croat *Cijevna*, q.v.		
Cenci (It.)	chĕn'-chē	chen'-chee
Cenciano (It.)	chĕn-chä'-nô	chen-chah'-no
Cenis, Mont (Fr., It., mt.)	sə-nē', môN	suh-nee', moN
Čenta (Yugosl.)	chĕn'-tä	chen'-tah
Centocelle (It.)	chĕn-tô-chĕl'-lĕ	chen-to-chel'-leh
Centrache (It.)	chĕn'-trä-kĕ	chen'-trah-keh
Centralia (Ill., Wash.)	sĕn-trā'-lyə	sen-tray'-lyuh
Centuripe (Sicily)	chĕn-tōō'-rē-pĕ	chen-too'-ree-peh
Ceos (Gr., isl.) See *Keos.*		
Čeotina (Yugosl., riv.)	chĕ'-ô'-tĭ-nä	cheh'-o'-ti-nah
Cepet (Fr., cape) See *Sépet.*		
Cephalonia (Gr., isl.)	*Eng.* sĕf-ə-lōn'-yə	sef-uh-lohn'-yuh
Greek *Kephalenia*, q.v.		
Cephissus (Gr., riv.)	*Eng.* sē'-fĭs-əs	see'-fis-uhs
Greek *Kephisos*, kē-fē-sôs' [kee-fee-sos'].		
Ceprano (It.)	chĕ-prä'-nô	cheh-prah'-no
Cer (Yugosl.)	tsĕr'	tsehr'
Ceram (NEI)	*Eng.* sē-răm'	see-ram'
	Du. sā'-räm	say'-rahm
Cerami (Sicily)	chĕ-rä'-mē	cheh-rah'-mee
Ceraunia (Alb.)	*Eng.* sĭ-rô'-nĭ-ə	si-ro'-ni-uh
Albanian *Karaburun*, q.v.		
Cerchio (It.)	chĕr'-kyô	chehr'-kyo
cerebral	sĕr'-ə-brəl	sehr'-uh-bruhl

No dictionary yet authorizes an accent on the second syllable, although the pronunciation sə-rē'-brəl [suh-ree'-bruhl] is not uncommon, especially in medical circles.

Ceremuşul (Pol., Rum., riv.) See *Czeremosz.*		
Cérences (Fr.)	sĕ-räNs'	seh-rahNs'
Çerevoda (Alb.) See *Çerevodë.*		
Çerevodë (Alb.)	chĕ-rĕ-vô'-də	cheh-reh-vo'-duh
Ceri (It.)	chĕ'-rē	cheh'-ree
Cerigo (Gr., isl.)	*It.* chĕ'-rē-gô	cheh'-ree-go
Greek *Kythera*, q.v. English *Cythera.*		

Cerisy la Salle (Fr.)	sĕ-rē-zē′ lä säl′	seh-ree-zee′ lah sahl′
Cerknica (Yugosl.)	tsĕrk′-nĭ-tsä	tsehrk′-ni-tsah
Cerna (Rum., riv.)	chĕr′-nä	chehr′-nah
Cernăuţi (Rum. > Rus.)	chĕr-nə-ōͦts′	chehr-nuh-uts′

Russian *Chernovitsy*, q.v. Polish *Czernowitz*, q. v.

Cerna Vodă (Rum.)	chĕr′-nä vô′-də	chehr′-nah vo′-duh
Černište (Yugosl.)	chĕr′-nĭ-shtĕ	chehr′-ni-shteh
Cerreto (It.)	chĕr-rĕ′-tô	chehr-reh′-to
Certosa (It.)	chĕr-tô′-zä	chehr-to′-zah
Cervara (It.)	chĕr-vä′-rä	chehr-vah′-rah
Cervaro (It., riv.)	chĕr-vä′-rô	chehr-vah′-ro
Cervia (It.)	chĕr′-vyä	chehr′-vyah
Cervino (Sicily)	chĕr-vē′-nô	chehr-vee′-no
Cesana (It.)	chĕ-sä′-nä	cheh-sah′-nah
Cesano (It., riv.)	chĕ-sä′-nô	cheh-sah′-no
Cesaro (It.)	chĕ′-zä-rô	cheh′-zah-ro
Cesarò (Sicily)	chĕ-zä-rô′	cheh-zah-ro′
Cesena (It.)	chĕ-zĕ′-nä	chee-zeh′-nah
Cesenatico (It.)	chĕ-zĕ-nä′-tē-kô	cheh-zeh-nah′-tee-ko
Cesima (It., mt.)	chĕ′-sē-mä	cheh′-see-mah
Cēsis (Latvia)	tsä′-sēs *or* -zēz	tsay′-sees *or* -zeez

Also spelled *Tseziz* and *Zehsis*. German *Wenden*, q.v.

Český See *Czech*.

Češljeva Bara (Yugosl.)	chĕsh′-lyĕ-vä bä′-rä	chesh′-lyeh-vah bah′-rah
Cessnock (Austral.)	sĕs′-nŏk	ses′-nok
Cetatea Albă (Rum. > Rus.)	chĕ-tä′-tyä äl′-bə	cheh-tah′-tyah ahl′-buh

Russian *Akkerman*, äk′-ər-män [ahk′-uhr-mahn].

Cetinje (Yugosl.)	tsĕ′-tĭ-nyĕ	tseh′-ti-nyeh
Četnik (Yugosl. guerrilla)	chĕt′-nĭk	chet′-nik
Cetraro (It.)	chĕ-trä′-rô	cheh-trah′-ro
Cette (Fr.)	sĕt′	set′

Now officially spelled *Sète*, q.v.

Ceuta (Sp. Mor.)	*Eng.* syōō′-tə	syoo′-tuh
	Sp. thĕ-ōō′-tä *or* sĕ-	theh-oo′-tah *or* seh-
Cévennes (Fr.)	sĕ-vĕn′	seh-ven′
Čevo (Yugosl.)	chĕ′-vô	cheh′-vo
Ceylon (India, isl.)	sĭ-lŏn′	si-lon′
Ceylonese	sē-lə-nēz′ *or* -nēs′	see-luh-neez′ *or* -nees′

As an adjective pertaining to Ceylon, *Singhalese*, q.v., is more common in some senses.

Cèze (Fr., riv.)	sĕz′	sez′

ch, kh, and often *h* are variants in Greek. If necessary see all three.

ch is an Anglicized spelling of Yugoslav č. It may be necessary to look up both spellings.

Chablais (Fr.)	shä-blĕ′	shah-bleh′
Chablis (Fr.)	shä-blē′	shah-blee′

As the name of a wine, often Anglicized to shăb′-lĭ [shab′-li].

Chabua (India)	chä′-bōō-ä′	chah′-boo-ah′
chaconne	*Fr.* shä-kôn′	shah-kon′

Spanish dance and musical form. Also called *chacon*, shä-kôN′ [shah-koN′]. Spanish *chacona*, chä-kô′-nä [chah-ko′-nah].

Chad (Afr., lake)	*Eng.* chăd′	chad′

Officially *Tchad*, chäd′ [chahd].

Chagny (Fr.)	shä-nyē′	shah-nyee′
Chagodoshcha (Rus.)	chä-gŏ-dô′-shchä	chah-go-do′-shchah
Chagos (India, isls.)	chä′-gōs	chah′-gohs
Chagres (Pan.)	chä′-grĕs	chah′-gres
Chahar (Ch., prov.)	chä-här	chah-hahr
Chahbar (Iran)	shä-bär′	shah-bahr′
Chaîne de Maures (Fr., mts.)	shĕn də môr′	shen duh mor′
Chaize le Vicomte, la (Fr.)	shĕz lə vē-kôNt′, lä	shez luh vee-koNt′, lah
Chalaines (Fr.)	shä-lĕn′	shah-len′
Chalcidice (Gr., pen.)	*Eng.* kăl-sĭd′-ĭ-sĭ	kal-sid′-i-si
Greek *Khalkidike*, q.v.		
Châlette (Fr.)	shä-lĕt′	shah-let′
Chalkis *or* Chalcis (Gr.)	See *Khalkis.*	
Challans (Fr.)	shä-läN′	shah-lahN′
Challis (Idaho)	chăl′-ĭs	chal′-is
Châlons sur Marne (Fr.)	shä-lôN sür märn′	shah-loN sür mahrn′
Chalon sur Saône (Fr.)	shä-lôN sür sōn′	shah-loN sür sohn′
Chalus (Iran)	chä-lōōs′	chah-loos′
Chambal (India)	chŭm′-bəl	chuhm′-buhl
Chambéry (Fr.)	shäN-bĕ-rē′	shahN-beh-ree′
Chamizal, el	chä-mē-säl′, ĕl	chah-mee-sahl′, el

Territory in dispute between U. S. and Mexico at El Paso.

chamois	*Eng.* shăm′-ĭ	sham′-i
	Fr. shä-mwä′	shah-mwah′
Chamorros	chä-mô′-rôs	chah-mo′-ros

The people of the Marianas or Ladrone Isls. (Oc.)

Champ de Mars (Fr.)	shäN də märs′	shahN duh mahrs′
Champetier de Ribes, August (Fr. polit.)	shäN-pə-tyĕ də rēb′, ô-güst′	shahN-puh-tyeh duh reeb′, o-güst′

Champigny (Fr.)	shäN-pē-nyē′	shahN-pee-nyee′
Champs Élysées (Fr., Paris)	shäN zĕ-lē-zĕ′	shahN zeh-lee-zeh′
Champtocé (Fr.)	shäN-tô-sĕ′	shahN-to-seh′
Champtoceaux (Fr.)	shäN-tô-sō′	shahN-to-soh′
Chanda (India)	chän′-də	chahn′-duh
Chandalar (Alaska)	shăn-də-lär′	shan-duh-lahr′
Chandernagor (India)	chŭn-dər-nə-gôr′	chuhn-duhr-nuh-gor′
Chandpur (India)	chänd′-pŏͦr	chahnd′-pur
Chandra Buri (Siam) See *Chanthaburi.*		
Ch'ang-an (Ch., Shansi) Also called *Si-an,* q.v.	chäng-än	chahng-ahn
Ch'ang-chih (Ch., Shansi)	chäng-jû	chahng-juh
Ch'ang-chow (Ch., Kiangsu) Also called *Wu-chin,* q.v.	*Eng.* chăng-chou *Ch.* chäng-jō	chang-chau chahng-joh
Ch'ang Ch'un (Ch. polit.)	chäng chŏͦn	chahng chun
Ch'ang-ch'un (Manchu.) Also called *Hsin-king* or *Hsin-ching,* shĭn-jĭng [shin-jing].	chäng-chŏͦn	chahng-chun
Changé (Fr.)	shäN-zhĕ′	shahN-zheh′
Ch'ang Hsüeh-liang (Ch. polit.) Also called the *Young Marshall.*	chäng shüĕ-lyäng	chahng shüeh-lyahng
Ch'ang-hua (Ch., Chekiang)	chäng-whä	chahng-whah
Ch'ang-mên (Ch., Fukien)	chäng-mŭn	chahng-muhn
Ch'ang-sha (Ch., Hunan)	chäng-shä	chahng-shah
Ch'ang-shan (Ch., Chekiang)	chäng-shän	chahng-shahn
Ch'ang-tê *or* -teh (Ch., Hunan)	chäng-dŭ	chahng-duh
Ch'ang-tsu (Ch., Shansi)	chäng-dzə	chahng-dzuh
Ch'ang-yang (Ch., Hupeh)	chäng-yäng	chahng-yahng
Chanthaburi (Siam) Also spelled *Chandra Buri.*	chän′-tə-bə-rē′	chahn′-tuh-buh-ree′
Chantilly (Fr.)	*Eng.* shăn-tĭl′-ĭ *Fr.* shäN-tē-yē′	shan-til′-i shahN-tee-yee′
Chantonnay (Fr.)	shäN-tô-nĕ′	shahN-to-neh′
Chao, Menam or River (Siam) Also called *Menam Chao Phraya,* q.v., or *Bhraya* or *Phya.*	chou′, mă-näm′	chau′, ma-nahm′
Chao-an (Ch., Fukien)	jou-än	jau-ahn

Ch'ao-an (Ch., Kwang-tung)	chou-än	chau-ahn

Also called *Ch'ao-chou*, q.v.

Ch'ao-chou (Ch., Kwangtung)	chou-jō	chau-joh
Chaouach (Tun.)	shä-wäsh'	shah-wahsh'
Chaouia (Mor.)	shä-wē'-yä	shah-wee'-ah

Also spelled *Shawiya*.

Ch'ao-yang (Ch., Kwangtung)	chou-yäng	chau-yahng
Ch'ao-yang (Manchu.)	chou-yäng	chau-yahng
Chapaev (Rus.)	chä-pä'-yĕf	chah-pah'-yef
Chapelle, la (Fr.)	shä-pĕl', lä	shah-pel', lah
Chaplinka (Rus.)	chäp'-lĭn-kä	chahp'-lin-kah
Chaplino (Rus.)	chäp'-lĭ-nŏ	chahp'-li-no
Chappaqua (N.Y.)	shăp'-ə-kwô or chăp'-ə-kwä	shap'-uh-kwaw chap'-uh-kwah
Chapultepec (Mex.)	chä-pōōl'-tĕ-pĕk'	chah-pool'-teh-pek'
Charan Konoa (Oc., Saipan)	chä-rän' kô-nô'-ä	chah-rahn' ko-no'-ah
Charente (Fr., riv.)	shä-räNt'	shah-rahNt'
Charenton (Fr.)	shä-räN-tôN'	shah-rahN-toN'
Charkhari (India)	chər-kä'-rē	chuhr-kah'-ree
charlatan	shär'-lə-tən	shahr'-luh-tuhn
Charlemont (Mass.)	chär'-lə-mŏnt	chahr'-luh-mont
Charleroi (Belg.)	shär-lə-rwä'	shahr-luh-rwah'
Charleville (Austral.)	chärl'-vĭl	chahrl'-vil
Charleville (Fr.)	shärl-vēl'	shahrl-veel'
Charlevoix (Can., Mich.)	*Eng.* shär'-lə-voi or chär'-lə-voi *Fr.* shär-lə-vwä'	shahr'-luh-voi chahr'-luh-voi shahr-luh-vwah'
Charlottenburg (Ger.)	*Eng.* shär-lŏt'-ən-bûrg *Ger.* shär-lŏt'-ən-bŏŏrk(h)	shahr-lot'-uhn-buhrg shahr-lot'-uhn-burk(h)
Charmes (Fr.)	shärm'	shahrm'
Chartres (Eng. name)	chär'-tərz	chahr'-tuhrz
Chartres (Fr.)	shär'tr	shahr'tr
Charybdis	*Eng.* kə-rĭb'-dĭs	kuh-rib'-dis

The ancient name of a whirlpool near Messina, Italy.

Chasovaya (Rus.)	chä-sŏ-vä'-yä	chah-so-vah'-yah
Chatalja (Turk.)	chä-täl'-jä	chah-tahl'-jah

Turkish spelling *Çatalca*, q.v.

Châteaubriant (Fr.)	shä-tō-brē-äN'	shah-toh-bree-ahN'

Châteaudun (Fr.)	shä-tō-dûN′	shah-toh-dœN′
Châteaugiron (Fr.)	shä-tō-zhē-rôN′	shah-toh-zhee-roN′
Château Gontier (Fr.)	shä-tō gôN-tyĕ′	shah-toh goN-tyeh′
Châteaulin (Fr.)	shä-tō-lăN′	shah-toh-laN′
Châteauroux (Fr.)	shä-tō-rōō′	shah-toh-roo′
Château Salins (Fr.)	shä-tō sä-lăN′	shah-toh sah-laN′
Château Thierry (Fr.)	*Eng.* shă-tō′ tē′-ə-rē	sha-toh′ tee′-uh-ree
	Fr. shä-tō tyĕ-rē′	shah-toh tyeh-ree′
Châtelet (Fr.)	shät-lĕ′	shaht-leh′
Châtellerault (Fr.)	shä-tĕl-rō′	shah-tel-roh′
Chatham (Eng. name)	chăt′-əm	chat′-uhm
	or chăt′-hăm	chat′-ham

Especially on Cape Cod, chăt′-hăm [chat′-ham].

Châtillon (Fr.)	shä-tē-yôN′	shah-tee-yoN′
Châtre, la (Fr.)	shä′tr, lä	shah′tr, lah
Chattanooga (Tenn.)	chăt′-ə-nōō′-gə	chat′-uh-noo′-guh
Chauk (Burma)	chouk′	chauk′
Chaumont (Fr.)	shō-môN′	shoh-moN′
Chautauqua (N.Y.)	shə-tô′-kwə	shuh-taw′-kwuh
Chaux de Fonds (Fr.)	shō də fôN′	shoh duh foN′
Chavagnac (Fr., fort)	shä-vä-nyäk′	shah-vah-nyahk′
Chavez, Dennis	*Sp.* chä′-vĕs	chah′-ves
(U.S. senator)	*Eng.* chăv′-ĭz	chav′-iz
Cheb (Cz.)	hĕb′ or hĕp′	heb′ or hep′

German *Eger*, ā′-gər [ay′-guhr].

Chebba (Tun.)	shĕb′-bä	sheb′-bah
Chebir (Libya)	kə-bēr′	kuh-beer′

Cf. *Kebir*.

Cheboksari (Rus.)	chĕ-bŏk-sä′-rĭ	cheh-bok-sah′-ri
Chechen (Rus. district)	chĕ′-chĕn′	cheh′-chen′

Also called *Chechna*, chĕch-nyä′ [chech-nyah′].

Chê-chiang (Ch., prov.)	jŭ-jyäng	juh-jyahng

Anglicized as *Chekiang*, q.v.

Chęciny (Pol.)	hăN-tsē′-nĭ	haN-tsee′-ni

Russian *Khentsini*, hĕn-tsē′-nĭ [hen-tsee′-ni].

Cheduba (Burma, isl.)	chĕ-dōō′-bə	cheh-doo′-buh
	or chĕ′-dŏŏ-bə	cheh′-du-buh
Chefoo (Ch., Shantung)	*Eng.* chē-fōō	chee-foo

Chinese *Chih-fu* and *Chih-fow*, q.v.

Cheguimi (Tun.)	shĕ-gē′-mĭ	sheh-gee′-mi
Chekchagirskoe	chĕk-chä-gēr′-	chek-chah-geer′-
(Rus., lake)	skŏ-yĕ	sko-yeh
Chekiang (Ch., prov.)	*Eng.* chĕ-kyăng	cheh-kyang

Chinese *Chê-chiang*, q.v.

Chelles (Fr.)	shĕl'	shel'
Chełm (Pol.)	hĕlm'	helm'
Russian *Kholm*, hôlm' [holm'].		
Chełmno (Pol.)	hĕlm'-nô	helm'-no
German *Kulm*, kŏŏlm' [kulm'].		
Chełmża (Pol.)	hĕlm'-zhä	helm'-zhah
German *Kulmsee*, kŏŏlm'-zä [kulm'-zay].		
Chelyabinsk (Rus.)	chĕ-lyä'-bĭnsk	cheh-lyah'-binsk
Chelyadz (Pol.) See *Czeladź*.		
Chemnitz (Ger.)	kĕm'-nĭts	kem'-nits
Chemulpo (Korea)	chĕ-mŏŏl-pô	cheh-mool-po
chemurgic	kĕ-mûr'-jĭk	keh-muhr'-jik
chemurgy	kĕm'-ûr-jĭ	kem'-uhr-jih
Chenango (N.Y.)	shə-năng'-gō	shuh-nang'-goh
Chên Chêng (Ch. general)	jŭn jŭng	juhn juhng
Chên-chiang (Ch., Kiangsu)	jŭn-jyäng	juhn-jyahng
Variant of *Chin-kiang*, q.v.		
Ch'ên-chow (Ch., Hunan)	chŭn-jō	chuhn-joh
Also called *Yuan-ling*, q.v.		
Chêng-chia-tun (Manchu.)	jŭng-jyä-dŏŏn	juhng-jyah-dun
Chêng-chow (Ch., Honan)	jŭng-jō	juhng-joh
Chêng-hai (Ch., Kwangtung)	jŭng-hī	juhng-hai
Ch'êng-hsien (Ch., Chekiang)	chŭng-shyĕn	chuhng-shyen
Ch'êng-teh (Manchu.)	chŭng-dŭ	chuhng-duh
Also called *Jehol*, q.v.		
Chêng T'ien-hsi (Ch. diplomat)	jŭng tyĕn-shē	juhng tyen-shee
Ch'êng-tu (Ch., Szechwan)	chŭng-dŏō	chuhng-doo
Chên-hsi (Ch., Sinkiang)	jŭn-shē	juhn-shee
Also called *Barkol*, q.v.		
Ch'ên K'uo-fu (Ch. polit.)	chŭn kwô-fŏō	chuhn kwo-foo
Ch'ên Li-fu (Ch. polit.)	chŭn lē-fŏō	chuhn lee-foo
Chên-nan (Ch., pass, Kwangsi; town, Yünnan)	jŭn-nän	juhn-nahn
Chennault, Claire Lee (Am. general)	shĕn'-nôlt'	shen'-nolt'

Chenoweth, J. Edgar	chĕn'-ə-wĕth	chen'-uh-weth
(U.S. representative)		
Ch'ên P'u-lei (Ch. polit.)	chŭn pōō lā	chuhn poo lay
Chenstokhov (Pol.) See *Częstochowa.*		
Chên-yüan (Ch., Kansu,	jŭn-yüän	juhn-yü-ahn
Kweichow, Yünnan)		
Cheops (Pharaoh)	kē'-ŏps	kee'-ops
Cher (Fr., riv.)	shĕr'	shehr'
Cheraw (S.C.)	chə-rô'	chuh-raw'
Cherbourg (Fr.)	*Eng.* shĕr'-bōorg	shehr'-burg
	Fr. shĕr-bōor'	shehr-boor'
Cherchen (Ch., Sinkiang)	chĕr-chĕn	chehr-chen
Chercher (Ethiopia)	chĕr'-chĕr'	chehr'-chehr'
Cheremkhovo (Rus.)	chĕ-rĕm-hô'-vŏ	cheh-rem-ho'-vo
Chérence le Roussel (Fr.)	shĕ-räNs' lə rōō-sĕl'	sheh-rahNs' luh
		roo-sel'
Cherepanovo (Rus.)	chĕ-rĕ-pä'-nŏ-vŏ	cheh-reh-pah'-no-vo
Cherepovets (Rus.)	chĕ-rĕ-pŏ-vĕts'	cheh-reh-po-vets'
Cheribon (NEI, Java)	*Eng.* chĕr-ĭ-bŏn'	chehr-i-bon'
	Du. chĕ-rē-bôn'	cheh-ree-bon'
Cherkasi (Rus.)	chĕr-kä'-sĭ	chehr-kah'-si
Cherkessk (Rus.)	chĕr-kĕsk'	chehr-kesk'
Cherkez Kermen (Rus.)	chĕr-kĕz' kĕr-mĕn'	chehr-kez' kehr-men'
Chern (Rus.)	chĕrn'(y)	chehrn'(y)
Chernaya (Pol., riv.) See *Czarna.*		
Cherniahovsk (Ger. >	chĕr-nyä-hôfsk'	chehr-nyah-hofsk'
Rus.)		
German *Insterburg,* q.v.		
Chernigov (Rus.)	chĕr-nē'-gŏf	chehr-nee'-gof
Chërnoe More	*Rus.* chôr'-nŏ-yĕ	chor'-no-yeh
	mô'-rĕ	mo'-reh
English the *Black* or *Euxine Sea.*		
Chernovitsy (Rum. >	chĕr'-nŏ-vĭ-tsĭ	chehr'-no-vi-tsi
Rus.)		
Commonly known by the Polish variant *Czernowitz,* chĕr'-nô-vĭts [chehr'-no-vits]. Rumanian *Cernăuţi,* q.v.		
Chernyaevo (Rus.)	chĕr-nyä'-yĕ-vŏ	chehr-nyah'-yeh-vo
Chernyakovski, David	chĕr-nyä-kôf'-skĭ	chehr-nyah-kof'-ski
(Rus. general)		
Chërny Rynok (Rus.)	chôr'-nĭ rwē'-nŏk	chor'-ni rwee'-nok
Chërny Yar (Rus.)	chôr'-nĭ yär'	chor'-ni yahr'
Chernyshevsk (Rus.)	chĕr-nĭ-shĕfsk'	chehr-ni-shefsk'
Cherso (It. > Yugosl., isl.)	kĕr'-sô	kehr'-so
Serb-Croat *Cres,* q.v.		

Chersonese (Turk., pen.)   *Eng.* kûr′-sə-nēz   kuhr′-suh-neez
    Also called *Gallipoli*, q.v. Greek *Khersonesos*, q.v.

Chertkovo (Rus.)   chĕrt-kô′-vŏ   chehrt-ko′-vo

Cheshkaya (Rus., bay)   chĕsh′-kä-yä   chesh′-kah-yah

Chetnik (Yugosl.   chĕt′-nĭk   chet′-nik
    guerrilla)

Chevigné, Pierre de   shə-vē-nyĕ′, pyĕr′   shuh-vee-nyeh′,
    (Fr. officer)   də   pyehr′ duh

Cheyenne (Wyo.)   shī-ĕn′   shai-ehn′

Cheylus (Tun.)   shā-lüs′   shay-lüs′

Chiaia *or* Chiaja (It., mt.) kyä′-yä   kyah′-yah

Chia-mu-ssu, -seh   jyä-mōō-sə   jyah-moo-suh
    (Manchu.)

Chi-an (Ch., Kiangsi,   jē-än   jee-ahn
    Manchu.)

chiang *or* kiang   jyäng *or* kyäng   jyahng *or* kyahng
    Chinese word meaning *river*.

Chiang-chin (Ch.,   jyäng-jĭn   jyahng-jin
    Szechwan)

Chiang Ching-k'uo   jyäng jĭng-kwô   jyahng jing-kwo
    (Ch. polit.)

Chiang Kai-shek   jyäng kī-shĕk   jyahng kai-shek
    (Ch. generalissimo)
    Chiang is also pronounced in English chyäng [chyahng] and chyăng
[chyang]. The Peiping Mandarin form is *Chiang Chieh-shih*, jyäng jyĕ-
shû [jyahng jyeh-shuh]. *Chiang Kai-shek* is a "courtesy name" or
nickname. The Generalissimo's real name is *Chiang Chung-chêng*,
jyäng jŏong-jŭng [jyahng jung-juhng]. Though put first in Chinese,
Chiang corresponds in use to an English "last name." Madame
Chiang is *Mei-ling Soong*, q.v.

Chiang Kee-yen *or* Ch'ee- jyäng chē-yĕn   jyahng chee-yen
    yen (Ch. general)

Chiang-ling (Ch., Hupeh) jyäng-lĭng   jyahng-ling

Chiang Mai (Siam)   chyĕng′ mī′   chyeng′ mai′
    Also spelled *Chiengmai* and *Kiang-mai*.

Chiangrai (Siam)   chyäng-rī′   chyahng-rai′

Chiang-shan (Ch.,   jyäng-shän   jyahng-shahn
    Chekiang)
    Ch'ang-shan and *Chiang-shan* should be distinguished.

Chianjur (NEI, Java)   chyän′-jōōr   chyahn′-joor
    Also spelled *Tjiandjoer*, q.v.

Chianti (It., mts.)   kyän′-tē   kyahn′-tee

Chiapas (Mex.)   chyä′-päs   chyah′-pahs

Chiasso (It.)   kyäs′-sô   kyahs′-so

Chiba (Jap.)	chē'-bä	chee'-bah
Chicacole (India)	chĭk-ə-kōl'	chik-uh-kohl'
Chichagof (Alaska, isl.)	*Eng.* chĭch'-ə-gŏf	chich'-uh-gof
	Rus. chĭ-chä'-gŏf	chi-chah'-gof
Chichén Itzá (Mex.)	chē-chĕn' ēt-sä'	chee-chehn' eet-sah'
Chichi Jima (Bonin isls.)	chĭ-chē' jē'-mä'	chi-chee' jee'-mah'

Formerly English *Beechey*, bēch'-ĭ [beech'-i].

Chickasaw (Iowa)	chĭk'-ə-sô	chick'-uh-saw
Chickasha (Okla.)	chĭk'-ə-shā	chik'-uh-shay
Chieh-yäng (Ch., Kwangtung)	jyĕ-yäng	jyeh-yahng
Chiem See (Ger.)	kēm' zā'	keem' zay'
Ch'ien-chiang (Ch., Kwangsi, Szechwan)	chyĕn-jyäng	chyen-jyahng

Variant of *Chien-kiang*, q.v.

Chiengmai (Siam)	*Eng.* chyĕng-mī	chyeng-mai

Officially *Chiangmai*, q.v.

Chien-kiang (Ch., Kwangsi, Szechwan)	*Eng.* chyĕn-kyăng	chyen-kyang

Variant of *Ch'ien-chiang*, q.v.

Chien-li (Ch., Hupeh)	jyĕn-lē	jyen-lee
Ch'ien-nan (Ch., Kiangsi)	chyĕn-nän	chyen-nahn
Chien-ow (Ch., Fukien)	jyĕn-ō	jyen-oh
Ch'ien-shan (Ch., Kiangsi)	chyĕn-shän	chyen-shahn
Ch'ien-t'ang (Ch., riv.)	chyĕn-täng	chyen-tahng
Chien-tê *or* -teh (Ch., Chekiang)	jyĕn-dŭ	jyen-duh

Also spelled *Kien-teh*.

Chienti (It., riv.)	kyĕn'-tē	kyen'-tee
Chiesuola (It., mt.)	kyĕ-swô'-lä	kyeh-swo'-lah
Chiete (It.)	kyĕ'-tĕ	kyeh'-teh
Chieti (It.)	kyĕ'-tē	kyeh'-tee
Chigi (It.)	kē'-jē	kee'-jee
Chigirin (Rus.)	chĭ-gē'-rĭn	chi-gee'-rin
Chih-chiang (Ch.) See *Chih-kiang*.		
Ch'ih-fêng (Manchu.)	chû-fŭng	chuh-fuhng
Chih-fu *or* Chih-fow (Ch., Shantung)	jû-fōō *or* jû-fō	juh-foo *or* juh-foh

Anglicized as *Chefoo*, q.v. Also called *Yen-t'ai*, q.v.

Chih-kiang *or* Chih-chiang (Ch., Hunan)	jû-jyäng	juh-jyahng

The present Anglicized forms are chĭk-yăng and chĭk-ĭ-ăng.

Chih-li (Ch., prov.) See *Hopeh.*

Chihuahua (Mex.) chē-wä'-wä chee-wah'-wah

Ch'i-k'ou (Ch., Chekiang) chē-kō chee-koh
The birthplace of Chiang Kai-shek. Also spelled *Kikow.*

Chilachap (NEI, Java) See *Tjilatjap.*

Chile (S.A.) *Eng.* chĭl'-ĭ chil'-i
Sp. chē'-lĕ chee'-leh

Chilia Nouǎ (Rum.>Rus.) kē-lē'-ä nô'-wə kee-lee'-ah no'-wuh
Russian *Kiliya*, kē'-lĭ-yä [kee'-li-yah].

Chilivani (Sard.) kē-lē-vä'-nē kee-lee-vah'-nee

Chillán (Chile) chē-yän' *or* -lyän' chee-yahn' *or* -lyahn'

Chimara (Alb.) *It.* kē-mä'-rä kee-mah'-rah
Albanian *Himarë*, q.v.

China *Eng.* chĭ'-nə chai'-nuh
Chinese *Ch'ung-hua Min-k'uo*, chŏōng-whä mĭn-kwô [chung-whah min-kwo], Republic of China.

Chi-nan (Ch., Shantung) jē-nän jee-nahn
Also spelled *Tsi-nan.* Also called *Li-cheng*, q.v.

Chin-ch'êng (Ch., Shansi) jĭn-chŭng jin-chuhng

Chin-ch'i (Ch., Kiangsi) jĭn-chē jin-chee

Chindit chĭn'-dĭt chin'-dit
The Chindits were air-borne, mixed United Kingdom, Indian Gurkha, Burman, and Chin troops operating in World War II, in the India-Burma theater. The name was expected to be, not *Chindit*, but *Chinthey*, chĭn'-thĕ [chin'-theh], a mythological beast—half lion, half griffin—who stands guard over Burmese temples to ward off evil spirits. Since the troops were to be used for Combined Operations—land and air, lion and griffin—the name was appropriate. However someone by mistake called them *chindits* and the name persisted.

Chindwin (Burma) chĭn'-dwĭn chin'-dwin

Chinese chĭ-nēz' *or* -nēs' chai-neez' *or* -nees'
The pronunciation chĭ-nēz' [chai-neez'] is preferable. See *Japanese.*

Ching-an (Ch., Kiangsi) jĭng-än jing-ahn

Ch'ing-chiang (Ch., chĭng-jyäng ching-jyahng
Kiangsi)

Ch'ing-hai (Ch., prov.) chĭng-hī ching-hai
Also called *Koko Nor*, q.v., and *Kuku Nor.*

Ching-hai (Ch., jĭng-hī jing-hai
Hopeh, Shantung)

Ching-mên (Ch., Hupeh) jĭng-mŭn jing-muhn

Chin Hills (Burma) chĭn' chin'

Chin-hsien (Ch., Kiangsi) jĭn-shyĕn jin-shyen

Chin-hwa (Ch., Chekiang) jĭn-whä jin-whah
  Also spelled *Kin-hwa*, q.v.

Ch'in-hwang-tao (Ch., chĭn-whäng-dou chin-whahng-dau
  Hopeh)

Chi-ning (Ch., jē-nĭng jee-ning
  Shantung, Suiyüan)

Ch'in-ju (Korea) chĭn-rōo *or* -jōo chin-roo *or* -joo

Ch'in-kai (Korea) chĭn-kī chin-kai

Chin-kiang (Ch., *Eng.* chĭn-kyăng chin-kyang
  Kiangsu)
  Variant of *Chên-chiang*, q.v.

Ch'in-nam-po (Korea) chĭn-näm-pô chin-nahm-po

Chinon (Fr.) shē-nôN′ shee-noN′

Chinook (Am. Indian) shĭ-nŏŏk′ *or* chĭ-nōŏk′ shi-nuk′ *or* chi-nook′
  Correspondents in Oregon and Washington prefer the first, dictionaries
  the second.

Chioggia (It.) kyôd′-jä kyod′-jah

Chios (Gr.) *Eng.* kī′-ŏs kai′-os
               Gr. hē′-ôs hee′-os

Chiperfield, Robert chĭp′-ər-fēld chip′-uhr-feeld
  (U.S. representative)

Chir (Rus., riv.) chēr′ cheer′

Chirico, Giorgio di kē′-rē-kô, kee′-ree-ko,
  (It. painter) jôr′-jô dē jor′-jo dee

Chirikof (Alaska, Attu) chē′-rĭ-kŏf chee′-ri-kof

Chiriquí (Pan., gulf) chē-rē-kē′ chee-ree-kee′

Chirpan (Bulg.) chĭr-pän′ chihr-pahn′

Chirskaya (Rus.) chēr′-skä-yä cheer′-skah-yah

Chishima(Jap.>Rus.,isls.)chē-shē-mä chee-shee-mah
  Russian *Kuril*, q.v.

Chisholm Trail (U.S.) chĭz′-əm chiz′-uhm

Ch'i-shui (Ch., Hupeh) chē-shwā chee-shway

Chi-shui (Ch., Kiangsi) jē-shwā jee-shway

Chişinău (Rum. > Rus.) kē-shē-nû′-ŏŏ kee-shee-nuh′-u
  Russian *Kishinëv*, q.v.

Chita (Rus.) chĭ-tä′ chi-tah′

Chitral (India) chĭ-träl′ chi-trahl′

Chittagong (India) chĭt′-ə-gŏng chit′-uh-gong

Chiu-chiang (Ch., Kiangsi) jyōo-jyäng jyoo-jyahng
  Also spelled *Kiu-kiang*, q.v.

Chiu-lung (Ch., Hongkong) See *Kowloon*.

Chiunzi (It., pass) kyōōn′-dzē kyoon′-dzee

Chiusa (It.) kyōō′-sä kyoo′-sah

Chiusi (It.) kyōō′-sē kyoo′-see

Ch'i-yang (Ch., Hunan)	chē-yäng	chee-yahng
Also called *K'i-yang*.		
Chkaloff (Rus.)	chkä'-lŏf	chkah'-lof
Chmielnik (Pol.)	k(h)myĕl'-nĭk	k(h)myel'-nik
Russian *Khmyelnik*.		
Chodzież (Pol.)	hô'-jĕsh	ho'-jesh
German *Kolmar*, q.v.		
Choiseul (Oc., Solomons)	shwä-zûl'	shwah-zœl'
Chojnica (Ger. > Pol.)	hoi-nē'-tsä	hoi-nee'-tsah
German *Koenigsberg*, *Neumark*, q.v.		
Chojnice (Pol.)	hoi-nē'-tsĕ	hoi-nee'-tseh
Chojnów (Ger. > ? Pol.)	hoi'-nŏŏf	hoi'-nuf
German *Haynau*, q.v.		
choleric	kŏl'-ə-rĭk	kol'-uh-rik
There is no dictionary authority for a stress on the second syllable.		
Cholet (Fr.)	shô-lĕ'	sho-leh'
Cholon (Indo-Ch.)	*Fr.* shô-lôN'	shaw-loN'
	Indo. chə-lûn'	chuh-luhn'
Chomudinza (Rus.)	chŏ-mŏŏ-dēn'-tsä	cho-mu-deen'-tsah
Chomůtov (Cz.)	hô'-mōō-tôf	ho'-moo-tof
Chortkov (Pol. > Rus.)	chôrt'-kôf	chort'-kof
Polish *Czortków*, q.v.		
Chorzele (Pol.)	hô-zhĕ'-lĕ	ho-zheh'-leh
Russian *Khorzhele*, hŏr-zhĕ'-lĕ [hor-zheh'-leh].		
Chorzów (Pol.)	hô'-zhŏŏf	ho'-zhuf
Chōsen (Asia)	chô'-sĕn	cho'-sen
The Japanese name for *Korea*, q.v.		
Chōshi (Jap.)	chô'-shē'	cho'-shee'
Choszczno (Ger. > Pol.)	hôsh'-chnô	hosh'-chno
German *Arnswalde*, q.v.		
chott	shŏt'	shot'
An element, meaning *salt lake* (more or less dried up), in Arabic names of Algeria and Tunisia. *Chott* is the French spelling, *shott*, the English.		
Chott Djerid (Tun.)	shŏt jĕ-rēd'	shot jeh-reed'
Chott el Fedjadj (Tun.)	shŏt ĕl fə-jăj'	shot el fuh-jaj'
Chott Melghir (Tun.)	shŏt mĕl-gēr'	shot mel-geer'
Also called *Chott Melrir*, shŏt mĕl-rēr' [shot mel-reer'].		
Chou En-lai (Ch. general)	*Eng.* chou ĕn-lī	chau en-lai
	Ch. jō ĕn-lī	joh en-lai
Chouigi (Tun.)	shwē'-gē	shwee'-gee
Chowan (N.C., riv.)	chŏ-wän'	choh-wahn'
Christiansund (Nor.)	krĭs'-tyän-sŏŏn'	kris'-tyahn-sun'
Variant spelling of *Kristiansund*.		

Christophe Henri	krēs-tôf′,	krees-tof′,
(Haitian ruler)	äN-rē′	ahN-ree′
Chrzanów (Pol.)	kshä′-nŏof	kshah′-nuf
Ch'uan-chow (Ch.,	chwän-jō	chwahn-joh
Fukien)		
Chubut (Arg.)	chōō-bōot′	choo-boot′
Chu-chi (Ch., Chekiang)	jōō-jē	joo-jee
Ch'ü-ching (Ch., Yünnan)	chü-jĭng	chü-jing
Ch'u-chow (Ch.,	*Eng.* chōō-chou	choo-chau
Chekiang)	*Ch.* chōō-jō	choo-joh
Chudovo (Rus.)	chōō′-dŏ-vŏ	choo′-do-vo
Chudskoye ozero	*Rus.* chŏod-skŏ′-yĕ	chud-sko′-yeh
(Rus., Est., lake)	ŏ′-zĕ-rŏ	o′-zeh-ro
Estonian *Peipsijärv*, q.v.		
Chūgoku (Jap.)	chōō′-gŏ-kōō	choo′-go-koo
	or chōō′-gôk	choo′-gok
Chuguchak (Ch.,	chōō′-gōō-chäk′	choo′-goo-chahk′
Sinkiang)		
Also called *Tah-ch'êng*, q.v., and *Tarbagatai*.		
Chuguev (Rus.)	chōō-gōō′-yĕf	chu-goo′-yef
Ch'ü-hsien (Ch.,	chü-shyĕn	chü-shyen
Chekiang)		
Chu Hsüeh-fan	jōō shü-ĕ fän	joo shü-eh fahn
(Ch. labor leader)		
Chu-ki Variant of *Chu-chi*, q.v.		
Chukok (Burma)	chōō-kōk′	chu-kohk′
Chumphon (Siam)	chŏom-pôn′	chum-pawn′.
Chumukan (Rus.)	chōō-mōō-kän′	choo-moo-kahn′
Ch'ung-i (Ch., Kiangsi)	chŏong-ē	chung-ee
Ch'ung-jin (Korea)	chŏong-jĭn	chung-jin
Ch'ung-ju (Korea)	chŏong-rōō *or* -jōō	chung-roo *or* -joo
Chungking (Ch.,	*Eng.* chŏong-kĭng	chung-king
Szechwan)		
Mandarin *Chung-ch'ing*, jŏong-chĭng [jung-ching]. Also called *Pa -hsien*, bä-shyĕn [bah-shyen].		
Chung-shan	jŏong-shän	jung-shahn
(Ch., Kwangtung)		
See also *Sun Yat-sen*.		
Chung-tien (Yünnan)	jŭng-dyĕn	juhng-dyen
Ch'ung-yàng (Ch.,	chŏong-yäng	chung-yahng
Hupeh)		
Chuniksak (Alaska, Attu)	chōō′-nĭk-săk′	choo′-nik-sak′
Chur (Switz.)	kōōr′	koor′
French *Coire*, kwär [kwahr].		

Churchill, Winston   chûrch'-ĭl *or* -əl   chuhrch'-il *or* -uhl
  (Br. polit.)
The pronunciation chûrch'-hĭll [chuhrch'-hill] is not recommended.
Ch'u Shih-ming (Ch.   chōō shû-mĭng   choo shuh-ming
  general)
Chust (Cz. >Rus.) See *Khust.*
Chu-têh (Ch. general)   jōō-dŭ   joo-duh
Ch'wan-shih (Ch.,   chwän-shû   chwahn-shuh
  Fukien, isl.)
Ciampino (It.)   chäm-pē'-nô   chahm-pee'-no
Ciano (It.)   chä'-nô   chah'-no
Cibola (N.M.)   sē'-bô-lä   see'-bo-lah
Čićevac (Yugosl.)   chē'-chĕ-väts   chee'-cheh-vahts
Čičevica (Yugosl., mts.)   chē'-chĕ'-vĭ-tsä   chee'-cheh'-vi-tsah
Čičevo, Gornje *and*   chē'-chĕ-vô,   chee'-cheh-vo,
  Dolnje (Yugosl.)   gôr'-nyĕ *and*   gor'-nyeh *and*
                 dôl'-nyĕ   dol'-nyeh
Ciciliano (It.)   chē-chē-lyä'-nô   chee-chee-lyah'-no
Ciechanów (Pol.)   chĕ-hä'-nōŏf   cheh-hah'-nuf
  Russian *Tsyekhanov,* tsĕ-hä'-nôf [tseh-hah'-nof].
Ciechanowski, Jan   chĕ-hä-nôf'-skĭ,   cheh-hah-nof'-ski,
  (Pol. polit.)   yän'   yahn'
Ciechocinek (Pol.)   chĕ-hô-chē'-nĕk   cheh-ho-chee'-nek
  Russian *Tsyekhotsinsk,* tsĕ-hŏ-tsēnsk' [tseh-ho-tseensk'].
Ciénaga (Colom.)   syĕ'-nä-gä   syeh'-nah-gah
Ciénega (Mex.)   syĕ'-nĕ-gä   syeh'-neh-gah
Cienfuegos (Cuba)   syĕn-fwĕ'-gôs   syehn-fweh'-gos
Cieszyn (Pol., Cz.)   *Pol.* chĕ'-shĭn   cheh'-shin
  German *Teschen,* q.v.
Čiflik (Yugosl.)   chē'-flĭk   chee'-flik
Cijevna (Balkan riv.)   *S.-C.* tsē'-yĕv-nä   tsee'-yev-nah
  Albanian *Cemi,* q.v.
Cilento (It.)   chē-lĕn'-tô   chee-len'-to
Cima (It.)   chē'-mä   chee'-mah
Cimiez (Fr.)   sē-myĕ'   see-myeh'
Cinapusan (P.I.)   sē-nä-pōō'-sän   see-nah-poo'-sahn
  Also called *Cinapuran,* sē-nä-pōō'-rän [see-nah-poo'-rahn].
Cincinnati (Ohio)   sĭn'-sĭ-năt'-ĭ *or* -ə   sin'-si-nat'-i *or* -uh
These embattled pronunciations seem equally matched. Cf. *Missouri.*
Cineto (It.)   chē-nĕ'-tô   chee-neh'-to
Ciney (Belg.)   sē-nĕ'   see-neh'
Cinglais (Fr., forest)   săN-glĕ'   saN-gleh'
Cinquefronde (It.)   chēn'-kwĕ-frôn'-dĕ   cheen'-kweh-fron'-
                                           deh

Cintheaux (Fr.)	săN-tō′	saN-toh′
Cinto (Corsica, mt.)	chēn′-tô	cheen′-to
Cintra (Port.)	sēn′-trə	seen′-truh
Ciotat, la (Fr.)	syô-tä′, lä	syo-tah′, lah
Čiovo (Yugosl.)	chē′-ô-vô	chee′-o-vo
Italian *Bua*, q.v.		
Circassia (Rus.)	*Eng.* sər-kăsh′-ə	suhr-kash′-uh
Circeo (It.,)	chēr-chĕ′-ô	cheer-cheh′-o
Cirene (Libya) See *Cyrene*.		
Cisneros, Guy Pérez	sēs-nĕ′-rôs, gē	sees-neh′-ros, gee
(Cuban diplomat)	pĕ′-rĕs	peh′-res
Cisneros, Villa	sēs-nĕ′-rôs, vē′-lyä	sees-neh′-ros,
(Rio de Oro)		vee′-lyah
Cisterna (It.)	chē-stĕr′-nä	chee-stehr′-nah
Citerna (It.)	chē-tĕr′-nä	chee-tehr′-nah
Čitluk (Yugosl.)	chĕt′-lōōk	cheet′-look
Citrine, Sir Walter	sĭ-trēn′	sih-treen′
(Br. polit.)		
Città (It.)│	chĕt-tä′	cheet-tah′
Cittaducale (It.)	chĕt-tä′-dōō-kä′-lĕ	cheet-tah′-doo-kah′-leh
Città Vecchia (It.,	chĕt-tä′ vĕk′-kyä	cheet-tah′ vek′-kyah
Yugosl.)		
Ciudad Juárez (Mex.)	syōō-däd′ hwä′-rĕs	syoo-dahd′ hwah′-res
Local English hwŏr′-ĭz [hwor′-iz].		
Ciudad Real (Sp.)	thyōō-däd′ (*or* syōō-) rĕ-äl′	thyoo-dahd′ (*or* syoo-) reh-ahl′
Ciudad Trujillo	syōō-däd′	syoo-dahd′
(Dom. Rep.)	trōō-hē′-yô	troo-hee′-yo
Civita (It.)	chē′-vē-tä	chee′-vee-tah
Civitavecchia (It.)	chē′-vē-tä-vĕk′-kyä	chee′-vee-tah-vek′-kyah
Civitella Roveto (It.)	chē-vē-tĕl′-lä rô-vĕ′-tô	chee-vee-tel′-lah ro-veh′-to
Cizre (Turk.)	jĭz′-rĕ′	jiz′-reh′
Claire (Fr., riv.)	klĕr′	klehr′
Clairefontaine (Fr.)	klĕr-fôN-tĕn′	klehr-foN-ten′
Clark Kerr, Sir	klärk′ kär′	klahrk′ kahr′
Archibald (Br. diplomat)		
Clason, Charles R.	klā′-sən	klay′-suhn
(U.S. representative)		
Claverhouse (Scot. name)	*BBC* klā′-vər-hous	klay′-vuhr-haus
Also pronounced klăv′-ərz [klav′-uhrz], klăv′-ər-əs [klav′-uhr-uhs],		

klăv'-ər-hoủs [klav'-uhr-haus], and klā'-vərz [klay'-vuhrz]. "Honey, ask the man how to pronounce his name." It is evidently three syllables in Sir Walter Scott's line: "To the lairds in convention 'twas Claverhouse spoke."

Clécy (Fr.)	klĕ-sē'	kleh-see'
Clefcy (Fr.)	klĕf-sē'	klef-see'
Cle Elum (Wash.)	klē' ĕl'-əm	klee' el'-uhm
Clemenceau, Georges	klĕ-mäN-sō',	kleh-mahN-soh',
(Fr. polit.)	zhôrzh'	zhorzh'
Clercken (Belg.)	klĕr'-kən	klehr'-kuhn
Clères (Fr.)	klĕr'	klehr'
Clermont Ferrand (Fr.)	klĕr-môN fĕ-räN'	klehr-moN feh-rahN'
Clermont l'Hérault (Fr.)	klĕr-môN lĕ-rō'	klehr-moN leh-roh'
Clervaux (Lux.)	klĕr-vō'	klehr-voh'
Cleve or Kleve (Ger.)	klā'-və	klay'-vuh

English *Cleves*, klēvz' [kleevz'].

Clevenger, Cliff	klĕv'-ən-jər	klev'-uhn-juhr
(U.S. representative)		
Clichy (Fr.)	klē-shē'	klee-shee'
Clinchamp (Fr.)	klăN-shäN'	klaN-shahN'
Clippinger, Roy	klĭp'-ĭng-ər	klip'-ing-uhr
(U.S. representative)		
Cliveden (Eng.)	klĭv'-dən	kliv'-duhn

The first syllable has the vowel of the verb, to *live*.

Cloete, Stuart	kloō'-tĭ	kloo'-ti
(S. Afr. author)		
Cloncurry (Austral.)	klŏn-kûr'-ɨ	klon-kuhr'-i
Cloquet (Minn.)	klō-kā'	kloh-kay'
Closon, Louis(Fr. polit.)	klô-zôN', lwē'	klo-zoN', lwee'
cloture	klō'-chər	kloh'-chuhr
Cluj (Rum.)	kloŏzh'	kluzh'

Hungarian *Kolozsvár*, kô'-lôzh-vär [ko'-lozh-vahr]. German *Klausen-burg*, klou'-zən-boŏrk(h) [klau'-zuhn-burk(h)].

Coahuila (Mex.)	kô-ä-wē'-lä	ko-ah-wee'-lah
Cobán (Guat.)	kô-bän'	ko-bahn'
Cóbh (Eire)	*Am. Eng.* kŏb'	kohb'
	Irish kōv' *or* kōf	kohv' *or* kohf

Formerly called *Queenstown*.

Coblenz (Ger.)	kō'-blĕnts	koh'-blents
Also spelled *Koblenz*, q.v.		
Cobleskill (N.Y.)	kō'-bəlz-kĭl	koh'-buhlz-kil
Cobourg (Austral.)	kō'-bûrg	koh'-buhrg
Cocanada (India)	kō-kə-nä'-də	koh-kuh-nah'-duh
Cochabamba (Bol.)	kô-chä-bäm'-bä	ko-chah-bahm'-bah

Cochem (Ger.)   kŏk(h)′-əm   kok(h)′-uhm
Cochin (India)   kō′-chĭn′   koh′-chin′
Cochin China (Indo-Ch.)   kō′-chĭn chĭ′-nə   koh′-chin chai′-nuh
   French *Cochinchine*, kô-shăN-shēn′ [ko-shaN-sheen′].
Cockburn (Canada, isl.)   kō′-bərn   koh′-buhrn
   This English name is sometimes spelled *Coburn*.
Cocos (Ind. Oc.)   kō′-kōs   koh′-kohs
   Also called *Keeling Isls.*, q.v.
Cocullo (It.)   kô-kōōl′-lô   ko-kool′-lo
Coelho dos Reis   kwĕ′-lyŏŏ dŏŏs rās′   kweh′-lyu dus rays′
   (Braz. polit.)
Coenties Slip   kwĭn′-sĭz′   kwin′-siz
   (New York City)   *or* kŭn′-tĭz   kun′-tiz
   The Dutch owner of the neighboring property was *Coenraet* (modern
   Koenraad) *Ten Eyck*, kōōn′-rät′ tĕn īk′. He was known by the di-
   minutive *Coentje*, kōōn′-tyə, which became in English kōōn′-chĭ.
   Under the influence of the spelling, two lines developed: (1) kwĕn′-
   chĭ, kwĭn′-chĭ, kwĭn′-sĭ, kwĭn′-tĭ and (2) kŭn′-tĭ, kŏn′-tĭ.
Coepernick (Ger.)   kû′-pər-nĭk   kœ′-puhr-nik
Coesfeld (Ger.)   kōs′-fĕlt   kohs′-felt
Coethen (Ger.)   kû′-tən   kœ′-tuhn
Coeur d'Alene (Am.   kŏŏr′ də-lĕn′   kur′-duh-len′
   Indian; Idaho)   *or* kûr′- *or* kōr′-   *or* kuhr′- *or* kohr′-
            or . . . . lān′   *or* . . . . layn′
Coevorden (Neth.) See *Koevorden*.
Cogolin (Fr.)   kô-gô-lăN′   ko-go-laN′
Cohoes (N.Y.)   kō′-hōz   koh′-hohz
Coimbra (Port.)   kwēm′-brə   kweem′-bruh
Coincy (Fr.)   kwăN-sē′   kwaN-see′
Coire (Switz.) See *Chur*.
Colasi (P.I.)   kô-lä′-sē   ko-lah′-see
Colban, Erik (Nor.   kōl′-bän   kohl′-bahn
   polit.)
Colby College (Me.)   kōl′-bĭ   kohl′-bi
Coldragone (It.)   kôl-drä-gô′-nĕ   kol-drah-go′-neh
Colijnsplaat (Neth.) See *Kolijnsplaat*.
Colima (Mex.)   kô-lē′-mä   ko-lee′-mah
Colindres, Vincente Mejía (Hond. polit.) See *Mejía Colindres*.
Collagna (It.)   kôl-lä′-nyä   kol-lah′-nyah
Collarmele (It.)   kôl-lär-mĕ′-lĕ   kol-lahr-meh′-leh
Colle Ferro (It.)   kôl′-lĕ fĕr′-rô   kol′-leh fehr′-ro
Colleville (Fr.)   kôl-vēl′   kol-veel′
Colli Euganei (It.) See *Euganean Hills*.

Colmar (Fr.)	*Eng.* kōl′-mär	kohl′-mahr
	Fr. kôl-mär′	kol-mahr′
Colmars (Fr.)	kôl-mär′	kol-mahr′
Colmer, William M.	kŏl′-mər	kol′-muhr
(U.S. representative)		
Colocontó (P.I.)	kô-lô-kôn-tô′	ko-lo-kon-to′
Cologne (Ger.)	*Eng.* kə-lōn′	kuh-lohn′
	Fr. kô-lôn′(y)	ko-lon′(y)
German *Koeln,* q.v.		
Colomb Béchar (Alg.)	kô-lôNb′ bĕ-shär′	ko-loNb′ beh-shahr′
Colombes (Fr.)	kô-lôNb′	ko-loNb′
Colombia (S. A.)	*Eng.* kə-lŭm′-bĭ-ə	kuh-luhm′-bi-uh
	Sp. kô-lôm′-byä	ko-lom′-byah
Colombo (Ceylon)	kə-lŭm′-bō	kuh-luhm′-boh
Colomea (Pol.) See *Kołomyja.*		
Colón (Panama)	kô-lôn′	ko-lon′
Colón, Cristóbal	*Sp.* kô-lôn′,	ko-lon′,
	krēs-tô′-bäl	krees-to′-bahl
English *Christopher Columbus.*		
Colonia Elena (It.)	kô-lô′-ynä	ko-lo′-nyah
	ĕ′-lĕ-nä	eh′-leh-nah
Colonna (It.)	kô-lôn′-nä	ko-lon′-nah
Colorado (U.S.)	kŏl′-ə-răd′-ə	kol′-uh-rad′-uh
Spanish kô-lô-rä′-dô [ko-lo-rah′-do].		
Colotlán (Mex.)	kô-lô-tlän′	ko-lo-tlahn′
Coltainville (Fr.)	kôl-tăN-vēl′	kol-taN-veel′
Colum, Padraic	kŏl′-əm, päd′-rĭk	kol′-uhm, pahd′-rik
(Irish-Am. poet)	*or* pô*th*′-rĭg	po*th*′-rig
Columbia	kə-lŭm′-bĭ-ə	kuh-luhm′-bi-uh

It is best to pronounce the *o* of the first syllable as schwa. The vowel should not disappear, leaving klŭm-bĭ-ə, nor should it be pronounced like the *o* of *go.* Acceptable variants of -bĭ-ə are -bĭ-yə and -byə.

column	kŏl′-əm	kol′-uhm

The pronunciation kŏl′-yəm (and the spelling *colyum*) should be reserved for a newspaper *column.* Both are, or were once, comic. Similarly *columnist,* kŏl′-əm-ĭst *or* -nĭst [kol′-uhm-ist *or* -nist]; comic -yəm- [-yuhm-].

Comacchio (It.)	kô-mäk′-kyô	ko-mahk′-kyo
Combermere (Burma)	kŭm′-bər-mĭr	kuhm′-buhr-mihr
Combourg (Fr.)	kôN-bōōr′	koN-boor′
Comines (Fr., Bel.)	kô-mēn′	ko-meen′
Comintern (Rus.)	*Eng.* kŏm′-ĭn-tûrn′	kom′-in-tuhrn′

The first syllable should not be pronounced kōm- [kohm-].

Comiso (Sicily)	kô′-mē-zô	ko′-mee-zo
Commercy (Fr.)	kô-mĕr-sē′	ko-mehr-see′

communique   *Eng.* kə-myōō'-nĭ-kā'   kuh-myoo'-ni-kay'
  The pronunciation kyōō-myōō'-nĭ-kā' [kyoo-myoo'-ni-kay'] tempts
many Americans. Cf. *coupon.*
Comores (E. Afr., isls.) See *Comoro Isls.*
Comorin (India, cape)   kŏm'-ə-rĭn   kom'-uh-rin
Comoro Isls. (E. Afr.)   *Eng.* kŏm'-ə-rō   kom'-uh-roh
  French *Archipel des Comores,* är-shē-pěl dě kô-môr' [ahr-shee-pel
deh ko-mor'].
Compiegne (Fr.)   kôN-pyěn'(y)   koN-pyen'(y)
Comrat (Rum. > Rus.)   kôm-rät'   kom-raht'
  Russian spelling, *Komrat.*
Comtat Venaissin (Fr.)   kôN-tä' və-ně-săN'   koN-tah' vuh-neh-
                                                       saN'
Conant, James B.   kō'-nənt   koh'nuhnt
  (Am. scientist)
Conca (It., riv.)   kôn'-kä   kon'-kah
Concarneau (Fr.)   kôN-kär-nō'   koN-kahr-noh'
Concepción (Chile)   kôn-sěp-syôn'   kon-sep-syon'
Conches (Fr.)   kôNsh'   koNsh'
Concord (Mass.)   kŏng'-kərd   kong'-kuhrd
Condado (P.R.)   kôn-dä'-dô   kon-dah'-do
Condé sur Noireau (Fr.)   kôN-dě' sür nwä-ro'   koN-deh' sür nwah-
                                                   roh'
Condobolin (Austral.)   kən-dō'-bə-lĭn   kuhn-doh'-buh-lin
condolence   kən-dō'-ləns   kuhn-doh'-luhns
                   or kŏn'-də-lens   kon'-duh-luhns
conduit   kŏn'-dōō-ĭt   kon'-du-it *or* kon'-dit
                   or kŏn'-dĭt
  The first is the pronunciation of engineers. Old-fashioned, kŭn'-dĭt.
Conejos (Col.)   *Eng.* kə-nä-əs   kuh-nay-uhs
                  Sp. kô-ně'-hôs   ko-neh'-hos
Conesus (N.Y.)   kə-nē'-səs   kuh-nee'-suhs
Conflans l'Archevêque   kôN-fläN lärsh-věk'   koN-flahN lahrsh-
  (Fr.)   vek'
Cönigsborn (Ger.) See *Königsborn.*
Conjeeveram (India)   kŏn-jē-və-rŭm'   kon-jee-vuh-ruhm'
Connacht (Eire)   *Eng.* kŏn'-ôt   kon'-awt
                   Irish kŏn'-ŭk(h)t   kon'-uhk(h)t
Connecticut (U.S.)   kə-nět'-ĭ-kət   kuh-net'-i-kuht
  The *c* of the second syllable has never been pronounced in the State,
but the curious spelling has given rise to kə-něk'-tĭ-kət [kuh-nek'-ti-
kuht] in England and other foreign countries.
Connemara (Eire)   kŏn'-ə-mă'-rə   kon'-uh-ma'-ruh
Čonoplja (Yugosl.)   chô'-nôp-lyä   cho'-nop-lyah
Constance (Ger.)   *Eng.* kŏn'-stəns   kon'-stuhns
  German *Konstanz,* q.v.   [115]

Constanţa (Rum.)   kôn-stän'-tsä   kon-stahn'-tsah
Constantine (Alg.)   *Eng.* kŏn'-stən-tēn'   kon'-stuhn-teen'
                          Fr. kôN-stäN-tēn'   koN-stahN-teen'
Constantinople (Turk.)   *Eng.* kŏn'-stăn-tĭ-   kon'-stan-ti-
                          nō'-pəl   noh'-puhl
Now officially known as *İstanbul,* q.v.
contact   kŏn'-tăkt   kon'-takt

As a verb meaning to get in touch with a person, this word was over-
used in the golden age of sales promotion. Though the word suggested
interesting metaphors of engineering, it excited objections from purists
and many ordinary speakers, probably because they heard it too often.
Now the verb seems likely to disappear with other foibles and symbols
of the Golden Era. It is best avoided in radio scripts except for
established technical phrases, such as *to contact the enemy.*

Conteville (Fr.)   kôNt-vēl'   koNt-veel'
controversial   kŏn'-trō-vûr'-shəl   kon'-troh-vuhr'-shuhl

The last syllables, *-sial,* should not be pronounced -sĭ-əl [-si-uhl], an
unidiomatic pronunciation based upon the spelling. Such false refine-
ments are often the result of bad instruction in stage and concert
diction. Radio must have idiomatic American English, and no arty
speech can take its place. Announcers must critically examine pronunciations which will leave them open to a charge of being pretentious, affected, and unreal. This -sĭ-əl [-si-uhl] pronunciation is not
listed in any dictionary, and it is not characteristic of any variety of
American speech. Cf. *crucial* and *issue.*

convoy   *noun* kŏn'-voi   kon'-voi
                          verb kŏn-voi'   kon-voi'

A principal stress on the first syllable of the verb still sounds awkward
to many listeners, although naval usage during the war may have
established it in the language.

Coo (Dodec.)   *It.* kô'-ô   ko'-o
Greek *Kos,* q.v.
Coolgardie (Austral.)   kōōl-gär'-dĭ   kool-gahr'-di
Cooma (Austral.)   kōō'-mä *or* -mə   koo'-mah *or* -muh
Cooper, Jere   kŏŏp'-ər, jĕr'-ĭ   kup'-uhr, jehr'-i
(U.S. representative)
Cooper, John S.   kŏŏp'-ər   kup'-uhr
(U.S. senator)
Cootamundra (Austral.)   kōō'-tə-mŭn'-drə   koo'-tuh-muhn'-druh
Čop (Cz.)   chôp'   chop'
Hungarian *Csap,* chŏp' [chop'].
Copacabana (Braz.,   *Port.* kô-pə-kə-bä'-nə ko-puh-kuh-bah'-nuh
Bol., Col.)   *Sp.* kô-pä-kä-bä'-nä   ko-pah-kah-bah'-nah
Not *Copacabanha* or *Copacabaña.*

Copanello (It.) kô-pä-nĕl'-lô ko-pah-nel'-lo
Copenhagen (Den.) *Eng.* kō-pən-hä'-gən koh-puhn-hay'-guhn
   Copenhagen is the English variant of the Danish *Köbenhavn.* It should
   be pronounced as English with long *a* as in *Haig and Haig.* A broad
   "ah", as in *Harvard,* does not give the native pronunciation, for
   Köbenhavn is pronounced kûpn-houn' [kœpn-haun'].
copra (coconut meat) kŏp'-rə kop'-ruh
Corab (Balkan mts.) See *Korab.*
Corabia (Rum.) kô-rä'-byä ko-rah'-byah
Corbeil (Fr.) kôr-bĕ'(y) kor-beh'(y)
Córdoba (Sp.) kôr'-dô-bä kor'-do-bah
   English *Cordova,* kôr'-də-və [kor'-duh-vuh].
Coreno (It.) kô-rĕ'-nô ko-reh'-no
Corfinio (It.) kôr-fē'-nyô kor-fee'-nyo
Corfù (Gr.) *Eng.* kôr'-fyoo kor'-fyoo
   It. kôr-fōō' kor-foo'
   Greek *Kerkyra,* q.v.
Cori (It.) kô'-rē ko'-ree
Cories (Attu, lake) kôr'-ĭz kor'-iz
Corigliano (It.) kô-rē-lyä'-nô ko-ree-lyah'-no
Corinth (Gr.) *Eng.* kŏr'-ĭnth kor'-inth
   Greek *Korinthos,* kŏ'-rĭn-thôs [ko'-rin-thos]. The gulf is also called
   Lepanto, (Eng.) lĭ-păn'-tō [li-pan'-toh].
Corizza (Alb.) *It.* kô-rēt'-sä ko-reet'-sah
   Albanian *Korrçë,* q.v.
Corleone (Sicily) kôr-lĕ-ô'-nĕ kor-leh-o'-neh
Çorlu (Turk.) chôr'-lōō' chor'-lu'
Cormeilles en Parisis (Fr.) kôr-mĕ(y) zäN kor-meh(y) zahN
                 pä-rē-zē' pah-ree-zee'
Cormeilles en Vexin (Fr.) kôr-mĕ(y) zäN kor-meh(y) zahN
                 vĕk-säN' vek-saN'
Corneliussen, Elias kōr-nä'-lĭ-ōōs'n, kohr-nay'-li-us'n,
   (Nor. admiral) ĕ-lē'-äs eh-lee'-ahs
Corniche (Fr., road) kôr-nēsh' kor-neesh'
Corogna (Sicily) kô-rô'-nyä ko-ro'-nyah
Coromandel (India) kŏr'-ō-măn'-dəl kor'-oh-man'-duhl
Corrêa, Jonas (Braz. kô-rä'-ə, zhô'-nəs ko-ray'-uh, zho'-nuhs
   polit.)
Corregidor (P.I.) *Eng.* kə-rĕg'-ĭ-dōr' kuh-reg'-i-dohr'
              Sp. kô-rĕ'-hē-dôr' ko-reh'-hee-dor'
   The first is favored by men who have served in the Philippines.
Correio da Manhã kô-rä'-ōō də mə- ko-ray'-u duh muh-
   (Braz. newspaper) nyäN' nyahN'
Correnti (Sicily, cape) kôr-rĕn'-tē kor-ren'-tee

Corrientes (Arg.)	kôr-ryĕn'-tĕs	kor-ryen'-tes
Corsica (Med., isl.)	*Eng.* kôr'-sĭ-kə	kor'-si-kuh
	It. kôr'-sē-kä	kor'-see-kah

French *Corse*, kôrs' [kors'].

Corte (Corsica)	kôr'-tĕ	kor'-teh
Cortina d'Ampezzo (It.)	kôr-tē'-nä	kor-tee'-nah
	däm-pĕt'-sô	dahm-pet'-so
Coruña (Sp.)	kô-rōō'-nyä	ko-roo'-nyah
Cos (Dodec.) See *Kos.*		
Cosel (Ger. > Pol.)	kō'-zəl	koh'-zuhl

Polish *Koźle*, q.v.

Cosenza (It.)	kô-zĕn'-tsä	ko-zen'-tsah
Cosina (It., riv.)	kô'-sē-nä	ko'-see-nah
Cosne (Fr.)	kōn'	kohn'
Costa, Arthur de Souza (Braz. polit.) See *Souza Costa.*		
Costa, Fernando	kôs'-tə, fĕr-näN'-dŏŏ	kos'-tuh, fehr-
(Braz. polit.)		nahN'-du

Fernando may approach fĕr-nĕN'-dŏŏ [fehr-neN'-du].

Costa Rica (C.A.)	*Eng.* kŏs'-tə rē'-kə	kos'-tuh ree'-kuh
	Sp. kôs'-tä rē'-kä	kos'-tah ree'-kah
Costa, Santos (Port. polit.) See *Santos Costa.*		
Costa, Souza (Braz. polit.) See *Souza Costa.*		
Costa, Zenóbio da	kôs'-tə, zĕ-nôb'-yŏŏ	kos'-tuh, zeh-nob'-yu
(Braz. general)	də	duh
Coswig (Ger.)	kôs'-vĭk(h)	kos'-vik(h)
Cotabato (P.I.)	kô-tä-bä'-tô	ko-tah-bah'-to
Côte d'Azure (Fr.)	kōt dä-zür'	koht dah-zür'
Côte d'Or (Fr.)	kōt dôr'	koht dor'
Côtes du Nord (Fr.)	kōt dü nôr'	koht dü nor'
Cöthen (Ger.)	kû-tən	kœ'-tuhn
Cotignola (It.)	kô-tē-nyô'-lä	ko-tee-nyo'-lah
Cottian Alps (Fr., Switz.)	kŏt'-ĭ-ən	kot'-i-uhn
Couckelaere (Belg.)	kōō'-kə-lä'-rə	koo'-kuh-lah'-ruh
Coudert, Frederick R.	kōō-dĕr'	koo-dehr'
(U.S. representative)		
Coulanges (Fr.)	kōō-läNzh'	koo-lahNzh'
coulee	kōō'-lĭ	koo'-li

A lava flow or a canyon. French *coulée*, kōō-lĕ' [koo-leh'].

Coulee City (Wash.)	kōō'-lĭ sĭt'-ĭ	koo'-li sit'-i
Coulvain (Fr.)	kōol-văN'	kool-vaN'
coup d'état	kōō-dĕ-tä'	koo-deh-tah'
Couperin (Fr. mus.)	kōō-prăN'	koo-praN'
coupon	kōō'-pŏn *or* kyōō'-pŏn	koo'-pon *or* kyoo'-pon

The pronunciation of *coupon* is hotly debated. The *Thorndike-Century*

Dictionary (1941) lists kōō'-pŏn [koo'-pon] first and kyōō'-pŏn [kyoo'-pon] second. *Webster's* (1934, 1936) gives kōō'-pŏn and adds, "in U.S. often, incorrectly, kyōō'-pŏn." However, soap dramas usually prefer kyōō'-pŏn [kyoo'-pon], and we hear it also from some of our most eloquent and most intelligent speakers. In time it may even win first place, but at present it is probably second to kōō'-pŏn [koo'-pon].

Courantine (Br. Guiana)	kō'-rən-tĭn	koh'-ruhn-tain
Dutch *Corantijn*, kō'-rän-tĭn [koh'-rahn-tain].		
Courcel, Geoffroy de	kōor-sĕl', zhô-	koor-sel', zho-
(Fr. polit.)	frwä' də	frwah' duh
Cournarie, Pierre Charles	kōor-nä-rē', pyĕr'	koor-nah-ree', pyehr'
(Fr. general)	shärl'	shahrl'
Coursan (Fr.)	kōor-säN'	koor-sahN'
Courseulles (Fr.)	kōor-sûl'	koor-sœl'
Courseulles sur Mer (Fr.)	kōor-sûl' sür mĕr'	koor-sœl' sür mehr'
Courtalain (Fr.)	kōor-tä-lăN'	koor-tah-laN'
Courtney, Wirt	kōrt'-nĭ, wûrt'	kohrt'-ni, wuhrt'
(U.S. representative)		
Courtrai (Belg.)	*Fr.* kōor-trĕ'	koor-treh'
Flemish *Kortrijk*, q.v.		
Coutances (Fr.)	kōō-täNs'	koo-tahNs'
Couterne (Fr.)	kōō-tĕrn'	koo-tehrn'
Coutras (Fr.)	kōō-trä'	koo-trah'
Couvron (Fr.)	kōō-vrôN'	koo-vroN'
Covent Garden (London)	kŏv'-ənt	kov'-uhnt
	or kŭv'-ənt	kuv'-uhnt

The BBC recommends the first pronunciation and it is preferred by Daniel Jones, who marks the second "old-fashioned." Nevertheless the second is probably the more usual in America, as Kenyon and Knott suggest.

Coventry (Eng., U.S.)	kŭv'-ən-trĭ *or* kŏv'-	kuhv'-uhn-tri *or* kov'-

The BBC prefers the latter, but the former, with its eighteenth-century flavor, is more common in the United States.

Cowanesque (Pa.)	kou'-ə-nĕs'-kĭ	kau'-uh-nes'-ki
Cowell (Austral.)	kou'-əl	kau'-uhl
Cowles, Russell	kōlz'	kohlz'
(Am. painter)		
"Pronounce like coals—long ō." R.C.		
Cozes (Fr.)	kôz'	koz'
Cozmeni (Rum. > Rus.)	kôz-mĕn'	koz-men'
Russian *Kitsman*, q.v.		
Cracow (Pol.)	*Eng.* krăk'-ou	krak'-au
	or krăk'-ō	*or* krak'-oh
	or krā'-kō	*or* kray'-koh
	Ger. krä'-kou	krah'-kau

Polish *Kraków*, krä′-kŏŏf [krah′-kuf]. Russian *Krakov*, krä′-kŏf [krah′-kof]. German *Krakau*, krä′-kou [krah′-kau].

Crailsheim (Ger.)	krīls′-hīm	krails′-haim
Craiova (Rum.)	krä-yô′-vä	krah-yo′-vah
Cranz (Ger.)	kränts′	krahnts′
Craon (Fr.)	kräN′	krahN′
Craonne (Fr.)	krän′	krahn′
Craponne (Fr., riv.)	krä-pôn′	krah-pon′
Crau (Fr.)	krō′	kroh′
Cravens, Fadjo (U.S. representative)	krā′-vənz, făd′-jō	kray′-vuhnz, fad′-joh
Crécy en Ponthieu (Fr.)	krĕ-sē äN pôN-tyû′	kreh-see ahN poN-tyœ′
credence	krē′-dəns *or* krēd′ns	kree′-duhns *or* kreed′ns

Not krā′-dəns [kray′-duhns].

credo	*Eng.* krē′-dō	kree′-doh
	Latin krā′-dō	kray′-doh
Creech Jones, Arthur (Br. polit.)	krēch′ jōnz′	kreech′ johnz′
Creil (Fr.)	krĕ′(y)	kreh′(y)
Crema (It.)	krĕ′-mä	kreh′-mah
Cremona (It.)	krĕ-mô′-nä	kreh-mo′-nah
Crepaja (Yugosl.)	tsrĕ′-pä-yä	tsreh′-pah-yah
Crèpy en Laonnois (Fr.)	krĕ-pē′ äN lä-nwä′	kreh-pee′ ahN lah-nwah′
Crerar, Henry Duncan Graham (Can. general)	krē′-rär	kree′-rahr
Cres (It. > Yugosl., isl.) Italian *Cherso*, q.v.	*S.-C.* tsrĕs′	tsres′
Crest (Fr.)	krĕst′	krest′
Crete (Gr., isl.)	*Eng.* krēt′	kreet′

Greek *Krete*, krē′-tē [kree′-tee].

Créteil (Fr.)	krĕ-tĕ′(y)	kreh-teh′(y)
Creteville (Tun.)	krĕt-vēl′	kret-veel′
Creully (Fr.)	krû-yē′	krœ-yee′
Creuse (Fr.)	krûz′	krœz′
Creusot, le (Fr.)	krû-zō′, lə	krœ-zoh′, luh
Crèvecoeur en Auge (Fr.)	krĕv-kûr′ äN ōzh′	krev-kœr′ ahN ohzh′
Crimea (Rus.)	*Eng.* krī-mē′-ə	krai-mee′-uh

Russian *Krim*, krĭm′ [krim′].

Crionero (Alb.)	*It.* krē-ô-nĕ′-rô	kree-o-neh′-ro

Albanian *Kaninë*, q.v.

[120]

Criquetot l'Esneval (Fr.)	krēk-tō′ lĕs-nə-väl′ *or* lĕ-nə-väl′	kreek-toh′ les-nuh- vahl′ *or* leh-nuh- vahl′
Cristobal (Canal Zone) Spanish *Cristóbal*, krēs-tô′-bäl [krees-to′-bahl].	*Eng.* krĭs-tō′-bəl	kris-toh′-buhl
Cristóbal Colón (Ven.)	krēs-tô′-bäl kô-lôn′	crees-to′-bahl ko-lon′
Crítica, la (Sp. title)	krē′-tē-kä, lä	kree′-tee-kah, lah
Crkvena planina (Yugosl., mt.)	tsər′-kvĕ-nä plä′-nē′-nä	tsuhr′-kveh-nah plah′-nee′-nah
Crkvenica (Yugosl.)	tsər′-kvĕ′-nĭ-tsä	tsuhr′-kveh′-ni-tsah
Crkvice (Yugosl.)	tsər′-kvĭ-tsĕ	tsuhr′-kvi-tseh
Crljenac (Yugosl.)	tsər′-lyĕ-näts	tsuhr′-lyeh-nahts
Crljeni, Veliki (Yugosl.)	tsər′-lyĕ-nĭ, vĕ′-lĭ-kĭ	tsuhr′-lyeh-ni, veh′-li-ki
Crna (Yugosl., riv.)	tsər′-nä	tsuhr′-nah
Crna Bara (Yugosl.)	tsər′-nä bä′-rä	tsuhr′-nah bah′-rah
Crna Gora (Yugosl., mts.) Italian *Montenegro*, q.v., former kingdom.	tsər′-nä gô′-rä	tsuhr′-nah go′-rah
Crnajka (Yugosl.)	tsər′-nĭ-kä	tsuhr′-nai-kah
Crniće, Veliko *and* Malo (Yugosl.)	tsər′-nĭ-chĕ, vĕ′-lĭ-kô *and* mä′-lô	tsuhr′-ni-cheh, veh′- li-ko *and* mah′-lo
Crni Drim (Balkan riv.) Albanian *Drin i zi*, q.v.	tsər′-nĭ drēm′	tsuhr′-ni dreem,
Crni Rt (Yugosl.)	tsər′-nĭ ərt′	tsuhr′-ni uhrt′
Crni Rzav (Yugosl.)	tsər′-nĭ ər′-zäv	tsuhr′-ni uhr′-ahv
Crnoljeva planina (Yugosl., mts.)	tsər′-nô′-lyĕ-vä plä′-nē′-nä	tsuhr′-no′-lyeh-vah plah′-nee′-nah
Črnomelj (Yugosl.)	chər′-nô-mĕl′(y)	chuhr′-no-mel′(y)
Crnook (Yugosl., mt.)	tsər′-nô-ôk′	tsuhr′-no-ok′
Croat Avoid krōt [kroht]. Serb-Croat *Hrvat*, q.v.	krō′-ăt	kroh′-at
Croatia (Yugosl.) Serb-Croat *Hrvatska*, q.v.	*Eng.* krō-ā′-shə	kroh-ay′-shuh
Croce, Benedetto (It. philosopher)	krô′-chĕ, bĕ-nĕ-dĕt′- tô	kro′-cheh, beh-neh- det′-to
Crocetta (It.)	krô-chĕt′-tä	kro-chet′-tah
Crocicchie (It.)	krô-chēk′-kyĕ	kro-cheek′-kyeh
Croia (Alb.) Albanian *Krujë*, q.v.	*It.* krô′-yä	kro′-yah
Crossen (Ger. >? Pol.) Polish *Krosno*, q.v.	krôs′-ən	kros′-uhn
Croton (N.Y.) The analogy of *Groton* (q.v.) is misleading.	krōt′n	kroht′n

Crotone (It.)	krô-tô′-nĕ	kro-to′-neh
Crotoy, le (Fr.)	krô-twä′, lə	kro-twah′, luh
Crowley (Col., La.)	krou′-lĭ	krau′-li
Crowley, Leo T. (Wis. polit.)	krou′-lĭ, lē′-ō	krau′-li, lee′-oh
Crozon (Fr.)	krô-zôN′	kro-zoN′
crucial	krōō′-shəl	kroo′-shuhl

Avoid krōō′-sĭ-əl [kroo′-si-uhl]. *controversial.*

Cruikshank, (Eng. name)	krŏŏk′-shănk	kruk′-shank
Crvena Jabuka (Yugosl.)	tsər′-vĕ-nä yä′-bōō-kä	tsuhr′-veh-nah yah′-boo-kah
Crvena Reka (Yugosl.)	tsər′-vĕ-nä rĕ′-kä	tsuhr′-veh-nah reh′-kah
Crvenka (Yugosl.)	tsər′-vĕn-kä	tsuhr′-ven-kah

Cs- For Serb-Croat names beginning with *Cs-*, see *C-* and *Č-*.

Csaba (Hung.)	chŏ′-bŏ	cho′-bo
Csallóköz (Cz., isl.)	*Hung.* chŏ′-lô-kûz	cho′-lo-kœz

Slovak *Veľký Žitný Ostrov*, q.v. German *Grosse Schütt-Insel.*

Csap (Cz.) See *Čop.*

Csepel (Hung., isl.)	chĕ′-pĕl	cheh′-pel

Village on island may also be called *Ráczkeve*, q.v.

Csongrád (Hung.)	chông′-gräd	chong′-grahd
Csorna (Hung.)	chôr′-nŏ	chor′-no
Cuba	*Eng.* kyōō′-bə	kyoo′-buh
	Sp. kōō′-bä	koo′-bah

See "Note on 'b' and 'v'," page 31.

Cúcuta (Colom.)	kōō′-kōō-tä	koo′-koo-tah
Cuddalore (India)	kŭd-ə-lōr′	kuhd-uh-lohr′
Cuenca (Sp.)	kwĕng′-kä	kweng′-kah
Cuernavaca (Mex.)	kwĕr-nä-vä′-kä	kwehr-nah-vah′-kah
Cuers (Fr.)	kwĕr′	kwehr′
Cues (Ger.)	kōōs′	koos′
Cuffiano (It.)	kōōf-fyä′-nô	koof-fyah′-no
Cufra (Libya)	kōō′-frə	koo′-fruh

Arabic *Kufara.*, q.v.

Cuges les Pins (Fr.)	küzh lĕ păN′	küzh leh paN′
Cuiabá (Brazil)	kōō-yə-bä′	koo-yuh-bah′
Čukarica (Yugosl.)	chōō′-kä′-rĭ-tsä	choo′-kah′-ri-tsah

Çukat (Alb., mt.) See *Tomor.*

Culemborg (Neth.) See *Kuilenburg.*

Culzean (Scot.)	kə-lān′	kuh-layn′
Cumaná (Ven.)	kōō-mä-nä′	koo-mah-nah′
Cum Burnu (Dodec., Rh., point)	*Turk.* kŏŏm bŏŏr-nŏŏ′	kum bur-nu′

Greek *Zonari*, zô-nä′-rē [zo-nah′-ree]. Italian *Punta Molino*, pōōn′-tä mô-lē′-nô [poon′-tah mo-lee′-no], and *Capo della Sabbia*, kä′-pô dĕl′-lä säb′-byä [kah′-po del′-lah sahb′-byah].

Cumhuriyet (Turkish newspaper)	jōŏm′-hŏŏ-rĭ-yĕt′	jum′-hu-ri-yet′
Cuneo (It.)	kōō′-nĕ-ô	koo′-neh-o

French *Coni*, kô-nē′ [ko-nee′].

Cunnamulla (Austral.)	kŭn′-ə-mŭl′-ə	kuhn′-uh-muhl′-uh
Čupino Brdo (Yugosl., mts.)	chōō′-pĭ-nô bər′-dô	choo′-pi-no buhr′-do
Ćuprija (Yugosl.)	chōō′-prĭ-yä	choo′-pri-yah
Curaçao (Du. W.I.)	*Eng.* kyŏŏr′-ə-sō′ *for.* kōō-rä-sou′	kyur′-uh-soh′ koo-rah-sau′
curator	kyŏŏ-rā′-tər	kyu-ray′-tuhr

In the sense of legal guardian often pronounced kyŏŏr′-ə-tər [kyur′-uh-tuhr].

Curie, Ève (author)	kü-rē′, ĕv′ (*Eng.* ēv′)	kü-ree′, ev′ (*Eng.*eev′)
Curie Joliot, Irène (Fr. scientist)	kü-rē zhô-lyō′, ē-rĕn′	kü-ree zho-lyoh′, ee-ren′
Curie, Marja Skłodowska (Pol. scientist)	kü-rē′ (*Eng.* kyōō-rē′), mär′-yä sklŏ-dôf′-skä	kü-ree′ (*Eng.* kyoo-ree′), mahr′-yah sklo-dof′-skah
Curitiba (Brazil)	kōō-rē-tē′-bə	koo-ree-tee′-buh
curmudgeon	kər-mŭj′-ən	kuhr-muj′-uhn
Currimao (P.I.)	kōōr-rē-mou′	koor-ree-mau′
Curtici (Rum.)	kŏŏr-tēch′	kur-teech′
Curúan (P.I.)	kōō-rōō′-än	koo-roo′-ahn
Čurug (Yugosl.)	chōō′-rōōg	choo′-roog
Curzola (Yugosl.)	*It.* kōōr-tsô′-lä	koor-tso′-lah

Serb-Croat *Korčula*, q.v.

Cutch (India)	kŭch′	kuhch′

Also spelled *Kutch*.

Cuttack (India)	kŭ-tăk′	kuh-tak′
Cuxhaven (Ger.)	kŏŏks′-hä-fən	kuks′-hah-fuhn
Cuyahoga (Ohio)	kī-hŏg′-ə *or* kī-ə-hō′-gə	kai-hog′-uh kai-uh-hoh′-guh

There are almost as many pronunciations of *Cuyahoga* as of *Los Angeles*. Citizens of Cleveland and the county may say, and fight for, kī′-ə-hŏg′-ə [kai′-uh-hog′-uh] or kə-hŏg′-ə [kuh-hog′-uh] or any of the variants with -hôg′-ə [-hawg′-uh] and -hō′-gə [hoh′-guh]. Dr. John S. Kenyon of Hiram College and *Webster's* place kī-hŏg′-ə [kai-hog′-uh] first and qualify kī′-ə-hō′-gə [kai-uh-hoh′-guh] as "old-fashioned" (Kenyon) or "rarely" (Webster's). However, a Cleveland correspondent writes: "There are many natives and long-time residents of the county who do not consider themselves old-fashioned, who use only the pronunciation kĭ'-ə-hō'-gə [kai'-uh-hoh'-guh].''

Cuyapó (P.I.)	kōō-yä-pô'	koo-yah-po'
Cuyuna (Minn., range)	kĭ-yōō'-nə	kai-yoo'-nuh
Cuzco (Peru)	koos'-kô	koos'-ko
Cuzgan (Rum.)	kŏŏz-gän'	kuz-gahn'
Cwmbwrla (Wales)	kŏŏm-bŏŏr'-lä	kum-bur'-lah
Cyclades (Gr., isls.)	*Eng.* sĭk'-lə-dēz	sik'-luh-deez
	Gr. kē-klä'-dĕs	kee-klah'-des
Cyclops (NEI, mts.)	*Eng.* sī'-klŏps	sai'-klops

Cyllene (Gr., mt.) See *Kyllene.*

Cyrankiewicz, Józef	tsĭ-rän-kyĕ'-vĭch,	tsi-rahn-kyeh'-vich,
(Pol. polit.)	yŏŏ'-zĕf	yu'-zef
Cyrenaica (Libya)	sĭ-rə-nä'-ĭ-kə	si-ruh-nay'-i-kuh
	or sī'-rə-nä'-ĭ-kə	sai'-ruh-nay'-i-kuh

Not sĭ-rə-nī'-ĭ-kə [si-ruh-nai'-i-kuh]. Italian *Cirenaica,* chē-rĕ-nä'-ē-kä [chee-reh-nah'-ee- kah].

Cyrene (Libya)	*Eng.* sī-rē'-nē	sai-ree'-nee

Italian *Cirene,* chē-rĕ'-nĕ [chee-reh'-neh].

Cythera (Gr., isl.) See *Kythera.*

Czarna (Pol., riv.)	chär'-nä	chahr'-nah

Russian *Chernaya,* chôr'-nä-yä [chor'-nah-yah].

Czech	*Eng.* chĕk'	chek'

Czech is the Polish spelling for Czechish *Čech,* chĕk(h)' [chek(h)'], "a Bohemian." The Bohemian language is *Český,* chĕs'-kē [ches'-kee].

Czechoslovak	chĕk'-ō-slō'-văk	chek'-oh-sloh'-vak
Czechoslovakia	chĕk'-ō-slō-văk'-yə	chek'-oh-sloh-vak'-yuh

Czech *Ceskoslovensko,* chĕs'-kô-slô'-vĕn-sko [ches'-ko-slo'-ven-sko].

Czeladź (Pol.)	chĕ'-läj	cheh'-lahj

German *Tscheliadz,* chĕl'-yädz [chel'-yahdz]. Russian spelling *Chelyadz.*

Czeremosz (Pol., Rum., riv.)	chĕ-rĕ'-môsh	cheh-reh'-mosh

Rumanian *Ceremuşul,* chĕ-rĕ'-mŏŏ-shŏŏl [cheh-reh'-mu-shul].

Czernowitz (Rum. >Rus.)	*Pol.* chĕr'-nô-vĭts	chehr'-no-vits

Russian *Chernovitsy,* q.v.

Czersk (Pol.)	chĕrsk'	chehrsk'
Częstochowa (Pol.)	chăN-stô-hô'-vä	chaN-sto-ho'-vah

Russian *Chenstokhov,* chĕn-stô'-hŏf [chen-sto'-hof]. German *Tschenstochau,* chĕn-shtō'-k(h)ou [chen-shtoh'-k(h)au].

Czortków (Pol. >Rus.)	chôrt'-kŏŏf	chort'-kuf

Russian *Chortkov,* chôrt'-kŏf [chort'-kof.]

Đ. See also *Dj-*, an alternative spelling in Yugoslav place names.

| daal | däl′ | dahl′ |

An element, meaning *valley*, in Dutch place names.

| Dąb (Ger. >Pol.) | dôNf′ | doNf′ |

German *Altdamm*, q.v.

Daba, el (Libya)	däb′-ä, ĕd	dahb′-ah, ed
Dabir Soula (Tun.)	dă′-bēr soō′-lä	da′-beer soo′-lah
Dąbrowa Górnicza (Pol.)	dôN-brô′-vä	doN-bro′-vah
	go͞or-nē′-chä	gur-nee′-chah

Russian *Dombrova*, dŏm-brô′-vä [dom-bro′-vah].

| Dąbrowica (Pol.) | dôN-brô-vē′-tsä | doN-bro-vee′-tsah |

Russian *Dombrovitsa*, dŏm-brô′-vĭ-tsä [dom-bro′-vi-tsah].

Dacar (Fr. W. Afr.)	dä′-kär′	dah′-kahr′
Dacca (India)	dăk′-ə	dak′-uh
Dachau (Ger.)	dä′-k(h)ou	dah′-k(h)au
dacoit	də-koit′	duh-koit′

An Indian or Burman gangster; *dacoity*, də-koit′-ĭ [duh-koit′-i], his profession.

Dáet (P.I.)	dä′-ĕt	dah′-et
Dafne (Gr.)	*Eng.* dăf′-nĭ	daf′-ni
	Gr. däf′-nē	dahf′-nee
Dafni (Gr.)	däf-nē′	dahf-nee′
Daftari, Akbar	däf-tə-rē′, ăk′-bər *or*	dahf-tuh-ree′,
(Iran. polit.)	-bär	ak′-buhr *or* -bahr
Dagami (P.I.)	dä-gä′-mē	dah-gah′-mee
Dage (Est., isl.)	*Rus.* dä′-gĕ	dah′-geh
Estonian *Hiiumaa*, q.v. German *Dagö*, q.v.		
Dagens Nyheter	dä′-yəns nü′-hĕ-tər	dah′-yuhns nü′-heh-
(Sw. paper)		tuhr
Daghestan (Rus.)	dä-gĕ-stän′	dah-geh-stahn′
Dagö *or* Dagoe (Est., isl.)	*Ger.* dä′-gû	dah′-gœ
Estonian *Hiiumaa*, q.v. Russian *Dage*, q.v.		
Dague, Paul B.	dāg′	dayg′
(U. S. representative)		
Dagupan (P.I.)	dä-go͞o′-pän	dah-goo′-pahn

Dagupan river is also called *Binmaley*, q.v.

Dahlem (Ger.)	dä′-ləm	dah′-luhm
dahlia	dăl′-yə *or* däl′-yə	dal′-yuh *or* dahl′-yuh
	or däl′-yə	*or* dayl′-yuh
Dahomey (Afr., Fr. col.)	*Eng.* də-hō′-mĭ	duh-hoh′-mi
	Fr. dä-ô-mĕ′	dah-o-meh′
Dail Eireann (Ir.)	dôl′ ĕr′-ən *or* ā′-rôn	dol′ ehr′-uhn *or* ay′-
		ron

Daiquirí (Cuba)   dī-kē-rē′   dai-kee-ree′
    As the name of a cocktail, it is usually accented on the first syllable.
Dairen (Manchu.)   dī-rĕn   dai-ren
    Also called *Ta-lien(-wan)*, q.v. Russian *Dalny*, däl′(y)-nĭ [dahl′(y)-ni].
dais   dā′-ĭs *or* dās′   day′-is *or* days′
    Plural daises, dā′-ĭ-sĭz [day′-i-siz] or dā′-sĭz [day′-siz].
Dajt (Alb., mt.)   dīt′   dait′
    Also called *Mal i Dajtit.*
Đak (Yugosl., mt.)   dyäk′   dyahk′
Dakar (Fr. W. Afr.)   dä′-kär′   dah′-kahr′
Đakovica (Yugosl.)   dyä′-kô-vĭ-tsä   dyah′-ko-vi-tsah
dal *or* dalen   däl′ *or* dä′-lən   dahl′ *or* dah′-luhn
    An element, meaning *valley*, in Norwegian place names.
Daladier, Édouard   *Fr.* dä-lä-dyĕ′,   dah-lah-dyeh′,
    (Fr. polit.)   ĕ-dwär′   eh-dwahr′
                 Eng. də-lăd′-yā   duh-lad′-yay
Dalagican (P.I.   dä-lä-hē′-kän   dah-lah-hee′-kahn
Dalaguete (P.I.)   dä-lä-gĕ′-tĕ   dah-lah-geh′-teh
Dalat (Indo-Ch.)   dä-lät′   dah-laht′
Dale (Nor.)   dä′-lə   dah′-luh
Dalen (Neth.)   dä′-lən   dah′-luhn
Dalen (Nor.)   dä′-lən   dah′-luhn
D'Alesandro, Thomas, Jr.   dăl′-ĭ-săn′-drō   dal′-i-san′-droh
    (U.S. representative)
Dalfsen (Neth.)   dälf′-sən   dahlf′-suhn
Dalhousie (Can., N.B.)   dăl-hou′-zĭ   dal-hau′-zi
Dalhousie, Port (Can.,   dăl-hōō′-zĭ   dal-hoo′-zi
    Ont.)
Đalica (Alb., mt.)   See *Gjalicĕ.*
Dalles, the (Ore.)   dălz′   dalz′
Dalmatia (Yugosl.)   *Eng.* dăl-mā′-shə   dal-may′-shuh
    Serb-Croat *Dalmacija*, däl′-mä′-tsĭ-yä [dahl′-mah′-tsi-yah].
Dalny (Manchu.)   See *Dairen.*
Daluege, Kurt (Ger. polit.) dä-lü′-gə, kŏŏrt′   dah-lü′-guh, kurt′
Daman *or* Damão (Port.   dä′-män′   dah′-mahn′
    India)   *or* dä-mouN′   dah-mauN′
Damanhur (Egypt)   dä-män-hŏŏr′   dah-mahn-hur′
Damaraland (S.W. Afr.)   dăm′-ə-rə-lănd′   dam′-uh-ruh-land′
Damascus (Syria)   də-măs′-kəs   duh-mas′-kuhs
    French *Damas*, dä-mäs′[dah-mahs′]. Arabic *Esh Sham*, ĕsh shäm′
    [esh shahm′].
Damaskenos (Gr. archbishop) dä-mä-skē-nôs′   dah-mah-skee-nos′
Damba Gavan (Latvia)   *Rus.* däm′-bä   dahm′-bah
                   gä′-vän(y)   gah′-vahn(y)

Dâmboviţa (Rum., riv.)	dûm'-bô-vē-tsä	duhm'-bo-vee-tsah
Damghan (Iran)	däm-gän'	dahm-gahn'
Damietta (Egypt)	dăm-ĭ-ĕt'-ə	dam-i-et'-uh
Also called *Dumyat*, q.v.		
Da Motta e Silva,	də mô'-tĭ sēl'-və,	duh mo'-ti seel'-vuh,
Álvaro Alberto	äl'-və-rōō	ahl'-vuh-ru
(Braz. diplomat)	äl-bĕr'-tōō	ahl-behr'-tu
Dampálit (P.I.) See *Puló Calamcá*.		
Dampier (Austral.)	dăm'-pĭr	dam'-pihr
Damulaan (P.I.)	dä-mōō-lä'-än	dah-moo-lah'-ahn
Danaher, John A.	dăn'-ə-hûr	dan'-uh-huhr
(U.S. senator)		
Danbi (Burma)	dən-bē'	duhn-bee'
Dandini (It.)	dän-dē'-nē	dahn-dee'-nee
Dangé (Fr.)	däN-zhĕ'	dahN-zheh'
Dangila (Ethiopia)	dän'-gû-lä'	dahn'-guh-lah'
Danilovgrad (Yugosl.)	dä'-nē'-lôf-gräd	dah'-nee'-lof-grahd
Dankov (Rus.)	dän'-kôf	dahn'-kof
Dannemarie (Fr.)	dän-mä-rē'	dahn-mah-ree'
Dannemora (N. Y.)	dăn'-ĭ-mô'-rə	dan'-i-mo'-ruh
D'Annunzio, Gabriele	dän-nōōn'-tsyô,	dahn-noon'-tsyo,
(It. poet)	gä-brē-ĕ'-lĕ	gah-bree-eh'-leh
Dansalan (P.I.)	dän-sä'-län	dahn-sah'-lahn
Dantumadeel (Neth.)	dän'-tü-mä-dāl'	dahn'-tü-mah-dayl'
Danube (Europ. riv.)	*Eng.* dăn'-yōōb	dan'-yoob
	Fr. dä-nüb'	dah-nüb'

The variations of the name of this great river are indicative of the problem of finding a "correct" pronunciation of any ancient landmark in Central Europe. We are fortunate when there is an established English form, in this instance as in many others derived from the French. Bulgarian *Dunav*, dōō'-näf [du'-nahf]. Czech and Polish *Dunaj*, dōō'-nĭ [du'-nai]. Italian *Danubio*, dä-nōō'-byô [dah-noo'-byo]. German *Donau*, dō'-nou [doh'-nau]. Greek *Dounabis*, dōō'-nä-vēs [doo'-nah-vees]. Hungarian *Duna*, dōō'-nǒ [du'-no]. Rumanian *Dunărea*, dōō'-nə-ryä [du'-nuh-ryah]. Russian *Dunai*, dōō-nĭ' [doo-nai'] Serb-Croat *Dunav*, dōō'-näv [doo'-nahv.] And the vowels here marked are, of course, polite fictions. There are two classical forms: Greek *Istros*, ē'-strôs [ee'-stros]; Latin *Danuvius*, dä-nōō'-wē-ōōs [dah-noo'-wee-oos] and *Ister* or *Hister*, (h)ē'-stĕr [(h)ee'-stehr].

Danzé (Fr.)	däN-zĕ'	dahN-zeh'
Danzig (Free City > Pol.)	*Eng.* dăn'-sĭg	dan'-sig
	Ger. dän'-tsĭk(h)	dahn'-tsik(h)
Polish *Gdańsk*, gdän(y)sk' [gdahn(y)sk'].		
Dao (P.I.)	dou'	dau'

| Daon (Fr.) | däN′ | dahN′ |
| Dapitan (P.I.) | dä-pē′-tän | dah-pee′-tahn |

Dar. For Arabic names with *Dar*, see also *Deir*.

Daram (P.I.)	dä-räm′	dah-rahm′
Đaravica (Yugosl., mt.)	dyä′-rä′-vĭ-tsä	dyah′-rah′-vi-tsah
Darband (Iran)	där-bănd′	dahr-band′
Darbėnai (Lith.)	där-bā′-nĭ	dahr-bay′-nai
Darda (Yugosl.)	där′-dä	dahr′-dah
Dardanelles (Turk., strait)	*Eng.* där′-də-nĕlz′	dahr′-duh-nelz′

Turkish *Çanakkale Boğazı*, chä-näk′-kä-lĕ′ bô-ä′-zĭ [chah-nahk′-kah-leh′ bo-ah′-zi]. Also called the *Hellespont*, (Eng.) hĕl′-əs-pŏnt [hel′-uhs-pont].

Dardha (Alb.)   See *Dardhë*.

Dardhë (Alb.)	där′-*th*ə	dahr′-*th*uh
Dar es Salaam	där′ ĕs sə-läm′	dahr′ es suh-lahm′
(Tanganyika)		
D'Argenlieu, Georges	där-zhän-lyû′,	dahr-zhahn-lyœ′,
Thierry (Fr. admiral)	zhôrzh′ tyĕ-rē′	zhorzh′ tyeh-ree′
Darial (Rus., pass)	där-yäl′	dahr-yahl′
Darien	*Eng.* dĕr′-ĭ-ĕn′	dehr′-i-ehn′
	Sp. dä-ryĕn′	dah-ryehn′
Darjeeling (India)	där-jē′-lĭng	dahr-jee′-ling
Darkehmen (Ger. > Rus.)	där-kā′-mən	dahr-kay′-muhn
Russian *Ozersk*, ô-zĕrsk′ [o-zehrsk′].		
Darlan, Jean François	där-läN′, zhäN′	dahr-lahN′, zhahN′
(Fr. admiral)	fräN-swä′	frahN-swah′
Darmand, Joseph	där-mäN′	dahr-mahN′
(Fr. polit.)		
Darmasatiawan	där-mä-sä′-chä-wän′	dahr-mah-sah′-
(Indo. polit.)		chah-wahn′
Darmawan (Indo. polit.)	där-mä-wän′	dahr-mah-wahn′
Darmstadt (Ger.)	*Eng.* därm′-stăt	dahrm′-stat
	Ger. därm′-shtät	dahrm′-shtaht
Darnétal (Fr.)	där-nĕ-täl′	dahr-neh-tahl′
Darrell's Island (Ber-	dăr′-əlz	dehr′-uhlz
muda)		
Daru (New Guinea)	dä′-rōō	dah′-roo
Daruvar (Yugosl.)	dä′-rōō-vär	dah′-roo-vahr
Daryal (Rus.)	där-yäl′	dahr-yahl′
Also spelled *Darial*, q.v.		
dasht	däsht′	dahsht′

An element, meaning *desert*, in Persian place names.

| Dasht-i-Kavir (Iran) | däsht′-ē-kə-vēr′ | dahsht′-ee-kuh-veer′ |
| Dasht-i-Lut (Iran) | däsht′-ē-lōōt′ | dahsht′-ee-loot′ |

Dasmariñas (P.I.)   däs-mä-rē′-nyäs   dahs-mah-ree′-nyahs
Dasol (P.I.)   dä-sôl′   dah-sol′
data   dā′-tə or dăt′-ə   day′-tuh or dat′-uh
   See *status*.
Datteln (Ger.)   dät′-əln   daht′-uhln
Daugava (Latvia,   dou′-gä-vä   dau′-gah-vah
   Rus., riv.)
   Russian *Dvina*, q.v. German *Düna*, q.v.
Daugavgrīva (Latvia)   dou′-gäf-grē-vä   dau′-gahf-gree-vah
   German *Dünamünde*, q.v. Russian *Ust Dvinsk*, q.v.
Daugavpils (Latvia)   dou′-gäf-pēls   dau′-gahf-peels
   Russian *Dvinsk*, q.v. German *Dünaburg*, q.v.
Daugherty, H. M.   dô′-ər-tĭ   daw′-uhr-ti
   (Am. polit.)
Daun (Ger.)   doun′   daun′
Dauphin, Port (Madag.)   *Eng.* dô′-fĭn   do′-fin
                           Fr. dō-făN′   doh-faN′
Dauphiné (Fr.)   dō-fē-ně′   doh-fee-neh′
Davao (P.I.)   *Eng.* dä-vou′   dah-vau′
                           native dä′-vou   dah′-vau
Daventry (Eng.)   dăv′-ən-trĭ   dav′-uhn-tri
                           or dān′-trĭ   dayn′-tri
David Gorodok   dä-vēd′   dah-veed′
   (Pol. >Rus.)   gŏ-rŏ-dôk′   go-ro-dok′
   Polish *Dawidgródek*, q.v.
Davies, Arthur B.   dā′-vēz or dā′-vĭs   day′-veez or day′-vis
   (Am. painter)
Dávila (Sp.)   dä′-vē-lä   dah′-vee-lah
Davos Platz (Switz.)   dä-vōs′ pläts′   dah-vohs′ plahts′
Dawidgródek (Pol. >Rus.) dä-vĭd-grŏŏ′-děk   dah-vid-gru′-dek
   Russian *David Gorodok*, dä-vēd′ gŏ-rŏ-dôk′ [dah-veed′ go-ro-dok′].
Dax (Fr.)   däks′   dahks′
Dáyap (P.I.)   dä′-yäp   dah′-yahp
Daye (Fr.) See *St. Jean de Daye*.
Deakin, Arthur   dē′-kĭn   dee′-kin
   (Br. polit.)
Déat, Marcel (Fr. polit.) dĕ-ä′, mär-sĕl′   deh-ah′, mahr-sel′
Deauville (Fr.)   *Eng.* dō′-vĭl   doh′-vil
                           Fr. dō-vēl′   doh-veel′
debacle   dĕ-bäk′-əl   deh-bahk′-uhl
                           or dĭ-băk′-əl   di-bak′-uhl
   French *débâcle*, dĕ-bäk′l [deh-bahk′l].
Debaltsevo (Rus.)   dĕ-bäl′(y)-tsĕ-vŏ   deh-bahl′(y)-tseh-vo

Debar (Yugosl.)	dĕ′-bär	deh′-bahr
	Albanian *Dibër*, q.v.	
Debeljača (Yugosl.)	dĕ′-bĕ′-lyä-chä	deh′-beh′-lyah-chah
Dębica (Pol.)	dăN-bē′-tsä	daN-bee′-tsah
De Bilt (Neth.)	də bĭlt′	duh bilt′
Dęblin (Pol.)	dăN′-blĭn	daN′-blin

Russian *Ivangorod*, ē-vän′-gŏ-rŏt [ee-vahn′-go-rot].

Debrc (Yugosl.)	dĕ′-bərts	deh′-buhrts
Debrecen (Hung.)	dĕ′-brĕ-tsĕn	deh′-breh-tsen
Debruyne, Edmond	də-brûĭn′	duh-brœin′
(Belg. polit.)		
Debussy (Fr. composer)	də-bü-sē′	duh-bü-see′

Dictionaries do not list the usual American pronunciation, də-byoo′-sē [duh-byoo′-see], although the French pronunciation (above) is very difficult, almost impossible, for us to say in the cadence of an American sentence. Most announcers compromise between the two in order to avoid fluffs. The first syllable should contain schwa (ə), not ā.

debut *or* début	*Eng.* dā′-byoo *or* dĕ-byoo′	day′-byoo *or* deh-byoo′
	Fr. dĕ-bü′	deh-bü′
Dečani (Yugosl.)	dĕ′-chä-nĭ	deh′-chah-ni
Dečanska Bistrica	dĕ′-chän-skä	deh′-chahn-skah
(Yugosl.)	bē′-strĭ-tsä	bee′-stri-tsah
Decatur (Ala., Ga.)	də-kāt′r	duh-kayt′r
De Chevigné, Pierre	də shə-vē-nyĕ′,	duh shuh-vee-nyeh′,
(Fr. officer)	pyĕr′	pyehr′
Decies (Eng. baron)	dē′-shēz	dee′-sheez
Decimomannu (Sard.)	dĕ′-chē-mô-mä′-noo	deh′-chee-mo-mah′-noo
Děčín (Cz.)	dyĕ′-chēn	dyeh′-cheen
	German *Tetschen*, q.v.	
Decoux, J. (Fr. admiral)	də-koo′	duh-koo′
Dede Agach (Gr.)	See *Alexandroupolis.*	
Dedeli (Yugosl.)	dĕ′-dĕ-lĭ	deh′-deh-li
De Gasperi, Alcide	dĕ gä′-spĕ-rē,	deh gah′-speh-ree,
(It. polit.)	äl-chē′-dĕ	ahl-chee′-deh
de Gaulle, Charles André	də gōl′, shärl′	duh gohl′, shahrl′
Joseph Marie	äN-drĕ′ zhō-zĕf′	ahN-dreh′ zhoh-
(Fr. polit.)	mä-rē′	zef′ mah-ree′
De Geer, Dirk Jan	də k(h)är′, dĭrk′	duh k(h)ayr′, dihrk′
(Du. polit.)	yän′	yahn′
De Grelle, Léon	də grĕl′, lĕ-ôN′	duh grel′, leh-oN′
(Belg. polit.)		
De Groot (Neth.)	də k(h)rōt′	duh k(h)roht′
Dehibat, el (Tun.)	dĕ-hĭ-băt′, ĕd	deh-hi-bat′, ed

Deil (Neth.)	dĭl'	dail'
Deir el Munassib (Egypt)	dār' ĕl mōō-năs'-sĭb	dayr' el moo-nas'-sib
Deir el Rahil (Egypt)	dār' ĕl ră'-hĭl	dayr' el ra'-hil
Also spelled *Dar* and *Ragil*.		
Dej (Rum.)	dĕzh'	dezh'
Hungarian *Dés*, dāsh' [daysh'].		
De Kruif, Paul	də krûîf' *or* də krīf'	duh krœif'
(Am. author)		duh kraif'
Delden (Neth.)	dĕl'-dən	del'-duhn
De Lemmer (Neth.)	də lĕm'-ər	duh lem'-uhr
Also called *Lemmer*, q.v.		
Delft (Neth.)	dĕlft'	delft'
Delfzijl (Neth.)	dĕlf-zīl'	delf-zail'
Delhi (India)	dĕl'-ĭ	del'-i

Our correspondents agree upon this pronunciation of the Indian city, *New Delhi*. In India, the English approximation "Dilly" is frequently heard. Of course the American place name is dĕl'-hĭ [del'-hai].

De Lier (Neth.)	də lēr'	duh leer'
Deligrad (Yugosl.)	dĕ'-lĭ-gräd	deh'-li-grahd
Deli Jovan (Yugosl., mts.)	dĕ'-lĭ yô'-vän	deh'-li yo'-vahn
Dellys (Alg.)	dĕ-lēs'	deh-lees'
Delmenhorst (Ger.)	dĕl'-mən-hôrst'	del'-muhn-horst'
Delnice (Yugosl.)	dĕl'-nĭ-tsĕ	del'-ni-tseh
Delphi (Gr.)	*Eng.* dĕl'-fī	del'-fai
Greek *Delphoi*, dĕl-fē' [del-fee'].		
Del Rio (Tex.)	dĕl rē'-ō	del ree'-oh
Delvina (Alb.) See *Delvinë*.		
Delvinë (Alb.)	dĕl-vē'-nə	del-vee'-nuh
Italian *Delvino*.		
Demarara (Br. Guiana)	dĕm'-ə-rär'-ə	dem'-uh-rehr'-uh
demagogic	dĕm-ə-gä'-jĭk	dehm-uh-gah'-jik
Demavend (Iran, mt.)	dĕ-mə-vĕnd'	deh-muh-vend'
Demestichas, Ioannis (Gr. polit.)	dĕ-mĕ'-stē-häs, yô-ä'-nēs	deh-meh'-stee-hahs, yo-ah'-nees
Demetrakakis, Stylianos (Gr. polit.)	dē-mē-trä-kä'-kēs, stē-lyä-nôs'	dee-mee-trah-kah'-kees, stee-lyah-nos'
Demir Hissar (Gr.)	dĕ-mēr' hē-sär'	deh-meer' hee-sahr'
The official name is *Siderokastron*, q.v.		
Demir Kapija (Yugosl.)	dĕ'-mĭr kä'-pĭ-yä	deh'-mihr kah'-pi-yah
Demotika (Gr.)	dē-mô-tē-kä'	dee-mo-tee-kah'
Officially called *Didymoteikhon*, q.v.		
Demta (NEI, New Guinea)	dĕm'-tä	dem'-tah
De Murville, Maurice Couve (Fr. diplomat)	də mür-vēl', mô-rēs' kōōv'	duh mür-veel', mo-rees' koov'

Demyansk (Rus.)   dĕm-yänsk′   dem-yahnsk′

Denain (Fr.)   də-năN′   duh-naN′

Denali (Alaska)   dĭ-nä′-lĭ *or* dĭ′-nä-lĭ   di-nah′-li *or* di′-nah-li

Den Bos (Neth.)   dən bôs′   duhn bos′

The full name is *'s Hertogenbosch*, q.v. French *Bois le Duc*, bwä lə dük′ [bwah luh dük′].

Den Briel (Neth.)   dən brēl′   duhn breel′

Also called *Brielle*, q.v.

Den Burg (Neth.)   dən bûrk(h)′   duhn bœrk(h)′

Dendrames, Vasili *or*   dĕn-drä-mēs′,   den-drah-mees′,

  Basileios   vä-sē′-lē *or*   vah-see′-lee *or*

  (Gr. diplomat)   vä-sē′-lē-ôs   vah-see′-lee-os

Denekamp (Neth.)   dā′-nə-kämp   day′-nuh-kahmp

Den Haag (Neth.)   dən häk(h)′   duhn hahk(h)′

English *The Hague*, q.v. The full name is *'s Gravenhage*, q.v.

Den Helder (Neth.)   dən hĕl′-dĕr   duhn hel′-dehr

Denia (Sp.)   dĕ′-nyä   deh′-nyah

De Nicola, Enrico   dĕ nē-kô′-lä,   deh nee-ko′-lä,

  (It. polit.)   ĕn-rē′-kô   ĕn-ree′-ko

De Noue, Jehan (Fr.   də nōō′, zhäN′   duh noo′, zhahN′

  diplomat)

Đenovići (Yugosl.)   dyĕ′-nô′-vĭ-chĭ   dyeh′-no′-vi-chi

Denpasar (NEI, Bali)   dĕn-pä′-sär   den-pah′-sahr

D'Entrecasteaux (Oc.)   däN-trə-käs-tō′   dahN-truh-kahs-toh′

Depok (Java)   dĕ-pôk′   de-pok′

deportation   dē′-pōr-tā′-shən   dee′-pohr-tay′-shuhn

Not dĕp′-ôr-tā′-shən [dep′-or-tay′-shuhn].

Depósito (P.I.)   dĕ-pô′-sē-tô   deh-po′-see-to

depot   dĕp′-ō *or* dē′-pō   dep′-oh *or* dee′-poh

The first, in various senses, is military usage. The second, meaning *railroad station*, was once common in civilian usage.

depravity   dĭ-prăv′-ĭ-tĭ   di-prav′-i-ti

The second syllable should not have the ā of *deprave*.

Dera Ismail Khan (India)   dā′-rä ĭs-mä-ēl′ kän′   day′-rah is-mah-eel′ kahn′

Derbent (Rus.)   dĕr-bĕnt′   dehr-bent′

Derby (horse race)   *Am.* dûr′-bĭ   duhr′-bi

         Eng. där′-bĭ   dahr′-bi

Derby (Conn., Vt., and   dûr′-bĭ   duhr′-bi

  also Austral.)

Derbyshire (Eng.)   där′-bĭ-shĭr *or* dûr′-   dahr′-bi-shihr *or* duhr′-

Dereva (Rus.)   dĕ′-rĕ-vä   deh′-reh-vah

Derevyanko, Kuzma   dĕ-rĕ-vyän′-kô   deh-reh-vyahn′-ko,
  (Rus. diplomat)   kŏŏz-mä′   kuz-mah′
Derg (Libya)   dĕrg′   dehrg′
De Ribes, Champetier (Fr. polit.) See *Champetier de Ribes.*
derision   dĭ-rĭzh′-ən   di-rizh′-uhn
derisive, derisory   dĭ-rī′-sĭv, -sə-rĭ   di-rai′-siv, -suh-ri
  Among lexicographers only Daniel Jones authorizes also the pro-
  nunciation dĭ-rĭz′-ĭv [di-riz′-iv].
Đerlap (Yugosl., Rum., gorge) See *Iron Gates.*
Derłów (Ger. >Pol.)   dĕr′-lŏŏf   dehr′-luf
  German *Ruegenwalde,* q.v.
Derna (Libya)   dĕr′-nä   dehr′-nah
Derrichsweiler (Ger.)   dĕr′-ĭk(h)s-vī′-lər   dehr′-ik(h)s-vai′-
                                   luhr
Der Tagesspiegel (Berlin   dĕr tä′-gəs-shpē′-gəl   dehr tah′-guhs-
  newspaper)   shpee′-guhl
Derval (Fr.)   dĕr-väl′   dehr-vahl′
Derventa (Yugosl.)   dĕr′-vĕn-tä   dehr′-ven-tah
Dés (Rum.) See *Dej.*
De Saint Hardouin,   də săN tär-dwăN′,   duh saN tahr-dwaN′,
  Jacques Tarbe   zhäk′ tärb′   zhahk′ tahrb′
  (Fr. diplomat)
De Sangroniz, José (Sp. polit.) See *Sangroniz, José de.*
Dešat (Yugosl., mts.)   dĕ′-shät   deh′-shaht
Desmael, Albert   dĕ-smäl′   deh-smahl′
  (Belg. polit.)
Des Moines (Iowa)   dĭ moin′   di moin′
Des Plaines (Ill.)   dĕs plānz′   des playnz′
Despoto planina (Balkan mts.) See *Rhodope.*
Despotovac (Yugosl.)   dĕ′-spô′-tô-väts   deh′-spo′-to-vahts
Dessau (Ger.)   dĕs′-ou   des′-au
Dessie (Ethiopia)   dĕ′-syĕ   deh′-syeh
Desterro (Brazil)   dĕs-tĕ′-rŏŏ   des-teh′-ru
  Officially called *Florianópolis,* q.v.
De Tassigny,   də tä-sē-nyē′,   duh tah-see-nyee′,
  Jean de Lattre   zhäN′ də lät′r   zhahN′ duh
  (Fr. general)   laht′r
Detinja (Yugosl., riv.)   dĕ′-tĭ-nyä   deh′-ti-nyah
detonator   dĕt′-ō-nā′-tər   det′-oh-nay′-tuhr
  Possible but uncommon is dē′-tō-nā′-tər [dee′-toh-nay′-tuhr].
Detskoe Selo (Rus.)   dĕt′-skŏ-yĕ sĕ-lô′   det′-sko-yeh seh-lo′
Deurne (Belg., Neth.)   dûr′-nə   dœr′-nuh
Deutekom (Neth.)   dŭ′-tə-kôm   dœ′-tuh-kom
  Also called *Doetinchem,* dōō′-tĭn-k(h)əm [doo′-tin-k(h)uhm].

Deutsche Allgemeine Zeitung (Ger. paper)	doi'-chə äl'-gə-mĭ'-nə tsĭ'-tŏŏng	doi'-chuh ahl'-guh-mai'-nuh tsai'-tung

Deutsch Eylau (Ger. >Pol.) doich' ĭ'-lou   doich' ai'-lau
Polish *Iława*, q.v.

Deutsch Krone (Ger. >Pol.) doich' krō'-nə   doich' kroh'-nuh
Polish *Wałcz*, q.v.

Deux Sévres (Fr.) dû sĕ'vr   dœ seh'vr

Deuz Magots (Paris) dû mä-gō'   dœ mah-goh'

Deva (Rum.) dĕ'-vä   deh'-vah
Hungarian *Déva*, dā'-vŏ [day'-vo].

De Valera, Eamon (Irish polit.) dĕ vä-lĕr'-ə, ā'-mən   deh vah-lehr'-uh, ay'-muhn

or Irish dĕ vä-lā'-rə deh vah-lay'-ruh
There are other pronunciations but these are probably the best.

Đevđelija (Yugosl.) dyĕv'-dyĕ'-lĭ-yä   dyev'-dyeh'-li-yah

Deve Bajir (Yugosl., mt.) dĕ'-vĕ bä'-yĭr   deh'-veh bah'-yihr

Deventer (Neth.) dā'-vən-tər   day'-vuhn-tuhr

Devereux (family name) *Am.* dĕv'-ə-rō   dev'-uh-roh
For British usage the BBC gives dĕv'-ə-rə, -rŏŏ, -rŏŏks *and* -rĕks [dev-uh-ruh, -roo, -rooks *and* -reks].

Devers, Jacob L. (U.S. general) dĕv'-ərz   dev'-uhrz

Devica (Yugosl., mts.) dĕ'-vĭ-tsä   deh'-vi-tsah

Devitt, Edward J. (U.S. representative) dĕv'-ĭt   dev'-it

Devoll (Alb.) dĕ'-vôl   deh'-vol
Devolli (Alb.)   See *Devoll.*

D'Ewart, Wesley A. (U.S. representative) dĭ-yŏŏ'-ärt *or* -ərt   di-yoo'-ahrt *or* -uhrt

De Wijk (Neth.) də wĭk'   duh waik'

Dezhnëv (Rus., cape) dĕzh-nyôf'   dezh-nyof'

Dhahran (Arabia) däk(h)-rän'   dahk(h)-rahn'
or dä-rän'   dah-rahn'

Dia (Crete, isl.) dē'-ä   dee'-ah
Also called *Standia*, stän-dē'-ä [stahn-dee'-ah].

Diaghilev, Sergei (Rus. ballet producer) dyä'-gĭ-lĕf, sĕr-gä'   dyah'-gi-lehf, sehr-gay'

Diamantina (Austral., riv.) dī'-ə-mən-tē'-nə   dai'-uh-muhn-tee'-nuh

Diarbekr (Turk.) See *Diyarbekır.*

Diário da Noite (Braz.   dē-är'-yŏŏ də noi'-tĭ   dee-ahr'-yu duh
  newspaper)   noi'-ti

Diário de Noticias   dē-är'-yŏŏ dĭ   dee-ahr'-yu di
  (Braz. newspaper)   nŏ-tēs'-yəs   no-tees'-yuhs

Dias, Antonio Gonçalves (Braz. poet) See *Gonçalves Dias*.

Díaz, Porfirio   dē'-äs, pôr-fē'-ryô   dee'-ahs, por-fee'-
  (Mex. polit.)   ryo

Dibër or Dibra (Alb.,   *Alb.* dē'-bər *or*   dee'-buhr *or*
  Yugosl.)   dē'-brä   dee'-brah
  Serb-Croat *Debar*, q.v.

Dibrugarh (India)   dĭb-rŏŏ-gär' *or* -gŭr'   dib-ru-gahr' *or*
                                                        -guhr'

Dičina (Yugosl., riv.)   dē'-chĭ-nä   dee'-chi-nah

Diciosânmărtin (Rum.)   dē'-chô-sûn-mûr'-tĭn   dee'-cho-suhn-muhr'-
                                                      tin

  Also called *Târnava* (q.v.) *Sânmărtin.*

Dickstein, Samuel   dĭk'-stēn   dik'-steen
  (U.S. representative)   *or* dĭk'-stīn   dik'-stain

Dicomano (It.)   dē-kô-mä'-nô   dee-ko-mah'-no

dictionary   dĭk'-shən-ĕr'-ĭ   dik'-shuhn-ehr'-i
  In American dictionaries the pronunciation dĭk'-shən-ər-ĭ [dik'-shuhn-
  uhr-i], if given at all, is an alternative and is marked *or especially
  British*. It is unsuitable for American radio.

Didam (Neth.)   dē'-däm   dee'-dahm

Didymoteikhon (Gr.)   dē-dē-mô'-tē-hô(n)   dee-dee-mo'-tee-
                                                      ho(n)

  Commonly called *Demotika*, q.v.

Die (Fr.)   dē'   dee'

Diedendorf (Fr.)   dē'-dən-dôrf'   dee'-duhn-dorf'

Diedenhofen (Fr.)   *Ger.* dē'-dən-hō'-fən   dee'-duhn-hoh'-fuhn
  French *Thionville*, tyôN-vēl' [tyoN-veel'].

Diégo Suarez (Madag.)   dyĕ'-gô swä'-rĕs   dyeh'-go swah'-res

Diekirch (Lux.)   dē'-kĭrk(h)   dee'-kihrk(h)

Diélette (Fr.)   dyĕ-lĕt'   dyeh-let'

Diember (NEI) See *Djember.*

Diemen (Neth.)   dē'-mən   dee'-muhn

Diepenveen (Neth.)   dēp'-ən-vān   deep'-uhn-vayn

Diepholz (Ger.)   dēp'-hôlts   deep'-holts

Dieppe (Fr.)   *Eng.* dĭ-ĕp'   di-ep'
                        Fr. dyĕp'   dyep'

Dierdorf (Ger.)   dēr'-dôrf   deer'-dorf

Dieren (Neth.)   dē'-rən   dee'-ruhn

Dies, Martin   dīz'   daiz'.
  (U.S. representative)

Dietz (Ger.) See *Diez*.

Dieuze (Fr.)	dyûz′	dyœz′
Diever (Neth.)	dē′-vər	dee′-vuhr
Diez *or* Dietz (Ger.)	dēts′	deets′
Difesa (It., riv.)	dē-fĕ′-sä	dee-feh′-sah
Differdange (Luxem.)	dē-fĕr-däNzh′	dee-fehr-dahNzh′
Digboi (India)	dĭg′-boi	dig′-boi
Digne (Fr.)	dēn′(y)	deen′(y)
Dilasac (P.I., bay)	dē-lä′-säk	dee-lah′-sahk
Dili *or* Dilli (Port. Timor)	dĭl′-ē	dil′-ee
Dillingen (Ger.)	dĭl′-ĭng-ən	dil′-ing-uhn
Dilweg, LaVern R. (U.S. representative)	dĭl′-wĭg	dil′-wig
Dimitrov, Georgi (Bulg. polit.)	dĭ-mē′-trŏf, gĕ-ôr′-gĭ	di-mee′-trof, geh-or′-gi
Dimitsana (Gr.)	dē-mē-tsä′-nä	dee-mee-tsah′-nah
Dimond, Antony J. (Alaskan polit.)	dĭ′-mənd	dai′-muhnd
Dinagat (P.I.)	dē-nä′-gät	dee-nah′-gaht
Dinajpur (India)	dĭ-näj′-po͝or	dih-nahj′-pur
Dinan (Fr.)	dē-näN′	dee-nahN′
Dinant (Belg.)	dē-näN′	dee-nahN′
Dinapore (India) Also called *Dinapur*.	dē′-nä-pôr′	dee′-nah-por′
dinar (coin)	dē-när′	dee-nahr′
Dinard (Fr.)	dē-när′	dee-nahr′
Dinaric Alps (Yugosl.)	*Eng.* dĭ-när′-ĭk	di-nehr′-ik

Serb-Croat *Dinarske Planine*, dē′-när-skĕ plä′-nē′-nĕ [dee′-nahr-skeh plah′-nee′-neh].

Dingalan (P.I., bay)	dēng-gä′-län	deeng-gah′-lahn
Dingell, John D. (U.S. representative)	dĭng′-gĕl	ding′-gel
dinghy *or* dingy	dĭng′-gĭ *or* dĭng′-ĭ *sometimes* dēngk′-ĭ *or* dēnk′	ding′-gi *or* ding′-i deengk′-i *or* deenk′

This is another fighting word. The local yachtsmen seem to prefer the second pronunciation. Producers leave *dinghy* in the script at their own risk.

Dingrás (P.I.)	dēn-gräs′	deen-grahs′
Dingsperloo (Neth.)	dĭngs′-pĕr-lō	dings′-pehr-loh
Di Nicola, Enrico (It. polit.) See *De Nicola*.		
Dinkelsbuehl *or* Dinkelsbühl (Ger.)	dĭnk′-əls-bül	dink′-uhls-bül

Dinnyés, Lajos (Hung.   dēn'-nyĕsh, lŏ'-yôsh   deen'-nyesh, lo'-yosh
polit.)

Dinslaken (Ger.)   dĭns'-lä-kən   dins'-lah-kuhn

diocesan   dī-ŏs'-ə-sən   dai-os'-uh-suhn

diocese   dī'-ə-sĭs *or* -sēs   dai'-uh-sis *or* -sees

For the plural *dioceses*, dictionaries recommend only dĭ'-ə-sĭ-sĭz [dai'-uh-si-siz] or -sē-sĭz [-see-siz], but general usage appears to be, with few exceptions, dĭ'-ə-sēz [dai'-uh-seez]. This popular pronunciation, avoiding multiple sibilants, may be preferable for radio.

Diosgyŏr (Hung.)   dĭ'-ôsh-dyûr   di'-osh-dyœr

Diphrys (Gr., mt.)   dē'-frēs   dee'-frees

diphtheria   dĭf-thĭr'-ĭ-ə   dif-thihr'-i-uh

The more recent dictionaries list as an alternative, dĭp-thĭr'-rĭ-ə [dip-thihr'-ri-uh], a pronunciation, once held incorrect, that illustrates *dissimilation*. See also *diphthong*.

diphthong   dĭf'-thông   dif'-thong

As in the case of *diphtheria*, a pronunciation of the first syllable as dĭp- now has dictionary authority.

Diredawa (Ethiopia)   *Eng.* dē'-rĕ-dä'-wä   dee'-reh-dah'-wah
     or dĭr'-ĭ-dou'-wə   dihr'-i-dau'-wuh
     native dē-rĕ-də-wä   dee-reh-duh-wah

Direk Chaiyanam   dē'-rĕk chī'-yə-näm'   dee'-rek chai'-yuh-
(Siamese polit.)   nahm'

Dirksen, Everett M.   dûrk'-sən   duhrk'-suhn
(U.S. representative)

Dirschau (Pol.)   See *Tczew*.

Disenka (Pol. > Rus., riv.) dĭ-sĕn'-kä   di-sen'-kah
Polish *Dzisna*, jēz'-nä [jeez'-nah].

Disko (Greenl., isl.)   dĭs'-kō   dis'-koh

Disna (Pol. > Rus.)   dĭs-nä'   dis-nah'
Polish *Dzisna*, jēz'-nä [jeez'-nah].

Dison (Belg.)   dē-zôN'   dee-zoN'

disparate   dĭs'-pə-rĭt   dis'-puh-rit

The analogy of the accent of *disparage*, dĭs-păr'-ĭj [dis-pehr'-ij] is misleading.

Dissay (Fr.)   dē-sĕ'   dee-seh'

Di Tremiti (It., isls.)   dē trĕ'-mē-tē   dee treh'-mee-tee

Dittaino (Sicily, riv.)   dēt-tī'-nô   deet-tai'-no

Diu (Port. India)   dē'-ŏŏ   dee'-u

Dives (Fr., riv.)   dēv'   deev'

Dives sur Mer (Fr.)   dēv sür mĕr'   deev sür mehr'

Divette (Fr., riv.)   dē-vĕt'   dee-vet'

Divnoe (Rus.)   dēv'-nŏ-yĕ   deev'-no-yeh

Dixmude (Belg.)   *Fr.* dēks-müd′   deeks-müd′
Flemish *Dixmuiden*, dēks-mûĭ′-də(n) [deeks-mœi′-duh(n)].
Diyarbekır (Turk.)   dē-yär-bĕ-kĭr′   dee-yahr-beh-kihr′
Dizful (Iran)   dĭz-fōōl′   diz-fool′
Dj-.   See also *Đ*, an alternative spelling in Yugoslav place names.
Djailolo (NEI, Halmahera) jĭ-lô′-lô   jai-lo′-lo
Djakovica (Yugosl.)   dyä′-kô′-vĭ-tsä   dyah′-ko′-vi-tsah
Djakovo (Yugosl.)   *Alb.* dyä′-kô-vô   dyah′-ko-vo
Serb-Croat *Đakovica*, q.v.
Djambi *or* Dyambi (NEI) jäm′-bē   jahm′-bee
Djanet (Alg.)   jă′-nĕt   ja′-net
Djapara (NEI, Java)   jä-pä′-rä   jah-pah′-rah
djebel *or* jebel   jĕb′-əl   jeb′-uhl
     These are alternative spellings for an element, meaning *hill*, in Arabic place names. The former is to be expected in French territory. It may be necessary to look up both.
Djebel Abiod (Tun.)   jĕb′-əl äb-yŏd′   jeb′-uhl ahb-yod′
Djebel Ainchouna (Tun.) jĕb′-əl ān-shōō′-nä   jeb′-uhl ayn-shoo′-
     nah
Djebel Ajred (Tun.)   jĕb′-əl äzh′-rĕd   jeb′-uhl ahzh′-red
Djebel Antra (Tun.)   jĕb′-əl än′-trä   jeb′-uhl ahn′-trah
Djebel Artoug el   jĕb′-əl är-tōōg′ ĕl   jeb′-uhl ahr-toog′ el
Hanech (Tun.)   hä′-nĕsh   hah′-nesh
Djebel Azag (Tun.)   jĕb′-əl ä′-zäg   jeb′-uhl ah′-zahg
Djebel Berda (Tun., mt.) jĕb′-əl bĕr′-dä   jeb′-uhl behr′-dah
Djebel Bou Aoukaz   jĕb′-əl bōō′ ou-kăz′   jeb′-uhl boo′ au-kaz′
(Tun.)
Djebel Bou Hadjar   jĕb′-əl bōō′ hä′-jär   jeb′-uhl boo′ hah′-
(Tun.)   jahr
Djebel Bou Kournine   jĕb′-əl bōō′ kôôr-nēn′ jeb′-uhl boo′ kur-
(Tun.)   neen′
Djebel Bou Kril (Tun.)   jĕb′-əl bōō′ krēl′   jeb′-uhl boo′ kreel′
Djebel Chirich (Tun.)   jĕb′-əl shĭ-rēsh′   jeb′-uhl shi-reesh′
Djebel Dardyss (Tun.)   jĕb′-əl där-dēs′   jeb′-uhl dahr-dees′
Djebel Edjehaf (Tun.)   jĕb′-əl ĕd-jə-hăf′   jeb′-uhl ed-juh-haf′
Also spelled *El Djehaf*.
Djebel el Ahmera (Tun.) jĕb′-əl ĕl ä′-mə-rä   jeb′-uhl el ah′-muh-
Also called *Long Stop Hill*.   rah
Djebel el Ang (Tun.)   jĕb′-əl ĕl äng′   jeb′-uhl el ahng′
Djebel el Bacouala   jĕb′-əl ĕl bä-kwä′-lä   jeb′-uhl el bah-
(Tun.)   kwah′-lah
Djebel el Menassir   jĕb′-əl ĕl   jeb′-uhl el muh-
(Tun.)   mə-năs′-sĭr   nas′-sihr
Djebel el Sema (Tun.)   jĕb′-əl ĕs sĕ′-mä   jeb′-uhl es seh′-mah

Djebel Garci (Tun.)	jĕb'-əl gär'-sē	jeb'-uhl gahr'-see
Djebel Kalaat el Senam (Tun.)	jĕb'-əl kä-lät' ĕs sĕ-năm'	jeb'-uhl kah-laht' es seh-nam'
Djebel Mansour (Tun.)	jĕb'-əl män-sōōr'	jeb'-uhl mahn-soor'
Djebel Menobab (Tun.)	jĕb'-əl mĕ-nô-băb'	jeb'-uhl meh-no-bab'
Djebel Mrata (Tun.)	jĕb'-əl mə-ră'-tä	jeb'-uhl muh-ra'-tah
Djebel Nechat el Maza (Tun.)	jĕb'-əl nə-shăt' ĕl mä'-zä	jeb'-uhl nuh-shat' el mah'-zah
Djebel Orbata (Tun., mt.)	jĕb'-əl ôr-bä'-tä	jeb'-uhl or-bah'-tah
Djebel Rmel (Tun.)	jĕb'-əl rə-māl'	jeb'-uhl ruh-mayl'
Djebel Sidi Meftah (Tun.)	jĕb'-əl sē'-dē məf-tä'	jeb'-uhl see'-dee muhf-tah'
Djebel Tahent (Tun.)	jĕb'-əl tä-hĕnt'	jeb'-uhl tah-hent'
Djebel Tangouch (Tun.)	jĕb'-əl tän-gōōsh'	jeb'-uhl tahn-goosh'
Also called *Tangoucha,* tän-gōō'-shä [tahn-goo'-shah].		
Djebel Tobaga (Tun., mt.)	jĕb'-əl tô-bä'-gä	jeb'-uhl to-bah'-gah
Djebel Zaghouan (Tun.)	*Ar.* jĕb'-əl zäg-wăn' *Fr.* zäg-wäN'	jeb'-uhl zahg-wan' zahg-wahN'
Djebibina (Tun.)	jĕ-bĭ-bē'-nä	jeh-bi-bee'-nah
Djebiniana (Tun.)	jĕ-bĭn-yă'-nä	jeh-bin-ya'-nah
Djedeida (Tun.)	jə-dä'-dä	juh-day'-dah
Djefna (Tun.)	jĕf'-nä	jef'-nah
Also spelled *Jefna,* q.v.		
Djem, el (Tun.)	jĕm', ĕd	jem', ed
Djember (NEI, Java)	jĕm-bûr'	jem-buhr'
Djeradou (Tun.)	jĕ-rä-dōō'	jeh-rah-doo'
Djerba (Tun., isl.)	jĕr'-bä	jehr'-bah
Djibouti (Fr. Som.)	jē-bōō'-tē	jee-boo'-tee
Also spelled *Jibuti.* French jē-bōō-tē' [jee-boo-tee'].		
Djidjelli (Alg.)	jē-jĕ-lē'	jee-jeh-lee'
Also spelled *Jijelli.*		
Djokjakarta (NEI, Java) See *Joggjakarta.*		
Djoumine (Tun., riv.)	jōō-mēn'	joo-meen'
Dmitrievsk (Rus.)	dmē'-trĭ-yĕfsk	dmee'-tri-yefsk
Dmitrov (Rus.)	dmē-trôf'	dmee-trof'
Dmitrovsk (Rus.)	dmē-trôfsk'	dmee-trofsk'
Dnepr (Rus., riv.)	*Eng.* nē'-pər *Rus.* dnĕ'-pər	nee'-puhr dneh'-puhr
Dneprodzerzhinsk (Rus.)	dnĕ'-prô-jĕr-zĭnsk' or *Eng.* nē'-pər-	dneh'-pro-jehr-zinsk' nee'-puhr-
Dnepropetrovsk (Rus.)	dnĕ'-prô-pĕ-trôfsk' or *Eng.* nē'-pər-	dneh'-pro-peh-trofsk' nee'-puhr-

Dneprostroi (Rus.)   dně'-prŏ-stroi'   dneh'-pro-stroi'

Dnestr (Europ. riv.)   See *Dniester.*

Dnieper (Rus., riv.)   *Eng.* nē'-pər   nee'-puhr
   Russian *Dnepr*, q.v.

Dniester (Europ. riv.)   *Eng.* nē'-stər   nee'-stuhr
   Polish *Dniestr*, dnyě'str [dnye'str]. Russian *Dnestr*, dně'str [dne'str].
   Ukrainian *Dnister*, dnē'-stər [dnee'-stuhr]. Rumanian *Nistrul*, nē-
   strŏol [nee'-strul].

Dno (Rus.)   dnô'   dno'

Dnyeprovsko-Bugski, Kanal (Pol.)   See *Królewski, Kanal.*

Döbeln (Ger.)   dû'-bəln   dœ'-buhln

Dobo (NEI, Aroe)   dô'-bô   do'-bo

Dobra (Yugosl.)   dô'-brä   do'-brah

Dobrič (Yugosl.)   dô'-brǐch   do'-brich

Dobrici (Rum.)   dô'-brēch'   do'-breech'
   Also called *Bazargic*, q.v.

Dobrogea (Rum.)   *Rum.* dô'-brô-jä   do'-bro-jah
   English and Bulgarian *Dobruja*, q.v.

Dobro Polje (Yugosl.)   dô'-brô pô'-lyě   do'-bro po'-lyeh

Dobrostica (Yugosl., mt.) dô'-brô'-stǐ-tsä do'-bro'-sti-tsah

Dobruja (Rum.)   *Eng.* dō'-brŏŏ'-jə doh'-broo'-juh
                  Bulg. dô'-brŏŏ-jä do'-bru-jah
   Rumanian *Dobrogea*, q.v.

Dobruševo (Yugosl.)   dô'-brŏŏ'-shě-vô do'-broo'-sheh-vo

Dodecanese (Aegean isls.) *Eng.* dō-děk'-ə-nēz' doh-dek'-uh-neez'
                 or nēs'   *or* nees'
   The second and last syllables should be accented, not the first and last.
   The adjective, however, is *Dodecanesian*—dō'-děk-ə-nē'-zhən *or* shən
   [doh'-dek-uh-nee'-zhuhn *or* shuhn]. Greek *Dodekanesos*, q.v., and *Dod-
   ekanesa*, dô-dě-kä'-nē-sä [do-deh-kah'-nee-sah].

Dodekanesos (Gr., isls.) dô-dě-kä'-nē-sô(s) do-deh-kah'-nee-so(s)

Dodewaard (Neth.)   dō'-də-wärt   doh'-duh-wahrt

Dodo Oninskoe (Rus.) dō'-dō ŏ-nǐn'-skŏ-yě doh'-doh o-nin'-sko-
                                     yeh

Dodsworth, Henrique   dädz'-wûrth,   dahdz'-wuhrth,
   (Braz. polit.)   ěN-rē'-kǐ   eN-ree'-ki

Doebeln (Ger.)   dû'-bəln   dœ'-buhln

Doenitz *or* Dönitz, Karl dû'-nǐts   dœ'-nits
   (Ger. admiral)

Doerane (Balkan lake)   *Gr.* dô-ē-rä'-nē do-ee-rah'-nee
   Also called *Limne Doeranes*, lēm'-nē dô-ē-rä'-nēs [leem'-nee do-ee-rah'-
   nees]. Serb-Croat *Dojran*, q.v.

Doesburg (Neth.)   dŏŏs'-bûrk(h)   doos'-bœrk(h)

Doetinchen (Neth.) See *Deutekom*.

Doganella (It.)   dô-gä-nĕl'-lä   do-gah-nel'-lah

Doganica (Yugosl., mts.)   dô'-gä'-nĭ-tsä   do'-gah'-ni-tsah

Dogra (India)   dô-grä'   doh-grah'

Doihara, Kenji   dô'-ē'-hä-rä, kĕn'-jē   do'-ee'-hah-rah,
(Jap. polit.)   ken'-jee

Dojo (NEI, New Guinea) dō'-yō   doh'-yoh

Dojran (Balkan lake)   S.-C. doi'-rän   doi'-rahn
Also called *Dojransko jezero*, doi'-rän-skô yĕ'-zĕ-rô [doi'-rahn-sko
yeh'-zeh-ro]. Greek *Doerane*, q.v.

Dokkum (Neth.)   dôk'-əm   dok'-uhm

Dol (Fr.)   dôl'   dol'

Dolban (Rus.)   dōl'-bän(y)   dohl'-bahn(y)

Dôle (Fr.)   dōl'   dohl'

Dolenji Logatec   dô'-lĕ-nyĭ lô'-gä-tĕts   do'-leh-nyi
(Yugosl.)   lo'-gah-tets

Dolgintsevo (Rus.)   dôl-gēn'-tsĕ-vŏ   dol-geen'-tseh-vo

Dolina (Pol. > Rus.)   dô-lē'-nä   do-lee'-nah

Dolinovka (Rus.)   dô-lē'-nŏf-kä   do-lee'-nof-kah

Doljevac (Yugosl.)   dô'-lyĕ-väts   do'-lyeh-vahts

Dollfuss, Engelbert   dôl'-fo͞os   dol'-foos
(Austrian polit.)

Dolon (Ch., Chahar)   *Eng.* dō'-lŏn'   doh'-lon'

Dolon Nor (Ch., Hopeh)   *Eng.* dō'-lŏn nôr'   doh'-lon nor'

Dolovo (Yugosl.)   dô'-lô-vô   do'-lo-vo

Dolya (Rus.)   dôl'-yä   dol'-yah

Dolzhik (Rus.)   dôl'-zhĭk   dol'-zhik

Domažlice (Cz.)   dô'-mäzh-lĭ-tsĕ   do'-mahzh-li-tseh
German *Taus*.

Dombaas (Nor.)   do͞om'-bôs   dum'-bos

Dombrova (Pol.) See *Dąbrowa Górnicza*.

Dombrovitsa (Pol.) See *Dąbrowica*.

Dombrowa (Ger.)   dôm-brô'-vä   dom-bro'-vah

Domburg (Neth.)   dôm'-bûrk(h)   dom'-bœrk(h)

Dōmei (Jap. news   dô'-mä   doh'-may
agency)

Domengeaux, James   dô-mäN-zhô'   doh-mahN-zhoh'
(U.S. representative)

Domfront (Fr.)   dôN-frôN'   doN-froN'

Dominican Republic   də-mĭn'-ə-kən   duh-min'-uh-kuhn
Spanish *República Dominicana*, rĕ-po͞o'-blē-kä dô-mē'-nē-kä'-nä [reh-
poo'-blee-kah do-mee'-nee-kah'-nah].

Dommel (Neth., riv.)   dôm'-əl   dom'-uhl

Domodossola (It.)   dô-mô-dôs'-sô-lä   do-mo-dos'-so-lah

Domozhirov (Rus.)	dŏ-mŏ-zhĭ'-rŏf	do-mo-zhi'-rof
Dömsöd (Hung.)	dûm'-shûd	dœm'-shœd
Dom Soyuzov (Rus.)	dôm sô-yōō'-zôf	dom so-yoo'-zof
Don (Fr., riv.)	dôN'	doN'
Don (Rus., riv.)	dôn' or Eng. dŏn'	don'
Donato (It.)	dô-nä'-tô	do-nah'-to
Donau (Europ. riv.)	See Danube.	
Donbaik (Burma)	dŏn'-bĭk'	dohn'-baik'
Donbas (Rus.)	dôn-bäs'	don-bahs'
Dondero, George A.	dŏn-dĕr'-ŏ	don-dehr'-oh
(U.S. representative)		
Dondon (Rus., riv.)	dŏn-dôn'	don-don'
Donegal (Eire)	dŏn'-ĭ-gôl'	don'-i-gawl'
Donets (Rus., riv.)	dŏ-nĕts'	do-nets'
Dongara (Austral.)	dŏn-gä'-rə	don-gah'-ruh
Dongen (Neth.)	dông'-ən	dong'-uhn
Donggala (NEI, Celebes)	dông-gä'-lä	dong-gah'-lah
Donghoi (Indo-Ch.)	dŏng-hoi'	dong-hoi'
Dongola (Sudan)	dŏng'-gə-lə	dong'-guh-luh
Dongón (P.I.)	dông-ôn'	dong-on'
Doniawerstal (Neth.)	dô'-nyä-wĕr'-stäl	doh'-nyah-wehr'-stahl
donja, -ji	dô'-nyä, -nyĭ	do'-nyah, -nyi

An element, meaning *lower*, in Yugoslav place names. *Gornja, -ji*, gôr'-nyä, -nyĭ [gor'-nyah, -nyi], means *upper*. It may be necessary to look up the other part of the name.

Donja Lendava (Yugosl.)	dô'-nyä lĕn'-dä-vä	do'-nyah len'-dah-vah
German *Unter-Limbach*.		
Donji Lapac (Yugosl.)	dô'-nyĭ lä'-päts	do'-nyi lah'-pahts
Donji Milanovac	dô'-nyĭ	do'-nyi
(Yugosl.)	mē'-lä'-nô-väts	mee'-lah'-no-vahts
Donji Vakuf (Yugosl.)	See *Vakuf, Donji*.	
Don Muang	dôn mōŏ'-äng	don mu'-ahng
(Bangkok, airport)		
Donon (Fr., pass)	dô-nôN'	do-noN'
Donskaya (Rus., riv.)	dŏn-skä'-yä	don-skah'-yah
Doorn (Neth.)	dōrn'	dohrn'
Doornspijk (Neth.)	dōrn'-spīk	dohrn'-spaik
Dordogne (Fr., riv.)	dôr-dôn'(y)	dor-don'(y)
Dordrecht (Neth.)	dôr'-drĕk(h)t	dor'-drek(h)t
English *Dort*.		
D'Orlando (Sicily, cape)	dôr-län'-dô	dor-lahn'-do
Dorlobos (Yugosl.)	dôr'-lô-bôs	dor'-lo-bos
Dornot (Fr.)	dôr-nō'	dor-noh'

Dorogobuzh (Pol. >Rus.)	dŏ-rŏ-gŏ-boōsh′	do-ro-go-boosh′
Polish *Drohobycz*, q.v.		
Dorohoi (Rum.)	dô-rô-hoi′	do-ro-hoi′
Dorozsma (Hung.)	dô′-rôzh-mŏ	do′-rozh-mo
Also called *Kiskundorozsma*, q.v.		
Dorpat (Est.)	*Ger.* dôr′-pät	dor′-paht
Estonian *Tartu*, q.v. Russian *Jurjev*, q.v.		
Dorscheid (Ger.)	dôr′-shīt	dor′-shait
Dorsten (Ger.)	dôrs′-tən	dors′-tuhn
Dortmund (Ger.)	*Eng.* dôrt′-münd	dort′-muhnd
	Ger. dôrt′-mŏŏnt	dort′-munt
Dorval (Montreal, airport)	dôr-väl′	dor-vahl′
Došnica (Yugosl., riv.)	dô′-shnĭ-tsä	do′-shni-tsah
Dostoevski, Feodor	dŏ-stŏ-yĕf′-skĭ,	do-sto-yef′-ski,
Mikhailovich	fyô′-dŏr	fyo′-dor
(Rus. author)	mĭ-hī′-lŏ-vĭch	mi-hai′-lo-vich
Dothan (Ala.)	dŏ′-thən *or* -thăn	doh′-thuhn *or* -than
Douai (Fr.)	*Eng.* doō-ā′	doo-ay′
	Fr. dwĕ′	dweh′
Douala (Fr. Cameroons)	dwä′-lä	dwah′-lah
Also spelled *Duala*, q.v.		
Douarnenez (Fr.)	dwär-nə-nĕz′ *or* -nĕ′	dwahr-nuh-nez′ *or* -neh′
Douaumont (Fr.)	dwō-môN′	dwoh-moN′
Doubs (Fr.)	doō′	doo′
Doughton, Robert L.	dout′n	daut′n
(U.S. representative)		
Douguay Trouin	doō-gĕ trwăN′	doo-geh trwaN′
Fr. cruiser		
Douirat (Tun.)	doō-ĭ-răt′	doo-i-rat′
Doullens (Fr.)	doō-läN′	doo-lahN′
Dounabis (Europ. riv.)	See *Danube*.	
Douro (Port., Sp., riv.)	*Port.* dŏ′-rŏŏ	doh′-ru
Spanish *Duero*, q.v.		
Douve (Fr., riv.)	doōv′	doov′
Douvres (Fr.)	doōv′r	doov′r
Douz (Tun.)	doōz′	dooz′
Dovezence (Yugosl.)	dŏ′-vĕ′-zĕn-tsĕ	do′-veh′-zen-tseh
Dovrefjell (Nor., mts.)	dŏ′-vrə-fyĕl	do′-vruh-fyel
Downey, Sheridan	dou′-nĭ	dau′-ni
(U.S. senator)		
Dozulé (Fr.)	dô-zü-lĕ′	do-zü-leh′
Dračevo (Yugosl.)	drä′-chĕ-vô	drah′-cheh-vo
Drachten (Neth.)	dräk(h)′-tən	drahk(h)′-tuhn

Draganov, Parvan (Bulg. polit.)	drä-gä′-nŏf, pär′-vän	drah-gah′-nof, pahr′-vahn
Draginac (Yugosl.)	drä′-gĭ-näts	drah′-gi-nahts
Dragoïcheva, Tzola (Bulg. polit.)	drä-gô′-ĭ-chĕ-vä, tsô′-lä	drah-go′-i-cheh-vah, tso′-lah
Dragoumis, Philip (Gr. polit.)	drä-gōō′-mēs	drah-goo′-mees
Draguignan (Fr.)	drä-gē-nyäN′	drah-gee-nyahN′
Drajinci (Yugosl.)	drä′-yĭn-tsĭ	drah′-yin-tsi
Drama (Gr.)	drä′-mä	drah′-mah
Drammen (Nor.)	dräm′-ən	drahm′-uhn
Dramonara (Crete, isl.)	drä-mô-nä′-rä	drah-mo-nah′-rah
Dramont (Fr.)	drä-môN′	drah-moN′
Drangedal (Nor.)	dräng′-ə-däl	drahng′-uh-dahl
Drapani (Crete, point)	drä-pä′-nē	drah-pah′-nee
Drapeau Rouge (Belg. newspaper)	drä-pō rōōzh′	drah-poh′ roozh′
Drava (Yugosl., riv.) German *Drau.*	drä′-vä	drah′-vah
Draveil (Fr.)	drä-vĕ′(y)	drah-veh′(y)
Dravina (Yugosl., riv.) German *Drann.*	drä′-vĭ-nä	drah′-vi-nah
Dravograd (Yugosl.)	drä′-vô-gräd	drah′-vo-grahd
Drawski Młyn (Pol.)	dräf′-skĭ mlĭn′	drahf′-ski mlin′
Dren (Yugosl.)	drĕn′	dren′
Drenica (Yugosl.)	drĕ′-nĭ-tsä	dreh′-ni-tsah
Drenova, Velika (Yugosl.)	drĕ′-nô-vä, vĕ′-lĭ-kä	dreh′-no-vah, veh′-li-kah
Drente (Neth.)	drĕn′-tə	dren′-tuh
Drepanon, Ak. (Crete, point)	drĕ′-pä-nô(n)	dreh′-pah-no(n)
Dresden (Ger.)	*Eng.* drĕz′-dən *Ger.* dräs′-dən	drez′-duhn drays′-duhn
Dreumel (Neth.)	drû′-məl	drœ′-muhl
Dreux (Fr.)	drû′	drœ′
Drewenz (Pol., riv.) See *Drwęca.*		
Drewitz (Ger.)	drä′-vĭts	dray′-vits
Drewry, Patrick H. (U.S. representative)	drŏŏr′-ĭ	drur′-i
Dreyfus	*Eng.* drā′-fəs *or* drī′-fəs *Fr.* drĕ-füs′	dray′-fuhs drai′-fuhs dreh-füs′
Driant (Fr., fort)	dryäN′	dryahN′
Driebergen (Neth.)	drē′-bĕr-k(h)ən	dree′-behr-k(h)uhn

Driel (Neth.)   drēl′   dreel′

Drigh Road (India,   drĭg′   **drig′**
   Karachi, airport)

Drina (Yugosl., riv.)   drē′-nä   dree′-nah

Drini (Balkan rivs.) See *Drin* . . . .

Drin i Bardhë   *Alb.* drēn′ ē bär′-*th*ə   dreen′ ee bahr′-*th*uh
   (Balkan riv.)
   Serb-Croat *Beli Drim*, q.v. English *White Drin*, drēn′ [dreen′].

Drin i Math (Alb., riv.)   drēn′ ē mäth′   dreen′ ee mahth′
   Italian *Drinasa*, drē′-nä-sä [dree′-nah-sah].

Drin i Zi (Balkan riv.)   *Alb.* drēn′ ē zē′   dreen′ ee zee′
   Serb-Croat *Crni Drim*, q.v. English *Black Drin*, drēn′ [dreen′].

Drinska (Yugosl.)   drēn′-skä   dreen′-skah

Drissa (Rus.)   drēs′-sä   drees′-sah

Drivyati (Pol., lake)   See *Drywiaty*.

Dröbak (Nor.)   drû′-bäk   drœ′-bahk

Drobner, Bolesław   drôb′-nĕr,   drob′-nehr,
   (Pol. polit.)   bô-lĕ′-släf   bo-leh′-slahf

Drobnjaci (Yugosl.)   drôb′-nyä′-tsĭ   drob′-nyah′-tsi

Droebak (Nor.)   drû′-bäk   drœ′-bahk

Drogheda (Eire)   drô′-hĭ-də   draw′-hi-duh

Drogichin (Pol. > Rus.)   drŏ-gē′-chĭn   dro-gee′-chin
   Polish *Drohiczyn*, q.v.

Drohiczyn (Pol. > Rus.)   drô-hē′-chĭn   dro-hee′-chin
   Russian *Drogichin*, drŏ-gē′-chĭn [dro-gee′-chin].

Drohobycz (Pol. > Rus.)   drô-hô′-bĭch   dro-ho′-bich
   Russian *Dorogobuzh*, dŏ-rŏ-gŏ-bōōsh′ [do-ro-go-boosh′].

Drôme (Fr.)   drôm′   drohm′

Dronrijp (Neth.)   drôn′-rīp   dron′-raip

Drossen (Ger.)   drôs′-ən   dros′-uhn

Drottningholm (Sw.)   drŏt′-nĭng-hôlm′   drot′-ning-holm′

Droué (Fr.)   drwĕ′   drweh′

Drove (Ger.)   drō′-və   droh′-vuh

Drugehnen (Ger. > Rus.)   drōō-gä′-nən   dru-gay′-nuhn

Druja (Pol. > Rus.) See *Druya*.

Drunen (Neth.)   drü′-nən   drü′-nuhn

Druse (Syrian people)   drōōz′   drooz′

Druskeniki (Pol. > Rus.)   drōō-skĕ-nē′-kĭ   dru-skeh-nee′-ki
   Polish spelling *Druskieniki*.

Druten (Neth.)   drü′-tən   drü′-tuhn

Druya (Pol. > Rus.)   drōō′-yä   droo′-yah
   Polish spelling *Druja*.

Drvenik (Yugosl.)   dər′-vĕ-nĭk   duhr′-veh-nik
   Italian *Zirona*, q.v.

Drventsa (Pol., riv.) See *Drwęca*.

Drwęca (Pol., riv.) dər-văN′-tsä duhr-vaN′-tsah
  Russian *Drventsa*, drvĕn′-tsä [drven′-tsah]. German *Drewenz*, drä̆′-
  vĕnts [dray′-vents].

Drywiaty (Pol., lake) drĭ-vyä′-tĭ dri-vyah′-ti
  Russian spelling *Drivyati*.

Duala (Fr. Cameroons) dŏŏ-ä′-lä du-ah′-lah

Duarte de Perón, Eva dwär′-tĕ dĕ pĕ-rôn′, dwahr′-teh deh peh-
  (Arg. polit.) ĕ′-vä ron′, eh′-vah

Dubbeldam (Neth.) dûb′-əl-däm′ dœb′-uhl-dahm′

Dubbo (Austral.) dŭb′-ŏ duhb′-oh

Dubiecko (Pol.) dŏŏ-byĕ′-tskô du-byeh′-tsko

Dublin (Eire) dŭb′-lĭn duhb′-lin
  Gaelic *Baile Átha Cliath*, q.v.

Dublje (Yugosl.) dŏŏb′-lyĕ doob′-lyeh

Dubois (Fr. name) *Eng.* dŏŏ-boiz′ du-boiz′
  Fr. dü-bwä′ dü-bwah′

Du Bois, Guy Pène (Am. painter) See *Pène du Bois*.

Dubos (Fr. name) dü-bōs′ dü-bohs′

Dubose (Am. name) dyŏŏ-bōz′ dyu-bohz′

Dubossary (Rus.) dŏŏ-bŏ-sä′-rĭ doo-bo-sah′-rĭ

Dubravica (Yugosl.) dŏŏ′-brä′-vĭ-tsä doo′-brah′-vi-tsah

Dubrovačka (Yugosl.) dŏŏ′-brô-väch-kä doo′-bro-vahch-kah

Dubrovnik (Yugosl.) dŏŏ′-brôv-nĭk doo′-brov-nik
  Italian *Ragusa*, q.v.

Dubuque (Iowa) dŏŏ-byŏŏk′ *or* də- du-byook′ *or* duh-

Duce, il (It.) dŏŏ′-chĕ, ēl doo′-cheh, eel
  Italian for *the leader*. Cf. *der Fuehrer* and *el Caudillo*.

Ducey (Fr.) dü-sĕ′ dü-seh′

Duclair (Fr.) dü-klĕr′ dü-klehr′

Duclos, Jacques dü-klō′, zhäk′ dü-kloh′, zhahk′
  (Fr. polit.)

Duda, el (Libya) dŏŏ′-dä, ĕd doo′-dah, ed

Dudelange (Lux.) dŏŏ′-də-läng′-ə doo′-duh-lahng′-uh
  Also called *Dudelingen*, dŏŏ′-də-lĭng′-ən [doo′-duh-ling′-uhn].

Dudica (Yugosl., Gr., mt.) dŏŏ′-dĭ-tsä doo′-di-tsah

Due (Rus.) dŏŏ′-ĕ doo′-eh

Duelken (Ger.) dül′-kən dül′-kuhn

Duelmen (Ger.) dül′-mən dül′-muhn

Duena *or* Düna (Rus., *Ger.* dü′-nä dü′-nah
  Latvia, riv.)
  Russian *Dvina*, q.v. Latvian *Daugava*, q.v.

Duenamuende (Latvia) *Ger.* dü′-nä-mün′-də dü′-nah-mün′-duh
  Latvian *Daugavgrīva*, q.v.

Duero (Sp., Port., riv.)   *Sp.* dwĕ′-rô   dweh′-ro
   Portuguese *Duoro,* q.v.
Dueren (Ger.)   dü′-rən   **dü′-ruhn**
Duerer, Albrecht   dü′-rər, äl′-brĕk(h)t   dü′-ruhr, ahl′-
   (Ger. painter)   brek(h)t
Duerwiss (Ger.)   dür′-vĭs   dür′-vis
Duesseldorf *or* Düsseldorf   *Eng.* dŏŏs′-əl-dôrf   dus′-uhl-dorf
   (Ger.)   *Ger.* düs′-əl-dôrf   düs′-uhl-dorf
Dugi Otok (Yugosl., isl.) dōō′-gĭ ô′-tôk   doo′-gi o′-tok
   Italian *Isola Lunga,* q.v., or *Isola Grossa.*
Dugny (Fr.)   dü-nyē′   dü-nyee′
Dugo Selo (Yugosl.)   dōō′-gô sĕ′-lô   doo′-go seh′-lo
Duhalde, Alfredo   dōō-äl′-dĕ, äl-frĕ′-dô   doo-ahl′-deh, ahl-
   (Chilean polit.)   freh′-do
Duisburg (Ger.)   *Eng.* dyōōz′-bûrg   dyooz′-buhrg
                   Ger. düs′-bŏŏrk(h)   düs′-burk(h)
Duiven (Neth.)   dûĭ′-vən   dœi′-vuhn
Duizend (NEI)   dûĭ′-zənt   dœi′-zuhnt
Dukat (Alb.)   dōō′-kät   doo′-kaht
Dukati (Alb.) See *Dukat.*
Dukhovshchina (Rus.)   dōō-hŏf-shchē′-nä   doo-hof-shchee′-nah
Dúlag (P.I.)   dōō′-läg   doo′-lahg
Dulcigno (Yugosl.)   *It.* dōōl-chē′-nyô   dool-chee′-nyo
   Serb-Croat *Ulcinj.*
Đulica (Yugosl., mt.)   dyōō′-lĭ-tsä   dyoo′-li-tsah
Dülken (Ger.)   dül′-kən   dül′-kuhn
Dulles, John Foster   dŭl′-əs   duhl′-uhs
   (Am. lawyer)
Dülmen (Ger.)   dül′-mən   dül′-muhn
Duluth (Minn.)   də-lōōth′ *or* dōō-   duh-looth′ *or* duh
Dulwich (Eng.)   dŭl′-ĭch   duhl′-ich
Dum Dum (India)   dŭm dŭm   duhm duhm
Dumaguete (P.I.)   dōō-mä-gĕ′-tĕ   doo-mah-geh′-teh
Dumanquilas (P.I.)   dōō-män-kē′-läs   doo-mahn-kee′-lahs
Dumarsais, Estimé   dü-mär-sĕ′,   dü-mahr-seh′,
   (Haitian polit.)   ĕs-tē-mĕ′   ehs-tee-meh′
Dumbarton (Scot., U.S.) dŭm-bärt′n   duhm-bahrt′n
Dumyat (Egypt)   dŏŏm-yät′   dum-yaht′
   Also spelled *Dumiat.* Also called *Damietta,* q.v.
Duna (Europ. riv.) See *Danube.*
Düna (Rus., Latvia, riv.) *Ger.* dü′-nä   dü′-nah
   Russian *Dvina,* q.v. Latvian *Daugava,* q.v.
Dünaburg (Latvia)   *Ger.* dü′-nä-bŏŏrk(h)   dü′-nah-burk(h)
   Latvian *Daugavpils,* q.v. Russian *Dvinsk,* q.v.

Dunaföldvár (Hung.)   dŏŏ'-nŏ-fúld'-vär   du'-no-fœld'-vahr
Dunaharaszti (Hung.)   dŏŏ'-nŏ-hŏ'-rŏs-tĭ   du'-no-ho'-ros-ti
Dunai *and* Dunaj (Europ. riv.) See *Danube*.
Dunajec (Pol., riv.)   dŏŏ-nä'-yĕts   du-nah'-yets
Dunakeszi (Hung.)   dŏŏ'-nŏ-kĕ'-sĭ   du'-no-keh'-si
Dunalmás (Hung.)   dŏŏ'-nŏl-mäsh   du'-nol-mahsh
Dünamünde (Latvia)   *Ger.* dü'-nä-mün'-də   dü'-nah-mün'-duh
   Latvian *Daugavgrĭva*, q.v.
Dunărea (Europ. riv.)   See *Danube*.
Dunav (Europ. riv.)   See *Danube*.
Dunavecse (Hung.)   dŏŏ'-nŏ-vĕ'-chĕ   du'-no-veh'-cheh
Dunavska (Yugosl.)   dŏŏ'-näv-skä   doo'-nahv-skah
Dunbar (Scot.)   dən-bär'   duhn-bahr'
   As an American name *Dunbar* is accented on the first syllable.
Dundalk (Eire)   dŭn-dôk'   duhn-dawk'
   Gaelic *Dúndealgan*, dōōn-dyăl'-găn [doon-dyal'-gan].
Dúndealgan (Eire) See *Dundalk*.
Dunedin (N.Z.)   dŭn-ē'-dĭn   duhn-ee'-din
Dungarvan (Eire)   dŭn-gär'-vən   dun-gahr'-vuhn
Dungen (Neth.)   dûng'-ən   dœng'-uhn
Dungeness (Eng.)   dŭnj'-nĕs'   duhnj'-nes'
Đunis (Yugosl.)   dyōō'-nĭs   dyoo'-nis
Dunkerque (Fr.)   dúN-kĕrk'   dœN-kehrk'
   English *Dunkirk*, dŭn'-kərk [duhn'-kuhrk].
Dúnlaoghaire (Eire)   dōōn-lă'-rĭ   doon-la'-ri
   Formerly *Kingstown*.
Duparc, M. Jacques Fouques (Fr. diplomat) See *Fouques Duparc*.
Dupnitsa (Bulg.)   dŏŏp'-nĭ-tsä   dup'-ni-tsah
Dupón (P.I.)   dōō-pôn'   doo-pon'
Duquesne (Pa.)   dyōō-kän'   dyoo-kayn'
Durakova (Rus.)   dŏŏ-rä-kô'-vä   du-rah-ko'-vah
Durance (Fr.)   dü-räNs'   dü-rahNs'
Durango (Col., Mex.)   *Eng.* dŏŏ-răng'-gō   du-rang'-goh
                             Sp. dōō-räng'-gô   doo-rahng'-go
Durazzo (Alb.)   *It.* dōō-rät'-sô   doo-raht'-so
   Albanian *Durrĕs*, q.v.
Durban (U. of S. Af.)   dûr'-bən   duhr'-buhn
Düren (Ger.)   dü'-rən   dü'-ruhn
Dürer, Albrecht   dü'-rər, äl'-brĕk(h)t   dü'-ruhr, ahl'-
   (Ger. painter)   brek(h)t
Durfuli (Yugosl.)   dōōr'-fōō-lĭ   door'-foo-li
Durham (N.C.)   dûr'-əm   duhr'-uhm
   Not dōōr'-əm [dur'-uhm].

Durham, Carl T. (U.S. senator)	dûr'-əm	duhr'-uhm
Durmitor (Yugosl., mts.)	dōōr'-mĭ-tôr	door'-mi-tor
Durostor (Rum.)	dŏŏ-rô-stôr'	du-ro-stor'
Durovo (Rus.)	dōō'-rŏ-vŏ	doo'-ro-vo
Durrës (Alb.)	dōōr'-rəs	door'-ruhs

Italian *Durazzo*, q.v.

Durrësi (Alb.)   See *Durrës*.

Durwiss (Ger.)	dür'-vĭs	dür'-vis
Düršanovac (Yugosl.)	dōō'-shä'-nô-väts	doo'-shah'-no-vahts

Duüsseldorf (Ger.)   See *Duesseldorf*.

Dussen (Neth.)	dûs'-ən	dœs'-uhn
Dutch Guiana (S.A.)	gē-ä'-nə	gee-ah'-nuh

Properly *Surinam*, sōōr-ĭ-näm' [sur-i-nahm']. Dutch *Suriname*, sü-rĭ-nä'-mə [sür-ri-nah'-muh].

Dutra, Eurico Gaspar (Braz. polit.)	dōō'-trə, ĕ-ōō-rē'-kŏŏ gäs-pär'	doo'-truh, eh-u-ree'-ku gahs-pahr'
Dvina (Rus., Latvia, riv.)	dvĭ-nä'	dvi-nah'

Latvian *Daugava*, q.v. German *Duena*, q.v.

Dvinsk (Latvia)	*Rus.* dvēnsk'	dveensk'

Latvian *Daugavpils*, q.v. German *Dünaburg*, q.v.

Dvořák, Anton (Cz. composer)	dvôr'-zhäk, än'-tôn	dvor'-zhahk, ahn'-ton
Dwedar (Libya)	dōō'-ĕ-där'	du'-eh-dahr'
Dwingeloo (Neth.)	dwĭng'-ə-lō	dwing'-uh-loh
Dworshak, Henry C. (U.S. senator)	dwôr'-shăk	dwohr'-shak
Dwyfor (Wales)	dōōĭ'-vōr	dui'-vohr

Dy-.See also *Dj-* and *Đ*, alternative spellings in Yugoslav place names.

Dyambi (NEI)   See *Djambi*.

Dyatkovo (Rus.)	dyät-kô'-vŏ	dyaht-ko'-vo
Dyaul (Oc., New Ireland)	joul'	jaul'
d'Yeu, Île (Fr.)	dyû', ēl'	dyœ', eel'
Dzanakakis, Emmanuel (Gr. polit.)	dzä-nä-kä'-kēs, ĕ-mä-nwēl'	dzah-nah-kah'-kees, eh-mah-nweel'
Džep (Yugosl.)	jĕp'	jep'
Dzhankoi (Rus.)	jän-koi'	jahn-koi'
Dzharkent (Rus.)	jär-kĕnt'	jahr-kent'

Also spelled *Jarkent*.

Dzherzinsk (Rus.)	jĕr-zĭnsk'	jehr-zinsk'
Dzhida (Rus., riv.)	jē'-dä	jee'-dah
Dzhizak (Rus.)	jē-zäk'	jee-zahk'
Dzhulfa (Rus.)	jōōl-fä'	jul-fah'

Działdówka (Pol., Ger.,   jäl-dŏŏf′-kä   jahl-duf′-kah
  riv.)
German *Soldau*, q.v. Also called *Wkra*, q.v.
Działdowo (Pol.)   jäl-dô′-vô   jahl-do′-vo
German *Soldau*, q.v.
Działoszyce (Pol.)   jä-lô-shǐ′-tsĕ   jah-lo-shi′-tseh
Dzisna (Pol. >Rus.) See *Disna* (village and lake). See *Disenka* (river).
Džuma Obasi (Yugosl.)   jōō′-mä ô′-bä-sǐ   joo′-mah o′-bah-si
Dzungaria (Ch.,   *Eng.* zŏŏn-gär′-ĭ-ə   zun-gehr′-i-uh
  Sinkiang)
Also spelled *Sungaria* and *Zungaria*.

Eady, Sir Wilfred   ē′-dǐ   ee′-di
  (Br. diplomat)
Eaker, Ira C.   ā′-kər   ay′-kuhr
  (Am. general)
Eakins, Thomas   ā′-kǐnz   ay′-kinz
  (Am. painter)
EAM (Gr.)   ĕ′-äm′   eh′-ahm′
The initials of the words for Greek Liberation Front.
Earthman, Harold H.   ûrth′-mən   uhrth′-muhn
  (U.S. representative)
Eastleigh (Eng.)   ēst′-lē   eest′-lee
Eauripik (Oc., Carolines) ĕ-ou′-rē-pēk   eh-au′-ree-peek
Ebadon (Oc., Kwajalein) ĕ-bä′-dôn   eh-bah′-don
Eben Emael (Belg., fort) *Fr.*   ĕ-bən ĕ-mäl′   eh-buhn eh-mahl′
                 Flem. ā′-bən ā′-mäl   ay′-buhn ay′-mahl
Ebenrode (Ger. >Rus.) See *Eydt Kuhnen*.
Eberharter, Herman P.   ĕb′-ər-här′-tər   eb′-uhr-hahr′-tuhr
  (U.S. representative)
Eberswalde (Ger.)   ā′-bərs-väl′-də   ay′-buhrs-vahl′-duh
Ebeye (Oc., Marshalls)   ĕ′-bĕ-yĕ   eh′-beh-yeh
Eboli (It.)   ĕ′-bô-lē   eh′-bo-lee
Ebon (Oc., Marshalls)   ĕ′-bôn   eh′-bon
Also called *Boston Isl.*
Éboué, Félix   ĕ-bwĕ′, fĕ-lēks′   eh-bweh′, feh-leeks′
  (Fr. col. polit.)
Ebro (Sp., riv.)   ĕ′-brô   eh′-bro
Eccles, Marriner   ĕk′-əlz, mär′-ə-nər ek′-uhlz, mehr′-uh-
  Stoddard (Am. banker) stŏd′-ərd   nuhr stod′-uhrd
Ečer, Bohuslav   ĕ′-chĕr, bô′-hŏŏ- eh′-chehr, bo′-hu-
  (Cz. polit.)   släf   slahf
Ech, Loch (Scot.)   ĕk′, lŏk(h)′   ek′, lok(h)′
Echagüe (P.I.)   ĕ-chä′-gwĕ   eh-chah′-gweh

echelon	*Eng.* ĕsh'-ə-lŏn	esh'-uh-lon
	or ĕch'-ə-lŏn	ech'-uh-lon
	Fr. ĕsh-lôN'	esh-loN'
Échiré (Fr.)	ĕ-shē-rĕ'	eh-shee-reh'
Echt (Neth.)	ĕk(h)t'	ek(h)t'
Echternach (Luxem.)	ĕk(h)'-tər-näk(h)	ek(h)'-tuhr-nahk(h)
Écija (Sp.)	ĕ'-thē-hä *or* -sē-	eh'-thee-hah *or* -see-
l'École (Fr.)	lĕ-kôl'	leh-kol'
economics	ē'-kə-nŏ'-mĭks	ee'-kuh-no'-miks
	or ĕk'-ə-nŏ'-mĭks	ek'-uh-no'-miks

Of nine authoritative dictionaries, eight list the pronunciation with ē- before that with ĕk-. While the order of placement is not decisive, it suggests the pronunciation ē'-kə-nŏ'-mĭks [ee'-kuh-no'-miks] for a program where agreement on the pronunciation is called for.

Écouché (Fr.)	ĕ-kōō-shĕ'	eh-koo-sheh'
Écouen (Fr.)	ĕ-kwäN'	eh-kwahN'
Ecrehou (Fr., isls.)	ĕ-krə-ōō'	eh-kruh-oo'
Ecton, Zales N.	ĕk'-tən, zālz'	ek'-tuhn, zaylz'
(U.S. representative)		
Ecuador (S.A.)	*Eng.* ĕk'-wə-dôr	ek'-wuh-dor
	Sp. ĕ-kwä-dôr'	eh-kwah-dor'
Ecueillé (Fr.)	ĕ-kû-yĕ'	eh-kœ-yeh'
Edam (Neth.)	*Eng.* ē'-dăm	ee'-dam
	Du. ā-däm'	ay-dahm'
Eddekhila (Tun.)	ĕd-dĕ-kē'-lä	ed-deh-kee'-lah

Also spelled *El Dekhila*.

Ede (Neth.)	ā'-də	ay'-duh
Ede, James Chuter	ēd', jāmz'	eed', jaymz'
(Br. polit.)	chōōt'-ər	choot'-uhr
Edenkoben (Ger.)	ā'-dən-kō'-bən	ay'-duhn-koh'-buhn
Eder (Ger., riv.)	ā'-dər	ay'-duhr
EDES (Gr.)	ĕ'-dĕs	eh'-des

The initials of the words for Greek Democratic National Army.

Edessa (Gr.)	ĕ'-dĕ-sä	eh'-deh-sah
Edinburgh (Scot.)	ĕd'-ĭn-bŭr'-ə	ed'-in-buhr'-uh

As an American place name, *Edinburg* is pronounced ĕd'-ĭn-bûrg [ed'-in-buhrg].

Edirne (Turk.)	ĕ-dēr'-nĕ	eh-deer'-neh

Also called *Adrianople*, q.v.

Edisto (S.C., isl.)	ĕd'-ĭ-stō	ed'-i-stoh
Edjehan (Tun.)	ĕd-jə-hăn'	ed-juh-han'

Also spelled *El Djehan*, q.v.

Edom (Trans-Jordan)	ē'-dəm	ee'-duhm
Eduskunta	ĕ'-dōōs-kōōn-tä	eh'-dus-kun-tah

Finnish parliament.

Eecloo (Belg.)	āk'-lō	ayk'-loh
Eelde (Neth.)	āl'-də	ayl'-duh
Eem (Neth., riv.)	ām'	aym'
Eenrum (Neth.)	ān'-rəm	ayn'-ruhm
Eersel (Neth.)	ār'-səl	ayr'-suhl
Efate (Oc., New Hebrides)	ĕ-fä'-tĕ	eh-fah'-teh

French *Vaté*, vä-tĕ' [vah-teh'].

effendi	ĕ-fĕn'-dĭ	eh-fehn'-di

A title or honorific in the Middle East, usually following the name. It is disregarded in alphabetical listing.

Efogi (Oc., New Guinea, Papua)	ĕ-fō'-gē	eh-foh'-gee
Egadi, Isole (Sicily)	ĕ'-gä-dē, ē'-zȯ-lĕ	eh'-gah-dee, ee'-zo-leh

English the *Aegadian Isles*, ĭ-gā'-dĭ-ən [i-gay'-di-uhn], or the *Aegates*, ĭ-gā'-tēz [i-gay'-teez].

Eger (Ger., Cz., riv.; Cz., town)	*Ger.* ā'-gər	ay'-guhr

See *Ohře* and *Cheb*.

Eger (Hung.)	ĕ'-gĕr	eh'-gehr

German *Erlau*, ĕr'-lou [ehr'-lau].

Egersund (Nor.)	āg-ər-sōͦn'	ayg-uhr-sun'
Eggedal (Nor.)	ĕg'-ə-däl	eg'-uh-dahl
L'Église de Grenneville (Fr.)	lĕ-glēz də grĕn-vēl'	leh-gleez duh gren-veel'
Egmond-aan-Zee (Neth.)	ĕk(h)'-mȏnt än zā'	ek(h)'-mont ahn zay
Egmond Binnen (Neth.)	ĕk(h)'-mȏnt bĭn'-ən	ek(h)'-mont bin'-uhn
Eguía (P.I.)	ĕ-gē'-ä	eh-gee'-ah
Egypt (Afr.)	ē'-jĭpt	ee'-jipt

Arabic *El Qutr el Masri*, ĕl kōͦ'tr ĕl mäs'-rĭ [el koo'tr el mahs'-ri] or *El Masr*, ĕl mäsr' [el mahsr'].

Ehime (Jap.)	ĕ-hē'-mĕ'	eh-hee'-meh'
Ehmen (Ger.)	ā'-mən	ay'-muhn
Ehrang (Ger.)	ā'-räng	ay'-rahng
Ehrenbreitstein (Ger.)	ā'-rən-brīt'-shtĭn	ay'-ruhn-brait'-shtain
Ehrenburg, Ilya Grigorievich (Rus. writer)	ā'-rən-bŏȯrk, ĭl-yä' grĭ-gôr'-yĕ-vĭch	ay'-ruhn-boork, il-yah' gri-gor'-yeh-vich
ei		

In Dutch *ei* is interchangeable with *ij* and *y*, though *ij* is usually preferred when initial. A consultant may have to look for all three forms before he finds his word. Dutch and German *ei* is pronounced approximately ī [ai]. In other languages, including Arabic, the pronunciation ā [ay] is usually required or preferable.

Eibergen (Neth.)	ī'-bĕrk(h)-ən	ai'-berk(h)-uhn

[152]

Eichelberger, Robert L. ĭ′-kəl-bûr′-gər ai′-kuhl-bûr′-guhr
(Am. general)
Eidanger (Nor.) ā-däng′-ər ay-dahng′-uhr
Eide (Nor.) ā′-də ay′-duh
Eidsbugaren (Nor.) āds-bōō-gä′-rən ayds-boo-gah′-ruhn
Eidsfoss (Nor.) āds′-fôs ayds′-fos
Eidsoera or āds′-û-rə ayds′-œ-ruh
 Eidsöra (Nor.)
Eidsvold (Nor.) āds′-vôl ayds′-vol
Eidt Kunen (Ger. >Rus.) See *Eydt Kuhnen.*
Eifel (Ger., mts.) ĭ′-fəl ai′-fuhl
 Also called *Schnee Eifel,* shnā′ ĭ′-fəl [shnay′ ai′-fuhl].
Eiffel Tower (Paris) *Eng.* ĭ′-fəl ai′-fuhl
 Fr. ĕ-fĕl′ eh-fel′
Eigelshoven (Neth.) ĭ′-k(h)əls-hō′-vən ai′-k(h)uhls-hoh′-
 vuhn
Eijsden or Eisden (Neth.) īs′-dən ais′-duhn
Eikesdal (Nor.) ā′-kəs-däl ay′-kuhs-dahl
Eildon (Scot., hills) ēl′-dən eel′-duhn
Eilendorf (Ger.) ĭ′-lən-dôrf ai′-luhn-dorf
Eil Malk (Oc., Carolines) āl′ mälk′ ayl′ mahlk′
ʻein ān′ ayn′
 An element, meaning *spring,* in Arabic and Hebrew place names. Also
 spelled ʻ*ain* and ʻ*en.*
Eina (Nor.) ā′-nä ay′-nah
Eindhoven (Neth.) īnt′-hō-vən aint′-hoh-vuhn
Ein Jidi (Pal.) ān jĭ-dē′ ayn ji-dee′
 Also called *Engedi,* q.v.
Einruhr (Ger.) īn′-rōōr ain′-roor
Einville (Fr.) ăN-vēl′ aN-veel′
Eire (= Ireland) ĕr′-ə ehr′-uh
 or *Irish* ā′-rə ay′-ruh
 The analogy should be *Erin* not *Ireland.*
Eireann ĕr′-ən or ā′-rôn ehr′-uhn or ay′-ron
 Adjective of *Eire.*
Eirene, Agia (Crete) ē-rē′-nē, ĭ′-yä ee-ree′-nee, ai′-yah
Eisden (Neth.) See *Eijsden.*
Eisenach (Ger.) ĭ′-zən-äk(h) ai′-zuhn-ahk(h)
Eisenberg (Ger.) ĭ′-zən-bĕrk(h) ai′-zuhn-behrk(h)
Eisenhower, Dwight D. ĭ′-zən-hou′-ər ai′-zuhn-hau′-uhr
(Am. general)
 The pronunciation ĭ′-sĕn-hou′-ər [ai′-sen-hau′-uhr] is exceptional.
Eisernes Tor (Rum., Yugosl., gorge) See *Iron Gates.*
Eisk (Rus.) āsk′ aysk′

Eisleben (Ger.)	īs'-lā-bən	ais'-lay-buhn
Eisteddfod (Welsh festi-val)	īs-tĕ*th*'-fəd	ais-teh*th*'-fuhd
Eitorf (Ger.)	ī'-tôrf	ai'-torf
Ekimchan (Rus.)	ĕ-kĭm-chän'	eh-kim-chahn'
EKKA (Gr.)	ĕ'-kä	eh'-kah

The initials of the words for National and Social Liberation of Greece.

| el *or* al | ĕl, äl | el, ahl |

The Arabic article complicates alphabetical listing. It may or may not be omitted; it may be spelled with *e* or *a*; the consonant *l* may be assimilated to that of the following word. Thus *El Kerak* and *Kerak* both occur. *El Djem* is pronounced and may be written *Ed Djem* or *Edjem*. *Alhambra* is from Arabic *al hamra'*; *Suez* from Arabic *Es Suweis*. The consultant may have to look for several forms or for the second element of the name.

Ela (Burma, riv.)	ā'-lä	ay'-lah
El Adem (Libya)	ĕl ă'-dĕm	el a'-dem
El Agelat (Libya)	ĕl ä-gĕ-lăt'	el ah-geh-lat'
El Agheila (Libya)	ĕl ä-gā'-lä	el ah-gay'-lah
El Akarit (Tun.)	ĕl ä-kä-rēt'	el ah-kah-reet'
El Alamein (Egypt)	ĕl ä-lä-mān'	el ah-lah-mayn'
El Alia (Tun.)	ĕl ä'-lĭ-ä	el ah'-li-ah
El Amine, Sidi Mohammed (Arab polit.)	ĕl ä-mēn', sē'-dē mŏŏ-häm'-mĕd	el ah-meen', see'-dee mu-hahm'-med
El Aouana (Tun.)	ĕl ä-wă'-nä	el ah-wa'-nah
El Aouaria (Tun.)	ĕl ä-wä-rē'-yä	el ah-wah-ree'-yah
Elaphonesi (Crete, isl.)	ĕ-lä-fô-nē'-sē	eh-lah-fo-nee'-see
Elaphonesos (Gr., isl.)	ĕ-lä-fô'-nē-sôs	eh-lah-fo'-nee-sos
El Arima (Tun.)	ĕl ä-rē'-mä	el ah-ree'-mah
El Arish (Egypt)	ĕl ä-rēsh'	el ah-reesh'
El Aroussa (Tun.)	ĕl ä-rōō'-sä	el ah-roo'-sah
ELAS (Gr.)	ĕ'-läs	eh'-lahs

The initials of the words for Greek Popular Liberation Army.

Elasa (Crete, isl.)	ĕ'-lä-sä	eh'-lah-sah
Elason (Gr.)	ĕ-lä-sôn'	eh-lah-son'
Elato (Oc., Carolines)	ĕ-lä'-tô	eh-lah'-to
El Auja (Pal.)	ĕl ou'-jä	el au'-jah
El Azaria (Pal.) See *Bethany*.		
El Azib (Tun.)	ĕl ä'-zĭb	el ah'-zib
El Azizia (Libya)	ĕl ă-zĭ-zē'-ä	el a-zi-zee'-ah
Elbach (Ger., riv.)	ĕl'-bäk(h)	el'-bahk(h)
Elbasan (Alb.)	ĕl-bä-sän'	el-bah-sahn'
Elbasani (Alb.) See *Elbasan*.		

Elbe (Europ. riv.)   *Ger.* ĕl'-bə   el'-buh
    Czech *Labe,* lä'-bĕ [lah'-beh].

El Belqa (Trans-Jordan) See *Moab* and *Gilead.*

Elberta (peach)   ĕl-bûr'-tə   el-bur'-tuh

Elbeuf (Fr.)   ĕl-bûf'   el-bœf'

Elbing (Ger. >Pol.)   ĕl'-bǐng   el'-bing
    Polish *Elbląg,* q.v.

Elbląg (Ger. >Pol.)   ĕl'-bläNk   el'-blahNk
    German *Elbing,* q. v.

Elborus (Rus., mt.)   ĕl-bŏ-rōōs'   el-bo-rus'
    English *Elbrus,* ĕl'-brōōs [el'-brus], *or* āl'-brōōs' [ayl'-broos'].

Elbrus (Rus., mt.) See *Elborus.*

Elburg (Neth.)   ĕl'-bûrk(h)   el'-bœrk(h)

Elburz (Iran, mts.)   ăl'-bōŏrz'   al'-burz'

El Caudillo (Sp.)   ĕl kou-dē'-lyô *or* -yô   el kau-dee'-lyo *or* -yo
    Spanish for *the leader.* Cf. *il Duce* and *der Fuehrer.*

El Daba (Libya)   ĕd däb'-ä   ed dahb'-ah

El Dehibat (Tun.)   ĕd dĕ-hǐ-băt'   ed deh-hi-bat'

El Dekhila (Tun.)   See *Eddekhila.*

El Djehaf (Tun.)   See *Djebel Edjehaf.*

El Djehan (Tun.)   ĕd jə-hăn'   ed juh-han'
    Also spelled *Edjehan,* q.v.

El Djem (Tun.)   ĕd jĕm'   ed jem'

El Dorado   *Sp.* ĕl dô-rä'-dô   el do-rah'-do
    In English the myth is pronounced ĕl də-rä'-dō [el duh-rah'-doh] or
    ĕl də-rā'-dō [el duh-ray'-doh] or, old fashioned (and in Poe's rhyme),
    ĕl də-răd'-ō [el duh-rad'-oh]. As a place name -rä'- [-rah'-] is reported
    for California and, oddly, for Arkansas; and -rā'- [-ray'-] for Illinois,
    Kansas, and Missouri. The final syllable *-do* may be pronounced -də
    [-duh]. Cf. *tomato.*

El Duda (Libya)   ĕd dōō'-dä   ed doo'-dah

Elena (Bulg.)   yĕ'-lĕ-nä   yeh'-leh-nah

Elena, Colonia (It.)   ĕ'-lĕ-nä, kô-lô'-nyä   eh'-leh-nah, ko-lo'-
                                                    nyah

El Erg (Alg., Tun.)   ĕl ĕrg'   el ehrg'

Eleusis (Gr.)   *Eng.* ē-lyōō'-sǐs   ee-lyoo'-sis
    Greek *Elevsis,* ĕ-lĕf-sēs' [eh-lef-sees'].

Eleuthera (Bahamas)   ǐ-lyōō'-thər-ə   i-lyoo'-thuhr-uh

Elevtheri Ellada (Gr.   ĕ-lĕf'-thĕ-rē ĕl-lä'-dä   eh-lef'-theh-ree el-
    newspaper)   lah'-dah

El Faiyum (Egypt)   ĕl fī-yōōm'   el fai-yoom'

El Faregh (Libya)   ĕl fä'-rĕg   el fah'-reg

El Ferrol (Sp.)   ĕl fĕ-rôl'   el feh-rol'

Elgar, Sir Edward   ĕl′-gər   el′-guhr
   (Br. musician)
   The pronunciation ĕl′-gär is inferior to ĕl′-gər.
El Gazala (Libya)   ĕl gä-zä′-lä   el gah-zah′-lah
El Ghami (Pal.)   ĕl k(h)ä′-mē   el k(h)ah′-mee
Elgin   *Ill.* ĕl′-jĭn   el′-jin
            elsewhere, ĕl′-gĭn   el′-gin
   The *g* is hard in Canada, Scotland, Texas, and the British Museum.
El Giza (Egypt)   ĕl gē′-zə   el gee′-zuh
   Also spelled *Gizeh.*
El Gubbi (Libya)   ĕl go͝o′-bē   el gu′-bee
El Guettar (Tun.)   ĕl gĕ-tär′   el geh-tahr′
El Gusbat (Libya)   ĕl go͝os-băt′   el gus-bat′
El Hamma (Tun.)   ĕl häm′-mä   el hahm′-mah
El Haouaria (Tun.)   ĕl hä-wä-rē′-ä   el hah-wah-ree′-ah
Elia (Gr.)   ĕ-lyä′   eh-lyah′
Elia ("Essays of Elia")   ē′-lĭ-ə   ee′-li-uh
   Pseudonym of Charles Lamb.
Elias (It., mt.)   ĕ-lē′-äs   eh-lee′-ahs
Elika (Gr.)   ĕ-lē′-kä   eh-lee′-kah
El Imayid Station (Egypt) ĕl ē-mă′-yĭd   el ee-ma′-yid
Elis (Gr.)   See *Achaia and Elis.*
Elisenvaara (Fin. > Rus.)   ĕ′-lĭ-sĕn-vä′-rä   eh′-li-sen-vah′-rah
Elista (Rus.)   ĕ′-lĭs-tä   eh′-lis-tah
Elizalde, Joaquín M.   ĕ-lē-säl′-dĕ,   eh-lee-sahl′-deh,
   (Fil. polit.)   hwä-kēn′   hwah-keen′
El Jelil (Pal.) See *Galilee.*
El Kerak (Trans-Jordan) ĕl kĕ′-räk *or* kĕ′-räk   el keh′-rahk *or* keh′-
El Khalil (Pal.) See *Hebron.*   rak
El Kharita (Egypt)   ĕl kä′-rē-tə   el kah′-ree-tuh
Elkhotovo (Rus.)   ĕl-hô′-tŏ-vŏ   el-ho′-to-vo
Elkhovo (Bulg.)   yĕl′-kŏ-vŏ   yel′-ko-vo
El Khudeira (Pal.) See *Hadera.*
Elle (Fr., riv.)   ĕl′   el′
Ellender, Allen J.   ĕl′-ən-dər   el′-uhn-duhr
   (U.S. senator)
Ellenikon (Gr.)   ĕ-lē-nē-kô(n)′   eh-lee-nee-ko(n)′
Ellenikon Aima (Gr.   ĕ-lē′-nē-kôn ĕ′-mä   eh-lee′-nee-kon eh′-
   newspaper)   mah
Ellice Isls. (Oc.)   ĕl′-ĭs   el′-is
El Mabtouha (Tun.)   ĕl məb-to͞o′-hə   el muhb-too′-huh
El Majdal (Pal.)   ĕl măj′-däl   el maj′-dahl
El Maou (Tun.)   ĕl mou′   el mau′
Elmas (Sard.)   ĕl′-mäs   el′-mahs

El Mekhili (Libya)	ĕl mĕ-kē′-lē	el meh-kee′-lee
El Miteiriya (Egypt)	ĕl mĭ-tä-rē′-yä	el mi-tay-ree′-yah
Elmshorn (Ger.)	ĕlms′-hôrn	elms′-horn
Elne (Fr.)	ĕln′	eln′

El Nokrashy (Egypt. polit.) See *Mahmoud Fahmy El Nokrashy.*

El Obeid (Sudan)	ĕl ô-bād′	el o-bayd′
El Paso (Tex.)	ĕl păs′-ō	el pas′-oh
El Rharsa (Tun.)	ĕr rär′-sä	ehr rahr′-sah
Elsaesser, Edward J.	ĕl′-sĕs-ər	el′-ses-uhr
(U.S. representative)		
El Salvador (C.A.)	ĕl säl-vä-dôr′	el sahl-vah-dor′
Elsene (Belg.)	*Flem.* ĕl′-sə-nə	el′-suh-nuh
French *Ixelles,* ĭk-sĕl′ [ik-sel′].		
Elsloo (Neth.)	ĕls′-lō	els′-loh
Elst (Neth.)	ĕlst′	elst′
Elster (Ger., riv.)	ĕl′-stər	el′-stuhr
El Taqa (Egypt)	ĕt tä′-kä	et tah′-kah
Eltegen (Rus.)	ĕl-tĕ′-gĕn	el-teh′-gen
Eltonskaya (Rus.)	ĕl-tôn′-skä-yä	el-ton′-skah-yah
Elvedalen (Nor.)	ĕl′-və-dä-lən	el′-vuh-dah-luhn
Elverum (Nor.)	ĕl′-və-rŏŏm	el′-vuh-rum
Elveseter (Nor.)	ĕl′-və-sä-tər	el′-vuh-say-tuhr
Emae (Oc.,	ĕng-mī′	eng-mai′
New Hebrides)		
French *Mai,* mī′ [mai′].		
Emau (Oc.,	ĕng-mou′	eng-mau′
New Hebrides)		
French *Maou,* mou′ [mau].		
Emba (Rus.)	ĕm′-bä	em′-bah
Emeny, Brooks	ĕm′-ə-nĭ	em′-uh-ni
(Am. educator)		
Emerainville (Fr.)	ĕm-răN-vēl′	em-raN-veel′
emir	ə-mēr′	uh-meer′

A title or honorific in the Middle East and Africa. It is disregarded in alphabetical listing.

Emirau (Oc., Bismarck	ĕ-mē-rou′	eh-mee-rau′
arch.)		
Emmen (Neth.)	ĕm′-ən	em′-uhn
Emmendingen (Ger.)	ĕm′-ən-dĭng′-ən	em′-uhn-ding′-uhn
Emmerich (Ger.)	ĕm′-ər-ĭk(h)	em′-uhr-ik(h)
Empedocle (It.)	ĕm-pĕ′-dô-klĕ	em-peh′-do-kleh

Also called *Porto Empedocle,* q.v.

Empoli (It.)	ĕm′-pô-lē	em′-po-lee
Empros (Gr. newspaper)	ĕm-brôs′	em-bros′

Ems (Ger.)	*Eng.* ĕmz'	emz'
	Ger. ĕms' *or* āms'	ems' *or* ayms'

'en. See '*ein.*

Encinitas (Calif.)	ĕn'-sĭ-nē'-təs	en'-si-nee'-tuhs
Enckell, Carl J. A.	ĕng'-kəl, kärl'	eng'-kuhl, kahrl'
(Fin. diplomat)		
Ende (NEI, Flores)	ĕn'-də	en'-duh
Enez (Turk.)	ĕ'-nĕz	eh'-nez

Greek *Ainos,* ĕ'-nôs [eh'-nos]. Bulgarian *Enos,* ĕ'-nŏs [eh'-nos].

Enfidaville (Tun.)	ĕn-fē-dä-vēl'	en-fee-dah-veel'
	or Fr. äN-fē-dä-vēl'	ahN-fee-dah-veel'
Engaño (P.I., cape)	ĕn-gä'-nyô	en-gah'-nyo
Engebi (Oc., Eniwetok)	ĕng'-gĕ'-bē	eng'-geh'-bee
Engedi (Pal.)	än-gĕ'-dē	ayn-geh'-dee

Also called *Ein Jidi,* q.v.

Engel, Albert J.	ĕng'-əl	eng'-uhl
(U.S. representative)		
Engelhardt, V. A.	ĕn-gĕl-gärt'	en-gel-gahrt'
(Rus. scientist)		
Engels (Ger.)	ĕng'-əls	eng'-uhls
Engels (Pokrovsk) (Rus.)	ĕng'-gĕls (pŏk-rôfsk')	eng'-gels (pok-rofsk')
Enggano (NEI)	ĕng-gä'-nô	eng-gah'-no
Englebright, Harry L.	ĕng'-gəl-brīt	eng'-guhl-brait
(U. S. representative)		
Enguinegatte (Fr.)	äN-gēn-gät'	ahN-geen-gaht'
Eniwetok (Oc., Marshalls)	*Eng.* ĕn-ĭ-wē'-tŏk	en-i-wee'-tok
	native ĕ-nē'-wĕ-tôk	eh-nee'-weh-tok

The first has been popularized by forces returning from the South
Pacific. The second is that given in the pamphlets of the PCGN,
Royal Geographical Society. Cf. *Tahiti* and *Tarawa.*

Enkhuizen (Neth.)	ĕnk-hûĭ'-zən	enk-hœi'-zuhn
Enna (Sicily)	ĕn'-nä	en'-nah

En Nasira (Pal.) See *Nazareth.*

Enniscorthy (Eire)	ĕn-ĭs-kôr'-*th*ĭ	en-is-kor'-*th*i
Enniskillen (No. Ire.)	ĕn-ĭs-kĭl'-ən	en-is-kil'-uhn
En Nofilia (Libya)	ĕn nô-fē'-lyä	en no-fee'-lyah
Enogai (Oc.)	ĕ-nô-gī'	eh-no-gai'

Enos (Turk.) See *Enez.*

Enoshima (Jap.)	ĕ-nô'-shē'-mä'	eh-no'-shee'-mah'
Enschede (Neth.)	ĕn'-sk(h)ə-dä'	en'-sk(h)uh-day'
ensemble	*Eng.* än-sŏm'-bəl	ahn-som'-buhl
	Fr. äN-säN'bl	ahN-sahN'bl

The English pronunciation is preferable for American radio because
the final *l* of our French pronunciation is usually lost in transmission.

Ensenade (Mex.)	ĕn-sĕ-nä'-dä	ehn-seh-nah'-dah

Entebbe (Uganda)	ĕn-tĕb′-bĕ	en-teb′-beh
entire	ĕn-tīr′	en-tair′

For emphasis the accent may occasionally shift to the first syllable; normally it should be placed on the final syllable.

Entizam, Nasrullah (Iran. polit.)	ĕn-tĭ-zäm′, näs-ro͝ol′-lä	ehn-ti-zahm′, nahs-rul′-lah
Entrammes (Fr.)	äN-träm′	ahN-trahm′
Entre Ríos (Arg.)	ĕn′-trĕ rē′-ôs	en′-treh ree′-os
envoy	ĕn′-voi	en′-voi

The first syllable should not be pronounced like the first syllable of French *enfant*, but like that of English *envy*.

Enz (Ger., riv.)	ĕnts′	ents′
Eolie, Isole (Sicily)	ĕ-ô′-lyĕ, ē′-zô-lĕ	eh-o′-lyeh, ee′-zo-leh

The *Aeolian Isls.*, usually called in English the *Lipari Isls*, q.v.

Epe (Neth.)	ā′-pə	ay′-puh
Épernay (Fr.)	ĕ-pĕr-nĕ′	eh-pehr-neh′
Épernon (Fr.)	ĕ-pĕr-nôN′	eh-pehr-noN′
Ephrata	*Pa.* ĕf′-rə-tə	ef′-ruh-tuh
	Wash. ĭ-frā′-tə	i-fray′-tuh
Épinal (Fr.)	ĕ-pē-näl′	eh-pee-nahl′
Épinay (Fr.)	ĕ-pē-nĕ′	eh-pee-neh′
Epirus *or* Epiros (Gr.)	*Eng.* ē-pī′-rəs	ee-pai′-ruhs
	Gr. ē′-pē-rôs	ee′-pee-ros
epitome	ĭ-pĭt′-ə-mĭ	i-pit′-uh-mi
Épône Mézières (Fr.)	ĕ-pōn mĕ-zyĕr′	eh-pohn meh-zyehr′
Epte (Fr., riv.)	ĕpt′	ept′
Équeurdreville (Fr.)	ĕ-kûr-drə-vēl′	eh-kœr-druh-veel′
l'Équille (Fr.)	lĕ-kēl′	leh-keel′
era	ĭr′-ə	ir′-uh

The pronunciation ĕr′-ə [ehr′-uh] is not recommended.

Erakleion (Crete)	ē-rä′-klē-ô(n)	ee-rah′-klee-o(n)

Also spelled *Herakleion*, q.v.

Ercegnovi (Yugosl.)	ĕr′-tsĕg-nô′-vĭ	ehr′-tseg-no′-vi
Erciyas (Turk., mt.)	ĕr-jē′-äs	ehr-jee′-ahs

Also called *Erceyiş*, ĕr-jä′-ĭsh [ehr-jay′-ish].

Ercsi (Hung.)	ĕr′-chĭ	ehr′-chih
Erdre (Fr., riv.)	ĕr′dr	ehr′dr
Erdželija (Yugosl.)	ĕr′-jĕ-lē′-yä	ehr′-jeh-lee′-yah
Ereğli (Turk.)	ĕ-rä′-lē	eh-ray′-lee

Greek *Herakleia*, ē-rä′-klē-ä [ee-rah′-klee-ah].

Erenik (Yugosl., riv.)	ĕ′-rĕ-nĭk	eh′-reh-nik
Eretria (Gr.)	*Eng.* ĭ-rē′-trĭ-ə	i-ree′-tri-uh
Erfelden (Ger.)	ĕr′-fĕl-dən	ehr′-fel-duhn
Erft (Ger., riv.)	ĕrft′	ehrft′
Erfurt (Ger.)	ĕr′-fo͝ort	ehr′-furt

Erg, el (Alg., Tun., dunes)	ĕrg′, ĕl	ehrg′, el
Erg Iguidi (Mor., Alg., dunes)	ĕrg ē-gē-dē′	ehrg ee-gee-dee′
Erickson, Leif (U.S. polit.)	ĕr′-ĭk-sən, lēf′ or *Nor.* lāf′	ehr′-ik-suhn, leef′ or *Nor.* layf′
Ericussa (Gr., isl.) Also called *Merlera.*	ĕ-rē-kōōs′-sä	eh-ree-koos′-sah
Eriksson, Herman (Sw. diplomat)	ā′-rĭk-sôn, hĕr′-män	ay′-rik-son, hehr′-mahn
Erikub (Oc., Marshalls)	ĕ-rē-kōōb′	eh-ree-koob′
Eritrea (Afr.)	*It.* ĕ-rē-trĕ′-ä *Eng.* ĕ-rĭ-trē′-ə	eh-ree-treh′-ah eh-ri-tree′-uh
Erivan (Rus.) Also called *Yerevan*, q.v.	ĕ′-rĭ-vän′(y)	eh′-ri-vahn′(y)
Erkelenz (Ger.)	ĕr′-kə-lĕnts	ehr′-kuh-lents
Erkner (Ger.)	ĕrk′-nər	ehrk′-nuhr
Erlangen (Ger.)	ĕr′-läng-ən	ehr′-lahng-uhn
Erlau (Hung.) See *Eger.*		
Erma (Balkan riv.) Serb-Croat *Jerma*, q.v.	*Bulg.* yĕr′-mä	yehr′-mah
Ermeloo (Neth.)	ĕr′-mə-lō	ehr′-muh-loh
Ermita (P.I.)	ĕr-mē′-tä	ehr-mee′-tah
Erne (Eire, riv.)	ûrn′	uhrn′
Ernée (Fr.)	ĕr-nĕ′	ehr-neh′
Ernes (Fr.)	ĕrn′	ehrn′
Ernici (It., mts.)	ĕr′-nē-chē	ehr′-nee-chee
Ernstfelde (Ger.)	ĕrnst′-fĕl-də	ehrnst′-fel-duh
Eromanga (Austral.)	ĕr′-ō-măng′-gə	ehr′-oh-mang′-guh
Erp (Neth.)	ĕrp′	ehrp′
Erpel (Ger.)	ĕr′-pəl	ehr′-puhl
Er Ramle (Pal.)	ĕr räm′-lə	er rahm′-luh
Erseka (Alb.) See *Ersekë.*		
Ersekë (Alb.)	ĕr-sĕ′-kə	ehr-seh′-kuh
Érsekújvár (Cz.) See *Nové Zámky.*		
Erstein (Fr.)	*Fr.* ĕr-stăN′ *Ger.* ĕr′-shtīn	ehr-staN′ ehr′-shtain
Erzen (Alb., riv.) Greek *Artzen.* Italian *Arzen.*	ĕr-zĕn′	ehr-zen′
Erzeni (Alb., riv.) See *Erzen.*		
Erzerum (Turk.)	ĕr′-zə-rōōm	ehr′-zuh-rum
Esbjærg *or* Esbjerg (Den.)	ĕs′-byĕr	es′-byehr
Escanaba (Mich.)	ĕs′-kə-nä′-bə	es′-kuh-nah′-buh
Escardó, Grace (Peru. artist)	ĕs-kär-dô′	ehs-kahr-do′

l'Escaut (Fr., Belg., Neth., riv.) See *Scheldt.*

Esch (Ger.) ĕsh′ esh′

Esch sur Altz (Luxem.) ĕsh sür älts′ esh sür ahlts′

Eschweiler (Ger.) esh′-vī-lər esh′-vai-luhr

Escoville (Fr.) ĕs-kô-vēl′ es-ko-veel′

Escuintla (Guat., Mex.) ĕs-kwēnt′-lä ehs-kweent′-lah

Esdraelon (Pal.) ĕz′-drə-ē′-lən ez′-druh-ee′-luhn
Also called the Plain of *Jezreel,* q.v.

Esel *or* Ezel (Est., isl.) *Rus.* ĕ′-zĕl(y) eh′-zel(y)
Also called *Ostrov Sarema,* q.v. Estonian *Saare(maa),* q.v.

Esino (It., riv.) ĕ′-sē-nô eh′-see-no

Eskişehir (Turk.) ĕs-kē′-shĕ-hēr es-kee′-sheh-heer

Esmé (Eng. name) ĕz′-mĭ ehz′-mi

Eso (Yugos., isl.) *It.* ĕ′-sô eh′-so
Serb-Croat *Iž,* q.v.

España (English *Spain*) ĕs-pä′-nyä es-pah′-nyah

Espedal (Nor., lake) ĕs′-pə-däl es′-puh-dahl

Esperance (Austral.) ĕs′-pə-rəns es′-puh-ruhns

Esperia (It.) ĕ-spĕ′-ryä eh-speh′-ryah

Espínola, Eduardo (ĭ)spē′-nô-lə, (i)spee′-no-luh,
(Braz. polit.) ĕ-dwär′-dŏŏ eh-dwahr′-du

Espirito Santo (Brazil) (ĭ)spē′-rē-tŏŏ (i)spee′-ree-tu
sän′-tŏŏ sahn′-tu

Esquay (Fr.) ĕs-kĕ′ es-keh′

Esquiline (It., Rome) *Eng.* ĕs′-kwĭ-līn es′-kwih-lain
Italian *Esquilino,* ĕs-kwē-lē′-nô [es-kwee-lee′-no].

Es Salt (Trans-Jordan) ĕs sält′ es sahlt′

Essarts, les (Fr.) ĕ-sär′, lĕz eh-sahr′, lez

Essen (Ger.) ĕs′-ən es′-uhn

Esserden (Ger.) ĕs′-ər-dən es′-uhr-duhn

Esslingen (Ger.) ĕs′-lĭng-ən es′-ling-uhn

Es Suweis (Egypt) See *Suez.*

Estado de São Paulo, O (ĭ)stä′-dŏŏ dĭ souN (i)stah′-du di sauN
(Braz. newspaper) pou′-lŏŏ, ŏŏ pau′-lu, u

Estanzuela (P.I.) ĕs-tän-swĕ′-lä es-tahn-sweh′-lah
Also called *Caridad,* q.v.

Esternay (Fr.) ĕs-tĕr-nĕ′ es-tehr-neh′

Esthonia (Rus.) See *Estonia.*

Estimé, Dumarsais (Haitian polit.) See *Dumarsais Estimé.*

Estlandia (Rus.) See *Estonia.*

Estonia (Rus.) ĕs-tō′-nyə es-toh′-nyuh
Also called *Esthonia,* ĕs-thō-nyə [es-thoh′-nyuh]. Estonian *Eestimaa,*
ās′-tĭ-mä [ays′-ti-mah]. Russian *Estlandia,* ĕst-län′-dĭ-yä [est-lahn′-di-yah].

Estoril (Port.)	ĭsh-tô-rēl′	ish-to-reel′
Estrées (Fr.)	ĕs-trĕ′	es-treh′
Estremadura (Port.)	ĕsh-trə-mə-dōō′-rə	esh-truh-muh-doo′-ruh
Estremadura (Sp.)	ĕs-trĕ-mä-dōō′-rä	es-treh-mah-doo′-rah
Esztergom (Hung.)	ĕs′-tĕr-gôm	es′-tehr-gom

German *Gran*, grän′ [grahn′].

Etal (Oc., Carolines)	ĕ-täl′	eh-tahl′
Étampes (Fr.)	ĕ-täNp′	eh-tahNp′
étang	ĕ-täN′	eh-tahN′

In French names an element meaning *lagoon*. Look up the other part of the name.

Étaples (Fr.)	ĕ-tä′pl	eh-tah′pl
Etchegoyen, Alcides	ĕ-chə-gô′-yən,	eh-chuh-go′-yuhn,
(Braz. polit.)	äl-sē′-dĭs	ahl-see′-dis
Eten (Neth.)	ā′-tən	ay′-tuhn
Eten (Oc., Truk)	ĕ′-tĕn	eh′-ten
Ethiopia (Afr.)	ē′-thĭ-ō′-pĭ-ə	ee′-thi-oh′-pi-uh

Also called Abyssinia, ăb′-ĭ-sĭn′-ĭ-ə [ab′-i-sin′-i-uh]. Abyssinian *Ityopya*, ē-tyô′-pyä [ee-tyo′-pyah].

Etienne (Alaska, Attu)	ĕ-tyĕn′	eh-tyen′
Etimesğut (Turk.,	ĕ-tē′-mĕs-yōōt	eh-tee′-mes-yut
Ankara, airport)		
Etna (Sicily)	*Eng.* ĕt′-nə	et′-nuh
	It. ĕt′-nä	et′-nah

Etna (Crete) is pronounced ĕt-nä′ [et-nah′].

l'Étoile (Fr.)	lĕ-twäl′	leh-twahl′
Étretat (Fr.)	ĕ-trə-tä′	eh-truh-tah′
Ettelbruck (Luxem.)	ĕt′-əl-brŏŏk	et′-uhl-bruk
Etten (Neth.)	ĕt′-ən	et′-uhn
Ettenheim (Ger.)	ĕt′-ən-hīm	et′-uhn-haim
Ettlingen (Ger.)	ĕt′-lĭng-ən	et′-ling-uhn
Eu (Fr.)	û′	œ′
Eu (Gr.)	û′	œ′

Euboea (Gr., isl.) See *Evvoia*.

| Eucla (Austral.) | yōō′-klə | yoo′-kluh |

Euganea (It.) See *Venezia Euganea*.

| Euganean Hills (It.) | yōō-gā′-nĭ-ən | yoo-gay′-ni-uhn |
| | *or* yōō′-gə-nē′-ən | yoo′-guh-nee′-uhn |

Italian *Colli Euganei*, kôl′-lē ĕ-ōō-gä′-nä [kol′-lee eh-oo-gah′-nay].

| Eugen, Prince (Ger.) | oi-gān′ *or* oi′-gän | oi-gayn′ *or* oi′-gayn |

Speakers of German would be inclined to use the first and older pronunciation in the phrase *Prince Eugen*, although the modern family name has the latter. The usual radio pronunciation has been oi'-gĕn [oi'-gen].

Eulenspiegel, Till   *Ger.* oi'-lən-shpē'-   oi'-luhn-shpee'-
                       gəl, tĭl'   guhl, til'
     This form occurs in the title of Strauss' tone poem, but see also *Ulenspiegel.*

Eupen (Belg.)   oi'-pən   oi'-puhn
Eure (Fr.)   ûr'   œr'
Eureka (Calif.)   yōō-rē'-kə   yoo-ree'-kuh
Euskirchen (Ger.)   ois'-kĭr-k(h)ən   ois'-kihr-k(h)uhn
Eutaw (Ala., S.C.)   yōō'-tô   yoo'-taw
Eutin (Ger.)   oi-tēn'   oi-teen'
Euxine Sea   yōōk'-sĭn *or* -sīn   yook'-sin *or* -sain
     Usually called the *Black Sea.* Russian *Chërnoe More,* q.v.

evacuee   ĭ-văk'-yōō-ē'   i-vak'-yoo-ee'
     Webster's (1934) gives only the French word and pronunciation, but the word has since been Englished.

Evangelista (It.)   ĕ-vän-jĕ-lē'-stä   eh-vahn-jeh-lee'-stah
Evatt, Herbert Vere   ĕv'-ət, vĭr'   ev'-uht, vihr'
     (Australian diplomat)
l'Évêque, Pont (Fr.)   lĕ-vĕk', pôN   leh-vek', poN
Evins, Joe L. (U.S.   ĕv'-ənz   ev'-uhnz
     representative)
Évora (Port.)   ĕ'-vô-rə   eh'-vo-ruh
Evoron (Rus., lake)   ĕ'-vŏ-rŏn   eh'-vo-ron
Évrecy (Fr.)   ĕ-vrə-sē'   eh-vruh-see'
Évreux (Fr.)   ĕ-vrû'   eh-vrœ'
Evripos (Gr., strait)   ĕ'-vrē-pôs   eh'-vree-pos
     See *Khalkis.*
Évron (Fr.)   ĕ-vrôN'   eh-vroN'
Evros (Balkan riv.)   ĕ'-vrôs   eh'-vros
     Also called *Maritsa,* q.v.
Evrotas (Gr., riv.)   ĕ-vrô'-täs   eh-vro'-tahs
Evstratios, Agios   ĕf-strä'-tē-ôs,   ef-strah'-tee-os,
     (Gr., isl.)   ī'-yôs   ai'-yos
     Commonly called *Aïstrates,* ī-strä'-tēs [ai-strah'-tees].
Evvoia (Gr., isl.)   ĕ'-vē-ä   eh'-vee-ah
     English *Euboea,* yōō-bē'-ə [yoo-bee'-uh].
evzone   *Eng.* ĕv'-zōn   ev'-zohn
     Plural *evzones,* ĕv'-zōnz [ev'-zohnz]. Greek *evzonos,* ĕv'-zô-nôs [ev'-zo-nos]; plural *evzoni,* ĕv'-zô-nē [ev'-zo-nee].
Ewiig (P.I., riv.) See *Iuálit.*
Ewijk (Neth.)   ā'-wīk   ay'-waik

Exintaris, Georgios   ĕ-ksēn-dä'-rēs,   eh-kseen-dah'-rees,
    (Gr. polit.)   yôr'-yôs   yor'-yos
Exmes (Fr.)   ĕm'   em'
Extremadura (Sp.) See *Estremadura*.
extremist   ĕks-trēm'-ĭst   eks-treem'-ist
    Short *e* in the second syllable is a mistake. The analogy should be
    extreme, not *extremity*.
Eya (Burma)   ā'-yä   ay'-yah
Eya (Rus., riv.)   ā'-yä   ay'-yah
    Also spelled *Yeya*, q.v.
Eydtkau (Ger.)   īt'-kou   ait'-kau
Eydt Kuhnen (Ger.>Rus.)   īt' kōō'-nən   ait'-koo'-nuhn
    Russian *Eidt Kunen*, āt' kōō'-nĕn [ayt' koo'-nen]. In Hitler's time
    called *Ebenrode*, ā'-bən-rō'-də [ay'-buhn-roh'-duh].
Eyguières (Fr.)   ĕ-gyĕr'   eh-gyehr'
Eylau, Deutsch- (Ger.) See *Deutsch Eylau*.
Eyre (Austral.)   ĕr'   ehr'
Eyskens, Gaston   īs'-kəns   ais'-kuhns
    (Belg. polit.)
Eziorka (Pol., riv.)   See *Jezierna*.
Ez Zauia (Libya)   ĕz zä'-wĭ-ä   ez zah'-wi-ah
Ez Zib (Pal.)   ĕz zēb'   ez zeeb'
    Hebrew *Akhziv* or *Achzib*, äk(h)-zēv' *or* -zēb' [ahk(h)-zeev' *or* -zeeb'].
Ez Zuetina (Libya)   ĕz zōō-ĕ-tē'-nä   ez zu-eh-tee'-nah

Faaberg (Nor.)   fô'-bĕr   fo'-behr
Faaborg (Den.)   fô'-bôr   fo'-bor
Fabbriche (It.)   fäb'-brē-kĕ   fahb'-bree-keh
Fabbricia (It.)   fäb-brē'-chä   fahb-bree'-chah
Fabriano (It.)   fä-bryä'-nô   fah-bryah'-no
Facchinetti, Cipriano   fäk-kē-nĕt'-tē,   fahk-kee-neht'-tee,
    (It. polit.)   chē-pryä'-nô   chee-pryah'-no
Fadhil Jamali (Iraqi   fäd'l jə-mä'-lĭ   fahd'l juh-mah'-li
    diplomat)
Faenza (It.)   fä-ĕn'-dzä   fah-en'-dzah
Færoeerne *or* Færöerne   fĕr-û'-ər-nə   fehr-œ'-uhr-nuh
    (Den., isls.)
    English the *Faeroes*, fär'-ōz [fehr'-ohz].
Făgăraş (Rum.)   fə-gə-räsh'   fuh-guh-rahsh'
    Hungarian *Fogaras*, fô'-gŏ-rŏsh [fo'-go-rosh].
Fagernes (Nor.)   fä'-gər-nĕs   fah'-guhr-nes
Făget (Rum.)   fə-jĕt'   fuh-jet'
Fahlun (Sw.) See *Falun*.
Faid (Tun., pass)   fä'-ēd   fah'-eed

Faifo (Indo-Ch.)   fä-fō′   fay-foh′

Fais (Oc., Carolines)   fä′-ēs *or* fīs′   fah′-ees *or* fais′
   Also called *Tromelin*, trô′-mĕ-lēn [tro′-meh-leen].

Faisal al Saud (Saudi Arabian prince) See *Feisal al Saud.*

Faisi (Oc., Solomons)   fä-ē′-sē   fah-ee′-see

Faito (It., mt.)   fä-ē′-tô   fah-ee′-to

Faiyum, el (Egypt)   fī-yōōm′, ĕl   fai-yoom′, el

Fakfak (NEI)   fäk′-fäk   fahk′-fahk

Falaise (Fr.)   fä-lĕz′   fah-lez′

Falam (Burma)   fə-läm′   fuh-lahm′

Falange(Sp.political party)   *Eng.* fä′-lănj′   fay′-lanj′
    Sp.   fä-län′-hĕ   fah-lahn′-heh

falangist   *Eng.* fä-län′-jĭst   fay-lan′-jist

Falangista   *Sp.*   fä-län-hēs′-tä   fah-lahn-hees′-tah
   See *Falange.*

Falconieri (It.)   fäl-kô-nyĕ′-rē   fahl-ko-nyeh′-ree

Falkland Isls. (S. Atlantic)   fôk′-lənd   fawk′-luhnd
   Also called *Islas Malvinas*, ēs′-läs mäl-vē′-näs [ees′-lahs mahl-vee′-nahs].

Falster (Den., isl.)   fäl′-stər   fahl′-stuhr

Falsterbo (Sw.)   fäl′-stər-bōō   fahl′-stuhr-boo

Fălticeni (Rum.)   fəl-tē-chĕn′   fuhl-tee-chen′

Falun (Sw.)   fä′-lōōn *or* fô′-lōōn   fah′-lun *or* fo′-lun

Falvaterra (It.)   fäl-vä-tĕr′-rä   fahl-vah-tehr′-rah

Famagusta (Cyprus)   fä-mä-gōōs′-tä   fah-mah-goos′-tah

Faneuil Hall (Boston)   făn′l *or* făn-yəl   fan′l *or* fan-yuhl
   Other pronunciations range from the old-fashioned fŭn′l [fuhn′l] to
   the literal făn′-yōō-əl [fan′-yu-uhl].

Fanò (Gr., isl.)   *It.* fä-nô′   fah-no′
   Also called *Othonoi*, ô′-thô-nē [o′-tho-nee].

Fano (It.)   fä′-nô   fah′-no

Fara (Oc., Solomons)   fä′-ra   fah′-rah

Farafra (Egypt)   fə-rä′-frä   fuh-rah′-frah

Farallón de Medinilla   fä-rä-lyôn′ dĕ   fah-rah-lyon′ deh
   (Oc., Marianas)   mĕ-dē-nē′-lyä   meh-dee-nee′-lyah

Farallón de Pájaros   fä-rä-lyôn′ dĕ pä′-hä-   fah-rah-lyon′ deh
   (Oc., Marianas)   rôs   pah′-hah-ros

Faraulep (Oc., Carolines)   fä-rou′-lĕp   fah-rau′-lep

Faregh, el (Libya)   fä′-rĕg, ĕl   fah′-reg, el

Fares El Khoury (Syrian   fä′-rĕs ĕl   fah′-res el
   diplomat)   k(h)ōō′-rē   k(h)oo′-ree

Faria, Gustavo   fə-rē′-ə, gōōs-tä′-vŏŏ   fuh-ree′-uh, goos-
   Cordeiro de   kôr-dā′-rŏŏ dĭ   tah′-vu kor-day′-
   (Braz. polit.)   ru di

Faria, Oswaldo Cordeiro de (Braz. general)	fə-rē'-ə, ôz-väl'-dŏŏ kŏr-dä'-rŏŏ dĭ	fuh-ree'-uh, oz-vahl'-du kor-day'-ru di
Farinacci, Roberto (It. polit.)	fä-rē-nät'-chē, rô-bĕr'-tô	fah-ree-naht'-chee, ro-behr'-to
Faro (Port.)	fä'-rŏŏ	fah'-ru
Farouk (King of Egypt)	fä-rŏŏk'	fah-rook'
Farrell, Edelmiro (Arg. polit.)	fä-rĕl', ĕ-dĕl-mē'-rô	fah-rel', eh-del-mee'-ro
Farrington, (Eng. name)	făr'-ĭng-tən	fehr'-ing-tuhn
Fars (Iran)	färs'	fahrs'
Farsund (Nor.)	fär'-sŏŏn	fahr'-sun

Faruk (King of Egypt) See the French spelling, *Farouk*.

Fas (Mor.) English *Fez*, q.v.	fäs'	fahs'
fascismo (It.)	fä-shēs'-mô	fah-shees'-mo
fascist	*Eng.* făsh'-ĭst	fash'-ist

Italian *fascista* (sg.), *-i* (pl.), fä-shē'-stä, -ē [fah-shee'-stah, -ee].

Fastov (Rus.)	fäs'-tŏf	fahs'-tof
Fatezh (Rus.)	fä'-tĕsh	fah'-tesh
Fauconnerie, la (Tun., airfield)	fō-kôn-rē', lä	foh-kon-ree', lah
Faughan (N. Ire., riv.)	fôn'	fawn'
Faulkner, John and William (Am. authors)	fôk'-nər	fawk'-nuhr
Faulquemont (Fr.)	fōk-môN'	fohk-moN'
Fauquemberques (Fr.)	fō-käN-bĕrk'	foh-kahN-behrk'
Făurei (Rum.)	fə-ŏŏ-rä'	fuh-u-ray'
Fauro (Oc., Solomons)	fä-ŏŏ'-rô	fah-oo'-ro
Fauske (Nor.)	fou'-skə	fau'-skuh
Fauteux, Gaspard (Can. polit.)	fō-tû', gäs-pär'	foh-tœ', gahs-pahr'
Fauville (Fr.)	fō-vēl'	foh-veel'
Fauzieh (Egypt. princess)	fou-zē'-ə	fau-zee'-uh
Favignana (Sicily, isl.)	fä-vē-nyä'-nä	fah-vee-nyah'-nah
Fayal (Azores)	fä-yäl'	fah-yahl'
Fayetteville	*N.Y.* fä-ĕt'-vĭl *Tenn.* fä'-ĭt-vĭl	fay-et'-vil fay'-it-vil
Fayu (Oc., Carolines)	fä'-yŏŏ	fah'-yoo
Fécamp (Fr.)	fĕ-käN'	feh-kahN'
Fedhala (Mor.) Also spelled *Fdala*.	fə-dä'-lä	fuh-dah'-lah
Fedjadj, Chott el (Tun.)	fə-jăj', shŏt' ĕl	fuh-jaj', shot' el

[166]

Fedorenko (Rus. name) fĕ-dŏ-rĕn'-kŏ feh-do-ren'-ko
Fëdorovka (Rus.) fyô'-dŏ-rŏf-kä fyo'-do-rof-kah
Fefan (Oc.) fĕ'-fän feh'-fahn
  Japanese *Aki Shima*, ä-kē'-shē'-mä' [ah-kee' shee'-mah'].
Feighan, Michael A. fē'-ăn fee'-an
  (U.S. representative)
Feisal al Saud fā'-səl äl sä-ōōd' fay'-suhl ahl sah-ood'
  (Saudi Arabian prince)
Feistritz (Austria, riv.) fī'-strĭts fai'-strits
Félegyháza (Hung.) fā'-lĕt(y)-hä'-zŏ fay'-let(y)-hah'-zo
  Also called *Kiskunfélegyháza*, q.v.
Felice Circeo (It.) fĕ-lē'-chĕ feh-lee'-cheh
    chēr-chĕ'-ô cheer-cheh'-o
Fellin (Est.) *Rus.* fĕl'-lĭn fel'-lin
  Estonian *Viljandi*, q.v.
Femmina Morta (It.) fĕm'-mē-nä môr'-tä fem'-mee-nah mor'-
    tah
Femund (Nor., lake) fĕ'-mŏŏn feh'-mun
Fên (Ch., Shansi, riv.) fŭn fuhn
Fenard, Raymond (Fr. fə-när', rĕ-môN' fuh-nahr', reh-moN'
  admiral)
Fêng-ch'êng (Ch., fŭng-chŭng fuhng-chuhng
  Kiangsi, Manchu.)
Fêng-hsin (Ch., Kiangsi) fŭng-shĭn fuhng-shin
Fêng-hua (Ch., Chekiang) fŭng-whä fuhng-whah
  The district in which Chiang Kai-shek was born.
Fêng-shun (Ch., fŭng-shŏŏn fuhng-shun
  Kwangtung)
Fêng-t'ien (Manchu., fŭng-tyĕn fuhng-tyen
  prov. and city)
  Also called *Mukden*, q.v.
Fên-i (Ch., Kiangsi) fŭn-ē fuhn-ee
Feni (Oc., Bismarck arch.) fĕ'-nē feh'-nee
  Also called *Anir*, q.v.
Fenny (India) fĕn'-nĭ fen'-ni
Fên-shui (Ch., Chekiang) fŭn-shwä fuhn-shway
Feodor (Alaska, Attu) fyô'-dŏr fyo'-dor
  English *Theodore*, q.v.
Feodosiya (Rus.) fĕ-ŏ-dŏ'-sĭ-yä feh-o-do'-si-yah
Feonov, Nikolai fĕ-ô'-nŏf, nĭ-kŏ-lī' feh-o'-nof, ni-ko-lai'
  (Rus. polit.)
Fère Champenoise, la fĕr shäN-pə-nwäz', fehr shahN-puh-
  (Fr.) lä nwahz', lah
Feriana (Tun.) fĕ-rĭ-ă'-nä feh-ri-a'-nah

Ferigh (Libya)	fĕ-rēg'	feh-reeg'
Fermanagh (N. Ire.)	fûr-măn'-ə	fuhr-man'-uh
Fermi, Enrico (It., Am. scientist)	fĕr'-mē, ĕn-rē'-kô	fehr'-mee, en-ree'-ko
Fernana (Tun.)	fĕr-nä'-nä	fehr-nah'-nah
Fernandes, Raoul (Braz. polit.)	fĕr-nän'-dĭs, rä-ōōl'	fehr-nahn'-dis, rah-ool'
Fernández (Sp. name)	*Am. Sp.* fĕr-nän'-dĕs *Sp.* fĕr-nän'-dĕth	fehr-nahn'-dehs fehr-nahn'-dehth
Fernandez, Antonio M. (U.S. representative)	fĕr-nän'-dĕs, än-tô'-nyô	fehr-nahn'-des, ahn-to'-nyo
Fernando Póo (Afr., Sp. isl.)	fĕr-nän'-dô pô'-ô	fehr-nahn'-do po'-o

English *Fernando Po*, fər-năn'-dō pō' [fuhr-nan'-doh poh'].

Fernós Isern, A. (Puerto Rican polit.)	fĕr-nôs' ē-sĕrn'	fehr-nos' ee-sehrn'
Ferrajoli (It.)	fĕr-rä-yô'-lē	fehr-rah-yo'-lee
Ferrara (It.)	fĕr-rä'-rä	fehr-rah'-rah
Ferrol, el (Sp.)	fĕ-rôl', ĕl	feh-rol', el
Ferryville (Tun.)	fĕ-rē-vēl'	feh-ree-veel'

Named after the French leader.

ferté	fĕr-tĕ'	fehr-teh'

An element, meaning *fort*, in the names of ancient fortified places of France.

Ferté Alais (Fr.)	fĕr-tĕ ä-lĕ'	fehr-teh ah-leh'
Ferté Bernard, la (Fr.)	fĕr-tĕ bĕr-när', lä	fehr-teh behr-nahr', lah
Ferté Gaucher (Fr.)	fĕr-tĕ gō-shĕ'	fehr-teh goh-sheh'
Ferté Macé (Fr.)	fĕr-tĕ mä-sĕ'	fehr-teh mah-seh'
Ferté Milon (Fr.)	fĕr-tĕ mē-lôN'	fehr-teh mee-loN'
Ferté sous Jouarre (Fr.)	fĕr-tĕ sōō zhwär'	fehr-teh soo zhwahr'
Ferté Vidam (Fr.)	fĕr-tĕ vē-däN'	fehr-teh vee-dahN'
Ferwerd (Neth.)	fĕr'-wərt	fehr'-wuhrt
Ferwerderadeel (Neth.)	fĕr-wĕr'-də-rä-dāl'	fehr-wehr'-duh-rah-dayl'
Fès (Mor.)	fĕs'	fehs'

English *Fez*, q.v.

feterita	fĕt'-ə-rē'-tə	fet-uh-ree'-tuh
Fetești (Rum.)	fĕ-tĕsht'	feh-tesht'
Feucht (Ger.)	foik(h)t'	foik(h)t'
Feudo (It.)	fĕ'-ōō-dô	feh'-oo-do
Feufeurolles (Fr.)	fû-gû-rôl'	fœ-gœ-rol'
Fez (Mor.)	*Eng.* fĕz'	fez'

French *Fès*, fĕs' [fes']. Arabic *Fas*, fäs' [fahs'].

[168]

Fezzan (Libya) fĕz-zăn' fez-zan'

Fianarantsoa (Madag.) fyə-nä'-rən-tsô'-ə fyuh-nah'-ruhn-tso'-uh

Fianna Fail (Irish party) fē'-ə-nə fôl' fee'-uh-nuh fol'

Fiddichow (Ger. >Pol.) fĭd'-ĭk(h)-ō fid'-ik(h)-oh
Polish *Widuchowo*, q.v.

Fier (Alb.) fyĕr' fyehr'

Fierlinger, Zdeněk fēr'-lĭng-ər, feer'-ling-uhr,
(Cz. polit.) zděn'-yĕk zdehn'-yehk

Fiersbach (Ger.) fērs'-bäk(h) feers'-bahk(h)

Figeac (Fr.) fē-zhäk' fee-zhahk'

Figl, Leopold fē'-gəl, lā'-ô-pôlt fee'-guhl, lay'-o-polt
(Austrian polit.)

Figueiredo, Assís de fē-gĕ-rĕ'-dŏŏ, ä-sēs' fee-geh-reh'-du,
(Braz. polit.) dĭ ah-sees' di
Both names should be used, thus: *Assís de Figueiredo*, not *Figueiredo* alone.

Figueroa, Manuel Mora (Sp. polit.) See *Mora Figueroa, Manuel*.

Fiji (Oc.) fē'-jē fee'-jee

Fijnaard (Neth.) fī'-närt fai'-nahrt

Filatov (Rus. scientist) fĭ-lä'-tŏf fi-lah'-tof

Filefjell (Nor., mt.) fē'-lə-fyĕl fee'-luh-fyel

Filene's (Boston store) fĭ-lēnz' fai-leenz'

filho fē'-lyŏŏ fee'-lyu
An element, meaning *son* or *junior*, in Portuguese names. Look up the other part of the name.

Filiaşi (Rum.) fē-lyäsh' fee-lyahsh'

Filicudi (It., isl.) fē-lē-kōō'-dē fee-lee-koo'-dee

Filyas (Turk.) fēl'-yäs' feel'-yahs'

Finale (Sicily) fē-nä'-lĕ fee-nah'-leh

Finistère (Fr.) fē-nē-stĕr' fee-nee-stehr'

Finisterre (Sp., point) *Eng.* fĭn'-ĭs-tĕr' fin'-is-tehr'
 Sp. fē-nēs-tĕ'-rĕ fee-nees-teh'-reh

Finland *Eng.* fĭn'-lənd fin'-luhnd
Finnish *Suomi*, sŏŏ'-ô'-mē [su'-o'-mee].

Finschhafen (N.E. New *Eng.* fĭnch'-hä-fən finch'-hah-fuhn
Guinea, Oc.) *Ger.* fĭnsh'-hä-fən finsh'-hah-fuhn

Finse (Nor.) fĭn'-sə fin'-suh

Finsterwolde (Neth.) fĭn'-stər-wôl'-də fin'-stuhr-wol'-duh

Fiojo (It., riv.) fyô'-yô fyo'-yo

Firdausi (Per. poet) *Eng.* fər-dou'-sē fuhr-dau'-see
 Pers. fər-dō-sē' fuhr-doh-see'

Firenze (It.) fē-rĕn'-dzĕ fee-ren'-dzeh
English *Florence*, q.v.

Firenzuola (It.)	fē-rĕn-tswô′-lä	fee-ren-tswo′-lah
Firuz, Mozaffar (Iran. polit.)	fē-rōōz′, mô-zä′-fär	fee-rooz′, mo-zah′-fahr
Firuzkuh (Iran)	fē-rōōz′-kōō	fee-rooz′-koo
Fischhausen (Ger. >Rus.)	fĭsh′-hou′-zən	fish′-hau′-zuhn

Russian *Primorsk*, prĭ-môrsk′ [pri-morsk′].

Fischsee (Pol., lake)	*Ger.* fĭsh′-zā	fish′-zay

Polish *Morskie Oko*, q.v.

Fiuggi (It.)	fyōōd′-jē	fyood′-jee
fiume	fyōō′-mĕ	fyoo′-meh

An element, meaning *river*, in Italian place names.

Fiume (It. >Yugosl.)	fyōō′-mĕ	fyoo′-meh

Serb-Croat *Rieka*, q.v.

Fiume Torto (Sicily)	fyōō′-mĕ tôr′-tô	fyoo′-meh tor′-to
Fiumicello (It., riv.)	fyōō-mē-chĕl′-lô	fyoo-mee-chel′-lo
Fiumicino (It.)	fyōō-mē-chē′-nô	fyoo-mee-chee′-no
Fivizzano (It.)	fē-vēt-sä′-nô	fee-veet-sah′-no
Fjærland (Nor.)	fyăr′-län	fyehr′-lahn
fjell	fyĕl′	fyel′

An element, meaning *mountain*, in Norwegian place names.

Fjelstad, Anders (Nor. diplomat)	fyĕl′-stä, än′-ərs *or* än′-dərs	fyel′-stah, ahn′-uhrs *or* ahn′-duhrs
Fjerland (Nor.)	fyăr′-län	fyehr′-lahn
fjord (Nor.)	fyōr′ *or* fyŏōr′	fyohr′ *or* fyur′

An element in Norwegian place names. The English variant is *fiord*, fyôrd [fyord].

Flaam (Nor.)	flôm′	flom′
Flamands, des (Fr., fort)	flä-mäN′, dĕ	flah-mahN′, deh
Flaminian Way (It., road)	*Eng.* flə-mĭn′-ĭ-ən	fluh-min′-i-uhn
Flammersfeld (Ger.)	fläm′-ərs-fĕlt	flahm′-uhrs-felt
Flandin, Pierre Étienne (Fr. polit)	fläN-dăN′, pyĕr′ ĕ-tyĕn′	flahN-daN′, pyehr′ eh-tyen′
Flèche, la (Fr.)	flĕsh′, lä	flesh′, lah
Flekkefjord (Nor.)	flĕk′-ə-fyōr	flek′-uh-fyohr
Flensburg (Ger.)	*Eng.* flĕnz′-bûrg *Ger.* flĕns′-bŏork(h)	flenz′-buhrg flens′-burk(h)
Flers (Fr.)	flĕr′	flehr′
Fleury (Fr.)	flû-rē′	flœ-ree′
Flinders (Austral., bay and mts.)	flĭn′-dərz	flin′-duhrz
Flins (Fr.)	fläN′	flaN′

Florac (Fr.)	flô-räk′	flo-rahk′
Florence (It.)	*Eng.* flŏr′-əns	flor′-uhns
Italian *Firenze*, q.v.		
Flores (Azores)	fiô′-rĭsh	flo′-rish
Flores (NEI)	flô′-rĕs	flo′-res
Florianópolis (Brazil)	flôr-yə-nô′-pŏŏ-lēs	flor-yuh-no′-pu-lees
Also called, unofficially, *Desterro*, q.v.		
Flórida Blanca (P.I.)	flô′-rē-dä bläng′-kä	flo′-re-dah blahng′-kah
Florina (Gr.) See *Phlorina*.		
Floroe *or* Florö *or*	flō′-rû *or* flō′-rûĭ	floh′-rœ *or* floh′-rœi
Floroey *or* Floröy (Nor.)		
flotsam	flŏt′-səm	flot′-suhm
Flottemanville (Fr.)	flôt-mäN-vēl′	flot-mahN-veel′
Flushing (Neth.)	*Eng.* flŭsh′-ĭng	fluhsh′-ing
Dutch *Vlissingen*, q.v.		
Fly (New Guinea, Papua, riv.)	flī′	flai′
Foča (Yugosl.)	fô′-chä	fo′-chah
Focke, Heinrich	fôk′-ə	fok′-uh
German designer of the airplane Focke-Wulf, fôk′-ə-vŏŏlf′ [fok′-uh-vulf′].		
Focşani (Rum.)	fôk-shän′	fok-shahn′
Foerde (Nor.)	fûr′-də	fœr′-duh
Fogaras (Rum.) See *Făgăraş*.		
Foggia (It.)	fôd′-jä	fod′-jah
Fogliano (It., lake)	fô-lyä′-nô	fo-lyah′-no
Foix (Fr.)	fwä′	fwah′
Fojnica (Yugosl.)	foi′-nĭ-tsä	foi′-ni-tsah
Folgefonnen (Nor.)	fôl′-gə-fôn-ən	fol′-guh-fon-uhn
A variant is *Folgefonna*.		
Foligny (Fr.)	fô-lē-nyē′	fo-lee-nyee′
Folke (Sw. name)	fôl′-kə	fol′-kuh
Follonica (It.)	fôl-lô′-nē-kä	fol-lo′-nee-kah
Fondi (It.)	fôn′-dē	fon′-dee
Fondouk el Aouareb (Tun.)	fŏn′-dōōk ĕl ä-wă′-rĕb	fon′-dook el ah-wa′-reb
Fon du Lac (Wis.)	fŏn′ də lăk′ *or* fŏn′ jə lăk′	fon′ duh lak′ fon′ juh lak′
Fontainebleau (Fr.)	fôN-tĕn-blō′	foN-ten-bloh′
Fontana (Calif., Tenn.)	fŏn-tăn′-ə	fon-tan′-uh
Fontechiari (It.)	fôn′-tĕ-kyä′-rē	fon′-teh-kyah′-ree
Fontenay (Fr.)	fôNt-nĕ′	foNt-neh′

| Foo-chow (Ch., Fukien) | *Eng.* fōō-chou | foo-chau |
| | *Ch.* fōō-jō | foo-joh |

Also called *Min-how*, q.v.

Foo-chow (Ch., Yünnan)	fōō-jō	foo-joh
Forand, Aime J.	fôr'-ănd', ā'-mĭ	fohr'-and', ay'-mi
(U.S. representative)		
Forbach (Fr.)	fôr-bäk'	for-bahk'
Forcalquier (Fr.)	fôr-käl-kyĕ'	for-kahl-kyeh'
Forchheim (Ger.)	fôrk(h)'-hīm	fork(h)'-haim
Förde (Nor.)	fûr'-də	fœr'-duh
Fordon (Pol.)	fôr'-dôn	for'-don
Forêt de Mont	fô-rĕ' də môN	fo-reh' duh moN
Castre (Fr.)	käs'tr	kahs'tr
Forges les Eaux (Fr.)	fôrzh lĕ zō'	forzh leh zoh'
Forlì (It.)	fôr-lē'	for-lee'
Formia (It.)	fôr'-myä	for'-myah
Formicola (It.)	fôr-mē'-kô-lä	for-mee'-ko-lah
formidable	fôr'-mĭ-də-bəl	for'-mi-duh-buhl

A stress on the second syllable is not recommended.

Formigny (Fr.)	fôr-mē-nyē'	for-mee-nyee'
Formosa (Jap.>Ch., isl.)	*Port., Eng.* fôr-mō'-	for-moh'-zuh
	zə *or* -sə	*or* -suh

Chinese and Japanese *T'ai-wan*, tī-wän [tai-wahn].

Fornebu (Nor.)	fôr'-nə-bōō	for'-nuh-boo
Fornoli (It.)	fôr'-nô-lē	for'-no-lee
Fornova di Taro (It.)	fôr-nô'-vô dē	for-no'-vo dee
	tä'-rô	tah'-ro
Forst (Ger.)	fôrst'	forst'

Polish *Barszcz*, bärshch' [bahrshch'].

| Fortaleza (Brazil) | fôr-tä-lĕ'-zə | for-tah-leh'-zuh |

Also called *Ceará*, q.v.

Fort Bayard (N.M.)	bī'-ərd	bai'-uhrd
Fort Huachuca (N.M.)	wä-chōō'-kə	wah-choo'-kuh
Fotić, Constantin	fô'-tĭch,	fo'-tich,
(Yugosl. diplomat)	kôn-stän-tēn'	kon-stahn-teen'
Fortino (It.)	fôr-tē'-nô	for-tee'-no
Fort Lamy (Fr. Eq. Afr.)	See *Lamy.*	
Fort Lauderdale (Fla.)	lô'-dər-dāl	law'-duhr-dayl
Foscari (It.)	fô'-skä-rē	fo'-skah-ree
Fosna (Nor.)	fōs'-nä	fohs'-nah
foss	fôs'	fos'

An element, meaning *waterfall* or *rapids*, in Norwegian place names.

| Fossheim (Nor.) | fôs'-hām | fos'-haym |
| Fossli (Nor.) | fôs'-lē | fos'-lee |

Fougères (Fr.)	fōō-zhĕr′	foo-zhehr′
Fougerolles (Fr.)	fōōzh-rôl′	foozh-rol′
Fouillard Thorigné (Fr.)	fwē-yär tô-rē-nyĕ′	fwee-yahr to-ree-nyeh′
Fou-liang (Ch., Kiangsi)	fō-lyäng	foh-lyahng
Foum Tatahouine (Tun.)	fōōm tä-tä-hwēn′	foom tah-tah-hween′
Fouques Duparc, M. Jacques (Fr. diplomat)	fōōk dü-pärk′, zhäk′	fook dü-pahrk′, zhahk′
Fouquières lès Lens (Fr.)	fōō-kyĕr′ lĕ läN′	foo-kyehr′ leh lahN′
Fourmies (Fr.)	fōōr-mē′	foor-mee′
Frachon, Benoît (Fr. polit.)	frä-shôN′, bə-nwä′	frah-shoN′, buh-nwah′
Franceschini (It. name)	frän-chĕs-kē′-nē	frahn-ches-kee′-nee
Franco, Francisco (Sp. dictator)	*Eng.* frăng′-kō *Sp.* fräng′-kô, frän-thēs′-kô	frang′-koh frahng′-ko, frahn-thees′-ko
Franc Tireur (Fr. newspaper)	*Eng.* frănk′ tĭ-rûr′ *Fr.* fräN tē-rûr′	frank′ ti-ruhr′ frahN tee-rœr′
Franeker (Neth.)	frä′-nə-kər	frah′-nuh-kuhr
Frankensteen, Richard T. (Am. labor leader)	frănk′-ən-stēn	frank′-uhn-steen
Frankenstein (Ger. >? Pol.) Polish Ząbkowice, q.v.	fränk′-ən-shtīn	frahnk′-uhn-shtain
Frankfort on Main; on Oder (Ger.)	*Eng.* frănk′-fərt ŏn mān; ŏn ō′-dər	frank′-fuhrt on mayn; on oh′-duhr
Frankfurt am Main; an der Oder (Ger.)	fränk′-fōōrt äm mīn′; än dər ō′-dər	frahnk′-furt ahm main′; ahn duhr oh′-duhr

English *Frankfort*, q.v. The Polish name of *Frankfurt an der Oder* is *Słubice*, slōō-bē′-tsĕ [slu-bee′-tseh].

Frankfurter Zeitung (Ger. newspaper)	fränk′-fōōr-tər tsī′-tŏŏng	frahnk′-fur-tuhr tsai′-tung
Frascati (It.)	frä-skä′-tē	frah-skah′-tee
Frashër (Alb.)	frä′-shər	frah′-shuhr

Greek *Phrasare*, frä′-sä-rē [frah′-sah-ree].

Frashëri (Alb.) See *Frashër.*

Frauwuellesheim *or* Frauwüllesheim (Ger.)	frou-vül′-əs-hīm	frau-vül′-uhs-haim
Frechen (Ger.)	frĕk(h)′-ən	frek(h)′-uhn
Fredenthal, David (Am. painter)	frēd′n-thôl	freed′n-thawl

Fredericia (Den.)　　　　*Eng.* frĕd'-ə-rĭsh'-yə　　fred'-uh-rish'-yuh
　　　　　　　　　　　　Dan. frĭ-*th*ə-rē'-tsĭ-ä　　fri-*th*uh-ree'-tsi-ah
Frederikshaap (Greenl.)　frĭ*th*'-rĭks-hôp'　　　frith'-riks-hop'
Frederikshavn (Den.)　　frĭ*th*'-rĭks-houn'　　frith'-riks-haun'
Fredrikshamn (Fin.) See *Hamina.*
Fredrikstad (Nor.)　　　frĕd'-rĭk-stä　　　　fred'-rik-stah
Freeman, Douglas
　　Southall (Va. editor)　sou'-*th*ôl　　　　　sau'-*th*ol
　　The last syllable of *Southall* has "th" as in *though.*
Freiberg (Ger.)　　　　frī'-bĕrk(h)　　　　frai'-behrk(h)
Freiburg (Ger.)　　　　frī'-bo͞ork(h)　　　frai'-burk(h)
　　An English pronunciation of both *Freiberg* and *Freiburg* is frī'-bûrg
　　[frai'-buhrg].
Freienwalde (Ger.)　　　frī'-ən-väl'-də　　frai'-uhn-vahl'-duh
Freire, Rómulo Gallegos (Ven. author and polit.) See *Gallegos Freire.*
Freistadt (Austria)　　　frī'-shtät　　　　frai'-shtaht
Fréjus (Fr.)　　　　　　frĕ-zhüs'　　　　freh-zhüs'
Fréjus, Col de (Fr., mt.)　frĕ-zhüs', kôl də　freh-zhüs', kol duh
Fremantle (Austral.)　　frē'-măn-tl　　　　free'-man-tl
French Guiana (S.A.)　　gē-ä'-nə　　　　gee-ah'-nuh
Frenz (Ger.)　　　　　frĕnts'　　　　　frents'
Fresnay (Fr.)　　　　　frĕ-nĕ'　　　　　freh-neh'
Fresnes (Fr.)　　　　　frĕn'　　　　　　fren'
Fresno (Calif.)　　　　frĕz'-nō　　　　　frez'-noh
Fret, le (Fr.)　　　　　frĕ', lə　　　　　freh', luh
Fréteval (Fr.)　　　　　frĕt-väl'　　　　fret-vahl'
Frévent (Fr.)　　　　　frĕ-väN'　　　　freh-vahN'
Freystadt (Ger.)　　　　frī'-shtät　　　　frai'-shtaht
Fribourg (Switz.)　　　frē-bo͞or'　　　　free-boor'
　　German *Freiburg,* frī'-bo͞ork(h) [frai'-burk(h)].
Friedenshütte (Pol.)　　*Ger.* frē'-dəns-hüt'-ə　free'-duhns-hüt'-uh
　　Polish *Nowy Bytom,* q.v.
Friedland (Ger. > Rus.)　frēt'-länt　　　　freet'-lahnt
　　Russian *Pravdinsk,* präv'-dĭnsk [prahv'-dinsk].
Friedrichshafen (Ger.)　frē'-drĭk(h)s-hä'-fən　free'-drik(h)s-hah'-
　　　　　　　　　　　　　　　　　　　　　　fuhn
Friedrichstadt (Latvia)　*Ger.* frē'-drĭk(h)-　　free'-drik(h)-shtaht
　　　　　　　　　　　　shtät
　　Latvian *Jaunjelgava,* q.v.
Friesche Meeren (Neth.)　frē'-sə mä'-rən　　free'-suh may'-ruhn
Friesland (Neth., prov.)　*Eng.* frēz'-lənd　　freez'-luhnd
　　　　　　　　　　　　Du. frēs'-länt　　frees'-lahnt
Friesoythe (Ger.)　　　frē'-zoi-tə　　　　free'-zoi-tuh
Friezenveen (Neth.)　　frē'-zən-vän'　　free'-zuhn-vayn'

Frigido (It., riv.)	frē'-jē-dô	free'-jee-do
Frihagen, Anders	frē'-hä-gən, än'-ərs	free'-hah-guhn, ahn'-
(Nor. polit.)	or än'-dərs	uhrs or ahn'-duhrs
Frisches Haff	frĭsh'-əs häf'	frish'-uhs hahf'

(Ger. >Pol., Rus., lagoon)
Polish *Mierzeja Wiślana,* myĕ-zhĕ'-yä vĕsh-lä'-nä [myeh-zheh'-yah veesh-lah'-nah] or *Zalew Wiślany,* zä'-lĕf vĕsh-lä'-nĭ [zah'-lef veesh-lah'-ni]. Russian *Frishes Gaf,* frē'-shĕs gäf' [free'-shes gahf'].

Friuli (It.)	frē-ōō'-lē	free-oo'-lee

German *Friaul,* frĭ-oul' [fri-aul'].

Frome (Eng.)	frōōm'	froom'
Fromentine (Fr.)	frô-mäN-tēn'	fro-mahN-teen'
Frosinone (It.)	frô-sē-nô'-nĕ	fro-see-no'-neh
Fruges (Fr.)	früzh'	früzh'
Frunze (Rus.)	frōōn'-zĕ	froon'-zeh
fu	fōō	foo

An element, meaning *metropolitan district,* in Japanese place names.

Fuad (Former King of Egypt)	fōō-ăd'	foo-ad'
Fu-chin (Manchu.)	fōō-jĭn	foo-jin
Fucine (It.)	fōō-chē'-nĕ	foo-chee'-neh
Fucino (It.)	foo'-chē-nô	foo'-chee-no

Also called Lake *Celano,* chĕ-lä'-nô [cheh-lah'-no].

Fuehrer, der (Ger.)	fü'-rər, dər	fü'-ruhr, duhr

German for *the leader.* Cf. *il Duce* and *el Caudillo.*

Fuenen (Den., isl.)	See *Fyn.*	
Fuenterrabía (Sp.)	fwĕn-tĕ-rä-bē'-ä	fwen-teh-rah-bee'-ah
Fuerstenwalde (Ger.)	für'-stən-väl'-də	für'-stuhn-vahl'-duh
Fuerth (Ger.)	fürt'	fürt'
Fuhlsbuettel	fōōls'-büt'-əl	fools'-büt'-uhl
or Fuhlsbüttel (Ger., Hamburg, airport)		
Fujita (Jap., zaibatsu)	fōō'-jē-tä	foo'-jee-tah
Fuka (Egypt)	fōō'-kä	foo'-kah
Fukien (Ch., prov.)	fōō-kyĕn	foo-kyen
Fukui (Jap.)	fōō-kōō'-ē	foo-koo'-ee
Fukukawa (Jap.)	fōō-kōō'-kä-wä	foo-koo'-kah-wah
Fukuoka (Jap.)	fōō-kōō'-ô-kä	foo-koo'-o-kah
Fukushima (Jap.)	fōō-kōō'-shē'-mä'	foo-koo'-shee'-mah'
	or fōō-kōō'-shē-mä	foo-koo'-shee-mah
Fulbright, J. W. (U.S. representative)	fŏŏl'-brīt	ful'-brait
Fulda (Ger., riv.)	fŏŏl'-dä	ful'-dah
Fullerton (Calif.)	fŏŏl'-ər-tən	ful'-uhr-tuhn

Fulmer, Hampton P. (U.S. representative)	fo͞ol'-mər	ful'-muhr
Fülöpszállás (Hung.)	fü'-lûp-säl'-läsh	fü'-luhp-sahl'-lahsh
Fu-min (Ch., Yünnan)	fo͞o-mĭn	foo-min
Fum Tatavin (Tun.) See *Foum Tatahouine*.		
Funafuti (Oc., Ellice)	fo͞o-nä-fo͞o'-tē	foo-nah-foo'-tee
Fu-ning (Ch., Fukien) See *Siapu*.		
Furka (Yugosl.)	fo͞or'-kä	foor'-kah
Furlong, Grant (U.S. representative)	fûr-lông'	fuhr-long'
Furneaux (Austral., isls.)	fûr'-nō	fuhr'-noh
Furnes (Belg.)	*Fr.* fürn'	fürn'

Flemish *Veurne*, q.v. If *Furnes* comes into the news, it will probably
be Anglicized to fûr'-nĭs [fuhr'-nis].

Fürstenfeld (Austria)	für'-stən-fĕlt	für'-stuhn-felt
Fürstenwalde (Ger.)	für'-stən-väl'-də	für'-stuhn-vahl'-duh
Fürth (Ger.)	fürt'	fürt'
Furtwaengler, Wilhelm (Ger. musician)	fo͞ort'-vĕng-lər, vĭl'-hĕlm	furt'-veng-luhr, vil'-helm
Also spelled *Furtwängler*.		
Fusan (Korea)	fo͞o-sän	foo-sahn
Fusaro (It.)	fo͞o-sä'-rô	foo-sah'-ro
Fuse (Ger., riv.)	fo͞o'-zə	foo'-zuh
fusha (Alb.) See *fushë*.		
fushë (Alb.)	fo͞o'-shə	foo'-shuh

An element, meaning *plain*, in Albanian place names. Look up the
other part of the name.

Fu-shun (Manchu.)	fo͞o-sho͞on	foo-shun
Fusignano (It.)	fo͞o-sē-nyä'-nô	foo-see-nyah'-no
Futa (It., pass)	fo͞o'-tä	foo'-tah
futile	*Am.* fyo͞ot'l *or* fyo͞o'-tĭl	fyoot'l *or* fyoo'-til
	Br. fyo͞o'-tĭl	fyoo'-tail
Futog (Yugosl.)	fo͞o'-tôg	foo'-tog
Fu-t'u (Ch., Fukien, isl.)	fo͞o-to͞o	foo-too
Fuyang (Ch., Chekiang)	fo͞o-yäng	foo-yahng
Fu-yüan (Manchu.)	fo͞o-yüän	foo-yü-ahn
Fyn (Den., isl.)	fün'	fün'
German *Fünen*, fü'-nən [fü'-nuhn].		
Gaasterland (Neth.)	k(h)äs'-tər-länt	k(h)ahs'-tuhr-lahnt
Gabas (P.I.)	gä'-bäs	gah'-bahs
Gabès (Tun.)	gä'-bĕs	gah'-bes
Arabic *Qabes*.		

Gablonz (Cz.)   *Ger.* gä'-blônts   gah'-blonts
   Czech *Jablonec*, q.v.
Gabon (Afr., Fr. col.)   gä-bôN'   gah-boN'
Gabrovo (Bulg.)   gä'-brŏ-vŏ   gah'-bro-vo
Gacé (Fr.)   gä-sĕ'   gah-seh'
Gacko (Yugosl.)   gäts'-kô   gahts'-ko
Gadames *or* Gedames (Libya) See *Ghadames.*
Gadaronesi (Dodec.) See *Gaidaro.*
Gadd el Ahmar (Libya)   gäd ĕl ä'-mär   gahd el ah'-mahr
                   or äk(h)'-mär   *or* ahk(h)'-mahr
Gadyach (Rus.)   gä'-dyäch   gah'-dyahch
Gaeta (It.)   gä-ĕ'-tä   gah-eh'-tah
Gaeta (Oc., Solomons)   gä'-ĕ-tä   gah'-eh-tah
Gaetano (Italian name)   gä-ĕ-tä'-nô   gah-eh-tah'-no
Gaferut (Oc., Carolines) gä'-fĕ-rо̄о̄t   gah'-feh-root
Gafsa (Tun.)   gäf'-sä   gaf'-sah
Gagi (Oc., Solomons)   gä'-gē   gah'-gee
   Both *g's* as in *get.*
Gagliano (It.)   gä-lyä'-nô   gah-lyah'-no
Gahagan, Helen M.   gä'-hā-gən   gay'-hay-guhn
   (U.S. representative)   *or* gə-hā'-gən   guh-hay'-guhn
   Miss Gahagan says that in Ohio the first syllable is usually accented
   and in New York the second.
Gaidaro (Dodec.)   *It.* gĭ-dä'-rô   gai-dah'-ro
   Greek *Gaïdouronesi,* gĭ-dо̄о̄-rô-nĕ'-sē [gai-doo-ro-nee'-see]; *Gaïda-*
   ronesi, gĭ-dä-rô-nĕ'-sē [gai-dah-ro-nee'-see], and *Gadaronesi,* gä-dä-
   rô-nĕ'-sē [gah-dah-ro-nee'-see].
Gaïdaronesi (Crete, isl.) gĭ-dä-rô-nĕ'-sē   gai-dah-ro-nee'-see
Gaïdouronesi (Gr., isl.; Dodec.) See *Gaidaro.*
Gailigenbail (Ger. >Rus.) See *Heiligenbeil.*
Gailleamh (Eire) See *Galway.*
Gaillard, David DuBose gĭl-yärd', dyо̄о̆-bōz' gil-yahrd', dyu-bohz'
   (U.S.A. engineer)
   This is the South Carolina pronunciation. French gä-yär' [gah-yahr'].
Gaillard Cut (Canal Zone) gĭl-yärd'   gil-yahrd'
   Named in honor of David DuBose Gaillard. Formerly *Culebra Cut,*
   kо̄о̄-lĕ'-brä [koo-leh'-brah].
Gaillon (Fr.)   gä-yôN'   gah-yoN'
Gainasch (Latvia)   *Rus.* gĭ'-näsh   gai'-nahsh
   Latvian *Ainaži*, q.v.
Gainovka (Pol.) See *Hajnówka.*
Galápagos (Pac., isls.)   gä-lä'-pä-gôs   gah-lah'-pah-gos
   Also called *Archipiélago de Colón,* är-kē-pyĕ'-lä-gô dĕ kô-lôn' [ahr-
   kee-pyeh'-lah-go deh ko-lon'].

Galata (Mont.)	gə-lăt′-ə	guh-lat′-uh
Galata (Turk.)	gä′-lä-tä	gah′-lah-tah
Galaţi (Rum.)	gä-läts′	gah-lahts′
Also spelled *Galatz.*		
Galato (Dodec., Rh.)	gä-lä′-tô	gah-lah′-to
Galdhoepiggen *or*	gäl′-hû-pĭg-ən	gahl′-hœ-pig-uhn
Galdhöpiggen (Nor., mt.)		
Galela (NEI)	gä-lä′-lä	gah-lay′-lah
Galena (Ill.)	gə-lē′-na	guh-lee′-nuh
Genghis Khan (Mongol	jĕng′-gĭs-kän′	jehng′-gis kahn′
leader)		
Galera (P.I.)	gä-lĕ′-rä	gah-leh′-rah
Galeria (It.)	gä-lĕ′-ryä	gah-leh′-ryah
Galich (Pol. >Rus.)	gä′-lĭch	gah′-lich
Polish *Halicz,* q.v.		
Galicia (Pol., dist.)	*Eng.* gə-lĭsh′-yə	guh-lish′-yuh
	Rus. gä-lē′-tsĭ-yä	gah-lee′-tsi-yah
Polish *Galicja,* gä-lē′-chä [gah-lee′-chah].		
Galicia (Sp., dist.)	*Eng.* gə-lĭsh′-ə	guh-lish′-uh
	Sp. gä-lē′-thyä *or*	gah-lee′-thyah *or*
	-syä	-syah
Galičica (Yugosl., mts.)	gä′-lē′-chĭ-tsä	gah′-lee′-chi-tsah
Galičnik (Yugosl.)	gä′-lĭch-nĭk	gah′-lich-nik
Galilee (Pal.)	găl′-ə-lē	gal′-uh-lee
Hebrew Hag Galil, häg gä′-lēl′ [hahg gah′-leel′]. Arabic *El Jelil,*		
ĕl jĕ-lēl′ [el jeh-leel′].		
Galion (Ohio)	găl′-yən	gal′-yuhn
Gallagher, James	găl′-ə-gər	gal′-uh-guhr
(U.S. representative)		
Gallardon (Fr.)	gä-lär-dôN′	gah-lahr-doN′
Gallatin (Am. name)	găl′-ə-tən *or* -tĭn	gal′-uh-tuhn *or* -tin
Galle (Ceylon)	gäl′	gahl′
Gallegos Freire, Rómulo	gä-yĕ′-gôs frä′-rĕ,	gah-yeh′-gos fray′-
(Ven. polit.)	rô′-mōō-lô	reh, ro′-moo-lo
Gallicano (It.)	gäl-lē-kä′-nô	gahl-lee-kah′-no
Gallipoli (It.)	gäl-lē′-pô-lē	gahl-lee′-po-lee
Gallipoli (Turk., pen.,	*Eng.* gə-lĭp′-ə-lĭ	guh-lip′-uh-li
town)		
Turkish *Gelibolu,* gə-lē′-bô-lŏŏ [guh-lee′-bo-lu]. The peninsula is also		
called the *Chersonese,* q.v.		
Gallipolis (Ohio)	găl′-ĭ-pō-lēs′	gal′-i-poh-lees′
Gallo (Gr., cape) See *Akritas.*		
Gallo (Sicily, cape)	gäl′-lô	gahl′-lo
Gallup (N.M.)	găl′-əp	gal′-uhp

| Galveston (Tex.) | găl'-vəs-tən | gal'-vuhs-tuhn |
| Galway (Eire) | gôl'-wā | gawl'-way |

Gaelic *Gailleamh,* or *Gaillimh,* găl'-yĭv [gal'-yiv].

Gambia (Afr., Brit. col.)	găm'-bĭ-ə	gam'-bi-uh
Gambier (Austral., Ohio)	găm'-bĭr'	gam'-bihr'
Gamboa (Canal Zone)	gäm-bô'-ä	gahm-bo'-ah
Gambut (Libya)	gäm'-bо̄о̄t'	gahm'-but'
Gamelin, Maurice	gäm-lăN',	gahm-laN',
Gustave (Fr. general)	mô-rēs' güs-täv'	mo-rees' güs-tahv'
Gamvik (Nor.)	gäm'-vēk	gahm'-veek
Gananoque (Can.)	găn'-ə-nŏk'-wĭ *or* -wə	gan'-uh-nok'-wi *or* -wuh
Gander (Newf.)	găn'-dər	gan'-duhr
Gandhi, Mahatma Mo-	gän'-dē, mə-hät'-mə	gahn'-dee, muh-haht'-
handas Karamchand	mô-hən-däs'	muh moh-huhn-
(Indian leader)	kə-rəm-chŭnd'	dahs' kuh-ruhm-
		chuhnd'
Gangaro (Yugosl., isl.)	*It.* gäng'-gä-rô	gahng'-gah-ro

Serb-Croat *Kankar,* q.v.

Gangelt (Ger.)	gäng'-əlt	gahng'-uhlt
Ganges (Fr.)	gäNzh'	gahNzh'
Ganges (India, riv.)	găn'-jēz	gan'-jeez

Sanskrit *Ganga,* gŭng'-gä [guhng'-gah].

Gangi (Sicily)	gän'-jē	gahn'-jee
Ganjam (India)	gŭn-jäm'	guhn-jahm'
Ganongga (Oc., Solomons)	gä-nông'-gä	gah-nong'-gah

Gantsevichi (Pol.) See *Hancewicze.*

| gaol | jāl' | jayl' |

A variant spelling of *jail.*

Gap (Fr.)	gäp'	gahp'
Gapán (P.I.)	gä-pän'	gah-pahn'
Gapeau (Fr.)	gä-pō'	gah-poh'
Gapsal (Est.)	*Rus.* gäp'-säl(y)	gahp'-sahl(y)

Estonian *Haapsalu,* q.v.

Garaet Achkel (Tun.,	gä-rä'-ət äsh'-kĕl	gah-rah'-uht ahsh'-kel
lake)		
Garakayo (Oc., Palau)	gä-rä-kä'-yô	gah-rah-kah'-yo
Garam (Hung., Cz., riv.)	*Hung.* gŏ'-rŏm	go'-rom

Czech *Hron,* q.v.

| Garand, John C. | găr'-ənd | gehr'-uhnd |

The inventor of the Garand rifle writes: "I have given different pronunciations of my name at various times but, right or wrong, I must live with it." These include gə-rănd' [guh-rand'] and gä-räN' [gah-rahN'], but găr'-ənd [gehr'-uhnd] is the pronunciation he prefers.

Garapan (Oc., Marianas)	gä'-rä-pän *or*-păng	gah'-rah-pahn *or*-pang
García (Spanish name)	*Eng.* gär'-shə	gahr'-shuh
	Am. Sp. gär-sē'-ä	gahr-see'-ah
	Sp. gär-thē'-ä	gahr-thee'-ah
. Gard (Fr., riv.)	gär'	gahr'
Gardemoen (Nor.)	gär'-də-mōn	gahr'-duh-mohn
Garešnica (Yugosl.)	gä'-rĕsh'-nĭ-tsä	gah'-resh'-ni-tsah
Gargaliani (*or* -noi) (Gr.)	gär-gä-lyä'-nē	gahr-gah-lyah'-nee
Garian (Libya)	gä-rē-yăn'	gah-ree-yan'
Garigliano (It.)	gä-rē-lyä'-nô	gah-ree-lyah'-no
Garitsa (Corfu)	gä-rē'-tsä	gah-ree'-tsah
Garnes (Nor.)	gär'-nĕs	gahr'-nes
Garonne (Fr., riv.)	gä-rôn'	gah-ron'
Garove (Oc.)	gä-rô'-vĕ	gah-ro'-veh
Gartok (India)	gär-tŏk'	gahr-tok'
Gartz (Ger.)	gärts'	gahrts'
Garwolin (Pol.)	gär-vô'-lĭn	gahr-vo'-lin

Russian spelling *Garvolin.*

Gasenpot (Latvia)	*Rus.* gä'-zĕn-pŏt	gah'-zen-pot

Latvian *Aizpute,* q.v. German *Hasenpoth,* q.v.

Gasmata(Oc.,New Britain)	gäs-mä'-tä	gahs-mah'-tah
Gaspé (Can., pen.)	*Eng.* găs-pā'	gas-pay'
	Fr. gäs-pĕ'	gahs-peh'
Gasperi, Alcide de	gä'-spĕ-rē,	gah'-speh-ree,
(It. polit.)	äl-chē'-dĕ dĕ	ahl-chee'-deh deh
gasr	gäsr'	gahsr'

An element, meaning *castle,* in Arabic place names.

Gasselte (Neth.)	k(h)äs'-əl-tə	k(h)ahs'-uhl-tuh

Gassicourt (Fr.) See *Mantes Gassicourt.*

Gastein (Austria)	gä'-stīn	gah'-stain
Gastel (Neth.)	k(h)äs'-təl	k(h)ahs'-tuhl
Gastouni (Gr.)	gä-stoo'-nē	gah-stoo'-nee
Gathings, E. C.	găth'-ĭngz	gath'-ingz
(U.S. representative)		
Gâtinais (Fr.)	gä-tē-nĕ'	gah-tee-neh'
Gatnya (Rus.)	gät'-nyä	gaht'-nyah
Gatow, (Berlin, airport)	gä'-tō	gah'-toh
Gatukai (Oc., Solomons)	gä-too-kī'	gah-too-kai'
Gatun (Canal Zone)	gä-toon'	gah-toon'
Gau	gou'	gau'

German meaning *district.* Gauleiter, gou'-lī-tər [gau'-lai-tuhr], *district leader.*

Gau Algesheim (Ger.)	gou' äl'-gəs-hīm	gau' ahl'-guhs-haim

Gauhati (India)	gou-hä'-tē	gau-hah'-tee
Gauja (Latvia, riv.)	gou'-yä	gau'-yah
Gaulle, Charles de (Fr. polit.)	gōl', shärl' də	gohl', shahrl' duh
Gausta (Nor., mt.)	gou'-stä	gau'-stah
Gavam Sultaneh (Iran. polit.) See *Ahmed Qavam*.		
Gavdos (Crete, isl.)	gäv'-dô(s)	gahv'-do(s)
Gavigan *or* Gavagan (Irish, Am. name)	găv'-ə-gən	gav'-uh-guhn
Gavignano (It.)	gä-vē-nyä'-nô	gah-vee-nyah'-no
Gavin, James M. (Am. general)	găv'-ĭn	gav'-in
Gavin, L. H. (U.S. representative)	găv'-ĭn	gav'-in
Gävle (Sw.)	yĕv'-lə	yev'-luh
Gavray (Fr.)	gä-vrĕ'	gah-vreh'
Gavrielidis, Kostas (Gr. polit.)	gä-vrē-lē'-dēs, kô'-stäs	gah-vree-lee'-dees, ko'-stahs
Gavrilović, Stoyan (Yugosl. diplomat)	gä-vrē'-lô'-vĭch, stô'-yän'	gah-vree'-lo'-vich, sto'-yahn'
Gavrilovo (Rus.)	gä-vrē'-lŏ-vŏ	gah-vree'-lo-vo
Gavrilovski Posad (Rus.)	gä-vrē'-lŏf-skĭ pŏ-säd'	gah-vree'-lof-ski po-sahd'
Gavrus (Fr.)	gä-vrüs'	gah-vrüs'
Gavutu (Oc.)	gä-vōō'-tōō	gah-voo'-too
gawa	gä-wä	gah-wah

An element, meaning *river*, in Japanese place names. See *-kawa*.

| Gaya (India) | gī'-ə | gai'-uh |
| Gaza (Pal.) | *Eng.* gä'-zə *or* gā'-zə | gah'-zuh gay'-zuh |

Webster's prefers gā'-zə [gay'-zuh], but gä'-zə [gah'-zuh] was probably more often said in the title of the Huxley novel, *Eyeless in Gaza*. Compare *Prague*, präg' [prahg'] and prāg' [prayg'].

Gazala, el (Libya)	gä-zä'-lä, ĕl	gah-zah'-lah, el
Gazi (Crete)	gä'-zē	gah'-zee
Gaziköy (Turk.)	gä-zē'-kûĭ	gah-zee'-kœi
Gaziman (Rus., riv.)	gä-zē-män'	gah-zee-mahn'
Gdańsk See *Danzig*.		
Gdov (Rus.)	gdôf'	gdof'
Gdynia (Pol.)	gdĭ'-nyä	gdi'-nyah
Gea (Oc., Kwajalein)	gĕ'-ä	geh'-ah
Gearhart, Bertrand W. (U.S. representative)	gĭr'-härt	gihr'-hahrt

Mr. Gearhart writes, "With a hard G and an e-a-r as in 'ear' . . . In other words, Gear is pronounced like the gears you shift in your automobile."

Gedames (Libya)   See *Ghadames*.

Geelan, James P. (U.S. representative)	gē′-lən	gee′-luhn
Geelong (Austral.)	jĭ-lông′	ji-long′
Geelvink (NEI, New Guinea)	k(h)āl′-vĭngk	k(h)ayl′-vingk

Geer, Dirk Jan de (Du. polit.)   See *De Geer*.

Geertruidenberg (Neth.)	k(h)ār-trûĭ′-dən-bĕrk(h)	k(h)ayr-trœi′-duhn-behrk(h)
Geffen (Neth.)	k(h)ĕf′-ən	k(h)ef′-uhn
Geg (Alb.)	*Eng.* gĕg′	geg′

Meaning *North Albanian*. Albanian *Gegë*, gĕ′-gə [geh′-guh], and *Gega*.

Geiger, Roy Stanley (Am. general)	gī′-gər	gai′-guhr
Geilenkirchen (Ger.)	gī′-lən-kĭr′-k(h)ən	gai′-luhn-kihr′-k(h)uhn
Geilo (Nor.)	yā′-lō	yay′-loh
Geiranger (Nor.)	gā′-räng-ər	gay′-rahng-uhr
Gela (Sicily)	*It.* jĕ′-lä	jeh′-lah
	Eng. jē′-lə	jee′-luh
Gelati (Sicily)	jĕ-lä′-tē	jeh-lah′-tee
Gelderland (Neth., prov.)	*Eng.* gĕl′-dər-lănd	gel′-duhr-land
	Du. k(h)ĕl′-dər-länt	k(h)el′-duhr-lahnt
Geldermalsen (Neth.)	k(h)ĕl′-dər-mäl′-sən	k(h)el′-duhr-mahl′-suhn
Geldrop (Neth.)	k(h)ĕl′-drôp	k(h)el′-drop
Geleen (Neth.)	k(h)ə-lān′	k(h)uh-layn′
Gelendzhik (Rus.)	gĕ-lĕn-jĭk′	geh-len-jik′

Gelibolu (Turk., pen., town)   See *Gallipoli*.

Gelsenkirchen (Ger.)	gĕl′-zən-kĭr′-k(h)ən	gel′-zuhn-kihr′-k(h)uhn
Gemert (Neth.)	k(h)ā′-mərt	k(h)ay′-muhrt
Gemuend *or* Gemünd (Ger.)	gə-münt′	guh-münt′
Gendringen (Neth.)	k(h)ĕn′-drĭng-ən	k(h)en′-dring-uhn
genealogy	jē-nĭ-ăl′-ə-jĭ	jee-ni-al′-uh-ji
	or jĕn-ĭ-	*or* jen-i-
	or -ŏl′-ə-jĭ	*or*-ol′-uh-ji

Among dictionaries only Kenyon and Knott list -ŏl′- as an alternative pronunciation, commenting: The ŏ "sound is found in all parts of the United States and in Canada. The *-ology* words have influenced it."

Genemuiden (Neth.) k(h)ā'-nə-mûĭ'-dən k(h)ay'-nuh-mœi'-duhn

Geneva (Switz.) *Eng.* jə-nē'-və juh-nee'-vuh
French *Genève*, zhə-nĕv' [zhuh-nev']. German *Genf*, gĕnf' [genf'].
Italian *Ginevra*, jē-nĕ'-vrä [jee-neh'-vrah].

Geneva, Lake (Switz.) *Eng.* jə-nē'-və juh-nee'-vuh
Also called *Lake Leman*, lē'-mən [lee'-muhn]. French *Lac de Léman*,
läk də lĕ-mäN' [lahk duh leh-mahN']. German *Genfer See*, gĕn'-fər
zā' [gen'-fuhr zay'].

Genève (Switz.) See *Geneva*.

Genf (Switz.) See *Geneva*.

Genghis Khan (Mongol jĕng'-gĭs kän' jehng'-gis kahn'
leader)

Genichesk (Rus.) gĕ-nĭ-chĕsk' geh-ni-chesk'

Génissiat (Fr.) zhĕ-nē-syä' zheh-nee-syah'

Genitsa *or* Gianitsa (Gr.) yĕ-nē-tsä' yeh-nee-tsah'
or yä-nē-tsä' yah-nee-tsah'
Serb-Croat *Janica*, yä'-nĭ-tsä [yah'-ni-tsah].

Gennargentu (Sard., jĕn'-när-jĕn'-tōō jen'-nahr-jen'-too
mts.)

Gennep (Neth.) k(h)ĕn'-əp k(h)en'-uhp

Gennes (Fr.) zhĕn' zhen'

Genoa (It.) *Eng.* jĕn'-ō-ə jen'-oh-uh

Genova (It.) jĕ'-nô-vä jeh'-no-vah
English *Genoa*, q.v.

Gensan (Korea) gĕn'-sän gen'-sahn

Genusus (Alb., riv.) See *Shkumbi.*

Genzano (It.) jĕn-tsä'-nô jen-tsah'-no

Geographe (Austral., bay) jĭ-ŏg'-rə-fĭ ji-og'-ruh-fi
Pronounced as if spelled *geography.*

Georgatos (Gr. name) yôr-gä'-tôs yor-gah'-tos

George, Alphonse Joseph zhôrzh', äl-fôNs' zhorzh', ahl-foNs'
(Fr. general) zhô-zĕf' zho-zef'

Georgiev, Kimon gĕ-ôr'-gĭ-yĕf, geh-or'-gi-yehf,
(Bulg. polit.) kĭ-môn' ki-mon'

Georgievsk (Rus.) gĕ-ôr'-gĭ-yĕfsk geh-or'-gi-yefsk

Georgioupolis (Crete) yôr-yōō'-pô-lē(s) yor-yoo'-po-lee(s)
Also called *Almyros*, äl-mē-rôs' [ahl-mee-ros'] *or* är-mē-rôs' [ahr-mee-ros'].

Ger (Fr.) zhĕr' zhehr'

Gera (Ger.) gā'-rä gay'-rah

Gerace (It.) jĕ-rä'-chĕ jeh-rah'-cheh

Gerano (It.) jĕ-rä'-nô jeh-rah'-no

Gérardmer (Fr.) zhĕ-rär-mĕ' zheh-rahr-meh'

Gerbini (Sicily)	jĕr-bē'-nē	jehr-bee'-nee
Gerbrandy, Pieter S. (Du. polit.)	k(h)ĕr-brän'-dĭ, pē'-tər	k(h)ehr-brahn'-di, pee'-tuhr
Gerhardsen, Einar (Nor. polit.)	gĕr'-härd-sən, ā'-när or ĭ'-när	gehr'-hahrd-suhn, ay'-nahr or ai'-nahr
geriatrician	jĕr'-ĭ-ə-trĭsh'-ən	jehr'-i-uh-trish'-uhn
geriatrics	jĕr'-ĭ-ăt'-rĭks	jehr'-i-at'-riks
geriatrist	jĕr'-ĭ-ăt'-rĭst	jehr'-i-at'-rist
Gerlach, Charles L. (U.S. representative)	gûr'-läk(h)'	guhr'-lahk(h)'
Geroldsby Kasbach (Ger.)	gā'-rôlts-bĭ käs'-bäk(h)	gay'-rolts-bih kahs'-bahk(h)
Gerolstein (Ger.)	gā'-rôl-shtīn	gay'-rol-shtain
Gerona (Sp.)	hĕ-rô'-nä	heh-ro'-nah
gerontology	jĕr'-ən-tŏl'-ə-jĭ	jehr'-uhn-tol'-uh-ji
Gerow, Leonard (Am. general)	gĕ-rō'	geh-roh'
Gerry, Peter G. (U.S. senator)	gĕr'-ĭ	gehr'-i
Gerunda (It.)	jĕ-rōōn'-dä	jeh-roon'-dah
Gesso (It.)	jĕs'-sô	jes'-so
Gestapo	gə-stä'-pō or gə-shtä'-pō	guh-stah'-poh guh-shtah'-poh

Also Englished as gĕs'-tə-pō [ges'-tuh-poh]. An abbreviation of *Geheime Staatspolizei*, the former German "secret state police."

Getulio Vargas See *Vargas, Getulio*.

Gevelsberg (Ger.)	gā'-fəls-bĕrk(h)	gay'-fuhls-behrk(h)
Gey (Ger.)	gī'	gai'
Ghadames (Libya)	gə-dä'-mĕs	guh-dah'-mes

Also spelled *Gadames* and *Gedames*.

Ghardimaou (Tun.)	gär-dĭ-mă'-ōō	gahr-di-ma'-oo
ghat	gôt' or gät'	gawt' or gaht'
Ghats (India, mts.)	gôts' or gäts'	gawts' or gahts'

Ghavam Sultaneh (Iran. polit.) See *Ahmed Qavam*.

ghazi	gä'-zē	gah'-zee

A title or honorific in the Middle East, usually following the name.

Ghazi, Mahmud Khan (Afghan leader) See *Mahmud Khan Ghazi*.

Ghazni (Afghan.)	gŭz'-nē	guhz'-nee
Gheel (Belg.)	*Eng.* gāl' *Flem.* k(h)äl'	gayl' k(h)ayl'
Ghent (Belg.)	*Eng.* gĕnt'	gent'

Flemish *Gent*, k(h)ĕnt' [k(h)ent']. French *Gand*, gäN' [gahN'].

Gheorgheni (Rum.)   gyôr-gĕn'   gyor-gen'
Hungarian *Gyergyószentmiklós,* dyĕr'-dyô-sĕnt'-mĭk-lôsh [dyehr'-dyo-sent'-mik-losh].

Gherla (Rum.)   gĕr'-lä   gehr'-lah

Ghiaia (It.)   gyä'-yä   gyah'-yah

Ghibelline   gĭb'-ə-lēn *or* -līn   gib'-uh-leen *or* -lain
Italian *Ghibellino,* gē-bĕl-lē'-nô [gee-bel-lee'-no].

Ghiczy, Jenő von   gĭ'-tsĭ, yĕ'-nû fôn   gi'-tsi, yeh'-nœ fon
(Hung. polit.)

Ghilan *or* Gilan   gē-län'   gee-lahn'
(Iran)

Ghimeş (Rum., pass)   gē-mĕsh'   gee-mesh'

Ghimeş Făget (Rum.)   gē-mĕsh' fə-jĕt'   gee-mesh' fuh-jet'

Ghisonaccia (Corsica)   gē-sô-nät'-chä   gee-so-naht'-chah

Giacomo   jä'-kô-mô   jah'-ko-mo
Italian form of *Jacob* and *James.* It should not be stressed on the second syllable.

Giadalla (Libya)   jä-däl'-lä   jah-dahl'-lah

Gialam (Indo-Ch.)   zhä-lŭm'   zhah-luhm'

Gialo (Libya)   jä'-lō   jah'-loh

Gialomonokhoron (Crete)   yä-lô-mô-nô'-hô-rô(n)   yah-lo-mo-no'-ho-ro(n)

Gianicolo (It., Rome) See *Janiculum.*

Giannesada (Crete, isl.)   yä-nē-sä'-dä   yah-nee-sah'-dah

Giannetto (It.)   jän-nĕt'-tô   jahn-net'-to

Giannini   *Eng.* jə-nē'-nē   juh-nee'-nee
(It. name)   *It.*   jän-nē'-nē   jahn-nee'-nee

Giannini, Guglielmo   jän-nē'-nē,   jahn-nee'-nee,
(It. polit.)   gōō-lyĕl'-mô   goo-lyel'-mo

Giarabub (Libya)   jä'-rä-bōōb'   jah'-rah-boob'
Also spelled *Jarabub.*

Giarre (Sicily)   jär'-rĕ   jahr'-reh

gibber, -ish   jĭb'-ər, -ĭsh   jib'-uhr, -ish
     or gĭb'-ər, -ĭsh   gib'-uhr, -ish

gibber   jĭb'-ər   jib'-uhr
An Australian word meaning *rock* or *stone.*

gibber (swelling)   gĭb'-ər   gib'-uhr

gibbous   gib'-əs   gib'-uhs

gibe *or* jibe   jīb'   jaib'

Gibostad (Nor.)   gē'-bō-stä   gee'-boh-stah

Gibraltar   *Eng.* jĭ-brôl'-tər   ji-brol'-tuhr
     Sp. hē-bräl-tär'   hee-brahl-tahr'

Gien (Fr.)   zhyăN'   zhyaN'

Giens (Fr., pen.)   zhyăN'   zhyaN'

Gier (Fr., riv.)	zhyĕ′	zhyeh′
Giessen (Ger.)	gēs′-ən	gees′-uhn
Gieten (Neth.)	k(h)ē′-tən	k(h)ee′-tuhn
Giethoorn (Neth.)	k(h)ēt′-hōrn	k(h)eet′-hohrn
Gifu (Jap.)	gē-fŏŏ′	gee-foo′
Giglio (It., isls.)	jē′-lyô	jee′-lyo
gigue	*Fr.* zhēg′	zheeg′
	Eng. jĭg′	jig′
Gijón (Sp.)	hē-hôn′	hee-hon′
Gijunabena (Oc., Solomons)	gē-jŏŏ-nä-bĕ′-nä	gee-joo-nah-beh′-nah
Gila (Ariz.)	*Eng.* hē′-lə	hee′-luh
	Sp. hē′-lä	hee′-lah
Gilan *or* Ghilan (Iran)	gē-län′	gee-lahn′
Gildersleeve, Virginia Crocheron (Am. educator)	gĭl′-dər-slēv, krŏ′-shə-rŏn	gil′-duhr-sleev, kroh′-shuh-ron
Gilead (Trans-Jordan)	gĭl′-ĭ-ăd	gil′-i-ad
Modern *Ajlun,* äj-lŏŏn′ [ahj-loon′], with a part of *El Belqa,* bĕl′-kä [bel′-kah].		
Giles (Tenn., Va.)	jīlz′	jailz′
Gilgit (India)	gĭl′-gĭt	gil′-git
Giljevo (Yugosl.)	gē′-lyĕ-vô	gee′-lyeh-vo
Gillette, Guy M. (U.S. senator)	jĭ-lĕt′	ji-let′
Gillie, George W. (U.S. representative)	gĭl′-ĭ	gil′-i
gillyflower	jĭl′-ĭ-flou′-ər	jil′-ih-flau′-uhr
Gilze en Reijen (Neth.)	k(h)ĭl′-zə ĕn rī′-ən	k(h)il′-zuh en rai′-uhn
Ginneken (Neth.)	k(h)ĭn′-ə-kən	k(h)in′-uh-kuhn
Ginza (Jap.)	gēn′-zä′	geen′-zah′
Gioia di Tauro (It.)	jô′-yä dē tou′-rô	jo′-yah dee tau′-ro
Gioiosa Ionica *or* Jonica (It.)	jô-yô′-sä yô′-nē-kä	jo-yo′-sah yo′-nee-kah
Gioja (It.)	jô′-yä	jo′-yah
Giojosa (It.)	jô-yô′-zä	jo-yo′-zah
Giolitti, Giovanni (It. polit.)	jô-lēt′-tē, jô-vän′-nē	jo-leet′-tee, jo-vahn′-nee
Giorgio (It.)	jôr′-jô	jor′-jo
Giornale della Sera (Rome newspaper)	jôr-nä′-lē dĕl-lä sĕ′-rä	jor-nah′-lee del-lah seh′-rah
Giornale d'Italia (Rome newspaper)	jôr-nä′-lē dē-tä′-lyä	jor-nah′-lee dee-tah′-lyah
Gioumoultzina (Gr.)	See *Komotine.*	

Gioura (Gr., isl.)	yōō'-rä	yoo'-rah
giovanezza (It.)	jô-vä-nĕt'-sä	jo-vah-net'-sah
Giovenco (It., riv.)	jô-vĕn'-kô	jo-ven'-ko
Girál y Pereira, José (Sp. polit.)	hē-räl' ē pĕ-rā'-rä, hô-sĕ'	hee-rahl' ee peh-ray'-rah, ho-seh'
Giraud, Henri Honoré (Fr. general)	zhē-rō', äN-rē' ô-nô-rĕ'	zhee-roh', ahN-ree' o-no-reh'
Girgenti (It.)	jēr-jĕn'-tē	jeer-jen'-tee

Officially *Agrigento,* q.v.

Gironde (Fr., riv.)	zhē-rôNd'	zhee-roNd'

Gishu (Korea) See *Shingishu.*

Gisors (Fr.)	zhē-zôr'	zhee-zor'
Gissi (It.)	jēs'-sē	jees'-see
Giulianello (It.)	jōō-lyä-nĕl'-lô	joo-lyah-nel'-lo
Giuliano (It. name)	jōō-lyä'-nô	joo-lyah'-no
Giulie, Alpi (It., Yugosl., mts.)	jōō'-lyĕ, äl'-pē	joo'-lyeh, ahl'-pee

English *Julian Alps.*

Giupana (Yugosl., isl.)	*It.* jōō-pä'-nä	joo-pah'-nah

Serb-Croat *Šipan,* q.v.

Giurgiu (Rum.)	jŏŏr'-jŏŏ	jur'-ju
Givet (Fr.)	zhē-vĕ'	zhee-veh'
Givors (Fr.)	zhē-vôr'	zhee-vor'
Giza, el (Egypt)	gē'-zə, ĕl	gee'-zuh, el

Also spelled *Gizeh.*

Gizeux (Fr.)	zhē-zû'	zhee-zœ'
Gizio (It., riv.)	jē'-tsyô	jee'-tsyo
gizmo	gĭz'-mō	giz'-moh

A word meaning *gadget,* used in the Navy air force; perhaps derived from the Arabic *gism,* gĭsm' [gism'], meaning *body, stature, strength.*

Gizo (Oc., Solomons)	gē'-zô	gee'-zo

Gj-. For names of Yugoslavia in *Gj-,* see also *D-, Đ,* and *Dj-.*

Gjalica (Alb., mt.) See *Gjalicë.*

Gjalicë (Alb., mt.)	gyä'-lē-tsə	gyah'-lee-tsuh

Also called *Mal i Gjalicës.* Serb-Croat *Đalica,* dyä'-lĭ-tsä [dyah'-li-tsah].

Gjendesheim (Nor.)	yĕn'-dəs-hām	yen'-duhs-haym
Gjinokastër (Alb.)	gyē-nô-kä'-stər	gyee-no-kah'-stuhr

Italian *Argirocastro,* är-jē-rô-kä'-strô [ahr-jee-ro-kah'-stro]. Greek *Argyrokastron,* q.v.

Gjinokastra (Alb.) See *Gjinokastër.*

Gjoevik or Gjövik (Nor.)	yû'-vēk	yœ'-veek
Gjöres or Gjoeres, Axel (Sw. diplomat)	yû'-rĭs, äk'-səl	yœ'-ris, ahk'-suhl

Gjuhëzës, Kep i (Alb., cape) English *Glossa,* q.v.

Gjurgjevac (Yugosl.)	dyo͞or'-dyĕ-väts	dyoor'-dyeh-vahts
Gjusevo (Bulg.)	gyo͞o'-sĕ-vŏ	gyoo'-seh-vo
Glackens, William (Am. painter)	glăk'-ənz	glak'-uhnz
Gladbach Rheydt (Ger.)	glät'-bäk(h) rīt'	glaht'-bahk(h) rait'
Glamoč (Yugosl.)	glä'-môch	glah'-moch
Glan (Ger., riv.)	glän'	glahn'
Glane (Fr., riv.)	glän'	glahn'
Glarus (Switz.)	glä'-ro͞os	glah'-rus
French *Glaris*, glä-rē' [glah-ree'].		
Glasgow (Scot.)	*Am.* glăs'-gō *or* -kō	glas'-goh *or* -koh
	Scot. gläs'-gō *or* -kō	glahs'-goh *or* -koh
Glatz (Ger. >Pol.)	gläts'	glahts'
Polish *Kładzko*, q.v.		
Głębokie (Pol. >Rus.)	glăN-bô'-kyĕ	glaN-bo'-kyeh
Russian *Glubokoe*, glo͞o-bô'-kŏ-yĕ [glu-bo'-ko-yeh].		
Gledićske planine (Yugosl., mts.)	glĕ'-dĭch-skĕ plä'-nē'-nĕ	gleh'-dich-skeh plah'-nee'-neh
Gleiwitz (Ger. >Pol.)	glī'-vĭts	glai'-vits
Polish *Gliwice*, q.v.		
Glibovac (Yugosl.)	glē'-bô-väts	glee'-bo-vahts
Glière, Reinhold (Rus. composer)	glĭ-yĕr', rän'-gŏlt	gli-yehr', rayn'-golt
Glittertind (Nor.)	glĭt'-ər-tĭn	glit'-uhr-tin
Gliwice (Ger. >Pol.)	glĭ-vē'-tsĕ	gli-vee'-tseh
German *Gleiwitz*, q.v.		
Globo, O (Braz. newspaper)	glô'-bŏ, ŏŏ	glo'-bu, u
Glogau (Ger. > ? Pol.)	glō'-gou	gloh'-gau
Polish *Głogów*, glô'-go͞of [glo'-guf].		
Głogówek (Ger. >Pol.)	glô-go͞o'-vĕk	glo-gu'-vek
German *Oberglogau*, q.v.		
Glomfjord (Nor.)	glôm'-fyōr	glom'-fyohr
Glomma (Nor., riv.)	glôm'-ä	glom'-ah
Gloška (Yugosl., mt.)	glôsh'-kä	glosh'-kah
Glossa (Alb., cape)	*Eng.* glôs'-ə	glos'-uh
Albanian *Kep i Gjuhëzës*, kĕp' ē gyo͞o-hə'-zəs [kep' ee gyoo-huh'-zuhs], and *Karaburun*, q.v.		
Gloucester	glŏs'-tər *or* glôs'-tər	glos'-tuhr glos'-tuhr
Głubczyce (Ger. >Pol.)	glo͞ob-chĭ'-tsĕ	glub-chi'-tseh
German *Leobschuetz*, q.v.		
Glubokoe (Pol. >Rus.)	glo͞o-bô'-kŏ-yĕ	glu-bo'-ko-yeh
Polish *Głębokie*, q.v.		

Glusk (Rus.)	gloōsk′	gloosk′
Glukhov (Rus.)	gloō′-hŏf	gloo′-hof
Gmuend *or* Gmünd (Ger.)	gmünt′	gmünt′
Gneisenau (Ger.)	gnī′-zə-nou	gnai′-zuh-nau
Gniew (Pol.)	gnyĕf′	gnyef′
Gniezna (Pol., riv.)	gnyĕz′-nä	gnyez′-nah
Gniezno (Pol.)	gnyĕz′-nô	gnyez′-no
Gnjilane (Yugosl.)	gnyē′-lä-nĕ	gnyee′-lah-neh
Gnome et Rhône (Fr., Le Mans, factory)	gnōm ĕ rōn′ *or* nōm...	gnohm eh rohn′ *or* nohm...
Goa *or* Gôa (Port. India)	gō′-ə	goh′-uh
Goarshausen, Sankt (Ger.) See *Sankt Goarshausen.*		
Göbbels, Joseph Paul (Ger. polit.)	gûb′-əls, yō′-zĕf poul′	gœb′-uhls, yoh′-zehf paul′
Goch (Ger.)	gôk(h)′	gok(h)′
Godavari (India, riv.)	gō-dä′-və-rē	goh-dah′-vuh-ree
Goderville (Fr.)	gô-dĕr-vēl′	go-dehr-veel′
Godesberg, Bad (Ger.)	gō′-dəs-bĕrk(h), bät′	goh′-duhs-behrk(h), baht′
Godhavn (Greenland)	gô*th*′-houn	go*th*′-haun
Godolesh (Alb.)	gô-dô′-lĕsh	go-do′-lesh
Godoleshi (Alb.) See *Godolesh.*		
Gödöllő (Hung.)	gû′-dûl-lû	gœ′-dœl-lœ
Godthaab (Greenl.)	gôt′-hôp′	got′-hop′
Goebbels, Joseph Paul (Ger. polit.)	gûb′-əls, yō′-zĕf poul′	gœb′-uhls, yoh′-zehf paul′
Goedereede (Neth., isl.)	k(h)oō′-də-rā′-də	k(h)oo′-duh-ray′-duh
The island is divided into *Goeree*, q.v., and *Overflakkee*, q.v.		
Goeding (Cz.) See *Hodonín.*		
Goeker, Muzaffer (Turk. diplomat) See *Göker.*		
Goerdeler, Karl (Ger. polit.)	gûr′-də-lər	gœr′-duh-luhr
Goeree (Neth., isl.) See *Goedereede.*	k(h)oō′-rā′	k(h)oo′-ray′
Goering, Hermann (Ger. polit.)	gû′-rĭng, hĕr′-män	gœ′-ring, hehr′-mahn
Goeritz (Ger.)	gû′-rĭts	gœ′-rits
Goerlitz (Ger. > Pol.) See *Görlitz.*		
Goerz (It.) See *Gorizia.*		
Goes (Neth.)	k(h)oōs′	k(h)oos′
Goeschenen (Switz.)	gû′-shĕn-ən	gœ′-shen-uhn
Góes Monteiro, Pedro Aurelio de (Braz. general)	gô′-ĭs môn-tā′-roŏ, pĕ′-droŏ ou-rĕ′-lē-oŏ də	go′-is mon-tay′-ru, peh′-dru au-rĕh-lee′-u duh

[189]

Goethals, George W. (U.S.A. engineer)	gō′-thəlz	goh′-thuhlz
Goethe, Johann Wolfgang von (Ger. poet)	gû′-tə, yō′-hän vôlf′-gäng fən	gœ′-tuh, yoh′-hahn volf′-gahng fuhn
Goettingen (Ger.)	gût′-ĭng-ən	gœt′-ing-uhn
Gogarty, Oliver St. John (Irish poet)	gō′-gər-tĭ	goh′-guhr-ti
Gogebic (Mich.)	gō-jē′-bĭk	goh-jee′-bĭk
Gogol, Nikolai Vasilievich (Rus. writer)	Eng. gō′-gŏl Rus. gô′-gŏl(y), nĭ-kŏ-lī′ vä-sē′-lyĕ-vĭch	goh′-gol gaw′-gol(y), ni-ko-lai′ vah-see′-lyeh-vich
Gogra (India, riv.)	gō′-grä	goh′-grah
Goiânia (Brazil)	gô-yä′-nyə	go-yah′-nyuh
Goiaz (Brazil)	gô-yäs′	go-yahs′
Goirle (Neth.) See Goorle.		
Göker, Muzaffer (Turk. diplomat)	gû-kĕr′, mōō-zäf-fĕr′	gœ-kehr′, moo-zahf-fehr′
Gokteik (Burma)	gōk′-tāk′	gohk′-tayk′
Gol (Nor.)	gōl′	gohl′
Golanowo (Ger. >Pol.) German Gollnow, q.v.	gô-lä-nô′-vô	go-lah-no′-vo
Gołdap (Ger. >Pol.) German spelling Goldap.	gôl′-däp	gol′-dahp
Goldingen (Latvia) Latvian Kuldiga, q.v.	Ger. gôl′-dĭng-ən Rus. gôl′(y)-dĭn-gĕn	gol′-ding-uhn gol′(y)-din-gen
Golema Rudina (Balkan mt.)	gô′-lĕ-mä rōō′-dĭ-nä	go′-leh-mah roo′-di-nah
Goleš (Yugosl., mt.)	gô′-lĕsh	go′-lesh
Golešnica (Yugosl.)	gô′-lĕsh′-nĭ-tsä	go′-lesh′-ni-tsah

golfo (It.) *Golfo* or *gulf* is often ignored in the alphabetical listing. Look for the name itself.

Goliad (Tex.)	gō′-lĭ-ăd	goh′-li-ad
Golightly (Eng. name)	gə-līt′-lĭ	guh-lait′-li
Golija (Yugosl., mts.)	gô′-lĭ-yä	go′-li-yah
Golikov, Filip (Rus. general)	gô′-lĭ-kôf, fĭ-lēp′	go′-li-kof, fi-leep′
Goljak planina (Yugosl., mts.)	gô′-lyäk plä′-nē′-nä	go′-lyahk plah′-nee′-nah
Gollnow (Ger. >Pol.) Polish Golanowo, q.v.	gôl′-nō	gol′-noh
Golova (Rus.)	gŏ-lŏ-vä′	go-lo-vah′

Golovanov, Aleksandr (Rus. general)	gŏ-lŏ-vä'-nŏf, ä-lĕ-ksän'-dər	go-lo-vah'-nof, ah-leh-ksahn'-duhr
Goltva (Rus.)	gôl'-tvä	gol'-tvah
Golub (Pol.)	gŏ'-lo͞op	go'-lup
Golubac (Yugosl.)	gŏ'-lo͞o'-bäts	go'-loo'-bahts
Golzheim (Ger.)	gôlts'-hīm	golts'-haim
Golzow (Ger.)	gôl'-tsō	gol'-tsoh
Gomel (Rus.)	gŏ'-mĕl(y)	go'-mel(y)
Gomera (Canary Isls.)	gô-mĕ'-rä	go-meh'-rah
Gómes, Eduardo (Braz. general)	gŏ'-mĭs, ĕ-dwär'-do͞o	go'-mis, eh-dwahr'-du
Gómez de Jordana (Sp. polit)	gŏ'-mĕth (or -mĕs) dĕ hôr-dä'-nä	go'-meth (or -mes) deh hor-dah'-nah
Gómez Pérez, Blas (Sp. polit)	gŏ'-mĕth (or -mĕs) pĕ'-rĕth (or -rĕs), bläs'	go'-meth (or -mes) peh'-reth (or -res), blahs'
Gomułka, Władysław (Pol. polit.)	gô-mo͞ol'-kä, vlä-dĭ'-släf	go-mul'-kah, vlah-di'-slahf
Gona (New Guinea, Papua)	gŏ'-nä	go'-nah
Gonaïves (Haiti)	gŏ-nä-ēv'	go-nah-eev'
Gonatas, Stylianos (Gr. polit.)	gŏ-nä-täs', stē-lē-ä-nôs'	go-nah-tahs', stee-lee-ah-nos'
Gonâve (Haiti, isl.)	gô-näv'	go-nahv'
Gonçalves Dias, Antonio (Braz. poet)	gŏn-säl'-vĭz dē'-əs, än-tô'-nyo͞o	gon-sahl'-viz dee'-uhs, ahn-to'-nyu
Gonneville (Fr.)	gôn-vēl'	gon-veel'
González (Sp., Am. name)	Eng. gən-zăl'-ĭz Am. Sp. gôn-sä'-lĕs Sp. gôn-thä'-lĕth	guhn-zal'-iz gon-sah'-les gon-thah'-leth
González Videla, Gabriel (Chilean polit.)	gôn-sä'-lĕs vē-dĕ'-lä, gä-brē-ĕl'	gon-sah'-les vee-deh'-lah, gah-bree-el'
Goodenough (Oc.) An English family name.	go͞od'-ĭ-nŭf	gud'-i-nuhf
Goor (Neth.)	k(h)ōr'	k(h)ohr'
Goorle (Neth.) Also spelled Goirle.	k(h)ōr'-lə	k(h)ohr'-luh
Gopło (Pol., lake)	gŏ'-plô	go'-plo
Gora (Rus., mt.)	gŏ-rä'	go-rah'
Góra Kalwarja (Pol.)	go͞o'-rä käl-vär'-yä	gu'-rah kahl-vahr'-yah
Russian Gora Kalvaria,	gŏ-rä' käl(y)-vä'-rĭ-yä	[go-rah' kahl(y)-vah'-
ri-yah].		
Goransko (Yugosl.)	gŏ'-rän-skô	go'-rahn-sko
Goražde (Yugosl.)	gŏ'-räzh-dĕ	go'-rahzh-deh

Gorbachovo (Rus.)	gŏr-bä-chŏ'-vŏ	gor-bah-cho'-vo
Gorbatov (Rus.)	gŏr-bä'-tŏf	gor-bah'-tof
Gorbitsa (Rus.)	gŏr'-bĭ-tsä	gor'-bi-tsah
Gördeler, Karl (Ger. polit.)	gûr'-də-lər	gœr'-duh-luhr
Goreloe (Rus.)	gŏ-rĕ'-lŏ-yĕ	go-reh'-lo-yeh
Gorgany (Pol., mts.)	gŏr-gä'-nĭ	gor-gah'-ni
Gorgona (It., isl.)	gŏr-gŏ'-nä	gor-go'-nah
Gori (Rus.)	gŏ'-rē	go'-ree
Goriano Sicoli (It.)	gô-ryä'-nô	go-ryah'-no
	sē'-kô-lē	see'-ko-lee

Gorica (Alb.)   See *Goricĕ*.

Gorica, Velika (Yugosl.)	gŏ'-rĭ-tsä, vĕ'-lĭ-kä	go'-ri-tsah, veh'-li-kah
Goricë (Alb.)	gô-rē'-tsə	go-ree'-tsuh
Gorin (Pol. >Rus., riv.)	gô'-rĭn(y)	go'-rin(y)

Ukrainian *Horin* and Polish *Horyń*, hô'-rĭn(y) [ho'-rin(y)].

Gorinchem (Neth.)	k(h)ō'-rĭ-kəm	k(h)oh'-ri-kuhm

Another form and the usual pronunciation is *Gorkum*, q.v.

Göring, Hermann	gû'-rĭng, hĕr'-män	gœ'-ring, hehr'-mahn
(Ger. polit.)		
Göritz (Ger.)	gû'-rĭts	gœ'-rits
Gorizia (It.)	gô-rē'-tsyä	go-ree'-tsyah

German *Goerz*, gûrts' [gœrts'].

Gorjanci (Yugosl., mts.)	gŏr'-yän-tsĭ	gor'-yahn-tsi
Gorki (Rus.)	gŏr'-kĭ	gor'-ki
Gorkum (Neth.)	k(h)ŏr'-kəm	k(h)or'-kuhm

Another form is *Gorinchem*, q.v.

Görlitz (Ger.)	gûr'-lĭts	gœr'-lits

Polish *Zgorzelice*, zgô-zhĕ-lē'-tsĕ [zgo-zheh-lee'-tseh].

Gorna Dzhumaya (Bulg.)	gŏr'-nä jŏŏ'-mä-yä'	gor'-nah ju'-mah-yah'
Gorna Orehovitsa	gŏr'-nä ŏ-rĕ-hŏ'-	gor'-nah o-reh-ho'-
(Bulg.)	vĭ-tsä	vi-tsah

gornja, -ji (an element in Yugoslav place names) See *donji*.

Gorodenka (Pol. >Rus.)	gŏ-rŏ-dĕn'-kä	go-ro-den'-kah

Polish *Horodenka*, q.v.

Gorodlo (Pol.)   See *Horodło*.

Gorodnitsa (Rus.)	gŏ-rŏd-nē'-tsä	go-rod-nee'-tsah

Gorodno (Pol.)   See *Horodno*.

Gorodok Yagellonski	gŏ-rŏ-dôk' yä-gĕl'-	go-ro-dok' yah-gel'-
(Pol. >Rus.)	lŏn-skĭ	lon-ski

Polish *Gródek Jagielloński*, q.v.

Gorontalo (NEI) See *Tomini*.

Gorredijk (Neth.)	k(h)ôr'-ə-dĭk'	k(h)or'-uh-daik'
Gorron (Fr.)	gô-rôN'	go-roN'
Gorsel (Neth.)	k(h)ôr'-səl	k(h)or'-suhl

Görz (It.) See *Gorizia*.

Gorzów (Ger. >Pol.)   gô′-zhōōf   go′-zhuf
    German *Landsberg*, q.v.

Göschenen (Switz.)   gû′-shĕn-ən   gœ′-shen-uhn

Goslar (Ger.)   gôs′-lär   gos′-lahr

Gospić (Yugosl.)   gô′-spĭch   go′-spich

Gossett, Ed   gŏs′-ĭt   gos′-it
    (U.S. representative)

Gostivar (Yugosl.)   gô′-stĭ-vär   gô′-sti-vahr

Gostyń (Pol.)   gô′-stĭn(y)   go′-stin(y)

Gostynin (Pol.)   gô-stĭ′-nĭn   go-sti′-nin
    Russian *Gostinin*, gŏ-stē′-nĭn [go-stee′-nin].

Göteborg (Sw.)   yû′-tə-bôr′(y)   yœ′-tuh-bor′(y)
    Often Englished as *Gothenburg*, q.v., especially in radio usage.

Gotha (Ger.)   gō′-tä   goh′-tah

Gothenburg (Sw.)   *Eng.* gŏt′n-bûrg′   got′n-buhrg′
    Swedish *Göteborg*, q.v.

Gotland *or* Gottland   *Eng.* gŏt′-lənd   got′-luhnd
    (Sw., isl.)   *Sw.* gôt′-lŭnd *or* gôl′-   got′-luhnd *or* gol′-

Gotnya (Rus.)   gôt′-nyä   got′-nyah

Gotovuše (Yugosl.)   gô′-tô′-vōō-shĕ   go′-to′-voo-sheh

Gotterswickerhamm   gôt′-ərs-vĭk′-ər-häm   got′-uhrs-vik′-uhr-
    (Ger.)   hahm

Gottesberg (Ger. > ?Pol.)   gôt′-əs-bĕrk(h)   got′-uhs-behrk(h)
    Polish *Boża Góra*, q.v.

Göttingen (Ger.)   gût′-ĭng-ən   gœt′-ing-uhn

Gottwald, Klement   gôt′-vält, klĕ′-mĕnt   got′-vahlt, kleh′-ment
    (Cz. polit.)

Goubellat (Tun.)   gōō-bəl-lăt′   goo-buhl-lat′

Goucherie (Fr.)   gōōsh-rē′   goosh-ree′

Gouda (Neth.)   k(h)ou′-dä   k(h)au′-dah

Gouillons (Fr.)   gwē-yôN′   gwee-yoN′

Gouin, Félix (Fr. polit.)   gwăn′, fĕ-lēks′   gwaN′, feh-leeks′

Goulburn (Austral.)   gōl′-bərn   gohl′-buhrn

Goulette, la (Tun.)   gōō-lĕt′, lä   goo-let′, lah

Goumenitsa (Gr.)   gōō-mĕ′-nē-tsä   goo-meh′-nee-tsah

Goumiers   gōō-myĕ′   goo-myeh′
    French Moroccan troops organized into units of 160 men called a
    goum, gōōm [goom]; Arabic meaning *tribe* or *family*.

Goura (Gr.)   gōō′-rä   goo′-rah

Gourgé (Fr.)   gōōr-zhĕ′   goor-zheh′

Gourin (Fr.)   gōō-răN′   goo-raN′

Gournay (Fr.)   gōōr-nĕ′   goor-neh′

Gousev, Fëdor (Rus. diplomat) See *Gusev*.

Gouvais (Crete)	gōō'-vĕs	goo'-ves
Govarljevo (Yugosl.)	gô'-vär'-lyĕ-vô	go'-vahr'-lyeh-vo
Govorov, Leonid A. (Rus. general)	gô'-vŏ-rŏf, lĕ-ŏ-nēt'	go'-vo-rof, leh-o-neet'
Gowanus (Brooklyn)	gə-wä'-nəs	guh-wah'-nuhs
Grabovica (Yugosl.)	grä'-bô-vĭ-tsä	grah'-bo-vi-tsah
Grabovnica (Yugosl.)	grä'-bôv-nĭ-tsä	grah'-bov-ni-tsah
Grabski, Stanisław (Pol. polit)	gräp'-skĭ, stä-nē'-släf	grahp'-ski, stah-nee'-slahf
Gračac (Yugosl.)	grä'-chäts	grah'-chahts
Gračanica (Yugosl.)	grä'-chä'-nĭ-tsä	grah'-chah'-ni-tsah
Gračanka (Yugosl., riv.)	grä'-chän-kä	grah'-chahn-kah
Grad (Yugosl.)	gräd'	grahd'
Gradačac (Yugusl.)	grä'-dä'-chäts	grah'-dah'-chahts
Gradec (Yugosl.)	grä'-dĕts	grah'-dets
Gradešnica (Yugosl.)	grä'-dĕsh'-nĭ-tsä	grah'-desh'-ni-tsah
Gradiška, Stara (Yugosl.)	grä'-dĭ-shkä, stä'-rä	grah'-di-shkah, stah'-rah
Gradište (Yugosl.)	grä'-dĭ-shtĕ	grah'-di-shteh
Gradizhsk (Rus.)	grä-dĭshk'	grah-dishk'
Graefenhausen *or* Gräfenhausen (Ger.)	grĕ'-fən-hou'-zən	greh'-fuhn-hau'-zuhn
Graevo (Pol.) See *Grajewo.*		
Graham, Louis E. (U.S. representative)	grĕ'-əm	greh'-uhm
Grahovo (Yugosl.)	grä'-hô-vô	grah'-ho-vo
Graiba (Tun.)	grä-ē'-bä	grah-ee'-bah
Grainville (Fr.)	gräN-vēl'	graN-veel'
Graivoron (Rus.)	grī'-vŏ-rŏn	grai'-vo-ron
Grajewo (Pol.)	grä-yĕ'-vô	grah-yeh'-vo
Russian *Graevo,* grä'-yĕ-vŏ [grah'-yeh-vo].		
Gramada (Yugosl.)	grä'-mä-dä	grah'-mah-dah
Grambouza (Crete, isl.)	gräm-bōō'-zä	grahm-boo'-zah
Gramsh (Alb.)	grämsh'	grahmsh'
Gramshi (Alb.) See *Gramsh.*		
Gran (Hung.) See *Esztergom.*		
Granada (Sp.)	*Eng.* grə-nä'-də *or* grə-nā'-də *Sp.* grä-nä'-dä	gruh-nah'-duh gruh-nay'-duh grah-nah'-dah
Granarolo (It.)	grä-nä-rô'-lô	grah-nah-ro'-lo
Grandcamp (Fr.)	gräN-käN'	grahN-kahN'
Grand Coulee (Wash., range and dam)	grănd' kōō'-lĭ	grand' koo'-li

Grand Dorsal (Tun., mts.)	*Eng.* gră̆nd dôr'-səl *Fr.* gräN dôr-säl'	grand dor'-suhl grahN dor-sahl'
Grand Gosier (Haiti)	gräN gô-syĕ'	grahN go-syeh'
Grandjean (Fr. name)	gräN-zhäN'	grahN-zhahN'
Grand Lieu (Fr., lake)	gräN lyû'	grahN lyœ'
Grandménil (Belg.)	gräN-mĕ-nēl'	grahN-meh-neel'
Grand Morin (Fr.)	gräN mô-ră̆N'	grahN mo-raN'
Grand Teton (Wyo., nat. pk.)	tē'-tŏn	tee'-tŏn
Granitola (Sicily, cape)	grä-nē'-tô-lä	grah-nee'-to-lah
Granterath (Ger.)	grän'-tə-rät	grahn'-tuh-raht
Granville (Fr.)	gräN-vēl'	grahN-veel'
Granvin (Nor.)	grän'-vĭn	grahn'-vin
Grasse (Fr.)	gräs'	grahs'
Gratang (Nor.)	grä'-täng	grah'-tahng
Gratangen (Nor.)	grä'-täng-ən	grah'-tahng-uhn
Graubünden (Switz.) See *Grisons*.		
Graudenz (Pol.) See *Grudziądz*.		
Grau San Martín, Ramón (Cuban polit.)	grou' sän mär-tēn', rä-môn'	grau' sahn mahr-teen,' rah-mon'
Grave (Fr.)	gräv'	grahv'
Gravehals (Nor., tunnel)	grä'-və-häls	grah'-vuh-hahls
Gravelines (Fr.)	gräv-lēn'	grahv-leen'
Gravelotte (Fr.)	gräv-lôt'	grahv-lot'
's Gravendeel (Neth.)	sk(h)rä'-vən-dāl'	sk(h)rah'-vuhn-dayl'
's Gravenhage (Neth.)	sk(h)rä'-vən-hä'-k(h)ə	sk(h)rah'-vuhn-hah'-k(h)uh

An abbreviated form and the common pronunciation is *Den Haag*, dən häk(h)' [duhn hahk(h)']. English The *Hague*, q.v.

's Gravenzande (Neth.)	sk(h)rä'-vən-zän'-də	sk(h)rah'-vuhn-zahn'-duh
Gray (Fr.)	grĕ'	greh'
Graz (Austria)	gräts'	grahts'
Graziani, Rodolfo (It. general)	grä-tsyä'-nē, rô-dôl'-fô	grah-tsyah'-nee, ro-dol'-fo
Grazzanise (It.)	grät-sä-nē'-zĕ	graht-sah-nee'-zeh
Grbalj (Yugosl.)	gər'-bäl(y)	guhr'-bahl(y)
Grčište (Yugosl.)	gər'-chĭ-shtĕ	guhr'-chi-shteh
Grdelica (Yugosl.)	gər'-dĕ'-lĭ-tsä	guhr'-deh'-li-tsah
Grebbe, the (Neth., line of defense)	k(h)rĕb'-ə	k(h)reb'-uh
Greben, Veliki (Yugosl., mts.)	grĕ'-bĕn, vĕ'-lĭ-kĭ	greh'-ben, veh'-li-ki

Grechaninov, Aleksandr T. (Rus. composer) grĕ-chä-nē'-nŏf, ä-lĕk-sän'-dər — greh-chah-nee'-nof, ah-lek-sahn'-duhr

Grefrath (Ger.) grĕf'-rät — gref'-raht

Grefsen (Nor.) grĕfs'n — grefs'n

Gregorio (It.) grĕ-gô'-ryô — greh-go'-ryo

Greifenberg (Ger. >Pol.) grī'-fən-bĕrk(h) — grai'-fuhn-behrk(h)
Polish *Gryfice*, q.v.

Greifenhagen (Ger.) grī'-fən-hä'-gən — grai'-fuhn-hah'-guhn

Greiz (Ger.) grīts' — graits'

Grejač (Yugosl.) grĕ'-yäch — greh'-yahch

Grenaa (Den.) grĕn'-ô — gren'-o

Grenada (Miss., W.I.) grə-nā'-də — gruh-nay'-duh

Grenadines (W.I.) grĕn'-ə-dēnz — gren'-uh-deenz

Grenchen (Switz.) grĕn'-k(h)ən — gren'-k(h)uhn

Grenneville (Fr.) grĕn-vēl' — gren-veel'

Grenoble (Fr.) *Eng.* grə-nō'-bəl — gruh-noh'-buhl
Fr. grə-nô'bl — gruh-no'bl

Gressenich (Ger.) grĕs'-ə-nik(h) — gres'-uh-nik(h)

Gretchaninoff, Aleksandr T. (Rus. composer) See *Grechaninov.*

Grevena (Gr.) grĕ-vĕ-nä' — greh-veh-nah'

Grevenbroich (Ger.) grā'-vən-broik(h) — gray'-vuhn-broik(h)

Grevenmacher (Luxem.) grā'-vən-mäk'-ər — gray'-vuhn-mahk'-uhr

Grèves, Pointes des (Fr.) grĕv', pwăNt' dĕ — grev', pwaNt' deh'

Grey of Fallodon (Br. statesman) făl'-ə-dən — fal'-uh-duhn

Gridino (Rus.) grē'-dĭ-nŏ — gree'-di-no

Griesheim (Ger.) grēs'-hīm — grees'-haim

grievous grēv'-əs — greev'-uhs

There is no such word as *grievious.* Cf. the erroneous forms *mischievious* for *mischievous, portentious* for *portentous, tremendious* for *tremendous.*

Grigoriopol (Rus.) grĭ-gŏ-rĭ-ô'-pŏl(y) — gri-go-ri-o'-pol(y)

Grijpskerk (Neth.) k(h)rīps'-kĕrk — k(h)raips'-kehrk

grimace grĭ-mās' — gri-mays'
or grĭm'-ĭs — grim'-is

If this somewhat literary word is uttered, the second pronunciation, though without dictionary authority, occurs more often than the first.

Grimbosq (Fr., forest) grăN-bôsk' — graN-bosk'

Grimstad (Nor.) grĭm'-stä — grim'-stah

Grini (Nor.) grē'-nē — gree'-nee

Gris Nez (Fr., cape) grē nĕ' — gree neh'

Grisons (Switz.) grē-zoN′   gree-zoN′
 German *Graubünden* grou-bün′-dən [grau-bün′-duhn].
Grīva (Latvia) grē′-vä   gree′-vah
 Russian *Kalkuny*, q.v.
Grljan (Yugosl.) gər′-lyän   guhr′-lyahn
Grocka (Yugosl.) gər′-ô-tskä   guhr′-o-tskah
Gródek Jagielloński grŏŏ′-dĕk yä-gyĕl- gru′-dek yah-gyel-
 (Pol. >Rus.) lôn′(y)-skĭ   lon′(y)-ski
 Russian *Gorodok Yagellonski*, gŏ-rŏ-dôk′ yä-gĕl′-lŏn-skĭ [go-ro-dok′
 yah-gel′-lon-ski].
Grodisk (Pol.) See *Grodzisk.*
Grodna (Pol. >Rus.) grôd′-nä   grod′-nah
 Polish *Grodno*, grôd′-nô [grod′-no].
Grodzisk (Pol.) grô′-jĭsk   gro′-jisk
 Russian *Grodisk*, grô′-dĭsk [gro′-disk].
Grodzyanka (Rus.) grôd-zyän′-kä   grod-zyahn′-kah
Groenloo (Neth.) k(h)rŏŏn′-lō   k(h)roon′-loh
Groenoey (Nor.) grûn′-ûĭ   grœn′-œi
Groesbeek (Neth.) k(h)rŏŏs′-bāk   k(h)roos′-bayk
Groitsi (Pol.) See *Grójec.*
Groix (Fr., isl.) grwä′   grwah′
Grójec (Pol.) grŏŏ′-yĕts   gru′-yets
 Russian *Groitsi*, groi′-tsĭ [groi′-tsi].
Grol, Milan grôl′, mē′-län   grol′, mee′-lahn
 (Yugosl. polit.)
Grombalia (Tun.) grŏm-bä′-lĭ-ä   grom-bah′-li-ah
Gromyko, Andrei A. grŏ-mĭ′-kō, än-drā′ gro-mih′-koh,
 (Rus. diplomat)   ahn-dray′
Grong (Nor.) grông′   grong′
Groningen (Neth.) *Eng.* grō′-nĭng-ən groh′-ning-uhn
   Du. k(h)rō′-nĭng-ən k(h)roh′-ning-uhn
Groningen Diep *Eng.* grō′-nĭng-ən groh′-ning-uhn deep′
 (Neth.)   dēp′
   Du. k(h)rō′-nĭng-ən k(h)roh′-ning-uhn
   dēp′   deep′
 Also called *Reit Diep*, q.v.
Grönöy (Nor.) grûn′-ûĭ   grœn′-œi
Grootebroek (Neth.) k(h)rō′-tə-brŏŏk′ k(h)roh′-tuh-brook′
Groote Eylandt (Austral.) grŏŏt ĭ′-lənd groot ai′-luhnd
 The earlier pronunciation was k(h)rō′-tə ĭ′-länt [k(h)roh′-tuh ai′-
 lahnt], but the name has been Englished.
Grootegast (Neth.) k(h)rō′-tə-k(h)äst′ k(h)roh′-tuh-
     k(h)ahst′
groschen (currency unit) grō′-shən groh′-shuhn

Grosny (Rus.)	grôz′-nĭ	groz′-ni
Gross Blumberg (Ger.)	grōs′ blōōm′-bĕrk(h)	grohs′ bloom′-behrk(h)
Grosseto (It.)	grôs-sĕ′-tô	gros-seh′-to

This name (among others) strains the phonetic system, for the *e* is close. However it should not be pronounced a diphthong.

Gross Gerau (Ger.)	grōs′ gā′-rou	grohs′ gay′-rau
Grosshau (Ger.)	grōs′-hou	grohs′-hau
Gross Rominten (Ger.)	grōs′ rō′-mĭn-tən	grohs′ roh′-min-tuhn
Gross Strehlitz (Ger.)	grōs′ shtrā′-lĭts	grohs′ shtray′-lits
Gross Tychow (Ger. > Pol.)	grōs tēk(h)′-ō	grohs teek(h)′-oh
Polish *Tychowo*, q.v.		
Grostenquin (Fr.)	grō-täN-kăN′	groh-tahN-kaN′
Grosvenor (family name)	grōv′-nēr	grohv′-nuhr
Grosz, George	grōs′	grohs′
(Ger.-,Am. painter)		
Grosz, Wiktor (Pol. polit.)	grôsh′, vík′-tôr	grosh′, vik′-tor
Grotewohl, Otto	grō′-tə-vōl	groh′-tuh-vohl
(Ger. polit.)		
Grotli (Nor.)	grōt′-lē	groht′-lee
Groton (Mass., school)	grŏt′-ən	grot′-uhn

The analogy of *Croton* is misleading. However, *Groton*, Conn., is often pronounced grōt′n [groht′n].

Grottaglie (It.)	grôt-tä′-lyĕ	grot-tah′-lyeh
Grotteria (It., Calab.)	grôt-tĕ-rē′-ä	grot-teh-ree′-ah
Grouw (Neth.)	k(h)rou′	k(h)rau′
Groza, Petru (Rum. polit.)	grô′-zä, pĕ′-trōō	gro′-zah, peh′-troo
Grubbenvorst (Neth.)	k(h)rûb′-ən-vôrst	k(h)rœb′-uhn-vorst
Gruber, Karl (Austrian polit.)	grōō′-bər, kärl′	groo′-buhr, kahrl′
Grubeshov (Pol.) See *Hrubieszów*.		
Grubišno Polje (Yugosl.)	grōō′-bĭsh-nô pôl′-yĕ	groo′-bish-no pol′-yeh
Grudziądz (Pol.)	grōŏ′-jôNts	gru′-joNts
German *Graudenz*, grou′-dĕnts [grau′-dents].		
Gruenberg, Grünberg	grün′-bĕrk(h)	grün′-behrk(h)
(Ger. > ? Pol.)		
Polish *Zielona Góra*, q.v.		
Grunau (Rus.)	grōō′-nou	groo′-nau
Grundernhausen (Ger.)	grŏŏn′-dərn-hou′-zən	grun′-duhrn-hau′-zuhn
Gruž (Yugosl.)	grōōzh′	groozh′
Gruža (Yugosl.)	grōō′-zhä	groo′-zhah
Gryazi (Rus.)	gryä′-zē	gryah′-zee

Gryfice (Ger. >Pol.)   grĭ-fē′-tsĕ   gri-fee′-tseh
German *Greifenberg*, q.v.

Grytviken (S. Georgia,   grüt′-vēk-ən   grüt′-veek-uhn
isl.)

Guadalajara (Sp., Mex.)   (g)wä-dä-lä-hä′-rä   (g)wah-dah-lah-hah′-rah

Guadalcanal (Oc.)   gwä-däl-kä-näl′   gwah-dahl-kah-nahl′
According to the Royal Geographical Society pamphlets the local pronunciation is kä-lä-kä′-nä [kah-lah-kah′-nah]. Another form is *Guadalcanar*.

Guadalquivir (Sp., riv.)   gwä-däl-kē-vēr′   gwah-dahl-kee-veer′

Guadalupe   *Sp.* gwä-dä-lōō′-pĕ   gwah-dah-loo′-peh
    Eng. gwä′-də-lōōp′   gwah′-duh-loop′
    or gô′-də-lōōp′   gaw′-duh-loop′

Guadarrama (Sp., mts.)   gwä-dä-rä′-mä   gwah-dah-rah′-mah

Guadeloupe   *Eng.* gô′-də-lōōp′   gaw′-duh-loop′
(Fr. W. Indies)   *Fr.* gwä-də-lōōp′   gwah-duh-loop′

Guadiana (Port., Sp.,   *Port.* gwä-dyä′-nə   gwah-dyah′-nuh
riv.)   *Sp.* gwä-dyä′-nä   gwah-dyah′-nah

Guadix (Sp.)   gwä′-dēsh   gwah′-deesh

Guagua (P.I.)   gwä′-gwä   gwah′-gwah

Guáimaro (Cuba)   gwĭ′-mä-rô   gwai′-mah-ro

Guam (Oc., Marianas)   gwäm′   gwahm′

Guanahuato (Mex.)   (g)wä-nä-hwä′-tô   (g)wah-nah-hwah′-to

Guani, Alberto   gwä′-nē, äl-bĕr′-tô   gwah′-nee, ahl-behr′-to
(Urug. polit.)

Guantánamo (Cuba)   gwän-tä′-nä-mô   gwahn-tah′-nah-mo

Guaporé (Bol., riv.)   guä-pô-rĕ′   guah-po-reh′
Also called *Iténez*, ē-tĕ′-nĕs [ee-teh′-nes].

Guarcino (It.)   gwär-chē′-nô   gwahr-chee′-no

Guariglia, Raffaele (It.   gwä-rē′-lyä,   gwah-ree′-lyah,
polit.)   räf-fä-ĕ′-lĕ   rahf-fah-eh′-leh

Guasti (Calif.)   gwäs′-tē   gwahs′-tee

Guatemala (C.A.)   *Eng.* gwät′-ə-mä′-lə   gwaht′-uh-mah′-luh
    Sp. gwä-tĕ-mä′-lä   gwah-teh-mah′-lah

Guayaquil (Ecuador)   gwä-yä-kēl′   gwah-yah-keel′

Guaymas (Mex.)   gwĭ′-mäs   gwai′-mahs

guayule (Sp.)   gwä-yōō′-lĕ   gwah-yoo′-leh

Gubbi, el (Libya)   gŏŏb′-bē, ĕl   gub′-bee, el

Gubbio (It.)   gōōb′-byô   goob′-byo

Guben (Ger. > ? Pol.)   gōō′-bən   goo′-buhn
Polish *Gubin*, gōō′-bĭn [gu′-bin].

Guča (Yugosl.)   gōō′-chä   goo′-chah

Gudbrandsdalen (Nor.)   gŏŏd′-bräns-däln   gud′-brahns-dahln

Gudermes (Rus.)	gōō-dĕr-mĕs′	goo-dehr-mes′
Gudjakovo (Yugosl.)	gōō′-dyä′-kô-vô	goo′-dyah′-ko-vo
Gudvangen (Nor.)	gŏŏd′-väng-ən	gud′-vahng-uhn
Guebwiller (Fr.)	gĕb-vē-lĕr′	geb-vee-lehr′
Guedalla, Philip	gwə-dăl′-ə	gwuh-dal′-uh
(Br. author)		
Guelman (Alg.)	gĕl-măn′	gel-man′
Guelph or Guelf	gwĕlf′	gwelf′
Italian Guelfo, gwĕl′-fô [gwel′-fo].		
Guérande (Fr.)	gĕ-räNd′	geh-rahNd′
Guéret (Fr.)	gĕ-rĕ′	geh-reh′
Guernica (Sp.)	gĕr-nē′-kä	gehr-nee′-kah
Guerrero (Mex.)	gĕr-rĕ′-rô	gehr-reh′-ro
Guerrero, José Gustavo	gĕr-rĕ′-rô, hô-sĕ′	gehr-reh′-ro, ho-seh′
(Salv. polit.)	gōōs-tä′-vô	goos-tah′-vo
Guerrero, Manuel Amador (Pan. polit.) See Amador Guerrero.		
Guesrand (Fr.)	gĕ-räN′	geh-rahN′
Guesten or Güsten (Ger.)	güs′-tən	güs′-tuhn
Guetaria Pass (Tun.)	gĕ-tä-rē′-ä	geh-tah-ree′-ah
Guetersloh (Ger.)	gü′-tərs-lō	gü′-tuhrs-loh
Guettar, el (Tun.)	gĕ-tär′, ĕl	geh-tahr′, el
Guffarini Guidi, Guido	gōōf-fä-rē′-nē	goof-fah-ree′-nee
(It. polit.)	gwē′-dē, gwē′-dô	gwee′-dee, gwee′-do
Guglionesi (It.)	gōō-lyô-nĕ′-zē	goo-lyo-neh′-zee
Guguan (Oc., Marianas)	gōō-gwän′	goo-gwahn′
Guhrau (Ger.)	gōō′-rou	goo′-rau
Guichen (Fr.)	gē-shăN′	gee-shaN′
Guidonia (It.)	gwē-dô′-nyä	gwee-do′-nyah
Guienne (Fr.)	gē-yĕn′	gee-yehn′
Guignes (Fr.)	gēn′(y)	geen′(y)
Guiguintó	gē-gēn-tô′	gee-geen-to′
Guildonia (It.)	gwēl-dô′-nyä	gweel-do′-nyah
Guilhem, Aristides	gē′-lyəm, ä-rēs-	gee′-lyuhm, ah-rees-
(Braz. admiral)	tē′-dĭs	tee′-dis
Guillaume (Fr.)	gē-yōm′	gee-yohm′
Guillén, Néstor	gē-yĕn′, nĕs′-tôr	gee-yehn′, nehs′-tor
(Bol. polit.)		
Guimba, San Juan de (P.I.) See San Juan de Guimba.		
Guiñazú, Enrique Ruiz	gē-nyä-sōō′, ĕn-rē′-	gee-nyah-soo′, en-
(Arg. polit.)	kĕ rōō-ēs′	ree′-keh roo-ees′
Correctly Ruiz Guiñazú rather than simply Guiñazú. However the latter has been the usage of our radio and press.		
Guinea (Afr.)	gĭn′-ĭ	gin′-i
Guînes (Fr.)	gēn′	geen′

Guingamp (Fr.)	găN-gäN′	gaN-gahN′
Guipúzcoa (Sp.)	gē-pōōth′-kô-ä	gee-pooth′-ko-ah
	or -pōōs′-	or -poos′-
Guise (Fr.)	Eng. gēz′	geez′
	Fr. gü-ēz′ or gēz′	gü-eez′ or geez′
Guisi (P.I., riv.)	gē′-sē	gee′-see
Guisto (It.)	gwē′-stô	gwee′-sto
Guiuan (P.I.)	gē′-wän	gee′-wahn

Guixols (Sp.) See *San Feliú de Guixols.*

Gulbene (Latvia)	gōōl′-bĕ-nĕ	gul′-beh-neh

German *Schwanenburg,* q.v.

Gulijanska planina	gōō′-lē′-yän-skä	goo′-lee′-yahn-skah
(Yugosl., mts.)	plä′-nē′-nä	plah′-nee′-nah
Gullo, Fausto	gōōl′-lô, fou′-stô	gool′-lo, fau′-sto
(It. polit.)		
Gulpen (Neth.)	k(h)ûl′-pən	k(h)œl′-puhn
Gulsvik (Nor.)	gōōls′-vēk	guls′-veek
Gulyui (Rus.)	gōō-lyōō′ĭ	gu-lyoo′i
Gumbinnen (Ger. >Rus.)	gōōm′-bĭn-ən	gum′-bin-uhn

Russian *Gusev,* gōō′-sĕf [goo′-sef].

Gumma (Jap.)	gōōm′-mä	goom′-mah
Gümüljene (Gr.)	*Turk.* gü-mül′-jə-nĕ	gü-mül′-juh-neh

Greek *Komotine,* q.v.

Gümüşhane (Turk.)	gü-müsh′-hä′-nĕ	gü-müsh′-hah′-neh
gun	gōōn	goon

An element, meaning *county,* in Japanese place names.

guntō	gōōn-tô	goon-to

An element, meaning *archipelago,* in Japanese place names.

Gura Humorului (Rum.)	gōō′-rä	gu′-rah
	hōō-mô′-rōō-lwĭ	hu-mo′-ru-lwi
Gurev (Rus.)	gōōr′-yĕf	goor′-yef
Gurevsk (Ger. >Rus.)	gōōr′-yĕfsk	goor′-yefsk

German *Neuhausen,* q.v.

Gurgan (Iran)	gōōr-gän′	goor-gahn′

Formerly *Asterabad,* äs-tə-rä-bäd′ [ahs-tuh-rah-bahd′].

Gurkha (India)	gōōr′-kä	gur′-kah
Gurney, Chan	gûr′-nē	guhr′-nee
(U.S. senator)		
Gurzuf (Rus.)	gōōr-zōōf′	gur-zoof′
Gus (Rus.)	gōōs′	goos′
Gusbat, el (Libya)	gōōs-băt′, ĕl	gus-bat′, el
Gusev, Fëdor	gōō′-sĕf, fyô′-dŏr	goo′-sef, fyo′-dor
(Rus. polit.)		

Gusev (Ger. >Rus.)	gōō'-sĕf	goo'-sef
German *Gumbinnen.*, q.v.		
Gusiatin (Pol. >Rus.)	gōō-syä'-tĭn	gu-syah'-tin
Polish *Husiatyn*, q.v.		
Gusinje (Yugosl.)	gōō'-sē'-nyĕ	goo'-see'-nyeh
Gusow (Ger.)	gōō'-zō	goo'-zoh
Gussev, Fëdor (Rus. polit.) See *Gusev, Fëdor.*		
Guštanj (Yugosl.)	gōō'-shtän(y)	goo'-shtahn(y)
Gustav Adolf Folke	gŭs'-täv ä'-dŏlf	guhs'-tahv ah'-dolf
Hubertus (Sw. prince)	fôl'-kə hü-bĕr'-tōōs	fol'-kuh hü-behr'-tus
Gütersloh (Ger.)	gü'-tərs-lō	gü'-tuhrs-loh
Gutiérrez (Sp. name)	*Am. Sp.* gōō-tyĕr'-rĕs	goo-tyehr'-res
	Sp. gōō-tyĕr'-rĕth	goo-tyher'-reth
Guyenne *or* Guienne (Fr.)	gē-yĕn'	gee-yehn'
Guyer, U.S.	gī'-ər	gai'-uhr
(U.S. representative)		
Guymon (Okla.)	gī'-mən	gai'-muhn
Guyos (P.I.)	gōō'-yôs	goo'-yos
Guzenko, Igor	gōō-zĕn'-kô, ē'-gôr	goo-zehn'-ko, ee'-gor
(Rus. diplomat)		
Guzmán (Mex.)	gōōs-män'	goos-mahn'
Gvardeisk (Ger. >Rus.)	gvär-dāsk'	gvahr-daysk'
German *Tapiau*, q.v.		
Gwa (Burma)	gwä'	gwah'
Gwadar (Baluch.)	gwä'-dər	gwah'-duhr
Gwalior (India)	gwä'-lĭ-ôr	gwah'-li-or
Gyaing (Burma)	jĭng'	jaing'
Gyergyószentmiklós (Rum.) See *Gheorgheni.*		
Gympie (Austral.)	gĭm'-pĭ	gim'-pi
Gyömrő (Hung.)	jûm'-rû	jœm'-rœ
Gyón (Hung.)	dyôn'	dyon'
Gyöngyös (Hung.)	dyûn'-dyûsh	dyœn'-dyœsh
Gyöngyösy, János	dyûn'-dyû-shĭ, yä'-nŏsh	dyœn'-dyœ-shi, yah'-nosh
(Hung. polit.)		
Győr' (Hung.)	dyûr'	dyœr'
gyro	jī'-rō	jai'-roh
gyroscope	jī'-rə-skōp	jai'-ruh-skohp
Gytheion (Gr.)	yē'-thē-ô(n)	yee'-thee-o(n)
Gyula (Hung.)	dyōō'-lŏ	dyu'-lo
Gyulafehérvár (Rum.) See *Alba Julia.*		
Gzhatsk (Rus.)	gzhätsk'	gzhahtsk'

H-. In Greek names initial *H-* is often omitted from the spelling. For example, it might be necessary to look up *Erakleion* instead of *Herakleion*. Also, instead of *H-*, one may find *Kh-* or *Ch-*.

Häädemeeste (Est.)	hă'-dĕ-mĕs-tĕ	ha'-deh-mes-teh
Haaften (Neth.)	häf'-tən	hahf'-tuhn
Haag, den (Neth.)	dən häk(h)'	duhn hahk(h)'

English *The Hague*, q.v. The full name is *'s Gravenhage*, q.v.

Haakon VII	hô'-kŏ͞on	ho'-kun
(King of Norway)		
Haaksbergen (Neth.)	häks'-bĕrk(h)-ən	hahks'-behrk(h)-uhn
Haamstede (Neth.)	häm'-stä-də	hahm'-stay-duh
Haapasaari (Fin., isl.)	hä'-pä-sä-rē	hah'-pah-sah-ree
Haapsalu (Est.)	häp'-sä-lŏͦ	hahp'-sah-loo
Russian *Gapsal*, q.v.		
Haarlem (Neth.)	här'-ləm	hahr'-luhm
Haarlemmerliede (Neth.)	här'-lĕm-ər-lē'-də	hahr'-lem-uhr-lee'-duh
Haarlemmermeer (Neth.)	här'-lĕm-ər-mär'	hahr'-lem-uhr-mayr'

Habana (Cuba) See *Havana*.

Habanero, -a (Sp.)	ä-bä-nĕ'-rô, -ä	ah-bah-neh'-ro, -ah

Adjective of *Habana*. Not *Habañero*.

Habbaniya (Iraq)	hăb-bä-nē'-yə	hab-bah-nee'-yuh

Locally həb-bä'-nē-yə [huhb-bah'-nee-yuh].

Habkirchen (Ger.)	häb'-kĭr-k(h)ən	hahb'-kihr-k(h)uhn
Habscheid (Ger.)	häp'-shīt	hahp'-shait
Hacha, Emil	hä'-hä, ĕ'-mĭl	hah'-hah, eh'-mil
(Cz. polit.)		

A possible Englishing is hä'-chä [hah'-chah].

Hachem, Ibrahim (Trans-Jordan polit.) See *Ibrahim Hashem*.

Hachenburg (Ger.)	*Eng.* häk'-ən-bûrg	hahk'-uhn-buhrg
	Ger. häk(h)'-ən-bŏͦork(h)	hahk(h)'-uhn-burk(h)
Hachiōji (Jap.)	hä-chē-ô'-jē	hah-chee-o'-jee
Hackzell, Antti	häk'-sĕl, änt'-tē	hahk'-sel, ahnt'-tee
(Fin. polit.)		
Hadamar (Ger.)	hä'-dä-mär	hah'-dah-mahr
Hadassah	hə-dăs'-ə	huh-das'-uh

An organization of Jewish women.

Hadeland (Nor.)	hä'-də-län	hah'-duh-lahn
Hadera (Pal.)	hĕ-dä'-rä	heh-day'-rah

Also spelled *Hedera*. Arabic *El Khudeira*, k(h)ŏͦo-dä'-rə [k(h)u-day'-ruh].

Hadjeb el Aioun (Tun.)	hä'-jĕb ĕl ī-yŏͦon'	hah'-jeb el ai-yoon'
Hadjes el Aiouth (Tun.)	hä'-jĕz ĕl ä-yŏͦot'	hah'-jez el ah-yoot'

Haehnlein (Ger.)   hĕn'-līn   hen'-lain

Haelsingborg (Sw.) See *Hälsingborg*.

Haemeenlinna (Fin.) See *Hämeenlinna*.

Hafez Afifi   hä'-fĕz ä-fē'-fē   hah'-fez ah-fee'-fee
    Pasha (Egypt. polit.)   pä'-shä   pah'-shah

Haffer (Ger.)   häf'-ər   hahf'-uhr

Haft Kel (Iran)   hăft' kĕl'   haft' kel'

Haga Castle (Sw.)   hô'-gä   haw'-gah

Haganah   hä-gä-nä'   hah-gah-nah'
    The name, meaning *defense*, of Jewish underground forces in Palestine.

Hagen (Ger.)   hä'-gən   hah'-guhn

Hagen, Harold C.   hā'-gən   hay'-guhn
    (U.S. representative)

hagios, hagioi (Gr.)   ī'-yôs, ī'-yē   ai'-yos, ai'-yee
    An element, meaning *saint(s)*, in Greek place names. Look up the
    other part of the name.

Hagnides (Gr. polit.)   ä-gnē'-dēs   ah-gnee'-dees

Hagonoy (P.I.)   hä-gô-noi'   hah-go-noi'

Hague, la (Fr., cape)   äg', lä   ahg', lah
    Cap de la Hague, käp' də lä äg' [kahp' duh lah ahg'].

Hague, The (Neth.)   *Eng.* hāg'   hayg'
    Dutch *'s Gravenhage*, q.v., commonly abbreviated to *Den Haag*, q.v.

Haguenau (Fr.)   äg-nō'   ahg-noh'

Hähnlein (Ger.)   hĕn'-līn   hen'-lain

Hai (Ch., riv.)   hī   hai

Haifa (Pal.)   hī'-fä   hai'-fah

Hai-fêng (Ch.,   hī-fŭng   hai-fuhng
    Kwangtung)

Hailar (Manchu.)   hī-lär   hai-lahr

Hailun (Manchu.)   hī-lōōn   hai-lun

Hailuoto (Fin., isl.)   hī'-lōō-ô-tô   hai'-lu-o-to
    Swedish *Karloe*, kärl'-û' [kahrl'-œ'].

Hai-mên (Ch.,   hī-mŭn   hai-muhn
    Kwangtung, bay)

Hainan (Ch. Kwangtung,   hī-nän   hai-nahn
    isl.)

Hainaut (Belg.)   ĕ-nō'   eh-noh'

Hainburg (Austria)   hīn'-bŏŏrk   hain'-burk

Haiphong (Indo-Ch.)   *Eng.* hī-fŏng'   hai-fong'
    Chinese *Hai-fang*.

Haiti (W.I.)   hā'-tĭ   hay'-ti
    French *Haiti*, ä-ē-tē' [ah-ee-tee']. The island which the Republic of
    Haiti shares with the Dominican Republic is called either *Hispaniola*,
    q.v. (once the official name), or more often *Haiti*.

Haitian	hā'-shən _or_ hā'-tĭ-ən	hay'-shuhn hay'-ti-uhn
Haj Amin el Husseini (Grand Mufti of Jerusalem)	häj' ä-mēn' ĕl hŏŏs-sā'-nĭ (mŭf'-tĭ _or_ mŏŏf'-tĭ)	hahj' ah-meen' ehl hus-say'-ni (muhf'-ti _or_ muf'-ti)
Hajduböszörmény (Hung.)	hoi'-dŏŏ-bû'-sûr- män(y)	hoi'-du-bœ'-sœr- mayn(y)
Hajdunánás (Hung.)	hoi'-dŏŏ-nä'-näsh	hoi'-du-nah'-nahsh
Hajduszoboszló (Hung.)	hoi'-dŏŏ-sô'-bôs-lô	hoi'-du-so'-bos-lo
Hajla (Yugosl., mts.)	hĭ'-lä	hai'-lah
Hajnemann, Jan (Pol. polit.)	hĭ'-nə-män, yän'	hai'-nuh-mahn, yahn'
Hajnówka (Pol.)	hĭ-nŏŏf'-kä	hai-nuf'-kah

Russian _Gainovka_, gĭ-nôf'-kä [gai-nof'-kah].

Hakadal (Nor.)	hä'-kä-däl	hah'-kah-dahl
Hakodate (Jap.)	hä-kô'-dä'-tĕ'	hah-ko'-dah'-teh'
Hakone (Jap.)	hä-kô'-nĕ'	hah-ko'-neh'
Halahala (P.I.) See _Jala_.		
Halas (Hung.)	hŏ'-lŏsh	ho'-losh

Also called _Kiskunhalas_, q.v.

Halberstadt (Ger.)	häl'-bər-shtät	hahl'-buhr-shtaht
Halden (Nor.)	häld'n	hahld'n
Halfaya (Libya)	häl-fä'-yä	hahl-fah'-yah
Halicz (Pol. >Rus.)	hä'-lĭch	hah'-lich

Russian _Galich_, gä'-lĭch [gah'-lich].

Halle (Ger.)	häl'-ə	hahl'-uh
Halleck, Charles A. (U.S. representative)	hăl'-lĕk	hal'-lek
Hallein (Austria)	häl'-īn	hahl'-ain
Hallingdal (Nor.)	häl'-lĭng-däl	hahl'-ling-dahl
Hallouf (Tun.)	häl-lōōf'	hahl-loof'
Hallugh (Libya)	häl-lōōg'	hahl-loog'
Halluin (Fr.)	äl-wăN'	ahl-waN'
Halmahera (NEI)	häl-mä-hĕ'-rä	hahl-mah-heh'-rah

Also called _Djailolo_, q.v.

Halovo (Yugosl., mts.)	hä'-lô-vô	hah'-lo-vo
Halsey, William F. (U.S. admiral)	hôl'-zĭ	hawl'-zi
Hälsingborg (Sw.)	hĕl'-sĭng-bôr'(y)	hel'-sing-bor'(y)
Halsteren (Neth.)	häl'-stər-ən	hahl'-stuhr-uhn
Ham, le (Fr.)	äm', lə	ahm', luh
hama	hä-mä	hah-mah

An element, meaning _beach_ or sometimes _fishing village_, in Japanese place names.

Hamadan (Iran)	*Per.* hă-mə-dän′	ha-muh-dahn′
	Eng. hăm′-ə-dăn	ham′-uh-dan
Hamamatsu (Jap.)	hä-mä′-mä-tsōō	hah-mah′-mah-tsoo
	or hä-mä′-mäts	hah-mah′-mahts
Hamar (Nor.)	hä′-mär	hah′-mahr
Hamaröy *or* Hamaroey	hä′-mär-ûĭ	hah′-mahr-œi
(Nor.)		
Hambach (Ger.)	häm′-bäk(h)	hahm′-bahk(h)
Hamborn (Ger.)	häm′-bôrn	hahm′-born
Hambro, Carl (Nor.	*Nor.* häm′-brōŏ	hahm′-bru
polit.)	*Eng.* häm′-brō	hahm′-broh
Hamburg (Ger.)	*Eng.* hăm′-bûrg	ham′-buhrg
	Ger. häm′-bōŏrk(h)	hahm′-burk(h)
Hambye (Fr.)	äN-bē′	ahN-bee′
Hamdi al Bajaji (Iraqi	häm-dĭl′ bə-chä′-chĭ	hahm-dil′ buh-chah′-
polit.)		chi
Also spelled *Bagehgi.*		
Hämeenlinna (Fin.)	hă′-mān-lĭn-nă	ha′-mayn-lin-nah
Ha-mi (Ch., Sinkiang)	hä-mē	hah-mee
Hamila (Tun.)	hä-mē′-lä	hah-mee′-lah
Hamina (Fin.)	hä′-mē-nä	hah′-mee-nah

Swedish *Fredrikshamn,* frä′-drĭks-hämn′ [fray′-driks-hahmn′]. *Hamina* is an element, meaning *harbor* or *haven*, in Finnish place names.

Hamm (Ger.)	häm′	hahm′
Hamma, el (Tun.)	häm′-mä, ĕl	hahm′-mah, el
Hammam (Egypt)	See *Al Hammam.*	
Hammamet (Tun.)	häm-mä-mĕt′	hahm-mah-met′
Hammam Lif (Tun.)	häm-măm′ lēf′	hahm-mam′ leef′
Hammerfest (Nor.)	hä′-mər-fĕst	hah′-muhr-fest
Hamminkeln (Ger.)	häm′-ĭn-kĕln	hahm′-in-keln
Hamtramck (Mich.)	hăm-trăm′-ĭk	ham-tram′-ik
	or hăm-trămk′	ham-tramk′
Hancewicze (Pol.)	hän-tsĕ-vē′-chĕ	hahn-tseh-vee′-cheh

Russian *Gantsevichi,* gän-tsĕ′-vĭ-chĭ [gahn-tseh′-vi-chi].

Haneda (Jap., Tokyo,	hä-nĕ′-dä′	hah-neh′-dah′
airport)		
hangar	hăng′-ər	hang′-uhr
	or hăng′-gär *or* -gēr	hang′-gahr *or* -guhr
French äN-gär′ [ahN-gahr′].		
Hang-chow (Ch.,	*Eng.* hăng-chou	hang-chau
Chekiang)	*Ch.* häng-jō	hahng-joh
Hangö (Fin.)	*Sw.* häng′-û	hahng′-œ
Finnish *Hanko,* q.v.		
Hanko (Fin.)	häng′-kô	hahng′-ko

Hankoe *or* Hankö (Nor.)	häng'-kû	hahng'-kœ
Han-k'ow (Ch., Hupeh)	*Eng.* hăn-kou	han-kau
	Ch. hän-kō	hahn-koh
Hannover (Ger.)	hän-ō'-vər	hahn-oh'-vuhr
	or hän-ō'-fər	hahn-oh'-fuhr
English *Hanover*, q.v.		
Hanoï (Indo-Ch.)	*Eng.* hăn'-oi'	han'-oi'
	Fr. ä-nô-ē'	ah-no-ee'
Hanover (Ger.)	*Eng.* hăn'-ō-vər	han'-oh-vuhr
German *Hannover*, q.v.		
Hansteen, Wilhelm (Nor. general)	hän'-stān, vĭl'-hĕlm	hahn'-stayn, vil'-helm
Hansweert (Neth.)	häns-wārt'	hahns-wayrt'
Hanthawaddy (Burma, riv.)	hăn-thə-wŏd'-ĭ	han-thuh-wod'-i
Hantz (Fr., pass)	änts'	ahnts'
Han-yang (Ch., Hupeh)	hän-yäng	hahn-yahng
Han-yüan (Ch., Sikang)	hän-yüän	hahn-yü-ahn
Haouaria, el (Tun.)	hä-wä-rē'-ä, ĕl	hah-wah-ree'-ah, el
Harada, Ken (Jap. diplomat)	hä'-rä-dä, kĕn'	hah'-rah-dah, ken'
hara-kiri	hä'-rä-kē'-rē	hah'-rah-kee'-ree
Variants are *hari-kari* and *hara-kari*.		
Harald (Nor. prince)	hä'-räl	hah'-rahl
English *Harold*.		
Harar (Ethiopia)	hä'-rər	hah'-ruhr
Harasztos (Rum.) See *Călăraşi*.		
Harbin (Manchu.)	här'-bēn' *or* här'-bĭn	hahr'-been' *or* hahr'-bin
Harburg (Ger.)	*Eng.* här'-bûrg	hahr'-buhrg
	Ger. här'-bo͞ork(h)	hahr'-burk(h)
Hardanger (Nor.)	här-däng'-ər	hahr-dahng'-uhr
Hardangerfjord (Nor.)	här-däng'-ər-fyōr	hahr-dahng'-uhr-fyohr
Hardangerjoeklen *or* Hardangerjöklen (Nor.)	här-däng'-ər-yûk-lən	hahr-dahng'-uhr-yœk-luhn
Hardangervidda (Nor.)	här-däng'-ər-vĭd-dä	hahr-dahng'-uhr-vid-dah
Hardelot (Fr.)	ärd-lō'	ahrd-loh'
Hardenberg (Neth.)	här'-dən-bĕrk(h)	hahr'-duhn-behrk(h)
Harderwijk (Neth.)	här'-dər-wīk	hahr'-duhr-waik
Hardingsveld (Neth.)	här'-dĭngs-vĕlt	hahr'-dings-velt
Haren (Belg., Brussels, airport)	hä'-rən	hah'-ruhn

Haren (Neth.)	hä'-rən	hah'-ruhn
Harenkarspel (Neth.)	hä'-rən-kär'-spəl	hah'-ruhn-kahr'-spuhl
Harewood (Eng. earl)	här'-wŏŏd	hahr'-wud
Harfleur (Fr.)	är-flûr'	ahr-flœr'
Hargarten (Ger.)	här'-gär-tən	hahr'-gahr-tuhn
Harijan (Gandhi's newspaper)	hŭ'-rĭ-jən	huh'-ri-juhn
Hari Rud (India, riv.)	hŭ'-rĭ rōōd'	huh'-ri rood'
Harlange (Belg.)	*Fr.* är-läNzh'	ahr-lahNzh'
	Ger. här'-läng-ə	hahr'-lahng-uh
Hârlău (Rum.)	hûr'-lû'-ŏŏ	huhr'-luh'-u
Harlingen (Neth.)	här'-lĭng-ən	hahr'-ling-uhn
Harmelen (Neth.)	här'-mə-lən	hahr'-muh-luhn
Harpefoss (Nor.)	här'-pə-fôs	hahr'-puh-fos
Harput (Turkey)	här'-pŏŏt	hahr'-put
Harriman, W. Averell (Am. diplomat)	här'-ə-mən, ā'-və-rəl	hehr'-uh-muhn, ay'-vuh-ruhl
Hârşova (Rum.)	hûr'-shô-vä	huhr'-sho-vah
Harstad (Nor.)	här'-stä *or* häsh'-tä	hahr'-stah *or* hahsh'-tah
Harwich (Eng.)	här'-ĭch *or* -ĭj	hehr'-ich *or* -ij.
Harwich (Mass.)	här'-wĭch	hahr'-wich
Harz (Ger., mts.)	härts'	hahrts'
Hasani (Gr.)	hä-sä'-nē	hah-sah'-nee
Hasanli (Yugosl.)	hä'-sän-lē	hah'-sahn-lee
Hasenpoth (Latvia)	*Ger.* hä'-zən-pôt	hah'-zuhn-pot

Latvian *Aizpute,* q.v. Russian *Gasenpot,* q.v.

Hashem, Ibrahim (Trans-Jordan polit.) See *Ibrahim Hashem.*

| hashi | hä-shē | hah-shee |

An element, meaning *bridge,* in Japanese place names. See *bashi.*

Hashimoto, Kingorō (Jap. polit.)	hä-shē'-mô'-tô', kēn'-gô-rô	hah-shee'-mo'-to', keen'-go-ro
Haskerland (Neth.)	häs'-kər-länt	hahs'-kuhr-lahnt
Hassani (Gr., Athens, airport)	hä-sä'-nē	hah-sah'-nee

Greek *Khassani.*

Hasselt (Belg.)	häs'-əlt	hahs'-uhlt
Hata, Shunroku (Jap. general)	hä'-tä, shōōn'-rô-kōō	hah'-tah, shoon'-ro-koo
Hatoyama, Ichirō (Jap. polit.)	hä-tô'-yä'-mä', ē-chē-rô'	hah-to'-yah'-mah', ee-chee-ro'
Hattem (Neth.)	hät'-əm	haht'-uhm
Hatten (Fr.)	ä-täN'	ah-tahN'

Hatteras (N. C.)	hăt'-ə-rəs	hat'-uh-ruhs
Hatvan (Hung.)	hŏt'-vŏn	hot'-von
Haubourdin (Fr.)	ō-bōōr-dăN'	oh-boor-daN'
Haugastoel *or* Haugastöl (Nor.)	hou'-gä-stûl	hau'-gah-stœl
Haugesund (Nor.)	hou'-gə-sŏŏn	hau'-guh-sun
Haukeliseter (Nor.)	hou'-kə-lē-sä-tər	hau'-kuh-lee-say-tuhr
Hauketo (Nor.)	hou'-kə-tō	hau'-kuh-toh
Hautes Alpes (Fr.)	ōt zälp'	oht zahlp'
Haute Saône (Fr., dept.)	ōt sōn'	oht sohn'
Haute Savoie (Fr., dept.)	ōt sä-vwä'	oht sah-vwah'
Hautmesnil (Fr.)	ō-mĕ-nēl'	oh-meh-neel'
Hautmont (Fr.)	ō-môN'	oh-moN'
Haut Rhin (Fr., dept.)	ō răN'	oh raN'
Havana (Cuba)	*Eng.* hə-văn'-ə	huh-van'-uh
	Sp. ä-vä'-nä	ah-vah'-nah
See "Note on 'b' and 'v'," page xliv.		
Havas (Fr. news service)	ä-väs'	ah-vahs'
Havasupai (Am. Indian)	hăv'-ə-sōō'-pī	hav'-uh-soo'-pai
Havel (Ger., riv.)	hä'-fəl	hah'-fuhl
Havelte (Neth.)	hä'-vəl-tə	hah'-vuhl-tuh
Havenner, Franck R. (U. S. representative)	hā'-vən-ər	hay'-vuhn-uhr
Havre (Mont.)	hăv'-ər	hav'-uhr
Havre, le (Fr.)	*Eng.* hävr', lə	hahvr', luh
	Fr. ävr', lə	ahvr', luh
Havre de Grace (Md.)	hăv'-ər də grăs' *or* grās'	hav'-uh rduh gras' *or* grays'
Hawaii (U. S., territory)	hä-wī'-ĭ	hah-wai'-i
Also called *Owyhee*, ō-wē'-hē [o-wee'-hee].		
Hawaiian	hə-wī'-yən	huh-wai'-yuhn
Haya de la Torre (Peru. polit.)	ä'-yä dĕ lä tôr'-rĕ	ah'-yah deh lah tor'-reh
Hayange (Fr.)	ä-yäNzh'	ah-yahNzh'
Hayden, Carl (U. S. senator)	hād'n	hayd'n
Haye, Gaston Henri (Fr. diplomat) See *Henri-Haye*.		
Haye, la (Fr.) See *La Haye*.		
Haynau (Ger. >? Pol.) Polish *Chojnów*, q.v.	hī'-nou	hai'-nau
Hazebrouck (Fr.)	äz-brōōk'	ahz-brook'
Hazerswoude (Neth.)	hä'-zərs-wou'-də	hah'-zuhrs-wau'-duh
Heathrow (London, airport)	hēth'-rō	heeth'-roh

Heber (Utah)	hē'-bər	hee'-buhr
Hebert, F. Edward (U.S. representative) "The word *ay* (long ā) plus the word *bear*."	ā-băr'	ay-behr'
Hebron (Pal.)	hē'-brən	hee'-bruhn
Arabic *El Khalil,* ĕl k(h)ä-lēl' [el k(h)ah-leel'] or *El Khulil,* ĕl k(h)o͞o-lēl' [el k(h)u-leel'].		
Hedera (Pal.) See *Hadera.*		
Hedmark (Nor.)	hĕd'-märk	hed'-mahrk
Hedrick, E. H. (U.S. representative)	hĕd'-rĭk	hed'-rik
Heeg (Neth.)	hāk(h)'	hayk(h)'
Heel (Neth.)	hāl'	hayl'
Heemskerk (Neth.)	hāms'-kĕrk	hayms'-kehrk
Heemstede (Neth.)	hām'-stā-də	haym'-stay-duh
's Heer Arendskerke (Neth.)	sär ä'-rənts-kĕr'-kə	sayr ah'-ruhnts-kehr'-kuh
Heerde (Neth.)	hār'-də	hayr'-duh
Heerenveen (Neth.)	hā'-rən-vān'	hay'-ruhn-vayn'
Heerhugowaard (Neth.)	hār-hü'-k(h)ō-wärt'	hayr-hü'-k(h)oh-wahrt'
Heerlen (Neth.)	hār'-lən	hayr'-luhn
Hees (Neth.)	hās'	hays'
Heesch (Neth.)	hās'	hays'
Heffernan, James J. (U.S. representative)	hĕf'-ər-năn	hef'-uhr-nan
Hegel, G. W. F. (Ger. philosopher)	hā'-gəl	hay'-guhl
Hegoumenitsa (Gr.)	ē-go͞o-mĕ-nē'-tsä	ee-goo-meh-nee'-tsah
Heho (Burma)	hā'-hō'	hay'-hoh'
Hei-an (Korea)	hā-än	hay-ahn
Heian Nan (Korea) See *P'yŏng-jang.*		
Heide (Ger.)	hī'-də	hai'-duh
Heidelberg (Ger.)	*Eng.* hī'-dəl-bûrg *Ger.* hī'-dəl-bĕrk(h)	hai'-duhl-buhrg hai'-duhl-behrk(h)
Heidenau (Ger.)	hī'-də-nou	hai'-duh-nau
Heidenheim (Ger.)	hī'-dən-hīm	hai'-duhn-haim
Heidinger, J. V. (U.S. representative)	hī'-dĭng-ər	hai'-ding-uhr
Heidous (Tun.)	hā-do͞os'	hay-doos'
Heijō (Korea) Korean *P'yŏng-jang,* q.v.	*Jap.* hā'-jô	hay'-jo
Heilbronn (Ger.)	hīl'-brôn	hail'-bron

Heiligenbeil (Ger. >Rus.) hī'-lǐ-gən-bīl'   hai'-li-guhn-bail'
  Russian *Gailigenbail*, gī'-lǐ-gən-bīl [gai'-li-guhn-bail].
Heiloo (Neth.)   hī'-lō   hai'-loh
Heilsberg (Ger. >Pol.) hĭls'-bĕrk(h)   hails'-behrk(h)
  Polish *Licbark*, q.v.
Hei-lung-kiang   hā-lŏŏng-jyäng   hay-lung-jyahng
  (Manchu., prov.)
  Also called *Amur*, q.v.
Heimbach (Ger.)   hīm'-bäk(h)   haim'-bahk(h)
Heinkel (Ger.)   hĭnk'-əl   haink'-uhl
Heinoo (Neth.)   hī'-nō   hai'-noh
Heinrichswalde (Ger. > hīn'-rĭk(h)s-väl'-də hain'-rik(h)s-vahl'-
  Rus.)   duh
  Russian *Slavsk*, släfsk' [slahfsk'].
Heistern (Ger.)   his'-tern   hais'-tuhrn
Heiterblick (Ger.)   hī'-tər-blĭk   hai'-tuhr-blik
Heithuizen (Neth.)   hīt'-hûĭ-zən   hait'-hœi-zuhn
Hejaz (Arabia)   hē-jăz'   hee-jaz'
Hekmat (Iran. polit.)   hĕk'-măt'   hek'-mat'
Hel (Pol.)   hĕl'   hel'
Helden (Neth.)   hĕl'-dən   hel'-duhn
Helder, den (Neth.)   hĕl'-dər, dən   hel'-duhr, duhn
Helena   *Ark., Mont.* hĕl'-ə-nə hel'-uh-nuh
                 Ohio   hĕ-lē'-nə heh-lee'-nuh
As a personal name *Helena* is usually stressed on the first syllable.
Helgoland (Ger.)   hĕl'-gô-länt   hel'-go-lahnt
  English *Heligoland*, q.v.
helicopter   hĕl'-ĭ-kŏp'-tər   hel'-i-kop'-tuhr
              or hē'-lĭ-kŏp'-tər hee'-li-kop'-tuhr

The second pronunciation, though without dictionary authority, is favored by aeronautical engineers. (Avoid *heliocopter*. *Helio-* [the sun] has no part in this word, which is made from *helico-pter[on]*, spiral-wing.) So with many compounds of *helic(o)-*, meaning *spiral-*. Except perhaps in *helical*, engineers prefer hē'-lĭ- [hee'-li-], the dictionary recommendation to the contrary notwithstanding. In technical copy the engineers' preference should probably be followed. Although the *e* of Greek *helic-* is short, there is warrant for lengthening in an English stressed open syllable. In long words one expects short vowels (compare *penal, penalty; holy, holiday*); nevertheless long words are often pronounced as if they were two or more short words. Compare the several correct pronunciations of *genealogy, hegemony, hemoglobin, ideology, bivalent, dictionary, necessary.*

Heligoland (Ger.)   *Eng.* hĕl'-ĭ-gō-lănd' hel'-i-goh-land'

Hell (Nor.)	hĕl′	hel′
Hellas	*Eng.* hĕl′-əs	hel′-uhs

Modern Greek *Ellas,* ĕl′-äs [el′-ahs].

Hellendoorn (Neth.)	hĕl′-ən-dōrn	hel′-uhn-dohrn

Hellenikon (Gr.)   See *Ellenikon.*

Hellenthal (Ger.)	hĕl′-ən-täl	hel′-uhn-tahl

Hellespont (Turk., strait)   See *Dardanelles.*

Hellesylt (Nor.)	hĕl′-ə-sült	hel′-uh-sült
Hellevoetsluis (Neth.)	hĕl′-ə-vōōt-slûĭs′	hel′-uh-voot-slœis′
Helmand (India, riv.)	hĕl′-mənd	hel′-muhnd
Helmond (Neth.)	hĕl′-mônt	hel′-mont
Helsingfors (Fin.)	*Eng.* hĕl′-sĭng-fôrz	hel′-sing-forz
	Sw. hĕl′-sĭng-fôrs′	hel′-sing-fors′

Finnish *Helsinki,* q.v.

Helsingoer *or*	hĕl′-sĭng-ûr′	hel′-sing-œr′
Helsingör (Den.)		

English *Elsinore,* ĕl′-sĭ-nôr′ [el′-si-nor′].

Helsinki (Fin.)	hĕl′-sĭng-kē	hel′-sing-kee
Helvoort (Neth.)	hĕl′-vōrt	hel′-vohrt
Hemsedal (Nor.)	hĕm′-sə-däl	hem′-suh-dahl
Hencha, la (Tun.)	hĕn′-shä, lä	hen′-shah, lah
Hendaye (Fr.)	äN-dī′	ahN-dai′
Hendrik Ido-Ambacht	hĕn′-drĭk ē′-dō äm′-	hen′-drik ee′-doh
(Neth.)	bäk(h)t	ahm′-bahk(h)t
Hengeloo (Neth.)	hĕng′-ə-lō	heng′-uh-loh
Hêng-fêng (Ch., Kiangsi)	hŭng-fŭng	huhng-fuhng
Hêng-shan (Ch., Hunan)	hŭng-shän	huhng-shahn
Hêng-yang (Ch., Hunan)	hŭng-yäng	huhng-yahng
Hénin Liétard (Fr.)	ĕ-năN lyĕ-tär′	eh-naN lyeh-tahr′
Hennaarderadeel (Neth.)	hĕ-när′-də-rä-däl′	heh-nahr′-duh-rah-dayl′
Henpan (Oc., Solomons)	hĕn′-pän	hen′-pahn
Henri, Robert	hĕn′-rī	hen′-rai
(Am. painter)		
Henriot, Philippe	äN-ryō′, fē-lēp′	ahN-ryoh′, fee-leep′
(Fr. polit.)		
Henry-Haye, Gaston	äN-rē′, gäs-tôN′	ahN-ree eh′, gahs-toN′
(Fr. diplomat)		
Henzada (Burma)	hĕn′-zə-dä′	hen′-zuh-dah′

Herakleia (Turk.)   See *Ereğli.*

Herakleion (Crete)	ē-rä′-klē-ô(n)	ee-rah′-klee-o(n)

In English usually called *Candia,* q.v.; in Greek *Megalo Kastro,* q.v., or *Khandax,* hän′-däks [hahn′-dahks].

Herald Tribune (N.Y. newspaper)   See *Tribune.*

Herat (Afghan.)	hĕr-ät′	hehr-aht′
Hérault (Fr., dept.)	ĕ-rō′	eh-roh′
Herbiers, les (Fr.)	ĕr-byĕ′, lĕz	ehr-byeh′, lez
Hercegovina (Yugosl.)	*Eng.* hĕr′-tsĭ-gō- vē′-nə	hehr′-tsi-goh- vee′-nuh
	S.-C. hĕr′-tsĕ-gô′- vĭ-nä	hehr′-tseh-go′- vi-nah

English *Herzegovina,* q.v.

herculean	hər-kyōō′-lĭ-ən *or* hûr′-kyə-lē′-ən	huhr-kyoo′-li-uhn huhr′-kyuh-lee′-uhn
Hereford (Eng.)	hĕr′-ĭ-fərd	hehr′-i-fuhrd
Herefoss (Nor.)	hĕr′-ə-fôs	hehr′-uh-fos
Hergenrath (Belg.)	hĕr′-gən-rät	hehr′-guhn-raht
Hergla (Tun.)	hĕr′-glä	hehr′-glah
Héricourt (Fr.)	ĕ-rē-kōōr′	eh-ree-koor′
Herisau (Switz.)	hā′-rĭ-zou	hay′-rih-zau
Hermosa (P.I.)	ĕr-mô′-sä	ehr-mo′-sah
Hermosa Beach (Calif.)	hûr-mō′-sə	huhr-moh′-suh
Hermosillo (Mex.)	ĕr-mô-sē′-yä	ehr-mo-see′-yah
Hermoupolis (Gr., Syros)	ĕr-mōō′-pô-lē(s)	ehr-moo′-po-lee(s)
Hernádnémeti (Hung.)	hĕr′-näd-nā′-mĕ-tĭ	hehr′-nahd-nay′- meh-ti
Hernández (Sp. name)	*Am. Sp.* ĕr-nän′-dĕs *Sp.* ĕr-nän′-dĕth	ehr-nahn′-des ehr-nahn′-deth
Hernani (P.I.)	ĕr-nä′-nē	ehr-nah′-nee
Herne (Ger.)	hĕr′-nə	hehr′-nuh
Herning (Den.)	hĕr′-nĭng	hehr′-ning
Heroeya *or* Heröya (Nor.)	hĕr′-û-yä	hehr′-œ-yah
Hérouville (Fr.)	ĕ-rōō-vēl′	eh-roo-veel′
Herrera (Sp.)	ĕ-rĕ′-rä	eh-reh′-rah
Herresbach (Luxem.)	hĕr′-əs-bäk(h)	hehr′-uhs-bahk(h)
Herriot, Édouard (Fr. polit.)	ĕ-ryō′, ĕ-dwär′	eh-ryoh′, eh-dwahr′
Hersey, John (Am. author)	hûr′-sĭ	huhr′-si

Mr. Hersey adds that it is not hûr′-shĭ [huhr′-shi] or hûr′-zĭ [huhr′-zi].

Hersin Coupigny (Fr.)	ĕr-säN kōō-pē-nyē′	ehr-saN koo-pee-nyee′
Herter, Christian A. (U.S. representative)	hûr′-tər	huhr′-tuhr
Hertford (Eng.)	härt′-fərd	hahrt′-fuhrd
's Hertogenbosch (Neth.)	sĕr′-tō-k(h)ən-bôs′	sehr′-toh-k(h)uhn-bos′

A common abbreviated form is *Den Bos,* dən bôs′ [duhn bos′]. French *Bois le Duc,* bwä lə dük′ [bwah luh dük′].

Herve (Belg.)	ĕrv′	ehrv′
Herwen (Neth.)	hĕr′-wən	hehr′-wuhn
Herzegovina (Yugosl.)	hĕr′-tsĭ-gō-vē′-nə	hehr′-tsi-goh-vee′-nuh

Serb-Croat *Hercegovina*, q.v.

Herzfelde (Ger.)	hĕrts′-fĕl-də	hehrts′-fel-duh
Herzogenrath (Ger.)	hĕr′-tsō-gən-rät′	hehr′-tsoh-guhn-raht′
Hesdin (Fr.)	ĕ-dăN′	eh-daN′
Hessen (Ger.)	hĕs′-ən	hes′-uhn

English *Hesse*, hĕs′ [hes′].

Hestmannen (Nor., isls.)	hĕst′-män-ən	hest′-mahn-uhn
Het Bilt (Neth.)	hĕt bĭlt′	het bilt′
Heteren (Neth.)	hā′-tə-rən	hay′-tuh-ruhn
Het Loo (Neth.)	hĕt lō′	het loh′
hetman	*Eng.* hĕt′-măn	het′-man

Ukrainian hāt′-män [hayt′-mahn]. Russian *getman*, gĕt′-män [get′-mahn]. A title disregarded in alphabetical listing.

Hetzerath (Ger.)	hĕts′-ə-rät	hets′-uh-raht
Heumen (Neth.)	hû′-mən	hœ′-muhn
Heusden (Neth.)	hûs′-dən	hœs′-duhn
hevea (rubber tree)	hē′-vĭ-ə	hee′-vi-uh
Heydrich, Reinhard	hĭ′-drĭk(h), rīn′-härt	hai′-drik(h), rain′-
(Ger. polit.)		hahrt
Heye Foundation (N.Y.)	hĭ′	hai′

Museum of the American Indian, New York.

Heze (Neth.)	hā′-zə	hay′-zuh
Hickenlooper, Bourke B.	hĭk′-ĭn-lōō′-pər	hik′-in-loo′-puhr
(U. S. senator)		
Hieralimen (Gr.)	yĕ-rä-lē-mēn′	yeh-rah-lee-meen′
Hierapetra (Crete)	yĕ-rä′-pĕ-trä	yeh-rah′-peh-trah
	or ē-ĕ-rä′-pĕ-trä	ee-eh-rah′-peh-trah

Also called *Kastelli*, kä-stĕ′-lē [kah-steh′-lee].

Hieropotamos (Crete)	yĕ-rô-pô′-tä-mô(s)	yeh-ro-po′-tah-mo(s)
	or ē-ĕ-rô-pô′-tä-	ee-eh-ro-po′-tah-
	mô(s)	mo(s)
Hierro (Canary Isls.)	yĕr′-rô	yehr′-ro
Hiesfeld (Ger.)	hēs′-fĕlt	hees′-felt
higashi	hē-gä-shē	hee-gah-shee

An element, meaning east, in Japanese place names.

Higashi (Jap., Iwo)	hē-gä′-shē′	hee-gah′-shee′
Higashi Kuni (Jap.	hē-gä′-shē′ kōō′-nē′	hee-gah′-shee′ koo′-
prince)		nee′
High Tatra (Europ. mts.)	*Eng.* hĭ′ tä′-trə	hai′ tah′-truh

Slovak *Vysoké Tatry*, vwĭ′-sŏ-kĕ tä′-trĭ [vwi′-so-keh tah′-tri]. Hungarian *Tátra*, tä′-trŏ (tah′-tro).

Hiitola (Fin.)	hē'-tô-lä	hee'-to-lah
Russian *Khitola*, q.v.		
Hiiu *or* Hiiumaa	hē'-ōō	hee'-oo
(Est., isl.)	*or* hē'-ōō-mä	hee'-oo-mah
Russian *Dage*, q.v. German *Dagö*, q.v.		
Hildburghausen (Ger.)	hĭlt'-bŏŏrk(h)-hou'-zən	hilt'-burk(h)-hau'-zuhn
Hildesheim (Ger.)	hĭl'-dəs-hīm	hil'-duhs-haim
Hillegersberg (Neth.)	hĭl'-ə-k(h)ərs-bĕrk(h)'	hil'-uh-k(h)uhrs-behrk(h)'
Hillegom (Neth.)	hĭl'-ə-k(h)ôm	hil'-uh-k(h)om
Hillenkoetter, Roscoe H.	hĭl'-ən-kût'-ər	hil'-uhn-kuht'-uhr
(U.S. admiral)		
Hilleroed *or* Hilleröd	hĭl'-ə-rû*th*	hil'-uh-rœ*th*
(Den.)		
Hillesheim (Ger.)	hĭl'-əs-hīm	hil'-uhs-haim
Hillscheid (Ger.)	hĭl'-shīt	hil'-shait
Hilo (Hawaii)	hē'-lō	hee'-loh
Hilvarenbeek (Neth.)	hĭl'-vä-rən-bāk'	hil'-vah-ruhn-bayk'
Hilversum (Neth.)	hĭl'-vər-səm	hil'-vuhr-suhm
Himalaya (Asia, mts.)	hĭ-mä'-lə-yə	hi-mah'-luh-yuh
	or hĭm-ə-lä'-yə	him-uh-lay'-yuh
Himara (Alb.) See *Himarē*.		
Himarë (Alb.)	hē-mä'-rə	hee-mah'-ruh
Italian *Chimara*, q.v. Greek *Kheimara*, hē-mä'-rä [hee-mah'-rah].		
Himeimat (Egypt)	hĭ-mā-măt'	hi-may-mat'
See *Qaret el Himeimat*.		
Himeji (Jap.)	hē-mĕ'-jē'	hee-meh'-jee'
Hindahl, Olav	hĭn'-däl, ō'-läv	hin'-dahl, oh'-lahv
(Nor. polit.)		
Hindang (P.I.)	hēn-däng'	heen-dahng'
Hindeloopen (Neth.)	hĭn'-də-lō'-pən	hin'-duh-loh'-puhn
Hindemith, Paul (Ger.	hĭn'-də-mĭt	hin'-duh-mit
Am. musician)		
Hindenburg (Ger. >Pol.)	hĭn'-dən-bŏŏrk(h)	hin'-duhn-burk(h)
Polish *Zabrze*, q.v.		
Hindenburg, Paul von	*Eng.* hĭn'-dən-bûrg,	hin'-duhn-buhrg,
(Ger. general)	vŏn	von
	Ger. hĭn'-dən-bŏŏrk(h), fôn	hin'-duhn-burk(h), fon
Hindu Kush (India,	hĭn'-dōō kŏŏsh'	hin'-doo kush'
mts.)		
Hinunangan (P.I.)	hē-nōō-näng'-än	hee-noo-nahng'-ahn
Hiraiwa (Jap.)	hē-rä'-ē'-wä'	hee-rah'-ee'-wah'

Hiranuma, Kiichiro (Jap. hē-rä'-nōō'-mä', kē'-   hee-rah'-noo'-mah',
  polit.)   ē'-chē-rô   kee'-ee'-chee-ro

Hirel (Fr.)   ē-rĕl'   ee-rel'

Hirohito (Jap. emperor)   *Eng.* hē'-rō-hē'-tō   hee'-roh-hee'-toh

A Japanese pronunciation is suggested by hē-rô'-hē-tô [hee-ro'-hee-to] or hē-rôsh'-tô [hee-rosh'-to].

Hirosaki (Jap.)   hē-rô'-sä-kē   hee-ro'-sah-kee

Hiroshige (Jap. name)   hē-rô'-shē-gĕ   hee-ro'-shee-geh

Hiroshima (Jap.)   *Eng.* hē'-rō-shē'-mə   hee'-roh-shee'-muh
                   Jap. hē-rô'-shē'-mä'   hee-ro'-shee'-mah'

Hirota, Kōki (Jap. polit.) hē'-rô-tä, kô'-kē   hee'-ro-tah, ko'-kee

Hirschberg (Ger. >? Pol.) hĭrsh'-bĕrk(h)   hirsh'-behrk(h)
  Polish *Jelenia Góra*, q.v.

Hirson (Fr.)   ēr-sôN'   eer-soN'

Hirtshals (Den.)   hĭrts'-häls   hihrts'-hahls

Hispaniola (W.I.)   *Eng.* hĭs'-păn-ĭ-ō'-lə his'-pan-i-oh'-luh
  Spanish *Española*, ĕs-pä-nyô'-lä [es-pah-nyo'-lah]. Usually called
  Haiti, hā'-tĭ [hay'-ti].

Hiss, Alger   hĭs', ăl'-jər   his', al'-juhr
  (Am. diplomat)

Hister *or* Ister (Europ. riv.) See *Danube.*

Hitachi (Jap.)   hē-tä'-chē   hee-tah'-chee

Hitler, Adolph (Ger.   hĭt'-lər, ăd'-ŏlf   hit'-luhr, ad'-olf
  dictator)   *Ger.* ä'-dôlf   ah'-dolf

Called *der Schickelgruber*, dər shĭk'-əl-grōō'-bər [duhr shik'-uhl-groo'-buhr].

Hitra (Nor.)   hĭt'-rä   hit'-rah

Hitzacker (Ger.)   hĭt'-säk-ər   hit'-sahk-uhr

Hitzdorf (Ger.)   hĭts'-dôrf   hits'-dorf

Hiw (Oc., New Hebrides) hē'ōō   hee'u

Hjelle (Nor.)   yĕl'-ə   yel'-uh

Hjelmtveit, Nils   yĕlm'-tvāt, nĭls'   yelm'-tvayt, nils'
  (Nor. polit.)

Hjerkinn (Nor.)   yĕr'-kĭn   yehr'-kin

Hjoerring *or*   yûr'-ĭng   yœr'-ing
  Hjörring (Den.)

Hjukseboe *or*   yōōk'-sə-bû   yuk'-suh-bœ
  Hjuksebö (Nor.)

Hlônd, Augustus   hlônd'   hlond'
  Cardinal (Pol. churchman)

Ho (Chinese word   *Eng.* hō   hoh
  meaning *river*)   *Ch.* hŭ   huh

Hoboken (N.J.)   hō'-bō'-kən   hoh'-boh'-kuhn

Hoch, Daniel K.	hōk(h)′	hohk(h)′
(U.S. representative)		
Ho-chiang (Ch., Szechwan)	hŭ-jyäng	huh-jyahng
Also spelled *Ho-kiang*.		
Ho-ch'ih (Ch., Kwangsi)	hŭ-chŭ	huh-chuh
Ho Chih-minh	hô′ chē-mĭn′	ho′ chee-min′
(Vietnamese polit.)		
Höchst (Ger.)	hûk(h)st′	hœk(h)st′
Hochwald (Ger.)	hôk(h)′-vält	hok(h)′-vahlt
Hódmezővásárhely	hôd′-mĕ-zû-vä′-	hod′-meh-zœ-vah′-
(Hung.)	shär-hā	shahr-hay
Hodonín (Cz.)	hô′-dô-nēn	ho′-do-neen
German *Göding*, gû′-dĭng [gœ′-ding].		
Hoduciszki (Pol.)	hô-dŏŏ-tsē′-shkĭ	ho-du-tsee′-shki
Hoechst (Ger.)	hûk(h)st′	hœk(h)st′
Hoefen (Ger.)	hû′-fən	hœ′-fuhn
Hoehr (Ger.)	hûr′	hœr′
Hoek van Holland	hōōk′ vän hôl′-änt	hook′ vahn hol′-
English *Hook of Holland*.		ahnt
Hoenefoss (Nor.)	hû′-nə-fôs	hœ′-nuh-fos
Hoengen (Ger.)	hûng′-ən	hœng′-uhn
Hoenningen (Ger.)	hûn′-ĭng-ən	hœn′-ing-uhn
Hoensbroek (Neth.)	hōōns′-brōōk	hoons′-brook
Hoerde (Ger.)	hûr′-də	hœr′-duh
Hoeven (Neth.)	hōō′-vən	hoo′-vuhn
Hoeven, Charles B.	hōō′-vən	hoo′-vuhn
(U.S. representative)		
Hoey, Clyde R.	hōō′-ĭ	hoo′-i
(U. S. senator)		
Ho-fei (Ch., Anhwei)	hŭ-fā	huh-fay
Also called *Lu-chow*, q.v.		
Höfen (Ger.)	hû′-fən	hœ′-fuhn
Hogland (Fin., isl.) See *Suursaari*.		
Hogue, la (Fr.)	ōg′, lä	ohg′, lah
Hohensalza (Pol.) See *Inowrocław*.		
Hohe Tauern (Austria,	hō′-ə tou′-ərn	hoh′-uh tau′-uhrn
mts.)		
Höhr (Ger.)	hûr′	hœr′
Hokiang Variant of *Ho-chiang*, q.v.		
Hokkaidō (Jap.)	hôk-kĭ′-dô	hok-kai′-do
Hokksund (Nor.)	hôk′-sŏŏn	hok′-sun
Hōko Rettō ,Guntō, Tō (Jap. >Ch., isls.) See *Pescadores*.		
Ho-kow (Ch., Yünnan)	*Eng.* hō-kou	hoh-kau
	Ch. hŭ-kō	huh-koh

hoku	hô-kōō	ho-koo

An element, meaning *north*, in Japanese place names.

Holbæk (Den.)	hôl'-bĕk	hol'-bek
Holborn (Eng., London)	hō'-bərn	hoh'-buhrn
Holbrook (Ariz.)	hōl'-brŏŏk	hohl'-bruk
Holguín (Cuba)	ôl-gēn'	ol-geen'
Holifield, Chet (U.S. representative)	hŏl'-ĭ-fēld', chĕt'	hol'-i-feeld', chet'
Holland, Spessard L. (U. S. representative)	hŏl'-ənd, spĕs'-ərd	hol'-uhnd, spes'-uhrd
Hollandia (NEI, New Guinea)	*Eng.* hŏ-lăn'-dĭ-ə *Du.* hôl-län'-dē-ä	ho-lan'-di-uh hol-lahn'-dee-ah
Hollandsch Diep (Neth., estuary)	hôl'-änts dēp'	hol'-ahnts deep'
Hollandsche Veld (Neth.)	hôl'-änt-sə vĕlt'	hol'-ahnt-suh velt'
Hollerath (Ger.)	hôl'-ə-rät	hol'-uh-raht
Holmenkollen (Nor.)	hôlm'n-kôl-ən	holm'n-kol-uhn
Holmestrand (Nor.)	hôl'-mə-strän	hol'-muh-strahn
holocaust	hŏl'-ə-kôst	hol'-uh-kost
Holstebro (Den.)	hôl'-stə-brō'	hol'-stuh-broh'
Holsteinsborg (Greenl.)	hôl'-stīns-bôr	hol'-stains-bor
Holtz (Alaska, Attu)	hôlts'	holts'
Holving (Fr.)	ôl-vĭng'	ol-ving'
Holyoke (Mass.)	hōl'-yōk	hohl'-yohk
Holzminden (Ger.)	hôlts'-mĭn-dən	holts'-min-duhn
Homalin (Burma)	hōm'-mə-lĭn'	hohm'-muh-lin'
Homma, Masaharu (Jap. general)	hôm-mä', mä-sä'-hä-rōō	hom-mah', mah-sah'-hah-roo
Hommet (Fr., fort)	ô-mĕ'	o-meh'
Homolje (Yugosl.)	hô'-mô-lyĕ	ho'-mo-lyeh
Homonhón (P.I.)	hô-môn-hôn'	ho-mon-hon'

Also called *Jomonhol*, hô-môn-hôl' [ho-mon-hol'] and *Malhón*, mäl-hôn' [mahl-hon'].

Homorod (Rum., riv.)	hô'-mô-rôd'	ho'-mo-rod'
Homs (Libya)	hôms'	homs'
Ho-nan (Ch., prov.)	*Eng.* hō-năn *Ch.* hŭ-nän	hoh-nan huh-nahn
Ho-nan-fu (Ch., Honan)	*Eng.* hō-năn-fōō *Ch.* hŭ-nän-fōō	hoh-nan-foo huh-nahn-foo

Also called *Lo-yang*, q.v.

Honduras (C.A.)	*Eng.* hŏn-dŏŏr'-əs *Sp.* ôn-dōō'-räs	hon-dur'-uhs on-doo'-rahs
Hönefoss (Nor.)	hü'-nə-fôs	hœ'-nuh-fos

Honegger, Arthur	*Ger.* hō′-nĕg-ər	hoh′-neg-uhr
(Swiss composer)	*Fr.* ô-nĕ-gĕr′	o-neh-gehr′
Honfleur (Fr.)	ôN-flûr′	oN-flœr′
Hongay (Indo-Ch.)	hông-gī′	hong-gai′
Höngen (Ger.)	hûng′-ən	hœng′-uhn
Hong Kong (Ch.,	*Eng.* hŏng kŏng	hong kong
Kwangtung)		
Honnef (Ger.)	hôn′-ĕf	hon′-ef
Hönningen (Ger.)	hûn′-ĭng-ən	hœn′-ing-uhn
Honningsvaag (Nor.)	hôn′-ĭngs-vôg	hon′-ings-vog
Honshū (Jap.)	hôn′-shoo͞	hon′-shoo
Honskirch (Fr.)	ôNs-kĭrsh′	oNs-kihrsh′
Hontenisse (Neth.)	hôn′-tə-nĭs′-ə	hon′-tuh-nis′-uh
Hoo, Victor	hoo͞′	hoo′
(Ch. diplomat). Chinese *Hu.*		
Hoofdplaat (Neth.)	hôft′-plät	hohft′-plaht
Hoogeloon (Neth.)	hō′-k(h)ə-lōn′	hoh′-k(h)uh-lohn′
Hoogeveen (Neth.)	hō′-k(h)ə-vān′	hoh′-k(h)uh-vayn′
Hoogezand (Neth.)	hō-k(h)ə-zänt′	hoh-k(h)uh-zahnt′
Hooghly *or* Hugli (India)	hoo͞g′-lē	hoog′-lee
Hoogkarspel (Neth.)	hōk(h)-kär′-spəl	hohk(h)-kahr′-spuhl
Hoogkerk (Neth.)	hōk(h)-kĕrk′	hohk(h)-kehrk′
Hoogwoud (Neth.)	hōk(h)-wout′	hohk(h)-waut′
Hoorn (Neth.)	hōrn′	hohrn′
Hopeh (Ch., prov.)	*Eng.* hō-pā	hoh-pay
	Ch. hŭ-bā	huh-bay
Formerly *Chih-li*, jû-lē [juh-lee].		
Ho P'ing Pao	hŭ pĭng bou	huh ping bau
(Ch. newspaper)		
Hopong (Burma)	hō′-pŏng′	hoh′-pong′
Hoppenot, Henri	ôp-nō′, äN-rē′	op-noh′, ahN-ree′
Etienne (Fr. polit.)	ĕ-tyĕn′	eh-tyen′
Hörde (Ger.)	hûr′-də	hœr′-duh
Hořice (Cz.)	hôr′-zhĭ-tsĕ	hor′-zhi-tsĕ
Hungarian *Hořitz*, hôr′-zhĭts [hor′-zhits]; German *Horitz*, hō′-rĭts [hoh′-rits].		
Horikiri, Zenjirō (Jap.	hô-rē′-kē′-rē′, zĕn′-	ho-ree′-kee′-ree′,
executive)	jē-rô	zen′-jee-ro
Horin (Pol. >Rus., riv.) See *Gorin.*		
Hornád (Cz., riv.)	hôr′-nät	hor′-naht
Horneck (Ger.)	hôr′-nĕk	hor′-nek
Hornoy (Fr.)	ôr-nwä′	or-nwah′
Horodenka (Pol. >Rus.)	hô-rô-dĕn′-kä	ho-ro-den′-kah
Russian *Gorodenka*, gŏ-rŏ-dĕn′-kä [go-ro-den′-kah].		

Horodło (Pol.)   hô-rôd′-lô   ho-rod′-lo
   Russian *Gorodlo*, gŏ-rôd′-lŏ [go-rod′-lo].
Horodno (Pol.)   hô-rôd′-nô   ho-rod′-no
   Russian *Gorodno*, gŏ-rôd′-nŏ [go-rod′-no].
Horovice (Cz.)   hôr′-zhô-vǐ-tsĕ   hor′-zho-vi-tseh
   German *Horowitz*.
Horrem (Ger.)   hôr′-əm   hor′-uhm
Horsens (Den.)   hôr′-səns   hor′-suhns
Horst (Neth.)   hôrst′   horst′
Hort (Hung.)   hôrt′   hort′
Horta (Azores)   ôr′-tə   or′-tuh
Horten (Nor.)   hôrt′n   hort′n
Horthy, Miklós (Hung.   hôr′-tǐ, mǐk′-lôsh   hor′-ti, mik′-losh
   polit.)
Horyń (Pol. > Rus., riv.)   hô′-rǐn(y)   ho′-rin(y)
   Russian *Gorin*, gô′-rǐn(y) [go′-rin(y)].
Hōryūji (Jap. temple)   hô′-ryōō-jē   ho′-ryoo-jee
Hoshijima, Jirō (Jap.   hô-shē′-jē′-mä′, jē′-rô   ho-shee′-jee′-mah′,
   polit.)   jee′ro
Hoshino (Jap.)   hô′-shē-nô   ho′-shee-no
Hoti (Yugosl., Alb.)   *S.-C.* hô′-tē   ho′-tee
Ho-t'ien (Ch.,   hŭ-tyĕn   huh-tyen
   Kwangtung)
Hotin (Rum. > Rus.)   hô′-tǐn   ho′-tin
   Russian spelling *Khotin*.
Hottot Les Baques (Fr.)   ô-tō′ lĕ bäk′   o-toh′ leh bahk′
Houaïlou (Oc., New Caledonia) See *Wailu*.
Houde, Camellien   ōōd′, kä-mĕ-lyăN′   ood′, kah-meh-lyaN′
   (Can. polit.)
Houdon (Fr.)   ōō-dôN′   oo-doN′
Houffalize (Belg.)   ōō-fä-lēz′   oo-fah-leez′
Hough (Eng. name)   hŭf′   huhf′
Houghwout (Am. name)   hou′-ǐt *or* -ət   hau′-it *or* -uht
Houlgate (Fr.)   ōōl′-gät′   ool-gaht′
Houlton (Me.)   hōlt′n   hohlt′n
Houmt Souk (Tun.)   hōō′-mət sōōk′   hoo′-muht sook′
Houplines (Fr.)   ōō-plēn′   oo-pleen′
Housman, Alfred E.   hous′-mən   haus′-muhn
   (Br. poet)
Houssaie, la (Fr.)   ōō-sĕ′, lä   oo-seh′, lah
Houston (Tex.)   hyōōs′-tən   hyoos′-tuhn
   Houston Street, New York, is pronounced hous′-tən [haus′-tuhn].
In England *Houston* is usually pronounced hōōs′-tən [hoos′-tuhn],
occasionally hous′-tən [haus′-tuhn].

Houtem (Neth.)	hou'-təm	hau'-tuhm
Hova (Madag.)	hŭ'-və	huh'-vuh
Hovde, Bryn J.	hŏv'-də, brĭn'	hov'-duh, brin'
(Am. educator)		
Hovden (Nor.)	hôvd'n	hovd'n
Hoven (Ger.)	hō'-fən	hoh'-fuhn
Hoxha, Envër	hô'-jä, ĕn'-vər	ho'-jah, en'-vuhr
(Albanian polit.)		
Howrah (India)	hou'-rä	hau'-rah
Ho Ying-chin (Ch.	hŭ yĭng-jĭn	huh ying-jin
general)		

Usually Anglicized to hō yĭng-chĭn [hoh ying-chin].

Hradčany	hrät'-chä-nĭ	hraht'-chah-ni
(Cz., Prague, palace)		
Hradec Králové (Cz.)	hrä'-dĕts	hrah'-dets
	krä'-lô-vĕ	krah'-lo-veh
Hrubecki, Jan	hrōō-bĕts'-kĭ, yän'	hru-bets'-ki, yahn'
(Pol. polit.)		
Hrubieszów (Pol.)	hrōō-byĕ'-shŏŏf	hru-byeh'-shuf

Russian *Grubeshov*, grōō-bĕ'-shŏf [gru-beh'-shof].

Hrvat (Croat)	hər'-vät	huhr'-vaht

Hrvatski, -*a*, hər'-vät'-ski, -ä [huhr'-vaht'-ski, -ah], adj., means *Croatian*.

Hrvatska (Yugosl.)	hər'-vät'-skä	huhr'-vaht'-skah

English *Croatia*, q.v.

Hs- See also names in *S*-.

Hsenwi (Burma)	shĕn'-wē'	shen'-wee'
Hsia-chiang (Ch.,	shyä-jyäng	shyah-jyahng
Kiangsi, Kweichow)		
Hsia-kwan (Ch.,	shyä-gwän	shyah-gwahn
Yünnan)		
Hsiang Chiang *or* River	shyäng	shyahng
(Ch., Hunan)		
Hsiang-Hsiang	shyäng-shyäng	shyahng-shyahng
(Ch., Hunan)		
Hsiang Kiang *or*	shyäng	shyahng
Hsiang River		
Hsiang-t'an	shyäng-tän	shyahng-tahn
(Ch., Hunan)		
Hsiang-yang (Ch.,	shyäng-yäng	shyahng-yahng
Hupeh)		
Hsiang-yin (Ch., Hunan)	shyäng-yĭn	shyahng-yin
Hsiang-yün (Ch.,	shyäng-yün	shyahng-yün
Yünnan)		
Hsiao-fêng (Ch.,	shyou-fŭng	shyau-fuhng
Chekiang)		

Hsiao-lin (Ch., Kiangsi)	shyou-lĭn	shyau-lin
Hsiao-shan (Ch., Chekiang)	shou-shän	shau-shahn
Hsia-p'u (Ch., Fukien) See *Siapu*.		
Hsi-ch'ang (Ch., prov.) See *Si-ch'ang*.		
Hsieh-mu-shan (Ch., Kwangtung)	shyĕ-mōō-shän	shyeh-moo-shahn
Hsien-ning (Ch., Kiangsi)	shyĕn-nĭng	shyen-ning
Hsin (Ch., Kiangsi, riv.)	shĭn	shin
Hsin-ching Variant spelling of *Hsin-king*, q.v.		
Hsin-fêng (Ch., Kiangsi)	shĭn-fŭng	shin-fuhng
Hsing-hsan-chên (Manchu.)	shĭng-shän-jŭn	shing-shahn-juhn
Hsing-kwo (Ch., Kiangsi)	shĭng-gwô	shing-gwo
Also called *Nan-kang*, q.v.		
Hsing-tzŭ (Ch., Kiangsi)	shĭng-dzə	shing-dzuh
Hsin-king (Manchu.)	shĭn-jĭng	shin-jing
Also spelled *Hsin-ching*. Also called *Ch'ang-ch'un* q.v.		
Hsin-ning (Ch., Hunan)	shĭn-nĭng	shin-ning
Hsin-têng (Ch., Chekiang)	shĭn-dŭng	shin-duhng
Hsin-ti (Ch., Hupeh)	shĭn-dē	shin-dee
Hsin-wu (Ch., Kiangsi)	shĭn-wōō	shin-woo
Hsin-yü (Ch., Kiangsi)	shĭn-yü	shin-yü
Hsipaw (Burma)	sē'-pô'	see'-paw'
Hsi-ts'ang (Ch. dependency) See *Si-ts'ang* and *Tibet*.		
Hsiung Shih-hui (Ch. polit.)	shyŏŏng shû-whā	shyung shuh-whay
Hsiu-shui (Ch., Kiangsi)	shyōō-shwā	shyoo-shway
Hsü-an T'ung (former Chinese Emperor) See *P'u-yi*.		
Hsü-ch'ang (Ch., Honan)	shü-chäng	shü-chahng
Hsü-chow (Ch., Szechwan)	shü-jō	shü-joh
Also called *I-p'in*, q.v.		
Hsüeh Yüeh (Ch. general)	shü-ĕ yü-ĕ	shü-eh yü-eh
Hsü Mo (Ch. polit.)	shü mô	shü maw
Htizwe (Burma)	tē'-zwĕ'	tee'-zweh'
Huachuca (N.M., mts.)	wä-chōō'-kə	wah-choo'-kuh
Huarás (Peru)	wä-räs'	wah-rahs'
Hua-yang (Ch., Anhwei)	whä-yäng	whah-yahng
Hua-yung (Ch., Hunan)	whä-yŏŏng	whah-yung
Huber, Walter B. (U.S. representative)	hyōō'-bər	hyoo'-buhr

Hubert, St. (Belg.) See *Saint Hubert*.

Hubli (India)	hŏŏb'-lĭ	hub'-li
Hu-chow (Ch., Chekiang)	*Eng.* hōō-chou *Ch.* hōō-jō	hoo-chau hoo-joh
Hucqueliers (Fr.)	ü-kə-lyĕ'	ü-kuh-lyeh'
Hué (Indo-Ch.)	hwĕ'	hweh'
Hüe, George Adolphe (Fr. composer)	ü'	ü'
Hueco Tanks (Tex.) Cf. *Waco*, Tex.	wā'-kō	way'-koh
Huedin (Rum.)	k(h)wĕ-dēn'	k(h)weh-deen'
Huelgoat (Fr.)	wĕl-gô-ät'	wel-go-aht'
Huels (Ger.)	hüls'	hüls'
Huelva (Sp.)	wĕl'-vä	wel'-vah
Huenxe (Ger.)	hün'-ksə	hün'-ksuh
Huerta, Victoriano (Mex. general)	wĕr'-tä, vēk-tô-ryä'- nô	wehr'-tah, veek-to- ryah'-no
Huertgen (Ger.)	hürt'-gən	hürt'-guhn
Huerth (Ger.)	hürt'	hürt'
Huesca (Sp., prov.)	wĕs'-kä	wes'-kah
Huettingen (Ger.)	hüt'-ĭng-ən	hüt'-ing-uhn
Huger (S.C. name)	yōō-jē'	yoo-jee'

Hugessen, Sir Hugh Montgomery Knatchbull (Br. diplomat) See
Knatchbull Hugessen.

Hughenden (Austral.)	hyōō'-ĭn-dən	hyoo'-in-duhn

Hugli (India) See *Hooghly*.

Hu-hsien (Ch.)	hōō-shyĕn	hoo-shyen
Hui-ch'ang (Ch., Kiangsi)	whā-chäng	whay-chahng
Hui-lai (Ch., Kwangtung)	whā-lī	whay-lai
Hui-li (Ch., Sikang) Also spelled *Hweili*.	whā-lē	whay-lee
Huisduinen (Neth.)	hûĭs-dûĭ'-nən	hœis-dœi'-nuhn
Huisen (Neth.)	hûĭ'-sən	hœi'-suhn
Huisne (Fr.)	wēn'	ween'
Huissen (Neth.)	hûĭ'-sən	hœi'-suhn
Huizen (Neth.)	hûĭ'-zən	hœi'-zuhn
Hukawng (Burma, valley)	hōō'-kông'	hoo'-kawng'
Hukbalahap (Fil. political party)	hŭk'-bä-lä-häp'	huhk'-bah-lah-hahp'
Hukong (Burma) Also spelled *Hukawng*, q.v.	hōō'-kông'	hoo'-kawng'

Hu-k'ou (Ch., Kiangsi)	hōō-kŏ	hoo-koh
Hu-lin (Manchu.)	hōō-lĭn	hoo-lin
Hulm (Ger.)	hŏŏlm′	hulm′
Hüls (Ger.)	hüls′	hüls′
Hulst (Neth.)	hûlst′	hœlst′
Hu-lu-t'ao (Manchu.)	hōō-lōō-tou	hoo-loo-tau
Hu-ma (Manchu.)	hōō-mä	hoo-mah

Humbert II (deposed King of Italy) See *Umberto.*

Humboldt (NEI, bay)	*Eng.* hŭm′-bōlt	huhm′-bohlt
	Ger. hŏŏm′-bôlt	hum′-bolt
Hummeloo (Neth.)	hûm′-ə-lō	hœm′-uh-loh
Hun (Libya)	hōōn′	hoon′
Hu-nan (Ch., prov.)	hōō-nän	hoo-nahn
Hun-ch'un (Manchu.)	hŏŏn-chŏŏn	hun-chun

hunda (Alb.) See *hundë.*

hundë (Alb.)	hŏŏn′-də	hoon′-duh

An element, meaning *cape,* in Albanian place names. Look up the other part of the name.

Hunder (Nor.)	hŏŏn′-ər	hun′-uhr
Hundorp (Nor.)	hŏŏn′-dôrp	hun′-dorp
Hunedoara (Rum.)	hŏŏ-nĕ-dwä′-rä	hu-neh-dwah′-rah

Hungarian *Hunyad,* hŏŏ′-nyŏd [hu′-nyod], and *Vajdahunyad,* voi′-dŏ- [voi′-do-].

Hungary	*Eng.* hŭng′-gə-rĭ	huhng′-guh-ri

Hungarian *Magyarország,* mŏ′-dyŏr-ôr′-säg [mo′-dyor-or′-sahg].

Huningue (Fr.)	ü-năNg′	ü-naNg′
Hunsrueck *or* Hunsrück	hŏŏns′-rük	huns′-rük
(Ger., mts.)		
Hunte (Ger., riv.)	hŏŏn′-tə	hun′-tuh
Hünxe (Ger.)	hün′-ksə	hün′-ksuh

Hunyad (Rum.) See *Hunedoara.*

Hunze (Neth., riv.)	hûn′-zə	hœn′-zuh
Huon (Oc., N.E. New	*Eng.* hyōō′-ŏn	hyoo′-on
Guinea, pen.)		
Hu-peh (Ch., prov.)	*Eng.* hōō-pā	hoo-pay
	Ch. hōō-bĕ	hoo-beh
Hünxe (Ger.)	hün′-ksə	hün′-ksuh
Hurbache (Fr.)	ür-bäk′	ür-bahk′
Hürtgen (Ger.)	hürt′-gən	hürt′-guhn
Hürth (Ger.)	hürt′	hürt′

Hüseyin Ragıp Baydur (Turk. diplomat) See *Baydur.*

Hu Shih (Ch. diplomat)	hōō shû	hoo shuh
Huşi (Rum.)	hŏŏsh′	hush′

Husiatyn (Pol >Rus.)   hŏŏ-shä'-tĭn   hu-shah'-tin
  Russian *Gusiatin,* gŏŏ-syä'-tĭn [gu-syah'-tin].

Hussein Ala   hŏŏ-sän' ä-lä'   hu-sayn' ah-lah'
  (Iran. polit.)

Husseini (Arab name) See *Jamal Effendi* and *Haj Amin.*

Hussein Sirry (Egyptian hŏŏs-sän' sĭr'-rĭ   hus-sayn' sihr'-ri
  leader)

Hust (Cz. >Rus.) See *Khust.*

Husum (Ger.,   hōō'-zŏŏm   hoo'-zum
  Schleswig-Holstein)

Husum (Nor.)   hōō'-sŏŏm   hoo'-sum

Huszt (Cz. >Rus.) See *Khust.*

Hüttingen (Ger.)   hüt'-ĭng-ən   hüt'-ing-uhn

Huveaune (Fr., riv.)   ü-vōn'   ü-vohn'

Huysmans, Camille   *Fl.* hûĭs'-mäns   hœis'-mahns
  (Belg. polit.)   *Fr.* ü-ēs-mäNs', ü-ees-mahNs',
                kä-mē'(y)   kah-mee'(y)

Hvar (Yugosl.)   hvär'   hvahr'
  Italian *Lesina,* q.v.

Hvittingfoss (Nor.)   vĭt'-ĭng-fôs   vit'-ing-fos

Hwai Ho *or* Hwai River whī   whai
  (Ch.)

Hwai-yang (Ch., Honan) whī-yäng   whai-yahng

Hwang Ho *or* River (Ch.) whäng   whahng
  Also called the *Yellow River.*

Hwang-k'ang (Ch.,   whäng-käng   whahng-kahng
  Hupeh)

Hwang-peh (Ch., Hupeh) whäng-bĕ   whahng-beh

Hwa-yan-k'ow   whä-yän-kō   whah-yahn-koh
  (Ch., Honan)

Hwa-yung (Ch., Hunan) whä-yŏŏng   whah-yung

Hwei-chow (Ch.,   *Eng.* whā-chou   whay-chau
  Anhwei)   *Ch.* whä-jō   whay-joh

Hweili (Ch.) See *Huili.*

Hyannis (Mass.)   hī-ăn'-ĭs   hai-an'-is

Hyderabad (India)   hī-drə-băd' *or* -bäd' hai-druh-bad' *or*
                                -bahd'

Hydra (Gr., isl.)   ē'-drä   ee'-drah

Hyenville (Fr.)   yäN-vēl'   yahN-veel'

Hyères (Fr.)   yĕr'   yehr'

hygiene   hī'-jēn   hai'-jeen
          or hī'-jĭ-ēn   hai'-ji-een

hygienic   hī'-jĭ-ĕn'-ĭc   hai'-ji-en'-ic
          or hī-jēn'-ĭk   hai-jeen'-ik

hygienist	hī′-jĭ-ə-nĭst	hai′-ji-uh-nist
	or hī′-jē-nĭst	hai′-jee-nist
Hymettus (Gr., mt.)	*Eng.* hī-mĕt′-əs	hai-met′-uhs
Hyōgo (Jap.)	hyô′-gô	hyo′-go
hypholin	hī′-fō-lĭn	hai′-foh-lin

A form of penicillin.

| Hyrynsalmi (Fin.) | hü′-rün-säl-mē | hü′-rün-sahl-mee |
| Hyvinkää (Fin.) | hü′-vĭng-kǎ | hü′-ving-ka |

| Iakkima (Fin. >Rus.) | yäk′-kĭ-mä | yahk′-ki-mah |

Finnish spelling *Jaakkima.*

Ialomiţa (Rum., riv.)	yä′-lô-mē′-tsä	yah′-lo-mee′-tsah
Ianina (Gr.) See *Ioannina.*		
Iaşi (Rum.)	yäsh′	yahsh′

German *Jassy,* yäs′-ē [yahs′-ee].

Iba (P.I.)	ē′-bä	ee′-bah
Ibaán (P.I.)	ē-bä-än′	ee-bah-ahn′
Ibar (Yugosl., riv.)	ē′-bär	ee′-bahr
Ibaraki (Jap.)	ē-bä′-rä′-kē′	ee-bah′-rah′-kee′

Ibarra, José María Velasco (Ecuador. polit.) See *Velasco Ibarra.*

Ibbenbueren *or*	ĭb′-ən-bü′-rən	ib′-uhn-bü′-ruhn
Ibbenbüren (Ger.)		
ibn	ĭb′n	ib′n

An element, meaning *son,* in Arabic personal names. Hebrew *ben,* q.v.

Ibn Saud, Abdul Aziz	ĭb′n sä-ōōd′, äb-dŏŏl′	ib′n sah-ood′, ahb-
(King of Saudi Arabia)	ä-zēz′	dul′ ah-zeez′
Ibrahim Hashem	ĭb-rä-hēm′ hǎsh′-əm	ib-rah-heem′ hash′-
Pasha (Trans-Jordan	pä′-shä	uhm pah′-shah
polit.)		

French spelling *Hachem.*

Icaria (Gr., isl.) See *Ikaria.*

Içel (Turk.)	ē′-chĕl	ee′-chel
I-ch'ang (Ch., Hupeh)	ē-chäng	ee-chahng
Ichinomiya (Jap.)	ē-chē′-nô′-mē-yä	ee-chee′-no′-mee-yah
Ichnya (Rus.)	ĭch-nyä′	ich-nyah′
I-chun (Ch., Kiangsi)	ē-jŏŏn	ee-jun
Ickes, Harold L.	ĭk′-əs *or* ĭk′-ĭz	ik′-uhs *or* ik′-iz
(Am. polit.)		
Idaarderadeel (Neth.)	ē′-där-də-rä-dāl′	ee′-dahr-duh-rah-
		dayl′
Idaho (U.S.)	ī′-də-hō	ai′-duh-hoh
Idenburg (NEI, riv.)	ĭd′-ən-bûrk(h)	id′-uhn-bœrk(h)
ideology	ī′-dĭ-ŏl′-ə-jĭ	ai′-di-ol′-uh-ji
	or ĭd′-ĭ-ŏl′-ə-jĭ	id′-i-ol′-uh-ji

The latter is placed first by *Webster's*, the former by Kenyon and Knott, *Thorndike Century*, and *Funk and Wagnalls*.

Ide Oros (Crete, mt.)   ē'-dē ô'-rôs   ee'-dee o'-ros
English *Mt. Ida*, ĭ'-də [ai'-duh]. Also called *Ypseloreites*, ē-psē-lô-rē'-tēs [ee-psee-lo-ree'-tees].

Idice (It.)   ē'-dē-chĕ   ee'-dee-cheh
Iditerod (Alaska)   ĭ-dĭt'-ə-räd   ai-dit'-uh-rahd
Idritsa (Rus.)   ē'-drĭ-tsä   ee'-dri-tsah
Ie Jima (Jap., isl.)   ē-ĕ' jē'-mä'   ee-eh' jee'-mah'
Ienne (It.)   yĕn'-nĕ   yen'-neh
Ieperen (Belg.)   ē'-pə-rən   ee'-puh-ruhn
    French *Ypres*, q.v.
Ieriki (Latvia)   ē'-ĕ'-rē-kē   ee'-eh'-ree-kee
Ierseke (Neth.)   ēr'-sə-kə   eer'-suh-kuh
Iesi (It.)   yĕ'-zē   yeh'-zee
Iewe (Est.)   *Rus.* yĕ'-vĕ   yeh'-veh
    Estonian *Jõhvi*, q.v.
Ifalik (Oc., Carolines)   ē'-fä-lēk   ee'-fah-leek
I-fêng (Ch., Kiangsi)   ē-fŭng   ee-fuhng
Iffendic (Fr.)   ē-fäN-dēk'   ee-fahN-deek'
Ifni (Mor., Rio de Oro)   ēf'-nē   eef'-nee
Ígat (P.I.)   ē'-gät   ee'-gaht
Iglau (Cz., riv., town)   See *Jihlava*.
Iglawa (Cz., riv., town)   See *Jihlava*.
Iglesias (Sard.)   ē-glĕ'-sĭ-äs   ee-gleh'-si-ahs
İgneada (Turk.)   ē-nĕ'-ä-dä   ee-neh'-ah-dah
Igorrotes (P.I., people)   ē-gôr-rô'-tĕs   ee-gor-ro'-tes
    Singular *Igorrote*, ē-gôr-rô'-tĕ [ee-gor-ro'-teh]. English *Igorrot*, ē-gō-rōt' [ee-goh-roht'], plural *Igorrots*, -rōts' [-rohts'].
Iguig (P.I.)   ē-gēg'   ee-geeg'
Igurin (Oc., Eniwetok)   ē-gōō'-rĭn   ee-goo'-rin
Ihna (Ger., riv.)   ē'-nä   ee'-nah
I-hwang (Ch., Kiangsi)   ē-whäng   ee-whahng
    Also spelled *Yi-hwang*.
Iijärvi (Fin., lakes)   ē'-yăr-vē   ee'-yehr-vee
Iisalmi (Fin.)   ē'-säl-mē   ee'-sahl-mee
ij
    In Dutch *ij* is interchangeable with *ei* and *y*. A consultant may have to look for all three forms before he finds his word.
IJlst (Neth.)   īlst'   ailst'
IJmuiden (Neth.)   ī-mûĭ'-dən   ai-mœi'-duhn
IJssel (Neth., riv.)   ī'-səl   ai'-suhl
    Also spelled *Ijsel* and *Yssel*.
IJsselmeer (Neth., lake)   ī'-səl-mār   ai'-suhl-mayr

IJsselmonde (Neth.) ĭ'-səl-môn'-də ai'-suhl-mon'-duh
IJsselstein (Neth.) ĭ'-səl-stīn ai'-suhl-stain
IJzendijke (Neth.) ĭ'-zən-dĭ'-kə ai'-zuhn-dai'-kuh
Ikaria (Gr., isl.) *Eng.* ē-kăr'-ĭ-ə ee-kehr'-i-uh
                Gr. ē-kä-rē'-ä ee-kah-ree'-ah
  Also called *Nicaria,* nē-kär-yä' [nee-kahr-yah'].
Ikeda, Seihin (Jap. ē-kĕ'-dä', sā'-hēn ee-keh-'dah', say'-
  executive) heen
Ikhthys (Gr., point) ēk(h)-thēs' eek(h)-thees'
  The point of *Katakolon,* q.v.
Ilagan (P.I.) ē-lä'-gän ee-lah'-gahn
Ilandža (Yugosl.) ē'-län-jä ee'-lahn-jah
Iława (Ger. >Pol.) ĭ-lä'-vä i-lah'-vah
  German *Deutsch Eylau,* q.v.

Île de la Cité (Fr.) ēl də lä sē-tĕ' eel duh lah see-teh'
Île d'Yeu (Fr.) ēl dyû' eel dyœ'
Îles d'Hyères (Fr.) ēl dyĕr' eel dyehr'
Ilich (Rus.) ĭl-yēch' il-yeech'
Iligan (P.I.) ē-lē'-gän ee-lee'-gahn
Iliisk (Rus.) ē-lēsk' ee-leesk'
Ilijina Glava (Balkan ē'-lē'-yĭ-nä ee'-lee'-yi-nah
  mt.) glä'-vä glah'-vah
Ilín (P.I.) ē-lēn' ee-leen'
  Also spelled *Ylin.*
Ilja (Pol.) See *Ilża.*
Ill (Fr., riv.) ēl' eel'
Illana (P.I., bay) ē-lyä'-nä *or* -yä'- ee-lyah'-nah *or* -yah'-
Ille (Fr., riv.) ēl' eel'
illegal ĭ-lē'-gəl i-lee'-guhl
  The pronunciation ĭ-lĭg'-əl [i-lig'-uhl] should be avoided.
Ille Rance (Fr., canal) ēl räNs' eel rahNs'
Illinois (U.S.) ĭl'-ə-noi *or* -noiz il'-uh-noi *or* -noiz
Illovaiskaya (Rus.) ĭl-lŏ-vĭ'-skä-yä il-lo-vai'-skah-yah
Ilmen (Rus. lake) *Eng.* ĭl'-mən il'-muhn
           Rus. ēl'(y)-mĕn(y) eel'(y)-men(y)
Il Messaggero (Rome ēl mĕs-säd-jĕ'-rô eel mes-sahd-jeh'-
  newspaper) ro
Ilocos Norte (P.I.) ē-lô'-kôs nôr'-tĕ ee-lo'-kos nor'-teh
Ilocos Sur (P.I.) ē-lô'-kôs sōor' ee-lo'-kos soor'
Ílog, Abra de (P.I.) See *Abra de Ílog.*
Iloilo (P.I.) ē'-lô-ē'-lô ee'-lo-ee'-lo
Ilok (Yugosl.) ē'-lôk ee'-lok
Iłowo (Pol.) ĭ-lô'-vô i-lo'-vo

Ilya Uksu (Fin. > Rus.)	ĭl-yä′ ōŏk′-sŏŏ	il-yah′ ook′-su
Finnish *Uuksu,* q.v.		
Iłża (Pol.)	ēl′-zhä	eel′-zhah
Russian *Ilja,* ē-lyä′ [ee-lyah′].		
Im (Rus.)	ēm′	eem′
imam	ĭ-mäm′	i-mahm′
A Moslem title, which is disregarded in alphabetical listing.		
Iman (Rus.)	ĭ-män′	i-mahn′
Imatra (Fin.)	ē′-mät-rä	ee′-maht-rah
Imbros (Turk., isl.)	*Gr.* ēm′-brôs	eem′-bros
Turkish *İmroz,* ēm′-rôz′ [eem′-roz′].		
Imele (It., riv.)	ē-mĕ′-lĕ	ee-meh′-leh
Imola (It.)	ē′-mô-lä	ee′-mo-lah
Imotski (Yugosl.)	ē′-môt-skĭ	ee′-mot-ski
Imphal (India)	ĭmp′-hŭl′	imp′-huhl′
Imrédy, Béla (Hung. polit.)	ĭm′-rä-dĭ, bā′-lŏ	im′-ray-di, bay′-lo
İmroz (Turk., isl.)	ēm′-rôz′	eem′-roz′
Greek *Imbros,* q.v.		
Imus (P.I.)	ē′-mōōs	ee′-moos
Inagua (Bahamas)	ē-nä′-gwä	ee-nah′-gwah
Inari (Fin., lake)	ē′-nä-rē	ee′-nah-ree
Incoronata (Yugosl., isl.)	*It.* ēn-kô-rô-nä′-tä	een-ko-ro-nah′-tah
Serb-Croat *Kornat,* q.v.		
Indainggyi (Burma)	ĭn-dīng-jē′	in-daing-jee′
Indán (P.I.)	ēn-dän′	een-dahn′
Indang (P.I.)	ēn-däng′	een-dahng′
Indaw (Burma)	ĭn′-dô′	in′-daw′
indecorous	ĭn-dĕk′-ə-rəs	in-dek′-uh-ruhs
	or ĭn-dĭ-kō′-rəs	in-di-koh′-ruhs

Similarly *decorous,* dĕk′-ə-rəs [dek′-uh-ruhs] *or* dĭ-kō′-rəs [di-koh′-ruhs]. The more realistic authorities, British and American, give this order of preference, the more conservative and old-fashioned stress the next to the last syllable. One would have expected the analogy of *decorum* to govern present-day usage, but for the last thirty years a recessive accent has seemed attractive to many Americans. Compare *pianist.*

Inden (Ger.)	ĭn′-dən	in′-duhn
Indiana (U.S.)	ĭn′-dĭ-ăn′-ə	in′-di-an′-uh
Indianapolis (Ind.)	ĭn′-dĭ-ə-năp′-ə-lĭs	in′-di-uh-nap′-uh-lis
Indies	ĭn′-dēz *or* -dĭz	in′-deez *or* -diz
Inđija (Yugosl.)	ēn′-dyĭ-yä	een′-dyi-yah
Indio (Calif.)	ĭn′-dĭ-ō	in′-di-oh
Indonesia	ĭn′-dŏ-nē′-zhə *or* -shə	in′-doh-nee′-zhuh *or* -shuh

Indore (India)	ĭn-dôr′	in-dor′
Indramajoe *or* Indra- mayu (NEI)	ĭn-drä-mä′-yōō	in-drah-mah′-yoo
Indre (Fr., riv.)	ăN′dr	aN′dr
Indret (Fr., isl.)	ăN-drĕ′	aN-dreh′
Indus (India, riv.)	ĭn′-dəs	in′-duhs
Inércskakucs (Hng.)	ĭ′-nārch-kŏ′-kōōch	i′-nayrch-ko′-kuch
Ineu (Rum.)	ē-nĕ′-ōō	ee-neh′-u
Infermeria (It.)	ēn-fĕr-mĕ-rē′-ä	een-fehr-meh-ree′-ah
Inge, William R. (Former Dean of St. Paul's, London)	ĭng′	ing′
Ingolstadt (Ger.)	ĭng′-gôl-shtät	ing′-gol-shtaht
Ingul (Rus., riv.)	ĭn-gōōl′	in-gul′
Ingulets (Rus., riv.)	ĭn-gōō′-lĕts	in-gu′-lets
Ingyin (Burma)	ĭn-jĭn′	in-jin′
Inkagahtawng (Burma)	ĭn′-kə-gä-tông′	in′-kuh-gah-tawng′
Inkerman (Rus.)	ĭng′-kər-män	ing′-kuhr-mahn
Inn (Europ. riv.)	ĭn′	in′
Innisfail (Austral.)	ĭn′-ĭs-fāl	in′-is-fayl
Innokentievka (Rus.)	ĭn-nŏ-kĕn′-tyĕf-kä	in-no-ken′-tyef-kah
Innsbruck (Austria)	*Eng.* ĭnz′-brōōk	inz′-bruk
	Ger. ĭns′-brōōk	ins′-bruk
Inogošte (Yugosl.)	ē′-nô-gô′-shtĕ	ee′-no-go′-shteh
İnönü, İsmet (Turk. polit.)	ē′-nû-nü′, ĭs-mĕt′	ee′-nœ-nü′, is-met′
Inopacan (P.I.)	ē-nô-pä′-kän	ee-no-pah′-kahn
Inowrocław (Pol.)	ĭ-nô-vrô′-tsläf	i-no-vro′-tslahf

German *Hohensalza*, hō′-ən-zäl-tsä [hoh′-uhn-zahl-tsah].

inquiry	ĭn-kwī′-rĭ	in-kwai′-ri
	or ĭn′-kwĭ-rĭ	in′-kwi-ri

Both pronunciations are acceptable although the second is recognized only in recent editions of American dictionaries. Presumably ĭn′-kwī-rĭ [in′-kwai-ri] is inferior to both.

Insam, Puló (P.I., isl.)	ĭn-säm′, pōō-lô′	in-sahm′, poo-lo′
Insterburg (Ger. >Rus.)	ĭn′-stər-bōōrk(h)	in′-stuhr-burk(h)

Russian *Cherniakhovsk*, chĕr-nyä-hôfsk′ [chehr-nyah-hofsk′].

interesting	ĭn′-tər-ĕs-tĭng	in′-tuhr-es-ting
	or ĭn′-trəs-tĭng	in′-truhs-ting

The alternative pronunciation of *interesting* has better standing in America than the similar pronunciations of *dictionary*, q.v., and *necessary*, q.v. The second vowel of *interest* is often lost, and this syncopation gives a native analogy, whereas the "British" pronunciations of *dictionary* and *necessary* sound alien to American ears.

Intramuros (P.I.)	ēn-trä-mōō′-rôs	een-trah-moo′-ros

Inza (Rus.)	ēn'-zä	een'-zah
Inzecca (Corsica)	ēn-dzĕk'-kä	een-dzek'-kah
Ioannes, Agios (Crete)	yô-ä'-nēs, ī'-yôs	yo-ah'-nees, ai'-yos
Ioannina (Gr.)	yô-ä'-nē-nä	yo-ah'-nee-nah
	or yä'-nē-nä	yah'-nee-nah

Serb-Croat *Janina,* yä'-nē-nä [yah'-nee-nah].

Ionia (Turk.)	*Eng.* ī-ō'-nyə	ai-oh'-nyuh
ionosphere	ī-ŏn'-ə-sfĭr	ai-ŏn'-uh-sfihr
Ios (Gr., isl.)	ē'-ô(s)	ee'-o(s)
Iowa (U.S.)	ī'-ə-wə	ai'-uh-wuh

A local and old-fashioned pronunciation is ī'-ə-wä' [ai'-uh-way'].

| I-p'in (Ch., Szechwan) | ē-pĭn | ee-pin |

Also called *Hsü-chow,* q.v.

Ipoh (Malaya)	ē'-pō	ee'-poh
Iput (Rus., riv.)	ē'-pŏŏt	ee'-put
I.Q.	ī' kyōō'	ai' kyoo'

The abbreviation of *intelligence quotient.*

Iran	*Eng.* ĭ-răn'	i-ran'
	Per. ē-rän'	ee-rahn'
Iranian	ĭ-rā'-nĭ-ən	ai-ray'-ni-uhn
'Iraq	*Eng.* ĭ-răk'	i-rak'
	Per. ē-räk'	ee-rahk'
Iraqi	*Eng.* ĭ-răk'-ĭ	i-rak'-i
	Per. ē-rä'-kē	ee-rah'-kee
Irazú (Costa Rica, mt.)	ē-rä-sōō'	ee-rah-soo'
Irbid (Trans-Jordan)	ĭr'-bĕd	ihr'-bed
Irgun Zvai Leumi	ĭr'-gōōn tsvä-ē'	ihr'-goon tsvah-ee'
	lĕ-yōō-mē'	leh-yoo-mee'

The name, meaning *National Military Organization,* of Jewish under-
ground forces in Palestine.

Irig (Yugosl.)	ē'-rĭg	ee'-rig
Irio (It.)	ē'-ryô	ee'-ryo
Iriron (P.I.)	ē-rē'-rôn	ee-ree'-ron
Irkutsk (Rus.)	ĭr-kōōtsk'	ihr-kootsk'
Irodouer (Fr.)	ē-rô-dwĕ'	ee-ro-dweh'
Iron Gates (Yugosl.,	ī'-ərn gäts'	ai'-uhrn gayts'
Rum., gorge)		

Serb-Croat *Đerlap,* dyĕr'-läp [dyehr'-lahp]. Rumanian *Porţile de Fier,*
pôr-tsē'-lĕ dĕ fyĕr' [por-tsee'-leh deh fyehr']. German *Eisernes Tor,*
ī'-zər-nəs tōr' [ai'-zuhr-nuhs tohr']. Hungarian *Vaskapu,* vŏsh'-kŏ-pōō
[vosh'-ko-poo].

| Iroquois (Am. Indian) | ĭr'-ə-kwoi *or* -kwoiz | ir'-uh-kwoi *or* -kwoiz |

As a river and place name pronounced ĭr'-ə-kwoi' [ir'-uh-kwoi'].

Irrawaddy (Burma, riv.)   ĭr-ə-wŏd'-ĭ   ihr-uh-wod'-i
Irredentist   *Eng.* ĭr'-ə-dĕn'-tĭst   ir'-uh-den'-tist
  Member of a political party pledged to redeem *Italia irredenta*, q.v.
irrevocable   ĭ-rĕv'-ə-kə-bəl   i-rehv'-uh-kuh-buhl
  Avoid ĭr'-ə-vō'-kə-bəl [ihr'-uh-voh'-kuh-buhl].
Irtish (Rus., riv.)   ĭr-tĭsh'   ihr-tish'
Irún (Sp.)   ē-rōōn'   ee-roon'
Isaacs, George (Br. polit.) ī'-zəks *or* -zĭks   ai'-zuhks *or* -ziks
Isac (Fr., riv.)   ē-zäk'   ee-zahk'
Isar (Ger., riv.)   ē'-zär   ee'-zahr
Isarco (It.)   ē-sär'-kô   ee-sahr'-ko
Isarog (P.I., mt.)   ē-sä-rôg'   ee-sah-rog'
Isaszeg (Hung.)   ĭ'-shŏ-sĕg   i'-sho-seg
Ischia (It., isl.)   ē'-skyä   ee'-skyah
Isdud (Pal.)   ĭs-dōōd'   is-dood'
Ise (Jap.)   ē'-sĕ   ee'-seh
Isefjord (Den.)   ē'-sə-fyōr   ee'-suh-fyohr
Iseghem (Belg.)   ĭz'-ə-k(h)əm   iz'-uh-k(h)uhm
Isère (Fr., riv.)   ē-zĕr'   ee-zehr'
Iserlohn (Ger.)   ē-zər-lōn'   ee-zuhr-lohn'
Isern, Fernós A. (P.R. resident commissioner) See *Fernós Isern.*
Isernia (It.)   ē-sĕr'-nyä   ee-sehr'-nyah
Isfahan (Iran)   ĭs-fə-hän'   is-fuh-hahn'
Ishibashi, Tanzan (Jap.   ē-shē'-bä-shē,   ee-shee'-bah-shee,
  executive)   tän'-zän   tahn'-zahn
Ishikawa (Jap.)   ē-shē'-kä'-wä'   ee-shee'-kah'-wah'
Ishim (Rus.)   ĭsh-ēm'   ish-eem'
Ishui (Ch., Shantung)   ē-shwä   ee-shway
Isigny (Fr.)   ē-zē-nyē'   ee-zee-nyee'
Isili (Sard.)   ē'-sē-lē   ee'-see-lee
İskenderun (Turk.)   ĭs-kĕn'-də-rōōn   is-ken'-duh-roon
  Also spelled *Iskanderon.* English *Alexandretta*, q.v.
Isker *or* Iskr (Bulg., riv.) ĭs'-kər   is'-kuhr
Isle Au Haut (Me.)   īl' (*or* ēl') ə hō'   ail' (*or* eel') uh hoh'
  "Natives" use the first pronunciation; "summer complaints," the
  second.
Isleta (N.M., Tex.)   *Eng.* ĭs-lĕt'-ə   is-let'-uh
                          Sp. ēs-lĕ'-tä   ees-leh'-tah
Ismail (Rum. >Rus.)   ēs-mä-ēl'   ees-mah-eel'
  Russian *Izmail*, q.v.
Ismailia (Egypt)   ēs'-mä-ĭ-lē'-yä   ees'-mah-i-lee'-yah
Ismail Sidky Pasha   ĭs-mä'-ēl sĭd'-kē   is-mah'-eel sid'-kee
  (Egyptian polit.)   pä'-shä   pah'-shah

isola   ē'-zô-lä *or* ē'-sô-lä   ee'-zo-lah *or* ee'-so-la

An element, meaning *island*, in Italian place names. It may be necessary to look up the other part of the name.

Isola Bella (It.)   ē'-zô-lä bĕl'-lä   ee'-zo-lah bel'-lah

Isola Farnese (It.)   ē'-zô-lä fär-nĕ'-zĕ   ee'-zo-lah fahr-neh'-zeh

Isola Lunga *or* Isola   *It.* ē'-zô-lä lōōn'-gä   ee'-zo-lah loon'-gah
  Grossa (Yugosl.)   *or* grôs'-sä   *or* gros'-sah
  Serb-Croat *Dugi Otok,* q.v.

Isonzo (It., Yugosl., riv.)   ē-zôn'-tsô   ee-zon'-tso
  Serb-Croat *Soča,* q.v.

Ispahan (Iran)   See *Isfahan.*

Ispica (Sicily)   ēs'-pē-kä   ees'-pee-kah

Israel (Pal.)   ĭz'-rĭ-əl   iz'-ri-uhl

Issayeff, Feodor (Rus.)   ĭ-sä'-yĕf, fyô'-dŏr   i-sah'-yef, fyo'-dor

Issei   ēs'-sā   ees'-say

Japanese subjects who have come to the United States and are living here. They are not eligible for citizenship. See *Kibei* and *Nisei.*

Issel (Ger., Neth. riv.)   ĭ'-səl   ai'-suhl
  A variant of *IJssel,* q.v.

Issole (Fr., riv.)   ē-sôl'   ee-sol'

Issoudun (Fr.)   ē-sōō-dûN'   ee-soo-dœN'

issue   ĭsh'-yōō *or* ĭsh'-ōō   ish'-yoo *or* ish'-oo

There is no dictionary authority for the pronunciation of "s" instead of "sh" in this word. The pronunciation with "s" is probably not dialect but an overrefinement, technically called a hyperurbanism.

Is sur Tille (Fr.)   ēs sür tē'(y)   ees sür tee'(y)

Ist (Yugosl)   ēst'   eest'

İstanbul (Turk.)   *Eng.* ĭs'-tăn-bōōl'   is'-tan-bool'
    Turk. ĭs-täm'-bŏŏl   is-tahm'-bul

Formerly *Constantinople* and also *Byzantium.*

Istein (Ger.)   ē'-shtīn   ee'-shtain

isthmian   ĭs'-mĭ-ən *or* ĭsth'-   is'-mi-uhn *or* isth'-

isthmus   ĭs'-məs *or* ĭsth'-   is'-muhs *or* isth'-

Istok (Yugosl.)   ē'-stôk   ee'-stok

Istranca Dağları (Turk.,   ĭs-trän'-jä dä'-lä-rĭ   is-trahn'-jah dah'-
  mts.)   lah-ri

Istres (Fr.)   ēs'tr   ees'tr

Istria (It. > Yugosl.)   *Eng.* ĭs'-trĭ-ə   is'-tri-uh

Istros (Europ. riv.)   See *Danube.*

Italia irredenta   ē-tä'-lyä   ee-tah'-lyah eer-reh-
  (It. polit. slogan)   ēr-rĕ-dĕn'-tä   den'-tah

Itasca (Minn., lake)   ī-tăs'-kə   ai-tas'-kuh

Ithaca (Gr., isl.)   *Eng.* ĭth′-ə-kə   ith′-uh-kuh

    Greek *Ithake*, ē-thä′-kē [ee-thah′-kee], or *Theaki*, thē-ä′-kē [thee-ah′-kee].

Itri (It.)   ē′-trē   ee′-tree

I-tu (Ch., Hupeh)   ē-dōō   ee-doo

Itzehoe (Ger.)   ĭt′-sə-hō   it′-suh-hoh

Iuálit (P.I., riv.)   ē-wä′-lĭt   ee-wah′-lit

    Also called *Ewiig*, ĕ′-wē′-ēg′ [eh′-wee′-eeg′].

Ivailovgrad (Bulg.)   ē-vī′-lŏf-grät   ee-vai′-lof-graht

Ivanča, Mala (Yugosl.)   ē′-vän-chä, mä′-lä   ee′-vahn-chah, mah′-lah

Ivančica (Yugosl., mts.)   ē′-vän′-chĭ-tsä   ee′-vahn′-chi-tsah

Ivanec (Yugosl.)   ē′-vä-nĕts   ee′-vah-nets

Ivangorod (Pol.)   See *Dęblin.*

Ivanjica (Yugosl.)   ē′-vä-nyĭ-tsä   ee′-vah′-nyi-tsah

Ivankovci (Yugosl.)   ē′-vän′-kŏv-tsĭ   ee′-vahn′-kov-tsi

Ivanovka (Rus.)   ĭ-vä′-nŏf-kä   i-vah′-nof-kah

Ivanovo (Rus.)   ĭ-vä′-nŏ-vŏ   i-vah′-no-vo

Ivat (Rus.)   ĭ-vät′   i-vaht′

Ivatsevichi (Pol.)   See *Iwacewicze.*

Ivins, Wm. M. (Am.   ī′-vĭnz   ai′-vinz
curator)

Ivry (Fr.)   ē-vrē′   ee-vree′

Iwacewicze (Pol.)   ĭ-vä-tsĕ-vē′-chĕ   i-vah-tseh-vee′-cheh

    Russian *Ivatsevichi*, ĭ-vä-tsĕ′-vĭ-chĭ [i-vah-tseh′-vi-chi].

Iwasaki (Jap., zaibatsu)   ē-wä′-sä-kē   ee-wah′-sah-kee

Iwate (Jap.)   ē′-wä′-tĕ   ee′-wah′-teh

Iwō Jima (Jap., isl.)   *Eng.* ē′-wô jē′-mə   ee′-wo jee′-muh
                        Jap. ē-ô′ jē′-mä′   ee-o′ jee′-mah′

I-wu (Ch., Chekiang)   ē-wōō   ee-woo

    Also spelled *Yi-wu.*

Ixelles (Belg.)   See *Elsene.*

I-yang (Ch., Kiangsi)   ē-yäng   ee-yahng

    Also spelled *Yi-yang.*

Iž (Yugosl., isl.)   ēzh′   eezh′

    Italian *Eso*, q.v.

Izac, Ed. V.   ē′-zăk′   ee′-zak′
    (U.S. representative)

Izbor (Yugosl.)   ēz′-bôr   eez′-bor

Izgrev (Bulg. newspaper)   ēz′-grĕf   eez′-gref

    Organ of the *Zveno* party, zvĕ′-nŏ [zveh′-no].

Izhevsk (Rus.)   ĭ-zhĕfsk′   i-zhefsk′

Izmail (Rum. >Rus.)   ĭz-mä-ēl′   iz-mah-eel′

    Rumanian *Ismail*, q.v. Also called *Tuchkov*, tōōch-kôf′ [tooch-kof′].

İzmir (Turk.) ĭz'-mĭr iz'-mihr
 English *Smyrna*, q.v.
Iztaccihuatl (Mex. mt.) ēs-täk-sē'-wätl ees-tahk-see'-wahtl
 Also called *Ixtacihuatl,* ēs-tä-sē'-wätl [ees-tah-see'-wahtl]. In American
 usage the accent may be placed on the last syllable. See *Popocatepetl.*
Izu Shichitō (Jap., isls.) ē-zōō shē-chē'-tô ee-zoo shee-chee'-to
Izvestia ĭz-vĕs'-tĭ-yä iz-ves'-ti-yah
 (Rus. newspaper)
Izyaslav (Rus.) ĭz-yä-släf' iz-yah-slahf'
Izyum (Rus.) ĭ-zyōōm' i-zyoom'

Jaakkima (Fin. > Rus.) yäk'-kĭ-mä yahk'-ki-mah
 Russian spelling *Iakkima.*
Jablanac (Yugosl.) yä'-blä-näts yah'-blah-nahts
Jablanica (Yugosl., yä'-blä-nĭ-tsä yah'-blah-ni-tsah
 mts., riv.)
Jablanov Vrh yä'-blä-nôv vərk(h)' yah'-blah-nov
 (Yugosl., mt.)   vuhrk(h)'
Jablonec (Cz.) yä'-blô-nĕts yah'-blo-nets
Jablonica (Cz.) yä'-blô-nē'-tsä yah'-blo-nee'-tsah
Jabłonowo (Pol.) yä-blô-nô'-vô yah-blo-no'-vo
Jabolčište (Yugosl.) yä'-bôl'-chĭ-shtĕ yah'-bol'-chi-shteh
Jabukovac (Yugosl.) yä'-bōō-kô-väts yah'-boo-ko-vahts
Jabwot (Oc., Marshalls) jäb'-wôt jahb'-wot
Jaca (Sp.) hä'-kä hah'-kah
Jáchymov (Cz.) yä'-hĭ-môf yah'-hi-mof
 German *Joachimsthal,* q.v.
Jackson, Robert Houghwout (Am. justice) See *Houghwout.*
Jacmel (Haiti) zhäk-mĕl' zhahk-mehl'
Jacomy, Henri Paul zhä-kô-mē', zhəh-ko-mee',
 (Fr. general) äN-rē' pôl' ahN-ree' pol'
Jadar (Yugosl., riv.) yä'-där yah'-dahr
Jadovnik (Yugosl., mts.) yä'-dôv-nĭk yah'-dov-nik
Jadre (Yugosl., isl.) yä'-drĕ yah'-dreh
 Italian *Peschiera,* q.v.
Jaeckle, Edwin F. jā'-kəl jay'-kuhl
 (N.Y. polit.)
Jaeger (Ger. name) *Eng.* yā'-gər yay'-guhr
      Ger. yĕ'-gər yeh'-guhr
Jaehnsdorf (Ger.) yĕns'-dôrf yens'-dorf
Jaemtland (Sw.) yĕmt'-länd yemt'-lahnd
Jaén (Sp.) hä-ĕn' hah-en'
Jaenisjaervi (Fin., dist.) See *Jänisjärvi.*
Jaeren (Nor.) yăr'-ən yehr'-uhn

Jafar Pishevari (Iran. polit.)	jä′-fär pē′-shĕ-vä-rē′	jah′-fahr pee′-sheh-vah-ree′
Jaffa *or* Yafa (Pal.)	*Eng.* jăf′-ə	jaf′-uh
	Ar. yä′-fä	yah′-fah
Ancient *Joppa,* jŏp′-ə [jop′-uh].		
Jaffna (Ceylon)	jăf′-nə	jaf′-nuh
Jagdführer *or* -fuehrer	yäkt′-fü′-rər	yahkt′-fü′-ruhr
German *fighter-commander.*		
Jägerndorf (Cz.) See *Krnov.*		
Jagiełło (Pol. dynasty)	yä-gyĕl′-lô	yah-gyel′-lo
Jagodina (Yugosl.)	yä′-gô-dĭ-nä	yah′-go-di-nah
Jagodnja (Yugosl., mts.)	yä′-gôd-nyä	yah′-god-nyah
Jagst (Ger., riv.)	yäkst′	yahkst′
Jähnsdorf (Ger.)	yĕns′-dôrf	yens′-dorf
Jahnsfelde (Ger.)	yäns′-fĕl-də	yahns′-fel-duh
Jahverbhai Patel (Indian polit.) See *Patel.*		
Jaime (Sp. name)	hī′-mĕ	hai′-meh
The English form is *James.*		
Jaintia (India)	jīn′-tē-ä	jain′-tee-ah
Jaipur (India)	jĭ′-pŏōr′	jai′-pur′
Jajce (Yugosl.)	yī′-tsĕ	yai′-tseh
Jakobstad (Fin.)	*Sw.* yä′-kôp-städ′	yah′-kop-stahd′
Jakobstadt (Latvia)	*Ger.* yä′-kôp-shtät	yah′-kop-shtaht
Latvian *Jēkabpils,* q.v.		
Jala (P.I.)	hä′-lä	hah′-lah
Also called *Jalajala,* hä-lä-hä′-la [hah-lah-hah′-lah].		
Jalaigai (Oc., Guam)	hä-lī-gī′	hah-lai-gai′
Jalajala (P.I.) See *Jala.*		
Jalalabad (Afghan.)	jə-lä-lä-bäd′	juh-lah-lah-bahd′
Jalapa (Mex.)	hä-lä′-pä	hah-lah′-pah
Jalaun (India)	jə-loun′	juh-laun′
Jalisco (Mex.)	hä-lēs′-kô	hah-lees′-ko
Jallaucourt (Fr.)	zhä-lō-kōor′	zhah-loh-koor′
Jalpaiguri (India)	jŭl-pī-gōō′-rē	juhl-pai-goo′-ree
Jaluit (Oc., Marshalls)	jä′-lŏō-ĭt	jah′-lu-it
Jamaica (W.I.)	jə-mā′-kə	juh-may′-kuh
Jamaja (Est., isl.)	yä′-mä-yä	yah′-mah-yah
Jamal Effendi Husseini (Arab polit.)	jə-mäl′ ĕ-fĕn′-dē hŏō-sä′-nē	juh-mahl′ eh-fehn′-dee hu-say′-nee
Jamali, Fadhil (Iraqi diplomat)	jə-mä′-lĭ, fäd′l	juh-mah′-li, fahd′l
Jamali, Mohammed (Iraqi polit.)	jə-mä′-lē, mŏō-häm′-mĕd	juh-mah′-lee, mu-hahm′-med
Jamalpur (India)	jə-mäl′-pŏōr′	juh-mahl′-pur′

[236]

Jamil Pasha Tutunji   jə-mēl' pä'-shä   juh-meel' pah'-shah
  (Trans-Jordan diplomat)   tŏo-tōōn'-jē   tu-toon'-jee
Jamkhandi (India)   jŭm'-k(h)ŭn-dē   juhm'-k(h)uhn-dee
Jammerbugt (Den.)   yäm'-ər-bŏokt   yahm'-uhr-bukt
Jammu (India)   jŭm'-ōō   juhm'-oo
Jamna or Yamna   yäm'-nä'   yahm'-nah'
  (NEI, isl.)
Jamnagar (India)   jăm-nŭg'-ər   jam-nuhg'-uhr
  Also called Navanagar, q.v.
Jamshedpur (India)   jăm-shĕd-pŏor'   jam-shed-pur'
Jämtland (Sw.)   yĕmt'-länd   yemt'-lahnd
Jamul (Calif.)   hä-mōol'   hah-mool'
Jamuna (India, riv.)   jŭm'-ōō-nä   juhm'-oo-nah
Janakpur (Nepal)   jŭ'-nək-pŏor'   juh'-nuhk-pur'
Janaojanao (P.I.)   hä-nou-hä-nou'   hah-nau-hah-nau'
Janica (Gr.)   See Genitsa.
Janiculum (It., Rome)   Eng. jə-nĭk'-yə-lŭm   juh-nik'-yuh-luhm
  Italian Gianicolo, jä-nē'-kô-lô [jah-nee'-ko-lo].
Janina (Gr.)   See Ioánnina.
Jänisjärvi (Fin., dist.) yă'-nĭs-yăr-vē   ya'-nis-yehr-vee
  Russian Yanisyarvi, q.v.
Janjevo (Yugosl.)   yä'-nyĕ-vô   yah'-nyeh-vo
Janjira (India)   jŭn'-jē-rä   juhn'-jee-rah
Jankoi (Rus.)   jän-koi'   jahn-koi'
Jánosháza (Hung.)   yä'-nŏsh-hä-zŏ   yah'-nosh-hah-zo
Janov (Lith.)   Rus. yä'-nŏf   yah'-nof
  Lithuanian Jonava, q.v.
Janów Podlaski (Pol.)   yä'-nŏof pôd-lä'-skĭ yah'nuf pod-lah'-ski
  Russian Yanov, yä'-nŏf [yah'-nof].
Janssteen, Sint (Neth.)   yäns'-stän, sĭnt   yahns'-stayn, sint
Janum (Oc., Guam)   hä'-nōom   hah'-noom
Janzé (Fr.)   zhäN-zĕ'   zhahN-zeh'
Jao-ho (Manchu.)   jou-hŭ or rou-hŭ   jau-huh or rau-huh
Jao-p'ing (Ch.,   jou-pĭng or rou-pĭng jau-ping or rau-ping
  Kwangtung)
Japan   jə-păn'   juh-pan'
  Officially Nippon, q.v., or Nihon.
Japanese   jăp'-ə-nēz' or -nēs' jap'-uh-neez' or -nees'
In names like Japanese and Chinese, either "-nēz" or "-nēs" is correct.
Of the two, -nēz is preferred by most speakers and by most dictionaries.
Certainly no announcer who naturally says -nēz should affect -nēs as
an elegance. For information on this and 1,100 other debatable pro-
nunciations, see the famous Section 277 of Webster's (p. lix). There
is a similar section in the New Standard Dictionary.

Japara (NEI, Java) jä-pä'-rä jah-pah'-rah
 Dutch spelling Djapara.
Japen (NEI, Schouten yä'-pĕn yah'-pen
 isls.)
Japtan (Oc., Eniwetok) jäp'-tän jahp'-tahn
Jarabub (Libia) jä'-rä-bōōb' jah'-rah-boob'
Jarkent (Rus.) See *Dzharkent.*
Jarkovac (Yugosl.) yär'-kô-väts yahr'-ko-vahts
Jarman, Pete jär'-măn jahr'-man
 (U.S. representative)
Jaro (P.I.) hä'-rô hah'-ro
Jarocin (Pol.) yä-rô'-chĭn yah-ro'-chin
Jarosław (Pol.) yä-rô'-släf yah-ro'-slahf
 Russian *Yaroslav,* yä-rŏ-släf' [yah-ro-slahf']
järvi yăr'-vē yehr'-vee
 An element, meaning *lake,* in Finnish place names.
Jasenica (Yugosl., riv.) yä'-sĕ'-nĭ-tsä yah'-seh'-ni-tsah
Jasenovac (Yugosl.) yä'-sĕ'-nô-väts yah'-seh'-no-vahts
Jasiňa (Cz. >Rus.) yä'-sĭ-nyä yah'-si-nyah
 Russian spelling *Yasinya.* Hungarian *Kőrösmezŏ,* kû'-rûsh-mĕ'-zû
 [kœ'-rœsh-meh'-zœ].
Jasiołda (Pol. >Rus., riv.) See *Yaselda.*
Jask (Iran) jäsk' jahsk'
Jasło (Pol.) yä'-slô yah'-slo
Jassy (Rum.) *Ger.* yäs'-ē yahs'-ee
 Rumanian *Iaşi,* q.v.
Jastrebac (Yugosl.) yä'-strĕ-bäts yah'-streh-bahts
Jastrebarsko (Yugosl.) yä'-strĕ-bär-skô yah'-streh-bahr-sko
 Magyar *Jaska.*
Jastrow (Ger.) yäs'-trō yahs'-troh
Jászapáti (Hung.) yäs'-ŏ'-pä-tĭ yahs'-o'-pah-ti
Jászberény (Hung.) yäs'-bĕ'-rān(y) yahs'-beh'-rayn(y)
Jászkarajenő (Hung.) yäs'-kŏ-rŏ-yĕ'-nû yahs'-ko-ro-yeh'-nœ
jato *USN* jä'-tō jay'-toh
  USA jăt'-ō jat'-oh
An abbreviation of *jet assist take off,* a device for assisting a plane to
take off from a restricted area. The Navy prefers the first pronuncia-
tion, the Army the second or jĕt'-ō [jet'-oh].
Jauer (Ger. >? Pol.) you'-ər yau'-uhr
 Polish *Jawor,* q.v.
Jaulnay (Fr.) zhōl-nĕ' zhohl-neh'
Jaunjelgava (Latvia) youn'-yĕl'-gä-vä yaun'-yel'-gah-vah
 German *Friedrichstadt,* q.v.

Jaunlatgale (Latvia)	youn'-lät-gä-lĕ	yaun'-laht-gah-leh
Russian *Pytalovo*, q.v.		
Jaunpur (India)	joun'-poōr'	jaun'-poor'
Java (NEI)	jä'-və	jah'-vuh
Javits, Jacob K.	jăv'-ĭts	jav'-its
(U.S. representative)		
Javor (Yugosl., mts.)	yä'-vôr	yah'-vor
Javorište (Yugosl.)	yä'-vô'-rĭsh-tĕ	yah'-vo'-rish-teh
Javron (Fr.)	zhä-vrôN'	zhah-vroN'
Jawor (Ger. >? Pol.)	yä'-vôr	yah'-vor
German *Jauer*, q.v.		
Jaz (Yugosl.)	yäz'	yahz'
jebel *or* djebel	jĕb'-əl	jeb'-uhl

These are alternative spellings for an element, meaning *hill*, in Arabic place names. The latter is to be expected in French territory. It may be necessary to look up both.

Jebel Ishkel (Tun.)	jĕb'-əl ĭsh'-kĕl	jeb'-uhl ish'-kel
Jebel Kalakh (Egypt)	jĕb'-əl kă-lăk'	jeb'-uhl ka-lak'
Jebel Kharuf (Pal.)	jĕb'-əl k(h)ä-roōf'	jeb'-uhl k(h)ah-roof'
Jebel Khirag (Egypt)	jĕb'-əl kĭ-răg'	jeb'-uhl ki-rag'
Jedabia (Libya)	jĕ-dä'-byä	jeh-dah'-byah
Italian *Agedabia*, q.v.		
Jedda (Saudi Arabia)	jĕd'-də	jed'-duh
Also called *Jidda*, q.v.		
Jędrzejów (Pol.)	yăN-jĕ'-yoōf	yaN-jeh'-yuf
Jędrzychowski, Stephan	yăN-jĭ-hôf'-skĭ,	yaN-ji-hof'-ski,
(Pol. polit.)	stĕ'-fän	steh'-fahn
Jeetze (Ger., riv.)	yä'-tsə	yay'-tsuh
Jefna (Tun.)	jĕf'-nä	jef'-nah
Also spelled *Djefna*, q.v.		
Jehol (Manchu., prov.,	*Eng.* jə-hŏl'	juh-hol'
town)	*Ch.* rŭ-hŭ	ruh-huh

It seems sensible to Anglicize this Jesuit spelling of a Chinese name almost unpronounceable in English sounds. Our dictionaries usually give rĕ-hō or rä-hō; BBC recommends jə-hŏl'. The city is also called *Ch'êng-teh*, q.v.

Jēkabpils (Latvia)	yä'-käb-pēls *or* yă'-	yay'-kahb-peels *or*
German *Jakobstadt*, q.v.		ya'-
Jelenia Góra	yĕ-lĕ'-nyä goō'-rä	yeh-leh'-nyah
(Ger. >? Pol.)		gu'-rah
German *Hirschberg*, q.v.		
Jelgava (Latvia)	yĕl'-gä-vä	yel'-gah-vah
Russian *Mitava*, q.v. German *Mitau*, mē'-tou [mee'-tau].		
Jelica (Yugosl., mts.)	yĕ'-lĭ-tsä	yeh'-li-tsah

Jelova (Yugosl., mts.)	yĕ'-lô-vä	yeh'-lo-vah
Jemo (Oc., Marshalls)	jĕ'-mô	jeh'-mo
Jena (Ger.)	yā'-nä	yay'-nah
Jenin (Pal.)	jĕ-nēn'	jeh-neen'
Jenison, Edward H.	jĕn'-ĭ-sən	jen'-i-suhn
(U.S. representative)		
Jenne (It.)	yĕn'-nĕ	yen'-neh
Jensen, Ben F.	jĕn'-sən	jen'-suhn
(U.S. representative)		

Jerba (Tun., isl.) French *Djerba*, q.v.

Jeren (Nor.)	yăr'-ən	yehr'-uhn
Jerez (Sp.)	hĕ-rĕth' *or* -rĕs'	heh-reth' *or* -res'

Formerly *Xeres*, shĕ'-rĕs [sheh'-res].

Jericho (Pal.)	jĕr'-ə-kō	jehr'-uh-koh
Jerid, Chott el (Tun.)	jĕ-rēd', shôt' ĕl	jeh-reed', shot' el
Jerma (Balkan riv.)	*S.-C.* yĕr'-mä	yehr'-mah

Bulgarian spelling *Erma*.

Jerusalem (Pal.)	jə-rōō'-sə-lĕm	juh-roo'-suh-lehm

Arabic *El Quds esh Sherif*, ĕl kŏŏds' ĕsh shĕ-rēf' [el kuds' esh sheh-reef'].

Jesenice (Yugosl.)	yĕ'-sĕ'-nĭ-tsĕ	yeh'-seh'-ni-tseh
Jesselton (Borneo)	jĕs'-əl-tən	jes'-uhl-tuhn
jetsam	jĕt'-səm	jet'-suhm
Jette (Belg.)	zhĕt'	zhet'
Jezierna (Pol., riv.)	yĕ-zhĕr'-nä	yeh-zhehr'-nah

Russian *Eziorka*, yĕ-zĭ-ôr'-kä [yeh-zi-or'-kah].

jezioro (Pol.)	yĕ-zhô'-rô	yeh-zho'-ro

A common element, meaning *lake*, in Polish place names. Look up the other part of the name.

Jezreel (Pal.)	jĕz'-rĭ-ĕl' *or* jĕz'-rēl'	jez'-ri-ehl' *or* jez'-reel'

Arabic *Zir'in*, zĭr-ēn'[zihr-een']. See also *Esdraelon*.

Jhansi (India)	jän'-sē	jahn'-see
Jhelum (India, riv.)	jā'-ləm	jay'-luhm
Jibuti (Fr. Som.)	jē-bōō'-tē	jee-boo'-tee

Also spelled *Djibouti*. French jē-bōō-tē' [jee-boo-tee'].

Jidda (Saudi Arabia)	*Eng.* jĭd'-dä'	jid'-dah'
	Arabic jäd'-dä	jahd'-dah
	or jŏŏd'-dä	jud'-dah
jihad *or* jehad	jĭ-häd'	ji-hahd
Jihlava (Cz., riv., town)	yĕ'-k(h)lä-vä	yee'-k(h)lah-vah

German *Iglawa* (river), ĭk(h)'-lä-vä [ik(h)'-lah-vah]; *Iglau* (town), ĭk(h)'-lou [ik(h)'-lau].

Jijelli (Alg.)	jē-jĕ-lē'	jee-jeh-lee'

Also spelled *Djidjelli*.

Jijiga (Ethiopia)	jē'-jē-gä	jee'-jee-gah
Jiji Shimpō (Jap., Tokyo newspaper)	jē-jē' shēm'-pô	jee-jee' sheem'-po
Jijona (Sp.)	hē-hô'-nä	hee-ho'-nah
Jiloca (Sp., riv.)	hē-lô'-kä	hee-lo'-kah
jima	jē-mä	jee-mah

An element, meaning *island*, in Japanese place names. See *shima*.

Jimbolea (Rum.)	zhēm-bô'-lyä	zheem-bo'-lyah

Serb-Croat *Žombolj*, q.v. Hungarian *Zsombolya*, zhôm'-bô-yŏ [zhom'-bo-yo].

Jiménez (Sp. name)	*Am. Sp.* hē-mĕ'-nĕs	hee-meh'-nes
	Sp. hē-mĕ'-nĕth	hee-meh'-neth
Jiménez, Enrique A. (Pan. polit.)	hē-mĕ'-nĕs, ĕn-rē'-kĕ	hee-meh'-nes, en-ree'-keh
Jinamoc (P.I.)	hē-nä-môk'	hee-nah-mok'
Jinatuan (P.I.)	hē-nä-tōō'-än	hee-nah-too'-ahn
Jinnah, Mohamed Ali (Indian polit.)	jĭn'-ə, mō-hăm'-ĭd ä'-lē	jin'-uh, moh-ham'-id ah'-lee
Jinotepe (Nicar.)	hē-nô-tĕ'-pĕ	hee-no-teh'-peh
Jinsen (Korea)	jĭn'-sĕn'	jin'-sen'

Japanese name of *Chemulpo*, q.v.

jisr	jĭs'r	jis'r

An element, meaning *dyke*, in Arabic place names. In Egypt *gisr*, gĭs'r [gis'r].

Jisr Damiya (Pal.)	jĭs'r däm'-yĕ	jis'r dahm'-yeh
Also spelled *Damye*.		
Jisr Sheik(h) Hussein (Pal.)	jĭs'r shāk(h) hŏŏs-sān'	jis'r shayk(h) hus-sayn'
Jiu (Rum., riv.)	zhē'-ŏŏ	zhee'-u
Jiwani (India)	jə-wä'-nē	juh-wəh'-nee
Joachimsthal (Cz.)	yō'-ä-k(h)ĭms-täl'	yoh'-ah-k(h)ims-tahl'
Czech *Jáchymov*, q.v.		
Joad, C. E. M. (Br. philosopher)	jōd'	johd'

"Pronounced to rhyme with TOAD, as they never ceased to remind me at school." C. E. M. J.

João (Port.)	zhŏŏ-ouN'	zhu-auN'
	or zhô-ouN'	zho-auN'

To an American ear, this name (*John*) often sounds like one syllable, zhwouN' [zhwauN'], zhouN' [zhauN'], or even zhôN' [zhoN'].

João Pessoa (Brazil)	zhŏŏ-ouN' pĕ-sô'-ə	zhu-auN' peh-so'-uh

Also called, unofficially, *Paraíba* or *Parahiba*, q.v.

Joaquín (Sp.)	hwä-kēn'	hwah-keen'
Jodhpur (India)	jōd'-pŏŏr	johd'-pur

Jodl, Alfred (Ger. general)	yōd'l	yohd'l
Joelster (Nor.)	yûl'-stər	yœl'-stuhr
Joenkoeping (Sw.)	yûn'-chû-pĭng	yœn'-chœ-ping
Joensuu (Fin.)	yô'-ĕn'-sōō	yo'-en'-soo
Joeuf (Fr.)	zhû-üf'	zhœ-üf'
Jõgeva (Est.)	yû'-gĕ-vä	yuh'-geh-vah
Jogjakarta or Jogyakarta (NEI, Java)	*Eng.* jŏg'-yä-kär'-tä	jog'-yah-kahr'-tah
	Du. jôk(h)'-yä-kär'-tä	jok(h)'-yah-kahr'-tah
Johannesburg (U. of S. Afr.)	*Eng.* jō-hăn'-ĭs-bûrg	joh-han'-is-burg
	Du. yô-hän'-əs-bûrk(h)	yo-hahn'-'uhs-burk(h)
Jóhannesson, Ólafur (Icel. diplomat)	yō'-hän-nəs-sôn, ō'-lä-vər	yoh'-hahn-nuhs-son, oh'-lah-vuhr
Johore (Malaya)	jə-hôr'	juh-hor'
Jõhvi (Est.)	yûk(h)'-vĭ	yuhk(h)'-vi
Russian *Iewe*, q.v.		
Joigny (Fr.)	zhwä-nyē'	zhwah-nyee'
Joinville (Fr.)	zhwăN-vēl'	zhwaN-veel'
joki	yô'-kē	yo'-kee
An element, meaning *river* or *stream*, in Finnish place names.		
Jokonga (Rus.)	yŏ-kôn'-gä	yo-kon'-gah
Jokyakarta (NEI, Java) See *Jogjakarta*.		
Joliet (Ill.)	jō'-lĭ-ĕt'	joh'-li-et'
Joliot Curie, Frédéric (Fr. scientist)	zhô-lyō kü-rē', frĕ-dĕ-rēk'	zho-lyoh kü-ree', freh-deh-reek'
Joló (P.I.)	*Eng.* hō'-lō *native* hô-lô'	hoh'-loh ho-lo'
Jölster (Nor.)	yûl'-stər	yœl'-stuhr
Jomonjol (P.I.)	hô-môn-hôl'	ho-mon-hol'
Also called *Homonhón*, hô-môn-hôn' [ho-mon-hon'], and *Malhón*, mäl-hôn' [mahl-hon'].		
Jonava (Lith.)	yô'-nä-vä	yo'-nah-vah
Russian *Janov*, q.v.		
Jones, Arthur Creech (Brit. polit.) See *Creech Jones*.		
Joniškis (Lith.)	yô'-nĭsh-kĭs	yo'-nish-kis
Jonkman, Bartel J. (U.S. representative)	yŏnk'-män, bär-tĕl'	yonk'-mahn, bahr-tel'
Jönköping (Sw.)	yûn'-chû-pĭng	yœn'-chœ-ping
Jónsson, Finnur (Icel. diplomat)	yōns'-sôn, fĭn'-nər	yohns'-son, fin'-nuhr
Joplin (Mo.)	jŏp'-lĭn	jop'-lin
Joppa (Pal.) See *Jaffa*.		

Joralemon (Brooklyn street)	jə-räl'-ə-mən	juh-rahl'-uh-muhn
Jorje, San (Col., riv., gulf)	hôr'-hĕ, sän	hor'-heh, sahn
Jornal, O (Braz. newspaper)	zhôr-näl', o͝o	zhor-nahl', u
Jornal do Brasil (Braz. newspaper)	zhôr-näl' do͝o brä-zēl'	zhor-nahl' du brah-zeel'
Jornal do Comércio (Braz. newspaper)	zhôr-näl' do͝o kô-mĕr'-syo͝o	zhor-nahl' du ko-mehr'-syu
Joro (P.I.)	hô'-rô	ho'-ro
José (Sp. name)	Eng. hō-zā' Sp. hô-sĕ'	hoh-zay' ho-seh'

In Webster's Unabridged and in the College Standard dictionaries the common European variants of Christian names are listed with pronunciations under the English entry. For *José*, see *Joseph;* for *Jorge*, see *George;* and so on. This feature can be very helpful to radio speakers, not all of whom are aware of the extraordinary resources of our magnificent American dictionaries.

Josselin (Fr.)	zhôs-lăN'	zhos-laN'
Jostedal (Nor.)	yôs'-tə-däl	yos'-tuh-dahls-
Jostedals Breen (Nor.)	yôs'-tə-däls-brā'-ən	yos'-tuh-dahls-bray'-uhn
Jotunheimen (Nor., mt. region)	yō'-to͝on-hā-mən	yoh'-tun-hav-muhn
Jouhaux, Léon (Fr. polit.)	zho͞o-ō', lĕ-ôN'	zhoo-oh', leh-oN'
Joure (Neth.)	you'-rə	yau'-ruh
Jovac (Yugosl.)	yô'-väts	yo'-vahts
Jovanovac (Yugosl.)	yô'-vä'-nô-väts	yo'-vah'-no-vahts
Juárez, Benito (Mex. hero)	hwä'-rĕs, bĕ-nē'-tô	hwah'-res, beh-nee'-to
Juba (Sudan)	jo͞o'-bä	joo'-bah
Jubbulpore (India)	jŭb-əl-pôr'	juhb-uhl-por'
Juby (Rio de Oro, cape)	jo͞o'-bĭ	joo'-bi

Spanish *Cabo Yubi*, kä'-bô yo͞o'-bē [kah'-bo yoo'-bee].

Ju-ch'êng (Ch., Hunan)	Eng. jo͞o-chŭng Ch. ro͞o-chŭng	joo-chuhng roo-chuhng
Judah (Pal.)	jo͞o'-də	joo'-duh
Judea *or* Judaea (Pal.)	jo͞o-dē'-ə	joo-dee'-uh
Juelich (Ger.)	yü'-lĭk(h)	yü'-lik(h)
Juengersdorf (Ger.)	yüng'-ərs-dôrf	yüng'-uhrs-dorf
Jueterbog (Ger.)	yü'-tər-bôk(h)	yü'-tuhr-bok(h)
Jugenheim (Ger.)	yo͞o'-gən-hīm	yoo'-guhn-haim

[243]

Juhor (Yugosl., mts.)	yōō′-hôr	yoo′-hor
Jui-an (Ch., Chekiang)	rwā-än	rway-ahn
Jui-ch'ang (Ch., Kiangsi)	rwā-chäng	rway-chahng
Jui-chin (Ch., Kiangsi)	rwā-jĭn	rway-jin
Jui-hung (Ch., Kiangsi)	rwā-hŏŏng	rway-hung
Juilliard (Foundation	jōōl′-ĭ-ärd	jool′-i-ahrd
and School of Music)	*or* jōōl′-yärd	jool′-yahrd
Juin, Alphonse (Fr. general)	zhwăN′, äl-fôNs′	zhwaN′, ahl-foNs′
Juine (Fr.)	zhwēn′	zhween′
Julfa (Iran)	jŏŏl′-fä	jul′-fah
Julianehaap (Greenl.)	yōō-lĭ-ä′-nə-hôp′	yoo-li-ah′-nuh-hop′
Jülich (Ger.)	yü′-lĭk(h)	yü′-lik(h)
Jullundur (India)	jŭl′-ən-dər	juhl′-uhn-duhr
Jumet (Belg.)	zhü-mĕ′	zhü-meh′
Jumna (India)	jŭm′-nə	juhm′-nuh
Juneau (Alaska)	jōō′-nō	joo′-noh
Jüngersdorf (Ger.)	yüng′-ərs-dôrf	yüng′-uhrs-dorf
Jungfernsee (Ger.)	yŏŏng′-fĕrn-zā	yung′-fehrn-zay
Also called *Kettwitz*, kĕt′-vĭts [ket′-vits].		
Junik (Yugosl.)	yōō′-nĭk	yoo′-nik
Junker (Ger. aristocrat)	*Ger.* yŏŏnk′-ər	yunk′-uhr
	Eng. jŭnk′-ər	juhnk′-uhr
Junkovci (Yugosl.)	yōōn′-kôv-tsĭ	yoon′-kov-tsi
junta ("council" or	*Eng.* jŭn′-tə	jun′-tuh
"clique")	*Sp.* hōōn′-tä	hoon′-tah
Also in English *junto*, jŭn′-tō [juhn′-toh].		
Jupilles (Fr.)	zhü-pē′(y)	zhü-pee′(y)
Jurjev *or* Yurev (Est.)	*Rus.* yōōr′-yĕf	yoor′-yef
Estonian *Tartu*, q.v. German *Dorpat*, q.v.		
Jurukluk (Yugosl.)	yōō′-rōōk-lōōk	yoo′-rook-look
Jüterbog (Ger.)	yü′-tər-bôk(h)	yü′-tuhr-bok(h)
Jutfaas (Neth.)	yût′-fäs	yœt′-fahs
Jutland (Den.)	*Eng.* jŭt′-lənd	juht′-luhnd
Danish *Jylland*, yül′-län [yül′-lahn].		
Juvigny (Fr.)	zhü-vē-nyē′	zhü-vee-nyee′
Južna Morava (Yugosl., riv.)	yōōzh′-nä mô′-rä-vä	yoozh′-nah mo′-rah-vah
Jylland (Den.) See *Jutland*.		
Jyväskylä (Fin.)	yü′-văs-kü-lă	yü′-vas-kü-la

k and *c* are interchangeable in Greek and other languages. It may be necessary to look up both spellings. In Greek *k* is officially preferred.

Kaa (Nor., fjord)	kä′	kah′

Kaala Djerda (Tun.) kä'-ä-lä jĕr'-dä kah'-ah-lah jehr'-dah

Kaap de Goede Hoop käp də k(h)ōō'-də kahp duh k(h)oo'-
(NEI, New Guinea) hōp' duh hohp'

English *Cape of Good Hope*. Native *Tanjong Jamoersba*, tän'-jông yä-mōōrs'-bä [tahn'-jong yah-moors'-bah]. Also called *Sansapor*, q.v.

Kaballa (Gr.) See *Kavalla*.

Kabanskoe (Rus.) kä-bän'-skŏ-yĕ kah-bahn'-sko-yeh

Kabardinka (Rus.) kä-bär-dēn'-kä kah-bahr-deen'-kah

Kabaw (Burma, valley) kə-bô' kuh-baw'

kabo (Gr.) kä'-vô kah'-vo

An element, meaning *cape*, in Greek place names. Look up the other part of the name.

Kabugao (P.I.) kä-bōō'-gou kah-boo'-gau

Kabuki kä-bōō'-kē' kah-boo'-kee'

A type of Japanese drama.

Kabul (Afghan.) kä'-bŏŏl kah'-bul

Kabungkut (P.I.) kä-bōōng-kōōt' kah-boong-koot'

Kabyu (Burma) kə-byōō' kuh-byoo'

Kać (Yugosl.) käch' kahch'

Kačanik (Yugosl.) kä'-chä-nĭk kah'-chah-nik

Kačer (Yugosl., riv.) kä'-chĕr kah'-chehr

Kachalino (Rus.) kä-chä'-lĭ-nŏ kah-chah'-li-no

Kachanovka (Rus.) kä-chä-nŏf'-kä kah-chah-nof'-kah

Kachin (Burma, hills) kə-chĭn' kuh-chin'

Kack Mały (Pol.) kätsk' mä'-lĭ kahtsk' mah'-li

Kaczynski, Zygmunt kä-chĭn'-skĭ, kah-chin'-ski,
(Pol. polit.) zĭg'-mŏŏnt zig'-munt

Kadijica (Balkan mt.) *S.-C.* kä'-dĭ-yĭ-tsä kah'-di-yi-tsah

Kadina (Yugosl., riv.) kä'-dĭ-nä kah'-di-nah

Kadnikov (Rus.) käd'-nĭ-kŏf kahd'-ni-kof

Kadovar (NEI, Schouten) kä-dô-vär' kah-do-vahr'

Kaeckenbeeck, kä'-kən-bāk kah'-kuhn-bayk
M. G. (Belg. diplomat)

Kaekisalmi (Fin. > Rus.) See *Käkisalmi*.

Kagalnitskaya (Rus.) kä-gäl'(y)-nĭt-skä-yä kah-gahl'(y)-nit-
skah-yah

Kaganovich, Lazar M. kä-gä-nô'-vĭch, kah-gah-no'-vich,
(Rus. polit.) lä'-zär lah'-zahr

Kagawa (Jap.) kä-gä'-wä' kah-gah'-wah'

Kagawa, Toyohiko (Jap. kä'-gä-wä, tô-yô'- kah'-gah-wah, to-yo'-
leader) hē-kô hee-ko

Kaggi (Sicily) käd'-jē kahd'-jee

Kagoshima (Jap.) kä-gô'-shē'-mä' kah-go'-shee'-mah'

Kagul (Rum. > Rus.) kä-gōōl' kah-gool'
Rumanian *Cahul*, q.v.

Kahili (Oc., Bougainville)	kä-hē'-lĭ	kah-hee'-li
Kahoolawe (Hawaii)	kä-hōō-lä'-wĕ	kah-hoo-lah'-weh
Kahuku (Hawaii)	kä-hōō'-kōō	kah-hoo'-koo
Kahului (Hawaii)	kä-hōō-lōō'-ē	kah-hoo-loo'-ee
kai	kī	kai

An element, meaning *sea*, in Japanese place names.

Kai (NEI)	kī'	kai'
K'ai-fêng (Ch., Honan)	kī-fŭng	kai-fuhng
kaikyō	kī-kyô	kai-kyo

An element, meaning *strait*, in Japanese place names.

K'ai-lu (Manchu.)	kī-lōō	kai-loo
Kaimana (NEI, New Guinea)	kī-mä'-nä	kai-mah'-nah
Kairiru (N.E., New Guinea)	kī-rē-rōō'	kai-ree-roo'
Kairouan (Tun.) Arabic *Qairwan*, q.v.	*Fr.* kĕr-wäN'	kehr-wahN'
Kaiserslautern (Ger.)	kī'-zərs-lou'-tərn	kai'-zuhrs-lau'-tuhrn
Kaišiadorys (Lith.) Russian *Koshedary*, q.v.	kī-shyä-dô-rēs'	kai-shyah-do-rees'
K'ai-yüan (Ch., Manchu.)	kī-yüän	kai-yü-ahn
Kajaani (Fin.)	kä'-yä-nē	kah'-yah-nee
Kajali (Yugosl.)	kä'-yä-lĭ	kah'-yah-li
Kajmakčalan (Balkan mt.)	kī'-mäk-chä'-län	kai'-mahk-chah'-lahn
Kakavia (Dodec., Rh.)	kä-kä-vyä'	kah-kah-vyah'
Kake Skala (Crete, coast)	kä-kē' skä'-lä	kah-kee' skah'-lah
Kakhovka (Rus.)	kä-hôf'-kä	kah-hof'-kah
Käkisalmi (Fin. >Rus.)	kă'-kē-säl-mē	ka'-kee-sahl-mee

Swedish *Kexholm*, chĕks'-hôlm' [cheks'-holm']. Russian *Keksgolm*, kĕks'-gŏl(y)m [keks'-gol(y)m].

Kalabak (Yugosl., Alb., mt.)	*S.-C.* kä'-lä-bäk	kah'-lah-bahk
Kalach (Rus.)	kä-läch'	kah-lahch'
Kaladan (Burma, riv.)	kə-lə-dăn' *or* kə-lə-dŭn'	kuh-luh-dan' kuh-luh-duhn'
Kalahari Desert (S. Afr.)	kä-lä-hä'-rē	kah-lah-hah'-ree
Kalamai (Gr.)	kä-lä'-mĕ	kah-lah'-meh

Also called *Kalamata*, kä-lä-mä'-tä [kah-lah-mah'-tah].

Kalamaki (Gr.)	kä-lä-mä'-kē	kah-lah-mah'-kee
Kalambaka (Gr.)	kä-lä-bä'-kä	kah-lah-bah'-kah
Kalamos (Gr., isl.)	kä'-lä-mô(s)	kah'-lah-mo(s)

Kalarash (Rum. >Rus.)   kä-lä-räsh'   kah-lah-rahsh'
   Rumanian *Călăraşi*, kə-lə-räsh' [kuh-luh-rahsh'].
Kalat *or* Khelat (Baluch.)   kə-lät'   kuh-laht'
Kalathos (Dodec., Rh.)   kä'-lä-thôs   kah'-lah-thos
Kalavryta (Gr.)   kä-lä'-vrē-tä   kah-lah'-vree-tah
Kalaw (Burma)   kə-lô'   kuh-law'
Kale (Burma, valley)   kə-lä'   kuh-lay'
Kalemyo (Burma)   kə-lä'-myō   kuh-lay'-myoh
Kalenborn (Ger.)   kä'-lən-bôrn   kah'-luhn-born
Kalenić (Yugosl.)   kä'-lĕ-nĭch   kah'-leh-nich
Kaleniéska (Yugosl., riv.)   kä'-lĕ'-nĭch-skä   kah'-leh'-nich-skah
Kalgachinskaya (Rus.)   käl-gä'-chĭn-skä-yä   kahl-gah'-chin-skah-yah
Kalgan (Ch., Chahar)   käl-gän   kahl-gahn
Kalgoorlie (Austral.)   kăl-gōōr'-lĭ   kal-goor'-li
Kalidjati (NEI, Java)   kä-lē-jä'-tē   kah-lee-jah'-tee
Kalinga (P.I.)   kä-lĭng'-gä   kah-ling'-gah
Kalinin, Mikhail   kä-lē'-nĭn, mĭ-hä-ēl'   kah-lee'-nin,
   (Rus. polit.)   mi-hah-eel'
Kaliningrad (Ger. >Rus.)   kä-lē'-nĭn-grät   kah-lee'-nin-graht
   German *Koenigsberg*, q.v.
Kalinkovichi (Rus.)   kä-lĭn-kô'-vĭ-chĭ   kah-lin-ko'-vi-chi
Kalispell (Mont.)   kăl'-ə-spĕl'   kal'-uh-spel'
Kalisz (Pol.)   kä'-lĭsh   kah'-lish
   Russian spelling *Kalish*.
Kalitva (Rus., riv.)   kä-lĭt-vä'   kah-lit-vah'
Kalitvenskaya (Rus.)   kä-lēt'-vĕn-skä-yä   kah-leet'-ven-skah-yah
Kalkuny (Latvia)   *Rus.* käl-kōō'-nĭ   kahl-koo'-ni
   Latvian *Grīva*, q.v.
Kallmet (Alb.)   käl'-mĕt   kahl'-met
Kallmeti (Alb.)   See *Kallmet*.
Kallone (Gr., Lesbos)   kä-lô-nē'   kah-lo-nee'
Kalmius (Rus., riv.)   käl'(y)-mē-ōōs   kahl'(y)-mee-oos
Kalmuck (Rus.)   kăl'-mŭk   kal'-muhk
Kalocsa (Hung.)   kŏ'-lô-chŏ   ko'-lo-cho
Kalogeri (Crete)   kä-lô-yĕ'-rē   kah-lo-yeh'-ree
Kalpaki (Gr.)   käl-pä'-kē   kahl-pah'-kee
Kaluga (Rus.)   kä-lōō'-gä   kah-loo'-gah
Kalundborg (Den.)   kä-lŏŏn-bôr'   kah-lun-bor'
Kałuszyn (Pol.)   kä-lōō'-shĭn   kah-lu'-shin
   Russian spelling *Kalushin*.
Kalvarija (Lith.)   *Lith.* käl-vä-rē'-yä   kahl-vah-ree'-yah
                      Rus. käl-vä'-rĭ-yä   kahl-vah'-ri-yah

Kalyazin (Rus.)	kä-lyä′-zĭn	kah-lyah′-zin
Kalymnos (Dodec.)	kä′-lēm-nô(s)	kah′-leem-no(s)

Italian *Calino,* kä-lē′-nô [kah-lee′-no]. The town is called *Kalymnos* or *Pothea,* pô′-thĕ-ä [po′-theh-ah].

Kalyvas, N. (Gr. polit.)	kä-lē′-väs	kah-lee′-vahs
Kamaing (Burma)	kə-mĭng′	kuh-maing′
Kamaishi (Jap.)	kä-mä′-ē-shē	kah-mah′-ee-shee

Near by is a famous iron mine.

Kamakura (Jap.)	kä-mä′-kōō′-rä′	kah-mah′-koo′-rah′

Kamâl Atatürk See *Kemal Atatürk.*

Kamara (Crete)	kä-mä′-rä	kah-mah′-rah
Kämärä (Fin.)	kä′-mä-rä	ka′-ma-ra
Kamauk (Burma)	kə-mouk′	kuh-mauk′
Kambata (Abys.)	käm-bä′-tä	kahm-bah′-tah
Kambeira (Oc.)	käm-bä′-rä	kahm-bay′-rah
Kambotorosh (Oc., New Ireland)	käm-bô-tô-rôsh′	kahm-bo-to-rosh′
Kamchatka (Rus.)	*Eng.* käm-chăt′-kə	kam-chat′-kuh
	Rus. käm-chät′-kä	kahm-chaht′-kah
Kamchia (Bulg., riv.)	käm′-chĭ-yä	kahm′-chi-yah
Kamen (Rus.)	kä′-mĕn(y)	kah′-men(y)
Kamen Kashirsky (Pol. >Rus.)	kä′-mĕn(y) kä-shĭr′-skĭ	kah′-men(y) kah-shihr′-ski

Polish *Kamień Koszyrski,* q.v.

Kamendol (Yugosl.)	kä′-mĕn-dôl′	kah′-men-dol′
Kamenets Podolsk (Rus.)	kä-mĕ-nĕts′ pŏ-dôlsk′	kah-meh-nets′ po-dolsk′
Kamenica (Yugosl.)	kä′-mĕ-nĭ-tsä	kah′-meh-ni-tsah
Kamennaya (Pol., riv.)	See *Kamienna.*	
Kamensk (Rus.)	kä′-mĕnsk	kah′-mensk
Kamieniogóra (Ger. > ?Pol.)	kä-myĕ-nyô-gŏŏ′-rä	kah-myeh-nyo-gu′-rah

German *Landeshut,* q.v.

Kamień Koszyrski (Pol. >Rus.)	kä′-myĕn(y) kô-shĭr′-skĭ	kah′-myen(y) ko-shihr′-ski

Russian *Kamen Kashirski,* kä′-mĕn(y) kä-shĭr′-skĭ [kah′-men(y) kah-shihr′-ski].

Kamienna (Pol., riv.)	kä-myĕn′-nä	kah-myen′-nah

Russian *Kamennaya,* kä′-mĕn-nä-yä [kah′-men-nah-yah].

Kamikaze	*Eng.* kä′-mē-kä′-zē	kah′-mee-kah′-zee
	Jap. kä-mē′-kä-zĕ	kah-mee′-kah-zeh

Japanese suicide plane, literally *divine wind.*

Kampanou (Crete)	kä(m)-bä-nōō′	kah(m)-bah-noo′
Kampen (Neth.)	käm′-pən	kahm′-puhn

[248]

Kamperduin (Neth.)	käm'-pər-dûĭn'	kahm'-puhr-dœin'
Kampoengbaroe (NEI, Celebes) Also called *Tolitoli*, q.v.	käm-pōōng-bä'-rōō	kahm-poong-bah'-roo
Kampot (Indo-Ch.)	käm-pôt'	kahm-pot'
Kamptee (India)	kämp-tē'	kahmp-tee'
Kamrang (Indo-Ch., bay)	See *Camranh*.	
Kamyshevatsk (Rus.)	kä-mĭ-shĕ-vätsk'	kah-mi-sheh-vahtsk'
Kamyshin (Rus.)	kä-mwē'-shĭn	kah-mwee'-shin
Kamyshly (Rus.)	kä-mwēsh'-lĭ	kah-mweesh'-li
Kanagawa (Jap.)	kä-nä'-gä-wä	kah-nah'-gah-wah
Kanaka (Oc. people)	kə-năk'-ə or kăn'-ə-kə	kuh-nak'-uh kan'-uh-kuh
Kanali (Gr.)	kä-nä'-lē	kah-nah'-lee
Kanamitsu, Tsuneo (Jap. polit.)	kä-nä'-mē-tsōō or kä-nä'-mēts, tsōō-nĕ'-ô'	kah-nah'-mee-tsoo or kah-nah'-meets, tsoo-neh'-o'
Kanamori, Eigoro (Jap. educator)	kä-nä'-mô-rē, ä'-gô-rô	kah-nah'-mo-ree, ay'-go-ro
Kanaung (Burma)	kăn-oung'	kan-aung'
Kanawha (U.S., riv.)	kə-nô'-wə	kuh-naw'-wuh
Kanazawa (Jap.)	kä-nä'-zä-wä	kah-nah'-zah-wah
Kanbalu (Burma)	kăn-bə-lōō'	kan-buh-loo'
Kanburi (Thai)	kän'-bōō-rē'	kahn'-bu-ree'
Kan Chiang *or* River (Ch., Kiangsi)	gän	gahn
Kan-chow (Ch., Kiangsi)	gän-jŏ	gahn-joh
Kandahar (Afghan.)	kən-də-här'	kuhn-duh-hahr'
Kandalaksha (Rus.)	kän-dä-läk'-shä	kahn-dah-lahk'-shah
Kandalakskaya Guba (Rus.)	kän-dä-läk'-skä-yä gōō-bä'	kahn-dah-lahk'-skah-yah goo-bah'
Kandy (Ceylon)	kăn'-dĭ	kan'-di
Kanelopoulos, Panagiotes (Gr. polit.)	kä-nĕ-lô'-pōō-lôs, pä-nä-yô'-tēs	kah-neh-lo'-poo-los, pah-nah-yo'-tees
Kangaung (Burma)	kăn-goung'	kan-gaung'
Kangean (NEI)	käng'-ĕ-än	kahng'-eh-ahn
K'ang Tê (former Chinese Emperor) See *P'u-yi*.		
K'ang-ting (Ch., Sikang)	käng-dĭng	kahng-ding
Kan-hsien (Ch., Kiangsi)	gän-shyĕn	gahn-shyen
Kaniet (Oc., Bismarck arch.)	kä-nē'-ĕt	kah-nee'-et
Kanina (Alb.) See *Kaninë*.		
Kaninë (Alb.) Italian *Crionero*, q.v.	kä-nē'-nə	kah-nee'-nuh

Kanjiža, Stara (Yugosl.)	kä'-nyĭ-zhä, stä'-rä	kah'-nyi-zhah, stah'-rah
Kankakee (Ill.)	kăng'-kə-kē'	kang'-kuh-kee'
Kankar (Yugosl.) Italian *Gangaro*, q.v.	kän'-kär	kahn'-kahr
Kan-kō (Korea)	käng-kô	kahng-ko
Kano (Nigeria)	kä'-nō	kah'-noh
Kansk (Rus.)	känsk'	kahnsk'
Kan-su (Ch., prov.)	*Eng.* kăn-sōō *Ch.* gän-sōō	kan-soo gahn-soo
Kantang (Thai)	kän'-täng'	kahn'-tahng'
Kantanos (Crete)	kän'-dä-nôs	kahn'-dah-nos
Kantemirovka (Rus.)	kän-tĕ-mē'-rŏf-kä	kahn-teh-mee'-rof-kah
Kantō (Jap.)	kän'-tô	kahn'-to
Kao-an (Ch., Kiangsi)	gou-än	gau-ahn
Kaoe (NEI, bay)	kou'	kau'
Kao-lan (Ch., Kangsu) Also called *Lan-chow*, q.v.	gou-län	gau-lahn
kaoliang (Chinese millet)	*Eng.* kou'-lĭ-ăng' *Ch.* gou-lyäng	kau'-li-ang' gau-lyahng
Kao-p'ing (Ch., Shansi)	gou-pĭng	gau-ping
Kao-t'ai (Ch., Kansu)	gou-tī	gau-tai
Kapela (Gr., Yugosl.)	kä-pĕ'-lä	kah-peh'-lah
Kapelle (Neth.) Also spelled *Capelle*, q.v.	kä-pĕl'-ə	kah-pel'-uh
Kapherevs (Gr., Euboea, point)	kä-fē-rĕfs'	kah-fee-refs'
Commonly called *Kabontoros*, kä-vô-dô'-rôs [kah-vo-do'-ros].		
Kapingamarangi (Oc., Carolines)	kä-pĭng'-ä-mä-räng'-ē	kah-ping'-ah-mah-rahng'-ee
Kapitza, Peter L. (Rus. scientist)	kä'-pĭ-tsä	kah'-pi-tsah
Kápolna (Hung.)	kä'-pôl-nŏ	kah'-pol-no
Kapos (Hung., riv.)	kŏ'-pôsh	ko'-posh
Kaposmérő (Hung.)	kŏ'-pôsh-mä'-rû	ko'-posh-may'-rœ
Kaposmezŏ (Hung.)	kŏ'-pôsh-mĕ'-zû	ko'-posh-meh'-zœ
Kaposvár (Hung.)	kŏ'-pôsh-vär	ko'-posh-vahr
Kaprije (Yugosl.) Italian *Capri*, q.v.	kä'-prĭ-yĕ	kah'-pri-yeh
Kapsalion (Gr.) See *Kythera*.		
Karabekir, Kâzim (Turk. polit.)	kä-rä'-bĕ-kĭr, kyä-zĭm'	kah-rah'-beh-kihr, kyah-zim'

Karaburun (Alb., pen.)   kä-rä-bōō'-rōōn   kah-rah-boo'-roon
  English *Acroceraunia*, q.v., and (the point) Cape *Glossa*, q.v.
Karaburuni (Alb., pen.)   See *Karaburun.*
Karachev (Rus.)   kä-rä-chôf'   kah-rah-chof'
Karachi (India)   kə-rä'-chē   kuh-rah'-chee
Karadeniz Boğazı   kä-rä'-dĕ-nēz   kah-rah'-deh-neez
  (Turk., strait)   bô-ä'-zĭ   bo-ah'-zi
  English Bosporus, q.v.
Karadžica planina   kä'-rä'-jĭ-tsä   kah'-rah'-ji-tsah
  (Yugosl., mts.)   plä'-nē'-nä   plah'-nee'-nah
Karafuto (Jap. > Rus.)   kä-rä'-fōō-tô *or* kah-rah'-foo-to
                          kä-räf'-tô   kah-rahf'-to
  The southern half of *Sakhalin Island.*
Karagach Limanı (Gr., bay) See *Lagos.*
Karahisar (Turk.)   kä'-rä'-hĭ-sär   kah'-rah'-hi-sahr
  Also called *Afyon Karahisar*, q.v.
Karaj (Iran)   kä-rĕj'   ka-rej'
Karakoram (India, mts.)   kä-rä-kō'-rəm   kah-rah-koh'-ruhm
Karantaon (Gr., mt.)   kä-rän-dä'-ô(n)   kah-rahn-dah'-o(n)
Karapanayotis, Byron (Gr. leader)   See *Carapanayotis.*
Karaš (Yugosl., riv.)   kä'-räsh   kah'-rahsh
Kara Sou (Balkan riv.)   See *Struma.*
Kara Ular (Yugosl.)   kä'-rä ōō'-lär   kah'-rah oo'-lahr
Karavasta (Alb., lake)   kä-rä-vä'-stä   kah-rah-vah'-stah
  Also called *Knetë e Karavastas.*
Karavoutas (Crete, point) kä-rä-vōō'-täs   kah-rah-voo'-tahs
  Also called *Khersonesos*, hĕr-sô'-nē-sôs [hehr-so'-nee-sos].
  See also *Chersonese.*
Karcag (Hung.)   kŏr'-tsŏg   kor'-tsog
Karczew (Pol.)   kär'-chĕf   kahr'-chef
  Russian spelling *Karchev.*
Kardamyli (Gr.)   kär-dä-mē'-lē   kahr-dah-mee'-lee
Kardelj, Edward   kär'-dĕl'(y), ĕd'-värt kahr'-del'(y), ed'-
  (Yugosl. polit.)   vahrt
Karditsa (Gr.)   kär-dē'-tsä   kahr-dee'-tsah
Kärdla (Est.)   kärd'-lä   kehrd'-lah
Karelia (Rus.)   *Eng.* kə-rēl'-yə kuh-reel'-yuh
                          Rus. kä-rĕ'-lĭ-yä kah-reh'-li-yah
  Finnish *Karjala*, q.v.
Karelian Isthmus (Rus.)   *Eng.* kə-rēl'-yən kuh-reel'-yuhn
Karelskaya (Rus.)   kä-rĕl'(y)-skä-yä kah-rel'(y)-skah-yah
Kariango (Borneo)   kä-rē-äng'-ō   kah-ree-ahng'-oh
Karikal (Fr. India)   kä-rē-käl'   kah-ree-kahl'
Karimata (NEI)   kä-rĭ-mä'-tä   kah-ri-mah'-tah

Karin, Abdul (Indo.   kä'-rĭn, äb'-dŏŏl   kah'-rin, ahb'-dool
  polit.)

Karjala (Fin. > Rus.)   kär'-yä-lä   kahr'-yah-lah
  English and Russian *Karelia*, q.v.

Karkar (N.E. New   kär'-kär   kahr'-kahr
  Guinea, isl.)

Karkinit (Rus., bay)   kär-kĭ-nēt'   kahr-ki-neet'

Karkinitski Zaliv (Rus.)   kär-kĭ-nēt'-skĭ   kahr-ki-neet'-ski
                       zä-lēf'   zah-leef'

Karla (Gr., lake)   See *Boibeis*.

Karlobag (Yugosl.)   kär'-lô-bäg   kahr'-lo-bahg

Karloe *or* Karlö (Fin., isl.)   See *Hailuoto*.

Karlovac (Yugosl.)   kär'-lô-väts   kahr'-lo-vahts

Karlovci Sremski   kär'-lôv-tsĭ srĕm'-skĭ   kahr'-lov-tsi
  (Yugosl.)   srem'-ski

Karlovka (Rus.)   kär'-lôf-kä   kahr'-lof-kah

Karlovo (Bulg.)   kär'-lô-vŏ   kahr'-lo-vo

Karlovo Selo (Yugosl.)   kär'-lô-vô sĕ'-lô   kahr'-lo-vo seh'-lo

Karlovy Vary (Cz.)   See *Carlsbad*.

Karlsbad (Cz.)   See *Carlsbad*.

Karlsruhe (Ger.)   *Eng.* kärlz'-rōō-ə   kahrlz'-roo-uh
                 Ger. kärls'-rōō-ə   kahrls'-roo-uh

Karmoey *or* Karmöy   kär'-mûĭ   kahr'-mœi
  (Nor.)

Karnabat (Bulg.)   kär'-nä-bät   kahr'-nah-baht

Karobka, Y. L. (Rus.   kä-rôb'-kä   kah-rob'-kah
  polit.)

Károlyi, Michael,   kä'-rô-lyĭ   kah'-ro-lyi
  Count (Hung. polit.)   *or* kä'-rô-yĭ   kah'-ro-yi

Karora (Sudan)   kä-rô'-rä   kah-ro'-rah

Karouva (Crete)   kä-rōō'-vä   kah-roo'-vah

Karpathos (Dodec.)   kär'-pä-thô(s)   kahr'-pah-tho(s)
  Also called *Skarpatho*, skär'-pä-thô [skahr'-pah-tho]. It. *Scarpanto*, q.v.

Karpenesion (Gr.)   kär-pĕ-nē'-sē(-ôn)   kahr-peh-nee'-
                                      see(-on)

Kars (Turkey)   kärs'   kahrs'

Kārsava (Latvia)   kär'-sä-vä   kahr'-sah-vah

Kartalis, Georgios   kär-tä'-lēs, yôr'-yôs   kahr-tah'-lees,
  (Gr. polit.)   yor'-yos

Karteros (Crete)   kär-tĕ-rôs'   kahr-teh-ros'

Kartuzskaya Berëza (Pol.)   See *Bereza Kartuska*.

Kartuzy (Pol.)   kär-tōō'-zĭ   kahr-too'-zi

Karuizawa (Jap.)   kä-rōō'-ē-zä-wä   kah-roo'-ee-zah-wah

Karumba (Austral.)   kä-rŭm'-bə   kah-ruhm'-buh

Karun (Iran, riv.)	kä-rōōn′	kah-roon′
Karuscia (Pantelleria, point)	kä-rōō′-shä	kah-roo′-shah
Karvasaras (Gr.)	kär-vä-sä-räs′	kahr-vah-sah-rahs′
Karydi (Crete)	kä-rē′-dē	kah-ree′-dee
Karystos (Gr.)	kä′-rē-stôs	kah′-ree-stos

Kasbach, Geroldsby (Ger.) See *Geroldsby Kasbach.*

Kashan (Iran)	kä-shän′	kah-shahn′
Kashgai (Per. tribe)	kăsh-gī′	kash-gai′
Kashgar (Ch., Sinkiang, riv. and town)	*Eng.* kăsh-gär	kash-gahr

Town also called *Shu-fu,* q.v.

Kashin (Rus.)	kä′-shĭn	kah′-shin
Kashino (Rus.)	kä′-shĭ-nŏ	kah′-shi-no
Kashira (Rus.)	kä-shĭ′-rä	kah-shi′-rah
Kashkina (Rus.)	käsh′-kĭ-nä	kahsh′-ki-nah
Kashmir (India)	kăsh-mĭr′	kash-mihr′
Kasimov (Rus.)	kä-sē′-mŏf	kah-see′-mof
Kaskinen (Fin.)	käs′-kē-nĕn	kahs′-kee-nen

Swedish *Kaskoe,* käsk′-û [kahsk′-œ].

Kaskoe *or* Kaskö (Fin.) See *Kaskinen.*

Kason (Yugosl., mt.)	kä′-sôn	kah′-son
Kasos (Dodec.)	kä′-sô(s)	kah′-so(s)

Kassa (Cz.) See *Košice.*

Kassandra (Gr.)	kä-sän′-drä	kah-sahn′-drah
Kassel (Ger.)	käs′-əl	kahs′-uhl

Also spelled *Cassel.* Often Englished as kăs′-əl [kas′-uhl].

Kasserine (Tun.)	*Eng.* kăs′-ə-rēn′	kas′-uh-reen′
	or käs-sĕ-rēn′	kahs-seh-reen′
Kastelia (Gr.)	kä-stĕ′-lyä	kah-steh′-lyah
Kastelli (Crete)	kä-stĕ′-lē	kah-steh′-lee

Also called *Kastelli Pediadas* or *-os,* pĕ-dē-ä′-däs *or* -ôs [peh-dee-ah′-dahs *or* -os].

Kastelorizon (Dodec.)	käs-tĕl-ô′-rē-zô(n)	kahs-tel-o′-ree-zo(n)

Also called *Megiste,* mĕ-yē′-stē [meh-yee′-stee]. Italian *Castelrosso,* q.v.

Kastoria (Gr.)	kä-stô-rē′-ä	kah-sto-ree′-ah
Kastornaya (Rus.)	käs-tôr′-nä-yä	kahs-tor′-nah-yah
Kastos (Gr., isl.)	kä-stôs′	kah-stos′
Kastrikum (Neth.)	käs′-trĭ-kəm	kahs′-trih-kuhm
Kastron (Gr.)	kä′-strô(n)	kah′-stro(n)
Kastrosikia (Gr.)	kä-strô-sē-kyä′	kah-stro-see-kyah′
Kastrup (Den., Copenhagen, airport)	kăs′-trŏŏp	kas′-trup
Kasvin (Iran)	kăz-vēn′	kaz-veen′

Also spelled *Kazvin* and *Qazvin.*

Katahdin (Me.)	kə-tä′-dĭn	kuh-tah′-din
Katakolon (Gr.)	kä-tä′-kô-lô(n)	kah-tah′-ko-lo(n)
Katanning (Austral.)	kə-tăn′-ĭng	kuh-tan′-ing
Katayama, Sen (Jap. polit.)	kä-tä′-yä′-mä′, sĕn′	kah-tah′-yah′-mah′, sen′
Katayama, Tetsu (Jap. polit.)	kä-tä′-yä′-mä′, tĕ′-tsōō	kah-tah′-yah′-mah′, teh′-tsoo
Katerine (Gr.)	kä-tĕ-rē′-nē	kah-teh-ree′-nee

Also called *Aikaterine,* ĕ-kä-tĕ-rē′-nē [eh-kah-teh-ree′-nee].

Katha (Burma)	kə-thä′	kuh-thah′
Kathemerini (Gr. news-paper)	kä-thē-mĕ-rē-nē′	kah-thee-meh-ree-nee′
Kathiawar (India)	kä-tĭ-ä-wär′	kah-ti-ah-wahr′
Katmandu (Nepal)	kät-män-dōō′	kaht-mahn-doo′
Katō, Shizuko (Jap. baroness)	kä′-tô, shē′-zōō-kô	kah′-to, shee-′zoo-ko
Kato Akhaia (Gr.)	kä′-tô ä-hĭ′-ä	kah′-to ah-hai′-ah

See *Achaia* and *Elis.*

Katoomba (Austral.)	kə-tōōm′-bə	kuh-toom′-buh
Katowice (Pol.)	kä-tô-vē′-tsĕ	kah-to-vee′-tseh
Katsuura (Jap.)	kä-tsōō′-ōō-rä	kah-tsoo′-oo-rah
Kattegat (Den., Sw., sea)	*Eng.* kăt′-ĭ-găt	kat′-i-gat
Kattendijke (Neth.)	kät′-ən-dĭ′-kə	kaht′-uhn-dai′-kuh
Katwijk aan Zee (Neth.)	kät′-wīk än zä′	kaht′-waik ahn zay′
Katyn (Rus., forest)	kä-tĭn′(y)	kah-tin′(y)
Katzbach (Ger. >? Pol., riv.)	käts′-bäk(h)	kahts′-bahk(h)

Polish *Kocaba,* q.v.

Kauai (Hawaii)	kou-ĭ′	kou-ai′
Kaub (Ger.)	koup′	kaup′
Kauimbei (N.E. New Guinea)	kou′-ĭm-bā	kau′-im-bay
Kaulwitz (Ger.)	koul′-vĭts	kaul′-vits
Kaunas (Lith.)	kou′-näs	kau′-nahs

Russian *Kovno,* q.v.

kaupunki	kou′-pŏŏng-kē	kau′-pung-kee

An element, meaning *town* or *borough,* in Finnish place names.

Kaut (Oc., New Ireland)	kout′	kaut′
Kautokeino (Nor.)	kou-tō-kā′-nō	kau-toh-kay′-noh
Kavadarci (Yugosl.)	kä′-vä′-där-tsĭ	kah′-vah′-dahr-tsi
Kavaganda (Rus.)	kä-vä-gän′-dä	kah-vah-gahn′-dah
Kavaja (Alb.) See *Kavajë.*		
Kavajë (Alb.)	kä-vä′-yə	kah-vah′-yuh

Italian *Cavaia,* q.v.

Kavak (Turk.)   kä′-väk′   kah′-vahk′

Kavalla (Gr.)   kä-vä′-lä   kah-vah′-lah

Kavam Sultaneh (Iran. polit.) See *Ahmed Qavam*.

Kavieng (Oc.,New Ireland) kĕ-vĭ-ĕng′   keh-vi-eng′

Kavkazskaya (Rus.)   käf-käz′-skä-yä   kahf-kahz′-skah-yah

Kavomalias (Gr., cape)   kä-vô-mä-lyä(s)′   kah-vo-mah-lyah(s)′
     Also called *Maleas*, q.v.

Kavontoros (Gr., Euboea, point) See *Kapherevs*.

Kavousi (Crete)   kä-vo͞o′-sē   kah-voo′-see

kawa   kä-wä   kah-wah
     An element, meaning *river*, in Japanese place names. See *-gawa*.

Kawanishi (Jap. name)   kä-wä′-nē-shē   kah-wah′-nee-shee

Kawlin (Burma)   kô′-lĭn′   kaw′-lin′

Kayangel (Oc., Carolines) kä-yäng′-ĕl   kah-yahng′-el

Kazak (Rus.)   kä-zäk′   kah-zahk′

Kazan (Rus.)   kä-zän′(y)   kah-zahn′(y)

Kazanlik (Bulg.)   kä′-zän-lĭk′   kah′-zahn-lik′

Kazatin (Rus.)   kä-zä′-tĭn   kah-zah′-tin

Kazbek (Rus., mt.)   käz-bĕk′   kahz-bek′

Kazemi (Iran. name)   kä-zə-mē′   kah-zuh-mee′

Kazvin *or* Kasvin   kăz-vēn′   kaz-veen′
     or Qazvin (Iran)

Kearney, Bernard W.   kär′-nĭ, bûr′-nûrd′   kahr′-ni, buhr′-nuhrd′
     (U.S. representative)

Kearns, Carroll D. (U.S.   kûrns′   kuhrns′
     representative)

Kebili (Tun.)   kə-bē′-lē   kuh-bee′-lee

Kebir (Alg.)   kə-bēr′   kuh-beer′
     An abbreviation of *Mers el Kebir*, q.v.

Kecskemét (Hung.)   kĕch′-kĕ-māt   kech′-keh-mayt

Kedah (Malaya)   kā′-dä   kay′-dah

Kédainiai (Lith.)   kä-dĭ′-nyī *or* -nĕ   kay-dai′-nyai *or* -neh
     Russian *Keidany*, q.v.

Kediri (NEI, Java)   kĕ-dē′-rē   keh-dee′-ree

Keeling Isls. (Ind. Oc.)   kē′-lĭng   kee′-ling
     Also called *Cocos*, q.v.

Keesler Field (Miss.)   kēs′-lər   kees′-luhr

Kef, le (Tun.)   kāf′, lə   kayf′, luh

Kefauver, Estes   kē′-fô-vər, ĕs′-tĕs   kee′-faw-vuhr, es′-tes
     (U.S. representative)

Kef el Goraa (Tun.)   kāf′ ĕl gŭ-rä′   kayf′ el guh-rah′

Keflavík (Iceland)   kĕf′-lä-vēk′   kef′-lah-veek′
     local kăb′-lä-vēk   kab′-lah-veek

Kef Touro (Tun.)   kāf′ to͞o′-rō   kayf′ too′-roh

Kegel (Est.)	*Rus.* kĕ'-gĕl(y)	keh'-gel(y)
	Ger. kā'-gəl	kay'-guhl
Estonian *Keila,* q.v.		
Kehl (Ger.)	kāl'	kayl'
Kehoe (Irish name)	kĕ'-ō *or* kyō'	kee'-oh *or* kyoh'
Kei (NEI)	kī'	kai'
Also spelled *Kai,* q.v.		
Keidany (Lith.)	*Rus.* kā-dä'-nĭ	kay-dah'-ni
Lithuanian *Kėdainiai,* q.v.		
Keijō (Korea) See *Seoul.*		
Keikino (Est.)	kā'-kĭ-nŏ	kay'-ki-no
Keila (Est.)	kā'-lä	kay'-lah
Russian *Kegel,* q.v.		
Keitel, Wilhelm (Ger. general)	kī'-təl, vĭl'-hĕlm	kai'-tuhl, vil'-helm
Keksgolm (Fin. >Rus.)	kĕks'-gŏl(y)m	keks'-gol(y)m
Finnish *Käkisalmi,* q.v.		
Kĕlcyra (Alb.) See *Kĕlcyrë.*		
Kĕlcyrë (Alb.)	kəl-tsü'-rə	kuhl-tsü'-ruh
Greek *Kleisoura,* klē-sōō'-rä [klee-soo'-rah].		
Kelibia (Tun.)	kə-lē'-bĭ-ä	kuh-lee'-bi-ah
Kem (Rus.)	kām'(y)	kaym'(y)
Kem, James P. (U.S. senator)	kĕm'	kem'
Kema (NEI, Celebes)	kā'-mä	kay'-mah
Kemal Atatürk (Turk. polit.)	kə-mäl' ä-tä-türk'	kuh-mahl' ah-tah-türk'
Formerly called *Mustapha Kemal Pasha,* mŏŏs'-tä-fä kə-mäl' pä'-shä' [mus'-tah-fah kuh-mahl' pah'-shah'].		
Kemara Rettō (Oc.)	*Jap.* kĕ-mä'-rä' rĕt'-tô'	keh-mah'-rah' ret'-to'
Kembs (Fr.)	kĕmps'	kemps'
Kemerovo (Rus.)	kĕ'-mĕ-rŏ-vŏ	keh'-meh-ro-vo
Kemi (Fin.)	kĕ'-mē	keh'-mee
Kemijärvi (Fin.)	kĕ'-mē-yär-vē	keh'-mee-yehr-vee
Kemmel (Belg.)	kĕm'-əl	kem'-uhl
Kemozersk (Rus.)	kām'-ŏ-zĕrsk'	kaym'-o-zehrsk'
Kempei (Jap. military police)	kĕm'-pä	kem'-pay
Kempen (Pol.) See *Kępno.*		
Kenali (Yugosl.)	kĕ'-nä-lĭ	keh'-nah-li
Kenayis (Egypt)	kĕ-nă'-yĭs	keh-na'-yis
Kendari (NEI, Celebes)	kĕn-dä'-rē	ken-dah'-ree

Kengtung (Burma) kāng'-tŏong' kayng'-tung'
  Also called *Chêng-tung*, jŭng-dŏong [juhng-dung].
Kennelly, Martin H. kə-nĕl'-lĭ kuh-nel'-li
  (Chicago polit.)
Kenosha (Wis.) kə-nō'-shə kuh-noh'-shuh
Kenya (Afr., Br. col.) kĕn'-yə *or* kĕn'-yə keen'-yuh *or* ken'-yuh
  The more correct (and the BBC) pronunciation is kĕn'-yə (keen'-yuh).
  Our efforts to inculcate this pronunciation at WCBS were enfeebled
  when Prime Minister Churchill repeatedly said "kĕn'-yə."
Kenzingen (Ger.) kĕn'-tsĭng-ən ken'-tsing-uhn
Keo(u)gh (Irish name) kē'-ō kee'-oh
Keogh, Eugene J. kē'-ō kee'-oh
  (U.S. representative)
Keos *or* Kea (Gr., isl.) kĕ'-ôs *or* kĕ'-ä keh'-os *or* keh'-ah
  English *Ceos*, sē'-ôs [see'-os]. Also called *Tzia*, dzē-ä' [dzee-ah'] *or*
  jä' [jah'], and *Zea*, q.v.
kep (Alb.) kĕp' kep'
  An element, meaning *cape*, in Albanian place names. Look up the
  other part of the name.
Kephalas (Crete) kĕ-fä-läs' keh-fah-lahs'
Kephalenia (Gr., isl.) kĕ-fä-lē-nē'-ä keh-fah-lee-nee'-ah
  Also called *Kephalonia*, kĕ-fä-lô-nyä' [keh-fah-lo-nyah']. English
  Cephalonia, q.v.
Kephisia (Gr.) kē-fē-syä' kee-fee-syah'
kepi (Alb.) See *kep*.
Kępno (Pol.) kăNp'-nô kaNp'-no
  German *Kempen*, kĕm'-pən [kem'-puhn].
Keppeln (Ger.) kĕp'-pəln kep'-puhln
Ker, Stari (Yugosl.) kĕr', stä'-rĭ kehr', stah'-ri
Kerak (Trans-Jordan) kĕ'-răk keh'-rak
  See *El Kerak*.
Kerch (Rus.) kĕrch' kehrch'
Kerchenski (Rus., straits) kĕr'-chĕn-skĭ kehr'-chen-ski
Kerecsend (Hung.) kĕ'-rĕ-chĕnd keh'-reh-chend
Kerékegyháza (Hung.) kĕ'-rä-kĕt(y)-hä'-zŏ keh'-ray-ket(y)-hah'-
        zo
Kerensk (Rus.) kĕ-rĕnsk' keh-rensk'
Kerensky, Alexander kĕ-rĕn'-skĭ, keh-rehn'-ski,
  Feodorovitch (Rus. ä-lĕ-ksän'-dĕr ah-leh-ksahn'-dehr
  polit.) fyô'-dŏ-rŏ-vĭch fyo'-do-ro-vich
Kereny (Yugosl.) *Mag.* kĕ'-rĕn(y) keh'-ren(y)
  Serb-Croat *Krnjaja*, q.v.
Kerintji (NEI) kə-rĭn'-chē kuh-rin'-chee
Kerkennah (Tun., isl.) kər-kĕn'-nä kuhr-ken'-nah

Kerkine (Balkan mts.)   *Gr.* kĕr-kē'-nē   kehr-kee'-nee
  Serb-Croat *Belasica planina*, q.v.
Kerkrade (Neth.)   kĕrk'-rä-də   kehrk'-rah-duh
Kerkyra (Gr.)   kĕr'-kē-rä   kehr'-kee-rah
  Italian *Corfù*, q.v.
Kermadek Isls. (N.Z.) kər-măd'-ĕk   kuhr-mad'-ek
Kerman (Iran)   kĕr-män'   kehr-mahn'
Kermanshah (Iran)   kĕr-män-shä'   kehr-mahn-shah'
Kerr (Eng. name)   *Am.* kûr' *or* kär' kuhr' *or* kahr'
               Br. kär' *or* kĕr' *or* kahr' *or* kehr' *or*
                 kûr'   kuhr'
Kerr, Sir Archibald Clark (Br. diplomat) See *Clark Kerr.*
Kerr, Deborah   kär', dĕb'-ə-rə   kahr', deb'-uh-ruh
  (Br. actress)
Kerr, John H.   kär'   kahr'
  (U.S. representative)
Kërrabë (Alb., pass) See *Krrabe.*
Kersa (Libya)   kĕr'-sä   kehr'-sah
Kersten, Charles J.   kûr'-stən   kuhr'-stuhn
  (U.S. representative)
Kerulen (Mongolia,   kĕr'-ōō-lĕn   kehr'-oo-len
  Rus., riv.; Mongol town)
Kessellingen (Ger.)   kĕs'-əl-ĭng-ən   kes'-uhl-ing-uhn
Kesteren (Neth.)   kĕs'-tə-rən   kes'-tuh-ruhn
Keszthely (Hung.)   kĕst'-hā   kest'-hay
Ketchikan (Alaska)   kĕch'-ĭ-kăn   kech'-i-kan
Ketel (Neth.)   kā'-təl   kay'-tuhl
Kettwig (Ger.)   kĕt'-vĭk(h)   ket'-vik(h)
Kettwitz (Ger.) See *Jungfernsee.*
Kevelaer (Ger.)   kā'-və-lär   kay'-vuh-lahr
Kewaunee (Wis.)   kĭ-wô'-nĭ   ki-waw'-ni
Kexholm (Fin. >Rus.) See *Käkisalmi.*
Keynes, John Maynard kānz', mā'-närd kaynz', may'-nahrd
  (Eng. economist)
kh, ch, and often *h* are variant spellings in Greek. The consultant may
  have to look for all three.
Khabarovsk (Rus.)   hä-bä'-rŏfsk   hah-bah'-rofsk
Khachatourian,   *Eng.* kăch'-ə-tōō'- kach'-uh-too'-ri-uhn
              rĭ-ən,
  Aram (Rus. composer) *Rus.* hä-chä-tōō-ryän', hah-chah-too-ryahn',
              ä-räm'   ah-rahm'
khaki   kăk'-ĭ *or* kä'-kĭ   kak'-i *or* kah'-ki
  The first is the general American and Army pronunciation.
Khalepa (Crete)   hä-lĕ'-pä   hah-leh'-pah

Khalke (Dodec.)   häl'-kē   hahl'-kee
   Also called *Khalkia*, häl-kyä' [hahl-kyah'], and *Kharkia*, här-kyä'
[hahr-kyah']. Italian *Calchi*, q.v.
Khalkidike (Gr., pen.)   häl-kē-dē'-kē   hahl-kee-dee'-kee
   English *Chalcidice*, kăl-sĭd'-ĭ-sĭ [kal-sid'-i-si].
Khalkis *or* Chalcis (Gr.)   *Eng.* kăl'-sĭs   kal'-sis
                             Gr. häl-kēs'   hahl-kees'
   Also called *Evripos*, ĕ'-vrē-pôs [eh'-vree-pos].
khan   *Eng.* kän' *or* kăn'   kahn' *or* kan'
                    Arabic k(h)än'   k(h)ahn'
   A title or honorific in the Middle East, usually following the name.
It is disregarded in alphabetical listing.
Khan, Liaquat Ali (Indian polit.) See *Liaquat Ali Khan*.
Khanaqin (Iraq)   *Per.* hä-nə-kēn'   hah-nuh-keen'
                   Eng. kăn'-ə-kĭn   kan'-uh-kin
Khandax (Crete)   hän'-däks   hahn'-dahks
   Also called *Herakleion*, q.v.
Khania (Crete)   *Eng.* kä-nē'-ə   kah-nee'-uh
                   Gr. hän-yä'   hahn-yah'
   Also spelled *Canea*, q.v.
Khanka (Rus., lake)   hän'-kä   hahn'-kah
Khantrinou (Gr.)   hän-drē-nōō'   hahn-dree-noo'
Khan Yunis (Pal.)   kän yōō'-nĭs   kahn yoo'-nis
Kharita, el (Egypt)   kä'-rē-tə, ĕl   kah'-ree-tuh, el
Kharitonov (Rus. name)   hä-rĭ-tô'-nŏf   hah-ri-to'-nof
Kharkia (Dodec.)   See *Khalke*.
Kharkov (Rus.)   *Eng.* kär'-kŏf *or* -kŏv   kahr'-kof *or* -kov
                   Rus. här'-kŏf   hahr'-kof
   The name acquired its English pronunciation centuries ago.
Kharokopeon (Gr.)   hä-rô-kô-pē-ô(n)'   hah-ro-ko-pee-o(n)'
Kharput (Turkey) See *Harput*.
Khartoum (Sudan)   *Eng.* kär-tōōm'   kahr-toom'
   Arabic *Khartum*, k(h)är-tōōm' [k(h)ahr-toom'].
Khasi (India)   k(h)ä'-sē   k(h)ah'-see
Khasia (Gr., mt.)   hä-syä'   hah-syah'
Khaskovo (Bulg.)   häs'-kŏ-vŏ   hahs'-ko-vo
Khassan (Rus., lake)   häs-sän'   hahs-sahn'
Khassani (Gr., Athens,   hä-sä'-nē   hah-sah'-nee
   airport)
Khatzchatourian, Aram (Rus. composer) See *Khachatourian*.
Kheimara (Alb.)   See *Himarë*.
Khelat (Baluch.)   See *Kalat*.
Khenchela (Alg.)   kĕn-shā'-lä   ken-shay'-lah
Kherson (Rus.)   hĕr-sôn'   hehr-son'

Khersonesos (Crete,   hĕr-sô'-nē-sôs   hehr-so'-nee-sos
cape; Turk., pen.)
English *Chersonese*, q.v.
Khiliodromia (Gr., isl.)   See *Alonesos*.
Khilok (Rus., riv.)   hĭ-lôk'   hi-lok'
Khios (Gr., isl.)   *Eng.* kĭ'-ŏs   kai'-os
                 Gr. hē'-ô(s)   hee'-o(s)
khirbet   k(h)ĭr'-bĕt   k(h)ihr'-bet
An element, meaning *ruin*, in Arabic place names.
Khirbet Deiran (Pal.) See *Rehovot*.
Khitola (Fin. >Rus.)   hē'-tŏ-lä   hee'-to-lah
Finnish *Hiitola*, q.v.
Khlebnikof (Alaska,   klĕb'-nĭ-kŏf   kleb'-ni-kof
Attu)
Khmelnik (Rus.)   k(h)mĕl'(y)-nĭk   k(h)mel'(y)-nik
Khmyelnik (Pol.)   See *Chmielnik*.
Khodorkov (Rus.)   hŏ-dŏr-kŏf'   ho-dor-kof'
Khoi (Iran)   k(h)oi'   k(h)oi'
Kholm (Pol.)   See *Chelm*.
Kholm (Rus.)   hôlm'   holm'
Khoms (Libya)   k(h)ôms'   k(h)oms'
Italian *Homs*, q.v.
Khondron (Crete, point)   hôn-drô(n)'   hon-dro(n)'
Khong (Indo-Ch.)   kŭm'   kuhm'
It would probably be Englished as kŏng' [kong'].
Khon Khen (Siam)   kôn'-kăn   kawn'-kan
Khopër (Rus., riv.)   hŏ-pyôr'   ho-pyor'
Khor (Rus., riv.)   hôr'   hor'
Khora Sphakion (Crete)   hô'-rä sfä-kē'-ô(n)   ho'-rah sfah-kee'-o(n)
Also called *Sphakia*, q.v.
Khorassan (Iran.)   k(h)ō-rä-sän'   k(h)oh-rah-sahn'
Also called *Khurasan*, q.v.
Khorog (Rus.)   hŏ'-rŏg   ho'-rog
Khorol (Rus.)   hŏ-rôl'   ho-rol'
Khorzhele (Pol.) See *Chorzele*.
Khotin (Rum. >Rus.)   hô'-tĭn   ho'-tin
Rumanian spelling *Hotin*.
Khotynets (Rus.)   hŏ-twē'-nĕts   ho-twee'-nets
Khoury, Fares El   k(h)ōō'-rē, fä'-rĕs ĕl   k(h)oo'-ree,
(Syrian diplomat)   fah'-res el
Khrushchov, Nikita   krōō-shchôf',   kru-schhof',
(Rus. polit.)   nĭ-kē'-tä   ni-kee'-tah
Khurasan (Iran.)   k(h)ōō-rä-sän'   k(h)u-rah-sahn'
Also called *Khorassan*, q.v.

Khurramabad (Iran)   k(h)ŏŏr-räm'-ə-bäd'   k(h)ur-rahm'-uh-
                                                     bahd'

Khurramshahr (Iran)   k(h)ŏŏr-räm'-shär'   k(h)ur-rahm'-shahr'
   Formerly called *Mohammereh*, q.v.

Khust (Cz. >Rus.)   hōōst'   hoost'
   Czech spellings *Chust* and *Hust*. Hungarian spelling *Huszt*.

Khyber Pass   kī'-bər   kai'-buhr
   (India, Afghan.)

Kiakhta (Rus.)   kyä'-k(h)tä   kyah'-k(h)tah

Ki-an (Ch., Kiangsi)   Variant spelling of *Chi-an*, q.v.

kiang   Chinese word meaning *river*. See *chiang*.

Kiangan (Luzon, P.I.)   kyäng-än'   kyahng-ahn'

Kiangmai (Siam)   kyäng-mī'   kyahng-mai'
   Officially *Chiangmai*, q.v.

Kiang-shan (Ch., Chekiang)   Variant of *Chiang-shan*, q.v.

Kiang-si (Ch., prov.)   *Eng.* kyăng-sē   kyang-see
                         Ch. jyäng-sē   jyahng-see

Kiang-su (Ch., prov.)   *Eng.* kyăng-sōō   kyang-soo
                         Ch. jyäng-sōō   jyahng-soo

Kiao-chow (Ch.,   *Eng.* kyou-chou   kyau-chau
   Shantung)   *Ch.* jyou-jō   jyau-joh

Kibei   *Eng.* kē'-bā   kee'-bay
                         Jap. kē-bā'   kee-bay'
   U. S. citizens of Japanese ancestry, who visited Japan and returned
   to this country. Kibeis stress the first syllable, although a stress on
   the second syllable is closer to the Japanese pronunciation.

Kičevo (Yugosl.)   kē'-chĕ-vô   kee'-cheh-vo

Kido, Kōichi (Jap. polit.)   kē-dô', kô'-ē'-chē   kee-do', ko'-ee'-chee

Kieferstädtel   kē'-fər-shtĕt'-əl   kee'-fuhr-shtet'-uhl
   (Ger. >Pol.)
     Polish *Sośnicowice*, q.v.

Kiel (Ger.)   kēl'   keel'

Kielce (Pol.)   kyĕl'-tsĕ   kyel'-tseh

Kienitz (Ger.)   kē'-nĭts   kee'-nits

Kien-ow (Ch., Fukien)   Variant spelling of *Chien-ow*, q.v.

Kien-teh   Variant spelling of *Chien-teh*, q.v.

Kierkegaard, Sören Aaby   kēr'-kə-gôr, sû'-rən   keer'-kuh-gor, sœ'-
   (Dan. philosopher)   ô'-bü   ruhn o'-bü

Kiernik, Władysław   kyĕr'-nĭk, vlä-dĭ'-släf   kyehr'-nik, vlah-di'-
   (Pol. polit.)   slahf

Kieta (Oc., Bougainville)   kē-ĕ'-tä   kee-eh'-tah

Kiev (Rus.)   kē'-yĕf   kee'-yef

Kihnu (Est., isl.)   kēk(h)'-nōō   keek(h)'-noo
   Russian *Kuno*, q.v.

Kijkduin (Neth.)   kĭk-dûĭn′   kaik-dœin′

Kikinda, Velika   kē′-kĭn-dä,   kee′-kin-dah,
  (Yugosl.)   vĕ′-lĭ-kä   veh′-li-kah

  Hungarian *Nagykikinda*, nŏt′(y)-kĭ′-kĭn-dŏ [not′(y)-ki′-kin-do].

Kikori (New Guinea,   kē′-kô′-rē   kee′-ko′-ree
  Papua)

Kilday, Paul J.   kĭl-dā′   kil-day′
  (U.S. representative)

Kildin (Rus.)   kēl′-dĭn   keel′-din

Kilgore, Harley M.   kĭl′-gōr, här′-lĭ   kil′-gohr, hahr′-li
  (U. S. senator)

Kili (Oc., Marshalls)   kē′-lē   kee′-lee

Kilinailau (Oc.)   kē′-lē-nĭ′-lou   kee′-lee-nai′-lau

Kiliya (Rum. >Rus.)   kē′-lĭ-yä   kee′-li-yah
  Rumanian *Chilia Nouă*, q.v.

Kilkis (Gr.)   kēl-kēs′   keel-kees′

Killelagh (No. Ire.)   kĭ-lā′-lĭ   ki-lay′-li

kilometer   kĭl′-ə-mē′-tər   kil′-uh-mee′-tuhr
              or kĭ-lŏm′-ə-tər   ki-lom′-uh-tuhr

Dictionaries prefer the first. The analogy should be *decimeter* and other terms of the metric system, not *barometer*. Cp. *altimeter*.

Kilraughts (No. Ire.)   kĭl-răts′   kil-rats′

Kimba (Austral.)   kĭm′-bə   kim′-buh

Kimkan (Rus.)   kĭm-kän′   kim-kahn′

Kim Koo (Korean polit.) *Eng.* kĭm kōō   kim koo
              Kor. gĭm gōō   gim goo

Kimpolung (Rum.) See *Câmpulung*.

Kimry (Rus.)   kēm′-rĭ   keem′-ri

Kimura (Jap. name)   kē-mōō′-rä′   kee-moo′-rah′

Kin (Burma)   kĭn′   kin′

Kinabalu (Br. Borneo) kĭn-ä-bä′-lōō   kin-ah-bah′-loo

Kindat (Burma)   kĭn-dăt′   kin-dat′

Kingisepp (Rus.)   kĭng′-gĭ-sĕp   king′-gi-sep

Kin-hwa (Ch., Chekiang) jĭn-whä   jin-whah
  Also spelled *Chin-hwa*, q.v.

Kinkaid, Thomas Cassin kĭn′-kād, kăs′-ĭn kin′-kayd,
  (Am. admiral)   kas′-in

Kingstown (Eire) See *Dúnlaoghaire*.

Kin-ki (Ch., Kiangsi) Variant spelling of *Chin-ch′i*, q.v.

Kintore (Austral., mt.) kĭn′-tôr   kin′-tor

Kinu (Burma)   kĭn-ōō′   kin-oo′

Kinzer, J. Roland   kĭn′-zər   kin′-zuhr
  (U.S. representative)

Kinzig (Ger., riv.)   kĭn′-tsĭk(h)   kin′-tsik(h)

Kir (Alb., riv.)	kēr'	keer'
Kircheib (Ger.)	kĭrk(h)'-ĭp	kihrk(h)'-aip
Kirghiz (Rus.)	kĭr-gēz'	kihr-geez'
Kiri (Alb., riv.) See *Kir.*		
Kirin (Manchu.)	kē-rĭn	kee-rin
Kirkenes (Nor.)	chēr'-kə-nĕs	cheer'-kuh-nes
Kırklareli (Turk.)	kĭrk-lä'-rĕ-lē	kihrk-lah'-reh-lee
Kirkuk (Iraq)	kĭr-kōōk'	kihr-kook'
Kirov, Sergei (Rus. polit.)	kē'-rŏf, sĕr-gā'	kee'-rof, sehr-gay'
Kirovabad (Rus.)	kē'-rŏ-vä-bät'	kee'-ro-vah-baht'
Kirovo (Rus.)	kē'-rŏ-vŏ	kee'-ro-vo
Kirovsk (Rus.)	kē'-rŏfsk	kee'-rofsk
Kirsanov (Rus.)	kĭr-sä'-nŏf	kihr-sah'-nof
Kirwan, Michael J. (U.S. representative)	kûr'-wän	kuhr'-wahn
Kiryū (Jap.)	kē'-ryōō	kee'-ryoo
Kisamos (Crete)	kē'-sä-môs	kee'-sah-mos
Kisbér (Hung.)	kĭsh'-bār	kish'-bayr
Kiselëv, Kuzma V. (Rus. polit.)	kĭ-sĕ-lyôf', kōōz-mä'	ki-seh-lyof', kuz-mah'
Kishinëv (Rum. >Rus.)	*Rus.* kĭ-shĭ-nyôf'	ki-shi-nyof'
	Eng. kĭ-shĭ-nyĕf'	ki-shi-nyef'
Rumanian *Chişinău,* q.v.		
Kishm (Iran, isl.)	kĭsh'm	kish'm
Kisiljevo (Yugosl.)	kē'-sē'-lyĕ-vŏ	kee'-see'-lyeh-vo
Kiska (Alaska, isl.)	kĭs'-kə	kis'-kuh
Kiskundorozsma (Hung.)	kĭsh'-kōōn-dŏ'-rôzh-mŏ	kish'-kun-do'-rozh-mo
Kiskunfélegyháza (Hung.)	kĭsh'-kōōn-fā'-lĕt(y)-hä'-zŏ	kish'-kun-fay'-let(y)-hah'-zo
Kiskunhalas (Hung.)	kĭsh'-kōōn-hŏ'-lŏsh	kish'-kun-ho'-losh
Kispest (Hung.)	kĭsh'-pĕsht	kish'-pesht
Kissavos (Gr., mt.)	kē'-sä-vôs	kee'-sah-vos
Kissimmee (Fla.)	kĭ-sĭm'-ĭ	ki-sim'-i
Kistna (India, riv.)	kĭst'-nə	kist'-nuh
Kistokaj (Hung.)	kĭsh'-tô-koi	kish'-to-koi
Kisumu (Kenya)	kĭ-sōō'-mōō	ki-soo'-moo
kita	kē-tä	kee-tah

An element, meaning *north,* in Japanese place names.

Kitsman (Rum. >Rus.)	kĭts'-män	kits'-mahn

Formerly *Kozmeni,* kôz-mĕ'-nĭ [koz-meh'-ni]. Rumanian *Cozmeni,* q.v.

Kitzbuehel *or* Kitzbühel (Austria)	kĭts'-bü-əl	kits'-bü-uhl

Kiu-kiang (Ch.,	*Eng.* kyōō-kyăng	kyoo-kyang
Kiangsi)	*Ch.* jyōō-jyäng	jyoo-jyahng

Also spelled *Chiu-chiang*, q.v.

Kiung-shan (Hainan)	kyŏŏng-shän	kyung-shahn

K'i-yang (Ch., Hunan) See *Ch'i-yang.*

Kiyose, Ichiro (Jap.	kē'-yô-sĕ, ē-chē'-rô'	kee'-yô-seh, ee-chee'-
executive)		ro'
Kizlar (Rus.)	kĭz-lyär'	kiz-lyahr'
Kjeller (Nor.)	kyĕl'-lər	kyel'-luhr
Kjoellefjord *or*	kyûl'-ə-fyōr	kyœl'-uh-fyohr
Kjöllefjord (Nor.)		
Kladanj (Yugosl.)	klä'-dän(y)	klah'-dahn(y)
Kladno (Cz.)	kläd'-nô	klahd'-no
Kladovo (Yugosl.)	klä'-dô-vô	klah'-do-vo
Kładzko (Ger. >Pol.)	kläts'-kô	klahts'-ko
German *Glatz*, q.v.		
Klagenfurt (Austria)	klä'-gən-fōŏrt	klah'-guhn-furt
Klaipéda (Lith.)	klī'-pĕ-dä	klai'-peh-dah
Russian and German *Memel*, q.v.		
Klamath Falls (Ore.)	klăm'-əth	klam'-uhth
Klanjec (Yugosl.)	klä'-nyĕts	klah'-nyets
Klaten (NEI, Java)	klä'-tĕn	klah'-ten
Klatovy (Cz.)	klä'-tô-vĭ	klah'-to-vi
German *Klattau.*		
Klausenburg (Rum.) See *Cluj.*		
Kleberg, R. M.	klā'-bûrg	klay'-buhrg
(U.S. representative)		
Kłecko (Pol.)	klĕts'-kō	klets'-koh
Kledia (Tun.)	klā'-dyä	klay'-dyah
Kleffens, Eelco Nicolaas van (Du. diplomat) See *Van Kleffens.*		
Klein (Ger.)	klīn'	klain'
Kleinhau (Ger.)	klīn'-hou	klain'-hau
Kleisoura (Alb.) See *Kĕlcyrĕ.*		
Klenike (Yugosl.)	klĕ'-nĭ-kĕ	kleh'-ni-keh
Klenje (Yugosl.)	klĕ'-nyĕ	kleh'-nyeh
Klesów (Pol. >Rus.)	klĕ'-sōŏf	kleh'-suf
Russian *Klesov*, klĕ'-sŏf [kleh'-sof].		
Kletnya (Rus.)	klĕt'-nyä	klet'-nyah
Kletskaya (Rus.)	klĕt'-skä-yä	klet'-skah-yah
Klevan (Pol.) See *Klewań.*		
Klewań (Pol.)	klĕ'-vän(y)	kleh'-vahn(y)
Russian spelling *Klevan.*		
Kličevac (Yugosl.)	klē'-chĕ-väts	klee'-cheh-vahts
Klin (Rus.)	klēn'	kleen'

Klina (Yugosl., riv.)	klē'-nä	klee'-nah
Klinci (Yugosl.)	klēn'-tsĭ	kleen'-tsi
Klinge (Neth.)	klĭng'-ə	kling'-uh
Klintsy (Rus.)	klĭn-tsĭ'	klin-tsi'
Ključ (Yugosl.)	klyōōch'	klyooch'
Kłodawa (Pol.)	klô-dä'-vä	klo-dah'-vah
Kloetinge (Neth.)	klōō'-tĭng-ə	kloo'-ting-uh
Kloosterburen (Neth.)	klōs'-tər-bü'-rən	klohs'-tuhr-bü'-ruhn
Klotzsche (Ger., riv.)	klôch'-ə	kloch'-uh
Kluczborek (Ger. >Pol.)	klōōch-bô'-rĕk	kluch-bo'-rek
German *Kreuzburg,* q.v.		
Kluge, Günther von	klōō'-gə, gün'-tər fən	kloo'-guh, gün'-tuhr
(Ger. general)		fuhn
Klukhor(ski) (Rus., pass)	klōō-hôr'(-skĭ)	kloo-hor'(-ski)
Klundert (Neth.)	klûn'-dərt	klœn'-duhrt
Klyazma (Rus., riv.)	klyäz'-mä	klyahz'-mah
Klyuchi (Rus.)	klyōō-chē'	klyoo-chee'
Knaben (Nor.)	knäb'n	knahb'n
Knatchbull Hugessen,	năch'-bŏŏl hyōō'-jə-	nach'-bul hyoo'-juh-
Sir Hugh Montgomery	sən	suhn
(Br. diplomat)		
kneta (Alb.) See *knetë.*		
knetë (Alb.)	knĕ'-tə	kneh'-tuh

An element, meaning *lagoon* or *lake,* in Albanian place names. Look up the other part of the name.

Knić (Yugosl.)	knēch'	kneech'
Knightsbridge (Libya)	nĭts'-brĭj	naits'-brij
Knishin (Pol.) See *Knyszyn.*		
Knjaževac (Yugosl.)	knyä'-zhĕ-väts	knyah'-zheh-vahts
Knocke (Belg.)	knôk-ə	knok-uh
Knoedler Galleries	*Eng.* nōd'-lər	nohd'-luhr
(New York)	*Ger.* knûd'-lər	knœd'-luhr
The firm itself uses the English pronunciation.		
Knopf, Alfred A.	knŭpf'	knupf'
(Am. publisher)		
Knud (Scandinavian	*Danish* knōōth'	knooth'
name)	*Nor.* knōōt'	knoot'
Knutson, Harold	knōōt'-sən	knoot'-suhn
(U.S. representative)		
Knyaz (Rus.)	knyäz'	knyahz'
Knyszyn (Pol.)	knĭ'-shĭn	kni'-shin
Russian spelling *Knishin.*		
kō	kô	ko

An element, meaning *harbor,* in Japanese place names.

Kobayashi (Jap. zaibatsu)	kô-bä'-yä'-shē'	ko-bah'-yah'-shee'
Kōbe (Jap.)	kô'-bĕ	ko'-beh
Kobelyaki (Rus.)	kŏ-bĕ-lyä'-kĭ	ko-beh-lyah'-ki
Köbenhavn (Den.) See *Copenhagen.*		
Kobilica (Yugosl., mt.)	kô'-bē'-lĭ-tsä	ko'-bee'-li-tsah
Kobišnica (Yugosl.)	kô'-bĭsh-nĭ-tsä	ko'-bish-ni-tsah
Koblenz (Ger.)	kō'-blĕnts	koh'-blents
Also spelled *Coblenz,* q.v.		
Kobrin (Pol. >Rus.)	kô'-brĭn(y)	ko'-brin(y)
Polish spelling *Kobryń.*		
Kocaba (Ger. >? Pol., riv.)	kô-tsä'-bä	ko-tsah'-bah
German *Katzbach,* q.v.		
Kočane (Yugosl.)	kô'-chä-nĕ	ko'-chah-neh
Koceljeva (Yugosl.)	kô'-tsĕ'-lyĕ-vä	ko'-tseh'-lyeh-vah
Kočevje (Yugosl.)	kô'-chĕ-vyĕ	ko'-cheh-vyeh
Kochalino (Rus.)	kŏ-chä'-lĭ-nŏ	ko-chah'-li-no
Kochanskoe (Rus.)	kŏ-chän'-skŏ-yĕ	ko-chahn'-sko-yeh
Kocher (Ger., riv.)	kôk(h)'-ər	kok(h)'-uhr
Kōchi (Jap.)	kô'-chē	ko'-chee
Kock (Pol.)	kôtsk'	kotsk'
Russian spelling *Kotsk.*		
Kodály, Zoltán (Hung. musician)	kô'-dĭ, zôl'-tän	ko'-dai, zol'-tahn
Kodiak (Alaska, isl.)	kŏ'-dĭ-ăk	koh'-di-ak
Kodža Balkan (Yugosl., mts.)	kô'-jä bäl'-kän	ko'-jah bahl'-kahn
Kodžadžik (Yugosl.)	kô'-jä-jĭk	ko'-jah-jik
Koedoes (NEI, Java)	kōō'-dōōs	koo'-doos
Koege (Den.)	kû'-gə	kœ'-guh
Koekelberg (Belg.)	kōō'-kəl-bĕrk(h)	koo'-kuhl-behrk(h)
Koeln (Ger.)	kûln'	kœln'
English *Cologne,* q.v.		
Koenig, Joseph Pierre (Fr. general)	kû-nēg', zhō-zĕf' pyĕr'	kœ-neeg', zhoh-zef' pyehr'
Koenigsberg (Ger. >Rus.)	kû'-nĭk(h)s-bĕrk(h)	kœ'-nik(h)s-behrk(h)
Russian *Kaliningrad,* q.v. Polish *Królewiec,* krōō-lĕ'-vyĕts [kru-leh'-vyets].		
Koenigsberg, Neumark (Ger. >Pol.)	kû'-nĭk(h)s-bĕrk(h), noi'-märk	kœ'-nik(h)s-behrk(h), noi-mahrk
Polish *Chojnica,* hoi-nē'-tsä [hoi-nee'-tsah]		
Koenigsborn (Ger.)	kû'-nĭk(h)s-bôrn	kœ'-nik(h)s-born
Koenigsmacher (Fr.)	kû'-nĭk(h)s-mä'-k(h)ər	kœ'-nik(h)s-mah'-k(h)uhr

Koenigs See (Ger.)	kû'-nĭk(h)s zā'	kœ'-nik(h)s zay'
Koenigstein (Ger.)	kû'-nĭk(h)-shtīn	kœ'-nik(h)-shtain
Koenigswinter (Ger.)	kû'-nĭk(h)s-vĭn'-tər	kœ'-nik(h)s-vin'-tuhr
Koeniz (Switz.)	kû'-nĭts	kœ'-nits
Koepang *or* Kupang (NEI, Timor)	*Eng.* kōō'-păng *Du.* kōō'-päng	koo'-pang koo'-pahng
Koepernick (Ger.)	kû'-pər-nĭk	kœ'-puhr-nik
Koermend (Hung.)	kûr'-měnd	kœr'-mend
Koesfeld (Ger.) See Coesfeld.		
Koeslin (Ger. >Pol.) See *Köslin*.		
Koetaradja *or* Kutaradya (NEI, Sumatra)	kōō'-tä-rä'-jä	koo'-tah-rah'-jah
Koethen (Ger.)	kût'-ən	kœt'-uhn
Koevorden (Neth.)	kōō'-vôr-dən	koo'-vor-duhn
Koewacht (Neth.)	kōō-wäk(h)t'	koo-wak(h)t'
Kōfu (Jap.)	kô'-fōō'	ko'-foo'
Köge (Den.)	kû'-gə	kœ'-guh
Kohima (India)	kô'-hē'-mä'	koh'-hee'-mah'
Kohlow (Ger.)	kô'-lō	koh'-loh
Kohlsheidt (Ger.)	kōl'-shīt	kohl'-shait
Koiso, Kuniaki (Jap. polit.)	kô-ē'-sô', kōō'-nē'-ä-kē	ko-ee'-so', koo'-nee'-ah-kee
Koitere (Fin., dist.)	koi'-tě-rě	koi'-teh-reh
Koivisto (Fin. >Rus.)	koi'-vĭs-tô	koi'-vis-to
Kokkalis (Gr. name)	kô-kä'-lēs	ko-kah'-lees
Kokkola (Fin.)	kôk'-kô-lä	kok'-ko-lah
Kokoda (New Guinea, Papua)	kô-kô'-dä	ko-ko'-dah
Koko Nor (Ch., prov., lake)	kō-kō nôr	koh-koh nor

Also called *Kuku Nor*, kōō-kōō. Prov. also called *Ch'ing-hai*, q.v.

Kokopo (Oc., New Britain)	kô'-kô-pô	ko'-ko-po
Kokos (NEI)	kô'-kôs	ko'-kos
Kokra (Yugosl., riv.)	kô'-krä	ko'-krah
Kokura (Jap.)	kô-kōō'-rä'	ko-koo'-rah'
Kola (Rus., pen.)	kô'-lä	ko'-lah
Kolaka (NEI, Celebes)	kô-lä'-kä	ko-lah'-kah
Kolari (Yugosl.)	kô'-lä-rĭ	ko'-lah-ri
Kolarov, Vasil (Bulg. polit.)	kŏ-lä'-rŏf, vä-sēl'	ko-lah'-rof, vah-seel'
Kolašin (Yugosl.)	kô'-lä'-shĭn	ko'-lah'-shin
Kolberg (Ger. >Pol.)	kôl'-běrk(h)	kol'-behrk(h)
Polish *Kołobrzeg*, q.v.		

Kolding (Den.)	kôl'-dǐng	kol'-ding
Kolhapur (India)	kōl'-hä-pŏor'	kohl'-hah-pur'
Kolijnsplaat (Neth.)	kō-līns'-plät	koh-lains'-plaht.
Kolín (Cz.)	kô'-lēn	ko'-leen
Kolkas Rags (Latvia, cape)	kôl'-käs rägs'	kol'-kahs rahgs'
Kollerthal (Ger.)	kôl'-ər-täl	kol'-uhr-tahl
Kollumerland (Neth.)	kôl'-əm-ər-länt'	kol'-uhm-uhr-lahnt'
Kolmar (Pol.)	Ger. kôl'-mär	kol'-mahr

Polish *Chodzież*, q.v.

| Köln (Ger.) | kûln' | kœln' |

English *Cologne*, q.v.

| Koło (Pol.) | kô'-lô | ko'-lo |

Russian *Kola*, kô'-lä [ko'-lah].

| Kołobrzeg (Ger. >Pol.) | kô-lô'-bzhĕk | ko-lo'-bzhek |

German *Kolberg*, q.v.

| Koločen (Yugosl., isl.) | kô'-lô-chĕn | ko'-lo-chen |

Italian *Calamotta*, q.v.

Kołodziej, Antoni (Pol. polit.)	kô-lô'-jǐ-ā, än-tô'-nǐ	ko-lo'-jih-ay, ahn-to'-ni
Kolombangara (Oc., Solomons)	kô-lôm-bäng'-ä-rä	ko-lom-bahng'-ah-rah
Kolomia (Pol. >Rus.)	kŏ-lŏ-mē'-yä	ko-lo-mee'-yah

Polish *Kołomyja*, kô-lô-mǐ'-yä [ko-lo-mi'-yah]. Rumanian *Colomea*, kô-lô-mĕ'-ä [ko-lo-meh'-ah]. German *Kolomea*.

Kolomna (Rus.)	kŏ-lôm'-nä	ko-lom'-nah
Kolosovka (Rus.)	kŏ-lŏ-sôf'-kä	ko-lo-sof'-kah
Kolozsvár (Rum.)	See *Cluj*.	
Kolpino (Rus.)	kôl'-pǐ-nŏ	kol'-pi-no
kolpos	kôl'-pôs	kol'-pos

An element, meaning *gulf*, in Greek place names. Look up the other part of the name.

Kolskaya Guba (Rus.)	kôl'(y)-skä-yä gōō-bä'	kol'(y)-skah-yah goo-bah'
Kolubara (Yugosl., riv.)	kô-lōō'-bä-rä	ko-loo'-bah-rah
Koluszki (Pol.)	kô-lŏŏsh'-kǐ	ko-lush'-ki
Kolymbari (Crete)	kô-lēm-bä'-rē	ko-leem-bah'-ree
Komandorskie (Rus., isls.)	kŏ-män-dôr'-skǐ-yĕ	ko-mahn-dor'-ski-yeh
Komarnicki, Wacław (Pol. polit.)	kô-mär-nē'-tskǐ, vä'-tsläf	ko-mahr-nee'-tski, vah'-tslahf
Komárno (Cz.)	kô'-mär'-nô	ko'-mahr'-no

Hungarian *Komárom*, kô'-mä-rôm [ko'-mah-rom].

Komárom (Cz.) See *Komárno*.

Komarów (Pol.)	kô-mä′-rŏof	ko-mah′-ruf
Komiža (Yugosl.)	kô′-mĭ-zhä	ko′-mi-zhah
Kommandantur (Ger.)	kôm′-än-dän-tōor′	kom′-ahn-dahn-toor′

Office of the highest military authority of a fort or other military station.

Kommerscheidt (Ger.)	kôm′-ər-shīt	kom′-uhr-shait
Kommunari (Rus.)	kŏm-mōo-nä′-rĭ	kom-moo-nah′-ri
Komolova (Rus.)	kŏ-mô′-lŏ-vä	ko-mo′-lo-vah
Komorowski, Tadeusz	kô-mô-rôf′-skĭ,	ko-mo-rof′-ski,
(Pol. polit.)	tä-dĕ′-ŏosh	tah-deh′-ush

Also called "General Bor."

Komotine (Gr.)	kô-mô-tē-nē′	ko-mo-tee-nee′

Also called *Gioumoultzina*, gyōō-mōol-dzē′-nä [gyoo-mool-dzee′-nah]; and *Gümüljene*, q.v.

Komovi (Yugosl., mts.)	kô′-mô-vĭ	ko′-mo-vi
Kompong Cham	kŏm-pŏng′ chäm′	kom-pong′ chahm′
(Indo-Ch.)		
Komrat (Rum. >Rus.)	kôm-rät′	kom-raht′

Rumanian spelling *Comrat*.

Komsomol	kŏm-sŏ-môl′	kom-so-mol′

Russian *Young Communists' League*.

Komsomolsk (Rus.)	kŏm-sŏ-môlsk′	kom-so-molsk′
Komsomolskaya Pravda	kŏm-sŏ-môl′(y)-skä-yä präv′-dä	kom-so-mol′(y)-skah-yah prahv′-dah

Newspaper of the *Komsomol*, q.v.

Konderski, Władysław	kôn-dĕr′-skĭ,	kon-dehr′-ski,
(Pol. diplomat)	vlä-dĭ′-släf	vlah-di′-slahf
Konev, Ivan (Rus.	kô′-nĕf, ē-vän′	ko′-nef, ee-vahn′
general)		
Kongsberg (Nor.)	kôngs′-bĕrg *or* -bĕr	kongs′-behrg *or* -behr
Kongsvinger (Nor.)	kôngs′-vĭng-ər	kongs′-ving-uhr

Königsberg (Ger. >Rus.) See *Koenigsberg* and *Kaliningrad*.

Königsberg, Neumark (Ger. >Pol.) See *Koenigsberg, Neumark*.

Königsborn (Ger.)	kû′-nĭk(h)s-bôrn	kœ′-nik(h)s-born
Königs See (Ger.)	kû′-nĭk(h)s zä′	kœ′-nik(h)s zay′
Königstein (Ger.)	kû′-nĭk(h)-shtīn	kœ′-nik(h)-shtain
Königswinter (Ger.)	kû′-nĭk(h)s-vĭn′-tər	kœ′-nik(h)s-vin′-tuhr
Konin (Pol.)	kô′-nĭn	ko′-nin
Konispol (Alb.)	kô-nēs′-pôl	ko-nees′-pol

Konispoli (Alb.) See *Konispol*.

Konitsa (Gr.)	kô′-nē-tsä	ko′-nee-tsah
Köniz (Switz.)	kû′-nĭts	kœ′-nits
Konjic (Yugosl.)	kô′-nyĭts	ko′-nyits
Konjice (Yugosl.)	kô′-nyĭ-tsĕ	ko′-nyi-tseh

Konjska (Yugosl., riv.)   kôn′(y)-skä   kon′(y)-skah

Konoa (Oc., Saipan) See *Charan Konoa*.

Konotop (Rus.)   kŏ-nŏ-tôp′   ko-no-top′

Konoye, Fumimaro (Jap.   kô-nŏ′-ĕ′, fōō′-mē′-   ko-no′-eh′, foo′-mee′-
   prince)   mä-rô   mah-ro

Końskie (Pol.)   kôn′(y)-skyĕ   kon′(y)-skyeh
   Russian *Konsk*, kônsk′ [konsk′].

Konstadt (Ger.)   kôn′-shtät   kon′-shtaht

Konstantinovka   kŏn′-stän-tē′-nŏf-kä   kon′-stahn-tee′-nof-
   Dimitrievka (Rus.)   dĭ-mē′-trĭ-yĕf-kä   kah di-mee′-tri-yef-
                           kah

Konstantynów (Pol.)   kôn-stän-tĭ′-nŏŏf   kon-stahn-ti′-nuf

Konstanz (Ger.)   kōn′-shtänts   kohn′-shtahnts
   English *Constance*, q.v.

Konya (Turk.)   kôn′-yä   kon′-yah

Konz (Ger.)   kônts′   konts′

Koo, Wellington   kōō′   koo′
   (Ch. diplomat)
   Chinese *Ku*, gōō [goo].

Koog aan de Zaan   kōk(h)′ än də zän′   kohk(h)′ ahn duh
   (Neth.)   zahn′

Kopač (Yugosl.)   kô′-päch   ko′-pahch

Kopanica (Pol.)   kô-pä-nē′-tsä   ko-pah-nee′-tsah

Kopanovka (Rus.)   kŏ-pä′-nŏf-kä   ko-pah′-nof-kah

Kopaonik (Yugosl., mts.)   kô′-pä′-ô-nĭk   ko′-pah′-o-nik

Kopeć Ogruszecki,   kô′-pĕch ô-grōō-   ko′-pech o-gru-shets′-
   Stanisław (Pol. polit.)   shĕts′-kĭ, stä-nē′-   ki, stah-nee′-slahf
                 släf

Köpernick (Ger.)   kû′-pər-nĭk   kœ′-puhr-nik

Kopervik (Nor.)   kō′-pər-vēk   koh′-puhr-veek

Koppang (Nor.)   kôp′-päng   kop′-pahng

Koprena (Gr.)   kô′-prĕ-nä   ko′-preh-nah

Koprivnica (Yugosl.)   kô′-prĭv′-nĭ-tsä   ko′-priv′-ni-tsah

Koprivnik (Yugosl., mt.)   kô′-prĭv-nĭk   ko′-priv-nik

Korab (Balkan mt.)   *Eng.* kô′-răb   ko′-rab
   Albanian *Mal i Korabit*. Serb-Croat *Korab*.

Kora Gahtaung (Burma)   kō′-rä gä′-toung   koh′-rah gah′-taung

Korat (Siam)   kō-rät′   koh-raht′

Korba (Tun.)   kôr′-bä   kor′-bah

Korbous (Tun.)   kôr-bōōs′   kor-boos′

Korcha (Alb.)   kôr′-chə   kor′-chuh
   Albanian spelling *Korrçë*, q.v.

Korčula (Yugosl., isl.)   kôr′-chōō-lä   kor′-choo-lah
   Italian *Curzola*, q.v.

Kordofan (Sudan)   kôr-dô-fän'   kor-do-fahn'

Korea (Asia)   kō-rē'-ə   koh-ree'-uh

    Chinese *K'ao-li*, kou-lē [kau-lee]. Korean *Chyosyŏn*, chyô-syûn [chyo-syœn]. Japanese *Chōsen*, chô'-sĕn [cho'-sen].

Koreish (Arab tribe)   kô-rāsh' *or* kô-rīsh'   ko-raysh' *or* ko-raish'

Korenevo (Rus.)   kô'-rĕ-nĕ-vŏ   ko'-reh-neh-vo

Korenica (Yugosl.)   kô'-rĕ'-nĭ-tsä   ko'-reh'-ni-tsah

Korijen (Yugosl., mts.)   kô'-rĭ-yĕn   ko'-ri-yen

Korinthos (Gr.)   See *Corinth*.

Koritnik (Balkan mt.)   *S.-C.* kô'-rĭt-nĭk   ko'-rit-nik

Körmend (Hung.)   kûr'-mĕnd   kœr'-mend

Kornat (Yugosl., isl.)   kôr'-nät   kor'-naht

    Italian *Incoronata*, q.v.

Korneichuk, Alexander   kŏr-nā-chŏŏk',   kor-nay-chuk',
  Yevdokimovich   yĕv-dŏ-kē'-mŏ-vĭch   yev-do-kee'-mo-
  (Rus. dramatist)   vich

Kórnik (Pol.)   kŏŏr'-nĭk   kur'-nik

    German spelling *Kurnik*.

Kornsjoe *or* Kornsjö   kōrn'-shû   kohrn'-shœ
  (Nor.)

Korocha (Rus.)   kŏ-rô'-chä   ko-ro'-chah

Korone (Gr.)   kô-rô'-nē   ko-ro'-nee

    Also called *Asine*, ä-sē'-nē [ah-see'-nee].

Korop (Rus.)   kô'-rŏp   ko'-rop

Koror (Oc., Carolines)   kô'-rôr   ko'-ror

Kőrös (Hung., riv.)   kû'-rûsh   kœ'-rœsh

Kőrösmező (Cz. > Rus.)   See *Yasinya*.

Korosten (Rus.)   kŏ-rŏ-stĕn'(y)   ko-ro-sten'(y)

Korotoyak (Rus.)   kŏ-rŏ-tŏ-yäk'   ko-ro-to-yahk'

Korrça *or* Korrçë (Alb.)   kôr'-chə   kor'-chuh

    Italian *Corizza*, q.v. Greek *Korytsa*, q.v. English *Korcha*, q.v.

Korsoer *or* Korsör (Den.)   kôrs-ûr'   kors-œr'

Korsun (Rus.)   kŏr-sōōn'(y)   kor-soon'(y)

Kortgene (Neth.)   kôrt'-k(h)ä'-nə   kort'-k(h)ay'-nuh

Kortrijk (Belg.)   *Flem.* kôrt'-rīk   kort'-raik

    French *Courtrai*, q.v.

Korytsa (Alb.)   *Gr.* kô-rē-tsä'   ko-ree-tsah'

    Albanian *Korrçë*, q.v.

Koryukovka (Rus.)   kŏr-yōō-kôf'-kä   kor-yoo-kof'-kah

Korzycki, Antoni   kô-zhĭts'-kĭ, än-tô'-nĭ   ko-zhits'-ki, ahn-to'-
  (Pol. polit.)   ni

Kos (Dodec.)   *Eng.* kŏs'   kos'
    Gr. kô(s)'   ko(s)'

    Italian *Coo*, kô'-ô [ko'-o].

Kosančić (Yugosl.)	kô'-sän-chĭch	ko'-sahn-chich
Kosanica (Yugosl., riv.)	kô'-sä'-nĭ-tsä	ko'-sah'-ni-tsah
Kosanović, Sava N.	kŏ-sä'-nŏ-vĭch,	ko-sah'-no-vich,
(Yugosl. diplomat)	sä'-vä	sah'-vah
Kościan (Pol.)	kô'-shchän	ko'-shchahn

German *Kosten*, kôs'-tən [kos'-tuhn].

Kościerzyna (Pol.)	kô-shchĕ-zhĭ'-nä	ko-shcheh-zhi'-nah
Kosciusko (Austral., mt.)	kŏz'-ĭ-ŭs'-kō	koz'-i-uhs'-koh
Kosciusko, Thaddeus	kŏs'-ĭ-ŭs'-kō,	kos'-i-uhs'-koh,
(Pol. patriot)	thăd'-ĭ-əs	thad'-i-uhs

Polish *Tadeusz Andrzej Kościuszko*, tä-dĕ'-ōōsh än'-jä kôsh-chyōōsh'-kô [tah-deh'-ush ahn'-jay kosh-chyush'-ko].

Koshchagil (Rus.)	kŏ-shchä-gĭl'	ko-shchah-gil'
Koshedary (Lith.)	*Rus.* kô'-shĕ-dä'-rĭ	ko'-sheh-dah'-ri

Lithuanian *Kaišiadorys*, q.v.

Košice (Cz.)	kô'-shĭ-tsĕ	ko'-shi-tseh

Hungarian *Kaṣsa*, kŏsh'-shŏ [kosh'-sho].

Košíře (Cz.)	kô'-shē-rzhĕ	ko'-shee-rzheh
Kosjerići (Yugosl.)	kôs'-yĕ'-rĭ-chĭ	kos'-yeh'-ri-chi
Koslar (Ger.)	kôs'-lär	kos'-lahr
Köslin (Ger. >Pol.)	kûs-lēn'	kœs-leen'

Polish *Koszalin*, q.v.

Kosmaj (Yugosl., hill)	kôs'-mī	kos'-mai
Kosovo Polje (Yugosl.)	kô'-sô-vô pô'-lyĕ	ko'-so-vo po'-lyeh
Kosów (Pol.)	kô'-sōōf	ko'-suf
Kossuth, Lajos	*Eng.* kŏs'-sōōth'	kos'-sooth'
(Hung. patriot)	*Hung.* kô'-shōŏt,	ko'-shut, lo'-yosh
	lŏ'-yôsh	
Kostajnica (Yugosl.)	kô'-stī'-nĭ-tsä	ko'-stai'-ni-tsah
Kosten (Pol.) See *Kościan*.		
Kostolac (Yugosl.)	kô'-stô-läts	ko'-sto-lahts
Kostroma (Rus.)	kŏ-strŏ-mä'	ko-stro-mah'
Kostrzyn (Ger. >Pol.)	kôs'-chĭn	kos'-chin
German *Küstrin*, q.v.	*or* -jĭn	*or* -jĭn
Kosturino (Yugosl.)	kô'-stōō'-rĭ-nô	ko'-stoo'-ri-no
Kosygin, Aleksei	kŏ-sī'-gĭn, ä-lĕ-ksä'	ko-si'-gin, ah-leh-
N. (Rus. polit.)		ksay'
Koszalin (Ger. >Pol.)	kô-shä'-lĭn	ko-shah'-lin
German *Köslin*, q.v.		
Kotabaroe *or* Kotabaru	kô'-tä-bä'-rōō	ko'-tah-bah'-roo
(NEI, Borneo)		
Kota Bharoe *or* Bharu	kô'-tä bä'-rōō	kaw'-tah bah'-roo
(Malaya)		
Kotel (Bulg.)	kô'-tĕl	ko'-tel

Kotelnikov (Rus.)	kŏ-tĕl(y)′-nĭ-kŏf	ko-tel(y)′-ni-kof
Köthen (Ger.)	kû′-tən	kœ′-tuhn
Kotikovo (Rus.)	kŏ′-tĭ-kŏ-vŏ	ko′-ti-ko-vo
Kotka (Fin.)	kŏt′-kä	kot′-kah
Kotlas (Rus.)	kŏt′-läs	kot′-lahs
Kotlenik (Yugosl., mts.)	kŏt′-lĕ-nĭk	kot′-leh-nik
Kotor (Yugosl.)	kŏ′-tôr	ko′-tor
Italian *Cattaro*, q.v.		
Kotor Varoš (Yugosl.)	kŏ′-tǫr vä′-rôsh	ko′-tor vah′-rosh
Kotronas (Gr.)	kŏ′-trô-näs	ko′-tro-nahs
Kotsk (Pol.) See *Kock*.		
Kottbus (Ger.)	kŏt′-bo͝os	kot′-bus
Koudekerke (Neth.)	kou′-də-kĕr′-kə	kau′-duh-kehr′-kuh
Kouloure (Gr., isl.) See *Salamis*.		
Kouphonesi (Crete, isl.)	ko͞o-fô-nē′-sē	koo-fo-nee′-see
Also called *Lefke*, lĕf′-kē [lef′-kee].		
Koussevitzky, Sergei	ko͞o′-sə-vĭt′-skĭ,	koo′-suh-vit′-ski,
(Rus. Am. musician)	sĕr-gä′	sehr-gay′
Sergei is sometimes Gallicized to *Serge*, sĕrzh′ [sehrzh′], or Englished		
as sûrj′ [suhrj′].		
Koutoulos (Crete, point)	ko͞o′-to͞o-lôs	koo′-too-los
Koutri (Crete, point)	ko͞o′-trē	koo′-tree
Kov (Rus., riv.)	kŏf′	kof′
Kovačevac (Yugosl.)	kŏ′-vä′-chĕ-väts	ko′-vah′-cheh-vahts
Kovačica (Yugosl.)	kŏ′-vä′-chĭ-tsä	ko′-vah′-chi-tsah
Kovács, Ferenc (Hung.	kŏ′-väch, fĕ′-rĕnts	ko′-vahch, feh′-rents
polit.)		
Kovács, Imre	kŏ′-väch, ĭm′-rĕ	ko′-vahch, im′-reh
(Hung. polit.)		
Kovda (Rus.)	kŏv′-dä	kov′-dah
Kovel (Pol. >Rus.)	kŏ′-vĕl(y)	ko′-vel(y)
Polish *Kowel*, q.v.		
Koviljača (Yugosl.)	kŏ′-vĭ-lyä-chä	ko′-vi-lyah-chah
Kovin (Yugosl.)	kŏ′-vĭn	ko′-vin
Kovno (Lith.)	*Rus.* kŏv′-nŏ	kov′-no
Lithuanian *Kaunas*, q.v.		
Kovrov (Rus.)	kŏv-rôf′	kov-rof′
Kovtun Stankevich,	kŏf-to͞on′ stän-kĕ′-	kof-toon′ stahn-keh′-
Andrei (Rus. general)	vĭch, än-drä′	vich, ahn-dray′
Kovzha (Rus.)	kŏv′-zhä	kov′-zhah
Kowel (Pol. >Rus.)	kŏ′-vĕl	ko′-vel
Russian *Kovel*, kŏ′-vĕl(y) [ko′-vel(y)].		
Kowloon (Ch., Hongkong)	kou-lo͞on	kau-loon
Chinese *Chiu-lung*, jyo͞o-lo͝ong [jyoo-lung].		

Kozane (Gr.)	kô-zä'-nē	ko-zah'-nee
Kozelsk (Rus.)	kŏ-zĕlsk'	ko-zelsk'
Kozenitse (Pol.) See *Kozienice*.		
Kozienice (Pol.)	kô-zhĕ-nē'-tsĕ	ko-zheh-nee'-tseh
Russian *Kozenitse*, kŏ-zĕ-nē'-tsĕ [ko-zeh-nee'-tseh].		
Kozjak (Yugosl., mt.)	kôz'-yäk	koz'-yahk
Koźle (Ger. >Pol.)	kôzh'-lĕ	kozh'-leh
German *Cosel*, q.v.		
Kozlov (Rus.)	kŏz-lôf'	koz-lof'
Koźłów (Pol.)	kôzh'-lŏof	kozh'-luf
Kozmeny (Rum. >Rus.)	kôz-mĕ'-nĭ	koz-meh'-ni
Rumanian *Cozmeni*, q.v.		
Koźmin (Pol.)	kôzh'-mĭn	kozh'-min
Kožuf (Balkan mts.)	S.-C. kô'-zhŏof	ko'-zhoof
Kra (Siam, isthmus)	krä'	krah'
Krabbendijke (Neth.)	kräb'-ən-dī'-kə	krahb'-uhn-dai'-kuh
Krageroe *or* Kragerö (Nor.)	krä'-gĕr-û	krah'-gehr-œ
Kragujevac (Yugosl.)	krä'-gŏo'-yĕ-väts	krah'-goo'-yeh-vahts
Krajina (Yugosl.)	krä'-yĭ-nä	krah'-yi-nah
Krajište (Yugosl.)	krä'-yĭ-shtĕ	krah'-yi-shteh
Krakatau (NEI)	krä-kä-tou'	krah-kah-tau'
Krakov *or* Kraków (Pol.) See *Cracow*.		
Kralje (Yugosl.)	krä'-lyĕ	krah'-lyeh
Kraljevica (Yugosl.)	krä'-lyĕ'-vĭ-tsä	krah'-lyeh'-vi-tsah
Kraljevo (Yugosl.)	krä'-lyĕ-vô	krah'-lyeh-vo
Kramatorsk (Rus.)	krä-mä-tôrsk'	krah-mah-torsk'
Kranj (Yugosl.)	krän'(y)	krahn'(y)
Krapina (Yugosl.)	krä'-pĭ-nä	krah'-pi-nah
Krasilnikov, Alexei (Rus. diplomat)	krä-sēl'(y)-nĭ-kôf, ä-lĕk-sā'	krah-seel'(y)-ni-kof, ah-lek-say'
Krāslava (Latvia)	kräs'-lä-vä	krahs'-lah-vah
Krasne (Pol. >Rus.)	kräs'-nĕ	krahs'-neh
Kraśnik (Pol.)	kräsh'-nĭk	krahsh'-nik
Russian *Krasnik*, kräs'-nĭk [krahs'-nik].		
Krasnoarmeisk (Rus.)	kräs'-nŏ-är-mäsk'	krahs'-no-ahr-maysk'
Krasnodar (Rus.)	kräs-nŏ-där'	krahs-no-dahr'
Krasnograd (Rus.)	kräs-nŏ-grät'	krahs-no-graht'
Krasnogvardeisk (Rus.)	kräs-nŏ-gvär-däsk'	krahs-no-gvahr-daysk'
Krasnovodsk (Rus.)	kräs-nŏ-vôdsk'	krahs-no-vodsk'
Krasnoyarsk (Rus.)	kräs-nŏ-yärsk'	krahs-no-yahrsk'
Krasnoye (Rus.)	kräs'-nŏ-yĕ	krahs'-no-yeh

Krasnoznamensk   kräs-nŏz-nä′-mĕnsk   krahs-noz-nah′-
(Ger. >Rus.)   mensk
German *Lasdehnen*, q.v.

Krasny Kholm (Rus.)   kräs′-nĭ hôlm′   krahs′-ni holm′
Krasny Liman (Rus.)   kräs′-nĭ lĭ-män′   krahs′-ni li-mahn′
Krasnystaw (Pol.)   kräs′-nĭ-stäf   krahs′-ni-stahf
Russian *Krasnostav*, kräs-nŏ-stäf′ [krahs-no-stahf′].

Kraste (Yugosl., hills)   krä′-stĕ   krah′-steh
Kratié (Indo-Ch.)   krä-tyĕ′   krah-tyeh′
Kratovo (Yugosl.)   krä′-tô-vô   krah′-to-vo
Krawang (NEI, Java)   krä-wäng′   krah-wahng′
Krčin, Donji (Yugosl.)   kər′-chĭn, dôn′-yĭ   kuhr′-chin, don′-yĭ
Krefeld (Ger.)   krā′-fĕlt   kray′-felt
Kreising (Pol.)   *Ger.* krī′-zĭng   krai′-zing
Polish *Krzesiny*, kshĕ-shē′-nĭ [ksheh-shee′-ni].

Kremenchug (Rus.)   krĕ-mĕn-chŏŏk′   kreh-men-chuk′
Kremenets (Pol. >Rus.)   krĕ-mĕ-nĕts′   kreh-meh-nets′
Polish *Krzemieniec*, q.v.

Krepoljin (Yugosl.)   krĕ′-pô′-lyĭn   kreh′-po′-lyin
Kreševo (Yugosl.)   krĕ′-shĕ-vô   kreh′-sheh-vo
Kresta (Alaska, Attu)   krĕs′-tä   kres′-tah
Kresttsi (Rus.)   krĕst-tsĭ′   krest-tsi′
Krete (Gr., isl.)   See *Crete*.
Kretinga (Lith.)   krĕ′-tĭng-gä   kreh′-ting-gah
Kreutzburg (Latvia)   *Ger.* kroits′-bŏŏrk(h) kroits′-burk(h)
                            Rus. kräts′-bŏŏrk   krayts′-burk
Latvian *Krustpils*, q.v.

Kreuz (Ger. >Pol.)   kroits′   kroits′
Polish *Krzyż*, q.v.

Kreuzburg (Ger. >Pol.)   kroits′-bŏŏrk(h)   kroits′-burk(h)
Polish *Kluczborek*, q.v.

Kreuzingen (Ger. >Rus.)   kroits′-ĭng-ən   kroits′-ing-uhn
Russian spelling *Kroitsingen*.

Kreuznach (Ger.)   kroits′-näk(h)   kroits′-nahk(h)
Kreymborg, Alfred (Am.   krām′-bôrg   kraym′-borg
poet)
Kriba (Tun.)   krē′-bə   kree′-buh
Krichev (Rus.)   krē′-chĕf   kree′-chef
Krim (Rus.)   krĭm′   krim′
English *Crimea*, q.v.

Krimpen (Neth.)   krĭm′-pən   krim′-puhn
Krios (Crete, point)   krē-ôs′   kree-os′
Kriou Metopon (Crete,   krē-ōō′ mĕ′-tô-pô(n)   kree-oo′ meh′-to-
point)   po(n)
Also called *Krios*, q.v.

[275]

Kristiansand (Nor.)	krĭs-tyän-sän'	kris-tyahn-sahn'
Kristiansund (Nor.)	krĭs-tyän-sŏōn'	kris-tyahn-sun'
Kristinestad (Fin.)	*Sw.* krĭs-tē'-nə-städ'	kris-tee'-nuh-stahd'

Finnish *Kristiinankaupunki*, krĭs'-tē-nän-kou'-pŏōng-kē [kris'-tee-nahn-kau'-pung-kee].

Kritsa (Crete)	krĕ-tsä'	kree-tsah'
Kriva (Yugosl., riv.)	krē'-vä	kree'-vah
Kriva Lakavica	krē'-vä lä'-kä-vĭ-tsä	kree'-vah lah'-kah-
(Yugosl., riv.)		vi-tsah
Kriva Palanka (Yugosl.)	krē'-vä pä'-län-kä	kree'-vah pah'-lahn-
		kah
Krivelj (Yugosl.)	krē'-vĕl(y)	kree'-vel(y)
Krivogaštani (Yugosl.)	krē'-vô-gä'-shtä-nĭ	kree'-vo-gah'-shtah-ni
Krivoi Rog (Rus.)	krĭ-voi' rôg'	kri-voi' rog'
Krivolak (Yugosl.)	krē'-vô-läk	kree'-vo-lahk
Krivomuzginskaya	krĭ-vŏ-mōōz'-gĭn-	kri-vo-mooz'-gin-
(Rus.)	skä-yä	skä-yä
Krivorozhe (Rus.)	krĭ-vŏ-rôzh'-yĕ	kri-vo-rozh'-yeh
Kriz (Tun.)	krēz'	kreez'
Križevci (Yugosl.)	krē'-zhĕv-tsĭ	kree'-zhev-tsi
Krk (Yugosl.)	kərk'	kuhrk'

Italian *Veglia*, q.v.

Krka (Yugosl., rivs.)	kər'-kä	kuhr'-kah
Krnjaja (Yugosl.)	kər'-nyä-yä	kuhr'-nyah-yah
Krnov (Cz.)	kər'-nôf	kuhr'-nof
Kroederen *or* Kröderen	krû'-də-rən	krœ'-duh-ruhn
(Nor.)		

Kroitsingen (Ger. >Rus.) See *Kreuzingen*.

| Krokowo (Pol.) | krô-kô'-vô | kro-ko'-vo |
| Krolevets (Rus.) | krŏ-lĕ'-vĕts | kro-leh'-vets |

Królewiec (Ger. >Pol.) See *Koenigsberg*.

| Królewska Huta (Pol.) | krŏō-lĕf'-skä hŏō'-tä | kru-lef'-skah hoo'-tah |
| Królewski, Kanal (Pol.) | krŏō-lĕf'-skĭ, kä'-näl | kru-lef'-ski, kah'-nahl |

Russian *Dnyeprovsko-Bugski Kanal*, dnĕ-prôf'-skŏ-bōōg'-skĭ kä-näl' [dneh-prof'-sko-boog'-ski kah-nahl'].

Kroll, Leon (Am. painter)	krōl'	krohl'
Kroměříž (Cz.)	krô'-myĕ-rzhēzh	kro'-myeh-rzheezh
Kromi (Rus.)	krô'-mĭ	kro'-mi
Krommenie (Neth.)	krôm'-ə-nē'	krom'-uh-nee'
Kronstadt (Rus.)	krŏn-shtät'	kron-shtaht'
Kropotkin (Rus.)	krŏ-pôt'-kĭn	kro-pot'-kin
Kropotkin, Prince Pëtr	krŏ-pôt'-kĭn, pyô'tr	kro-pot'-kin, pyo'tr
A. (Rus. writer)		
Krośniewice (Pol.)	krôsh-nyĕ-vē'-tsĕ	krosh-nyeh-vee'-tseh

Krosno (Ger. >? Pol.) krôs′-nô kros′-no
  German *Crossen*, q.v.
Krotoszyn (Pol.) krô-tô′-shǐn kro-to′-shin
Krraba (Alb., pass) See *Krrabë.*
Krrabë (Alb., pass) krä′-bə krah′-buh
  Also called *Qafe e Krrabës.*
Kršs, Veliki *and* Mali kərsh′, vĕ′-lǐ-kǐ kuhrsh′, veh′-li-ki
  (Yugosl., mts.) *and* mä′-lǐ *and* mah′-li
Krševica (Yugosl.) kər′-shĕ′-vǐ-tsä kuhr′-sheh′-vi-tsah
Krško (Yugosl.) kərsh′-kô kuhrsh′-ko
Krsna, Velika *and* Mala kərs′-nä, vĕ′-lǐ-kä kuhrs′-nah, veh′-li-
  (Yugosl.) *and* mä′-lä kah *and* mah′-lah
Krtole (Yugosl.) kər′-tô-lĕ kuhr′-to-leh
Krug, Julius Albert krōōg′ kroog′
  (Am. administrator)
Kruif, Paul de (Am. author) See *De Kruif.*
Kruiningen (Neth.) krûǐ′-nǐng-ən krœi′-ning-uhn
Kruja (Alb.) See *Krujë.*
Krujë (Alb.) krōō′-yə kroo′-yuh
  Italian *Croia*, q.v. Formerly (Turkish) *Akçehisar.*
Krung Thep *or* Krungdheb (Siam) See *Bangkok.*
Krupanj (Yugosl.) krōō′-pän(y) kroo′-pahn(y)
Krupp (Ger.) *Eng.* krŭp′ kruhp′
  Ger. krōōp′ krup′
Kruščica (Yugosl., mts.) krōōsh′-chǐ-tsä kroosh′-chi-tsah
Kruševac (Yugosl.) krōō′-shĕ-väts kroo′-sheh-vahts
Kruševica (Yugosl.) krōō′-shĕ′-vǐ-tsä kroo′-sheh′-vi-tsah
Kruševo (Yugosl.) krōō′-shĕ-vô kroo′-sheh-vo
Krustpils (Latvia) krōōst′-pēls krust′-peels
  Russian and German *Kreutzburg*, q.v.
Kruszwica (Pol.) krōōsh-vē′-tsä krush-vee′-tsah
Krvavi Kamik (Balkan *S.-C.* kər′-vä-vǐ kuhr′-vah-vi
  mt.) kä′-mǐk kah′-mik
Krylov, Sergei krǐ-lôf′, sĕr-gā′ kri-lof′, sehr-gay′
  Borisovich (Rus. polit.) bŏ-rē′-sŏ-vǐch bo-ree′-so-vich
Krymskaya (Rus.) krǐm′-skä-yä krim′-skah-yah
Krynica (Pol.) krǐ-nē′-tsä kri-nee′-tsah
Kryoneri (Gr.) krē-ô-nĕ′-rē kree-o-neh′-ree
Krzemieniec (Pol. >Rus.) kshĕ-myĕ′-nyĕts ksheh-myeh′-nyets
  Russian *Kremenets*, krĕ-mĕ-nĕts′ [kreh-meh-nets′].
Krzesiny (Pol.) kshĕ-shē′-nǐ ksheh-shee′-ni
  German *Kreising*, krǐ′-zǐng [krai′-zing].
Krzyż (Ger. >Pol.) kshǐsh′ kshish′
  German *Kreuz*, q.v.

Krzyżatka (Pol.)	kshĭ-zhät′-kä	kshi-zhaht′-kah
Ksar (Tun.)	kə-sär′	kuh-sahr′
Ksar Rhilane (Tun.)	kə-sär′ rĭ-lăn′	kuh-sahr′ ri-lan′
Ksar Tyr (Tun.)	kə-sär′ tēr′	kuh-sahr′ teer′
Ksenievskaya (Rus.)	ksĕ′-nĭ-yĕf-skä-yä	kseh′-ni-yef-skah-yah
Książ (Pol.)	kshôNsh′	kshoNsh′
Ksour Essaf (Tun.)	kə-sōōr′ ĕs-săf′	kuh-soor′ es-saf′
ku	kōō	koo

An element, meaning *city ward* or *quarter*, in Japanese place names.

Kuala Lumpur (Malaya)	kwä′-lə lōōm′-pōōr′	kwah′-luh lum′-pur′
Kuang- (Ch.) See *Kwang-*.		
Kuaua (Oc., New Caledonia)	kōō-ä-ōō′-ä	koo-ah-oo′-ah
Kuba (Rus.)	kōō′-bä	koo′-bah
Kuban (Rus., riv.)	kōō-bän′(y)	ku-bahn′(y)
Kuberle (Rus)	kōō-bĕr-lĕ′	koo-behr-leh′
Kubršnica (Y ugosl., riv.)	kōō′-bərsh′-nĭ-tsä	koo′-buhrsh′-ni-tsah
Kubuleti (Rus.)	kōō-bōō-lĕ′-tĭ	koo-boo-leh′-ti
Kuç (Alb.)	kōōch′	kooch′
Kučaj (Yugosl.)	kōō′-chī	koo′-chai
Kučajna (Yugosl.)	kōō′-chī-nä	koo′-chai-nah
Kučevo (Yugosl.)	kōō′-chĕ-vô	koo′-cheh-vo
Kuchan *or* Quchan (Iran)	kōō-chän′	koo-chahn′
Kuching (Sarawac)	kōō′-chĭng	koo′-ching
Kučkovo (Yugosl.)	kōōch′-kô-vô	kooch′-ko-vo
Kuçova (Alb.) See *Kuçovë*.		
Kuçovë (Alb.)	kōō-chô′-və	koo-cho′-vuh

Also called *Vajguras*, q.v. Italian *Petrolia*, q.v.

Kudat (Br. Borneo)	kōō-dät′	koo-daht′
Kuei- (Ch.) See *Kwei-*.		
Kuenga (Rus.)	kōō-ĕn-gä′	koo-en-gah′
Kufara (Libya)	kōō′-frə	koo′-fruh
Italian *Cufra*, q.v.		
Kuibyshev (Rus.)	*Eng.* kwē′-bĭ-shĕf	kwee′-bi-shef
	Rus. kōō′ĭ-bwē-shĕf	koo′i-bwee-shef
	or kōōĭ-bwē′-shĕf	kui-bwee′-shef
Kuik (Neth.)	kûĭk′	kœik′
Kuilenburg (Neth.)	kûĭ′-lən-bûrk(h)	kœi′-luhn-bœrk(h)

Also called *Culemborg*, kü′-ləm-bôrk(h) [kü′-luhm-bork(h)].

Kukës (Alb.)	kōō′-kəs	koo′-kuhs
Kukësi (Alb.) See *Kukës*.		
Kukiel, Marian (Pol. general)	kōō′-kyĕl, mär′-yän	koo′-kyel, mahr′-yahn
Ku-Klux, Kuklux	kyōō′-klŭks	kyoo′-kluks
	or kōō′-klŭks	koo′-kluks

Kukui (Rus.)	kŏŏ-kōō′ĭ	ku-koo′i
Kuku Nor (Ch., prov., lake)	See *Koko Nor*.	
Kula (Oc., Solomons, gulf)	kōō′-lä	koo′-lah
Kula (Yugosl.)	kōō′-lä	koo′-lah
Kulamadau (Oc., Woodlark)	kōō-lä-mä′-dou	koo-lah-mah′-dau
Kuldiga (Latvia)	kŏŏl′-dē-gä	kul′-dee-gah
Russian and German *Goldingen*, q.v.		
Ku-ling (Ch., Kiangsi)	gōō-lĭng	goo-ling
Kuliviu (Oc., New Hebrides)	kōō-lē′-vē-ōō	koo-lee′-vee-oo
Kulm (Pol.) See *Chełmno*.		
Kulmbach (Ger.)	kŏŏlm′-bäk(h)	kulm′-bahk(h)
Kulmsee (Pol.) See *Chełmża*.		
Kum *or* Qum (Iran)	kŏŏm′	kum′
Kuma (Rus., riv.)	kōō′-mä	koo′-mah
Kumamoto (Jap.)	kōō-mä′-mô′-tô′	koo-mah′-mo′-to′
Kumaničevo (Yugosl.)	kōō′-mä-nē′-chĕ-vô	koo′-mah-nee′-cheh-vo
Kumanovo (Yugosl.)	kōō′-mä-nô-vô	koo′-mah-no-vo
Kumanovska (Yugosl., riv.)	kōō′-mä-nôf-skä	koo′-mah-nof-skah
Kumbur (Yugosl.)	kŏŏm′-bōōr	koom′-boor
Kumodraž (Yugosl.)	kōō′-mô-dräzh	koo′-mo-drahzh
Kumusi (New Guinea, Papua, riv.)	kōō-mōō′-sē	koo-moo′-see
Kuni, Higashi (Jap. prince) See *Higashi Kuni*.		
Kunda (Est.)	kŏŏn′-dä	koon′-dah
Kunersdorf (Ger.)	kōō′-nərs-dôrf	koo′-nuhrs-dorf
K′ung, Dr. Hsiang Hsi (Chinese polit.)	kŏŏng, shyäng shē	kung, shyahng shee
Mme. K′ung is *Ai-ling Soong*, q.v.		
Kung-an (Ch., Hupeh)	gŏŏng-än	gung-ahn
Kungur (Rus.)	kŏŏn-gōōr′	kun-gur′
Kunkel, John C. (U.S. representative)	kŏŏng′-kĕl′	kung′-kel′
Kunlong (Burma)	kŏŏn-lŏng′	kun-long′
K′un-lun (Ch., Sinkiang, mts.)	kŏŏn-lōōn	kun-lun
K′un-ming (Ch., Yünnan)	kŏŏn-mĭng	kun-ming
Also called *Yün-nan-fu*, q.v.		
Kuno (Est., isl.)	*Rus.* kōō′-nŏ	koo′-no
Estonian *Kihnu*, q.v.		

[279]

Kunora (Alb., mt.)   See *Kunorë*.

Kunorë (Alb., mt.)	kōō-nô'-rə	koo-no'-ruh
Kunszentmiklós (Hung.)	kŏŏn'-sĕnt-mē-klôsh'	kun'-sent-mee-klosh'
Kuomintang (Ch.	*Eng.* kwŏ-mĭn-tăng	kwoh-min-tang
political party)	*Ch.* gwô-mĭn-däng	gwo-min-dahng
Kuop (Oc., Carolines)	kōō'-ôp	koo'-op
Kuopio (Fin.)	kŏŏ'-ô'-pē-ô	ku'-o'-pee-o
Kupa (Yugosl., riv.)	kōō'-pä	koo'-pah

German *Kulpa*.

Kupang (NEI, Timor) See *Koepang*.

Kupci (Yugosl.)	kŏŏp'-tsĭ	koop'-tsi
Ku-pe-k'ou (Ch., Hopeh)	gōō-bā-kō	goo-bay-koh
Kupyansk (Rus.)	kōō'-pyänsk	koo'-pyahnsk
Kur (Rus., riv.)	kōōr'	koor'
Kura (Rus., riv.)	kōō-rä'	koo-rah'
Kurd (Per. tribe)	*Eng.* kûrd'	kuhrd'
	Per. kōōrd'	koord'
Kurdistan (Iran)	*Per.* kōōr-dĭs-tän'	koor-dis-tahn'
	Eng. kûr'-dĭs-tăn	kuhr'-dis-tan
Kure (Jap.)	kōō'-rĕ	koo'-reh
Kuressaare (Est.)	kōō'-rĕs-sä'-rĕ	koo'-res-sah'-reh

Also called *Kuresaari*, kōō-rĕ-sä'-rĭ [koo-reh-sah'-ri]. German *Arensburg*, q.v.

Kurgan (Rus.)	kŏŏr-gän'	kur-gahn'
Kurgannaya (Rus.)	kŏŏr-gän'-nä-yä	kúr-gahn'-nah-yah
Kuria (Oc., Gilberts)	kōō'-rē-ä	koo'-ree-ah
Kuril (Rus., str., isls.)	kōō-rēl' *or* kōō'-rĭl	koo-reel' *or* koo'-ril

The islands, formerly Japanese, were called *Chishima*, chē-shē'-mä [chee-shee'-mah].

Kurische Nehrung (Ger.)	kōō'-rĭsh-ə nā'-rŏŏng	koo'-rish-uh nay'-rung
Kurisches Haff (Ger. >	kōō'-rĭsh-əs häf'	koo'-rish-uhs hahf'
Rus., lagoon)		

Russian *Kurishes Gaf*, kōō'-rĭ-shĕs gäf [koo'-ri-shes gahf].

Kurishi (Rus.)	kōō'-rĭ-shĭ	koo'-ri-shi
Kurjače (Yugosl.)	kōōr'-yä-chê	koor'-yah-cheh
Kurnik (Pol.) See *Kórnik*.		
Kurnub (Pal.)	kŏŏr'-nŏŏb'	kur'-nub'
Kursk (Rus.)	kŏŏrsk'	koorsk'
Kuršumlija (Yugosl.)	kŏŏr'-shōōm'-lĭ-yä	koor'-shoom'-li-yah
Kurum, Ras en (Pal.) See *Ras en Kurum*.		
Kurume (Jap.)	kōō'-rōō-mĕ	koo'-roo-meh
Kusadak (Yugosl.)	kōō'-sä-däk	koo'-sah-dahk
Kusaie (Oc., Carolines)	kōō-sī'-ĕ	koo-sai'-eh

Kush (India, mts.)　See *Hindu Kush.*

Kushchëvka (Rus.)　koo-shchôf'-kä　koo-shchof'-kah
Kushiro (Jap.)　koo-shē'-rô　koo-shee'-ro
Kušijevo (Yugosl.)　koo'-shē'-lyĕ-vô　koo'-shee'-lyeh-vo
Kustlanai (Rus.)　koo-stä-nĭ'　koo-stah-nai'
Küstrin (Ger. > Pol.)　küs-trēn'　küs-treen'
　Polish *Kostrzyn*, q.v.
Kutais (Rus.)　koo-tä-ēs'　koo-tah-ees'
Kutaradya (NEI, Sumatra) See *Koetaradja.*
Kutch (India)　See *Cutch.*
Kutina (Yugosl., riv.)　koo'-tĭ-nä　koo'-ti-nah
Kutkai (Burma)　koot-kĭ'　kut-kai'
Kutná Hora (Cz.)　koot'-nä hô'-rä　koot'-nah ho'-rah
Kutno (Pol.)　koot'-nô　kut'-no
Kuty (Pol.)　koo'-tĭ　koo'-ti
Kuusamo (Rus.)　koo'-sä-mō　koo'-sah-moh
Kuusinen Leino, Herrta　koo'-sē-nĕn　koo'-see-nen
　(Fin. polit.)　lä'-nô, hĕr'-tä　lay'-no, her'-tah
Kuvshinovo (Rus.)　koof-shĭ'-nŏ-vô　koof-shi'-no-vo
Kuwatly, Shukry el (Syrian polit.) See *Shukry el Kuwatly.*
Kuweit *or* Kuwait　koo-wät' *or* koo-wīt'　ku-wayt' *or* ku-wait'
　(Arabia)
Kuznetsk (Rus.)　kooz-nĕtsk'　kooz-netsk'
Kuznetsova (Rus.)　kooz-nĕ-tsô'-vä　kooz-neh-tso'-vah
Kvam (Nor.)　kväm'　kvahm'
Kvanne (Nor.)　kvän'-nə　kvahn'-nuh
Kvarner (Yugosl., inlets) See *Mali Kvarner* and *Veliki Kvarner.*
Kvaroey *or* Kvaröy　kvär'-ûĭ　kvahr'-œi
　(Nor.)
Kvédarna (Lith.)　kvä'-där-nä　kvay'-dahr-nah
Kvesmenes (Nor.)　kvĕs'-mə-nĕs　kves'-muh-nes
Kvisvik (Nor.)　kvĭs'-vēk　kvis'-veek
Kviteseid (Nor.)　kvĭt'-sā　kvit'-say
　　　or kvĭt'-ə-sād　kvit'-uh-sayd
Kwajalein　kwä'-jä-län　kwah'-jah-layn
　(Oc., Marshalls)
　Also pronounced by the American forces kwä'-jə-lēn' [kwah'-juh-leen']
　and kwä'-jə-lĭn [kwah'-juh-lin]. Formerly Russian *Menshikov*, mĕn'-
　shĭ-kôf [men'-shi-kof].
Kwakea (Oc., New　kwä-kĕ'-ä　kwah-keh'-ah
　Hebrides)
Kwang-ch'ang (Ch.,　gwäng-chäng　gwahng-chahng
　Kiangsi)
Kwang Chow Wan (Ch.,　gwäng jō wän　gwahng joh wahn
　Kwangtung, Fr. colony)

Kwang-fêng (Ch., Kiangsi)	gwäng-fŭng	gwahng-fuhng
Kwang-si (Ch., prov.)	*Eng.* kwăng-sē	kwang-see
	Ch. gwäng-sē	gwahng-see
Kwang-tung (Ch., prov.)	*Eng.* kwăng-tŏŏng	kwang-tung
	Ch. gwäng-dŏŏng	gwahng-dung
K'wan-t'o (Manchu.)	See *Kwantung.*	
Kwan-tung (Manchu.)	*Eng.* kwăn-tŏŏng	kwan-tung
	Ch. gwän-dŏŏng	gwahn-dung
Also called *K'wan-t'o,* kwän-tô [kwahn-to].		
Kwapinski, Jan	kvä-pēn'-skĭ, yän'	kvah-peen'-ski, yahn'
(Pol. polit.)		
Kwa-tsa (Ch., Yünnan)	gwä-dzä	gwah-dzah
Kwazon (Burma)	kwä-zōn'	kwah-zohn'
Kwei-ch'i (Ch., Kiangsi)	gwä-chē	gway-chee
Also spelled *Kwei-ki.*		
K'wei-ch'ieh (Burma)	kwä-chyĕ	kway-chyeh
Kwei-chow (Ch., prov.)	*Eng.* kwä-chou	kway-chau
	Ch. gwä-jō	gway-joh
Kwei-hwa (Ch., Suiyüan)	gwä-whä	gway-whah
Kwei-hwa Sui-yüan	gwä-whä swä-yüän	gway-whah sway-
(Ch., prov.)		yü-ahn
Also called *Sui-yüan,* q.v.		
Kwei-ki (Ch.) Variant spelling of *Kwei-ch'i,* q.v.		
Kwei-lin (Ch., Kiangsi)	gwä-lĭn	gway-lin
Kwei-sui (Ch., Suiyüan)	gwä-swä	gway-sway
Kwei-yang (Ch.,	gwä-yäng	gway-yahng
Kweichow)		
Kwidzyń (Ger. >Pol.)	kvē'-dzĭn(y)	kvee'-dzin(y)
German *Marienwerder,* q.v.		
Kwisa (Ger. >? Pol.,	kvē'-sä	kvee'-sah
riv.)		
German *Queis,* q.v.		
Kwo Ho *or* Kwo River	gwô	gwo
(Ch.)		
Kwomintang (Ch. polit. party) See *Kuomintang.*		
Kyaikkami (Burma)	chĭk'-kə-mē'	chaik'-kuh-mee'
Kyaikthin (Burma)	chĭk'-thĭn'	chaik'-thin'
Kyakhta (Rus.)	kyäk(h)'-tä	kyahk(h)'-tah
Kyamon (Crete, point)	See *Melekhas.*	
Kyangin (Burma)	chăn'-gĭn'	chan'-gin'
Kyaukkyi (Burma)	chouk'-chē'	chauk'-chee'
Kyaukpadaung (Burma)	chouk'-pə-doung'	chauk'-puh-daung'
Kyaukpyu (Burma)	chouk'-pyōō'	chauk'-pyoo'
Kyaukse (Burma)	chouk'-sĕ'	chauk'-seh'

Kyauktaw (Burma)	chouk'-tô'	chauk'-taw'
Kybartai (Lith.)	kē-bär'-tī	kee-bahr'-tai
Kyelce (Pol.) See *Kielce*.		
Kyklades (Gr., isls.) See *Cyclades*.		
Kyll (Ger., riv.)	kĭl'	kil'
Kyllburg (Ger.)	*Eng.* kĭl'-bûrg	kil'-buhrg
	Ger. kĭl'-bŏŏrk(h)	kil'-burk(h)
Kyllene (Gr.)	kē-lē'-nē	kee-lee'-nee

Also called *Zyria* or *Zerea*, zē'-rē-ä [zee'-ree-ah]. English *Cyllene*, sĭ-lē'-nē [si-lee'-nee].

Kyme (Gr.)	kē'-mē *or* kōō'-mē	kee'-mee *or* koo'-mee
Kyōdō (Jap. news agency)	kyô'-dô'	kyo'-do'
Kyōto (Jap.)	kyô'-tô	kyo'-to
Kyparisi (Gr.)	kē-pä-rē'-sē	kee-pah-ree'-see
Kyparissia (Gr.)	kē-pä-rē-sē'-ä	kee-pah-ree-see'-ah

Also some villages of this name accent the last syllable, and some the antepenult. For the noun (*cypress tree*) the accent is on the antepenult.

Kythera (Gr., isl., town)	kē'-thē-rä	kee'-thee-rah

English *Cythera*, sĭ-thē'-rä [si-thee'-rah]. The island is also called *Tserigo*, tsĕ-rē'-gô [tseh-ree'-go]; the town, *Kapsali(on)*, kä-psä'-lē [kah-psah'-lee].

Kythnos (Gr., isl.)	kēth'-nô(s)	keeth'-no(s)

English *Cythnus*, sĭth'-nəs [sĭth'-nuhs].

Kyukok (Burma) See *Chukok*.		
Kyungon (Burma)	chŏŏn'-gōn'	chun'-gohn'
Kyūshū (Jap.)	kyōō'-shōō	kyoo'-shoo
Kyustendil (Bulg.)	kyōō'-stĕn-dĭl'	kyoo'-sten-dil'
Laagendal (Nor.)	lô'-gən-däl	lo'-guhn-dahl
Laaland (Den., isl.)	lô'-län	lo'-lahn
Laatefoss (Nor.)	lô'-tə-fôs	lo'-tuh-fos
Laba (Rus., riv.)	lä'-bä	lah'-bah
Lababia (N.E. New Guinea)	lä-bä'-bē-ä	lah-bah'-bee-ah
Labarca, Amanda (Chilean diplomat)	lä-bär'-kä, ä-män'-dä	lah-bahr'-kah, ah-mahn'-dah
Labe (Europ. riv.) See *Elbe*.		
Labiau (Ger. >Rus.)	lä'-bĭ-ou	lah'-bi-au

Russian *Polessk*, pŏ-lĕsk' [po-lesk'].

Labico (It.)	lä-bē'-kô	lah-bee'-ko
Labinskaya (Rus.)	lä-bēn'-skä-yä	lah-been'-skah-yah
Łabiszyn (Pol.)	lä-bē'-shĭn	lah-bee'-shin

German spelling *Labischin*.

Labó (P.I)	lä-bô'	lah-bo'

Laboeha *or* Labuha (NEI, Moluccas)	lä-bōō'-hä	lah-boo'-hah
Labrador (P.I.)	lä-brä-dôr'	lah-brah-dor'
Labuan (Br. Borneo)	lä-bŏŏ-än'	lah-bu-ahn'
La Buy, Walter J. (Am. judge)	lə bī'	luh bai'
La Calle (Alg.)	lä käl'	lah kahl'
La Camargue (Fr., isl.)	lä kä-märg'	lah kah-mahrg'
Laccadive (India, isls.)	lăk'-ə-dīv	lak'-uh-daiv
La Chapelle (Fr.)	lä shä-pĕl'	lah shah-pel'
La Ciotat (Fr.)	lä syô-tä'	lah syo-tah'
Lacis, Vilis (Latvian polit.)	lä'-tsēs, vē'-lēs	lah'-tsees, vee'-lees

Lac Léman (Switz.) See *Geneva, Lake.*

Laconia (Gr.)	*Eng.* lə-kōn'-yə	luh-kohn'-yuh
	Ger. lä-kô-nē'-ä	lah-ko-nee'-ah
Lacroma (Yugosl., isl.)	*It.* lä-krô'-mä	lah-kro'-mah

Serb-Croat *Lokrum*, q.v.

Ladoga (Indiana)	lə-dō'-gə	luh-doh'-guh
Ladoga (Rus., lake)	lä'-dŏ-gä	lah'-do-gah

Russian *Ladozhskoe Ozero*, q.v. Finnish *Laatokka*, lä'-tôk-kä [lah'-tok-kah].

Ladozhskoe Ozero (Rus., lake)	lä'-dŏzh-skô-yĕ ô'-zĕ-rŏ	lah'-dozh-sko-yeh o'-zeh-ro

Also called *Ladoga*, q.v.

Ladrones (Oc.)	*Eng.* lə-drōnz'	luh-drohnz'
	Sp. lä-drô'-nĕs	lah-dro'-nes

Usually called the *Marianas*, q.v.

Ladushkin (Ger. >Rus.)	lä'-dŏŏ-shkĭn	lah'-du-shkin

German *Ludwigsort*, q.v.

Lae (N.E. New Guinea)	lä'-ĕ *or* lī'	lah'-eh *or* lai'
Laeken (Belg.)	lä'-kən	lah'-kuhn
Lærdal (Nor.)	lĕr'-däl	lehr'-dahl
Læsoe *or* Læsö (Den., isl.)	lĕs'-û	les'-œ
La Fauconnerie (Tun., airfield)	lä fō-kôn-rē'	lah foh-kon-ree'
La Follette, Robert M., Jr. (U. S. senator)	lə fŏl'-ĭt	luh fol'-it
Laghetto (It.)	lä-gĕt'-tô	lah-get'-to
Lagny (Fr.)	lä-nyē'	lah-nyee'
lago	lä'-gô	lah'-go

An element, meaning *lake*, in Italian place names. It may be necessary to look up the other part of the name.

Lagonoy (P.I.)	lä-gô'-noi	lah-go'-noi

Lagos (Gr., bay) lä'-gôs lah'-gos
  Turkish *Karagach Limanı*, kä-rä-gäch' lē-mä-nĭ' [kah-rah-gahch'
  lee-mah-ni'].
Lagos (Mex.) lä'-gôs lah'-gos
Lagos (Nigeria) lä'-gôs lah'-gos
  or lā'-gŏs lay'-gos
Lagos (Port.) lä'-gōōsh lah'-gush
Lagosta (It. > Yugosl., isl.) lä-gô'-stä lah-go'-stah
  Serb-Croat *Lastovo*, lä'-stô-vô [lah'-sto-vo].
La Goulette (Tun.) lä gōō-lĕt' lah goo-let'
La Guardia, Fiorello *Eng*. lə gwär'-dĭ-ə luh gwahr'-di-uh
  (Am. polit.) *or* lə gär'-dĭ-ə luh gahr'-di-uh
  It. lä gwär'-dyä lah gwahr'-dyah
Before broadcasting from a WCBS studio on October 20, 1942, Mr.
La Guardia said that he had pronounced his name lə gwär'-dĭ-ə
[luh gwahr'-di-uh] for over fifty years and saw no reason to change it
to lə gär'-dĭ-ə [luh gahr'-di-uh].
La Hague (Fr., cape) *Eng*. lä häg' lah hahg'
  Fr. lä äg' lah ahg'
La Haye (Fr.) lä ĕ' lah eh'
La Haye du Puits (Fr.) lä ĕ dü pwē' lah eh dü pwee'
La Haye Pesnel (Fr.) lä ĕ pĕ-nĕl' lah eh peh-nel'
Lahdenpohja (Fin. > Rus.) See *Lakhdenpokhia*.
La Hencha (Tun.) lä hĕn'-shä lah hen'-shah
Lahn (Ger., riv.) län' lahn'
Lahore (India) lə-hôr' luh-hor'
Lahti (Fin.) lä'-tē lah'-tee
Laibach (Yugosl.) *Ger*. lĭ'-bäk(h) lai'-bahk(h)
  Serb-Croat *Llubljana*, q.v., and *Ljubljanica*, q.v.
Laigle (Fr.) lĕ'gl leh'gl
Laika (Oc., New Hebrides) lä-ē'-kä lah-ee'-kah
Lajkovac (Yugosl.) lĭ'-kô-väts lai'-ko-vahts
Lajos lŏ'-yôsh lo'-yosh
  The Hungarian form of *Lewis*.
Lajosmizse (Hung.) lŏ'-yôsh-mē'-zhĕ lo'-yosh-mee'-zheh
Lakatos Géza, Vitéz lŏ'-kŏ-tôsh gä'-zŏ, lo'-ko-tosh gay'-zo,
  (Hung. polit.) vē'-täz vee'-tayz
Lakchang (Burma) läk-chăng' lak-chang'
Lakhdenpokhia läk(h)'-dĕn- lahk(h)'-den-
  (Fin. > Rus.) pôk(h)'-yä pok(h)'-yah
  Finnish spelling *Lahdenpohja*.
Lakonikos Kolpos (Gr., lä-kô-nē-kôs' lah-ko-nee-kos'
  gulf) kôl'-pôs kol'-pos
  English Gulf of *Laconia*, q.v.

La Línea (Sp.)	lä lē'-nĕ-ä	lah lee'-neh-ah
Lallemand, Fort (Alg.)	läl-mäN'	lahl-mahN'
Lalmand, Edgar (Belg. polit.)	läl-mäN'	lahl-mahN'
La Maddalena (Sard., isl.)	lä mä-dä-lĕ'-nä	lah mah-dah-leh'-nah
La Marsa (Tun.)	lä mär'-sä	lah mahr'-sah
Lamballe (Fr.)	läN-bäl'	lahN-bahl'
Lambayeque (Peru)	läm-bä-yĕ'-kĕ	lahm-bah-yeh'-keh
Lambersart (Fr.)	läN-bĕr-sär'	lahN-behr-sahr'
Lambézellec (Fr.)	läN-bĕ-zĕ-lĕk'	lahN-beh-zeh-lek'
Lambom (Oc., New Ireland)	läm-bôm'	lahm-bom'
Lamensk (Rus.)	lä'-mĕnsk	lah'-mensk
Lamia (Gr.)	lä-mē'-ä	lah-mee'-ah
Lamnay (Fr.)	läm-nĕ'	lahm-neh'
Lamone (It., riv.)	lä-mô'-nĕ	lah-mo'-neh
Lamotrec (Oc.)	lä'-mô-trĕk	lah'-mo-trek
Lampedusa (It., isl.)	läm'-pĕ-dōō'-zä	lahm'-peh-doo'-zah
Lampione (It., isl.)	läm-pyô'-nĕ	lahm-pyo'-neh
Lampriniadis (Gr. name)	läm-brē-nyä'-dēs	lahm-bree-nyah'-dees
Lamy, Fort (Fr. Eq. Afr.)	Fr. lä-mē'	lah-mee'
	Eng. lā'-mĭ	lay'-mi
Lan (Pol. >Rus., riv.) Polish spelling Łań.	län'(y)	lahn'(y)
Lanai (Hawaii)	lä-nī'	lah-nai'
Lancaster (Eng.)	lănk'-əs-tər	lank'-uhs-tuhr
Lancaster (U.S.)	lănk'-əs-tər	lank'-uhs-tuhr
	or lăn'-kăs-tər	lan'-kas-tuhr
Lan-ch'i (Ch., Chekiang)	län-chē	lahn-chee
Lan-chow (Ch., Kangsu) Also called Kao-lan, q.v.	län-jō	lahn-joh
Lanciano (It.)	län-chä'-nô	lahn-chah'-no
Łańcut (Pol.)	län'(y)-tsŏŏt	lahn'(y)-tsut
-land	-lənd or -lănd	-luhnd or -land

In short compounds such as *Iceland, Greenland, Finland* the vowel of *land* should be schwa, not short *a*. This is generally recognized for *England* and *Poland*, but often an overemphatic radio pronunciation is ĭs'-lănd', grēn'-lănd'; preferable are ĭs'-lənd, grēn'-lənd, for they suggest speech instead of reading. In long compounds, such as Somaliland, Newfoundland, *-land* has a stress and the correct vowel is short *a*.

Landau (Ger.)	län'-dou	lahn'-dau
Landerneau (Fr.)	läN-dĕr-nō'	lahN-dehr-noh'
Landes (Fr., dept.)	läNd'	lahNd'

Landeshut (Ger. >? Pol.)   län'-dəs-hōōt   lahn'-duhs-hoot
  Polish *Kamieniogóra*, q.v.

Landsberg (Ger. >Pol.)   länts'-bĕrk(h)   lahnts'-behrk(h)
  Polish *Gorzów*, q.v.

Landshut (Ger.)   länts'-hōōt'   lahnts'-hoot'

Landskrona (Sw.)   läns-krōō'-nä   lahns-kroo'-nah

Landsmeer (Neth.)   läns-mär'   lahns-mayr'

Landwarów (Pol.)   län-dvä'-rōōf   lahn-dvah'-ruf
  Russian *Landvarovo*, län-dvä'-rŏ-vŏ [lahn-dvah'-ro-vo].

Lange, Halvard M.   läng'-ə, häl'-vär'   lahng'-uh, hahl'-vahr'
  (Nor. polit.)

Lange, Oscar (Pol. polit.) län'-gĕ *or* läng'-gĕ   lahn'-geh *or* lahng'-
  Often Anglicized to lăng'.   geh

Langeais (Fr.)   läN-zhĕ'   lahN-zheh'

Langeland (Den., isl.)   läng'-ə-län   lahng'-uh-lahn

Langen (Ger.)   läng'-ən   lahng'-uhn

Langenbielau   läng'-ən-bē'-lou   lahng'-uhn-bee'-lau
  (Ger. >? Pol.)
  Polish *Bielawa*, q.v.

Langensalza (Ger.)   läng'-ən-zäl'-tsä   lahng'-uhn-zahl'-
                                  tsah

Langensoultzbach (Fr.) läng'-ən-sōōlts'-bäk lahng'-uhn-sults'-
                                  bahk

Langer, William   lăng'-ər   lang'-uhr
  (U.S. senator)

Langerwehe (Ger.)   läng'-ər-vä'-ə   lahng'-uhr-vay'-uh

Langesund (Nor.)   läng'-ə-sōōn   lahng'-uh-sun

Langfuhr (Danzig > Pol.) See *Wrzeszcz*.

Langres (Fr.)   läN'gr   lahN'gr

Langrune sur Mer (Fr.) läN-grün sür mĕr'   lahN-grün sür mehr'

Langson (Indo-Ch.)   läng-sŭn'   lahng-suhn'
  French läN-sôN' [lahN-soN']. English lăng'-sŭn' [lang'-suhn'].

Languedoc (Fr.)   läNg-dôk'   lahNg-dok'

Lanham, Fritz G.   lăn'-əm   lan'-uhm
  (U.S. representative)

Lanham, Henderson   lăn'-əm   lan'-uhm
  (U.S. representative)

Lanište (Yugosl.)   lä'-nĭ-shtĕ   lah'-ni-shteh

Lanisy (Fr.)   lä-nē-zē'   lah-nee-zee'

Lankada (Gr.)   läng-gä'-dä   lahng-gah'-dah

Lankadas (Gr.)   läng-gä-däs'   lahng-gah-dahs'

Lan-ki (Ch., Chekiang) län-chē   lahn-chee
  Also spelled *Lan-ch'i*, q.v.

Lannion (Fr.)   lä-nyôN'   lah-nyoN'

Lan-tsang (S.E. Asia, riv.)	län'-tsäng'	lahn'-tsahng'
Also called the *Mekong,* q.v.		
Lanusei (Sard.)	lä-nōō-sä'	lah-noo-say'
Lanuvio (It.)	lä-nōō'-vyô	lah-noo'-vyo
Lanvaux, Landes de	läN-vō', läNd' də	lahN-voh', lahNd'
(Fr., heath)		duh
Lanvéoc Poulmic (Fr.)	läN-vĕ-ôk' pōōl-mēk'	lahN-veh-ok' pool-
		meek'
Laoag (P.I.)	lä-wäg'	lah-wahg'
Laoet (NEI) See *Laut.*		
Laoighise *or* Leix (Eire)	lä'-ĭsh *or* läks'	lay'-ish *or* layks'
Formerly *Queen's.*		
Laokay (Indo-Ch.)	lou-kī'	lau-kai'
Laole (Yugosl.)	lä'-ô-lĕ	lah'-o-leh
Laon (Fr.)	läN'	lahN'
Laos (Indo-Ch.)	*Eng.* lä'-ŏs	lay'-os
	Fr. lä-ôs'	lah-os'
Lao-shan (Ch., bay)	lou-shän	lau-shahn
Lao-yao (Ch., Kiangsu)	lou-you	lau-yau
Lapac (P.I.)	lä-päk'	lah-pahk'
La Pallice (Fr.)	lä pä-lēs'	lah pah-lees'
La Palma (Canary Isls.)	lä päl'-mä	lah pahl'-mah
Laparán (P.I.)	lä-pä-rän'	lah-pah-rahn'
Also called *Paragua,* pä-rä'-gwə [pah-rah'-gwuh].		
La Paz (Bolivia)	*Eng.* lä päz'	lah pahz'
	Sp. lä päs'	lah pahs'
La Perouse (Rus., Jap.,	lä pĕ-rōōz'	lah peh-rooz'
str.)		
Lapham, Roger Dearborn	lăp'-əm	lap'-uhm
(Calif. polit.)		
Lapide (It.)	lä'-pē-dĕ	lah'-pee-deh
La Plata (Arg.)	lä plä'-tä	lah plah'-tah
Lapovo (Yugosl.)	lä'-pô-vô	lah'-po-vo
Lappeenranta (Fin.)	läp'-pän-rän-tä	lahp'-payn-rahn-tah
Swedish *Villmanstrand,* vĭl'-män-stränd' [vil'-mahn-strahnd'].		
Łapy (Pol.)	lä'-pĭ	lah'-pi
Russian spelling *Lapi.*		
Larache (Mor.)	*Fr.* lä-räsh'	lah-rahsh'
Arabic *El 'Araish.*		
Laramie (Wyo.)	lăr'-ə-mĭ	lehr'-uh-mi
Larcade, Henry D.	lär-kād'	lahr-kayd'
(U.S. representative)		
Laredo (Mex.)	lä-rĕ'-dô	lah-reh'-do
Laredo (Tex.)	lə-rä'-dō	luh-ray'-doh

Laren (Neth.)   lä′-rən   lah′-ruhn
Lariano (It.)   lä-ryä′-nô   lah-ryah′-no
Larisa or Larissa (Gr.)   lä′-rē-sä   lah′-ree-sah
    There is also an English pronunciation lə-rĭs′-ə [luh-ris′-uh].
Larkana (India)   lär-kä′-nə   lahr-kah′-nuh
Larnaca (Cyprus)   lär′-nä-kä   lahr′-nah-kah
Laroche (Belg.)   lä-rôsh′   lah-rosh′
La Rochelle (Fr.)   lä rô-shĕl′   lah ro-shel′
La Roche sur Yon (Fr.)   lä rôsh sür yôN′   lah rosh sür yoN′
Larrea, Lelo de (Mex. diplomat) See Lelo de Larrea.
Larvik (Nor.)   lär′-vēk   lahr′-veek
Lašče, Velike (Yugosl.)   läsh′-chĕ, vĕ′-lĭ-kĕ   lahsh′-cheh,veh′-li-keh
Las Cruces (N.M.)   Eng. läs krōōs′-ĭs   lahs kroos′-is
    Sp. läs krōō′-sĕs   lahs kroo′-sehs
Lasdehnen (Ger. >Rus.)   läs-dä′-nən   lahs-day′-nuhn
    Russian Krasnoznamensk, kräs-nŏz-nä′-mĕnsk [krahs-noz-nah′-mensk].
La Sebala (Tun.)   lä sə-bă′-lä   lah suh-ba′-lah
La Senia (Alg.)   lä sä′-nyä   lah say′-nyah
Lasethion (Crete)   lä-sē′-thē(-ôn)   lah-see′-thee(-on)
    Also called Nikolaos, Agios, q.v.
La Seyne sur Mer (Fr.)   lä sĕn sür mĕr′   lah sen sür mehr′
Lashio (Burma)   lăsh′-yō   lash′-yoh
    or lŭ′-shyō′   luh′-shyoh′
Lashkar (India)   lŭsh′-kər   luhsh′-kuhr
Łask (Pol.)   läsk′   lahsk′
La Skhirra (Tun.)   lä sə-kĭr′-rä   lah suh-kihr′-rah
    Often spelled Cekhira, q.v.
Laski, Harold Joseph   lăs′-kĭ   las′-ki
    (Br. economist)
Laško (Yugosl.)   läsh′-kô   lahsh′-ko
Lasovačka planina   lä′-sô-väch-kä   lah′-so-vahch-kah
    (Yugos., mts.)   plä′-nē′-nä   plah′-nee′-nah
La Spezia (It.)   lä spĕ′-tsyä   lah speh′-tsyah
Lastovo (It. >Yugosl.,   lä′-stô-vô   lah′-sto-vo
    isl.)
    Italian Lagosta, q.v.
Las Vegas (N.M., Nev.)   Eng. lŏs vĕg′-əs   los veg′-uhs
    Sp. lôs vĕ′-gäs   los veh′-gahs
Latimodjong (NEI,   lä-tē-mô′-jŏng   lah-tee-mo′-jong
    Celebes, mt.)
La Tortue (Haiti, isl.)   lä tôr-tü′   lah tor-tü′
Latronico (It.)   lä-trô′-nē-kô   lah-tro′-nee-ko
Latvia (Rus.)   lăt′-vĭ-ə   lat′-vi-uh
    Lettish Latvija, lät′-vĭ-yä [laht′-vi-yah]. Russian spelling Latviya.

Lauban (Ger. >? Pol.)   lou'-bän   lau'-bahn
  Polish *Lubań*, q.v.
Laudara (Yugosl., isl.)   *It.* lou-dä'-rä   lau-dah'-rah
  Serb-Croat *Lavdara*, q.v.
Lauderdale (Miss.)   lô'-dər-dāl   law'-duhr-dayl
Lauenberg (Ger. >Pol.)   lou'-ən-bĕrk(h)   lau'-uhn-behrk(h)
  Polish *Lębork*, q.v.
Laugier, Henri   lō-zhyĕ',   loh-zhyeh',
  (Fr. diplomat)   äN-rē'   ahN-ree'
Laulau (Oc., Saipan)   lou'-lou'   lau'-lau'
Launceston (Austral.)   lŏn'-sĕs-tən   lon'-ses-tuhn
Laurel, José P.   lou-rĕl', hô-sĕ'   lau-rel', ho-seh'
  (Fil. polit.)
Laurentians (Can., mts.)   lô-rĕn'-shənz   lo-rehn'-shuhnz
Lauria (It.)   lou-rē'-ä   lau-ree'-ah
Lauritsala (Fin.)   lou'-rĭt-sä-lä   lau'-rit-sah-lah
Lausanne (Switz.)   *Eng.* lō-zăn'   loh-zan'
                Fr. lō-zän'   loh-zahn'
Lausche, F. J.   lou'-shē   lau'-shee
  (Am. polit.)
Laut *or* Laoet (NEI)   lä'-ōot   lah'-oot
Lauta (Ger.)   lou'-tä   lau'-tah
Lauterbourg (Fr.)   lou'-tər-bōor'   lau'-tuhr-boor'
Lauterbourg (Ger.)   lou'-tər-bōork(h)   lau'-tuhr-burk(h)
Laval (Fr.)   lä-väl'   lah-vahl'
Laval, Pierre (Fr. polit.)   lä-väl', pyĕr'   lah-vahl', pyehr'
  The usual French *a* is rather like that of New England. It is between
  the *a* of *father* and the *a* of *fat.*
Lavandou (Fr.)   lä-väN-dōo'   lah-vahN-doo'
Lavansaari (Fin., isl.)   lä'-vän-sä-rē   lah'-vahn-sah-ree
Lavdara (Yugosl., isl.)   läv'-dä-rä   lahv'-dah-rah
Laverton (Austral.)   lăv'-ər-tən   lav'-uhr-tuhn
Lavongai (Oc., New   lä-vông'-ī   lah-vong'-ai
  Ireland)
  Also called *New Hanover.*
Lavrentyev, A. I.   lä-vrĕn'-tyĕf   lah-vren'-tyef
  (Rus. polit.)
Lavrion (Gr.)   lä'-vrē-ô(n)   lah'-vree-o(n)
  English *Laurium*, lô'-rĭ-əm [lo'-ri-uhm].
Lawolai (Oc., New   lä'-wô-lī   lah'-wo-lai
  Ireland)
Lawrence, Lord Pethick (Br. polit.) See *Pethick Lawrence.*
Laye (Fr., riv.)   lĕ'   leh'
Layon (Fr., riv.)   lä-yôN'   lah-yoN'

Lazarevac (Yugosl.)	lä′-zä′-rĕ-väts	lah′-zah′-reh-vahts
Lead (S.D.)	lēd′	leed′
Leahy, Wm. Daniel (Am. admiral)	lā′-hĭ	lay′-hi
Leathers, Lord (Br. polit.)	lĕ*th*′-ərz	le*th*′-uhrz
Leba (Ger. >Pol.)	lā′-bä	lay′-bah

Polish *Łeba*, lĕ′-bä [leh′-bah].

Lebadeia (Gr., isl.)	lĕ-vä′-dyä *or* lē-vä-dyä′	leh-vah′-dyah lee-vah-dyah′
Lebane (Yugosl.)	lĕ′-bä-nĕ	leh′-bah-neh
Lebanon (Syria)	*Eng.* lĕb′-ə-nən	leb′-uh-nuhn

Also called *Lebanese Republic*, lĕb′-ə-nēz′ *or* -nēs′ [leb′-uh-neez′ *or* -nees′]. French *République Libanaise*, rĕ-pü-blēk′ lē-bä-nĕz′ [reh-pü-bleek′ lee-bah-nez′]. Arabic *Libnan*, lēb-năn′ [leeb-nan′].

Le Bardo (Tun.)	lə bär′-dō	luh bahr′-doh
Lebedin (Rus.)	lĕ-bĕ-dēn′	leh-beh-deen′
Lebedyan (Rus.)	lĕ-bĕ-dyän′(y)	leh-beh-dyahn′(y)
Lębork (Ger. >Pol.)	lăN′-bôrk	laN′-bork

German *Lauenberg*, q.v.

Le Bourget (Fr., airport near Paris)	lə bōōr-zhĕ′	luh boor-zheh′
Lebrun, Albert (Fr. polit.)	lə-brûN′, äl-bĕr′	luh-brœN′, ahl-behr′
Lebus (Ger.)	lā′-bŏŏs	lay′-bus
Lec (Ger. >Pol.)	lĕts′	lets′

German *Loetzen*, q.v.

Le Catene (Yugosl., It., str.)	*It.* lĕ kä-tĕ′-nĕ	leh kah-teh′-neh

Serb-Croat *Verige*, q.v.

Lecce (It.)	lĕt′-chĕ	let′-cheh
Lecco (It.)	lĕk′-kô	lek′-ko
Lech (Ger., riv.)	lĕk(h)′	lek(h)′
LeClerc, Jacques (Fr. general)	lə klĕr′, zhäk′	luh klehr′, zhahk′
l'École (Fr.)	lĕ-kôl′	leh-kol′
Le Compte, Karl M. (U.S. representative)	lə kount′	luh kaunt′
Le Creusot (Fr.)	lə krû-zō′	luh krœ-zoh′
Le Crotoy (Fr.)	lə krô-twä′	luh kro-twah′
Łęczyca (Pol.)	lăN-chĭ′-tsä	laN-chi′-tsah

Russian *Lenchitsa*, lĕn-chē′-tsä [len-chee′-tsah].

Ledo (India)	lē′-dō	lee′-doh

This station on the new Burma Road is pronounced by the Indian

Information Service in Washington, and by the office of the Indian Trade Commissioner in New York, and by General Sewell of the British Information Service as lē'-dō [lee'-doh], not lā'-dō [lay'-doh]. The Indians that I talked with are not familiar with the language of the frontier region, but their guess is that *Ledo* is an English spelling of the native sounds and so should be pronounced as English. In any case, being in ignorance of the local pronunciation they feel safer in Anglicizing the name than in reaching for an uncertain localism.

Leek (Neth.)	lāk'	layk'
Leende (Neth.)	lān'-də	layn'-duh
Leens (Neth.)	lāns'	layns'
Leerdam (Neth.)	lār-däm'	layr-dahm'
Leeuwarden (Neth.)	lā'-wär-dən	lay'-wahr-duhn
	local lā'-ōŏ-wärt	lay'-u-wahrt
Leeuwarderadeel (Neth.)	lā-wär'-də-rä-dāl'	lay-wahr'-duh-rah-dayl'
Leeuwin (Austral., cape)	lōō'-ĭn	loo'-in
Le Fevre, Jay	lə fē'-vər	luh fee'-vuhr
(U.S. representative)		
Lefke (Crete, isl.) See *Kouphonesi*.		
Legaspi (P.I.)	lĕ-gäs'-pĭ	leh-gahs'-pi
Leghorn (It.)	lĕg'-hôrn	leg'-horn
Italian *Livorno*, q.v.		
Legião (Port. legion)	lĭ-zhyouN'	li-zhyauN'
Leh (India)	lā'	lay'
Le Havre (Fr.)	*Eng.* lə hävr'	luh hahvr'
	Fr. lə ävr'	luh ahvr'

A pronunciation lə ärv' [luh ahrv'] should be avoided.

Lehi (Utah)	lē'-hĭ	lee'-hai
Lehman, Herbert H.	lē'-mən	lee'-muhn
(Am. polit.)		
lei	lā'	lay'

The plural of the Rumanian currency unit. Singular *leu* lĕ'-ōŏ [leh'-u].

Leicester (Eng., Mass.)	lĕs'-tər	les'-tuhr
Lei Chiang *or* Lei River	lā'	lay'
(Ch., Hunan, riv.)		
Leichlingen (Ger.)	līk(h)'-lĭng-ən	laik(h)'-ling-uhn
Leiden (Neth.)	lĭ'-dən	lai'-duhn
Leiderdorp (Neth.)	lĭ'-dər-dôrp'	lai'-duhr-dorp'
Leigh, Vivien	lē'	lee'
(Br. actress)		
Leigh Mallory, T. L.	lē' mäl'-ə-rĭ	lee' mal'-uh-ri
(Br. general)		
Leighton (Eng. name)	lā'-tən *or* lāt'n	lay'-tuhn *or* layt'n

Leili (Oc., Solomons)	lā'-lē	lay'-lee
Leimok (NEI)	lā'-môk'	lay'-mok'
Leïmona (Gr.)	lā'-mô-nä	lay'-mo-nah
Leimuiden (Neth.)	lī-mûï'-dən	lai-mœi'-duhn
Leine (Ger., riv.)	lī'-nə	lai'-nuh
Leino, Yrjö (Fin. polit.)	lā'-nô, ür'-yû	lay'-no, ür'-yœ
Leinster (Eire)	lĕn'-stər	len'-stuhr
	or lēn'- or lĭn'-	or leen'- or lĭn'-

Leipsig Mockau (Ger.) See *Mockau.*
Leipsig Taucha (Ger.) See *Taucha.*

Leipzig (Ger.)	*Eng.* lĭp'-sĭg	laip'-sig
	Ger. lĭp'-tsĭk(h)	laip'-tsik(h)
leisure	lē'-zhər or lĕzh'-ər	lee'-zhuhr or lezh'-uhr

"But the best is lā'-zhər [lay'-zhuhr]," the Irishman said.

Leith (Scot.)	lēth'	leeth'
Leitha (Austria, riv.)	lī'-tä	lai'-tah
Leitmeritz (Cz.)	līt'-mĕ-rĭts	lait'-meh-rits
Czech *Litoměřice,* q.v.		
Leitrim (Eire)	lē'-trĭm	lee'-trim
Leix (Eire) See *Laoighise.*		
Lei-yang (Ch., Hunan)	lā-yäng	lay-yahng
Lek (Neth., riv.)	lĕk'	lek'
Le Kef (Tun.)	lə kāf'	luh kayf'
Lekhena (Gr.)	lĕ'-hĕ-nä	leh'-heh-nah
Lekkerkerk (Neth.)	lĕk'-ər-kĕrk	lek'-uhr-kehrk
Lele (Oc., Carolines)	lə-lŭ'	luh-luh'
German *Lölö Hafen.*		
Lelle (Est.)	lĕl'-lĕ	lel'-leh
Le Locle (Switz.)	lə lôk'l	luh lok'l
Lelo de Larrea, José	lĕ'-lô dĕ lä-rĕ'-ä,	leh'-lo deh lah-reh'-
(Mex. diplomat)	hô-sĕ'	ah, ho-seh'
Lelova (Gr.)	lĕ'-lô-vä	leh'-lo-vah
Lelushenko (Rus. name)	lĕ-lyōō-shĕn'-kŏ	leh-lyoo-shen'-ko
Lemaigre Dubreuil,	lə-mĕ'gr dü-brûï',	luh-me'gr dü-brœi',
Jacques (Fr. polit.)	zhäk'	zhahk'
Leman, Lake (Switz.) See *Geneva, Lake.*		
Le Mans (Fr.)	lə mäN'	luh mahN'
Le May, Curtis	lə mā'	luh may'
(Am. general)		
Lembeh (NEI)	lĕm'-bĕ	lem'-beh
Lemberg (Pol. >Rus.) See *Lvov.*		
Lemery (P.I.)	lĕ-mĕ-rē'	leh-meh-ree'
Le Mesnil Durand (Fr.)	lə mĕ-nēl' dü-räN'	luh meh-neel' dü-
		rahN'

Le Mesnil Vigot (Fr.)	lə mĕ-nēl′ vē-gō′	luh meh-neel′ vee-goh′
Lemmer (Neth.)	lĕm′-ər	lem′-uhr
Also called *De Lemmer*, q.v.		
Lemnos (Gr., isl.)	*Eng.* lĕm′-nŏs	lem′-nos
	Gr. lĕm′-nô(s)	leem′-no(s)
Lemsterland (Neth.)	lĕm′-stər-länt	lem′-stuhr-lahnt
Lemvig (Den.)	lĕm′-vēk(h)	lem′-veek(h)
Lenchitsa (Pol.) See *Łęczyca*.		
Lengerich (Ger.)	lĕng′-ə-rĭk(h)	leng′-uh-rik(h)
Lengyel, Menyhért	lĕn′-dyĕl, mĕn′(y)-	len′-dyel, men′(y)-
(Hung. writer)	härt	hayrt
Lenin (Rus. polit.)	lĕ′-nĭn	leh′-nin
Real name *Vladimir Ilyich Ulyanov*, vlä-dē′-mĭr ĭl-yēch′ ōōl-yä′-nŏf [vlah-dee′-mihr il-yeech′ ool-yah′-nof].		
Leninakan (Rus.)	lĕ′-nĭ-nä-kän′	leh′-ni-nah-kahn′
Leningrad (Rus.)	*Eng.* lĕn′-ĭn-grăd	len′-in-grad
	Rus. lĕ′-nĭn-grät′	leh′-nin-graht′
Leninsk (Rus.)	lĕ′-nĭnsk	leh′-ninsk
Leninsk Kuznetski (Rus.)	— kōōz-nĕt′-skĭ	— kuz-net′-ski
Lenola (It.)	lĕ′-nô-lä	leh′-no-lah
Lens (Fr.)	läNs′	lahNs′
Lentini (Sicily)	lĕn-tē′-nē	len-tee′-nee
Leoben (Austria)	lĕ-ō′-bən	leh-oh′-buhn
Leobschuetz, Leobschütz	lā′-ôp-shüts	lay′-op-shüts
(Ger. >Pol.)		
Polish *Głubczyce*, q.v.		
Leominster (Eng.)	lĕm′-stər	lem′-stuhr
Leominster (Mass.)	lĕm′-ĭn-stər	lem′-in-stuhr
León (Sp., prov.)	lĕ-ôn′	leh-on′
Leone (Pantelleria)	lĕ-ô′-nĕ	leh-o′-neh
Leonideion (Gr.)	lĕ-ô-nē′-dē(-ôn)	leh-o-nee′-dee(-on)
Leovo (Rum. >Rus.)	lĕ-ô′-vô	leh-o′-vo
Rumanian *Leova*, lĕ-ô′-vä [leh-o′-vah].		
Lepanto (Gr., gulf)	*Eng.* lĭ-păn′-tō	li-pan′-toh
	It. lĕ′-pän-tô	leh′-pahn-to
Also called the Gulf of *Corinth*, q.v.		
Lepel (Rus.)	lĕ′-pĕl(y)	leh′-pel(y)
Lepenac (Yugosl., riv.)	lĕ′-pĕ′-näts	leh′-peh′-nahts
Lepenica (Yugosl.)	lĕ′-pĕ′-nĭ-tsä	leh′-peh′-ni-tsah
Lepini (It., mts.)	lĕ-pē′-nē	leh-pee′-nee
Le Pollet (Fr.)	lə pô-lĕ′	luh po-leh′
Lepontine Alps (Switz.,	lə-pŏn′-tĭn	luh-pon′-tin
Italy)		
Le Puy de Dôme (Fr.)	lə pwē də dōm′	luh pwee duh dohm′

Lercara (Sicily)	lĕr-kä′-rä	lehr-kah′-rah
Lérida (Sp.)	lĕ′-rē-dä	leh′-ree-dah
Lérins (Fr., isls.)	lĕ-răNs′	leh-raNs′
According to *Larousse*.		
Leros (Dodec.)	lĕ′-rô(s)	leh′-ro(s)
Les Baux (Fr.)	lĕ bō′	leh boh′
Lesbos (Gr., isl.)	*Eng.* lĕz′-bŏs	lez′-bos
	Gr. lĕz′-vô(s)	lez′-vo(s)
Usually called *Mytilene*, q.v.		
Lešće (Yugosl.)	lĕsh′-chĕ	lesh′-cheh
Lescot, Élie	lĕs-kō′, ĕ-lē′	les-koh′, eh-lee′
(Haitian polit.)		
Lesh (Alb.)	lĕsh′	lesh′
Also Leshë. Italian *Alessio*, q.v.		
Les Halles (Fr., Paris)	lĕ äl′	leh ahl′
Leshi (Alb.) See *Lesh*.		
Lesina (Yugosl.)	*It.* lĕ′-sĭ-nä	leh′-si-nah
Serb-Croat *Hvar*, q.v.		
Lesinski, John	lĕ-sĭn′-skĭ	leh-sin′-ski
(U.S. representative)		
Lesja (Nor.)	lĕsh′-ä	lesh′-ah
Leskovac (Yugosl.)	lĕs′-kô-väts	les′-ko-vahts
Leskovik (Alb.)	lĕ-skô-vēk′	leh-sko-veek′
Leskoviku (Alb.) See *Leskovik*.		
Les Milleries (Fr.)	lĕ mēl-rē′	leh meel-ree′
Lešnica (Yugosl.)	lĕsh′-nĭ-tsä	lesh′-ni-tsah
Lesozavodsk (Rus.)	lĕ′-sŏ-zä-vôtsk′	leh′-so-zah-votsk′
lespedeza	lĕs′-pə-dē′-zə	les′-puh-dee′-zuh
Les Pieux (Fr.)	lĕ pyû′	leh pyœ′
Les Sables d'Olonne (Fr.)	lĕ sä′bl dô-lôn′	leh sah′bl do-lon′
Les Salines (Tun.)	lĕ sä-lēn′	leh sah-leen′
Lessay (Fr.)	lĕ-sĕ′	leh-seh′
Leszno (Pol.)	lĕsh′-nô	lesh′-no
Letarf (Alg.)	lə-tärf′	luh-tahrf′
lethal	lē′-thəl	lee′-thuhl
Avoid lē′-thôl [lee′-thol].		
Le Touquet (Fr.)	lə tōō-kĕ′	luh too-keh′
Letpadan (Burma)	lĕp′-pə-dän′	lep′-puh-dahn′
Le Tréport (Fr.)	lə trĕ-pôr′	luh treh-por′
Leubsdorf (Ger.)	loips′-dôrf	loips′-dorf
Leuca (It.)	lĕ′-ōō-kä	leh′-u-kah
Leucate (Fr.)	lû-kät′	lœ-kaht′
Leucate, Étang de (Fr.)	lû-kät′, ĕ-täN′ də	lœ-kaht′,eh-tahN′duh

Leucio (It., mt.)	lĕ'-ōō-chô	leh'-oo-cho
Leukas (Gr.) See *Levkas*.		
Leuna (Ger.)	loi'-nä	loi'-nah
Leuna Odendorf (Ger.)	loi'-nä ŏ'-dən-dôrf	loi'-nah oh'-duhn-dorf
Leusden (Neth.)	lûs'-dən	lœs'-duhn
Leuven (Belg.)	*Flem.* lû'-vən	lœ'-vuhn
French *Louvain*, q.v.		
Léva (Cz.) See *Levice*.		
Levač (Yugosl.)	lĕ'-väch	leh'-vahch
Levallois Perret (Fr.)	lə-vä-lwä pĕ-rĕ'	luh-vah-lwah peh-reh'
Levan (Alb.)	lĕ'-vän	leh'-vahn
Levanger (Nor.)	lĕ-väng'-ər	leh-vahng'-uhr
Levani (Alb.) See *Levan*.		
Levant, the	lə-vănt'	luh-vant'
Levant (Fr.)	lə-väN'	luh-vahN'
Levantine	lə-văn'-tĭn	luh-van'-tin
	or lĕv'-ən-tīn	lev'-uhn-tain
Levanzo (It., isl.)	lĕ'-vän-tsô	leh'-vahn-tso
l'Évêque, Pont	lĕ-vĕk', pôN'	leh-vek', poN'
Leverano (It.)	lĕ-vĕ-rä'-nô	leh-veh-rah'-no
Leverkusen (Ger.)	lā'-vər-kōō'-zən	lay'-vuhr-koo'-zuhn
Lévi (Fr., cape)	lĕ-vē'	leh-vee'
Levice (Cz.)	lĕ'-vĭ-tsĕ	leh'-vi-tseh
Hungarian *Léva*, lā'-vŏ [lay'-vo].		
Levitha (Dodec.)	lĕ-vē'-thä	leh-vee'-thah
Levkas (Gr.)	lĕf-käs'	lef-kahs'
English *Leucas*, lyōō'-kəs [lyoo'-kuhs].		
Levoča (Cz.)	lĕ'-vô-chä	leh'-vo-chah
Lewes (Del.)	lōō'-ĭs	lu'-is
A variant spelling of *Lewis*. A family name and the name of a town.		
Ley, Robert (Ger. polit.)	lī'	lai'
Leye (Fr., Belg., riv.) See *Lys*.		
Leyte (P.I.)	*Eng.* lā'-tĭ	lay'-ti
	Sp. lā'-tĕ	lay'-teh
Ležaky (Cz.)	lĕ'-zhä-kĭ	leh'-zhah-ki
Lgov (Rus.)	lgôf' (lə-gôf')	lgof' (luh-gof')
Lhasa (Tibet)	*Eng.* lă'-sə *or* lä'-sä	la'-suh *or* lah'-sah
Lhoknga (NEI, Sumatra)	lô'-nä' *or* -ngä	loh'-nah' *or* -ngah
Li (Ch., Hunan)	lē	lee
Liadromia (Gr., isl.) See *Alonesos*.		
liaison	*Eng.* lē-ā-zôN' *or* lē'-ə-zən *or* lĭ-ā'-zən	lee-ay-zoN' *or* lee'-uh-zuhn *or* li-ay'-zuhn
	Fr. lyĕ-zôN'	lyeh-zoN'
Also reported by an officer of the Marines, lī'-ə-zən [lai'-uh-zuhn].		

Liakoura (Gr., mt.)   See *Parnassus*.

Lian (P.I.)	lē-än′	lee-ahn′
Liang-chow (Ch., Kansu)	lyäng-jō	lyahng-joh
Liano (Crete, point)	lyä-nô′	lyah-no′
Lianokladi (Gr.)	lē-ä-nô-klä′-dē	lee-ah-no-klah′-dee
Liao-ning (Manchu., prov.)	lyou-nĭng	lyau-ning
Liaqat Ali Khan (Indian polit.)	lē-ä′-kət ä′-lē kän′	lee-ah′-kuht ah′-lee kahn′

Sometimes preceded by his title, *nawabzada*, nə-wŏb′-zä-dä [nuh-wob′-zah-dah].

Lib (Oc., Marshalls)	lēb′	leeb′

Liban (Syria)   See *Lebanon*.

Libau (Latvia)	*Ger.* lē′-bou	lee′-bau

Latvian *Liepāja*, q.v. Russian *Libava*, q.v.

Libava (Latvia)	*Rus.* lĭ-bä′-vä	li-bah′-vah

Latvian *Liepāja*, q.v. German *Libau*, q.v.

Liberdad (Peru)	lē-bĕr-däd′	lee-behr-dahd′
Liberec (Cz.)	lē′-bĕ-rĕts	lee′-beh-rets
Liblar (Ger.)	lĭb′-lär	lib′-lahr

Libnan (Syria)   See *Lebanon*.

Libohova (Alb.)   See *Libohovë*.

Libohovë (Alb.)	lē-bô′-hô-və	lee-bo′-ho-vuh

Greek *Limpokhovon*, lē-bô′-hô-vô(n) [lee-bo′-ho-vo(n)].

Libongao (P.I.)	lē-bông′-ou	lee-bong′-au
Libramont (Belg.)	lē-brä-môN′	lee-brah-moN′
Librazhd (Alb.)	lē′-bräzhd	lee′-brahzhd

Librazhdi (Alb.)   See *Librazhd*.

Libúnao (P.I.)	lē-bōō′-nou	lee-boo′-nau
Libútab (P.I.)	lē-bōō′-täb	lee-boo′-tahb
Libya (Afr.)	lĭb′-ĭ-ə	lib′-i-uh

Italian *Libia*.

Licab (P.I.)	lē-käb′	lee-kahb′
Licata (Sicily)	lē-kä′-tä	lee-kah′-tah
Licbark (Ger. >Pol.)	lĭts′-bärk	lits′-bahrk

German *Heilsberg*, q.v.

Licenza (It.)	lē-chĕn′-tsä	lee-chen′-tsah
Li-ch'êng (Ch., Shantung)	lē-chŭng	lee-chuhng
Lichtenberg (Ger.)	lĭk(h)′-tən-bĕrk(h)	lik(h)′-tuhn-behrk(h)
Lichtenfels (Greenl.)	lĭk(h)′-tən-fĕls	lik(h)′-tuhn-fels
Lichtenvoorde (Neth.)	lĭk(h)′-tən-vōr′-də	lik(h)′-tuhn-vohr′-duh
Li-ch'wan (Ch., Kiangsi)	lē-chwän	lee-chwahn

Licosa (It., cape)   lē-kô'-zä   lee-ko'-zah

Lida (Pol. >Rus.)   lē'-dä   lee'-dah

Lidda (Pal.) See *Lydda*.

Lidice (Cz.)   lē'-dĭ-tsĕ   lee'-di-tseh

Sometimes anglicized to lĭd'-ĭ-chĭ [lid'-i-chi] or lĭd'-ĭ-sĭ [lid'-i-si]. *Lidice*, Illinois, is pronounced locally lē'-dĭ-shā [lee'-di-shay] according to J. Walter Lowrey, postmaster of the Joliet district, which includes this American namesake of the Bohemian village.

Lido di Roma (It.)   lē'-dô dē rô'-mä   lee'-do dee ro'-mah

Near the ancient *Ostia*, q.v.

Lie, Trygve Halvdan   lē', trüg'-və *or*   lee', trüg'-vuh *or*

(Nor. diplomat)   *Eng.* trĭg'-və,   *Eng.* trig'-vuh,

hälv'-dän   hahlv'-dahn

Liebenow (Ger.)   lē'-bə-nō   lee'-buh-noh

Liebeslied   lē'-bəs-lēt'   lee'-buhs-leet'

German meaning *love song*. *Lied*, song, must be distinguished from *Leid*, līt' [lait'], sorrow.

Liechtenstein   *Eng.* lĭk'-tən-stĭn   lik'-tuhn-stain

(principality)   *Ger.* lēk(h)'-tən-shtĭn   leek(h)'-tuhn-shtain

Lied, *pl.* Lieder (Ger.)   lēt', lē'-dər   leet', lee'-duhr

See *Liebeslied*.

Liége (Belg.)   *Fr.* lyezh'   lyezh'

    Eng. lĭ-āzh'   li-ayzh'

Flemish *Luik*, lûĭk' [lœik'].

Liegnitz (Ger. >? Pol.)   lēg'-nĭts   leeg'-nits

Polish *Lignica*, q.v.

Lieksa (Fin.)   lē'-ĕk'-sä   lee'-ek'-sah

Lielupe (Latvia, riv.)   lē'-ĕ'-lo͞o-pĕ   lee'-eh'-lu-peh

Lienden (Neth.)   lēn'-dən   leen'-duhn

Lien-hua (Ch., Kiangsi)   lyĕn-whä   lyen-whah

Lienz (Austria)   lĭ-ĕnts'   li-ents'

Liepāja (Latvia)   lē'-ĕ'-pä-yä   lee'-eh'-pah-yah

Russian *Libava*, q.v. German *Libau*, q.v.

Lier (Belg.)   lēr'   leer'

French *Lierre*, lyĕr' [lyehr'].

Lier (Nor.)   lē'-ər   lee'-uhr

Lier, de (Neth.)   lēr', də   leer', duh

Liesching, Percivale   lē'-shĭng   lee'-shing

(Br. diplomat)

Lieshout (Neth.)   lēs'-hout   lees'-haut

Liestal (Switz.)   lēs'-täl   lees'-tahl

Lieurey (Fr.)   lyû-rĕ'   lyœ-reh'

Lieve Vrouwen Parochie   lē'-və vrou'-ən   lee'-vuh vrau'-uhn

(Neth., Het Bilt)   pä-rôk(h)'-ē   pah-rok(h)'-ee

Liévin (Fr.)	lyĕ-văN′	lyeh-vaN′
Liffey (Ire., riv.)	lĭf′-ĭ	lif′-ĭ
Liffré (Fr.)	lē-frĕ′	lee-freh′
Lignica (Ger. >? Pol.)	lĭg-nē′-tsä	lig-nee′-tsah
German *Liegnitz,* q.v.		
Ligny en Barrois (Fr.)	lē-nyē äN bä-rwä′	lee-nyee ahN bah-rwah′
Ligurian Sea	lĭ-gyo͝or′-ĭ-ən	li-gyur′-i-uhn
Lihir (Oc., Bismarck arch.)	lē′-hēr	lee′-heer
Lihons (Fr.)	lē-ôN′	lee-oN′
Liinahamari (Fin. >Rus.)	lē′-nä-hä′-mä-rē	lee′-nah-hah′-mah-ree
Lijeva Rijeka (Yugosl.)	lē′-yĕ-vä rĭ-yĕ′-kä	lee′-yeh-vah ri-yeh′-kah
Likhaya (Rus.)	lĭ-hä′-yä	li-hah′-yah
Likhoslavl (Rus.)	lĭ-hŏ-slävl′(y)	li-ho-slahvl′(y)
Likhvin (Rus.)	lēk(h)′-vĭn	leek(h)′-vin
Likiep (Oc., Marshalls)	lē′-kē-ĕp	lee′-kee-ep
Lilibeo (Sicily, cape)	lē-lē-bĕ′-ô	lee-lee-beh′-o
Also called *Boeo,* q.v.		
Lilienthal, David E. (Am. administrator)	lĭl′-yən-thôl	lil′-yuhn-thawl
Lille (Fr.)	lēl′	leel′
Lillebaelt (Den., sound)	lĭl′-ə-bĕlt	lil′-uh-belt
Lillebonne (Fr.)	lēl-bôn′	leel-bon′
Lillehammer (Nor.)	lĭl′-ə-hä-mər	lil′-uh-hah-muhr
Lillers (Fr.)	lē-lĕr′	lee-lehr′
Lillesand (Nor.)	lĭl′-ə-sän	lil′-uh-sahn
Lillestroem *or* Lilleström (Nor.)	lĭl′-ə-strûm	lil′-uh-strœm
Liloan (P.I.)	lē-lô′-än	lee-lo′-ahn
Lim (Yugosl., riv.)	lēm′	leem′
Lima, Mendonça (Braz. polit.) See *Mendonça Lima.*		
Limassol (Cyprus)	lē-mä-sôl′	lee-mah-sol′
Limay (P.I.)	lē-mī′	lee-mai′
Limbones (P.I.)	lēm-bô′-nĕs	leem-bo′-nes
Also called *Carabao,* kä-rä-bou′ [kah-rah-bau′].		
Limbourg (Fr.)	*Fr.* lăN-bo͞or′	laN-boor′
	Eng. lĭm′-bûrg	lim′-buhrg
Limburg (Ger.)	*Eng.* lĭm′-bûrg	lim′-buhrg
	Ger. lĭm′-bo͝ork(h)	lim′-burk(h)
Limburg (Neth., prov.)	*Eng.* lĭm′-bûrg	lim′-buhrg
	Du. lĭm′-bûrk(h)	lim′-bœrk(h)

[299]

limen	lē-mēn'	lee-meen'

A common element, meaning *harbor*, in Greek place names.

Limen Setias (Crete)	lē-mēn' sē-tē'-äs	lee-meen' see-tee'-ahs
Limerick (Eire)	lĭm'-ər-ĭk	lim'-uhr-ik
	colloq. lĭm'-rĭk	lim'-rik

Gaelic *Luimneach*, lĭm'-yăk(h) [lim'-yak(h)].

Lim Fjord (Den.)	lēm'	leem'
Limljani (Yugosl.)	lēm'-lyä-nĭ	leem'-lyah-ni
Limne (Gr., Euboea)	lēm'-nē	leem'-nee

A common element, meaning *lake*, in Greek place names.

Limoges (Fr.)	*Eng.* lĭ-mōzh'	li-mohzh'
	Fr. lē-môzh'	lee-mozh'
Limón (P.I.)	lē-môn'	lee-mon'
Limousin (Fr.)	lē-mōō-zăN'	lee-moo-zaN'
Limoux (Fr.)	lē-mōō'	lee-moo'
Lin-an (Ch., Chekiang)	lĭn-än	lin-ahn
Línao (P.I.)	lē'-nou	lee'-nau
Linares (Sp., Chile)	lē-nä'-rĕs	lee-nah'-res
Lin-ch'wan (Ch., Kiangsi)	lĭn-chwän	lin-chwahn
Lindesnes (Nor.)	lĭn'-dəs-nĕs	lin'-duhs-nes

Also called The *Naze*, nāz [nayz].

Lindi (Tanganyika)	lĭn'-dĭ	lin'-di
Lindre, Étang de (Fr.,)	läN'dr, ĕ-täN' də	laN'dr, eh-tahN' duh
Lindsay, Vachel (Am. poet)	lĭn'-zĭ, vā'-chəl	lin'-zi vay'-chuhl
Línea, la (Sp.)	lē'-nĕ-ä, lä	lee'-neh-ah, lah
Lineinoye (Rus.)	lĭ-nā'-nŏ-yĕ	li-nay'-no-yeh
Lingayen (P.I.)	lĭng-gä'-yĕn	ling-gah'-yen

The form recorded in several gazetteers is *Lingayén*, lĭng-gä-yĕn' [ling-gah-yen'], but I have never heard it so stressed by American soldiers and sailors or by Filipinos.

Ling-ch'uan (Ch., Shansi)	lĭng-chwän	ling-chwahn
Lingeh (Iran)	lĭng'-gĕ'	ling'-geh'
Lingen (Ger.)	lĭng'-ən	ling'-uhn
Linggadjati (NEI)	lĭng'-gä-jä'-tē	ling'-kah-jah'-tee
Linguaglossa (Sicily)	lēn-gwä-glôs'-sä	leen-gwah-glos'-sah
Linguetta, Capo (Alb. cape)	*It.* lĭn-gwĕt'-tä	lin-gwet'-tah

English *Glossa*, q.v. Albanian *Kep i Gjuhëzës* and *Karaburum*, q.v.

Linhares, José (Braz. polit.)	lē-nyä'-rĭs, zhô-zĕ'	lee-nyah'-ris, zho-zeh'
Lin-hsiang (Ch., Hunan)	lĭn-shyäng	lin-shyahng
Lin-hsien (Ch., Hopeh)	lĭn-shyĕn	lin-shyen

Linkomies, Edwin (Fin. lǐng'-kô-mē-ĕs, ling'-ko-mee-es,
   polit.) ĕd'-vǐn ed'-vin
Linlithgow (Scot.) lǐn-lǐth'-gō lin-lith'-goh
linna lǐn'-nä lin'-nah
  An element, meaning *fort* or *castle*, in Finnish place names.
Linnich (Ger.) lǐn'-ǐk(h) lin'-ik(h)
Linosa (It., isl.) lē-nô'-zä lee-no'-zah
Lins de Barros, lēns' dǐ bär'-rŏ͝os, leens' di bahr'-rus,
  João Alberto zhwoun' äl-bĕr'-tŏ͝o zhwaun' ahl-behr'-
  (Braz. polit.) tu
Lin Sên (Ch. polit.) lǐn sŭn lin suhn
Lintían (P.I.) lǐn-tē'-än lin-tee'-ahn
Linz (Ger.) lǐnts' lints'
Linzhausen (Ger.) lǐnts'-hou'-zən lints'-hau'-zuhn
Lion sur Mer (Fr.) lyôN sür mĕr' lyoN sür mehr'
Lious (Gr., isl.) See *Aigila*.
Lipá (P.I.) lē-pä' lee-pah'
Lipari (Sicily, isls.) *Eng.* lǐp'-ə-rē lip'-uh-ree
          It. lē'-pä-rē lee'-pah-ree
  Italian *Isole Eolie*, q.v. A local pronunciation is reported, lǐ'-pä-rē
  [li'-pah-ree].
Lipcani (Rum. >Rus.) See *Lipkany* .
Lipec (Yugosl.) lē'-pĕts lee'-pets
Lipkany (Rum. >Rus.) lǐp-kä'-nǐ lip-kah'-ni
  Rumanian *Lipcani*, lēp-kän' [leep-kahn'].
Lipljan (Yugosl.) lēp'-lyän leep'-lyahn
Lipolist (Yugosl.) lē'-pô-lēst' lee'-po-leest'
Lippe (Ger., riv.) lǐp'-ə lip'-uh
Lippedorf (Ger.) lǐp'-ə-dôrf lip'-uh-dorf
Lippstadt (Ger.) lǐp'-shtät lip'-shtaht
Lipse (Hung.) lǐp'-shĕ lip'-sheh
Lipsi (Dodec.) See *Lipsos*.
Lipso(s) (Dodec.) *Eng.* lǐp'-sō *or* lip'-soh *or* lip'-sos
          lǐp'-sŏs
          Gr. lē-psô(s)' lee-pso(s)'
  Also called *Lisso*, lǐs'-sō [lis'-soh].
liqen lē-kyĕn' lee-kyen'
  An element, meaning *lake*, in Albanian place names. Look up the
  other part of the name.
liqeni (Alb.) See *liqen*.
Liri (It., riv.) lē'-rē lee'-ree
Lisac (Yugosl., mt.) lē'-säts lee'-sahts
Lisboa (Port.) lēzh-bô'-ə leezh-bo'-uh
  English *Lisbon*, q.v.

Lisbon (Port., U.S.)   *Eng.* lĭz'-bən   liz'-buhn
Li-shih (Ch., Shansi)   lē-shû   lee-shuh
Li-shui (Ch., Chekiang)   lē-shwā   lee-shway
Lisichansk (Rus.)   lĭ-sĭ-chänsk'   li-si-chahnsk'
Lisický, Karel   lē'-sĭ-tskē, kä'-rĕl   lee'-si-tskee, kah'-rel
(Cz. diplomat)
Lisieux (Fr.)   lē-zyû'   lee-zyœ'
Lisinj (Yugosl., mt.)   lē'-sĭn(y)   lee'-sin(y)
Liski (Rus.)   lēs'-kĭ   lees'-ki
Lismore (Austral.)   lĭz'-môr   liz'-mor
Lison (Fr.)   lē-zôN'   lee-zoN'
Lissa (Yugosl., isl.)   *It.* lēs'-sä   lees'-sah
Serb-Croat *Vis*, q.v.
Lisse (Neth.)   lĭs'-ə   lis'-uh
Lisso (Dodec.)   See *Lipso.*
Literno (It.)   lē-tĕr'-nô   lee-tehr'-no
Lithgow (Austral.)   lĭth'-gō   lith'-goh
Lithuania (Rus.)   lĭth'-ŏŏ-ā-nyə   lith'-u-ay-nyuh
   Lithuanian *Lietuva,* lĭ-ĕ-tōō'-vä [li-eh-too'-vah]. Russian *Litva,* lĭt-vä'
   [lit-vah'].
Litija (Yugosl.)   lē'-tĭ-yä   lee'-ti-yah
Litoměřice (Cz.)   lē'-tô-myĕ'-rzhĭ-tsĕ   lee'-to-myeh'-rzhi-tseh

German *Leitmeritz*, q.v.
Littoria (It.)   lēt-tô'-ryä   leet-to'-ryah
Litvinov, Maxim (Rus.   lĭt-vē'-nŏf, mäk-sēm'   lit-vee'-nof, mahk-
polit.)   seem'
Liu-ch'iu (Jap.) See *Ryūkyū.*
Liu-chow (Ch., Kwangsi)   lyōō-jō   lyoo-joh
Liu-wang-lou (Ch.,   lyō-wäng-lō   lyoh-wahng-loh
Kiangsu)
Livadia (Rus.)   lĭ-vä'-dĭ-yä   lih-vah'-dih-yah
Livarot (Fr.)   lē-vä-rō'   lee-vah-roh'
Liverdun (Fr.)   lē-vĕr-dûN'   lee-vehr-dœN'
Livergnano (It.)   lē-vĕr-nyä'-nô   lee-vehr-nyah'-no
Livno (Yugosl.)   lēv'-nô   leev'-no
Livny (Rus.)   lēv'-nĭ   leev'-ni
Livonia (Rus.)   lĭ-vō'-nyə   li-voh'-nyuh
Livorno (It.)   lē-vôr'-nô   lee-vor'-no
English *Leghorn*, q.v.
Livry (Rus.)   lē'-vrĭ   lee'-vri
Ljig (Yugosl.)   lyēg'   lyeeg'
Ljubičevac (Yugosl.)   lyōō'-bē'-chĕ-väts   lyoo'-bee'-cheh-vahts

Ljubljana (Yugosl.)	lyōō'-blyä'-nä	lyoo'-blyah'-nah
German *Laibach*, q.v.		
Ljubljanica (Yugosl., riv.)	lyōō'-blyä'-nĭ-tsä	lyoo'-blyah'-ni-tsah
German *Laibach*, q.v.		
Ljubljanska (Yugosl.)	lyōō'-blyän'-skä	lyoo'-blyahn'-skah
Ljuboten (Yugosl., mt.)	lyōō'-bô-tĕn	lyoo'-bo-ten
Ljubovija (Yugosl.)	lyōō'-bô'-vĭ-yä	lyoo'-bo'-vi-yah
Ljubuški (Yugosl.)	lyōō'-bōō-shkĭ	lyoo'-boo-shki
Ljutomer (Yugosl.)	lyōō'-tô-mĕr	lyoo'-to-mehr
Llanafan (Wales)	län-ä'-vän	lahn-ah'-vahn

In Welsh *ll* is pronounced as a *voiceless l*, similar to a final *l* sound in French or to *hl* of the nonce word *hleap* in contrast to the *l* of *leap*.

Llandaff (Wales)	län'-däf	lahn'-dahf
Llanelly (Wales)	län-ĕ'-lĭ	lahn-eh'-li
Llanfaethlu (Anglesey)	län-vĭth'-lĭ	lahn-vaith'-li
Llano (Tex.)	lăn'-ō	lan'-oh
Llanquihue (Chile)	lyän-kē'-wĕ	lyahn-kee'-weh
Llixha (Alb.) See *Llixhë*.		
Llixhë (Alb.)	lē'-jə	lee'-juh
Lo-an (Ch., Kiangsi)	lô-än	lo-ahn
Loanda (S.W. Afr.)	lōō-än'-də	lu-ahn'-duh

Also called *São Paulo de Loanda*, souN pou'-lōō də lōō-än'-də [sauN pau'-lu duh lu-ahn'-duh].

Löbau (Pol.) See *Lubawa*.

Loboó (P.I.)	lô-bô-ô'	lo-bo-o'
Locarno (Switz.)	lô-kär'-nô	lo-kahr'-no
Loch an Eilean (Scot.)	lôk(h)' ən ē'-lən	lok(h)' uhn ee'-luhn
Lochem (Neth.)	lôk(h)'-əm	lok(h)'-uhm
Loches (Fr.)	lôsh'	losh'
Lo-chia-tu (Ch., Kwangtung)	lô-jyä-dōō	lo-jyah-doo
Loch Lomond (Scot., lake)	lôk(h)' lō'-mən	lok(h)' loh'-muhn
Locle, le (Switz.)	lô'kl, lə	lo'kl, luh
Locminé (Fr.)	lôk-mē-nĕ'	lok-mee-neh'
Lodeinoe Pole (Rus.)	lŏ-dä'-nŏ-yĕ pô'-lĕ	lo-day'-no-yeh po'-leh
Lodi (Calif., N.J.)	lō'-dī'	loh'-dai'
Lodi (It.)	lô'-dē	lo'-dee
Lödingen (Nor.)	lû'-dĭng-ən	lœ'-ding-uhn
Łódź (Pol.)	lōōdzh'	ludzh'

Russian *Lodz*, lôdz' [lodz'].

Lœbau (Pol.) See *Lubawa*.

Loedingen (Nor.)	lû'-dĭng-ən	lœ'-ding-uhn
Loeffler (Ger., Am. name)	*Eng.* lĕf'-lər	lef'-luhr
	Ger. lûf'-lər	lœf'-luhr

Loekken (Nor.)	lŭk'-kən	luhk'-kuhn
Loen (Nor.)	lō'-ən	loh'-uhn
Loenen (Neth.)	lōō'-nən	loo'-nuhn
Loeningen (Ger., riv.)	lû'-nĭng-ən	lœ'-ning-uhn
Loerrach (Ger.)	lû'-räk(h)	lœ'-rahk(h)
Loetzen (Ger. >Pol.)	lût'-sən	lœt'-suhn
Polish *Lec*, q.v.		
Loev (Rus.)	lō'-yĕf	lo'-yef
Loevenich (Ger.)	lû'-və-nĭk(h)	lœ'-vuh-nik(h)
Loevoe (Hung.) See *Lövö*.		
Lofoten (Nor., isls.)	*Eng.* lō-fō'-tən	loh-foh'-tuhn
	Nor. lōō'-fōōtn	loo'-footn
Lofthus (Nor.)	lôft'-hōōs	loft'-hoos
Loges, les (Fr.)	lôzh', lĕ	lozh', leh
Logothetopoulos,	lô-gô-thĕ-tô'-pōō-lôs,	lo-go-theh-to'-poo-los,
Konstantinos	kôn-stän-dē'-	kon-stahn-dee'-
(Gr. polit.)	nôs	nos
Logroño (Sp.)	lô-grô'-nyô	lo-gro'-nyo
Logtak (India, lake)	lôg'-täk	log'-tahk
Also spelled *Loktak*.		
Lohe (Ger. >? Pol., riv.)	lō'-ə	loh'-uh
Lohja (Fin.)	lō'-yä	lo'-yah
Lohmen (Ger.)	lō'-mən	loh'-muhn
Lo-ho (Ch., Anhwei)	lô-hô	lo-ho
Loikaw (Burma)	loi'-kô'	loi'-kaw'
Loilem (Burma)	loi'-lĕm'	loi'-lem'
Loimola (Fin.)	loi'-mô-lä	loi'-mo-lah
Loing (Fr., riv.)	lwăN'	lwaN'
Loire (Fr., riv.)	lwär'	lwahr'
Loire Inférieure (Fr.)	lwär ăN-fĕ-ryûr'	lwahr aN-feh-rycer'
Lokalanzeiger, Berliner	lō-käl'-än'-tsī-gər,	loh-kahl'-ahn'-tsai-
(Ger. newspaper)	bĕr-lē'-nər	guhr, behr-lee'-
		nuhr
Lokeren (Belg.)	lō'-kə-rən	loh'-kuh-ruhn
Lokhvitsa (Rus.)	lôk(h)'-vĭ-tsä	lok(h)'-vi-tsah
Lökken (Nor.)	lŭk'-kən	luhk'-kuhn
Lokrum (Yugosl., isl.)	lô'-krōōm	lo'-kroom
Italian *Lacroma*, q.v.		
Loktak (India, lake) See *Logtak*.		
Lolland (Den., isl.) See *Laaland*.		
Lolobau (Oc., Bismarck	lô'-lô-bou	lo'-lo-bau
arch.)		
Lo Lung-chi (Ch. polit.)	lô lōŏng-jē	lo lung-jee
Lom (Bulg.)	lôm'	lom'

Lom (Nor.)   lŏŏm′   lum′

Lombardo Toledano,   lôm-bär′-dô tô-lĕ-   lom-bahr′-do to-leh-
   Vincente (Mex. labor   dä′-nô, vēn-sĕn′-tĕ   dah′-no, veen-sen′-
   leader)   teh

Lombok (NEI)   lŏm-bŏk′   lom-bok′

Łomża (Pol.)   lôm′-zhä   lom′-zhah
   Russian spelling *Lomzha.*

Lomzha (Pol.)   See *Łomża.*

Londos, Demetrios   lôn′-dôs, dē-mē′-   lon′-dos, dee-mee′-
   (Gr. polit.)   trē-ôs   tree-os

Longa (Gr.)   lông-gä′   long-gah′

Longeville (Fr.)   lôNzh-vēl′   loNzh-veel′

Longjumeau (Fr.)   lôN-zhü-mō′   loN-zhü-moh′

Longny au Perche (Fr.)   lôN-nyē ō pĕrsh′   loN-nyee oh pehrsh′

Longos (Gr., pen.)   lông′-gôs   long′-gos
   Also called *Sithonia,* sē-thô-nē′-ä [see-tho-nee′-ah].

Longué (Fr.)   lôN-gĕ′   loN-geh′

Longwy (Fr.)   lôN-wē′   loN-wee′

Longxuyen (Indo-Ch.)   lŭm-swĭn′   luhm-swin′
    Siam. lôŭm-swēn′   lo-uhm-sween′

Löningen (Ger., riv.)   lû′-nĭng-ən   lœ′-ning-uhn

Lonkin (Burma)   *Eng.* lŏn′-kĭn′   lon′-kin′
    Bur. lōn′-tĭn′   lohn′-tin′

Lonoy (P.I.)   lô-noi′   lo-noi′

Lons le Saunier (Fr.)   lôN lə sō-nyĕ′   loN luh soh-nyeh′

Loo, Het (Neth.)   lō′, hĕt   loh′, het

Loochoo (Jap.)   See *Okinawa Gunto.*

Loog (P.I., bay)   lô-ôg′   lo-og′

Loon op Zand (Neth.)   lōn′ ôp zänt′   lohn′ op zahnt′

Loosdrecht (Neth.)   lōs′-drĕk(h)t   lohs′-drek(h)t

Loosduinen (Neth.)   lōs-dûĭ′-nən   lohs-dœi′-nuhn

Loparskaya (Rus.)   lŏ-pär′-skä-yä   lo-pahr′-skah-yah

Lopatka (Rus., cape)   lŏ-pät′-kä   lo-paht′-kah

Lopburi (Siam)   lŏp′-bŏŏ-rē′   lohp′-bu-ree′

Lopes, Simões (Braz. polit.) See *Simões Lopes.*

López (Sp. name)   *Am. Sp.* lô′-pĕs   lo′-pehs
    Sp.   lô′-pĕth   lo′-pehth

López, Alfonzo (Colom.   lô′-pĕs, äl-fôn′-sô   lo′-pes, ahl-fon′-so
   diplomat)

López, Francisco Solano (Para. polit.) See *Solano López.*

Lo-p'ing (Ch., Kiangsi)   lô-pĭng   lo-ping

Loppersum (Neth.)   lôp′-ər-səm   lop′-uhr-suhm

Lopud (Yugosl., isl.)   lô′-pōōd   lo′-pood
   Italian *Mezzo,* q.v.

loran   lō-răn′ *or* lôr′-ən   loh-ran′ *or* lor′-uhn
  An abbreviation of *long range navigation.*

Lorca (Sp.)	lôr′-kä	lor′-kah
Lorch (Ger.)	lôrk(h)′	lork(h)′

Lorengau (Oc., Admiralties) See *Lorungau.*

Lorentzweiler (Luxem.)	lō′-rĕnts-vī′-lər	loh′-rents-vai′-luhr
Loreto (It.)	lô-rĕ′-tô	lo-reh′-to
Lorgues (Fr.)	lôrg′	lorg′
Lorient (Fr.)	lô-ryäN′	lo-ryahN′
Lörrach (Ger.)	lû′-räk(h)	lœ′-rahk(h)
Lorris (Fr.)	lô-rēs′	lo-rees′
Lorungau (Oc., Admiralties)	lô-rōōng-ou′	lo-roong-au′

  Also called *Lorengau,* lô-rĕng-ou′ [lo-reng-au′].

Los Alamitos (Calif.)	lôs ä-lä-mē′-tôs	los ah-lah-mee′-tos
Los Álamos (N.M.)	lôs ä′-lä-môs	los ah′-lah-mos
Los Angeles (Calif.)	lŏs *or* lōs ăng′-gə-ləs	los *or* lohs ang′-guh-luhs
	or lŏs ăn′-jə-ləs	los an′-juh-luhs
	or -lēz	-leez

Thorndike Century (1941), Holt (1938), and the Columbia Encyclopedia (1935) prefer lŏs (*not* lōs) ăng′-gə-ləs; but Webster's (1934) prefers lōs. The Standard prefers lŏs ăn′-jə-lēz. The pronunciation in the city itself is far from settled. It is said that the place-name studies of the University of California will show that the present younger generation favors lŏs ăn′-jə-ləs [los an′-juh-luhs]. If so, this is in my opinion a return to the pronunciation of their grandfathers, before the great real estate agitation for "something different—Spanish-like." The Spanish is lôs äng′-hĕ-lĕs [los ahng′-heh-les].

Losap (Oc., Carolines)	lô′-säp	lo′-sahp
Los Baños (P.I.)	lôs bä′-nyôs	los bah′-nyos
Los Gatos (Calif.)	lŏs găt′-əs	los gat′-uhs
Lo-shan (Ch., Honan)	lô-shän	lo-shahn
Los Indios (Cuba)	lôs ēn′-dyôs	los een′-dyos
Lošinj (It. > Yugosl., isl.)	*S.-C.* lô′-shĭn(y)	lo′-shin(y)

  Italian *Lussino,* q.v.

Los Negros (Mex.)	lôs nĕ′-grôs	los neh′-gros

Losoncz (Cz.) See *Lučenec.*

Los Reyes (Oc., Admiralties)	lôs rĕ′-yĕs	los reh′-yes
Losser (Neth.)	lôs′-ər	los′-uhr
Lot (Fr., riv.)	lôt′	lot′

Lotfi, Ahmed (Egypt. polit.) See *Ahmed Lotfi el Seyed.*

Lötzen (Ger. >Pol.)	lût′-sən	lœt′-suhn
Polish *Lec*, q.v.		
Loudéac (Fr.)	lōō-dĕ-äk′	loo-deh-ahk′
Loudon, Alexander	loud′n	laud′n
(Du. diplomat)		
Lough Neagh (N. Ire.)	lôk(h) nā′	lawk(h) nay′
Louhans (Fr.)	lwäN′	lwahN′
Louisiade (Oc., isls.)	lōō-ē′-zĭ-ăd′	loo-ee′-zi-ad′
Louisiana (U.S.)	lōō′-ĭz-ĭ-ăn′-ə	lu′-iz-i-an′-uh
	or lōō-(w)ē′-zĭ-ăn-ə	lu-(w)ee′-zi-an′-uh
Louisville (Ky.)	lōō′-ĭ-vĭl	loo′-i-vil
	or lōō′-ə-vəl	lu′-uh-vuhl

As a place name in other states, lōō′-ĭs-vĭl [loo′-is-vil].

Loup (Fr., riv.)	lōō′	loo′
Lourenço Marques	*Eng.* lō-rĕn′-sō	loh-ren′-soh
(Mozambique, Afr.)	mär′-kĕs	mahr′-kes
	Port. lō-rĕN′-sŏō	loh-reN′-su
	mär′-kĭsh	mahr′-kish
Louros (Gr.)	lōō′-rôs	loo′-ros
Louroux Béconnais, le	lōō-rōō bĕ-kô-nĕ′, lə	loo-roo beh-ko-neh′,
(Fr.)		luh
Loutra (Gr., Lesbos)	lōō-trä′	loo-trah′

A common element, meaning *baths*, in Greek place names.

Loutron (Crete)	lōō-trô(n)′	loo-tro(n)′
Loutros (Gr.)	lōō-trôs′	loo-tros′
Loutsa (Gr.)	lōō′-tsä	loo′-tsah
Louvain (Belg.)	*Eng.* lōō-vān′	loo-vayn′
	Fr. lōō-văN′	loo-vaN′
Flemish *Leuven*, q.v.		
Louvaris (Gr. collab.)	lōō′-vä-rēs	loo′-vah-rees
Louviers (Fr.)	lōō-vyĕ′	loo-vyeh′
Louvigné du Désert (Fr.)	lōō-vē-nyĕ dü dĕ-zĕr′	loo-vee-nyeh dü
		deh-zehr′
Louvigny (Fr.)	lōō-vē-nyē′	loo-vee-nyee′
Louvre (Fr., palace)	lōō′vr	loo′vr
Lovćen (Yugosl., mt.)	lôv′-chĕn	lov′-chen
Lovech (Bulg.)	lô′-vĕch	lo′-vech
Lövenich (Ger.)	lû′-və-nĭk(h)	lœ′-vuh-nik(h)
Lovich (Pol.) See *Łowicz.*		
Lovisa *or* Loviisa (Fin.)	lô′-vē-sä	lo′-vee-sah

The length of the second vowel may give the effect of an accent.

Lövö (Hung.)	lû′-vû	lœ′-vœ
Lowestoft (Eng.)	lōs′-tŏft *or* lōs′-təf	lohs′-toft *or* lohs′-tuhf

Łowicz (Pol.)	lŏ′-vĭch	lo′-vich
Russian spelling *Lovich*.		
Lowman (N.Y.)	lou′-mən	lau′-muhn
Lowville (N.Y.)	lou′-vĭl	lau′-vil
Lo-yang (Ch., Honan)	lŏ-yäng	lo-yahng
Also called *Honanfu*, q.v.		
Lož (Yugosl.)	lŏzh′	lozh′
German *Laas*.		
Lozère (Fr.)	lŏ-zĕr′	lo-zehr′
Loznica (Yugosl.)	lŏz′-nĭ-tsä	loz′-ni-tsah
Lozovaya (Rus.)	lŏ-zŏ-vä′-yä	lo-zo-vah′-yah
Lozovik (Yugosl.)	lŏ′-zŏ-vĭk	lo′-zo-vik
Lozovsky (Rus.)	lŏ-zŏf′-skĭ	lo-zof′-ski
luang	lwäng′	lwahng′
A Siamese title. Look up the other part of the name.		
Luang Prabang	lwäng′ prə-bäng′	lwahng′ pruh-bahng′
(Indo-Ch.)		
Lubań (Ger. >? Pol.)	lōō′-bän(y)	loo′-bahn(y)
German *Lauban*, q.v.		
Lubānas (Latvia)	lōō′-bä-näs	lu′-bah-nahs
Lubang (P.I.)	lōō-bäng′	loo-bahng′
Lubao (P.I.)	lōō-bou′	loo-bau′
Lubartów (Pol.)	lōō-bär′-tŏōf	lu-bahr′-tuf
Russian *Lyubartov*, lyōō-bär′-tŏf [lyoo-bahr′-tof].		
Lubawa (Pol.)	lōō-bä′vä	lu-bah′-vah
German *Löbau*, lŭ′-bou [lœ′-bau].		
Lübben (Ger.)	lüb′-ən	lüb′-uhn
Lübeck (Ger.) See *Luebeck*.		
Lüben (Ger. >? Pol.)	lü′-bən	lü′-buhn
Polish *Lubiń*, lōō′-bĭn(y) [lu′-bin(y)].		
Lubiana (Yugosl.)	*It.* lōō-bē-ä′-nä	loo-bee-ah′-nah
Serb-Croat *Ljubljana*, q.v.		
Lublin (Pol.)	lyŏō′-blĭn	lyu′-blin
Russian *Lyublin*, lyōō′-blĭn [lyoo′-blin].		
Lubny (Rus.)	lōōb′-nĭ	loob′-ni
Luboml (Pol. >Rus.)	lōō′-bŏml	loo′-boml
Russian *Lyuboml*, lyŏō-bôml′(y) [lyu-boml′(y)].		
Lubuagan (P.I.)	lōō-bwä′-gän	loo-bwah′-gahn
Luc, le (Fr.)	lük′, lə	lük′, luh
Lucca (It.)	lōōk′-kä	look′-kah
Lucch (Libya)	lōōk(h)′	luk(h)′
Luce, Clare Boothe	lōōs′	loos′
(Am. playwright)		
Lucena (P.I.)	lōō-thĕ′-nä- *or* -sĕ′-	loo-theh′-nah *or* -seh′-

Lu šenec (Cz.)	lōō'-chĕ-nĕts	loo'-cheh-nets
Hungarian *Losoncz*, lô'-shônts [lo'-shonts].		
Luchaire, Jean	lü-shăr', zhäN'	lü-shehr', zhaN'
(Fr. polit.)		
Luché (Fr.)	lü-shĕ'	lü-sheh'
Lu-chow (Ch., Anhwei)	*Eng.* lōō-chou	loo-chau
	Ch. lōō-jō	loo-joh
Also called *Ho-fei*.		
Lucia (girl's name)	*Eng.* lyōō'-shə	lyoo'-shuh
	It. lōō-chē'-ä	loo-chee'-ah
Lucia (Sicily)	lōō-chē'-ä	loo-chee'-ah
Lučica (Yugosl.)	lōō'-chĭ-tsä	loo'-chi-tsah
Lucien (Fr.)	lü-syĕN'	lü-syeN'
Łuck (Pol. > Rus.)	lōōtsk'	lootsk'
Russian *Lutsk*, q.v.		
Lucknow (India)	lŭk'-nou	luhk'-nau
Luçon (Fr.)	lü-sôN'	lü-soN'
Luc Ouistreham (Fr.)	lük wēs-träN'	lük wees-trahN'
Ludas (Hung.)	lōō'-dŏsh	loo'-dosh
Ludbreg (Yugosl.)	lōōd'-brĕg	lood'-breg
Ludington (Mich.)	lŭd'-ĭng-tən	luhd'-ing-tuhn
Ludwigshafen (Ger.)	lōōt'-vĭk(h)s-hä'-fən	loot'-vik(h)s-hah'-fuhn
Ludwigslust (Ger.)	lōōt'-vĭk(h)s-lōōst'	lut'-vik(h)s-lust'
Ludwigsort (Ger. > Rus.)	lōōt'-vĭk(h)s-ôrt'	loot'-vik(h)s-ort'
Russian *Ladushkin*, lä'-dōō-shkĭn [lah'-du-shkin].		
Ludze (Latvia)	lōōd'-zĕ	lud'-zeh
Russian *Luzen*, q.v.		
Luebben (Ger.)	lüb'-ən	lüb'-uhn
Luebeck *or* Lübeck	*Eng.* lōō'-bĕk'	loo'-bek'
(Ger.)	*Ger.* lü'-bĕk	lü'-bek
Lueben (Ger >? Pol.) See *Lüben*.		
Lueneburg (Ger.)	lü'-nə-bōōrk(h)	lü'-nuh-burk(h)
Lueneburger Heide	lü'-nə-bōōr-gər hī'-də	lü'-nuh-bur-guhr hai'-duh
English *Lueneburg Heath*.		
Luetzendorf (Ger.)	lüt'-sən-dôrf	lüt'-suhn-dorf
Lu-fêng (Ch., Kwangtung)	lōō-fŭng	loo-fuhng
Luftwaffe	lōōft'-väf-ə	luft'-vahf-uh
German word meaning *air force*.		
Ług (Pol., riv.)	lōōk'	look'
Russian *Luga*, lōō'-gä [loo'-gah].		
Luga (Rus., riv.)	lōō'-gä	loo'-gah
Lugano (Switz.)	lōō-gä'-nô	loo-gah'-no

Lugavčina (Yugosl.)	lōō'-gäv'-chĭ-nä	loo'-gahv'-chi-nah
Lugny (Fr.)	lü-nyē'	lü-nyee'
Lugo (Sp.)	lōō'-gô	loo'-go
Lugoj (Rum.)	lōō'-gôzh	lu'-gozh

Hungarian *Lugos*, lōō'-gôsh [lu'-gosh].

Lugomir (Yugosl., riv.)	lōō'-gô-mĭr	loo'-go-mihr
Luigny (Fr.)	lwē-nyē'	lwee-nyee'

Luik (Belg.)   See *Liége*.

Luimneach (Eire) See *Limerick*.

Luino (It.)	lwē'-nô	lwee'-no
Luizet, Charles (Fr. polit.)	lwē-zĕ', shärl'	lwee-zeh', shahrl'
Lukirski, P. I. (Rus. scientist)	lōŏ-kēr'-skĭ	lu-keer'-ski
Lu-k'ou (Ch., Hunan)	lōō-kō	loo-koh
Lukovica (Balkan riv.)	S.-C. lōō'-kô-vĭ-tsä	loo'-ko-vi-tsah
Lukovo (Yugosl.)	lōō'-kô-vô	loo'-ko-vo
Łuków (Pol.)	lōō'-kŏŏf	lu'-kuf

Russian *Lukov*, lōō'-kŏf [loo'-kof].

Luks, George (Am. painter)	lōōks'	looks'

"*Luke* plus *s*," on the testimony of Everett Shinn, Alfred G. B. Steel, and Mahonri M. Young. Not lŭks or lŏŏks.

Lukunor (Oc., Carolines)	lōō-kōō-nôr'	loo-koo-nor'
Luleå *or* Luleaa (Sw.)	lü'-lĕ-ō	lü'-leh-oh
Lüleburgaz (Turk.)	lü-lĕ'-bŏŏr-gäz	lü-leh'-bur-gahz
Luling (Tex.)	lōō'-lĭng	loo'-ling
lum	lōōm'	loom'

An element, meaning *river*, in Albanian place names. Look up the other part of the name. The definite for is *lumi*.

Luma (Alb.)   See *Lumë*.

Lumë (Alb.)	lōō'-mə	loo'-muh
Lumintan (P.I.)	lōō-mēn'-tän	loo-meen'-tahn
Lumíntao (P.I.)	lōō-mēn'-tou	loo-meen'-tau
Lund (Sw.)	lŏŏnd'	lund'
Lunde (Nor.)	lŏŏn'-də	lun'-duh
Lüneburg (Ger.)	lü'-nə-bŏŏrk(h)	lü'-nuh-burk(h)

Lüneburger Heide (Ger.) See *Lueneburger Heide*.

Lunel (Fr.)	lü-nĕl'	lü-nel'
Lunéville (Fr.)	lü-nĕ-vēl'	lü-neh-veel'
Lunga (Oc., Guadalcanal)	lōōng'-ä	loong'-ah

Americanized as lŏŏng'-gä [lung'-gah].

Lung-ch'i (Ch., Fukien)	lŏŏng-chē	lung-chee

Also called *Lung-ki*, q.v.

Lung-chiang (Manchu.) See *Tsitsihar*.

Lung-ch'üan (Ch.,   lо̄о̆ng-chüän   lung-chü-ahn
  Chekiang)

Lung-hai (Ch., railroad) lо̄о̆ng-hī   lung-hai

Lunghezza (It.)   lо̄о̆ng-gĕd'-sä   loong-ged'-zah

Lung-ki (Ch., Fukien) lо̄о̆ng-kē   lung-kee
  Also called *Lung-ch'i*, q.v.

Lung-kow (Ch.,   *Eng.* lо̄о̆ng-kou   lung-kau
  Shantung)   *Ch.* lо̄о̆ng-kō   lung-koh

Lung-ling (Ch., Yünnan) lо̄о̆ng-lĭng   lung-ling

Lung-nan (Ch., Kiangsi) lо̄о̆ng-nän   lung-nahn

Lung-yu (Ch., Chekiang) lо̄о̆ng-yо̄о   lung-yoo

Luninets (Pol. > Rus.) lо̄о̄-nē'-nĕts   lu-nee'-nets
  Polish *Łuniniec*, lо̄о̄-nē'-nyĕts [lu-nee'-nyets].

L'Unità (Rome,   lо̄о̄-nē-tä'   loo-nee-tah'
  newspaper)

L'Uomo Qualunque   lwô'-mô   lwo'-mo
  (Rome, newspaper)   kwä-lо̄о̄n'-kwĕ   kwah-loon'-kweh

Lupao (P.I.)   lо̄о̄-pou'   loo-pau'

Lur (Per. tribe)   lо̄о̄r'   loor'

Lure (Fr.)   lür'   lür'

Lushnja (Alb.) See) *Lushnje*.

Lushnje (Alb.)   lо̄о̄sh'-nyĕ   loosh'-nyeh
  Serb-Croat *Lušnje*.

Lü-shun-k'ow (Manchu.) See *Port Arthur*.

Lussino (It. > Yugosl., isl.) lо̄о̄s-sē'-nô   loos-see'-no
  Serb-Croat *Lošinj*, q.v.

Luštica (Yugosl.)   lо̄о̄'-shtĭ-tsä   loo'-shti-tsah

Lutsk (Pol. > Rus.) lо̄о̄tsk'   lootsk'
  Polish *Łuck*, q.v.

Luttrebois (Belg.)   lü-trə-bwä'   lü-truh-bwah'

Lützen (Ger.)   lüt'-sən   lüt'-suhn

Lutzerath (Ger.)   lо̄о̄t'-sə-rät   lut'-suh-raht

Luuk (P.I.)   lо̄о̄-о̄о̄k'   loo-ook'

Luxembourg   *Fr.* lük-säN-bо̄о̄r'   lük-sahN-boor'

Luxemburg   *Eng.* lŭk'-səm-bûrg   luhk'-suhm-buhrg
    Ger. lо̄о̆k'-səm-   luk'-suhm-burk(h)
        bо̄о̆rk(h)

  French *Luxembourg*, q.v.

Luxeuil les Bains (Fr.) lük-sûi' lĕ băN   lük-sœi' leh baN'

Luxor (Egypt)   lŭk'-sôr *or* lо̄о̆k'-   luk'-sor *or* look'-
  Arabic *El Aqsur*, ĕl äk'-sо̄о̄r [el ahk'-sur].

luxurious   lŭg-zhо̄о̄r'-rĭ-əs   luhg-zhur'-ri-uhs
    or lŭks-yо̄о̄'-rĭ-əs   luhks-yoo'-ri-uhs

luxury   lŭk'-shŏŏr-ĭ   luhk'-shur-i

The pronunciation lŭg'-zhŏŏr-ĭ [luhg'-zhur-i] is not recommended.

Lužane (Yugosl.)   lŏŏ'-zhä-nĕ   loo'-zhah-neh

Luzarches (Fr.)   lü-zärsh'   lü-zahrsh'

Luzen (Latvia)   *Rus.* lyŏŏ'-tsĕn   lyoo'-tsen

   Latvian *Ludze*, q.v.

Luzón (P.I.)   *Eng.* lŏŏ-zŏn'   loo-zon'

          Sp. lŏŏ-sôn'   loo-son'

Lvov (Pol. >Rus.)   lvôf'   lvof'

   Polish *Lwów*, lvŏŏf' [lvoof']. German *Lemberg*, lĕm'-bĕrk(h) [lem'-
   behrk(h)].

Lwów (Pol.>Rus.) See *Lvov*.

Lyangra (Rus.)   lyän-grä'   lyahn-grah'

Lyautey (Mor.)   *Eng.* lē-ō-tā'   lee-oh-tay'

   Named after the French marshal, lyō-tĕ' [lyoh-teh'].

Lyck (Ger.)   lĭk'   lik'

Lyda (Pol.>Rus.) Lithuanian spelling of *Lida*, q.v.

Lydda (Pal.)   lĭd'-ə   lid'-uh

Lyon (Fr.)   lyôN'   lyoN'

   English *Lyons*, q.v.

Lyons (Fr.)   *Eng.* lī'-ənz   lai'-uhnz

   For the French City, the French form *Lyon*, q.v., is more common
   even in English contexts. The English form occurs as an American
   name.

Lyons la Forêt (Fr.)   lyôN lä fô-rě'   lyoN lah fo-reh'

Lys (Fr., Belg., riv.)   lēs'   lees'

   Flemish *Leye*, lī'-ə [lai'-uh].

Lysaker (Nor.)   lüs'-ä-kər   lüs'-ah-kuhr

Lysefjord (Nor.)   lü'-sə-fyŏr   lü'-suh-fyohr

Lysekloster (Nor.)   lü'-sə-klôs-tər   lü'-suh-klos-tuhr

Lysk (Ger.)   lĭsk'   lisk'

Lyubartov (Pol.)   See *Lubartów*.

Lyublin (Pol.)   See *Lublin*.

Lyuboml (Pol.>Rus.)   lyŏŏ-bôml'(y)   lyu-boml'(y)

   Polish *Luboml*, q.v.

Lyubytino (Rus.)   lyŏŏ-bwē'-tĭ-nŏ   lyu-bwee'-ti-no

Lyudinovo (Rus.)   lyŏŏ-dē'-nŏ-vŏ   lyu-dee'-no-vo

Maaloey *or* Maalöy (Nor.)   môl'-ûĭ   mol'-œi

Ma'an (Trans-Jordan)   mə-än'   muh-ahn'

Maarheeze (Neth.)   mär-hā'-zə   mahr-hay'-zuh

Maarianhamina (Fin.)   mä'-rĕ-än-hä'-mĕ-nä   mah'-ree-ahn-hah'-
                     mee-nah

   Swedish *Mariehamn*, q.v.

Maarsen (Neth.)   mär'-sən   mahr'-suhn
Maarseveen (Neth.)   mär'-sə-vān'   mahr'-suh-vayn'
Maartensdijk (Neth.)   mär'-təns-dīk'   mahr'-tuhns-daik'
    Also called *Sint Maartensdijk,* q.v.
Maas *or* Maes (Europ.   *Du., Flem.* mäs'   mahs'
    riv.)
    French *Meuse,* q.v. See also *Nieuwe Maas, Oude Maas,* and *Merwede.*
Maas, Melvin J.   mäs'   mahs'
    (U.S. representative)
Maasälkä (Fin., isth.)   mä'-săl-kă   mah'-sel-keh
Maasbree (Neth.)   mäs'-brā   mahs'-bray
Maashees (Neth.)   mäs-hās'   mahs-hays'
Maasin (P.I.)   mä-ä'-sēn   mah-ah'-seen
Maasniel (Neth.)   mäs'-nēl   mahs'-neel
Maassluis (Neth.)   mäs-slûĭs'   mahs-slœis'
Maastricht (Neth.)   mäs'-trĭk(h)t'   mahs'-trik(h)t'
Maaten Bagush (Egypt)   mä'-tĕn bä-gōōsh'   mah'-ten bah-goosh'
Mabalácat (P.I.)   mä-bä-lä'-kät   mah-bah-lah'-kaht
Mabtouha, el (Tun.)   məb-tōō'-hə, ĕl   muhb-too'-huh, el
Macabebe (P.I.)   mä-kä-bĕ'-bĕ   mah-kah-beh'-beh
Macajalar (P.I.)   mä-kä-hä-lär'   mah-kah-hah-lahr'
Macao (Ch., Kwangtung,   mə-kou'   muh-kau'
    Port. col.)
Macatí (P.I.) See *San Pedro Macatí.*
Maccarese (It.)   mäk-kä-rĕ'-zĕ   mahk-kah-reh'-zeh
McCarran, Pat   mə-kăr'-ən   muh-kehr'-uhn
    (U.S. senator)
Macchia (It.)   mäk'-kyä   mahk'-kyah
McConaughy, James   mə-kŏn'-ə-hĭ,   muh-kon'-uh-hi,
    Lukens (Am. educator)   lōō'-kĭnz   loo'-kinz
McCowen, Edward O.   mə-kou'-ĕn   muh-kau'-en
    (U.S. representative)
Mac Crohón (P.I.)   mäk krô-hôn'   mahk kro-hon'
McDonough, Gordon   mək-dŏn'-ə   muhk-don'-uh
    L. (U.S. representative)
Macedonia (Bulg.,   *Eng.* măs-ĭ-dō'-nyə   mas-i-doh'-nyuh
    Gr., Yugosl.)
    Bulgarian *Makedoniya,* mä-kĕ-dô'-nē-yä [mah-keh-do'-nee-yah]. Greek
    Makedonea, mä-kĕ-dô-nē'-ä [mah-keh-do-nee'-ah]. Serb-Croat *Maće-*
    donija, mä'-chĕ-dô'-nē-yä [mah'-cheh-do'-nee-yah].
Maceió (Brazil)   mä-sä-ô'   mah-say-o'
Macerata (It.)   mä-chĕ-rä'-tä   mah-cheh-rah'-tah
McEwen (Scot. name)   mə-kyōō'-ən   muh-kyoo'-uhn
McGeagh (Irish name)   mə-gā'   muh-gay'

McGehee, Dan R. (U.S. representative)	mə-gē'-hē	muh-gee'-hee
McGeough (Irish name)	mə-gō'	muh-goh'
McGranery, James P. (Former U.S. representative)	mə-grăn'-ər-ĭ	muh-gran'-uhr-i
Machecoul (Fr.)	mäsh-kōōl'	mahsh-kool'
machi	mä-chē	mah-chee

An element, meaning *town*, in Japanese place names.

Machias (Me., N.Y.)	mə-chī'-əs	muh-chai'-uhs
Machichaco (Sp., cape)	mä-chē-chä'-kô	mah-chee-chah'-ko
machination	măk'-ĭ-nā'-shən	mak'-i-nay'-shuhn
Maciejowice (Pol.)	mä-chĕ-yô-vē'-tsĕ	mah-cheh-yo-vee'-tseh

Russian *Matseyevitse*, mä-tsĕ-yĕ'-vĭ-tsĕ [mah-tseh-yeh'-vi-tseh].

MacKaye, Percy (Am. author)	mə-kī'	muh-kai'
Mackinac (Mich.)	măk'-ĭ-nô	mak'-ih-naw

However, the pronunciation măk'-ĭ-năk' is common on the island. The adjective is spelled *Mackinaw*.

McLean (Scot. name)	mə-klān'	muh-klayn'

In America occasionally pronounced mə-klēn' [muh-kleen'].

Macleod, Fiona	mə-kloud', fĭ-ō'-nə *or* fē'-nə	muh-klaud', fi-oh'-nuh *or* fee'-nuh

Pseudonym of William Sharp, Scottish poet.

McLeod, James (S.C. polit.)	mə-kloud'	muh-klaud'
McMahon, Brien (U.S. senator)	mək-măn'	muhk-man'
McMein, Neysa (Am. illustrator)	măk-mēn', nē'-sə	mak-meen', nee'-suh

Mrs. *Baragwanath*, bär'-ə-gwän'-äth [bahr'-uh-gwahn'-ahth].

Mâcon (Fr.)	mä-kôN'	mah-koN'
Macon (Ga., Ala., etc.)	mā'-kən	may'-kuhn
Macorís (Dom. Rep.)	mä-kô-rēs'	mah-ko-rees'
Mactan (P.I.)	mäk-tän'	mahk-tahn'
Mačva (Yugosl.)	mäch'-vä	mahch'-vah
MacVeagh, Lincoln (Am. diplomat)	mək-vā'	muhk-vay'
Madagascar (Afr., isl.)	măd'-ə-găs'-kər	mad'-uh-gas'-kuhr

In English usage, though not in French, the final syllable is better -kər than -kär.

madame	*Eng.* măd'-əm	mad'-uhm
	Fr. mä-däm'	mah-dahm'

In English contexts, the English pronunciation should be used. For the

plural, however, even in English contexts, *madams* is probably less
common than *mesdames*, pronounced mĕ-däm′ [meh-dahm′].

Madang (N.E. New Guinea)	mä′-däng	mah′-dahng
Maddalena (Libya)	mäd-dä-lĕ′-nä	mahd-dah-leh′-nah
Maddalena, la (Sard.)	mä-dä-lĕ′-nä, lä	mah-dah-leh′-nah, lah
Made (Neth.)	mä′-də	mah′-duh
Madeira (Port., isl.)	*Eng.* mə-dĭr′-ə	muh-dihr′-uh
	Port. mä-dā′-rə	mah-day′-ruh
Madeleine	*Eng.* măd′-ə-lĭn	mad′-uh-lin
	or măd′-lĭn	mad′-lin
	Fr. mä-dlĕn′	mah-dlen′
Madeleine, la (Fr.)	mäd-lĕn′, lä	mahd-len′, lah
Madero, Francisco Indalecio (Mex. polit.)	mä-dĕ′-rô, frän-sēs′-kô ēn-dä-lĕ′-syô	mah-deh′-ro, frahn-sees′-ko een-dah-leh′-syo
Madhe, Fand i (Alb., riv.)	mä′-*th*ĕ, fänd′ ē	mah′-*th*eh, fahnd′ ee

The larger tributary of the *Mat,* q.v.

Madioen *or* Madiun (NEI, Java)	mä-dē-ōōn′ *or* mä′-jōōn′	mah-dee-oon′ mah′-joon′
Madjene *or* Madyene (NEI, Celebes)	mä-jĕ′-nĕ	mah-jeh′-neh
Madoera *or* Madura (NEI)	mä-dōō′-rä	mah-doo′-rah
Madras (India)	mə-drăs′ *or* -dräs′	muh-dras′ *or* -drahs′
Madrid (Sp.)	*Eng.* mə-drĭd′	muh-drid′
	Sp. mä-*th*rē′	mah-*th*ree′
Madura (India)	mä′-jōō-rə	ma′-ju-ruh

Madura (NEI)   See *Madoera.*

Madyene (NEI)   See *Madjene.*

Madyun (NEI)   See *Madjoen.*

Maebashi (Jap.)	mä-ĕ′-bä-shē	mah-eh′-bah-shee
Maeda, Tamon (Jap. educator)	mä-ĕ′-dä′, tä′-môn	mah-eh′-dah′, tah′-mon
Mæl (Nor.)	măl′	mal′
Maenza (It.)	mä-ĕn′-tsä	mah-en′-tsah
Mærtha	măr′-tä	mehr′-tah

(Crown Princess of Norway)
English *Martha.*

Maes (Neth.) See *Maas.*

Maeseyck (Belg.)	mäs′-īk	mahs′-aik
Mafeking (U. of S. Afr.)	măf′-ĭ-kĭng	maf′-i-king
Maffia	mäf′-fē-ä	mahf′-fee-ah

Illegal Sicilian secret society.

Maffin (NEI, New Guinea, bay)	măf'-ĭn *or* mä'-fĭn	maf'-in mah'-fin
Magálang (P.I.)	mä-gä'-läng	mah-gah'-lahng
Magalhães, Gonçalves de (Braz. author)	mə-gə-lyĭNs', gôn-säl'-vĭz dĭ	muh-guh-lyaiNs', gon-sahl'-viz di
Magallanes (P.I.)	mä-gä-yä'-nĕs	mah-gah-yah'-nes
Maganik (Yugosl., mts.)	mä'-gä-nĭk	mah'-gah-nik
Magat (P.I., riv.)	mä-gät'	mah-gaht'
Magdagachi (Rus.)	mäg-dä-gä'-chĭ	mahg-dah-gah'-chi
Magdala (Ethiopia)	mäg'-dä-lä	mahg'-dah-lah
Magdalen, Magdalene (fem. name) See *Migdal.*	măg'-də-lən	mag'-duh-luhn
Magdalen College (Oxford)	môd'-lĭn	mod'-lin
Magdalena (Mex.)	mäg-dä-lä'-nä *or* mä-dä-lä'-nä	mahg-dah-lay'-nah mah-dah-lay'-nah
English măg'-də-lē'-nə [mag'-duh-lee'-nuh].		
Magdalene College (Cambridge)	môd'-lĭn	mod'-lin
Magdeburg (Ger.)	*Eng.* măg'-də-bûrg *Ger.* mäg'-də-bŏŏrk(h)	mag'-duh-buhrg mahg'-duh-burk(h)
Magelang (NEI, Java)	mä-gə-läng'	mah-guh-lahng'
Maggiore (It.)	mäd-jô'-rĕ	mahd-jo'-reh
Magiadag (Gr.) See *Phanos.*		
Magicienne (Oc., Saipan)	*Eng.* mə-jĭs'-ĭ-ĕn *Fr.* mä-zhē-syĕn'	muh-jis'-i-en mah-zhee-syen'
Maginot (Fr. line of defense)	*Eng.* măj'-ĭ-nō *Fr.* mä-zhē-nō'	maj'-i-noh mah-zhee-noh'
Maglaj (Yugosl.)	mä'-glĭ	mah'-glai
Maglakob (P.I.)	mäg-lä-kôb'	mahg-lah-kob'
Maglianella (It.)	mä-lyä-nĕl'-lä	mah-lyah-nel'-lah
Magliano (It.)	mä-lyä-nô	mah-lyah'-no
Maglić (Yugosl., mts.)	mä'-glĭch	mah'-glich
Magnitogorsk (Rus.)	mäg-nĭ-tŏ-gôrsk'	mahg-ni-to-gorsk'
Magnor (Nor.)	mäng'-nōr	mahng'-nohr
Magnuson, Warren G. (U.S. representative)	măg'-nə-sən	mag'-nuh-suhn
Magnuszew (Pol.)	mäg-nōō'-shĕf	mahg-noo'-shef
Magoffin (Ky.)	mə-gŏf'-ĭn	muh-gof'-in
Magog (Can.)	mä'-gŏg	may'-gog
Magresina (Yugosl., isl.) Serb-Croat *Planik,* q.v.	*It.* mä-grĕ-sē'-nä	mah-greh-see'-nah

Magusaiai (Oc., Solomons)	mä-gōo-sī'-ĭ	mah-goo-sai'-ai
Magwe (Burma)	mə-gwā'	muh-gway'
Magyar	*Hung.* mŏ'-dyŏr	mo'-dyor
	Eng. măg'-yär	mag'-yahr
Magyaróvár (Hung.)	mŏ'-dyŏr-ô'-vär	mo'-dyor-o'-vahr
Magyarpolány (Hung.)	mŏ'-dyŏr-pô'-län(y)	mo'-dyor-po'-lahn(y)
Mahalla el Kubra	mə-häl'-lə ĕl	muh-hahl'-luh el
(Egypt)	kōō'-brə	koo'-bruh
Mahan, Alfred Thayer	mə-hăn'	muh-han'
(U.S. admiral)		
Mahanadi (India, riv.)	mə-hä'-nŭ'-dĭ	muh-hah'-nuh'-di
maharajah	*Eng.* mä'-hä-rä'-jə	mah'-hah-rah'-juh
	Sans. mə-hä'-rä'-jə	muh-hah'-rah'-juh
Mahares (Tun.)	mə-hä-rĕs'	muh-hah-res'
Mahdia (Tun.)	mä-dē'-yä	mah-dee'-yah
Also called *Mahedia*, mä-hə-dē'-yä [mah-huh-dee'-yah].		
Mahé (Fr. India)	mä-ĕ'	mah-eh'
Mahedia (Tun.) See *Mahdia*.		
Mahige (Oc., Solomons)	mä-hē'-gĕ	mah-hee'-geh
Mahmoud Fahmy en	mä-mōōd' fä'-mē ĕn	mah-mood' fah'-mee
Nokrashy Pasha	nô'-krä-shē pä'-	en no'-krah-shee
(Egypt. polit.)	shä	pah'-shah
Mahmoud Hassan	mä-mōōd' hăs-săn'	mah-mood' has-san'
Pasha (Egypt. polit.)	pä'-shä	pah'-shah
Mahmoud Khan Ghazi	mä-mōōd' kän' gä'-zē	mah-mood' kahn'
(Afghan leader)		gah'-zee
Or k(h)än k(h)ä'-zē [k(h)ahn k(h)ah'-zee].		
Mahon, George	mā'-hŏn'	may'-hon'
(U.S. representative)		
Mahouin (Tun.)	mä-hwēn'	mah-hween'
Mahur (Oc., New Ireland)	mä-hōōr'	mah-hoor'
Mai (Oc.) See *Emae*.		
Maidanek (Pol.)	mī-dä'-nĕk	mai-dah'-nek
Maidan-i-Naftun (Iran)	mä-dän'-ē-năft'-ōōn	may-dahn'-ee-naft'-
		oon
Maikop (Rus.)	mī-kôp'	mai-kop'
Maillezais (Fr.)	mī-zĕ'	mai-zeh'
Mailly (Fr.)	mä-yē'	mah-yee'
Main (Ger., riv.)	mīn'	main'
Mainaga (P.I.)	mī-nä'-gä	mai-nah'-gah
Maine (Fr.)	*Eng.* män'	mayn'
	Fr. mĕn'	men'
Maine et Loire (Fr.)	mĕn ĕ lwär'	men eh lwahr'
Maingkwan (Burma)	mīng-kwän'	maing-kwahn'

Mainichi (Jap., Tokyo newspaper)	mä-ē'-nē'-chē'	mah-ee'-nee'-chee'
Maintenon (Fr.)	măNt-nôN'	maNt-noN'
Maintirano (Madag.)	mīn'-tē-rä'-nô	main'-tee-rah'-no
Mainz (Ger.)	mīnts'	maints'

An English pronunciation, mānts' [maynts'], is not recommended.

Maio (It., mt.)	mä'-yô	mah'-yo
Maiori (It.)	mä-yô'-rē	mah-yo'-ree
Maipo (Chile)	mī'-pô	mai'-po

Also called *Maipu*, mī'-pōō [mai'-poo].

Maipu (Arg.)	mī'-pōō	mai'-poo
Maisi (Cuba)	mī'-sē	mai'-see
Maisky, Ivan M. (Rus. polit.)	mī'-skǐ, ē-vän'	mai'-ski, ee-vahn'
Maisons Alfort (Fr.)	mě-zôN zäl-fôr'	meh-zoN zahl-for'
Maisons Laffitte (Fr.)	mě-zôN lä-fēt'	meh-zoN lah-feet'
Maisontiers (Fr.)	mě-zôN-tyě'	meh-zoN-tyeh'

Maixent (Fr.) See *Saint Maixent*.

Maizières (Fr.)	mě-zyěr'	meh-zyehr'
Maizuru (Jap.)	mī'-zōō-rōō	mai'-zoo-roo
Maja Streoc (Yugosl.)	mä'-yä strě'-ôts	mah'-yah streh'-ots

Majdal (Pal.) See *El Majdal*.

Majdanpek (Yugosl.)	mī'-dän-pěk'	mai'-dahn-pek'
Majella (It., mts.)	mä-yěl'-lä	mah-yel'-lah
Majilovac (Yugosl.)	mä'-yē'-lô-väts	mah'-yee'-lo-vahts
Majlis (Iran. parliament)	măj-lǐs'	maj-lis'
Majo (It., mt.)	mä'-yô	mah'-yo
Majorca (Sp.)	*Eng.* mə-jôr'-kə	muh-jor'-kuh

Spanish *Mallorca*, q.v.

Majunga (Madag.)	mə-jŭng'-gä	muh-juhng'-gah
Majuro (Oc., Marshalls)	mä-jōō'-rô	mah-joo'-ro
Makada (Oc., New Britain)	mä-kä-dä'	mah-kah-dah'
Makarovo (Rus.)	mä-kä'-rǒ-vǒ	mah-kah'-ro-vo
Makarska (Yugosl.)	mä'-kär-skä	mah'-kahr-skah
Makassar (NEI, Celebes)	*Eng.* mə-kăs'-ər	muh-kas'-uhr
Makci (Yugosl.)	mäk'-tsǐ	mahk'-tsi

Makedonea (Gr.) See *Macedonia*.

Makeevka (Rus.)	mä-kě'-yěf-kä	mah-keh'-yef-kah
Makhach Kala (Rus.)	mä-häch' kä-lä'	mah-hahch' kah-lah'
Makin (Oc., Gilberts)	*Eng.* mā'-kǐn	may'-kin
	native mŭg'-gǐn	mug-gin
	or mŭk'-kǐn	muk'-kin

Mr. H. E. Maude, Acting Commissioner of the Gilbert and Ellice

Islands, wrote, November 6, 1946, "I wish you could persuade the broadcasting world to stop calling *Makin Island* 'May'-kin' instead of the correct 'Mug'-gin' with hard 'gs': that is how the people of Makin call it, though further south the island is termed 'Muk'-kin,' the reason being that the Northern Gilberts (under the influence of the Marshall Island language) have a harsher pronunciation than the Southern Gilberts (which comes under the influence of Polynesia). The island is, in any case, universally known throughout the Pacific (by both natives and Europeans) as Butaritari [q.v.] and not Makin at all, but I imagine that is beyond your province."

Mr. Edward Steers, historian of the U.S. Board on Geographical Names, points out that Pitt's Island is the early English name of Makin Atoll and that Butaritari has a common variant *Taritari*. In Charles Wilkes's Narrative of the U.S. Exploring Expedition, 1838-1842, Captain Hudson wrote, "There are two islands known under this name (Pitt's Island): the largest is called by the natives Taritari, and the smallest, Makin." Mr. Steers adds, "Robert Louis Stevenson devoted several chapters of his book *In the South Seas* to his sojourn in the Gilbert Islands during the year 1889. He resided for some weeks on Taritari, or Butaritari. He refers to this island as 'Great Makin' and to the natives as 'Butaritarians'." In short the atoll contains two principal islands: *Makin* and *Butaritari* (Taritari). Either name may be given to the atoll as a whole and, evidently, may apply loosely to either island.

Makin, Norman J. (Austral. polit.)	mā'-kĭn	may'-kin
Makkum (Neth.)	mäk'-əm	mahk'-uhm
Maknassy (Tun.)	mək-näs'-sĭ	muhk-nahs'-si
Maknine (Tun.)	mək-nēn'	muhk-neen'
Makó (Hung.)	mŏ'-kō	mo'-koh
Makoshino (Rus.)	mä-kô'-shĭ-nŏ	mah-ko'-shi-no
Makou (Iran) See *Maku*.		
Makovo (Rus.)	mä'-kŏ-vŏ	mah'-ko-vo
Makram Ebeid Pasha (Egypt. polit.)	mäk'-räm ĕ-bād' pä'-shä	mahk'-rahm eh-bayd' pah'-shah
Makreteikhos (Crete)	mä-krē'-tē-hôs	mah-kree'-tee-hos
Makršane (Yugosl.)	mä'-kər'-shä-nĕ	mah'-kuhr'-shah-neh
Makrysgialos (Crete, bay)	mä-krēs'-yä-lôs'	mah-krees'-yah-los'
Maksatikha (Rus.)	mäk-sä-tē'-hä	mahk-sah-tee'-hah
Maksimos, Demetrios (Gr. polit.) See *Maximos, Demetrios*.		
Maktar (Tun.)	mŭk'-tär	muhk'-tahr
Maku *or* Makou (Iran)	mä-kōō'	mah-koo'

mal   mäl'   mahl'

An element, meaning *mountain*, in Albanian place names. Look up the other part of the name.

mala, -li, -lo   mä'-lä, -lĭ, -lô   mah'-lah, -li, -lo

An element, meaning *little*, in Slavic place names. It may be necessary to look up the other part of the name.

Malabang (P.I.)	mä-lä-bäng'	mah-lah-bahng'
Malabolo (P.I., riv.)	mä-lä-bô'-lô	mah-lah-bo'-lo
Malabón (P.I.)	mä-lä-bôn'	mah-lah-bon'

Also called *Tambóbong*, täm-bô'-bông [tahm-bo'-bong].

Malacañán (Manila, palace)	mä-lä-kä-nyän'	mah-lah-kah-nyahn'
Malacca (Malay)	*Eng.* mə-lăk'-ə	muh-lak'-uh
Malad City (Idaho)	mə-lăd'	muh-lad'
Málaga (Sp.)	*Eng.* măl'-ə-gə	mal'-uh-guh
	Sp. mä-lä-gä	mah'-lah-gah
Malagasy (Madag.)	*Eng.* măl'-ə-găs'-ĭ	mal'-uh-gas'-i
Malagi, Puló (P.I., isl.)	mä-lä'-hē, pōō-lô'	mah-lah'-hee, poo-lo'
Malaita (Oc., Solomons)	mä-lĕ'-tä	mah-leh'-tah
Malakal (Oc., Palau)	mä'-lä-käl	mah'-lah-kahl
Malampaya (P.I., bay)	mä-läm-pä'-yä	mah-lahm-pah'-yah
Malang (NEI, Java)	mä-läng'	mah-lahng'
Malasiquí (P.I.)	mä-lä-sē-kē'	mah-lah-see-kee'
Malate (P.I.)	mä-lä'-tĕ	mah-lah'-teh
Malaya Vishera (Rus.)	mä'-lä-yä vē'-shĕ-rä	mah'-lah-yah vee'-sheh-rah

Malbork (Ger. >Pol.)   mäl'-bôrk   mahl'-bork

German *Marienburg*, q.v.

Malbug (P.I.) See *Villalón*.

Malče (Yugosl.)	mäl'-chĕ	mahl'-cheh
Maldive (Ceylon, isls.)	măl'-dīv	mal'-daiv
Malea (Crete, gulf)	mä'-lē-ä	mah'-lee-ah
Maleas (Gr., cape)	mä-lĕ'-ä(s)	mah-leh'-ah(s)
	or mä-lyä(s)'	mah-lyah(s)'

Also called *Kavomalias*, q.v.

malefactor	măl'-ə-făk'-tər	mal'-uh-fak'-tuhr
Maleme (Crete)	mä'-lĕ-mĕ	mah'-leh-meh
Malenkov, Georgi M. (Rus. polit.)	mä-lĕn'-kŏf, gĕ-ôr'-gĭ	mah-len'-kof, geh-or'-gi
Maleš (Yugosl.)	mä'-lĕsh	mah'-lesh
Malestroit (Fr.)	mä-lĕ-trwä'	mah-leh-trwah'
Maletto (Sicily)	mä-lĕt'-tô	mah-let'-to
Malhón (P.I.)	mäl-hôn'	mahl-hon'

Also called *Homonhón*, hô-môn-hôn′ [ho-mon-hon′], and *Jomonhol*,
hô-môn-hôl′ [ho-mon-hol′].

mali (Alb.)   See *mal.*

Malíbay (P.I.)	mä-lē′-bī	mah-lee′-bai
Malícay (P.I.)	mä-lē′-kī	mah-lee′-kai
Malígay (P.I.)	mä-lē′-gī	mah-lee′-gai
Malik, Charles (Syrian diplomat)	măl′-ĭk	mal′-ik
Malik, Yakov (Rus. polit.)	mä′-lĭk, yä′-kŏf	mah′-lik, yah′-kof
Mali Kvarner (Yugosl. channel) Italian *Quarnerolo,* q.v.	mä′-lĭ kvär′-nĕr	mah′-li kvahr′-nehr
Malin (Rus.)	mä′-lĭn	mah′-lin
Malindang (P.I.)	mä-lĭn-däng′	mah-lin-dahng′
Malines (Belg.)	*Fr.* mä-lēn′	mah-leen′
	Eng. mə-lēnz′	muh-leenz′
Flemish *Mechelen,* q.v.		
malinger	mə-lĭng′-gər	muh-ling′-guhr
Malinovsky, R. Y. (Rus. general)	mä-lĭ-nôf′-skĭ	mah-li-nof′-ski
Maliq (Alb., lake)	*Eng.* mä′-lēk	mah′-leek

Albanian *Liqen(i) i Maliqit,* lē-kyĕn′ ē mä-lē′-kyēt [lee-kyen′ ee
mah-lee′-kyeet].

Małkinia (Pol.)	mäl-kē′-nyä	mahl-kee′-nyah

Russian *Malkin,* mäl′-kĭn [mahl′-kin].

Malko Tarnovo (Bulg.)	mäl′-kŏ tär′-nŏ-vŏ	mahl′-ko tahr′-no-vo
Mallawi (Egypt)	məl-lä′-wē	muhl-lah′-wee
Also spelled *Mellawi.*		
Mallorca (Sp.)	mä-lyôr′-kä *or* -yôr-	mah-lyor′-kah *or* -yor-
English *Majorca,* q.v.		
Malmédy (Belg.)	mäl-mĕ-dē′	mahl-meh-dee′
Malmoe *or* Malmö (Sw.)	*Eng.* măl′-mō	mal′-moh
	Sw. mälm′-û′	mahlm′-œ′
Malmyzh (Rus.)	mäl-mwēsh′	mahl-mweesh′
Malo Arkhangelsk (Rus.)	mä′-lŏ är-hän′-gĕlsk	mah′-lo ahr-hahn′-gelsk
Maloelap (Oc., Marshalls)	mä′-lô-ĕ-läp′	mah′-lo-eh-lahp′
Malolo (N.E. New Guinea)	mä-lô′-lô	mah-lo′-lo
Malolos (P.I.)	mä-lô′-lôs	mah-lo′-los
Malona (Dodec., Rh.)	mä-lô′-nä	mah-lo′-nah
Malone, Dumas (Am. historian)	mə-lōn′, dyōō′-mä′	muh-lohn′, dyoo′-mah′

Maloney, Paul H. (U.S. representative)	mə-lō′-nĭ	muh-loh′-ni
Malošište (Yugosl.)	mä′-lô-shĭ-shtĕ	mah′-lo-shi-shteh
Malo Tymovsk (Rus.)	mä′-lŏ twē′-mŏfsk	mah′-lo twee′-mofsk
Maloyaroslavets (Rus.)	mä′-lŏ-yä-rŏ-slä′-vĕts	mah′-lo-yah-ro-slah′-vets
Maltot (Fr.)	mäl-tō′	mahl-toh′

Malvinas, Islas (S. Atlantic) See *Falkland Islands*.

Mamaybanay (P.I.) See *Pastrana*.

Mambán (P.I., mt.)	mäm-bän′	mahm-bahn′
Mamberamo (NEI, New Guinea)	mäm-bĕ-rä′-mô	mahm-beh-rah′-mo
Mambúlao (P.I.)	mäm-bōō′-lou	mahm-boo′-lau
Mambúrao (P.I.)	mäm-bōō′-rou	mahm-boo′-rau
Mamers (Fr.)	mä-mĕr′	mah-mehr′
Ma-mien-kwan (Ch., Yünnan)	mä-myĕn-gwän	mah-myen-gwahn
Mamison (Rus., pass)	mä-mĭ-sôn′	mah-mi-son′
Mammola (It.)	mäm′-mô-lä	mahm′-mo-lah
Ma-mo-i (Ch., Fukien)	mä-mô-ē	mah-mo-ee
Mamoré (Bol., riv.)	mä-mô-rĕ′	mah-mo-reh′
Manado (NEI, Celebes)	mä-nä′-dō	mah-nah′-doh
Managua (Nicar.)	mä-nä′-gwä	mah-nah′-gwah
Manakara (Madag.)	mä′-nə-kä′-rə	mah′-nuh-kah′-ruh
Manam (N.E. New Guinea)	mä-näm′	mah-nahm′
Mananjary (Madag.)	mä′-nän-zhä′-rē	mah′-nahn-zhah′-ree
Manáoag (P.I.)	mä-nä′-wäg	mah-nah′-wahg
Manaoba (Oc., Solomons)	mä-nä-ô′-bä	mah-nah-o′-bah
Manasco, Carter (U.S. representative)	mə-năs′-kō	muh-nas′-koh

Manastir (Yugosl.) See *Monastir*.

Manastir Morački (Yugosl.)	mä′-nä-stĭr mô′-räch-kĭ	mah′-nah-stihr mo′-rahch-ki
Manaus *or* Manáos (Brazil)	mä-nous′	mah-naus′
Manay (P.I.)	mä-nĭ′	mah-nai′
Manche (Fr., prov.)	mäNsh′	mahNsh′
Mancheno, Carlos (Equador. polit.)	män-chĕ′-nô, kär′-lôs	mahn-cheh′-no, kahr′-los
Man-chu-k'uo (Manchu state)	*Eng.* măn-chōō-kwō *Ch.* män-jō-kwô	man-choo-kwoh mahn-joh-kwo

Also spelled *Man-ch'ou-k'uo*.

Man-ch'u-li (Manchu.)	män-chōō-lē	mahn-choo-lee

Mandakas, Manolis	män'-dä-käs,	mahn'-dah-kahs,
(Gr. polit.)	mä-nồ'-lēs	mah-no'-lees
Mandal (Nor.)	män'-däl	mahn'-dahl
Mandalay (Burma)	măn'-də-lä'	man'-duh-lay'
Mandalóyong (P.I.) See *San Felipe Nery*.		
Mandan (N.D.)	măn'-dăn'	man'-dan'
Mandoliana (Oc.,	män-dồ-lē-ä'-nä	mahn-do-lee-ah'-nah
Solomons)		
Manduria (It.)	män-dōō'-ryä	mahn-doo'-ryah
Manfredonia (It.)	män-frĕ-dồ'-nyä	mahn-freh-do'-nyah
Mangaldán (P.I.)	mäng-gäl-dän'	mahng-gahl-dahn'
Mangalia (Rum.)	män-gä'-lyä	mahn-gah'-lyah
Mangareva (Oc.,	mäng'-ä-rĕ'-vä	mahng'-ah-reh'-vah
Tuamotu)		
Mangarín (P.I.)	män-gä-rēn'	mahn-gah-reen'
Mangas (P.I.)	mäng'-gäs	mahng'-gahs
Mangataren (P.I.)	män-gä-tä'-rĕn	mahn-gah-tah'-ren

There is also authority for stressing the last syllable and for spelling the word with final *m* instead of *n*.

Manggar (NEI, Billiton)	mäng'-gär	mahng'-gahr
Maniadakis (Gr. name)	mä-nyä-dä'-kēs	mah-nyah-dah'-kees
Manila (P.I.)	*Eng.* mə-nĭl'-ə	muh-nil'-uh

Tagalog mī-nē'-lä [mai-nee'-lah]. Spanish mä-nē'-lä [mah-nee'-lah].

Manipur (India)	mŭn'-ĭ-pŏ͞or'	muhn'-i-pur'

Also called *Manipore*, mŭn'-ĭ-pồr' [muhn'-i-por'].

Manisa (Turk.)	mä'-nĭ-sä	mah'-ni-sah
Manitowok (Wis.)	măn'-ĭ-tō-wŏk'	man'-i-toh-wok'
Maniu, Iuliu (Rum.	mä-nyōō', yōō'-lyŏ͞o	mah-nyoo', yoo'-lyu
polit.)		
Manizales (Colom.)	mä-nē-sä'-lĕs	mah-nee-sah'-lehs
Mankato (Minn.)	măn-kā'-tō	man-kay'-toh
Mankovo (Rus.)	män'(y)-kŏ-vŏ	mahn'(y)-ko-vo
Mannar (India, gulf)	măn-när' *or* mə-när'	man-nahr' *or* muh-nahr'
Mannay (Belg.)	mä-nĕ'	mah-neh'
Mannes, David	măn'-əs	man'-uhs
(Am. musician)		
Mannheim (Ger.)	män'-hīm	mahn'-haim
Manokwari (NEI, New	mä-nồ-kwä'-rē	mah-no-kwah'-ree
Guinea)		
Manosque (Fr.)	mä-nồsk'	mah-nosk'
Manouba (Tun.)	mə-nōō'-bä	muh-noo'-bah
Manpin (Burma)	män'-pĭn'	mahn'-pin'
Mans, le (Fr.)	mäN', lə	mahN', luh

Mansalay (P.I.)	män-sä-lī′	mahn-sah-lai′
Mansiol (P.I.)	män-sē-ôl′	mahn-see-ol′
Mansum (Burma)	män′-sŏŏm′	mahn′-sum′
Mansur (Libya)	män-sŏŏr′	mahn-sur′
Mansur, Ali Khan (Iran. polit.)	män′-sŏŏr′, ä′-lē	mahn′-soor′, ah′-lee
Mansura, el (Egypt)	män-sŏŏ′-rä, ĕl	mahn-soo′-rah, el
Manteo (N.C.)	măn′-tĭ-ō	man′-ti-oh
Mantes (Fr.)	mäNt′	mahNt′
Mantes Gassicourt (Fr.)	mäNt gä-sē-kŏŏr′	mahNt gah-see-koor′
Also called *Mantes la Jolie*, . . . lä zhô-lē′ [. . . lah zho-lee′].		
Manthelan (Fr.)	mäNt-läN′	mahNt-lahN′
Manti (Utah)	măn′-tī	man′-tai
Mantova (It.) See *Mantua*.		
Mantsurov (Rus.)	män-tsŏŏ′-rŏf	mahn-tsoo′-rof
Mantua (It.)	*Eng.* măn′-tyŏŏ-ə	man′-tyu-uh
Italian *Mantova*, män′-tô-vä [mahn′-to-vah].		
Mantzavinos, Georgios (Gr. polit.)	män-dzä-vē′-nôs, yôr′-yôs	mahn-dzah-vee′-nos, yor′-yos
Manu (Oc., Admiralties)	mä′-nŏŏ	mah′-noo
Manuc Mancá (P.I.)	mä-nŏŏk′ män-kä′	mah-nook′ mahn-kah′
Manuilski, Dimitri (Ukrain. polit.)	mä′-nŏŏ-ēl′-skĭ, dĭ-mē′-trĭ	mah-nu-eel′-ski, di-mee′-tri
Manuk Manukan (P.I.)	mä-nŏŏk′ mä-nŏŏ′-kän	mah-nook′ mah-noo′-kahn
Manus (Oc., Admiralties)	mä′-nŏŏs	mah′-noos
Many, Fernand de (Belg. polit.)	mä-nē′, fĕr-näN′ də	mah-nee′, fehr-nahN′ duh
Manych (Rus., riv.)	mä-nwēch′	mah-nweech′
Manzanillo (Mex.)	*Eng.* măn′-zə-nē′-yə *Sp.* män-sä-nē′-yô	man′-zuh-nee′-yuh mahn-sah-nee′-yo
Maori (N.Z.)	mou′-rĭ *or* mä′-ô-rē	mau′-ri *or* mah′-o-ree
Mao Tsê-tung (Ch. general)	mou dzŭ-dŏŏng	mau dzuh-dung
Maou, el (Tun.)	mou′, ĕl	mau′, el
Mapandán (P.I.)	mä-pän-dän′	mah-pahn-dahn′
Mapao (India)	mä-pou′	mah-pau′
Mapia (NEI)	mä′-pĭ-ə	mah′-pi-uh
Mappach (Ger.)	mäp′-äk(h)	mahp′-ahk(h)
Maquis, le (Fr.)	mä-kē′, lə	mah-kee′, luh

The literal translation of *Maquis* is "underbrush." The name was applied in World War II to those groups of French patriots who left their homes to take up a nomadic existence as guerrillas in isolated regions. These groups belonged to what was called the FFI (French Forces of the Interior). The individual member of *le Maquis* is *un Maquisard*, ûN mä-kē-zär' [œN mah-kee-zahr'].

Marabang (P.I., riv.)	mä-rä'-bäng	mah-rah'-bahng
Marabao (P.I., mt.)	mä-rä-bou'	mah-rah-bau'
Maracaibo (Ven.)	mä-rä-kī'-bô	mah-rah-kai'-bo
Maracás (Brazil)	mä-rä-käs'	mah-rah-kahs'
Maracas (Trinidad)	mä-rä'-käs	mah-rah'-kahs
Maragheh (Iran)	mä-rä-gĕ'	mah-rah-geh'
Maraghi (Egypt. name)	mä-rä'-gē	mah-rah'-gee
Maragondón (P.I.)	mä-rä-gôn-dôn'	mah-rah-gon-don'
Marakei (Oc., Gilberts)	mä-rä'-kā	mah-rah'-kay
Maramasike (Oc., Solomons)	mä-rä-mä-sē'-kĕ	mah-rah-mah-see'-keh
Maranajt (Alb., mt.)	mä-rä'-nīt	mah-rah'-nait
Marangay (P.I.)	mä-räng'-ī	mah-rahng'-ai
Maranhão (Brazil)	mä-rə-nyouN'	mah-ruh-nyauN'
Mărăşeşti (Rum.)	mə-rə-shĕsht'	muh-ruh-shesht'
Marassi (It.)	mä-räs'-sē	mah-rahs'-see
Marathon (Gr.)	*Eng.* mǎr'-ə-thŏn	mehr'-uh-thon
	Gr. mä-rä-thôn'	mah-rah-thon'
Maraua (Libya)	mä'-rə-wä	mah'-ruh-wah
Marburg (Ger.)	*Eng.* mär'-bûrg	mahr'-buhrg
	Ger. mär'-bŏŏrk(h)	mahr'-burk(h)
Marcali (Hung.)	mŏr'-tsŏ-lĭ	mor'-tso-lih
Marcantonio, Vito (U.S. representative)	märk-ăn-tō'-nĭ-ō, vē'-tō	mahrk-an-toh'-ni-oh, vee'-toh
Marcellina (It.)	mär-chĕl-lē'-nä	mahr-chel-lee'-nah
March (Europ. riv.)	See *Morava.*	
Marche (Belg.)	märsh'	mahrsh'
Marcigliana, la (It.)	mär-chē-lyä'-nä, lä	mahr-chee-lyah'-nah, lah
Marcondes Filho, Alexandre (Braz. polit.)	mär-kôn'-dĭs fē'-lyŏŏ, ä-lĭ-shän'-drə	mahr-kon'-dis fee'-lyu, ah-li-shahn'-druh
Marcus (Oc.)	mär'-kəs	mahr'-kuhs
Marennes (Fr.)	mä-rĕn'	mah-ren'
Mareth (Tun.)	mǎ'-rĕt *or* mǎ'-rĕth	ma'-ret *or* ma'-reth
Marettimo (Sicily, isl.)	mä-rĕt'-tē-mô	mah-ret'-tee-mo
Mareuil (Fr.)	mä-rû'(y)	mah-rœ'(y)
margarine	mär'-jə-rēn *or* -rĭn	mahr'-juh-reen *or* -rin
	or mär'-gə-rēn *or* -rĭn	mahr'-guh-reen *or* -rin

The second and older pronunciation is now less common than the first.

Margariti (Gr.)	mär-gä-rē'-tē	mahr-gah-ree'-tee

Mărghita (Rum.)	mər-gē′-tä	muhr-gee′-tah
Margil (Iran, airport)	mär-gĭl′	mahr-gil′
Margitsziget (Hung., isl.)	mŏr′-gĭt-sĭ′-gĕt	mor′-git-si′-get
Margrabowa (Ger. >Pol.)	mär-grä-bô′-vä	mahr-grah-bo′-vah
German *Treuburg*, q.v.		
Mariampolė (Lith.)	mä-rĭ-äm-pô′-lĕ	mah-ri-ahm-po′-leh
Russian *Mariampol*, mä-rĭ-äm′-pŏl(y) [mah-ri-ahm′-pol(y)].		
Marianas (Oc.)	mä-rē-ä′-näs	mah-ree-ah′-nahs
Also called the *Ladrones*, q.v.		
Mariaweiler (Ger.)	mä-rē′-ä-vī′-lər	mah-ree′-ah-vai′-luhr
Mariazell (Austria)	mä-rē′-ä-tsĕl′	mah-ree′-ah-tsel′
Maribo (Den.)	mä′-rē-bō	mah′-ree-boh
Maribor (Yugosl.)	mä′-rĭ-bôr	mah′-ri-bor
German *Marburg*.		
Maricabán (P.I., isl.)	mä-rē-kä-bän′	mah-ree-kah-bahn′
Mariehamn (Fin.)	*Sw.* mä-rē̟′-ə-hämn′	mah-ree′-uh-hahmn′
Finnish *Maarianhamina*, q.v.		
Marienberg (N.E. New Guinea)	mə-rē′-ən-bûrg	muh-ree′-uhn-buhrg
Marienburg (Ger. >Pol.)	mä-rē′-ən-bo͆rk(h)	mah-ree′-uhn-burk(h)
Polish *Malbork*, q.v.		
Marienburg (Latvia)	*Ger.* mä-rē′-ən-bo͆rk(h)	mah-ree′-uhn-b(hurk)
	Rus. mä-rē′-yĕn-bo͆rk	mah-ree′-yen-burk
Latvian *Alūksne*, q.v.		
Marienwerder (Ger. > Pol.)	mä-rē′-ən-vĕr′-də	mah-ree′-uhn-vehr′-duh
Polish *Kwidzyń*, q.v.		
Marifjord (Nor.)	mä′-rē-fyōr	mah′-ree-fyohr
Marignane (Fr. airport near Marseilles)	mä-rē-nyän′	mah-ree-nyahn′
Marigny (Fr.)	mä-rē-nyē′	mah-ree-nyee′
Mari(i)nsk (Rus.)	mä-rē′-yĭnsk	mah-ree′-yinsk
Marikina (P.I.)	mä-rē-kē′-nä	mah-ree-kee′-nah
Also spelled *Mariquina*.		
Marilao (P.I.)	mä-rē-lou′	mah-ree-lau′
Marin, John (Am. painter)	mär′-ĭn	mehr′-in
Marín, Luis Muñoz (P.R. polit.) See *Muñoz Marín*.		
Marina (Christian name)	*Eng.* mə-rē′-nə	muh-ree′-nuh
Marina (Yugosl.)	mä′-rĭ-nä	mah′-ri-nah
Marina di Catanzaro (It.)	mä-rē′-nä dē kä-tän-dzä′-rô	mah-ree′-nah dee kah-tahn-dzah′-ro

Marina di Paola (Sicily) mä-rē'-nä dē   mah-ree'-nah dee
                          pä'-ô-lä   pah'-o-lah
Marinduque (P.I.)   mä-rĭn-dōō'-kĕ   mah-rin-doo'-keh
Marines (Fr.)   mä-rēn'   mah-reen'
Mariquina (P.I.) See *Marikina*.
Maristova (Nor.)   mä'-rē-stô-vä   mah'-ree-sto-vah
Maritsa (Balkan riv.)   *Bulg.* mä-rē'-tsä mah-ree'-tsah
                          S.-C. mä'-rē-tsä mah'-ree-tsah
    Turkish *Meriç*, mĕ'-rēch' [meh'-reech']. Greek *Evros*, q.v.
Maritsa (Dodec., Rh.)   mä-rē-tsä'   mah-ree-tsah'
Mariupol (Rus.)   mä-rĭ-ōō'-pŏl(y)   mah-ri-oo'-pol(y)
Marival (Fr., fort)   mä-rē-väl'   mah-ree-vahl'
Mariveles (P.I.)   mä-rē-vĕ'-lĕs   mah-ree-veh'-les
Marjesson, Henry D. R.,   mär'-jə-sən,   mahr'-juh-suhn,
    Viscount (Br. polit.)   vī'-kount   vai'-kaunt
Markeloo (Neth.)   mär'-kə-lō   mahr'-kuh-loh
Marken (Neth., isl.)   mär'-kən   mahr'-kuhn
Markham (N.E. New   mär'-kəm   mahr'-kuhm
    Guinea, valley)
Markovac (Yugosl.)   mär'-kô-väts   mahr'-ko-vahts
Marmagao *and* Marmagoa (Port. India)   See *Mormugão*.
Marmande (Fr.)   mär-mäNd'   mahr-mahNd'
Mármarossziget (Rum.)   See *Sighet*.
Marne (Fr., riv.)   märn'   ,   mahrn'
Marolles les Braults (Fr.) mä-rôl lĕ brō'   mah-rol leh broh'
Marons (Fr.)   mä-rôN'   mah-roN'
Maros (Rum., Hung., riv.) See *Mureş*.
Marosvásárhely (Rum.)   See *Târgul Mureş*.
Marovo (Oc., Solomons)   mä-rô'-vô   mah-ro'-vo
Marovoa (Madag.)   mä'-rô-vô'-ə   mah'-ro-vo'-uh
Marpi (Oc., Saipan)   mär'-pē'   mahr'-pee'
Marquand, John P.   mär-kwänd'   mahr-kwahnd'
    (Am. author)
Marquart, Edward J.   mär'-kärt   mahr'-kahrt
    (U.S. admiral)
Marquesas (Oc.,   mär-kā'-säs   mahr-kay'-sahs
    Polynesia)
    French *Îles Marquises*, ēl mär-kēz' [eel mahr-keez'].
marquess   mär'-kwĭs   mahr'-kwis
    An English variant of *marquis*.
marquis   *Eng.* mär'-kwĭs   mahr'-kwis
                          Fr. mär-kē'   mahr-kee'
Marrakesh (Mor.)   mär-rä'-kĕsh   mahr-rah'-kesh
    Also called *Morocco*, q.v.

Marrane, Georges (Fr. polit.)	mä-rän′, zhôrzh′	mah-rahn′, zhorzh′
Marree (Austral.)	mə-rē′	muh-ree′
Mars (Fr.) See *Champ de Mars.*		
Marsa, la (Tun.)	mär′-sä, lä	mahr′-sah, lah
Marsala (Sicily)	mär-sä′-lä	mahr-sah′-lah
Marsa Matruh (Egypt) See *Mersa Matruh.* Cf. *La Marsa* (Tun.)		
Marseillan (Fr.)	mär-sĕ-yäN′	mahr-seh-yahN′
Marseille (Fr.)	mär-sĕ′(y) *or* -sä′	mahr-seh′(y) *or* -say′
Marseilles (Fr.)	*Eng.* mär-sālz′	mahr-saylz′

For the French city, the French form, *Marseille*, q.v., is more common even in English contexts. The English form occurs as an American place name.

Maršić (Yugosl.)	mär′-shĭch	mahr′-shich
Marstein (Nor.)	mär′-stān *or* mäsh′-tān	mahr′-stayn mahsh′-tayn
Martaban (Burma)	mär′-tə-bǎn′	mahr′-tuh-ban′
Martelon (Crete, point)	mär′-tĕ-lô(n)	mahr′-teh-lo(n)
Märtha (Crown Princess of Norway)	mĕr′-tä	mehr′-tah

English *Martha*, mär′-thə [mahr′-thuh].

Martigné Forchaud (Fr.)	mär-tē-nyĕ fôr-shō′	mahr-tee-nyeh for-shoh′
Martigny (Switz.)	mär-tē-nyē′	mahr-tee-nyee′
Martigues (Fr.)	mär-tēg′	mahr-teeg′
Martin, St. (Cz.) See *Turčiansky Svätý Martin.*		
Martínez (Sp. name)	mär-tē′-nĕth *or* -nĕs	mahr-tee′-neth *or* -nes
Martinez (Calif.)	mär-tē′-nĭz	mahr-tee′-niz
Martínez Barrio, Diego (Sp. polit.)	mär-tē′-nĕth bä′-ryô, dyĕ′-gô	mahr-tee′-neth bah′-ryo, dyeh′-go
Martínez Cabañas, Gustavo (Mex. diplomat)	mär-tē′-nĕs kä-bä′-nyäs, gōōs-tä′-vô	mahr-tee′-nes kah-bah′-nyahs, goos-tah′-vo
Martuba (Libya)	mär′-tōō′-bä	mahr′-too′-bah
Marty, André (Fr. polit.)	mär-tē′, äN-drĕ′	mahr-tee′, ahN-dreh′
Marugame (Jap.)	mä-rōō′-gä′-mĕ	mah-roo′-gah′-meh
Marum (Neth.)	mä′-rəm	mah′-ruhm
Marunouchi (Jap.)	mä′-rōō-nô-ōō′-chē	mah′-roo-no-oo′-chee
Marur (New Guinea)	mä′-rōōr′	mah′-roor′
Marzeno (It.)	mär-tsĕ′-nô	mahr-tseh′-no
Masahet (Oc., New Ireland)	mä-sä-hĕt′	mah-sah-het′
Masapílit (P.I.)	mä-sä-pē′-lĭt	mah-sah-pee′-lit

Masaryk, Jan Garrigue (Cz. polit.)   mä'-sä-rĭk, yän' gä-rēg'   mah'-sah-rik, yahn' gah-reeg'

Masaryk, Tomáš Garrigue (Cz. polit.)   mä'-sä-rĭk, tô'-mäsh gä-rēg'   mah'-sah-rik, to'- mahsh gah-reeg'

Masbate (P.I.)   mäs-bä'-tĕ   mahs-bah'-teh

Mascalucia (Sicily)   mäs-kä-lōō-chē'-ä   mahs-kah-loo-chee'-ah

Maseru (Afr., Basutoland)   măz'-ə-rōō   maz'-uh-roo

Masin (P.I.)   mä'-sēn   mah'-seen

Masingloc (P.I.)   mä-sēng-lôk'   mah-seeng-lok'

Masinloc (P.I.)   mä-sēn-lôk'   mah-seen-lok'

Masjid-i-Sulaiman (Iran)   măs-jēd'-ē-sōō-lā- män'   mas-jeed'-ee-su-lay- mahn'

Maslay, Puló (P.I., isl.)   mäs-lī', pōō-lô'   mahs-lai', poo-lo'

Maslinica (Yugosl.)   mä'-slē'-nĭ-tsä   mah'-slee'-ni-tsah

masochism   măz'-ə-kĭsm   maz'-uh-kizm

masochist   măz'-ə-kĭst   maz'-uh-kist

Masoedji or Masudyi (NEI, Sumatra, riv.)   mä-sōō'-jē   mah-soo'-jee

Massa d'Albe (It.)   mäs'-sä däl'-bĕ   mahs'-sah dahl'-beh

Massawa (Eritrea) Italian Massaua.   mäs-sä'-wä   mahs-sah'-wah

Massicault (Tun.)   mäs-sē-kō'   mahs-see-koh'

Massico (It., mt.)   mäs'-sē-kô   mahs'-see-ko

Massillon (Ohio)   măs'-ə-lən   mas'-uh-luhn

Mastanli (Bulg.)   See Momtchilovgrad.

Mastekhon, Ak. (Gr., Chios)   See Phanai.

Masulipatam (India)   mə-sōō'-lĭ-pə-tăm'   muh-soo'-li-puh-tam'

Masuria (Ger., region)   Eng. mə-zŏŏr'-ĭ-ə   muh-zur'-i-uh
German Masuren, mä-zōō'-rən [mah-zoo'-ruhn].

Mat (Alb., riv.)   mät'   maht'
Also called Mati and Matja, mä'-tyä, and Lum i Matit. Greek Mathis, mä'-thēs [mah'-thees].

Matagob (P.I.)   mä-tä-gôb'   mah-tah-gob'

Matagug (P.I.)   mä-tä-gōōg'   mah-tah-goog'

Matanatamberam (Oc., New Ireland)   mä-tä-nä-täm'-bĕ- räm   mah-tah-nah-tahm'- beh-rahm

Matanzas (Cuba)   Eng. mə-tăn'-zəs Sp. mä-tän'-säs   muh-tan'-zuhs mah-tahn'-sahs

Matapan (Gr., cape)   Eng. măt'-ə-păn   mat'-uh-pan
Greek Matapas or Tainaron, q.v.

Matara (Ceylon)   mä'-tə-rə   mah'-tuh-ruh

Mataram (NEI, Lombok)   mä-tä'-räm   mah-tah'-rahm

Matejča (Yugosl.)	mä'-tā-chä	mah'-tay-chah
Matejevac (Yugosl.)	mä'-tĕ'-yĕ-väts	mah'-teh'-yeh-vahts
Matera (It.)	mä-tĕ'-rä	mah-teh'-rah
matériel	*Eng.* mə-tĭr'-ĭ-ĕl'	muh-tir'-i-el'
	Fr. mä-tĕ-ryĕl'	mah-teh-ryehl'
Mateševo (Yugosl.)	mä'-tĕ'-shĕ-vô	mah'-teh'-sheh-vo
Mateur (Tun.)	mä-tûr'	mah-tœr'
Mati (P.I.)	mä'-tē	mah'-tee
Matina (P.I.)	mä-tē'-nä	mah-tee'-nah
Matjë (Alb., riv.) See *Mat.*		
Matmata (Tun.)	mät-mä'-tä	maht-mah'-tah
Mato Grosso (Brazil)	mä'-tŏŏ grô'-sŏŏ	mah'-tu gro'-su
Mátra (Hung.)	mä'-trŏ	mah'-tro
Matratin (Libya)	mă-trə-tēn'	ma-truh-teen'
Matrice (It., riv.)	mä-trē'-chĕ	mah-tree'-cheh
Matruh (Egypt)	mä-trŏŏ'	mah-troo'
Also called *Mersa Matruh*, q.v.		
Matsudaira, Yoshitami	mä-tsŏŏ'-dä'-ē-rä,	mah-tsoo'-dah'-ee-
(Jap. polit.)	yô-shē'-tä-mē	rah, yo-shee'-tah-
		mee
Matsumoto (Jap.)	mä-tsŏŏ'-mô'-tô'	mah-tsoo'-mo'-to'
Matsuoka, Yōsuke (Jap.	mä-tsŏŏ'-ô-kä, yô'-	mah-tsoo'-o-kah, yo'-
polit.)	sŏŏ-kĕ *or* yôs'-kĕ	soo-keh *or* yos'-keh
Matsuyama (Jap.)	mä-tsŏŏ'-yä-mä	mah-tsoo'-yah-mah
Matsuye (Jap.)	mä-tsŏŏ-ĕ	mah-tsoo-eh
Matteawan (N.Y., N.J.)	măt'-ə-wän	mat'-uh-wahn
Matzavinos, G.	mä-dzä-vē'-nôs	mah-dzah-vee'-nos
(Gr. polit.)		
Maubeuge (Fr.)	mō-bûzh'	moh-bœzh'
Maubin (Burma)	mə-ōō'-bĭn'	muh-oo'-bin'
Mauch Chunk (Pa.)	mô chŭnk'	maw chuhnk'
Maug (Oc., Marianas)	moug'	maug'
Maui (Hawaii)	mou'-ē	mou'-ee
Maulana Abul Kalam Azad (Indian polit.) See *Azad Maulana.*		
Maulbronn (Ger.)	moul'-brôn	maul'-bron
Maulmain (Burma) See *Moulmein.*		
Mauna Kea (Hawaii, mt.)	mou'-nä kĕ'-ä	mou'-nah keh'-ah
Mauna Loa	mou'-nä lô'-ä	mau'-nah lo'-ah
(Hawaii, volcano)		
Maungdaw (Burma)	moung'-dô'	maung'-daw'
Maupertuis (Fr.)	mō-pĕr-twē'	moh-pehr-twee'
Maupertus (Fr.)	mō-pĕr-tüs'	moh-pehr-tüs'
Maura, Miguel (Sp.	mou'-rä, mē-gĕl'	mau'-rah, mee-gel'
polit.)		

Maurik (Neth.)	mou'-rĭk	mau'-rik
Mauritania (Afr.)	mô-rə-tä'-nĭ-ə	mo-ruh-tay'-ni-uh
French *Mauritanie,* mô-rē-tä-nē' [mo-ree-tah-nee'].		
Mauritius (Br., isl.)	mô-rĭsh'-əs	mo-rish'-uhs
	or mô-rĭsh'-ĭ-əs	mo-rish'-i-uhs
Maury (Va.)	môr'-ĭ	mawr'-i
Mauthausen (Ger.)	mout'-hou'-zən	maut'-hau'-zuhn
Mauvromati (Gr.)	mä-vrô-mä'-tē	mah-vro-mah'-tee
Mavia (Oc., New Hebrides)	mä-vē'-ä	mah-vee'-ah
Mavrovouni (Gr.)	mä-vrô-vōō'-nē	mah-vro-voo'-nee
Mawchi (Burma)	mô'-chē'	maw'-chee'
Mawlaik (Burma)	mô'-līk'	maw'-laik'
Mawlu (Burma)	mô'-lōō'	maw'-loo'
Maximos, Demetrios (Gr. polit.)	mäk'-sē-môs, dē-mē'-trē-ôs	mahk'-see-mos, dee-mee'-tree-os
May (Fr.)	mĕ'	meh'
Mayagüez (P.R.)	mä-yä-gwĕs'	mah-yah-gwes'
Mayantoc (P.I.)	mä-yän-tôk'	mah-yahn-tok'
Mayavaram (India)	mä'-yŭv'-ə-rəm	mah'-yuhv'-uh-ruhm
Maycauayán (P.I.) See *Meycauayán.*		
Mayen (Ger.)	mī'-ən	mai'-uhn
Mayenne (Fr.)	mä-yĕn'	mah-yen'
Mayet (Fr.)	mä-yĕ'	mah-yeh'
Maymyo (Burma)	mā'-myō'	may'-myoh'
Named after the English General May. Burman *myo* means *town.*		
Mayo (Eire)	mā'-ō	may'-oh
Mayón (Fil., volcano)	mä-yôn'	mah-yon'
Mayonga (P.I.)	mä-yông'-ä	mah-yong'-ah
Mayotte (Comoro isls.)	mä-yôt'	mah-yot'
Mayu (Burma, riv.)	mə-yōō'	muh-yoo'
Mayumo (P.I.) See *San Miguel de Mayumo.*		
Mazagan (Mor.)	mä-zä-gän'	mah-zah-gahn'
Mazanderan (Iran, prov.)	mä-zăn'-də-rän'	mah-zan'-duh-rahn'
Mazaraki (Gr.)	mä-zä-rä'-kē	mah-zah-rah'-kee
Mazatlán (Mex.)	*Eng.* măz'-ət-lăn'	maz'-uht-lan'
	Sp. mä-sä-tlän'	mah-sah-tlahn'
Mažeikiai (Lith.)	mä-zhä'-kyī	mah-zhay'-kyai
Russian *Muravyevo,* q.v.		
Mazzara (Sicily)	mäd-zä'-rä	mahd-zah'-rah
Mbalu Mbalu (Oc., Solomons)	mbä'-lōō mbä'-lōō	mbah'-loo mbah'-loo
Mboli (Oc., Solomons)	mbô'-lē	mbo'-lee

Mbretit, Fushë e (Alb.)   mbrĕ'-tēt, fōō'-shə ĕ   mbreh'-teet, foo'-
                                                                     shuh eh

     English Plain of *Elbasan,* q.v.

Mbuke (Oc., Admiralties) mbōō'-kĕ   mboo'-keh

Mbulo (Oc., Solomons)   mbōō'-lô   mboo'-lo

Meath (Eire)   mē*th'* or mēth'   mee*th'* or meeth'

Meau (Fr.)   mō'   moh'

Meauffe, la (Fr.)   mōf', lä   mohf', lah

Méaulte (Fr.)   mĕ-ōlt'   meh-ohlt'

Meaux (Fr.)   mō'   moh'

Mecca (Arabia)   *Eng.* mĕk'-ə   mek'-uh
                       Arabic mək'-kə   muhk'-kuh

Mechelen (Belg.)   *Flem.* mĕk(h)'-ə-lən   mek(h)'-uh-luhn

     French *Malines,* q.v. English *Mechlin,* mĕk'-lĭn [mek'-lin].

Mechernich (Ger.)   mĕk(h)'-ər-nĭk(h)   mek'(h)-uhr-nik(h)

Mechetinskaya (Rus.)   mĕ-chĕ'-tĭn-skä-yä   meh-cheh'-tin-skah-
                                                                   yah

Mechili (Libya)   mĕ-kē'-lē   meh-kee'-lee

Mecklenburg (Ger.)   *Eng.* mĕk'-lən-bûrg   mek'-luhn-buhrg
                       Ger. mĕk'-lən-   mek'-luhn-burk(h)
                                bŏŏrk(h)

——Schwerin (Ger.)   ——shvĕ-rēn'   ——shveh-reen'

——Strelitz (Ger.)   ——shtrā'-lĭts   ——shtray'-lits

Mečkujevci (Yugosl.)   mĕch'-kōō'-yĕv-tsĭ   mech'-koo'-yev-tsi

Medalie, George G.   mĭ-däl'-yə   mi-dahl'-yuh
     (Am. lawyer)

Medan (NEI, Sumatra)   mĕ-dän'   meh-dahn'

Medeia (Turk.)   See *Midye.*

Medelana (It.)   mĕ-dĕ-lä'-nä   meh-deh-lah'-nah

Medellín (Colom.)   mĕ-dĕ-yēn'   meh-deh-yeen'

Medemblik (Neth.)   mä'-dəm-blĭk   may'-duhm-blik

Medenine (Tun.)   mĕ-dĕ-nēn'   meh-deh-neen'

Mediaş (Rum.)   mĕ-dyäsh'   meh-dyahsh'

Medici (It.)   mĕ'-dē-chē   meh'-dee-chee

Medicina (It.)   mĕ-dē-chē'-nä   meh-dee-chee'-nah

Medina (Arabia)   mĕ-dē'-nä   meh-dee'-nah

Medina, Harold (Am.   mə-dē'-nə   muh-dee'-nuh
     judge)

Medina Angarita, Isaías   mĕ-dē'-nä äng-gä-   meh-dee'-nah ahng-
     (Ven. polit.)   rē'-tä, ē-sä-ē'-äs   gah-ree'-tah,
                                                          ee-sah-ee'-ahs

Medinilla (Oc.,   mĕ-dĕ-nē'-yä   meh-dee-nee'-yah
     Marianas)

Médis (Fr.)   mĕ-dē'   meh-dee'

Medjerda (Tun., riv.)	mə-jĕr'-dä	muh-jehr'-dah
Medjes el Bab (Tun.)	mĕ'-jĕz ĕl băb'	meh'-jez el bab'
Medjidia (Rum.)	mĕ-jē-dē'-ä	meh-jee-dee'-ah
Medouina (Mor.)	mĕd-wē'-nä	med-wee'-nah
Medvedovsk (Rus.)	mĕd-vĕ'-dôfsk	med-veh'-dofsk
Medvegja (Yugosl.)	mĕd'-vĕ-dyä	med'-veh-dyah
Medvegje (Yugosl.)	mĕd'-vĕ-dyĕ	med'-veh-dyeh
Medvezhya Gora (Rus.)	mĕd-vĕzh'-yä gŏ-rä'	med-vezh'-yah go-rah'
Medyn (Rus.)	mĕ-dwēn'(y)	meh-dween'(y)
Meekatharra (Austral.)	mē'-kə-thăr'-ə	mee'-kuh-thehr'-uh
Meenen (Belg.)	*Flem.* mā'-nən	may'-nuhn
French *Menin*, mə-năN' [muh-naN'].		
meer	*Du.* mār'	mayr'
	Eng. mĭr'	mihr'

An element, meaning *lake*, in Dutch place names. Cf. *Harlem Meer* in Central Park.

Meerloo (Neth.)	mār'-lō	mayr'-loh
Meersch, Ganshof van den (Belg. general)	mārs', gäns'-hôf vän dən	mayrs', gahns'-hof vahn duhn
Meersen (Neth.)	mār'-sən	mayr'-suhn
Meerut (India)	mē'-rət	mee'-ruht
Megalo Kastro (Crete)	mĕ-gä'-lô käs'-trô	meh-gah'-lo kahs'-tro
English *Candia*, q.v. Also called *Herakleion*, q.v.		
Megalopolis (Gr.)	mĕ-gä-lô'-pô-lē(s)	meh-gah-lo'-po-lee(s)
Meganesi (Gr.)	mĕ-gä-nē'-sē	meh-gah-nee'-see
Megara (Gr.)	mĕ'-gä-rä	meh'-gah-rah
Megiddo (Pal.)	mə-gĭd'-ō	muh-gid'-oh
Megiste (Dodec.) See *Kastelorizon*.		
Mehamn (Nor.)	mā'-hämn	may'-hahmn
Mehdia (Mor.)	mĕ-dē'-yä	meh-dee'-yah
Also called *Mehediya*, mĕ-hə-dē'-yä [meh-huh-dee'-yah].		
Mehr (Ger.)	mār'	mayr'
Meiji (Jap. era name)	mā'-jē	may'-jee
Meijel *or* Meiel (Neth.)	mī'-əl	mai'-uhl
Meiktila (Burma)	mēk'-tĭ-lə	meek'-ti-luh
Mei-ling (Ch., Kiangsi, Kwangtung, pass)	mā-lĭng	may-ling
Mei-ling Soong (Mme. Chiang Kai-shek)	mā-lĭng sŏŏng	may-ling sung
Meiningen (Ger.)	mī'-nĭng-ən	mai'-ning-uhn
Meiringen (Switz.)	mī'-rĭng-ən	mai'-ring-uhn
Meissen (Ger.)	mī'-sən	mai'-suhn
Meissner, Otto (Ger. polit.)	mīs'-nər, ôt'-ō	mais'-nuhr, ot'-oh

Meitner, Lise (Ger. scientist)	mīt′-nər, lē′-zə	mait′-nuhr, lee′-zuh
Mejatto (Oc., Kwajalein)	mĕ-jät′-tô	meh-jaht′-to
Mejía Colindres, Vincente (Hond. polit.)	mĕ-hē′-a kô-lēn′-drĕs, vēn-sĕn′-tĕ	meh-hee′-ah ko-leen′-drehs, veen-sehn′-teh
Mejit (Oc., Marshalls)	mĕ′-jĕt	meh′-jeet
Mekhili, el (Libya)	mĕ-kē′-lē, ĕl	meh-kee′-lee, el
Mekhov (Pol.) See *Miechów*.		
Meklong (Siam, riv.)	mă-klông′	ma-klawng′
Meknès (Mor.)	mĕk-nĕs′	mek-nes′
Mekong (S.E. Asia, riv.)	*Eng.* mā′-kŏng′ *Siam.* mă-kōng′	may′-kong′ ma-kohng′
Chinese *Lan-ts'ang*, q.v.		
Melada (Yugosl.)	*It.* mĕ-lä′-dä	meh-lah′-dah
Serb-Croat *Mulat*, q.v.		
Melbourne (Austral.)	mĕl′-bərn	mel′-buhrn
The pronunciation mĕl′-bôrn [mel′-born] is not recommended.		
Melbu (Nor.)	mĕl′-bo͞o	mel′-boo
Melchers, J. Gari (Am. painter)	mĕl′-chərz, gär′-ĭ	mel′-chuhrz, gehr′-i
Mêle, le (Fr.)	mĕl′, lə	mel′, luh
Meleda (Yugosl., isl.)	*It.* mĕ′-lĕ-dä	meh′-leh-dah
Serb-Croat *Mljet*, q.v.		
Melekhas (Crete, point)	mĕ-lĕ′-häs	meh-leh′-hahs
Also called *Kyamon*, kē′-ä-môn [kee′-ah-mon].		
Melenci (Yugosl.)	mĕ′-lĕn-tsĭ	meh′-len-tsi
Melfa (It., riv.)	mĕl′-fä	mel′-fah
Melfa (Libya)	mĕl′-fä	mel′-fah
Also called *Bir el Melfa*.		
Melghir, Chott (Tun.)	mĕl-gēr′, shŏt′	mel-geer′, shot′
Meli (Tun.)	mā′-lē	may′-lee
Meligala (Gr.)	mĕ-lē-gä-lä′	meh-lee-gah-lah′
Meliha (Libya)	mā-lē′-hä	may-lee′-hah
Melilla (Sp. Mor.)	mĕ-lē′-lyä	meh-lee′-lyah
Melissa (Crete, point)	mĕ′-lē-sä	meh′-lee-sah
Also called *Psykhion*, psē′-hē-ôn [psee′-hee-on].		
Melito (It.)	mĕ-lē′-tô	meh-lee′-to
Melitopol (Rus.)	mĕ-lĭ-tô′-pŏl(y)	meh-li-to′-pol(y)
Meljine (Yugosl.)	mĕ′-lyĭ-nĕ	meh′-lyi-neh
Melk (Austria)	mĕlk′	melk′
Melnica (Yugosl.)	mĕl′-nĭ-tsä	mel′-ni-tsah
Melnik (Bulg.)	mĕl′-nĭk	mel′-nik
Mělník (Cz.)	myĕl′-nēk	myel′-neek

Melnik (Pol.)   See *Mielnik.*

Melos (Gr., isl.)	mē′-lô(s)	mee′-lo(s)
Melrir, Chott (Tun.)	mĕl-rēr′, shŏt′	mel-reer′, shot′
Melun (Fr.)	mə-lûN′	muh-lœN′
Memel (Lith., city, riv.)	*Ger.* mā′-məl	may′-muhl
	Eng. mĕm′-əl	mem′-uhl

The city is called in Russian *Memel*, mā′-mĕl(y) [may′-mel(y)]; in Lithuanian *Klaipėda*, klī′-pĕ-dä [klai′-peh-dah]. For names of the river, see *Niemen.*

Memešli (Yugosl.)	mĕ′-mĕsh-lĭ	meh′-mesh-li
Memphremagog (Vt., Que.)	mĕm′-frə-mā′-gŏg	mem′-fruh-may′-gog
Menai (Wales, str.)	mĕ′-nĭ	meh′-nai
Menaldumadeel (Neth.)	mĕ-näl′-dü-mä-dāl′	meh-nahl′-dü-mah-dayl′
menam	mă-näm′	ma-nahm′

Siamese word meaning *river.* It may be necessary to look up the other part of the name.

Menam Chao Phraya (Siam, riv.)	mă-näm′ chou prä-yä′	ma-nahm′ chau prah-yah′

Bhraya and *Phya* are variants of *Praya.*

Menassir (Tun.)   See *Djebel el Menassir.*

Mencken, H. L. (Am. author)	mĕng′-kĭn *or* -kən	meng′-kin *or* -kuhn

The Sage of Baltimore writes: "The colored folk here in Baltimore always call me *Meekins.* It seems to them more rational and Christian."

Mendes de Morãis (Braz. polit.)	mān′-dĭs dĭ mô-rīNs′	mayn′-dis di mo-raiNs′
Mendèz France, Pierre (Fr. polit.)	măN-dĕz fräNs′, pyĕr′	maN-dez frahNs′, pyehr′
Méndez Núñez (P.I.)	mĕn′-dĕs noō′-nyĕs	men′-des noo′-nyes
Mendola (It.)	mĕn′-dô-lä	men′-do-lah
Mendonça Lima, João de (Braz. polit.)	mĕn-dôn′-sə lē′-mə, zhŏō-ouN′ də	men-don′-suh lee′-muh, zhu-auN′ duh
Mendoza (Sp. name)	*Am. Sp.* mĕn-dô′-sä *Sp.* mĕn-dô′-thä	men-do′-sah mehn-do′-thah
Mendre (Yugosl.)	mĕn′-drĕ	men′-dreh
Menemencioǧlu, Numan (Turk. polit.)	mĕ-nĕ-mĕn-jĭ′-ô-loō, noō′-män′	meh-neh-men-ji′-o-lu, nu′-mahn′
Menfi (Sicily)	mĕn′-fē	men′-fee
Mêng-ma (Ch., Yünnan)	mŭng-mä	muhng-mah
Mêng-shui (Ch., Kansu)	mŭng-shwä	muhng-shway
Mêng-t'ing (Ch., Yünnan)	mŭng-tĭng	muhng-ting

Mêng-tzŭ (Ch., Yünnan)   mŭng-dzə   muhng-dzuh

Menidi (Gr.)   mĕ-nē′-dē   meh-nee′-dee

Menin (Belg.) See *Meenen.*

Menninger, Karl A.   mĕn′-ĭng-ər   men′-ing-uhr
  (Am. psychiatrist)

Menominee (Mich.)   mə-nŏm′-ə-nē   muh-nom′-uh-nee

Menominie (Wis.)   mə-nŏm′-ə-nē   muh-nom′-uh-nee

Mentawai (NEI)   mĕn-tä′-wĭ   men-tah′-wai

Menton (Fr.)   *Eng.* mĕn-tōn′   men-tohn′
                Fr.   mäN-tôN′   mahN-toN′

  Italian *Mentone,* mĕn-tô′-nĕ [men-to′-neh], *or Eng.* mĕn-tō′-nĭ [men-toh′-ni].

Menzel Bou Zelfa (Tun.) mĕn′-zĕl bōō zĕl′-fä men′-zel boo zel′-fah

Menzel Djemil (Tun.)   mĕn′-zĕl jə-mēl′   men′-zel juh-meel′

Menzel Temime (Tun.) mĕn′-zĕl tə-mēm′   men′-zel tuh-meem′

Menzies (Scot. name)   *Austral.* mĕn′-zĭz   men′-ziz
                Br.   mĕng′-ĭz   meng′-iz
                or mĭng′-ĭs   *or* ming′-is

Menzies, Robert Gordon mĕn′-zĭz   men′-ziz
  (Austral. polit.)

Meppel (Neth.)   mĕp′-əl   mep′-uhl

Merak (NEI, Java)   mŭ′-räk   moe′-rahk

Merauke (NEI, New   mĕ-rou′-kĕ   meh-rau′-keh
  Guinea)

Merced (Calif.)   *Eng.* mər-sĕd′   muhr-sed′
                Sp. mĕr-sĕd′   mehr-sed′

Mercurea (Rum.)   mĕr′-kōō-ryä   mehr′-ku-ryah

Merderet (Fr., riv.)   mĕr-də-rĕ′   mehr-duh-reh′

Merdrignac (Fr.)   mĕr-drē-nyäk′   mehr-dree-nyahk′

Meretskov, Kiryl (Rus. mĕ-rĕts-kôf′,   meh-rets-kof′,
  general)   kĭ-rēl′   ki-reel′

Mergui (Burma)   mər-gwē′   muhr-gwee′

Mérida (Sp., Mex.)   mĕ′-rē-dä   meh′-ree-dah

Mérignac (Fr., airport   mĕ-rē-nyäk′   meh-ree-nyahk′
  near Bordeaux)

Merizo (Oc., Guam)   mĕ-rē′-sô   meh-ree′-so

Merode (Ger.)   mā′-rō-də   may′-roh-duh

  As a French name, *Mérode* is pronounced mĕ-rōd′ [meh-rohd′].

Merrow, Chester E.   mĕr′-ō   mehr′-oh
  (U.S. representative)

Mersa Matruh (Egypt) mĕr′-sä mä-trōō′ mehr′-sah mah-troo′

Mersch (Luxem.)   mĕrsh′   mehrsh′

Merseburg (Ger.)   mĕr′-zə-bōŏrk(h) mehr′-zuh-burk(h)

Mers el Kebir (Alg.)   mĕrs′ ĕl kə-bēr′ mehrs′ el kuh-beer′

Mersig (Ger.)	mĕr′-zĭk(h)	mehr′-zik(h)
Mersin (Turk.)	mĕr′-sĭn′	mehr′-sin′

Also called *Mersina*, mĕr-sē′-nä [mehr-see′-nah].

Méru (Fr.)	mĕ-rü′	meh-rü′
Merville (Fr.)	mĕr-vēl′	mehr-veel′
Merwede (Neth., riv.)	mĕr′-wā-də	mehr′-way-duh
Merxem (Belg.)	mĕrk′-səm	mehrk′-suhm
Méry (Fr.)	mĕ-rē′	meh-ree′
Merzig (Ger.)	mĕr′-tsĭk(h)	mehr′-tsik(h)
Merzighausen (Ger.)	mĕr′-tsĭk(h)-hou′-zən	mehr′-tsik(h)-hau′-zuhn
Merzinich (Ger.)	mĕr′-tsĭn-ĭk(h)	mehr′-tsin-ik(h)
Mesabi (Minn., range)	mə-sä′-bĭ	muh-sah′-bi

Variants are *Missabe* and *Mesaba*, reminiscent of the controversy of *Missouri*: Shall the unstressed vowels be ĭ or ə?

Mesara (Crete)	mĕ-sä-rä′	meh-sah-rah′
Meschede (Ger.)	mä′-shä-də	may′-shay-duh
Mesemvria (Bulg.)	See *Nesebar*.	
Meseritz (Ger. >Pol.)	mĕ′-zə-rĭts	meh′-zuh-rits

Polish *Międzyrzecz*, q.v.

Meševište (Yugosl.)	mĕ′-shĕ-vĭ-shtĕ	meh′-sheh-vi-shteh
Meshchersk (Rus.)	mĕ-shchĕrsk′	meh-shchehrsk′
Meshchovsk (Rus.)	mĕ-shchŏfsk′	meh-shchofsk′
Meshed (Iran)	*Per.* măsh-hăd′	mash-had′
	Eng. mĕsh′-hĕd	mesh′-hed
Mesilla (N.M.)	*Eng.* mə-sē′-yə	muh-see′-yuh
	Sp. mĕ-sē′-yä	meh-see′-yah
Meslay (Fr.)	mĕ-lĕ′	meh-leh′
Mesnil Durand, le (Fr.)	mĕ-nēl dü-räN′, lə	meh-neel dü-rahN′, luh
Mesnil Vigot, le (Fr.)	mĕ-nēl vē-gō′, lə	meh-neel vee-goh′, luh
Mesolongion (Gr.)	mĕ-sô-lông′-gē(-ôn)	meh-so-long′-gee(-on)
meson	mĕz′-ŏn	mez′-on

This is probably the commonest pronunciation among physicists, but the word is also pronounced mĕs′-ən [mes′-uhn], mē′-sŏn[mee′-son], mē′-zən [mee′-zuhn].

mesotron	mĕz′-ə-trŏn	mez′-uh-tron

Also pronounced mē′-zə-trŏn [mee-zuh-tron], mĕs′-ə-trŏn [mes′-uh-tron], and mē′-sə-trŏn [mee′-suh-tron].

Messagère d'Athènes (Gr. weekly paper)	mĕ-sä-zhĕr dä-tĕn′	meh-sah-zhehr dah-ten′
Messaggero, Il (Rome newspaper)	mĕs-säd-jĕ′-rô, ēl	mes-sahd-jeh′-ro, eel

Messe (Sard.)	měs'-sě	mes'-seh
Messene (Gr.)	mě-sē'-nē	meh-see'-nee
Messenia (Gr.)	mě-sē-nē'-ä	meh-see-nee'-ah
Messeniakos Kolpos	mě-sē-nē-ä-kôs'	meh-see-nee-ah-kos'
(Gr., gulf)	kôl'-pôs	kol'-pos

English Gulf of *Messenia*, q.v.

Messiaen, Olivier (Fr.	mě-syäN', ô-lē-vyě'	meh-syahN', o-lee-
composer)		vyeh'
Messina (Sicily)	měs-sē'-nä	mes-see'-nah
Mesta (Balkan riv.)	*Bulg.* mě'-stä	meh'-stah

Greek *Nestos*, q.v.

Mestre (It.)	mě'-strě	meh'-streh
Metalanim (Oc., Ponape)	mě-tä-lä'-nǐm	meh-tah-lah'-nim
Metamer (Tun.)	mě-tă'-měr	meh-ta'-mehr
metamorphosis	mět'-ə-môr'-fə-sǐs	met'-uh-mor'-fuh-sis

Plural *metamorphosez*, mět'-ə-môr'-fə-sēz [met'-uh-mor'-fuh-seez].

Metaponto (It.)	mě-tä-pôn'-tô	meh-tah-pon'-to
Methone (Gr.)	mě-thô'-nē	meh-tho'-nee
Metković (Yugosl.)	mět'-kô-vǐch	met'-ko-vich
Metlaoui (Tun.)	mět-lä'-wē	met-lah'-wee
Metline (Tun.)	mět-lēn'	met-leen'
Metlire (Tun.)	mět-lēr'	met-leer'
Metohija (Yugosl.)	mě'-tô'-hǐ-yä	meh'-to'-hi-yah
Metslawier (Neth.)	mět-slä-wēr'	met-slah-weer'
Metsovon (Gr.)	mě'-tsô-vô(n)	meh'-tso-vo(n)
Mettarheni (Tun.)	mět-tär-hă'-nē	met-tahr-hay'-nee
Metz (Fr.)	*Eng., Ger.* měts'	mets'
	Fr. měs'	mes'
Meudon (Fr.)	mû-dôN'	mœ-doN'
Meulaboh (NEI,	mû-lä'-bô	mœ-lah'-bo
Sumatra)		
Meulan les Mureaux	mû-läN lě mü-rō'	mœ-lahN leh
(Fr.)		mü-roh'
Meung (Fr.)	mûN'	mœN'
Meurice, Paul	mû-rēs'	mœ-rees'
(Fr. dramatist)		
Meurthe (Fr., riv.)	mûrt'	mœrt'
Meuse (Europ. riv.)	*Eng.* mūz'	myooz'
	Fr. mûz'	mœz'

Dutch and Flemish *Maas*, q.v.

Meux, le (Fr.)	mû', lə	mœ', luh
Mexia (Tex.)	*local* mə-hä'-ə	muh-hay'-uh
	Sp. mě-hē'-ä	meh-hee'-ah
Mexicali (Mex.)	měk-sē-kä'-lē	mehk-see-kah'-lee

Mexico   *Eng.* měk′-sǐ-kō   mek′-si-koh
   Spanish *México* (officially) or *Méjico*, mě′-hē-kô [meh′-hee-ko].
Meximieux (Fr.)   měk-sē-myû′   mek-see-myœ′
Meycauayán (P.I.)   mā-kä-wä-yän′   may-kah-wah-yahn′
   Also called *Maycauayán*, mī-kä-wä-yän′ [mai-kah-wah-yahn′].
Mèze (Fr.)   měz′   mez′
Mézidon (Fr.)   mě-zē-dôN′   meh-zee-doN′
Mézières (Fr.)   mě-zyěr′   meh-zyehr′
Mezőberény (Hung.)   mě′-zû-bě′-rān(y)   meh′-zœ-beh′-rayn(y)
Mezőkövesd (Hung.)   mě′-zû-kû′-vězhd   meh′-zœ-kœ′-vezhd
Mezőtúr (Hung.)   mě′-zû-tōōr   meh′-zœ-toor
Mezzano (It.)   měd-zä′-nô   med-zah′-no
Mezzo (Yugosl., isl.)   *It.* měd′-zô   med′-zo
   Serb-Croat *Lopud*, q.v.
Mezzocammino (It.)   měd′-zô-käm-mē′-nô   med′-zo-kahm-mee′-
                                                       no
Mezzolara (It.)   měd-zô-lä′-rä   med-zo-lah′-rah
Mezzouna (Tun.)   měz-zōō′-nä   mez-zoo′-nah
Mga (Rus.)   mgä′   mgah′
Mglin (Rus.)   mglēn′   mgleen′
Mhow (India)   mou′   mau′
Miagao (P.I.)   myä-gou′   myah-gau′
Miami (Ariz., Fla.)   mī-ăm′-ǐ *or* -ə   mai-am′-i *or* -uh
Mianeh (Iran)   mē-ä-ně′   mee-ah-neh′
Miangas (NEI) See *Palmas.*
Miaskovsky, Nikolai   myäs-kôf′-skǐ,   myahs-kof′-ski,
   (Rus. composer)   nǐ-kǒ-lī′   ni-ko-lai′
Michael (King of   mī′-kəl   mai′-kuhl
   Rumania)
   Rumanian *Mihai*, mē-hī′ [mee-hai′].
Michałowski, Jerzy   mǐ-hä-lôf′-skǐ,   mi-hah-lof′-ski,
   (Pol. diplomat)   zhě′-zhǐ   zheh′-zhi
Michener, Earl C.   mǐch′-ə-nər   mich′-uh-nuhr
   (U.S. representative)
Michoacán (Mex.)   mē-chô-ä-kän′   mee-cho-ah-kahn′
Michurin (Rus. scientist)   mē-chōō′-rǐn   mee-choo′-rin
Michurinsk (Rus.)   mē-chōō′-rǐnsk   mee-choo′-rinsk
Middelburg (Neth.)   *Eng.* mǐd′-əl-bûrg   mid′-uhl-buhrg
             Du. mǐd′-əl-bûrk(h)   mid′-uhl-bœrk(h)
Middelharnis (Neth.)   mǐd′-əl-här′-nǐs   mid′-uhl-hahr′-nis
Middlesbrough (Eng.)   mǐd′lz-brə   mid′lz-bruh
Midi, le (Fr.)   mē-dē′, lə   mee-dee′, luh
   The *South* of France.
Midoun (Tun.)   mǐ-dōōn′   mi-doon′

Midwolde (Neth.)   mĭd-wôl′-də   mid-wọl′-duh

Midye (Turk.)   mēd′-yĕ′   meed′-yeh′
     Greek *Medeia*, mē′-dē-ä [mee′-dee-ah].

Midžor (Balkan mt.)   mē′-jôr   mee′-jor

Miechów (Pol.)   myĕ′-kŏŏf   myeh′-kuf
     Russian *Mekhov*, mĕ′-hŏf [meh′-hof].

Mie (Jap.)   mē′-ĕ   mee′-eh

Międzychód (Pol.)   myăN-zĭ′-hŏŏd   myaN-zi′-hud
     German *Birnbaum*, bĭrn′-boum [bihrn′-baum].

Międzylesie (Ger. >Pol.)   myăN-dzĭ-lĕ′-shĕ   myaN-dzi-leh′-sheh
     German *Mittelwalde*, q.v.

Międzyrzec (Pol.)   myăN-jĭ′-zhĕts   myaN-ji′-zhets
     Russian *Mezhireche*, mĕ-zhĭ-rĕ′-chyĕ [meh-zhi-reh′-chyeh].

Międzyrzecz (Ger. >Pol.)   myăN-jĭ′-zhĕch   myaN-ji′-zhech
     German *Meseritz*, q.v.

Mielec (Pol.)   myĕ′-lĕts   myeh′-lets

Mielnik (Pol.)   myĕl′-nĭk   myel′-nik
     Russian *Melnik*, mĕl′(y)-nĭk [mel′(y)-nik].

Mielziner, Jo   mĕl-zē′-nər   mel-zee′-nuhr
     (Am. stage designer)

Mierloo (Neth.)   mēr′-lō   meer′-loh

Mierzeja Wiślana   *Pol.* myĕ-zhĕ′-yä   myeh-zheh′-yah
     (Ger. >Pol., Rus.,   vēsh-lä′-nä   veesh-lah′-nah
     lagoon)
     German *Frisches Haff*, q.v. Russian *Frishes Gaf*, frē′-shĕs gäf [free′-shuhs gahf].

Mietzel (Ger.)   mē′-tsəl   mee′-tsuhl

Migdal (Pal.)   mĭg′-däl   mig′-dahl
     Arabic *El Majdal*, q.v. Ancient *Magdala*, măg′-də-lə [mag′-duh-luh], whence "The Magdalene."

Mignano (It.)   mē-nyä′-nô   mee-nyah′-no

Miguel (Sp. name)   mē-gĕl′   mee-gel′

Migulinsk (Rus.)   mĭ-gŏŏ′-lĭnsk   mi-goo′-linsk

Migyaungye (Burma)   mē-joung-yĕ′   mee-jaung-yeh′

Mihai (King of Rumania)   mē-hī′   mee-hai′
     English *Michael*, q.v.

Mihajlovac (Yugosl.)   mē-hī′-lô-väts   mee-hai′-lo-vahts

Miholjac, Donji   mē′-hô-lyäts, dôn′-yĭ   mee′-ho-lyahts,
     (Yugosl.)   don′-yi

Mijajlovica (Yugosl.,   mē-yĭ′-lô-vĭ-tsä   mee-yai′-lo-vi-tsah
     mt.)

Mijdrecht (Neth.)   mĭ′-drĕk(h)t   mai′-drek(h)t

Mikashevichi (Pol.)   See *Mikaszewicze*.

Mikaszewicze (Pol.)   mĭ-kä-shĕ-vē'-chĕ   mi-kah-sheh-vee'-cheh

Russian *Mikashevichi*, mĭ-kä-shĕ-vē'-chĭ [mi-kah-sheh-vee'-chi].

Mikhailo-Semenovskaya   mĭ-hī'-lŏ-sĕ-myô'-nŏf-skä-yä   mi-hai'-lo-seh-myo'-nof-skah-yah
(Rus.)

Mikhailović, Draža   mĭ-hī'-lô-vĭch, drä'-zhä   mi-hai'-lo-vich, drah'-zhah
(Yugosl. general)

Also spelled *Mihailovitch, Draja*. The familiar *Draža* is short for *Dragoljub*, drä'-gô-lyōōb' [drah'-go-lyoob']. *Mihailovitch* (however spelled) as a Serbian name is stressed on the second syllable; as a Polish name on the third syllable; as a Russian name on the second or the third syllable.

Mikhailovka (Rus.)   mĭ-hī'-lŏf-kä   mi-hai'-lof-kah

Mikhalopoulos, A. (Gr. polit.)   mē-hä-lô'-pōō-lôs   mee-hah-lo'-poo-los

Mikołajczyk, Stanislaw   mĭ-kô-lĭ'-chĭk, stä-nē'-släf   mi-ko-lai'-chik, stah-nee'-slahf
(Pol. polit.)

Mikoyan, Anastas (Rus. polit.)   mĭ-kô'-yän, ä-nä'-stäs   mi-ko'-yahn, ah-nah'-stahs

Mikoyan Shakhar (Rus.)   mĭ-kŏ-yän' shä'-här'   mi-ko-yahn' shah'-hahr'

Mikra Mantinea (Gr.)   mē-krä' män-dē'-nē-ä   mee-krah' mahn-dee'-nee-ah

Mil (Neth.)   mĭl'   mil'

Milan (It.)   *Eng.* mĭ-lăn' *or* mĭl'-ən   mi-lan' mil'-uhn
    It. mē-lä'-nô   mee-lah'-no

Milan (Mich., Mo., Tenn.)   mĭ'-lən   mai'-luhn

Milanovac, Gornji   mē'-lä'-nô-väts, gôr'-nyĭ   mee'-lah'-no-vahts, gor'-nyi
(Yugosl.)

Milatos (Crete)   mē'-lä-tôs   mee'-lah-tos

Milatovac (Yugosl.)   mē'-lä'-tô-väts   mee'-lah'-to-vahts

Milazzo (Sicily)   mē-lät'-sô   mee-laht'-so

Mileškovo (Yugosl.)   mē'-lĕ'-shkô-vô   mee'-leh'-shko-vo

Milesse, la (Fr.)   mē-lĕs'   mee-les'

Milhaud, Darius   mē-lō', dä-ryüs'   mee-loh', dah-ryüs'
(Fr. composer)

Mili (Crete, isl.)   See *Pontikonesi*.

Mili (Oc., Marshalls)   mē'-lē   mee'-lee

Miliana (Tun., riv.)   mĭl-yă'-nä   mil-ya'-nah

Miliane (Tun., riv.)   mĭl-yăn'   mil-yan'

Miljevska planina   mē'-lyĕv-skä plä'-nē'-nä   mee'-lyev-skah plah'-nee'-nah
(Yugosl.)

Millau (Fr.)	mē-yō′	mee-yoh′
Millay, Edna St. Vincent (Am. poet)	mǐ-lā′	mi-lay′
Milleries, les (Fr.)	mĕl-rē′, lĕ	meel-ree′, leh
Millerovo (Rus.)	mǐl′-lĕ-rŏ-vŏ	mil′-leh-ro-vo
Millikin, Eugene D. (U.S. senator)	mǐl′-ǐ-kǐn	mil′-i-kin
Millingen (Neth.)	mǐl′-ǐng-ən	mil′-ing-uhn
Milne (New Guinea, Papua, bay)	mǐln′ or mǐl′	miln′ or mil′
Named after the English geographer.		
Milo (Sicily)	mē′-lô	mee′-lo
Miloševac (Yugosl.)	mē′-lô′-shĕ-väts	mee′-lo′-sheh-vahts
Milošević, Sima (Yugosl. polit.)	mē′-lô′-shĕ-vǐch, sē′-mä	mee′-lo′-sheh-vich, see′-mah
Miloševo (Yugosl.)	mē′-lô′-shĕ-vô	mee′-lo′-sheh-vo
Milot (Alb.)	mē′-lôt	mee′-lot
Milot (Haiti)	mē-lō′	mee-loh′
Miloti (Alb.) See *Milot*.		
Milparinka (Austral.)	mǐl′-pər-ēngk′-ə	mil′-puhr-eengk′-uh
Minalin (P.I.)	mē-nä′-lǐn	mee-nah′-lin
minami	mē-nä-mē	mee-nah-mee
An element, meaning *south*, in Japanese place names.		
Minami, Jiro (Jap. polit.)	mē′-nä-mē, jē′-rô	mee′-nah-mee, jee′-ro
Minas Gerais (Brazil)	mē′-nəs zhĕ-rīs′	mee′-nuhs zheh-rais′
minato	mē-nä-tô	mee-nah-to
An element, meaning *port*, in Japanese place names.		
Minbu (Burma)	mǐm′-bōō	mim′-boo
Minbya (Burma)	mǐm-byä′	mim-byah′
Minc, Hilary (Pol. diplomat)	mēnts′, hǐl′-ə-rǐ	meents′, hil′-uh-ri
Min Chiang or Min River (Ch., Fukien)	mǐn	min
Also called *Min-kong*, q.v.		
Mindanao (P.I.)	mǐn-dä-nou′	min-dah-nau′
Minden (Ger.)	mǐn′-dən	min′-duhn
Mindoro (P.I.)	mǐn-dô′-rô	min-do′-ro
Mindszenty, József, Cardinal (Hung.)	mǐnd′-sĕn-tǐ, yô′-zhĕf	mind′-sen-ti, yo′-zhef
Mineralnye Vody (Rus.)	mǐ-nĕ-räl′(y)-nǐ-yĕ vô′-dǐ	mi-neh-rahl′(y)-ni-yeh vo′-di
Mingaladon (Burma)	mǐng′-gə-lə-dōn′	ming′-guh-luh-dohn′
Minho (Port., Sp., riv.) Spanish *Miño*, q.v.	mē′-nyōō	mee′-nyu

Min-how (Ch., Fukien)　mĭn-hō　　　　min-hoh
　Also called *Foo-chow*, q.v.

Min-kong (Ch., Fukien,　mĭn-jŏng　　　min-jong
　riv.)
　Also called *Min Chiang*, q.v.

Miño (Sp., Port., riv.)　mē'-nyô　　　mee'-nyo
　Portuguese *Minho*, q.v.

Minobe, Tatsukichi　mē'-nô-bĕ, tä-tsōō'-　mee'-no-beh, tah-
　(Jap. educator)　kē'-chē'　　　　tsoo'-kee'-chee'

Minsk (Rus.)　mēnsk'　　　　　meensk'

Mińsk Mazowiecki (Pol.)　mēn(y)sk' mä-zô-　meen(y)sk' mah-zo-
　　　　　　vyĕ'-tskĭ　　　　vyeh'-tski
　Russian *Novominsk*, nô'-vŏ-mēnsk' [no'-vo-meensk'].

Minthami (Burma)　mĭn'-*th*ə-mē'　　min'-*th*uh-mee'

Minusinsk (Rus.)　mĭ-nōō-sēnsk'　　mi-noo-seensk'

Mioko (Oc., New Britain)　mē-ô'-kô　　　mee-o'-ko

Mionica (Yugosl.)　mē'-ô'-nĭ-tsä　　mee'-o'-ni-tsah

Miramas (Fr.)　mē-rä-mä'　　　mee-rah-mah'

Mirambello (Crete, gulf)　mē-rä(m)-bĕ'-lô　mee-rah(m)-beh'-lo

Mirandola (It.)　mē-rän'-dô-lä　　mee-rahn'-do-lah

Miravci (Yugosl.)　mē'-räv-tsĭ　　　mee'-rahv-tsi

Mirdita (Alb.)　See *Mirditë*.

Mirditë (Alb.)　mēr-dē'-tə　　　meer-dee'-tuh

Mirecourt (Fr.)　mēr-kōōr'　　　meer-koor'

Mirgorod (Rus.)　mēr'-gŏ-rŏt　　meer'-go-rot

Miri (Borneo)　mē'-rē　　　　mee'-ree

Mirjaweh (Iran)　mēr-jä'-vĕ　　　meer-jah'-veh

Mirkovce (Yugosl.)　mēr'-kôv-tsĕ　　meer'-kov-tseh

Mirna (Yugosl., riv.)　mēr'-nä　　　　meer'-nah

Miros, Agios (Crete)　mē'-rôs, ĭ'-yôs　　mee'-ros, ai'-yos

Miruša (Yugosl., riv.)　mē'-rōō-shä　　mee'-roo-shah

Misa (It., riv.)　mē'-zä　　　　mee'-zah

misaki　mē-sä-kē　　　　mee-sah-kee
　An element, meaning *cape*, in Japanese place names.

Misamis (P.I.)　mē-sä'-mēs　　　mee-sah'-mees

misandry　mĭs'-ăn-drĭ　　　mis'-an-dri
　Presumably the noun agent is *misandrist*, mĭs'-ăn-drĭst [mis'-an-drist],
　a female hater of men.

Misburg (Ger.)　mĭs'-bōŏrk(h)　　mis'-burk(h)

mischievous.　See *grievous*.

Misilmeri (Sicily)　mē-zēl-mĕ'-rē　　mee-zeel-meh'-ree

Misima (Oc., Louisiade　mē-sē'-mä　　　mee-see'-mah
　arch.)

Miskolc (Hung.)　mĭsh'-kôlts　　　mish'-kolts

Mislinja (Yugosl., riv.)   mĕ'-slĭ-nyä   mee'-slĭ-nyah
Mišljenovac (Yugosl.)   mĕsh'-lyĕ'-nô-väts   meesh'-lyeh'-no-vahts
Misoöl (NEI)   mĕ'-sō'-əl   mee'-soh'-uhl
Missolonghi (Gr.)   See *Mesolongion.*
Missoula (Mont.)`   mə-zōō'-lə   muh-zoo'-lah
Missouri   mə-zōōr'-ĭ *or* -ə   muh-zur'-i *or* -uh

American Speech once printed an article of 17 pages on the historical disputes about the pronunciation of this name. My impression is that three out of four Missourians today favor mə-zōōr'-ə [muh-zur'-uh], but that the fourth preferring mə-zōōr'-ĭ [muh-zur'-i] regards it as socially superior. The -ĭ pronunciation is stronger in St. Louis than in Kansas City. If mĭ-zōō'-rĭ is more respectable than mĭ-zōōr'-ə, this is contrary to the social standing of "Louisy" as compared with *Louisa,* "Marthy" with *Martha,* and even the familiar "Annie" as a variant of *Anna* and *Anne.* For *Cincinnati,* final ĭ and final ə seem at present equally matched.

Misterbianco (Sicily)   mē-stĕr-byän'-kô   mee-stehr-byahn'-ko
Misurata (Libya)   mē-zōō-rä'-tä   mee-zoo-rah'-tah
Mitau (Latvia)   *Ger.* mē'-tou   mee'-tau
   Latvian *Jelgava,* q.v. Russian *Mitava,* q.v.
Mitava (Latvia)   *Rus.* mĭ-tä'-vä   mi-tah'-vah
   Latvian *Jelgava,* q.v. German *Mitau,* mē'-tou [mee'-tau].
Miteiriya, el (Egypt)   mĭ-tä-rē'-yä, ĕl   mi-tay-ree'-yah, el
Mitikas (Gr.)   mē'-tē-käs   mee'-tee-kahs
Mito (Jap.)   mē-tô'   mee-to'
Mitropoulos, Dimitri   mē-trô'-pōō-lôs,   mee-tro'-poo-los,
   (Gr. musician)   dē-mē'-trē   dee-mee'-tree
Mitrovica (Yugosl.)   mē'-trô-vĭ-tsä   mee'-tro-vi-tsah
Mitscher, Mark Andrew   mĭch'-ər   mich'-uhr
   (Am. admiral)
Mitsubishi (Jap.)   mē-tsōō'-bē-shē   mee-tsoo'-bee-shee
Mitsuchi, Chūzō (Jap.   mē-tsōō'-chĕ', chōō'-   mee-tsoo'-chee',
   polit.)   zô'   choo'-zo'
Mitsui (Jap., zaibatsu)   mē'-tsōō-ē   mee'-tsoo-ee
Mittelbronn (Fr.)   mĭt-əl-brôn'   mit-uhl-bron'
Mittelwalde (Ger. >Pol.)   mĭt'-əl-väl'-də   mit'-uhl-vahl'-duh
   Polish *Międzylesie,* q.v.
Mi-tu (Ch., Yünnan)   mē-dōō   mee-doo
Mius (Rus., riv.)   mē-ōōs'   mee-oos'
Miyagi (Jap.)   mē-yä'-gē'   mee-yah'-gee'
Miyake (Jap.)   mē-yä'-kĕ'   mee-yah'-keh'
Miyandoab (Iran)   mē-ăn-dō-äb'   mee-an-doh-ahb'
Miyazaki (Jap.)   mē-yä'-zä-kē   mee-yah'-zah-kee
Miye (Jap.)   mē'-ĕ   mee'-eh

Mizda (Libya)	mĭz'-dä	miz'-dah
Mizil (Rum.)	mē-zēl'	mee-zeel'
Mizner, Wilson (Am. author)	mīz'-nər	maiz'-nuhr
Mjoesa or Mjösa (Nor., lake)	myû'-sä	myœ'-sah
Mladá Boleslav (Cz.)	mlä'-dä bô'-lĕ-släf	mlah'-dah bo'-leh-slahf
Mladenovac (Yugosl.)	mlä'-dĕ'-nô-väts	mlah'-deh'-no-vahts
Mlava (Yugosl., riv.)	mlä'-vä	mlah'-vah
Mława (Pol.)	mlä'-vä	mlah'-vah
Russian spelling *Mlava*.		
Mljet (Yugosl., isl.)	mlyĕt'	mlyet'
Italian *Meleda*, q.v.		
Mo (Nor.)	mō'	moh'
The Norwegian is close to mŏŏ [mu].		
Moab (Trans-Jordan)	mō'-ăb	moh'-ab
Modern *El Belqa*, ĕl bĕl'-kä [el bel'-kah].		
Mobile (Ala.)	mō-bēl'	moh-beel'
Moçambique (Afr.) See *Mozambique*.		
Mocha (Arabia)	*Eng.* mō'-kə	moh'-kuh
Arabic *Mucha*, mŏŏ'-k(h)ä [mu'-k(h)ah].		
Mockau (Ger.)	môk'-ou	mok'-au
Also called *Leipsig Mockau*.		
Mocsa (Hung.)	mô'-chŏ	mo'-cho
Modane (Fr.)	mô-dän'	mo-dahn'
Model, Walter von (Ger. polit.)	mō'-dəl, väl'-tər fən	moh'-duhl, vahl'-tuhr fuhn
Modena (It.)	mô'-dĕ-nä	mo'-deh-nah
Moder (Fr., riv.)	*Fr.* mô-dĕr'	mo-dehr'
	Ger. mō'-dər	moh'-duhr
Modica (Sicily)	mô'-dĕ-kä	mo'-dee-kah
Modion (Crete)	mô'-dē(-ôn)	mo'-dee(-on)
Modlin (Pol.)	mô'-dlĭn	mo'-dlin
Russian *Novogeorgievsk*, nô'-vô-gĕ-ôr'-gĭ-yĕfsk [no'-vo-geh-or'-gi-yefsk].		
Modzelewski, Zygmunt (Pol. polit.)	mô-jĕ-lĕf'-skĭ, zĭg'-mŏŏnt	mo-jeh-lef'-ski, zig'-munt
Moeara (Br. Borneo) See *Muara*.		
Moearatewa or Muratewa (NEI, Borneo)	mwä'-rä-tĕ'-wä	mwah'-rah-teh'-wah
Moedling or Mödling (Austria)	mûd'-lĭng	mœd'-ling
Moedrath or Mödrath (Ger.)	mût'-rät	mœt'-raht

Moeen *or* Möen (Den., isl.)   mŭ'-ən   mœ'-uhn

Moehlen (Ger.)   mŭ'-lən   mœ'-luhn

Moehne (Ger., dam)   mŭ'-nə   mœ'-nuh

Moelfre (Wales)   moil'-vrā   moil'-vray

Moen (NEI, Kai)   mōōn'   moon'

Moen (Oc., Truk)   mô'-ĕn   mo'-en

Moena *or* Muna (NEI, Celebes)   mōō'-nä   moo'-nah

Moerdijk (Neth.)   mōōr-dīk'   moor-daik'

Moergestel (Neth.)   mōōr-k(h)ĕs'-təl   moor-k(h)es'-tuhl

Moerkerke (Belg.)   mōōr'-kĕr-kə   moor'-kehr-kuh

Moers (Ger.)   mûrs'   mœrs'

Moesia (ancient Danubian country)   mē'-shə   mee'-shuh

Moeskroen (Belg.)   *Flem.* mōōs'-krōōn   moos'-kroon
French *Mouscron*, q.v.

Moesvatn (Nor., dam)   mûs'-vätn   mœs'-vahtn

Mogadishu (Somaliland)   mô-gə-dē'-shōō   mo-guh-dee'-shoo
Italian *Mogadiscio*, mô-gä-dē'-shô [mo-go-dee'-sho].

Mogador (Mor.)   mô-gä-dôr'   mo-gah-dor'
There is also an English pronunciation, mŏg'-ə-dôr' [mog'-uh-dor'].

Mogaung (Burma)   mō'-goung'   moh'-gaung'

Mogelnitsa (Pol.)   See *Mogielnica*.

Moghrane (Tun.)   mŭg-răn'   muhg-ran'

Mogielnica (Pol.)   mô-gyĕl-nē'-tsä   mo-gyel-nee'-tsah
Russian *Mogelnitsa*, mŏ-gĕl'(y)-nĭ-tsä [mo-gel'(y)-ni-tsah].

Mogila (Yugosl.)   mô'-gĭ-lä   mo'-gi-lah

Mogilëv (Rus.)   mô-gĭ-lyôf'   mo-gi-lyof'
The name is Anglicized mô'-gĭ-lĕf' [moh'-gi-lef'].

Mogilëv Podolski (Rus.)   mô-gĭ-lyôf' pŏ-dôl'(y)-skĭ   mo-gi-lyof' po-dol'(y)-ski

Mogilyani (Pol.)   See *Mohylany*.

Mogollon (Ariz.)   mô-gô-yôn'   mo-go-yon'

Mogzon (Rus.)   mŏg-zôn'   mog-zon'

Mohács (Hung.)   mô'-häch   mo'-hahch

Mohammed   *Eng.* mə-hăm'-ĭd   muh-ham'-id
Also called *Mahomed*, -*t*, mə-hŏm'-ĕd, -ĭt [muh-hom'-ed, -it]. Arabic mōō-häm'-mĕd [mu-hahm'-med] *and* mōō-häm'-məd [mu-ham'-muhd].

Mohammed Hussein Heikal Pasha (Egypt. polit.)   mōō-häm'-mĕd hōōs-sān' hā'-käl pä'-shä   mu-hahm'-med hus-sayn' hay'-kahl pah'-shah

Mohammed Kabir Ludin (Afghan polit.)   mōō-häm'-mĕd kə-bēr' lōō-dēn'   mu-hahm'-med kuh-beer' lu-deen'

Mohammed Zahir Shah (King of Afghanistan)	mŏŏ-häm′-mĕd zä′-hər shä′	mu-hahm′-med zah′-huhr shah′
Mohammedia (Tun.)	mŏŏ-häm-mə-dē′-ä	mu-hahm-muh-dee′-ah
Mohammereh (Iran)	mŏŏ-häm′-mə-rə	mu-hahm′-muh-ruh

Now called *Khurramshahr*, q.v.

Möhlen (Ger.)	mû′-lən	mœ′-luhn
Möhne (Ger., dam)	mû′-nə	mœ′-nuh
Mohrungen (Ger.)	mō′-rŏŏng-ən	moh′-rung-uhn
Mohylany (Pol.)	mô-hĭ-lä′-nĭ	mo-hi-lah′-ni

Russian *Mogilyani*, mŏ-gĭ-lyä′-nĭ [mo-gi-lyah′-ni].

Moi (Nor.)	mō′-ē	moh′-ee
Moircy (Belg.)	mwär-sē′	mwahr-see′
Moires (Crete)	mē′-rĕs	mee′-res
Mõisaküla (Est.)	mûĭ′-sä-kü′-lä	muh(y)′-sah-kü-lah

Russian *Moisekul*, q.v.

Moisdon (Fr.)	mwä-dôN′	mwah-doN′
Moisekul (Est.)	*Rus.* moi′-zĕ-kyōōl(y)	moi′-zeh-kyool(y)

Estonian *Mõisaküla*, q.v.

Mojan (Balkan mt.)	mô′-yän	mo′-yahn
Mojave Desert (Calif.)	mô-hä′-vĕ	mo-hah′-veh
Moji (Jap.)	mô′-jē	mo′-jee
Mokmer (NEI, Biak)	môk′-mĕr	mok′-mehr
Mokotów (Pol., airport)	mô-kô′-tŏŏf	mo-ko′-tuf
Mokpalin (Burma)	môk′-pə-lĭn′	mohk′-puh-lin′
Mokpo (Korea)	môk-pô	mok-po
Mokranja (Yugosl.)	mô′-krä-nyä	mo′-krah-nyah
Mokrin (Yugosl.)	mô′-krĭn	mo′-krin
Mokshany (Rus.)	mŏk-shän′-ĭ	mok-shahn′-i
Mol (Yugosl.)	môl′	mawl′
Molakobi (Oc., Solomons)	mô-lä-kô′-bē	mo-lah-ko′-bee
Moldau (Cz., riv.)	*Ger.* môl′-dou	mol′-dau

Czech *Vltava*, q.v.

Moldava (Cz.)	môl′-dä-vä	mol′-dah-vah
Moldavia (Rum.)	*Eng.* mŏl-dā′-vyə	mol-day′-vyuh

Rumanian *Moldova*, q.v.

Molde (Nor.)	môl′-də *or* môl′-lə	mol′-duh *or* mol′-luh
Moldova (Rum.)	môl-dô′-vä	mol-do′-vah

English *Moldavia*, q.v.

Molenbeek (Belg.)	mō′-lən-bāk	moh′-luhn-bayk
Moletta (It.)	mô-lĕt′-tä	mo-let′-tah

Molina, Rafael Leonidas Trujillo (Dom. polit.) See *Trujillo Molina*.

Moline (Ill.)	mō-lēn′	moh-leen′

| Molino (It.) | mô-lē′-nô | mo-lee′-no |
| Molodechno (Pol. >Rus.) | mô-lô-dĕch′-nô | mo-lo-dech′-no |

Polish spelling *Mołodeczno.*

Mologa (Rus., riv.)	mô-lô′-gä	mo-lo′-gah
Molokai (Hawaii)	mô-lô-kī′	mo-lo-kai′
Molonta (Yugosl., pen.)	*It.* mô-lôn′-tä	mo-lon′-tah

Serb-Croat *Molunat,* q.v.

| Molotov, Vyacheslav M. | mô′-lŏ-tŏf, vyä-chĕ- | mo′-lo-tof, vyah- |
| (Rus. diplomat) | släf′ | cheh-slahf′ |

Born *Skryabin,* skryä′-bĭn [skryah′-bin].

Molotovo (Rus.)	mô′-lŏ-tŏ-vŏ	mo′-lo-to-vo
Molsheim (Fr.)	*Fr.* môl-zĕm′	mol-zem′
	Ger. môls′-hīm	mols′-haim
Moluccas (NEI)	*Eng.* mŏ-lŭk′-əz	moh-luhk′-uhz
Molunat (Yugosl., pen.)	mô′-lōō-nät	mo′-loo-naht
Molyvos (Gr., Lesbos)	mô′-lē-vôs	mo′-lee-vos
Mombasa (Kenya)	mŏm-bä′-sä	mom-bah′-sah
Momein (Ch., Yünnan)	mô-mān	mo-mayn

Also called *T'êng-ch'ung,* q.v.

| Mommenheim (Fr.) | mô-mə-nĕm′ | mo-muh-nem′ |
| Momtchilovgrad (Bulg.) | mŏm-chē′-lŏf-grät | mom-chee′-lof-graht |

Also called *Mastanli,* mä′-stän-lē′ [mah′-stahn-lee′].

| Mon (Est., isl.) | *Rus.* môn′ | mon′ |
| | *Ger.* mōn′ | mohn′ |

Estonian *Muhu,* q.v.

| Monaco (It.) | mô′-nä-kô | mo′-nah-ko |
| Monaco (principality) | mô′-nä-kô | mo′-nah-ko |

There is no dictionary authority for the American pronunciation accenting the second syllable.

| Monasterace (It.) | mô-nä-stĕ-rä′-chĕ | mo-nah-steh-rah′-cheh |
| Monastir (Yugosl.) | *Turk.* mô-nä-stēr′ | mo-nah-steer′ |

Yugoslav *Bitolj,* q.v. Greek *Monastéri(on),* mô-nä-stē′-rē(-ôn) [mo-nah-stee′-ree(-on)].

Moncado (P.I.)	môn-kä′-dô	mon-kah′-do
Moncay (Indo-Ch.)	môn-kī′	mon-kai′
Monceau sur Sambre (Belg.)	môN-sō sür säN′br	moN-soh sür sahN′ br
Monck (Eng. name)	mŭnk′	muhnk′
Moncoutant (Fr.)	môN-kōō-täN′	moN-koo-tahN′
Moncton (Can.)	mŭnk′-tən	muhnk′-tuhn
mond	mônt′	mont′

An element, meaning *river mouth,* in Dutch place names.

| Mondego (Port., riv.) | môn-dĕ′-gŏ͞o | mon-deh′-gu |
| Mondeville (Fr.) | môNd-vēl′ | moNd-veel′ |

Mondidier (Fr.)	môN-dē-dyě′	moN-dee-dyeh′
Mondoubleau (Fr.)	môN-dōō-blō′	moN-doo-bloh′
Mondragone (It.)	môn-drä-gô′-ně	mon-drah-go′-neh
Mondriaan, Piet (Du. painter)	môn′-drĭ-än, pēt′	mon′-dri-ahn, peet′
Also spelled *Mondriaan*.		
Monemvasia (Gr.)	mô-něm-vä-sē′-ä	mo-nem-vah-see′-ah
Monfestino (It.)	môn-fěs-tē′-nô	mon-fes-tee′-no
monger	mŭng′-gər	muhng′-guhr
Mongmau (Burma)	mŏng′-mou′	mong′-mau′
Mongolia	*Eng.* mŏn-gō′-lĭ-ə	mon-goh′-li-uh
Mongsit (Burma)	mŏng′-sĭt′	mong′-sit′
Mongkut (former King of Siam)	mông′-gōŏt	mong′-gut
Monheim (Ger.)	môn′-hĭm	mon′-haim
Moniz, Júlio Botelho (Port. polit.) See *Botelho Moniz*.		
Monkiewicz, B. J. (U.S. representative)	mŭn′-kě-vēts′	muhn′-keh-veets′
Monnai (Fr.)	mô-ně′	mo-neh′
Monnet, Jean (Fr. polit.)	môn-ně′, zhäN′	mon-neh′, zhahN′
Monnikendam (Neth.)	môn′-ĭ-kən-däm′	mon′-i-kuhn-dahm′
Mono (Oc., Solomons)	mô′-nô	mo′-no
Monongahela (U.S., riv.)	mō-nŏng′-gə-hē′-lə	moh-nong′-guh-hee′-luh
Monopoli (It.)	mô-nô′-pô-lē	mo-no′-po-lee
Monor (Hung.)	mô′-nôr	mo′-nor
Monoštor (Yugosl.)	mô′-nô-shtôr	mo′-no-shtor
Monroney, Mike (U.S. representative)	mən-rō′-nĭ	muhn-roh′-ni
Monrovia (Liberia)	mən-rō′-vĭ-ə	muhn-roh′-vi-uh
Mons (Belg.)	*Eng.* mŏnz′	monz′
	Fr. môNs′	moNs′
Monsalvat (in Wagner's "Parsifal") Cf. *Montserrat*.	môn-zäl-vät′	mon-zahl-vaht′
Monschau (Ger.)	mōn′-shou	mohn′-shau
Mons en Baroeul (Fr.)	môN säN bä-rûl′	moN sahN bah-rœl′
Monserrato (It.)	môn-sěr-rä′-tô	mon-sehr-rah′-to
Monster (Neth.)	môn′-stər	mon′-stuhr
Montabaur (Ger.)	môn′-tä-bour	mon′-tah-baur
Montagnana Togliatti, Rita (It. polit.)	môn-tä-nyä′-nä tô-lyät′-tē, rē′-tä	mon-tah-nyah′-nah to-lyaht′-tee, ree′-tah
Montaigu (Fr.)	*Eng.* mŏn′-tə-gyōō	mon′-tuh-gyoo
	Fr. môN-tě-gü′	moN-teh-gü′

Montalbán (P.I.)	môn-täl-bän′	mon-tahl-bahn′
Montalbano (It.)	môn-täl-bä′-nô	mon-tahl-bah′-no
Montalegre (Port.)	môn-tə-lĕ′-grə	mon-tuh-leh′-gruh
Montana (U.S.)	mŏn-tăn′-ə	mon-tan′-uh
Mont Argis (Fr.)	môN tär-zhē′	moN tahr-zhee′
Montauban (Fr.)	môN-tō-bäN′	moN-toh-bahN′
Montbéliard (Fr.)	môN-bĕ-lyär′	moN-beh-lyahr′
Montbertrand (Fr.)	môN-bĕr-träN′	moN-behr-trahN′
Mont Castre, Forêt de (Fr.)	môN käs′tr, fô-rĕ də	moN kahs′tr, fo-re duh
Montceaux (Fr.)	môN-sō′	moN-soh′
Mont Cenis (Fr., It., mt.)	môN sə-nē′	moN suh-nee′
Montchanin les Mines (Fr.)	môN-shä-năN lĕ mēn′	moN-shah-naN leh meen′
Montcornet (Fr.)	môN-kôr-nĕ′	moN-kor-neh′
Mont de Marsan (Fr.)	môN də mär-säN′	moN duh mahr-sahN′
monte	môn′-tĕ	mon′-teh

An element, meaning *mount*, in Italian place names. It may be necessary to look up the other part of the name.

Montebourg (Fr.)	môNt-bo͞or′	moNt-boor′
Monte Carlo (Mon.)	*Eng.* mŏn′-tĭ kär′-lō	mon′-ti kahr′-loh
	It. môn′-tĕ kär′-lô	mon′-teh kahr′-lo
Montecilfone (It.)	môn-tĕ-chēl-fô′-nĕ	mon-teh-cheel-fo′-neh
Montego (Jamaica, bay)	*Eng.* mŏn-tē′-gō	mon-tee′-goh
Monteiro, Goes (Braz. general) See *Goes Monteiro*.		
Montelanico (It.)	môn-tĕ-lä′-nē-kô	mon-teh-lah′-nee-ko
Montélimar (Fr.)	môN-tĕ-lē-mär′	moN-teh-lee-mahr′
Montelungo (It.)	môn-tĕ-lo͞ong′-gô	mon-teh-loong′-go
Montenegro (Yugosl.)	*Eng.* mŏn′-tĭ-nē′-grô	mon′-ti-nee′-gro
	It. môn′-tĕ-nĕ′-grô	mon′-teh-neh′-gro

Serb-Croat *Crna Gora*, q.v.

Monte Pedral (Port.)	môn′-tĭ pĭ-dräl′	mon′-ti pi-drahl′
Montepescali (It.)	môn′-tĕ-pĕ-skä′-lē	mon′-teh-peh-skah′-lee
Montereau Faut Yonne (Fr.)	môNt-rō fō yôn′	moNt-roh foh yon′
Monterrey (Calif., Mex.)	*Eng.* mŏn-tə-rā′	mon-tuh-ray′
	Sp. môn-tĕ-rā′	mon-teh-ray′
Monte San Biagio (It.)	môn′-tĕ sän byä′-jô	mon′-teh sahn byah′-jo
Montevideo (Urug.)	*Eng.* mŏn′-tĭ-vĭd′-ĭ-ō	mon′-ti-vid′-i-oh
	Sp. môn′-tĕ-vē-dĕ′-ô	mon′-teh-vee-deh′-o
Montfaucon (Fr.)	môN-fō-kôN′	moN-foh-koN′

Montferrat (Fr.)	môN-fĕ-rä′	moN-feh-rah′
Montfoort (Neth.)	mônt′-fōrt	mont′-fohrt
Montfort (Fr.)	môN-fôr′	moN-for′
Montgomery	mən(t)-gŭm′-(ə-)rĭ	muhn(t)-guhm′-(uh-)ri
	or mŏn(t)-gŭm′-(ə-)rĭ	mon(t)-guhm′-(uh-)ri

In America and England mən-gŭm′-rĭ [muhn-guhm′-ri] is both old-
fashioned genteel and popular. As the most idiomatic pronunciation
it is probably preferable for radio, although pronunciations according
to the spelling are as common.

Monthermé (Fr.)	môN-tĕr-mĕ′	moN-tehr-meh′
Monticelli (It.)	môn-tē-chĕl′-lē	mon-tee-chel′-lee
Monticello (N.Y., Ark.,	mŏn′-tĭ-sĕl′-ō	mon′-ti-sel′-oh
etc.)	*or* mŏn′-tə-sĕl′-ə	mon′-tuh-sel′-uh

Jefferson's home near Charlottesville, Va., is so pronounced, the
pronunciation mŏn′-tĭ-chĕl′-ō [mon′-ti-chel′-oh] being rare locally.

Montivilliers (Fr.)	môN-tē-vē-yĕ′	moN-tee-vee-yeh′
Montlhéry (Fr.)	môN-lĕ-rē′	moN-leh-ree′
Montluçon (Fr.)	môN-lü-sôN′	moN-lü-soN′
Montmartre (Fr., Paris)	môN-mär′tr	moN-mahr′tr
Montmédy (Fr.)	môN-mĕ-dē′	moN-meh-dee′
Montmirail (Fr.)	môN-mē-rī′	moN-mee-rai′
Montmorency (Fr.)	*Eng.* mŏnt′-mə-rĕn′-sĭ	mont′-muh-ren′-si
	Fr. môN-mô-räN-sē′	moN-mo-rahN-see′
Montorio (It.)	môn-tô′-ryô	mon-to′-ryo
Montparnasse (Fr., Paris)	môN-pär-näs′	moN-pahr-nahs′
Montpelier (Vt.)	mŏnt-pē′-lyər	mont-pee′-lyuhr
Montpellier (Fr.)	môN-pĕ-lyĕ′	moN-peh-lyeh′
Montrabot (Fr.)	môN-trä-bō′	moN-trah-boh′
Montreal (Can.)	mŏn′-trĭ-ôl′	mon′-tri-awl′

French *Montréal,* môN-rĕ-äl′ [moN-reh-ahl′].

Montreuil (Fr.)	môN-trû′(y)	moN-trœ′(y)
Montreuil Bellay (Fr.)	môN-trû(y) bĕ-lĕ′	moN-trœ(y) beh-leh′
Montreux (Switz.)	môN-trû′	moN-trœ′
Montrevault (Fr.)	môN-trə-vō′	moN-truh-voh′
Montrichard (Fr.)	môN-rē-shär′	moN-ree-shahr′
Montserrat (Sp., mts.	*Eng.* mŏnt-sə-răt′	mont-suh-rat′
and monastery)	*Sp.* mônt-sĕ-rät′	mont-seh-raht′
Montsurs (Fr.)	môN-sür′	moN-sür′
Montvilliers (Fr.)	môN-vē-lyĕ′	moN-vee-lyeh′
Monywa (Burma)	mōn-yo͝o-ä′	mohn-yu-ah′
Mook (Neth.)	mōk′	mohk′
Moordrecht (Neth.)	mōr′-drek(h)t	mohr′-drek(h)t
Moppo (Korea)	môp-pô	mop-po

Morača (Yugosl., riv.)   mô′-rä-chä   mo′-rah-chah

Moradabad (India)   mō-rə-də-băd′   moh-ruh-duh-bad′
                  or mō-rä-dä-bäd′   moh-rah-dah-bahd′

Mora Figueroa, Manuel mô′-rä fē-gĕ-rô′-ä,   mo′-rah fee-geh-ro′-
  (Sp. polit.)   mä-nwĕl′   ah, mah-nwel′

Morãis, Mendes de (Braz. polit.) See *Mendes de Morãis.*

Morava (Europ. riv.)   *Cz.* mô′-rä-vä   mo′-rah-vah
  German *March,* märk(h)′ [mahrk(h)′]. Hungarian *Morva,* môr′-vŏ
  [mor′-vo].

Morava (Yugosl., riv.)   mô′-rä′-vä   mo′-rah′-vah

Moravia (Cz., prov.)   *Eng.* mō-rā′-vĭ-ə   moh-ray′-vi-uh
  Czech *Morava,* mô′-rä-vä [mo′-rah-vah]. German *Mähren,* mĕ′-rən
  [meh′-ruhn].

Moravica (Yugosl., riv.) mô′-rä′-vĭ-tsä   mo′-rah′-vi-tsah

Moravice, Staro   mô′-rä′-vĭ-tsĕ,   mo′-rah′-vi-tseh,
  (Yugosl.)   stä′-rô   stah′-ro

Moravská, -é, -ý (Cz.)   mô′-räf-skä, -ĕ, -ĭ   mo′-rahf-skah, -eh, -i
  A common element, meaning *Moravian,* in Czech place names. It may
  be necessary to look up the other part of the name.

Moravska (Yugosl.)   mô′-räv′-skä   mo′-rahv′-skah

Moravská Ostrava (Cz.) mô′-räf-skä   mo′-rahf-skah
                 ô′-strä-vä   o′-strah-vah
  German *Mährisch Ostrau,* mĕ′-rĭsh ôs′-trou [meh′-rish os′-trau].

Morawski, Edward Osubka (Pol. polit.) See *Osubka Morawski*

Moray (Scot.)   mŭr′-ĭ   muhr′-i

Morbihan (Fr., dept.)   môr-bē-äN′   mor-bee-ahN′

Mordelles (Fr.)   môr-dĕl′   mor-del′

Morea (Gr.)   *Eng.* mō-rē′-ə   moh-ree′-uh
  Greek *Moreas,* mô-rĕ′-äs [mo-reh′-ahs] *or* môr-yäs′ [mor-yahs′]. See
  Peloponnesos.

Moree (Austral.)   mō-rē′   moh-ree′

Moreel, Ben (Am. admiral) mô-rēl′   mo-reel′

Morelia (Mex.)   mô-rĕ′-lyä   mo-reh′-lyah

Morelos (Mex.)   mô-rĕ′-lôs   mo-reh′-los

Moret (Fr.)   mô-rĕ′   mo-reh′

Moreton (Austral., bay) môrt′n   mort′n

Moreuil (Fr.)   mô-rû′(y)   mo-rœ′(y)

Morge, la (Fr., riv.)   môrzh′, lä   morzh′, lah

Morgenstierne, Wilhelm môr′-gən-styĕr′-nə, mor′-guhn-styehr′-
  (Nor. diplomat)   vĭl′-hĕlm   nuh, vil′-helm

Morgenthau, Henry, Jr. môr′-gən-thô   mor′-guhn-thaw
  (Am. polit.)

Morgenthau, Henry, Sr. môr′-gən-tou   mor′-guhn-tau
  (Am. diplomat)

Morgon Tidningen (Sw. newspaper)	môr'-gôn tēd'-nĭng-ən	mor'-gon teed'-ning-uhn
Morhange (Fr.)	môr-äNzh'	mor-ahNzh'
Moriches (New York)	mô-rĭch'-ĭz	mo-rich'-iz
Moricone (It.)	mô-rē-kô'-nĕ	mo-ree-ko'-neh
Morin (Fr.)	mô-răN'	mo-raN'
Morínigo, Higinio (Para. polit.)	mô-rē'-nē-gô, ē-hē'-nyô	mo-ree'-nee-go, ee-hee'-nyo
Morinj (Yugosl.)	mô'-rĭn(y)	mo'-rin(y)
Morioka (Jap.)	mô-rē'-ô-kä	mo-ree'-o-kah
Moriones (P.I.)	mô-rē-ô'-nĕs	mo-ree-o'-nes
Morlacca Channel (Yugosl.)	*Eng.* môr-lăk'-ə *It.* môr-läk'-kä	mor-lak'-uh mor-lahk'-kah
Serb-Croat *Planinski Kanal,* q.v.		
Morlaix (Fr.)	môr-lĕ'	mor-leh'
Morlupo (It.)	môr-lōō'-pô	mor-loo'-po
Mormanno (It.)	môr-män'-nô	mor-mahn'-no
Mormugão (Port. India)	môr-mōō-gouN'	mor-moo-gauN'
Also called *Marmagao,* mär-mə-gou' [mahr-muh-gau'], and *Marmagoa,* mär-mə-gō'-ə [mahr-muh-goh'-uh].		
Morobe (N.E. New Guinea)	mô-rô'-bĕ	mo-ro'-beh
Morocco (Afr.)	mə-rŏk'-ō	muh-rok'-oh
French *Maroc,* mä-rôk' [mah-rok']. See *Marrakech.*		
Morombe (Madag.)	mô-rôm-bĕ'	mo-rom-beh'
Moro Palawan (P.I.)	mô'-rô pä-lä'-wän	mo'-ro pah-lah'-wahn
Morotai (NEI)	mô-rô-tī'	mo-ro-tai'
Morova planina (Alb., mts.)	mô'-rô-vä plä'-nē'-nä	mo'-ro-vah plah'-nee'-nah
Morozov, Alexandr P. (Rus. economist)	mŏ-rô'-zôf, ä-lĕ-ksän'-dər	mo-ro'-zof, ah-leh-ksahn'-duhr
Morozovskaya (Rus.)	mŏ-rô'-zôf-skä-yä	mo-ro'-zof-skah-yah
Mörs (Ger.)	mûrs'	mœrs'
Morshansk (Rus.)	môr-shänsk'	mor-shahnsk'
Morskie Oko (Pol., lake)	môr'-skyĕ ô'-kô	mor'-skyeh o'-ko
German *Fischsee,* q.v.		
Morsott (Alg.)	mŏr-sŏt'	mor-sot'
Mortagne (Fr.)	môr-tän'(y)	mor-tahn'(y)
Mortain (Fr.)	môr-tăN'	mor-taN'
Mortcerf (Fr.)	môr-sĕr'	mor-sehr'
Morteaux (Fr.)	môr-tō'	mor-toh'
Morvillars (Fr.)	môr-vē-yär'	mor-vee-yahr'
Mosalsk (Rus.)	mŏ-sälsk'	mo-sahlsk'

Moscow (Idaho) mŏs'-kō mos'-koh
According to John Gunther, *Inside U.S.A.*, p. 114, named for an
Indian tribe, the Masco.

Moscow (Rus.) mŏs'-kō mos'-koh
This is the pronunciation usually recorded in dictionaries, and radio
speakers should therefore adopt it as probably the most convenient.
However, a spelling pronunciation, mŏs'-kou [mos'-kau], is very common in the United States and deserves dictionary recognition. The
Russian is *Moskva*, pronounced mŏs-kvä' [mos-kvah']. English derivatives are *Muscovy* and *Muscovite*—mŭs'-kō-vĭ [muhs'-koh-vi] and
mŭs'-kō-vīt [muhs'-koh-vait].

Moscow (Pa.) mŏs'-kou mos'-kau
Moselle (Fr., Ger., riv.) mô-zĕl' mo-zel'
German *Mosel*, mō'-zəl [moh'-zuhl].

Mosher, Ira mō'-zhər moh'-zhuhr
(Am. executive)

Mosjoeen *or* Mosjöen mō'-shû-ən moh'-shœ-uhn
(Nor.)

Moskenes (Nor., isl.) mŏŏs'-kĕ-nĕs mus'-keh-nes
Moskva (Rus., riv.) mŏs-kvä' mos-kvah'
Moslem mŏz'-ləm moz'-luhm
  or mŏs'-ləm *or* mos'-luhm
Also *Muslem, -lim*, mŭz'-ləm, -lĭm [muhz'-luhm, -lim].

Moson (Hung.) mō'-shôn mo'-shon
Mosori (Hung.) mō'-shô-rĭ mo'-sho-rih
Moss (Nor.) mŏs' mos'
Mossadegh, F. (Iran. polit.) See *Musaddik*.

Most (Cz.) môst' most'
German *Brüx*, brüks' [brüks'].

Mostaganem (Alg.) môs-tä-gä-nĕm' mos-tah-gah-nem'
Moštanica (Yugosl.) mô'-shtä'-nĭ-tsä mo'-shtah'-ni-tsah
Mostar (Yugosl.) mô'-stär mo'-stahr
Mosul (Iraq) mō'-səl moh'-suhl
Arabic *Al Mūsil*.

Mösvatn (Nor., dam) mûs'-vätn mœs'-vahtn
Mothe Achard, la (Fr.) môt ä-shär', lä mot ah-shahr', lah
Motovski Zaliv (Rus.) mô-tôf'-skĭ zä-lēf' mo-tof'-ski zah-leef'
Motta e Silva, Álvaro mô'-tĭ sēl'-və, mo'-ti seel'-vuh,
  Alberto da äl'-və-rŏŏ ahl'-vuh-ru
  (Braz. diplomat) äl-bĕr'-tŏŏ də ahl-behr'-tu duh
Motteville (Fr.) môt-vēl' mot-veel'
Mouen (Fr.) mwäN' mwahN'
Mouliana (Crete) mŏŏ-lyä-nä' moo-lyah-nah'
Moulins (Fr.) mŏŏ-lăN' moo-laN'

Moulmein (Burma)   mо̄о̆l-mān′   mul-mayn′
  The first syllable is also pronounced *môl-* and *mōl-*. The native pro-
nunciation is approximately mô′-lə-myīng′ [maw′-luh-myaing′].
Moult (Fr.)   mо̄о̄lt′   moolt′
Mount Carmel (Pal., Ill.,) kär′-məl   kahr′-muhl
Mount Desert (Me.)   mount dĕ-zûrt′   maunt dĕh-zuhrt′
                 or dĕz′-ərt   *or* dez′-uhrt
Mount Etna (Sicily)   *Eng.* ĕt′-nə   et′-nuh
Mount Rainier (Wash.)   rā-nĭr′   ray-nihr′
                 or rā′-nĭr   ray′-nihr
  Also called Mount *Tacoma,* tə-kō′-mə [tuh-koh′-muh].
Mouscron (Belg.)   mо̄о̄-skrôN′   moo-skroN′
  Flemish *Moeskroen,* q.v.
Moustier (Belg.)   mо̄о̄s-tyĕ′   moos-tyeh′
Moustiers Ste. Marie   mо̄о̄-tyĕ săNt mä-rē′ moo-tyeh saNt
  (Fr.)   mah-ree′
Moûtiers (Fr.)   mо̄о̄-tyĕ′   moo-tyeh′
Mouy (Fr.)   mwē′   mwee′
Mouzaki (Gr.)   mо̄о̄-zä′-kē   moo-zah′-kee
Moxee City (Wash.)   mŏk-sē′ sĭt′-ĭ   mok-see′ sit′-i
Moyenvic (Fr.)   mwä-yăN-vēk′   mwah-yaN-veek′
Mozaffar Firuz   mô-zä′-fär fē-rо̄о̄z′ mo-zah′-fahr fee-
  (Iran. polit.)   rooz′
Mozambique (Afr.)   mō′-zəm-bēk′   moh′-zuhm-beek′
  Portuguese *Moçambique,* mô′-səm-bē′-kĭ [mo′-suhm-bee′-ki].
Mozart, Wolfgang   mô′-tsärt, vôlf′-gäng mo′-tsahrt, volf′-
  Amadeus (Austrian   ä-mä-dä′-о̄о̆s   gahng ah-mah-
  musician)   day′-us
Mozdok (Rus.)   mŏz-dŏk′   moz-dok′
Mozgovo (Yugosl.)   mô̆z′-gô-vô   moz′-go-vo
Mozhaisk (Rus.)   mô-zhĭsk′   mo-zhaisk′
Mozirje (Yugosl.)   mô′-zĭr-yĕ   mo′-zihr-yeh
Mozyr (Rus.)   mô-zwēr′   mo-zweer′
Mramorak (Yugosl.)   mrä′-mô-räk   mrah′-mo-rahk
Mrčajevci (Yugosl.)   mər′-chä′-yĕv-tsĭ muhr′-chah′-yev-tsi
Mrkonjićgrad (Yugosl.) mər′-kô′-nyĭch-gräd muhr′-ko′-nyich-
                                     grahd
Mrsać (Yugosl.)   mər′-säch   muhr′-sahch
Mruk, Joseph   mə-rŭk′   muh-ruhk′
  (U.S. representative)
Mrzen (Yugosl.)   mər′-zĕn   muhr′-zen
Mrzenci (Yugosl.)   mər′-zĕn-tsĭ   muhr′-zen-tsi
Msaken (Tun.)   mə-sä′-kĕn   muh-sa′-ken
Mshchonov (Pol.)   See *Mszczonów.*

Mshinskaya (Rus.)	mshĭn′-skä-yä	mshin′-skah-yah
Msta (Rus., riv.)	mstä′	mstah′
Msus (Libya)	mə-sōōs′	muh-soos′
Mszczonów (Pol.)	mshchô′-nŏŏf	mshcho′-nuf
Russian *Mshchonov,* mshchô′-nŏf [mshcho′-nof].		
Mtsensk (Rus.)	mtsĕnsk′	mtsensk′
Muara (Br. Borneo)	mwä′-rä	mwah′-rah
Muaratewa (NEI, Borneo) See *Moeratewa.*		
Mubo (N.E. New Guinea)	mōō′-bô	moo′-bo
Muckey (Scot. name)	mə-kē′	muh-kee′
Mudaliar, Sir Rama- swami (Indian polit.)	mə-dä′-lyär, rä′-mä-swä′-mē	muh-dah′-lyahr, rah′-mah-swah′- mee
Muelheim (Ger.)	mül′-hĭm	mül′-haim
Muellrose (Ger.)	mül′-rō-zə	mül′-roh-zuh
Muencheberg (Ger.)	mün′-k(h)ə-bĕrk(h)	mün′-k(h)uh- behrk(h)
Muenchen (Ger.) English *Munich,* q.v.	mün′-k(h)ən	mün′-k(h)uhn
Muenchen Gladback (Ger.)	mün′-k(h)ən glät′-bäk(h)	mün′-k(h)uhn glaht′-bahk(h)
muende *or* münde	mün′-də	mün′-duh
An element, meaning *river mouth,* in German place names.		
Muenster (Ger.)	mün′-stər	mün′-stuhr
Muenstereifel (Ger.)	mün′-stər-ĭ′-fəl	mün′-stuhr-ai′-fuhl
Mueritz See (Ger.)	mü′-rĭts zä′	mü′-rits zay′
Mufta (Libya)	mŏŏf′-tä	muf′-tah
mufti	*Eng.* mŭf′-tĭ	muhf′-ti
	Ar. mŏŏf′-tĭ	muf′-ti
Mugil (N. E. New Guinea)	mōō′-gēl	moo′-geel
Muğla (Turk.)	mōō′-lä′	moo′-lah′
Muhlenberg, Frederick A. (U.S. representative)	myōō′-lən-bûrg	myoo′-luhn-buhrg
Muhu(maa) (Est., isl.) Russian and German *Mon,* q.v.	mōō′-hōō(-mä)	moo′-hoo(-mah)
Muiden (Neth.)	mœĭ′-dən	mœi′-duhn
Muir, John (Am. naturalist)	myōōr′	myoor′
Mujeres (Mex., isls.)	mōō-hĕ′-rĕs	moo-heh′-rehs
Muka (Sarawak)	mōō′-kä	moo′-kah
Mukachevo (Cz. >Rus.)	mōō-kä-chĕ′-vŏ *or* mōō-kä-chô′-vŏ	mu-kah-cheh′-vo mu-kah-cho′-vo

Czech spelling *Mukačevo*. Hungarian *Munkacs*, mŏŏng'-käch [mung'-kahch].

Mukden (Manchu., prov., city)	mŏŏk-dĕn *or* mōōk-dĕn	muk-den *or* mook-den

Also called *Fêng-t'ien*, q.v.

Mulat (Yugosl.)	mōō'-lät	moo'-laht

Italian *Melada*, q.v.

mulct, -ed	mŭlkt', mŭlk'-tĭd	muhlkt', muhlk'-tid
Mulde (Ger., riv.)	mōōl'-də	mul'-duh
Mulebbis (Pal.) See *Petah Tiqva*.		
mulga (Australian tree)	mŭl'-gə	muhl'-guh
Mülheim (Ger.)	mül'-hīm	mül'-haim
Mulhouse (Fr.)	mü-lōōz'	mü-looz'

German *Mülhausen*, mül'-hou'-zən [mül'-hau'-zuhn].

Mullingar (Eire)	mŭl-ĭn-gär'	muhl-in-gahr'
Müllrose (Ger.)	mül'-rō-zə	mül'-roh-zuh
Multan (India)	mōōl-tän'	mul-tahn'
Multnomah (Ore.)	mŭlt-nō'-mə	muhlt-noh'-muh
Münch, Charles (Fr. musician)	münsh', shärl'	münsh', shahrl'
Munchar (Tun.)	mōōn-shär'	mun-shahr'
Müncheberg (Ger.)	mün'-k(h)ə-bĕrk(h)	mün'-k(h)uh-behrk(h)
München (Ger.)	mün'-k(h)ən	mün'-k(h)uhn

English *Munich*, q.v.

München Gladbach (Ger.)	mün'-k(h)ən-gläd'-bäk(h)	mün'-k(h)uhn-glahd'-bahk(h)
Muncie (Ind.)	mŭn'-sĭ	muhn'-si
Munda (Oc., Solomons)	mōōn'-dä	moon'-dah
Mundt, Karl (U.S. representative)	mŭnt'	muhnt'
Muni (Afr., riv.)	mōō'-nē	moo'-nee
Munich (Ger.)	*Eng.* myōō'-nĭk	myoo'-nik

German *Muenchen*, q.v.

Munkács (Cz. >Rus.) See *Mukachevo*.

Muñoz (Sp. name)	*Am. Sp.* mōō-nyôs'	moo-nyos'
	Sp. mōō-nyôth'	moo-nyoth'
Muñoz Marín, Luis (P. R. polit.)	mōō-nyôs' mä-rēn', lwēs'	moo-nyos' mah-reen', lwees'
Münster (Ger.)	mün'-stər	mün'-stuhr

To be distinguished from *Munster*, Eire, mŭn'-stər [muhn'-stuhr].

Münstereifel (Ger.)	mün'-stər-ī'-fəl	mün'-stuhr-ai'-fuhl
Muntendam (Neth.)	mûn'-tən-däm'	mœn'-tuhn-dahm'
Muntenia (Rum.) See *Walachia*.		

Muntí, Puló (P.I., isl.)	mōōn-tē′, pōō-lô′	moon-tee′, poo-lo′
Muntinlupa (P.I.)	mōōn-tĭn-lōō′-pä	moon-tin-loo′-pah
Mur (Austria,Yugosl.,riv.)	mōōr′	moor′
Mûr (Fr.)	mür′	mür′
mura	mōō-rä	moo-rah

An element, meaning *village*, in Japanese place names.

Mura (Yugosl., riv.)	mōō′-rä	moo′-rah
Murakami (Jap. name)	mōō-rä′-kä-mē	moo-rah′-kah-mee
Muraszombat (Yugosl.)	See *Murska Sobota*.	
Muraviev, Konstantin	mōō-rä′-vĭ-yĕf,	moo-rah′-vi-yef,
(Bulg. polit.)	kŏn-stän-tēn′	kon-stahn-teen′
Muravyëvo (Lith.)	*Rus.* mōō-rä-vyô′-vŏ	mu-rah-vyo′-vo
Lithuanian *Mažeikiai*, q.v.		
Murcia (Sp.)	*Eng.* mōōr′-shə	mur′-shuh
	Sp. mōōr′-thyä *or*	moor′-thyah *or*
	-syä	-syah
Mureş *or* Mureşul	mōō′-rĕsh *or* mōō′-	mu′-rehsh *or* mu′-
(Rum., Hung., riv.)	rĕ′-shŏŏl	reh-shul
Hungarian *Maros*, mä′-rôsh [mah′-rosh].		
Murg (Ger., riv.)	mŏŏrk(h)′	murk(h)′
Murilo (Oc., Carolines)	mōō-rē-lô′	moo-ree-lo′
Müritz See (Ger.)	mü′-rĭts zä′	mü′-rits zay′
Murmansk (Rus.)	mōōr′-mänsk′	moor′-mahnsk′
Muroc (Calif., airfield)	myōō′-rŏk′	myoo′-rok′
Murom (Rus.)	mōō′-rŏm	moo′-rom
Muroran (Jap.)	mōō-rô′-rän	moo-ro′-rahn
Murro di Porco *or*	mōōr′-rô dē pôr′-kô	moor′-ro dee por′-ko
Porto (Sicily, cape)	*or* pôr′-tô	*or* por′-to
Murska Sobota (Yugosl.)	mōōr′-skä sô′-bô-tä	moor′-skah so′-bo-tah
Hungarian *Muraszombat*, mōō′-rŏ-sôm′-bŏt [mu′-ro-som′-bot]. German		
Olsnitz.		
Murua (Oc.)	mōō′-rōō-ä	moo′-roo-ah
Also called *Woodlark*.		

Murville, Maurice Couve de (Fr. diplomat) See *De Murville*.

Murzuch (Libya)	mōōr′-zōōk	moor′-zook
Also spelled *Murzuq, Murzuk, Mourzouk*.		
Musacchia (Alb.)	*It.* mōō-säk′-kyä	moo-sahk′-kyah
Albanian *Myzeqe*, q.v.		
Musaddik, F.	mōō′-sä′-dēk′	moo′-sah′-deek′
(Iran. polit.)		
Also called Mossadegh, mô′-sä′-dēk′ [mo-sah-deek].		
Muscel (Rum.)	mŏŏs-chĕl′	mus-chel′
Mushu (N.E. New	mōō-shōō′	moo-shoo′
Guinea)		

Musi (NEI)   See *Moesi*.

Muskegon (Mich.)	mŭs-kē'-gən	muhs-kee'-guhn
Muskogee (Okla.)	mŭs-kō'-gĭ	mus-koh'-gi

Muslem, Muslim. See *Moslem*.

Mussau (Oc., New Ireland)	mōōs-sou'	moos-sau'
Mussolini, Benito (It. dictator) See *Duce*.	mōōs-sô-lē'-nē, bĕ-nē'-tô	moos-so-lee'-nee, beh-nee'-to
Mussulman	mŭs'-əl-mən	muhs'-uhl-muhn

Mustafa el Nahas Pasha (Egypt. polit.) See *Nahas Pasha*.

Mustapha Kemal Pasha (Turk. polit.)   See *Kemal Atatürk*.

Mušutište (Yugosl.)	mōō'-shōō'-tĭ-shtĕ	moo'-shoo'-ti-shteh
Mutnica (Yugosl.)	mōōt'-nĭ-tsä	moot'-ni-tsah
Mutupina (Oc., Bougainville)	mōō-tōō-pē'-nä	moo-too-pee'-nah
Muy, le (Fr.)	mwē', lə	mwee', luh

Muzaffer Göker (Turk. diplomat) See *Göker*.

Muzhëll (Alb.)	mōō'-zhəl	moo'-zhuhl

Muzhlli (Alb.)   See *Muzhëll*.

Muzillac (Fr.)	mü-zē-yäk'	mü-zee-yahk'
Myanaung (Burma)	myän-oung'	myahn-aung'
Myebon (Burma)	myĕ-bōn'	myeh-bohn'
Myingyan (Burma)	myĭn'-jän'	myin'-jahn'
Myitkyina (Burma)	myĭt'-chĭ-nä *or* myĭt-chē-nä'	myit'-chi-nah myit-chee-nah'
Myittha (Burma)	myĭt-thä'	myit-thah'
Mykonos (Gr., isl.)	mē'-kô-nô(s)	mee'-ko-no(s)
Mylonas, Alexandros (Gr. polit.)	mē-lô-näs', ä-lĕ'-ksän-drôs	mee-lo-nahs', ah-leh'-ksahn-dros
Myohaung (Burma)	myō-houng'	myoh-haung'
Myrdal (Nor.)	mür'-däl	mür'-dahl
Myrdal, Gunnar (Sw. sociologist)	mür'-däl *or* -dôl, gŭn'-är	mur'-dahl *or* -dôl, gun'-ahr
Anglicized as mĭr'-däl [mihr'-dahl].		
Myrtos (Crete)	mēr'-tôs	meer'-tos
Mysen (Nor.)	müs'n	müs'n
Myślenice (Pol.)	mĭsh-lĕ-nē'-tsĕ	mish-leh-nee'-tseh
Mysore (India)	mĭ-sōr'	mai-sohr'
Mysovaya (Rus.)	mĭ-sŏ-vä'-yä	mi-so-vah'-yah
Mytho (Indo-Ch.)	mē-tô'	mee-taw'
Mytilene (Gr., isl., city)	*Eng.* mĭt'-ĭ-lē'-nĭ *Gr.* mē-tē-lē'-nē	mit'-i-lee'-ni mee-tee-lee'-nee

Also called *Lesbos*, q.v.

Myzeqe (Alb.)	mü-zĕ′-kyĕ	mü-zeh′-kyeh

Italian *Musacchia*, q.v.

Myzeqeja (Alb.) See *Myzeqe*.

Naaldwijk (Neth.)	nält′-wĭk	nahlt′-waik
Naarden (Neth.)	när′-dən	nahr′-duhn
Naba (Burma)	nə-bä′	nuh-bah′
Nabao Grande *and* Chico (P.I., rivs.)	nä-bou′ grän′-dĕ *and* chē′-kô	nah-bau′ grahn′-deh *and* chee′-ko
Nabeul (Tun.)	nä-bûl′	nah-bœl′
Nabeur (Tun.)	nä-bûr′	nah-bœr′
Nablus (Pal.)	nä-blo͞os′	nah-bloos′

nabob (title) See *nawab*.

nacelle	nə-sĕl′	nuh-sel′
Náchod (Cz.)	nä′-hôd	nah′-hod
Nacogdoches (Tex.)	năk′-ə-dō′-chĭz	nak′-uh-doh′-chiz
Nădlac (Rum.)	nəd-läk′	nuhd-lahk′
Nadvoitsy (Rus.)	nä-dvoi′-tsĭ	nah-dvoi′-tsi
Nadvornaya (Pol. > Rus.)	nä-dvôr′-nä-yä	nah-dvor′-nah-yah

Polish *Nadwórna*, nä-dvo͞or′-nä [nah-dvur′-nah].

Nadzab (New Guinea)	näd′-zäb	nahd′-zahb
Nærofjord (Nor.)	när′-û-fyôr	nehr′-œ-fyohr
Næstved (Den.)	nĕst′-vĕ*th*	nest′-ve*th*
Naft Safid (Iran)	năft′ sä-fēd′	naft′ sa-feed′
Nafutan (Oc., Saipan)	nä-fo͞o-tän′	nah-foo-tahn′
Naga (Burma, hills)	nə-gä′	nuh-gah′
Naga (P.I.)	nä′-gä	nah′-gah
Nagai, Ryūtarō (Jap. polit.)	nä′-gä-ē, ryo͞o′-tä-rô	nah′-gah-ee, ryoo′-tah-ro
Nagano (Jap.)	nä-gä′-nô′	nah-gah′-no′

Nagara Patom (Siam) See *Nakhon Phanom*.

Nagara Sawarn (Siam) See *Nakhon Sawan*.

Nagasaki (Jap.)	*Eng.* năg′-ə-säk′-ĭ *Jap.* nä-gä′-sä-kē	nag′-uh-sak′-i nah-gah′-sah-kee
Nagato (Jap. battleship)	nä′-gä-tô	nah′-gah-to
Nagornoe (Rus.)	nä-gôr′-nŏ-yĕ	nah-gor′-no-yeh

Nagorn Sridharmarat (Siam) See *Nakhon Si Thammarat*.

Nagorn Svagara (Siam) See *Nakhon Sawan*.

Nagoya (Jap.)	nä′-gô-yä	nah′-go-yah
Nagpartían (P.I.)	näg-pär-tē′-än	nahg-pahr-tee′-ahn
Nagpur (India)	năg-po͞or′	nag-pur′
nagy (Hung.)	nŏd′(y) *or* nŏt′(y)	nod′(y) *or* not′(y)

An element, meaning *great* or *large*, in Hungarian place names. It may be necessary to look up the other part of the name. *Nagy* should be pronounced as one syllable approaching nŏj′ or nŏch′.

Nagy, Costa   nä′-gĭ, kô′-stä   nah′-gi, ko′-stah
  (Yugosl. polit.)
Probably the same name as Hungarian *Nagy* but pronounced as Slavic.

Nagy, Ferenc (Hung.   nŏd′(y), fĕ′-rĕnts   nod′(y), feh′-rents
  polit.)   *or Eng.* nŏj′   noj′
Nagybánya (Rum.)   See *Baia Mare.*
Nagybecskerek (Yugosl.)   See *Bečkerek, Veliki.*
Nagykanizsa (Hung.)   nŏt′(y)-kŏ′-nĭ-zhŏ   not′(y)-ko′-ni-zho
Nagykároly (Rum.)   See *Carei.*
Nagykikinda (Yugosl.)   See *Kikinda, Velika.*
Nagykőrös (Hung.)   nŏt′(y)-kû′-rûsh   not′(y)-kœ′-rœsh
Nagyszalonta (Rum.)   See *Salonta.*
Nagyszeben (Rum.)   See *Sibiu.*
Nagyvárad (Rum.)   See *Oradea.*
Nahas Pasha, Mustafa el   nä-häs′ pä′-shä,   nah-hahs′ pah′-shah,
  (Egypt. polit.)   mŏŏs′-tä-fä ĕn   mus′-tah-fah en
Nahe (Ger., riv.)   nä′-ə   nah′-uh
nahr   när′   nahr′
  An element, meaning *river*, in Arabic place names.
Nahuatl   nä′-wätl   nah′-wahtl
  The language of the Aztecs.
nai   nī′   nai′
  A Siamese honorific comparable to English *mister.* Look up the other part of the name.
Naic *or* Naig (P.I.)   nīk′ *or* nīg′   naik′ *or* naig′
Naidu, Sarojini   nī′-dŏŏ, sə-rô′-jĭ-nē   nai′-du, suh-ro′-ji-
  (Indian polit.)   nee
  Also called *Sarojini Nayadu,* nä′-yə-dŏŏ [nah′-yuh-du].
Naig (P.I.) See *Naic.*
Naim Antaki Bey   nä′-ĭm än′-tä-kĭ bā′   nah′-im ahn′-tah-ki
  (Syrian polit.)   bay′
Nairobi (Kenya)   nī-rō′-bĭ   nai-roh′-bi
Naistenjärvi (Fin. >Rus.)   nīs′-tĕn-yär-vĭ   nais′-ten-yehr-vi
  Russian *Naistenyarvi.*
Nájera, Francisco Castillo (Mex. diplomat) See *Castillo Nájera.*
Najjada   nəj-jăd′-ə   nuhj-jad′-uh
  An Arab political party in Palestine.
Nakajima (Jap., zaibatsu) nä-kä′-jē′-mä′   nah-kah′-jee′-mah′
Nakano, Seigo (Jap.   nä-kä′-nô′, sä′-gô   nah-kah′-no′, say′-go
  polit.)

Nakhichevan (Rus.)	nä-hĭ-chĕ-vän′(y)	nah-hi-cheh-vahn′(y)
Nakhon Phanom (Siam)	nə-kôn′ pə-nōm′	nuh-kon′ puh-nohm′
Nakhon Sawan (Siam)	nə-kôn′ sə-wän′	nuh-kon′ suh-wahn′
Nakhon Si Thammarat (Siam)	nə-kôn′ sē′ tŭm-mə-rät′	nuh-kon′ see′ tuhm-muh-raht′
Nakło (Pol.)	nä′-klô	nah′-klo
Nakta (Tun.)	näk′-tä	nahk′-tah
Nalchik (Rus.)	näl′(y)-chĭk	nahl′(y)-chik
Nalut (Libya)	nä-lōōt′	nah-loot′
Nambara, Shigeru (Jap. polit.)	näm′-bä-rä, shē-gĕ′-rōō	nahm′-bah-rah, shee-geh′-roo
Namdalen (Nor.)	näm′-dä-lən	nahm′-dah-luhn
Namdinh (Indo-Ch.)	näm-dĭn′	nahm-din′
Namlea (NEI, Boeroe)	näm′-lĕ-ä	nahm′-leh-ah
Namoluk (Oc., Carolines)	nä′-mô-lōōk	nah′-mo-look
Namonuito (Oc., Carolines)	nä-mô-nōō-ē′-tô	nah-mo-noo-ee′-to
Japanese *Ororu Shotō*, q.v.		
Namorik (Oc., Marshalls)	nä′-mô-rēk	nah′-mo-reek
Nampa (Idaho)	năm′-pə	nam′-puh
Nampicúan (P.I.)	näm-pē-kōō′-än	nahm-pee-koo′-ahn
Namslau (Ger. >Pol.)	näms′-lou	nahms′-lau
Polish *Namysłów*, nä-mĭ′-slōōf [nah-mi′-sluf].		
Namsos (Nor.)	näm′-sōs	nahm′-sohs
Nam-t'ing (Ch., Yünnan)	näm-tĭng	nahm-ting
Namtu (Burma)	nəm-tōō′	nuhm-too′
Namu (Oc., Marshalls)	nä′-mōō	nah′-moo
Namur (Belg.)	*Eng.* nä-mōōr′	nah-moor′
	Fr. nä-mür′	nah-mür′
Namur (Oc., Kwajalein)	nä′-mōōr	nah′-moor
nan	nän	nahn
An element, meaning *south*, in Japanese place names.		
Nan, Menam (Siam, riv.)	nän′, mă-näm′	nahn′, ma-nahm′
Nanaimo (Can.)	nă-nī′-mō	na-nai′-moh
Nan-ch'ang (Ch., Kiangsi)	nän-chäng	nahn-chahng
Nan-ch'êng (Ch., Kiangsi)	nän-chŭng	nahn-chuhng
Nan-chêng (Ch., Shansi)	nän-jŭng	nahn-juhng
Nan-ch'i (Ch., Szechwan)	nän-chē	nahn-chee
Nan-ching (Ch., Fukien)	nän-jĭng	nahn-jing
Nancy (Fr.)	*Eng.* năn′-sĭ	nan′-si
	Fr. näN-sē′	nahN-see′
Nan-fêng (Ch., Kiangsi)	nän-fŭng	nahn-fuhng

Nangis (Fr.)   näN-zhē′   nahN-zhee′
Nan-hsien (Ch., Hunan)   nän-shyĕn   nahn-shyen
Nan-k'ang (Ch., Kiangsi)   nän-käng   nahn-kahng
  Also called *Hsing-tzu*, q.v. This city is north of Lake Poyang.
Nan-k'ang (Ch., Kiangsi)   nän-chäng   nahn-chahng
  A variant spelling of *Nan-ch'ang*, q.v. This city is south of Lake
  Poyang.
Nan-king (Ch., Kiangsu)   *Eng.* nän-kĭng   nan-king
                           Ch.   nän-kĭng   nahn-king
Nan-ling (Ch., mt. range)   nän-lĭng   nahn-ling
  Also called *Nan-shan*, q.v.
Nan Lui (Ch., Yünnan,   nän lōō-ē   nahn loo-ee
  riv.)
Nan-ning (Ch., Kwangsi)   *Eng.* nän-nĭng   nan-ning
                           Ch.   nän-nĭng   nahn-ning
Nan-pên-chiang (Ch.,   nän-pŭn-jyäng   nahn-puhn-jyahng
  Yünnan)
Nan-shan (Ch., mt. range)   nän-shän   nahn-shahn
  Also called *Nan-ling*, q.v.
Nantes (Fr.)   *Eng.* nănts′   nants′
                           Fr.   näNt′   nahNt′
Nantua (Fr.)   näN-twä′   nahN-twah′
Nanumanga (Oc., Ellice)   nä′-nōō-mäng′-ä   nah′-noo-mahng′-ah
Nanumea (Oc., Ellice)   nä-nōō-mĕ′-ä   nah-noo-meh′-ah
Nanyaseik (Burma)   nän′-yä-sāk′   nahn′-yah-sayk′
Nan-yo (Ch., Hunan)   nän-yō   nahn-yoh
Naoetsu (Jap.)   nä-ô′-ĕ′-tsōō′   nah-o′-eh′-tsoo′
Naousa *or* Niaousta   nou′-sä   nau′-sah
  (Gr.)   *or* nyou′-stä   nyau′-stah
Napa (Calif.)   năp′-ə   nap′-uh
Naples (It.)   *Eng.* nā′-pəlz   nay′-puhlz
Napoli (It.)   nä′-pô-lē   nah′-po-lee
  English *Naples*, q.v.
Napoule, la (Fr.)   nä-pōōl′, lä   nah-pool′, lah
Napula (P.I., point)   nä-pōō′-lä   nah-poo′-lah
  There is also authority for *Napulá*.
Naqura, Ras en (Pal.) See *Ras en Naqura*.
Nara (Jap.)   nä′-rä   nah′-rah
Narage (Oc., Bismarck   nä-rä′-gĕ   nah-rah′-geh
  arch.)
Narbada (India, riv.)   nər-bŭd′-ə   nuhr-buhd′-uh
Narbefontaine (Fr.)   närb-fôN-tĕn′   nahrb-foN-ten′
Narbonne (Fr.)   när-bôn′   nahr-bon′
Nardi, Luigi (It. polit.)   när′-dē, lwē′-jē   nahr′-dee, lwee′-jee

Nares (Eng. name)	nărz'	nehrz'
Narew (Pol.)	nä'-rĕf	nah'-ref

Russian spelling *Narev.*

Narik (Oc., Marshalls)	nä'-rēk	nah'-reek
Narkomvnudel (Rus.)	när-kôm'-vnŏŏ-dĕl'	nahr-kom'-vnu-del'

A telescope word from *Narodni Kommisariat Vnutrennikh Del* (People's Commisariat for Internal Affairs), nä-rôd'-nĭ kŏm-mĭ-sä-ryät' vnŏŏ'-trĕn-nĭk(h) dĕl' [nah-rod'-ni kom-mi-sah-ryaht' vnoo'-tren-nik(h) del'].

Narocz (Pol.)	nä'-rôch	nah'-roch

Russian spelling *Naroch.*

Narodichi (Rus.)	nä-rô'-dĭ-chĭ	nah-ro'-di-chi
Naro Fominsk (Rus.)	nä'-rŏ fŏ-mēnsk'	nah'-ro fo-meensk'
Narova (Est., riv.)	nä-rô'-vä	nah-ro'-vah
Narromine (Austral.)	năr'-ə-mĭn'	nehr'-uh-main'
Nartë (Alb.) See *Arta.*		
Narva (Est.)	när'-vä	nahr'-vah
Narváez (Sp. name)	*Am. Sp.* när-vä'-ĕs	nahr-vah'-ehs
	Sp. när-vä'-ĕth	nahr-vah'-ehth
Narvik (Nor.)	*Eng.* när'-vĭk	nahr'-vik
	Nor. när'-vēk	nahr'-veek

The analogy of the English pronunciation of *Narvik* with "short *i*" will probably govern other place names with *-vik* if they come into the news.

Năsăud (Rum.)	nə-sə-ŏŏd'	nuh-suh-ud'

Hungarian *Naszod,* nŏ'-sôd [no'-sod].

Naselsk (Pol.) See *Nasielsk.*		
Nashchi (Rus.)	nä'-shchĭ	nah'-shchi
Nashimoto (Jap. prince)	nä-shē'-mô'-tô'	nah-shee'-mo'-to'
Našice (Yugosl.)	nä'-shĭ-tsĕ	nah'-shi-tseh
Nasielsk (Pol.)	nä'-syĕlsk	nah'-syelsk

Russian *Naselsk,* nä-sĕl(y)sk' [nah-sel(y)sk'].

Nasik (India)	nä'-sĭk	nah'-sik
Nasrullah Entizam	näs-rŏŏl'-lä ĕn-tĭ-zäm'	nahs-rul'-lah en-ti-
(Iran. polit.)		zahm'
Nassa (Gr., Paros)	nä'-sä	nah'-sah
Nassau	*Eng.* năs'-ô	nas'-aw
	Ger. nä'-sou	nah'-sau
Nasu (Jap.)	nä'-sŏŏ *or* näs'	nah'-soo *or* nahs'
Nasugbú (P.I.)	nä-sŏŏg-bŏŏ'	nah-soog-boo'
Nászaly (Hung.)	nä'-sī	nah'-sai
Naszod (Rum.) See *Năsăud.*		
Natal (Brazil)	nä-täl'	nah-tahl'

Almost nä-toul' [nah-taul'] or nä-tôl' [nah-tawl'].

Natal (U. of S. Afr.)	nə-täl'	nuh-tal'

Natalinci (Yugosl.)	nä′-tä′-lĭn-tsĭ	nah′-tah′-lin-tsi
Natches (Miss.)	năch′-ĭz	nach′-iz
Natchitoches (La.)	năk′-ĭ-tŏsh	nak′-i-tosh
Natmaw (Burma)	nət′-mô′	nuht′-maw′
Natoena or Natuna (NEI)	nä-tōō′-nä	nah-too′-nah
Naturaliste (Austral., cape)	năch′-rə-lĭst or năch′-ə-rə-lĭst	nach′-ruh-list nach′-uh-ruh-list

Pronounced like *naturalist*.

Natzweiler (Ger.)	näts′-vī-lər	nahts′-vai-luhr
Nauján (P.I.)	nou-hän′	nau-hahn′
Naumiestis (Lith.)	nou′-myĕs-tĭs	nau′-myes-tis
Nauna (Oc., Admiralties)	nä-ōō′-nä	nah-oo′-nah
Nauplia (Gr.) See *Navplion*.		
Naura (Oc., Gilberts)	nä-ōō′-rä	nah-oo′-rah
Nauroz (Iran)	nŏ-rōōz′	noh-rooz′

The great spring holiday of Persia.

Nauru (Oc.)	nä-ōō′-rōō	nah-oo′-roo
Nauvoo (Ill.)	nô-vōō′	naw-voo′
Navaho (Am. Indian)	*Eng.* năv′-ə-hō	nav′-uh-hoh

Spanish *Navajó*, nä-vä-hô′ [nah-vah-ho′].

Naval (P.I.)	nä-väl′	nah-vahl′
Navanagar (India)	nŭv-ə-nŭg′-ər	nuhv-uh-nuhg′-uhr

Also spelled *Nawanagar*; also called *Jamnagar*, q.v.

Navarino (Gr.)	*It.* nä-vä-rē′-nô	nah-vah-ree′-no
	Gr. nä-vä-rē′-nô(n)	nah-vah-ree′-no(n)

The official name is *Pylos*, q.v.

Navarra (Sp.)	nä-vä′-rä	nah-vah′-rah

English *Navarre*, nə-vär′ [nuh-vahr′].

Navesink Hills (N.J.)	năv′-ə-sĭnk′	nav′-uh-sink′
Naviglio (It.)	nä-vē′-lyô	nah-vee′-lyo
Navlya (Rus.)	näv′-lyä	nahv′-lyah
Navotas (P.I.)	nä-vô′-täs	nah-vo′-tahs

Also called *San José de Navotas*, sän hô-sĕ′ dĕ nä-vô′-täs [sahn ho-seh′ deh nah-vo′-tahs].

Navpaktos (Gr.)	năf′-pä-ktôs	nahf′-pah-ktos
Navplion (Gr.)	näf′-plē-ô(n)	nahf′-plee-o(n)

English *Nauplia*, nô′-plĭ-ə [naw′-pli-uh].

nawab	nə-wŏb′	nuh-wob′

A title in India which is disregarded in alphabetical listing. So also *nawabzada*, nə-wŏb′-zä-dä [nuh-wob′-zah-dah], son of the nawab. English *nabob*, nä′-bŏb [nay′-bob].

Nawanagar (India) See *Navanagar*.		
Naxos (Gr.)	*Eng.* năk′-sŏs	nak′-sos
	Gr. nä′-ksô(s)	nah′-kso(s)

Nayadu, Sarojini (Indian polit.) See *Naidu.*

Nayarit (Mex.)	nä-yä-rēt′	nah-yah-reet′
Nayo Grande (P.I., riv.)	nä′-yô grän′-dĕ	nah′-yo grahn′-deh
Nayon (P.I., riv.)	nä′-yôn	nah′-yon
Nazaré (Port.)	nä-zə-rĕ′	nah-zuh-reh′
Nazareth (Pal.)	năz′-ə-rĕth	naz′-uh-reth

Arabic *En Nasira,* ĕn nä′-sə-rä [en nah′-suh-rah]. Hebrew *Natsrat,* nä-tsĕ′-rĕt [nah-tseh′-ret].

Naze, the (Nor.)	*Eng.* nāz′	nayz′

Norwegian *Lindesnes,* q.v.

Nazi	nä′-tsĭ *or* năt′-sĭ	nah′-tsi *or* nat′-si
	or năz′-ĭ *or* nä′-zĭ	naz′-i *or* nah′-zi

An abbreviation of German *Nationalsozialistische* Partei. The first pronunciation is probably the most common, but it may be displaced by the second or third.

Ndawara (Oc., Manus)	ndä-wä′-rä	ndah-wah′-rah
Ndruval (Oc., Manus)	ndrōō′-väl	ndroo′-vahl
Nduke (Oc., Solomons)	ndōō′-kĕ	ndoo′-keh
Neagh, Lough (N. Ire.)	nä′, lôk(h)	nay′, lawk(h)
Neai Kalamai (Gr.)	nĕ′-ĕ kä-lä′-mĕ	neh′-eh kah-lah′-meh
Neapolis (Crete)	nĕ-ä′-pô-lēs	neh-ah′-po-lees
nebelwerfer	nä′-bəl-vĕr′-fər	nay′-buhl-vehr′-fuhr

German six-barreled rocket gun.

Nebe Musa	nĕ′-bĕ mōō′-sə	neh′-beh moo′-suh

Arabic meaning *Prophet Moses.*

Nebeur (Tun.)	nĕ-bûr′	neh-bœr′
necessary	nĕs′-ə-sĕr′-ĭ	nes′-uh-sehr′-i

The pronunciation nĕs′-ə-sər-ĭ [nes′-uh-suhr-i] is listed (as an alternative marked *or, especially British*) by only one of five American dictionaries. It is not suited to American radio use.

Neches (Tex., riv.)	nĕch′-ĭz	nech′-iz
Neckar (Ger., riv.)	nĕk′-är	nek′-ahr
Nede (Neth.)	nä′-də	nay′-duh
Nederbrakel (Belg.)	nä′-dər-brä′-kəl	nay′-duhr-brah′-kuhl
Neder Rijn (Neth., riv.)	nä′-dər rīn′	nay′-duhr rain′

See *Rhein.*

Nederweerd (Neth.)	nä′-dər-wärt	nay′-duhr-wayrt
Nedrigaylov (Rus.)	nĕ-drĭ-gī′-löf	neh-dri-gai′-lof
Neer (Neth.)	när′	nayr′
Neerpelt (Belg.)	när′-pĕlt	nayr′-pelt
Nefta (Tun.)	nĕf′-tä	nef′-tah
Negapatam (India)	nĕ′-gə-pə-tăm′	neh′-guh-puh-tam′
Negeb (Pal.)	nĕg′-ĕb	neg′-eb

Negoi *or* Negoiul (Rum., mt.)	nĕ-goi′ *or* nĕ-goi′-ŏŏl	neh-goi′ *or* neh-goi′-ul
Hungarian *Negoj*, nĕ′-goi [neh′-goi].		
Negotin (Yugosl.)	nĕ′-gô-tĭn	neh′-go-tin
Negrades (Gr.)	nĕ-grä′-dĕs	neh-grah′-des
Negrais (Burma)	nĕ-grā′-ĭs	neh-gray′-is
Nègre (Fr., cape)	nĕ′gr	neh′gr
Negrín, Juan (Sp. polit.)	nĕ-grēn′, hwän′	neh-green′, hwahn′
Negroni (It.)	nĕ-grô′-nē	neh-gro′-nee
Negros (P.I.)	nĕ′-grôs	neh′-gros
Néhou (Fr.)	nĕ-ōō′	neh-oo′
Nehru, Pandit Jawaharlal (Indian polit.)	nĕ′-rōō, pŭn′-dĭt jə-wä-hər-läl′	neh′-roo, puhn′-dit juh-wah-huhr-lahl′
Neidenburg (Ger.)	nī′-dən-bŏŏrk(h)	nai′-duhn-burk(h)
Neikban (Burma)	nāk′-băn′	nayk′-ban′
Neisse (Ger.,? Pol., riv.)	nīs′-ə	nais′-uh
Polish *Nisa Łuzycka*, q.v.		
Neisse, Glatzer (? Ger., Pol., riv.)	nīs′-ə, gläts′-ər	nais′-uh, glahts′-uhr
Polish *Nisa Kładzka*, q.v.		
Nejd (Saudi Arabia)	nĕjd′	nejd′
Nelidovo (Rus.)	nĕ-lē′-dŏ-vŏ	neh-lee′-do-vo
Nellore (India)	nĕl-lôr′	nel-lor′
Neman (Europ. riv.) See *Niemen*.		
Nemanjinci (Yugosl.)	nĕ′-mä′-nyĭn-tsĭ	neh′-mah′-nyin-tsi
Nĕmec, František (Cz. polit.)	nyĕ′-mĕts, frän′-chĭ-shĕk	nyeh′-mets, frahn′-chi-shek
Nemenikuće (Yugosl.)	nĕ′-mĕ-nē′-kōō-chĕ	neh′-meh-nee′-koo-cheh
Nemi (It., lake)	*Eng.* nā′-mĭ	nay′-mi
	It. nĕ′-mē	neh′-mee
Nemirov (Rus.)	nĕ-mē′-rŏf	neh-mee′-rof
Nemours (Fr.)	nə-mōōr′	nuh-moor′
Nemunas (Europ. riv.) See *Niemen*.	*Lith.* nyĕ′-mōō-näs	nyeh′-mu-nahs
Nemuro (Jap.)	nĕ′-mōō-rô	neh′-moo-ro
Nemuro Kaikyō *or* Nemuro Straits (Jap.)	nĕ′-mōō-rô kĭ′-kyô	neh′-moo-ro kai′-kyo
Nenana (Alaska)	nĭ-năn′-ə	ni-nan′-uh
Nĕnerçka (Alb., mts.) See *Nĕnerçkë*.		
Nĕnerçkë (Alb., mts.)	nə-nĕrch′-kə	nuh-nehrch′-kuh
Nenni, Pietro (It. polit.)	nĕn′-nē, pyĕ′-trô	nen′-nee, pyeh′-tro
neoprene	nē′-ō-prēn′	nee′-oh-preen′
Nepal (Asia)	nə-pôl′	nuh-pawl′

Nephi (Utah)	nē′-fī	nee′-fai
Nercha (Rus., riv.)	nĕr′-chä	nehr′-chah
Nerchinsk (Rus.)	nĕr′-chĭnsk	nehr′-chinsk
Nerchinski Zavod (Rus.)	nĕr′-chĭn-skĭ zä-vôd′	nehr′-chin-ski zah-vod′
Nère (Fr., riv.)	nĕr′	nehr′
Neresnica (Yugosl.)	nĕ′-rĕs′-nĭ-tsä	neh′-res′-ni-tsah
Neretva (Yugosl.)	nĕ′-rĕ-tvä	neh′-reh-tvah

Italian *Narenta*.

Neris (Rus., riv.) See *Viliya*.

Nerodimka (Yugosl., riv.)	nĕ′-rô′-dĭm-kä	neh′-ro′-dim-kah
Neroefjord (Nor.)	nĕr′-û-fyōr	nehr′-œ-fyohr
Nerola (It.)	nĕ′-rô-lä	neh′-ro-lah

Nervo, Luis Padilla (Mex. diplomat) See *Padilla Nervo*.

| nes | nĕs′ | nes′ |

An element, meaning *headland*, in Norwegian place names.

| Nesebar (Bulg.) | nĕ′-sĕ-bär | neh′-seh-bahr |

Also called *Mesemvria*, mĕ-sĕm′-vrē-yä [meh-sem′-vree-yah].

| Nesflaten (Nor.) | nĕs′-flätn | nes′-flahtn |

Neshava (Pol.) See *Nieszawa*.

| Nesterov (Ger. >Rus.) | nĕ′-stĕ-rŏf | neh′-steh-rof |

German *Stallupoehnen*, q.v.

| Nestos (Balkan riv.) | nĕ′-stôs | neh′-stos |

Bulgarian *Mesta*, q.v.

| Nesvizh (Pol. >Rus.) | nĕs′-vĭzh | nes′-vizh |

Polish *Nieśwież*, q.v.

Nethe (Belg., riv.)	nā′-tə	nay′-tuh
Nettuno (It.)	nĕt-tōō′-nô	net-too′-no
Netze (Ger., Pol., riv.)	*Ger.* nĕt′-sə	net′-suh

Polish *Noteć*, q.v.

Neubourg, le (Fr.)	nû-bōōr′, lə	nœ-boor′, luh
Neubrandenburg (Ger.)	noi-brän′-dən-bōŏrk(h)	noi-brahn′-duhn-burk(h)
Neuchâtel (Switz.)	nû-shä-tĕl′	nœ-shah-tel′
Neudamm (Ger.)	noi′-däm	noi′-dahm
Neuenahr (Ger.)	noi′-ən-är	noi′-uhn-ahr
Neuenhagen (Ger.)	noi′-ən-hä′-gən	noi′-uhn-hah′-guhn
Neufbrisach (Fr.)	nû-brē-zäsh′	nœ-bree-zahsh′

German *Neubreisach*, noi-brī′-zäk(h) [noi-brai′-zahk(h)].

Neufchateau (Fr.)	nû-shä-tō′	nœ-shah-toh′
Neufchâtel en Bray (Fr.)	nû-shä-tĕl äN brĕ′	nœ-shah-tel ahN breh′
Neufmesnil (Fr.)	nû-mĕ-nēl′	nœ-meh-neel′
Neuhausen (Ger. >Rus.)	noi-hou′-zən	noi-hau′-zuhn

Russian *Gurevsk*, gōōr′-yĕfsk [goor′-yefsk].

Neuillé (Fr.)	nû-yĕ′	nœ-yeh′
Neuilly (Fr.)	nû-yē′	nœ-yee′
Neuilly Plaisance (Fr.)	nû-yē plĕ-zäNs′	noe-yee pleh-zahNs′
Neukoelln or Neukölln (Ger.)	noi′-kûln	noi′-kœln
Neumuenster or Neumünster (Ger.)	noi′-mün-stər	noi′-mün-stuhr
Neung (Fr.)	nûN′	nœN′
Neunkirchen (Ger.)	noin′-kĭr′-k(h)ən	noin′-kihr′-k(h)uhn
Neuquén (Arg., prison)	nĕ-ōō-kĕn′	neh-u-ken′
Neuruppin (Ger.)	noi-rŏŏp-pēn′	noi-rup-peen′
Neusalz (Ger. >? Pol.) Polish *Nowasól*, q.v.	noi′-zälts	noi′-zahlts
Neu Sandec (Pol.) See *Nowy Sącz*.		
Neuse (N.C., riv.)	nyōōs′	nyoos′
Neuss (Ger.)	nois′	nois′
Neustadt Oberschlesien (Ger. >Pol.) Polish *Prudnik*, q.v.	noi′-shtät ō′-bər-shlä′-zĭ-ən	noi′-shtaht oh′-buhr-shlay′-zi-uhn
Neustrelitz (Ger.)	noi-shtrā′-lĭts	noi-shtray′-lits
Neuwied (Ger.)	noi′-vēt	noi′-veet
Neuzen (Neth.) See *Terneuzen*.		
Neuzen Hulst (Neth.)	nû′-zən hûlst′	nœ′-zuhn hœlst′
Neva (Rus., riv.)	*Eng.* nē′-və	nee′-vuh
	Rus. nĕ-vä′	neh-vah′
Nevada (U.S.)	nə-văd′-ə	nuh-vad′-uh
	or nə-vä′-də	nuh-vah′-duh

As a place name in Iowa, Missouri, and Arkansas, pronounced nə-vä′-də [nuh-vay′-duh].

Nevada, Sierra (Calif., Sp.)	*Eng.* nə-văd′-ə, sĭ-ĕr′-ə	nuh-vad′-uh, si-ehr′-uh
	Sp. nä-vä′-dä, syĕr′-rä	nah-vah′-dah, syehr′-ah
Nevel (Rus.)	nĕ′-vĕl(y)	neh′-vel(y)
Nevers (Fr.)	nə-vĕr′	nuh-vehr′
Nevesinje (Yugosl.)	nĕ′-vĕ′-sĭ-nyĕ	neh′-veh′-si-nyeh
Nevidiskof (Alaska, Attu)	nĕ-vē′-dĭs-kŏf	neh-vee′-dis-kof
Néville (Fr.)	nĕ-vēl′	neh-veel′
Nevinnomyssk (Rus.)	nĕ-vĭn-nŏ-mwēsk′	neh-vin-no-mweesk′

Also called *Nevinnomysskaya*, nĕ-vĭn-nŏ-mwēs′-skä-yä [neh-vin-no-mwees′-skah-yah].

Nevrokop (Bulg.)	nĕ′-vrŏ-kŏp	neh′-vro-kop
New Delhi (India) See *Delhi*.		

Newfoundland   nyōō'-fənd-lănd'   nyoo'-fuhnd-land'
    Note that the second syllable is normally not stressed and has the vowel schwa. However, as an attribute in *Newfoundland dog*, the second syllable is stressed and is pronounced "found."

New Guinea (Oc.)   nyōō gĭn'-ĭ   nyoo gin'-i

New Orleans (La.)   nyōō ôr'-lyənz   nyoo or'-lyuhnz
    or nyōō ôr'-lĭ-ənz   nyoo or'-li-uhnz

    Elsewhere in the South, the city is often called nyōō ôr'-lənz [nyoo or'-luhnz]. The minstrel show pronunciation rhyming with *jeans*, nyōō' ôr-lēnz' [nyoo' or-leenz'] should be avoided. Cf. *Orleans*.

Nezhin (Rus.)   nĕ'-zhĭn   neh'-zhin

Nez Percé (Am. Indian)   *Eng.* nĕz' pûrs'   nez' puhrs'
    Fr. nĕ-pĕr-sĕ'   neh pehr-seh'

    English plural *Nez Percés*, nĕz' pûr'-sĭz [nez puhr'-siz]. See *Nezperce*.

Nezperce, Nez Perce   nĕz-pûrs'   nez-puhrs'
    (Idaho)

    Miss Marion Orr of Idaho Falls writes that the older pronunciation nĭ-pûr'-sĭ [ni-puhr'-si] is still occasionally heard.

Ngan-hwei (Ch., prov.) See *An-hwei*.

Ngesebus (Oc., Palau)   ngĕ'-sĕ-bōōs   ngeh'-seh-boos

Nggela (Oc., Solomons)   ng-gĕ'-lä   ng-geh'-lah

Ngulu (Oc., Carolines)   ngōō-lōō'   ngoo-loo'

Nguna (Oc., New   ngōō'-nä   ngoo'-nah
    Hebrides)

Nha Trang (Indo-Ch.)   nyä-träng'   nyah-trahng'

Niagara (N.Y., Can.)   nĭ-ăg'-ə-rə   nai-ag'-uh-ruh

Niamţ (Rum.)   nyämts'   nyahmts'

Nias (NEI)   nē'-äs   nee'-ahs

Nicaragua (C.A.)   *Eng.* nĭk'-ə-rä'-gwə   nik'-uh-rah'-gwuh
    Sp. nē-kä-rä'-gwä   nee-kah-rah'-gwah

Nicaria (Gr., isl.)   See *Ikaria*.

Nicobar (India, isls.)   nĭk-ō-bär'   nik-oh-bahr'

Nicola, Enrico de   nē-kô'-lä, ĕn-rē'-kô   nee-ko'-lah, ehn-ree'-
    (It. polit.)   dĕ   ko deh

Nicosia (Sicily)   nē-kô-zē'-ä   nee-ko-zee'-ah

Nicoya (Costa Rica)   nē-kô'-yä   nee-ko'-yah

Nida (Pol., riv.)   nē'-dä   nee'-dah

Nidaros (Nor.)   nē'-dä-rōs   nee'-dah-rohs
    Officially called *Trondheim*, q.v.

Nidda (Ger., riv.)   nĭd'-ä   nid'-ah

Nidže (Balkan mt.)   nē'-jĕ   nee'-jeh

Nidzica (Pol., riv.)   nē-jē'-tsä   nee-jee'-tsah

Niebuhr, Reinhold (Am.   nē'-bŏŏr, rīn'-hōld   nee'-bur rain'-hold
    theologian)

Niedere Tauern (Austria, mts.) — nē'-də-rə tou'-ərn — nee'-duh-ruh tau'-uhrn

Nieder Schlettenbach (Ger.) — nē'-dər shlĕt'-ən-bäk(h) — nee'-duhr shlet'-uhn-bahk(h)

Nielsen, Sven (Nor. diplomat) — nĕl'-sən, svĕn' — neel'-suhn, sven'

Nieman (Europ. riv.) — *Eng.* nē'-mən — nee'-muhn
Pol. nyĕ'-mĕn — nyeh'-men

Russian *Neman* (formerly *Nyeman*), nĕ'-män [neh'-mahn]. Lithuanian *Nemunas*, nyĕ'-mōō-näs [nyeh'-mu-nahs]. German *Memel*, q.v., and *Russ*, rōōs' [rus'].

Niemcewicz, Julian Ursyn (Pol. patriot) — nyĕm-tsĕ'-vĭch, yōō'-lyän ōōr'-sĭn — nyehm-tseh'-vich, yoo'-lyahn ur'-sin

niemi — nē'-ĕ'-mē — nee'-eh'-mee

An element, meaning *cape* or *point*, in Finnish place names.

Niemoeller, Martin (Ger. pastor) — nē'-mûl-ər — nee'-mœl-uhr

Nienburg (Ger.) — nēn'-bŏŏrk(h) — neen'-burk(h)

Nieppe (Fr.) — nyĕp' — nyep'

Niers (Ger., riv.) — nērs' — neers'

Nieśwież (Pol. >Rus.) — nyĕsh'-vyĕsh — nyesh'-vyesh

Russian *Nesvizh*, nĕs'-vĭzh [nes'-vizh].

Nieszawa (Pol.) — nyĕ-shä'-vä — nyeh-shah'-vah

Russian *Neshava*, nĕ-shä'-vä [neh-shah'-vah].

Nietzsche, F. W. (Ger. philosopher) — nē'-chə — nee'-chuh

Nieul (Fr.) — nyûl' — nyœl'

Nieuport (Belg.) — nē'-ōō-pôrt — nee'-u-port

Inevitable English nyōō'-pôrt [nyoo'-port].

Nieuwe Maas (Neth., riv.) — nē'-wə mäs' — nee'-wuh mahs'

Nieuwenhagen (Neth.) — nē'-wən-häk(h)'-ən — nee'-wuhn-hahk(h)'-uhn

Nieuwe Pekela (Neth.) — nē'-wə pä'-kə-lä — nee'-wuh pay'-kuh-lah

Nieuwer Amstel (Neth.) — nē'-wər äm'-stəl — nee'-wuhr ahm'-stuhl

Nieuwerkerk aan den IJssel (Neth.) — nē'-wər-kĕrk' än dən ī'-səl — nee'-wuhr-kehrk' ahn duhn ai'-suhl

Nieuwe Schans (Neth.) — nē'-wə sk(h)äns' — nee'-wuh sk(h)ahns'

Nieuwe Tonge (Neth.) — nē'-wə tông'-ə — nee'-wuh tong'-uh

Nieuw Hellevoet (Neth.) — nē'-ōō hĕl'-ə-vōōt — nee'-u hel'-uh-voot

Nieuwkoop (Neth.) — nē'-ōō-kōp' — nee'-u-kohp'

Nieuw Lekkerland (Neth.) — nē'-ōō lĕk'-ər-länt — nee'-u lek'-uhr-lahnt

Nieuw Leuzen (Neth.)	nē'-ŏŏ lû'-zən	nee'-u lœ'-zuhn
Nièvre (Fr.)	nyĕ'vr	nyeh'vr
Niger (Afr., riv.)	nī'-jər	nai'-juhr
Nigeria (Afr.)	nĭ-jĭr'-ĭ-ə	nai'-jihr'-i-uh
Nigrita (Gr.)	nē-grē'-tä	nee-gree'-tah

Nihon. See *Nippon*.

Niigata (Jap.)	*Eng.* nē'-gä-tä	nee'-gah-tah
	Jap. nē-ē'-gä'-tä	nee-ee'-gah'-tah
Niihau (Hawaii)	nē-ē-hou'	nee-ee-hau'
Nijkerk (Neth.)	nī'-kĕrk	nai'-kehrk
Nijmegen (Neth.)	*Eng.* nī'-mä-gən	nai'-may-guhn
	Du. nī'-mä-k(h)ən	nai'-may-k(h)uhn

For the usual Dutch pronunciation see *Nimwegen*. Cf. *Nimeguen*.

Nikitinka (Rus.)	nĭ-kē'-tĭn-kä	ni-kee'-tin-kah
Nikitovka (Rus.)	nĭ-kē'-tŏf-kä	ni-kee'-tof-kah
Nikkō (Jap.)	nēk'-kô	neek'-ko
Nikolaev (Rus.)	nĭ-kŏ-lä'-yĕf	ni-ko-lah'-yef
Nikolaeva, Klavdia I.	nĭ-kŏ-lä'-yĕ-vä,	ni-ko-lah'-yeh-vah,
(Rus. polit.)	kläv'-dĭ-yä	klahv'-di-yah
Nikolaevskaya (Rus.)	nĭ-kŏ-lä'-yĕf-skä-yä	ni-ko-lah'-yef-skah-yah
Nikolaos, Hagios	nē-kô'-lä-ôs, ī'-yôs	nee-ko'-lah-os, ai'-yos
(Gr., Crete)		

Also called *Lasethion*, lä-sē'-thē(-ôn) [lah-see'-thee(-on)].

Nikolinci (Yugosl.)	nē'-kô'-lĭn-tsĭ	nee'-ko'-lin-tsi
Nikoloudes (Gr. name)	nē-kô-lōō'-dēs	nee-ko-loo'-dees
Nikolsk Ussuriski	nĭ-kôl(y)sk' ōōs-sōō-	ni-kol(y)sk' oos-soo-
(Rus.)	rē'-skĭ	ree'-ski

Now called *Voroshilov*, vŏ-rŏ-shĭ'-lŏf [vo-ro-shi'-lof].

Nikopol (Bulg.)	nē'-kŏ-pŏl(y)	nee'-ko-pol(y)
Nikopol (Rus.)	nē'-kŏ-pŏl(y)	nee'-ko-pol(y)
Nikšić (Yugosl.)	nēk'-shĭch	neek'-shich
Nilgiri (India)	nĭl'-gĭ-rĭ	nil'-gi-ri
Nimeguen (Neth.)	nĭm'-ā-gən	nim'-ay-guhn

For an English pronunciation, see *Nijmegen*. For the usual Dutch pronunciation see *Nimwegen*.

Nîmes (Fr.)	*Eng.* nēmz'	neemz'
	Fr. nēm'	neem'
Nims (Ger., riv.)	nĭms'	nims'
Nimwegen (Neth.)	nĭm'-vä-k(h)ən	nim'-vay-k(h)uhn

This pronunciation is the most common in the Netherlands, however the name is spelled. Cf. *Nijmegen* and *Nimeguen*. For an English pronunciation see *Nijmegen*.

| Nin (Yugosl.) | nēn' | neen' |

Ning-kang (Ch., Kiangsi)	nĭng-gäng	ning-gahng
Ning-p'o (Ch., Chekiang)	nĭng-pô	ning-po
Ning-sia (Ch., prov., town)	nĭng-shyä	ning-shyah

Also spelled *Ning-hsia*.

Ning-tu (Ch., Kiangsi)	nĭng-dōō	ning-doo
Ninian (Fr., riv.)	nē-nyäN′	nee-nyahN′
Ninigo (Oc., Admiralties)	nē′-nē-gô	nee′-nee-go
Niobrara (U.S., riv.)	nĭ′-ō-brăr′-ə	nai′-oh-brehr′-uh
Niokastro (Gr.) See *Pylos*.		
Niort (Fr.)	nyôr′	nyor′
Nipigon (Can., lake)	nĭp′-ĭ-gŏn	nip′-i-gon
Nipissing (Can., lake)	nĭp′-ĭ-sĭng	nip′-i-sing
Nippon	*Eng.* nĭp′-ŏn	nip′-on
	Jap. nēp-pôn′	neep-pon′

Nippon or *Nihon*, nē-hôn′ [nee-hon′], is the official name of *Japan*.
Dai Nippon or *Nihon*, dä-ē nēp-pôn′ or nē-hôn, means *Great Japan*.

Niš (Yugosl.)	nēsh′	neesh′
Nisa (Ger. > Pol.)	nē′-sä	nee′-sah
German *Neisse*, q.v.		
Nisa Kładzka (? Ger., Pol., riv.)	nē′-sä kläts′-kä	nee′-sah klahts′-kah
German *Neisse, Glatzer*, q.v.		
Nisa Łużycka (Ger., ? Pol., riv.)	nē′-sä lōō-zĭts′-kä	nee′-sah lu-zits′-kah

Also called *Nisa Zachodnia* (or *Western Nisa*), zä-hôd′-nyä [zah-hod′-nyah]. German *Neisse*, q.v.

Nišava (Yugosl., riv.)	nē′-shä-vä	nee′-shah-vah
Niscemi (Sicily)	nē-shĕ′-mē	nee-sheh′-mee
Nisei	nē′-sä	nee′-say

U.S. citizens by birth, born of Japanese subjects living in this country.
See *Issei* and *Kibei*.

Niseros (Dodec.) See *Nisyros*.		
Niševac (Yugosl.)	nē′-shĕ-väts	nee′-sheh-vahts
Nishapur (Iran)	nē-shä-pōōr′	nee-shah-pur′
	or nē-shä-bōōr′	nee-shah-bur′
nishi	nē-shē	nee-shee

An element, meaning *west*, in Japanese place names.

Niška Banja (Yugosl.)	nēsh′-kä bän′-yä	neesh′-kah bahn′-yha
Nisot, Joseph (Belg. diplomat)	nē-zō′, zhō-zĕf′	nee-zoh′, zhoh-zef′
Nissan (Oc., Bismarck arch.)	nĭs-sän′	nis-sahn′

Nissen hut	nĭs'-ən	nis'-uhn
Nisser (Nor., riv.)	nĭs'-ər	nis'-uhr
Nistelrode (Neth.)	nĭs'-təl-rō'-də	nis'-tuhl-roh'-duh
Nistrul (Europ. riv.)	See *Dniester.*	
Nisyros (Dodec.)	nē'-sē-rô(s)	nee'-see-ro(s)
Niterói (Brazil)	nē-tĕ-roi'	nee-teh-roi'
Nitobe, Inazō (Jap. educator)	nē'-tô-bĕ, ē-nä-zô'	nee'-to-beh, ee-nah-zo'
Nitra (Cz.)	nē'-trä	nee'-trah
Nitti, Francesco Saverio (It. polit.)	nēt'-tē, frän-chĕ'-skô sä-vĕ'-ryô	neet'-tee, frahn-cheh'-sko sah-veh'-ryo
Niutao (Oc., Ellice)	nē-ōō-tä'-ô	nee-oo-tah'-o
Nivelles (Belg.)	nē-vĕl'	nee-vel'
Nizhne Tambovskoe (Rus.)	nēzh'-nĕ täm-bôf'-skŏ-yĕ	neezh'-neh tahm-bof'-sko-yeh
Nizhneudinsk (Rus.)	nēzh'-nĕ-ōō-dēnsk'	neezh'-neh-oo-deensk'
Nizhny Lomov (Rus.)	nēzh'-nĭ lô'-môf	neezh'-ni lo'-mof
Nizkovka (Rus.)	nēz'-kŏf-kä	neez'-kof-kah
Nizza (Sicily)	nēt'-sä	neet'-sah
Njeguši (Yugosl.)	nyĕ'-gōō-shĭ	nyeh'-goo-shi
Nmai (Burma, riv.)	nmĭ'	nmai'
Noailles (Fr.)	nô-ĭ'	no-ai'
Noakhali (India)	nô-ə-kä'-lē	no-uh-kah'-lee
Also called *Sudharam,* q.v.		
Nobel prizes	nō-bĕl'	noh-bel'
Established by Alfred Bernhard Nobel, Swedish philanthropist.		
Nobeoka (Jap.)	nô-bĕ'-ô-kä	no-beh'-o-kah
Nobuhito, Takamatsu no Miya (Jap. prince)	nô-bōō'-hē-tô, tä-kä'-mä'-tsōō' nô mē-yä	no-boo'-hee-to, tah-kah'-mah'-tsoo' no mee-yah
Nocera (It.)	nô-chĕ'-rä	no-cheh'-rah
Nodar, Robert, Jr. (U.S. representative)	nō'-där	noh'-dahr
Noe (name)	*Eng.* nō'-ĭ	noh'-i
	Fr. nô-ĕ'	no-eh'
Noehoetjoet (NEI, Kai)	nōō-hōō'-chōot	noo-hoo'-choot
Noel Baker, Philip (Br. polit.)	nō'-əl bā'-kər	noh'-uhl bay'-kuhr
Noemfoor *or* Numfoor (NEI, Schouten isls.)	nōōm'-fōr	noom'-fohr
Noeux les Mines (Fr.)	nû lĕ mēn'	nœ leh meen'
Nofilia (Libya)	See *Zauta en Nofilia.*	
Nogaisk (Rus.)	nŏ-gĭsk'	no-gaisk'

Nogales (Ariz.)	nō-găl'-ĭs	noh-gal'-is
Nogales (Mex.)	nô-gä'-lĕs	no-gah'-lehs
Nogent (Fr.)	nô-zhäN'	no-zhahN'
Noginsk (Rus.)	nŏ-gēnsk'	no-geensk'
Noguès, Auguste (Fr. general)	nô-gĕs', ô-güst'	no-ges', o-güst'
Noirmoutier (Fr., isl.)	nwär-mōō-tyĕ'	nwahr-moo-tyeh'
Noirterre (Fr.)	nwär-tĕr'	nwahr-tehr'
Noisy le Sec (Fr.)	nwä-zē lə sĕk'	nwah-zee luh sek'
Nojima Zaki or Nojima Cape (Jap.)	nô-jē-mä' zä-kē	no-jee-mah' zah-kee
Nokrashy (Egypt. polit.) See *Mahmoud Fahmy El Nokrashy.*		
Nomoi (Oc., Carolines)	nô'-moi	no'-moi
Nomura (Jap., zaibatsu)	nô-mōō'-rä'	no-moo'-rah'
Nomura, Kichisaburō (Jap. diplomat)	nô-mōō'-rä', kē'-chē'-sä'-bōō-rô	no-moo'-rah', kee'-chee'-sah'-boo-ro
Nomwin (Oc., Carolines)	nôm'-wĭn	nom'-win
Nonant le Pin (Fr.)	nô-näN lə päN'	no-nahN luh paN'
Non-ni (Manchu., riv.)	nŏn-nē	non-nee
Nonouti (Oc., Gilberts)	nô-nô-ōō'-tē	no-no-oo'-tee
Noon, Firozkhan (Indian polit.)	nōōn', fē-rôz-k(h)än'	noon', fee-roz-k(h)ahn'
Noord Beveland (Neth.)	nōrt bä'-və-länt	nohrt bay'-vuh-lahnt
Noord Brabant (Neth.)	nōrt brä'-bänt	nohrt brah'-bahnt
For English pronunciations, see *Brabant.*		
Noorddijk (Neth.)	nōr-dĭk'	nohr-daik'
Noordgouwe (Neth.)	nōrt-k(h)ou'-wə	nohrt-k(h)au'-wuh
Noord Holland (Neth., prov.)	nōrt hôl'-änt	nohrt hol'-ahnt
Noordscharwoude (Neth.)	nōrt'-sk(h)är-wou'-də	nohrt'-sk(h)ahr-wau'-duh
Noordwijk (Neth.)	nōrt'-wĭk	nohrt'-waik
Noordwijkerhout (Neth.)	nōrt'-wī-kər-hout'	nohrt'-wai-kuhr-haut'
Norblad, Walter (U.S. representative)	nôr'-blăd	nor'-blad
Nordagutu (Nor.)	nō'-rä-gōō'-tŏŏ	noh'-rah-goo'-tu
Nordbreitbach (Ger.)	nôrt'-brīt'-bäk(h)	nort'-brait'-bahk(h)
Norden (Ger.)	nôr'-dən	nor'-duhn
Norderney (Ger., isl.)	nôr'-dər-nī'	nor'-duhr-nai'
Nordfjord (Nor.)	nōr'-fyōr	nohr'-fyohr
Nordhordland (Nor.)	nōr'-hôr-län	nohr'-hor-lahn
Nordkapp (Nor.)	nōr'-käp	nohr'-kahp
English *North Cape* is usually preferable for American radio.		
Nordmarka (Nor.)	nōr'-mär-kä	nohr'-mahr-kah

Nordmoere *or*   nŏr′-mû-rə   nohr′-mœ-ruh
  Nordmöre (Nor.)

Nordreisa (Nor.)   nŏr′-rā-sä   nohr′-ray-sah

Nore (Nor.)   nŏ′-rə   noh′-ruh

Noreanlegget (Nor.)   nŏ′-rə-än-lĕg-ə   noh′-ruh-ahn-leg-uh

Norfolk (Va.)   nŏr′-fək   nor′-fuhk

Normanton (Austral.)   nŏr′-mən-tən   nor′-muhn-tuhn

Norodom   nô-rô-dôm′   no-ro-dom′
  (King of Cambodia)

Norodom Sianuk (Cambodian prince) See *Sianuk.*

Noroton (Conn.)   nə-rōt′n   nuh-roht′n

Norrell, W. F.   nŏr′-əl   nor′-uhl
  (U.S. representative)

Northam (Austral.)   nŏr′-thəm   nor′-thuhm

Northeim (Ger.)   nôrt′-hīm   nort′-haim

Norwich (Eng.)   nŏr′-ĭch   nor′-ich

Norzagaray (P.I.)   nôr-sä-gä-rī′   nor-sah-gah-rai′

Nosaka, Sanji (Jap.   nŏ′-sä-kä, sän′-jē   no′-sah-kah, sahn′-
  polit.)   jee

Noteć (Pol., Ger., riv.)   *Pol.* nŏ′-tĕch   no′-tech
  German *Netze,* q.v.

Noto (Sicily)   nŏ′-tô   no′-to

Notodden (Nor.)   nōt′-ôdn   noht′-odn

Notre Dame (Ind.)   *Eng.* nŏ′-trə dãm′   noh′-truh daym′
  In rapid speech often nōt′r dãm′ [noht′r daym′]. French nô′tr däm′
  [no′tr dahm′].

Nouméa (Oc., New   *Eng.* nōō-mē′-ə   noo-mee′-uh
  Caledonia)   *Fr.* nōō-mĕ-ä′   noo-meh-ah′
  Also spelled *Numea* and pronounced nōō-mĕ′-ä [noo-meh′-ah]. There
  is some evidence to support *Noumea* pronounced nô-ōō-mĕ′-ä [no-
  oo-meh′-ah].

nová, -é, -ý (Cz.)   nô′-vä, -ĕ, -ĭ   no′-vah, -eh, -i
  A common element, meaning *new,* in Czech place names. It may be
  necessary to look up the other part of the name.

Nova Gradiška (Yugosl.)   nô′-vä grä′-dĭsh-kä   no′-vah grah′-dish-kah

Novaliches (P.I.)   nô-vä-lē′-chĕs   no-vah-lee′-ches

Novalja (Yugosl.)   nô-vä′-lyä   no-vah′-lyah

Nová Ves (Cz.)   nô′-vä vĕs′   no′-vah ves′

Nova Zagora (Bulg.)   nô′-vä zä′-gŏ-rä   no′-vah zah′-go-rah

Noveleta (P.I.)   nô-vĕ-lĕ′-tä   no-veh-leh′-tah

Nové Zámky (Cz.)   nô′-vĕ zäm′-kĭ   no′-veh zahm′-ki
  Hungarian *Érsekújvár,* är′-shĕk-ōō′ĭ-vär [ayr′-shek-oo′(y)-vahr].

Novgorod Severski   nôv′-gŏ-rŏt sĕ′-vĕr-   nov′-go-rot seh′-
  (Rus.)   skĭ   vehr-ski

Novi, Bosanski (Yugosl.) nô'-vĭ, bô'-sän-skĭ   no'-vi, bo'-sahn-ski

Novikov, Alexander   nô'-vĭ-kŏf, ä-lĕk-   no'-vi-kof, ah-lek-
  (Rus. general)   sän'-dǝr   sahn'-duhr

Novikov, Nikolai   nô'-vĭ-kŏf, nĭ-kŏ-lĭ'   no'-vi-kof, ni-ko-lai'
  (Rus. polit.)

Novi Pazar (Yugosl.)   nô'-vĭ pä'-zär   no'-vi pah'-zahr

Novi Sad (Yugosl.)   nô'-vĭ säd'   no'-vi sahd'
  Hungarian *Újvidék*, ōō'ĭ-vĭ-dāk [oo'(y)-vi-dayk].

Novi Vileisk (Pol.)   See *Nowa Wilejka.*

Novoaleksandriya (Pol.)   See *Puławy.*

Novocherkassk (Rus.)   nô'-vŏ-chĕr-käsk'   no'-vo-chehr-kahsk'

Novodugino (Rus.)   nô'-vŏ-dōō'-gĭ-nŏ   no'-vo-doo'-gi-no

Novogeorgievsk (Pol.)   See *Modlin.*

Novograd (Rus.)   nô'-vŏ-grät'   no'-vo-graht'

Novogrudok (Pol. >Rus.) nô'-vŏ-grōō'-dŏk   no'-vo-groo'-dok
  Polish *Nowogródek*, q.v.

Novoierusalimskaya   nô'-vŏ-yĕ-rōō-sä-   no'-vo-yeh-roo-sah-
  (Rus.)   lēm'-skä-yä   leem'-skah-yah

Novominsk (Pol.)   See *Mińsk Mazowiecki.*

Novoradomsk (Pol.)   See *Radomsko.*

Novorossisk (Rus.)   nô'-vŏ-rŏ-sēsk'   no'-vo-ro-seesk'

Novorzhev (Rus.)   nô'-vŏ-rzhĕf'   no'-vo-rzhef'

Novo Selo (Yugosl.)   nô'-vô sĕ'-lô   no'-vo seh'-lo

Novosibirsk (Rus.)   nô'-vŏ-sĭ-bērsk'   no'-vo-si-beersk'

Novosil (Rus.)   nô'-vŏ-sēl'   no'-vo-seel'

Novosokolniki (Rus.)   nô'-vŏ-sŏ-kôl'(y)-   no'-vo-so-kol'(y)-
                nē-kĭ   nee-ki

Novosvyentsyani (Pol.)   See *Nowe Święciany.*

Novoukrainka (Rus.)   nô'-vŏ-ōō-krĭn'-kä   no'-vo-oo-krain'-kah

Novozybkov (Rus.)   nô'-vŏ-zĭp'-kŏf   no'-vo-zip'-kof

Novy Bug (Rus.)   nô'-vĭ bōōg'   no'-vi boog'

Novy Oskol (Rus.)   nô'-vĭ ŏs-kôl'   no'-vi os-kol'

Nowasól (Ger. >? Pol.) nô'-vä-sŏŏl'   no'-vah-sul'
  German *Neusalz*, q.v.

Nowa Wilejka (Pol.)   nô'-vä vĭ-lā'-kä   no'-vah vi-lay'-kah
  Russian *Novi Vileisk*, nô'-vĭ vĭ-lāsk' [no'-vi vi-laysk'].

Nowemiasto (Pol.)   nô'-vĕ-myä'-stô   no'-veh-myah'-sto

Nowe Święciany (Pol.)   nô'-vĕ shvyăN-   no'-veh shvyaN-
                chä'-nĭ   chah'-ni
  Russian *Novosventsyani*, nô'-vŏ-svĕn-chä'-nĭ [no'-vo-sven-chah'-ni].

Nowgong (India)   nou-gŏng'   nau-gong'

Nowogródek (Pol. >Rus.) nô-vô-grōō'-dĕk   no-vo-gru'-dek
  Russian *Novogrudok*, nô'-vŏ-grōō'-dŏk [no'-vo-groo'-dok].

Nowy Bytom (Pol.)   nô'-vĭ bĭ'-tôm   no'-vi bi'-tom
  German *Friedenshütte*, q.v.

| Nowy Dwór (Pol.) | nô'-vĭ dvŏŏr' | no'-vih dvur' |
| Nowy Sącz (Pol.) | nô'-vĭ sôNch' | no'-vi soNch' |

German *Neu Sandec,* noi zän'-dĕts [noi zahn'-dets].

Nowy Targ (Pol.)	nô'-vĭ tärk'	no'-vi tahrk'
Nowy Tomyśl (Pol.)	nô'-vĭ tô'-mĭshl	no'-vi to'-mishl
Noyal sur Vilaine (Fr.)	nwä-yäl sür vē-lĕn'	nwah-yahl sür vee-len'
Noyen (Fr.)	nwä-yăN'	nwah-yaN'
Noyers (Fr.)	nwä-yĕ'	nwah-yeh'
Noyon (Fr.)	nwä-yôN'	nwah-yoN'
Nozay (Fr.)	nô-zĕ'	no-zeh'
Nsawam (Gold Coast)	nsä'-wäm	nsah'-wahm
Nsopzup (Burma)	nsôp-zŏŏp'	nsawp-zup'
Nuan-shui-chieh (Ch., Hupeh)	nwän-shwā-jyĕ	nwahn-shway-jyeh
Nubia (Sicily)	nŏŏ'-byä	noo'-byah
Nuernberg *or* Nürnberg (Ger.) English *Nuremberg,* q.v.	nürn'-bĕrk(h)	nürn'-behrk(h)
Nueva Cáceres (P.I.)	nwĕ'-vä kä'-sĕ-rĕs	nweh'-vah kah'-seh-res
Nueva Écija (P.I., prov.)	nwĕ'-vä ĕ'-sē-hä	nweh'-vah eh'-see-hah
Nuevo Laredo (Mex.)	nwĕ'-vô lä-rĕ'-dô	nweh'-vo lah-reh'-do
Nuevo León (Mex.)	nwĕ'-vô lĕ-ôn'	nweh'-vo leh-on'
Nuguria (Oc., Bismarck arch.)	nŏŏ-gŏŏ-rĕ'-ä	noo-goo-ree'-ah
Nui (Oc., Ellice)	nŏŏ'-ē	noo'-ee
Nukha (Rus.)	nŏŏ'-hä	noo'-hah
Nukufetau (Oc., Ellice)	nŏŏ'-kŏŏ-fĕ-tou'	noo'-koo-feh-tau'
Nukulaelae (Oc., Ellice)	nŏŏ'-kŏŏ-lä'-ĕ-lä'-ĕ	noo'-koo-lah'-eh-lah'-eh
Nukunau (Oc., Gilberts)	nŏŏ'-kŏŏ-nou'	noo'-koo-nau'
Nukuoro (Oc., Carolines)	nŏŏ-kwô'-rô	noo-kwo'-ro
Nullarbor (Austral.)	nŭl'-ə-bōr'	nuhl'-uh-bohr'

An amusing Latinism, or so it is said.

Numansdorp (Neth.)	nü'-mäns-dôrp	nü'-mahns-dorp
Numea (Oc.) See *Nouméa.*		
Numedal (Nor.)	nŏŏ'-mə-däl	noo'-muh-dahl
Numfoor (NEI) See *Noemfoor.*		
nuncio	nŭn'-shĭ-ō	nuhn'-shi-oh
Nunen (Neth.)	nü'-nən	nü'-nuhn
Nunivak (Alaska, isl.)	nŏŏ'-nĭ-văk	noo'-ni-vak
Nunspeet (Neth.)	nûn'-spāt	nuhn'-spayt
Nuremberg (Ger.)	*Eng.* nyŏŏr'-əm-bûrg	nyur'-uhm-buhrg

German *Nuernberg,* q.v.

Nurmi, Paavo (Fin. athlete)	nōōr'-mē, pä'-vô	nur'-mee, pah'-vo
Nurri (Sard.)	nōōr'-rē	noor'-ree
Nut (Neth.)	nût'	nuht'
Nyasaland (E. Afr.)	nī-ăs'-ə-lănd	nai-as'-uh-land
Nyaungbinwun (Burma)	nyoung'-bĭn-wōōn'	nyaung'-bin-wun'
Nyaungywe (Burma)	See *Yawnghwe*.	
Nyborg (Den.)	nü'-bôr	nü'-bor
Nyeman (Europ. riv.)	See *Niemen*.	
Nygaardsvold, Johan (Nor. polit.)	nü'-gôrs-vôl, yōō-hän'	nü'-gors-vol, yu-hahn'
Nyiregyháza (Hung.)	nyĭ'-rĕd(y)-hä'-zŏ	nyi'-red(y)-hah'-zo
Nykoebing *or* Nyköbing (Den.)	nü'-kû-bĭng	nü'-kœ-bing
Nymburk (Cz.)	nĭm'-bōōrk	nim'-burk
Nyons (Fr.)	nyôN'	nyoN'
Nystad (Fin.)	See *Uusikaupunki*.	
Nystua (Nor.)	nü'-stōō-ä	nü'-stoo-ah
Nyukzha (Rus.)	nyōōk'-zhä'	nyook'-zhah'

ø is commonly used in Norwegian orthography for *ö* or *æ*. In this book spellings with both *ö* and *æ* are listed, for each may occur in the English spelling of Norwegian names. The use of ø did not seem important enough, from the English point of view, to justify the listing of a third spelling.

Oahu (Hawaii)	ô-ä'-hōō	o-ah'-hoo
Oaxaca (Mex.)	wä-hä'-kä	wah-hah'-kah
Ob (Rus., riv.)	ôp'	op'
Obando (P.I.)	ô-bän'-dô	o-bahn'-do
Oberammergau (Ger.)	ō'-bər-äm'-ər-gou	oh'-buhr-ahm'-uhr-gau
Oberembt (Ger.)	ō'-bər-ĕmpt	oh'-buhr-empt
Oberesch (Ger.)	ō'-bər-ĕsh	oh'-buhr-esh
Oberglogau (Ger. > Pol.) Polish *Głogówek*, q.v.	ō'-bər-glō'-gou	oh'-buhr-gloh'-gau
Oberhausen (Ger.)	ō'-bər-hou'-zən	oh'-buhr-hau'-zuhn
Oberhunnefeld (Ger.)	ō'-bər-hōōn'-ə-fĕlt	oh'-buhr-hun'-uh-felt
Oberleuken (Ger.)	ō'-bər-loi'-kən	oh'-buhr-loi'-kuhn
Ober Maubach (Ger., dam)	ō'-bər mou'-bäk(h)	oh'-buhr mau'-bahk(h)
Obernai (Fr.)	ō-bĕr-nĕ'	oh-behr-neh'
Obernburg (Ger.)	ō'-bərn-bōōrk(h)	oh'-buhrn-burk(h)
Oberramstadt (Ger.)	ō'-bər-räm'-shtät	oh'-buhr-rahm'-shtaht

Obilić (Yugosl.)	ŏ′-bĭ-lĭch	o′-bi-lich
Obluche (Rus.)	ŏ-blōō′-chĕ	o-bloo′-cheh
Obot (Alb.)	ŏ′-bôt	o′-bot
Oboti (Alb.) See *Obot.*		
Oboyan (Rus.)	ŏ-bŏ-yän′(y)	o-bo-yahn′(y)
Obra (Ger., Pol. riv.)	ôb′-rä	ob′-rah
Obrenovac (Yugosl.)	ŏ′-brĕ′-nŏ-väts	o′-breh′-no-vahts
Obrež (Yugosl.)	ŏ′-brĕzh	o′-brezh
Obrovac (Yugosl.)	ŏ′-brŏ-väts	o′-bro-vahts
Obruchev, V. A. (Rus. scientist)	ŏ′-brōō-chĕf	o′-broo-chef
Oca (Oc., Guam)	ŏ′-kä	o′-kah
Ocala (Fla.)	ŏ-kăl′-ə	oh-kal′-uh
Ocampo, Victoria (Arg. writer)	ŏ-käm′-pô	o-kahm′-po
occipital	ŏk-sĭp′-ə-təl	ok-sip′-uh-tuhl
Ochakov (Rus.)	ŏ-chä′-kŏf	o-chah′-kof
Ochemchiri (Rus.)	ŏ-chĕm-chē′-rĭ	oh-chem-chee′-ri
Ochoa (Sp. name)	ô-chŏ′-ä	o-cho′-ah
Ochrida (Yugosl., city; Balkan lake) See *Ohrid.*		
Ochten (Neth.)	ôk(h)′-tən	ok(h)′-tuhn
Oconomowoc (Wis.)	ŏ-kŏn′ə-mō-wôk′	oh-kon′-uh-moh-wok′
Ócsa (Hung.)	ŏ′-chŏ	o′-cho
Octeville (Fr.)	ôk-tə-vēl′	ok-tuh-veel′
Odda (Nor.)	ôd′-ä	od′-ah
Odense (Den.)	ŏ′-dən-sĕ	oh′-duhn-seh
Oder (Europ. riv.)	ŏ′-dər	oh′-duhr
Czech and Polish *Odra,* ŏ′-drä [o′-drah].		
Odessa (Rus.)	*Eng.* ŏ-dĕs′-ə	oh-des′-uh
	Rus. ŏ-dĕ′-sä	o-deh′-sah
Odilienberg, Sint (Neth.) See *Sint Odilienberg.*		
Odnes (Nor.)	ôd′-nĕs	od′-nes
Odoevo (Rus.)	ŏ-dô′-yĕ-vŏ	o-do′-yeh-vo
Ōdomari (Jap.)	ŏ-dô′-mä-rē	o-do′-mah-ree
Odon (Fr., riv.)	ô-dôN′	o-doN′
Odoorn (Neth.)	ŏ-dōrn′	oh-dohrn′
Odorhei (Rum.)	ô-dôr-hä′	o-dor-hay′
Hungarian *Székelyudvarhely,* sä′-kĕĭ-ŏŏd′-vŏr-hĕĭ [say′-kei-ud′-vor-hei].		
Odra (Europ. riv.) See *Oder.*		
Odžaci (Yugosl.)	ŏ′-jä-tsĭ	o′-jah-tsi
Oedelem (Belg.)	ōō′-də-lĕm	oo′-duh-lem
Oedenburg (Hung.) See *Sopron.*		
Oedenrode, Sint (Neth.)	ōō′-dən-rŏ′-də, sĭnt	oo′-duhn-roh′-duh, sint

Oegstgeest (Neth.)	ōōk(h)st-k(h)āst′	ook(h)st-k(h)ayst′
Oeksfjord (Nor.)	ûks′-fyōr	œks′-fyohr
Oeland (Sw., isl.)	û-länd′	œ-lahnd′
Oelen (Nor.)	û′-lən	œ′-luhn
Oels (Ger. >Pol.)	ûls′	œls′
Polish *Oleśnica*, q.v.		
Oema (Oc., Solomons)	ô-ĕ′-mä	o-eh′-mah
Oeresund (Sw., Den., sound)	û′-rə-sôōn	œ′-ruh-sun
Oerskog (Nor.)	ûr′-skōg	œr′-skohg
	or ûsh′-kōg	œsh′-kohg
Oesel (Est., isl.)	*Ger.* û′-zəl	œ′-zuhl

Estonian *Saare*, q.v. Russian *Esel*, q.v., or *Ostrov Sarema*, q.v.

O Estado de São Paulo (Braz. newspaper)   See *Estado de São Paulo, O.*

Oesterdalen (Nor.)	ûs′-tər-dä′-lən	œs′-tuhr-dah′-luhn
Oestfold (Nor.)	ûst′-fôl	œst′-fol
Oestvaagoe (Nor., isl.)	ûst′-vôg-û′	œst′-vog-œ′
Oetzthal (Austria, mts.)	ûts′-täl	œts′-tahl
Oeye (Nor.)	ûï′-ə	œï-uh
Oeyjord (Nor.)	ûï′-yōr	œï-yohr
Offaly (Eire)	ôf′-ə-lĭ	of′-uh-li
Offenburg (Ger.)	ôf′-ən-bôōrk(h)	of′-uhn-burk(h)
Ōgaki (Jap.)	ô′-gä-kē	o′-gah-kee
Ogasawara Jima (Oc.)	ô-gä′-sä-wä′-rä jē-mä	o-gah′-sah-wah′-rah jee-mah

The Japanese name of the *Bonins*, bō′-nĭnz [boh′-ninz].

Ogińskiego, Kanał (Pol.)	ô-gĭn(y)-skyĕ′-gô, kä′-näl	o-gin(y)-skyeh′-go, kah′-nahl

Russian *Oginski Kanal*, ŏ-gĭn′-skĭ kä-näl′ [o-gin′-ski kah-nahl′].

ogle	ō′-gəl	oh′-guhl

The pronunciation ŏg′-əl [og′-uhl] is not recommended.

Ogliastro (It.)	ô-lyäs′-trô	o-lyahs′-tro

O Globo (Braz. newspaper)   See *Globo, O.*

Ognon (Fr., riv.)	ô-nyôN′	o-nyoN′
Ogowe (Fr. Eq. Afr.)	*Eng.* ō-gō-wä′	oh-goh-way′

French *Ogooué* ô-gô-wĕ′ [o-go-weh′].

Ogražden (Yugosl., mt.)	ô′-gräzh-dĕn	o′-grahzh-den
Ogulin (Yugosl.)	ô′-gôō-lĭn	o′-goo-lin
Oguni (Jap.)	ô-gôō′-nē	o-goo′-nee
Ohio (U.S.)	ō-hī′-ō	oh-hai′-oh

Often reduced by natives to ə-hī′-ə [uh-hai′-uh].

Ohlau (Ger. >? Pol.)	ō′-lou	oh′-lau
Polish *Olawa*, q.v.		

Ohlenberg (Ger.)	*Eng.* ō'-lən-bûrg	oh'-luhn-buhrg
	Ger. ō'-lən-běrk(h)	oh'-luhn-behrk(h)
Ohligs (Ger.)	ō'-lĭk(h)s	oh'-lik(h)s
Ohře (Cz., Ger., riv.)	*Cz.* ô'-rzhě	o'-rzheh

German *Eger,* ā'-gər [ay'-guhr].

| Ohri (Yugosl.) | *Alb.* ô'-hrē | o'-hree |

Serb-Croat *Ohrid,* q.v.

| Ohrid (Yugosl., city; | *Eng.* ŏk'-rĭd | ok'-rid |
| Balkan lake) | *S.-C.* ôk(h)'-rĭd | ok(h)'-rid |

The lake is called *Ohridsko Jezero,* ôk(h)'-rĭd-skô yě'-zě-rô [ok(h)'-
rid-sko yeh'-zeh-ro]. Albanian *Liqen i Ohrit,* lē-kyěn' ē ô'-hrēt [lee-
kyen' ee o'-hreet]. Greek *Limne Achridos,* lēm'-nē äk(h)-rē'-dôs
[leem'-nee ahk(h)-ree'-dos], or *Achris,* äk(h)-rēs' [ahk(h)-rees'].

Oirat Tula (Rus.)	oi-rät' tōō'-lä	oi-raht' too'-lah
Oise (Fr., riv.)	wäz'	wahz'
Oisemont (Fr.)	wäz-môN'	wahz-moN'
Oissel (Fr.)	wä-sěl'	wah-sel'
Ōita (Jap.)	ô'-ē-tä	o'-ee-tah
Oituz (Rum.)	oi-tōōz'	oi-tōōz'
O Jornal (Braz. newspaper)	See *Jornal, O.*	
Oka (Rus., riv.)	ŏ-kä'	o-kah'
Okaba (NEI, New	ô-kä'-bä	o-kah'-bah
Guinea)		
Okada, Keisuke (Jap.	ô-kä'-dä', kā'-sōō-kě	o-kah'-dah', kay'-soo-
polit.)		keh
Ōkawa, Shūmei (Jap.	ô'-kä-wä, shōō'-mä	o'-kah-wah, shoo'-
polit.)		may
Okayama (Jap.)	ô-kä'-yä-mä	o-kah'-yah-mah
Okeechobee (Fla.)	ō'-kĭ-chō'-bĭ	oh'-ki-choh'-bi
Oker (Ger., riv.)	ō'-kər	oh'-kuhr
Okhotsk (Rus., sea)	*Eng.* ō-kŏtsk'	oh-kotsk'
	Rus. ŏ-hôtsk'	o-hotsk'

Okhrida (Yugosl., city; Balkan lake) See *Ohrid.*

Okhtokanda (Rus.)	ŏk(h)-tŏ-kän'-dä	ok(h)-to-kahn'-dah
Okinawa Guntō (Jap.)	ô'-kē-nä-wä gōōn'-tô	o'-kee-nah-wah
		goon'-to

English ō'-kĭ-nä'-wə [oh'-ki-nah'-wuh], in the *Ryūkyū* archipelago, q.v.

Okmulgee (Okla.)	ŏk-mŭl'-gĭ	ohk-mul'-gi
Okol (Alb.)	ô-kôl'	o-kol'
O'Konski, Alvin E.	ō-kŏn'-skĭ	oh-kon'-ski
(U.S. representative)		
Öksfjord (Nor.)	ûks'-fyōr	œks'-fyohr
Okulicki, Bronisław,	ô-kōō-lēts'-kĭ,	o-ku-leets'-kih,
(Pol. polit.)	brô-nē'-släf	bro-nee'-slahf

Ōkura (Jap., zaibatsu)   ô-ô'-kōō'-rä'   o-o'-koo'-rah'
Okusi Ambeno (Port.   ô-kōō'-sē äm-bĕ'-nô   o-koo'-see ahm-beh'-
  Timor)   no
Öland (Sw., isl.)   û-länd'   œ-lahnd'
Olav   ô'-läv   oh'-lahv
  (Crown Prince of Norway)
Olawa (Ger. >? Pol.)   ô-lä'-vä   o-lah'-vah
  German *Ohlau*, q.v.
Olbia (Sard.)   ôl'-byä   ol'-byah
  Also called *Terranova*, q.v.
old age, changes of. See *geriatrics* and *gerontology*.
Oldebroek (Neth.)   ôl'-də-brōōk   ol'-duh-brook
Oldehove (Neth.)   ôl-də-hō'-və   ol'-duh-hoh'-vuh
Olden (Nor.)   ôl'-dən   ol'-duhn
Oldenburg (Ger.)   *Eng.* ōl'-dən-bûrg   ohl'-duhn-buhrg
    Ger. ōl'-dən-   ohl'-duhn-burk(h)
      bōŏrk(h)
Oldenzaal (Neth.)   ôl'-dən-zäl   ol'-duhn-zahl
Olean (N.Y.)   ō'-lĭ-ăn   oh'-li-an
Olekma (Rus., riv.)   ŏ-lĕk'-mä   o-lek'-mah
Ölen (Nor.)   û'-lən   œ'-luhn
Olenino (Rus.)   ŏ-lĕ'-nĭ-nŏ   o-leh'-ni-no
Olenya (Rus.)   ŏ-lĕ'-nyä   o-leh'-nyah
Oleśnica (Ger. >Pol.)   ô-lĕsh-nē'-tsä   o-lesh-nee'-tsah
  German *Oels*, q.v.
Oléron (Fr.)   ô-lĕ-rôN'   o-leh-roN'
Olevano (It.)   ô-lĕ'-vä-nô   o-leh'-vah-no
Olevsk (Rus.)   ŏ-lĕfsk'   o-lefsk'
Olevuga (Oc., Solomons)   ô-lĕ-vōō'-gä   o-leh-voo'-gah
Olga (Rus.)   ôl(y)-gä'   ol(y)-gah'
  Not the same as the girl's name *Olga*, ôl'-gä [ol'-gah].
Olgopol (Rus.)   ôl(y)-gô'-pôl(y)   ol(y)-go'-pol(y)
Olhão (Port.)   ô-lyouN'   o-lyauN'
Olib (Yugosl.)   ô'-lĭb   o'-lib
  Italian *Ulbo*, q.v.
Olika (Pol.)   See *Ołyka*.
Olimarao (Oc., Carolines)   ô-lē-mä-rou'   o-lee-mah-rau'
Olita (Lith.)   *Rus.* ŏ-lē'-tä   o-lee'-tah
  Lithuanian *Alytus*, q.v.
Oliva (It.)   ô-lē'-vä   o-lee'-vah
Oliveira Salazar, Antonio de (Port. dictator) See *Salazar, de Oliveira*.
Oliwa (Danzig >Pol.)   ô-lē'-vä   o-lee'-vah
  German *Oliva*, ô-lē'-fä [o-lee'-fah].
Olkusz (Pol.)   ôl'-kōŏsh   ol'-kush

Ollioules (Fr.)   ô-lyōōl'   o-lyool'

Olmütz (Cz.)   See *Olomouc.*

Olomouc (Cz.)   ô'-lô-mōts   o'-lo-mohts
German *Olmütz,* ôl'-müts [ol'-müts].

Olonets (Rus.)   ŏ-lô'-nĕts   o-lo'-nets

Olongapó (P.I.)   ô-lông-gä-pô'   o-long-gah-po'

Olonne (Fr.)   ô-lôn'   o-lon'

Olovyannaya (Rus.)   ŏ-lŏ-vyän'-nä-yä   o-lo-vyahn'-nah-yah

Olsau (Pol.)   See *Olza.*

Olst (Neth.)   ôlst'   olst'

Olsztyn (Ger. >Pol.)   ôl'-shtĭn   ol'-shtin
German *Allenstein,* q.v.

Olten (Switz.)   ôl'-tən   ol'-tuhn

Oltenia (Rum.)   ôl-tĕ'-nyä   ol-teh'-nyah

Olteniţa (Rum.)   ôl-tĕ'-nē-tsä   ol-teh'-nee-tsah

Oltul (Rum., riv.)   ôl'-tōōl   ol'-tul
Hungarian *Olt,* ôlt' [olt']. German *Alt,* ält' [ahlt'].

Olu Malau (Oc.,   ô'-lōō mä-lou'   o'-loo mah-lau'
Solomons)

Olutanga (P.I.)   ô-lōō-täng'-gä   o-loo-tahng'-gah

Ołyka (Pol.)   ô-lĭ'-kä   o-li'-kah
Russian spelling *Olika.*

Olympia (Gr.)   *Eng.* ō-lĭm'-pyə   oh-lim'-pyuh
     Gr. ô-lē(m)-bē'-ä   o-lee(m)-bee'-ah

Olympos (Gr., mt.)   *Eng.* ō-lĭm'-pəs   oh-lim'-puhs
     Gr. ô'-lēm-bôs   o'-leem-bos

Olza (Pol.)   ôl'-zä   ol'-zah
German *Olsau,* ôl'-zou [ol'-zau].

Omagh (N. Ire.)   ō'-mə   oh'-muh

Omaha (Neb.)   ō'-mə-hô *or* -hä   oh'-muh-haw *or* -hah

O'Mahoney, Joseph C.   ō-mă'-hə-nĭ   oh-ma'-huh-ni
(U.S. senator)
The *a* of the second syllable is properly pronounced between the usual *ä* of *father* and the *ă* of *fat.* The Senator's father described his name thus:

> "Oh, the bleat of the lamb
> And the fruit of the bee
> Make the name of the man
> Who's speaking to thee—
> OH-MA'-HONEY."

'Oman (Arabia)   ô-män'   o-mahn'

Omanville (Fr.)   ô-mäN-vēl'   o-mahN-veel'

Omdurman (Sudan)   ŏm-dər-män'   om-duhr-mahn'

Ōminato (Jap.)   ô'-mē'-nä-tô   o'-mee'-nah-to

Omiš (Yugosl.)	ồ'-mĭsh	o'-mish
Omišalj (Yugosl.)	ồ'-mĭ-shäl(y)	o'-mi-shahl(y)
Ommen (Neth.)	ồm'-ən	om'-uhn
Omoljica (Yugosl.)	ồ'-mồ'-lyĭ-tsä	o'-mo'-lyi-tsah
Omsk (Rus.)	ồmsk'	omsk'
Ōmura (Jap.)	ồ'-mōō-rä	o'-moo-rah
Onda (Rus., riv.)	ồn'-dä	on'-dah
Ondava (Cz., riv.)	ồn'-dä-vä	on'-dah-vah
Ondefontaine (Fr.)	ồNd-fồN-tĕn'	oNd-foN-ten'
Ondozero (Rus.)	ŏn-dồ'-zĕ-rồ	on-do'-zeh-ro
Onega (Rus., lake)	*Eng.* ō-nē'-gə	oh-nee'-guh
	Rus. ŏ-nĕ'-gä	o-neh'-gah
Onegin, Eugene	ŏ-nĕ'-gĭn, yōō-jēn'	o-neh'-gin, yoo-jeen'

(Tchaikovsky's opera)

In this title *Eugene* is commonly Anglicized. French *Eugène*, û-zhĕn' [œ-zhen']. Russian *Evgeni*, yĕv-gĕ'-nĭ [yev-geh'-ni]. As I remember, FPA in the old days took pains to point out that it was not "Eugene, one gin, and be quick about it."

Oneida (N.Y.)	ō-nī'-də	oh-nai'-duh
Onezhskoe (Rus., lake)	ŏ-nĕsh'-skŏ-yĕ	o-nesh'-sko-yeh
Onofrio (It.)	ồ-nồ'-fryồ	o-no'-fryo
Onomichi (Jap.)	ồ-nồ'-mē-chē	o-no'-mee-chee
Onondaga (N.Y.)	ŏn-ŏn-dä'-gə	on-on-dah'-guh
	or ŏn-ŏn-dồ'-gə	on-on-daw'-guh
Onstwedde (Neth.)	ồnst-wĕd'-ə	onst-wed'-uh
Ontong Java (Oc., Solomons)	ồn'-tồng jä'-vä	on'-tong jah'-vah
Onykhas (Crete, mt.)	ồ'-nē-häs	o'-nee-hahs
Oodnadatta (Austral.)	ōōd'-nə-dăt'-ə	ood'-nuh-dat'-uh
Ooldea (Austral.)	ōōl-dē'-ə	ool-dee'-uh
Ooltgensplaat (Neth.)	ōlt'-k(h)əns-plät'	ohlt'-k(h)uhns-plaht'
Oorschot (Neth.)	ồr'-sk(h)ồt	ohr'-sk(h)ot
oost *and* ooster	ōst' *and* ōs'-tər	ohst' *and* ohs'-tuhr

An element, meaning *east*, in Dutch place names. It may be necessary to look up the other part of the name.

Oostburg (Neth.)	ōst'-bûrk(h)	ohst'-bœrk(h)
Oostdongeradeel (Neth.)	ōst-dồng'-ə-rä-dāl'	ohst-dong'-uh-rah-dayl'
Oosterbeek (Neth.)	ōs'-tər-bāk	ohs'-tuhr-bayk
Oosterhesselen (Neth.)	ōs'-tər-hĕs'-ə-lən	ohs'-tuhr-hes'-uh-luhn
Oosterhout (Neth.)	ōs'-tər-hout	ohs'-tuhr-haut
Oosterwijk (Neth.)	ōs'-tər-wĭk	ohs'-tuhr-waik
Oostmahorn (Neth.)	ōst-mä-hồrn'	ohst-mah-horn'

Ooststellingwerf (Neth.)	ōst-stĕl′-ĭng-wĕrf′	ohst-stel′-ing-wehrf′
Oostvoorne (Neth.)	ōst-vōr′-nə	ohst-vohr′-nuh
Oostzaan (Neth.)	ōst-zän′	ohst-zahn′
Ootacamund (India)	ōō′-tə-kə-mŭnd′	oo′-tuh-kuh-muhnd′
Opatów (Pol.)	ô-pä′-tŏof	o-pah′-tuf
Opava (Cz.)	ô′-pä-vä	o′-pah-vah

German *Troppau*, trôp′-ou [trop′-au].

Opdal (Nor.)	ôp′-däl	op′-dahl
Opelika (Ala.)	ō′-pə-lī′-kə	oh′-puh-lai′-kuh
Opelousas (La.)	ŏp′-ə-lōō′-səs	op′-uh-loo′-suhs
opéra bouffe	*Eng.* ŏp′-ə-rə bōōf′	op′-uh-ruh bōōf′
	Fr. ô′-pĕ-rä bōōf′	o′-peh-rah boof′
Opladen (Ger.)	ôp′-lä-dən	op′-lah-duhn
Oploo (Neth.)	ôp′-lō	op′-loh
Opochinskoe (Rus.)	ô-pô′-chĭn-skŏ-yĕ	o-po′-chin-sko-yeh
Opochka (Rus.)	ô-pôch′-kä	o-poch′-kah
Opoczno (Pol.)	ô-pôch′-nô	o-poch′-no

Russian spelling *Opochno*.

Opole (Ger. > Pol.)	ô-pô′-lĕ	o-po′-leh

German *Oppeln*, q.v.

Oporto (Port.)	*Eng.* ō-pôr′-tō	oh-por′-toh

Portuguese *Porto*, q.v.

Oppeln (Ger. > Pol.)	ôp′-əln	op′-uhln

Polish *Opole*, q.v.

Oppenheimer, J. R.	ŏp′-ən-hī′-mər	op′-uhn-hai′-muhr
(Am. scientist)		
Oppido (It.)	ôp′-pē-dô	op′-pee-do
Oppio (It.)	ôp′-pyô	op′-pyo
Opsterland (Neth.)	ôp′-stər-länt	op′-stuhr-lahnt
opus	ō′-pəs	oh′-puhs

The plural of *opus* is *opera*. The plural *opuses* is badly needed but not yet authorized by the dictionaries. Cp. *octopuses* alongside of *octopodes* and *octopi*—all plurals of *octopus*.

Opuzen (Yugosl.)	ô′-pōō-zĕn	o′-poo-zen
Oradea (Rum.)	ô-rä′-dyä	o-rah′-dyah

Hungarian *Nagyvárad*, nŏd′(y)-vä′-rŏd [nod′(y)-vah′-rod].

Oradour sur Glane (Fr.)	ô-rä-dōōr sür glän′	o-rah-door sür glahn′
Orahovac (Yugosl.)	ô′-rä′-hô-väts	o′-rah′-ho-vahts
Orahovica (Yugosl.)	ô′-rä′-hô-vĭ-tsä	o′-rah′-ho-vi-tsah
Oran (Alg.)	*Eng.* ō′-răn′	oh′-ran′
	Fr. ô-räN′	o-rahN′
Orange (Fr.)	ô-räNzh′	o-rahNzh′
Orani (P.I.)	ô-rä′-nē	o-rah′-nee

Orani (Pol. >Rus.)	ô-rä'-nĭ	o-rah'-ni
Polish spelling *Orany*.		
Oranienbaum (Rus.)	ŏ-rän'-yĕn-boum	o-rahn'-yen-baum
Oranienburg (Ger.)	ô-rä'-nyən-bŏŏrk(h)	o-rah'-nyuhn-burk(h)
Oranjestad (NWI)	ô-rän'-yə-stät	o-rahn'-yuh-staht'
Orás (P.I.)	ô-räs'	o-rahs'
Orašac (Yugosl.)	ô'-rä'-shäts	o'-rah'-shahts
Orašje (Yugosl.)	ô'-räsh'-yĕ	o'-rahsh'-yeh
Orăştie (Rum.)	ô-rûsh'-tyĕ	o-ruhsh'-tyeh
Oraviţa (Rum.)	ô-rä'-vē-tsä	o-rah'-vee-tsah
Orbec (Fr.)	ôr-bĕk'	or-bek'
Orbetello (It.)	ôr-bĕ-tĕl'-lô	or-beh-tel'-lo
Ord (Austral., riv.)	ôrd'	ord'
Ordos (Ch., Suiyuan)	*Eng.* ôr'-dŏs	ohr'-dos
Ordzhonikidzegrad	ŏr-jŏ-nĭ-kēd'-zĕ-	or-jo-ni-keed'-zeh-
(Rus.)	grät	graht
Orebić (Yugosl.)	ô'-rĕ-bĭch	o'-reh-bich
Oregon (U.S.)	ŏr'-ə-gŏn *or* -gən	or'-uh-gon *or* -guhn
Orekhovo (Bulg.)	ŏ-rĕ'-hŏ-vŏ	o-reh'-ho-vo
Orekhovo Zuevo (Rus.)	ŏ-rĕ'-hŏ-vŏ	o-reh'-ho-vo
	zŏŏ'-yĕ-vŏ	zoo'-yeh-vo
Orël (Rus.)	*Eng.* ō-rĕl'	oh-rel'
	Rus. ŏr-yôl'	or-yol'
Orenburg (Rus.)	ŏ-rĕn-bŏŏrk'	o-ren-burk'
Orense (Sp.)	ô-rĕn'-sĕ	o-ren'-seh
Oreovica (Yugosl.)	ô'-rĕ'-ô-vĭ-tsä	o'-reh'-o-vi-tsah
Öresund (Sw., Den.,	û'-rə-sŏŏn	œ'-ruh-sun
sound)		
English the *Sound*.		
Orgãos, Serra dos	ôr-gouNs', sĕ'-rə	or-gauNs', sĕ'-rə duz
(Brazil, mts.)	dŏŏz	
Orgeev (Rum. >Rus.)	ôr-gĕ'-yĕf	or-geh'-yef
Rumanian *Orhei*, ôr-hä' [or-hay'].		
Orhei (Rum. >Rus.) See *Orgeev*.		
Oriente (Cuba)	ô-ryĕn'-tĕ	o-ryehn'-teh
Orillia (Can.)	ō-rĭl'-ĭ-ə	oh-ril'-i-uh
Orinoco (Ven., Col., riv.)	*Eng.* ō-rə-nō'-kō	oh-ruh-noh'-koh
	Sp. ô-rē-nô'-kô	o-ree-no'-ko
Orio (It.)	ô'-ryô	o'-ryo
Orión (P.I.)	ô-ryôn'	o-ryon'
Oriskany (N.Y.)	ə-rĭs'-kə-nĭ	uh-ris'-kuh-ni
Orissa (India)	ə-rĭs'-ə	uh-ris'-uh
Oristano (Sard.)	ô-rē-stä'-nô	o-ree-stah'-no
Orizaba (Mex.)	ô-rē-sä'-bä	o-ree-sah'-bah

Orjen (Yugosl., mt.)	ôr'-yĕn	or'-yen
Orkdalsoeyra or Ork-dalsöyra (Nor.)	ôrk'-däls-û'-rä	ork'-dahls-œ'-rah
Örkény (Hung.)	ûr'-kän(y)	œr'-kayn(y)
Orkney Islands (Eng.)	ôrk'-nĭ	ork'-ni

The *Orkneys*, ôrk'-nĭz [ork'-niz].

D'Orlando (Sicily, cape)	dôr-län'-dô	dor-lahn'-do
Orléans, Orleans	*Fr.* ôr-lĕ-äN'	or-leh-ahN'
	Eng. ôr-lēnz'	or-leenz'

For the French city the French pronunciation is probably the more common among American radio speakers. The American place name is pronounced ôr-lēnz' [or-leenz'] except for *New Orleans*, Louisiana, where the pronunciation is ôr'-lyənz [or'-lyuhnz] or ôr'-lĭ-ənz [or'-li-uhnz].

Orlov, Pavel (Rus. polit.)	ŏr-lôf', pä'-vĕl	or-lof', pah'-vel
Orlovka (Rus.)	ŏr-lôf'-kä	or-lof'-kah
Orly (Fr.)	*Eng.* ôr'-lĭ	or'-li
	Fr. ôr-lē'	or-lee'
Ormanli (Yugosl.)	ôr'-män-lĭ	or'-mahn-li
Ormoc (P.I.)	ôr-môk'	or-mok'
Ormož (Yugosl.)	ôr'-môzh	or'-mozh
Orne (Fr., riv.)	ôrn'	orn'
Oroluk (Oc., Carolines)	ô'-rô-lōōk	o'-ro-look
Orono (Me.)	ō'-rə-nō	oh'-ruh-noh
Ororu Shotō (Oc.)	*Jap.* ô-rô'-rōō sho-tô'	o-ro'-roo sho-to'

Also called *Namonuito*, q.v.

Ororutō (Oc., Carolines) See *Ulul.*

Oros, Agion (Gr., mt.) See *Athos.*

Orosh (Alb.)	ô'-rôsh	o'-rosh
Orosháza (Hung.)	ô'-rôsh-hä'-zŏ	o'-rosh-hah'-zo

Oroshi (Alb.) See *Orosh.*

Orote (Oc., Guam)	ô-rô'-tĕ	o-ro'-teh
Orozco, José Clemente (Mex. painter)	ô-rôs'-kô, hô-sĕ' klĕ-mĕn'-tĕ	o-ros'-ko, ho-seh' kleh-mehn'-teh
Orsk (Rus.)	ôrsk'	orsk'
Örskog (Nor.)	ûr'-skōg or ûsh'-kōg	œr'-skohg or œsh'-kohg

Officially *Aurskog*, q.v.

Orsogna (It.)	ôr-sô'-nyä	or-so'-nyah
Orşova (Rum.)	ôr'-shô-vä	or'-sho-vah

Hungarian *Orsova*, ôr'-shô-vŏ [or'-sho-vo].

Orte (It.)	ôr'-tĕ	or'-teh
Ortega (Sp., cape)	ôr-tĕ'-gä	or-teh'-gah
Ortegal (Sp., cape)	ôr-tĕ-gäl'	or-teh-gahl'

Ortelsburg (Ger. >Pol.)	ôr′-təls-bŏŏrk(h)	or′-tuhls-burk(h)
Polish *Szczytno,* q.v.		
Ortona (It.)	ôr-tô′-nä	or-to′-nah
Ortucchio (It.)	ôr-tōōk′-kyô	or-took′-kyo
Orvieto (It.)	ôr-vyĕ′-tô	or-vyeh′-to
Orvinio (It.)	ôr-vē′-nyô	or-vee′-nyo
Os *or* Oss (Neth.)	ôs′	os′
Ōsaka (Jap.)	ô′-sä-kä	o′-sah-kah
Osawatomie (Kans.)	ô′-sə-wät′-ə-mǐ *or*	oh′-suh-waht′-uh-mi
	ŏs′-ə-	*or* os′-uh-
Osceola (Fla.)	ŏs′-ǐ-ô′-lə	os′-i-oh′-luh
Oschersleben (Ger.)	ôsh′-ərs-lā′-bən	osh′-uhrs-lay′-buhn
	or ô′-shərs-lā′-bən	oh′-shuhrs-lay′-buhn
Osečina (Yugosl.)	ô′-sĕ′-chǐ-nä	o′-seh′-chi-nah
Ösel (Est., isl.)	*Ger.* û′-zəl	œ′-zuhl
Estonian *Saare,* q.v. Russian *Esel,* q.v., or *Ostrov Sarema,* q.v.		
Osen (Nor.)	ô′-sən	oh′-suhn
Osh (Rus.)	ôsh′	osh′
Ōshima, Hiroshi (Jap.	ô′-shē-mä, hē-rô′-shē	o′-shee-mah, hee-ro′-
diplomat)		shee
Oshmyana (Pol. >Rus.)	ŏsh-myä′-nä	osh-myah′-nah
Polish *Oszmiana,* q.v.		
Osiječka (Yugosl.)	ô′-sǐ-yĕch-kä	o′-si-yech-kah
Osijek (Yugosl.)	ô′-sǐ-yĕk	o′-si-yek
Osipaonica (Yugosl.)	ô′-sē-pä′-ô-nǐ-tsä	o′-see-pah′-o-ni-tsah
Osipovichi (Rus.)	ô-sǐ-pô′-vǐ-chǐ	o-si-po′-vi-chi
Oskol (Rus., riv.)	ŏs-kôl′	os-kol′
Oslo (Nor.)	*Eng.* ŏz′-lō *or* ŏs′-lō	oz′-loh *or* ohs′-loh
	Nor. ōŏs′-lōŏ	us′-lu
Oslofjord (Nor.)	*Eng.* ŏz′-lō-fyôrd′	oz′-loh-fyohrd′
	or ŏs′-lō-fyôrd′	ohs′-loh-fyohrd′
	Nor. ōŏs′-lōŏ-fyōr	us′-lu-fyohr
Osma (Bulg., riv.)	ôs′-mä	os′-mah
Also called *Osam,* ô′-säm [o′-sahm].		
Osmeña, Sergio (Fil.	ôs-mĕ′-nyä, sĕr′-hyô	os-meh′-nyah, sehr′-
polit.)		hyo
Osnabrueck *or* Osna-	*Eng.* ŏz′-nə-brŏŏk	oz′-nuh-bruk
brück (Ger.)	*Ger.* ôs-nä-brük′	os-nah-brük′
Osoeyra *or* Osöyra (Nor.)	ōs′-ûǐ-rä	ohs′-œi-rah
Osogovska planina	ô′-sô-gôv-skä	o′-so-gov-skah
(Balkan mts.)	plä′-nē′-nä	plah′-nee′-nah
Osoyoos (Can.)	ō-sōō′-yəs	oh-soo′-yuhs
Ospina Pérez, Mariano	ôs-pē′-nä pĕ′-rĕs,	os-pee′-nah peh′-res,
(Colom. polit.)	mä-ryä′-nô	mah-ryah′-no

Oss (Neth.) See *Os*.

Ossa (Gr., mt.) *Eng.* ŏs′-ə os′-uh
　　　　　　Gr. ô′-sä o′-sah

Osservatore Romano ôs-sĕr-vä-tô′-rĕ os-sehr-vah-to′-reh
　(Vatican newspaper) rô-mä′-nô ro-mah′-no

Ossetia (Rus.) ŏ-sĕt′-ĭ-ə o-set′-i-uh

Ossola (It.) ôs′-sô-lä os′-so-lah

Ostashkov (Rus.) ŏs-täsh′-kŏf os-tahsh′-kof

Ostend (Belg.) *Eng.* ŏs-tĕnd′ os-tend′
French *Ostende*, ôs-täNd′ [os-tahNd′]. Flemish *Oostende*, ōs-tĕn′-də [ohs-ten′-duh].

Österdalen (Nor.) ûs′-tər-dä′-lən œs′-tuhr-dah′-luhn

Osteriaccia (It.) ô-stĕ-ryät′-chä o-steh-ryaht′-chah

Osterode (Ger. >Pol.) ôs′-tə-rō′-də os′-tuh-roh′-duh
Polish *Ostród*, q.v.

Östfold (Nor.) ûst′-fôl œst′-fol

Osthofen (Ger.) ôst′-hō-vən ost′-hoh-vuhn

Ostia (It.) *Eng.* ŏs′-tĭ-ə os′-ti-uh
　　　　　It. ô′-styä o′-styah

Ostiglia (It.) ô-stē′-lyä o-stee′-lyah

Ostrau (Cz.) See *Moravská Ostrava*.

Ostród (Ger. >Pol.) ôs′-trŏŏt os′-trut
German *Osterode*, q.v.

Ostrog (Pol. >Rus.) ŏ-strôg′ o-strog′
Polish *Ostróg*, ô′-strŏŏk [o′-struk].

Ostrogozhsk (Rus.) ŏs-trŏ-gôshsk′ os-tro-goshsk′

Oštro Koplje (Yugosl.) ô′-shtrô kôp′-lyĕ o′-shtro kop′-lyeh

Ostrołęka (Pol.) ô-strô-lăN′-kä o-stro-laN′-kah
Russian *Ostrolenka*, ŏ-strŏ-lĕn′-kä [o-stro-len′-kah].

Ostrov Sarema (Est., isl.) *Rus.* ô′-strŏf sä′-rĕ-mä o′-strof sah′-reh-mah
Also called *Esel*, q.v. Estonian *Saare(maa)*, q.v.

Ostrów (Pol.) ô′-strŏŏf o′-struf
Russian *Ostrov*, ô′-strŏf [o′-strof]. German *Ostrowo*, ôs-trō′-vō [os-troh′-voh].

Ostrowiec (Pol.) ô-strô′-vyĕts o-stro′-vyets
Russian *Ostrovets*, ŏ-strŏ′-vĕts [o-stro′-vets].

Ostrów Mazowiecki ô′-strŏŏf mä-zô- o′-struf mah-zo-
　(Pol.) vyĕ′-tskĭ vyeh′-tski
Russian *Ostrov*, ô′-strŏf [o′-strof].

Ostružnica (Yugosl.) ô′-strŏŏzh′-nĭ-tsä o′-stroozh′-ni-tsah

Ostrvo (Yugosl., isl.) ô′-stər-vô o′-stuhr-vo

Östvaagö (Nor., isl.) ûst′-vôg-û′ œst′-vog-œ′

Osubka Morawski, ô-sŏŏb′-kä mô-räf′- o-sub′-kah mo-rahf′-
　Edward (Pol. polit.) skĭ, ĕd′-värt skih, ed′-vahrt

Oświęcim (Pol.) ôsh-vyăN′-tsĭm osh-vyaN′-tsim
 German *Auschwitz*, oush′-vĭts [aush′-vits].
Oszmiana (Pol. > Rus.) ôsh-myä′-nä osh-myah′-nah
 Russian *Oshmyana*, ŏsh-myä′-nä [osh-myah′-nah].
Otabato (P.I.) ô-tä-bä′-tô o-tah-bah′-to
Otaru (Jap.) ô′-tä-rōō o′-tah-roo
Othonoi (Gr., isl.). See *Fanô*.
Otočac (Yugosl.) ô′-tô-chäts o′-to-chahts
Otórola, Oscar Escudero ô-tô′-rô-lä, ôs-kär′ o-to′-ro-lah, os-kahr′
 (Chilean general) ĕs-kōō-dĕ′-rô es-koo-deh′-ro
Otra (Nor., riv.) ōt′-rä oht′-rah
Otranto (It., town, strait) *Eng.* ō-trän′-tō oh-trahn′-toh
   It. ô′-trän-tô o′-trahn-to
Otsego (N.Y.) ŏt-sē′-gō ot-see′-goh
Otsu (Jap.) ô′-tsōō o′-tsoo
Otta (Nor.) ŏŏt′-ä ut′-ah
Ottavio (It.) ôt-tä′-vyô ot-tah′-vyo
Ottawa (U.S. and Can.) ŏt′-ə-wə ot′-uh-wuh
Ottersum (Neth.) ôt′-ər-səm ot′-uhr-suhm
Ottmuth (Ger.) ôt′-mŏŏt ot′-mut
Ottumwa (Idaho) ŏ-tŭm′-wə o-tum′-wuh
Otwock (Pol.) ô′-tvôtsk o′-tvotsk
Ötzthal (Austria, mts.) ûts′-täl œts′-tahl
Ou-ch'ih-k′ou (Ch., ō-chû-kō oh-chuh-koh
 Hupeh)
Oucques (Fr.) ōōk′ ook′
Oud Beijerland (Neth.) out bī′-yər-länt aut bai′-yuhr-lahnt
Ouddorp (Neth.) oud′-dôrp aud′-dorp
Oude Ijssel (Neth., riv.) ou′-də ī′-səl au′-duh ai′-suhl
Oude Maas (Neth., riv.) ou′-də mäs′ au′-duh mahs′
Oude Pekela (Neth.) ou′-də pä′-kə-lä au′-duh pay′-kuh-lah
Oudenbosch (Neth.) ou′-dən-bôs′ au′-duhn-bos′
Ouder Amstel (Neth.) ou′-dər äm′-stəl au′-duhr ahm′-stuhl
Oude Rhein (Neth., riv.) ou′-də rīn′ au′-duh rain′
Ouderkerk (Neth.) ou′-dər-kĕrk au′-duhr-kehrk
Oude Tonge (Neth.) ou′-də tông′-ə au′-duh tong′-uh
Oudewater (Neth.) ou′-də-wä′-tər au′-duh-wah′-tuhr
Oud Gastel (Neth.) out′ k(h)äs′-təl aut′ k(h)ahs′-tuhl
Oudon (Fr., riv.) ōō-dôN′ oo-doN′
Oudref (Tun.) ōō′-drĕf oo′-dref
Oud Vosmeer (Neth.) out′ vôs′-mār aut′ vos′-mayr
Oued Zarga (Tun.) wĕd zär′-gä wed zahr′-gah
Ouessant (Fr., isl.) wĕ-säN′ weh-sahN′
 English *Ushant*, q.v.

Ouilly le Tesson (Fr.)	ōō-yē lə tĕ-sôN′	oo-yee luh teh-soN′
Ouistreham (Fr.)	wēs-träN′	wees-trahN′
Oulu (Fin.)	ō′-lōō	oh′-lu
Swedish *Uleåborg*, ü′-lĕ-ō-bôr′(y) [ü′-leh-oh-bor′(y)].		
Oumont, St. (Belg.) See *Saint Oumont*.		
Ounas Selkä (Fin., mts.)	ō′-näs sĕl′-kă	oh′-nahs sel′-ka
Our (Belg., riv.)	ōōr′	oor′
Ourcq (Fr., riv.)	ōōrk′	oork′
Ourthe (Belg., riv.)	ōōrt′	oort′
Ousseltia (Tun.)	ōō-sĕl′-tĭ-ä	oo-sel′-ti-ah
Oust (Fr., riv.)	ōōst′	oost′
Outland, George E.	out′-lənd	aut′-luhnd
(U.S. representative)		
Ouve (Fr., riv.)	ōōv′	oov′
Ouzouer le Marché (Fr.)	ōō-zwĕ lə mär-shĕ′	oo-zweh luh mahr-sheh′
Ovau (Oc., Solomons)	ô-vou′	o-vau′
Ovče Polje (Yugosl.)	ôv′-chĕ pôl′-yĕ	ov′-cheh pol′-yeh
Over Asselt (Neth.)	ō-vər äs′-əlt	oh-vuhr ahs′-uhlt
Overbroek (Neth.)	ō-vər-brōōk′	oh-vuhr-brook′
Overflakkee (Neth., isl.)	ō′-vər-flä-kä′	oh′-vuhr-flah-kay′
See *Goedereede*.		
Overloon (Neth.)	ō-vər-lōn′	oh-vuhr-lohn′
Overschie (Neth.)	ō-vər-sk(h)ē′	oh-vuhr-sk(h)ee′
Overysel (Neth.)	ō′-vər-ī′-səl	oh′-vuhr-ai′-suhl
Also spelled *Overyssel*.		
Ovid (Roman poet)	ŏv′-ĭd	ov′-id
As an American place name in New York and Michigan, pronounced ō′-vĭd [oh′-vid].		
Ovidiopol (Rus.)	ŏ-vĭ-dĭ-ô′-pŏl(y)	o-vi-di-o′-pol(y)
Oviedo (Sp.)	ô-vyĕ′-dô	o-vyeh′-do
Ovindoli (It.)	ô-vēn′-dô-lē	o-veen′-do-lee
Ovinishche (Rus.)	ŏ-vē′-nĭ-shchĕ	o-vee′-ni-shcheh
Ovruch (Rus.)	ôv′-rōōch	ov′-rooch
Ow-ch'ih-k'ow (Ch.) See *Ou-ch'ih-k'ou*.		
Owyhee (Hawaii) See *Hawaii*.		
Owyhee (Idaho)	ō-wī′-hē	oh-wai′-hee
Oxia (Gr., isl.)	ô-ksē′-ä	o-ksee′-ah
Oxya (Gr., mt.)	ô-ksē-ä′	o-ksee-ah′
Öye (Nor.)	ûĭ′-ə	œi′-uh
Öyjord (Nor.)	ûĭ′-yōr	œi′-yohr
Oza (Gr., mt.) See *Parnes*.		
Ozaki, Yukio (Jap. polit.)	ô′-zä-kē, yōō-kē′-ô′	o′-zah-kee, yoo-kee′-o′

ozero ô′-zĕ-rŏ o′-zeh-ro

A common element, meaning *lake*, in Russian place names. Look up the other part of the name.

Ozersk (Ger. >Rus.) ô-zĕrsk′ o-zehrsk′

German *Darkehmen*, q.v.

Ozëry (Rus.) ŏ-zyô′-rĭ o-zyo′-ri

Ozieri (Sard.) ô-dzyĕ′-rē o-dzyeh′-ree

Ozrinići (Yugosl.) ôz′-rē′-nĭ-chĭ oz′-ree′-ni-chi

Paama (Oc., New Hebrides) pä-ä′-mä pah-ah′-mah

French *Paou Ouma*, pä′-o͞o o͞o′-mä [pah′-oo oo′-mah].

Paan (Burma) pä-än′ pah-ahn′

Pa-an (Ch., Sikang) bä-än bah-ahn

Also called *Batang*, q.v.

Paarl (U. of S. Afr.) pärl′ pahrl′

Paasikivi, Juho Kusti (Fin. polit.) pä′-sē-kē-vē, yo͞o′-hô ko͝os′-tē pah′-see-kee-vee, yoo′-ho kus′-tee

Pabjanice (Pol.) pä-byä-nē′-tsĕ pah-byah-nee′-tseh

Pacciardi, Randolfo (It. polit.) pät-chär′-dē, rän-dôl′-fô paht-chahr′-dee, rahn-dol′-fo

Pacelli, Eugenio See *Pope Pius XII*.

Pachino (Sicily) pä-kē′-nô pah-kee′-no

Pachuca (Mex.) pä-cho͞o′-kä pah-choo′-kah

Pacijan (P.I.) pä-sē′-hän pah-see′-hahn

Paco (P.I., Manila) pä′-kô pah′-ko

Also called *San Fernando de Dilao*, sän fĕr-nän′-dô dĕ dē-lou′ [sahn fehr-nahn′-do deh dee-lau′]

Pacusan păk′-kyo͞o′-săn′ pak′-kyoo′-san′

A coinage formed by the initial letters of *Pacific Air Command, United States Army* plus "a euphonious *n*," as the Army's news bulletin put it. There is no standard of correctness for so recent a coinage but this pronunciation seems to be the favorite of CBS broadcasters.

Pacy (Fr.) pä-sē′ pah-see′

Padalung (Siam) See *Phatthalung*.

Padang (NEI, Sumatra) pä-däng′ pah-dahng′

Paderborn (Ger.) pä-dər-bôrn′ pah-duhr-born′

Paderewski, Ignacy Jan (Pol. leader) pä-dĕ-rĕf′-skĭ, ĭg-nä′-tsĭ yän′ pah-deh-ref′-ski, ig-nah′-tsi yahn′

Popular English păd′-ə-ro͞os′-kĭ [pad′-uh-roos′-ki].

Padiglione (It.) pä-dē-lyô′-nĕ pah-dee-lyo′-neh

Padilla, Ezequiel (Mex. polit.) pä-dē′-yä, ĕ-sĕ-kyĕl′ pah-dee′-yah, eh-seh-kyel′

Padilla Nervo, Luis   pä-dē′-yä nĕr′-vô,   pah-dee′-yah nehr′-
   (Mex. polit.)   lwēs′   vo, lwees′
Padina (Yugosl.)   pä′-dĭ-nä   pah′-di-nah
Padova (It.)   See *Padua*.
Padua (It.)   *Eng.* păd′-yōō-ə   pad′-yoo-uh
   Italian *Padova*, pä′-dô-vä [pah′-do-vah].
Paducah (Ky.)   pə-dyōō′-kə   puh-dyoo′-kuh
Paestum (It.)   *Eng.* pĕs′-təm   pes′-tuhm
   Italian *Pesto*, pĕ′-stô [peh′-sto].
Pag (Yugosl.)   päg′   pahg′
   Italian *Pago*, pä′-gô [pah′-go].
Pagaï (NEI, Mentawai)   pä-gä′-ē   pah-gah′-ee
Pagan (Burma)   pə-gän′   puh-gahn′
Pagan (Oc., Marianas)   pä-gän′   pah-gahn′
Pagán, Bolívar   pä-gän′, bô-lē′-vär   pah-gahn′, bo-lee′-
   (P.R. polit.)   vahr
Pagapas (P.I., riv.)   pä-gä′-päs   pah-gah′-pahs
   Also called *San Pedriño*, sän pĕ-drē′-nyô [sahn peh-dree′-nyo].
Pagėgiai (Lith.)   pä-gā′-gyī   pah-gay′-gyai
Paget (Eng. name)   păj′-ĭt   paj′-it
Pago Pago (Oc., Samoa)   päng′-ô päng′-ô   pahng′-o pahng′-o
   Also spelled *Pango Pango*. Also pronounced păng′-ō [pang′-oh],
   päng′-gō [pahng′-goh], pä′-gō [pah′-goh], and pā′-gō [pay′-goh].
Pagsán (P.I., riv.)   päg-sän′   pahg-sahn′
Pahlavi, Muhammad   pä-lä-vē′, mŏŏ-häm′-   pah-lah-vee′ mu-
   Riza (Shah of Iran)   məd rē′-zə   hahm′-muhd ree′-
                                            zuh
Pa-hsien (Ch., Szechwan) See *Chungking*.
Paide (Est.)   pī′-dĕ   pai′-deh
   Russian and German *Weissenstein*, q.v.
P′ai-ling-miao (Ch.,   pī-lĭng-myou   pai-ling-myau
   Suiyüan)
Paimboeuf (Fr.)   păN-bûf′   paN-bœf′
Paimpol (Fr.)   păN-pôl′   paN-pol′
Pai-sê (Ch., Kwangsi)   bī-sŭ   bai-suh
   Also called *Po-seh*, q.v.
Paita (Oc., New   pä-ē′-tä   pah-ee′-tah
   Caledonia)
Paiute (Am. Indian) See *Piute*.
Pájaros (Pan., isls.)   pä′-hä-rôs   pah′-hah-ros
Pakenham (Eng. name)   *Am.* păk′-ən-hăm   pak′-uhn-ham
                     Br. păk′-ən-əm   pak′-uhn-uhm
Pakhoi (Ch.,   *Eng.* păk-hoi   pak-hoi
   Kwangtung)   *Ch.* bäk-hoi   bahk-hoi
Pakin (Oc., Carolines)   pä′-kēn   pah′-keen

| Pakistan | păk'-ĭs-tăn | pak'-is-tan |
| | or päk'-ĭs-tän | pahk'-is-tahn |

"The work PAK—pure, clean . . . . stands for all that is noble and sacred in life for a Muslim. The name Pakistan, which has come to be applied . . . to the five Muslim provinces in the north-west of present-day India, is composed of letters taken from the names of its components: Punjab, North-West Frontier (of which the inhabitants are mainly Afghan), Kashmire, Sind, and Baluchistan. These territories were christened Pakistan by C. Rahmat Ali, founder of the Pakistan National Movement, in 1933." (Encyclopedia of Islam).

Paklay (Indo-Ch.)	päk-lĭ'	pahk-lai'
Pakleni Otoci (Yugosl.)	pä'-klĕ-nĭ ô'-tô-tsĭ	pah'-kleh-ni o'-to-tsi
Italian *Spalmadori*, q.v.		
Paknam (Siam)	päk-näm'	pahk-nahm'
	or păk-năm'	pak-nam'
Paknampo (Siam)	päk-näm'-pō'	pahk-nahm'-poh'
Pakokku (Burma)	pə-kōk'-kōō'	puh-kohk'-koo'
Pakrac (Yugosl.)	pä'-kräts	pah'-krahts
Paks (Hung.)	pŏksh'	poksh'
Pakse (Indo-Ch.)	päk-sĕ'	pahk-seh'
Palagonia (Sicily)	pä-lä-gô-nē'-ä	pah-lah-go-nee'-ah
Palagruža (It. > Yugosl., isl.)	S.-C. pä'-lä-grōō'-zhä	pah'-lah-groo'-zhah
Italian *Pelagosa*, q.v.		
Palaiseau (Fr.)	pä-lĕ-zō'	pah-leh-zoh'
Palanan (P.I., bay)	pä·lä'-nän	pah-lah'-nahn
Palanas (P.I.)	pä-lä'-näs	pah-lah'-nahs
Palanga (Lith.)	pä'-läng-gä	pah'-lahng-gah
Russian *Polangen*, q.v.		
Palanka (Yugosl.)	pä'-län-kä	pah'-lahn-kah
Palápag (P.I.)	pä-lä'-päg	pah-lah'-pahg
Palata (It.)	pä-lä'-tä	pah-lah'-tah
Palatinate, the (Ger.)	*Eng.* pə-lăt'-ə-nāt	puh-lat'-uh-nayt
German *Pfalz*, pfälts' [pfahlts'].		
Palatine (It., Rome)	*Eng.* păl'-ə-tīn	pal'-uh-tain
Italian *Palatino*, pä-lä-tē'-nô [pah-lah-tee'-noh].		
Palau (Oc., Carolines)	pä-lou'	pah-lau'
Also called *Pelew*, pē-lōō' [pee-loo'].		
Palaui (P.I.)	pä-lä'-wē	pah-lah'-wee
Paláuig (P.I.)	pä-lä'-wĭg	pah-lah'-wig
Palawan (P.I.)	pä-lä'-wän	pah-lah'-wahn
Palawit (P.I.)	pä-lä-wēt'	pah-lah-weet'
Palazzo (Sicily)	pä-lät'-sô	pah-laht'-so
Palazzolo (It.)	pä-lät-sô'-lô	pah-laht-so'-lo
Palembang (NEI, Sumatra)	pä-lĕm-bäng'	pah-lem-bahng'

Palencia (Sp.)	pä-lĕn'-thyä *or* -syä	pah-len'-thyah *or* -syah

Paleokhora (Crete) See *Selinon.*

Palermo (Alb.) Also called *Porto Palermo.* Albanian *Portë e Palermos,* q.v.

Palermo (Sicily)	*Eng.* pə-lûr'-mō	puh-luhr'-moh
	It. pä-lĕr'-mô	pah-lehr'-mo
Palestine	păl'-əs-tīn'	pal'-uhs-tain'

As the name of a Texas town, pronounced păl'-əs-tēn' [pal'-uhs-teen'].

Palestrina (It.)	pä-lĕ-strē'-nä	pah-leh-stree'-nah
Paletwa (Burma)	pə-lĕt'-wä	puh-let'-wah'
Pali (Alb., cape)	*Eng.* pä'-lē	pah'-lee

Albanian *Kep i Palit.*

Paliano (It.)	pä-lyä'-nô	pah-lyah'-no
Paliki (Rus.)	pä-lē'-kĭ	pah-lee'-ki
Palinuro (It., cape)	pä-lē-nōō'-rô	pah-lee-noo'-ro
Paliros (Gr.)	pä'-lē-rôs	pah'-lee-ros
Palk (India, str.)	pôk'	pawk'
Pallene (Gr., point)	pä-lē'-nē	pah-lee'-nee

The point of *Kassandra,* q.v.

Pallës, Bisht i *or* Hundë e (Alb.) Local names for cape *Pali,* q.v.

Pallice, la (Fr.)	pä-lēs', lä	pah-lees', lah

Palma, Arturo Alessandri (Chilean polit.) See *Alessandri Palma.*

Palma, la (Canary Isls.)	päl'-mä, lä	pahl'-mah, lah
Palmarola Vecchia (It.)	päl-mä-rô'-lä vĕk'-kyä	pahl-mah-ro'-lah vek'-kyah
Palmas (NEI)	päl'-mäs	pahl'-mahs

Also called *Miangas,* myäng'-gäs [myahng'-gahs].

Palmi (It.)	päl'-mē	pahl'-mee
Palmietfontein (U. of S. A., Johannesburg, airport)	päl-mēt'-fôn-tān'	pahl-meet'-fon-tayn'
Palmyra (place name)	păl-mī'-rə	pal-mai'-ruh
Palo (P.I.)	pä'-lô	pah'-lo
Palokastro, Nos (Bulg., cape)	pä-lŏ-kä'-strŏ, nôs'	pah-lo-kah'-stro, nos'
Palombara (It.)	pä-lôm-bä'-rä	pah-lom-bah'-rah
Palompón (P.I.)	pä-lôm-pôn'	pah-lom-pon'
Palos (Sp.)	pä'-lôs	pah'-los
Paltiski (Est.)	päl'-tĭs-kĭ	pahl'-tis-ki

Russian *Baltiski Port,* q.v.

Palúan (P.I.)	pä-lōō'-än	pah-loo'-ahn
Pamaloean (Borneo)	pä-mä-lōō'-än	pah-mah-loo'-ahn
Pameungpeuk (NEI, Java)	pä-mûng'-pûk	pah-mœng'-pœk

Pamlico (N.C., sound) păm′-lĭ-kō pam′-li-koh
Pampanga Grande *and* päm-päng′-gä grän′- pahm-pahng′-gah
 Chico (P.I., rivs.) dĕ *and* chē′-kô grahn′-deh *and*
  chee′-ko

Pana (Rus., riv.) pä′-nä pah′-nah
Panaccioni (It.) pä-nät-chyô′-nē pah-naht-chyo′-nee
Panagyurishte (Bulg.) pä-nä-gyōō′-rĭsh-tĕ pah-nah-gyoo′-rish-
  teh
Panama (C.A.) *Eng.* păn′-ə-mä pan′-uh-mah
 Spanish *Panamá*, pä-nä-mä′ [pah-nah-mah′].
Panamanian păn′-ə-mā′-nyən pan′-uh-may′-nyuhn
Panaón (P.I.) pä-nä-ôn′ pah-nah-on′
Panaria (It., isl.) pä-nä-rē′-ä pah-nah-ree′-ah
Panaro (It., riv.) pä-nä′-rô pah-nah′-ro
Panaroekan (NEI) pä-nä-rōō′-kän pah-nah-roo′-kahn
Panay (P.I.) pä-nī′ pah-nai′
Pančevo (Yugosl.) pän′-chĕ-vô pahn′-cheh-vo
 Hungarian *Pancsova*, pŏn′-chô-vô [pon′-cho-vo].
Pandacan (P.I.) pän-dä′-kän pahn-dah′-kahn
Pandán (P.I.) pän-dän′ pahn-dahn′
Pandarochan (P.I.) pän-dä-rô′-chän pahn-dah-ro′-chahn
Panderma (Turk.) pän-dĕr′-mä pahn-dehr′-mah
 Also called *Bandırma*, q.v.
Pandi (P.I.) See *Santa María de Pandi*.
pandit *or* pundit pŭn′-dĭt puhn′-dit
 Pandit and *pundit* are variants and should be pronounced alike. This
 is an example of the Indian "short *a*," which is close to schwa or
 "short *u*" (as in *but*), but which is often Angliziced to "short *a*" (as
 in *bat*). *Pandit* as an honorific tends to retain the more conservative
 pronunciation.
Panevėžys (Lith.) pä-nyĕ-vĕ-zhēs′ pah-nyeh-veh-zhees′
 Russian *Ponevezh*, q.v.
Pangasinán (P.I.) päng-gä-sē-nän′ pahng-gah-see-nahn′
Pange (Fr.) päNzh′ pahNzh′
Pangkal-pinang (NEI, päng′-käl-pē′-näng pahng′-kahl-pee′-
 Bangka) nahng

 or Eng. pē-năng′ pee-nang′
Pango Pango (Oc.) See *Pago Pago*.
Panguitch (Utah) păn′-gwĭch pan′-gwich
Pangutaran (P.I.) päng-ōō-tä′-rän pahng-oo-tah′-rahn
Paniqui (P.I.) pä-nē′-kē pah-nee′-kee
 There is also authority for *Paniquí*.
Panjim (Port. India) pän-zhēN′ pahn-zheeN′
Pannerden (Neth.) pän′-ər-dən pahn′-uhr-duhn

Pannerdensche Canal (Neth.)	pän'-ər-dən-sə	pahn'-uhr-duhn-suh
Panorm (Alb.)	pä'-nôrm	pah'-norm
Also called *Portë e Palermos*, q.v.		
Panormi (Alb.) See *Panorm*.		
Pansípit (P.I., riv.)	pän-sē'-pĭt	pahn-see'-pit
Pantano (It.)	pän-tä'-nô	pahn-tah'-no
Pantelimon, Agios (Crete)	pän-dĕ-lē'-môn, ĭ'-yôs	pahn-deh-lee'-mon, ai'-yos
Pantelleria (It., isl.)	pän-tĕl'-lĕ-rē'-ä	pahn-tel'-leh-ree'-ah
Pantin (Fr.)	päN-tăN'	pahN-taN'
Pantocrator (Corfù, mt.)	pän-tô-krä'-tôr	pahn-to-krah'-tor
Pánuco (Mex.)	pä'-nōō-kô	pah'-noo-ko
Panyushkin, Alexandr S. (Rus. diplomat)	pä-nyōōsh'-kĭn, ä-lĕ-ksän'-dər	pah-nyoosh'-kin, ah-leh-ksahn'-duhr
Paoay (P.I.)	pou-ī'	pau-ai'
Pao-ch'i (Ch., Shensi)	bou-chē	bau-chee
Pao-ch'ing (Ch., Hunan)	bou-chĭng	bau-ching
Also called *Shao-yang*, q.v.		
Paoli (Pa.)	pā-ō'-lĭ	pay-oh'-li
Paoli, Pasquale di (It. patriot)	pä-ô'-lē, päs-kwä'-lĕ dē	pah-o'-lee, pahs-kwah'-leh dee
Paombong (P.I.)	pä-ôm-bông'	pah-om-bong'
Pao-shan (Ch., Yünnan)	bou-shän	bau-shahn
Also called *Yung-ch'ang*, q.v.		
Pao-t'ou (Ch., Suiyüan)	bou-tō	bau-toh
Pápa (Hung.)	pä'-pŏ	pah'-po
Papandreou, Georgios (Gr. polit.)	pä-pän-drĕ'-ōō, yôr'-yôs	pah-pahn-dreh'-oo, yor'-yos
Papeete (Oc., Tahiti)	pä-pĕ-ā'-tĕ	pah-peh-ay'-teh
Papenburg (Ger.)	pä'-pən-bŏŏrk(h)	pah'-puhn-burk(h)
Papendrecht (Neth.)	pä'-pən-drĕk(h)t	pah'-puhn-drek(h)t
Papialou (Oc., Admiralties)	pä-pē'-ä-lô'-ōō	pah-pee'-ah-lo'-oo
Papitalai (Oc., Admiralties)	pä-pē-tä-lī'	pah-pee-tah-lai'
Papua (New Guinea)	păp'-yŏŏ-ə or pä'-pōō-ä	pap'-yu-uh pah'-poo-ah
Pará (Brazil)	pä-rä'	pah-rah'
Paracale (P.I.)	pä-rä-kä'-lĕ	pah-rah-kah'-leh
Paracel (Fr., isls.)	pä-rä-sĕl'	pah-rah-sel'
Japanese *Hirata Guntō*, hē-rä'-tä' gōōn'-tô [hee-rah'-tah 'goon'-to].		
Paraćin (Yugosl.)	pä'-rä-chĭn	pah'-rah-chin
Paragua (P.I.) See *Laparán*.		

Paragua (Ven., riv.)	pä-rä'-gwä	pah-rah'-gwah
Paraguaná (Ven., pen.)	pä-rä-gwä-nä'	pah-rah-gwah-nah'
Paraguarí (Para.)	pä-rä-gwä-rē'	pah-rah-gwah-ree'
Paraguassú (Brazil, riv.)	pä-rə-gwä-sōō'	pah-ruh-gwah-soo'
Paraguay	*Eng.* păr'-ə-gwā	par'-uh-gway
	Sp. pä-rä-gwī'	pah-rah-gwai'
Paraíba *or* Parahiba	pä-rə-ē'-bə	pah-ruh-ee'-buh
or Parahyba (Brazil)		
Officially *João Pessoa*, q.v.		
Param (Oc., Truk)	pä'-räm	pah'-rahm
Paramaribo (Du. Guiana)	*Eng.* păr'-ə-măr'-ĭ-bō	par'-uh-mar'-i-boh
	Du. pä-rä-mä'-rĭ-bô	pah-rah-mah'-ri-bo
Paramushiro (Jap. >Rus.)	pä-rä-mōō'-shē-rô	pah-rah-moo'-shee-ro
Russian *Paramusir*, pä-rä-mōō-sēr' [pah-rah-moo-seer'].		
Paramythia (Gr.)	pä-rä-mē-thē'-ä	pah-rah-mee-thee'-ah
Paraná (S.A., riv.)	pä-rə-nä'	pah-ruh-nah'
Paranaguá (Brazil)	pä-rä-nə-gwä'	pah-rah-nuh-gwah'
Parañaque (P.I.)	pä-rä-nyä'-kě	pah-rah-nyah'-keh
Parandova (Rus.)	pä-rän'-dŏ-vä	pah-rahn'-do-vah
Párang (P.I.)	pä'-räng	pah'-rahng
Pardubice (Cz.)	pär'-dōō-bĭ-tsě	pahr'-doo-bi-tseh
Paredes, Quintín	pä-rě'-děs, kēn-tēn'	pah-reh'-des, keen-
(Fil. polit.)		teen'
Parennes (Fr.)	pä-rěn'	pah-ren'
Parenzo (It.)	pä-rěn'-tsô	pah-ren'-tso
Pares, Sir Bernard	părz', bûr'-nərd	pehrz', bur-nuhrd
(Br. diplomat)		
Pareto, Vilfredo	pä-rě'-tô, vĭl-frě'-dô	pah-reh'-to, vil-freh'-
(It. author)		do
Parga (Gr.)	pär'-gä	pahr'-gah
Parham (Eng. name)	păr'-əm	pehr'-uhm
pariah	pə-rī'-ə *or* păr'-ĭ-ə *or*	puh-rai'-uh *or* par'-i-
	pä'-rĭ-ə	uh *or* pah'-ri-uh
Parichi (Rus.)	pä'-rĭ-chĭ	pah'-ri-chi
Paricutín (Mex.)	pä-rē-kōō-tēn'	pah-ree-koo-teen'
This is the usual spelling and pronunciation in Mexico City. Perhaps nearer to the Tarascan is *Parícutin*, pä-rē'-kōō-tēn [pah-ree'-koo-teen]. Also called *Parácutin* and *Paracutín*, q.v.		
Pari Pari (NEI)	pä'-rē pä'-rē	pah'-ree pah'-ree
Paris (Fr.)	*Eng.* păr'-ĭs	pehr'-is
	Fr. pä-rē'	pah-ree'
Parisis (Fr.)	pä-rē-zē'	pah-ree-zee'
Parma (It.)	pär'-mä	pahr'-mah

Parnassus (Gr., mt.)   *Eng.* pär-năs'-əs   pahr-nas'-uhs
   Greek *Parnasos,* pär-nä-sôs' [pahr-nah-sos']. Also called *Liakoura,*
   lyä'-kōō-rä [lyah'-koo-rah].

Parnes (Gr., mt.)   *Eng.* pär'-nēz   pahr'-neez
                  Gr. pär'-nēs   pahr'-nees
   Also called *Oza,* ô-zä' [o-zah'].

Pärnu (Est.)   pär'-nōō   pehr'-noo
   Russian *Pernov,* q.v. German *Pernau,* q.v.

Parodi, Alexandre	pä-rô-dē', ä-lĕk-	pah-ro-dee', ah-lek-
(Fr. diplomat)	säN'dr	sahN'dr
Parona (It.)	pä-rô'-nä	pah-ro'-nah
Paros (Gr., isl.)	pä'-rô(s)	pah'-ro(s)
Parowan (Utah)	păr'-rə-wän	pa'-ruh-wahn
Parpatsch (Rus.)	pär-päch'	pahr-pahch'
Parri, Ferruccio	pär'-rē, fĕr-rōōt'-chô	pahr'-ree, fehr-root'-
(It. polit.)		cho
Parroy (Fr.)	pä-rwä'	pah-rwah'
Parry (Oc., Eniwetok)	păr'-ĭ	pehr'-i
Parthenay (Fr.)	pär-tə-nĕ'	pahr-tuh-neh'
Partinico (Sicily)	pär-tē-nē'-kô	pahr-tee-nee'-ko
partisan *or* partizan	pär'-tĭ-zən	pahr'-ti-zuhn
	or pär'-tĭ-zăn'	pahr'-ti-zan'

   The latter spelling and pronunciation is sometimes associated with the
   military sense of the word.

Paruao (P.I., riv.)	pä-rōō-ou'	pah-roo-au'
Pásay (P.I.)	pä'-sī	pah'-sai

   Also called *Pineda,* pē-nĕ'-dä [pee-neh'-dah].

Pascagoola (Miss.)	păs'-kə-gōō'-lə	pas'-kuh-goo'-luh
Paşcani (Rum.)	päsh-kän'	pahsh-kahn'
Pasco (Wash.)	păs'-kō	pas'-koh
Pas de Calais (Fr.)	pä də kä-lĕ'	pah duh kah-leh'
pasha	păsh'-ə *or* päsh'-ä	pash'-uh *or* pahsh'-ah
	Turk. pä'-shä'	pah'-shah'

   A title or honorific in the Middle East, usually following the name. It
   is disregarded in alphabetical listing.

Pasha (Rus., riv.)	pä'-shä	pah'-shah
Pashmakli (Bulg.)	See *Smolian.*	
Pásib (P.I.)	pä'-sĭb	pah'-sib
Pásig (P.I.)	pä'-sĭg	pah'-sig
Pasjača (Yugosl., mts.)	päs'-yä-chä	pahs'-yah-chah
Pasjane (Yugosl.)	päs'-yä-nĕ	pahs'-yah-neh
Pasley (Austral., cape)	păz'-lĭ	payz'-li
Pašman (Yugosl.)	päsh'-män	pahsh'-mahn

Pasoeroean *or* Pasuruan   pä-sōō-rōō-än'   pah-soo-roo-ahn'
  (NEI, Java)
Pasquale (It.)   pä-skwä'-lĕ   pah-skwah'-leh
Pasquel, Jorje   päs-kĕl', hôr'-hĕ   pahs-kel', hor'-heh
  (Mex. promoter.)
passacaglia   *It.* päs-sä-kä'-lyä   pahs-sah-kah'-lyah
  Spanish dance and musical form. Spanish *pasacalle*, pä'-sä-kä'-lyĕ
  [pah'-sah-kah'-lyeh].
Passarowitz (Yugosl.)   See *Požarevats.*
Pass Christian (Miss.)   păs' krĭs'-chĭ-ăn'   pas' kris'-chi-an'
Passeri, Torre di (It.)   päs'-sĕ-rē, tôr'-rĕ dē   pahs'-seh-ree, tor'-
                                      reh dee
Passero (Sicily, cape)   päs'-sĕ-rô   pahs'-seh-ro
Pastrana (P.I.)   päs-trä'-nä   pahs-trah'-nah
  Also called *Mamaybanay*, mä-mī-bä-nī' [mah-mai-bah-nai'].
Paštrik (Balkan mt.)   *S.-C.* päsh'-trĭk   pahsh'-trik
  English *Pushtrik*, q.v.
Pasuquín (P.I.)   pä-sōō-kēn'   pah-soo-keen'
Pasvolsky, Leo   päs-vŏl'-skĭ   pahs-vol'-skih
  (Am. diplomat)
Patani (Siam)   pät'-ə-nē'   paht'-uh-nee'
Patapsko (Md., riv.)   pə-tăp'-skō   puh-tap'-skoh
Patarica (Yugosl., mt.)   pä'-tä-rĭ-tsä   pah'-tah-ri-tsah
Patay (Fr.)   pä-tĕ'   pah-teh'
Patel, (Sirdar)   pə-tĕl', (sər-där')   puh-tel', (suhr-dahr')
  Vallabhbhai Jahverbhai vŭl'-ləb-bī jə-vĕr'-   vul'-luhb-bai juh-
  (Indian polit.)   bī   vehr'-bai
Patel, Viththalbhai   pə-tĕl', vĭt'-təl-bī', puh-tel', vit'-tuhl-
  Jahverbhai (Indian   jə-vĕr'-bī   bai', juh-vehr'-bai
  polit.)
Paterno   *Sicily* pä-tĕr-nô'   pah-tehr-no'
                 Italy pä-tĕr'-nô   pah-tehr'-no
  As a family name in America, usually Anglicized pə-tûr'-nō [puh-
  tuhr'-noh].
Pateros (P.I.)   pä-tĕ'-rôs   pah-teh'-ros
Pathan (India)   pə-tän'   puh-tahn'
                or pət-hän'   puht-hahn'
Patiala (India)   pŭt'-ĭ-ä'-lə   puht'-i-ah'-luh
Patinos (Dodec.)   pä'-tē-nô(s)   pah'-tee-no(s)
  Also called *Patmos*, q.v.
patio   *Eng.* păt'-ĭ-ō   pat'-i-oh
                 Sp. pä'-tyô   pah'-tyo
Patjitan (NEI, Java)   pä'-chē-tän   pah'-chee-tahn

Patmos (Dodec.)	pät′-mô(s)	paht′-mo(s)
Also called *Patinos*, q.v.		
Patna (India)	păt′-nə *or* pŭt′-nä′	pat′-nuh *or* puht′-nah′
Pátoc (P.I.)	pä′-tôk	pah′-tok
Patrai (Gr.)	pä′-trĕ	pah′-treh
Patras (Gr.)	pä-träs′	pah-trahs′
Officially *Patrai*, q.v.		
Pătrăşcanu, Lucreţiu	pə-trəsh-kä′-nŏŏ,	puh-truhsh-kah′-nu,
(Rum. polit.)	lŏŏ-krĕ′-tsyŏŏ	lu-kreh′-tsyu
Patrica (It.)	pä′-trē-kä	pah′-tree-kah
Patron Kolpos (Gr., gulf)	pä-trôn′ kôl′-pôs	pah-tron′ kol′-pos
English Gulf of *Patras*, q.v.		
Patti (Sicily)	păt′-tē	paht′-tee
Patungan (P.I.)	pä-tōōng′-än	pah-toong′-ahn
Pau (Fr.)	pō′	poh′
Paukkan (Burma)	pouk′-kän	pauk′-kahn
Paul Boncour, Joseph	pôl bôN-kōōr′, zhō-	pol boN-koor′, zhoh-
(Fr. polit.)	zĕf′	zef′
Paulushof (Ger.)	pou′-lŏŏs-hōf	pau′-lus-hohf
Paungde (Burma)	poung′-dĕ′	paung′-deh′
Pavelets (Rus.)	pä-vĕ-lĕts′	pah-veh-lets′
Pavelić, Ante (Serb-	pä′-vĕ-lĭch, än′-tĕ	pah′-veh-lich, ahn′-
Croat polit.)		teh
Pavia (It.)	pä-vē′-ä	pah-vee′-ah
Pavilly (Fr.)	pä-vē-yē′	pah-vee-yee′
Păvilosta (Latvia)	pä′-vē-lôs-tä	pah′-vee-los-tah
Pavlof (Alaska, volcano)	pä′-vlŏf	pah′-vlof
Pavlograd (Rus.)	pä-vlŏ-grät′	pah-vlo-graht′
Pavlova, Anna	*Eng.* pä-vlō′-və	pah-vloh′-vuh
(Rus. dancer)	*Rus.* pä′-vlŏ-vä	pah′-vlo-vah
Pavsk (Rus.)	päfsk′	pahfsk′
Pavuvu (Oc., Solomons)	pä-vōō′-vōō	pah-voo′-voo
Paximadi (Gr., Euboea,	pä-ksē-mä′-dē	pah-ksee-mah′-dee
cape; Crete, isl.)		
Paximadia (Crete, isls.)	pä-ksē-mä′-dyä	pah-ksee-mah′-dyah
Paxinou, Katina	pä-ksē-nōō,′ kä-tē′-	pah-ksee-noo′, kah-
(Am. actress)	nä	tee′-nah
Paxos *or* Paxoi (Gr.)	pä-ksôs′ *or* pä-ksē′	pah-ksos′ *or* pah-ksee′
Payagyi (Burma)	pə-yä-jē′	puh-yah-jee′
Payette (Idaho)	pā-ĕt′	pay-et′
Paz, la (Bol.)	päs′, lä	pahs′, lah
Pazova, Stara (Yugosl.)	pä′-zô-vä, stä′-rä	pah′-zo-vah, stah′-rah
Pčinja (Yugosl., riv.)	pchē′-nyä	pchee′-nyah

Peć (Yugosl.)   pĕch'   pech'
Formerly *Ipek*.

Pečenjevce (Yugosl.)   pĕ'-chĕ'-nyĕv-tsĕ   peh'-cheh'-nyev-tseh

Pechenga (Fin. >Rus.)   pĕ'-chĕng-gä   peh'-cheng-gah
See *Petsamo*.

Pechora (Rus., riv.)   pĕ-chô'-rä   peh-cho'-rah

Pechory (Est.)   *Rus.* pĕ-chô'-rĭ   peh-cho'-ri
Estonian *Petseri*, q.v.

Pecka (Yugosl.)   pĕts'-kä   pets'-kah

Pecos (N.M., Tex., riv.)   pā'-kəs   pay'-kuhs

Pécs (Hung.)   pāch'   paych'

Pećska Bistrica   pĕch'-skä bē'-strĭ-tsä   pech'-skah bee'-stri-
(Yugosl., riv.)   tsah

Peden, Peter E.   pē'-dən *or* pēd'n   pee'-duhn *or* peed'n
(U.S. representative)

Pedro Miguel (Pan.   pĕ'-drô mē-gĕl'   peh'-dro mee-gel'
Canal, locks)
Called by engineers "Peter McGill."

PEEA   pĕ-ĕ-ä   peh-eh-ah
The abbreviation of the Greek words for *Political Committee for National Liberation*.

Peenemuende *or*   pā'-nə-mün'-də   pay'-nuh-mün'-duh
Peenemünde (Ger.)

Pege (Crete)   pē'-yĕ   pee'-yee

Pegram, George B.   pē'-grəm   pee'-gruhm
(Am. scientist)

Pegu (Burma)   *Burman* pĕ-gōō'   peh-goo'
                      Eng.   pē'-gyōō'   pee'-gyoo'

Pegu Yoma (Burma, mts.)   . . . yō'-mə   . . . yoh'-muh

Pehčevo (Yugosl.)   pĕk(h)'-chĕ-vô   pek(h)'-cheh-vo

Pehle, John W.   pā'-lĭ   pay'-li
(Am. fiscal expert)

Pei Chiang *or* Pei River   bā   bay
(Ch., Kwangtung, riv.)

Peine (Ger.)   pī'-nə   pai'-nuh

Pei-p'ing (Ch., Hopeh)   bā-pĭng   bay-ping
Formerly *Peking*, q.v.

Peipsi järv (Est., Rus.,   pā'-psĭ järv'   pay'-psi jehrv'
lake)
Russian *Chudskoye ozero*, q.v. English Lake *Peipus*, q.v.

Peipus (Est., Rus., lake)   *Eng.* pī'-pəs   pai'-puhs
                      Ger. pī'-pŏŏs   pai'-pus
Estonian *Peipsi järv*, q.v. Russian *Chudskoye ozero*, q.v.

Peiraievs (Gr.) See *Piraeus.*

Peixoto, Amaral (Braz. polit.) See *Amaral Peixoto.*

Peize (Neth.)	pī'-zə	pai'-zuh
Pek (Yugosl., riv.)	pĕk'	pek'
Pekalongan (NEI, Java)	pĕ'-kä-lông'-gän	peh'-kah-long'-gahn
Peker, Recep *or* Redjep (Turk. polit.)	pĕ-kĕr', rĕ-jĕp'	peh-kehr', reh-jep'
Peking (Ch., Hopeh)	*Eng.* pē-kǐng	pee-king
	Ch. bā-jǐng	bay-jing

Now officially *Pei-p'ing,* q.v.

Pekkala, Mauno (Fin. polit.)	pĕk'-kä-lä, mou'-nô	pek'-kah-lah, mau'-no
Pelagian (Sicily, isls.)	*Eng.* pə-lā'-jən	puh-lay'-juhn
Pelagonesi (Gr., isl.)	pĕ-lä-gô-nē'-sē	peh-lah-go-nee'-see
Pelagonia (Yugosl.)	*Gr.* pĕ-lä-gô-nē'-ä	peh-lah-go-nee'-ah

Serb-Croat *Bitoljsko Polje,* q.v.

Pelagosa (It. > Yugosl., isl.)	pĕ-lä-gô'-sä	peh-lah-go'-sah

Serb-Croat *Palagruža,* pä'-lä-grōō-zhä [pah'-lah-groo-zhah].

Pelée (Fr., fort)	pə-lĕ'	puh-leh'
Peleliu (Oc., Palau)	pĕ'-lĕ-lyōō	peh'-leh-lyoo
Pelew (Oc.) See *Palau.*		
Pelion (Gr., mt.)	*Eng.* pē'-lǐ-ən	pee'-li-uhn
	Gr. pē'-lē-ô(n)	pee'-lee-o(n)
Pelješac (Yugosl., pen.)	pĕ'-lyĕ-shäts	peh'-lyeh-shahts

Italian *Sabbioncello,* q.v.

Pellaro (It.)	pĕl'-lä-rô	pel'-lah-ro
pellg (Alb.)	pĕlg'	pelg'

An element, meaning *bay* or *gulf,* in Albanian place names.

pellgu (Alb.) See *pellg.*

Peloponnesos (Gr.)	*Eng.* pĕl'-ə-pə-nē'-səs	pel'-uh-puh-nee'-suhs
	Gr. pĕ-lô-pô'-nē-sôs	peh-lo-po'-nee-sos

Also called the *Morea,* q.v.

Pelusium (Egypt)	*Eng.* pə-lōō'-zǐ-əm	puh-loo'-zi-uhm

Peña, Eugenio Silva (Guat. diplomat) See *Silva Peña.*

Penang (Malaya)	*Eng.* pē'-năng'	pee'-nang'

Malay *Pulau Pinang.*

Peñaranda (P.I.)	pĕ-nyä-rän'-dä	peh-nyah-rahn'-dah
Peñaranda, Enrique (Bol. polit.)	pĕ-nyä-rän'-dä, ĕn-rē'-kĕ	peh-nyah-rahn'-dah, en-ree'-keh
Peñas, de (Sp., cape)	pĕ'-nyäs, dĕ	peh'-nyahs, deh
Pend Oreille (Idaho, Wash.)	pŏn'-də-rā'	pon'-duh-ray'

Mining engineers call it "Pond O'Reilly."

Penedo (Brazil)	pĭ-nĕ′-dŏŏ	pi-neh′-du
Pène du Bois,	pĕn dü bwä′, gē′	pen dü bwah′, gee′
Guy (Am. painter)		
Peneios (Gr., rivs.)	*Eng.* pē-nē′-əs	pee-nee′-uhs
	Gr. pē-nē-ôs′	pee-nee-os′

The Thessalian *Peneus* is also called *Salambrias*, sä-läm-brē-äs′ [sah-lahm-bree-ahs′].

pengö	pĕn′-gû	pen′-gœ

Hungarian currency unit. Anglicized as pĕn′-gō [pen′-goh].

Pêng-p'u (Ch., Anhwei)	bŭng-pōō	buhng-poo
P'êng-shih (Ch., Hupeh, riv.)	pŭng-shû	puhng-shuh
P'êng-tsê (Ch., Kiangsi)	pŭng-dzŭ	puhng-dzuh
Pên-hsi-hu (Manchu.)	bŭn-shē-hōō	buhn-shee-hoo
penicillin	pĕn′-ə-sĭl′-ən	pen′-uh-sil′-uhn
	or pĕn-ĭs′-ə-lən	pen-is′-uh-luhn

The doctors have not yet agreed upon the pronunciation of their new remedy. One should expect the first because the source, a mold of the *Penicillium* genus, is always pronounced pĕn′-ĭ-sĭl′-ĭ-əm [pen′-i-sil′-i-uhm], and similarly *pénicillate*, *pénicilliform*, *pénicillum*, and *pénicillus*. However, to the contrary is the analogy of *insulin*, *peninsula*, *peninsulate*, and *penniferous*. The American Illustrated Medical Dictionary places the accent on the second syllable. Black's dictionary (British) has the word but has not a pronunciation. Steadman's (1942) does not list the word. The New York Academy of Medicine reports that the doctors seem evenly divided between the two pronunciations, perhaps those who work on molds preferring pĕn′-ə-sĭl′-ən [pen′-uh-sil′-uhn]. However, Dr. Chester S. Keefer, Chairman of the National Research Committee on Chemotherapeutics, wrote, Dec. 7, 1943: "As is often the case with technical terms, and this is particularly true when something is introduced in England, the emphasis is frequently placed on the second syllable rather than the first. It is my understanding that the British pronounce *penicillin* as *penicillin*. By common usage in the U.S., the pronunciation has been *penicillin*." But Mr. Edward R. Murrow cabled from London, Dec. 20, 1943, that Mr. Alexander Fleming [since knighted], the British doctor who originated the treatment, says pĕn′-ə-sĭl′-ən [pen′-uh-sil′-uhn]. Is this another instance where Americans consider an odd pronunciation "British" and the British think it "American"? Cf. the phenomena of *Caribbean.*—From the phonetic point of view a similar problem is *salicylate* pronounced săl′-ə-sĭl′-ĭt [sal′uh-sil′-it] *or* sə-lĭs′-ə-lāt′ [suh-lis′-uh-layt′]. And the pronunciations of *helicopter* and *depot* show that professional usage may depart from conventional expectations.

Penne (It.)	pĕn′-nĕ	pen′-neh

Penong (Austral.)	pē'-nông'	pee'-nong'
Penza (Rus.)	pĕn'-zä	pen'-zah
Penzance (Eng.)	pĕn-zăns'	pen-zans'
Penzig (Ger.)	pĕn'-tsĭk(h)	pen'-tsik(h)
Peoria (Ill.)	pĭ-ō'-rĭ-ə	pi-oh'-ri-uh
Pepin (Minn., Wis.)	pĕp'-ĭn	pep'-in
	local pĭp'-ĭn	pip'-in
Pepys (Eng. name)	pĕp'-ĭs or pēps'	pep'-is or peeps'

The second is preferred for Samuel Pepys, the diarist.

Peqin (Alb.)	pĕ'-kyēn	peh'-kyeen
Peqini (Alb.) See Peqin.		
Perak (Malaya)	Eng. pā'-răk'	pay'-rak'
	Malay pĕ'-rä	peh'-rah
Perama (Crete)	pĕ'-rä-mä	peh'-rah-mah
Përat (Alb.)	pər'-ät	puhr'-aht
Përati (Alb.) See Përat.		
Percé Rock (Can.)	pĕr-sĕ'	pehr-seh'
Percile (It.)	pĕr-chē'-lĕ	pehr-chee'-leh
Percy (Fr.)	Eng. pûr'-sĭ	pœr'-si
	Fr. pĕr-sē'	pehr-see'
Pereira, José Girál y (Sp. polit.) See Girál y Pereira.		
Perekop (Rus.)	pĕ-rĕ-kôp'	peh-reh-kop'
Perelazovsky (Rus.)	pĕ-rĕ-lä'-zŏf-skĭ	peh-reh-lah'-zof-ski
Peremishl (Pol.) See Przemyśl.		
Peremyshl (Rus.)	pĕ-rĕ-mwēshl'(y)	peh-reh-mweeshl'(y)
Pereto (It.)	pĕ-rĕ'-tô	peh-reh'-to
Pérez Dasmariñas (P.I.)	pĕ'-rĕs däs-mä-rē'-	peh'-res dahs-mah-
	nyäs	ree'-nyahs
Pergola (It.)	pĕr'-gô-lä	pehr'-go-lah
Perguba (Rus.)	pĕr-gōō-bä'	pehr-goo-bah'
Périers (Fr.)	pĕ-ryĕ'	peh-ryeh'
Périgueux (Fr.)	pĕ-rē-gû'	peh-ree-gœ'
Peristeri (Gr., isl.)	pĕ-rē-stĕ'-rē	peh-ree-steh'-ree
Peristeri (Yugosl., mts.)	pĕ'-rĭ-stĕ-rĭ	peh'-ri-steh-ri
Perl (Ger.)	pĕrl'	pehrl'
Perlez (Yugosl.)	pĕr'-lĕz	pehr'-lez
Perm (Rus.)	pĕrm'(y)	pehrm'(y)
Përmet (Alb.)	pər'-mĕt	puhr'-met

Also called Prëmet, prə'-mĕt [pruh'-met].

Permeti (Alb.) See Përmet.		
Pernambuco (Brazil)	Eng. pûr'-nəm-bōō'-	puhr'-nuhm-boo'-koh
	kō	
	Port. pĕr-nəm-bōō'-	pehr-nuhm-boo'-ku
Officially Recife, q.v.	kŏŏ	

Pernau (Est.)   *Ger.* pĕr′-nou   pehr′-nau
   Estonian *Pärnu*, q.v. Russian *Pernov*, q.v.
Pernay (Fr.)   pĕr-nĕ′   pehr-neh′
Pernelle, la (Fr.)   pĕr-nĕl′, lä   pehr-nel′, lah
Pernov (Est.)   *Rus.* pĕr′-nŏf   pehr′-nof
   Estonian *Pärnu*, q.v. German *Pernau*, q.v.
Perón, Eva Duarte de   pĕ-rôn′, ĕ′-vä dwär-   peh-ron′, eh′-vah
   (Arg. polit.)   tĕ dĕ   dwahr′-teh deh
   Wife of Juan Domingo Perón.
Perón, Juan Domingo   pĕ-rôn′, hwän′ dô-   peh-ron′, hwahn′
   (Arg. polit.)   mēng′-gô   do-meeng′-go
Péronne (Fr.)   pĕ-rôn′   peh-ron′
Pérouse, la (Rus., Jap.,   pĕ-rōōz′, lä   peh-rooz′, lah
   str.)
   Japanese *Sōya Kaikyō*, sô′-yä kä′-ē-kyô [so′-yah kah′-ee-kyo].
Perpignan (Fr.)   pĕr-pē-nyäN′   pehr-pee-nyahN′
Perpoli (It.)   pĕr′-pô-lē   pehr′-po-lee
Perros Guirec (Fr.)   pĕ-rôs′ gē-rĕk′   peh-ros′ gee-rek′
Pertuis (Fr.)   pĕr-twē′   pehr-twee′
Perú (S.A.)   *Eng.* pə-rōō′   puh-roo′
              Sp. pĕ-rōō′   peh-roo′
Perugia (It.)   pĕ-rōō′-jä   peh-roo′-jah
Perušić (Yugosl.)   pĕ′-rōō-shĭch   peh′-roo-shich
Pervicchio (Yugosl., isl.)   *It.* pĕr-vĕk′-kyô   pehr-veek′-kyo
   Serb-Croat *Prvić*, q.v.
Pervomaisk (Rus.)   pĕr-vŏ-mīsk′   pehr-vo-maisk′
Pervozvanovka (Rus.)   pĕr-vŏ-zvä′-nŏf-kä   pehr-vo-zvah′-nof-kah
Perzyce (Ger. >Pol.)   pĕ-zhĭ′-tsĕ   peh-zhi′-tseh
   German *Pyritz*, q.v.
Pesa (It., riv.)   pĕ′-zä   peh′-zah
Pescadores   pĕs-kä-dô′-rĕs   pes-kah-do′-res
   (Jap. >Ch., isls.)
   Japanese, *Hōko Guntō*, hô-kô gōōn′-tô [ho-ko goon′-to]; *Hōko Rettō*,
   hô-kô rĕt′-tô [ho-ko ret′-to]; *Hōko Tō*, hô-kô tô′ [ho-ko to′].
Pescara (It.)   pĕ-skä′-rä   peh-skah′-rah
Pescasseroli (It.)   pĕ-skäs-sĕ′-rô-lē   peh-skahs-seh′-ro-lee
Peschici (It.)   pĕ′-skē-chē   peh′-skee-chee
Peschiera (Yugosl., isl.)   *It.* pĕ-skyĕ′-rä   peh-skyeh′-rah
   Serb-Croat *Jadre*, q.v.
Pescia (It.)   pĕ′-shä   peh′-shah
Pescina (It.)   pĕ-shē′-nä   peh-shee′-nah
Peshawar (India)   pĕ-shä′-wər   peh-shah′-wuhr
Peshkopi (Alb.)   pĕ-shkô′-pē   peh-shko′-pee
   Italian *Piscopeia*, q.v.

Peshkopija (Alb.)   See *Peshkopi*.

Peshtera (Bulg.)	pĕ'-shtĕ-rä	peh'-shteh-rah
Pesjak (Yugosl., mts.)	pĕs'-yäk	pes'-yahk
Peski (Rus.)	pĕs-kē'	pes-kee'
Pesnica (Yugosl., riv.)	pĕs'-nĭ-tsä	pes'-ni-tsah
Pessoa, Alfredo (Braz. polit.)	pĕ-sô'-ə, äl-frĕ'-dŏŏ	peh-so'-uh, ahl-freh'-du
Pešter (Yugosl.)	pĕsh'-tĕr	pesh'-tehr
Pesto (It.)	pĕ'-stô	peh'-sto

English *Pestum* (or *Paestum*), pĕs'-təm [pes'-tuhm].

Petacci, Claretta (Mussolini's mistress)	pĕ-tät'-chē, klä-rĕt'-tä	peh-taht'-chee, klah-reht'-tah
Petacciato (It.)	pĕ-tät-chä'-tô	peh-taht-chah'-to
Petah Tiqva (Pal.)	pĕ-tä' tēk'-vä	peh-tah' teek'-vah

Also spelled *Petah Tikvah*. Arabic *Mulebbis*, mŏŏ-lĕb'-bĭs [mu-leb'-bis].

Pétain, Henri Philippe (Fr. marshall)	pĕ-tăN', äN-rē' fē-lēp'	peh-taN', ahN-ree' fee-leep'
Petalas (Gr., isl.)	pĕ-tä-läs'	peh-tah-lahs'
Petalidi (Gr.)	pĕ-tä-lē'-dē	peh-tah-lee'-dee
Petange (Luxem.)	pə-täNzh'	puh-tahNzh'
Pethick Lawrence, Lord (Br. polit.)	pĕth'-ĭk lô'-rəns	peth'-ik law'-ruhns
Petkanov, Konstantin (Bulg. author)	pĕt-kä'-nŏf, kŏn-stän-tēn'	pet-kah'-nof, kon-stahn-teen'
Petkov, Nikola (Bulg. polit.)	pĕt'-kŏf, nē'-kô-lä	pet'-kof, nee'-ko-lah

Petra Velikogo, Zaliv   See *Zaliv*. . . .

Petrace (It., riv.)	pĕ-trä'-chĕ	peh-trah'-cheh
Petrella (It.)	pĕ-trĕl'-lä	peh-trel'-lah
Petrescu, Constantin (Rum. polit.)	pĕ-trĕs'-kŏŏ	peh-tres'-ku
Petrich (Bulg.)	pĕ'-trĭch	peh'-trich
Petrinja (Yugosl.)	pĕ'-trĭ-nyä	peh'-tri-nyah
Petrograd (Rus.)	*Eng.* pĕt'-rō-grăd	pet'-roh-grad
	Rus. pĕ-trŏ-grät'	peh-tro-graht'

Officially *Leningrad*, q.v.

Petrokov (Pol.)   See *Piotrków*.

Petrolia (Alb.)	*It.* pĕ-trô'-lyä	peh-tro'-lyah

Albanian *Vajguras*, q.v., and *Kuçovë*, q.v.

Petropavlovsk Kamchat-ski (Rus.)	pĕ-trŏ-päv'-lŏfsk käm-chät'-skĭ	peh-tro-pahv'-lofsk kahm-chaht'-ski
Petropolis (Brazil)	*Eng.* pə-trŏp'-ə-lis	puh-trop'-uh-lis
	Por. pĕ'-trô-pô-lēs'	peh'-tro-po-lees'

Petroşani (Rum.)   pĕ-trô-shän′   peh-tro-shahn′
   Hungarian *Petrozsény*, pĕ′-trô-zhän(y) [pe′-tro-zhayn(y)].
Petrovac (Yugosl.)   pĕ′-trô-väts   peh′-tro-vahts
Petrovaradin (Yugosl.)   pĕ′-trô-vä-rä′-dĭn   peh′-tro-vah-rah′-din
Petrovo Selo (Yugosl.)   pĕ′-trô-vô sĕ′-lô   peh′-tro-vo seh′-lo
Petrovsk (Rus.)   pĕ-trôfsk′   peh-trofsk′
Petrovskoe (Rus.)   pĕ-trôf′-skŏ-yĕ   peh-trof′-sko-yeh
Petrozavodsk (Rus.)   pĕ′-trô-zä-vôdsk′   peh′-tro-zah-vodsk′
Petrozsény (Rum.)   See *Petroşani*.
Petsamo (Fin. > Rus.)   pĕt′-sä-mô   pet′-sah-mo
   Petsamo is now the name of a Soviet republic. The port formerly
   called *Petsamo* is now officially *Pechenga*, pĕ′-chĕng-gä [peh′-cheng-gah].
Petseri (Est.)   pĕ′-tsĕ-rĭ   peh′-tseh-ri
   Russian *Pechory*, q.v.
Petten (Neth.)   pĕt′-ən   pet′-uhn
Peurifoy, John E.   pyŏŏr′-ə-foi   pyur′-uh-foi
   (Am. gov. official)
Peyrolles (Fr.)   pĕ-rôl′   peh-rol′
Pezzalonga (It.)   pĕt-sä-lông′-gä   pet-sah-long′-gah
Pfalz (Ger.)   See *Palatinate*.
Pfeifer, Joseph L.   fī′-fər   fai′-fuhr
   (U.S. representative)
Pforzheim (Ger.)   pfôrts′-hīm   pforts′-haim
Pfungstadt (Ger.)   pfŏŏng′-shtät   pfung′-shtaht
Phanai, Ak. (Gr., Chios)   fä′-nĕ   fah′-neh
   Also called *Mastekhos*, mä′-stē-hôs [mah′-stee-hos], or *Mastikhis*, mä-
   stē′-hē(s) [mah-stee′-hee(s)].
Phangnga (Siam)   päng′-(ng)ä′   pahng′-(ng)ah′
   Also spelled *Bhangnga*
Phanos (Gr.)   fä-nôs′   fah-nos′
   Also called *Magiadag*, mī-yä-däg′ [mai-yah-dahg′].
Phanrang (Indo-Ch.)   fän-räng′   fahn-rahng′
Pharsala (Gr.)   fär′-sä-lä   fahr′-sah-lah
   Also called *Phersala*, fĕr′-sä-lä [fehr′-sah-lah].
Phatthalung (Siam)   pät′-ə-lŏŏng′   paht′-uh-lung′
   Also spelled *Padalung* and *Bhadhalung*.
Pherai (Gr.)   fĕ-rĕ′ *or* fĕ′-rĕ   feh-reh′ *or* feh′-reh
   English *Pherae*, fē′-rē [fee′-ree]. Also called *Bęlestinon*, q.v.
Pherrai (Gr.)   fĕ′-rĕ   feh′-reh
   This Thracian town is distinguished from the Thessalian *Pherai*, q.v.
Phersala (Gr.)   See *Pharsala*.
Phet Buri (Siam)   pĕt′ bŏŏ-rē′   pet′ bu-ree′
                     or pĕch′-ə-bŏŏ-rē′   pech′-uh-bu-ree′
   Also spelled *Bejraburi* and *Bhejburi*.

Philbin, Philip (U.S. representative)	fĭl'-bĭn	fil'-bin
Philiates (Gr.)	fē-lyä'-tĕs	fee-lyah'-tes
Philiatra (Gr.)	fē-lyä-trä'	fee-lyah-trah'
Philip, André (Fr. polit.)	fē-lēp', äN-drĕ'	fee-leep', ahN-dreh'
Philipias (Gr.)	fē-lē-pyäs'	fee-lee-pyahs'
Philippeville (Alg.)	*Eng.* fĭl'-ĭp-vĭl	fil'-ip-vil
	Fr. fē-lēp-vēl'	fee-leep-veel'
Phillipopolis (Bulg.)	See *Plovdif.*	
Phitsanulok (Siam)	pĭt'-sə-nŏŏ-lōk' *or* pĭs'-nŏŏ-lōk'	pit'-suh-nu-lohk' pis'-nu-lohk'

Also spelled *Bisnulok* and *Bhisanulok.*

Phlorina (Gr.)	flô'-rē-nä	flo'-ree-nah
Phnom Penh (Indo-Ch.)	See *Pnompenh.*	
Phodelai (Crete)	fô'-dĕ-lĕ	fo'-deh-leh
Phoenicia	fĭ-nĭsh'-ə	fi-nish'-uh

The pronunciation fĭ-nē'-shə [fi-nee'-shuh], though common, is not recommended by dictionaries.

Phoinikias (Crete)	fē-nĕ-kyäs'	fee-nee-kyahs'
Pholegandros (Gr., isl.)	fô-lĕ'-gän-drô(s)	fo-leh'-gahn-dro(s)

Also called *Polykantro,* pô-lē'-kän-drô [po-lee'-kahn-dro].

Phourni (Gr.)	fōōr'-nē	foor'-nee
Phrae (Siam)	prä'	pra'
Phrankokastelli (Crete)	fräng-gô-kä-stĕ'-lē	frahng-go-kah-steh'-lee

Phrasare (Alb.) See *Frashër.*

Phratabong (Indo-Ch.) See *Battambang.*

Phraya, Menam or River (Siam)	prä-yä', mă-näm'	prah-yah', ma-nahm'

Also called *Menam Chao Phraya,* q.v. *Bhraya* and *Phya* are variants of *Phraya.*

Phumiphon Adulet (King of Siam)	pōō-mĭ'-pôn ä-dōōn'-dĕt	poo-mih'-pon ah-doon'-det
Phuquoc (Indo-Ch., isl.)	fōō-kwŏŏk'	foo-kwuk'

Also spelled *Phukok.*

Piacenza (It.)	pyä-chĕn'-tsä	pyah-chehn'-tsah
pianist	pĭ-ăn'-ĭst *or* pē'-ə-nĭst	pi-an'-ist pee'-uh-nist

American dictionaries prefer the first pronunciation; British dictionaries are divided. However, the situation is unstable; for instance, the precious novelty of the stressed *pi* as spoken by Paderewski's advanceman in 1912 or 1913 turned El Paso, Texas, overnight from a pi*a*nist town to a *pi*anist town.

Piano (It., mt.)	pyä'-nô	pyah'-no

Pianoro (It.)	pyä-nô′-rô	pyah-no′-ro
Pianosa (It., isls.)	pyä-nô′-sä	pyah-no′-sah
Piansinatico (It.)	pyän-sē-nä′-tē-kô	pyahn-see-nah′-tee-ko
Piaseczno (Pol.)	pyä-sĕch′-nô	pyah-sech′-no

Russian spelling *Pyasechno.*

Piatra Neamţ (Rum.)	pyä′-trä nyämts′	pyah′-trah nyahmts′
Piauí (Brazil)	pē-ə-wē′	pee-uh-wee′
Piave (It., riv.)	pyä′-vĕ	pyah′-veh
Pibul Songkram (Siam. polit.)	pē′-bŏŏn sōng-kräm′	pee′-bun sohng-krahm′
Picasso, Pablo Ruiz (Sp., Fr. painter)	pē-kä′-sô, pä′-blô rōō-ēth′	pee-kah′-so, pah′-blo roo-eeth′
Piccia (It.)	pēt′-chä	peet′-chah
Pi-chieh (Ch., Kweichow)	bē-jyĕ	bee-jyeh
Pichon (Tun.)	pē-shôN′	pee-shoN′
Picinisco (It.)	pē-chē-nē′-skô	pee-chee-nee′-sko
Pico (It.)	pē′-kô	pee′-ko
Pico Peak (Vt.)	pī′-kō	pai′-koh
Piddig (P.I.)	pĭd-dĭg′	pid-dig′
Pieck, Wilhelm (Ger. polit.)	pēk′	peek′
Piedimonte Etneo (Sicily)	pyĕ-dē-môn′-tĕ ĕt-nĕ′-ô	pyeh-dee-mon′-teh et-neh′-o
Pieksämäki (Fin.)	pē′-ĕk′-sä-mä-kē	pee′-ek′-sa-ma-kee

Pielinin (Fin.) See *Pielisjärvi.*

Pielisjärvi (Fin., lake)	pē′-ĕ′-lĭs-yär-vē	pee′-eh′-lis-yehr-vee

Also called *Pielinin,* pē′-ĕ′-lē-nĭn [pee′-eh′-lee-nin].

P'ien-mä (Ch., Yünnan)	pyĕn-mä	pyen-mah
Pierlot, Hubert (Belg. polit.)	pyĕr-lō′, ü-bĕr′	pyehr-loh′, ü-behr′

Piero della Francesca (It. painter) See *Francesca, Piero della.*

Pierre (S.D.)	pĭr′	pihr′
Piešt'any (Cz.)	pyĕsh′-tyä-nĭ	pyesh′-tyah-ni
Pieta, la (It.)	pyĕ′-tä, lä	pyeh′-tah, lah
Pietarsaari (Fin.)	pē′-ĕ′-tär-sä-rē	pee′-eh′-tahr-sah-ree

Swedish *Jakobstad,* q.v.

Pieterszoon, Jan (Du. musician) See *Sweelinck, Jan Pieterszoon.*

Pieux, les (Fr.)	pyû′, lĕ	pyœ′-leh
Pieve (It.)	pyĕ′-vĕ	pyeh′-veh
Pievepelago (It.)	pyĕ′-vĕ-pĕ′-lä-gô	pyeh′-veh-peh′-lah-go
Piglio (It.)	pē′-lyô	pee′-lyo
Pignataro (It.)	pē-nyä-tä′-rô	pee-nyah-tah′-ro
Pijnakker (Neth.)	pīn′-äk-ər	pain′-ahk-uhr

[411]

Pikela (Oc., Carolines)	pē'-kĕ-lä	pee'-keh-lah
Pikelot (Oc., Carolines)	pē'-kĕ-lôt	pee'-keh-lot
Piła (Ger. > Pol.)	pē'-lä	pee'-lah
German *Schneidermuehl*, q.v.		
Pilar (P.I.)	pē-lär'	pee-lahr'
Pilatovica (Yugosl., mt.)	pē'-lä'-tô-vĭ-tsä	pee'-lah'-to-vi-tsah
Pilica *or* Pilitsa (Pol., riv.)	pĭ-lē'-tsä	pi-lee'-tsah
Pililla (P.I.)	pē-lē'-yä	pee-lee'-yah
Pilis (Hung.)	pĭ'-lĭsh	pi'-lish
Pillau (Ger. > Rus.)	pĭl'-ou	pil'-au
Russian *Baltiisk*, bäl-tēsk' [bahl-teesk'].		
Pillauer Tief (Ger. > Rus., Frisches Haff)	pĭl'-ou-ər tēf'	pil'-au-uhr teef'
Pillkallen (Ger. > Rus.)	pĭl'-käl-ən	pil'-kahl-uhn
In Hitler's time called *Schlossberg*, shlôs'-bĕrk(h) [shlos'-behrk(h)].		
Pilsen (Cz.)	*Ger.* pĭl'-zən	pil'-zuhn
Czech *Plzeň*, pəl'-zĕn(y) [puhl'-zen(y)].		
Piłsudski, Józev (Pol. marshall)	pĭl-sōōt'-skĭ, yōō'-zĕf	pil-soot'-ski, yu'-zef
Pimlico (Eng. and Md.)	pĭm'-lĭ-kō	pim'-li-koh
Pina (Pol., riv.)	*Pol.* pē'-nä	pee'-nah
	Rus. pĭ-nä'	pi-nah'
Pinac de Candaba (P.I., lagoon)	pē-nŭk' dĕ kän-dä'-bä	pee-nuhk' deh kahn-dah'-bah
Pinamopoan (P.I.)	pē-nä-mô-pô'-än	pee-nah-mo-po'-ahn
Pinar del Río (Cuba)	pē-när' dĕl rē'-ô	pee-nahr' dehl ree'-o
Pin Chaung (Burma, riv.)	pĭn' choung'	pin' chaung'
Pinchot, Gifford (Am. polit.)	pĭn'-sho, gĭf'-ərd	pin'-sho, gif'-uhrd
Pincian (It., Rome)	pĭn'-chən	pin'-chuhn
Italian *Pincio*, pēn'-chô [peen'-cho]; *Pinciana*, *-no*, pēn-chä'-nä, -nô [peen-chah'-nah, -no].		
Pińczów (Pol.)	pēn'(y)-chŏŏf	peen'(y)-chuf
Russian *Pinchov*, pĭn-chôf' [pin-chof'].		
Pindus (Gr., mts.)	*Eng.* pĭn'-dəs	pin'-duhs
Greek *Pindos*, pēn'-dôs [peen'-dos].		
Pineda (P.I.) See *Pásay*.		
Pinepil (Oc., New Ireland)	pē-nĕ-pēl'	pee-neh-peel'
Pinero, Sir Arthur Wing (Br. dramatist)	pĭ-nĭr'-ō	pi-nihr'-oh
Piñero, Jesús T. (P.R. polit.)	pē-nyĕ'-rô, hĕ-sōōs'	pee-nyeh'-ro, heh-soos'
Pingelap (Oc., Carolines)	pĭng'-ĕ-läp	ping'-eh-lahp

P'ing-hsiang (Ch., Kiangsi)	pǐng-shyäng	ping-shyahng
P'ing-jang (Korea) See *P'yŏng-jang*.		
P'ing-lo (Ch., Kwangsi)	pǐng-lô	ping-lo
P'ing T'an (Ch., Fukien, isls.)	pǐng tän	ping tahn
P'ing-yang (Ch., Chekiang)	pǐng-yäng	ping-yahng
Pinlebu (Burma)	pǐn'-lĕ-bōō'	pin'-leh-boo'
Pinsk (Pol. >Rus.)	pēnsk'	peensk'
Polish *Pińsk,* pēn(y)sk' [peen(y)sk']		
Pinson (Fr., mt.)	păN-sôN'	paN-soN'
Pintugan (P.I.)	pēn-tōō'-gän	peen-too'-gahn
Piombino (It.)	pyôm-bē'-nô	pyom-bee'-no
Piotrków (Pol.)	pyô'tr-kōōf	pyo'tr-kuf
Russian *Petrokov,* pĕ-trŏ-kôf' [peh-tro-kof'].		
Piperi (Gr., isl.)	pē-pĕ'-rē	pee-peh'-ree
Piraeus (Gr.)	*Eng.* pī-rē'-əs	pai-ree'-uhs
Greek *Peiraievs,* pē-rĕ-ĕfs' [pee-reh-efs']. The English form should be preceded by the article *the.*		
Piraino (Sicily)	pē-rī'-nô	pee-rai'-no
piranha (fish)	pǐ-rä'-nyə	pi-rah'-nyuh
Piriac (Fr.)	pē-ryäk'	pee-ryahk'
Pirmasens (Ger.)	pǐr-mä-zĕns'	pihr-mah-zens'
Piroe *or* Piru (NEI, Ceram)	pē'-rōō	pee'-roo
Pirot (Yugosl.)	pē'-rôt	pee'-rot
Piryatin (Rus.)	pǐ-ryä'-tǐn	pi-ryah'-tin
Pisa (It.)	*Eng.* pē'-zə	pee'-zuh
	It. pē'-sä	pee'-sah
Pisciatello (It., riv.)	pē-shä-tĕl'-lô	pee-shah-tel'-lo
Pisciotta (It.)	pē-shôt'-tä	pee-shot'-tah
Piscopeia (Alb.)	*It.* pē-skô'-pĕ-yä	pee-sko'-peh-yah
Albanian *Peshkopi,* q.v.		
Piscopi (Dodec.)	*It.* pē'-skô-pē	pee'-sko-pee
Greek *Tilos,* q.v.		
Písek (Cz.)	pē'-sĕk	pee'-sek
Pishevari (Iran. polit.) See *Jafar Pishevari.*		
Pisida (Libya)	pē-sē'-dä	pee-see'-dah
Pisigan (P.I.)	pē-sē'-gän	pee-see'-gahn
Pistoia (It.)	pē-stô'-yä	pee-sto'-yah
Piteşti (Rum.)	pē-tĕsht'	pee-tesht'
Pithiviers (Fr.)	pē-tē-vyĕ'	pee-tee-vyeh'

Pittenger, Wm. A. (U.S. representative)	pĭt′n-jər	pit′n-juhr
Pitugu (P.I.)	pē-tōō′-gōō	pee-too′-goo
Pityilu (Oc., Admiralties)	pē-tyē′-lōō	pee-tyee′-loo
Pius XII (Pope) See *Pope Pius XII.*		
Piute (Am. Indian) Also spelled *Paiute.*	pĭ′-yōōt′	pai′-yoot′
Piyade, Mosha (Yugosl. polit.)	pē′-yä-dĕ, mô′-shä	pee′-yah-deh, mo′-shah
Pizzo (It.)	pēt′-sô	peet′-so
Pješivci (Yugosl.)	pyĕ′-shĭv-tsĭ	pyeh′-shiv-tsi
Placentia (Newf.)	plə-sĕn′-shə	pluh-sen′-shuh
Placerville (Calif.)	plăs′-ər-vĭl	plas′-uhr-vil
Plancher les Mines (Fr.)	pläN-shĕ lĕ mēn′	plahN-sheh leh meen′
Plancoët (Fr.)	pläN-kô-ĕt′	plahN-ko-et′
Plane (Ger., riv.)	plä′-nə	plah′-nuh
Planik (Yugosl., isl.) Italian *Magresina,* q.v.	plä′-nĭk	plah′-nik
Planinica (Yugosl.)	plä′-nē′-nĭ-tsä	plah′-nee′-ni-tsah
Planinski Kanal (Yugosl.) English and Italian *Morlacca* (Channel), q.v.	plä′-nēn′-skĭ kä′-näl	plah′-neen′-ski kah′-nahl
Plaquemine (La.)	plăk′-ə-mĭn or plăk′-min	plak′-uh-min plak′-min
Plaridel (P.I.)	plä-rē-dĕl′	plah-ree-del′
Plastiras, Nicholas (Gr. polit.)	plä-stē′-räs, nē′-kô-läs	plah-stee′-rahs, nee′-ko-lahs
Plastun (Rus., bay)	plä-stōōn′	plah-stoon′
Plata *or* Plate (S. A., estuary) See *Río de la Plata.*		
Platamon (Gr.)	plä-tä-môn′	plah-tah-mon′
Platamon, Rt (Yugosl.) Italian *Punta Platamone,* q.v.	plä′-tä-môn, ərt′	plah′-tah-mon, uhrt′
Plataria (Gr.)	plä-tär-yä′	plah-tahr-yah′
Platsa (Gr.)	plä′-tsä	plah′-tsah
Plauen (Ger.)	plou′-ən	plau′-uhn
Plauen im Vogtland (Ger.)	plou′-ən ĭm fōkt′-länt	plau′-uhn im fohkt′-lahnt
Plavinas (Latvia) German *Stockmanshof,* q.v.	plä′-vē-nyäs	plah′-vee-nyahs
Plavnica (Yugosl.)	pläv′-nĭ-tsä	plahv′-ni-tsah
Plavnik (Yugosl., isl.)	pläv′-nĭk	plahv′-nik
Plavsko Blato (Yugosl., lake)	pläv′-skô blä′-tô	plahv′-sko blah′-to

Pleisse (Ger., riv.)   plīs'-ə   plais'-uh

plenary   plĕn'-ə-rĭ *or* plē'-nə-rĭ   plen'-uh-ri *or* plee'-nuh-ri

Both pronunciations are correct, but this was the order of frequency among CBS correspondents in 1945 and 1946. The year 1947 has seen an advance by No. 2, but No. 1 is still the Editor's favorite.

Plérin (Fr.)   plĕ-răN'   pleh-raN'

Plešivec (Cz.)   plĕ'-shē-vĕts   pleh'-shee-vets

Pless (Pol.)   See *Pszczyna.*

Plessis (Fr., canal)   plĕ-sē'   pleh-see'

Pleubian (Fr.)   plû-byäN'   plœ-byahN'

Pleven (Bulg.)   *Eng.* plĕv'-ĕn   plev'-en

               Bulg. plĕ'-vĕn(y)   pleh'-ven(y)

Also called *Plevna*, plev'-nä [plev'-nah].

Pléven, René (Fr. polit.)   plĕ-vĕn', rə-nĕ',   pleh-ven', ruh-neh'

Pljačkovica (Yugosl.,   plyäch'-kô'-vĭ-tsä   plyahch'-ko'-vi-tsah

  mts.)

Pljevlja (Yugosl.)   plyĕv'-lyä   plyev'-lyah

Ploče, Rt (Yugosl.)   plô'-chĕ, ərt'   plo'-cheh, uhrt'

  Italian *Punta Planca*, q.v.

Płock (Pol.)   plôtsk'   plotsk'

  Russian spelling *Plotsk.*

Ploëmeur (Fr.)   plô-ə-mûr'   plo-uh-mœr'

Ploërmel (Fr.)   plô-ĕr-mĕl'   plo-ehr-mel'

Ploeser, Walter C.   plā'-zər   play'-zuhr

  (U.S. representative)

Ploeşti (Rum.)   plô-yĕsht'   plo-yesht'

Płońsk (Pol.)   plôn(y)sk'   plon(y)sk'

Plonton, Jacques   plôN-tôN', zhäk'   ploN-toN', zhahk'

  (Fr. polit.)

Plora (Crete)   plô'-rä   plo'-rah

Plotsk (Pol.)   See *Płock.*

Ploudalmézeau (Fr.)   plōō-däl-mĕ-zō'   ploo-dahl-meh-zoh'

Plouescat (Fr.)   plōō-ĕs-kä'   ploo-es-kah'

Plougastel Daoulas (Fr.)   plōō-gä-stĕl' dou-läs'   ploo-gah-stel' dau-lahs'

Plouguerneau (Fr.)   plōō-gĕr-nō'   ploo-gehr-noh'

Plouhinec (Fr.)   plōō-ē-nĕk'   ploo-ee-nek'

Plovdiv (Bulg.)   plôv'-dĭf   plov'-dif

  Greek *Phillipopolis*, (Eng.) fĭl'-ĭ-pŏp'-ə-lĭs [fil'-i-pop'-uh-lis].

Plumaudan (Fr.)   plü-mō-däN'   plü-moh-dahN'

Plyusa (Rus.)   plyōō'-sä   plyoo'-sah

Plzeň (Cz.)   See *Pilsen.*

Pnompenh (Indo-Ch.)	*Eng.* nŏm'-pĕn'	nom'-pen'
	local pnŏŏm-pĕn'(y)	pnum-pen'(y)
Siamese *Phnom Penh*, pnōm pĕn' [pnohm pen'].		
P'o (Ch., gulf) See *P'o-hai*.		
Poage, W. R.	pōg'	pohg'
(U.S. representative)		
Pobijenik (Yugosl., mts.)	pô'-bĭ-yĕ'-nĭk	po'-bi-yeh'-nik
Pocantico Hills (N.Y.)	pō-kăn'-tĭ-kō	poh-kan'-ti-koh
Pocatello (Idaho)	pō'-kə-tĕl'-ō *or* -ə	poh'-kuh-tel'-oh *or* -uh
Počekovina (Yugosl.)	pô'-chĕ'-kô-vĭ-nä	po'-cheh'-ko-vi-nah
Pochep (Rus.)	pô'-chĕp	po'-chep
Pochinok (Rus.)	pŏ-chē'-nŏk	po-chee'-nok
Pöchlarn (Austria)	pûk(h)'-lärn	pœk(h)'-lahrn
Pocomoke (Md.)	pō'-kə-mōk	poh'-kuh-mohk
Pocono (Pa., mts.)	pō'-kə-nō	poh'-kuh-noh
Podareš (Yugosl.)	pô'-dä-rĕsh	po'-dah-resh
Podena (NEI, isl.)	pô-dā'-nä	po-day'-nah
Podgorac (Yugosl.)	pôd'-gô-räts	pod'-go-rahts
Podgorica (Yugosl.)	pôd'-gô'-rĭ-tsä	pod'-go'-ri-tsah
Podhum (Yugosl.)	pôd'-hōōm	pod'-hoom
Po di Primaro (It.)	pô' dē prē-mä'-rô	po' dee pree-mah'-ro
Podlec (Yugosl.)	pôd'-lĕts	pod'-lets
Podmokly (Cz.)	pôd'-mô-klĭ	pod'-mo-kli
Podolsk (Rus.)	pŏ-dôl(y)sk'	po-dol(y)sk'
Podujevo (Yugosl.)	pô'-dōō'-yĕ-vô	po'-doo'-yeh-vo
Podunavci (Yugosl.)	pô'-dōō'-näv-tsĭ	po'-doo'-nahv-tsi
Podunavska (Yugosl.)	pô'-dōō'-näv-skä	po'-doo'-nahv-skah
Podwołoczyska (Pol.)	pôd-vô-lô-chĭ'-skä	pod-vo-lo-chi'-skah
Poechlarn (Austria)	pûk(h)'-lärn	pœk(h)'-lahrn
Poelitz (Ger.)	pû'-lĭts	pœ'-lits
Poerwakarta (NEI, Java)	pōōr-wä-kär'-tä	poor-wah-kahr'-tah
Poerwokerto (NEI, Java)	pōōr-wô-kĕr'-tô	poor-wo-kehr'-to
Poetoehena (Indo. polit.)	See *Putuhena*.	
Pogany, Willy (Hung.	*Eng.* pō-gä'-nĭ, wĭl'-ĭ	poh-gah'-ni, wil'-i
Am. artist)	*Hung.* pô'-gän(y)	po'-gahn(y)
Poggiardo (It.)	pôd-jär'-dô	pod-jahr'-do
Poggibonsi (It.)	pôd-jē-bôn'-sē	pod-jee-bon'-see
Poggio (It.)	pôd'-jô	pod'-jo
Pogled (Yugosl., mt.)	pô'-glĕd	po'-gled
Pogodinsk (Rus.)	pŏ-gô'-dĭnsk	po-go'-dinsk
Pogoryeloye Gorodishche	pŏ-gŏ-rĕ'-lŏ-yĕ	po-go-reh'-lo-yeh
(Rus.)	gŏ-rŏ-dē'-shchĕ	go-ro-dee'-shcheh
Pogradea (Alb.) See *Pogradec*.		

Pogradec (Alb.)   pô-grä′-dĕts   po-grah′-dets
Also called *Pogradea*, pô-grä′-dĕ-ä [po-grah′-deh-ah].

Pogranichnaya (Rus.)   pŏ-grä-nĕch′-nä-yä   po-grah-neech′-nah-yah

pogrom   pō′-grəm *or* pō-grŏm′   poh′-gruhm *or* poh-grom′

Recent American dictionaries accent the first syllable. Russian pŏ-grôm′ [po-grom′].

P'o-hai (Ch., gulf)   pô-hī   po-hai

Pohorje (Yugosl., mts.)   pô′-hŏr-yĕ   po′-hor-yeh

poilu (French private soldier)   pwä-lü′   pwah-lü′

point. Compounds with *point* are listed under the second element of the name.

Pointe de Grave (Fr.)   pwăNt də gräv′   pwaNt duh grahv′

Poissy (Fr.)   pwä-sē′   pwah-see′

Poitiers (Fr.)   pwä-tyĕ′   pwah-tyeh′

Poix (Fr.)   pwä′   pwah′

Pojan (Alb.)   pô′-yän   po′-yahn

Pojani (Alb.)   See *Pojan.*

Pokaakku (Oc., Marshalls)   pô′-kä-äk′-kōō   po′-kah-ahk′-koo
Also called *Taongi*, q.v.

Pola (It. >Yugosl.)   pô′-lä   po′-lah
Serb-Croat, *Pulj.*

Polá (P.I.)   pô-lä′   po-lah′

Polangen (Lith.)   *Rus.* pŏ-län′-gĕn   po-lahn′-gen
Lithuanian *Palanga*, q.v.

Polesia (Pol.)   *Eng.* pō-lē′-shə   poh-lee′-shuh
Polish *Polesie*, pô-lĕ′-syĕ [po-leh′-syeh].

Polessk (Ger. >Rus.)   pŏ-lĕsk′   po-lesk′
German *Labiau*, q.v.

Po-li (Manchu.)   bô-lē   bo-lee

Poliçan (Alb.)   pô-lē′-chän   po-lee′-chahn

Poliçani (Alb.)   See *Poliçan.*

Policastro (It., gulf)   pôl-ē-kä′-strô   pol-ee-kah′-stro

Polillo (P.I.)   pô-lē′-lyô *or* -yô   po-lee′-lyo *or* -yo

polio (disease)   pō′-lĭ-ō   poh′-li-oh
    or pŏl′-ĭ-ō   pol′-i-oh
See *poliomyelitis.*

poliomyelitis   pŏl′-ĭ-ō-mī′-ə-lī′-tĭs   pol′-ih-oh-mai′-uh-lai′-tis

Doctors, however, frequently say pō′-lĭ-ō-mī′-ə-lē′-təs [poh′-li-oh-mai′-

uh-lee'-tuhs]. The common abbreviation *polio* is usually pronounced pō'-lǐ-ō [poh'-li-oh], although pŏl'-ǐ-ō [pol'-i-oh] is also heard.

Politburo   *Eng.* pə-lĭt'-byŏŏr'-ō   puh-lit'-byur'-oh
       Rus. pŏ-lēt'-byŏŏ-rô'   po-leet'-byu-ro'
Russian Communist Executive Committee.

Pölitz (Ger.)   pů'-lĭts   pœ'-lits
Poljana (Yugosl.)   pô'-lyä'-nä   po'-lyah'-nah
Poljčane (Yugosl.)   pôl(y)'-chä-ně   pol(y)'-chah-neh
Pollenza (It.)   pôl-lěn'-tsä   pol-len'-tsah
Pollet, le (Fr.)   pô-lě', lə   po-leh', luh
Polnoe (Rus.)   pôl'-nŏ-yě   pol'-no-yeh
Polo (P.I.)   pô'-lô   po'-lo
Pologi (Rus.)   pŏ-lô'-gĭ   po-lo'-gi
Polotsk (Rus.)   pô'-lŏtsk   po'-lotsk
Poltava (Rus.)   pŏl-tä'-vä   pol-tah'-vah
Poltavka (Rus.)   pŏl-täf'-kä   pol-tahf'-kah
Polygyros (Gr.)   pô-lē'-yē-rôs   po-lee'-yee-ros
Polykantro (Gr., isl.)   See *Pholegandros.*
Pombelaa (NEI)   pôm'-bě-lä'   pom'-beh-lah'
Pomerania (Ger., Pol.)   *Eng.* pŏm-ə-rā'-nyə   pom-uh-ray'-nyuh
    Polish *Pomorze,* q.v. German *Pommern,* pôm'-ərn [pom'-uhrn].
Pomigliano d'Arco (It.)   pô-mē-lyä'-nô   po-mee-lyah'-no
       där'-kô   dahr'-ko
Pommern (Ger., Pol., provs.)   See *Pomerania.*
Pomorie (Bulg.)   pŏ-mô'-ryě   po-mo'-ryeh
Pomorze (Pol., Ger.,   *Pol.* pô-mô'-zhě   po-mo'-zheh
    provs.)
    See *Pomerania.*
pompano (fish)   pŏm'-pä-nō   pom'-pah-noh
Pompei(i) (It.)   *Eng.* pŏm-pā'   pom-pay'
       It. pôm-pě'-yē   pom-peh'-yee
Ponape (Oc., Carolines)   pô'-nä-pě   po'-nah-peh
Ponce (P.R.)   pôn'-sě   pon'-seh
Ponce, Federico   pôn'-sě, fě-dě-rē'-kô   pon'-seh, feh-deh-
    (Guat. polit.)   ree'-ko
Ponchielli, Amilcare   pôn-kyěl'-lē,   pon-kyel'-lee,
    (It. composer)   ä-mēl'-kä-rě   ah-meel'-kah-
                                                    reh
Pondichéry (Fr. India)   *Eng.* pŏn'-dĭ-chěr'-ĭ   pon'-di-chehr'-i
       Fr. pôN-dě-shě-rě'   poN-dee-sheh-ree'
Ponevezh (Lith.)   *Rus.* pŏ-ně-vězh'   po-neh-vezh'
    Lithuanian *Panevėžys,* q.v.
Pongoma (Rus., riv.)   pŏn-gô'-mä   pon-go'-mah
Pons, Lily (singer)   *Eng.* pŏnz, lĭl'-ĭ   ponz, lil'-i
       Fr. 'pôNs', lē-lē'   poNs', lee-lee'

Ponsón (P.I.)	pôn-sôn′	pon-son′
pont	pôN′	poN′

An element, meaning *bridge*, in French place names. It may be necessary to look up the other part of the name.

Ponta Delgada (Azores)	pôn′-tə děl-gä′-də	pon′-tuh del-gah′-duh
Pont à Mousson (Fr.)	pôN tä mōō-sôN′	poN tah moo-soN′
Pontarlier (Fr.)	pôN-tär-lyě′	poN-tahr-lyeh′
Pontassieve (It.)	pôn-täs-syě′-vě	pon-tahs-syeh′-veh
Pontaubault (Fr.)	pôN-tō-bō′	poN-toh-boh′
Pont Audemer (Fr.)	pôN tōd-měr′	poN tohd-mehr′
Pont Authou (Fr.)	pôN tō-tōō′	poN toh-too′
Pontchâteau (Fr.)	pôN-shä-tō′	poN-sha-toh′
Pont de Roide (Fr.)	pôN də rwäd′	poN duh rwahd′
Pont du Fahs (Tun.)	pôN dü fäs′	poN dü fahs′
Pontecorvo (It.)	pôn-tě-kôr′-vô	pon-teh-kor′-vo
Pontedera (It.)	pôn-tě-dě′-rä	pon-teh-deh′-rah
Pontelagoscuro (It.)	pôn′-tě-lä′-gô-skōō′-rô	pon′-teh-lah′-go-skoo′-ro
Ponte Olivo (Sicily)	pôn′-tě ô-lē′-vô	pon′-teh o-lee′-vo
Pontet, le (Fr.)	pôN-tě′, lə	poN-teh′, luh
Pontevedra (Sp.)	pôn-tě-vě′-drä	pon-teh-veh′-drah
Pontianak (NEI, Borneo)	pôn-tē-ä′-näk	pon-tee-ah′-nahk
Pontikonesi (Crete, isl.)	pôn-dē-kô-nē′-sē	pon-dee-ko-nee′-see

Also called *Mili*, mē′-lē [mee′-lee].

Pontine Marshes (It.)	*Eng.* pŏn′-tĭn *or* -tīn	pon′-tin *or* -tain
Pontivy (Fr.)	pôN-tē-vē′	poN-tee-vee′
Pont l'Abbé (Fr.)	pôN lä-bě′	poN lah-beh′
Pont l'Évêque (Fr.)	pôN lě-věk′	poN leh-vek′
Pontoise (Fr.)	pôN-twäz′	poN-twahz′
pontoon	pŏn-tōōn′	pon-toon′

Military *ponton*, pŏnt′n.

Pontorson (Fr.)	pôN-tôr-sôN′	poN-tor-soN′
Pontotoc (Miss.)	pŏn′-tə-tŏk′	pon′-tuh-tok′
Pontremoli (It.)	pôn-trě′-mô-lē	pon-treh′-mo-lee
Ponts de Cé, les (Fr.)	pôN də sě′, lě	poN duh seh′, leh
Ponyri (Rus.)	pŏ-nû-rē′	po-nuh-ree′
Ponza (It., isl.)	pôn′-tsä	pon′-tsah
Ponziane (It., isls.)	pôn-tsyä′-ně	pon-tsyah′-neh
Poona (India)	pōō′-nə	poo′-nuh
Poopó (Bol., lake)	pô-ô-pô′	po-o-po′
Popayán (Colom.)	pô-pä-yän′	po-pah-yahn′
Pope Pius XII, Eugenio Pacelli	ě-ōō-jě′-nyô pä-chěl′-lē	eh-u-jeh′-nyo pah-chel′-lee

Poperinghe (Belg.)	*Eng.* pŏp'-ər-ĭng	pop'-uhr-ing
	Flem. pō-pə-rĭnk'-k(h)ə	poh-puh-rink'-k(h)uh
	Fr. pô-pə-răNg'	po-puh-raNg'
Popiel, Karol (Pol. polit.)	pô'-pyĕl, kä'-rôl	po'-pyel, kah'-rol
Popocatepetl (Mex., vol.)	*Eng.* pō'-pə-kăt'-ə-pĕt'l	poh'-puh-kat'-uh-pet'l
	Sp. pô-pô-kä-tĕ'-pĕtl	po-po-kah-teh'-petl
Popoli (It.)	pô'-pô-lē	po'-po-lee
Popolo (It.)	pô'-pô-lô	po'-po-lo
Poporang (Oc., Solomons)	pô-pô-räng'	po-po-rahng'
Popovac (Yugosl.)	pô'-pô-väts	po'-po-vahts
Popović (Yugosl.)	pô'-pô-vĭch	po'-po-vich
Popovo (Bulg.)	pô'-pŏ-vŏ	po'-po-vo
Poppendorf (Ger.)	pôp'-ən-dôrf	pop'-uhn-dorf
Poprad (Cz.)	pô'-prät	po'-praht
Pórac (P.I.)	pô'-räk	po'-rahk
Porbandar (India)	pôr-bŭn'-dər	por-buhn'-duhr
Porcareccia (It.)	pôr-kä-rĕt'-chä	por-kah-ret'-chah
Porcher (S.C. name)	pôr-shä' *or* pə-shä'	por-shay' *or* puh-shay'
Porchia (It., mt.)	pôr'-kyä	por'-kyah
Porečka (Yugosl., riv.)	pô'-rĕch-kä	po'-rech-kah
Pori (Fin.)	pô'-rē	po'-ree

Swedish *Bjoerneborg,* byûr'-nə-bôr'(y) [byœr'-nuh-bor'(y)].

| Porkhov (Rus.) | pôr'-hŏf | por'-hof |
| Porkkala Udd (Fin. >Rus., pen.) | pôrk'-kä-lä ŏŏd' | pork'-kah-lah ud' |

This Finno-Swedish form the Russians prefer to the Finnish *Porkkalaniemi,* pôrk'-kä-lä-nē'-ĕ'-mē [pork'-kah-lah-nee'-eh'-mee]. Also called *Porkkala Udde,* ŏŏd'-ə [ud'-uh].

Pornic (Fr.)	pôr-nēk'	por-neek'
Porphyrogenis (Gr. name)	pôr-fē-rô-yĕ'-nēs	por-fee-ro-yeh'-nees
Porquerolles (Fr., isl.)	pôr-kə-rôl'	por-kuh-rol'
Porrentruy (Fr.)	pô-räN-trwē'	po-rahN-trwee'
Porsgrunn (Nor.)	pôrs'-grŏŏn	pors'-grun
	or pôsh'-grŏŏn	posh'-grun

port. Compounds with *port* may be listed under the second element of the name.

Porta e Palermos (Alb.)	See *Portë e Palermos.*	
Portalegre (Port.)	pôr-tə-lĕ'-grə	por-tuh-leh'-gruh
Port Angeles (Wash.)	pōrt ăn'-jə-ləs	pohrt an'-juh-luhs
Port Arthur (Manchu.)	pôrt är'-thər	port ahr'-thuhr

Chinese *Lü-shun-k'ow,* lü-shŏŏn-kō [lü-shun-koh]. Japanese *Ryojun-ko,* ryô-jōōn'-kô [ryo-joon'-ko].

Port au Prince (Haiti)	*Eng.* pôr′ tə prĭns′	por′ tuh prins′
	Fr. pôr tō prăNs′	por toh praNs′
Port Bail (Fr.)	pôr bĭ′	por bai′
Port Cros (Fr., isl.)	pôr krō′	por kroh′
Port Dalhousie (Can., Ont.)	dăl-hou′-zĭ	dal-hau′-zi
Port de Bouc (Fr.)	pôr′ də bōōk′	por′ duh book′
Portë e Palermos (Alb.)	pôr′-tə ĕ pä-lĕr′-môs	por′-tuh eh pah-lehr′-mos

Also called *Panorm,* q.v. Italian *Palermo,* q.v., or *Porto Palermo.*

Portela (Port.)	pôr-tĕ′-lä	por-teh′-lah
Portela de Sacavem	pôr-tĕl′-ə də sä′-kä-vĕN	por-tel′-uh duh sah′-kah-veN
Port en Bassin (Fr.)	pôr täN bĕ-săN′	por tahN beh-saN′
portentous. See *grievous.*		
Port Étienne (Fr. W. Afr.)	pôr tĕ-tyĕn′	por teh-tyehn′
Portimão (Port.)	pôr-tĭ-mouN′	por-ti-mauN′
Port Moresby (New Guinea, Papua)	*Eng.* mōrz′-bĭ	mohrz′-bi
Port Neches (Tex.)	nĕch′-ĭz	nech′-iz
Porto (Port.)	pôr′-tōō	por′-tu

English *Oporto,* ō-pôr′-tō [oh-por′-toh].

Porto Alegre (Brazil)	pôr′-tōō ä-lĕ′-grĭ	por′-tu ah-leh′-gri
Porto Caldo (Yugosl.)	*It.* pôr′-tô käl′-dô	por′-to kahl′-do
Serb-Croat *Teplo Pristanište,* q.v.		
Porto da Praia (Port., Cape Verde Isls.)	pôr′-tōō də prĭ′-ə	por′-tu duh prai′-uh
Porto Edda (Alb.)	*It.* pôr′-tô ĕd′-dä	por′-to ed′-dah

Mussolini's name for *Santi Quaranta,* q.v., Albanian *Sarandë,* q.v.

Porto Empedocle (Sicily)	pôr′-tô ĕm-pĕ′-dô-klĕ	por′-to em-peh′-do-kleh
Porto Farina (Tun.)	pôr′-tô fä-rē′-nä	por′-to fah-ree′-nah
Portoferraio (It.)	pôr′-tô-fĕr-rä′-yô	por′-to-fehr-rah′-yo
Porto Lago (Dodec., bay)	pôr′-tô lä′-gô	por′-to lah′-go
Porto Maggiore (It.)	pôr′-tô mäd-jô′-rĕ	por′-to mahd-jo′-reh
Porto Ponte Romano (It.)	pôr′-tô pôn′-tĕ rô-mä′-nô	por′-to pon′-teh ro-mah′-no
Porto Re (Yugosl.)	*It.* pôr′-tô rĕ′	por′-to reh′
Serb-Croat *Kraljevica,* q.v.		
Porto Rico (W.I.) Now officially called *Puerto Rico,* q.v.		
Portoscuso (Sard.)	pôr′-tô-skōō′-zô	por′-to-skoo′-zo
Porto Torres (Sard.)	pôr′-tô tôr′-rĕs	por′-to tor′-res
Porto Vecchio (It. and Corsica)	pôr′-tô vĕk′-kyô	por′-to vek′-kyo

Port Said (Egypt)   sä-ēd′   sah-eed′

It is perhaps as well to aim at the Arabic pronunciation so long as the English variants are numerous: BBC′s sīd′ [said′], Kenyon and Knott′s sād′ [sayd′], and the Editor′s sĕd′ [sed′].

Portugal	*Eng.* pôr′-chə-gəl	por′-chuh-guhl
	Port. pôr-tŏŏ-gäl′	por-tu-gahl′
Port Vendres (Fr.)	pôr väN′dr	por vahN′dr
Porya (Rus.)	pōr′-yä	pohr′-yah
Posad (Rus.)	pŏ-säd′	po-sahd′

An element, meaning *settlement*, in Russian place names.

Poschiavo (It.)	pô-skyä′-vô	po-skyah′-vo
Po-seh (Ch., Kwangsi)	bô-sŭ	bo-suh

Also called *Pai-seh*, q.v.

Posen (Pol.)	*Ger.* pō′-zən	poh′-zuhn

Polish *Poznań*, pôz′-nän(y) [poz′-nahn(y)].

Posillipo (It.)	pô-zēl′-lē-pô	po-zeel′-lee-po
Postumia (It.)	pô-stŏŏ′-myä	po-stoo′-myah
Postyshevo (Rus.)	pŏs-twē′-shĕ-vŏ	pos-twee′-sheh-vo
Potamos (Gr.)	pô-tä-môs′	po-tah-mos′
Poteat (Am. name)	pō-tēt′	poh-teet′
Potëmkin, Prince Grigori	pŏ-tyôm′-kĭn, grĭ-	po-tyom′-kin, gri-
(Rus. polit.)	gô′-rĭ	go′-ri
Potëmkinsk (Rus.)	pŏ-tyôm′-kĭnsk	po-tyom′-kinsk
Potenza (It.)	pô-tĕn′-tsä	po-ten′-tsah
Pothea (Dodec., Kalymnos)	See *Kalymnos*.	
Potinville (Tun.)	pô-tăN-vēl′	po-taN-veel′
Potocki, -a (Pol. name)	pô-tô′-tskĭ, -ä	po-to′-tski, -ah
Potomac (U.S., riv.)	pə-tō′-mək	puh-toh′-muhk

The pronunciation pə-tō′-mĭk [puh-toh′-mik] should be avoided.

Potony (Hung.)	pô′-tôn(y)	po′-ton(y)
Potosí (Bol.)	pô-tô-sē′	po-to-see′
Poughkeepsie (N.Y.)	pə-kĭp′-sĭ	puh-kip′-si
Pouilly (Fr.)	pŏŏ-yē′	poo-yee′
Poulitsas, Panayotis	pŏŏ-lē′-tsäs,	poo-lee′-tsahs,
(Gr. polit.)	pä-nä-yô′-tēs	pah-nah-yo′-tees
Poulson, Norris	pōl′-sən	pohl′-suhn
(U.S. representative)		
Pournaras, D. (Gr. polit.)	pŏŏr-nä′-räs	poor-nah′-rahs
Pourtalet (Fr.)	pŏŏr-tä-lĕ′	poor-tah-leh′
Pouzauges (Fr.)	pŏŏ-zōzh′	poo-zohzh′
Povenets (Rus.)	pŏ-vĕ-nĕts′	po-veh-nets′
Povorino (Rus.)	pŏ-vô′-rĭ-nŏ	po-vo′-ri-no
Powell, Baden (Eng. name)	See *Baden Powell*.	
Pownal (Vt.)	pou′-nəl	pau′-nuhl

P'o-yang (Ch.,   pô-yäng   po-yahng
  Kiangsi, lake)

Požarevac (Yugosl.)   pô'-zhä'-rĕ-väts   po'-zhah'-reh-vahts
  German *Passarowitz*, pä-sä'-rō-vĭts [pah-sah'-roh-vits].

Požega (Yugosl.)   pô'-zhĕ-gä   po'-zheh-gah

Požežena (Yugosl.)   pô'-zhĕ'-zhĕ-nä   po'-zheh'-zheh-nah

Poznań (Pol.)   pôz'-nän(y)   poz'-nahn(y)
  German *Posen*, pō'-zən [poh'-zuhn].

Pozorrubio (P.I.)   pô-sôr-rōō'-byô   po-sor-roo'-byô

Pozzaglia (It.)   pôt-sä'-lyä   pot-sah'-lyah

Pozzallo (Sicily)   pôt-sä'-lô   pot-sah'-lo

Pozzuoli (It.)   pôt-swô'-lē   pot-swo'-lee

Prabuty (Ger. > Pol.)   prä-bōō'-tĭ   prah-boo'-ti
  German *Riesenburg*, q.v.

Pracht, C. Frederick   präkt'   prahkt'
  (U.S. representative)

Prachuap Khiri Khan   prä'-chwŭp'   prah'-chwuhp'
  (Siam)   kē-rē kän'   kee-ree kahn'

Pradist Manudharm   prə-dĭt' mä-nōō'-täm pruh-dit' mah-nu'-
  (Siam. polit.)   tahm

Prądnik (Pol., riv.)   prôNd'-nĭk   proNd'-nik
  Russian *Prondnik*, prônd'-nĭk [prond'-nik].

Praga (Pol.)   prä'-gä   prah'-gah

Pragersko (Yugosl.)   prä'-gĕr-skô   prah'-gehr-sko

Prague (Cz.)   *Eng.* präg'   prahg'
This pronunciation has been adopted from the French. The older
English pronunciation is prāg' [prayg']. Czech *Praha*, prä'-hä [prah'-
hah]. German *Prag*, präk(h)' [prahk(h)'].

Praha (Cz.)   See *Prague*.

Prahecq (Fr.)   prä-ĕk'   prah-ek'

Prahovo (Yugosl.)   prä'-hô-vô   prah'-ho-vo

Prairie du Chien (Wis.)   prĕr'-ĭ də chēn'   prehr'-i duh cheen'

Prajadhipok   prə-chä'-tĭ-pôk   pruh-chah'-ti-pok
  (Former king of Siam)

praline   prä'-lēn   prah'-leen
"*Praline* is pronounced prah'-leen by the best people of New Orleans
and Louisiana generally. They frown upon praw'-leen as you would
frown upon chaw'-co-late; and they would have the horrors to hear
any lexicographer defend pray'-leen."—F. H.

Prasnish (Pol.) See *Przasnysz*.

Prasonesi (Dodec., Rh., point) See *Prasso*.

Prasso (Dodec., Rh.,   *It.* präs'-sô   prahs'-so
  point)
  Greek *Prasonesi*, prä-sô-nē'-sē [prah-so-nee'-see].

Pratas (Ch., isls.)	prä'-täs	prah'-tahs
Pratica di Mare (It.)	prä'-tē-kä dē mä'-rĕ	prah'-tee-kah dee mah'-reh
Pratola (It.)	prä'-tô-lä	prah'-to-lah
Pratorotondo (It.)	prä'-tô-rô-tôn'-dô	prah'-to-ro-ton'-do
Pravda (Rus. newspaper)	präv'-dä	prahv'-dah
Pravdinsk (Ger. >Rus.)	präv'-dĭnsk	prahv'-dinsk
German *Friedland*, q.v.		
Prčanj (Yugosl.)	pər'-chän(y)	puhr'-chahn(y)
Prĕja Glava (Yugosl., mt.)	pər'-chyä glä'-vä	puhr'-chyah glah'-vah
Prdejci (Yugosl.)	pər'-dä-tsĭ	puhr'-day-tsi
Preca (Alb.) See *Precĕ*.		
Precĕ (Alb.)	prĕ'-tsə	preh'-tsuh
Italian *Preza*.		
precedence	prĭ-sēd'-əns	pri-seed'-uhns
precedent, -s (noun)	prĕs'-ĭ-dənt, -s	pres'-i-duhnt, -s

To be distinguished from *precedence*, q.v., and from the adjective *precedent*, which is pronounced prĭ-sēd'-ənt [pri-seed'-uhnt].

Predborzh (Pol.) See *Przedbórz*.		
Predejane (Yugosl.)	prĕ'-dĕ-yä-nĕ	preh'-deh-yah-neh
Pré en Pail (Fr.)	prĕ äN pī'	preh ahN pai'
Pregel (Ger. >Rus., riv.)	*Ger.* prā'-gəl	pray'-guhl
	Rus. prĕ'-gĕl(y)	preh'-gel(y)
Prekestolen (Nor.)	prä'-kə-stō-lən	pray'-kuh-stoh-luhn
Prekornica (Yugosl., mts.)	prĕ'-kôr'-nĭ-tsä	preh'-kor'-ni-tsah
Prekoruplje (Yugosl.)	prĕ'-kô-rōōp'-lyĕ	preh'-ko-roop'-lyeh
prelate	prĕl'-ĭt	prel'-it
Preljina (Yugosl.)	prĕ'-lyĭ-nä	preh'-lyi-nah
Prelog (Yugosl.)	prĕ'-lôg	preh'-log
prelude	*Eng.* prĕl'-yōōd	prel'-yood
	or prē'-lyōōd	pree'-lyood
	Fr. prĕ-lüd'	preh-lüd'

One of the English pronunciations should be used except in French contexts. "The prĕ-lüd' [preh-lüd'] to the battle" sounds curious to English ears, though this pronunciation may be preferred when speaking of a *prélude* by Chopin.

Prëmet (Alb.) See *Përmet*.		
premier	prē'-mĭ-ər	pree'-mi-uhr
	or prĭ-mĭr'	pri-mihr'
	or prĕm'-yər	prem'-yuhr

Here is a wealth of choice. The word should not be confused with *première* prə-myĕr' [pruh-myehr'].

Premuda (Yugosl.)	prĕ'-mōō-dä	preh'-moo-dah
Premyo (Burma) See *Prome*.		
Prentzlau (Ger.)	prĕnts'-lou	prents'-lau

Přerov (Cz.)	przhě'-rôf	przheh'-rof
presage (noun)	prĕs'-ĭj	pres'-ij
presage (verb)	prĭ-sāj'	pri-sayj'

Presaging should be pronounced prĭ-sā'-jĭng [pri-say'-jing].

Preševo (Yugosl.)	prĕ'-shĕ-vô	preh'-sheh-vo
Presicce (It.)	prĕ-sēt'-chĕ	preh-seet'-cheh
presidio (Sp. "army	*Eng.* prə-sĭd'-ĭ-ō	pruh-sid'-i-oh
post")	*Sp.* prĕ-sē'-dyô	preh-see'-dyo
Preslav (Bulg.)	prĕ'-släf	preh'-slahf
Prešov (Cz.)	prĕ'-shôf	preh'-shof
Prespa (Balkan lake)	*Eng.* prĕs'-pə	pres'-puh
	S.-C. prĕs'-pä	pres'-pah

Also called *Prespansko jezero*, prĕs'-pän-skô yĕ'-zĕ-rô [pres'-pahn-sko yeh'-zeh-ro]. Albanian *Liqen i Presbĕs*, lē-kyĕn' ē prĕs'-bəs [lee-kyen' ee pres'-buhs]. Greek *Limne Prespa*, lēm'-nē prĕs'-pä [leem'-nee pres'-pah].

Presque Isle	*Me.* prĕs-kīl'	pres-kail'
	Mich. prĕs-kēl'	pres-keel'
Pressburg (Cz.)	See *Bratislava.*	
Prestes, Luis	prĕs'-tĭs, lōō-ēs'	pres'-tis, lu-ees'
Carlos (Braz. polit.)	kär'-lōōs	kahr'-lus
Prestwick (Scot.)	prĕst'-wĭk	prest'-wik
Pretoria (U. of S. Afr.)	prĭ-tō'-rĭ-ə	pri-toh'-ri-uh
Prétot (Fr.)	prĕ-tō'	preh-toh'
Preussen (Ger.)	proi'-sən	proi'-suhn
English *Prussia*, q.v.		
Preussisch Eylau	proi'-sĭsh ĭ'-lou	proi'-sish ai'-lau
(Ger. >Rus.)		

Russian *Bagrationovsk*, bä-grä-tĭ-ô'-nôfsk [bah-grah-ti-o'-nofsk].

Prevalje (Yugosl.)	prĕ'-vä-lyĕ	preh'-vah-lyeh
Preveza (Gr.)	prĕ'-vĕ-zä	preh'-veh-zah
Prevlaka (Yugosl.)	prĕ'-vlä'-kä	preh'-vlah'-kah
Preza (Alb.)	See *Precĕ.*	
PRI (Mex. political	prē'	pree'
party)		
Pribilci (Yugosl.)	prē'-bĭl-tsĭ	pree'-bil-tsi
Pribilof (Alaska, isl.)	prĭb'-ĭ-lôf'	prib'i-lof'
Priboj (Yugosl.)	prē'-boi	pree'-boi
Příbor (Cz.)	przhē'-bôr	przhee'-bor
Přibram (Cz.)	przhē'-bräm	przhee'-brahm
Pričinović (Yugosl.)	prē'-chĭ'-nô-vĭch	pree'-chi'-no-vich
Pridi Panomyong (Siam.	prē'-dē' pä-nôm'-	pree'-dee' pah-nom'-
polit.)	yông'	yong'
Priebe, Karl	prē'-bĭ	pree'-bi
(Am. painter)		

Prieto, Indalecio	pryĕ'-tô,	pryeh'-to,
(Sp. polit.)	ēn-dä-lĕ'-thyô	een-dah-leh'-thyo
Prijedor (Yugosl.)	prē'-yĕ-dôr	pree'-yeh-dor
Prijepolje (Yugosl.)	prē'-yĕ-pô'-lyĕ	pree'-yeh·po'-lyeh
Prikubansky (Rus.)	prĭ-kŏŏ-bän'-skĭ	pri-ku-bahn'-ski
Prilep (Yugosl.)	prē'-lĕp	pree'-lep
Priluki (Rus.)	prĭ-lōō'-kĭ	pri-loo'-ki
Prilužje (Yugosl.)	prē'-lōōzh-yĕ	pree'-loozh-yeh
primarily	prī'-mĕr-ĭ-lĭ	prai'-mehr-i-li

An emphatic pronunciation with principle accent on the second syllable is often heard, but all dictionaries prefer a recessive accent as in *primary*.

Primorsk (Ger. > Rus.)	prĭ-môrsk'	pri-morsk'
German *Fischhausen*, q.v.		
Primorsko Akhtarskaya	prĭ-môr'-skŏ äk(h)-	pri-mor'-sko ahk(h)-
(Rus.)	tär'-skä-yä	tahr'-skah-yah
Primorsko Krajiška	prē'-môr-skô	pree'-mor-sko
(Yugosl.)	krä'-yĭsh-kä	krah'-yish-kah
Primošten (Yugosl.)	prē'-mô-shtĕn	pree'-mo-shten
Prims (Ger., riv.)	prĭms'	prims'
Principe (Gulf of Guinea)	prēn'-sĭ-pĕ	preen'-si-peh
Prinsenhage (Neth.)	prĭn'-sən-hä'-k(h)ə	prin'-suhn-hah'-k(h)uh
Priora (It.)	pryô'-rä	pryo'-rah

Pripet (Pol. > Rus., riv.) See *Pripyat*.

Pripyat (Pol. > Rus., riv.)	prē'-pyät(y)	pree'-pyaht(y)

Polish *Prypeć*, q.v. English *Pripet*, prĭp'-ĕt [prip'-et].

Prisăcani (Rum.)	prē-sə-kän'	pree-suh-kahn'
Also called *Tulgheş*, q.v.		
Přísečnice (Cz.)	przhē'-sĕch'-nĭ-tsĕ	przhee'-sech'-ni-tseh
Prishibskaya (Rus.)	prĭ-shĭp'-skä·yä	pri-ship'-skah-yah
Priština (Yugosl.)	prē'-shtĭ-nä	pree'-shti-nah

Prisukha (Pol.) See *Przysucha*.

Priverno (It.)	prē-vĕr'-nô	pree-vehr'-no
Přívoz (Cz.)	przhē'-vôs	przhee'-vos
Prizren (Yugosl.)	prē'-zrĕn	pree'-zren
Prnjavor (Yugosl., near	pər'-nyä-vôr	puhr'-nyah-vor
Banjaluka)		
Prnjavor (Yugosl., near	pər-nyä'-vôr	puhr-nyah'-vor
Sarajevo)		
Proastion (Gr.)	prô-ä'-stē(-ôn)	pro-ah'-stee(-on)
Probolinggo (NEI, Java)	prô-bô-lĭng'-gô	pro-bo-ling'-go
Procida (It., isl.)	prô'-chē-dä	pro'-chee-dah
procurator	prŏk'-yŏŏ-rā'-tər	prok'-yu-ray'-tuhr

The accent on the first syllable accounts for its derivative *proctor*.

program   prō'-grăm   proh'-gram

Announcers are asked to follow the dictionaries and say prō'-grăm [proh'-gram], but everyone else in radio says prō'-grəm [proh'-gruhm]. The spelling has been simplified from *programme* and the new pronunciation prō'-grəm [proh'-gruhm] has developed. It will probably gain authority, but so far it is allowed as a second pronunciation by only Kenyon and Knott, *A Pronouncing Dictionary* (1944).

Prokhladnaya (Rus.)   prō-hläd'-nä-yä   pro-hlahd'-nah-yah
Also called *Prokhladnenski*, q.v.

Prokhladnenski (Rus.)   prō-hläd'-něn-skǐ   pro-hlahd'-nen-ski
Also called *Prokhladnaya*, q.v.

Prokletija (Yugosl., mts.) prō'-klě'-tǐ-yä   pro'-kleh'-ti-yah
Prokofiev, Sergei S.   prŏ-kô'-fyĕf, sĕrg-gā' pro-ko'-fyef, sehr-
(Rus. composer)   gay'
Prokuplje (Yugosl.)   prô'-kōōp'-lyě   pro'-koop'-lyeh
Proletarskaya (Rus.)   prŏ-lě-tär'-skä-yä   pro-leh-tahr'-skah-
                                              yah
Prome (Burma)   prōm'   prohm'

An English spelling; pronounce as one syllable, not two. Kipling rhymes *Prome* and *home*, as many will remember. The Burman is *Pyemyo*, pyā-myō' [pyay-myoh'].

Prondnik (Pol., riv.) See *Prądnik*.

Pronsfeld (Ger.)   prôns'-fĕlt   prons'-felt
Pronsk (Rus.)   prônsk'   pronsk'
Prosenikovo (Yugosl.)   prô'-sě-nē'-kô-vô   pro'-seh-nee'-ko-vo
Proskurov (Rus.)   prŏ-skōō'-rŏf   pro-skoo'-rof
Prossedi (It.)   prôs-sě'-dē   pros-seh'-dee
Prostějov (Cz.)   prô'-styě-yôf   pro'-styeh-yof
German *Prossnitz*, prôs'-nǐts [pros'-nits].

protégé, protégée   *Eng.* prō-tə-zhā',   proh-tuh-zhay'
                          Fr.   prô-tě-zhě'   pro-teh-zheh'
proteid   prō'-tēd *or* -tīd   proh'-teed *or* -taid
                      or prō'-tē-ǐd *or* -īd proh'-tee-id *or* -aid
Also spelled *proteide*. See note under *protein*.

protein   prō'-tēn   proh'-teen
                    or prō'-tē-ǐn   proh'-tee-in

This appears to be the order of preference among most American scientists, although the dictionaries gainsay it, holding to the logic of etymology. Similarly, *proteid*, q.v., but not *proteic*, which is pronounced prō-tē'-ik [proh-tee'-ik]. Cp. *hygiene* and *hygienic*.

Proti (Gr., isl.)   prô'-tē   pro'-tee
protocol   prō'-tə-kŏl   proh'-tuh-kol
Protville (Tun.)   prôt-vēl'   prot-veel'
Proust, Marcel (Fr.   prōōst', mär-sěl'   proost', mahr-sel'
author)

Provence (Fr.)	prô-väNs′	pro-vahNs′
Provins (Fr.)	prô-văN′	pro-vaN′
Provo (Utah)	prō′-vō	proh′-voh
Provo(o)st (Am. name)	prō′-vōst	proh′-vohst
provost	*military* prō′-vō′	proh′-voh′
	civilian prŏv′-əst	prov′-uhst
Prozor (Yugosl.)	prô′-zôr	pro′-zor
Prsten (Yugosl.)	pər′-stĕn	puhr′-sten
Prudnik (Ger. >Pol.)	prŏŏd′-nĭk	prud′-nik

German *Neustadt Oberschlesien*, q.v.

Pruem *or* Prüm (Ger.)	prüm′	prüm′
Prussia (Ger.)	*Eng.* prŭsh′-ə	pruhsh′-uh

German *Preussen*, q.v.

Pruszków (Pol.)	prŏŏsh′-kŏŏf	prush′-kuf

Russian *Prushkov*, prŏŏsh-kôf′ [prush-kof′].

Prut (Europ. riv.)	*Pol.* prŏŏt′	prut′

Russian *Prut*, prŏŏt′ [proot′]. Rumanian *Prutul*, prŏŏ′-tŏŏl [pru′-tul].

Prvić (Yugosl., isl.)	pər′-vĭch	puhr′-vich

Italian *Pervicchio*, q.v.

Prypeć (Pol. >Rus., riv.)	prĭ′-pĕch	pri′-pech

Russian *Pripyat*, prē′-pyät(y) [pree′-pyaht(y)]. English *Pripet*, prĭp′-ĕt [prip′-et].

Przasnysz (Pol.)	pshä′-snĭsh	pshah′-snish

Russian *Prasnish*, prä′-snĭsh [prah′-snish].

Przedbórz (Pol.)	pshĕd′-bŏŏzh	pshed′-buzh

Russian *Predborzh*, prĕd′-bŏrsh [pred′-borsh].

Przemyśl (Pol.)	pshĕ′-mĭshl	psheh′-mishl

Russian *Peremyshl*, pĕ-rĕ-mwēshl′(y) [peh-reh-mweeshl′(y)].

Przesecki, Stanisław	pshĕ-sĕt′-skĭ,	psheh-set′-ski,
(Pol. polit.)	stä-nē′-släf	stah-nee′-slahf
Przeworsk (Pol.)	pshĕ′-vôrsk	psheh′-vorsk

Przh-. See the variant spelling, Př-.

Przysucha (Pol.)	pshĭ-sŏŏ′-hä	pshi-soo′-hah

Russian *Prisukha*, prĭ-sŏŏ′-hä [pri-soo′-hah].

Psakon (Crete, pen.)	psä′-kô(n)	psah′-ko(n)

Also called *Rodopou*, q.v.

Psara (Gr., isl.)	psä-rä′	psah-rah′
Psaros (Gr. name)	psä-rôs′	psah-ros′
Psathoura (Gr.)	psä-thŏŏ′-rä	psah-thoo′-rah
Psël (Rus., riv.)	psyôl′	psyol′
Psira (Crete, isl.)	psē′-rä	psee′-rah
Pskov (Rus.)	pskôf′	pskof′
Psykhion (Crete, point)	See *Melissa*.	

Pszczyna (Pol.)   pshchĭ'-nä   pshchi'-nah
  German *Pless*, plĕs' [ples'].
Ptich (Rus., riv.)   ptĕch'   pteech'
Ptuj (Yugosl.)   ptōō'(y) *or* ptōō'ĭ   ptoo'(y) *or* ptoo'i
P'u-ch'êng (Ch., Fukien) pōō-chŭng   poo-chuhng
Pucheu, Pierre (Fr. polit.) pü-shû', pyĕr'   pü-shœ', pyehr'
P'u-chiang (Ch.,   pōō-jyäng   poo-jyahng
  Chekiang)
Puck (Pol.)   pŏŏtsk'   putsk'
  German *Putsig*, pŏŏt'-sĭk(h) [put'-sik(h)].
Pudozh (Rus.)   pōō'-dŏsh   poo'-dosh
Puebla (Mex.)   pwĕ'-blä   pweh'-blah
Pueblo (Col.)   pwĕb'-lō   pwehb'-loh
Puerto Barrios (Guat.) pwĕr'-tô bär'-ryôs pwehr'-to bahr'-ryos
Puerto Galera (P.I.)   pwĕr'-tô gä-lĕ'-rä pwehr'-to gah-leh'-
                                          rah
Puerto Princesa (P.I.) pwĕr'-tô prēn-sĕ'-sä pwehr'-to preen-seh'-
  Also called *Port Royalist*.   sah
Puerto Rico (W.I.)   pwĕr'-tô rē'-kô   pwehr'-to ree'-ko
  Preferable to the English form *Porto Rico*, pōr'-tə rē'-kō [pohr'-tuh
  ree'-koh].
Puetzlohn (Ger.)   püts'-lōn   püts'-lohn
Puget Sound (Wash.)   pyōō'-jĭt   pyoo'-jit
Puget Théniers (Fr.)   pü-zhĕ tĕ-nyĕ'   pü-zheh teh-nyeh'
Pugh(e) (Welsh name)   pyōō'   pyoo'
Puglia (It.)   pōō'-lyä   poo'-lyah
  English *Apulia*, q.v.
Pühalepa (Est.)   pü'-hä-lĕ'-pä   pü'-hah-leh'-pah
Puisaye (Fr.)   pwē-zĕ'   pwee-zeh'
Puka (Alb.) See *Pukë*.
Pukë (Alb.)   pōō'-kə   poo'-kuh
P'u-kiang (Ch., Chekiang) Variant of *P'u-chiang*, q.v.
Pukovac (Yugosl.)   pōō'-kô-väts   poo'-ko-vahts
P'u-k'ow (Ch., Kiangsu) pōō-kō   poo-koh
Pulap (Oc., Carolines)   pōō'-läp   poo'-lahp
  Also called *Tamatam*, q.v.
Pulaski, Kazimierz   pōō-lä'-skĭ,   pu-lah'-ski,
  (Pol. patriot)   kä-zē'-myĕsh   kah-zee'-myesh
  English *Casimir*, kăz'-ĭ-mĭr [kaz'-i-mihr]. As an American place name,
  Pulaski in New York, New Jersey and the Middle West is usually
  pronounced pə-lăs'-kī [puh-las'-kai]; in Tennessee and elsewhere in
  the South, pyŏŏ-lăs'-kĭ [pyu-las'-ki]. However, the *Pulaski* Sky High-
  way in northern New Jersey is generally pə-lăs'-kĭ [puh-las'-ki].
Pulau Pinang (Malaya) See *Penang*.

Puławy (Pol.)   pōō-lä'-vĭ   pu-lah'-vi
Russian *Novoaleksandriya*, nô'-vŏ-ä-lĕk-sän-drē'-yä [no'-vo-ah-lek-sahn-dree'-yah].

Pulicat (India)   pōō'-lĭ-kăt   poo'-li-kat
Pulilan (P.I.)   pōō-lē'-län   poo-lee'-lahn
Pulitzer, Joseph   pyōō'-lĭt-sər   pyoo'-lit-suhr
(Am. publisher)   *or* pŏŏl'-ĭt-sər   pul'-it-suhr
The first is the usual pronunciation in New York. It is used at Columbia University when the Pulitzer Prizes are awarded. The Pulitzer family, however, tend to prefer the older pronunciation pŏŏl'-ĭt-sər [pul'-it-suhr].

Pulj (It. > Yugosl.)   pōōl'(y)   pool'(y)
Usually called *Pola*, q.v.

puló   pōō-lô'   poo-lo'
A Malay word meaning *island*. It may be necessary to look up the other part of the name.

Pulo Anna (Oc.,   pōō'-lô än'-nä   poo'-lo ahn'-nah
Carolines)
Also called *Puru*, pōō'-rōō [poo'-roo].

Pulozero (Rus.)   pŏŏl-ô'-zĕ-rŏ   pul-o'-zeh-ro
Pułtusk (Pol.)   pŏŏl'-tōōsk   pul'-tusk
Pulusuk (Oc., Carolines)   pōō-lōō-sōōk'   poo-loo-sook'
Puluwat (Oc., Carolines)   pōō-lōō-wät'   poo-loo-waht'
Punaka (Bhutan)   pōō-nŭk'-ə   pu-nuhk'-uh
Puncán (P.I.)   pōōn-kän'   poon-kahn'
P'u-ning (Ch.,   pōō-nĭng   poo-ning
Kwangtung)
Punjab (India)   pŭn'-jäb'   puhn'-jahb'
Punjabi (India)   pŭn-jä'-bē   puhn-jah'-bee
punta (It., Sp.) *Punta* or *Point* is often ignored in the alphabetical listing. Look up the other part of the name.

Punta Arenas (Chile)   pōōn'-tä ä-rĕ'-näs   poon'-tah ah-reh'-nahs

Punta d'Arza (Yugosl.)   *It.* pōōn'-tä d'är'-tsä   poon'-tah d'ahr'-tsah
Serb-Croat Rt *Arca*, q.v.

Punta di Stilo (It.)   pōōn'-tä dē stē'-lô   poon'-tah dee stee'-lo
Puntadura (Yugosl.)   *It.* pōōn-tä-dōō'-rä   poon-tah-doo'-rah
Serb-Croat *Vir*, q.v.

Punta Planca (Yugos.)   *It.* pōōn'-tä plän'-kä   poon'-tah plahn'-kah
Serb-Croat Rt *Ploče*, q.v.

Punta Platamone   *It.* pōōn'-tä plä-tä-mô'-nĕ   poon'-tah plah-tah-mo'-neh
(Yugosl.)
Serb-Croat Rt *Platamon*, q.v.

[430]

Puntarenas (Costa Rica)	pōōn-tä-rĕ'-näs	poon-tah-reh'-nahs
Punxsutawney (Pa.)	pŭnk'-sə-tô'-nĭ	puhnk'-suh-taw'-ni
Puracé (Colom., volcano)	pōō-rä-sĕ'	poo-rah-seh'
Purcell, Henry (17th cent. Brit. composer)	pûr'-sĕl	puhr'-sel

As an American family name the last syllable is often accented.

Puri (India)	pōō'-rē'	poo'-ree'
Purič, Božidar (Yugosl. polit.)	pōō'-rĭch, bô'-zhĭ-där	poo'-rich, bo'-zhi-dahr
Purmerend (Neth.)	pûr'-mə-rĕnt'	pœr'-muh-rent'
Puru (Oc.) See *Pulo Anna.*		
Purwakarta (NEI, Java)	pōōr-wä-kär'-tä	poor-wah-kahr'-tah
Purwokerto (NEI, Java)	pōōr-wô-kĕr'-tô	poor-wo-kehr'-to
Pushkino (Rus.)	pōōsh'-kĭ-nŏ	poosh'-ki-no
Pushtrik (Balkan mt.)	*Eng.* pŏŏsh'-trĭk	push'-trik

Albanian *Mal i Pushtrikut* or *Bështriq,* q.v. Serb-Croat *Paštrik,* q.v.

Pusta (Yugosl.)	pōō'-stä	poo'-stah
Puteaux (Fr.)	pü-tō'	pü-toh'
P'u-t'ien (Ch., Fukien)	pōō-tyĕn	poo-tyen
Putivl (Rus.)	pōō-tēvl'(y)	poo-teevl'(y)
Putscheid (Ger.)	pŏŏt'-shīt	put'-shait
Putsig (Pol.) See *Puck.*		
Pütslohn (Ger.)	püts'-lōn	püts'-lohn
Putten (Neth.)	pût'-ən	pœt'-uhn
Puttershoek (Neth.)	pût-ərs-hōōk'	pœt-uhrs-hook'
Putuhena *or* Poetoehena (Indo. polit.)	pōō'-tōō-hĕ'-nä	poo'-too-heh'-nah
Puy, le (Fr.)	pwē', lə	pwee', luh
Puy de Dôme (Fr.)	pwē də dōm'	pwee duh dohm'
P'u-yi, Henry (Former Chinese emperor)	pōō-yē	poo-yee

Called as Manchu Emperor of China, *Hsü-an T'ung,* shü-än tŏŏng [shü-ahn tung]; as Japanese puppet Emperor, *K'ang Tê,* käng dŭ [kahng duh].

Pyapon (Burma)	pyä'-pŏn	pyah'-pohn
Pyasechno (Pol.) See *Piaseczno.*		
Pyatigorsk (Rus.)	pyä-tĭ-gôrsk'	pyah-ti-gorsk'
Pyawbwe (Burma)	pyô-bwĕ'	pyaw-bweh'
Pyinmana (Burma)	pyĭn'-mə-nä'	pyin'-muh-nah'
Pylos (Gr.)	*Eng.* pī'-lŏs	pai'-los
	Gr. pē'-lôs	pee'-los

Also called *Navarino,* q.v., and *Niokastro,* nyô'-kä-strô [nyo'-kah-stro].

Pyrgi (Gr.)	pēr'-yē	peer'-yee
Pyrgos (Gr., Crete)	pēr'-gôs	peer'-gos
Pyritz (Ger. > Pol.)	pē'-rĭts	pee'-rits

Polish *Perzyce*, q.v.

Pytalovo (Latvia)	*Rus.* pĭ-tä'-lŏ-vŏ	pi-tah'-lo-vo

Latvian *Jaunlatgale*, q.v.

qafa (Alb.) See *qafë*.

qafë (Alb.)	kyä'-fə	kyah'-fuh

An element, meaning *pass*, in Albanian place names. Look up the other part of the name.

Qain (Iran)	kīn'	kain'
Qainat (Iran)	kī-nät'	kai-naht'
Qairwan (Tun.)	kīr-wän'	kair-wahn'

French *Kairouan*, q.v.

Qais (Iran)	kīs	kais
qal'at	käl-ät'	kahl-aht'

An element, meaning *fortress*, in Arabic place names.

Qantara (Egypt)	kän'-tə-rə	kahn'-tuh-ruh

Also spelled *Kantara*.

Qaret el Himeimat (Egypt)	kă'-rĕt ĕl hĭ-mā-măt'	ka'-ret el hi-may-mat'
Qashquai (Iran. tribe)	gäsh'-gī'	gahsh'-gai'
qasr	käsr'	kahsr'

An element, meaning *castle*, in Arabic place names. See *gasr*.

Qasr-i-Shirin (Iran)	kăzr'-ē-shē-rēn'	kazr'-ee-shee-reen'
Qatiya (Egypt)	kä-tē'-yä	kah-tee'-yah
Qattara (Egypt)	kä-tä'-rä	kah-tah'-rah

Qavam Sultaneh (Iran. polit.) See *Ahmed Qavam*.

Qazvin (Iran)	kăz-vēn'	kaz-veen'

Also spelled *Kasvin* or *Kazvin*.

Qisarya (Pal.) See *Caesarea*.

Quaderna (It., canal)	kwä-dĕr'-nä	kwah-dehr'-nah
Quai d'Orsay	*Eng.* kā' dôr-sā'	kay' dor-say'
	Fr. kĕ dôr-sĕ'	keh dor-seh'
Quangngai (Indo-Ch.)	*Eng.* kwäng-nĭ'	kwahng-nai'
	local kwäng-ngĭ'	kwahng-ngai'
Quarnero (Yugosl., inlet)	*It.* kwä-nĕ'-rô	kwah-neh'-ro

Serb-Croat *Veliki Kvarner*, q.v.

Quarnerolo (Yugosl., channel)	*It.* kwär-nĕ-rô'-lô	kwahr-neh-ro'-lo

Serb-Croat *Mali Kvarner*, q.v.

quay	*Eng.* kē'	kee'
	Fr. kĕ'	keh'

Modern French spelling *quai*.

Quayle, Frank (N.Y. polit.).	kwāl′	kwayl′
Quchan (Iran) Also spelled *Kuchan*.	kōō-chän′	koo-chahn′
Quebec (Can.) French *Québec*, kĕ-bĕk′ [keh-bek′].	*Eng.* kwĭ-bĕk′	kwi-bek′
Queenstown (Eire) See *Cóbh*.		
Queis (Ger. >? Pol., riv.) Polish *Kwisa*, q.v.	kvīs′	kvais′
Quejo (Sp., cape)	kĕ′-hô	keh′-ho
Quelimane (Mozambique)	kĕl-ĭ-mä′-nĭ	kel-i-mah′-ni
Querétaro (Mex.)	kĕ-rĕ′-tä-rô	keh-reh′-tah-ro
Querqueville (Fr.)	kĕr-kə-vēl′	kehr-kuh-veel′
Quesada, E. R. *or* "Pete" (Am. general)	kĕ-sä′-dä *or* k(w)ə-sä′-də	keh-sah′-dah k(w)uh-sah′-duh
Quesnay (Fr.)	kĕ-nĕ′	keh-neh′
Quesne (Fr., mt.)	kĕn′	ken′
Questehou (Fr.)	kĕs-tōō′	kes-too′
Quetta (-Pishin) (Baluch.)	kwĕt′-ä (pĭ-shēn′)	kwet′-ah (pi-sheen′)
Quezaltenango (Guat.)	kĕ-säl′-tĕ-näng′-gô	keh-sahl′-teh-nahng′-go
Quezon, Manuel (Fil. polit.)	*Eng.* kā′-zŏn′, mǎn′-yōō-əl	kay′-zon′, man′-yu-uhl
	Sp. kĕ′-sôn (*or* -thôn), mä-nwĕl′	keh′-son (*or* -thon), mah-nwel′

One might expect Spanish *Quezon* to bear an accent on the final syllable. In a broadcast in honor of President Quezon, President Ávila Camacho of Mexico so stressed it. However, this seems not to be the usage of the Philippines. The name is usually Anglicized by American speakers.

Quiapo (P.I.)	kē-ä′-pô	pee-ah′-po
Quiberon (Fr.)	kē-brôN′	kee-broN′
quiescent	kwĭ-ĕs′-ənt	kwai-es′-uhnt
Quilbignon (Fr.)	kēl-bē-nyôN′	keel-bee-nyoN′
Quillebeuf (Fr.)	kē(y)-bûf′	kee(y)-bœf′
Quimper (Fr.)	kăN-pĕr′	kaN-pehr′
Quimperlé (Fr.)	kăN-pĕr-lĕ′	kaN-pehr-leh′
Quincé (Fr.)	kăN-sĕ′	kaN-seh′
Quinéville (Fr.)	kē-nĕ-vēl′	kee-neh-veel′
Quingua (P.I.)	kēng′-wä	keeng′-wah
Quinhon (Indo-Ch.)	kwē-nyŭn′	kwee-nyuhn′
Quintana Roo (Mex.)	kēn-tä′-nä rô′-ô	keen-tah′-nah ro′-o

Quintanilla, Luis (Mex. polit.)	kēn-tä-nē'-yä, lōō-ēs'	keen-tah-nee'-yah, loo-ees'
Quinto (It.)	kwēn'-tô	kween'-to
Quirinal (It., Rome)	*Eng.* kwĭr'-ĭ-nəl	kwihr'-ih-nuhl

Italian *Quirinale*, kwē-rē-nä'-lĕ [kwee-ree-nah'-leh].

Quirino, Elpidio (Fil. polit.)	kē-rē'-nô, ĕl-pē'-dyô	kee-ree'-no, el-pee'-dyo
Quisling, Vidkun Abraham (Nor. polit.)	*Eng.* kwĭz'-lĭng *Nor.* kvĭs'-lĭng, vĭd'-kŏŏn	kwiz'-ling kvis'-ling, vid'-kun
Quisquina (Sicily)	kwēs-kwē'-nä	kwees-kwee'-nah
Quitandinha (Brazil, Petropolis hotel)	kē-tän-dē'-nyə	kee-tahn-dee'-nyuh
Quito (Ecuador)	kē'-tô	kee'-to
Quittebœuf (Fr.)	kēt-bûf'	keet-bœf'
Qum *or* Kum (Iran)	kŏŏm'	kum'
Quoile (N. Ire., riv.)	koil'	koil'
Quonset hut	kwŏn'-sĭt	kwon'-sit
Quonset Point (R.I.)	kwŏn'-sĭt	kwon'-sit
Quo T'ai-ch'i (Ch. diplomat)	gwo tĭ-chē	gwo tai-chee
Raab (Austria, Hung., riv.)	*Ger.* räp'	rahp'

Hungarian *Rába*, rä'-bŏ [rah'-bo].

Raadhusplads (Den.)	rôth'-hōōs-pläs	roth'-hoos-plahs
Raahe (Fin.)	rä'-hĕ	rah'-heh
Raalte (Neth.)	räl'-tə	rahl'-tuh
Raamsdonk (Neth.)	räms'-dônk	rahms'-donk
Rab (Yugosl.)	räb'	rahb'

Italian *Arbe*, q.v.

Rába (Hung., Austria, riv.) See *Raab*.

Raba (NEI, Soembawa)	rä'-bä	rah'-bah
Raba (Pol., riv.)	rä'-bä	rah'-bah
rabar	rä'-bär	ray'-bahr

An abbreviation of *radar bearing*.

Rabat (Mor.)	rä-bät'	rah-baht'
Rabaul (Oc., New Britain)	rä-boul' *or* rä'-boul	rah-baul' *or* rah'-baul

See *Tahiti*.

Rabaut, Louis C. (U.S. representative)	răb'-ō	rab'-oh
Rabi, I. I. (Am. scientist)	rä'-bĭ	rah'-bi

rabies	rā'-bēz	ray'-beez

The pronunciation rā'-bǐ-ēz [ray'-bi-eez] once standard is now rare. The first syllable is occasionally rǎb'- [rab'-].

Rabin, Benjamin J. (U.S. representative)	rā'-bǐn	ray'-bin
Rabón (P.I., riv.)	rä-bôn'	rah-bon'
Rabotnichesko Delo (Bulg. newspaper)	rä'-bôt'-nǐ-chě-skô dě'-lô	rah'-bot'-ni-cheh-sko deh'-lo
Rabrovo (Yugosl.)	rä'-brô-vô	rah'-bro-vo
Rača (Yugosl.)	rä'-chä	rah'-chah
Raccuja (Sicily)	räk-kōō'-yä	rahk-koo'-yah
Rachgia (Indo-Ch.)	rä-zhä'	rah-zhah'
Rachov (Cz. >Rus.) See *Rakhov.*		
Racibórz (Ger. >Pol.) German *Ratibor,* q.v.	rä-chě'-bŏŏzh	rah-chee'-buzh
Racine (Wis.)	rə-sēn'	ruh-seen'
Ráckeve (Hung.)	räts'-kě-vě	rahts'-keh-veh
racon	rā'-kŏn	ray'-kon
An abbreviation of *radar beacon.*		
Ráczkeve (Hung.)	räts'-kě-vě	rahts'-keh-veh
Also called *Csepel,* q.v.		
Raczkiewicz, Wladyslaw (Pol. polit.)	räch-kyě'-vǐch, vlä-dǐ'-släf	rahch-kyeh'-vich, vlah-di'-slahf
Radac (Oc., Marshalls)	rä'-däk	rah'-dahk
radar	rā'-där	ray'-dahr
An abbreviation of *radio detecting and ranging.*		
Rădăuţi (Rum.) German *Radautz,* rä'-douts [rah'-dauts].	rə-də-ōŏts'	ruh-duh-uts'
Raddon (Fr.)	rä-dôN'	rah-doN'
Radebeul (Ger.)	rä'-də-boil	rah'-duh-boil
Räder, Erich (Ger. admiral) See *Raeder, Erich.*		
Rades (Tun.)	rä'-děs	rah'-des
Radescu (Rum. name)	rä-děs'-kŏŏ	rah-des'-ku
Radicofani (It.)	rä-dē-kô'-fä-nē	rah-dee-ko'-fah-nee
Radin (Pol.) See *Radzyń.*		
Radkiewicz, Stanisław (Pol. polit.)	rät-kyě'-vēch, stä-nē'-släf	raht-kyeh'-veech, stah-nee'-slahf
Radłowo (Pol.)	rä-dlô'-vô	rah-dlo'-vo
Radočelo (Yugosl., mts.)	rä'-dô-chě-lô	rah'-do-cheh-lo
Radom (Pol.)	rä'-dôm	rah'-dom
Radomir (Bulg.)	rä'-dŏ-mēr'	rah'-do-meer'
Radomka (Pol., riv.)	rä-dôm'-kä	rah-dom'-kah
Radomsko (Pol.)	rä-dôm'-skô	rah-dom'-sko
Russian *Novoradomsk,* nô'-vô-rä'-dŏmsk [no'-vo-rah'-domsk].		

Radomysl (Rus.)	rä-dŏ-mwĕshl′(y)	rah-do-mweeshl′(y)
Radoštak (Yugosl., mt.)	rä′-dô-shtäk	rah′-do-shtahk
Radovište (Yugosl.)	rä′-dô′-vǐ-shtĕ	rah′-do′-vi-shteh
Radovljica (Yugosl.)	rä′-dôv′-lyǐ-tsä	rah′-dov′-lyi-tsah
Radujevac (Yugosl.)	rä′-dōō′-yĕ-väts	rah′-doo′-yeh-vahts
Raduša (Yugosl.)	rä′-dōō-shä	rah′-doo-shah
Radziwiłł (Pol. name)	rä-jē′-vēl	rah-jee′-veel
Russian *Radzivill*, rä-dzǐ-vēl′ [rah-dzi-veel′].		
Radziwiłłów (Pol.)	rä-jǐ-vē′-lōōf	rah-ji-vee′-luf
Russian *Radzivilov*, rä-dzǐ-vē′-lŏf [rah-dzi-vee′-lof].		
Radzymin (Pol.)	rä-dzǐ′-mǐn	rah-dzi′-min
Radzyń (Pol.)	rä′-jǐn(y)	rah′-jin(y)
Russian *Radin*, rä′-dǐn [rah′-din].		
Raeder, Erich (Ger. admiral)	rä′-dər, ā′-rǐk(h)	reh′-duhr, ay′-rik(h)
Raetia (Austria, Switz.) See *Rhaetia*.		
Raffia, la (It., riv.)	räf′-fyä, lä	rahf′-fyah, lah
Ragay (P.I.)	rä-gī′	rah-gai′
Rager, Edward (N.Y. polit.)	rä′-gər	rah′-guhr
Ragnhild (Nor. princess)	räng′n-hǐl	rahng′n-hil
	or rägn′-hǐl	rahgn′-hil
Ragnit (Ger. >Rus.)	räg′-nǐt	rahg′-nit
Ragusa (Sicily)	rä-gōō′-zä	rah-goo′-zah
Ragusa (Yugosl.)	*It.* rä-gōō′-zä	rah-goo′-zah
Serb-Croat *Dubrovnik*, q.v.		
Rahó (Cz. >Rus.) See *Rakhow*.		
Rahway (N.J.)	rô′-wĕ	raw′-weh
Raiatea (Oc., Society isls.)	rī-ä-tĕ′-ä	rai-ah-teh′-ah
Raihu (New Guinea, riv.)	rī′-hōō	rai′-hoo
Raincy, le (Fr.)	räN-sē′, lə	raN-see′, luh
Rainier (Wash., national park)	rä-nǐr′	ray-nihr′
	or rä′-nǐr	ray′-nihr
Rainò (It.)	rī-nô′	rai-no′
Raipur (India)	rī′-pŏŏr′	rai′-pur′
Raivavae (Oc., Tubuai)	rī′-vä-vä′-ĕ	rai′-vah-vah′-eh
Rajagopalachari, C. (Indian polit.)	rä-jə-gô-pä-lə-chä′-rē	rah-juh-go-pah-luh-chah′-ree
Rajburi (Siam)	rät′-bŏŏ-rē′	raht′-bu-ree′
	or räj′-ə-bŏŏ-rē′	rahj′-uh-bu-ree′
Also spelled *Rajaburi* and recently *Rat Buri*, q.v.		
Rajistovac (Yugosl.)	rä′-yǐs-tô-väts	rah′-yis-to-vahts
Rajkot (India)	räj′-kōt	rahj′-koht
Rajpipla (India)	räj-pē′-plə	rahj-pee′-pluh

Rajput (India)   räj′-po͝ot   rahj′-put
Rajputana (India)   räj′-po͝o-tä′-nə   rahj′-pu-tah′-nuh
Rakhov (Cz. >Rus.)   rä′-hŏf   rah′-hof
    Czech spelling *Rachov.* Hungarian *Rahó,* rä′-hô [rah′-ho].
Rakinac (Yugosl.)   rä′-kĭ-näts   rah′-ki-nahts
Rakitno (Pol.)   See *Rokitno.*
Rákóczy (Hung. name)   rä′-kô-tsĭ   rah′-ko-tsi
Rákosi, Mátyás   rä′-kô-shĭ, mä′-tyäsh   rah′-ko-shi, mah′-
    (Hung. polit.)   tyahsh
Rákoskeresztur (Hung.)   rä′-kôsh-kĕ′-rĕs-to͝or   rah′-kosh-keh′-res-tur
Raków (Pol.)   rä′-ko͝of   rah′-kuf
    Russian *Rakov,* rä′-kŏf [rah′-kof].
Rakusha (Rus.)   rä′-ko͞o-shä   rah′-koo-shah
Rakvere (Est.)   räk′-vĕ-rĕ   rahk′-veh-reh
    German *Wesenberg,* q.v.
Raleigh (N.C., Va.)   rô′-lĭ   raw′-li
Ralik (Oc., Marshalls)   rä′-lĭk   rah′-lik
Ralinna (Austral.)   rə-lĭn′-ə   ruh-lin′-uh
Ralja (Yugosl.)   rä′-lyä   rah′-lyah
Rallis, Joannes   rä′-lēs, yô-ä′-nēs   rah′-lees, yo-ah′-nees
    (Gr. polit.)
Rallis, Petros   rä′-lēs, pĕ′-trôs   rah′-lees, peh′-tros
    (Gr. polit.)
Ramadan (Mohameddan   răm′-ə-dän   ram′-uh-dahn
    ninth month)
    Also *Ramazan,* răm′-ə-zän′ [ram′-uh-zahn′].
Ramadier, Paul   rä-mä-dyĕ′, pôl′   rah-mah-dyeh′, pol′
    (Fr. polit.)
Ramallah (Pal.)   rä-mäl′-ä   rah-mahl′-ah
Rambervillers (Fr.)   räN-bĕr-vē-lĕ′   rahN-behr-vee-leh′
    The above is the local pronunciation given in the *Larousse* dictionary.
    Webster's, however, gives -vē-yĕ′ [-vee-yeh′], a pronunciation which is
    also current in France.
Rambouillet (Fr.)   räN-bo͞o-yĕ′   rahN-boo-yeh′
Rambutyo (Oc.,   räm-bo͞o′-tyô   rahm-boo′-tyo
    Admiralties)
Rameswaram *or* Ramis-   rä-mĕs′-wə-rŭm′   rah-mes′-wuh-ruhm′
    seram (India)   *or* rä-mĭs′-ə-räm′   rah-mis′-uh-rahm′
Ramírez, Pedro   rä-mē′-rĕs, pĕ′-drô   rah-mee′-res, peh′-dro
    (Arg. polit.)
Râmnicul Sărat (Rum.)   rûm′-nē-ko͞ol sə-rät′   ruhm′-nee-kul suh-
                                                  raht′
Râmnicul Vâlcea   rûm′-nē-ko͞ol vûl′-   ruhm′-nee-kul vuhl′-
    (Rum.)   chä   chah

Ramón (Sp. name)	rä-môn′	rah-mon′
Ramon (Rus.)	rä-môn′(y)	rah-mon′(y)
Ramree (Burma)	răm-rē′	ram-ree′
Ramscheid (Ger.)	räm′-shīt	rahm′-shait
Ramu (N.E. New Guinea, riv.)	rä′-mōō	rah′-moo
Rance (Fr., riv.)	räNs′	rahNs′
Ranchi (India)	rän′-chē′	rahn′-chee′
Randazzo (Sicily)	rän-dät′-sô	rahn-daht′-so
Randers (Den.)	rän′-ərs	rahn′-uhrs
Randsfjord (Nor.)	räns′-fyōr	rahns′-fyohr
Ranenburg (Rus.)	rä′-nĕn-bŏŏrk	rah′-nen-burk
Rangoon (Burma)	răng-gōōn′	rang-goon′

Rann (Yugosl.)   See *Brežice*.

| Ranong (Siam) | rə-nông′ | ruh-nawng′ |
| ranta | rän′-tä | rahn′-tah |

An element, meaning *shore* or *strand*, in Finnish place names.

| Rapallo (It.) | rä-päl′-lô | rah-pahl′-lo |
| Rapido (It., riv.) | rä′-pē-dô | rah′-pee-do |

In radio reports of the bloody fighting on the Rapido, the name was often pronounced with accent on the second syllable despite the analogy of the English cognate *rapid*. This is additional evidence of the current penultimate fallacy: that all foreign words ending in a vowel should be stressed on the next to the last syllable. In contrast is the shifting of the Spanish accent in early borrowings such as *Florida*.

| Rarotonga (Oc., Cook isls.) | rä-rô-tông′-ä | rah-ro-tong′-ah |
| ras | räs′ | rahs′ |

An element, meaning *head* or *cape*, in Arabic place names.

Ras Abu Laho (Egypt)	räs′ ä′-bōō lä′-hô	rahs′ ah′-boo lah′-ho
Ras Alam el Rum (Egypt)	räs′ ä-lăm′ ĕr rōōm′	rahs′ ah-lam′ ehr room′
Ras at Tannura (Saudi Arabia)	räs′ ät tän-nōō′-rə	rahs′ aht tahn-noo′-ruh
Rašče (Yugosl.)	räsh′-chĕ	rahsh′-cheh
Raseiniai (Lith.)	rä-syā′-nyī	rah-syay′-nyai

Russian *Rossieny*, q.v.

| Ras el ʿAin *or* ʿEin (Pal.) | räs′ ĕl än′ | rahs′ el ayn′ |
| Ras el Kurum (Pal.) | räs′ ĕl kōō-rōōm′ | rahs′ el ku-room′ |

Also called *Cape Carmel*.

Ras el Milh (Libya)	räs′ ĕl mĭl(kh)′	rahs′ el mil(kh)′
Ras en Naqura (Pal.)	räs′ ĕn nä-kōō′-rə	rahs′ en nah-koo′-ruh
Rashid (Egypt)	rä-shēd′	rah-sheed′

Also called *Rosetta*, q.v.

Rashidi *or* Rasjidi,	rä'-shē'-dē', hä'-jē	rah'-shee'-dee',
Hadji (Indo. polit.)		hah'-jee
Rashin (Korea)	rä-shĭn	rah-shin
Rasht *or* Resht (Iran)	rǎsht'	rasht'
Rasina (Yugosl., riv.)	rä'-sĭ-nä	rah'-si-nah
Rasjidi, Hadji (Indo. polit.) See *Rashidi, Hadji.*		
Raška (Yugosl.)	rä'-shkä	rah'-shkah
Raspopinsk (Rus.)	räs-pô'-pĭnsk	rahs-po'-pinsk
Rasputin, Grigori	rä-spōō'-tĭn,	rah-spoo'-tin,
(Rus. monk)	grĭ-gô'-rĭ	gri-go'-ri
Rass ben Sekka (Tun.)	räs' bĕn sĕk'-kä	rahs' ben sek'-kah
Rastatt (Ger.)	rä'-shtät	rah'-shtaht
Rastembork (Ger. >Pol.)	rä-stĕm'-bôrk	rah-stem'-bork
German *Rastenburg*, q.v.		
Rastenburg (Ger. >Pol.)	räs'-tən-bŏŏrk(h)	rahs'-tuhn-burk(h)
Polish *Rastembork*, q.v.		
Rat Buri (Siam)	rät' bŏŏ-rē'	raht' bu-ree'
Formerly spelled *Rajburi*, q.v.		
Rathedaung (Burma)	rə-thä'-doung'	ruh-thay'-daung'
Rathenau, Walther	rä'-tə-nou, väl'-tər	rah'-tuh-nau, vahl'-
(Ger. polit.)		tuhr
Rathenow (Ger.)	rä'-tə-nō	rah'-tuh-noh
Ratibor (Ger. >Pol.)	rä'-tĭ-bôr	rah'-ti-bor
Polish *Racibórz*, q.v.		
ration (noun and verb)	rǎsh'-ən *or* rā'-shən	rash'-uhn *or* ray'-
		shuhn

Probably nine out of ten Americans in all walks of life use a pronunciation illustrated by *national* and *rational* rather than by *nation*. It is interesting that this general American usage is better reflected in British dictionaries, which are inclined to ignore rā'-shən [ray'-shuhn], than in American dictionaries, which list both pronunciations but place rǎsh'-ən [rash'-uhn] second. *Ration* is one of a number of instances where our dictionaries show a preference for a New England schoolmaster's pronunciation in contrast to an all-American usage. (However, it should be said that dictionary makers when they set down two pronunciations are required by two-dimensional space to place one either before or above the other and frequently mean nothing by the order. Fortunately, each new edition of our dictionaries shows a greater awareness of America west of the Connecticut River, though there are still corrections to be made.) There is no doubt that in military usage rǎsh'-ən [rash'-uhn] is preferred. It is likewise the pronunciation of President Roosevelt, Prime Minister Churchill, James F. Byrnes, Leon Henderson, Elmer Davis, and Eddie Rickenbacker. From the historical point of view, rǎsh'-ən [rash'-uhn] is the

Englishing of a French pronunciation and corresponds nicely to *depot* pronounced dĕ'-pō [deh'-poh] in military circles. Both words in technical senses were borrowed by the English army from the French. On the other hand rā'-shən [ray'-shuhn] follows the rules of the English pronunciation of Latin. It is natural that officers should favor the first and schoolmasters the latter. See Prof. Kemp Malone's article, "Ration," *American Speech*, vol. 18, pp 128-30, April, 1943. Other romance words appear in English with "short *a*" before a single consonant: *palace, satire, salad, fashion.* P.S.: The pronunciation răsh'-ən [rash'-uhn] is placed first in Kenyon and Knott, *A Pronouncing Dictionary* (1944), and in Funk and Wagnalls, *New Practical Standard Dictionary* (1946) and *College Standard Dictionary* (1947).

Ratisbon (Ger.)	*Eng.* răt'-ĭs-bŏn	rat'-is-bon
German *Regensburg*, q.v.		
Ratlam (India)	rət-läm'	ruht-lahm'
Ratmirovichi (Rus.)	rät-mē'-rŏ-vĭ-chĭ	raht-mee'-ro-vi-chi
Raton (N.M.)	*Eng.* ră-tōn'	ra-tohn'
Spanish *Ratón*, rä-tôn' [rah-ton'].		
Raubach (Ger.)	rou'-bäk(h)	rau'-bahk(h)
Rauma (Fin.; Nor., riv.)	rou'-mä	rau'-mah
Rauwederhem (Neth.)	rou'-wər-dər-hĕm'	rau'-wuhr-duhr-hem'
Rava Russkaya (Pol. > Rus.)	rä'-vä rōōs'-skä-yä	rah'-vah roos'-skah-yah
Polish *Rawa Ruska*, q.v.		
raven, ravening	răv'-ən, -ĭng	rav'-uhn, -ĭng
For the "short a," compare *ration*.		
Ravenga (Oc., New Hebrides)	rä-vĕng'-ä	rah-veng'-ah
Ravenna (It.)	*Eng.* rə-vĕn'-ə	ruh-ven'-uh
	It. rä-vĕn'-nä	rah-ven'-nah
Ravensbruck (Ger.)	rä'-vəns-brōōk(h)	rah'-vuhns-brook(h)
Raver, Paul J. (Am. administrator)	rā'-vər	ray'-vuhr
Raviscanina (It.)	rä-vē-skä-nē'-nä	rah-vee-skah-nee'-nah
Rawalpindi (India)	rä-wəl-pĭn'-dē	rah-wuhl-pin'-dee
Rawa Ruska (Pol. > Rus.)	rä'-vä rōō'-skä	rah'-vah roo'-skah
Russian *Rava Russkaya*, q.v.		
Rawicz (Pol.)	rä'-vĭch	rah'-vich
German spelling *Rawitsch*.		
Rawka (Pol., riv.)	räf'-kä	rahf'-kah
Russian spelling *Ravka*.		
Rawson (Arg.)	rou'-sôn	rau'-son
Inevitably Englished as rô'-sən [raw'-suhn].		

Rawson, Arturo (Arg. general)	rou'-sôn, är-tōō'-rô	rau'-son, ahr-too'-ro
Rayfiel, Leo F. (U.S. representative)	rā'-fĭ-ĕl, lē'-ō	ray'-fi-el, lee'-oh
Rayong (Siam)	rə-yông'	ruh-yawng'
Raz (Fr., point)	räz'	rahz'
Ražanj (Yugosl.)	rä'-zhän(y)	rah'-zhahn(y)
Razdelnaya (Rus.)	räz-dĕl'(y)-nä-yä	rahz-del'(y)-nah-yah
Razelm (Rum., lake)	rä'-zĕlm	rah'-zelm
Razgrad (Bulg.)	räs'-grät	rahs'-graht
Razliv (Rus.)	räz-lēf'	rahz-leef'
Razzolo (It.)	rät-sô'-lô	raht-so'-lo
Ré (Fr., isl.)	rĕ'	reh'
Reading	rĕd'-ĭng	red'-ing

This is the pronunciation in England, Massachusetts, Ohio, and Pennsylvania. From Michigan, however, rē'-dĭng [ree'-ding] is reported.

Recata (Oc., Solomons, bay)	*Eng.* rə-kăt'-ə	ruh-kat'-uh
	native rĕ-kä'-tä	reh-kah'-tah
Rechitsa (Rus.)	rĕ'-chĭ-tsä	reh'-chi-tsah
Recife (Brazil)	rĕ-sē'-fĭ	reh-see'-fi

Also called, unofficially, *Pernambuco*, q.v.

| Reciţa (Rum.) | rĕ'-chē-tsä | reh'-chee-tsah |

Hungarian *Resiczabánya*, rĕ'-shĭ-tsŏ-bä'-nyŏ [reh'-shi-tso-bah'-nyo].

Recklinghausen (Ger.)	rĕk'-lĭng-hou'-zən	rek'-ling-hau'-zuhn
Recouvrance (Fr.)	rə-kōō-vräNs'	ruh-koo-vrahNs'
Recto, Claro M. (Fil. polit.)	rĕk'-tô, klä'-rô	rek'-to, klah'-ro
Redange (Luxem.)	rə-däNzh'	ruh-dahNzh'
Redden, Monroe M. (U.S. representative)	rĕd'n	red'n
Reden (Neth.)	rā'-dən	ray'-duhn
Redeyef (Tun.)	rə-dä'-yĕf	ruh-day'-yef
Redin, Nicolai Gregorovich (Rus. officer)	rā'-dĭn, nĭ-kŏ-lī' grĭ-gôr'-yĕ-vĭch	ray'-din, ni-ko-lai' gri-gor'-yeh-vich
Redon (Fr.)	rə-dôN'	ruh-doN'
Redondo Beach (Calif.)	*Eng.* rə-dŏn'-dō	ruh-don'-doh
Rees (Ger.)	räs'	rays'
Reewijk (Neth.)	rä'-wĭk	ray'-waik
Regalbuto (Sicily)	rĕ-gäl-bōō'-tô	reh-gahl-boo'-to
Regensburg (Ger.)	*Eng.* rā'-gənz-bûrg	ray'-guhnz-buhrg
	Ger. rā'-gəns-bŏŏrk(h)	ray'-guhns-burk(h)

Also English *Ratisbon*, q.v.

| Regge (Neth., riv.) | rĕk(h)′-ə | rek(h)′-uh |
| Reggio Calabria (It.) | rĕd′-jô kä-lä′-brē-ä | red′-jo kah-lah′-bree-ah |

American speakers may follow the example of Italians and call it simply *Reggio*, rĕd′-jô [red′-jo].

Reggio Emilia (It.)	rĕd′-jô ĕ-mē′-lyä	red′-jo eh-mee′-lyah
Reghin (Rum.)	rĕ-gĕn′	reh-geen′
Regina Coeli (It.)	rĕ-jē′-nä chĕ′-lē	reh-jee′-nah cheh′-lee
Reglitz (Ger., riv.)	rĕg′-lĭts	reg′-lits
Regneville (Fr.)	rĕn(y)-vēl′	ren(y)-veel′
Rehovot (Pal.)	rĕ′-hō-vōt	reh′-hoh-voht

Also spelled *Rechobot*. Arabic *Khirbet Deiran*, k(h)ĭr′-bĕt dä-rän′ [k(h)ihr′-bet day-rahn′].

| Reichenbach (Ger. > ? Pol.) | rī′-kən-bäk(h) | rai′-kuhn-bahk(h) |

Polish *Rychbach*, q.v.

| Reichstag | *Eng.* rĭks′-täg | raiks′-tahg |
| | *Ger.* rĭk(h)s′-täk(h) | raik(h)s′-tahk(h) |

The pronunciation rĭk′-shtäg [raik′-shtahg] is incorrect. The *s*, as a genitive inflection, belongs to the first syllable, not to the second.

Reichswald (Ger.)	rĭk(h)s′-vält	raik(h)s′-vahlt
Reichwalde (Ger.)	rĭk(h)′-väl-də	raik(h)′-vahl-duh
Reims (Fr.)	*Eng.* rēmz′	reemz′
	Fr. răNs′	raNs′
Reinovo (Rus.)	rĕ′-ĭ-nŏ-vŏ	reh′-i-no-vo
Reiovets (Pol.) See *Rejowiec*.
Reipzig (Ger.)	rīp′-tsĭk(h)	raip′-tsik(h)
Reis, Coelho dos (Braz. polit.) See *Coelho dos Reis*.
Reisdorf (Luxem.)	rīs′-dôrf	rais′-dorf
Reisholz (Ger.)	rīs′-hôlts	rais′-holts
Reistad, Ole (Nor. officer)	rä′-stä, ō′-lə	ray′-stah, oh′-luh
Reit Diep (Neth.)	rīt′ dēp′	rait′ deep′
Also called *Groningen Diep*, q.v.
Rejowiec (Pol.)	rĕ-yô′-vyĕts	reh-yo′-vyets
Russian spelling *Reiovets*.
Rekovac (Yugosl.)	rĕ′-kô-väts	reh′-ko-vahts
Remada (Tun.)	rə-mă′-dä	ruh-ma′-dah
Remagen (Ger.)	rä′-mä-gən	ray′-mah-guhn
	or rä-mä′-gən	ray-mah′-guhn
Remagne (Belg.)	rə-män′(y)	ruh-mahn′(y)
Rembang (NEI, Java)	rĕm′-bäng′	rem′-bahng′
Rembs (Fr.)	räN′	rahN′
Remich (Luxem.)	rä′-mĭk(h)	ray′-mik(h)
Remscheid (Ger.)	rĕm′-shīt	rem′-shait

[442]

Rena (Nor.) rā'-nä ray'-nah
Renaix (Belg.) See *Ronse*.
Renault (Fr.) rə-nō' ruh-noh'
Renault, Abgar (Braz. rĕ-nō', äb-gär' reh-noh', ahb-gahr'
polit.)
Renchen (Ger.) rĕn'-k(h)ən ren'-k(h)uhn
Rendova (Oc., Solomons) rĕn-dô'-vä ren-do'-vah
or rĕn'-dô-vä ren'-do-vah
renege ("to deny") rĭ-nĭg' ri-nig'
This popular pronunciation has all but displaced the older rĭ-nēg'
[ri-neeg'].
Renen (Neth.) rā'-nən ray'-nuhn
Renesse (Neth.) rə-nĕs'-ə ruh-nes'-uh
Renfrew (Scot.) rĕn'-frōō ren'-froo
Reni (Rum. >Rus.) *Rus.* rĕ'-nĭ reh'-ni
Rum. rĕn' ren'
"renig." A popular spelling of *renege*, q.v.
Renkum (Neth.) rĕng'-kəm reng'-kuhm
Rennell (Oc., Solomons) rĕn'-əl ren'-uhl
Probably named after the English geographer.
Renner, Karl rĕn'-ər ren'-uhr
(Austrian polit.)
Rennes (Fr.) rĕn' ren'
Reno (It., riv.) rĕ'-nô reh'-no
Rensselaer (N.Y.) rĕn'-sə-lər ren'-suh-luhr
The Polytechnique Institute is often called rĕn'-sə-lĭr' [ren'-suh-lihr'].
Rentis, Konstantinos rĕn'-dēs, kôn-stän- ren'-dees, kon-stahn-
(Gr. polit.) dē'-nôs dee'-nos
Renton (Wash.) rĕn'-tən ren'-tuhn
Reppen (Ger.) rĕp'-ən rep'-uhn
Resa, Alexander J. rē'-sə ree'-suh
(U.S. representative)
Resan (Yugosl.) rĕ'-sän reh'-sahn
Resava (Yugosl., riv.) rĕ'-sä-vä reh'-sah-vah
Reschenscheideck rĕsh'-ən-shĭ'-dĕk resh'-uhn-shai'-dek
(Austria, It., pass)
research rĭ-sûrch' *or* rē'-sûrch ri-suhrch' *or* ree'-
suhrch
A campus joke is that those who talk about it say rĭ-sûrch' [ri-suhrch'];
those who do it, say rē'-sûrch [ree'-suhrch]. Though this isn't true,
the usage of many if not most scientists has made the pronunciation
rē'-sûrch [ree'-suhrch] acceptable. It was admitted by Webster's
(1934) and the Thorndike Century (1941).
Reshidiya (Libya) rĕ-shĭ-dē'-yä reh-shi-dee'-yah

Reshitsa (Rus.)	rĕ′-shĭ-tsä	reh′-shi-tsah
Resht *or* Rasht (Iran)	răsht′	rasht′
Resiczabánya (Rum.)	See *Recița.*	
Resistencia (Arg.)	rĕ-sēs-tĕn′-syä	reh-sees-tehn′-syah
Restelica (Yugosl.)	rĕ′-stĕ′-lĭ-tsä	reh′-steh′-li-tsah
Restinga (P.I.)	rĕs-tēng′-gä	res-teeng′-gah
Rethel (Fr.)	rə-tĕl′	ruh-tel′
Rethymne (Crete)	rĕ-thēm′-nē	reh-theem′-nee
Rethymnon (Crete)	rĕ′-thēm-nô(n)	reh′-theem-no(n)

Also called *Rethymne,* q.v., and *Rethymnos,* rĕ′-thēm-nôs [reh′-theem-nos].

Retiers (Fr.)	rə-tyĕ′	ruh-tyeh′
Retournemer (Fr.)	rə-tōōr-nə-mĕr′	ruh-toor-nuh-mehr′
	or -mĕ′	*or* -meh′
rettō	rĕt-tô	ret-to

An element, meaning *chain of islands,* in Japanese place names.

Reuter's (Br. news agency)	roi′-tərz	roi′-tuhrz
Reuther, Walter P. (Am. labor leader)	rōōth′-er	rooth′-uhr
Reutlingen (Ger.)	roit′-lĭng-ən	roit′-ling-uhn
Reuzel (Neth.)	rû′-zəl	rœ′-zuhl
Reval *or* Revel (Est.)	*Eng.* rĕv′-əl	rev′-uhl
	Rus. rĕ′-vĕl(y)	reh′-vel(y)
Estonian *Tallinn,* q.v.		
Revercomb, Chapman (U.S. senator)	rĕv′-ər-kŏm, chăp′-mən	rev′-uhr-kohm, chap′-muhn
Revest, le (Fr.)	rə-vĕ′	ruh-veh′
Reykjavík (Icel.)	rā′-kyə-vēk	ray′-kyuh-veek
Reynaud, Paul (Fr. polit.)	rĕ-nō′, pôl′	reh-noh′, pol′
Reza Shah Pahlevi (Iran)	See *Pahlevi, Shah Riza.*	
Rezayeh (Iran) See *Rizaigeh.*		
Rēzekne (Latvia)	rā′-zĕk-nĕ	ray′-zek-neh
Russian *Ryezhitsa,* q.v. German *Rositten,* q.v.		
Rezina (Rum. >Rus.)	rĕ-zē′-nä	reh-zee′-nah
Rēznas (Latvia, lake)	rāz′-näs	rayz′-nahs
Rgotina (Yugosl.)	ər′-gô′-tĭ-nä	uhr′-go′-ti-nah
Rhaetia (Austria, Switz.)	*Eng.* rē′-shə	ree′-shuh
Also spelled *Raetia.*		
Rhaetian Alps (Austria, Switz.)	rē′-shən	ree′-shuhn
Rharsa, el (Tun.)	rär′-sä, ĕr	rahr′-sah, ehr

Rhee Syngman (Korean   rē so͝ong-män   ree sung-mahn
   polit.)

Though put first, *Rhee* corresponds to an English "last name."

Rheindahlen (Ger.)   rĭn'-däl-ən   rain'-dahl-uhn

Rheine (Ger.)   rī'-nə   rai'-nuh

Rhein-Main (Ger.,   *Ger.* rĭn' mĭn'   rain' main'
   Frankfurt, airport)   *Eng.* rĭn' män'   rain' mayn'

Rheydt (Ger.)   rīt'   rait'

Rhine (Europ. riv.)   *Eng.* rīn'   rain'

Dutch spelling *Rijn.* German spelling *Rhein.* French *Rhin*, răN'
[raN'].

Rhio (NEI)   Variant spelling of *Riouw*, q.v.

Rhodes (Dodec.)   *Eng.* rōdz'   rohdz'

Greek *Rodos*, q.v. Italian *Rodi*, rô'-dē [ro'-dee].

Rhodesia (Br. Afr.)   rō-dē'-zhə   roh-dee'-zhuh

Rhodope (Balkan mts.) *Eng.* rŏd'-ə-pĭ   rod'-uh-pi
                        Gr. rô-*th*ô'-pē   ro-*tho*'-pee

Bulgarian *Despoto planina*, dĕ'-spŏ-tŏ plä'-nē'-nä [deh'-spo-to plah'-
nee'-nah].

Rhoendt *or* Rhöndt (Ger.) rûnt'   rœnt'

Rhône (Fr., Switz., riv.) rōn'   rohn'

Rhys (Welsh name)   rēs'   rees'

Riano (It.)   ryä'-nô   ryah'-no

Rians (Fr.)   ryäNs'   ryahNs'

Ribachi, the (Rus., pen.) rĭ-bä'-chĭ   ri-bah'-chi

Ribarci (Yugosl.)   rē'-bär-tsĭ   ree'-bahr-tsi

Ribe (Den.)   rē'-bə   ree'-buh

Ribera (Sicily)   rē-bĕ'-rä   ree-beh'-rah

Ribnica (Yugosl.)   rēb'-nĭ-tsä   reeb'-ni-tsah

Ricarte, Artemio   rē-kär'-tĕ, är-tĕ'-myô ree-kahr'-teh, ahr-
   (Fil. polit.)   teh'-myo

Richelieu (Fr.)   *Eng.* rĭsh'-ə-lo͞o   rish'-uh-loo
                      Fr. rē-shə-lyû'   ree-shuh-lœ'

Ridderkerk (Neth.)   rĭd'-ər-kĕrk   rid'-uhr-kehrk

Riegel (Ger.)   rē'-gəl   ree'-guhl

Riehlman, R. Walter   rēl'-mən   reel'-muhn
   (U.S. representative)

Rieka (It. > Yugosl.)   rē'-yĕ'-kä   ree'-yeh'-kah
   Italian *Fiume*, q.v.

Riesenburg (Ger. > Pol.) rē'-zən-bo͝ork(h)   ree'-zuhn-burk(h)
   Polish *Prabuty*, q.v.

Riesi (Sicily)   ryĕ'-zē   ryeh'-zee

Rieti (It.)   ryĕ'-tē   ryeh'-tee

Riez (Fr.)	ryĕz′	ryez′
Riff (Berber tribe)	rĭf′	rif′
Riga (Latvia)	rē′-gä	ree′-gah
Riis, Jacob A.	rēs′	rees′
(Dan. Am. author)		
Riiser-Larsen, Hjalmar	rē-sər-lär′-sən,	ree-suhr-lahr′-suhn,
(Nor. admiral)	yäl′-mär	yahl′-mahr
Rijeka Crnojevića	rĭ-yĕ′-kä tsər′-	ri-yeh′-kah tsuhr′-
(Yugosl.)	nô′-yĕ-vĭ-chä	no′-yeh-vi-chah
Rijen (Neth.)	rī′-ən	rai′-uhn
Rijn (Europ. riv.) See *Rhein.*		
Rijnsburg (Neth.)	rīns′-bûrk(h)	rains′-bœrk(h)
Rijsbergen (Neth.)	rīs′-bĕrk(h)-ən	rais′-behrk(h)-uhn
Rijssen (Neth.)	rīs′-ən	rais′-uhn
Rijswijk (Neth.)	rīs′-wīk	rais′-waik
English *Ryswick,* rĭz′-wĭk [riz′-wik].		
Riksdag	rēks′-däg	reeks′-dahg
Swedish parliament.		
Rila (Bulg., mts.)	rē′-lä	ree′-lah
Greek *Rilos,* rē′-lôs [ree′-los]. Turkish *Rilo.*		
Rille (Fr., riv.) See *Risle.*		
Rimaszombat (Cz.) See *Rimavská Sobota.*		
Rimavská Sobota (Cz.)	rē′-mäf-skä	ree′-mahf-skah
	sô′-bô-tä	so′-bo-tah
Hungarian *Rimaszombat,* rē′-mŏ-sôm′-bät [ree′-mo-som′-baht].		
Rimini (It.)	*Eng.* rĭm′-ĭ-nĭ	rim′-i-ni
	It. rē′-mē-nē	ree′-mee-nee
Rimske Toplice (Yugosl.)	rēm′-skĕ tôp′-lĭ-tsĕ	reem′-skeh top′-li-tseh
Rimski-Korsakov,	*Eng.* rĭm′-skĭ kôr′-sə-kôf	rim′-ski kor′-suh-kof
Nikolai Andreevivich		
(Rus. composer)	*Rus.* rēm′-skĭ kôr′-sä-kôf, nĭ-kŏ-lī′ än-drĕ′-yĕ-vĭch	reem′-ski kor′-sah-kof, ni-ko-lai′ ahn-dreh′-yeh-vich
Rincon (N.M.)	*Eng.* rĭn-kŏn′	rin-kon′
Spanish *Rincón,* rēn-kôn′ [reen-kon′].		
Rindjani (NEI)	rĭn-jä′-nē	rin-jah′-nee
Ringebu (Nor.)	rĭng′-ə-boo	ring′-uh-boo
Ringerike (Nor.)	rĭng′-ə-rē-kə	ring′-uh-ree-kuh
Ringkoebing *or* Ringkö-bing (Den.)	rĭng′-kû-bĭng	ring′-kœ-bing
Ringsaker (Nor.)	rĭng′-sä-kər	ring′-sah-kuhr
Ringsted (Den.)	rĭng′-stĕth	ring′-steth
Rio Branco (Brazil)	rē′-oo bräng′-koo	ree′-u brahng′-ku

Rio de Janeiro (Brazil)   *Eng.* rē′-ō də zhə-   ree′-oh duh zhuh-
                                 něr′-ō   nehr′-oh
                      Port. rē′-ŏŏ dĭ zhə-   ree′-u di zhuh-
                                   nā′-rŏŏ   nay′-ru

Río de la Plata (S. A.)   rē′-ô dĕ lä plä′-tä   ree′-o deh lah plah′-
                                                         tah
   British *River Plate*, plāt′ [playt′].

Río de Oro (Afr., Sp. col.)   rē′-ô dĕ ô′-rô   ree′-o deh o′-ro

Rio Grande   *Eng.* rē′-ō grăn′-dĭ   ree′-oh gran′-di
   (U.S., Mex., riv.)   *Sp.* rē′-ô grän′-dĕ   ree′-o grahn′-deh
   Old-fashioned English, rī′-ō grănd′ [rai′-oh grand′].

Rio Grande do Norte   rē′-ŏŏ grän′-dĭ dŏŏ   ree′-u grahn′-di du
   (Brazil)   nôr′-tĭ   nor′-ti

Rio Grande do Sul   rē′-ŏŏ grän′-dĭ dŏŏ   ree′-u grahn′-di du
   (Brazil)   sŏŏl′   sool′

Riom (Fr.)   *Fr.* ryôN′   ryoN′

Río Muni (Afr.)   rē′-ô mŏŏ′-nē   ree′-o moo′-nee
   Also called *Spanish Guinea*, gĭn′-ĭ [gin′-i].

Rion (Gr., cape)   rē′-ôn   ree′-on

Rion (Rus., riv.)   rĭ-ōn′   ri-ohn′

Ríos, Juan Antonio   rē′-ôs, hwän′   ree′-os, hwahn′
   (Chilean polit.)   än-tô′-nyô   ahn-to′-nyo

Riouw *or* Rhio (NEI)   rē′-ō   ree′-oh

Rioz (Fr.)   ryô′   ryo′

Ripanj (Yugosl.)   rē′-pän(y)   ree′-pahn(y)

Ripiglio (It.)   rē-pē′-lyô   ree-pee′-lyo

Ripoli (It.)   rē′-pô-lē   ree′-po-lee

Risan (Yugosl.)   rē′-sän   ree′-sahn
   Italian *Risano*, rē-sä′-nô [ree-sah′-no].

Risle (Fr., riv.)   rēl′   reel′
   Also spelled *Rille*.

Risoer (Nor.)   rē′-sûr   ree′-sœr

Risoeyhavn (Nor.)   rē′-sûĭ-hävn   ree′-sœi-hahvn

Risör (Nor.)   rē′-sûr   ree′-sœr

Risovon (Gr.)   rē′-sô-vô(n)   ree′-so-vo(n)

Risöyhavn (Nor.)   rē′-sûĭ-hävn   ree′-sœi-hahvn

Ristna (Est., Hiiu)   rĭst′-nä   rist′-nah

Risto Ryti (Fin. polit.)   See *Ryti, Risto*.

Rivadeo (Sp.)   rē-vä-dĕ′-ô   ree-vah-deh′-o

Rivera, Diego   rē-vĕ′-rä, dyĕ′-gô   ree-veh′-rah, dyeh′-go
   (Mex. painter)

Rivers, L. Mendel   rĭv′-ərz, mĕn′-dəl   riv′-uhrz, men′-duhl
   (U.S. representative)

Rives (Mo., Va.)   rēvz′   reevz′

Rizaiyeh (Iran, lake)   rē'-zä-ē'-yə   ree'-zah-ee'-yuh
   Formerly called *Urmiah*, English, ŏŏr'-mĭ-ə [ur'-mi-uh].
Rizal, José (Fil. polit.)   rē-säl', hô-sĕ'   ree-sahl', ho-seh'
Rizospastis (Gr. news-   rē'-zô-späs'-tēs   ree'-zo-spahs'-tees
   paper)
Rizzuto (It., cape)   rĕd-zōō'-tô   reed-zoo'-to
Rjukan (Nor.)   ryōō'-kän   ryoo'-kahn
Roa (Nor.)   rō'-ä   roh'-ah
Roatta, Mario   rô-ät'-tä, mä'-ryô   ro-aht'-tah, mah'-ryo
   (It. general)
Robles, Gil (Sp. polit.)   rô'-blĕs, hēl'   ro'-bles, heel'
robot (a mechanical man)   rō'-bət *or* rŏb'-ət   roh'-buht *or* rob'-uht
Robsion, John M.   rŏb'-sĭ-ən   rob'-si-uhn
   (U.S. representative)
Roccacasale (It.)   rôk'-kä-kä-sä'-lĕ   rok'-kah-kah-sah'-leh
Rocca Corneta (It.)   rôk'-kä kôr-nĕ'-tä   rok'-kah kor-neh'-tah
Rocca D'Arce (It.)   rôk'-kä där'-chĕ   rok'-kah dahr'-cheh
Rocca Giovane (It.)   rôk'-kä jô'-vä-nĕ   rok'-kah jo'-vah-neh
Rocca Massima (It.)   rôk'-kä mäs'-sē-mä   rok'-kah mahs'-see-mah
Roccella (It.)   rôt-chĕl'-lä   rot-chel'-lah
Rocchetto, la (It.)   rôk-kĕt'-tô   rok-ket'-to
Rochefort (Belg.)   rôsh-fôr'   rosh-for'
Rochefort (Fr.)   rôsh-fôr'   rosh-for'
Rochelle, la (Fr.)   rô-shĕl', lä   ro-shel', lah
Roche Qui Boît, la (Fr.)   rôsh kē bwä', lä   rosh kee bwah', lah
Rocheservière (Fr.)   rôsh-sĕr-vyĕr'   rosh-sehr-vyehr'
Rocio (Port.)   rōō-sē'-ōō   ru-see'-u
Rodakinon (Gr.)   rô-dä'-kē-nô(n)   ro-dah'-kee-no(n)
Rödberg (Nor.)   rû'-bĕrg   rœ'-behrg
Rod el Farag   rôd' ĕl fä-räg'   rod' el fah-rahg'
   (Egypt, Cairo, airport)
Roden (Neth.)   rō'-dən   roh'-duhn
rodeo   *Eng.* rō'-dĭ-ō   roh'-di-oh
        Sp. rô-dĕ'-ô   ro-deh'-o
Except occasionally on the Mexican border, cowmen use the English
   pronunciation.
Röder (Ger., riv.)   rû'-dər   rœ'-duhr
Rodi (Dodec.)   See *Rhodes*.
Rödingen (Ger.)   rû'-dĭng-ən   rœ'-ding-uhn
Rodionov, Konstantin K.   rô-dĭ-ô'-nŏf, kŏn-stän-   ro-di-o'-nof, kon-
   (Rus. admiral)   tēn'   stahn-teen'

Rodoni (Alb., cape)   rô-dô'-nē   ro-do'-nee
  Albanian *Kep i Rodonit.*

Rodopou (Crete,   rô-dô-pōō'   ro-do-poo'
  pen., mt.)
  Also called *Tityron*, tē'-tē-rôn [tee'-tee-ron]; *Spada*, spä'-dä [spah'-
  dah; and *Psakon*, q.v.

Rodos (Dodec.)   rô'-dôs   ro'-do(s)
  English *Rhodes*, rōdz' [rohdz'].

Rodosto (Turk.)   *It.* rô-dô'-stô   ro-do'-sto
  Turkish *Tekirdağ*, q.v.

Rodríguez (Sp. name)   *Am. Sp.* rô-drē'-gĕs ro-dree'-ges
                Sp. rô-drē'-gĕth   ro-dree'-geth

Rodríguez Larreta,   rô-drē'-gĕs lä-rĕ'-tä, ro-dree'-ges lah-
  Eduardo (Urug. polit.)   ĕ-dwär'-dô   reh'-tah, eh-
                                     dwahr'-do

Rodzinski, Artur   *Eng.* rō-jĭn'-skĭ,   roh-jin'-skih,
  (Am. musician)   är'-tōōr   ahr'-tur
                Pol. rô-jēn'-skĭ, ro-jeen'-skih,
                  är'-tōōr   ahr'-tur

Roebourne (Austral.)   rō'-bûrn'   roh'-buhrn'
Roedberg (Nor.)   rû'-bĕrg   roe'-behrg
Roeder (Ger., riv.)   rû'-dər   roe'-duhr
Roedingen (Ger.)   rû'-dĭng-ən   roe'-ding-uhn
Roehe (Ger.)   rû'-hə   roe'-huh
Roeldal (Nor.)   rûl'-däl   roel'-dahl
Roem (Den., isl.)   rûm'   roem'
  Also called *Roemoe*, rûm'-û [roem'-œ].

Roemer (Ger., Frankfurt) rû'-mər   roe'-muhr
Roemoe (Den., isl.) See *Roem*.
Roer (Neth., Ger. riv.) *Eng.* rōr' *or* rûr' rohr' *or* ruhr'
                 Ger., Du. rōōr'   roor'

Roer is the Dutch spelling. On German maps this river is spelled *Rur*
or *Ruhr*. This tributary of the Maas and the better-known *Ruhr*,
tributary of the Rhine, are pronounced exactly alike by Germans,
rōōr'. However, for American radio, a spelling pronunciation of *Roer*,
rōr' or rûr', has the advantage of distinguishing the two rivers for our
audience. *Ruhr* in standard German means dysentery and it may be
compared to English *stream* and *run.*

Roermond (Neth.)   rōōr-mônt'   roor-mont'
Roeros (Nor.)   rû'-rōs   roe'-rohs
Roervik (Nor.)   rûr'-vēk   roer'-veek
Roesvann (Nor., lake)   rûs'-vän   roes'-vahn
Roetgen (Ger.)   rût'-gən   roet'-guhn
Roeykenvik (Nor.)   rûĭ'-kən-vēk   roei'-kuhn-veek

Roeysheim (Nor.)	rûĭs′-hām	rœis′-haym
Rogachevsky (Rus. name)	rŏ-gä-chĕf′-skĭ	ro-gah-chef′-ski
Rogačica (Yugosl.)	rô′-gä′-chĭ-tsä	ro′-gah′-chi-tsah
Rogatica (Yugosl.)	rô′-gä′-tĭ-tsä	ro′-gah′-ti-tsah
Rogers, Edith Nourse (U.S. representative)	rŏj′-ərz, nûrs′	roj′-uhrz, nuhrs′
Roggel (Neth.)	rôk(h)′-əl	rok(h)′-uhl
Rognac (Fr.)	rô-nyäk′	ro-nyahk′
Rogozna (Yugosl., mts.)	rô′-gôz-nä	ro′-goz-nah
Rogoznica (Yugosl.)	rô′-gôz′-nĭ-tsä	ro′-goz′-ni-tsah
Röhe (Ger.)	rû′-hə	rœ′-huh
Rohrbough, E. G. (U.S. representative)	rôr′-bô	rohr′-baw
Roi (Oc., Kwajalein)	rô′-ē *or* roi′	ro′-ee *or* roi′
Roi Et (Siam)	roi′ ĕt	roi′ et
Rojate (It.)	rô-yä′-tĕ	ro-yah′-teh
Rokeach, Israel (Pal. polit.)	rô-kĕ′-äk(h), ĭz′-rĭ-əl	ro-keh′-ahk(h), iz′-ri-uhl
Rokietnica (Pol.)	rô-kyĕt-nē′-tsä	ro-kyet-nee′-tsah
Rokiškis (Lith.)	rŏ′-kĭsh-kĭs	ro′-kish-kis
Rokitno (Pol.)	rô-kēt′-nô	ro-keet′-no

Russian *Rakitno*, rä-kēt′-nŏ [rah-keet′-no].

Rokkanje (Neth.)	rôk-kän′(y)	rok-kahn′(y)
Rokossovsky, K. (Rus. general)	rŏ-kŏs-sôf′-skĭ	ro-kos-sof′-ski
Rola Zeliński, Michał (Pol. polit.)	rô′-lä zĕ-lēn′-skĭ, mē′-häl	ro′-lah zeh-leen′-ski, mee′-hahl
Rola Zymierski, Michał (Pol. polit.)	rô′-lä zĭ-myĕr′-skĭ, mē′-häl	ro′-lah zi-myehr′-ski, mee′-hahl
Röldal (Nor.)	rûl′-däl	rœl′-dahl
Rollesbroich (Ger.)	rôl′-əs-broik(h)	rol′-uhs-broik(h)
Rollingen (Luxem.)	rôl′-ĭng-ən	rol′-ing-uhn
Rolph, Thomas (U.S. representative)	rŏlf′	rolf′
Rölvaag, Ole Edvart (Nor. Am. writer)	rûl′-vôg, ō′-lə ĕd′-värt	rœl′-vog, oh′-luh ed′-vahrt
Röm (Den., isl.)	rûm′	rœm′

Also called *Römö*, rûm′-û [rœm′-œ].

| Roma (It.) | rô′-mä | ro′-mah |

English *Rome*, q.v.

Roman (Rum.)	rô′-män	ro′-mahn
România	*Eng.* rō-mān′-yə	roh-mayn′-yuh
	Rum. rô-mû′-nyä	ro-muh′-nyah

The common English form is *Rumania*, rōō-mā′-nyə [roo-may′-nyuh].

Romanov (Rus. name)	*Eng.* rō′-mä-nôf	roh′-mah-nof
	Rus. rŏ-mä′-nôf	ro-mah′-nof
Romanovce (Yugosl.)	rŏ′-mä′-nôv-tsĕ	ro′-mah′-nov-tseh
Romanovka (Rus.)	rŏ-mä′-nôf-kä	ro-mah′-nof-kah
Romblón (P.I.)	rôm-blôn′	rom-blon′
Rome (It.)	rōm′	rohm′
Italian *Roma,* q.v.		
Römer (Ger., Frankfurt)	rû′-mər	rœ′-muhr
Romer, Tadeusz	rô′-mĕr, tä-dĕ′-ōōsh	ro′-mehr, tah-deh′-
(Pol. polit.)		ush
Romerike (Nor.)	rō′-mə-rĭ-kə	roh′-muh-ri-kuh
Romilly (Fr.)	rô-mē-yē′	ro-mee-yee′
Romilly sur Seine (Fr.)	rô-mē-yē sür sĕn′	ro-mee-yee sür sen′
Rominten Heath (Ger.)	*Eng.* rō′-mĭn-tən	roh′-min-tuhn

German *Rominter Heide,* rō′-mĭn-tər hĭ′-də [roh′-min-tuhr hai′-duh].

Rommel, Erwin	rôm′l *or* rŭm′l,	rom′l *or* ruhm′l,
(Ger. general)	ĕr′-vēn	ehr′-veen
Romny (Rus.)	rôm′-nĭ	rom′-ni
Römö (Den., isl.) See *Roem.*		
Romola (It.)	rô′-mô-lä	ro′-mo-lah
Romorantin (Fr.)	rô-mô-räN-tăN′	ro-mo-rahN-taN′
Romsdal (Nor.)	rŏŏms′-däl	rums′-dahl
Romsdalsfjord (Nor.)	rŏŏms′-däls-fyōr	rums′-dahls-fyohr
Romsdalshorn (Nor.,	rŏŏms′-däls-hōrn	rums′-dahls-hohrn
mt.)		
Rómulo, Carlos P.	rô′-mōō-lô, kär′-lôs	ro′-moo-lo, kahr′-los
(Fil. polit.)		
Roncador (Oc., Solomons)	rôn-kä-dôr′	ron-kah-dor′
Roncaglia (It.)	rôn-kä′-lyä	ron-kah′-lyah
Rongelap (Oc., Marshalls)	rông′-ĕ-läp	rong′-eh-lahp
Rongerik (Oc., Marshalls)	rông′-ĕ-rĭk	rong′-eh-rik

Also pronounced rŏn′-jə-rĭk [ron′-juh-rik] by the American forces.

Ronne (Am., Nor. name)	rŭn′-ə *or* rĕn′-ə	ruhn′-uh *or* ren′-uh
Ronse (Belg.)	*Flem.* rôn′-sə	ron′-suh
French *Renaix,* rə-nĕ′ [ruh-neh′].		
Roodeschool (Neth.)	rō′-də-sk(h)ōl′	roh′-duh-sk(h)ohl′
Rook *or* Rooke (Oc.,	rŏŏk′	ruk′
Bismarck arch.)		

Named for Sir George Rooke. Also called *Umboi,* ōōm′-boi [oom′-boi].

Roosenburg (Neth.)	rō′-zən-bûrk(h)	roh′-zuhn-bœrk(h)
Roosendaal (Neth.)	rō′-zən-däl	roh′-zuhn-dahl
Also spelled *Rozendaal,* q.v.		
Roosevelt	rō′-zə-vĕlt	roh′-zuh-velt

The pronunciation with ō has been preferred by the families of both

Presidents, and it is the only pronunciation given in our dictionaries. However, a pronunciation rōō′-zə-vĕlt [roo′-zuh-velt] is also current. In certain stress patterns the name has two syllables—rōz′-vĕlt [rohz′-velt] or rōōs′-vĕlt. This same principle holds true of words like *president, governor, government, rationing.*)

Roquebrussane, la (Fr.)	rôk-brü-sän′, lä	rok-brü-sahn′, lah
Röros (Nor.)	rû′-rōs	rœ′-rohs
Rorschach (Switz.)	rôr′-shäk(h)	ror′-shahk(h)
Rörvik (Nor.)	rûr′-vēk	rœr′-veek
Rosales (P.I.)	rô-sä′-lĕs	ro-sah′-les
Rosario (Arg.)	rô-sä′-ryô	ro-sah′-ryo
Rosario (P.I.)	rô-sä′-ryô	ro-sah′-ryo

Also called *Salinas,* sä-lē′-näs [sah-lee′-nahs].

Rosarno (It.)	rô-sär′-nô	ro-sahr′-no
Roscoff (Fr.)	rôs-kôf′	ros-kof′
Rosenau (Fr.)	rō-zə-nou′	roh-zuh-nau′
Rosenborg (Den.)	rō′-sən-bôr	roh′-suhn-bor
Rosendal (Nor.)	rō′-sən-däl	roh′-suhn-dahl
Rosenovskaya (Latvia)	*Rus.* rô′-zĕ-nŏf-skä-yä	ro′-zeh-nof-skah-yah

Latvian *Zilupe,* q.v.

Rosetta (Egypt)	*Eng.* rō-zĕt′-ə	roh-zet′-uh

Also called *Rashid,* q.v.

Rosignano (It.)	rô-sē-nyä′-nô	ro-see-nyah′-no
Roşiorii de Vede (Rum.)	rô-shyô′-rē dĕ vĕ′-dĕ	ro-shyo′-ree deh veh′-deh
Rositten (Latvia)	*Ger.* rô-zĭt′-ən	ro-zit′-uhn

Latvian *Rēzekne,* q.v. Russian *Ryezhitsa,* q.v.

Roskilde (Den.)	rôs′-kĭl-ə	ros′-kil-uh
Roslavl (Rus.)	rŏs-lävl′(y)	ros-lahvl′(y)
Rosmalen (Neth.)	rôs′-mä-lən	ros′-mah-luhn
Rosolini (It.)	rô-sô-lē′-nē	ro-so-lee′-nee
Rossieny (Lith.)	*Rus.* rôs′-sĭ-yĕ-nĭ	ros′-si-yeh-ni

Lithuanian *Raseiniai,* q.v.

Rossosh (Rus.)	rôs′-sŏsh	ros′-sosh
Rostock (Ger.)	*Eng.* rŏs′-tŏk	ros′-tok
	Ger. rôs′-tôk	ros′-tok
Rostov (Rus.)	rŏ-stôf′	ro-stof′
Rostrenen (Fr.)	rôs-trə-näN′	ros-truh-nahN′
Roşu (Rum., pass)	rô′-shŏō	ro′-shu

Also called *Turnu Roşu,* tŏŏr′-nŏō [tur′-nu]. German *Roten Turm.*

Rösvann (Nor., lake)	rûs′-vän	rœs′-vahn
Rosyth (Scot.)	rō-sĭth′	roh-saith′
Rota (Oc., Marianas)	*Eng.* rō′-tə	roh′-tuh
	native rô′-tä′	ro′-tah′

[452]

Roten Turm (Rum., pass) rō'-tən tŏŏrm'　　roh'-tuhn turm'
　Rumanian Roşu and Turnu Roşu, q.v.
Rötgen (Ger.)　　　　　　rût'-gən　　　　　rœt'-guhn
Roth (Ger.)　　　　　　　rōt'　　　　　　roht'
Rothaar (Ger., mts.)　　　rōt'-här'　　　　roht'-hahr'
Rothenburg (Ger.)　　　Eng. rō'-tən-bûrg　roh'-tuhn-buhrg
　　　　　　　　　　　Ger. rō'-tən-　　　roh'-tuhn-burk(h)
　　　　　　　　　　　　　bŏŏrk(h)
Rotmistrof (Rus. name)　rôt'-mǐ-strŏf　　rot'-mi-strof
Rotterdam (Neth.)　　　Eng. rŏt'-ər-dăm　rot'-uhr-dam
　　　　　　　　　　　Du. rôt'-ər-däm'　rot'-uhr-dahm'
Rottumeroog (Neth., isl.)　rôt'-ə-mə-rōk(h)'　rot'-uh-muh-rohk(h)'
Rotuma (Oc., Fiji)　　　rô-tōō'-mä　　　ro-too'-mah
Rouault, Georges　　　　rwō', zhôrzh'　　rwoh', zhorzh'
　(Fr. painter)
Roubaix (Fr.)　　　　　rōō-bĕ'　　　　roo-beh'
Rouen (Fr.)　　　　　　rwäN'　　　　　rwahN'
Roule, du (Fr., fort)　　rōōl', dü　　　　rool', dü
Roulers (Belg.)　　See Rouselare.
Roumele, Agia (Crete)　rōō-mĕ'-lē,　　　roo-meh'-lee,
　　　　　　　　　　　ä-yē'-ä　　　　　ah-yee'-ah
Rouselare (Belg.)　　　rōō'-sə-lär　　　roo'-suh-lahr
　French Roulers, rōō-lĕrs' [roo-lehrs'], and rōō-lĕr' [roo-lehr'].
Rousseau, Jean Jacques　rōō-sō', zhäN' zhäk'　roo-soh', zhahN'
　(Fr. author)　　　　　　　　　　　　zhakh'
Roussos, Georgios　　　rou'-sôs, yôr'-yôs　rau'-sos, yor'-yos
　(Gr. polit.)
route　　　　　　　　　rōōt' or rout'　　root' or raut'
In military use and in all traffic departments, the pronunciation is
"raut." This is also the popular, old-fashioned American pronuncia-
tion. Dictionaries and purists, however, prefer "root," a Gallicism.
Certainly en route is a French phrase, the English equivalent being
in route. Like ration, route is a fighting word.
Routot (Fr.)　　　　　rōō-tō'　　　　roo-toh'
Rov (Rus., riv.)　　　　rôf'　　　　　rof'
Rovaniemi (Fin.)　　　rô'-vä-nē'-ĕ'-mē　ro'-vah-nee'-eh'-mee
Rovenki (Rus.)　　　　rŏ-vĕn(y)-kē'　ro-ven(y)-kee'
Rovigno (It.)　　　　　rô-vē'-nyô　　ro-vee'-nyo
　Serb-Croat Rovinj, q. v.
Rovigo (It.)　　　　　rô-vē'-gô　　　ro-vee'-go
Rovinj (It. > Yugosl.)　rô'-vēn(y)　　ro'-veen(y)
　Italian Rovigno, q.v.
Rovno (Pol. > Rus.)　　rôv'-nŏ　　　rov'-no
　Polish Równe, rŏŏv'-nĕ [ruv'-neh].

Rowan, William A.   rō'-ən   roh'-uhn
    (U.S. representative)

Rowayton (Conn.)   rō-wāt'n   roh-wayt'n

Rowe (family name)   rō' *or* rou'   roh' *or* rau'
    The first is the usual pronunciation, but David N. Rowe and Leo S.
    Rowe, both in the field of international relations, wish the name
    rhymed with *how* and *cow*.

Równe (Pol. > Rus.) See *Rovno*.

Roxas, Manuel A.   rô'-häs, mä-nwĕl'   ro'-hahs, mah-nwel'
    (Fil. polit.)

Royan (Fr.)   rwä-yäN'   rwah-yahN'

Röykenvik (Nor.)   rûĭ'-kən-vēk   rœi'-kuhn-veek

Röysheim (Nor.)   rûĭs'-hām   rœis'-haym

Rožaj (Yugosl.)   rô'-zhĭ   ro'-zhai

Roze (Yugosl.)   rô'-zĕ   ro'-zeh

Rozendaal (Neth.)   rō'-zən-däl   roh'-zuhn-dahl
    Also spelled *Roosendaal*, q.v.

Rožňava (Cz.)   rôzh'-nyä-vä   rozh'-nyah-vah
    Hungarian *Rozsnyó*, rôzh'-nyô [rozh'-nyo].

Rozsnyó (Cz.)   See *Rožňava*.

Rozwadów (Pol.)   rô-zvä'-dōof   ro-zvah'-duf

rt   ərt'   uhrt'
    In the case of compounds with *rt*, such as *Rt Arca*, look up the other
    part of the name, e.g., *Arca*. *Rt* is Serb-Croat meaning *point*.

Rtanj (Yugosl., mts.)   ər'-tän(y)   uhr'-tahn(y)

Rtkovo (Yugosl.)   ərt'-kô-vô   uhrt'-ko-vo

Rua Sura (Oc., Solomons)   rōō'-ä sōō'-rä   roo'-ah soo'-rah

Rubezhnoye (Rus.)   rōō-bĕzh'-nŏ-yĕ   roo-bezh'-no-yeh

Rublëvka (Rus.)   rōōb-lyôf'-kä   rub-lyof'-kah

Ruddervoorde (Belg.)   rŭd'-ər-vôr'-də   ruhd'-uhr-vohr'-duh

Rudenko, Roman   rōō-dĕn'-kô, rô-män'   roo-dehn'-ko, ro-
    (Rus. general)   mahn'

Rüdersdorf (Ger.)   rü'-dərs-dôrf   rü'-duhrs-dorf

Rüdesheim (Ger.)   rü'-dəs-hīm   rü'-duhs-haim

Rudkoebing *or* Rud-   rōō'-kû-bĭng   roo'-kœ-bing
    köbing (Den.)

Rudnik (Yugosl.)   rōōd'-nĭk   rood'-nik

Rudnitsa (Rus.)   rōōd'-nĭ-tsä   rood'-ni-tsah

Rue (Fr.)   rü'   rü'

Ruedersdorf (Ger.)   rü'-dərs-dôrf   rü'-duhrs-dorf

Ruedesheim (Ger.)   rü'-dəs-hīm   rü'-duhs-haim

Ruegen (Ger., isl.)   rü'-gən   rü'-guhn

Ruegenwalde (Ger. > Pol.)   rü'-gən-väl'-də   rü'-guhn-vahl'-duh
    Polish *Derłów*, q.v.

Rueil (Fr.)	rü-ĕ′(y) *or* -ā′	rü-eh′(y) *or* -ay′
Ruetenbrock (Ger.)	rü′-tən-brôk(h)	rü′-tuhn-brok(h)
Ruethen (Ger.)	rü′-tən	rü′-tuhn
Rügen (Ger., isl.)	rü′-gən	rü′-guhn
Rügenwalde (Ger. >Pol.) See *Ruegenwalde* and *Derłów*.		
Rugles (Fr.)	rü′gl	rü′gl
Rugozero (Rus.)	rōō-gô′-zĕ-rŏ	roo-go′-zeh-ro
Ruhnu (Est., isl.)	rōōk(h)′-nōō	rook(h)′-noo
Russian *Runo*, rōō′-nŏ [roo′-no].		
Ruhr (Ger., riv.)	rōōr′	roor′
Ruhrberg (Ger.)	rōōr′-bĕrk(h)	roor′-behrk(h)
Ruhrort (Ger.)	rōōr′-ôrt	roor′-ort
Ruinen (Neth.)	rûĭ′-nən	rœi′-nuhn
Ruini, Meuccio (It. polit.)	rwē′-nē, mĕ-ōōt′-chô	rwee′-nee, meh-oot′-cho
Ruislip (Eng.)	rīs′-lĭp	rais′-lip
Ruj (Balkan mt.)	rōō′(y) *or* rōō′ĭ	roo′(y) *or* roo′i
Rujen (Balkan, mt.)	rōō′-yĕn	roo′-yen
Rukfen (Neth.)	rûk′-fən	rœk′-fuhn
Rukhlovo (Rus.)	rōōk(h)-lô′-vŏ	ruk(h)-lo′-vo
Rumania	*Eng.* rōō-mān′-yə	roo-mayn′-yuh
The English variant of *Românĭa*, q.v.		
Rumija (Yugosl., mt.)	rōō′-mē-yä	roo′-mee-yah
Rundstedt, Gerd von (Ger. general)	rŏont′-shtĕt, gĕrt fən	runt′-shtet, gehrt fuhn
Ruokojaervi *or* -järvi (Fin., lake)	rōō′-ô′-kô-yăr-vē	ru′-o′-ko-yehr-vee
Rupel (Belg., riv.)	rü′-pəl	rü′-puhl
Ruschuk (Bulg.)	rōōs′-chōōk	rus′-chuk
Officially *Russe*, q.v.		
Russ (Europ. riv.) See *Niemen*.		
Russe *or* Ruse (Bulg.)	rōōs′-sĕ	rus′-seh
Rütenbrock (Ger.)	rü′-tən-brôk(h)	rü′-tuhn-brok(h)
Rutevce (Yugosl.)	rōō′-tĕv-tsĕ	roo′-tev-tseh
Rüthen (Ger.)	rü′-tən	rü′-tuhn
Ruthenia (Rus.)	rōō-thē′-nyə	roo-thee′-nyuh
Ruunitto (Oc., Eniwetok)	rōō′-ōō-nēt′-tô	roo′-oo-neet′-to
Ruurloo (Neth.)	rür′-lō	rür′-loh
Ruweisat (Egypt)	rōō-wā-săt′	roo-way-sat′
Ruysbroek (Belg.)	rûĭs′-brōōk	rœis′-brook
Ruysselede (Belg.)	rûĭs′-ə-lä′-də	rœis′-uh-lay′-duh
Ruza (Rus.)	rōō′-zä	roo′-zah
Ruzaevka (Rus.)	rōō-zä′-yĕf-kä	roo-zah′-yef-kah
Ružomberok (Cz.)	rōō′-zhôm-bĕ-rôk	roo′-zhom-beh-rok

Ruzýně (Cz., Prague airport)	rōō'-zē'-nyě	roo'-zee'-nyeh
Ryall, William Bolitho (Br. author)	rī'-əl, bō-lī'-*thō*	rai'-uhl, boh-lai'-*thoh*
Ryashev (Pol.) See *Rzeszów*.		
Ryazan (Rus.)	ryä-zän'(y)	ryah-zahn'(y)
Ryazhsk (Rus.)	ryäshsk'	ryahshsk'
Rybachi (Rus.)	rĭ-bä'-chĭ	ri-bah'-chi
Rybinsk (Rus.)	rwē'-bĭnsk	rwee'-binsk
Rybnik (Pol.)	rĭb'-nĭk	rib'-nik
Rybnitsa (Rus.)	rĭb'-nĭ-tsä	rib'-ni-tsah
Rychbach (Ger. >? Pol.) German *Reichenbach*, q.v.	rĭk(h)'-bäk(h)	rik(h)'-bahk(h)
Ryes (Fr.)	rē'	ree'
Ryezhitsa (Latvia) Latvian *Rēzekne*, q.v. German *Rositten*, q.v.	*Rus.* rě'-zhĭ-tsä	reh'-zhi-tsah
Ryfylke (Nor.)	rü'-fül-kə	rü'-fül-kuh
Rylsk (Rus.)	rĭl(y)sk'	ril(y)sk'
Rynda (Rus.)	rĭn'-dä	rin'-dah
Ryojun-kō (Manchu.) See *Port Arthur*.		
Rypin (Pol.)	rĭ'-pĭn	rih'-pin
Ryswick (Neth.) See *Rijswijk*.		
Ryti, Risto (Fin. polit.)	rü'-tē, rĭs'-tô *or Eng.* rĭt'-ĭ	rü'-tee, rĭs'-to rit'-i
Ryūkyū (Jap.) Chinese *Liu-Ch'iu*, lyōō-chyōō [lyoo-chyoo].	ryōō-kyōō	ryoo-kyoo
Rzeszów (Pol.) Russian *Ryashev*, ryä'-shěf [ryah'-shef].	zhě'-shōōf	zheh'-shuf
Rzhava (Rus.)	rzhä'-vä	rzhah'-vah
Rzhev (Rus.)	rzhěf'	rzhef'
Rzymowski, Wincenty (Pol. polit.)	zhĭ-môf'-skĭ, vĭn-tsěn'-tĭ	zhi-mof'-ski, vin-tsen'-ti

S—For Chinese names beginning in *S*- see also names in *Hs*-.

saadist	săd'-ĭst *or* sä'-dĭst	sad'-ist *or* sah'-dist

A member of the Egyptian political party founded by *Sa'ad Zaghloul Pasha*, säd' zäg-lōōl' [sahd' zahg-lool'].

Saale (Ger., riv.)	zä'-lə	zah'-luh
Saales (Fr., pass)	sä-äl'	sah-ahl'
Saalfeld (Ger.)	zäl'-fělt	zahl'-felt
Saanich (Can.)	să'-nĭch	sa'-nich
Saar (Ger., Fr., riv.)	zär'	zahr'

French *Sarre*, sär' [sahr'].

Saarbruecken *or* Saar-	*Eng.* zär-brŏŏk′-ən	zahr-bruk′-uhn
brücken (Ger.)	*Ger.* zär-brük′-ən	zahr-brük′-uhn
Saarburg (Ger.)	zär′-bŏŏrk(h)	zahr′-burk(h)
Saare(maa) (Est., isl.)	sä′-rĕ(-mä)	sah′-reh(-mah)

Russian *Ostrov Sarema*, q.v., or *Esel*, q.v. German *Oesel*, q.v.

| saari | sä′-rē | sah′-ree |

An element, meaning *island*, in Finnish place names.

Saari Selkä (Fin., mts.)	sä′-rē sĕl′-kă	sah′-ree sel′-ka
Saarlautern (Ger.)	zär′-lou′-tərn	zahr′-lau′-tuhrn
Šabac (Yugosl.)	shä′-bäts	shah′-bahts
Sabang (NEI, New	sä′-bäng	sah′-bahng
Guinea)		
Sabath, A. J.	săb′-əth	sab′-uhth
(U.S. representative)		
Sabaudia (It.)	sä-bou′-dyä	sah-bau′-dyah

A Pontine town and the old form of *Savoy*.

Sabbia (Dodec., Rh., point) See *Cum Burnu*.

| Sabbia (It.) | säb′-byä | sahb′-byah |
| Sabbioncello (Yugosl.) | *It.* säb-byôn-chĕl′-lô | sahb-byon-chel′-lo |

The Italian name of a Yugoslav town, *Orebić*, q.v., and the peninsula
Pelješac, q.v.

Sabine (La., Tex.)	sə-bēn′	suh-ben′
Sabine Hills (It.)	*Eng.* sā′-bīn	say′-bain
	or săb′-īn	sab′-ain

Italian *Monti Sabini*, môn′-tē sä-bē′-nē [mon′-tee sah-bee′-nee].

Sablán (P.I.)	sä-blän′	sah-blahn′
Also spelled *Zablán*.		
Sablayán (P.I.)	sä-blä-yän′	sah-blah-yahn′
Sables d'Olonne, les (Fr.)	sä′bl dô-lôn′, lĕ	sah′bl do-lon′, leh
Sablé sur Sarthe (Fr.)	sä-blĕ sür särt′	sah-bleh sür sahrt′
Sablon (Fr.)	sä-blôN′	sah-bloN′
saboteur	săb-ə-tûr′	sab-uh-tœr′

This word keeps usually its French final syllable; the pronunciation
săb-ə-tyŏŏr′ [sab-uh-tyoor′] is not recommended. In contrast *amateur*
has been completely Englished, and Webster's (q.v.) allows -tûr or
-tyŏŏr with accent on the final or on the first syllable.

Sabria (Tun.)	sä′-brĭ-ä	sah′-bri-ah
Sabsko (Rus.)	säp′-skŏ	sahp′-sko
Sabzawar (Iran)	săb-zə-vär′	sab-zuh-vahr′
Sacco (It., riv.)	säk′-kô	sahk′-ko
Sachsen (Ger.)	zäk′-sən	zahk′-suhn
English *Saxony*, q.v.		
Sachsendorf (Ger.)	zäk′-sən-dôrf	zahk′-suhn-dorf

Sachsenhausen (Ger.)	zäk(h)'-sən-hou'-zən	zahk(h)'-suhn-hau'-zuhn
Saco (Me.)	sô'-kō	saw'-koh
Sadaguia (Tun.)	să-dă-gē'-yä	sa-da-gee'-yah
Sadchikov, Ivan W. (Rus. polit.)	sät'-chǐ-kǒf	saht'-chi-kof
Sadiya (India)	sə-dē'-yä'	suh-dee'-yah'
Sadlak, Antoni N. (U.S. representative)	săd'-lăk, ăn'-tə-nǐ	sad'-lak, an'-tuh-ni
Sado (Jap.)	sä'-dô	sah'-do
Sadowski, George G. (U.S. representative)	să-dŭs'-kǐ	sa-duhs'-ki
Sae (Oc., Admiralties)	sä'-ĕ	sah'-eh
Sæby (Den.)	sĕ'-bü	seh'-bü
Safad (Pal.)	sä'-fəd	sah'-fuhd

Also called *Safed*. Hebrew *Zefat* or *Tsefat*, tsə-fät' [tsuh-faht'].

Saffré Joué (Fr.)	sä-frĕ zhwĕ'	sah-freh zhweh'
Safi *or* Saffi (Mor.)	sä'-fē	sah'-fee
Safid Rud (Iran, riv.)	să-fēd' rōōd'	seh-feed' rood'
Safrana (Dodec.) See *Zafrana*.		
Saga (Jap.)	sä'-gä	sah'-gah
Sagaing (Burma)	sə-gīng'	suh-gaing'
Sagami (Jap.)	sä'-gä-mē	sah'-gah-mee
Sagan (Ger. >? Pol.)	zä'-gän	zah'-gahn
Polish *Żegań*, q.v.		
Sagiada (Gr.)	sǐ-yä'-dä	sai-yah'-dah
Sagittario (It., riv.)	sä-jēt-tä'-ryô	sah-jeet-tah'-ryo
Sagone (Corsica, gulf)	sä-gô'-nĕ	sah-go'-neh
Saguenay (Can., riv.)	săg'-ə-nā	sag'-uh-nay
Saharanpur (India)	sə-hä'-rən-pōōr'	suh-hah'-ruhn-pur'
sahib	sä'-ĭb	sah'-ib

Also *saheb*, sä'-ĕb [sah'-eb]. A title or honorific in India, usually following the name. It is disregarded in alphabetical listing.

Šahovići (Yugosl.)	shä'-hô-vǐ-chǐ	shah'-ho-vi-chi
sai	sä-ē	sah-ee

An element, meaning *west*, in Japanese place names. See also *sei*.

Saida (Lebanon)	sä'-ē-dä	sah'-ee-dah
Also called *Sidon*, q.v.		
Saidor (N.E. New Guinea)	sä-ē-dôr'	sah-ee-dor'
Said Tadjeddin (Afghan diplomat)	sä-ēd' tä'-jĕd-dēn	sah-eed' tah'-jed-deen

Said Zia ed Din Tabatabai (Iran. polit.) See *Zia ed Din Tabatabai*.
Saif el Islam (Yemen leader) See *Seif el Islam*.

Saïgon (Indo-Ch.)	*Eng.* sī-gŏn'	sai-gon'
	Fr. sä-ē-gôN'	sah-ee-goN'
Sailly Saillisel (Fr.)	sä-yē sä-yē-sĕl'	sah-yee sah-yee-sel'
Saimaa (Fin., lake)	sī'-mä	sai'-mah
Saincaize Meauce (Fr.)	săN-kĕz môs'	saN-kez mos'
Saint Aignan (Fr.)	săN tĕ-nyäN'	saN teh-nyahN'
Saint Amand (Fr.)	săN tä-mäN'	saN tah-mahN'
Saint André (Fr.)	săN täN-drĕ'	saN tahN-dreh'
Saint André de l'Eure (Fr.)	săN täN-drĕ də lûr'	saN tahN-dreh duh loer'
Saint Aubin d'Aubigné (Fr.)	săN tō-băN dō-bē-nyĕ'	saN toh-baN doh-bee-nyeh'
Saint Aubin sur Mer (Fr.)	săN tō-băN sür mĕr'	saN toh-baN sür mehr'
Saint Avold (Fr.)	săN tä-vôl'	saN tah-vol'
Saint Benoît (Fr.)	săn bə-nwä'	saN buh-nwah'
Saint Berthevin (Fr.)	săN bĕr-tə-văN'	saN behr-tuh-vaN'
Saint Brice en Coglès (Fr.)	săN brēs äN kô-glĕs'	saN brees ahN ko-gles'
Saint Brieuc (Fr.)	săN brē-û'	saN bree-œ'
Saint Cannat (Fr.)	săN kä-nä'	saN kah-nah'
Saint Clair (Eng. name)	sănt klĕr' *or* sin'-klĕr *or* sĭng'-klər	saynt klehr' *or* sin'-klehr *or* sing'-kluhr
Also spelled *Sinclair.*		
Saint Clair sur l'Elle (Fr.)	săN klĕr sür lĕl'	saN klehr sür lel'
Saint Cosme de Vair (Fr.)	săN kōm də vĕr'	saN kohm duh vehr'
Saint Croix Hague (Fr.)	săNt krwä äg'	saNt krwah ahg'
Saint Cyprien (Tun.)	*Eng.* sänt sĭp'-rĭ-ən	saynt sip'-ri-uhn
	Fr. săN sē-prē-ăN'	saN see-pree-aN'
Saint Cyr (Fr.)	săN sēr'	saN seer'
Saint Denis (Fr.)	săN də-nē'	saN duh-nee'
Saint Didier (Fr.)	săN dē-dyĕ'	saN dee-dyeh'
Saint Dié (Fr.)	săN dyĕ'	saN dyeh'
Saint Dizier (Fr.)	săN dē-zyĕ'	saN dee-zyeh'
Saint Donat (Fr.)	săN dô-nä'	saN do-nah'
Sainte Baume (Fr.)	săNt bōm'	saNt bohm'
Sainte Hermine (Fr.)	săNt ĕr-mēn'	saNt ehr-meen'
Sainte Menehould (Fr.)	săNt mĕ-nōō'	saNt meh-noo'
Sainte Mère Église (Fr.)	săNt mĕr ĕ-glēz'	saNt mehr eh-gleez'
Sainteny (Fr.)	săNt-nē'	saNt-nee'
Saintes (Fr.)	săNt'	saNt'
Saint Florent (Corsica)	săN flô-räN'	saN flo-rahN'

Saint Gallen (Switz.)   sānt gäl′-ən   saynt gahl′-uhn
French *Saint Gall,* săN gäl′ [saN gahl′]. German *Sankt Gallen,* zänkt
gäl′-ən [zahnkt gahl′-uhn].

Saint Gatien (Fr.)	săN gä-syăN′	saN gah-syaN′
Saint Gelais (Fr.)	săN zhə-lĕ′	saN zhuh-leh′
Saint Germain de Près (Fr., Paris)	săN zhĕr-măN də prĕ′	saN zhehr-maN duh preh′
Saint Germain en Laye (Fr.)	săN zhĕr-măN äN lĕ′	saN zhehr-maN ahN leh′
Saint Gervais (Fr.)	săN zhĕr-vĕ′	saN zhehr-veh′
Saint Gildas (Fr.)	săN zhēl-däs′	saN zheel-dahs′
Saint Gilles (Belg.)	săN zhēl′	saN zheel′
Saint Gilles (Fr.)	săN zhēl′	saN zheel′
Saint Gingolph (Fr.)	săN zhăN-gôlf′	saN zhaN-golf′
Saint Goar (Ger.)	*Eng.* sānt gōr′	saynt gohr′

German *Sankt Goar,* zängkt gō-är′ [zahngkt goh-ahr′].

Saint Gotthard (Switz.)	*Eng.* sānt gŏt′-ərd	saynt got′-uhrd
	Fr. săN gô-tär′	saN go-tahr′
Saint Hardouin, Jacques Tarbe de (Fr. diplomat)	săN tär-dwăN′, zhäk′ tärb′ də	saN tahr-dwaN′, zhahk′ tahrb′ duh
Saint Helena (S. Atlantic)	sānt hĕ-lē′-nə	saynt heh-lee′-nuh
Saint Hélier (Eng., Jersey)	sānt hĕl′-yər *Fr.* săN-tĕ-lyĕ′	saynt hel′-yuhr saN-teh-lyeh′
Saint Hubert (Belg.)	săN tü-bĕr′	saN tü-behr′
Saint Ingbert (Ger.)	*Eng.* sānt ĭng′-bərt	saynt ing′-buhrt

German *Sankt Ingbert,* zängkt ĭng′-bərt [zahngkt ing′-buhrt].

Saint Jacques de Néhou (Fr.)	săN zhäk də nĕ-ōō′	saN zhahk duh neh- oo′
Saint James (Fr.)	*Eng.* sānt jāmz′ *Fr.* săN zhäm′	saynt jaymz′ saN zhahm′
Saint Jean de Daye (Fr.)	săN zhäN də dī′	saN zhahN duh dai′
Saint Jean de Luz (Fr.)	săN zhäN də lüz′	saN zhahN duh lüz′
Saint John (Eng. name)	sānt jŏn′ *or* sĭn′-jən	saynt jon′ sin′-juhn
Saint Jorès (Fr.)	săN zhô-rĕ′	saN zho-reh′
Saint Julien le Faucon (Fr.)	săN zhü-lyăN lə fō-kôN′	saN zhü-lyaN luh foh-koN′
Saint Just (Fr.)	săN zhüst′	saN zhüst′
Saint Laurent de la Salanque (Fr.)	săN lô-räN də lä sä-läNk′	saN lo-rahN duh lah sah-lahNk′
Saint Leger (Eng. name, race)	sānt lĕj′-ər *or* sĕl′-ĭn-jər	saynt lej′-uhr sel′-in-juhr
Saint Léger sous Beuvray (Fr.)	săN lĕ-zhĕ sōō bû-vrĕ′	saN leh-zheh soo bœ-vreh′

Saint Lô (Fr.)	săN lō′	saN loh′
Saint Lô d'Ourville (Fr.)	săN lō dōōr-vēl′	saN loh door-veel′
Saint Louis (Mo.)	sānt lōō′-ĭs	saynt lu′-is

The pronunciation sĭnt lōō′-ĭ [sint lu′-i] is seldom heard locally.

Saint Loup (Fr.)	săN lōō′	saN loo′
Saint Lucia (W. Indies)	sānt lyōō′-shĭ-ə	saynt lyoo′-shi-uh
	or lōō-sē′-ə	or loo-see′-uh

As a British colony the name has been Anglicized.

Saint Maclou (Fr.)	săN mä-klōō′	saN mah-kloo′
Saint Maixent (Fr.)	săN mĕk-säN′	saN mek-sahN′
Saint Malo (Fr.)	săN mä-lō′	saN mah-loh′
Saint Mars la Jaille (Fr.)	săN mär lä zhī′	saN mahr lah zhai′
Saint Martin de Varreville (Fr.)	săN mär-tăN də vär-vēl′	saN mahr-taN duh vahr-veel′
Saint Matthias (Oc., Bismarck arch.)	sānt′ mə-thī′-əs	saynt′ muh-thai′-uhs
Saint Maur (Eng. name)	sānt môr′ or sē′-môr	saynt mor′ or see′-mor

Also spelled Seymour.

Saint Maur des Fossés (Fr.)	săN môr dĕ fô-sĕ′	saN mor deh fo-seh′
Saint Maxime (Fr.)	săN mäk-sēm′	saN mahk-seem′
Saint Maximin (Fr.)	săN mäk-sē-măN′	saN mahk-see-maN′
Saint Méin (Fr.)	săN mĕ-ăN′	saN meh-aN′
Saint Mesmin (Fr.)	săN mĕs-măN′	saN mes-maN′
Saint Michel (Fr.)	săN mē-shĕl′	saN mee-shel′
Saint Mihiel (Fr.)	săN mē-yĕl′	saN mee-yel′
Saint Nazaire (Fr.)	săN nä-zĕr′	saN nah-zehr′
Saint Omer (Fr.)	săN-tô-mĕr′	saN-to-mehr′
Saintonge (Fr.)	săN-tôNzh′	saN-toNzh′
Saint Osyth (Essex, Eng.)	tōō′-zĭ	too′-zi
Saint Ouen (Fr.)	săN twäN′	saN twahN′
Saint Oumont (Belg.)	săN tōō-môN′	saN too-moN′
Saint Pierre Église (Fr.)	săN pyĕr ĕ-glēz′	saN pyehr eh-gleez′
Saint Pierre et Miquelon (Fr. isls.)	săN pyĕr ĕ mē-klôN′	saN pyehr eh mee-kloN′

English Saint Pierre and Miquelon, sānt pĭ-ĕr′ . . . . mĭk′-ə-lŏn [saynt pi-ehr′ . . . . mik′-uh-lon].

Saint Poelten (Austria)	Eng. sānt pûl′-tən	saynt puhl′-tuhn

German Sankt Poelten or Pölten, zängkt pûl′-tən [zahngkt pœl′-tuhn].

Saint Pois (Fr.)	săN pwä′	saN pwah′
Saint Poix (Fr.)	săN pwä′	saN pwah′
Saint Pol (Fr.)	săN pôl′	saN pol′

Saint Pol de Léon (Fr.)	săN pôl də lĕ-ôN′	saN pol duh leh-oN′
Saint Quai (Fr.)	săN kĕ′	saN keh′
Saint Quentin (Fr.)	*Eng.* sănt kwĕnt′n	saynt kwent′n
	Fr. săN käN-tăN′	saN kahN-taN′
Saint Raphael (Fr.)	săN rä-fä-ĕl′	saN rah-fah-el′
Saint Rémy (Fr.)	săN rĕ-mē′	saN reh-mee′
Saint Renan (Fr.)	săN rə-näN′	saN ruh-nahN′
Saint Saëns (Fr.)	săN säNs′	saN sahNs′
Saint Saëns, Camille	săN säNs′, kä-mē′(y)	saN sahNs′, kah-
(Fr. musician)		mee′(y)
Saint Sauveur (Fr.)	săN sō-vûr′	saN soh-vœr′
Saint Servan (Fr.)	săN sĕr-väN′	saN sehr-vahN′
Saint Sever (Fr.)	săN sə-vĕr′	saN suh-vehr′
Saint Séverin (Fr., Paris)	săN sĕ-vrăN′	saN seh-vraN′
Saint Tropez (Fr.)	săN trô-pĕ′	saN tro-peh′
Saint Vaast la Hougue	săN väst lä ōōg′	saN vahst lah oog′
(Fr.)		
Saint Valéry (Fr.)	săN vä-lĕ-rē′	saN vah-leh-ree′
Saint Vallier (Fr.)	săN vä-lyĕ′	saN vah-lyeh′
Saint Veit (Austria)	*Eng.* sănt vīt′	saynt vait′
German *Sankt Veit*, zängkt fīt′ [zahngkt fait′].		
Saint Vith (Belg.)	săN vēt′	saN veet′
Saint Vivien (Fr.)	săN vē-vyăN′	saN vee-vyaN′
Saipan (Oc.)	*Eng.* sĭ′-păn′	sai′-pan′
	native sĭ-pän′	sai-pahn′
Saire (Fr., riv.)	sĕr′	sehr′
Saitama (Jap.)	sä-ē′-tä′-mä′	sah-ee′-tah′-mah′
Saitō, Takao (Jap.	sä-ē′-tô′, tä-kä′-ô	sah-ee′-to′, tah-
polit.)		kah′-o
Sajo (Cz., riv.) See *Sland.*		
Sajólád (Hung.)	shŏ′-yô-läd	sho′-yo-lahd
Sakai (Jap.)	sä′-kä-ē	sah′-kah-ee
Sakalava (Madag.)	sä′-kə-lä′-və	sah′-kuh-lah′-vuh
Sakales, Georgios	sä-kä-lēs′, yôr′-yôs	sah-kah-lees′, yor′-
(Gr. polit.)		yos
Sakar (Oc., Bismarck	sä′-kär	sah′-kuhr
arch.)		
Sakəri (Jap.)	sä-kä′-rē	sah-kah′-ree
Sakellariou, A. (Gr. polit.)	sä-kĕ-lä′-rē-ōō	sah-keh-lah′-ree-oo
Sakhalin (Rus.)	sä-hä-lēn′	sah-hah-leen′
Saki (Rus.)	sä′-kĭ	sah′-ki
Saksin, Georgi F.	säk′-sĭn, gĕ-ôr′-gĭ	sahk′-sin, geh-or′-gi
(Rus. diplomat)		
Sala (P.I., point)	sä′-lä	sah′-lah

Salaj, Juro (Yugosl. polit.)   sä'-lī, yōō'-rŏ   sah'-lai, yoo'-ro

Salajar (NEI)   sä-lä'-yər   sah-lah'-yuhr
    Also Dutch *Saleier*, sä-lī'-ər [sah-lai'-uhr].

Salakhora (Gr.)   sä-lä-hô'-rä   sah-lah-ho'-rah

Salamanca (Sp., N.Y.)   *Eng.* săl'-ə-măng'-kə   sal'-uh-mang'-kuh
                       Sp. sä-lä-mäng'-kä   sah-lah-mahng'-kah

Salamaua (N. E. New   sä-lä-mou'-ä   sah-lah-mau'-ah
  Guinea)

Salambrias (Gr., riv.)   See *Peneios.*

Salamis (Gr., isl.)   *Eng.* săl'-ə-mĭs   sal'-uh-mis
                       Gr. sä-lä-mēs'   sah-lah-mees'
    Also called *Kouloure*, kōō'-lōō-rē [koo'-loo-ree].

Salangen (Nor.)   sä'-läng-ən   sah'-lahng-uhn

Salaroe *or* Selaru   sě-lä'-rōō   seh-lah'-roo
  (NEI, Tanimbar)

Salaš (Yugosl.)   sä'-läsh   sah'-lahsh

Salasa (P.I.)   sä-lä'-sä   sah-lah'-sah

Salayer (NEI) See *Salajar.*

Salazar, Antonio de   sə-lə-zär', än-tô'-nyŏŏ suh-luh-zahr', ahn-
  Oliveira (Port. dictator) dĭ ô-lĭ-vä'-rə   to'-nyu di o-li-vay'-
                                           ruh

Salbris (Fr.)   säl-brē'   sahl-bree'

Salcedo (P.I.)   säl-sě'-dô   sahl-seh'-do

Salcha (Alaska)   sôl'-chə   sol'-chuh

Sale (Austral.)   säl'   sayl'

Sale (Burma)   sə-lä'   suh-lay'

Saleh (Per. name)   sä'-lě   sah'-leh

Saleier (NEI) See *Salajar.*

Salernes (Fr.)   sä-lěrn'   sah-lehrn'

Salerno (It.)   sä-lěr'-nð   sah-lehr'-no

Sales, Apolônio (Braz.   sä'-lĭs, ä-pô-lô'-nyŏŏ sah'-lis, ah-po-lo'-nyu
  polit.)

Salgado Filho, Joaquim   səl-gä'-dŏŏ fē'-lyŏŏ, suhl-gah'-du fee'-lyu,
  Pedro (Braz. polit.)   zhwə-kēN' pě'-drŏŏ zhwuh-keeN peh'-
                                          dru

Salgótarján (Hung.)   shŏl'-gô-tŏr-yän   shol'-go-tor-yahn

Salida (Col.)   sə-lī'-də   suh-lai'-duh

salient   sā'-lĭ-ənt   say'-li-uhnt
    The mispronunciation săl'-ɪ-ənt [sal'-i-uhnt] is sometimes carried
  over from childhood when the spelling of such words is more familiar
  than the sound.

Salikana (Oc., Solomons) sä-lē-kä'-nä   sah-lee-kah'-nah

Salina (It., isl.)   sä-lē'-nä   sah-lee'-nah

Salina (Kan.)   sə-lī'-nə   suh-lai'-nuh

Salinas (Calif.)	sə-lē′-nəs	suh-lee′-nuhs
Salinas (Ecuador)	sä-lē′-näs	sah-lee′-nahs
Salinas (P.I.) See *Rosario*.		
Salins les Bains (Fr.)	sä-lăN lĕ băN′	sah-laN leh baN′
Salisbury (Eng., Am. name)	sôlz′-bĕr-ĭ *or* -bə-rĭ *or* -brĭ	solz′-behr-i *or* -buh-ri *or* -bri
Salla (Rus.)	säl′-lä	sahl′-lah
Sallaumines (Fr.)	sä-lō-mēn′	sah-loh-meen′
Salm (Belg., riv.)	sälm′	sahlm′
salmi	säl′-mē	sahl′-mee

An element, meaning *inlet* or *sound*, in Finnish place names.

Salome	*Eng.* sə-lō′-mĭ	suh-loh′-mi
	Fr. sä-lô-mĕ′	sah-lo-meh′
	Ger. zä′-lō-mĕ	zah′-loh-meh

There is no reason for avoiding the English pronunciation, although the foreign pronunciations are appropriate in foreign contexts.

Salomon (Crete, point)	sä-lô-môn′	sah-lo-mon′
Salon (Fr.)	sä-lôN′	sah-loN′
Salona (Gr.) See *Amphissa*.		
Salonica (Gr.) See *Saloniki*.		
Saloniki (Gr.)	sä-lô-nē′-kē	sah-lo-nee′-kee

The common abbreviation of *Thessalonike*, q.v. English *Salonica*, commonly pronounced sä-lŏn′-ĭ-kə [sah-lon′-i-kuh], although dictionaries authorize only sä-lô-nē′-kä [sah-lo-nee′-kah].

Salonta (Rum.)	sä-lôn′-tä	sah-lon′-tah

Also called Ṣalonta, shä-lôn′-tä [shah-lon′-tah]. Hungarian *Nagyszalonta*, nŏt′(y)-sŏ′-lôn-tä [not′(y)-so′-lon-tah].

Salpaus Selkä (Fin., mts.)	säl′-pous sĕl′-kă	sahl′-paus sel′-ka
Salsette (India, isl.)	säl′-sĕt′	sal′-set′
Salsk (Rus.)	säl(y)sk′	sahl(y)sk′
Salso (Sicily)	säl′-sô	sahl′-so
saltaneh (a title or honorific in the Middle East). See *sultaneh*.		
Saltdal (Nor.)	sält′-däl	sahlt′-dahl
Saltillo (Mex.)	säl-tē′-yô	sahl-tee′-yo

Border English sô-tē′-yə [saw-tee′-yuh].

Sal(l)um *or* Sol(l)um (Egypt)	säl-lōōm′	sahl-loom′
Salvador, El (C.A.)	säl-vä-dôr′, ĕl	sahl-vah-dor′, el
Salvemini, Gaetano (It. author)	säl-vĕ′-mē-nē, gä-ĕ-tä′-nô	sahl-veh′-mee-nee, gah-eh-tah′-no
Salween (Burma, Ch., riv.)	säl′-wēn′	sal′-ween′
Salza (Ger., riv.)	zäl′-tsä	zahl′-tsah
Salzach (Austria, riv.)	zäl′-tsäk(h)	zahl′-tsahk(h)
Salzburg (Austria)	*Eng.* sôlz′-bûrg	solz′-buhrg
	Ger. zälts′-bŏŏrk(h)	zahlts′-burk(h)

Salzkammergut (Austria)	zälts'-käm'-ər-gōōt'	zahlts'-kahm'-uhr-goot'
Šamac, Bosanski (Yugosl.)	shä'-mäts, bô'-sän-skĭ	shah'-mahts, bo'-sahn-ski
Sámal (P.I.)	sä'-mäl	sah'-mahl
Samaná (Dom. Rep.)	sä-mä-nä'	sah-mah-nah'
Samanjac (Yugosl., mts.)	sä'-mä-nyäts	sah'-mah-nyahts
Sámar (P.I.)	sä'-mär	sah'-mahr
Samara (Rus., riv.)	sä-mä'-rã	sah-mah'-rah
Samarai (New Guinea, Papua)	sä-mä-rī'	sah-mah-rai'
Samarang (NEI) See *Semarang*.		
Samaria (Pal.)	sə-mär'-ĭ-ə	suh-mehr'-i-uh
Samarinda (Borneo)	sä-mä-rĭn'-dä	sah-mah-rin'-dah
Samaritis, Myron (Gr. polit.)	sä-mä-rē'-tēs, mē'-rôn	sah-mah-ree'-tees, mee'-ron
Samarkand (Rus.)	*Eng.* săm'-ər-kănd' *Rus.* sä'-mär-känt'	sam'-uhr-kand' sah'-mahr-kahnt'
Sambeek (Neth.)	säm'-bāk	sahm'-bayk
Sambodja (Borneo)	säm-bô'-jä	sahm-bo'-jah
Sambor (Pol. > Rus.)	säm'-bôr	sahm'-bor
Ukrainian *Sambir*, säm'-bĭr [sahm'-bihr].		
Sambre (Fr., Belg., riv.)	säN'br	sahN'br
Sambucheto (It.)	säm-bōō-kĕ'-tô	sahm-boo-keh'-to
Sambuci (It.)	säm-bōō'-chē	sahm-boo'-chee
Samikon (Gr.)	sä-mē-kô(n)'	sah-mee-ko(n)'
Samland (Ger., pen.)	zäm'-länt	zahm'-lahnt
Samnan (Iran)	sĕm-nän'	sem-nahn'
Samoa (Oc.)	*Eng.* sä-mō'-ə *native* sä'-mô'-ä	sah-moh'-uh sah'-mo'-ah
Samobor (Yugosl.)	sä'-mô-bôr	sah'-mo-bor
Samoggia (It.)	sä-môd'-jä	sah-mod'-jah
Samokov (Bulg.)	sä'-mŏ-kŏf	sah'-mo-kof
Samonion (Crete, point)	sä-mô'-nē(-ôn)	sah-mo'-nee(-on)
Samos (Gr., isl.)	*Eng.* sā'-mŏs *Gr.* sä'-mô(s)	say'-mos sah'-mo(s)
Samothrace (Gr., isl.)	*Eng.* săm'-ō-thrās'	sam'-oh-thrays'
Greek *Samothrake*, sä-mô-thrä'-kē [sah-mo-thrah'-kee].		
Sampáloc (P.I.)	säm-pä'-lôk	sahm-pah'-lok
Sampang (NEI, Madoera)	säm'-päng	sahm'-pahng
Samsoe *or* Samsö (Den., isl.)	säms'-û	sahms'-œ

| Samsun (Turk.) | säm'-sōon' | sahm'-sun' |
| san | sän | sahn |

An element, meaning *mountain*, in Japanese place names. See *zan*.

San (Pol., riv.)	sän'	sahn'
San'a *or* Sanaa (Yemen)	sä-nä'	sah-nah'
San Agustín (P.I.)	sän ä-gōōs-tēn'	sahn ah-goos-teen'

English *Saint Augustin*.

Sanananda (New Guinea,	sä-nä-nän'-dä	sah-nah-nahn'-dah
Papua)		
Sanandaj (Iran)	sĕ-nən-däj'	seh-nuhn-dahj'

Also called *Sehneh*, q.v.

San Biagio (It.)	sän byä'-jô	sahn byah'-jo
San Carlos (P.I.)	sän kär'-lôs	sahn kahr'-los
Sancerre (Fr.)	säN-sĕr'	sahN-sehr'
Sánchez (Sp. name)	*Eng.* sän'-chĭz	san'-chiz
	Am. Sp. sän'-chĕs	sahn'-ches
	Sp. sän'-chĕth	sahn'-cheth
San Cipriano (It.)	sän chĕ-prē-ä'-nô	sahn chee-pree-ah'-no
San Clemente (P.I.)	sän klĕ-mĕn'-tĕ	sahn kleh-men'-teh
Sancoins (Fr.)	säN-kwăN'	sahN-kwaN'
San Cosimo (It.)	sän kô'-sē-mô	sahn ko'-see-mo
San Cristóbal (Oc. and	*Eng.* sän krĭs-tō'-bəl	san kris-toh'-buhl
elsewhere)	*Sp.* sän krēs-tô'-bäl	sahn krees-to'-bahl
sand	sän'	sahn'

Norwegian meaning *sand* (often the delta sand at a river mouth); an element in place names.

Sand (Nor.)	sän'	sahn'
Sandakan (Brit. Borneo)	săn-dä'-kən	san-dah'-kuhn
San Damyano (It.)	sän dä-myä'-nô	sahn dah-myah'-no
Sandane (Nor.)	sän'-ä-nə	sahn'-ah-nuh
Sandefjord (Nor.)	sän'-ə-fyōr	sahn'-uh-fyohr
Sandhaug (Nor.)	sän'-hou	sahn'-hau
Sandia (N. Mex., mts.)	*Eng.* săn-dē'-ə	san-dee'-uh
	Sp. sän-dē'-ä	sahn-dee'-ah
San Diego (Calif., Cuba)	*Eng.* săn dĭ-ā'-gō	san di-ay'-goh
	Sp. sän dyĕ'-gô	sahn dyeh'-go
Sandıklı (Turk.)	sän'-dĭk-lĭ	sahn'-dik-li
Sandjak (Yugosl.)	sän'-jäk	sahn'-jahk
Sandnes (Nor.)	sän'-nĕs	sahn'-nes
Sandnessjoeen *or*	sän'-nĕs-shû'-ən	sahn'-nes-shœ'-uhn
Sandnessjöen (Nor.)		
Sandomierz (Pol.)	sän-dô'-myĕzh	sahn-do'-myezh

Russian *Sandomir*, sän-dŏ-mēr' [sahn-do-meer'].

Sandos, Georgios (Gr. polit.) See *Siandos, Georgios*.

Sandoway (Burma)	săn'-dō-wā'	san'-doh-way'

Burman *Thandwe*, thən-dwĕ' [thuhn-dweh'].

Sandstroem, Emil (Sw. diplomat)	sän'-strûm, ā'-mĭl	sahn'-strœm, ay'-mil
Sandvika (Nor.)	sän'-vē-kä	sahn'-vee-kah
Sandys, Duncan (Br. polit.)	săndz'	sandz'
San Fabián (P.I.)	*Eng.* săn fā'-bĭ-ən	san fay'-bih-uhn
	Sp. sän fä-byän'	sahn fah-byahn'
San Felipe Nery (P.I.)	sän fĕ-lē'-pĕ nĕ'-rē	sahn feh-lee'-peh neh'-ree

Also called *Mandalóyong*, män-dä-lô'-yông [mahn-dah-lo'-yong], and *Mandaluyon*, män-dä-lōō'-yôn [mahn-dah-loo'-yon].

San Feliú de Guixols (Sp.)	sän fĕ-lyōō' dĕ gē'-shôls *or* -hôls	sahn feh-lyoo' deh gee'-shols *or* -hols
San Fernando (Calif.)	săn' fər-năn'-dō	san' fuhr-nan'-doh
San Fernando de Dilao (P.I.) See *Paco*.		
San Francisco (Calif.)	săn frən-sĭs'-kō	san fruhn-sis'-koh
San Francisco del Monte (P.I.)	sän frän-sēs'-kô dĕl môn'-tĕ	sahn frahn-sees'-ko del mon'-teh
San Fratello (Sicily)	sän frä-tĕl'-lô	sahn frah-tel'-lo
San Gaetano (It.)	sän gä-ĕ-tä'-nô	sahn gah-eh-tah'-no
Sangamon (Ill., county)	săng'-gə-mən	sang'-guh-muhn
Sangá Sangá (P.I.)	säng-ä' säng-ä'	sahng-ah' sahng-ah'
Sangatte (Fr.)	säN-gät'	sahN-gaht'
Sangi (NEI)	säng'-ē	sahng'-ee

Dutch *Sangihe*, säng-gē'-ĕ [sahng-gee'-eh].

San Giorgio (It.)	sän jôr'-jô	sahn jor'-jo
San Giovanni di Medua (Alb.)	*It.* sän jô-vän'-nē dē mĕ'-dōō-ä	sahn jo-vahn'-nee dee meh'-doo-ah

Albanian *Shëngjin*, q.v.

San Giuliano (It.)	sän jōō-lyä'-nô	sahn joo-lyah'-no
Sangro (It., riv.)	säng'-grô	sahng'-gro
Sangroniz, José de (Sp. polit.)	sän-grô-nēth', hô-sĕ' dĕ	sahn-gro-neeth', ho-seh' deh
Sanguigna (It., riv.)	säng-gwē'-nyä	sahng-gwee'-nyah
San Ildefonso (P.I.)	sän ēl-dĕ-fôn'-sô	sahn eel-deh-fon'-so
San Isidro (P.I.)	sän ē-sē'-drô	sahn ee-see'-dro
San Jacinto (Calif., Tex.)	săn' jə-sĭn'-tə	san' juh-sin'-tuh

Spanish sän hä-sēn'-tô [sahn hah-seen'-to].

San Joaquin (Calif.)	săn wä-kēn'	san wah-keen'

Spanish *San Joaquin*, sän hwä-kēn' [sahn hwah-keen'].

San Jorge (Oc., Solomons)	*Sp.* sän hôr'-hĕ	sahn hor'-heh

English *Saint George*.

San José (Calif.)	*Eng.* săn′ ə-zā′	san′ uh-zay′
	Sp. sän′ hô-sĕ′	sahn′ ho-seh′
San José de Navotas (P.I.) See *Navotas.*		
San Juan (P.R.)	sän hwän′	sahn hwahn′
San Juan Capistrano (Calif.)	sän hwän′ kăp-ĭs-trä′-nō	san hwahn′ kap-is-trah′-noh
San Juan de Guimba (P.I.)	sän hwän′ dĕ gēm′-bä	sahn hwan′ deh geem′-bah
San Juanico (P.I.)	sän hwä-nē′-kô	sahn hwah-nee′-ko
San Juan Teotihuacán (Mex.)	sän hwän′ tĕ-ô-tē-wä-kän′	sahn hwahn′ teh-o-tee-wah-kahn′
Sankovo (Rus.)	sän′-kŏ-vŏ	sahn′-ko-vo
Sankt Georgen (Cz.) See *Svätý Jur.*		
Sankt Goar (Ger.) See *Saint Goar.*		
Sankt Goarshausen (Ger.)	zänkt gō-ärs′-hou′-zən	zahnkt goh-ahrs′-hau′-zuhn
Sankt Poelten *or* Pölten (Austria) See *Saint Poelten.*		
Sankt Veit (Austria) See *Saint Veit.*		
San Lázaro (Mex.)	sän lä′-sä-rô	sahn lah′-sah-ro
San Leonardo (Pantelleria, point)	sän lĕ-ô-när′-dô	sahn leh-o-nahr′-do
San Lorenzo fuori le Mura (Rome)	sän lô-rĕn′-tsô fwô′-rē lĕ mōō′-rä	sahn lo-ren′-tso fwo′-ree leh moo′-rah
San Luis (P.I.)	sän lwēs′	sahn lwees′
San Luis Potosí (Mex.)	sän lwēs′ pô-tô-sē′	sahn lwees′ po-to-see′
San Manuel (P.I.)	sän mä-nwĕl′	sahn mah-nwel′
San Marcelino (P.I.)	sän mär-sĕ-lē′-nô	sahn mahr-seh-lee′-no
San Marcos (Tex.)	săn mär′-kəs	san mahr′-kuhs
San Marino (It.)	*Eng.* săn mə-rē′-nō	san muh-ree′-noh
	It. sän mä-rē′-nô	sahn-mah ree′-no
Sânmărtin (Rum.)	sûn-mûr′-tĭn	suhn-muhr′-tin
San Martín, Grau (Cuban polit.) See *Grau San Martín.*		
San Mateo (Calif.)	săn′ mə-tā′-ō	san′ muh-tay′-oh
San Mateo (Ven.)	sän mä-tĕ′-ô	sahn mah-teh′-o
San Matías (Arg., gulf)	sän mä-tē′-äs	sahn mah-tee′-ahs
San Michele (It.)	sän mē-kĕ′-lĕ	sahn mee-keh′-leh
San Miguel (Sp.)	sän mē-gĕl′	sahn mee-gel′
San Miguel de Mayumo (P.I.)	sän mē-gĕl′ dĕ mä-yōō′-mô	sahn mee-gel′ deh mah-yoo′-mo
San Miniato (It.)	sän mē-nyä′-tô	sahn mee-nyah′-to
San Narciso (P.I.)	sän när-sē′-sô	sahn nahr-see′-so
San Niccolò (It.)	sän nēk-kô-lò′	sahn neek-ko-lo′

San Nicola (It.)	sän nĕ-kô'-lä	sahn nee-ko'-lah
San Nicolai (It.)	sän nĕ-kô-lī'	sahn nee-ko-lai'
San Nicolao (It.)	sän nĕ-kô-lou'	sahn nee-ko-lau'
San Nicolás (P.I.)	sän nĕ-kô-läs'	sahn nee-ko-lahs'
San Nicolaus (It.)	sän nĕ-kô-lous'	sahn nee-ko-laus'
San Nicolò (It.)	sän nĕ-kô-lô'	sahn nee-ko-lo'
San Paolo (Sicily)	sän pä'-ô-lô	sahn pah'-o-lo

San Pedriño (P.I., riv.) See *Pagapas*.

San Pedro (Calif.)	sän pē'-drō	san pee'-droh

An exception to the usual California preference for a Spanish or quasi-Spanish pronunciation. However, săn pā'-drō [san pay'-droh] is also heard.

San Pedro de Lloc (Haiti)	sän pĕ'-drô dĕ lyôk'	sahn peh'-dro deh lyok'
San Pedro de Macorís (Dom. Rep.)	sän pĕ'-drô dĕ mä-kô-rēs'	sahn peh'-dro deh mah-ko-rees'
San Pedro Macatí (P.I.)	sän pĕ'-drô mä-kä-tē'	sahn peh'-dro mah-kah-tee'
San Pietro (It.; Sard., isl.)	sän pyĕ'-trô	sahn pyeh'-tro
San Quintín (P.I.)	sän kēn-tēn'	sahn keen-teen'
San Quirico (It.)	sän kwē'-rē-kô	sahn kwee'-ree-ko
San Rafael	*Calif.* săn rə-fĕl'	san ruh-fel'
	Sp. sän rä-fä-ĕl'	sahn rah-fah-el'
San Rafael (P.I.)	sän rä-fä-ĕl'	sahn rah-fah-el'
San Ramón (P.I.)	sän rä-môn'	sahn rah-mon'
San Remo (It.)	sän rĕ'-mô	sahn reh'-mo

Often anglicized to săn rē'-mō [san ree'-moh].

San Roque (P.I.)	sän rô'-kĕ	sahn ro'-keh
Sansapor (NEI, New Guinea)	sän-sä-pôr'	sahn-sah-por'

For Cape Sansapor, see *Kaap de Goede Hoop*.

San Sebastián (Sp.)	*Eng.* săn' sə-băs'-chən	san' suh-bas'-chuhn
	Sp. sän' sĕ-bäs-tyän'	sahn' seh-bahs-tyahn'
Sansego (It. > Yugosl., isl.)	sän-sĕ'-gô	sahn-seh'-go

Serb-Croat *Sušak*, sōō'-shäk [soo'-shahk].

San Severo (It.)	sän sĕ-vĕ'-rô	sahn seh-veh'-ro
San-shui (Ch., Kwantung)	sän-shwä	sahn-shway
San Simón (P.I.)	sän sē-môn'	sahn see-mon'
Sans Sousi (Ger., palace)	*Eng.* sănz' sōō-sē'	sanz' soo-see'
	Fr. säN sōō-sē'	sahN soo-see'

San Stefano di Camastra (Sicily)	sän stě'-fä-nô dē kä-mäs'-trä	sahn steh'-fah-no dee kah-mahs'-trah
Santa Ana (Calif.)	săn'-tə ăn'-ə	san'-tuh an'-uh
Santa Ana (P.I.)	sän'-tä ä'-nä	sahn'-tah ah'-nah
Santa Barbara (Calif.)	săn'-tə bär'-bə-rə	san'-tuh bahr'-buh-ruh
Santa Bárbara (P.I.)	sän'-tä bär'-bä-rä	sahn'-tah bahr'-bah-rah
Santa Chiara (It.)	sän'-tä kyä'-rä	sahn'-tah kyah'-rah
Santa Comba Dão (Port.)	sän'-tə kôm'-bə douN'	sahn'-tuh kom'-buh dauN'
Santa Croce (It.)	sän'-tä krô'-chě	sahn'-tah kro-'cheh
Santa Cruz	*Eng.* săn'-tə krōōz' *Sp.* sän'-tä krōōth'	san'-tuh krooz' sahn'-tah krooth'
Santa Fe (N.M.)	săn'-tə fā'	san'-tuh fay'

Spanish *Santa Fé,* sän'-tä fě' [sahn'-tah feh']. Old-fashionedEnglish, săn'-tə fē' [san'-tuh fee'].

Sant' Agata di Militello (Sicily)	sän tä'-gä-tä dē mě-lē-těl'-lô	sahn tah'-gah-tah dee mee-lee-tel'-lo
Santa Ignacia (P.I.)	sän'-tä ēg-nä'-syä	sahn'-tah eeg-nah'-syah

Also called *Binaco,* bē-nä'-kô [bee-nah'-ko].

Santa Isabel (P.I.)	sän'-tä ē-sä-běl'	sahn'-tah ee-sah-bel'
Santa María de Pandi (P.I.)	sän'-tä mä-rē'-ä dě pän'-dē	sahn'-tah mah-ree'-ah deh pahn'-dee
Santa Maria Maggiore (It., Rome)	sän'-tä mä-rē'-ä mäd-jô'-rě	sahn'-tah mah-ree'-ah mahd-jo'-reh
Santa Monica (Calif.)	săn'-tə mŏn'-ə-kə	san'-tuh mon'-uh-kuh
Santander (Sp.)	sän-tän-děr'	sahn-tahn-dehr'
Sant' Ansano (It.)	sän' tän-sä'-nô	sahn' tahn-sah'-no
Sant' Antioco (Sard., isl.)	sän' tän-tē'-ô-kô	sahn' tahn-tee'-o-ko
Santarém (Port.)	sän-tə-rěN'	sahn-tuh-reN'
Sant' Elia (It.)	sän' tě-lē'-ä	sahn' teh-lee'-ah
Santerno (It., riv.)	sän-těr'-nô	sahn-tehr'-no
Sant' Eufemia (It., gulf)	sän' tě-ōō-fě'-myä	sahn' teh-oo-feh'-myah
Santeuil (Fr.)	säN-tû'(y)	sahN-tœ'(y)
Santiago	*Eng.* săn'-tǐ-ā'-gô *Sp.* sän-tyä'-gô	san'-ti-ay'-go sahn-tyah'-go
Santi Quaranta (Alb.)	*It.* sän'-tē kwä-rän'-tä	sahn'-tee kwah-rahn'-tah

Also called *Porto Edda,* q.v. Albanian *Sarandē,* q.v.

Santo Domingo (Dom. Rep.)	*Sp.* sän'-tô dô-mēng'-gô	sahn'-to do-meeng'-go
	Eng. săn'-tə də-mǐng'-gō	san'-tuh duh-ming'-goh
Santomè (It.)	sän-tô-mĕ'	sahn-to-meh'
Santorini (Gr., isl.) See *Thera.*		
Santos (Brazil)	sän'-tōōs *or* -tōōsh	sahn'-tus *or* -tush
Santo Tomás (P.I.)	sän'-tô tô-mäs'	sahn'-to to-mahs'
San Vincente (P.I.)	sän vēn-sĕn'-tĕ	sahn veen-sen'-teh
San Vito (Sicily, cape)	sän vē'-tô	sahn vee'-to
San Vittorio (It.)	sän vēt-tô'-ryô	sahn veet-to'-ryo
São Jorge (Azores)	souN zhôr'-zhǐ	sauN zhor'-zhi
São Luiz do Maranhão (Brazil)	souN lwēs' dōō mä-rə-nyouN'	sauN lwees' du mah-ruh-nyauN'
Saône (Fr., riv.)	sōn'	sohn'
São Paulo (Brazil)	souN pou'-lōō	sauN pau'-lu
São Paulo de Loanda (S.W. Afr.) See *Loanda.*		
São Salvador (Brazil)	souN' säl-və-dôr'	sauN' sahl-vuh-dor'
Also called, unofficially, *Bahía* or *Baía,* q.v.		
Sapeloe (Ga.)	săp'-ē-lō	sap'-ee-loh
Sapientza (Gr., isl.)	sä-pyĕn'-dzä	sah-pyen'-dzah
Šapina (Yugosl.)	shä'-pǐ-nä	shah'-pi-nah
Sapoedi *or* Sapudi (NEI)	sä-pōō'-dē	sah-poo'-dee
Sappemeer (Neth.)	säp'-ə-mär'	sahp'-uh-mayr'
Sapporo (Jap.)	säp-pô'-rô	sahp-po'-ro
Sapri (It.)	sä'-prē	sah'-pree
Sapru, Tej Bahadur (Indian polit.)	sä'-prōō, tĕj' bə-hä'-dōōr	sah'-proo, tej' buh-hah'-dur
Sapudi (NEI) See *Sapoedi.*		
Sapulpa (Okla.)	sə-pŭl'-pə	suh-puhl'-puh
Saqqiz (Iran)	säk-kǐz' *or* -kĕz'	sahk-kiz' *or* -kez'
Sarabuz (Rus.)	sä-rä'-bōōs	sah-rah'-bus
Saracinesco (It.)	sä'-rä-chē-nĕ'-skô	sah'-rah-chee-neh'-sko
Saracoğlu, Şükrü (Turk. polit.)	sä-rä'-jô-lōō, shü'-krü'	sah-rah'-jo-lu, shü'-krü'
Sarafis, Stefanos (Gr. polit.)	sä-rä'-fēs, stĕ'-fä-nôs	sah-rah'-fees, steh'-fah-nos
Saragat, Giuseppe (It. polit.)	sä-rä-gät', jōō-sĕp'-pĕ	sah-rah-gaht', joo-sep'-peh
Saragossa (Sp.)	*Eng.* săr'-ə-gŏs'-ə	sehr'-uh-gos'-uh
Spanish *Zaragoza,* q.v.		
Sarajevo (Yugosl.)	sä'-rä'-yĕ-vô	sah'-rah'-yeh-vo

Sarajevska (Yugosl.)   sä'-rä'-yĕf-skä   sah'-rah'-yef-skah

Sarakhs (Iran)   sä-räk(h)s'   sah-rahk(h)s'

Sarana (Alaska, Attu)   sä-rä'-nä   sah-rah'-nah

Šaranci (Yugosl.)   shä'-rän-tsĭ   shah'-rahn-tsi

Saranda (Alb.) See *Sarandë*.

Sarandë (Alb.)   sä-rän'-də   sah-rahn'-duh
  Greek *Saranta*, sä-rän'-tä [sah-rahn'-tah].

Sarang (N.E. New   sä'-räng   sah'-rahng
  Guinea)

Saransk (Rus.)   sä-ränsk'   sah-rahnsk'

Saranta (Alb.) See *Sarandë*

Saraorci (Yugosl.)   sä-rä'-ôr-tsĭ   sah'-rah'-or-tsi

Sarapul (Rus.)   sä-rä'-pŏͦl   sah-rah'-pul

Sarapulskoe (Rus.)   sä-rä'-pŏͦl(y)-skŏ-yĕ   sah-rah'-pul(y)-sko-
                                        yeh

Saratov (Rus.)   sä-rä'-tŏf   sah-rah'-tof

Sarawak (Br. Borneo)   *Eng.* sə-rä'-wäk   suh-rah'-wahk
                     native sə-rä'-wä   suh-rah'-wah

Sarbacher, George W., Jr. sär'-bŏk-ər   sahr'-bok-uhr
  (U.S. representative)

Šarbanovac (Yugosl.)   shär'-bä'-nô-väts   shahr'-bah'-no-vahts

sardar *or* sirdar   sər-där'   suhr-dahr'
  A title or honorific in the Middle East. It is disregarded in alphabetical
  listing.

Sardasht (Iran)   sär-däsht'   sahr-dahsht'

Sardinia   *Eng.* sär-dĭn'-yə   sahr-din'-yuh
  Italian *Sardegna*, sär-dĕ'-nyä [sahr-deh'-nyah].

Sareyannis, Ptolemaios   sä-rē-yä'-nēs,   sah-ree-yah'-nees,
  (Gr. general)   ptô-lĕ-mĕ'-ôs   pto-leh-meh'-os

Sári (Hung.)   shä'-rĭ   shah'-ri

Saria (Dodec.) See *Saros*.

Sariguan (Oc., Marianas) sä-rē-gwän'   sah-ree-gwahn'

Sarmi (NEI, New Guinea) sär'-mē   sahr'-mee

Sarni (Pol. > Rus.)   sär'-nĭ   sahr'-ni
  Polish spelling *Sarny*.

Sarnia (Can.)   sär'-nĭ-ə   sahr'-ni-uh

Sarojini Naidu (Indian polit.) See *Naidu, Sarojini*.

Saronic Gulf (Gr.)   *Eng.* sə-rŏn'-ĭk   suh-ron'-ik
  Greek *Saronikos Kolpos*, sä-rô-nē-kôs' kôl'-pôs [sah-ro-nee-kos' kol'-
  pos].

Saros (Dodec.)   sä'-rô(s)   sah'-ro(s)
  Also called *Saria*, sä-rē'-ä [sah-ree'-ah] and sär-yä' [sahr-yah'].

Šar planina (Yugosl.,   shär' plä'-nĕ'-nä   shahr' plah'-nee'-nah
  mts.)

Sarpsborg (Nor.)	särps'-bôr	sahrps'-bor
Sarralbe (Fr.)	sä-rälb'	sah-rahlb'
Sarre (Fr., Ger., riv.)	sär'	sahr'
German *Saar*, zär' [zahr'].		

Sarre, Count of. See *Umberto.*

Sarrebourg (Fr.)	*Eng.* sär'-bo͞org	sahr'-burg
	Fr. sär-bo͞or'	sahr-boor'
Sarreguemines (Fr.)	sär-gə-mēn'	sahr-guh-meen'
Sartène (Corsica)	sär-těn'	sahr-ten'
Sarthe (Fr., riv.)	särt'	sahrt'
Sartre, Jean Paul (Fr. author)	sär'tr, zhän' pôl'	sahr'tr, zhahN' pol'
Sarych (Rus.)	sä-rǐch'	sah-rich'
Sarzana (It.)	sär-tsä'-nä	sahr-tsah'-nah
Sasebo (Jap.)	sä'-sě-bô	sah'-seh-bo
Saseno (It., isl.)	sä'-sě-nô	sah'-seh-no

Albanian *Sazan*, q.v. Greek *Sasson*, sä'-sôn [sah'-son].

Saskatchewan (Can.)	säs-kăch'-ə-wän	sas-kach'-uh-wahn
Saskatoon (Can.)	säs'-kə-to͞on'	sas'-kuh-toon'
Šasko Blato (Yugosl.)	shä'-skô blä'-tô	shah'-sko blah'-to
Sassari (Sard.)	säs'-sä-rē	sahs'-sah-ree
Sasscer, L. G. (U.S. representative)	säs'-ər	sas'-uhr
Sassenheim (Neth.)	säs'-ən-hǐm	sahs'-uhn-haim
Sassnitz (Ger.)	zäs'-nǐts	zahs'-nits
Sas van Gend (Neth.)	säs' vän k(h)ěnt'	sahs' vahn k(h)ent'

Satar (Arab polit.) See *Abul Mo-iz Abdul Satar.*

Satara (India)	sä-tä'-rə	sah-tah'-ruh
Sataria (Pantelleria, bay)	sä-tä-rē'-ä	sah-tah-ree'-ah
Satawal (Oc., Carolines)	sä'-tä-wäl	sah'-tah-wahl
Satawan (Oc., Carolines)	sä'-tä-wän	sah'-tah-wahn
Sátoraljaujhely (Hung.)	shä'-tôr-oi-yǒ-o͝o'ǐ-hä	shah'-tor-oi-yo-u'(y)-hay
Šatornja, Donja (Yugosl.)	shä'-tôr-nyä, dô'-nyä	shah'-tor-nyah, do'-nyah
Satul (Rum., riv.)	sä'-to͝ol	sah'-tul
Satul Mare (Rum.)	sä'-to͝ol mä'-rě	sah'-tul mah'-reh
Satul Nou (Rum.)	sä'-to͝ol nô'	sah'-tul noh'
Sauckel, Fritz (Ger. polit.)	zou'-kəl, frǐts'	zau'-kuhl, frits'
Sauda (Nor.)	sou'-dä	sau'-dah
Saudi (Arabia)	sä-o͞o'-dē	sah-oo'-dee
Sauer (Ger., riv.)	*Eng.* sou'-ər	sau'-uhr
	Ger. zou'-ər	zau'-uhr

Saugerties (N.Y.)   sô'-gər-tĭz   saw'-guhr-tiz
Saugor or Sagar (India)   sô-gōr' or sä'-gər   so-gohr' or sah'-guhr
Saugus (Mass.)   sô'-gəs   saw'-guhs
Saujon (Fr.)   sō-zhôN'   soh-zhoN'
Sauk Centre (Minn.)   sôk' sĕn'-tər   sawk' sen'-tuhr
   Is the change from *Center* to *Centre* a sign of sophistication?
Saulieu (Fr.)   sō-lyû'   soh-lyœ'
Sault (Fr.)   sō'   soh'
Sault Ste. Marie (Mich.)   soo' sānt mə-rē'   soo' saynt muh-ree'
   French sō săNt mä-rē' [soh saNt mah-ree'].
Saulx (Fr.)   sō'   soh'
Saulxures (Fr.)   sō-sür'   soh-sür'
Saumlakki (Oc., Tanim-   soum-läk'-kē   saum-lahk'-kee
   bar)
Saumur (Fr.)   sō-mür'   soh-mür'
Sauthoff, Harry   sôt'-hŭf   sawt'-huhf
   (U.S. representative)
Sava (Yugosl., riv.)   sä'-vä   sah'-vah
Savenay (Fr.)   säv-nĕ'   sahv-neh'
Saverne (Fr.)   sä-vĕrn'   sah-vehrn'
Savignano (It.)   sä-vē-nyä'-nô   sah-vee-nyah'-no
Savina (Yugosl., riv.)   sä'-vĭ-nä   sah'-vi-nah
Savio (It.)   sä'-vyô   sah'-vyo
Šavnik (Yugosl.)   shäv'-nĭk   shahv'-nik
Savo (Oc., Solomons)   *Eng.* sä'-vō   say'-voh
                           native sä'-vô   sah'-vo
Savoe or Savu (NEI)   See Sawoe or Sawu.
Savona (It.)   sä-vô'-nä   sah-vo'-nah
Savonlinna (Fin.)   sä'-vôn-lĭn-nä   sah'-von-lin-nah
Savran (Rus.)   sä-vrän'(y)   sah-vrahn'(y)
Saw, U (Burman polit.) See *U Saw.*
Sawoe or Sawu;   sä'-voo   sah'-voo
   Savoe or Savu (NEI)
Saxe-Coburg-Gotha   *Eng.* săks' kō'-bûrg saks' koh'-buhrg
   (Ger.)   gō'-thə   goh'-thuh
   German *Sachsen-Coburg und Gotha.*
Saxony (Ger.)   *Eng.* săk'-sə-nĭ   sak'-suh-ni
   German *Sachsen*, q.v.
Sayed, Ahmed Lotfi el (Egypt. polit.) See *Ahmed Lotfi el Seyed.*
Sazan (It., isl.)   *Alb.* sä'-zän   sah'-zahn
   Italian *Saseno*, q.v.
Sazani (It., isl.)   See *Sazan.*
Sbeitla (Tun.)   sbät'-lä   sbayt'-lah
Sbiba (Tun.)   sbē'-bä   sbee'-bah

[474]

Scalari (It., mt.)	skä-lä′-rē	skah-lah′-ree
Scalea (It.)	skä-lĕ′-ä	skah-leh′-ah
Scanderbeg (Alb., mt.)	*Eng.* skăn′-dər-bĕg	skan′-duhr-beg

Albanian *Mal i Skanderbeut.* Named after an Albanian hero whose Turkish name was *Iskander Bey* (or *Beğ*).

Scandriglia (It.)	skän-drē′-lyä	skahn-dree′-lyah
Scanlon, Thomas E.	skăn′-lŏn	skan′-lon
(U.S. representative)		
Scanno (It.)	skän′-nô	skahn′-no
Scaramia (Sicily, cape)	skä-rä′-myä	skah-rah′-myah
Scarpanto (Dodec.)	*It.* skär′-pän-tô	skahr′-pahn-to

Greek *Karpathos,* q.v.

Scavenius, Erik	skä-vā′-nĭ-ŏ̄os,	skah-vay′-ni-us,
(Dan. polit.)	ĭ′-rēk	i′-reek
Ščavnica (Yugosl., riv.)	shchäv′-nĭ-tsä	shchahv′-ni-tsah
Sceaux (Fr.)	sō′	soh′
Šćedro (Yugosl., isl.)	shchĕ′-drô	shcheh′-dro
	or shtyĕ′-drô	shtyeh′-dro

Italian *Torcola,* q.v.

Sch-. Alfred H. Holt makes the interesting observation that in place names of New York state, initial *Sch-* is pronounced *sk* because of Dutch tradition. Elsewhere in America, he adds, *Sch-* of place names is treated as German and pronounced *sh* with the exceptions of *sk* in *Schofield, Schuyler, Schuylkill,* and the many compounds with *school.* (See *American Place Names,* pp. 174–5.) The *sk* or "Dutch" tradition in New York has its exception in *Schultzville,* Dutchess County.

Schaaik (Neth.)	sk(h)īk′	sk(h)aik′
Schaarsbergen (Neth.)	sk(h)ärs′-bĕr-k(h)ən	sk(h)ahrs′-behr-k(h)uhn
Schacht, Hjalmar (Ger. banker)	shäk(h)t′, yäl′-mär	schahk(h)t′, yahl′-mahr

Baptized *Horace Greeley Hjalmar Schacht.*

Schaerbeek (Belg.)	sk(h)är′-bāk	sk(h)ahr′-bayk
Schaffhausen (Switz.)	shäf-hou′-zən	shahf-hau′-zuhn

French *Schaffhouse,* shä-fōōz′ [shah-fooz′].

Schagen (Neth.)	sk(h)ä′-k(h)ən	sk(h)ah′-k(h)uhn
Schaghticoke (N.Y.)	skăt′-ĭ-kōk	skat′-i-kohk
Scharendijke (Neth.)	sk(h)ä′-rən-dī′-kə	sk(h)ah′-ruhn-dai′-kuh
Scharnhorst (Ger.)	shärn′-hôrst	shahrn′-horst
Schaulen (Lith.)	*Ger.* shou′-lən	shau′-luhn

Lithuanian *Šiauliai,* q.v. Russian *Shavli,* q.v.

Scheemda (Neth.)	sk(h)äm′-dä	sk(h)aym′-dah
Scheggia (It.)	skĕd′-jä	sked′-jah

Scheldt (Neth., Belg.,   *Eng.* skĕlt′   skelt′
Fr., riv.)
  Dutch *Schelde*, sk(h)ĕl′-də [sk(h)el′-duh]. French *Escaut*, ĕs-kō′
[es-koh′].
Schenectady (N.Y.)   skə-nĕk′-tə-dĭ   skuh-nek′-tuh-di
Schenevus (N.Y.)   skə-nē′-vəs   skuh-nee′-vuhs
Scherfelde (Ger.)   shĕr′-fĕl-də   shehr′-fel-duh
Schermerhorn (N.Y.   *N.Y.* skûr′-mər-hôrn skuhr′-muhr-horn
  name, Neth. town)   *Neth.* sk(h)ĕr′-mər- sk(h)ehr′-muhr-horn
                         hôrn
Schermerhorn, Willem   sk(h)ĕr′-mər-hôrn, sk(h)ehr′-muhr-horn,
  (Du. polit.)   vĭl′-əm   vil′-uhm
Scheuenhuette (Ger.)   shoi′-ən-hüt′-ə   shoi′-uhn-hüt′-uh
Scheveningen (Neth.)   sk(h)ā′-və-nĭng-ən sk(h)ay′-vuh-ning-
                               uhn
Schiavonia (Yugosl.)   *It.* skyä-vô′-nyä   skyah-vo′-nyah
  English *Slavonia*, q.v.
Schiebroek (Neth.)   sk(h)ē′-brōōk   sk(h)ee′-brook
Schiedam (Neth.)   sk(h)ē′-däm′   sk(h)ee′-dahm′
Schiermonnikoog   sk(h)ēr′-môn-ĭ-   sk(h)eer′-mon-i-
  (Neth., isl.)   kōk(h)′   kohk(h)′
Schiffler, Andrew C.   shĭf′-lər   shif′-luhr
  (U.S. representative)
Schijndel (Neth.)   sk(h)īn′-dəl   sk(h)ain′-duhl
Schinnen (Neth.)   sk(h)ĭn′-ən   sk(h)in′-uhn
Schio (It.)   skē′-ô   skee′-o
Schiphol (Neth., Amster- sk(h)ĭp-hôl′   sk(h)ip-hol′
  dam, airport)
Schipluiden (Neth.)   sk(h)ĭp-lûĭ′-dən   sk(h)ip-lœi′-duhn
Schirmer, G. (Ger. Am.   *Eng.* shûr′-mər   shuhr′-muhr
  music publisher)   *Ger.* shĭr′-mər   shihr′-muhr
Schleiden (Ger.)   shlī′-dən   shlai′-duhn
Schlesien (Ger., Pol., Cz.) See *Silesia.*
Schleswig (Den., Ger.)   *Eng.* slĕs′-wĭk   sles′-wik
                Ger. shlās′-vĭk(h)   shlays′-vik(h)
  Danish *Slesvig*, q.v.
——Holstein (Ger.)   *Eng.* hōl′-stīn   hohl′-stain
                Ger. hôl′-shtīn   hol′-shtain
Schley (Am. family   slī′   slai′
  and place name)
Schlok (Latvia)   *Ger.* shlôk′   shlok′
  Latvian *Sloka*, q.v.
Schlossberg (Ger. >Rus.) See *Pillkallen.*
Schloss Rominten (Ger.) shlôs′ rō′-mĭn-tən shlos′ roh′-min-tuhn

[476]

Schlucht (Fr., pass)   shlükt'   shlükt'

Schlusselburg (Rus.)   shlēs'-sĕl-bŏŏrk'   shlees'-sel-burk'
    German *Schluesselburg* or *Schlüsselburg*, shlüs'-əl-bŏŏrk(h) [shlüs'-uhl-burk(h)].

Schnee Eifel (Ger.) See *Eifel*.

Schneidermuehl, -mül   shnī'-dər-mül   shnai'-duhr-mül
    (Ger.> Pol.)
    Polish *Piła*, q.v.

Schodack (N.Y.)   skō'-dăk   skoh'-dak

Schofield Barracks   skō'-fēld   skoh'-feeld
    (Oahu, Hawaii)

Schoharie (N.Y.)   skō-hăr'-ĭ   skoh-hehr'-i

Schoondijke (Neth.)   sk(h)ōn'-dī-kə   sk(h)ohn'-dai-kuh

Schoonebeek (Neth.)   sk(h)ō'-nə-bāk   sk(h)oh'-nuh-bayk

Schoonhoven (Neth.)   sk(h)ōn'-hō-vən   sk(h)ohn'-hoh-vuhn

Schoorl (Neth.)   sk(h)ōrl'   sk(h)ohrl'

Schophoven (Ger.)   shôp'-hō-fən   shop'-hoh-fuhn

Schouten (NEI)   sk(h)ou'-tən   sk(h)au'-tuhn

Schouwen (Neth.)   sk(h)ou'-wən   sk(h)au'-wuhn

Schram, Emil (Am.   shrăm, ā'-məl   shram, ay'-muhl
    banker)

Schrimm (Pol.)   See *Śrem*.

Schroda (Pol.)   See *Środa*.

Schroon Lake (N.Y.)   skrōōn'   skroon'

Schuschnigg, Kurt von   shŏŏs'-nĭk(h), kŏŏrt'   shus'-nik(h), kurt'
    (Austrian polit.)   fən   fuhn

Schuyler (Am., Du.   *Eng.* skī'-lər   skai'-luhr
    name)   *Du.* sk(h)ûĭ'-lər   sk(h)œi'-luhr

Schuylkill (Pa., riv.)   skōōl'-kĭl   skool'-kil
    Locally sometimes skōō'-kəl [skoo'-kuhl].

schwa   shwä' *or* shvä'   shwah' *or* shvah'
    No matter how spelt, the vowels of unstressed syllables in English tend to become an obscured "uh" sound. Its phonetic symbol is ə. Its name is *schwa*, which seems a comical word to speakers of English but is very useful as the name of the commonest vowel in spoken English. This is the sound spelled a in *about* and *sofa*, e in *taken*, i in *evil*, o in *connect*, u in *circus*.

Schwabe, Max   swä'-bĕ   swah'-beh
    (U.S. representative)

Schwammenauel (Ger.,   shväm'-ə-nou'-əl   shvahm'-uh-nau'-uhl
    dam)

Schwanenburg (Latvia)   *Ger.* shvä'-nən-   shvah'-nuhn-burk(h)
                 bŏŏrk(h)
    Latvian *Gulbene*, q.v.

Schwedt (Ger.)	shvĕt′	shvet′
Schweidnitz (Ger. > ? Pol.)	shvīt′-nĭts	shvait′-nits
Polish *Świdnica*, q.v.		
Schweinfurt (Ger.)	shvĭn′-fŏŏrt	shvain′-furt
Schwellenbach, Lewis Baxter (Am. polit.)	shwĕl′-ən-bäk	shwel′-uhn-bahk
Schwerte (Ger.)	shvār′-tə	shvayr′-tuh
Schwetzingen (Ger.)	shvĕts′-ĭng-ən	shvets′-ing-uhn
Schwiebus (Ger. >Pol.)	shvē′-bŏŏs	shvee′-bus
Polish *Świebodzin*, q.v.		
Sciacca (Sicily)	shäk′-kä	shahk′-kah
Sciaccazze (Pantelleria, point)	shäk-kät′-sĕ	shahk-kaht′-seh
Scicli (Sicily)	shē′-klē	shee′-klee
Scido (It.)	shē′-dô	shee′-do
Scilla (It.)	shēl′-lä	sheel′-lah

English *Scylla*, sĭl′-ə [sil′-uh]. Probably the English pronunciation is preferable for American speakers.

Ścinawa (Ger. >Pol.)	shtsĭ-nä′-vä	shtsi-nah′-vah
German *Steinau*, q.v.		
Sciota (N.Y.)	sī-ō′-tə	sai-oh′-tuh
Scipio (N.Y., Okla.)	sĭp′-ĭ-ō	sip′-i-oh
Scituate (Mass.)	sĭch′-ŏŏ-āt	sich′-u-ayt
Scoblick, James P. (U.S. representative)	skō′-blĭk	skoh′-blik
Scoccimarro, Mauro (It. polit.)	skôt-chē-mär′-rô, mou′-rô	skot-chee-mahr′-ro, mau′-ro
Scoglitti (Sicily)	skô-lyē′-tē	sko-lyee′-tee
Scordia (Sicily)	skôr-dē′-ä	skor-dee′-ah
Scorff (Fr., riv.)	skôrf′	skorf′
Scorza, Carlo (It. polit.)	skôr′-dzä, kär′-lô	skor′-dzah, kahr′-lo
Scotia (N.Y.)	skō′-shə	skoh′-shuh
Scrugham, James C. (U.S. senator)	skrŭg′-hăm	skruhg′-ham
Scurcola (It.)	skŏŏr′-kô-lä	skoor′-ko-lah
Scutari (Alb., city; Balkan lake)	*Eng.* skŏŏ′-tä-rē	skoo′-tah-ree

Albanian *Shkodër*, shkô′-dər [shko′-duhr]. Serb-Croat *Skadar*, skä′-där [skah′-dahr]. English *Lake Scutari*. Albanian *Liqen i Shkodrës*, lē-kyĕn′ ē shkô′-drəs [lee-kyen′ ee shko′-druhs]. Serb-Croat *Skadarsko Jezero*, skä′-där-skô yĕ′-zĕ-rô [skah′-dahr-sko yeh′-zeh-ro]. Turkish *Üskûdar*, q.v.

[478]

Scylla (It.)	*Eng.* sĭl'-ə	sil'-uh

Italian *Scilla*, shēl'-lä [sheel'-lah]. The English pronunciation is preferable for American speakers, especially when speaking of *Scylla* and *Charybdis*, q.v.

Seattle (Wash.)	sē-ăt'l	see-at'l
Seay (Am. name)	sē'	see'
Sebakoeng (Borneo)	sĕ-bä'-kŏong	seh-bah'-kung
Sebala, la (Tun.)	sə-bă'-lä, lä	suh-ba'-lah, lah
Sebastopol See *Sevastopol*.		
Sebenico (Yugosl.)	*It.* sĕ-bĕ'-nē-kô	seh-beh'-nee-ko
Serb-Croat *Šibenik*, q.v.		
Sebeş *or* Sebeşul (Rum., riv.)	sĕ-bĕsh' *or* sĕ-bĕ'-shŏol	seh-behsh' *or* seh-beh'-shul
Sebezh (Rus.)	sĕ'-bĕsh	seh'-besh
Sebkra Sidi Khalifa (Tun.)	sĕb'-krä sē'-dē kä-lē'-fä	seb'-krah see'-dee kah-lee'-fah
Sebkret Djaber (Tun.)	sĕb'-krĕt jă'-bər	seb'-kret ja'-buhr
Sebkret el Kourzia (Tun.)	sĕb'-krĕt ĕl kŏor-zē'-ä	seb'-kret el kur-zee'-ah
Seboekoe *or* Sebuku (NEI)	sä-bŏo'-kŏo	say-boo'-koo
Secchia (It., riv.)	sĕk'-kyä	sek'-kyah
Secinaro (It.)	sĕ-chē-nä'-rô	seh-chee-nah'-ro
Secine (It., mt.)	sĕ'-chē-nĕ	seh'-chee-neh
secretary	sĕk'-rə-tĕr-ĭ *or* sĕk'-ə-tĕr-ĭ	sehk'-ruh-tehr-i sehk'-uh-tehr-i

The latter pronunciation has lost an *r* by dissimilation. Compare *association*. See Kenyon and Knott, Section 121.

secretive	sĭ-krē'-tĭv	si-kree'-tiv

Secretive does double duty as an adjective for *se'cret*, noun, and *secrete'*, verb. In the first instance there is a popular tendency to stress the first syllable, though the shift of accent is not authorized by dictionaries. This pronunciation sē'-krĭ-tĭv [see'-kri-tiv] is perhaps ultra-refined, but it may become established what with the analogy of the recessive accent of the noun and the tabooed suggestion of the second-syllable accent of *secrete* and *secretion*. Well established in the language is the effort to distinguish senses and functions—to create new words—by more or less arbitrary devices of pronunciation and spelling. Compare *se'cret* and *secrete'*; *of* and *off*; *pat'ent* and *pa'tent*; *ad'dress* and *address'*.

Secunderabad (India)	sĭ-kŭn'-drə-băd' *or* sē-kŭn'-drä-bäd'	si-kuhn'-druh-bad' see-kuhn'-drah-bahd'
Sedan (Fr.)	*Eng.* sə-dăn'	suh-dan'
	Fr. sə-däN'	suh-dahN'

Séderon (Fr.)	sĕ-drôN'	seh-droN'
Sedes (Gr.)	sĕ'-dĕs	seh'-des
Sedjenane (Tun.)	sĕ-jĕ-năn'	seh-jeh-nan'
Sedjouna (Tun.)	sə-jōō'-nä	suh-joo'-nah
Šeduva (Lith.)	shĕ'-dōō-vä	sheh'-doo-vah
Sée (Fr., riv.)	sĕ'	seh'
Seelow (Ger.)	zā'-lō	zay'-loh
Seely Brown, Horace (U.S. representative)	sē'-lĭ broun'	see'-li braun'
Sées (Fr.)	sĕ'	seh'

Also spelled *Séez.*

Seg (Rus.)	sĕg'	seg'
Segesta (Sicily)	sĕ-jĕs'-tä	seh-jes'-tah

Segesvár (Rum.) See *Sighişoara.*

Segna (Yugosl.) See *Senj.*

Segnali (Libya)	sĕ-nyä'-lē	seh-nyah'-lee
Segni (It.)	sĕ'-nyē	seh'-nyee
Segovia (Sp.)	sĕ-gô'-vyä	seh-go'-vyah
Segré (Fr.)	sə-grĕ'	suh-greh'
Seguin (Tex.)	sə-gēn'	suh-geen'
Sehneh (Iran)	sĕ'-nĕ'	seh'-neh'

Also called *Sanandaj,* q.v.

sei	sā	say

An element, meaning *west,* in Japanese place names. See also *sai.*

Seibersdorf (Pol.) See *Zebrzydowice.*

Seiches (Fr.)	sĕsh'	sesh'
Seif el Islam (Yemen polit.)	sāf' ĕl ĭs-läm'	sayf' el is-lahm'
Seille (Fr., riv.)	sā'	say'
Seim (Rus., riv.)	sām'	saym'
Seine (Fr., riv.)	*Eng.* sān'	sayn'
	Fr. sĕn'	sen'
Seine Inférieure (Fr.)	sĕn ăN-fĕ-ryûr'	sen aN-feh-rycer'
Seishin (Korea)	sā-shĭn	say-shin
Seiskari (Fin.)	sās'-kä-rē	says'-kah-ree
Seitler (Rus.)	*Rus.* sāt'-lər	sayt'-luhr
	Ger. zīt'-lər	zait'-luhr
Sekeris, Evangelos (Gr. polit.)	sĕ'-kĕ-rēs, ĕ-väng'-gĕ-lôs	seh'-keh-rees, eh-vahng'-geh-los
Sekurić (Yugosl.)	sĕ'-kōō-rĭch	seh'-koo-rich
Selapiu (Oc., Bismarck arch.)	sĕ-lä-pē'-ōō	seh-lah-pee'-oo
Selbu (Nor.)	sĕl'-bōō	sel'-boo
Selce (Yugosl.)	sĕl'-tsĕ	sel'-tseh

Sele (It., riv.)	sĕ'-lĕ	seh'-leh
Sele (NEI, str.)	sĕ'-lĕ	seh'-leh
Selečka planina	sĕ'-lĕch-kä	seh'-lech-kah
(Yugosl., mts.)	plä'-nĕ'-nä	plah'-nee'-nah
Selemdzha (Rus., riv.)	sĕ-lĕm-jä'	seh-lem-jah'
Selenga (Rus., riv.)	sĕ-lĕn-gä'	seh-len-gah'
Selenginskaya Duma	sĕ-lĕn-gĭn'-skä-yä	seh-len-gin'-skah-yah
(Rus.)	dōō'-mä	doo'-mah
Seleo (New Guinea, isl.)	sĕ-lĕ'-ô	seh-leh'-o
Sélestat (Fr.)	sĕ-lə-stä'	seh-luh-stah'
Selevac (Yugosl.)	sĕ'-lĕ-väts	seh'-leh-vahts
Seličevica (Yugosl., mts.)	sĕ-lē'-chĕ-vĭ-tsä	seh-lee'-cheh-vi-tsah
Seliger (Rus.)	sĕ'-lĭ-gĕr	seh'-li-gehr
Selinon (Crete)	sĕ'-lē-nô(n)	seh'-lee-no(n)

Also called *Paleokhora*, pä-lyô-hô'-rä [pah-lyo-ho'-rah].

Selinou Kastelli (Crete, cape)	sĕ-lē'-nōō kä-stĕ'-lē	seh-lee'-noo kah-steh'-lee
Selizharovo (Rus.)	sĕ-lĭ-zhä'-rŏ-vŏ	seh-li-zhah'-ro-vo
Seljestad (Nor.)	sĕl'-yə-stä	sel'-yuh-stah
Seljord (Nor.)	sĕl'-yŏr	sel'-yohr
selkä	sĕl'-kă	sel'-ka

An element, meaning *ridge* or *range* of mountains, sometimes *bay* or *channel*, in Finnish place names.

Seloe *or* Selu (NEI, Tanimbar)	sĕ'-lōō	seh'-loo
Seltz (Fr.)	sĕlts'	selts'
Sélune (Fr., riv.)	sĕ-lün'	seh-lün'
Selva (It.)	sĕl'-vä	sel'-vah
Selve (Yugosl.)	*It.* sĕl'-vĕ	sel'-veh

Serb-Croat *Silba*, q.v.

Seman *or* Semen (Alb., riv., cape)	sĕ'-män	seh'-mahn

Semani *or* Semeni (Alb., riv., cape)   See *Seman*.

Semarang (NEI, Java)	sə-mä'-räng	suh-mah'-rahng
Sembodjalama (Borneo)	sĕm-bô-jä-lä'-mä	sem-bo-jah-lah'-mah

Semën (Rus. name) See *Simeon*.

Semënov, Grigori	sĕ-myô'-nôf,	seh-myo'-nof,
(Rus. general)	grĭ-gô'-rĭ	gri-go'-ri
Semerara (P.I.)	sĕ-mĕ-rä'-rä	seh-meh-rah'-rah
Semeroe *or* Semeru (NEI)	sĕm'-ə-rōō	sem'-uh-roo
	or smĕ'-rōō	smeh'-roo
Semidi (Alaska, isls.)	sĕ'-mĭ-dĭ	seh'-mi-di
Semijaj (Yugosl.)	sĕ'-mĭ-yī'	seh'-mi-yai'

Semiostrovskoe (Rus.)	sĕ-mĭ-ôs'-trŏf-skŏ-yĕ	seh-mi-os'-trof-sko-yeh
Semipalatinsk (Rus.)	sĕ-mĭ-pä-lä'-tĭnsk	seh-mi-pah-lah'-tinsk
Semki (Rus.)	sĕm-kē'	sem-kee'
Semois (Fr., riv.)	sə-mwä'	suh-mwah'
Sémussac (Fr.)	sĕ-mü-säk'	seh-mü-sahk'
Sendai (Jap.)	sĕn'-dä-ē	sen'-dah-ee
Seneca (N.Y.)	sĕn'-ə-kə	sen'-uh-kuh
Sened (Tun.)	sĕ'-nĕd	seh'-ned
Senegal (Fr. W. Afr.)	*Eng.* sĕn'-ə-gôl'	sen'-uh-gawl'

French *Sénégal*, sĕ-nĕ-gäl' [seh-neh-gahl'].

Senegalese	sĕn'-ə-gə-lēz'	sen'-uh-guh-leez'
	or sĕn'-ə-gô-lēz'	sen'-uh-gaw-leez'
Senegambia (Fr. W. Afr.)	sĕn-ə-găm'-bĭ-ə	sen-uh-gam'-bi-uh

French *Sénégambie*, sĕ-nĕ-gäN-bē' [seh-neh-gahN-bee'].

senhor, senhora,	sĭ-nyôr', sĭ-nyô'-rə,	si-nyor', si-nyo'-ruh,
senhorita	sĭ-nyô-rē'-tə	si-nyo-ree'-tuh

Portuguese courtesy titles, comparable to English *Mr.*, *Mrs.*, and *Miss*.

Senia, la (Alg.)	sĕ'-nyä, lä	seh'-nyah, lah
Senigallia (It.)	sĕ-nē-gäl'-lyä	seh-nee-gahl'-lyah
Senio (It.)	sĕn'-yô	sen'-yo
Senj (Yugosl.)	sĕn'(y)	sen'(y)

Italian *Segna*, sĕ'-nyä [seh'-nyah]. Hungarian *Zengg*, zĕng' [zeng'].

Senja (Nor., isl.)	sĕn'-yä	sen'-yah
Senjski Rudnik (Yugosl.)	sĕn'(y)-skĭ	sen'(y)-ski
	rōōd'-nĭk	rood'-nik
Senlis (Fr.)	*Eng.* sĕn'-lĭs	sen'-lis
	Fr. säN-lēs'	sahN-lees'
Senonches (Fr.)	sə-nôNsh'	suh-noNsh'
señor, señora, señorita	sĕ-nyôr', sĕ-nyô'-rä,	seh-nyor', seh-nyo'-
	sĕ-nyô-rē'-tä	rah, seh-nyo-ree'-
		tah

Spanish courtesy titles, comparable to English *Mr.*, *Mrs.*, and *Miss*.

Sens (Fr.)	säNs'	sahNs'
Senta (Yugosl.)	sĕn'-tä	sen'-tah

Hungarian *Zenta*, zĕn'-tŏ [zen'-to].

Sentani (NEI, lake)	sĕn-tä'-nē	sen-tah'-nee
Senyavin (Oc., Carolines)	sĕ'-nyä-vĭn	seh'-nyah-vin
Seoul (Korea)	*Eng.* sōl'	sohl'

Séoul is the French spelling, and American dictionaries have accordingly recommended the pronunciation sĕ-ōōl' [seh-ool']. To the contrary, missionaries born there, returned service men, and Mr. William Costello, CBS correspondent in Korea, insist that the English pronunciation is, and has been, simply sōl' [sohl'], like the words *soul* and *sole*. Korean sô-ŏ͞ol' [saw-ul'] or sô'əl [saw'-uhl]. (PCGN lists "Korean Syöul" and German *Söul*, but my Korean informants did not front the vowel.) Often called by Koreans kyŭng sŭng [kyuhng suhng], the Korean pronunciation of a Chinese name of the city. Japanese *Keijō*, kā'-jō [kay'-joh]. Chinese *Han-ch'êng*, hän-chŭng [hahn-chuhng].

Sépet (Fr., cape)	sĕ-pĕ'	seh-peh'
Also spelled *Cepet*.		
Sepik (N.E. New Guinea, riv.)	sĕ'-pēk	seh'-peek
Sepinggan (Borneo)	sĕ-pĭng'-gän	seh-ping'-gahn
Sepoy (India)	sē'-poi	see'-poi
Sepsiszentgyörgy (Rum.)	See *Sfântul Gheorghe*.	
Septeuil (Fr.)	sĕp-tû'(y)	sep-tœ'(y)
Sepulveda (Calif.)	*Eng.* sə-pŭl'-və-də	suh-puhl'-vuh-duh
	Sp. sĕ-pōol'-vĕ-dä	seh-pool'-veh-dah
Serafimovich (Rus.)	sĕ-rä-fĭ-mô'-vĭch	seh-rah-fi-mo'-vich
Seraing (Belg.)	sə-räN'	suh-raN'
Serajevo (Yugosl.) See *Sarajevo*.		
Serang (NEI)	sĕ-räng'	seh-rahng'
Serbariu (Sard.)	sĕr-bä-rē'-ōo	sehr-bah-ree'-oo
Serbia (Yugosl.)	*Eng.* sûr'-bĭ-ə	suhr'-bi-uh
Serb-Croat *Srbija*, sər'-bĭ-yä [suhr'-bi-yah].		
Serbino (Rus.)	sĕr'-bĭ-nŏ	sehr'-bi-no
Serchio (It., riv.)	sĕr'-kyô	sehr'-kyo
Serdobol (Fin. >Rus.)	sĕr'-dŏ-bŏl(y)	sehr'-do-bol(y)
Finnish *Sortavala*, q.v.		
Seret (Pol. >Rus., riv.)	sĕ'-rĕt	seh'-ret
Sergiopol (Rus.)	sĕr-gĭ-ô'-pŏl(y)	sehr-gi-o'-pol(y)
Sergipe (Brazil)	sĕr-zhē'-pĭ	sehr-zhee'-pi
Sergo (Rus.)	sĕr'-gŏ	sehr'-go
Sergo Ivanovskaya (Rus.)	sĕr'-gô ē-vä'-nŏf-skä-yä	sehr'-go ee-vah'-nof-skah-yah
Seria (Borneo)	sĕ-rē'-ä	seh-ree'-ah
Seriphos (Gr., isl.)	sĕ'-rĭ-fô(s)	seh'-ri-fo(s)
Sermaises (Fr.)	sĕr-mĕz'	sehr-mez'
Sermenin (Yugosl.)	sĕr'-mĕ-nĭn	sehr'-meh-nin
Sermoneta (It.)	sĕr-mô-nĕ'-tä	sehr-mo-neh'-tah
Serock (Pol.)	sĕ'-rôtsk	seh'-rotsk
Seroei (NEI)	sĕ-rōo'-ē	seh-roo'-ee
Also spelled *Serui*.		
Serpets (Pol.) See *Sierpc*.		
Serpukhov (Rus.)	sĕr'-pōo-hŏf	sehr'-poo-hof
Serqueux (Fr.)	sĕr-kû'	sehr-kœ'

Serrai (Gr.)	sĕ'-rĕ	seh'-reh
Also called *Serres*, sĕ'-rĕs [seh'-res].		
Serrano, Carlos I.	sĕr-rä'-nô,	sehr-rah'-no,
(Mex. polit.)	kär'-lôs	kahr'-los
Serrano Suñer, Ramón	sĕ-rä'-nô sōō-nyĕr',	se-rah'-no soo-nyehr',
(Sp. polit.)	rä-môn'	rah-mon'
Serres (Fr.)	sĕr'	sehr'
Serres (Gr.) See *Serrai*.		
Serrone (It.)	sĕr-rô'-nĕ	sehr-ro'-neh
Serui (NEI) See *Seroei*.		
Servech (Pol., riv.) See *Serwecz*.		
Serwecz (Pol., riv.)	sĕr'-vĕch	sehr'-vech
Russian spelling *Servech*.		
Sessano (It.)	sĕs-sä'-nô	ses-sah'-no
Sète (Fr.)	sĕt'	set'
Setesdal (Nor.)	sä'-təs-däl	say'-tuhs-dahl
Setia (Crete, town, gulf)	sĕ-tē'-ä	see-tee'-ah
Sétif (Alg.)	sĕ-tēf'	seh-teef'
Setterich (Ger.)	zĕt'-ə-rĭk(h)	zet'-uh-rik(h)
Setúbal (Port.)	sĕ-tōō'-bäl	seh-too'-bahl
Seudre (Fr., riv.)	sû'dr	sœ'dr
Seulimeum (NEI,	sû-lē-mä'-əm	sœ-lee-may'-uhm
Sumatra)		
Seulles (Fr., riv.)	sûl'	sœl'
Sevastopol (Rus.)	*Eng.* sĭ-väs'-tə-pōl	si-vahs'-tuh-pohl
	Rus. sĕ-väs-tô'-pŏl(y)	seh-vahs-to'-pol(y)
Sevenum (Neth.)	sä'-və-nəm	say'-vuh-nuhm
Sévérac (Fr.)	sĕ-vĕ-räk'	seh-veh-rahk'
Severnaya (Rus.)	sĕ'-vĕr-nä-yä	seh'-vehr-nah-yah
Severnaya Dvina (Rus.,	sĕ'-vĕr-nä-yä dvĭ-nä'	seh'-vehr-nah-yah
riv.)		dvi-nah'
Sevilla (Sp.)	sĕ-vē'-lyä *or* -yä	seh-vee'-lyah *or* -yah
English *Seville*, sə-vĭl' [suh-vil'] *or* sĕ'-vĭl [seh'-vil].		
Sevlievo (Bulg.)	sĕ'-vlĭ-yĕ-vŏ	seh'-vli-yeh-vo
Sèvre (Fr., riv.)	sĕ'vr	seh'vr
Sèvres (Fr.)	sĕ'vr	seh'vr
Sevsk (Rus.)	sĕfsk'	sefsk'
Sewanee (Tenn.)	sĭ-wô'-nĭ	si-waw'-ni
Seward (Alaska)	syōō'-ərd	syoo'-uhrd
Sexmoán (P.I.)	sĕks-mwän'	seks-mwahn'
Seychelles (Ind. Oc.)	sä-shĕl' *or* sä-shĕlz'	say-shel' *or* say-shelz'
Seyne, la (Fr.)	sĕn', lä	sen', lah
Seyss Inquart, Artur	*Eng.* sīs' ĭng'-kwärt	sais' ing'-kwahrt
von (Ger. polit.)	*Ger.* zīs' ĭng'-kvärt	zais' ing'-kvahrt

Sézanne (Fr.)	sĕ-zän′	seh-zahn′
Sezzè (It., north of Milan)	sĕt-sĕ′	set-seh′
Sezze (It., south of Rome)	sĕt′-sĕ	set′-seh
Sfântul Gheorghe (Rum.)	sfûn′-tōōl gyôr′-gĕ	sfuhn′-tul gyor′-geh

Hungarian *Sepsiszentgyörgy*, shĕp′-shĭ-sĕn′-dyûrd(y) [shep′-shi-sen′-dyœrd(y)].

Sfax (Tun.)	sfäks′	sfahks′
Sforza, Carlo (It. polit.)	sfôr′-tsä, kär′-lô	sfor′-tsah, kahr′-lo
Sgouritsas, Constantinos (Gr. polit.)	zgōō-rē′-tsäs, kô-stän-dē′-nôs	zgoo-ree′tsahs, ko-stahn-dee′-nos
's Gravendeel (Neth.)	sk(h)rä′-vən-dāl′	sk(h)rah′-vuhn-dayl′
's Gravenhage (Neth.)	sk(h)rä′-vən-hä′-k(h)ə	sk(h)rah′-vuhn-hah′-k(h)uh

The common abbreviated form is *Den Haag*, dən häk(h)′ [duhn hahk(h)′]. English *The Hague*, q.v.

's Gravenzande (Neth.)	sk(h)rä′-vən-zän′-də	sk(h)rah′-vuhn-zahn′-duh
Sgurgola (It.)	zgōōr′-gô-lä	zgoor′-go-lah
Shabelsk (Rus.)	shä-bĕl(y)sk′	shah-bel(y)sk′
Shaduzup (Burma)	shä′-dōō-zŭp′	shah′-doo-zuhp′
Shafaat Ahmed Khan (Indian polit.)	shä-fät′ ä′-mĕd kän′	sha-faht′ ah′-med kahn′
shah	shä′	shah′

A title, usually of a supreme ruler, in the Middle East. It may be disregarded in alphabetical listing.

Shah Mamud Khan (Afghan polit.)	shä′ mä-mōōd′ kän′	shah′ mah-mood′ kahn′
Shah Muhammad Pahlavi (Ruler of Iran)	shä′ mŏŏ-häm′-məd pä-lä-vē′	shah′ mu-hahm′-muhd pah-lah-vee′
Shah Riza Pahlavi (Former ruler of Iran)	shä′ rē′-zə pä-lä-vē′	shah′ ree′-zuh pah-lah-vee′
Shahi (Iran)	shä′-hē′	shah′-hee′

Shahrir, Sutan (Indo. polit.) See *Sjahrir, Soetan*.

Shahrud (Iran)	shä-rōōd′	shah-rood′
Shakhnovo (Rus.)	shäk(h)′-nŏ-vŏ	shahk(h)′-no-vo
Shakhty (Rus.)	shäk(h)′-tĭ	shahk(h)′-ti
Shang Chên (Ch. general)	shäng jŭn	shahng juhn
Shang-hai (Ch., Kiangsu)	*Eng.* shăng-hī *Ch.* shäng-hī	shang-hai shahng-hai
Shang-jao (Ch., Kiangsi)	shäng-rou	shahng-rau

Shang-kao (Ch., Kiangsi) shäng-gou   shahng-gau

Shangri La   shăng-grĭ lä'   shang-gri lah'

Questioned by newspaper reporters, President Roosevelt humorously replied that the planes that bombed Tokio, April 18, 1942, might have flown from *Shangri La*, the imaginary land of James Hilton's *Lost Horizon*. The author writes, August 23, 1946, ". . . accent on the last syllable, and the syllables as follows: 'Shang' to rhyme with 'hang,' 'gri' as in 'grisly' and the 'La' like the French definite article. This is the pronunciation I intended for it from the outset and also the way most other people have pronounced it, including, I believe, the late President."

Shang-yü (Ch., Chekiang)	shäng-yü	shahng-yü
Shang-yu (Ch., Kiangsi)	shäng-yō	shahng-yoh
Shan-hsien (Ch., Shantung)	shän-shyĕn	shahn-shyen
Shannon (Eire, riv.)	shăn'-ən	shan'-uhn
Shan-si (Ch., prov.)	*Eng.* shăn-sē	shan-see
	Ch. shän-sē	shahn-see
Shan States (Burma)	shăn' *or* shän'	shan' *or* shahn'
Shan-t'ow (Ch., Kwangtung)	shän-tō	shahn-toh
Also called *Swatow*, q.v.		
Shan-tung (Ch., prov.)	*Eng.* shăn-tŏong	shan-tung
	Ch. shän-dŏong	shahn-dung
Shao-hsing *or* Shao-hing (Ch., Chekiang)	shou-shĭng *or* shou-hĭng	shau-shing shau-hing
Shao-yang (Ch., Hunan)	shou-yäng	shau-yahng
Also called *Pao-ching*, q.v.		
Shaposhnikov, Boris (Rus. general)	shä'-pŏsh-nĭ-kŏf, bŏ-rēs'	shah'-posh-ni-kof, bo-rees'
Sharifudin Amir (Indo. polit.)	shä'-rē-foo'-dĭn ă-mēr'	shah'-ree-foo'-din a-meer'
Also spelled *Sjarifoedin*.		
Sharon (Pal.)	shăr'-ən	shehr'-uhn
Sharq el Urdunn (Arabia)	See *Trans-Jordan*.	
Sha-shih (Ch., Hupeh)	shä-shû	shah-shœ
Sha-si *or* Sha-shih (Ch., Hupeh)	*Eng.* shä-sē *Ch.* shä-shû	shah-see shah-shuh
shatt (Arabic, "salt lake")	See *chott*.	
Shatt al Arab (Iran, Iraq, riv.)	shăt' əl ä'-räb	shat' uhl ah'-rahb
Shavli (Lith.)	*Rus.* shäv'-lĭ	shahv'-li
Lithuanian *Šiauliai*, q.v.		

Shawiya (Mor.) French *Chaouia*, q.v.

Sha-yang (Ch., Hupeh)	shä-yäng	shah-yahng
Shchara (Pol. >Rus., riv.)	shchä'-rä	shchah'-rah

Polish spelling *Szczara*.

Shcherbakov, Aleksei	shchĕr-bä-kŏf',	shchehr-bah-kof',
(Rus. polit.)	ä-lĕk-sā'	ah-lek-say'
Shchigry (Rus.)	shchē'-grĭ	shchee'-gri
Shchuchin (Pol. >Rus.)	shchoo'-chĭn	shchoo'-chin

Polish spelling *Szczuczyn*.

Shebekino (Rus.)	shĕ-bĕ'-kĭ-nŏ	sheh-beh'-ki-no
's Heer Arendskerke (Neth.)	sär ä'-rənts-kĕr'-kə	sayr ah'-ruhnts-kehr'-kuh
sheik, sheikh	shēk' *or* shāk'	sheek' *or* shayk'

The first pronunciation is usual in American English, the second in British English. Arabic *shaykh* or *sheykh*. A title or honorific which is disregarded in alphabetical listing.

Shek-lung (Ch., Kwangtung)	shû-lŏŏng	shœ-lung

Also spelled *Shih-lung*.

Shelikof (Alaska, str.)	shĕl'-ə-kŏf'	shel'-uh-kof'
Shëngjin (Alb.)	shən'-gyĭn	shuhn'-gyin

Italian *San Giovanni di Medua*, q.v.

Shëngjini (Alb.) See *Shëngjin*.

Shenjt, Mal i (Alb., mt.)	shĕn(y)t', mäl' ē	shen(y)t', mahl' ee
Shên-si (Ch., prov.)	*Eng.* shĕn-sē	shen-see
	Ch. shŭn-shē	shuhn-shee
Shên-yang (Manchu.)	shŭn-yäng	shuhn-yahng
Shepetovka (Rus.)	shĕ-pĕ-tôf'-kä	sheh-peh-tof'-kah
's Hertogenbosch (Neth.)	sĕr'-tō-k(h)ən-bôs'	sehr'-toh-k(h)uhn-bos'

The common abbreviated form is *Den Bos*, dən bôs' [duhn bos']. French *Bois le Duc*, bwä lə dük' [bwah luh dük'].

shi	shē	shee

An element, meaning *city*, in Japanese place names.

Shibertui (Rus.)	shĭ-bĕr-tŏŏ'ĭ	shi-behr-too'i
Shibin el Kom (Egypt)	shĭ-bēn' ĕl kôm'	shi-been' el kom'
Shibusawa, Masao (Jap. executive)	shē-bŏŏ'-sä'-wä', mä-sä'-ô'	shee-boo'-sah'-wah', mah-sah'-o'
Shibuya (Jap.)	shē'-bŏŏ-yä	shee'-boo-yah
Shidehara, Kijirō (Jap. polit.)	shē-dĕ'-hä-rä, kē-jē'-rô'	shee-deh'-hah-rah, kee-jee'-ro'
Shidlovets (Pol.) See *Szydłowiec*.		
Shiga (Jap.)	shē'-gä	shee'-gah
Shigatse (Tibet)	shē-gä'-tsĕ	shee-gah'-tseh

Shigemitsu, Mamoru (Jap. diplomat)	shē-gĕ'-mē-tsōō or shē-gĕ'-mēts, mä-mô'-rōō'	shee-geh'-mee-tsoo shee-geh'-meets, mah-mo'-roo'
Shih-ch'êng (Ch., Kiangsi)	shû-chŭng	shuh-chuhng
Shih-chia-chwang (Ch., Hopeh)	shû-jyä-jwäng	shuh-jyah-jwahng

Also spelled *Shih-kia-chwang.*

Shih-fêng (Manchu.)	shû-fŭng	shuh-fuhng

Shih-kia-chwang (Ch., Hopeh)   See *Shih-chia-chwang.*

Shih-li-miao (Ch., Honan)	shû-lē-myou	shuh-lee-myau
Shih-mên (Ch., Hunan)	shû-mŭn	shuh-muhn
Shih-p'ai (Ch., Hupeh)	shû-pī	shuh-pai
Shih-shou (Ch., Hupeh)	shû-shŏ	shuh-shoh
Shih-wei (Manchu.)	shû-wä	shuh-way
Shijak (Alb.)	shē'-yäk	shee'-yahk

Shijaku (Alb.)   See *Shijak.*

Shikapur (India)	shē-kä'-pŏŏr'	shee-kah'-pur'
Shikoku (Jap.)	shē-kô'-kōō or shkôk'	shee-ko'-koo shkok'
Shilka (Rus., riv.)	shĭl'-kä	shil'-kah
Shillong (India)	shĭl-lông'	shil-long'
shima	shē-mä	shee-mah

An element, meaning *island*, in Japanese place names. See *jima.*

Shimane (Jap.)	shē-mä'-nĕ'	shee-mah'-meh'
Shimbashi (Jap.)	shēm'-bä-shē	sheem'-bah-shee
shimbun	shēm-bōōn'	sheem-boon'

A Japanese word meaning *newspaper.* In compounds the accent shifts to the first syllable.

Shimizu (Jap.)	shē'-mē-zōō	shee'-mee-zoo
Shimonoseki (Jap.)	*Eng.* shĭm'-ə-nə-sä'-kĭ *Jap.* shē-mô'-nô'-sĕ-kē	shim'-uh-nuh-say'-ki shee-mo'-no'-seh-kee
Shimsk (Rus.)	shĭmsk'	shimsk'
Shingishū (Korea)	shĭng-gē'-shōō	shing-gee'-shoo
Shintō (Japanese religion)	*Eng.* shĭn'-tō *Jap.* shēn'-tô	shin'-toh sheen'-to
Shipka (Bulg., pass)	shĭp'-kä	ship'-kah
Shiraz (Iran)	shē-räz'	shee-rahz'
Shizuoka (Jap.)	shē-zōō'-ô-kä	shee-zoo'-o-kah
Shklov (Rus.)	shklôf'	shklof'
Shkodër *or* Shkodra (Alb., city; Balkan lake)		See *Scutari.*
Shkumbi (Alb., riv.)	shkōōm'-bē	shkoom'-bee

Latin *Genusus.*

Shkumbini (Alb., riv.) See *Shkumbi*.

Shkva (Pol., riv.) See *Szkwa*.

Sholapur (India) shō-lə-pŏŏr' shoh-luh-pur'

Sholokhov, M. A. shŏ'-lŏ-hŏf · sho'-lo-hof
(Rus. writer)

Shoshone (Am. Indian) shō-shō'-nĭ shoh-shoh'-ni
A place name in Idaho and Wyoming. The pronunciation of two
syllables, shō'-shōn' [shoh'-shohn'] is not recommended.

Shostakovich, Dmitri shŏ-stä-kŏ'-vĭch, sho-stah-ko'-vich,
Dmitriyevich dmē'-trē dmee'-tree
(Rus. composer) dmē'-trĭ-yĕ-vĭch dmee'-tri-yeh-vich

shotō shŏ-tô sho-to
An element, meaning *archipelago*, in Japanese place names.

shott (Arabic, "salt lake") See *chott*.

Shqipni (or *Albania*) shkyēp'-nē shkyeep'-nee
Also called *Shqipnija*, *Shqipri*, and *Shqiprija*. English *Albania*, q.v.

Shubashich, Ivan (Yugosl. polit.) See *Šubašić*.

Shu-fu (Ch., Sinkiang) shōō-fōō shoo-foo
Also called *Kashgar*, q.v.

Shukairy *or* Shukri (Arab. polit.) See *Ahmed Shukairy*.

Shukry el Kuwatly shŏŏ-krē' ĕl kŏŏ-wät'- shu-kree' el ku-waht'-
(Syrian polit.) lē lee

Shumagin (Alaska, isl.) shōō'-mə-gĭn shoo'-muh-gin

Shumen (Bulg.) shōō'-mĕn(y) shu'-men(y)

Shushica (Alb., riv.) See *Shushicĕ*.

Shushicĕ (Alb., riv.) shōō-shē'-tsə shoo-shee'-tsuh

Shuya (Rus., riv.) shōō'-yä shoo'-yah

Shvernik, Nikolai M. shvĕr'-nĭk, nē-kŏ-lī' shvehr'-nik, nee-ko-
(Rus. polit.) lai'

Shwebo (Burma) shwā'-bō' shway'-boh'

Shwedaung (Burma) shwā'-doung' shway'-daung'

Shweli (Burma, riv.) shwā'-lē' shway'-lee'

Siagne (It., riv.) syä'-nyĕ syah'-nyeh

Sialkot (India) sĭ-äl'-kōt' si-ahl'-koht'

Siam *or* Thai sī-ăm' *or* tī' sai-am' *or* tai'

Si-an *or* Hsi-an (Ch., sē-än *or* shē-än see-ahn *or* shee-ahn
Shensi)
Also called *Ch'ang-an*, q.v.

Siandos *or* Sandos, sē-än'-dôs *or* see-ahn'-dos *or*
Georgios (Gr. polit.) sän'-dôs, yôr'-yôs sahn'-dos, yor'-yos

Siang- (Ch.) See *Hsiang-*.

Sianuk, Norodom sē-ä-nōōk', see-ah-nook'
(Cambodian prince) nô-rô-dôm' no-ro-dom'

Siapón (P.I.) syä-pôn' syah-pon'

Siapu (Ch., Fukien)   syä-po͞o   syah-poo
    Mandarin *Hsia-p'u*, approximately shyä-po͞o [shyah-poo]. Also called
    Fu-ning, fo͞o-nĭng [foo-ning].

Siasi (P.I.)   sē-ä'-sē   see-ah'-see

Siatista (Gr.)   sē-ä'-tē-stä   see-ah'-tee-stah

Šiauliai (Lith.)   shyou'-lyī   shyau'-lyai
    Russian *Shavli*, q.v. German *Schaulen*, shou'-lən [shau'-luhn].

Sibanicú (Cuba)   sē-bä-nē-ko͞o'   see-bah-nee-koo'.

Sibari (It.)   sē'-bä-rē   see'-bah-ree
    The ancient form is *Sybaris*, pronounced in *Eng.* sĭb'-ə-rĭs [sib'-uh-ris].

Sibelius, Jean (Fin.   sĭ-bā'-lyo͝os, zhäN'   si-bay'-lyus, zhahN'
    composer)

Šibenik (Yugosl.)   shē'-bĕ'-nĭk   shee'-beh'-nik
    Italian *Sebenico*, q.v.

Siberut *or* Siberoet (NEI,   sē-bə-ro͞ot'   see-buh-root'
    Mentawai)

Sibiu (Rum.)   sē-byo͝o'   see-byu'
    Hungarian *Szeben*, sĕ'-bĕn [seh'-ben], and *Nagyszeben*, nŏt'(y)-
    [not'(y)-].

Sibnica (Yugosl.)   sēb'-nĭ-tsä   seeb'-ni-tsah

Sibolga (NEI, Sumatra)   sē-bôl'-gä   see-bol'-gah

Sibret (Belg.)   sē-brĕ'   see-breh'

Sibu (Sarawak)   sē'-bo͞o   see'-boo

Sibug (P.I., riv.)   sē-bo͞og'   see-boog'

Sibuguey (P.I.)   sē-bo͞o-gä'   see-boo-gay'

Sibulan (P.I.)   sē-bo͞o'-län   see-boo'-lahn

Sibutú (P.I.)   sē-bo͞o-to͞o'   see-boo-too'

Sibuyán (P.I.)   *Eng.* sē-bo͞o'-yän   see-boo'-yahn
                        native sē-bo͞o-yän'   see-boo-yahn'

Sibylla (Swedish princess) sē-bül'-ä   see-bül'-ah

Sićevo (Yugosl.)   sē'-chĕ-vô   see'-cheh-vo

Si-ch'ang (Ch., Sikang)   sē-chäng   see-chahng
    Also called *Hsi-ch'ang*, shē-chäng [shee-chahng].

Sicily (It., isl.)   *Eng.* sĭs'-ĭ-lĭ   sis'-i-li
    Italian *Sicilia*, sē-chē'-lyä [see-chee'-lyah].

Siculiania (Sicily)   sē-ko͞o-lyä'-nä   see-koo-lyah'-nah

Šid (Yugosl.)   shēd'   sheed'

Sidari (Corfù)   sē-dä'-rē   see-dah'-ree

Siderno Marina (It.)   sē-dĕr'-nȯ mä-rē'-nä   see-dehr'-no mah-ree'-
                                                 nah

Siderokastron (Gr.)   sē-dĕ-rô'-kä-strô(n)   see-deh-ro'-kah-
                                                 stro(n)

    Also called *Demir Hissar*, q.v.

Sideron (Crete, point)   sē'-dĕ-rȯ(n)   see'-dee-ro(n)

Sideville (Fr.)	sēd-vēl′	seed-veel′
sidi	sē′-dē	see′-dee

In Arabic names an element, sometimes omitted, meaning *saint*.

Sidi Abdallah *or* Abdullah (Tun.)	sē′-dē äb-dŭl′-lə	see′-dee ahb-duhl′-luh
Sidi Abu el Rahman (Egypt)	sē′-dē ä′-boō ĕr rä-măn′	see′-dee ah′-boo ehr ra-man′
Sidi Ahmed (Tun.)	sē′-dē ä′-mĕd	see′-dee ah′-med
Sidi Atman (Tun.)	sē′-dē ät-măn′	see′-dee aht-man′
Sidi Barrani (Egypt)	sē′-dē bä-rä′-nē	see′-dee bah-rah′-nee
Sidi-bel-Abbès (Alg.)	sē′-dē-bĕl-ä-bĕs′	see′-dee-bel-ah-bes′
Sidi Belgasem (Libya)	sē′-dē bĕl-gä′-sĕm	see′-dee bel-gah′-sem
Sidi Bou Zid (Tun.)	sē′-dē boō zēd′	see′-dee boo zeed′
Sidi Ferruch (Alg.)	sē′-dē fĕr-roōk′	see′-dee fehr-rook′
Sidi Haneish (Egypt)	sē′-dē hä-nāsh′	see′-dee hah-naysh′
Sidi Mar(r)our (Tun.)	sē′-dē mä-roōr′	see′-dee mah-rur′
Sidi Nair (Tun.)	sē′-dē nä-ēr′	see′-dee nah-eer′
Sidi Nsir (Tun.)	sē′-dē nə-sēr′	see′-dee nuh-seer′
Sidi Omar (Libya)	sē′-dē ō′-mär	see′-dee oh′-mahr
Sidi Rezegh (Libya)	sē′-dē rĕ-zĕg′	see′-dee reh-zeg′

Sidky Pasha, Ismail (Egypt. polit.) See *Ismail Sidky Pasha*.

Sidon (Lebanon)	*Eng.* sīd′n	said′n

Also called *Saida*, q.v.

Sidra (Libya)	sĭd′-rə	sid′-ruh

Also called *Sirte*, q.v.

Siedlce (Pol.)	shĕ′dl-tsĕ	she′dl-tseh

Russian *Sedlets*, sĕd′-lĕts [sed′-lets].

Sieg (Ger., riv.)	zēk(h)′	zeek(h)′
Siegburg (Ger.)	zēk(h)′-boŏrk(h)	zeek(h)′-burk(h)
Siegen (Ger.)	zē′-gən	zee′-guhn
Siegenheim (Ger.)	zē′-gən-hīm	zee′-guhn-haim
Siegfried (Ger.)	*Eng.* sēg′-frēd	seeg′-freed
	Ger. zēk′(h)-frēt	zeek′(h)-freet
Siegmar (Ger.)	zēk(h)′-mär	zeek(h)′-mahr
Siemreap (Indo-Ch.)	sē′-əm-rĭ′-əp	see′-uhm-ri′-uhp
Siena (It.)	*Eng.* sĭ-ĕn′-ə	si-en′-uh
	It. syĕ′-nä	syeh′-nah
Sienne (Fr., riv.)	syĕn′	syen′
Sieradz (Pol.)	shĕ′-räts	sheh′-rahts
Sieraków (Pol.)	shĕ-rä′-koŏf	sheh-rah′-kuf
Sierentz (Fr.)	sē-rĕnts′	see-rents′
Sierpc (Pol.)	shĕrpts′	shehrpts′

Russian *Serpets*, sĕr′-pĕts [sehr′-pets].

Sierra Leone (Br. Afr.)	sĭ-ĕr′-ə lĭ-ō′-nĭ	si-ehr′-uh li-oh′-ni

Sierra Madre (Mex., mts.)	syĕr'-rä mä'-drĕ	syehr'-rah mah'-dreh
Sierra Morena (Sp., mts.)	syĕ'-rä mŏ-rĕ'-nä	syeh'-rah mo-reh'-nah
Sierra Nevada (Calif., Sp., mts.)	*Eng.* sĭ-ĕr'-ə nə-văd'-ə *or* nə-väd'-ə	si-ehr'-uh nuh-vad'-uh *or* nuh-vahd'-uh
	Sp. syĕ'-rä nĕ-vä'-dä	syeh'-rah neh-vah'-dah
Siersdorf (Ger.)	zērs'-dôrf	zeers'-dorf
Sieve (It., riv.)	syĕ'-vĕ	syeh'-veh
Sigale (Alg., cape)	sē-gäl'	see-gahl'
Sigdal (Nor.)	sĭg'-däl	sig'-dahl
Sigean, Étang de (Fr., lagoon)	sē-zhäN', ĕ-täN' də	see-zhahN', eh-tahN' duh
Sighet (Rum.)	sē-gĕt'	see-get'

Hungarian *Mármarossziget*, mär'-mŏ-rôsh-sĭ'-gĕt [mahr'-mo-rosh-si'-get].

Sighişoara (Rum.)	sē-gē-shwä'-rä	see-gee-shwah'-rah

Hungarian *Segesvár*, shĕ'-gĕsh-vär [sheh'-gesh-vahr].

Sigli (NEI, Sumatra)	sē'-glē	see'-glee
signor, signora, signorina	sē-nyôr', sē-nyô'-rä, sē-nyô-rē'-nä	see-nyor', see-nyo'-rah, see-nyo-ree'-nah

Italian courtesy titles, comparable to English *Mr.*, *Mrs.*, and *Miss.*

Sikaiana (Oc., Solomons)	sē-kī-ä'-nä	see-kai-ah'-nah
Si-k'ang *or* Hsi-k'ang (Ch., prov.)	*Eng.* sē-käng	see-kang
	Ch. shē-käng	shee-kahng
Sikes, Bob (U.S. representative)	sīks'	saiks'
Sikh (India, sect)	sēk'	seek'
Sikinos (Gr.)	sē'-kē-nôs	see'-kee-nos
Sikirica (Yugosl.)	sē'-kĭ-rĭ-tsä	see'-ki-ri-tsah
Sikorsky, Igor I. (Rus. Am. engineer)	sĭ-kôr'-skĭ, ē'-gôr	si-kor'-ski, ee'-gor
Sikorsky, Władysław (Pol. polit.)	sĭ-kôr'-skĭ, vlä-dĭ'-släf	si-kor'-ski, vlah-di'-slahf
Silang (P.I.)	sē-läng'	see-lahng'
Silba (Yugosl.)	sēl'-bä	seel'-bah

Italian *Selve*, q.v.

Silchar (India)	sēl'-chär'	seel'-chahr'
Silesia (Ger., Pol., Cz.)	*Eng.* sĭ-lē'-shə *or* sī-	si-lee'-shuh *or* sai-

German *Schlesien*, shlä'-zĭ-ən [shlay'-zi-uhn]. Polish *Śląsk*, shlôNsk' [shloNsk']. Czech *Slezsko*, slĕs'-kô [sles'-ko].

Siliana (Tun.)	sēl-yă'-nä	seel-ya'-nah
Silistra (Rum.)	*Eng.* sĭ-lĭs'-trə	si-lis'-truh
	Rum. sē-lē'-strä	see-lee'-strah

Bulgarian *Silistria*, (Eng.) sĭ-lĭs'-trĭ-ə [si-lis'-tri-uh]; (Bulg.) sĭ-lē'-strĭ-yä [si-lee'-stri-yah].

Silistria (Rum.)   See *Silistra*.

Silivri (Turk.)	sē-lēv'-rē'	see-leev'-ree'
Šiljegovac (Yugosl.)	shē'-lyĕ'-gô-väts	shee'-lyeh'-go-vahts
Sillé le Guillaume (Fr.)	sē-yĕ lə gē-yōm'	see-yeh luh gee-yohm'
Šilutė (Lith.)	shē-lōō'-tĕ	shee-loo'-teh

Silva, Álvaro Alberto da Motta e (Braz. diplomat) See *Da Motta e Silva*.

Silva Peña, Eugenio (Guat. diplomat)	sēl'-vä pĕ'-nyä, ĕ-ōō-hĕ'-nyô	seel'-vah peh'-nyah, eh-oo-heh'-nyo
Silva, Valentim Benicio (Braz. polit.)	sēl'-və, vä-lən-tēN' bĕ-nē'-syōō	seel'-vuh, vah-luhn-teeN' beh-nee'-syu

Simalac *or* Simaluc (P.I.) See *Tataán*.

Simara (P.I.)	sē-mä'-rä	see-mah'-rah
Simbirsk (Rus.)	sĭm-bĕrsk'	sim-beersk'
Simbo (Oc., Solomons)	sĭm'-bô	sim'-bo
Simeon (Former king of Bulgaria)	*Eng.* sĭm'-ĭ-ən *Bulg.* sĭ-mĕ-ôn'	sim'-i-uhn si-meh-on'

Russian variant *Semën*, sĕ-myôn' [seh-myon'].

Simeria (Rum.)	sē-mĕ-rē'-ä	see-meh-ree'-ah
Simeto (Sicily, riv.)	sē-mĕ'-tô	see-meh'-to
Simeuloee *or* Simeulue (NEI)	sē-mû-lōō'-ĕ	see-mœ-loo'-eh
Simferopol (Rus.)	sĭm-fĕ-rô'-pŏl(y)	sim-feh-ro'-pol(y)

Also called *Ak Mechet*, äk' mĕ-chĕt' [ahk' meh-chet'].

Simi (Dodec.)   See *Syme*.

Simić, Stanoye (Yugosl. polit.)	sē'-mĭch, stä'-nô'-yĕ	see'-mich, stah'-no'-yeh

Also spelled *Simich* and *Simitch*.

Simich, *or* Simitch, Stanoye (Yugosl. polit.) See *Simić, Stanoye*.

Simla (India)	sĭm'-lə	sim'-luh
Simmerath (Ger.)	zĭm'-ə-rät	zim'-uh-raht
Simmern (Ger.)	zĭm'-ərn	zim'-uhrn
Simões Lópes (Braz. polit.)	sē-moiNs' lô'-pĭs	see-moiNs' lo'-pis
Simola (Fin.)	sē'-mô-lä	see'-mo-lah
Simpelveld (Neth.)	sĭm'-pəl-vĕlt	sim'-puhl-velt
Simplon (Switz.)	*Eng.* sĭm'-plŏn *Fr.* säN-plôN'	sim'-plon saN-ploN'
Simrishamn (Sw.)	sēm'-rēs-hämn	seem'-rees-hahmn
Sin (Fr.)	säN'	saN'

Sinaia (Rum.)	*Eng.* sə-nĭ′-yə	suh-nai′-yuh
	Rum. sē-nä′-yä	see-nah′-yah
Sinaloa (Mex.)	*Eng.* sĭn′-ə-lō′-ə	sin′-uh-loh′-uh
	Sp. sē-nä-lô′-ä	see-nah-lo′-ah
Sinauen (Libya)	sĭ-nä′-wĕn	si-nah′-wen
Sinbaungwe (Burma)	sĭn-boung-wĕ′	sin-baung-weh′
Sind (India)	sĭnd′	sind′
Sindol (P.I.)	sēn-dôl′	seen-dol′
Sindorf (Ger.)	zĭn′-dôrf	zin′-dorf
Sinelnikovo (Rus.)	sĭ-nĕl′(y)-nĭ-kŏ-vŏ	si-nel′(y)-ni-ko-vo
Singapore (Straits Settlements)	sĭng′-gə-pôr′	sing′-guh-por′

The pronunciation sĭng′-ə-pôr [sing′-uh-por] is common, though not authorized by the dictionaries. Malaysian sĭng-ä-pōō′-rə [sing-ah-poo′-ruh].

Singaradja (NEI, Bali)	sĭng′-gä-rä′-jä	sing′-gah-rah′-jah
Singen (Ger.)	zĭng′-ən	zing′-uhn
Singhalese (Ceylonese)	sĭng-gə-lēz′ *or* -lēs′	sing-guh-leez′ *or* -lees′
Singora (Siam)	sĭng-gô′-rä	sing-gaw′-rah

Siamese *Songkhla*, sŏng-klä′ [song-klah′].

Sing-sing-sia *or* Hsing-hsing-hsia (Ch., Sinkiang-Kansu)	shĭng-shĭng-shyä	shing-shing-shyah
Singu (Burma)	sĭn-gōō′	sin-goo′
Sining *or* Hsining (Ch., Chinghai)	shē-nĭng	shee-ning
Sinj (Yugosl.)	sēn′(y)	seen′(y)
Sinjajevina planina (Yugosl., mts.)	sē′-nyä′-yĕ-vĭ-nä plä′-nē′-nä	see′-nyah′-yeh-vi-nah plah′-nee′-nah
Sin-kiang *or* Hsin-kiang (Ch., prov.)	*Eng.* sĭn-kyăng	sin-kyang
	Ch. shĭn-jyäng	shin-jyahng
Sinn Fein (Irish party)	shĭn′ fān′	shin′ fayn′
Sinopoli (It.)	sē-nô′-pô-lē	see-no′-po-lee
Sint Anna Parochie (Neth., Het Bilt)	sĭnt än′-ä pä-rôk(h)′-ē	sint ahn′-ah pah-rok(h)′-ee
Sint Filipsland (Neth.)	sĭnt fĭ-lĭps′-länt	sint fi-lips′-lahnt
Sint Jacobi Parochie (Neth.,, Het Bilt)	sĭnt yä-kō′-bē pä-rôk(h)′-ē	sint yah-koh′-bee pah-rok(h)′-ee
Sint Janssteen (Neth.)	sĭnt yäns′-stän	sint yahns′-stayn
Sint Maartensdijk (Neth.)	sĭnt mär′-təns-dīk′	sint mahr′-tuhns-daik′
Sint Michielsgestel (Neth.)	sĭnt mē′-k(h)ēls-k(h)ĕs′-təl	sint mee′-k(h)eels-k(h)es′-tuhl
Sint Niklaas (Belg.)	sĭnt nē′-kläs	sint nee′-klahs

[494]

Sint Odilienberg (Neth.)	sĭnt ô-dē′-lyən-bĕrk(h)	sint′ o-dee′-lyuhn-behrk(h)
Sint Oedenrode (Neth.)	sĭnt ōō′-dən-rō′-də	sint oo′-duhn-roh′-duh
Sin-yang *or* Hsin-yang (Ch., Honan)	shĭn-yäng	shin-yahng
Sinz (Ger.)	zĭnts′	zints′
Sinzig (Ger.)	zĭn′-tsĭk(h)	zin′-tsik(h)
Siófok (Hung.)	shĭ′-ô-fôk	shi′-o-fok
Sioto (Ohio)	sī-ō′-tə	sai-oh′-tuh
Sioux (Am. Indian)	sōō′	soo′

An element in many place names.

Šipan (Yugosl.)	shē′-pän(y)	shee′-pahn(y)

Italian *Giupana*, q.v.

Siphnos (Gr., isl.)	sēf′-nô(s)	seef′-no(s)
Sipócot (P.I.)	sē-pô′-kôt	see-po′-kot
Sira (Nor., riv.)	sē′-rä	see′-rah
Siracusa (Sicily)	sē-rä-kōō′-zä	see-rah-koo′-zah

American *Syracuse*, sĭr′-ə-kyōōs [sihr′-uh-kyoos] is preferable for American radio.   British sĭ′-rə-kyōōz [sai′-ruh-kyooz].

Sirakovo (Yugosl.)	sē′-rä′-kô-vô	see′-rah′-ko-vo
sirdar *or* sardar	sər-där′	suhr-dahr′

A title or honorific in the Middle East. It is disregarded in alphabetical listing.

Siredalen (Nor.)	sē′-rə-dä-lən	see′-ruh-dah-luhn
Siret (Rum.)	sĭ-rĕt′	si-ret′
Siretul (Rum., riv.)	sĭ-rĕ′-tōōl	si-reh′-tul
Sirot (Oc., Bismarck arch.)	sē-rôt′	see-rot′
Sirte (Libya)	sĭr′-tĕ	sihr′-teh

Also called *Sidra*, q.v., and *Zaafran*, q.v.

Sisevac Vrčić (Yugosl.)	sē′-sĕ-väts vər′-chĭch	see′-seh-vahts vuhr′-chich
Siskiyou (Calif.)	sĭs′-kĭ-yōō	sis′-ki-yoo
Sison, Teófilo (Fil. polit.)	sē′-sôn, tyô′-fē-lô	see′-son, tyo′-fee-lo
Sissano (N. E. New Guinea)	sĭs-sä-nô′	sis-sah-no′
Sisteron (Fr.)	sēs-tə-rôN′	sees-tuh-roN′
Şiştov (Bulg.) See *Svishtov*.		
Sithonia (Gr., pen.) See *Longos*.		
Sitka (Alaska)	sĭt′-kə	sit′-kuh
Sitnica (Yugosl., riv.)	sēt′-nĭ-tsä	seet′-ni-tsah
Si-ts'ang (Ch. dependency)	sē-tsäng	see-tsahng

Also called *Hsi-ts'äng*, shē-tsäng [shee-tsahng]. English *Tibet*, q.v.

Sittang (Burma, riv.)	sĭt'-tăng'	sit'-tang'
Sittard (Neth.)	sĭt'-ärt	sit'-ahrt
Sittaung (Burma)	sĭt'-toung'	sit'-taung'
Sivac (Yugosl.)	sē'-väts	see'-vahts
Sivash (Rus., lagoons)	sĭ-väsh'	si-vahsh'
Also called the *Putrid Sea*.		
Siwa (Egypt)	sē'-wä	see'-wah
Sjaelland (Den., isl.) See *Zealand*.		
Sjahrir, Soetan	shä'-rēr', sōō'-tän	shah'-reer', soo'-tahn
(Indo. polit.)		
Also spelled *Shahrir, Sutan*.		
Sjarifoedin Amir (Indo. polit.) See *Sharifudin Amir*.		
Sjenica (Yugosl.)	syĕ'-nĭ-tsä	syeh'-ni-tsah
Sjoa (Nor.)	shō'-ä	shoh'-ah
Skadar (Alb.) See *Scutari*.		
Skadovsk (Rus.)	skä-dôfsk'	skah-dofsk'
Skagen (Den., cape)	skä'-gən	skah'-guhn
English the *Skaw*, skô' [skaw'].		
Skagerrak (Nor., Den., sea)	*Eng.* skăg'-ə-răk	skag'-uh-rak
Skagit (Wash.)	skăj'-ĭt	skaj'-it
Skalani (Crete)	skä-lä'-nē	skah-lah'-nee
Skanderbeut, Mal i (Alb., mt.) See *Scanderbeg*.		
Skantzoura (Gr., isl.)	skä'-dzōō-rä	skah'-dzoo-rah
Skaramangas (Gr.)	skä-rä-mä(ng)-gäs'	skah-rah-mah(ng)-gahs'
Škarda (Yugosl., isl.)	shkär'-dä	shkahr'-dah
Skarsfoss (Nor., dam)	skärs'-fôs	skahrs'-fos
	or skäsh'-fôs	skahsh'-fos
Skarżysko (Pol.)	• skär-zhĭ'-skô	skahr-zhi'-sko
Skaugum (Nor.)	skou'-gŏŏm	skau'-gum
Skaw, the (Den., cape) See *Skagen*.		
Skawa (Pol., riv.)	skä'-vä	skah'-vah
Skawina (Pol.)	skä-vē'-nä	skah-vee'-nah
Skei (Nor.)	shä'	shay'
Skerda (Yugosl., isl.)	skĕr'-dä	skehr'-dah
Skernevitsi (Pol.) See *Skierniewice*.		
Skhirra, la (Tun.)	sə-kĭr'-rä, lä	suh-kihr'-rah, lah
Often spelled *Cekhira*.		
ski	*Eng.* skē'	skee'
	Nor. shē'	shee'
Skiathos (Gr., isl.)	skē'-ä-thô(s)	skee'-ah-tho(s)
Skidel (Pol.)	skē'-dĕl(y)	skee'-del(y)
Skien (Nor.)	shä'-ən	shay'-uhn
	or shē'-ən	shee'-uhn

Skierniewice (Pol.)   skyĕr-nyĕ-vē'-tsĕ   skyehr-nyeh-vee'-tseh
   Russian *Skernevitsi*, skĕr-nĕ-vē'-tsĭ [skehr-neh-vee'-tsi].
skijoring   *Eng.* skē-jôr'-ĭng   skee-jor'-ing
Skive (Den.)   skē'-və   skee'-vuh
Skiza (Gr., isl.)   skē'-zä   skee'-zah
Skjeggedalsfoss (Nor.,   shĕg'-ə-däls-fôs'   sheg'-uh-dahls-fos'
   lake)
Skjervoei *or* Skjervöi   shĕrv'-ûĭ   shehrv'-œi
   (Nor.)
Skjoenstaa *or*   shûn'-stô   shœn'-sto
   Skjönstaa (Nor.)
Skjolden (Nor.)   shôl'-dən   shol'-duhn
Skobeltsyn, D. V.   skŏ-bĕl-tsĭn'   sko-bel-tsin'
   (Rus. scientist)
Škofja Loka (Yugosl.)   shkô'-fyä lô'-kä   shko'-fyah lo'-kah
Skogfoss (Nor.)   skôg'-fôs   skohg'-fos
Skopelos (Gr., isl.)   skô'-pĕ-lô(s)   sko'-peh-lo(s)
Skopin (Rus.)   skŏ-pēn'   sko-peen'
Skoplje (Yugosl.)   skôp'-lyĕ   skop'-lyeh
   Greek *Skopia*, skô'-pē-ä [sko'-pee-ah].
Skoppum (Nor.)   skôp'-ŏŏm   skop'-um
Skoupitsa (Gr.)   skōō-pē'-tsä   skoo-pee'-tsah
Skrapež (Yugosl., riv.)   skrä'-pĕzh   skrah'-pezh
Skreia (Nor.)   skrā'-ä   skray'-ah
Skrwa (Pol., riv.)   skər-vä'   skuhr-vah'
Skudeneshavn (Nor.)   skōō'-də-nĕs-hävn'   skoo'-duh-nes-hahvn'
Skulerud (Nor.)   skōō'-lə-rōōd'   skoo'-luh-rood'
Skvira (Rus.)   skvē'-rä   skvee'-rah
Skyros (Gr., isl.)   skē'-rô(s)   skee'-ro(s)
Slack (Fr., riv.)   släk'   slahk'
Slaná (Cz., riv.)   slä'-nä   slah'-nah
   Hungarian *Sajó*, shô'-yô [sho'-yo].
Slănic (Rum.)   slə-nēk'   sluh-neek'
Śląsk (Pol.)   See *Silesia*.
Slatina (Rum.)   slä'-tē-nä   slah'-tee-nah
Slatino (Rus.)   slä'-tĭ-nŏ   slah'-ti-no
Slavik, Juray   slä'-vĭk, yōō'-rī   slah'-vik, yoo'-rai
   (Cz. polit.)
Slaviště (Yugosl.)   slä'-vĭsh-tĕ   slah'-vish-teh
Slavkov (Cz.)   See *Austerlitz*.
Slavnoe (Rus.)   släv'-nŏ-yĕ   slahv'-no-yeh
Slavonia (Yugosl.)   *Eng.* slə-vōn'-yə   sluh-vohn'-yuh
   Serb-Croat *Slavonija*, slä-vô'-nĭ-yä [slah-vo'-ni-yah].
Slavsk (Ger. >Rus.)   släfsk'   slahfsk'
   German *Heinrichswalde*, q.v.

Slavyanoserbsk (Rus.)   slä-vyä-nŏ-sĕrpsk'   slah-vyah-no-sehrpsk'
Slavyansk (Rus.)   slä'-vyänsk   slah'-vyahnsk
Sleen (Neth.)   slān'   slayn'
Slesvig (Den.)   *Dan.* slĕs'-vĭk(h)   sles'-vik(h)
   German *Schleswig*, q.v.
Slezsko (Ger., Pol., Cz.)   See *Silesia.*
Slidell (La.)   slĭ-dĕl'   slai-del'
Slidre (Nor.)   slē'-rə   slee'-ruh
Sliedrecht (Neth.)   slē'-drĕk(h)t   slee'-drek(h)t
Sligo (Eire)   slĭ'-gō   slai'-goh
Slišane (Yugosl.)   slē'-shä-nĕ   slee'-shah-neh
Sliven (Bulg.)   slē'-vĕn(y)   slee'-ven(y)
   Also called *Slivno*, slĕv'-nŏ [sleev'-no].
Slivno (Bulg.)   See *Sliven.*
Slochteren (Neth.)   slôk(h)'-tə-rən   slok(h)'-tuh-ruhn
Sloka (Latvia)   slô'-kä *or* slwŏ'-   slo'-kah *or* slwo'-
   German *Schlok*, q.v.
Słomniki (Pol.)   slôm-nē'-kĭ   slom-nee'-ki
Slonim (Pol. > Rus.)   slô'-nĭm   slo'-nim
   Polish spelling *Słonim.*
Sloten *or* Slooten (Neth.)   slō'-tən   sloh'-tuhn
Slovakia (Cz.)   *Eng.* slō-vä'-kĭ-ə   sloh-vah'-ki-uh
   Czech *Slovensko*, slô'-vĕn-skô [slo'-ven-sko]. The English pronuncia-
   tion might well be slō-vā'-kĭ-ə [sloh-vay'-ki-uh] or slō-văk'-ĭ-ə [sloh-
   vak'-i-uh], but the seeming-foreign slō-vä'-kĭ-ə [sloh-vah'-ki-uh] is
   the most common.
Slovenia (Yugosl.)   *Eng.* slō-vēn'-yə   sloh-veen'-yuh
   Serb-Croat *Slovenija*, slô-vĕ'-nĭ-yä [slo-veh'-ni-yah].
Slovenjgradec (Yugosl.)   slô'-vĕn(y)-grä'-dĕts   slo'-ven(y)-grah'-dets
Słubice (Ger.) See *Frankfurt an der Oder.*
Sluch (Pol. > Rus., riv.)   slōōch'   sluch'
   Polish *Słucz.*
Słucz (Pol., riv.)   slōōch'   slooch'
Sluis (Neth.)   slûĭs'   slœis'
Sluiskil (Neth.)   slûĭs'-kĭl   slœis'-kil
Slunj (Yugosl.)   slōōn'(y)   sloon'(y)
Słupca (Pol.)   slōōp'-tsä   slup'-tsah
   Russian *Sluptsi*, slōōp'-tsĭ [sloop'-tsi].
Słupsk (Ger. > Pol.)   slōōpsk'   slupsk'
   German *Stolp*, q.v.
Sluptsi (Pol.)   See *Słupca.*
Slyudyanka (Rus.)   slyōō-dyän'-kä   slyoo-dyahn'-kah
Smaalenene *or*
   Smålenene (Nor.)   smô'-lĕ-nə-nə   smo'-leh-nuh-nuh

Smallingerland (Neth.)   smäl'-ĭng-ər-länt'   smahl'-ing-uhr-lahnt'

Smathers, George   smăth'-ərz   smath'-uhrz
(U.S. representative)

Smederevo (Yugosl.)   smĕ'-dĕ-rĕ-vô   smeh'-deh-reh-vo

Smela (Rus.)   smĕ'-lä   smeh'-lah

Smertenko, Johan J.   smĕr'-tĕn-kô, yō'-hän   smehr'-ten-ko, yoh'-
(Am. Zionist)   hahn

Smilde (Neth., canal)   smĭl'-də   smil'-duh

Smiltene (Latvia)   smĕl'-tĕ-nĕ   smeel'-teh-neh
Russian *Smilten*, smĕl'(y)-tĕn [smeel'(y)-ten].

Smindja (Tun.)   smĭn'-jä   smin'-jah

Smith, Walter Bedell   bĭd-dĕl' *or* bēd'l   bid-del' *or* beed'l
(Am. general)

His secretary wrote, Sept. 4, 1946, "General Smith himself prefers
the accent on the second syllable, but the other pronunciation has become so widespread that it has become accepted, even by the General
himself on occasion."

Smolensk (Rus.)   smŏ-lĕnsk'   smo-lensk'

Smolian (Bulg.)   smô'-lĭ-yän   smo'-li-yahn
Also called *Pashmakli*, päsh'-mä-klē' [pahsh'-mah-klee'].

Smoljinac (Yugosl.)   smô'-lyĭ-näts   smo'-lyi-nahts

Smorgon (Pol. > Rus.)   smŏr-gôn'(y)   smor-gon'(y)
Polish *Smorgonie*, smôr-gô'-nyĕ [smor-go'-nyeh].

Smuts, Jan C. (S. Afr.   smŭts', yän'   smuhts', yahn'
polit.)

Smyrna (Turk.)   *Eng.* smûr'-nə   smuhr'-nuh
Turkish *İzmir*, q.v.

Sneek (Neth.)   snäk'   snayk'

Sniatin (Pol. > Rus.)   snyä'-tĭn   snyah'-tin
Polish *Śniatyn*, shnyä'-tĭn [shnyah'-tin].

Snigirëvka (Rus.)   snĭ-gĭ-ryôf'-kä   sni-gi-ryof'-kah

Snoehetta *or* Snöhetta   snû'-hĕt-ä   snœ'-het-ah
(Nor., mt.)

Sobolev, Arkadi A.   sô'-bŏ-lĕf, är-kä'-dĭ   so'-bo-lef, ahr-kah'-di
(Rus. diplomat)

Sobótka (Ger. >? Pol.)   sô-bŏŏt'-kä   so-but'-kah
German *Zobten*, q.v.

Soča (It., Yugosl., riv.)   sô'-chä   so'-chah
Italian *Isonzo*, q.v.

Sochaczew (Pol.)   sô-hä'-chĕf   so-hah'-chef
Russian spelling *Sokhachev*.

Sochi (Rus.)   sô'-chĭ   so'-chi

Socna (Libya)   sŏk'-nä   sok'-nah

Socotra (Afr., isl.)   sō-kō'-trə   soh-koh'-truh
Also spelled *Soqotra*.

Söderhamn (Sw.)	sû'-dər-hämn'	sœ'-duhr-hahmn'
Södertälje (Sw.)	sû'-dər-tĕl'-yə	sœ'-duhr-tel'-yuh
Sodražica (Yugosl.)	sộ-drä'-zhĭ-tsä	so-drah'-zhi-tsah
Soebang or Subang (NEI, Java)	sōō'-bäng	soo'-bahng
Soebardjo (Indo. polit.)	sōō'-bär'-jộ'	soo'-bahr'-jo'
Soeburg (Neth.)	sōō'-bûrk(h)	soo'-bœrk(h)
Soederhamn (Sw.)	sû'-dər-hämn'	sœ'-duhr-hahmn'
Soedertälje (Sw.)	sû'-dər-tĕl'-yə	sœ'-duhr-tel'-yuh
Soedirman (Indo. polit.)	sōō'-dĭr-män	soo'-dihr-mahn
Soekaboemi or Sukabumi (NEI, Java)	sōō-kä-bōō'-mē	soo-kah-boo'-mee
Soekarno, Achmed (Indo. polit.)	sōō'-kär'-nộ', äk(h)-mĕt'	soo'-kahr'-no', ahk(h)-met'
Soela or Sula (NEI)	sōō'-lä	soo'-lah
Soemba or Sumba (NEI)	sōōm'-bä	soom'-bah
Soembawa or Sumbawa (NEI, Java)	sōōm-bä'-wä	soom-bah'-wah
Soember or Sumber (NEI, Borneo, riv.)	sōōm'-bĕr	soom'-behr
Soenda (NEI) See Sunda.		
Soengaitiram or Sungaitiram (NEI, Borneo)	sōŏng-ĭ-tē'-räm	sung-ai-tee'-rahm
Soepiori (NEI, Schouten isls.)	sōō-pĭ-ộ'-rĭ	soo-pi-oh'-ri
Soerabaja or Surabaya (NEI, Java)	sōō-rä-bä'-yä	soo-rah-bah'-yah
Soerakarta or Surakarta (NEI, Java)	sōō-rä-kär'-tä	soo-rah-kahr'-tah
Soerfold (Nor.)	sûr'-fộl	sœr'-fol
Soerumsand (Nor.)	sû'-rōŏm-sän	sœ'-rum-sahn
Soervaranger (Nor.)	sûr'-vä-räng'-ər	sœr'-vah-rahng'-uhr
Soest (Ger.)	zōst'	zohst'
Soest (Neth.)	sōōst'	soost'
Soestdijk (Neth.)	sōōst-dīk'	soost-daik'
Soeste (Ger., riv.)	zōs'-tə	zohs'-tuh
Soesterberg (Neth.)	sōōs'-tər-bĕrk(h)	soos'-tuhr-behrk(h)
Sofia (Bulg.)	Eng. sō'-fĭ-ə	soh'-fi-uh
	Bulg. sộ'-fĭ-yä	so'-fi-yah

Also spelled *Sofiya.* There is also an English pronunciation sō-fē'-ə [soh-fee'-uh]. Formerly called *Sredets*, srĕ'-dĕts [sreh'-dets].

Sofiskoe (Rus.)	sŏ-fē'-skŏ-yĕ	so-fee'-sko-yeh
Sofoulis, Emmanuel (Gr. polit.)	sộ-fōō'-lēs, ĕ-mä-nōō-ēl'	so-foo'-lees, eh-mah-noo-eel'

Sofoulis, Themistokles (Gr. polit.)	sô-fōō'-lēs, thĕ-mē-stô-klēs' *or Eng.* thə-mĭs'-tə-klēz	so-foo'-lees, theh-mee-sto-klees' *or Eng.* thuh-mis'-tuh-kleez
Sogn (Nor.)	sông'n *local* sôg'-ən	song'n sog'-uhn
Sogndal (Nor.)	sông'n-däl	song'n-dahl
Sognefjord (Nor.)	sông'-nə-fyōr	song'-nuh-fyohr
Sógod (P.I.)	sô'-gôd	so'-god
Soheily (Iran. name)	sô-hā'-lē	so-hay'-lee
Soignies (Belg.)	swä-nyē'	swah-nyee'
Soissons (Fr.)	swä-sôN'	swah-soN'
Sokal (Pol. > Rus.)	sô'-käl	so'-kahl
Sokhachev (Pol.) See *Sochaczew.*		
Soko Banja (Yugosl.)	sô'-kô bä'-nyä	so'-ko bah'-nyah
Sokolnikov, Grigori Yakovlevich (Rus. polit.)	sŏ-kôl'-nĭ-kôf, grĭ-gô'-rĭ yä'-kŏv-lĕ-vĭch	so-kol'-ni-kof, gri-go'-ri yah'-kov-leh-vich
Sokolovski, Vasili (Rus. general)	sŏ-kŏ-lôf'-skĭ, vä-sē'-lĭ	so-ko-lof'-ski, vah-see'-li
Sokolsky, George E. (Am. columnist)	sə-kŏl'-skĭ,	suh-kol'-skih
Sola (Nor.)	sō'-lä	soh'-lah
Sola (Pol., riv.)	sô'-lä	so'-lah
Solano López, Francisco (Para. polit.)	sô-lä'-nô lô'-pĕs, frän-sēs'-kô	so-lah'-no lo'-pes, frahn-sees'-ko
Solari, Marcello (It. polit.)	sô-lä'-rē, mär-chĕl'-lô	so-lah'-ree, mahr-chel'-lo
Soldau (Pol.)	*Ger.* zôl'-dou	zol'-dau
Polish *Działdówka* and *Działdówo*, q.v.		
Soldin (Ger.)	zôl-dēn'	zol-deen'
Solesmes (Fr.)	sô-lĕm'	so-lem'
Solenzara (Corsica)	sô-lĕn-tsä'-rä	so-len-tsah'-rah
Soleure (Switz.) See *Solothurn.*		
Soliman (Tun.)	*Eng.* sŏl'-ə-mən *Fr.* sô-lē-mäN'	sol'-uh-muhn so-lee-mahN'
Solimões (Brazil, riv.)	sô-lĭ-moiNsh'	so-li-moiNsh'
Solingen (Ger.)	zō'-lĭng-ən	zoh'-ling-uhn
Sol(l)um (Egypt) See *Sal(l)um.*		
Soloer *or* Solör (Nor.)	sō'-lûr	soh'-lœr
Solothurn (Switz.)	zō'-lô-tōŏrn	zoh'-lo-turn
French *Soleure* sô-lûr' [so-lœr'].		
Solovets (Rus.)	sŏ-lŏ-vĕts'	so-lo-vets'
Solovetskie Ostrova (Rus.)	sŏ-lŏ-vĕt'-skĭ-yĕ ŏs-trŏ-vä'	so-lo-vet'-ski-yeh os-tro-vah'

Solovtsy (Rus.)	sŏ-lŏf-tsē′	so-lof-tsee′
Solsk (Rus.)	sôl(y)sk′	sol(y)sk′
Solsona (P.I.)	sôl-sô′-nä	sol-so′-nah
Solstrand (Nor.)	sôl′-strän	sohl′-strahn
Solta (Yugosl., isl.)	*It.* sôl′-tä	sol′-tah

Serb-Croat *Sulet*, q.v.

Soltau (Ger.)	zôl′-tou	zol′-tau
Soltsi (Rus.)	sôl(y)-tsē′	sol(y)-tsee′
Soluch (Libya)	sô-lŏŏk′	so-luk′
So-lun (Manchu.)	sô-lŏŏn	so-lun
Somain (Fr.)	sô-măN′	so-maN′
Somaliland (E. Afr.)	sō-mä′-lĭ-lănd	soh-mah′-li-land
Sombor (Yugosl.)	sôm′-bôr	som′-bor

Hungarian *Zombor*, zôm′-bôr [zom′-bor].

Somers, Andrew L.	sŭm′-ərz	suhm′-uhrz
(U.S. representative)		
Somervell, Brehon	sŭm′-ər-vəl,	suhm′-uhr-vuhl,
(U.S. general)	brä′-hŏn	bray′-hon
Someş (Rum.)	sô′-měsh	so′-mesh
Someşul (Rum., riv.)	sô-mě′-shŏŏl	so-meh′-shul
Somino (Rus.)	sô′-mĭ-nŏ	so′-mi-no
Somme (Fr.)	sôm′	som′
Sommelsdijk (Neth.)	sôm′-əls-dīk′	som′-uhls-daik′
Somoza, Anastasio	sô-mô′-sä,	so-mo′-sah,
(Nicar. polit.)	ä-näs-tä′-syô	ah-nahs-tah′-syo
Somra (Burma, hills)	sŏŏn′-mə-yä′	sun′-muh-yah′

Suggested English pronunciation sŏŏm′-rä′ [sum′-rah′].

Šomrda (Yugosl., mts.)	shô′-mər′-dä	sho′-muhr′-dah
Son (India, riv.)	sōn′	sohn′
Songcau (Indo-Ch.)	sŏng′-kou′	song′-kau′
Songkhla (Siam)	See *Singora.*	
Sonnino (It.)	sôn-nē′-nô	son-nee′-no
Sónog (P.I.)	sô′-nôg	so′-nog
Sonoma (Calif.)	sə-nō′-mə	suh-noh′-muh
Sonora (Mex.)	sô-nô′-rä	so-no′-rah
sonorous	sə-nō′-rəs	suh-noh′-ruhs
	or sŏn′-ə-rəs	son′-uh-ruhs
Sonsorol (Oc., Carolines)	sôn′-sô-rôl	son′-so-rol
Sontay (Indo-Ch.)	sŭn-tī′	suhn-tai′
Son Telegraf (Turkish	sôn těl-gräf′	son tel-grahf′
newspaper)		
Soo-chow (Ch., Kiangsu)	*Eng.* sōō-chou	soo-chau
	Ch. sōō-jô	soo-joh

Near Shanghai. Also spelled *Su-chow.*

Soong, Ai-ling   sŏŏng, ī-lĭng   sung, ai-ling
The wife of *H. H. Kung*, q.v.
Soong, Ch'ing-ling   sŏŏng, chĭng-lĭng   sung, ching-ling
The wife of *Sun Yat-sen*, q.v.
Soong, Meiling   sŏŏng, mā-lĭng   sung, may-ling
The wife of *Chiang Kai-shek*, q.v.
Soong, T. L.   sŏŏng′   sung′
(Ch. financier)
"T.L." are the English initials of *Ts'u-liang*, tsə-lyäng [tsuh-lyahng].
Soong, T. V.   sŏŏng′   sung′
(Ch. financier)
"T.V." are the English initials of *Ts'u-wên* (or *-ven*), tsə-wŭn [tsuh-wuhn].
Soong Hsi-lien (Ch.   sŏŏng shē-lyĕn   sung shee-lyen
general)
Sophali (Gr.)   See *Souphli*.
Sophianopoulos   sô-fyä-nô′-pōō-lôs   so-fyah-no′-poo-los
(Gr. name)
Sophoulis, Emmanuel   sô-fōō′-lēs, ĕ-mä-   so-foo′-lees, eh-mah-
(Gr. polit.)   nōō-ēl′   noo-eel′
Sophoulis, Themistocles   sô-fōō′-lēs, thĕ-mē-   so-foo′-lees, theh-mee-
(Gr. polit.)   stô-klēs′ *or Eng.*   sto-klees′ *or Eng.*
     thə-mĭs′-tə-klēz   thuh-mis′-tuh-kleez
Sopot (Danzig > Pol.)   sô′-pôt   so′-pot
German *Zoppot*, tsôp′-ôt [tsop′-ot].
Sopot (Yugosl.)   sô′-pôt   so′-pot
Sopron (Hung.)   shôp′-rôn   shop′-ron
German *Oedenburg* or *Ödenburg*, û′-dən-bōŏrk(h) [œ′-duhn-burk(h)].
Soqotra (Afr., isl.) See *Socotra*.
Sora (It.)   sô′-rä   so′-rah
Sorarù (It.)   sô-rä-rōō′   so-rah-roo′
Sorau (Ger. >? Pol.)   zô′-rou   zo′-rau
Polish *Żarów*, q.v.
Sorba (Corsica)   sôr′-bä   sor′-bah
Sörfold (Nor.)   sûr′-fôl   sœr′-fol
Sorgenfri (Den.)   sôr′-gən-frē   sor′-guhn-free
Sorgono (Sard.)   sôr′-gô-nô   sor′-go-no
Soria (Sp.)   sô′-ryä   so′-ryah
Sorido (NEI)   sō-rē′-dō   soh-ree′-doh
Sormovo (Rus.)   sôr′-mŏ-vŏ   sor′-mo-vo
Soroca (Rum.)   sô-rô′-kä   so-ro′-kah
Russian *Soroki*, sŏ-rô′-kĭ [so-ro′-ki].
Soroe *or* Sorö (Nor.)   sô′-rû   soh′-rœ
Soroki (Rum. > Rus.)   sŏ-rô′-kĭ   so-ro′-ki
Rumanian *Soroca*, q.v.

Sorokin, Pitirim A.   sŏ-rô'-kĭn, pĭ-tĭ-rēm'   so-ro'-kin, pi-ti-reem'
  (Rus. Am. sociologist)
Soroksár (Hung.)   shô'-rôk-shär   sho'-rok-shahr
Sorol (Oc., Carolines)   sŏ'-rôl   so'-rol
Sorong (NEI, New   sŏ'-rông   so'-rong
  Guinea)
Sorot (Rus., riv.)   sŏ'-rŏt   so'-rot
Sorsogón (P.I.)   sôr-sô-gôn'   sor-so-gon'
Sortavala (Fin. >Rus.)   sôr'-tä-vä-lä   sor'-tah-vah-lah
  Russian *Serdobol*, q.v.
Sortland (Nor.)   sŏŏrt'-län   surt'-lahn
Sörumsand (Nor.)   sû'-rŏŏm-sän   sœ'-rum-sahn
Sörvaranger (Nor.)   sûr'-vä-räng'-ər   sœr'-vah-rahng'-uhr
Sośnicowice (Ger. >Pol.)   sôsh-nĭ-tsô-vē'-tsĕ   sosh-ni-tso-vee'-tseh
  German *Kieferstädtel*, q.v.
Sosnitsa (Rus.)   sŏs-nē'-tsä   sos-nee'-tsah
Sosnkowski, Kazimierz   sôsn-kôf'-skĭ,   sosn-kof'-ski, kah-
  (Pol. general)   kä-zē'-myĕsh   zee'-myesh
Sosnowiec (Pol.)   sô-snô'-vyĕts   so-sno'-vyets
  Russian spelling *Sosnovets*.
Šoštanj (Yugosl.)   shô'-shtän(y)   sho'-shtahn(y)
Sosunov (Rus., cape)   sŏ-sōō-nôf'   so-soo-nof'
Sosyka (Rus.)   sŏ-swē'-kä   so-swee'-kah
Sotteville (Fr.)   sôt-vēl'   sot-veel'
Souda (Crete)   sōō'-dä   soo'-dah
  Gulf of Souda, *Kolpos Soudas*, kôl'-pôs sōō'-däs [kol'-pos soo'-dahs].
Soufli (Gr.) See *Souphli*.
souk *or* suq *or* suk   sōōk'   sook'
  In Arabic names an element, sometimes omitted, meaning *market*.
Souk Ahras (Alg.)   sōōk ă-răs'   sook a-ras'
Souk el Arba (Tun.)   sōōk ĕl är'-bä   sook el ahr'-bah
Souk el Khemis (Tun.)   kə-mēs'   kuh-mees'
Souliasi (Gr.)   sōō'-lyä-sē   soo'-lyah-see
Soultz (Fr.)   sōōlts'   soolts'
Souphli (Gr.)   sōō-flē'   soo-flee'
  Also called *Sophali*, sô-fä-lē' [so-fah-lee'].
Souphlion (Gr.)   sōō-flē'(-ôn)   soo-flee'(-on)
Souppes (Fr.)   sōōp'   soop'
Sourdeval (Fr.)   sōōr-də-väl'   soor-duh-vahl'
Sousse (Tun.)   *Fr.* sōōs'   soos'
  Also called *Susa*, q.v.
Souza Costa, Arthur de   sō'-zə kôs'-tə,   soh'-zuh kos'-tuh,
  (Braz. polit.)   ər-tōōr' dĭ   uhr-toor' di
Soveria (It.)   sô-vĕ-rē'-ä   so-veh-ree'-ah

Sovetsk (Ger. >Rus.)   sŏ-vĕtsk′   so-vetsk′
   German *Tilsit*, q.v.

Sovetskaya Gavan   sŏ-vĕt′-skä-yä   so-vet′-skah-yah
   (Rus.)   gä′-vän(y)   gah′-vahn(y)

Soviet (Rus.)   *Eng.* sō′-vĭ-ĕt′   soh′-vi-et′
   Russian *Sovet*.

Sōya Kaikyō (Jap.,   sô′-yä kä′-ē-kyô   so′-yah kah′-ee-kyo
   Rus., str.)
   Also called *La Pérouse*, q.v.

Sozh (Rus., riv.)   sôzh′   sozh′

Sozopol (Bulg.)   sô′-zŏ-pŏl(y)   so′-zo-pol(y)

Spaak, Paul Henri   späk′, poul′ äN-rē′   spahk′, paul′ ahN-ree′
   (Belg. polit.)

Spaatz, Carl (U.S.   späts′   spahts′
   general)
   Airforce headquarters in the Tunisian campaign had the nickname, according to *Time*, March 22, 1943, of *Souk el Spaatz*, sōōk′ ĕl späts′ [sook′ el spahts′]. The General's nickname is *Tooey*, tōō′-ĭ [too′-i].

Spaccio (It.)   spät′-chô   spaht′-cho

Spada (Crete, pen., mt.)   See *Rodopou*.

Spadillo (Pantelleria,   spä-dēl′-lô   spah-deel′-lo
   point)

Spaeth, Sigmund (Am.   späth′, sĭg′-mənd   spayth′, sig′-muhnd
   musician)

Spahi   spä′-hē   spah′-hee
   A variant of *sepoy*, a native soldier.

Spain   See *España*.

Spakenburg (Neth.)   spä′-kən-bûrk(h)   spah′-kuhn-bœrk(h)

Spalato (Yugosl.)   *It.* spä′-lä-tô   spah′-lah-to
   Serb-Croat *Split*, q.v.

Spalmadori (Yugosl., isls.)   *It.* späl-mä-dô′-rĭ   spahl-mah-do′-ri
   Serb-Croat *Pakleni Otoci*, q.v.

Spančevo (Yugosl.)   spän′-chĕ-vô   spahn′-cheh-vo

Spandau (Ger.)   shpän′-dou   shpahn′-dau

Sparanise (It.)   spä-rä-nē′-zĕ   spah-rah-nee′-zeh

Sparkman, John J.   spärk′-mən   spahrk′-muhn
   (U.S. senator)

Sparta (Gr.)   *Eng.* spär′-tə   spahr′-tuh
   Greek *Sparte*, spär′-tē [spahr′-tee].

Spartivento (It., Sard.,   spär-tē-vĕn′-tô   spahr-tee-ven′-to
   cape)

Spas Demensk (Rus.)   späs′ dĕ-mĕnsk′   spahs′ deh-mensk′

Spassk (Rus.)   späsk′   spahsk′

Spatha (Crete, cape)   spä′-thä   spah′-thah
   Also called *Psakon*, q.v.

Speer, Albert (Ger. polit.) *Eng.* spĭr' spihr'
  Ger. shpār shpayr'
Spelea (Crete) spē-lyä' spee-lyah'
Speli (Crete) spē'-lē spee'-lee
Sperillen (Nor.) spĕr'-ĭl-ən spehr'-il-uhn
Sperlonga (It.) spĕr-lông'-gä spehr-long'-gah
Spetsai (Gr., isl.) spĕt'-sĕ spet'-seh
  Italian *Spezzia*, spĕt'-syä [spet'-syah].
Speyer (Ger.) shpĭ'-ər shpai'-uhr
  English *Spires*, spĭrz' [spairz'].
Spezia, la (It.) spĕ'-tsyä, lä speh'-tsyah, lah
Spezzia (Gr., isl.) See *Spetsai*.
Sphakia (Crete) sfä-kyä' sfah-kyah'
  Also called *Khora Sphakion*, q.v.
Sphakteria (Gr., isl.) sfä-ktē-rē'-ä sfah-ktee-ree'-ah
Sphenari (Crete) sfē-nä'-rē sfee-nah'-ree
Spič, Zaliv (Yugosl., bay) spēch', zä'-lĭv speech', zah'-liv
  Italian *Valle Spizza*, väl'-lĕ spēt'-sä [vahl'-leh speet'-sah].
Spielfeld (Austria) shpēl'-fĕlt shpeel'-felt
Spigno (It.) spē'-nyô spee'-nyo
Spigolino (It., mt.) spē-gô-lē'-nô spee-go-lee'-no
Spijkenisse (Neth.) spĭ'-kə-nĭs-ə spai'-kuh-nis-uh
Spinalonga (Crete, spē-nä-lông'-gä spee-nah-long'-gah
  point, isl.)
Spinazzola (Italy) spē-nät-sô'-lä spee-naht-so'-lah
Spires (Ger.) See *Speyer*.
Spiridonovka (Moscow, spĭ-rĭ-dô'-nŏf-kä spih-rih-do'-nof-kah
  palace)
Spirovo (Rus.) spē'-rŏ-vŏ spee'-ro-vo
Spiš (Cz.) spēsh' speesh'
  Hungarian *Szepes*, sĕ'-pĕsh [seh'-pesh].
Spiška, -é spēsh'-kä, -ĕ speesh'-kah, -eh
  An element, meaning *of Spiš*, q.v., in Czech place names. Look up the
  other part of the name.
Spital (Austria) shpē'-täl shpee'-tahl
Spitsbergen (Nor., isls.) spĭts'-bûrg-ən spits'-buhrg-uhn
  Included in the Norwegian polar territory *Svalbard*, sväl'-bär [svahl'-
  bahr].
Split (Yugosl.) splēt' *or* splĭt' spleet' *or* split'
  Italian *Spalato*, q.v.
Splügen (Switz., pass) shplü'-gən shplü'-guhn
Spokane (Wash.) spō-kăn' spoh-kan'
Spoleto (It.) spô-lĕ'-tô spo-leh'-to

spontaneity   spŏn'-tə-nē'-ə-tĭ   spon'-tuh-nee'-uh-ti

An erroneous pronunciation rhyming with *gaiety* is sometimes heard, echoing the stressed vowel of *spontaneous*.

Sporades (Gr., isls.)	*Eng.* spôr'-ə-dēz	spor'-uh-deez
	Gr. spô-rä'-dĕs	spo-rah'-des
Sprang (Neth.)	spräng'	sprahng'
Spratly (Ch. Sea, isl.)	sprăt'-lĭ	sprat'-li
Spree (Ger., riv.)	shprā'	shpray'
Sprendlingen (Ger.)	shprĕnd'-lĭng-ən	shprend'-ling-uhn
Sprottau (Ger. >? Pol.)	shprôt'-ou	shprot'-au

Polish *Szprotawa*, q.v.

Spuž (Yugosl.)	spōōzh'	spoozh'

sqep *or* sqepi (Alb.)   See *kep.*

squalid	skwŏl'-ĭd	skwol'-id
squall	skwŏl'	skwawl'
squalor	skwŏl'-ər	skwol'-uhr
	or skwā'-lər	skway'-luhr
Squillace (It., gulf)	skwēl-lä'-chĕ	skweel-lah'-cheh
squirrel	skwûr'-əl	skwuhr'-uhl

There are many other pronunciations less common, particularly skwĭr'-əl [skwihr'-uhl].

Srbica (Yugosl.)	sər'-bĭ-tsä	suhr'-bi-tsah
Srbobran (Yugosl.)	sər'-bô-brän'	suhr'-bo-brahn'
Srebrenica (Yugosl.)	srĕ'-brĕ-nĭ-tsä	sreh'-breh-ni-tsah
Srebrna Glava (Yugosl., mt.)	srĕ'-bər-nä glä'-vä	sreh'-buhr-nah glah'-vah

Sredets (Bulg.)   See *Sofia.*

Srednjevo (Yugosl.)	srĕd'-nyĕ-vô	sred'-nyeh-vo
Šrem (Pol.)	shrĕm'	shrem'

German *Schrimm*, shrĭm' [shrim'].

Srem (Yugosl.)   See *Syrmia.*

Sremčica (Yugosl.)	srĕm'-chĭ-tsä	srem'-chi-tsah
Sretensk (Rus.)	srĕ'-tĕnsk	sreh'-tensk
Srinagar (India)	srĕ-nŭg'-ər	sree-nuhg'-uhr
Šroda (Pol.)	shrô'-dä	shro'-dah
srpska, -e, -i, -o	sərp'-skä, -ĕ, -ĭ, -ŏ	suhrp'-skah, -eh, -i, -o

An element, meaning *Serbian*, in Yugoslav place names. It may be necessary to look up the other part of the name.

Srpska Crnja (Yugosl.)	sərp'-skä tsər'-nyä	suhrp'-skah tsuhr'-nyah
Srpski Elemir (Yugosl.)	sərp'-skĭ ĕ'-lĕ-mĭr	suhrp'-ski eh'-leh-mihr
Srpski Itebej (Yugosl.)	sərp'-skĭ ē'-tĕ-bä	suhrp'-ski ee'-teh-bay

Srpski Krstur (Yugosl.)   sərp'-skĭ kər'-sto͞or   suhrp'-ski kuhr'-stoor
Ssŭ-p'ing-chieh (Ch., Manchu.) See *Szê-ping Kai*.

St .... For compounds with *St.*, *Ste.*, see *Saint* (English); *Saint*, *Sainte*
(French); *San*, *Santo*, *-a* (Italian, Spanish); *Santi* (Italian); *Sân*
(Rumanian); *Sankt* (German); *São* (Portuguese); *Sint* (Dutch);
Szent (Hungarian), etc.

Stabekk (Nor.)   stä'-běk   stah'-bek
Stablo (Belg.) See *Stavelot*.

Stachouwer, Tjarda   stä'-k(h)ou-ər,   stah'-k(h)au-uhr,
  van Starkenborgh   chär'-dä vän   chahr'-dah vahn
  (Du. polit.)   stär'-kən-bôrk(h)   stahr'-kuhn-bork(h)

Stad (Nor.)   städ'   stahd'
Stadskanaal (Neth.)   stäts'-kä-näl'   stahts'-kah-nahl'
Stagnone (Sicily, isl.)   stän-yô'-ně   stahn-yo'-neh
Staiti (It.)   stĭ'-tē   stai'-tee
Stalać (Yugosl.)   stä'-läch   stah'-lahch
Stalheim (Nor.)   stäl'-hām   stahl'-haym
Stalin, Joseph (Rus.   stä'-lĭn   stah'-lin
  polit.)

  Real name, *Iosif Vissarionovich Dzhugashvili*, yô'-sĭf vĭs-sä-rĭ-ô'-nŏ-
  vĭch jo͞o-gä-shvē'-lē [yo'-sif vis-sah-ri-o'-no-vich joo-gah-shvee'-lee].

Stalinabad (Rus.)   stä-lĭ-nä-bät'   stah-li-nah-baht'
Stalingrad (Rus.)   *Eng.* stä'-lĭn-grăd   stah'-lin-grad
    Rus. stä-lĭn-grät'   stah-lin-graht'
Stalino (Rus.)   stä'-lĭ-nŏ   stah'-li-no
Stalinsk (Rus.)   stä'-lĭnsk   stah'-linsk
Stallupoehnen *or* Stal-   shtäl'-oͦ-pû'-nən   shtahl'-u-pœ'-nuhn
  lupöhnen (Ger. >Rus.)

  Russian *Nesterov*, ně'-stě-rŏf [neh'-steh-rof].

Stampalia (Dodec.)   *It.* stäm-pä-lē'-ä   stahm-pah-lee'-ah
  Greek *Astypalea*, q.v.
Stamsund (Nor.)   stäm'-soͦn   stahm'-sun
Stanczyk, Jan (Pol. polit.)   stän'-chĭk, yän   stahn'-chik, yahn
Standia (Crete, isl.)   See *Dia*.
Staničenje (Yugosl.)   stä'-nĭ-chě-nyě   stah'-ni-cheh-nyeh
Stanišić (Yugosl.)   stä'-nĭ-shĭch   stah'-ni-shich
Stanislavov (Pol. >Rus.)   stä-nĭ-slä'-vôf   stah-ni-slah'-vof
  Polish *Stanisławów*, stä-nē-slä'-voͦf [stah-nee-slah'-vuf].
Stankevich, Andrei Kovtun (Rus. general) See *Kovtun Stankevich*.
Stanleyville (Belg. Congo) stăn'-lĭ-vĭl   stan'-li-vil
Staphorst (Neth.)   stäp'-hôrst   stahp'-horst
stara, -ri, -ro   stä'-rä, -rĭ, -rŏ   stah'-rah, -ri, -ro
  An element, meaning *old*, in Yugoslav and Bulgarian place names. It
  may be necessary to look up the second part of the name.

Starace, Achille	stä-rä'-chĕ, ä-kēl'-lĕ	stah-rah'-cheh, ah-
(It. polit.)		keel'-leh
Stara planina (Balkan	stä'-rä plä'-nē'-nä	stah'-rah plah'-nee'-
mts.)		nah
Staraya Russa (Rus.)	stä'-rä-yä rōō'-sä	stah'-rah-yah roo'-sah
Stara Zagora (Bulg.)	stä'-rä zä'-gŏ-rä	stah'-rah zah'-go-rah
Starčevo (Yugosl.)	stär'-chĕ-vô	stahr'-cheh-vo
Stargard (Ger. >Pol.)	shtär'-gärt	shtahr'-gahrt
Polish *Starogród*, q.v.		
Stari Grad (Yugosl.)	stä'-rĭ gräd'	stah'-ri grahd'
Italian *Citta Vecchia*, q.v.		
Starii Oskol (Rus.)	stä'-rĭ ŏs-kôl'	stah'-ri os-kol'
Staritsa (Rus.)	stä'-rĭ-tsä	stah'-ri-tsah
Stari Vlah (Yugosl.)	stä'-rĭ vläk(h)'	stah'-ri vlahk(h)'
Starobelsk (Rus.)	stä-rŏ-bĕl(y)sk'	stah-ro-bel(y)sk'
Starodub (Rus.)	stä-rŏ-dōōp'	stah-ro-doop'
Starogard (Pol.)	stä-rŏ'-gärt	stah-ro'-gahrt
Starogród (Ger. >Pol.)	stä-rä'-grŏŏt	stah-rah'-grut
German *Stargard*, q.v.		
Starojineţ (Rum.)	stä-rô-zhē-nĕts'	stah-ro-zhee-nets'
Staro Konstantinov	stä'-rŏ kŏn-stän-	stah'-ro kon-stahn-
(Rus.)	tē'-nŏf	tee'-nof
Staro Minskaya (Rus.)	stä'-rŏ mēn'-skä-yä	stah'-ro meen'-skah-
		yah
Staro Tsurukhaituevsk	stä'-rŏ tsōō-rōō-hĭ-	stah'-ro tsoo-roo-hai-
(Rus.)	tōō'-yĕfsk	too'-yefsk
Stassen, Harold E.	stăs'n *or* stäs'n	stas'n *or* stahs'n
(Am. polit.)		

The pronunciation stăs'n was preferred in the reply, July 12, 1946, to
our query addressed to the Hon. Harold E. Stassen. However, only
the pronunciation stäs'n is given in *Webster's Biographical Dictionary*
(1943) and *Who's Who in America*, Vol. 23 (1944).

Stathelle (Nor.)	stät'-hĕl-ə	staht'-hel-uh
status	stā'-təs	stay'-tuhs

Many Americans say stăt'-əs [stat'-uhs] but radio speakers can play
safe by following the dictionary recommendation, as above. Webster's
(1934) allows short ă, as well as ā [ay], in *stratum, strata, apparatus*,
probably because so many scientists have the ă-pronunciation. But
datum and *data*, according to Webster's, should have ā [ay] or ä [ah].
Of course it would be reasonable to treat all such words alike and, I
believe, to admit ā [ay] and ă for the group.

Staunton (Eng., Ill., Ind.)	stŏn'-tən	ston'-tuhn
Staunton (Va.)	stăn'-tən	stan'-tuhn

Locally so called, but Tidewater Virginians may refer to this valley
town as stŏn'-tən [ston'-tuhn].

Stavanger (Nor.)	stä-väng'-ər	stah-vahng'-uhr
Stavelot (Belg.)	stä-vlō'	stah-vloh'

Flemish *Stablo,* stä'-blō [stah'-bloh].

Stavern (Nor.)	stä'-vĕrn	stah'-vehrn
Staviski (Pol.) See *Stawiski.*		
Stavoren (Neth.)	stä'-vô-rən	stah'-vo-ruhn
Stavros (Gr., point)	stä-vrôs'	stah-vros'
Staw (Pol.)	stäf'	stahf'
Stawiski (Pol.)	stä-vē'-skĭ	stah-vee'-ski

Russian spelling *Staviski.*

Ste. . . . See *Sainte* . . . . .

Steagall, Henry B.	stē-gôl'	stee-gawl'
(U.S. representative)		
stede	stä'-də	stay'-duh

An element, meaning *place,* in Dutch place names.

Steenbergen (Neth.)	stān'-bĕr-k(h)ən	stayn'-behr-k(h)uhn
Steenderen (Neth.)	stān'-də-rən	stayn'-duh-ruhn
Steenkerke (Belg.)	stān'-kĕr-kə	stayn'-kehr-kuh

Also called *Steenkerque,* stān'-kĕrk [stayn'-kehrk] and French *Stein-kerque,* stăN-kĕrk [staN-kehrk'].

Steenvoorde (Fr.)	stĕn-vōrd'	sten-vohrd'
Steenwerck (Fr.)	stĕn-vĕrk'	sten-vehrk'
Steenwijk (Neth.)	stān'-wīk	stayn'-waik
Steenwijkerwold (Neth.)	stān'-wī-kər-wôlt'	stayn'-wai-kuhr-wolt'
Stefan, Carl	stĕf'-ən	stef'-uhn
(U.S. representative)		
Stefano (It.)	stĕ'-fä-nô	steh'-fah-no

As a personal name and as a place name, *Stefano* should be stressed on the first, not on the second syllable. Cp. *Rapido.*

Stefansson, Vilhjalmur	*Eng.* stĕf'-ən-sən	stef'-uhn-suhn
(Can. explorer)	*Ice.* stĕ'-fäns-sōn,	steh'-fahns-sohn,
	vĭl'-hyoul-mər	vil'-hyaul-muhr
Stein (Neth.)	stīn'	stain'
Steinau (Ger. > Pol.)	shtī'-nou	shtai'-nau

Polish *Ścinawa,* q.v.

Steinkerque (Belg.) See *Steenkerke.*

Steinkjer (Nor.)	stān'-chĕr	stayn'-chehr
Stendal (Ger.)	shtĕn'-däl	shten'-dahl
Stepanakert (Rus.)	stĕ'-pä-nä-kĕrt'	steh'-pah-nah-kehrt'
Stephanopoulos,	stĕ-fä-nô'-pōō-lôs,	steh-fah-no'-poo-los,
Stephanos (Gr. polit.)	stĕ'-fä-nôs	steh'-fah-nos
Stepinatz, Aloysius	stĕp'-ĭ-näts,	step'-i-nahts,
(Yugosl. bishop)	ăl'-ō-ĭsh'-əs	al'-oh-ish'-uhs

Serb-Croat *Alojzije Stepinac*, ä-loi'-zē-ĕ stĕ'-pĭ-näts [ah-loi'-zee-eh steh'-pi-nahts].

Stepojevac (Yugosl.)	stĕ'-pô'-yĕ-väts	steh'-po'-yeh-vahts
Sterkrade (Ger.)	shtĕrk'-rä-də	shtehrk'-rah-duh
Sterlitamak (Rus.)	stĕr'-lĭ-tä-mäk'	stehr'-li-tah-mahk'
Sternes (Crete)	stĕr'-nĕs	stehr'-nes
Stettin (Ger. > Pol.)	shtĕ-tēn'	shteh-teen'
Polish *Szczecin*, q.v.		
Stettinius, Edward R.	stə-tĭn'-ĭ-əs	stuh-tin'-i-uhs
(U.S. diplomat)		
Stevens, Risë (Am.	stē'-vənz, rē'-sə	stee'-vuhnz, ree'-suh
singer)		
Steyr (Austria)	shtĭr'	shtair'
Stiens (Neth.)	stēns'	steens'
Štimlje (Yugosl.)	shtēm'-lyĕ	shteem'-lyeh
Stinica (Yugosl.)	stē'-nĭ-tsä	stee'-ni-tsah
Štip (Yugosl.)	shtēp'	shteep'
Stir (Pol. > Rus., riv.)	stĭr'	stir'
Polish spelling *Styr*.		
Štirovica (Yugosl.)	shtē'-rô-vĭ-tsä	shtee'-ro-vi-tsah
St. Niklaas (Belg.) See *Sint Niklaas*.		
Sto (Yugosl., mt.)	stô'	staw'
Stockerau (Austria)	shtôk'-ə-rou	shtok'-uh-rau
Stockholm (Sw.)	*Eng.* stŏk'-hōm	stok'-hohm
	Sw. stôk'-hôlm'	stok'-holm'
Stockmanshof (Latvia)	*Ger.* shtôk'-mäns-hôf	shtok'-mahns-hof
Latvian *Plaviņas*, q.v.		
Stoczek (Pol.)	stô'-chĕk	sto'-chek
Russian spelling *Stochek*.		
Stoeren (Nor.)	stû'-rən	stœ'-ruhn
Stoestad, Sverre (Nor.	stû'-stä, svĕr'-ə	stœ'-stah, svehr'-uh
diplomat)		
Stojakovo (Yugosl.)	stô'-yä'-kô-vô	sto'-yah'-ko-vo
Stojnik (Yugosl.)	stoi'-nĭk	stoi'-nik
Stokhod (Pol. > Rus.,	stŏ-hôt'	sto-hot'
riv.)		
Polish *Stochód*, stô'-hŏŏt [sto'-hut].		
Stokmarksnes (Nor.)	stôk'-märks-nĕs	stok'-mahrks-nes
Stokowski, Leopold	stô-kôf'-skĭ, lē'-ə-pōld	sto-kof'-ski, lee'-uh-
Antoni Stanisław	än-tô'-nē stä-nē'-	pohld ahn-to'-nee
Bolesławowicz (Eng.	släf bô-lĕ-slä-vô'-	stah-nee'-slahf bo-
Am. musician)	vĭch	leh-slah-vo'-vich
Stolac (Yugosl.)	stô'-läts	sto'-lahts
Stolberg (Ger.)	shtôl'-bĕrk(h)	shtol'-behrk(h)

Stolbtsi (Pol. >Rus.)	stôlp′-tsĭ	stolp′-tsi
Polish *Stołpce*, stôlp′-tsĕ [stolp′-tseh].		
Stolp (Ger. >Pol.)	shtôlp′	shtolp′
Polish *Słupsk*, q.v.		
Stolpmuende,	shtôlp′-mün-də	shtolp′-mün-duh
Stolpmünde (Ger. > Pol.)		
Polish *Ustka*, q.v.		
Stolwijk (Neth.)	stôl′-wīk	stol′-waik
stomach	stŭm′-ək	stuhm′-uhk

The pronunciation stŭm′-ĭk [stuhm′-ik] is common, but it isn't recommended.

Stompwijk (Neth.)	stômp′-wīk	stomp′-waik
Ston (Yugosl.)	stôn′	ston′
Stopanja (Yugosl.)	stô′-pä-nyä	sto′-pah-nyah
Stopnica (Pol.)	stôp-nĕ′-tsä	stop-nee′-tsah
Stord (Nor., isl.)	stŏŏrd′	sturd′
Storebaelt (Den., sound]	stô′-rə-bĕlt	sto′-ruh-belt
Stören (Nor.)	stŭ′-rən	stœ′-ruhn
Storfjord (Nor.)	stōr′-fyŏr	stohr′-fyohr
Storfosshei (Nor.)	stōr′-fôs-hā′	stohr′-fos-hay′
Storkow (Ger.)	shtôr′-kō	shtor′-koh
Storlien (Sw.)	stōr′-lē-ən	stohr′-lee-uhn
Storni, Ramón (Arg. polit.)	stôr′-nē, rä-môn′	stor′-nee, rah-mon′
Stöstad, Sverre (Nor. polit.)	stŭ′-stä, svĕr′-ə	stœ′-stah, svehr′-uh
Stotsenburg (P.I.)	stŏt′-sən-bûrg	stot′-suhn-buhrg
Stoumont (Belg.)	stōō-môN′	stoo-moN′
Stožac (Yugosl., mt.)	stô′-zhäts	sto′-zhahts
Strabane (N. Ire.)	strə-băn′	struh-ban′
Strabolgi, Lord (Br. polit.)	strə-bō′-gĭ	struh-boh′-gi
Strachan (Scot. name)	străk(h)′-ən *or* strôn′	strak(h)′-uhn *or* strawn′
Strachey, John (Br. polit.)	strā′-chĭ	stray′-chi
Stradiotti (Yugosl., isl.)	*It.* strä-dē-ôt′-tē	strah-dee-ot′-tee
Serb-Croat *Sveti Marko*, q.v.		
strafe, strafed, strafing	sträf′ *or* sträf′, -t, -ĭng	strayf′ *or* strahf′, -t, -ing

Because *strafe* is freely inflected as an English verb, the completely Anglicized pronunciation with ā [ay] is preferable to ä [ah] in all forms; sträf′ [strahf′] is not difficult to say, but to many people, sträft′ [strahft′] and sträf′-ĭng [strahf′-ing] seem unidiomatic. In contrast is *suave*, q.v., which as an adjective has only one form and more easily maintains an exotic pronunciation.

Stragari (Yugosl.)	strä'-gä-rĭ	strah'-gah-ri
Strait of Messina (Sicily)	mĕs-sē'-nä	mes-see'-nah
Strakonice (Cz.)	strä'-kô-nĭ-tsĕ	strah'-ko-ni-tseh
Strasbourg (Fr.)	*Eng.* sträz'-bŏŏrg	strahz'-burg
	Fr. sträz-bŏŏr'	strahz-boor'

As an American place name, it is pronounced strás'-bûrg [stras'-buhrg]. German *Strassburg*, shträs'-bŏŏrk(h) [shtrahs'-burk(h)].

Stratoni (Gr.)	strä-tô'-nē	strah-to'-nee
stratosphere	străt'-ə-sfĭr	strat'-uh-sfir
	or strā'-tə-sfĭr	stray'-tuh-sfir

Webster's prefers the second pronunciation but the first is more usual and is preferred by Kenyon and Knott, and by Thorndike Century dictionaries. For *strata*, all dictionaries prefer strā'-tə to străt'-ə, but the case for the short *a* in *stratosphere* rests upon the length of the word. Compare *holy* and *holiday*.

Strausberg (Ger.)	strous'-bĕrk(h)	straus'-behrk(h)
Štrba (Cz.)	shtər'-bä	shtuhr'-bah
Štrbac (Yugosl., mts.)	shtər'-bäts	shtuhr'-bahts
Strehlen (Ger. >? Pol.)	shträ'-lən	shtray'-luhn
Polish *Strzelin*, q.v.		
Strehlitz, Gross (Ger.) See *Gross Strehlitz*.		
Streicher, Julius (Ger. polit.)	shtrĭ'-k(h)ər, yŏŏ'-lĭ-ŏŏs	shtrai'-k(h)uhr, yoo'-li-us
Strelac (Yugosl.)	strĕ'-läts	streh'-lahts
strengthen	strĕng'-thən	streng'-thuhn

The pronunciation strĕn'-thən [stren'-thuhn], probably an infantilism, is not uncommon. It should, of course, be avoided.

Streoci (Yugosl.)	strĕ'-ô-tsĭ	streh'-o-tsi
streptomycin (drug)	strĕp-tə-mĭ'-sĭn	strep-tuh-mai'-sin
streptothricin (drug)	strĕp-tə-thrĭ'-sĭn	strep-tuh-thrai'-sin
	or -thrĭs'-ĭn	*or* -thris'-in

This seems to be the order of preference among American doctors.

Stresemann, Gustav (Ger. statesman)	shträ'-zə-män, gŏŏs'-täf	shtray'-zuh-mahn, gus'-tahf
Strešer (Yugosl., mt.)	strĕ'-shĕr	streh'-shehr
Strezlecki (Austral., mts.)	strĕz-lĕk'-ĭ	strez-lek'-i
Stri (Pol. > Rus.)	strē'	stree'
Polish spelling *Stryi*.		
Štrice (Yugosl.)	shtrĕ'-tsĕ	shtree'-tseh
Striegau (Ger. >? Pol.)	shtrē'-gou	shtree'-gau
Polish *Strzegom*, q.v.		
Strijen (Neth.)	strĭ'-ən	strai'-uhn

Strojkovce (Yugosl.)	stroi'-kôv-tsĕ	stroi'-kov-tseh
Stromberg (Ger.)	*Eng.* strŏm'-bərg	strom'-buhrg
	Ger. shtrōm'-bĕrk(h)	shtrohm'-behrk(h)
Stromboli (It., isl.)	strôm'-bô-lē	strom'-bo-lee
Stroobos (Neth.)	strō'-bôs	stroh'-bos
Strophades (Gr., isls.)	*Eng.* strō'-fə-dēz	stroh'-fuh-deez
	Gr. strô-fä'-dĕs	stro-fah'-des
Struer (Den.)	strōō'-ər	stroo'-uhr
Struga (Yugosl.)	strōō'-gä	stroo'-gah
Strugi (Rus.)	strōō'-gĭ	stroo'-gi
Struma (Balkan riv.)	strōō'-mä	stroo'-mah

Greek *Strouma* and *Strymon*, strē-môn' [stree-mon']. Turkish *Kara Sou*, kä-rä' sōō' [kah-rah' soo'].

Strumica (Yugosl.)	strōō'-mĭ-tsä	stroo'-mi-tsah

Stryi (Pol. >Rus.) See *Stri*.

Strypa (Pol. >Rus., riv.)	strĭ'-pä	stri'-pah
Strzałkowo (Pol.)	stchäl-kô'-vô	stchahl-ko'-vo
Strzegom (Ger. >? Pol.)	stchĕ'-gôm	stcheh'-gom
German *Striegau*, q.v.		
Strzelin (Ger. >? Pol.)	stchĕ'-lĭn	stcheh'-lin
German *Strehlen*, q.v.		
Stubica (Yugosl.)	stōō'-bĭ-tsä	stoo'-bi-tsah
Štubik (Yugosl.)	shtōō'-bĭk	shtoo'-bik
Studenica (Yugosl.)	stōō'-dĕ'-nĭ-tsä	stoo'-deh'-ni-tsah
Studeničane (Yugosl.)	stōō'-dĕ-nē'-chä-nĕ	stoo'-deh-nee'-chah-neh
Stuka (Ger. plane)	*Eng.* styōō'-kə	styoo'-kuh
	Ger. shtōō'-kä	shtoo'-kah
Šturac (Yugosl., mt.)	shtōō'-räts	shtoo'-rahts
Stuttgart (Ger.)	*Eng.* stŭt'-gärt	stuht'-gahrt
	Ger. shtōŏt'-gärt	shtut'-gahrt
Styer, W. D.	stī'-ər	stai'-uhr
(Am. general)		
Styr (Pol. >Rus., riv.)	stĭr'	stihr'
Russian spelling *Stir*.		
Styria (Austria)	stĭr'-ĭ-ə	stihr'-i-uh

German *Steiermark*, shtīr'-märk [shtair'-mahrk].

Sual (P.I.)	swäl'	swahl'
Suárez Veintimilla,	swä'-rĕs vān'-tĭ-mē'-	swah'-res vayn'-ti-
Mariano (Ecuador	yä, mä-ryä'-nô	mee'-yah, mah-
polit.)		ryah'-no
suave	swäv' *or* swāv'	swahv' *or* swayv'

The pronunciation swäv' [swahv'] is more common in America, swāv' [swayv'] in England. Cf. *strafe*.

[514]

Subaang (P.I.)	sōō-bä-äng′	soo-bah-ahng′
Subardjo (Indo. polit.)	sōō′-bär′-jô′	soo′-bahr′-jo′
Šubašić, Ivan (Yugosl. polit.)	shōō′-bä-shĭch, ē′-vän	shoo′-bah-shich, ee′-vahn

Also spelled *Subasitch* and *Shubashich*.

Subiaco (It.)	sōō-byä′-kô	soo-byah′-ko
Súbic (P.I.)	sōō′-bĭk	soo′-bik
Subotica (Yugosl.)	sōō′-bô′-tĭ-tsä	soo′-bo′-ti-tsah

Hungarian *Szabadka*, sŏ′-bŏt-kŏ [so′-bot-ko].

Subotinac (Yugosl.)	sōō′-bô′-tĭ-näts	soo′-bo′-ti-nahts
subpoene, subpene	sə-pē′nə *or* səb-pē′-nə	suh-pee′-nuh *or* suhb-pee′-nuh

In the South and East the pronunciation sə-pē′-nĭ [suh-pee′-nĭ] is common. Compare the interchange of ĭ and ə in *Missouri*.

Suceava (Rum.)	sōō-chä′-vä	su-chah′-vah
Suchan (Rus.)	sōō-chän′	soo-chahn′
Su-chow (Ch., Kansu)	sōō-jō	soo-joh
Su-chow (Ch., Kiangsu, near Shanghai)	See *Soo-chow*.	
Sü-chow (Ch., N. Kiangsu)	shü-jō	shü-joh

Also spelled *Hsü-chow*.

Süchteln (Ger.)	zük(h)′-tĕln	zük(h)′-teln
Sucre (Bol., Ven.)	sōō′-krĕ	soo′-kreh
Suda (Crete, bay)	sōō′-dä	soo′-dah

Also spelled *Souda*, q.v.

Sudab (P.I.)	sōō-däb′	soo-dahb′
Sudak (Rus.)	sōō-däk′	soo-dahk′
Sudan (Afr.)	sōō-dăn′	soo-dan′
Sudeten (Cz., Ger.)	*Eng.* sōō-dāt′n	soo-dayt′n
	Ger. zōō-dä′-tən	zoo-day′-tuhn

English *Sudetes* (noun), sōō-dē′-tēz [su-dee′-teez], and *Sudetic* (adj.), sōō-dĕt′-ĭk [su-det′-ik]. The noun *Sudetens* was coined in 1938. For the history of this interesting word see the article by Prof. Franz H. Mautner in *American Speech*, XVIII (October, 1943), 200-207.

Sudharam (India)	sōō-dä′-räm	su-dah′-rahm

Also called *Noakhali*, q.v.

Sudzha (Rus.)	sōō-jä′	su-jah′
Suechteln (Ger.)	zük(h)′-tĕln	zük(h)′-teln
Suetsugu, Nobumasa (Jap. polit.)	sōō-ĕ′-tsōō-gōō, nô-bōō′-mä-sä	soo-eh′-tsoo-goo, no-boo′-mah-sah
Suez (Egypt)	sōō-ĕz′	soo-ez′

Arabic *Es Suweis*, q.v.

Sugamo (Jap., Tokyo, prison)	sōō′-gä-mô	soo′-gah-mo

Sugrue, Thomas   shōō-grōō'   shoo-groo'
  (Am. author)

  Mr. Sugrue writes: "The name is encountered in America in various spellings: Shugrue, Sughrue, Sughroe, Sugru, Shugrew, etc."

Sui-an (Ch., Chekiang)   swĕ-än   swee-ahn

Sui-ch'ang (Ch., Che-   swĕ-chäng   swee-chahng
  kiang)

Sui-ch'wan (Ch.,   swĕ-chwän   swee-chwahn
  Kiangsi)

Sui-fên(-ho) (Manchu.)   swä-fŭn(-hŭ)   sway-fuhn(-huh)

Sui-fu (Ch., Szechwan)   swä-fōō   sway-foo

Sui-hua (Manchu.)   swä-whä   sway-whah

suite   swĕt' or syōōt', sōōt'   sweet' or syoot', soot'

  Suit and *suite* are the same word, a borrowing from Old French *siute*, later *suite*. The older pronunciation syōōt or sōōt is associated with the first spelling, and a quasi-French pronunciation, swĕt', may or may not be called for by the second. Examples: "the king and his suite (swĕt) or retinue"; "a piano suite" (swĕt); "This suit (syōōt) is trumps"; "This suit (syōōt) of clothes"; "this suite (syōōt or swĕt) of furniture"; "this suite (swĕt or syōōt) of rooms." In the last two examples, usage is divided, and preference for one or the other should not be permitted to divide friends or to separate wedded sweets in bridal suites.

Sui-yüan (Ch., prov.)   swä-yüän   sway-yü-ahn

  Webster's, soi'-ywän'; BBC, swä-yōō-ăn'. This province is also known as *Kweihwa-Suiyuan*, q.v.

Sukabumi (NEI, Java)   sōō-kä-bōō'-mē   soo-kah-boo'-mee

Sukarno, Achmed   sōō'-kär'-nộ',   soo'-kahr'-no',
  (Indo. polit.)   äk(h)-mĕt'   ahk(h)-met'

Sukhinichi (Rus.)   sōō-hē'-nĭ-chĭ   soo-hee'-ni-chi

Sukhum (Rus.)   sōō-hōōm'   soo-hoom'

sukiyaki   *Eng.* sōō'-kĭ-yä'-kĭ   soo'-ki-yah'-ki
    Jap. sōō-kē'-yä'-kē'   soo-kee'-yah'-kee'

  Japanese dish popular among Americans.

Sukkertoppen (Greenl.)   sŏŏk'-ər-tôp'n   suk'-uhr-top'n

Sukkur (India)   sŭk'-ər   suhk'-uhr

Sukošan (Yugosl.)   sōō'-kộ-shän   soo'-ko-shahn

Sula (Rus., riv.)   sōō'-lä   soo'-lah

Sulayman, Abdullah al (Arab. polit.) See *Abdullah al Suleiman.*

Suldal (Nor.)   sŏŏl'-däl   sul'-dahl

Sulechów (Ger. >Pol.)   sōō-lĕ'-hŏŏf   su-leh'-huf

  German *Zuellichau*, q.v.

Suleev (Pol.) See *Sulejów.*

Suleiman, Abdullah al (Arab. polit.) See *Abdullah al Suleiman.*

Sulejów (Pol.)　　　　　　soo-lĕ'-yoof　　　　su-leh'-yuf
　　Russian *Suleev,* soo-lĕ'-yĕf [su-leh'-yef].
Sulet (Yugosl.)　　　　　　soo'-lĕt　　　　　　soo'-let
　　Italian *Solta,* q.v.
Sulina (Rum.)　　　　　　soo-lē'-nä　　　　　su-lee'-nah
Sulitjelma (Nor.)　　　　　sool-ē-tyĕl'-mä　　　sul-ee-tyel'-mah
Sulmona (It.)　　　　　　sool-mô'-nä　　　　　sool-mo'-nah
Sultanabad (Iran)　　　　sool-tä'-nə-bäd'　　　sul-tah'-nuh-bahd'
　　Also called *'Iraq,* ē-räk' [ee-rahk'].
sultaneh *or* saltaneh　　　səl-tä-nĕ'　　　　　suhl-tah-neh'
　　A Persian title or honorific that follows the name. It is disregarded in
　　alphabetical listing.
Sulu (P.I.)　　　　　　　soo'-loo　　　　　　soo'-loo
Sulúan (P.I.)　　　　　　soo-loo'-än　　　　　soo-loo'-ahn
Sulyok, Dezső　　　　　　shool'-yôk, dĕ'-zhû　shul'-yok, deh'-zhœ
　　(Hung. polit.)
Šumadija (Yugosl.)　　　　shoo'-mä'-dĭ-yä　　　shoo'-mah'-di-yah
Sumatra (NEI)　　　　　soo-mä'-trə　　　　　su-mah'-truh
Sumay (Oc., Guam)　　　soo-mĭ'　　　　　　soo-mai'
Sumba (NEI)　　See *Soemba.*
Sumbawa (NEI)　　See *Soembawa.*
Sumitomo (Jap., zaibatsu) soo-mē'-tô'-mô'　　soo-mee'-to'-mo'
Sumprabum (Burma)　　soom'-prä-boom'　　　sum'-prah-bum'
Sumy (Rus.)　　　　　　soo'-mĭ　　　　　　soo'-mi
Sunario (Indo. polit.)　　soo'-nä'-ryô'　　　　soo'-nah'-ryo'
sund　　　　　　　　　soon'　　　　　　　sun'
　　An element, meaning *strait,* in Norwegian place names.
Sunda *or* Soenda (NEI)　*Eng.* sŭn'-də　　　suhn'-duh
　　　　　　　　　　　Du. soon'-dä　　　soon'-dah
Sundalsoeyra *or*　　　　soon'-däls-ûĭ'-rä　　sun'-dahls-œi-rah
　　Sundalsöyra (Nor.)
Sunde, Arne (Nor.　　　　soon'-də, är'-nə　　sun'-duh, ahr'-nuh
　　diplomat)
Sundstrom, Frank L.　　　sŭnd'-strəm　　　　suhnd'-struhm
　　(U.S. representative)
Sundsvall (Sw.)　　　　　soons'-väl　　　　　suns'-vahl
Sundvollen (Nor.)　　　　soon'-vôl-ən　　　　sun'-vol-uhn
Suñer, Ramón Serrano (Sp. polit.)　　See *Serrano Suñer.*
Sun Fo (Ch. polit.)　　　soon fô　　　　　　sun fo
　　Mandarin *Sun K'o,* soon kŭ [sun kuh].
Sungari (Manchu., riv.)　*Eng.* soong'-gə-rē'　soong'-guh-ree'
Sungaria (Ch., Sinkiang)　　See *Dzungaria.*
Sungi (P.I., point)　　　　soong'-ē　　　　　soong'-ee
Sung-tzŭ (Ch., Hupeh)　　soong-dzə　　　　　sung-dzuh
　　Also spelled *Sung-tze.*

Sung-yang (Ch.,   sŏong-yäng   sung-yahng
  Chekiang)

Sunnhordland (Nor.)   sŏon'-hôr-län   sun'-hor-lahn

Sunnmoere or Sunnmöre   sŏon'-mû-rə   sun'-mœ-ruh
  (Nor.)

Sun Wên (Ch. patriot) See *Sun Yat-sen.*

Sun Yat-sen (Ch. patriot) *Eng.* sŭn yăt-sĕn   suhn yat-sen
  Cantonese sŏon yät-sĕn [sun yaht-sen]. Mandarin *Sun I-hsien,* sŏon
  yē-shyĕn [sun yee-shyen]. Also called *Sun Chung-shan,* jŏong-shän
  [jung shahn] from his home town. These are "courtesy names" or
  nicknames, his real name being *Sun Wên* sŏon wŭn [sun wuhn].
  Madame Sun is *Ch'ing-ling Soong,* q.v.

Suojärvi (Fin. > Rus.)   sŏo'-ô'-yăr-vĕ   su'-o'-yehr-vee
  Russian *Suoyarvi,* sŏo-ô-yär'-vĭ [su-o-yahr'-vi].

Suomenlinna (Fin.)   sŏo'-ô'-mĕn-lĭn-nä   su'-o'-men-lin-nah
  Swedish *Sveaborg,* svĕ'-ä-bôr'(y) [sveh'-ah-bor'(y)].

Suomi   See *Finland.*

Suomussalmi (Fin.)   sŏo'-ô'-mŏos-säl-mē   su'-o'-mus-sahl-mee

Supetar (Yugosl.)   sŏo'-pĕ'-tär   soo'-peh'-tahr
  Italian *San Pietro della Brazza.*

Suphli (Gr.)   See *Souphlion.*

Supino (It.)   sŏo-pē'-nô   soo-pee'-no

Supiori (NEI) See *Soepiori.*

Sura (Rus., riv.)   sŏo-rä'   soo-rah'

Surabaya or Soerabaja   sŏo-rä-bä'-yä   soo-rah-bah'-yah
  (NEI, Java)

Surakarta (NEI)   See *Soerakarta.*

Surat (India, riv.)   sŏo-răt' *or* sŏo'-rət   su-rat' *or* soo'-ruht

Surazh (Rus.)   sŏo-räzh'   soo-rahzh'

Surcouf (Fr.)   sür-kōof'   sür-koof'

Surdulica (Yugosl.)   sŏor'-dōo'-lĭ-tsä   soor'-doo'-li-tsah

Sure (Belg., Luxem., riv.) sür'   sür'

Suribachi (Jap., Iwo, mt.) sŏo-rē-bä'-chē   soo-ree-bah'-chee

Surigao (P.I.)   sŏo-rĭ-gou'   soo-ri-gau'

Surinam (S.A.)   sŏor-ĭ-näm'   sur-i-nahm'
  Dutch *Suriname,* sü-rĭ-nä'-mə [sü-ri-nah'-muh]. Also called Dutch
  Guiana, gē-ä'-nə [gee-ah'-nuh].

Surovikino (Rus.)   sŏo-rŏ-vē'-kĭ-nŏ   su-ro-vee'-ki-no

Susa (Tun.)   sŏo'-sä   soo'-sah
  French *Sousse,* q.v.

Sušac (It. > Yugosl., isl.) *S.-C.* sŏo'-shäts   soo'-shahts
  Italian *Cazza,* q.v.

Sušak (It. > Yugosl., isl.) *S.-C.* sŏo'-shäk   soo'-shahk
  Italian *Sansego,* q.v.

Susitna (Alaska)	sōō-sĭt′-nə	soo-sit′-nuh
Susteren (Neth.)	sü′-stə-rən	sü′-stuh-ruhn
Sutlej (India, riv.)	sŭt′-lĕj	suht′-lej
Suursaari (Fin., isl.)	sōōr′-sä-rē	soor′-sah-ree

Swedish *Hogland*, hōōg′-länd [hoog′-lahnd].

Suva (Oc., Fiji)	sōō′-vä	soo′-vah
Suvorov (Oc.)	sōō-vô′-rŏf	su-vo′-rof
Suvorov, Aleksandr V.	sōō-vô′-rŏf,	su-vo′-rof, ah-leh-
(Rus. marshal)	ä-lĕ-ksän′-dər	ksahn′-duhr
Suvo Rudište (Yugosl.,	sōō′-vô rōō′-dĭ-shtĕ	soo′-vo roo′-di-shteh
mt.)		
Suwałki (Pol.)	sōō-väl′-kĭ	su-vahl′-ki

Russian spelling *Suvalki*.

Suzdal (Rus.)	sōōz′-däl(y)	sooz′-dahl(y)
Suze, la (Fr.)	süz′, lä	süz′, lah
Suzuki, Kantarō (Jap.	sōō-zōō′-kē′,	soo-zoo′-kee′,
polit.)	kän-tä-rô′	kahn-tah-ro′

Svalbard (Nor. polar territory) See *Spitsbergen*.

Svalyava (Cz. >Rus.)	svä′-lyä-vä	svah′-lyah-vah

Czech spelling *Svalava*. Hungarian *Szolyva*, sô′ĭ-vŏ [so′i-vo].

Svanvik (Nor.)	svän′-vēk	svahn′-veek
Svartisen (Nor., glacier)	svärt′-ē-sən	svahrt′-ee-suhn
Svätý Jur (Cz.)	svä′-tĭ yōōr′	sveh′-ti yoor′

German *Sankt Georgen*, English *St. George's*.

Sveaborg (Fin.) See *Suomenlinna*.

Svecha (Rus.)	svĕ-chä′ (locally	sveh-chah′ (locally
	-tsä′)	-tsah′)
Svelvik (Nor.)	svĕl′-vēk	svel′-veek
Svendborg (Den.)	svĕn′-bôr	sven′-bor
Svenska Dagbladet	svĕns′-kä däg′-blä-	svens′-kah dahg′-
(Sw. newspaper)	dət	blah′-duht
Šventoyi (Lith., riv.)	shvĕn-tô′-yē	shven-to′-yee
Šventsyani (Pol. >Rus.)	svĕn-chä′-nĭ	sven-chah′-ni
Polish *Święciany*, q.v.		
Sverdlovsk (Rus.)	svĕrd-lôfsk′	svehrd-lofsk′
Sveti Grgur (Yugosl., isl.)	svĕ′-tĭ gər′-gōōr	sveh′-ti guhr′-goor

Italian *Gregorio*, grĕ-gô′-ryô [greh-go′-ryo].

Sveti Juraj (Yugosl.)	svĕ′-tĭ yōō′-rī	sveh′-ti yoo′-rai

Italian *San Giorgio*, sän jôr′-jô [sahn jor′-jo].

Sveti Lovrenc (Yugosl.)	svĕ′-tĭ lô′-vrĕnts	sveh′-ti lo′-vrents
Sveti Marko (Yugosl.,	svĕ′-tĭ mär′-kô	sveh′-ti mahr′-ko
isl.)		
Italian *Stradiotti*, q.v.		
Sveti Naum (Yugosl.)	svĕ′-tĭ nä′-ōōm	sveh′-ti nah′-oom

Sveti Petar (It. > Yugosl., svĕ'-tĭ pĕ'-tär   sveh'-ti peh'-tahr
   isl.)
   Italian *Asinello*, q.v.

Sveto Brdo (Yugosl.)	svĕ'-tô bər'-dô	sveh'-to buhr'-do
Svilajnac (Yugosl.)	svē'-lĭ-näts	svee'-lai-nahts

Svir (Pol.)   See *Świr*.

Svirstroi (Rus.)	svēr'-stroi'	sveer'-stroi'
Svishtov (Bulg.)	svĭsh'-tŏf	svish'-tof

   Rumanian *Şiştov*, shĭsh'-tôf [shish'-tof].

Svisloch (Pol.)   See *Świsłocz*.

Svityaz (Pol.)   See *Świtaź*.

Sviyagino (Rus.)	svĭ-yä'-gĭ-nŏ	svi-yah'-gi-no
Svoboda (Rus.)	svŏ-bô'-dä	svo-bo'-dah
Svobodny (Rus.)	svŏ-bôd'-nĭ	svo-bod'-ni
Svojinovo (Yugosl.)	svô'-yĭ-nô-vô	svo'-yi-no-vo
Svolos, Alexandros	zvô'-lôs, ä-lĕ'-	zvo'-los, ah-leh'-
(Gr. polit.)	ksän-drôs	ksahn-dros
Svolvær (Nor.)	svôl'-văr	svol'-vehr
Svrljig (Yugosl.)	svər'-lyĭg	svuhr'-lyig
Svrljiški Timok	svər'-lyĭsh-kĭ tē'-môk	svuhr'-lyish-ki tee'-
(Yugosl., riv.)		mok
Swa (Burma, riv.)	swä'	swah'
Swaraj (Indian "home	swə-räj'	swuh-rahj'
rule")		
Swatow (Ch., Kwang-	*Eng.* swä-tou	swah-tau
tung)		

   Chinese *Shan-t'ow*, q.v.

Sweelinck, Jan	swä'-lĭnk, yän	sway'-link, yahn
Pieterszoon (Du.	pē'-tər-sōn	pee'-tuhr-sohn
musician)		

   Also spelled *Swelinck*.

Swevezeele (Belg.)	swä'-və-zā'-lə	sway'-vuh-zay'-luh
Świca (Pol., riv.)	shvē'-tsä	shvee'-tsah
Świdnica (Ger. > ? Pol.)	shvĭd-nē'-tsä	shvid-nee'-tsah

   German *Schweidnitz*, q.v.

Świebodzin (Ger. > Pol.)   shvyĕ-bô'-jĭn   shvyeh-bo'-jin

   German *Schwiebus*, q.v.

Swieçiany (Pol. > Rus.)   shvyăN-chä'-nĭ   shvyaN-chah'-ni

   Russian *Sventsyani*, svĕn-chä'-nĭ [sven-chah'-ni].

Swinemuende *or*	svē'-nə-mün'-də	svee'-nuh-mün'-duh
Swinemünde (Ger.)		
Świnica (Pol., Cz., mt.)	*Pol.* shvĭ-nē'-tsä	shvi-nee'-tsah
Świr (Pol.	shvēr'	shveer'

   Russian *Svir*, svēr' [sveer'].

Świsłocz (Pol.) shvē′-slôch shvee′-sloch
Russian *Svisloch*, svē′-slôch [svee′-sloch].
Świtaź (Pol.) shvē′-täzh shvee′-tahzh
Russian *Svityaz*, svē′-tyäz [svee′-tyahz].
Sychëvka (Rus.) sĭ-chôf′-kä si-chof′-kah
Sydenham (Eng. name) sĭd′n-əm sid′n-uhm
Syevernaya (Rus.) Variant of *Severnaya*, q.v.
Sylt (Ger., isl.) sĭlt′ silt′
Syme (Dodec.) sē′-mē see′-mee
Synge, John M. sĭng′ sing′
(Irish poet)
Syngman Rhee (Korean sŏŏng-män rē sung-mahn ree
polit.)
Syosset (N.Y., L.I.) sī-ŏs′-ĭt sai-os′-it
Syracuse, (N.Y.) sĭr′-ə-kyōōs sihr′-uh-kyoos
or sĭr′-ə-kyōōz sihr′-uh-kyooz
Italian *Siracusa*, q.v.
Syriam (Burma) sĭ′-rĭ-ăm si′-ri-am
Syrmia (Yugosl.) *Eng.* sûr′-myə suhr′-myuh
Serb-Croat *Srem*, srĕm′ [srem′]. Hungarian *Szerém*, sĕ′-rām [seh′-raym].
Syros (Gr., isl.) sē′-rô(s) see′-ro(s)
Syzran (Rus.) sĭz-rän′(y) siz-rahn′(y)
Szabadka (Yugosl.) See *Subotica.*
Szabadszállás (Hung.) sŏ′-bŏd-säl′-läsh so′-bod-sahl′-lahsh
Szálasi, Ferenc sä′-lŏ-shĭ, fĕ′-rĕnts sah′-lo-shi, feh′-rents
(Hung. polit.)
Szamos (Hung., Rum., sŏ′-môsh so′-mosh
riv.)
Szamotuły (Pol.) shä-mô-tōō′-lĭ shah-mo-too′-li
Szarvas (Hung.) sŏr′-vŏsh sor′-vosh
Szczakowa (Pol.) shchä-kô′-vä shchah-ko′-vah
Szczara (Pol. >Rus., riv.) See *Shchara.*
Szczawnica (Pol.) shchäv-nē′-tsä shchahv-nee′-tsah
Szczecin (Ger. >Pol.) shchĕ′-tsĭn shcheh′-tsin
German *Stettin*, q.v.
Szczekowski, Jan shchĕ-kôf′-skĭ, yän′ shcheh-kof′-ski, yahn′
(Pol. polit.)
Szczuczyn (Pol. >Rus.) shchōō′-chĭn shchoo′-chin
Russian spelling *Shchuchin.*
Szczytno (Ger. >Pol.) shchĭt′-nô shchit′-no
German *Ortelsburg*, q.v.
Szeben (Rum.) See *Sibiu.*
Szê-ch'wan (Ch., prov.) *Eng.* sĕ-chwän seh-chwahn
Ch. sŭ-chwän suh-chwahn

Szeged (Hung.)	sĕ'-gĕd	seh'-ged
Székelyudvarhely (Rum.)	See *Odorhei*.	
Székesfehérvar (Hung.)	sā'-kĕsh-fĕ'-hār-vär	say'-kesh-feh'-hayr-vahr
Szekszárd (Hung.)	sĕk'-särd	sek'-sahrd
Szelków (Pol.)	shĕl'-kōōf	shel'-kuf
Szê-ming (Ch., Fukien) See *Amoy*.		
Szentes (Hung.)	sĕn'-tĕsh	sen'-tesh
Szentgotthárd (Hung.)	sĕnt-gôt'-härt	sent-got'-hahrt
English *Saint Gotthard*, q.v.		
Szentgyörgyi, Albert	sĕn'-dyûr-dyĭ,	sen'-dyœr-dyi,
(Hung. polit.)	ŏl'-bĕrt	ol'-behrt
Szepesh (Cz.) See *Spiš*.		
Szê-ping Kai (Ch.,	*Eng.* sĕ-pĭng kī	seh-ping kai
Manchu.)	*Ch.* sŭ-pĭng gī	suh-ping gai
Mandarin, *Ssŭ-p'ing-chieh*, sŭ-pĭng-jyĕ [suh-ping-jyeh].		
Szerencs (Hung.)	sĕ'-rĕnch	seh'-rench
Szigeti, Joseph	*Eng.* sĭ-gĕt'-ĭ	si-get'-i
(Hung. violinist)	*Hung.* sĭ'-gĕ-tĭ	si'-geh-ti
Szigetvár (Hung.)	sĭ'-gĕt-vär	si'-get-vahr
Szikszó (Hung.)	sĭk'-sô	sik'-so
Szilard, Leo	sĭ-lärd'	si-lahrd'
(Hung. Am. scientist)		
Hungarian *Szilárd*, sē'-lärd [see'-lahrd].		
Szkwa (Pol., riv.)	shkvä'	shkvah'
Russian spelling *Shkva*.		
Szolnok (Hung.)	sôl'-nôk	sol'-nok
Szombathely (Hung.)	sôm'-bät-hā *or* -hĕ(y)	som'-baht-hay
Szopienice (Pol.)	shô-pyĕ-nē'-tsĕ	sho-pyeh-nee'-tseh
Szprotawa (Ger. >? Pol.)	shprô-tä'-vä	shpro-tah'-vah
Sztojay, Döme	stô'-yoi, dû'-mĕ	sto'-yoi, dœ'-meh
(Hung. polit.)		
Szwalbe, Stanisław	shväl'-bĕ, stä-nē'-släf	shvahl'-be, stah-nee'-slahf
(Pol. polit.)		
Szydłowiec (Pol.)	shĭ-dlô'-vyĕts	shi-dlo'-vyets
Russian *Shidlovets*, shĭ-dlô'-vĕts [shi-dlo'-vets].		
Szymczak, M. S.	sĭm'-chăk	sim'-chak
(Am. economist)		
Taal (P.I., lake)	tä-äl'	tah-ahl'
Tabanovci (Yugosl.)	tä'-bä'-nôv-tsĭ	tah'-bah'-nov-tsi
Tabar (Oc., Bismarck arch.)	tä-bär'	tah-bahr'

Tabarca (Tun.)   tä-bär'-kä   tah-bahr'-kah
   The accent of the ancient *Thabraca* was on the first syllable.
Tabariya (Pal.) See *Tiberias.*
Tabasco (Mex.)   *Eng.* tə-băs'-kō   tuh-bas'-koh
                Sp. tä-bäs'-kô   tah-bahs'-ko
Tabatabai, Säid Zia ed Din (Iran. polit.) See *Zia ed Din Tabatabai.*
Taber, John   tā'-bər   tay'-buhr
   (U.S. representative)
Tabín (P.I.)   tä-bēn'   tah-been'
Tabiteuea (Oc., Gilberts)   tä'-bē-tĕ'-ōō-ĕ'-ä   tah'-bee-teh'-oo-eh'-
                                       ah
Tabontabón (P.I.)   tä-bôn-tä-bôn'   tah-bon-tah-bon'
Tabor (Cz.)   tä'-bôr   tah'-bor
Tabriz (Iran)   tä-brēz'   tah-breez'
Tachiiwa (Jap.)   tä-chē'-ē-wä   tah-chee'-ee-wah
Tacloban (P.I.)   tä-klô'-bän   tah-klo'-bahn
Tacna (Peru)   täk'-nä   tahk'-nah
Tacoma (Wash)   tə-kō'-mə   tuh-koh'-muh
Tadjerouine (Tun.)   tä-jĕr-wēn'   tah-jehr-ween'
Tadji (New Guinea, isl.)   tä'-jē   tah'-jee
Tafaraoui (Alg.)   tä-fä-rä'-wē   **tah-fah-rah'-wee**
Tafilelt (Mor.)   tä-fē'-lĕlt   tah-fee'-lelt
Tagalog (P.I.)   tä-gä'-lŏg   tah-gah'-log
   Also called *Tagal,* tä-gäl' [tah-gahl'].
Taganrog (Rus.)   tä-gän-rôk'   tah-gahn-rok'
Tagawa, Daikichirō   tä'-gä-wä, dä-ē'-kē'-   tah'-gah-wah, dah-
   (Jap. educator)   chē'-rô   ee'-kee'-chee'-ro
Tagaytay (P.I.)   tä-gī-tī'   tah-gai-tai'
Tagbilaran (P.I.)   täg-bē-lä'-rän   tahg-bee-lah'-rahn
Tagiura (Libya)   tä-jōō'-rä   tah-joo'-rah
Tagliacozzo (It.)   tä-lyä-kôt'-sô   tah-lyah-kot'-so
Taguían (P.I.)   tä-gē'-än   tah-gee'-ahn
Taguig (P.I.)   tä-gēg'   tah-geeg'
Tagus (Port., Sp., riv.)   *Eng.* tā'-gəs   tay'-guhs
   Portuguese *Tejo,* tĕ'-zhŏŏ [teh'-zhu]. Spanish *Tajo,* tä'-hô [tah'-ho].
Taguús (P.I.)   tä-gōō-ōōs'   tah-goo-oos'
Tah-ch'êng (Ch.,   dä-chŭng   dah-chuhng
   Sinkiang)
   Also spelled *Ta-ch'eng.* Also called *Chuguchak,* q.v., and *Tarbagatai.*
Ta-hei-ho (Manchu.)   dä-hā-hŭ   dah-hay-huh
Tahiti (Oc., Society isls.)   tä-hē'-tē   tah-hee'-tee
                   or tī'-tē   tai'-tee
   The former is the older pronunciation, but by 1903, according to

Prof. Henry E. Crampton, the accent had shifted to the first syllable in the natives' pronunciation, the intervocalic *h* had weakened, and the word in effect became dissyllabic with a very long first syllable. The name of Chief *Opuhara* changed in the same way from ô-pōō-hä'-rä [o-poo-hah'-rah] to ô-pōō'-hä-rä [o-poo'-hah-rah] *or* ô-pōō'-rä [o-poo'-rah]. The great King *Pomare*, once called pô-mä'-rĕ [po-mah'-reh] was referred to as pô'-mä-rĕ [po'-mah-reh]. Such shifting of accent in native speech may account for the contradictory information we receive, as for instance, in the case of *Rabaul* and *Tarawa*. And it is always well to remember that in most languages of the world, including the Austronesian, the stress accent of English is quite out of place. For one thing it is much too heavy. Usually what we would consider a level stressing of all the vowels approaches a native pronunciation more closely than undue emphasis upon any one of them. Still over the American radio we must speak American English! Of the two pronunciations of *Tahiti*, the older, stressed on the second syllable, is probably what most of our listeners expect to hear.

Tahitian	tä-hē'-tǐ-ən	tah-hee'-ti-uhn
	or tä-hē'-shən	tah-hee'-shuhn
Tahoe (Cal., Nev., lake)	tä'-hō	tah'-hoh
T'ai Chi-t'ao (Ch. leader)	dī jē-tou	dai jee-tau
Tai-chow (Ch.,	*Eng.* tī-chou	tai-chau
Chekiang)	*Ch.* tī-jō	tai-joh
Taif (Saudi Arabia)	tīf'	taif'
Tai Hang Shan *or* Tai	tī-häng	tai-hahng
Hang Mts. (Ch.,		
Shansi, Hopei, Honan)		
T'ai-ho-k'u (Formosa)	*Eng.* tī-hō'-kōō	tai-hoh'-koo
	Ch. tī-hǔ-kōō	tai-huh-koo
Chinese *T'ai-p'eh*, tī-pĕ [tai-peh].		
T'ai-hǔ (Ch., Kiangsi)	tī-hǔ	tai-huh
Taikkyi (Burma)	tīk'-chē'	taik'-chee'
Taikyū (Korea)	tī-kyōō	tai-kyoo
Tainaron (Gr., cape)	tĕ'-nä-rô(n)	teh'-nah-ro(n)
Also called *Kavo Matapas*, kä'-vô mä-tä-päs' [kah'-vo mah-tah-pahs'].		
T'ai-p'eh (Formosa) See *T'ai-ho-k'u.*		
Taipha Ga (Burma)	tä'-pə gä'	tay'-puh gah'
Taira (Jap.)	tī'-rä	tai'-rah
Taishet (Rus.)	tī-shĕt'	tai-shet'
Taitsy (Rus.)	tī'-tsǐ	tai'-tsi
T'ai-wan (Jap.>Ch., isl.) See *Formosa.*		
T'ai-yüan (Ch., Shansi)	tī-yüän	tai-yü-ahn
Also called *Yang-ch'ü*, q.v.		
Taja (P.I.)	tä'-hä	tah'-hah

Tajo (Port., Sp., riv.)	See *Tagus*.	
Takahito, Mikasa no	tä-kä'-hē-tô, mē-kä'-	tah-kah'-hee-to, mee-
Miya (Jap. prince)	sä' nô mē-yä	kah'-sah' no mee-
		yah

Takahito may approach tä-käsh'-tô [tah-kahsh'-to].

Takamatsu (Jap.)	tä-kä'-mä-tsōō	tah-kah'-mah-tsoo
	or tä-kä'-mäts	tah-kah'-mahts
Takamatsu no Miya	tä-kä'-mä'-tsōō nô'	tah-kah'-mah'-tsoo
(Jap. prince)	mē-yä	no' mee-yah
Takaoka (Jap.)	tä-kä'-ô-kä	tah-kah'-o-kah
Takil (Rus.)	tä-kēl'	tah-keel'
Takoradi (Afr., Gold	tä-kô-rä'-dē	tah-ko-rah'-dee
Coast)		
Takrouna (Tun.)	täk-rōō'-nä	tahk-roo'-nah
Ta-ku (Ch., Hopei)	dä-gōō	dah-goo
Takuapa (Thai)	tŭ'-kwä-pä'	tuh'-kwah-pah'
Ta Kung Pao	dä gōōng bou	dah gung bau
(Shanghai newspaper)		
Talang Ga (Burma)	tə-län' gä'	tuh-lahn' gah'
Talara (Peru)	tä-lä'-rä	tah-lah'-rah
Talasea (Oc., New	tä-lä-sĕ'-ä	tah-lah-seh'-ah
Britain)		
Talaud (NEI)	tä'-lout	tah'-laut

Also called *Talaur*, tä-lour' [tah-laur'].

Talbot (Austral., cape)	tôl'-bət	tol'-buht
Taldom (Rus.)	täl-dôm'	tahl-dom'
Ta-li (Ch., Shansi,	dä-lē	dah-lee
Yünnan)		
Talibón (P.I.)	tä-lē-bôn'	tah-lee-bon'
Ta-lien(-wan) (Manchu.)	dä-lyĕn(-wän)	dah-lyen(-wahn)

Also called *Dairen*, q.v.

Talim (P.I.)	tä-lēm'	tah-leem'
Talísay (P.I.)	tä-lē'-sī	tah-lee'-sai
Talkeetna (Alaska)	tăl'-kēt'-nə	tal'-keet'-nuh
Talladega (Ala.)	tăl'-ə-dē'-gə	tal'-uh-dee'-guh
Talle, Henry O.	tä'-lē	tah'-lee
(U.S. representative)		
Tallinn (Est.)	täl'-lĭn	tahl'-lin
Russian *Revel*, q.v.		
Talmadge, Herman	tăl'-mĭj	tal'-mij
(Ga. polit.)		

Herman: hŭm'-ən [huhm'-uhn].

Talmud	tăl'-mŭd	tal'-muhd
Talovaya (Rus.)	tä-lŏ-vä'-yä	tah-lo-vah'-yah

Talsi (Latvia)   täl′-sē   tahl′-see
  Russian *Talsen*, täl(y)′-sĕn [tahl(y)′-sen].
Tamalpais (Calif., mt.)   tăm′-əl-pä′-ĭs   tam′-uhl-pah′-is
Taman (Rus., pen.)   tä-män′(y)   tah-mahn′(y)
Tamanthi (Burma)   tə-män′-*thē*′   tuh-mahn′-*thee*′
Tamási (Hung.)   tŏ′-mä-shĭ   to′-mah-shih
Tamatam (Oc., Carolines)   tä′-mä-täm   tah′-mah-tahm
  Also called *Pulap*, q.v.
Tamatave (Madag.)   tä-mä-täv′   tah-mah-tahv′
  Probably in English it will become tăm′-ə-tāv′ [tam′-uh-tayv′].
Tamaulipas (Mex.)   tä-mou-lē′-päs   tah-mou-lee′-pahs
Tamazunchale (Mex.)   tä′-mä-sōōn-chä′-lĕ   tah′-mah-soon-chah′-
                                                              leh

  Becoming famous as "Thomas and Charlie."
Tambagan (P.I.)   täm-bä′-gän   tahm-bah′-gahn
Tambóbong (P.I.) See *Malabón*.
Tamborini, José P.   täm-bô-rē′-nē, hô-sĕ′   tahm-bo-ree′-nee,
  (Arg. polit.)   ho-seh′
Tambov (Rus.)   täm-bôf′   tahm-bof′
Tambuco (P.I.)   täm′-bōō′-kô   tahm-boo′-ko
Tamezred (Tun.)   tä-mĕz-rĕd′   tah-mez-red′
Tamil (India)   tăm′-ĭl   tam′-il
Tamiš (Balkan riv.)   *S.-C.* tä′-mĭsh   tah′-mish
  Rumanian *Timişul*, q.v.
Tampere (Fin.)   täm′-pĕ-rĕ   tahm′-peh-reh
  Swedish *Tammerfors*, täm′-mər-fôrs′ [tahm′-muhr-fors′].
Tampico (Mex.)   *Eng.* tăm-pē′-kō   tam-pee′-koh
                                  Sp. täm-pē′-kô   tahm-pee′-ko
The English pronunciation is so well established that it should be
preferred in English reports.
Tamsalu (Est.)   täm′-sä-lōō   tahm′-sah-loo
Tana (Nor.)   tä′-nä   tah′-nah
Tanabuli (Oc., Solomons)   tä-nä-bōō′-lē   tah-nah-boo′-lee
Tanahmerah (NEI,   tä-nä-mĕ′-rä   tah-nah-meh′-rah
  New Guinea)
Tanaka, Giichi (Jap.   tä-nä′-kä′, gē′-ē-chē   tah-nah′-kah′, gee′-
  polit.)   ee-chee
Tanaka, Kōtarō (Jap.   tä-nä′-kä′, kô′-tä-rô   tah-nah′-kah′, ko′-
  educator)   tah-ro
Tanana (Alaska)   tăn′-ə-nô   tan′-uh-naw
Tananarive (Madag.)   tä-nä-nä-rēv′   tah-nah-nah-reev′
  Also called *Tananarivo*, tä-nä′-nä-rē′-vô [tah-nah′-nah-ree′-vo], and
  English *Antananarivo*, q.v.
Tanapag (Oc., Saipan)   tä′-nä-päg   tah′-nah-pahg

Tanaru (NEI, Java)	tä-nä'-rōō	tah-nah'-roo
Tanauan (P.I.)	tä-nä'-wän	tah-nah'-wahn
Tanay (P.I.)	tä-nī'	tah-nai'
Tan-chuk (Ch.,	Eng. tän'-chŏŏk'	tahn'-chuk'
Kwangsi)	Ch. dän-jōō	dahn-joo
Ţăndăre (Rum.)	tsən-də-rā'	tsuhn-duh-ray'

tandjoeng (Du.). An element, meaning *cape*, in East Indian place names. See also *tanjong*, the usual form in English.

Tandjoengpandan (NEI,	tän'-jōōng-pän'-dän	tahn'-jung-pahn'-
Billiton)		dahn
Tandjoengpinang	tän'-jōōng-pē'-näng	tahn'-jung-pee'-
(NEI, Riouw)	or *Eng.* -năng	nahng or -nang
Tandjoengpriok	tän'-jōōng-prē'-ŏk	tahn'-jung'pree'-ok
(NEI, Java)		

Also called *Tanjong Priok*, q.v.

Tandjoeng Selor (NEI,	tän'-jōōng sĕ'-lôr	tahn'-jung seh'-lor
Borneo)		
Tandú Bató (P.I.)	tän-dōō' bä-tô'	tahn-doo' bah-to'
Tane ga Shima (Jap., isl.)	tä-nĕ gä' shē-mä	tah-neh gah' shee-mah
Tanga (Oc., Bismarck arch.)	täng'-ä	tahng'-ah
Tanganyika (E. Afr.)	*Eng.* tăn-găn-yē'-kə	tan-gan-yee'-kuh
	native täng-gä-nyē'-kä	tahng-gah-nyee'-kah
Tangermuende *or* Tangermünde (Ger.)	täng'-ər-mün'-də	tahng'-uhr-mün'-duh
Tanghás (P.I.)	täng-häs'	tahng-hahs'

Also spelled *Tangjás*.

Tangier (Sp. Mor.)	tăn-jĭr'	tan-jihr'
Tangkoebang Prahoe	täng'-kōō-bäng	tahng'-koo-bahng
(NEI)	prä'-ōō	prah'-oo
T'ang-ku (Ch., Hopei)	täng-gōō	tahng-goo
Tangoucha (Tun.)	tän-gōō'-shä	tahn-goo'-shah

Also called *Djebel Tangouch*, q.v.

Tang-shan (Ch., Kiangsu)	däng-shän	dahng-shahn
Tang-yang (Ch., Hupeh)	däng-yäng	dahng-yahng
Tanimbar (NEI)	tä-nĭm'-bär	tah-nim'-bahr

Also spelled *Tenimbar*, q.v.

Tanin (Turkish news-paper)	tä-nĭn'	tah-nin'

tanjong. An element meaning *cape*. See also *tandjoeng*.

Tanjong Baram (Borneo)	tän'-jŏng bä'-räm	tahn'-jong bah'-rahm

Tanjong Jamoersba (NEI) See *Kaap de Goede Hoop*.

Tanjong Pinang (NEI, Riouw)	tän'-jŏng pē'-näng *or Eng.* -năng	tahn'-jong pee'-nahng *or* -nang
Tanjong Priok (NEI, Java)	tän'-jŏng prē'-ŏk	tahn'-jong pree'-ok
Tanner, Väinö A. (Fin. polit.)	tän'-nĕr, vī'-nû	tahn'-nehr, vai'-nœ
Tannura (Saudi Arabia) See *Ras at Tannura.*		
Tannu Tuva (Rus. protec.)	tän'-nŏŏ tŏŏ-vä'	tahn'-nu tu-vah'
Tanta (Egypt)	tän'-tä	tahn'-tah
T'ao-hwa-p'ing (Ch., Hunan)	tou-whä-pĭng	tou-whah-ping
Taongi (Oc., Marshalls) Also called *Pokaakku,* q.v.	tä-ông'-ē	tah-ong'-ee
Taormina (Sicily)	tä'-ôr-mē'-nä	tah'-or-mee'-nah
Taos (N.M.)	tä'-ôs	tah'-os
Colloquially pronounced tous' [taus'], rhyming with *mouse* and *house.*		
Tap (Rus., lake)	täp'	tahp'
Tapa (Est.) Russian *Taps,* q.v.	tä'-pä	tah'-pah
Tapiau (Ger. > Rus.) Russian *Gvardeisk,* gvär-dāsk' [gvahr-daysk'].	tä'-pĭ-ou	tah'-pi-au
Tápiószele (Hung.)	tä'-pyô-sĕ'-lĕ	tah'-pyo-seh'-leh
Tapolcafö (Hung.)	tŏ'-pôl-tsŏ'-fû	to'-pol-tso'-fœ
Tapoly (Cz., Hung., riv.)	See *Topľa.*	
Tapotchau (Oc., Saipan, mt.)	tä-pô-chou'	tah-po-chau'
Taps (Est.) Estonian *Tapa,* q.v.	*Rus.* täps'	tahps'
Taptugara (Rus.)	täp-tŏŏ-gä'-rä	tahp-too-gah'-rah
Tapuaemanu (Oc., Society isls.)	tä-pŏŏ-ä-ĕ-mä'-nŏŏ	tah-poo-ah-eh-mah'-noo
Tapul (P.I.)	tä-pŏŏl'	tah-pool'
Taqa, el (Egypt)	tä'-kä, ĕt	tah'-kah, et
Taquián (P.I.)	tä-kē-än'	tah-kee-ahn'
Taquizadeh, Seyed Hasan (Iran. polit.)	tä-kē-zä'-dĕ, sĕ-yĕd' häs'-än	tah-kee-zah'-deh, seh-yehd' hahs'-ahn
Tarakan (NEI, Borneo)	tä-rä-kän'	tah-rah-kahn'
Taranto (It.)	tä'-rän-tô	tah'-rahn-to
Classical *Tarentum,* tä-rĕn'-tŏŏm [tah-ren'-tum].		
Tarapacá (Chile)	tä-rä-pä-kä'	tah-rah-pah-kah'
Tarasco, Tarascan (Mex. Indian)	tä-räs'-kô, tä-räs'-kän	tah-rahs'-ko, tah-rahs'-kahn
Tarascon (Fr.)	tä-räs-kôN'	tah-rahs-koN'

Tarawa (Oc., Gilberts)	*native* tä'-rä'-wä'	tah'-rah'-wah'
	or tä'-rä-wä	tah'-rah-wah
	Eng. tăr'-ə-wä	tar'-uh-wah
	or tə-rä'-wä	tuh-rah'-wah

For the native pronunciation the Royal Geographical Society places an accent on the last syllable and the U.S. Board on Geographical names follows suit. Former Senator Hiram Bingham in a letter to the New York Times, Nov. 28, 1943 says that while his father was missionary to the islands the accent was on the first syllable. Lippincott's New Gazetteer places a secondary accent on the first syllable and a primary accent on the last syllable. It remains to be seen whether the recent Englishing with accent on the second syllable is the form that will persist in the English-speaking world. See the remarks on *Tahiti*. Note also that *Kanaka* may be accented on the first or on the second syllable.

To these notes of the first edition can be added the following extracts from the *Tarawa* file. Mr. Robert Sherrod, author of *Tarawa, The Story of a Battle*, August 24, 1946: "The nearest I can come to it in print is 'tare-a-wa' evenly accented." The former Resident Commissioner of the Gilbert and Ellice Islands, July 15, 1946: "I myself stress the word on the first syllable; and because I am an Englishman I suspect that I tend, in ordinary conversation, to pronounce Tarawa very like the English word 'narrower' . . . . The natives, I firmly believe, stress each syllable equally. This is nearly impossible of attainment by the average Westerner who, when he hears the word thus pronounced is apt to *think* that the stress is on the *last* syllable, simply because the word sounds so different from his own 'narrower' sound, and does not fade away at the end as does that word. (There used to be much argument, in India, about the pronunciation of Pipariya, a placename of the Central Provinces; the natives put an equal stress on each syllable). I have never heard the pronunciation Ta-RA-wa used by anyone whom I should suspect of knowing the right pronunciation; and my opinion is that this now very popular way is as wrong as can be. I would therefore advise broadcasters and others to get as near to the equal-stress-on-each-syllable way as they can; but it will help them, and not be too inaccurate, if they allow themselves a very slight extra stress on the first syllable; our old friend 'narrower' again, but with the vowels of the native word given their true values more generously than is, I fear done by, Yours sincerely, V. Fox-Strang-ways."

The Acting Resident Commissioner, Mr. H. E. Maude, an anthropologist, November 6, 1946: "Personally, having lived in the Central Pacific for some seventeen years, I should have sworn that there was no accent on any of the three syllables of Tarawa but I am bound to defer to the opinion of the islanders themselves, whom I have duly consulted, and who are unanimous that there is a slight accent on the first syllable and that it should be pronounced Tah'-rah-wah. Indeed, after listening to them carefully, I find it is even so. In his letter to me Mr. Fox-Strangways laments the modern American pronunciation of Tarawa with an accent on the second syllable. It is certainly quite new and incorrect, but as an American Marine said to one of our officers who voiced the same complaint: 'Listen, Buddy, we captured this gol-darned island and if we say it's called Tah-rah'-wah, Tah-rah'-wah's its name.'" [This story is told also of a Marine and Bougainville.]

Tarawasi (NEI)	tä-rä-wä'-sē	tah-rah-wah'-see
Tarbagatai (Ch.) See *Chuguchak*.		
Tarbes (Fr.)	tärb'	tahrb'
Tarchiani, Alberto	tär-kyä'-nē,	tahr-kyah'-nee, ahl-
(It. polit.)	äl-bĕr'-tô	behr'-to
Tarcoola (Austral.)	tär-kōō'-lə	tahr-koo'-luh
Tarentum (It.)	tä-rĕn'-tōōm	tah-ren'-tum
Italian *Taranto*, tä'-rän-tô [tah'-rahn-to].		
Targhee (Idaho)	tär'-gē	tahr'-gee
Târgovişte (Rum.)	tûr'-gô-vēsh'-tĕ	tuhr'-go-veesh'-teh
Târgul Jiu (Rum.)	tûr'-gōōl zhē'-ŏŏ	tuhr'-gul-zhee'-u
Târgu and *Târgul* are variants, the -*l* being the article.		
Târgul Mureş (Rum.)	tûr'-gōōl mŏŏ'-rĕsh	tuhr'-gul mu'-resh
Hungarian *Marosvásárhely*, mŏ'-rôsh-vä'-shär-hā [mo'-rosh-vah'-shahr-hay].		
Târgul Ocna (Rum.)	tûr'-gōōl ôk'-nä	tuhr'-gul ok'-nah
Târgul Săcuesc (Rum.)	tûr'-gōōl sə-kwĕsk'	tuhr'-gul suh-kwesk'
Tarhuna (Libya)	tär-hōō'-nä	tahr-hoo'-nah
Tarifa (Sp.)	tä-rē'-fä	tah-ree'-fah
Taritari (Oc., Makin)	tä'-rē-tä'-rē	tah'-ree-tah'-ree
Usually called *Butaritari*, q.v.		
Tárlac (P.I.)	tär'-läk	tahr'-lahk
Tarle, Evgenii E.	tär'-lĕ, yĕv-gĕ'-nĭ	tahr'-leh, yev-geh'-ni
(Rus. historian)		
Tarn (Fr., riv.)	tärn'	tahrn'
Tarnobrzeg (Pol.)	tär-nôb'-zhĕk	tahr-nob'-zhek
Tarnopol (Pol. >Rus.)	*Rus.* tär-nŏ-pŏl(y)	tahr'-no-pol(y)
	Pol. tär-nô'-pôl	tahr-no'-pol
Tarnów (Pol.)	tär'-nōōf	tahr'-nuf
Tarnowitz (Pol.) See *Tarnowskie Góry*.		
Tarnowskie Góry (Pol.)	tär-nôf'-skyĕ gōō'-rĭ	tahr-nof'-skyeh gu'-ri
German *Tarnowitz*, tär'-nô-vĭts [tahr'-no-vits].		

Tarquinia (It.)   tär-kwē'-nyä   tahr-kwee'-nyah
Tarragona (Sp.)   tä-rä-gô'-nä   tah-rah-go'-nah
Tartu (Est.)   tär'-tōō   tahr'-too
    Russian *Jurjev*, q.v., or *Yurev*. German *Dorpat*, q.v.
Tashkent (Rus.)   täsh-kĕnt'   tahsh-kent'
Tasman Sea   tăz'-mən   taz'-muhn
Tasmania (Austral.)   tăz-mā'-nĭ-ə   taz-may'-ni-uh
Tass (Rus. news service)   täs'   tahs'
Tassigny, Jean de Lattre de (Fr. general). See *De Tassigny, Jean de Lattre*.
Tataán (P.I.)   tä-tä-än'   tah-tah-ahn'
    Also called *Simaluc*, sē-mä-lōōk' [see-mah-look'] and *Simalac*, sē-mä-läk' [see-mah-lahk'].
Tatán (P.I.)   tä-tän'   tah-tahn'
Tatar Bunar (Rum. >   tä-tär' bŏŏ-när'   tah-tahr' bu-nahr'
    Rus.)
    Rumanian *Tătărăşti*, tə-tə-rûsht' [tuh-tuh-ruhsht'].
Tatar Pazardzhik (Bulg.)   tä-tär' pä-zär-jēk'   tah-tahr' pah-zahr-jeek'
Tatarski (Rus., strait)   tä-tär'-skĭ   tah-tahr'-ski
Tatau (Oc., Bismarck   tä-tou'   tah-tau'
    arch.)
Tateyama (Jap.)   tä-tĕ'-yä-mä   tah-teh'-yah-mah
Tateyamahōjō (Jap.)   tä-tĕ'-yä-mä-hô'-jô   tah-teh'-yah-mah-ho'-jo
Tatoï (Gr.)   tä-toi'   tah-toi'
Tatra Mountains (Europe) See *High Tatra*.
Tatsinskaya (Rus.)   tä-tsĭn'-skä-yä   tah-tsin'-skah-yah
Ta-t'ung (Ch., Chinghai,   dä-tŏŏng   dah-tung
    Shansi)
Ta-tung-kow (Manchu.)   *Eng.* tä-tŏŏng-kou   tah-tung-kau
               Ch. dä-dŏŏng-gō   dah-dung-goh
Taucha (Ger.)   tou'-k(h)ä   tau'-k(h)ah
    Also called *Leipsig Taucha*.
Taungbaw (Burma)   toung'-bô'   taung'-baw'
Taungdwingyi (Burma)   toung-dwĭn-jē'   taung-dwin-jee'
Taunggyi (Burma)   toung'-jē'   taung'-jee'
Taungup (Burma)   toung'-ŏŏp'   taung'-up'
Taunton (Eng.)   tôn'-tən *or* tän'-   tawn'-tuhn *or* tahn'-
Taunton (Mass.)   tänt'n   tahnt'n
Taunus (Ger., mts.)   tou'-nŏŏs   tau'-nus
Tauragė (Lith.)   tou-rä-gā'   tau-rah-gay'
    German *Tauroggen*, tou-rôg'-ən [tau-rog'-uhn].
Tauris   tô'-rĭs   taw'-ris
    An ancient name of the Crimea.

Tauroggen (Lith.)   See *Tauragė*, q.v.

Taus (Cz.)   See *Domažlice*.

Taute (Fr., riv.)	tōt′	toht′
Tauu (Oc., Solomons)	tou′-ōō	tau′-oo
Tavanatangir (Oc., New Britain)	tä-vä-nä-täng′-ēr	tah-vah-nah-tahng′-eer
Tavernucole, le (It.)	tä-vĕr-nōō′-kô-lĕ, lĕ	tah-vehr-noo′-ko-leh, leh
Tavolzhanka (Rus.)	tä-vŏl-zhän′-kä	tah-vol-zhahn′-kah
Tavoularis, G. (Gr. polit.)	tä-vōō-lä′-rēs	tah-voo-lah′-rees
Tavoy (Burma)	tə-voi′	tuh-voi′
Tawi Tawi (P.I.)	tä′-wē tä′-wē	tah′-wee tah′-wee

Commonly simplified to tä′-wē [tah′-wee].

Tawngpeng (Burma)	tông′-pĕng′	tawng′-peng′
Taxco (Mex.)	täs′-kô	tahs′-ko
Tayabas (P.I.)	tä-yä′-bäs	tah-yah′-bahs
Taygetos (Gr., mt.)	tī′-yĕ-tôs	tai′-yeh-tos
Taysán (P.I.)	tī-sän′	tai-sahn′
Taytay (P.I.)	tī′-tī	tai′-tai
Ta-yü (Ch., Kiangsi)	dä-yü	dah-yü
Tayug (P.I.)	tä-yōōg′	tah-yoog′
Tazov (Rus.)	tä′-zŏf	tah′-zof

Tbilisi (Rus.)   See *Tiflis*.

Tchad (Afr. lake)	chäd′	chahd′

English *Chad*, chăd′ [chad′].

Tczew (Pol.)	tchĕf′	tchef′

German *Dirschau*, dĭr′-shou [dihr′-shau].

Teaktebang (Borneo)	tĕ-äk-tĕ′-bäng	teh-ahk-teh′-bahng
T'ê-an (Ch., Kiangsi)	tŭ-än	tuh-ahn
Tebessa (Alg.)	*Eng.* tĕ-bĕs′-ə	teh-bes′-uh
	Fr. tĕ-bĕ-sä′	teh-beh-sah′
Teboulba (Tun.)	tə-bōōl′-bä	tuh-bool′-bah
Tebourba (Tun.)	tə-bōōr′-bä	tuh-boor′-bah
Teboursouk (Tun.)	tə-bōōr-sōōk′	tuh-boor-sook′
Techa (Libya)	tĕ′-kä	teh′-kah
Tê-ch'ing (Ch., Chekiang)	dŭ-chĭng	duh-ching
Tecuci (Rum.)	tĕ-kōōch′	teh-kuch′
Tegal (NEI, Java)	tĕ-gäl′	teh-gahl′
Tegelen (Neth.)	tä′-k(h)ə-lən	tay′-k(h)uh-luhn
Tegernsee (Ger., lake)	tä′-gərn-zä′	tay′-guhrn-zay′
Tegucigalpa (Hond.)	tĕ-gōō′-sē-gäl′-pä	teh-goo′-se-gahl′-pah
Tehachapi (Calif., mts.)	tə-hăch′-ə-pĭ	tuh-hach′-uh-pi

Tehran _or_ Teheran   _Per._ tĕ-hrän′   teh-hrahn′
  (Iran)   _Eng._ tĕ-ə-rän′ _or_ -răn′   teh-uh-rahn′ _or_ -ran′
              _or_ tĭ-ə-răn′ _or_ -rän′   ti-uh-ran′ _or_ -rahn′
  Our forces in Iran commonly called it tĕ-rän′ [teh-rahn′].

T'ê-hsing (Ch., Kiangsi)   tŭ-shĭng   tuh-shing
Tehuantepec (Mex.)   tĕ-wän′-tĕ-pĕk′   teh-wahn′-teh-pehk′
Teillé (Fr.)   tĕ-yĕ′   teh-yeh′
Teilleul, le (Fr.)   tĕ-yûl′, lə   teh-yœl′, luh
Teiteiripucchi (Oç.,   tā′-tā-rē-pōōk′-chē   tay′-tay-ree-pook′-
  Eniwetok)   chee
Teitgen, Henri   tĕd-jĕn′, äN-rē′   ted-jen′, ahN-ree′
  (Fr. polit.)
Tejo (Port., Sp., riv.)   See _Tagus._
Tekija (Yugosl.)   tĕ′-kĭ-yä   teh′-ki-yah
Tekirdaǧ (Turk.)   tĕ-kĕr′-dä   teh-keer′-dah
  Greek _Rodosto,_ q.v.
Tel Aviv (Pal.)   tĕl ă-vēv′ _or_ ä-vēv′   tel a-veev′ _or_ ah-
                               veev′
Telechany (Pol.)   tĕ-lĕ-hä′-nĭ   teh-leh-hah′-ni
  Russian spelling _Telekhani._
Telemark (Nor.)   tĕl′-ə-märk   tel′-uh-mahrk
Teleneshty (Rum. >Rus.)   tĕ-lĕ-nĕsh′-tĭ   teh-leh-nesh′-ti
  Rumanian _Teleneşti,_ tĕ-lĕ-nĕsht′ [teh-leh-nesht′].
Teleorman (Rum.)   tĕ′-lyôr-män′   teh′-lyor-mahn′
Télepte Algiers. See _Thélepte._
tell _or_ tel   tĕl′   tel′
  An element, meaning _mound_ or _small hill,_ in Arabic and Hebrew place
  names.
Tell el Eisa (Egypt)   tĕl′ ĕl ä-ē′-sä   tel′ el ah-ee′-sah
Tell el Makh Khad   tĕl′ ĕl mäk′ käd′   tel′ el mahk′ kahd′
  (Egypt)
Teloek-betoeng _or_   tə-lōōk′-bĕ-tōōng′   tuh-look′-beh-tung′
  Telok-betong (NEI,   _or_ tə-lŏk′-bĕ-tŏng′   tuh-lok′-beh-tong′
  Sumatra)
Telschi (Lith.)   See _Telšiai._
Telšiai (Lith.)   tĕl-shyĭ′   tel-shyai′
  Russian _Telschi,_ tĕl′(y)-shĭ [tel′(y)-shi].
Teltow (Ger.)   tĕl′-tō   tel′-toh
temblor   tĕm-blôr′   tem-blor′
Temerin (Yugosl.)   tĕ′-mĕ-rĭn   teh′-meh-rin
Temerza (Tun.)   tĕ-mĕr′-zä   teh-mehr′-zah
Temes (Balkan riv.)   See _Timişul._
Temesvár (Rum.)   _Hung._ tĕ′-mĕsh-vär   teh′-mesh-vahr
  Rumanian _Timişoara,_ q.v.

Temišvar (Rum.)   See *Timişoara*.

Temnac (Alaska, Attu)   těm'-năk'   tem'-nak'

Temnić (Yugosl.)   těm'-nĭch   tem'-nich

Tempe (Gr., valley)   těm'-pĭ   tem'-pi

Tempelhof (Ger., Berlin)   těm'-pəl-hōf   tem'-puhl-hohf

tempura   *Eng.* těm-pōō'-rə   tem-poo'-ruh

   Jap. těm-pōō'-rä'   tem-poo'-rah'

Japanese dish popular among Americans.

Temryuk (Rus.)   těm-ryōōk'   tem-ryook'

Temryukski Zaliv (Rus.)   těm-ryook'-skĭ zä-lēf'   tem-ryook'-ski zah-leef'

Temštica (Yugosl.)   těm'-shtĭ-tsä   tem'-shti-tsah

Tenaru (Oc., riv.)   tě-nä'-rōō   teh-nah'-roo

Tenasserim (Burma)   těn-ăs'-ə-rĭm   ten-as'-uh-rim

Ten Boer (Neth.)   těn bōōr'   ten boor'

Tendanye (New Guinea)   těn-dän'-yě   ten-dahn'-yeh

Tenerife   *Eng.* těn'-ə-rĭf   ten'-uh-rif

   (Canary Isls.)   *Sp.* tě-ně-rē'-fě   teh-neh-ree'-feh

T'êng-ch'ung (Ch., Yünnan)   tŭng-chōŏng   tuhng-chung

Also called *T'êng-yüeh*, q.v., and *Momein*, q.v.

Tengeder (Libya)   těn-jě-děr'   ten-jeh-dehr'

T'êng-yüeh (Ch., Yünnan)   tŭng-yüě   tuhng-yü-eh

Also called *T'êng-ch'ung*, q.v., and *Momein*, q.v.

Tenimbar (NEI)   tě-nĭm'-bär   teh-nim'-bahr

Also spelled *Tanimbar*, q.v.

Tenochtitlán (Mex.)   tě-nôch-tē-tlän'   teh-noch-tee-tlahn'

Tenos (Gr , isl.)   tē'-nô(s)   tee'-no(s)

Teotihuacán (Mex.)   tě-ô-tē-wä-kän'   teh-o-tee-wah-kahn'

Also called *San Juan Teotihuacán*, q.v.

Tepelena (Alb.)   See *Tepelenë*.

Tepelenë (Alb.)   tě-pě-lě'-nə   teh-peh-leh'-nuh

Tepic (Mex.)   tě-pēk'   teh-peek'

Teplice Šanov (Cz.)   tě'-plĭ-tsě shä'-nôf   teh'-pli-tseh shah'-nof

Teplo Pristanište   tě'-plô prē'-stä-   teh'-plo pree'-stah-

   (Yugosl.)   nĭ-shtě   ni-shteh

Ter Aar (Neth.)   tər är'   tuhr ahr'

Teramo (It.)   tě'-rä-mô   teh'-rah-mo

Ter Apel (Neth.)   tər ä'-pəl   tuhr ah'-puhl

Terbuf (Alb., lake)   *Eng.* tûr'-bōōf   tuhr'-boof

Albanian *Knetë e Tërbufit.*

Terceira (Azores)   těr-sä'-rə   tehr-say'-ruh

Terebovlia (Pol. >Rus.)   tě-rě-bô'-vlyä   teh-reh-bo'-vlyah

   Polish *Trembowla*, q.v.

Teregova (Rum.)	tĕ-rĕ-gô'-vä	teh-reh-go'-vah
Terek (Rus., riv.)	tĕ'-rĕk	teh'-rek
Terelle (It.)	tĕ-rĕl'-lĕ	teh-rel'-leh
Teresa (P.I.)	tĕ-rĕ'-sä	teh-reh'-sah
Teresina (Brazil)	tĕ-rĭ-zē'-nə	teh-ri-zee'-nuh
Terespol (Pol.)	tĕ-rĕ'-spôl	teh-reh'-spol
Terezin (Cz.)	tĕ'-rĕ-zĭn	teh'-reh-zin
Tergnier (Fr.)	tĕr-nyĕ'	tehr-nyeh'
Terheide (Neth.)	tər-hī'-də	tuhr-hai'-duh
Terijoki (Fin. >Rus.)	tĕ'-rē-yô-kē	teh'-ree-yo-kee

Russian spelling *Terioki*.

Terkoz (Turk., lagoon)	tĕr'-kôz'	tehr'-koz'
Termini Imerese (Sicily)	tĕr'-mē-nē	tehr'-mee-nee
	ē-mĕ-rĕ'-zĕ	ee-meh-reh'-zeh
Termoli (It.)	tĕr'-mô-lē	tehr'-mo-lee
Termunten (Neth.)	tər-mûn'-tən	tuhr-mœn'-tuhn

Also called *Termunterzijl*, tər-mûn'-tər-zīl' [tuhr-mœn'-tuhr-zail'].

Ternate (NEI)	tĕr-nä'-tĕ	tehr-nah'-teh
Ternate (P.I.)	tĕr-nä'-tĕ	tehr-nah'-teh
Terneuzen (Neth.)	tər-nû'-zən	tuhr-nœ'-zuhn

Also called *Neuzen*, nû'-zən [nœ'-zuhn].

Ter Poorten, Hein	tər pōr'-tən, hīn'	tuhr pohr'-tuhn, hain'
(Du. polit.)		
Terpsithea (Gr.)	tĕr-psē-thĕ'-ä	tehr-psee-theh'-ah
Terracina (It.)	tĕr-rä-chē'-nä	tehr-rah-chee'-nah
Terralba (Sard.)	tĕr-räl'-bä	tehr-rahl'-bah
Terranova (It.)	tĕr-rä-nô'-vä	tehr-rah-no'-vah
Terravecchia (It.)	tĕr-rä-vĕk'-kyä	tehr-rah-vek'-kyah
Terre Haute (Ind.)	tĕr'-ə hōt'	tehr'-uh hoht'
	or tĕr'-ĭ hŭt'	tehr'-i huht'
Terschelling (Neth., isl.)	tər-sk(h)ĕl'-ĭng	tuhr-sk(h)el'-ing
Tertre, le (Fr.)	tĕr'tr, lə	tehr'tr, luh
Teruel (Sp.)	tĕr-wĕl'	tehr-wel'
Tešanj (Yugosl.)	tĕ'-shän(y)	teh'-shahn(y)
Teschen (Cz., Pol.)	*Ger.* tĕsh'-ən	tesh'-uhn

Czech *Těšín*, q.v., Polish *Cieszyn*, q.v.

Tešica (Yugosl.)	tĕ'-shĭ-tsä	teh'-shi-tsah
Těšín (Cz., Pol.)	*Cz.* tyĕ'-shēn	tyeh'-sheen

German *Teschen*, q.v.

Tessel (Neth., isl.)	tĕs'-əl	tes'-uhl

For another spelling and an English pronunciation, see *Texel*.

Tessy sur Vire (Fr.)	tĕ-sē sür vēr'	teh-see sür veer'
Testour (Tun.)	tĕs-tōōr'	tes-toor'
Teterboro (N.J.)	tēt'r-bŭr'-ə	teet'r-buhr'-uh

Teterev (Rus., riv.)	tĕ'-tĕ-rĕf	teh'-teh-ref
Teteringen (Neth.)	tā'-tə-rĭng'-ən	tay'-tuh-ring'-uhn
Teteven (Bulg.)	tĕ'-tĕ-vĕn(y)	teh'-teh-ven(y)
Tetipari (Oc., Solomons)	tĕ-tē-pä'-rē	teh-tee-pah'-ree
Teton (Idaho, Mont.)	tē'-tŏn	tee'-ton

Only this pronunciation is current in Driggs, the county seat of Teton County, Idaho.

Tetschen (Cz.)	*Ger.* tĕt'-shən	tet'-shuhn

Czech *Děčín*, q.v.

Tettingen (Ger.)	tĕt'-ĭng-ən	tet'-ing-uhn
Tetuán (P.I.)	tĕ-twän'	teh-twahn'
Tetyukhi (Rus.)	tĕ-tyo͞o'-hĭ	teh-tyoo'-hi
Teupitz (Ger.)	toi'-pĭts	toi'-pits
Teutuán (Sp. Mor.)	tĕ-twän'	teh-twahn'
Tevai (Oc., Solomons)	tĕ-vī'	teh-vai'
Tevere (It., riv.)	tĕ'-vĕ-rĕ	teh'-veh-reh

English *Tiber*, tī'-bər [tai'-buhr], should be preferred in an English context.

Tewa (Am. Indian)	tē'-wä	tee'-wah
Texel (Neth., isl.)	*Eng.* tĕk'-səl	tek'-suhl
	Du. tĕs'-əl	tes'-uhl

Also spelled *Tessel*, q.v.

Thai *or* Siam	tī' *or* sī-ăm'	tai' *or* sai-am'
Thakhek (Indo-Ch.)	tä-kĕk'	tah-kek'
Thala (Tun.)	tä'-lä	tah'-lah
Thalia	*given name* thāl'-yə	thayl'-yuh
	Muse thə-lī'-ə	thuh-lai'-uh
Thames (Eng., riv.)	tĕmz'	temz'

The Connecticut river is usually thāmz' [thaymz'].

Thanbyuzayat (Burma)	thən-byo͞o-zə-yŭt'	thuhn-byoo-zuh-yuht'

Meaning *corrugated-iron rest-house*. In contrast is *Shwedaung*, q.v., meaning *golden peacock*.

Thanh-hoa (Indo-Ch.)	tän(y)-whä'	tahn(y)-whah'
Thann (Fr.)	tän'	tahn'
Thaon (Fr.)	tôn'	tohn'
Thar (India, desert)	tär' *or* tŭr'	tahr' *or* tuhr'
Thargominda (Austral.)	thär'-gō-mĭn'-də	thahr'-goh-min'-duh
Tharnes (Alb., pass)	*Eng.* thär'-nĕs	thahr'-nes
Tharrawaddy (Burma)	thă-rə-wŏd'-ĭ	tha-ruh-wod'-i
Thasos (Gr., isl.)	thä'-sȯ(s)	thah'-so(s)
Thaton (Burma)	thə-tŏn'	thuh-tohn'
Thau, Étang de (Fr.)	tō, ĕ-täN' də	toh, eh-tahN' duh
Thaungdut (Burma)	thoung-do͞ot'	thaung-dut'

Thayetkon (Burma)	thə-yĕt′-kōn′	thuh-yet′-kohn′
Thayetmyo (Burma)	thə-yĕt′-myō′	thuh-yet′-myoh′
Thazi (Burma)	thä′-zē′	thah′-zee′
the before consonants	*thə*	*thuh*
before yōō *or* ū	*thə*	*thuh*
before vowels	*thĭ*	*thi*

Avoid the overemphatic "thee." Compare the remarks on the indefinite article, *a*.

| Thebes (Gr.) | thēbs′ | theebs′ |

Greek *Thevai*, thē′-vĕ [thee′-veh].

The Dalles (Ore.)	dălz′	dalz′
Theil, le (Fr.)	tĕ(y)′, lə	teh(y)′, luh
Theiss (Europ. riv.)	See *Tisza.*	
Thélepte (Algiers)	tĕ-lĕpt′	teh-lept′
Thelepte (Tun.)	tĕ-lĕp′-tĕ	teh-lep′-teh
Thénezay (Fr.)	tĕn-zĕ′	ten-zeh′
Theodore (Alaska, Attu)	thē′-ə-dōr	thee′-uh-dohr

Russian *Feodor.*

| Theodoroi, Agioi (Crete) | thĕ-ô′-dô-rē, ĭ′-yē | theh-o′-do-ree, ai′-yee |

Also called *Thodoroi*, thô′-dô-rē [tho′-do-ree].

| Theodoros, Agios | thĕ-ô′-dô-rôs, ĭ′-yôs | theh-o′-do-ros, ai′- |
| (Crete, isl.) | | yos |

Also called *Thodorou*, thô-dô-rōō′ [tho-do-roo′].

Theofanides, Stavros	thĕ-ô-fä-nē′-dēs,	theh-o-fah-nee′-dees,
(Gr. polit.)	stä′-vrôs	stah′-vros
Theophilou (Crete, point)	thĕ-ô-fē′-lōō	theh-o-fee′-loo
Theotokis, Ioannis	thĕ-ô-tô′-kēs,	theh-o-to′-kees,
(Gr. polit.)	yô-ä′-nēs	yo-ah′-nees
Theotokis, Spyros	thĕ-ô-tô′-kēs, spē′-rôs	theh-o-to′-kees,
(Gr. polit.)		spee′-ros
Thera (Gr., isl.)	thē′-rä	thee′-rah

Also called *Santorini*, sän-dô-rē′-nē [sahn-do-ree′-nee].

| theremin | thĕr′-ə-mĭn | thehr′-uh-min |

The inventor of this musical instrument is described variously as *Leo Theremin*, lē′-ō thĕr′-ə-mĭn [lee′-oh thehr′-uh-min], *Lev Terĕmin*, lĕf′ tĕ-ryô′-mĭn [lef′ teh-ryo′-min], and *Léon Thérémin*, lĕ-ôN tĕ-rĕ-măN′ [leh-oN teh-reh-maN′].

| Thermaic Gulf (Gr.) | *Eng.* thər-mā′-ĭk | thuhr-may′-ik |

Greek *Thermaikos Kolpos*, thĕr-mä-ē-kôs′ kôl′-pôs [thehr-mah-ee-kos′ kol′-pos].

Theron, Frank H.	tûr-rŏn′	tuhr-ron′
(S. Afr. general)		
Thessalonike (Gr.)	thĕ-sä-lô-nē′-kē	theh-sah-lo-nee′-kee

Usually called *Saloniki*, q.v., or *Salonica.*

Thessaly (Gr.)   *Eng.* thĕs'-ə-lĭ   thes'-uh-li
  Greek *Thessalia,* thĕ-sä-lē'-ä [theh-sah-lee'-ah].
Thevai (Gr.)   See *Thebes.*
Thibar (Tun.)   tē-bǎr'   tee-behr'
Thiberville (Fr.)   tē-bĕr-vēl'   tee-behr-veel'
Thibica (Tun.)   tē'-bē-kä   tee'-bee-kah
Thielt (Belg.)   tēlt'   teelt'
Thienen (Belg.)   *Flem.* tē'-nən   tee'-nuhn
  French *Tirlemont,* tēr-lə-môN' [teer-luh-moN'].
Thiers (Fr.)   tyĕr'   tyehr'
Thiess (Ger. name)   tēs'   tees'
Thiganousa (Gr., isl.)   thē-gä-noō'-sä   thee-gah-noo'-sah
  Also called *Venetiko,* vĕ-nĕ'-tē-kô [veh-neh'-tee-ko].
Thilliers, les (Fr.)   tē-lyĕ', lĕ   tee-lyeh', leh
Thionville (Fr.)   tyôN-vēl'   tyoN-veel'
  German *Diedenhofen,* dē'-dən-hō'-fən [dee'-duhn-hoh'-fuhn].
Thisted (Den.)   tē'-stĕth   tee'-steth
Thodoroi (Crete)   See *Theodoroi.*
Thodorou (Crete, isl.)   See *Theodoros.*
Tholen (Neth., isl.)   tō'-lən   toh'-luhn
Tholon (Fr., riv.)   tô-lôN'   to-loN'
Thom, William R.   tŏm'   tom'
  (U.S. representative)
Thomason, Ewing   tŏm'-ə-sən, yoō'-ĭng   tom'-uh-suhn, yoo'-
  (U.S. representative)   ing
Thonon (Fr.)   tô-nôN'   to-noN'
Thonon les Bains (Fr.)   tô-nôN lĕ bǎN'   to-noN leh baN'
Thorée (Fr.)   tô-rĕ'   to-reh'
Thorez, Jeanette Vermeersch (Fr. polit.) See *Vermeersch Thorez.*
Thorez, Maurice   tô-rĕz', mô-rēs'   to-rez', mo-rees'
  (Fr. polit.)
Thorigné (Fr.)   tô-rē-nyĕ'   to-ree-nyeh'
Thorn (Pol.)   See *Toruń.*
Thórs, Thór (Icel.   tôrs', tôr'   tors', tor'
  diplomat)
Thorshavn (Den.)   tôrs-houn'   tors-haun'
Thouarcé (Fr.)   twär-sĕ'   twahr-seh'
Thouars (Fr.)   twär'   twahr'
Thouet (Fr., riv.)   twĕ'   tweh'
Thourout (Belg.)   *Fr.* toō-roō'   too-roo'
  Flemish *Torhout,* q.v.
Thrace (Gr.)   *Eng.* thrās'   thrays'
  Greek *Thrake,* thrä'-kē [thrah'-kee].

Thueringen *or*   tü'-rĭng-ən   tü'-ring-uhn
   Thüringen (Ger.)
   English *Thuringia,* thyo͝o-rĭn'-jə [thyu-rin'-juh].

Thule (Greenland)   thyo͞o'-lĭ *or* tho͞o'-   thyoo'-li *or* thoo'-

Thun (Switz.)   to͞on'   toon'

Thunersee (Switz., lake) to͞o'-nər-zā   too'-nuhr-zay

Thuringia (Ger.)   *Eng.* thyo͝o-rĭn'-jə   thyu-rin'-juh
   German *Thüringen,* tü'-rĭng-ən [tü'-ring-uhn].

Thury Harcourt (Fr.)   tü-rē är-ko͞or'   tü-ree ahr-koor'

Thye, Edward J.   thī'   thai'
   (Minn. polit.)

Thyssen, Fritz   tĭs'-ən   tis'-uhn
   (Ger. industrialist)

Tia Juana (Calif.)   tē'-ə hwä'-nə   tee'-uh hwah'-nuh

Tiangzup (Burma)   tyäng-zo͝op'   tyahng-zup'

Tiaret (Alg.)   tyä-rĕ'   tyah-reh'

Tibao (P.I.) See *Calapán.*

Tiber (It., riv.)   *Eng.* tī'-bər   tai'-buhr
   Italian *Tevere,* q.v.

Tiberias (Pal.)   tĭ-bĭr'-ĭ-əs   tai-bir'-i-uhs
   Arabic *Tabariya,* tä-bä-rē'-yä [tah-bah-ree'-yah]. Hebrew *Tevarya,*
   tĕ-vär'-yä [teh-vahr'-yah].

Tibet (Ch. dependency) *Eng.* tĭ-bĕt'   ti-bet'
   Chinese *Hsi-ts'ang,* shē-tsäng [shee-tsahng] *or* Si-ts'ang, q.v.

Tiburon (Calif.)   tĭb'-ə-rŏn   tib'-uh-ron

Tiburón (Colom., cape) tē-bo͞o-rôn'   tee-boo-ron'

Ticino (It., riv.)   tē-chē'-nô   tee-chee'-no

Ticino (Switz.)   tē-chē'-nô   tee-chee'-no

Tiddin (Burma)   tĭd'-dĭn   tid'-din

Tidore (NEI)   tĭ-dôr'-ĕ   tih-dor'-eh

Tiel (Neth.)   tēl'   teel'

Tien-pai (Ch.,   dyĕn-bī   dyen-bai
   Kwangtung)
   Also called *Tinpak,* q.v.

T'ien-shui (Ch., Kansu) tyĕn-shwä   tyen-shway

Tientsin (Ch., Hopeh)   *Eng.* tĭn-sĭn   tin-sin
   Chinese *T'ien-chin,* tyĕn-jĭn [tyen-jin].

Tiercé (Fr.)   tyĕr-sĕ'   tyehr-seh'

Tierra del Fuego   tyĕr'-rä dĕl fwĕ'-gô   tyehr'-rah dehl
   (Arg., Chile, isl.)   fweh'-go

Tietjens (Du. name)   tēt'-yəns   teet'-yuhns

Tietjens, Eunice Strong tē'-jəns   tee'-juhns
   (Am. poet)

Tietjerksteradeel (Neth.)   tēt-yĕrk'-stə-rä-däl'   teet-yehrk'-stuh-rah-
                                                      dayl'
Tiflis (Rus.)   *Eng.* tĭf'-lĭs   tif'-lis
                         Rus. tĭf-lēs'   tif-lees'
  Georgian *Tbilisi*, tbĭ-lē-sē' [tbi-lee-see'].
Tighina (Rum. > Rus.)   tē-gē'-nä   tee-gee'-nah
  Russian and German *Bender*, bĕn'-dər [ben'-duhr].
Tiglione (It.)   tē-lyô'-nĕ   tee-lyo'-neh
Ti-hwa (Ch., Sinkiang)   dē-whä   dee-whah
  Also called *Urumchi*, q.v.
Tijesno (Yugosl.)   tē'-yĕ'-snô   tee'-yeh'-sno
Tijuana (Mex.)   tē-hwä'-nä   tee-hwah'-nah
Tikhoretsk (Rus.)   tĭ-hŏ-rĕtsk'   ti-ho-retsk'
Tikhvin (Rus.)   tēk(h)'-vĭn   teek(h)'-vin
Tikopia (Oc., Solomons)   tē-kô-pē'-ä   tee-ko-pee'-ah
Tikotsin (Pol.)   See *Tykocin.*
Tikveš (Yugosl.)   tēk'-vĕsh   teek'-vesh
Tilburg (Neth.)   tĭl'-bûrk(h)   til'-bœrk(h)
Tildy, Zoltán   tĭl'-dĭ, zôl'-tän   til'-di, zol'-tahn
  (Hung. polit.)
Tilig (P.I., bay)   tē-lēg'   tee-leeg'
Till Eulenspiegel (folk hero) See *Eulenspiegel, Till.*
Tillon, Charles (Fr. polit.) tē-yôN', shärl' tee-yoN', shahrl'
Tilly la Campagne (Fr.)   tē-yē lä käN-pän'(y) tee-yee lah kahN-
                                          pahn'(y)
Tilly sur Seulles (Fr.)   tē-yē sür sûl'   tee-yee sür sœl'
Tilos (Dodec.)   tē'-lô(s)   tee'-lo(s)
  Italian *Piscopi*, q.v.
Tilsit (Ger. > Rus.)   tĭl'-zĭt   til'-zit
  Russian *Sovetsk*, sŏ-vĕtsk' [so-vetsk'].
Tim (Rus.)   tēm'   teem'
Timashevskaya (Rus.)   tĭ-mä'-shĕf-skä-yä   ti-mah'-shef-skah-yah
Timbaki (Crete)   tēm-bä'-kē   teem-bah'-kee
Timbuktu (Fr. W. Afr.)   tĭm-bŭk'-tōō   tim-buk'-too
  Also Anglicized as *Timbuctoo* and pronounced tĭm-bŭk-tōō' [tim'-
  buhk-too']. French *Tombouctou*, tôN-bōōk-tōō' [toN-book-too'].
Time (Rus.)   tē'-mĕ   tee'-meh
Timişoara (Rum.)   tē-mē-shwä'-rä   tee-mee-shwah'-rah
  Hungarian *Temesvár*, q.v. Serb-Croat *Temišvar*, tĕ'-mē-shvär [teh'-
  mee-shvahr].
Timişul (Balkan riv.)   *Rum.* tē'-mē-shōōl tee'-mee-shul
  Serb-Croat *Tamiš*, q.v. Hungarian *Temes*, tĕ'-mĕsh [teh'-mesh].
Timok (Yugosl., riv.)   tē'-môk   tee'-mok

Timor (NEI and Port.   tē'-môr   tee'-mor
cols.)

A recommendation that the principal accent be placed on the last syllable appears to be not well founded.

Timoshenko, Semyon K. (Rus. marshal)	tē-mŏ-shĕn'-kŏ, sĕm-yôn'	tee-mo-shen'-ko, sem-yon'
Tinagó (P.I.)	tē-nä-gô'	tee-nah-go'
Tinakula (Oc., Solomons)	tē-nä-kōō'-lä	tee-nah-koo'-lah
Tinchebray (Fr.)	tăNsh-brĕ'	taNsh-breh'
Tindja (Tun.)	tĭn'-jä	tin'-jah
Tine (Tun., riv.)	tēn'	teen'
Tinée (Fr., riv.)	tē-nĕ'	tee-neh'
Ting-hai (Ch., Chekiang)	dĭng-hī	ding-hai
Ting-nan (Ch., Kiangsi)	dĭng-nän	ding-nahn
Tinguianes (P.I., people)	tēn-gyä'-nĕs	teen-gyah'-nes
Tinian (Oc., Marianas)	Eng. tĭn-ĭ-ăn' or tē-nē-än'	tin-i-an' tee-nee-ahn'
Tinn (Nor.)	tĭn'	tin'
Tinnoset (Nor.)	tĭn'-ŏ-sə	tin'-oh-suh
Tinpak (Ch., Kwantung)	Eng. tĭn-păk	tin-pak

Chinese *Tien-pai*, q.v.

Tinsukia (India)	Eng. tĭn'-sōō'-kē	tin'-soo'-kee
Tinténiac (Fr.)	tăN-tĕ-nyäk'	taN-teh-nyahk'
Tioucha (Tun.)	tē-ōō'-shä	tee-yoo'-shah
Tippera (India)	tĭp'-ə-rä	tip'-uh-rah

Indian *Tripura*, trĭ-pōō-rä [tri-pu-rah], with level accent.

Tirana (Alb.)   See *Tiranë*.

Tiranë (Alb.)	tē-rä'-nə	tee-rah'-nuh
Tiraspol (Rus.)	tĭ-räs'-pŏl(y)	ti-rahs'-pol(y)
Tiriolo (It.)	tē-ryô'-lô	tee-ryo'-lo

Tirlemont (Belg.)   See *Thienen*.

Tirnovo (Bulg.)   See *Trnovo*.

Tirol (Austria)	Eng. tĭr'-ŏl Ger. tē-rōl'	tihr'-ol tee-rohl'
Tisa (Europ. riv.)	S.-C. tē'-sä	tee'-sah

Hungarian *Tisza*, q.v. German *Theiss*.

Tishovtsi (Pol.)   See *Tyszowce*.

Tisza (Europ. riv.)	Hung. tē'-sŏ	tee'-so

German *Theiss*, tīs' [tais']. Serbian *Tisa*, q.v.

Titerno (It., riv.)	tē-tĕr'-nô	tee-tehr'-no
Titicaca (S.A., lake)	Eng. tĭt'-ĭ-kä'-kə Sp. tē-tē-kä'-kä	tit'-i-kah'-kuh tee-tee-kah'-kah
Tito, Marshal	tē'-tō	tee'-toh

Nickname of Josip *Broz*, q.v.

Tittigarh (India)	tĭt-ĭ-gär′ *or* -gŭr′	tit-i-gahr′ *or* -guhr′
Tityron (Crete, pen., mt.)	See *Rodopou.*	
Tiulenev, I. V. (Rus. general)	tyōō-lĕ′-nĕf	tyoo-leh′-nef
Tivar (Yugosl.) Serb-Croat *Bar,* q.v.	*Alb.* tē′-vär	tee′-vahr
Tivoli (It.)	*Eng.* tĭv′-ə-lĭ	tiv′-uh-li
	It. tē′-vô-lē	tee′-vo-lee
Tiznit (Mor.)	tĭz′-nĭt	tiz′-nit
Tjapoe *or* Tjapu (NEI)	chä-pōō′	chah-poo′
Tjiamis (Java)	chē-ä′-mĭs	chee-ah′-mis
Tjiandjoer (NEI, Java)	chyän′-jōōr	chyahn′-joor
Also spelled *Chianjur,* q.v.		
Tjilatjap (NEI, Java)	chē-lä′-chäp	chee-lah′-chahp
Tlaxcala (Mex.)	tläs-kä′-lä	tlahs-kah′-lah
Tmimi (Libya)	tmē′-mē	tmee′-mee
tō	tô	to

An element in Japanese place names, meaning *east* or *island.* As *east,* it more often precedes than follows another form; as *island,* it usually follows another form.

Toau (Oc., Tuamotu)	tô-ou′	to-au′
Tobermore (N. Ire.)	tŭb-ər-mōr′	tuhb-uhr-mohr′
Toberoi *or* Toberei (Oc., Bougainville) See *Toboroi.*		
Tobey, Charles W. (U.S. senator)	tō′-bĭ	toh′-bi
Tobi (Oc., Carolines)	tô′-bē	to′-bee
Also called *Tokobi,* tô-kô′-bē [to-ko′-bee].		
Tobiishi (Jap.)	tô-bē′-ē-shē	to-bee′-ee-shee
Tobolsk (Rus.)	tô-bôl(y)sk′	to-bol(y)sk′
Toboroi (Oc., Bougain- ville)	tô′-bô-roi	to′-bo-roi
Tobruk (Libya)	tō′-brŏŏk′	toh′-bruk′
Also spelled *Tobruch* and *Tobrukh.*		
Toburba (Tun.) See *Tebourba.*		
Tochigi (Jap.)	tô-chē′-gē′	to-chee′-gee′
Todi (It.)	tô′-dē	to′-dee
Todmorden (Austral.)	tŏd′-môr-dən	tod′-mor-duhn
Todt, Fritz (Ger. engineer)	tōt′, frĭts′	toht′, frits′
Todtenhuegel *or* Todtenhügel (Ger.)	tōt′-ən-hüg-əl	toht′-uhn-hüg-uhl
Toem Wadke (NEI)	tōōm′ wät′-kə	toom′ waht′-kuh
Toender (Den.)	tûn′-ər	tœn′-uhr
Toensberg (Nor.)	tûns′-bĕr	tœns′-behr

Toenset (Nor.)   See *Tynset.*

Togliatti, Palmiro   tô-lyät′-tē, päl-mē′-rô   to-lyaht′-tee, pahl-
(It. polit.)   mee′-ro

Togliatti, Rita   tô-lyät′-tē, rē′-tä   to-lyaht′-tee, ree′-tah
Montagnana (It. polit.)   môn-tä-nyä′-nä   mon-tah-nyah′-nah

Tōhoku (Jap.)   tô′-hô-kōo   to′-ho-koo
                            or tô′-hôk   to′-hok

Tohopekaliga (Fla., lake)   tô′-hō-pē′-kə-lĭ′-gə   toh′-hoh-pee′-kuh
                           or -lē′-gə   lai′-guh *or* -lee′-guh

Toiokh (Ch.)   tô′-yôk(h)   to′-yok(h)

Tōjō, Hideki (Jap. polit.)   tô′-jô, hē-dĕ′-kē′   to′-jo, hee-deh′-kee′
   Eiki, ā′-kē [ay′-kee], is a variant of *Hideki.*

Tōkaidō (Jap.)   tô-kĭ′-dô   to-kai′-do

Tokay (Hung.)   *Eng.* tō-kā′   toh-kay′
   Hungarian *Tokaj,* tô′-koi [tô′-koi].

Tokelau (Oc.)   tô-kĕ-lou′   to-keh-lau′
   Also called *Union.*

Tokio (Jap.) See *Tōkyō.*

Tokmak (Rus.)   tŏk-mäk′   tok-mahk′

Tokobi (Oc.)   See *Tobi.*

Tököl (Hung., airport)   tû′-kûl′   tœ′-kœl′

Tokowinai (Oc., Bougain-   tô-kô-wē′-nī   to-ko-wee′-nai
ville, mt.)

Tokuda, Gen (Jap. polit.)   tô-kōo′-dä′, gĕn′   to-koo′-dah′, gen′

Tokugawa, Kuniyoshi   tô′-kōo′-gä-wä,   to′-koo′-gah-wah,
(Jap. prince)   kōo-nē′-yô-shē   koo-nee′-yo-shee

Tokushima (Jap.)   tô-kōo′-shē′-mä′   to-koo′-shee′-mah′
                  or tô-kōo′-shē′-mä   to-koo′-shee′-mah

Tokutomi, Iichirō (Jap.   tô-kōo′-tô-mē,   to-koo′-to-mee,
author)   ē-ē′-chē-rô   ee-ee′-chee-ro

Tōkyō (Jap.)   *Eng.* tō′-kĭ-ō   toh′-ki-oh
   The Japanese pronunciation has level stress and both syllables are long.

Tōkyō Mimpō (Jap.   tô-kyô mēm′-pô   to-kyo meem′-po
newspaper)

Tolan, John H.   tō′-lən   toh′-luhn
(U.S. representative)

Tolbukhin, Feodor I.   tŏl-bōo′-hĭn,   tol-boo′-hin,
(Rus. general)   fyô′-dŏr   fyo′-dor

Toledano, Vincente Lombardo (Mex. polit.) See *Lombardo Toledano.*

Toledo (Sp., U.S.)   *Eng.* tə-lē′-dō   tuh-lee′-doh
                    Sp. tô-lĕ′-dô   to-leh′-do

Tolitoli (NEI, Celebes)   tô′-lē-tô′-lē   to′-lee-to′-lee
   Also called *Kampoengbaroe,* q.v.

Tolkien (Eng. name)	tŏl′-kēn	tol′-keen
Tollefson, Thor C. (U.S. representative)	tŏl′-ĕf-sən	tol′-ef-suhn
Tollemache (Eng. name)	tŏl′-măsh	tol′-mash
Tollevast (Fr.)	tôl-väst′	tol-vahst′
Tolman, Richard C. (Am. scientist)	tŏl′-mən	tohl′-muhn
Tolón (P.I.)	tô-lôn′	to-lon′
Tolosa (P.I.)	tô-lô′-sä	to-lo′-sah
Tolovana (Alaska)	tō′-lə-văn′-ə	toh′-luh-van′-uh
Tolstoi, Aleksei N. (Rus. author)	tŏl-stoi′, ä-lĕ-ksā′	tol-stoi′, ah-leh-ksay′
Tolstoi, Lev Nikola-evich (Rus. author)	tŏl-stoi′, lĕf′ nĭ-kŏ-lä′-yĕ-vĭch	tol-stoi′, lef′ ni-ko-lah′-yeh-vich
Toluca (Mex.)	tô-loō′-kä	to-loo′-kah
Tolvajaervi or -järvi (Fin., lake)	tôl′-vä-yăr-vē	tol′-vah-yar-vee
Tomaszów (Pol.)	tô-mä′-shoōf	to-mah′-shuf

Russian *Tomashov*, tŏ-mä′-shŏf [to-mah′-shof].

| tomato | tə-mā′-tō | tuh-may′-toh |
| | or tə-mä′-tō | tuh-mah′-toh |

American dictionaries agree on this order. The first is without doubt the general American pronunciation. On a particular program, however, there may be a reason for preferring the pronunciation with the "broad ah." There is also an old-fashioned pronunciation, tə-măt′-ə [tuh-mat′-uh].

Tombouctou (Fr. W. Afr.) See *Timbuktu*.

| Tomil (Oc., Yap) | tô′-mēl | to′-meel |
| Tomini (NEI, Celebes) | tô-mē′-nē | to-mee′-nee |

Also called *Gorontalo*, gô-rôn-tä′-lô [go-ron-tah′-lo].

| Tomor (Alb., mt.) | *Eng.* tô′-môr | to′-mor |

Albanian *Mal i Tomorrit*; locally *Çukat*, choō′-kät [choo′-kaht].

Tomorrica (Alb.) See *Tomorricë*.

Tomorricë (Alb.)	tô-môr-rē′-tsə	to-mor-ree′-tsuh
Tomsk (Rus.)	tômsk′	tomsk′
Tonawanda (Pa.)	tŏn′-ə-wän′-də	ton′-uh-wahn′-duh
Tönder (Den.)	tûn′-ər	tœn′-uhr
Tondo (P.I.)	tôn′-dô	ton′-do
Tongres (Belg.)	tôN′gr	toN′gr
Tonkin (Indo-Ch.)	tŏn′-kĭn′	ton′-kin′

Also English *Tonking*. Chinese *Tung-ching*, doōng-jĭng [dung-jing].

Tonnerre (Fr.)	tô-nĕr′	to-nehr′
Tonopah (Nev.)	tō′-nə-pä′	toh′-nuh-pah′
Tonsaasen (Nor.)	toōns′-ôs-ən	tuns′-os-uhn

Tönsberg (Nor.)	tûns'-bĕr	tœns'-behr
Tönset (Nor.) See *Tynset*.		
Tooele (Utah)	tōō-wĭl'-ə	too-wil'-uh

Wayne Kearl of KSL, Salt Lake City, gives this as "the common pronunciation out here, in fact the only one I have ever heard among the natives." One dictionary, however, gives tōō-ĕl'-ə [too-el'-uh], and another tōō-ĕl'-ĕ [tu-el'-eh].

Toole (Mont.)	tōōl'	tool'
Toowoomba (Austral.)	tə-wōōm'-bə	tuh-woom'-buh
Topčider (Yugosl.)	tôp'-chĭ-dĕr	top'-chi-dehr
Topeka (Kans.)	tə-pē'-kə	tuh-pee'-kuh
Topl'a (Cz., Hung., riv.)	*Cz.* tô'-plyä	to'-plyah

Hungarian *Tapoly*, tä'-pôl(y) [tah'-pol(y)].

Toplica (Yugosl.)	tô'-plĭ-tsä	to'-pli-tsah
Toplou (Crete)	tô-plōō'	to-ploo'
Topola (Yugosl.)	tô'-pô-lä	to'-po-lah
Topoli (Rus.)	tô'-pŏ-lĭ	to'-po-li
Toponica (Yugosl.)	tô'-pô'-nĭ-tsä	to'-po'-ni-tsah
Torcola (Yugosl., isl.)	*It.* tôr'-kô-lä	tor'-ko-lah

Serb-Croat *Šćedro*, q.v.

Torda (Rum.) See *Turda*.

Torfinnsbu (Nor.)	tōōr'-fĭns-bōō	tur'-fins-boo
Torhout (Belg.)	*Flem.* tōr'-hout	tohr'-haut

French *Thourout*, q.v.

Torigni sur Vire (Fr.)	tô-rē-nyē sür vēr'	to-ree-nyee sür veer'
Torino (It.)	tô-rē'-nô	to-ree'-no

English *Turin*, q.v.

Torlonia (It.)	tôr-lô'-nyä	tor-lo'-nyah
tornadic	tôr-năd'-ĭk	tor-nad'-ik

Note the short *a* of the second syllable in contrast to the long *a* of *tornado*—tôr-nā'-dō [tor-nay'-doh].

Tornese, Colle (It.)	tôr-nĕ'-zĕ, kôl'-lĕ	tor-neh'-zeh, kol'-leh
Tornio (Fin.)	tôr'-nē-ô	tor'-nee-o
Tornya (Rum.) See *Turnu*.		
Törökszentmiklós (Hung.)	tû'-rûk-sĕnt'-mĭ-klôsh	tœ'-rœk-sent'-mi-klosh
Torontál (Hung.)	tô'-rôn-täl	to'-ron-tahl
Toropets (Rus.)	tŏ-rô'-pĕts	to-ro'-pets
Torraccia (It., mt.)	tôr-rät'-chä	tor-raht'-chah
Torre Annunziata (It.)	tôr'-rĕ än-nōōn'-tsyä'-tä	tor'-reh ahn-noon'-tsyah'-tah
Torre Archirafi (Sicily)	tôr'-rĕ är-kē-rä'-fē	tor'-reh ahr-kee-rah'-fee
Torre Cajetani (It.)	tôr'-rĕ kä-yĕ-tä'-nē	tor'-reh kah-yeh-tah'-nee

[545]

Torrens (Austral., lake, riv.)	tŏr′-ənz	tor′-uhnz
Torreón (Mex.)	tôr-rĕ-ôn′	tor-reh-on′
Torres (Austral., strait)	tŏr′-ĭz	tor′-iz
Torrès, Henri (Fr. lawyer)	tô-rĕs′, äN-rē′	to-res′, ahN-ree′
Torrèz, Maurice (Fr. polit.) See *Thorez.*		
Torrice (It.)	tôr′-rē-chĕ	tor′-ree-cheh
Torslanda (Sw., Gothenburg, airport)	tōōrs′-län-dä	toors′-lahn-dah
tortilla ("corn cake")	*Eng.* tôr-tē′-yə	tor-tee′-yuh
	Sp. tôr-tē′-yä	tor-tee′-yah
Torto, Fiume (Sicily)	tôr′-tô, fyōō′-mĕ	tor′-to, fyoo′-meh
Tortorici (Sicily)	tôr-tô-rē′-chĕ	tor-to-ree′-chee
Tortue, la (Haiti, isl.)	tôr-tü′, lä	tor-tü′, lah
Tortuga (W.I.)	tôr-tōō′-gä	tor-too′-gah
Toruń (Pol.)	tô′-rŏŏn(y)	to′-run(y)
German *Thorn*, tôrn′ [torn′].		
Torzhok (Rus.)	tŏr-zhôk′	tor-zhok′
Tosk (Alb.)	*Eng.* tôsk′	tosk′
Southern Albanian. Albanian *Toskë*, tôs′-kə [tos′-kuh], and *Toska.*		
Tosno (Rus.)	tôs′-nŏ	tos′-no
Tossignano (It.)	tôs-sē-nyä′-nô	tos-see-nyah′-no
Tószeg (Hung.)	tô′-sĕg	to′-seg
Tôtes (Fr.)	tōt′	toht′
Totonicapán (Guat.)	tô-tô′-nē-kä-pän′	to-to′-nee-kah-pahn′
Tottori (Jap.)	tôt′-tô′-rē	tot′-to′-ree
Totvázsony (Hung.)	tôt′-vä-zhôn(y)	tot′-vah-zhon(y)
Touareg (Sahara tribes) See *Tuareg.*		
Touggourt (Alg.)	*Fr.* tōō-gōōr′	too-goor′
Also called *Tug(g)urt*, q.v.		
Toujane (Tun.)	tōō-zhän′	too-zhahn′
Toul (Fr.)	tōōl′	tool′
Toulon (Fr.)	tōō-lôN′	too-loN′
Toulouse (Fr.)	tōō-lōōz′	too-looz′
Toum (Tun.)	tōōm′	toom′
Toungoo (Burma)	toung′-gōō′	taung′-goo′
	or toung′-ōō′	taung′-oo′
Touques (Fr., riv.)	tōōk′	took′
Touquet, le (Fr.)	tōō-kĕ′, lə	too-keh′, luh
Tourane (Indo-Ch.)	tōō-răn′ *or* tōō-rän′	too-ran′ *or* too-rahn′
Tourcoing (Fr.)	tōōr-kwăN′	toor-kwaN′
Tourlaville (Fr.)	tōōr-lä-vēl′	toor-lah-veel′
Tourloti (Crete)	tōōr-lô-tē′	toor-lo-tee′
Tournai (Belg.)	tōōr-nĕ′	toor-neh′
Flemish *Doornik*, dōr′-nĭk [dohr′-nik]		

Tournon (Fr.)	tōͦr-nôN′	toor-noN′
Tourouvre (Fr.)	tōō-rōō′vr	too-roo′vr
Tours (Fr.)	*Eng.* tōͦrz′	toorz′
	Fr. tōͦr′	toor′

The French pronunciation is common in English contexts.

Touyo (Oc.) See *Tuyio.*

tovarishch	tŏ-vä′-rĭsh	to-vah′-rish

Russian word meaning *comrade.*

Towe, Harry L.	tō′-ē	toh′-ee
(U.S. representative)		
Toyama (Jap.)	tô′-yä-mä	to′-yah-mah
Toynbee (family name)	toin′-bĭ	toin′-bi
Toyoda, Minoru (Jap.	tô′-yô-dä, mē-nô′-rōō	to′-yo-dah, mee-no′-
educator)		roo
Toyohashi (Jap.)	tô-yô′-hä-shē	to-yo′-hah-shee
Tōyō Keizai Shimpō	tô-yô kā′-zä-ē shēm′-	to-yo kay′-zah-ee
(Jap., Tokyo, news-	pô	sheem′-po
paper)		
Tozeur (Tun.)	tô-zûr′	to-zœr′
Trabzon (Turk.)	träb′-zôn′	trahb′-zon′

Also called *Trebizond,* q.v.

Trafalgar (Sp., cape)	*Eng.* trə-făl′-gər	truh-fal′-guhr
	Sp. trä-fäl-gär′	trah-fahl-gahr′
Traisen (Austria, riv.)	trī′-zən	trai′-zuhn
Trajano (It.)	trä-yä′-nô	trah-yah′-no
Trakhoulas (Crete, point)	trä′-hōō-läs	trah′-hoo-lahs
Trakya (Turk.)	trä′-kyä′	trah′-kyah′
Trälleborg (Sw.)	trĕl′-ə-bôr′(y)	trel′-uh-bor′(y)
Trang (Siam)	träng′	trahng′
Tranquebar (India)	träng-kwĭ-bär′	trang-kwi-bahr′
Trans-Jordan	trăns- *or* trănz-	trans- *or* tranz-
(Arab Kingdom)	jôr′-dən	jor′-duhn

Formerly *Transjordania,* trănz-jôr-dä′-nĭ-ə *or* trăns- [tranz-jor-day′-ni-uh *or* trans-]. Arabic *Sharq el Urdunn,* shärk′ ĕl ŏͦr′-dŏͦn [shahrk′-el ur′-dun]. Also called *Kerak,* kĕ′-răk [keh′-rak].

Transkei (U. of S. Afr.)	träns-kī′	trans-kai′
Transvaal (U. of S. Afr.)	träns-väl′	trans-vahl′
Transylvania (Rum.)	*Eng.* trăn′-sĭl-vā′-nyə	tran′-sil-vay′-nyuh
Trapani (Sicily)	trä′-pä-nē	trah′-pah-nee
Trappes (Fr.)	träp′	trahp′
Trasimeno (It., lake)	trä-sē-mĕ′-nô	trah-see-meh′-no
Traspontine (It.)	trä-spôn-tē′-nĕ	trah-spon-tee′-neh
Trašte (Yugosl.)	trä′-shtĕ	trah′-shteh
Trastevere (It., Rome)	trä-stĕ′-vĕ-rĕ	trah-steh′-veh-reh

Trau (Yugosl.) See *Trogir*.

Trautenau (Cz.)　See *Trutnov*.

Travancore (India)	trăv-ən-kôr′	trav-uhn-kor′
Travnička (Yugosl.)	träv′-nĭch-kä	trahv′-nich-kah
Trebbin (Ger.)	trĕb-bēn′	treb-been′
Třebíč (Cz.)	trzhĕ′-bēch	trzheh′-beech
Trebinje (Yugosl.)	trĕ′-bĭ-nyĕ	treh′-bi-nyeh
Trebisacce (It.)	trĕ-bē-sät′-chĕ	treh-bee-saht′-cheh
Trebišov (Cz.)	trĕ′-bĭ-shôf	treh′-bih-shof
Trebizond (Turk.)	*Eng.* trĕb′-ĭ-zŏnd′	treb′-i-zond′

Now officially *Trabzon*, q.v.

Trebnitz (Ger.)	trĕb′-nĭts	treb′-nits
Trebnje (Yugosl.)	trĕb′-nyĕ	treb′-nyeh
Trecastagni (Sicily)	trĕ-kä-stä′-nyē	treh-kah-stah′-nyee
Tréguier (Fr.)	trĕ-gyĕ′	treh-gyeh′
Tremblade, la (Fr.)	träN-bläd′	trahN-blahd′
Trembowla (Pol. > Rus.)	trĕm-bô′-vlä	trem-bo′-vlah

Russian *Terebovlia*, tĕ-rĕ-bô′-vlyä [teh-reh-bo′-vlyah].

tremendous.　See *grievous*.

Tremiti (It., isls.)	trĕ′-mē-tē	treh′-mee-tee
tremor	trĕm′-ər *or* trē′-mər	trehm′-uhr *or* tree′-muhr
Trenčín (Cz.)	trĕn′-chēn	tren′-cheen
Trento (It.)	trĕn′-tô	tren′-to

English *Trent*, trĕnt′ [trent′] .

Trentola (It.)	trĕn′-tô-lä	tren′-to-lah
Tre Pietre (It.)	trĕ′ pyĕ′-trĕ	treh′ pyeh′-treh
Tréport, le (Fr.)	trĕ-pôr′, lə	treh-por′, luh
Treptow (Ger. > Pol.)	trĕp′-tō	trep′-toh

Polish *Trzebiatów*, q.v.

Trets (Fr.)	trĕ′	treh′
Tretten (Nor.)	trĕt′n	tret′n
Treuburg (Ger. > Pol.)	troi′-bŏŏrk(h)	troi′-burk(h)

Polish *Margrabowa*, q.v.

Treungen (Nor.)	trä′-ŏŏng-ən	tray′-ung-uhn
Trèves (Ger.)	*Fr.* trĕv′	trev′

German *Trier*, q.v.

Trevi (It.)	trĕ′-vē	treh′-vee
Trévière (Fr.)	trĕ-vyĕr′	treh-vyehr′
Trevignano (It.)	trĕ-vē-nyä′-nô	treh-vee-nyah′-no
Treviso (It.)	trĕ-vē′-zô	treh-vee′-zo
Treysa (Ger.)	trī′-zä	trai′-zah
Trgoviški Timok (Yugosl.)	tər′-gô-vĭsh-kĭ tē′-môk	tuhr′-go-vish-ki tee′-mok

Triada, Agia (Crete)   trē-ä'-dä, ĭ'-yä   tree-ah'-dah, ai'-yah
Triaga (Tun.)   trē-ä'-gä   tree-a'-gah
tribunal   trĭ-byoo'-nəl or trĭ-   trai-byoo'-nuhl or tri-
tribune   trĭb'-yoon'   trib'-yoon'

As a word in unemphatic speech the first syllable usually has more stress than the second. As the name of a newspaper the second syllable may have the heavier stress. The pronunciation trī'-byoon [trai'-byoon] occurs in British speech, but trĭb'-byoon [trib'-byoon] is the BBC choice.

Trichinopoly (India)   trĭch-ĭ-nŏp'-ə-lĭ   trich-i-nop'-uh-li
Tricqueville (Fr.)   trēk-vēl'   treek-veel'
tridione (drug)   trĭ-dī'-ōn   trai-dai'-ohn
Triebel (Ger.)   trē'-bəl   tree'-buhl
Trier (Ger.)   trēr'   treer'
  French *Trèves*, q.v.
Trieste (It. >free terri-   *Eng.* trĭ-ĕst'   tri-est'
  tory)   *It.* trē-ĕs'-tĕ   tree-es'-teh
Trigno (It., riv.)   trē'-nyô   tree'-nyo
Trikala (Gr.)   trē'-kä-lä   tree'-kah-lah
Trincomali (Ceylon)   trĭng-kŭm'-mə-lē'   tring-kuhm'-muh-lee'
Trinidad (Colom.)   trĭn'-ə-dăd   trin'-uh-dad
  Spanish *Trinidád*, trē-nē-däd' [tree-nee-dahd'].
tripartite   trī'-pär'-tīt   trai'-pahr'-tait
    or trĭp'-ər-tīt   trip'-uhr-tait
Tripoli (Iowa)   trĭ-pō'-lĭ   tri-poh'-li
Tripoli (Libya)   *Eng.* trĭp'-ə-lĭ   trip'-uh-li
    It. trē'-pô-lē   tree'-po-lee
Tripolis (Gr.)   *Eng.* trĭp'-ə-lĭs   trip'-uh-lis
    Gr. trē'-pô-lē(s)   tree'-po-lee(s)
  Also called *Tripolitsa*, trē-pô-lē-tsä' [tree-po-lee-tsah'].
Tripolitania (Afr.)   *Eng.* trĭp'-ə-lĭ-tā'-   trip'-uh-li-tay'-ni-uh
      nĭ-ə
    It. trē'-pô-lē-tä'-   tree'-po-lee-tah'-nyah
      nyä
Tripsrath (Ger.)   trĭps'-rät   trips'-raht
Tripura (India)   trĭ-poo'-rə   tri-poo'-ruh
Tristan da Cunha   trĭs'-tăn dä koon'-yə   tris'-tan dah koon'-
  (S. Atlantic)   yuh
  Portuguese *Tristão da Cunha*, trēsh-touN' də koo'-nyə [treesh-tauN' duh koo'-nyuh].
Triton (Crete, cape) See *Vouxa*.
Trivandrum (India)   trĭ-văn'-drəm   tri-van'-druhm
Trivigliano (It.)   trē-vē-lyä'-nô   tree-vee-lyah'-no

Trn (Bulg.)	tərn'	tuhrn'
Trnava (Cz., riv.)	tər'-nä-vä	tuhr'-nah-vah
Trnjane (Yugosl.)	tər'-nyä-ně	tuhr'-nyah-neh
Trnovac (Yugosl.)	tər'-nô-väts	tuhr'-no-vahts
Trnovo (Bulg.)	tər'-nŏ-vŏ	tuhr'-no-vo

Also called *Tirnovo*, tēr'-nŏ-vŏ [teer'-no-vo].

Troarn (Fr.)	trô-ärn'	tro-ahrn'
Trobriand (Oc.)	trō'-brĭ-ănd'	troh'-bri-and'
Trocchio (It.)	trôk'-kyô	trok'-kyo
Troclet, Léon Émile	trô-klě', lě-ôN' ě-mēl'	tro-kleh', leh-oN'
(Belg. polit.)		eh-meel'
Trogir (Yugosl.)	trô'-gĭr	tro'-gihr

Italian *Trau*, trou' [trau'].

Troina (Sicily)	trô-ē'-nä	tro-ee'-nah
Troisdorf (Ger.)	trois'-dôrf	trois'-dorf
Troitsk (Rus.)	trô'-ĭtsk	tro'-itsk
Troitskoe (Rus.)	trô'-ĭts-kŏ-yě	tro'-its-ko-yeh
Troitskosavsk (Rus.)	trô'-ĭts-kŏ-säfsk'	tro'-its-ko-sahfsk'
Trojan (Balkan mts.)	*S.-C.* trô-yän	tro'-yahn

Albanian *Mal i Trojanit*, mäl' ē trô-yä'-nět [mahl' ee tro-yah'-neet].

Trojan (Bulg.)	trô'-yän	tro'-yahn
Trollheimen (Nor., mts.)	trôl'-hā-mən	trol'-hay-muhn
Trolltinnene (Nor., mt.)	trôl'-tĭn'-ə-nə	trol'-tin'-uh-nuh
Tromelin (Oc., Carolines) See *Fais*.		
Tromsoe *or* Tromsö (Nor.)	trŏŏms'-û	trums'-œ

Popular English trŏmz'-ō [tromz'-oh].

Trondheim (Nor.)	trôn'-hām	tron'-haym

Formerly called *Trondhjem*, trôn'-yěm [tron'-yem] and at one time *Nidaros*, nē'-dä-rōs [nee'-dah-rohs]. Avoid trôn'-hīm [tron'-haim].

Tronfjell (Nor., mt.)	trōn'-fyěl	trohn'-fyel
Tropea (It.)	trô-pě'-ä	tro-peh'-ah
Troppau (Cz.) See *Opava*.		
Trottebec (Fr.)	trôt-běk'	trot-bek'
Trouche, la (Fr.)	trŏŏsh', lä	troosh', lah
Troutman, Wm. I.	trout'-mən	traut'-muhn
(U.S. representative)		
Trouville (Fr.)	trŏŏ-vēl'	troo-veel'
Troyan (Balkan mt.)	*Eng.* troi'-ən	troi'-uhn

Albanian *Mal i Trojanit*. Serb-Croat *Trojan*, q.v.

Troyes (Fr.)	trwä'	trwah'
Trpanj (Yugosl.)	tər'-pän(y)	tuhr'-pahn(y)
Trstenik (Yugosl.)	tər'-stě-nĭk	tuhr'-steh-nik
Trsteno (Yugosl.)	tər'-stě-nô	tuhr'-steh-no
Italian *Cannosa*, q.v.		

Trubchevsk (Rus.)	trōōp-chĕfsk'	troop-chefsk'
Trujillo (Sp. name)	*Am. Sp.* trōō-hē'-yô	troo-hee'-yo
	Sp. trōō-hē'-lyô	troo-hee'-lyo
Trujillo Molina, Rafael	trōō-hē'-yô mô-lē'-nä,	troo-hee'-yo mo-lee'-
Leonidas (Dom. polit.)	rä-fä-ĕl' lĕ-ô-nē'-däs	nah, rah-fah-el'
		leh-o-nee'-dahs
Truk (Oc., Carolines)	*Eng.* trōōk' *or* trŭk'	truk' *or* truhk'
	native trōōk'	trook'
Trun (Fr.)	trûN'	trœN'
Trutnov (Cz.)	trōōt'-nôf	troot'-nof
German *Trautenau,* trou'-tə-nou [trau'-tuh-nau].		
Trypiti (Crete, cape)	trē-pē-tē'	tree-pee-tee'
Trysil (Nor.)	trü'-sĭl	trü'-sil
Trzcieniec (Pol.)	*Eng.* chĕ'-nyĕts	cheh'-nyets
	Pol. chtsyĕ'-nyĕts	chtsyeh'-nyets
Trzebiatów (Ger. > Pol.)	chĕ-byä'-tŏŏf	cheh-byah'-tuf
German *Treptow,* q.v.		
Tržič (Yugosl.)	tər'-zhĭch	tuhr'-zhich
Tsaldaris, Konstantinos	tsäl-dä'-rēs,	tsahl-dah'-rees,
(Gr. polit.)	kôn-stän-dē'-nôs	kon-stahn-dee'-nos
Tsarapkin, Semyon K.	tsä-räp'-kĭn, sĕm-yôn'	tsah-rahp'-kin,
(Rus. diplomat)		sem-yon'
Tsatsos, Themistocles	tsä'-tsôs,	tsah'-tsos, theh-
(Gr. polit.)	thĕ-mē-stô-klēs'	mee-sto-klees'
Tscheliadz (Pol.) See *Czeladź.*		
Tschenstochau (Pol.) See *Częstochowa.*		
Tsefat (Pal.) See *Safad.*		
Tserigo (Gr., isl.) See *Kythera.*		
Tserigoto (Gr., isl.) See *Aigila.*		
Tseziz (Latvia) See *Cēsis.*		
Ts'ien-t'ang (Ch.,	chyĕn-täng	chyen-tahng
Chekiang, riv.)		
Also spelled *Ch'ien-t'ang.*		
Tsimlyanskaya *or*	tsĭm-lyän'-skä-yä	tsim-lyahn'-skah-yah
Tsymlyansk (Rus.)	*or* tsĭm-lyänsk'	*or* tsim-lyahnsk'
Tsi-nan (Ch., Shantung) See *Chi-nan.*		
Ts'in-an (Ch., Kansu)	tsĭn-än	tsin-ahn
Tsin-chow (Ch., Kansu)	jĭn-jō	jin-joh
Also spelled *Chin-chow.*		
Ts'ing-hai (Ch., prov.)	chĭng-hī	ching-hai
Also spelled *Ch'ing-hai,* q.v.		
Tsing-kiang (Ch.,	*Eng.* tsĭng-kyäng	tsing-kyang
Fukien)	*Ch.* jĭng-jyäng	jing-jyahng
Also spelled *Tsin-chiang.* Also called *Ch'uan-chow,* q.v.		

Ts'ing-tao (Ch., Shan- tung)	*Eng.* tsĭng-tou *Ch.* chĭng-dou	tsing-tau ching-dau
Ts'ing-tien (Ch., Chekiang)	chĭng-dyĕn	ching-dyen
Tsi-ning (Ch., Shantung)	See *Chi-ning*.	
Tsin-yün (Ch., Chekiang)	dzĭn-yün	dzin-yün
Tsirimokos, Elias (Gr. polit.)	tsē-rē-mô'-kôs, ē-lē'-äs	tsee-ree-mo'-kos, ee-lee'-ahs
Tsironikos, N. (Gr. polit.)	tsē-rô'-nē-kôs	tsee-ro'-nee-kos
Tsitsihar (Manchu.)	tsē-tsē-här *or* chē-chē-här	tsee-tsee-hahr chee-chee-hahr

Chinese *Lung-chiang*, lŏŏng-jyäng [lung-jyahng].

Tsolakoglu (Gr. polit.)	tsô-lä'-kô-glŏŏ	tso-lah'-ko-gloo

Hellenizing of a Turkish name.

Tsouderos, Emmanuel (Gr. polit.)	tsŏŏ-dĕ-rôs', ĕ-mä-nŏŏ-ēl'	tsoo-deh-ros', eh-mah-noo-eel'
Tsugaru (Jap., str.)	tsŏŏ-gä'-rŏŏ	tsoo-gah'-roo
Tsugu-no-Miya Akihito (Jap. prince) See *Akihito*.		
Tsuruga (Jap.)	tsŏŏ'-rŏŏ-gä	tsoo'-roo-gah
Tsurupinsk (Rus.)	tsŏŏ-ryŏŏ'-pĭnsk	tsoo-ryoo'-pinsk
Tsushima (Jap., isl.)	tsŏŏ'-shē-mä	tsoo'-shee-mah
Tsyekhotsinsk (Pol.)	See *Ciechocinek*.	
Tsymlyansk (Rus.)	See *Tsimlyanskaya*.	
Tuamotu (Oc., Polynesia)	tōō-ä-mô'-tōō	too-ah-mo'-too
Tuao (P.I.)	twou'	twau'
Tuapse (Rus.)	tōō-äp-sĕ'	too-ahp-seh'
Tuareg (Sahara tribes)	twä'-rĕg	twah'-reg

French *Touareg*.

Tubbergen (Neth.)	tûb'-bĕrk(h)-ən	tœb'-behrk(h)-uhn
Tubile (P.I.)	tōō-bē'-lĕ	too-bee'-leh
Tübingen (Ger.)	tü'-bĭng-ən	tü'-bing-uhn
Tubuai (Oc.)	tōō-bōō-ĭ'	too-boo-ai'

Also called *Austral Islands*, ôs'-trəl [os'-truhl].

Tubuai Manu (Oc., Society isls.)	tōō-bōō-ĭ' mä'-nōō	too-boo-ai' mah'-noo
Tuburan (P.I.)	tōō-bōō'-rän	too-boo'-rahn
T'u-ch'ang (Ch., Kiangsi)	tōō-chäng	too-chahng
Tuchkov (Rum.)	See *Izmail*.	
Tuchola (Pol.)	tōō-hô'-lä	tu-ho'-lah
Tucumán (Arg.)	tōō-kōō-män'	too-koo-mahn'
Tucumcari (N.M.)	tyōō'-kəm-kăr'-ĭ	tyoo'-kuhm-kehr'-i

[552]

Tudeh (Iran. party)　　　toō'-dĕ'　　　　　　too'-deh'
A Persian word meaning *the people*.

Tuđemile (Yugosl.)　　　toō'-dyĕ'-mĭ-lĕ　　too'-dyeh'-mi-leh
Tuebingen (Ger.)　　　　tü'-bĭng-ən　　　　tü-bing-uhn
Tuffé (Fr.)　　　　　　　tü-fĕ'　　　　　　tü-feh'
Tufi (New Guinea,　　　toō'-fē　　　　　　too'-fee
　　Papua)
Tug(g)urt (Alg.)　　　　toō-goort'　　　　tu-goort'
French *Touggourt*, q.v.

Tuglie (It.)　　　　　　toō'-lyĕ　　　　　too'-lyeh
Tuguegarao (P.I.)　　　toō-gĕ-gä-rou'　　too-geh-gah-rau'
Tugurski (Rus., bay)　　toō-goōr'-skĭ　　tu-goor'-ski
Tuileries (Paris, palace)　*Eng.* twē'-lə-rĭz　　twee'-luh-riz
　　　　　　　　　　　　Fr.　twēl-rē'　　　tweel-ree'
Tujna (Yugosl.)　　　　toō'ĭ-nä *or* toō'(y)-　too'i-nah *or* too'(y)-
Tukhachevsky, Mikhail　toō-hä-chĕf'-skĭ,　tu-hah-chehf'-ski,
　　N. (Rus. general)　　　mĭ-hä-ēl'　　　mi-hah-eel'
Tukum (Latvia)　　　　*Rus.* toō-koōm'　　tu-koom'
Latvian *Tukums*, q.v.

Tukums (Latvia)　　　　toō'-koŏms　　　　tu'-kums
Russian *Tukum*, q.v.

Tula (Rus.)　　　　　　toō'-lä　　　　　too'-lah
Tulagi (Oc., Solomons)　toō-lä'-gē　　　　too-lah'-gee
　　Mr. Johannes Anderson, a New Zealand authority, writes that *Tulagi*
is an early missionary spelling of *Tulangai*, toō-läng-ä-ē [too-lahng-
ah-ee]. The letter *i* was used for *ai*, and *g* for *ng*. (Compare *Pago Pago*
for *Pango Pango*.) So when we believe we are going native with
toō-lä'-gē, instead of using a possible English tyoō-lä'-gī [tyoo-lay'-gai]
or tyoō-lăg'-ĭ [tyoo-lag'-i], we are probably still wrong though con-
scientious.

Tulare (Calif.)　　　　toō-lăr'-ĭ　　　　too-lehr'-i
Tularosa (N.M.)　　　　toō-lä-rô'-sä　　too-lah-ro'-sah
Tulcea (Rum.)　　　　　toŏl'-chä　　　　tul'-chah
Tulchin (Rus.)　　　　　toōl'(y)-chĭn'　　tool'(y)-chin'
Tule (Calif., Ore., lake)　toō'-lĭ　　　　too'-li
Tulear (Madag.)　　　　tü-lĕ-är'　　　　tü-leh-ahr'
Tulgheş (Rum.)　　　　toŏl-gĕsh'　　　tul-gesh'
　　Also called *Prisăcani*, q.v.

Tulkarm (Pal.)　　　　toōl'-kärm　　　tool'-kahrm
Tullahoma (Tenn.)　　　tŭl'-ə-hō'-mə　　tuhl'-uh-hoh'-muh
Tullamore (Eire)　　　　tŭl-ə-mōr'　　　tuhl-uh-mohr'
Tuloma (Rus., riv.)　　　toō'-lŏ-mä　　　too'-lo-mah
Tulsa (Okla.)　　　　　tŭl'-sə　　　　　tuhl'-suh
Tumanni (Rus., cape)　　toō-män'-nĭ　　too-mahn'-ni

Tumbes (Peru)	tōōm′-bĕs	toom′-behs
Tumleo (New Guinea)	tōōm-lĕ′-ô	toom-leh′-o
Tundzha (Balkan riv.)	tŏŏn′-jä	tun′-jah
T'ung-chow (Ch., Hopeh)	*Eng.* tŏŏng-chou *Ch.* tŏŏng-jō	tung-chau tung-joh
Tung-hsiang (Ch., Kiangsi)	dŏŏng-shyäng	dung-shyahng
T'ung-ku (Ch., Kiangsi)	tŏŏng-gōō	tung-goo
T'ung-kwan (Ch., Shensi)	tŏŏng-gwän	tung-gwahn
T'ung-liao (Manchu.)	tŏŏng-lyou	toong-lyau
T'ung-lu (Ch., Chekiang)	tŏŏng-lōō	tung-loo
Tung Pi-wu (Ch. polit.)	dŏŏng bē-wōō	dung bee-woo
T'ung-shan (Ch., Kiangsu)	tŏŏng-shän	tung-shahn
Tung-t'ing (Ch., Hunan, lake)	dŏŏng-tĭng	dung-ting
Tung-yang (Ch., Chekiang)	dŏŏng-yäng	dung-yahng
Tunis (Tun.)	tyōō′-nĭs	tyoo′-nis
Tunisia (Afr.)	tyōō-nĭsh′-(y)ə	tyoo-nish′-(y)uh

A quasi-foreign pronunciation, tyōō-nē′-shə, -zhə [tyoo-nee′-shuh, -zhuh] is also heard.

Tunja (Balkan riv.)   See *Tundzha*.

Tunnell, James M. (U.S. senator)	tŭn′-əl	tuhn′-uhl
Tuolumne (Calif.)	twŏl′-əm-nĭ	twol′-uhm-ni
Tura (Hung.)	tōō′-rŏ	tu′-ro
Turanj (Yugosl.)	tōō′-rän(y)	too′-rahn(y)
turbine	tûr′-bĭn *or* tûr′-bĭn	tuhr′-bain *or* tuhr′-bin

American engineers prefer tûr′-bĭn [tuhr′-bain]. As the word is a technical one, it may be wise to follow their example, especially on technical programs.

Turčiansky Svätý Martin (Cz.)	tōōr′-chyän-skĭ svă′-tĭ mär′-tĭn	toor′-chyahn-ski sva′-ti mahr′-tin
Turda (Rum.)	tŏŏr′-dä	tur′-dah

Hungarian *Torda*, tôr′-dŏ [tor′-do].

Turek (Pol.)	tōō′-rĕk	tu′-rek
T'ur-fan (Ch., Sinkiang)	tŏŏr-fän	tur-fahn
Türi (Est.)	tü′-rĭ	tü′-ri

Russian *Allenkul*, q.v.

Turija (Yugosl., riv.)	tōō′-rĭ-yä	too′-ri-yah
Turin (It.)	tyōō′-rĭn *or* tyōō-rĭn′	tyoo′-rin *or* tyoo-rin′

Avoid tōō-rēn′ [too-reen′]. Italian *Torino*, q.v.

Turirog (Rus.)	tōō'-rĭ-rôg'	too'-ri-rog'
Turkestan *or* Turkistan	tûr'-kĭ-stän' *or* -stän'	tuhr'-ki-stan' *or* -stahn'
Turkey	tûr'-kĭ	tuhr'-ki

Turkish *Türkiye Cumhuriyeti* (Republic of Turkey), tür-kĭ-yě' jōōm-hōō-rĭ-yě'-tē [tür-ki-yeh' jum-hu-ri-yeh'-tee].

Turkinsk (Rus.)	tōōr'-kĭnsk	toor'-kinsk
Turkmanchai (Iran)	tōōrk-män-chä'-ē	turk-mahn-chah'-ee
Turkmen (Rus.)	*Eng.* tûrk'-měn	tuhrk'-men
	Rus. tōōrk-měn'	turk-měn'

Also called Turkomen, tûr'-kō-měn [tuhr'-koh-men], and *Turkmenistan*, tûrk'-měn-ĭ-stän' *or* -stän' [tuhrk'-men-i-stan' *or* -stahn'].

Turku (Fin.)	tōōr'-kōō	tur'-ku

Swedish *Åbo*, q.v.

Turnhout (Belg.)	tûrn'-hout	tœrn'-haut
Turnu (Rum.)	tōōr'-nōō	tur'-nu

Hungarian *Tornya*, tôr'-nyŏ [tor'-nyo].

Turnu Măgurele (Rum.)	tōōr'-nōō mû'-gōō-rě'-lě	tur'-nu muh'-gu-reh'-leh
Turnu Roşu (Rum., pass)	tōōr'-nōō rô'-shōō	tur'-nu ro'-shu

German *Roten Turm*, q.v.

Turnu Severin (Rum.)	tōōr'-nōō sě-vě-rēn'	tur'-nu seh-veh-reen'
Turtagroe *or* Turtagrö (Nor.)	tōōr'-tä-grû	tur'-tah-grœ
Turtucaia (Rum.)	tōōr-tōō-kä'-yä	tur-tu-kah'-yah

Bulgarian *Tutracan*, tōō'-trä-kän' [tu'-trah-kahn'].

tushonka (Rus. stew)	tōō-shôn'-kä	tu-shon'-kah
Tuskegee (Ala.)	tŭs-kē'-gĭ	tuhs-kee'-gi
Tutow (Ger.)	tōō'-tō	too'-toh
Tuttlingen (Ger.)	tōōt'-lĭng-ən	tut'-ling-uhn
Tútú (P.I.)	tōō-tōō'	too-too'
Tutuba (Oc., New Hebrides)	tōō-tōō-bä'	too-too-bah'
Tutuila (Oc., Samoa)	tōō-tōō-ē'-lä	too-too-ee'-lah
Tuxpan (Mex.)	tōōs'-pän	toos'-pahn
Tuxtla (Mex.)	tōōs'-tlä	toos'-tlah
Tuy (P.I.)	twē'	twee'
Tuyio (Oc., New Hebrides, mt.)	tōō-yē'-ô	too-yee'-o

French *Touyo*, tōō-yō' [too-yoh'].

Tuzla (Yugosl.)	tōōz'-lä	tooz'-lah
Tuzlanska (Yugosl.)	tōō'-zlän-skä	too'-zlahn-skah
Tvedestrand (Nor.)	tväd'-ə-strän	tvayd'-uh-strahn
Tveitsund (Nor.)	tvät'-sōōn	tvayt'-sun

Tvertsa (Rus., riv.)	tvĕr-tsä'	tvehr-tsah'
Twyman, Robert J. (U.S. representative)	twĭ'-mən	twai'-muhn
Tychowo (Ger. >Pol.) German *Gross Tychow*, q.v.	tĭ-hộ'-vô	ti-ho'-vo
Tyin (Nor.)	tü'-ĭn	tü'-in
Tyinholmen (Nor.)	tü'-ĭn-hôl-mən	tü'-in-hol-muhn
Tykocin (Pol.) Russian spelling *Tikotsin.*	tĭ-kô'-tsĭn	ti-ko'-tsin
Tympaki(on) (Crete)	tēm-bä'-kē(-ôn)	teem-bah'-kee(-on)
Tynset *or* Toenset *or* Tönset (Nor.)	tün'-sĕt *or* tŭn'-sĕt	tün'-set tuhn'-set
Tyrifjord (Nor.)	tü'-rē-fyōr	tü'-ree-fyohr
Tyrma (Rus., riv.)	twēr'-mä	tweer'-mah
Tyrnavos (Gr.)	tēr'-nä-vôs *or* tōōr'-nä-vôs	teer'-nah-vos toor'-nah-vos
Tyrol (Austria) See *Tirol.*		
Tyrone (Ga., Pa.)	tĭ'-rōn'	tai'-rohn'
Tyrone (N. Ire.)	tĭ-rōn'	ti-rohn'
tyrothricin	tĭ'-rô-thrĭ'-sĭn *or* -thrĭs'-ĭn	tai'-ro-thrai'-sin *or* -thris'-in

The first is the preference of an originator of the treatment, Dr. René Dubos, rə-nā' dyŏŏ-bōs' *or* dü-bôs' [ruh-nay' dyu-bohs' *or* dü-bohs'].

Tyrrhenian Sea	*Eng.* tĭ-rē'-nĭ-ən	ti-ree'-ni-uhn

Italian *Mare Tirreno*, mä'-rĕ tĭr-rĕ'-nô [mah'-reh tihr-reh'-no].

Tyszowce (Pol.)	tĭ-shôf'-tsĕ	ti-shof'-tseh

Russian *Tishovtsi*, tĭ-shôf'-tsĭ [ti-shof'-tsi].

Tytärsaari (Fin., isl.)	tü'-tăr-sä-rē	tü'-tehr-sah-ree
Tyumen (Rus.)	tyŏŏ-mĕn'(y)	tyoo-men'(y)
Tzarevo (Bulg.)	tsä'-rĕ-vŏ	tsah'-reh-vo

Also called *Vasiliko*, vä-sē-lē'-kŏ [vah-see-lee'-ko].

Tzê-ch'i (Ch., Kiangsi) Also spelled *Tzŭ-ch'i.*	dzŭ-chē	dzuh-chee
Tz'ê-k'u (Ch., Sikang) Also spelled *Tz'ŭ-k'u.*	tsŭ-kōō	tsuh-koo
Tzia (Gr., isl.) See *Keos.*		
Tzoutzouras (Crete, point)	dzōō'-dzōō-räs	dzoo'-dzoo-rahs
Tz'ŭ-ch'i (Ch., Chekiang)	tsŭ-chē	tsuh-chee

u and *v* are interchangeable in Greek after *e* and *a*. It may be necessary to look up both spellings.

Uaddan (Libya)	wäd-dăn'	wahd-dan'

Ub (Yugosl.)	ōōb'	oob'
Übach or Uebach (Ger.)	ü'-bäk(h)	ü'-bahk(h)
Ubach Over Worms (Neth.)	ü'-bäk(h) ō'-vər wôrms'	ü'-bahk(h) oh'-vuhr worms'
Ubay (P.I.)	ōō'-bī	oo'-bai
Ubbergen (Neth.)	ûb'-bĕrk(h)-ən	œb'-behrk(h)-uhn
Úbeda (Sp.)	ōō'-bĕ-dä	oo'-beh-dah
Ubián (P.I.)	ōō-bē-än'	oo-bee-ahn'
Ubico, Jorge (Guat. polit.)	ōō-bē'-kô, hôr'-hĕ	oo-bee'-ko, hor'-heh
Ubili (Oc.)	ōō-bē'-lē	oo-bee'-lee
Ubol or Ubon (Siam)	ŏō-bōn'	u-bohn'
Ubonraj Dhani (Siam)	ŏō-bōn'-räj'-ə tä'-nē'	u-bohn'-rahj'-uh tah'-nee'
Ubort (Rus., riv.)	ōō-bôrt'	oo-bort'
Ude (Mongolia)	ōō-dĕ	oo-deh
Üdem or Uedem (Ger.)	ü'-dəm	ü'-duhm
Uden (Neth.)	ü'-dən	ü'-duhn
Udenhout (Neth.)	ü'-dən-hout	ü'-duhn-hout
Udine (It.)	ōō'-dē-nĕ	oo'-dee-neh
Udmurt (Rus.)	ŏōd'-mŏōrt'	ud'-murt'
Udomlya (Rus.)	ōō'-dŏm-lyä	oo'-dom-lyah
Udorndhani (Siam)	ŏō-dôn'-tä'-nē'	u-dawn'-tah'-nee'
Udovice (Yugosl.)	ōō'-dô'-vĭ-tsĕ	oo'-do'-vi-tseh
Udskaya Guba (Rus.)	ōōd'-skä-yä gōō-bä'	ood'-skah-yah goo-bah'
Udski Ostrog (Rus.)	ōōd'-skĭ ŏs-trôg'	ood'-ski os-trog'
Udyl (Rus., lake)	ōō-dĭl'	oo-dil'
Uea (Oc.)	ōō-ĕ'-ä	oo-eh'-ah
Uelzen (Ger.)	ül'-tsən	ül'-tsuhn
Uerdingen (Ger.)	ür'-dĭng-ən	ür'-ding-uhn
Ufa (Rus.)	ōō-fä'	oo-fah'
Ugaki, Kazushige (Jap. polit.)	ōō'-gä-kē, kä-zōō'-shē-gĕ	oo'-gah-kee, kah-zoo'-shee-geh
Uganda (Afr.)	Eng. yōō-găn'-də native ōō-gän'-dä	yoo-gan'-duh oo-gahn'-dah
Ugliano (Yugosl., isl.) See Uljan.		
Uglovka (Rus.)	ōō-glôf'-kä	oo-glof'-kah
Ugra (Rus., riv.)	ōō'-grä	oo'-grah
Uihlein (Wis. family)	ē'-līn	ee'-lain
Uilenspiegel, Tyl (folk hero) See Ulenspiegel.		
Uinta (Wyo.)	yōō-ĭn'-tə	yoo-in'-tuh
Uintah (Utah)	yōō-ĭn'-tə	yoo-in'-tuh
Uitgeest (Neth.)	ûĭt-k(h)äst'	œit-k(h)ayst'

[557]

Uithoorn (Neth.)	ûĭt-hōrn'	œit-hohrn'
Uithuizen (Neth.)	ûĭt-hûĭ'-zən	œit-hœi'-zuhn
Uithuizermeden (Neth.)	ûĭt'-hûĭ-zər-mā'-dən	œit'-hœi-zuhr-may'-duhn
Ujae (Oc., Marshalls)	ōō-jä'-ĕ	oo-jah'-eh
Ujelang (Oc., Marshalls)	ōō'-jĕ-läng	oo'-jeh-lahng
Ujhartyán (Hung.)	ōō'ĭ-hŏr'-tyän	u'i-hor'-tyahn
Ujpest (Hung.)	ōō'ĭ-pĕsht' or ōō'(y)-.	u'i-pesht' or u'(y)-
Újvidék (Yugosl.) See *Novi Sad.*		
Ukhrul (India)	ōŏk'-hrōŏl	uk'-hrul
Ukmergė (Lith.)	ōōk'-mĕr-gĕ	ook'-mehr-geh
Russian *Wilkomir,* q.v.		
Ukraine (Rus.)	*Eng.* yōō'-krān'	yoo'-krayn'
Russian *Ukraina,* ōō-krä'-ĭ-nä [oo-kraah'-i-nah].		
Ukrainian	yōŏ-krān'-yən	yu-krayn'-yuhn
Ulak (Alaska)	yōō'-lăk	yoo'-lak
Ulan Bator (Mongolia)	ōō-län bä-tôr	oo-lahn bah-tor
Ulan Ude (Rus.)	ōō'-län ōō'-dĕ	oo'-lahn oo'-deh
Ulbanski (Rus., bay)	ōŏl-bän'-skĭ	ul-bahn'-ski
Ulbo (Yugosl.)	*It.* ōōl'-bô	ool'-bo
Serb-Croat *Olib,* q.v.		
Ulcinj (Yugosl.)	ōōl'-tsĭn(y)	ool'-tsin(y)
Italian *Dulcigno,* q.v.		
Uleåborg (Fin.) See *Oulu.*		
Ulefoss (Nor.)	ōō'-lə-fôs	oo'-luh-fos
Ulenspiegel, Thyl	ü'-lən-spē'-gəl, tēl'	ü'-luhn-spee'-guhl, teel'

Under this title Charles de Coster wrote his famous epic in archaic French, published 1867. It became even more popular in an unauthorized Flemish translation (1904) by Jan Bruylants, q.v., entitled *Tyl Uilenspiegel,* tĭl' ûĭ'-lən-spē'-gəl [til' œi'-luhn-spee'-guhl]. An English variant of the name is *Till Owlglass,* tĭl' oul'-glăs [til aul'-glas]. German *Till Eulenspiegel,* oi'-lən-shpē'-gəl [oi'-luhn-shpee'-guhl].

Uliagan (New Guinea)	ōō-lē-ä'-gän	oo-lee-ah'-gahn
Uliassutai (Mongolia)	ōō-lyä-sōō-tī'	oo-lyah-su-tai'
Ulithi (Oc., Carolines)	ōō-lē'-thē or ōō-lē'-tē	oo-lee'-thee or oo-lee'-tee

Often pronounced yōō-lē'-thē [yoo-lee'-thee] by the American forces.

Uljan (Yugosl.)	ōō'-lyän	oo'-lyahn
Italian *Ugliano,* ōō-lyä'-nô [oo-lyah'-no].		
Uljma (Yugosl.)	ōōl'(y)-mä	ool'(y)-mah
Ullensvang (Nor.)	ōŏl'-əns-väng	ul'-uhns-vahng
Ulm (Ger.)	ōŏlm'	ulm'
Ulmin (Rus.)	ōōl-mĭn'	ool-min'

Ulrich, Vassily (Rus. polit.)	ōōl′-rĭk(h), vä-sē′-lĭ	ool′-rik(h), vah-see′-lih
Ulrum (Neth.)	ûl′-rəm	œl′-ruhm
Ulugan (P.I.)	ōō-lōō′-gän	oo-loo′-gahn
Also called *Banog*, bä-nôg′ [bah-nog′].		
Ulul (Carolines, Oc.)	ōōl′-ōōl	ool′-ool
Japanese *Ororutō*, ô-rô′-rōō-tô′ [o-ro′-roo-to′].		
Ulus (Turk. newspaper)	ōō′-lŏŏs′	u′-lus′
Ulvik (Nor.)	ŏŏl′-vēk	ul′-veek
Ulyanovsk (Rus.)	ōō-lyä′-nŏfsk	oo-lyah′-nofsk
Ülzen (Ger.)	ül′-tsən	ül′-tsuhn
Uman (Oc.)	ōō′-män′	oo′-mahn′
Japanese *Fuyu Shima*, fōō-yōō′ shē′-mä [foo-yoo′ shee′-mah′].		
Umanday (P.I.)	ōō-män-dī′	oo-mahn-dai′
Umba (Rus., riv.)	ōōm′-bä	oom′-bah
Umberto	*It.* ōōm-bĕr′-tô	oom-behr′-to
English *Humbert*. Italian King Humbert II in exile is called *Count of Sarre*, sär′-rĕ [sahr′-reh].		
Umboi (Oc., Bismarck arch.) See *Rook*.		
Umčari (Yugosl.)	ōōm′-chä-rĭ	oom′-chah-ri
Umeaa (Sw.)	ü′-mĕ-ō	ü′-meh-oh
Umnak (Alaska, isl.)	ōōm′-năk	oom′-nak
Umstead, William B. (U.S. senator)	ŭm′-stĕd	um′-sted
Unalaska (Alaska, isl.)	ŭn′-ə-lăs′-kə *or* ōōn′-ə-lăs′-kə	uhn′-uh-las′-kuh oon′-uh-las′-kuh
Unalga (Alaska, isl.)	ə-näl′-gə	uh-nahl′-guh
Unden, Bo Oesten (Sw. diplomat)	ŏŏn-dĭn′, bōō′ ûs′-tən	un-din′, boo′ œs′-tuhn
Also spelled *Bo Östen Undén*. Also pronounced ŏŏn-dān′ [un-dayn′].		
Unea (Oc., Bismarck arch.)	ōō-nĕ′-ä	oo-neh′-ah
Unecha (Rus.)	ōō-nĕ′-chä	oo-neh′-chah
UNESCO	yōō-nĕs′-kō *or* ōō-nĕs′-kō	yoo-nehs′-koh oo-nehs′-koh
Abbreviation of *United Nations Educational, Scientific and Cultural Organization*.		
Ungvár (Cz. >Rus.) See *Uzhgorod*.		
Unie (It. >Yugosl., isl.)	ōō′-nyĕ	oo′-nyeh
Serb-Croat *Unije*, ōō′-nĭ-yĕ [oo′-ni-yeh].		
Unije (It. >Yugosl., isl.) See *Unie*.		
Unimak (Alaska, isl.)	ōō′-nĭ-măk	oo′-ni-mak
Unión (P.I.)	*Eng.* yōōn′-yən *Sp.* ōō-nyôn′	yoon′-yuhn oo-nyon′

L'Unità (Rome, news- paper)	lōō-nē-tä′	loo-nee-tah′
university	yōō-nə-vûr′-sə-tĭ	yoo-nuh-vur′-suh-ti
	or yōō-nə-vûrs′-tĭ	yoo-nuh-vurs′-ti

The second pronunciation, with syncopation, is probably more common than the first. See *varsity*, a derivative.

Unkel (Ger.)	ŏŏng′-kəl	ung′-kuhl
Unna (Ger.)	ŏŏn′-ä	un′-ah
Unzen (Jap.)	ōōn′-zĕn	oon′-zen
L'Uomo Qualunque	lwô′-mô kwä-lōōn′-	lwo′-mo kwah-loon′-
(Rome, newspaper)	kwĕ	kweh
Upolu (Samoa)	ōō-pô′-lōō	oo-po′-loo
Uppsala (Sw.)	*Eng.* ŭp′-sä-lə	uhp′-sah-luh
	Sw. ŭp′-sä′-lä	uhp′-sah′-lah
ura	ōō-rä	oo-rah

An element, meaning *bay* or *cove*, in Japanese place names.

Uracas (Oc., Marianas)	ōō-rä′-käs	oo-rah′-kahs
Ural (Rus., mts.)	*Eng.* yōō′-rəl	yoo′-ruhl
	Rus. ōō-räl′	oo-rahl′
Uralova (Rus. name)	ōō-rä′-lô-vä	oo-rah′-lo-vah
Urawa (Jap.)	ōō-rä′-wä′	oo-rah′-wah′
Urbakh (Rus.)	ōōr′-bäk(h)	oor′-bahk(h)
Urbiztondo (P.I.)	ōōr-bēs-tôn′-dô	oor-bees-ton′-do
Urdaneta (P.I.)	ōōr-dä-nĕ′-tä	oor-dah-neh′-tah
Urdapilleta, Felipe	ōōr-dä-pē-yĕ′-tä,	oor-dah-pee-yeh′-tah,
(Arg. polit.)	fĕ-lē′-pĕ	feh-lee′-peh
Ürdingen (Ger.)	ür′-dĭng-ən	ür′-ding-uhn
Urey, Harold C.	yŏŏr′-ĭ	yur′-i
C. (Am. scientist)		
Urft (Ger., riv.)	ŏŏrft′	urft′
Urft Talsperre (Ger., dam)	ŏŏrft′ täl′-spĕr′-ə	urft′ tahl′-spehr′-uh
Uriarte (Sp. name)	ōō-ryär′-tĕ	oo-ryahr′-teh
Uritsky (Rus.)	ōō-rĭts′-kĭ	oo-rits′-ki

A square in Leningrad named after a murdered commissar.

Urk (Neth.)	ûrk′	œrk′
Urmi (Rus., riv.)	ōōr′-mĭ	oor′-mi
Urmiah (Iran, lake)	*Eng.* ōōr′-mĭ-ä	oor′-mi-ah
Uroševac (Yugosl.)	ōō′-rô′-shĕ-väts	oo′-ro′-sheh-vahts
Ursinus College (Pa.)	ûr-sī′-nəs	uhr-sai′-nuhs
Uruguay	*Eng.* yŏŏr′-ə-gwä	yur′-uh-gway
	Sp. ōō-rōō-gwī′	oo-roo-gwai′

yōō′-rōō-gwĭ [yoo′-roo-gwai] is neither English nor Spanish.

Uruguayan	yŏŏr′-ə-gwä′-ən	yur′-uh-gway′-uhn
	or ōō′-rōō-gwī′-ən	oo′-roo-gwai′-uhn

Urumchi (Ch., Sinkiang)	ōō-rōōm′-chē	oo-room′-chee
Also called *Urumtsi* and *Ti-hwa*, q.v.		
Urupinsk (Rus.)	ōō-ryōō′-pĭnsk	oo-ryoo′-pinsk
Urusan (Korea)	ōō′-rōō-sän	oo′-roo-sahn
Urusha (Rus.)	ōō-rōō′-shä	oo-roo′-shah
Uryumkansk (Rus.)	ōō-ryōōm-känsk′	oo-ryoom-kahnsk′
Urziceni (Rum.)	ŏŏr-zē-chĕn′	ur-zee-chen′
U Saw (Burman polit.)	*Eng.* yōō′ sô′	yoo′ saw′
In Burman, *U* pronounced ōō and meaning *uncle* is a title of respect.		
Usedom (Ger., isl.)	ōō′-zə-dōm	oo′-zuh-dohm
Ushant (Fr.)	*Eng.* ŭsh′-ənt	uhsh′-uhnt
French *Ouessant*, q.v.		
Ushba (Rus., mt.)	ŏŏsh′-bä	ush′-bah
Ushumun (Rus.)	ōō-shōō-mōōn′	oo-shoo-moon′
Uskoci (Yugosl.)	ōō′-skô-tsĭ	oo′-sko-tsi
Üsküdar (Turk.)	üs-kü′-där	üs-kü′-dahr
Also called *Scutari*, q.v.		
Usman (Rus.)	ōōs-män′(y)	oos-mahn′(y)
Ussuri (Rus.)	ōōs-sōō′-rē	oos-soo′-ree
Ustachi (Croat fascist party) A variant of *Ustaši*, q.v.		
Ustaoset (Nor.)	ŏŏs′-tä-ô′-sə	us′-tah-oh′-suh
Ustaši (Croat fascist party)	ōō-stä′-shĭ	oo-stah′-shi
Ust Busulutsk (Rus.)	ōōst′ bōō-zōō-lōōtsk′	oost′ boo-zoo-lootsk′
Ust Dvinsk (Latvia)	*Rus.* ōōst′ dvēnsk′	oost′ dveensk′
Latvian *Daugavgrīva*, q.v.		
Ústí (Cz.)	ōō′-stē	oo′-stee
Ustica (It., isl.)	ōō′-stē-kä	oo′-stee-kah
Ustka (Ger. > Pol.)	ŏŏst′-kä	ust′-kah
German *Stolpmuende*, q.v.		
Ustyuzhna (Rus.)	ōōs-tyōōzh′-nä	oos-tyoozh′-nah
Usuki (Jap.)	ōō-sōō′-kē	oo-soo′-kee
Utah (U.S.)	yōō′-tô	yoo′-taw
Ute (Am. Indian)	yōōt′ *or* yōō′-tĭ	yoot′ *or* yoo′-ti
Utėna (Lith.)	ōō′-tä-nä	oo′-tay-nah
Russian *Utseny*, q.v.		
Utica (Tun., U.S.)	*Eng.* yōō′-tĭ-kə	yoo′-ti-kuh
Utingeradeel (Neth.)	ü′-tĭng-ə-rä-däl′	ü′-ting-uh-rah-dayl′
Utique (Tun.)	*Fr.* ü-tēk′	ü-teek′
The English form, preferable in radio usage, is *Utica*, q.v.		
Utirik (Oc., Marshalls)	ōō′-tē-rēk	oo′-tee-reek
Utrata (Pol., riv.)	ŏŏ-trä′-tä	u-trah′-tah
Utrecht (Neth.)	*Eng.* yōō′-trĕkt	yoo′-trekt
	Du. ü′-trĕk(h)t	ü′-trek(h)t

Utrillo, Maurice (Fr. painter)	ōō-trē-lō', mô-rēs'	oo-tree-loh', mo-rees'

In the United States often pronounced ōō-trē'-yô [oo-tree'-yo].

Utseny (Lith.)	*Rus.* ōō-tsĕ'-nĭ	u-tseh'-ni
Lithuanian *Utèna*, q.v.		
Utsunomiya (Jap.)	ōō-tsōō-nô'-mē-yä	oo-tsoo-no'-mee-yah
Uttaradit (Thai)	ŏŏt'-ə-rə-dĭt'	ut'-uh-ruh-dit'
Uudenmaa (Fin.)	ōō'-dĕn-mä	oo'-den-mah
Uuksu (Fin. > Rus.)	ōōk'-sōō	ook'-su
Russian *Ilya Uksu*, q.v.		
Uuksujaervi *or* -järvi (Fin., lake)	ōōk'-sōō-yăr'-vē	ook'-su-yehr-vee
uusi	ōō'-sē	oo'-see

An element, meaning *new*, in Finnish place names.

Uusikaupunki (Fin.)	ōō'-sē-kou'-pōŏng-kē	oo'-see-kau'-pung-kee
Swedish *Nystad*, nü'-städ [nü'-stahd].		
Uusikirkko (Fin.)	ōō'-sē-kĭrk-kô	oo'-see-kihrk-ko
Uvac (Yugosl., riv.)	ōō'-väts	oo'-vahts
Uvalde (Tex.)	yōō-văl'-dĭ	yoo-val'-di
Uzbek (Rus.)	ŏŏz-bĕk'	uz-bek'
Also called *Uzbekistan*, ŏŏz-bĕ-kĭ-stän' [uz-beh-ki-stahn'].		
Uzerthe (Fr.)	ü-zĕrt'	ü-zehrt'
Uzès (Fr.)	ü-zĕs'	ü-zes'
Uzh (Rus., riv.)	ōōzh'	oozh'
Uzhgorod (Cz. > Rus.)	ōōzh'-gŏ-rŏt	oozh'-go-rot
Czech *Užhorod*, ōōzh'-hô-rôt [oozh'-ho-rot]. Hungarian *Ungvár*,		
ōōng'-vär [oong'-vahr].		
Užice (Yugosl.)	ōō'-zhĭ-tsĕ	oo'-zhi-tseh
Uzlovaya (Rus.)	ōōz-lŏ-vä'-yä	ooz-lo-vah'-yah
Uzunköprü (Turk.)	ōō-zōŏn'-kûp-rü	u-zun'-kœp-rü

v, *b*, and *bh* are interchangeable in Greek, and *b* and *v* in Spanish and other languages. It may be necessary to look up all these spellings.

v and *u* are interchangeable in Greek after *e* and *a*. It may be necessary to look up both spellings.

Vaad Leumi (Jewish council general)	väd' lĕ-ōō-mē'	vahd' leh-oo-mee'
Vaals (Neth.)	väls'	vahls'
vaara	vä'-rä	vah'-rah

An element, meaning *barren mountain*, in Finnish place names.

Vaas (Fr.)	väs'	vahs'
Vaasa (Fin.)	vä'-sä	vah'-sah
Vác (Hung.)	väts'	vahts'

[562]

Vaccarès, Etang de (Fr.)	vä-kä-rĕ', ĕ-täN' də	vah-kah-reh', eh-tahN' duh

Also called *Valcarès*.

Vacchereccia (It.)	väk-kĕ-rĕt'-chä	vahk-keh-ret'-chah
Vaccheria (It.)	väk-kĕ-rē'-ä	vahk-keh-ree'-ah
Vadheim (Nor.)	väd'-hām	vahd'-haym
Vadino (Rus.)	vä'-dĭ-nŏ	vah'-di-no
Vadsoe *or* Vadsö (Nor.)	väds'-û	vahds'-œ
Vaduz (Liecht.)	vä'-dōōts	vah'-duts
Værnes *or* Vernes (Nor.)	vär'-nĕs	vehr'-nes
Vaertsilae (Fin. > Rus.)	See *Värtsilä*.	
vagary	və-gĕr'-ĭ	vuh-gehr'-i

A pronunciation with accent on the first syllable is not recommended.

vagrant	vā'-grənt	vay'-gruhnt
Váh (Cz., riv.)	väk(h)'	vahk(h)'

German spelling *Waag*. Hungarian *Vág*, väg' [vahg'].

Vaiges (Fr.)	vĕzh'	vezh'
Vailele (Samoa)	vī-lĕ'-lĕ	vai-leh'-leh
Vailly (Fr.)	vä-yē'	vah-yee'
Vaitolahti (Fin. > Rus.)	vī'-tō-läk(h)-tē	vai'-toh-lahk(h)-tee
Vaitupu (Oc., Ellice)	vī-tōō'-pōō	vai-too'-poo
Vajdahunyad (Rum.)	See *Hunedoara*.	
Vajguras (Alb.)	vī-gōō'-räs	vai-goo'-rahs

Also called *Kuçovë*, q.v. Italian *Petrolia*, q.v.

Vakuf, Donji (Yugosl.)	vä'-kōōf, dôn'-yĭ	vah'-koof, don'-yi
Valanziera (It.)	vä-län-tsyĕ'-rä	vah-lahn-tsyeh'-rah
Valbona (Alb., riv.)	See *Valbonë*.	
Valbonë (Alb., riv.)	väl-bô'-nə	vahl-bo'-nuh
Valburg (Neth.)	väl'-bûrk(h)	vahl'-bœrk(h)
Valchetta (It.)	väl-kĕt'-tä	vahl-ket'-tah
Valckenaar (NEI, bay)	See *Walckenaer*.	
Vâlcov (Rum. > Rus.)	vûl'-kôv	vuhl'-kov

Russian *Vilkovo*, vēl'-kŏ-vŏ [veel'-ko-vo].

Valdai (Rus.)	väl-dĭ'	vahl-dai'
Valdepeñas (Sp.)	väl-dĕ-pĕ'-nyäs	vahl-deh-peh'-nyahs
Valdés, Basilio J. (Fil. polit.)	väl-dĕs', bä-sē'-lyô	vahl-des', bah-see'-lyo
Valdez (Alaska)	väl'-dĕz	val'-dez
Val d'Izé (Fr.)	väl dē-zĕ'	vahl dee-zeh'
Valdres (Nor.)	väl'-drəs	vahl'-druhs
Valea lui Mihai (Rum.)	vä'-lyä lōōĭ mē-hĭ'	vah'-lyah lui mee-hai'
Valence (Fr.)	vä-läNs'	vah-lahNs'

Valencia (Sp.)	*Eng.* və-lĕn'-chə *or*	vuh-len'-chuh *or*
	-shĭ-ə	-shi-uh
	Sp. vä-lĕn'-thyä	vah-len'-thyah *or*
	or -syä	-syah
Valensole (Fr.)	vä-läN-sôl'	vah-lahN-sol'
Valga (Est., Latvia)	väl'-gä	vahl'-gah

Latvian *Valka*, väl'-kä [vahl'-kah]. Russian *Valk*, q.v.

| Valjevo (Yugosl.) | vä'-lyĕ-vô | vah'-lyeh-vo |
| Valk (Est., Latvia) | *Rus.* välk' | vahlk' |

Estonian *Valga*, q.v. German spelling *Walk*. Latvian *Valka*.

Valka (Est., Latvia)   See *Valga*.

Valkenburg (Neth.)	väl'-kən-bûrk(h)	vahl'-kuhn-bœrk(h)
Valkenswaard (Neth.)	väl'-kəns-wärt'	vahl'-kuhns-wahrt'
Valki (Rus.)	väl'-kĭ	vahl'-ki
Valkó (Hung.)	vŏl'-kô	vol'-ko
Valladolid (Sp.)	*Eng.* vǎl'-ə-dō'-lĭd	val'-uh-doh'-lid
	Sp. vä-lyä-dô-lēd'	vah-lyah-do-leed'
Vallebuona (It.)	väl-lĕ-bwô'-nä	vahl-leh-bwo'-nah
Vallecchio (It.)	väl-lĕk'-kyô	vahl-lek'-kyo
Vallejo (Calif.)	vǎ-lā'-hō	va-lay'-hoh
	or və-lā'-ō	vuh-lay'-oh

Spanish vä-yĕ'-hô [vah-yeh'-ho].

Valleluce (It.)	väl-lĕ-lōō'-chĕ	vahl-leh-loo'-cheh
Vallendar (Ger.)	fäl'-ən-där	fahl'-uhn-dahr
Vallerotonda (It.)	väl'-lĕ-rô-tôn'-dä	vahl'-leh-ro-ton'-dah
Valle Spizza (Yugosl., bay)	*It.* väl'-lĕ spēt'-sä	vahl'-leh speet'-sah

Serb-Croat Zaliv *Spič*, q.v.

Vallet (Fr.)	vä-lĕ'	vah-leh'
Vallombrosa (It.)	väl-lôm-brô'-sä	vahl-lom-bro'-sah
Valmiera (Latvia)	väl'-myĕ-rä	vahl'-myeh-rah

Russian and German *Wolmar*, q.v.

Valmontone (It.)	väl-môn-tô'-nĕ	vahl-mon-to'-neh
Valmy (Fr., Alg.)	väl-mē'	vahl-mee'
Valognes (Fr.)	vä-lôn'(y)	vah-lon'(y)
Valona (Alb.)	*It.* vä-lô'-nä	vah-lo'-nah

Albanian *Vlonë*, q.v.

Valparaiso (Chile)	*Eng.* vǎl'-pə-rī'-zō	val'-puh-rai'-zoh
	or -rā'-zō	*or* -ray'-zoh
	Sp. väl-pä-rä-ē'-sô	vahl-pah-rah-ee'-so
Valparaiso (Ind.)	vǎl'-pə-rā'-zō	val'-puh-ray'-zoh
Valsch (NEI, New Guinea)	väls'	vahls'
Valuiki (Rus.)	vä-lōō'-ĭ-kĭ	vah-loo'-i-ki

Valverde (place name)	*Eng.* văl-vûr'-dĭ	val-vur'-di
	Sp. väl-vĕr'-dĕ	vahl-vehr'-deh
Vamos (Crete)	vä'-môs	vah'-mos
Van Acker, Achille (Belg. polit.)	vän ä'-kər, ä-shēl'	vahn ah'-kuhr, ah-sheel'
Van Boetzelaer van Oosterhout, Carel G. W. F. (Neth. polit.)	vän bōōt'-sə-lär vän ō'-stər-hout, kä'-rəl	vahn boot'-suh-lahr vahn oh'-stuhr-haut, kah'-ruhl

If the name is simplified, it becomes *Van Boetzelaer*, not *Van Ooster-hout.*

Van Cauwelaert, Frans (Belg. polit.)	vän kou'-wə-lärt', fräns'	vahn kau'-wuh-lahrt', frahns'
Vancouver (Can.)	văn-kōō'-vər	van-koo'-vuhr
Van den Meersch, Ganshof (Belg. general)	vän dən märs', gäns'-hôf	vahn duhn mayrs', gahns'-hof
Van Diemen (Austral., gulf)	văn dē'-mən	van dee'-muhn
Van Gogh, Vincent (Du. painter)	*Eng.* văn gō' *Du.* vän k(h)ôk(h)', vĭn-sĕnt'	van goh' vahn k(h)ok(h)', vin-sent'
Vangunu (Oc., Solomons)	väng'-ōō-nōō	vahng'-oo-noo
Vanikoro (Oc., Solomons)	vä-nē-kô'-rô	vah-nee-ko'-ro
Vanimo (N.E. New Guinea)	vä'-nē-mô	vah'-nee-mo
Van Keuren, A. H. (Am. admiral)	văn kyōō'-rən	van kyoo'-ruhn
Van Kleffens, Eelco Nicolaas (Du. diplomat)	vän klĕf'-əns, āl'-kō nē'-kō-läs	vahn klef'-uhns, ayl'-koh nee'-koh-lahs
Van Langenhove, Fernand (Belg. diplomat)	vän läng'-ən-hō'-və, fĕr-näN'	vahn lahng'-uhn-hoh'-vuh, fehr-nahN'
Van Loon, Hendrik (Am. author)	văn lōn', hĕn'-drĭk	van lohn', hen'-drik
Van Mook, Hubertus (Du. polit.)	vän mōk', hŏŏ-bĕr'-tŏŏs	vahn mohk', hu-behr'-tus
Vanne (Fr., riv.)	vän'	vahn'
Vannes (Fr.)	vän'	vahn'
Van Nuys (Calif.)	văn nīz'	van naiz'
Van Nuys, Frederick (U.S. senator)	văn nēs'	van nees'

Van Oosterhout, van Boetzelaer (Neth. polit.) See *Van Boetzelaer.*

Van Riper, Walter D. (N. J. polit.)	văn rī'-pər	van rai'-puhr

Van Roey, Joseph Ernest (Belg. cardinal)	văn rōō′-ĭ	van roo′-i
Vansittart, Sir Robert Gilbert, Baron Denham (Br. diplomat)	văn-sĭt′-ərt, . . . děn′-əm	van-sit′-uhrt, . . . den′-uhm
Van Staveren, J. J. A. (Du. polit.)	văn stä′-və-rən	vahn stah′-vuh-ruhn
Van Sweringen (Cleveland financiers)	văn swĕr′-ĭn-jən	van swehr′-in-juhn
Vanua Levu (Oc., Fiji)	vä-nōō′-ä lĕ′-vōō	vah-noo′-ah leh′-voo
Vanves (Fr.)	väNv′	vahNv′
Van Zandt, James E. (U.S. representative)	văn zănt′	van zant′
vár	vär′	vahr′

An element, meaning *castle* or *fortress*, in Hungarian place names.

Var (Fr.)	vär′	vahr′
Varadero (Cuba)	vä-rä-dě′-rô	vah-rah-deh′-ro
Varangerfjord (Nor.)	vä-räng′-ər-fyōr	vah-rahng′-uhr-fyohr
Varaždin (Yugosl.)	vä′-räzh′-dĭn	vah′-rahzh′-din

Italian *Varasdino*, vä-räs-dē′-nô [vah-rahs-dee′-no].

| Vardar (Balkan riv.) | vär′-där | vahr′-dahr |

Greek *Vardaris*, vär-dä′-rēs [vahr-dah′-rees]; *Vardarios*, vär-dä′-rē-ôs [vahr-dah′-ree-os]; and *Axios*, q.v.

Varde (Den.)	vär′-də	vahr′-duh
Vardoe *or* Vardö (Nor.)	värd′-û	vahrd′-œ
Varela, José Enrique (Sp. polit.)	vä-rě′-lä, hô-sě′ ěn-rē′-kě	vah-reh′-lah, ho-seh′ en-ree′-keh
Vargas, Getulio (Braz. polit.)	vär′-gəs, zhě-tōō′-lyōō	vahr′-guhs, zheh-too′-lyu
Vargas, Jorge B. (Fil. polit.)	vär′-gäs, hôr′-hě	vahr′-gahs, hor′-heh
Variš (Yugosl.)	vä′-rĭsh	vah′-rish
Varna (Bulg.)	vär′-nä	vahr′-nah
Varnsdorf (Cz.)	värns′-dôrf	vahrns′-dorf
Varnutka (Rus.)	vär-nōōt′-kä	vahr-noot′-kah
Varoš (Yugosl.)	vä′-rôsh	vah′-rosh
Városlöd (Hung.)	vä′-rôsh-lûd	vah′-rosh-lœd

Varreville (Fr.) See *St. Martin de Varreville*.

Varshava (Pol.) See *Warsaw*.

| varsity | vär′-sə-tĭ *or* värs′-tĭ | vahr′-suh-ti vahrs′-ti |

The second pronunciation, with syncopation, is probably more common than the first. See *university*.

Varta (Pol.) See *Warta*.

Värtsilä (Fin.)	värt′-sē-lǎ	vehrt′-see-la
Russian *Vyartsilya*, q.v.		
Varvaressos, Kyriakos	vär-vä-rĕs′-sôs,	vahr-vah-res′-sos,
(Gr. polit.)	kē-ryä′-kôs	kee-ryah′-kos
Varvarin (Yugosl.)	vär′-vä′-rĭn	vahr′-vah′-rin
Varvasena (Gr.)	vär-vä′-sĕ-nä	vahr-vah′-seh-nah
Varzuga (Rus., riv.)	vär-zōō′-gä	vahr-zoo′-gah
Vasas (Hung.)	vŏ′-shŏsh	vo′-shosh
Vaşcău (Rum.)	väsh-kû′-ŏŏ	vahsh-kœ′-u
Vasilevichi (Rus.)	vä-sĭ-lĕ′-vĭ-chĭ	vah-si-leh′-vi-chi
Vasilevka (Rus.)	vä-sē′-lyĕf-kä	vah-see′-lyef-kah
Vasilevsky, Alexander	vä-sĭ-lĕf′-skĭ,	vah-si-lef′-ski,
Mikhailovich (Rus.	ä-lĕk-sän′-dər	ah-lek-sahn′-duhr
general)	mĭ-hī′-lŏ-vĭch	mi-hai′-lo-vich
Vasiliadis, Gerasimos	vä-sē-lyä′-dēs,	vah-see-lyah′-dees,
(Gr. polit.)	yĕ-rä′-sē-môs	yeh-rah′-see-mos
Vasiliadis, Theodoros	vä-sē-lyä′-dēs,	vah-see-lyah′-dees,
(Gr. polit.)	thĕ-ô′-dô-rôs	theh-o′-do-ros
Vasiliev (Rus. name)	vä-sē′-lyĕf	vah-see′-lyehf
Vasiliko (Bulg.) See *Tzarevo*.		
Vasilkov (Rus.)	vä-sĭl(y)-kôf′	vah-sil(y)-kof′
Vaslui (Rum.)	vä-slŏŏ′ĭ	vah-slu′i
Vasojevići (Yugosl.)	vä′-sô′-yĕ-vĭ-chĭ	vah′-so′-yeh-vi-chi
Vassenden (Nor.)	väs′-ĕn-ən	vahs′-en-uhn
Vatan (Turkish news-	vä-tän′	vah-tahn′
paper)		
Vatheos Lemen (Gr.)	vä-thĕ′-ô(s) lē-mēn′	vah-theh′-o(s) lee-
		meen′
Also called *Vathy*, q.v.		
Vathy (Gr.)	vä-thē′	vah-thee′
Vatilau (Oc., Solomons)	vä-tē-lou′	vah-tee-lau′
Vatra Dornei (Rum.)	vä′-trä dôr′-nä	vah′-trah dor′-nay
Vatutin, Nikolai (Rus.	vä-tōō′-tĭn, nĭ-kŏ-lĭ′	vah-too′-tin, ni-ko-
general)		lai′
Vaucluse (Fr.)	vō-klüz′	voh-klüz′
Vauville (Fr.)	vō-vēl′	voh-veel′
Vauxhall (London)	vŏks′-hôl	voks′-hawl
Veaugues (Fr.)	vōg′	vohg′
Vecchiarelli, Carlo (It.	vĕk-kyä-rĕl′-lē,	vek-kyah-rel′-lee,
general)	kär′-lô	kahr′-lo
Vechel (Neth.)	vĕk(h)′-əl	vek(h)′-uhl
Also spelled *Veghel*.		
Vechelde (Ger.)	fĕk(h)′-əl-də	fek(h)′-uhl-duh
Vecht (Neth., riv.)	vĕk(h)t′	vek(h)t′

[567]

Vecsés (Hung.)	vĕ'-chäsh	veh-chaysh
Vedea (Rum., riv.)	vĕ'-dyä	veh'-dyah
Veendam (Neth.)	vän-däm'	vayn-dahm'
Veere (Neth.)	vā'-rə	vay'-ruh
Vegesack (Ger.)	vā'-gə-zäk	vay'-guh-zahk

Veghel (Neth.) See *Vechel.*

Veglia (Yugosl.)	*It.* vĕ'-lyä	veh'-lyah
Serb-Croat *Krk,* q.v.		
Vehčane (Yugosl.)	vĕk(h)'-chä-nĕ	vek(h)'-chah-neh
vehement	vē'-ə-mənt	vee'-uh-muhnt
	or vē'-hĭ-mənt	vee'-hi-muhnt

For *vehement, vehemence,* and *vehicle* all dictionaries prefer a pronunciation without *h.* Moreover an attempt to pronounce an *h* customarily silent may develop a stress on the second syllable, a hypercorrect or comic pronunciation. But note *vehicular.*

vehicle	vē'-ĭ-kəl	vee'-i-kuhl
	or vē'-hĭ-kəl	vee'-hi-kuhl
vehicular	vē-hĭk'-yə-lər	vee-hik'-yuh-luhr

Veintimilla, Mariano Suárez (Ecuador polit.) See *Suárez Veintimilla.*

Vejano (It.)	vĕ-yä'-nô	veh-yah'-no
Vejle (Den.)	vī'-lə	vai'-luh
Velasco Ibarra, José	vĕ-läs'-kô ē-bär'-rä,	veh-lahs'-ko ee-bahr'-
María (Ecuador. polit.)	hô-sĕ' mä-rē'-ä	rah, ho-seh' mah-
		ree'-ah
Velázquez (Sp. name)	*Eng.* və-lăs'-kwĭz	vuh-las'-kwiz
	Am. Sp. vĕ-läs'-kĕs	veh-lahs'-kehs
	Sp. vĕ-läth'-kĕth	veh-lahth'-kehth

Also spelled *Velásquez.*

Veldhoven (Neth.)	vĕlt'-hō-vən	velt'-hoh-vuhn
Velenje (Yugosl.)	vĕ'-lĕ-nyĕ	veh'-leh-nyeh
Veles (Yugosl.)	vĕ'-lĕs	veh'-les
Veleŝte (Yugosl.)	vĕ'-lĕ-shtĕ	veh'-leh-shteh
velika, -e, -i, -o	vĕ'-lĭ-kä, -ĕ, -ĭ, -ô	veh'-li-kah, -eh, -i, -o

An element, meaning *large* or *great,* in Yugoslav place names. It may be necessary to look up the other part of the name. The similar word in Czech is stressed on the first syllable; in Bulgarian, Polish, and Russian, on the second syllable.

Velikaya (Rus., riv.)	vĕ-lē'-kä-yä	veh-lee'-kah-yah
Veliki Burluk (Rus.)	vĕ-lē'-kĭ bōōr-lōōk'	veh-lee'-ki boor-look'
Veliki Kvarner (Yugosl.,	vĕ'-lĭ-kĭ kvär'-nĕr	veh'-li-ki kvahr'-nehr
inlet)		
Italian *Quarnero,* q.v.		
Velikie Luki (Rus.)	vĕ-lē'-kĭ-yĕ lōō'-kĭ	veh-lee'-ki-yeh loo'-ki
Velikii Tokmak (Rus.)	vĕ-lē'-kĭ tŏk-mäk'	veh-lee'-ki tok-mahk'

Velizh (Rus.)   vĕ'-lĭsh   veh'-lish

Vel'ký Žitný Ostrov   vēl'-kē zhēt'-nē   veel'-kee zheet'-nee
(Cz., isl.)   ô'-strôf   o'-strof
     Hungarian *Csallóköz*, q.v. German *Grosse Schütt-Insel*, grŏs'-ə shüt'
ĭn'-zəl [grohs'-uh shüt' in'-zuhl].

Vella Lavella (Oc., Solo-   vĕl'-ä lä-vĕl'-ä   vel'-ah lah-vel'-ah
mons)

Velletri (It.)   vĕl-lĕ'-trē   vel-leh'-tree
     See *Grosseto*, note.

Velloso, Pedro Leão   vĕ-lō'-sŏŏ, pā'-drŏŏ   veh-loh'-su, pay'-dru
(Braz. polit.)   lĭ-ouN'   lih-auN'

Velluire (Fr.)   vĕ-lwēr'   veh-lweer'

Velyun (Pol.)   See *Wieluń*.

Velzen (Neth.)   vĕl'-zən   vel'-zuhn

Vena Fiorita (Sard.)   vĕ'-nä fyô-rē'-tä   veh'-nah fyo-ree'-tah

Venafro (It.)   vĕ-nä'-frô   veh-nah'-fro

Venaissin (Fr.)   və-nĕ-săN'   vuh-neh-saN'

Venčane (Yugosl.)   vĕn'-chä-nĕ   ven'-chah-neh

Vendée, la (Fr.)   väN-dĕ', lä   vahN-deh', lah
     There is also an English variant, *the Vendee*, vĕn̤-dē' [ven-dee'].

Venden (Latvia)   See *Wenden*.

Vendeuvre (Fr.)   väN-dû'vr   vahN-dœ'vr

Vendôme (Fr.)   väN-dōm'   vahN-dohm'

Vendsyssel Thy (Den.,   vĕn'-süs-əl tü'   ven'-süs-uhl tü'
isl.)

Venendaal (Neth.)   vā'-nən-däl   vay'-nuhn-dahl

Venetia (It.)   *Eng.* və-nē'-shə   vuh-nee'-shuh
     or   və-nĭsh'-ə   vuh-nish'-uh
     Italian *Venezia*, vĕ-nĕ'-tsyä [veh-neh'-tsyah].

Venetia Euganea (It.)   və-nē'-shə (*or* və-   vuh-nee'-shuh (*or*
     nĭsh'-ə) yŏŏ-gā'-   vuh-nish'-uh)
     nĭ-ə (*or* yŏŏ-gə-nē'-ə)   yu-gay'-ni-uh (*or*
         yoo-guh-nee'-uh)

     Italian *Venezia Euganea*, q.v., or *Veneto*, q.v.

Venetian   və-nē'-shən   vuh-nee'-shuhn
     or və-nĭsh'-ən   vuh-nish'-uhn

Venetiko (Gr., isl.)   See *Thiganousa*.

Veneto (It.)   vĕ'-nĕ-tô   veh'-neh-to

Venezia (It.)   vĕ-nĕ'-tsyä   veh-neh'-tsyah
     English *Venice*, q.v., and *Venetia*, q.v.

Venezia Euganea (It.,   vĕ-nĕ'-tsyä   veh-neh'-tsyah
dept.)   ĕ-ŏŏ-gä'-nĕ-ä   eh-oo-gah'-neh-ah
     Also called *Veneto*, q.v. English *Venetia Euganea*, q.v.

Venezia Giulia (It.)   vĕ-nĕ'-tsyä jōō'-lyä   veh-neh'-tsyah joo'-
                                               lyah

Venezia Giulia e Zara, . . . ĕ dzä'-rä [eh dzah'-rah].

Venezia Tridentina (It.)   vĕ-nĕ'-tsyä trē-dĕn-   veh-neh'-tsyah tree-
                               tē'-nä   den-tee'-nah

Venezuela (S.A.)   *Eng.* vĕn'-ĭ-zwē'-lä   ven'-i-zwee'-lah
                 Sp. vĕ-nĕ-swĕ'-lä   veh-neh-sweh'-lah
                 or -thwĕ'-   *or* -thweh'-

Vengrov (Pol.)   See *Węgrów*.

Venhuizen (Neth.)   vĕn'-hûĭ-zən   ven'-hœi-zuhn

Venice (It.)   *Eng.* vĕn'-ĭs   ven'-is
   Italian *Venezia*, q.v.

Venizelos, Sophocles   vĕ-nē-zĕ'-lôs,   veh-nee-zeh'-los,
  (Gr. polit.)   sô-fô-klēs'   so-fo-klees'

Venlo *or* Venloo (Neth.) vĕn'-lō   ven'-loh

Venraai (Neth.)   vĕn'-rī   ven'-rai
   Also spelled *Venraij* and *Venray*.

Venraij (Neth.) See *Venraai*.

Venta (Latvia, riv.)   vĕn'-tä   ven'-tah

Ventena (It., riv.)   vĕn-tĕ'-nä   ven-teh'-nah

Ventotene (It., isl.)   vĕn-tô-tĕ'-nĕ   ven-to-teh'-neh

Ventspils (Latvia)   vĕnts'-pēls   vents'-peels
   Russian *Vindava*, q.v. German *Windau*, q.v.

Vera, Victoriano Benítez (Para. polit.) See *Benítez Vera*.

Veracruz (Mex.)   *Eng.* vĕr'-ə-krōōz'   vehr'-uh-krooz'
                 Sp. vĕ'-rä-krōōs'   veh'-rah-kroos'

Veraval (India)   vē'-rə-vəl   vee'-ruh-vuhl

Verberie (Fr.)   vĕr-bə-rē'   vehr-buh-ree'

Vercelli (It.)   vĕr-chĕl'-lē   vehr-chel'-lee

Vercors (Fr.)   vĕr-kôr'   vehr-kor'

Verde (Afr., cape;   *Eng.* vûrd'   vuhrd'
  Port. isls.)
  See *Cape Verde*.

Verde (P.I.)   vĕr'-dĕ   vehr'-deh

Verdon (Fr., riv.)   vĕr-dôN'   vehr-doN'

Verdun (Fr.)   vĕr-dûN'   vehr-dœN'

Vergato (It.)   vĕr-gä'-tô   vehr-gah'-to

Vergemoli (It.)   vĕr-jĕ'-mô-lē   vehr-jeh'-mo-lee

Vergennes (Vt.)   vûr-jĕnz'   vuhr-jenz'

Verige (Yugosl., str.)   vĕ'-rē-gĕ   veh'-ree-geh
   Also called *Boka Kotorska*, q.v. Italian *Le Catene*, q.v.

Verkhne Dneprovsk   vĕr'-k(h)nĕ dnĕ-   vehr'-k(h)neh dneh-
  (Rus.)   prôfsk'   profsk'

Verkhne Tambovskoe (Rus.)	vĕr′-k(h)nĕ tämbôf′-skŏ-yĕ	vehr′-k(h)neh tahmbof′-sko-yeh
Verkhne Udinsk (Rus.)	vĕr′-k(h)nĕ ōō-dēnsk′	vehr′-k(h)neh oo-deensk′
Verkhove (Rus.)	vĕr-hô′-vyĕ	vehr-ho′-vyeh
Verma (Nor.)	vĕr′-mä	vehr′-mah
Vermeer, Jan (Du. painter)	*Eng.* vər-mĭr′ *Du.* vər-mār′, yän′	vuhr-mihr′ vuhr-mayr′, yahn′
Vermeersch Thorez, Jeannette (Fr. polit.) Flemish vər-mārs′ [vuhr-mayrs′].	vĕr-mĕrsh′ tô-rĕz′, zhä-nĕt′	vehr-mehrsh′ torez′, zhah-neht′
Vern (Fr.)	vĕrn′	vehrn′
Vernadovka (Rus.)	vĕr-nä′-dŏf-kä	vehr-nah′-dof-kah
Vernes *or* Værnes (Nor.)	vär′-nĕs	vehr′-nes
Verneuil (Fr.)	vĕr-nû′(y)	vehr-nœ′(y)
Vernon (Fr.)	vĕr-nôN′	vehr-noN′
Verny (Fr.)	vĕr-nē′	vehr-nee′
Veroia (Gr.)	vĕ′-rē-ä	veh′-ree-ah
Veroli (It.)	vĕ′-rô-lē	veh′-ro-lee
Verona (It.)	*Eng.* və-rō′-nə *It.* vĕ-rô′-nä	vuh-roh′-nuh veh-ro′-nah
Verre (Belg.)	vĕr′	vehr′
Versailles (Fr.)	*Fr.* vĕr-sī′ *or* -sä′(y) *Eng.* vər-sālz′	vehr-sai′ *or* -sah′(y) vuhr-saylz′
Versailles (Ind.)	vər-sālz′	vuhr-saylz′
Versec (Yugosl.) See *Vršac*.		
Verson (Fr.)	vĕr-sôN′	vehr-soN′
Verviers (Belg.)	vĕr-vyĕ′	vehr-vyeh′
Vervins (Fr.)	vĕr-văN′	vehr-vaN′
Vesegonsk (Rus.)	vĕ-syĕ-gônsk′	veh-syeh-gonsk′
Vesoul (Fr.)	və-zōōl′	vuh-zool′
Vest-Agder (Nor.)	vĕst′-äg-dər	vest′-ahg-duhr
Vesteraalen (Nor., isls.)	vĕs′-tər-ô-lən	ves′-tuhr-o-luhn
Vestfjorden (Nor.)	vĕst′-fyŏr-ən	vest′-fyohr-uhn
Vestfold (Nor.)	vĕst′-fôl	vest′-fol
Vestnes (Nor.)	vĕst′-nĕs	vest′-nes
Vestvaagoe *or* Vestvågö (Nor., isl.)	vĕst′-vôg-û	vest′-vog-œ
Veszprém (Hung.)	vĕs′-präm	ves′-praym
Veternica (Yugosl., riv.)	vĕ′-tĕr-nĭ-tsä	veh′-tehr-ni-tsah
Veulen (Neth.)	vû′-lən	vœ′-luhn
Veur (Neth.)	vûr′	vœr′

Veurne (Belg.)	*Flem.* vûr′-nə	vœr′-nuh
French *Furnes*, fürn′.		
Vevey (Switz.)	və-vĕ′(y)	vuh-veh′(y)
German *Vivis*, vē′-vĭs [vee′-vis].		
Vexin (Fr.)	vĕk-săN′	vek-saN′
Vézelay (Fr.)	vĕ-zə-lĕ′	veh-zuh-leh′
Vézins (Fr.)	vĕ-zăN′	veh-zaN′
Via Appia (It., road)	vē′-ä äp′-pyä	vee′-ah ahp′-pyah
English the *Appian Way*, ăp′-ĭ-ən [ap′-i-uhn].		
Via Casilina (It., road)	vē′-ä kä-sē-lē′-nä	vee′-ah kah-see-lee′-nah
Via Flaminia (It., road)	vē′-ä flä-mē′-nyä	vee′-ah flah-mee′-nyah
English the *Flaminian Way*, flə-mĭn′-ĭ-ən [fluh-min′-i-uhn].		
Vianden (Luxem.)	vē-än′-dən	vee-ahn′-duhn
Vianen (Neth.)	vē-ä′-nən	vee-ah′-nuhn
Vianos (Crete)	vyä′-nôs	vyah′-nos
Viareggio (It.)	vyä-rĕd′-jô	vyah--red′-jo
Viborg (Den.)	vē′-bôr	vee′-bor
Viborg (Fin. > Rus.)	See *Viipuri*.	
Vibo Valentia (It.)	vē′-bô vä-lĕn′-tyä	vee′-bo vah-len′-tyah
Vibraye (Fr.)	vē-brĕ′	vee-breh′
Vicalvi (It.)	vē-käl′-vē	vee-kahl′-vee
Vicenza (It.)	vē-chĕn′-tsä	vee-chen′-tsah
vice versa	vī′-sə (*or* -sĭ) vûr′-sə	vai′-suh (*or* -si) vuhr′-suh

The pronunciation vīs vûr′-sə [vais vuhr′-suh] is not recommended.

Vichuga (Rus.)	vĭ-choō′-gä	vi-choo′-gah
Vichy (Fr.)	*Eng.* vĭsh′-ĭ	vish′-i
	Fr. vē-shē′	vee-shee′
Vicovaro (It.)	vē-kô-vä′-rô	vee-ko-vah′-ro
Victor Emmanuel	*Eng.* vĭk′-tər ĭ-măn′-yoō-əl	vik′-tuhr i-man′-yu-uhl

Italian *Vittorio Emanuele*, vēt-tô′-ryô ĕ-mä-nwĕ′-lĕ [veet-to′-ryo eh-mah-nweh′-leh]. Italian King Victor Emmanuel III in exile is called *Count of Pollenza*, pôl-lĕn′-tsä [pol-len′-tsah].

victual (n. and v.)	vĭt′l	vit′l

There is no dictionary authority for the spelling pronunciation vĭk′-tyoō-əl [vik′-tyu-uhl]. If vĭt′l seems homespun, vĭk′-tyoō-əl is worse.

Vidauban (Fr.)	vē-dō-bäN′	vee-doh-bahN′
Videla, Gabriel González (Chilean polit.) See *González Videla*.		
Videseter (Nor.)	vē′-də-sä-tər	vee′-duh-say-tuhr
Vidin (Bulg.)	vē′-dĭn	vee′-din
Vidlič (Yugosl., mts.)	vēd′-lĭch	veed′-lich

Vidlitsa (Rus.)	vēd'-lĭ-tsä	veed'-li-tsah
Vidrnjak (Yugosl., riv.)	vē'-dər'-nyäk	vee'-duhr'-nyahk
Vidzeme (Latvia, prov.)	vēd'-zĕ-mĕ	veed'-zeh-meh
Vielsalm (Belg.)	vyĕl-sälm'	vyel-sahlm'
Vienna (Austria)	*Eng.* vĭ-ĕn'-ə	vi-en'-uh
German *Wien*, q.v.		
Vienne (Fr.)	vyĕn'	vyen'
Vientiane (Indo-Ch.)	vē'-ən-tyĕn'	vee'-uhn-tyen'
Vieques (P.R., isl.)	vyĕ'-kĕs	vyeh'-kes
Vierlingsbeek (Neth.)	vēr'-lĭngs-bāk'	veer'-lings-bayk'
Vierraden (Ger.)	fēr'-rä'-dən	feer'-rah'-duhn
Viersen (Ger.)	fēr'-zən	feer'-zuhn
Vierville (Fr.)	vyĕr-vēl'	vyehr-veel'
Vierzon (Fr.)	vyĕr-zôN'	vyehr-zoN'
Viest, Rudolf	vyĕst'	vyest'
(Cz. general)		

Vietinghoff, Heinrich von (Ger. general) See *Von Vietinghoff.*

Viet Nam	vē-ĕt' näm'	vee-et' nahm'

The native "republic" of Tonkin and the northern part of Annam.

Vietnamese	vē-ĕt'-nä-mēz'	vee-et'-nah-meez'
Vigan (P.I.)	vē'-gän	vee'-gahn
Vigerie, Astier de la	vē-zhĕ-rē', äs-tyĕ' də	vee-zheh-ree', ahs-
(Fr. polit.)	lä	tyeh' duh lah
Vigne (It.)	vē'-nyĕ	vee'-nyeh
Vigo (Sp.)	vē'-gồ	vee'-go
Vigri (Pol.) See *Wigry.*		
Vigy (Fr.)	vē-zhē'	vee-zhee'
Vihiers (Fr.)	vē-yĕ'	vee-yeh'
Viipuri (Fin. >Rus.)	vē'-pŏŏ-rē	vee'-pu-ree

Swedish *Viborg*, vē'-bồr(y) [vee'-bor(y)]. Russian *Vyborg*, vwē'-bồrk [vwee'-bork].

Vijniţa (Rum.)	vēzh'-nē-tsä	veezh'-nee-tsah
Vijosa (Alb., riv.) See *Vijosë.*		
Vijosë (Alb., riv.)	vē-yồ'-sə	vee-yo'-suh

Greek *Voïousa*, voi-ōō'-sä [voi-oo'-sah], and *Aoos*, q.v.

vik	vēk'	veek'

Norwegian meaning *small bay* or *inlet*; an element in place names. In compounds like *Narvik*, vēk' [veek'] Anglicized to vĭk' [vik'].

Vikesund (Nor.)	vē'-kə-soõn	vee'-kuh-sun
Vila (Balkan mt.)	*S.-C.* vē'-lä	vee'-lah

Albanian *Mal i Vilës*, mäl' ē vē'-ləs [mahl' ee vee'-luhs].

Vilaine (Fr., riv.)	vē-lĕn'	vee-len'
Vileika (Pol. >Rus.)	vĭ-lā'-kä	vi-lay'-kah

Polish spelling *Wilejka.*

Vilich (Ger.) See *Beuel.*

Viliya (Pol. >Rus.,   vē'-lĭ-yä   vee'-li-yah
   Lith., riv.)
   Polish *Wilja,* vēl'-yä [veel'-yah]. Lithuanian *Neris,* nĕ'-rĭs [neh'-ris].

Viljandi (Est.)   vĭl'-yän-dĭ   vil'-yahn-di
   Russian *Fellin,* q.v.

Vilkaviškis (Lith.)   vĭl-kä-vēsh'-kĭs   vil-kah-veesh'-kis
   Russian *Wilkowischki,* q.v.

Vilkovo (Rum. >Rus.)   vēl'-kŏ-vŏ   veel'-ko-vo
   Rumanian *Vâlcov,* q.v.

Villa, Francisco *or*   vē'-yä, frän-sēs'-kô   vee'-yah, frahn-
   Pancho (Mex. outlaw)   *or* pän'-chô   sees'-ko *or* pahn'-cho

Villaba (Sp.)   vē-lyä'-bä   vee-lyah'-bah

Villach (Austria)   fĭl'-äk(h)   fil'-ahk(h)
   Serb-Croat *Beljak,* bĕl'-yäk [bel'-yahk].

Villacidro (Sard.)   vēl-lä-chē'-drô   veel-lah-chee'-dro

Villa Cisneros   vē'-lyä sēs-nĕ'-rôs   vee'-lyah sees-neh'-
   (Rio de Oro)   ros

Villacoublay (Fr.)   vēl-lä-kōō-blĕ'   veel-lah-koo-bleh'

Villaines la Juhel (Fr.)   vē-lĕn lä zhü-ĕl'   vee-len lah zhü-el'

Villa Latina (It.)   vēl'-lä lä-tē'-nä   veel'-lah lah-tee'-nah

Villa Lobos, Heitor   vē'-lä lô'-bôs, ā'-tôr   vee'-lah lo'-bos,
   (Braz. composer)   ay'-tor

Villamagna (It.)   vēl-lä-mä'-nyä   veel-lah-mah'-nyah

Villamor, Jesús (Fil.   vē-lyä-môr', hĕ-sōōs'   vee-lyah-mor', heh-
   polit.)   sōōs'

Villampuy (Fr.)   vē-läN-pwē'   vee-lahN-pwee'

Villarroel, Gualberto   vē-lyär'-rô-ĕl'   vee-lyahr'-ro-el'
   (Bol. polit.)   (*or* -yär'-),   (*or* -yahr'-),
                   gwäl-bĕr'-tô   gwahl-behr'-to

Villa San Giovanni (It.)   vēl'-lä sän jô-vän'-nē   veel'-lah sahn jo-
                                     vahn'-nee

Villasis (P.I.)   vē-lyä'-sēs   vee-lyah'-sees

Villedieu les Poèles (Fr.)   vēl-dyû lĕ pwĕl'   veel-dy œ leh pwel'

Villejuif (Fr.)   vēl-zhwēf'   veel-zhweef'

Villeneuve (Fr.)   vēl-nûv'   veel-nœv'

Viller Cotterets (Fr.)   vē-lĕr kô-trĕ'   vee-lehr ko-treh'

Villers Bocage (Fr.)   vē-lĕr bô-käzh'   vee-lehr bo-kahzh'

Villersexel (Fr.)   vē-lĕr-sĕk-sĕl'   vee-lehr-sek-sel'

Villers sur Mer (Fr.)   vē-lĕr sür mĕr'   vee-lehr sür mehr'

Villetta (It.)   vēl-lĕt'-tä   veel-let'-tah

Villetta Barrea (It.)   vēl-lĕt'-tä bär-rĕ'-ä   veel-let'-tah bahr-
                                     reh'-ah

Villiers (Fr.)   vē-yĕ'   vee-yeh'

Villiers Fossard (Fr.)   vē-yĕ fô-sär′   vee-yeh fo-sahr′
Villmanstrand (Fin.) See *Lappeenranta.*
Villy (Fr.)   vē-yē′   vee-yee′
Vilna (Pol. >Rus.)   *Eng.* vĭl′-nə   vil′-nuh
                    Rus. vēl′(y)-nä   veel′(y)-nah
  Lithuanian *Vilnyus,* vĭl′-nĭ-ŏŏs [vil′-ni-us]. Polish *Wilno,* vēl′-nô
  [veel′-no].
Vilyanov (Pol.) See *Wilanów.*
Viminal (It., Rome)   *Eng.* vĭm′-ə-nəl   vim′-uh-nuhl
  Italian *Viminale,* vē-mē-nä′-lĕ [vee-mee-nah′-leh].
Vimoutiers (Fr.)   vē-mōō-tyĕ′   vee-moo-tyeh′
Vinalhaven (Me.)   vī′-nəl-hā′-vən   vai′-nuhl-hay′-vuhn
Vinča (Yugosl.)   vēn′-chä   veen′-chah
Vincennes (Fr., Ind.)   *Eng.* vĭn-sĕnz′   vin-senz′
                    Fr. văN-sĕn′   vaN-sen′
Vinchiaturo (It.)   vēn-kyä-tōō′-rô   veen-kyah-too′-ro
Vinci (Yugosl.)   vēn′-tsĭ   veen′-tsi
Vindava (Latvia)   *Rus.* vĭn-dä′-vä   vin-dah′-vah
  Latvian *Ventspils,* q.v. German *Windau,* q.v.
Vinh (Indo-Ch.)   vĭn′ *or* vĭn′(y)   vin′ *or* vin′(y)
Vinica (Yugosl.)   vē′-nĭ-tsä   vee′-ni-tsah
Viničani (Yugosl.)   vē′-nĭ-chä-nĭ   vee′-ni-chah-ni
Vinje (Nor.)   vĭn′-yə   vin′-yuh
Vinjetinnene (Nor., mts.) vĭn′-yə-tĭn′-ə-nə   vin′-yuh-tin′-uh-nuh
Vinkeveen (Neth.)   vĭnk′-ə-vān′   vink′-uh-vayn′
Vinkovci (Yugosl.)   vēn′-kôv-tsĭ   veen′-kov-tsi
Vinnitsa (Rus.)   vēn′-nĭ-tsä   veen′-ni-tsah
Vinstra (Nor.)   vĭn′-strä   vin′-strah
Vintar (P.I.)   vēn-tär′   veen-tahr′
Vir (Yugosl.)   vēr′   veer′
  Italian *Puntadura,* q.v.
Virbalis (Lith.)   vēr-bä′-lĭs   veer-bah′-lis
  Russian *Werzhbolovo,* q.v.
Vire (Fr., riv.)   vēr′   veer′
Virovitica (Yugosl.)   vē′-rô-vē′-tĭ-tsä   vee′-ro-vee′-ti-tsah
Virpazar (Yugosl.)   vēr′-pä-zär   veer′-pah-zahr
Virts järv (Est.)   vĭrts′ yärv′   vihrts′ yehrv′
Viru (Oc., Solomons)   vē′-rōō   vee′-roo
Virzhbnik (Pol.) See *Wierzbnik.*
Vis (Yugosl.)   vēs′   vees′
  Italian *Lissa,* q.v.
visa (n. and v.)   vē′-zə   vee′-zuh
  Past tense *visaed,* vē′-zəd [vee′-zuhd]. See synonym *visé.*
visage   vĭz′-ĭj   viz′-ij

Visalia (Calif.)	vǐ-sāl'-yə	vi-sayl'-yuh
Vişăul de Jos (Rum.)	vē-shû'-ŏŏl dĕ zhôs'	vee-shœ'-ul deh zhos'
Vişăul de Sus (Rum.)	vē-shû'-ŏŏl dĕ sŏŏs'	vee-shœ'-ul deh sus'
Visayan Isls. (P.I.)	vē-sä'-yən	vee-sah'-yuhn

Spanish *Bisayas*, bē-sä'-yäs [bee-sah'-yahs].

| viscount | vǐ'-kount | vai'-kaunt |
| visé (n. and v.) | vē'-zā *or* vē-zā' | vee'-zay *or* vee-zay' |

Past tense, *viséed*, vē'-zād [vee'-zayd] *or* vē-zād' [vee-zayd']. See synonym *visa*.

| Višegrad (Yugosl.) | vē'-shĕ-gräd | vee'-sheh-grahd |
| Vishinski, Andrei Y. (Rus. polit.) | vǐ-shǐn'-skǐ, än-drā' | vi-shin'-ski, ahn-dray' |

Vishkov (Pol.) See *Wyszków.*

Vishogrod (Pol.) See *Wyszogród.*

Visla (Pol., riv.) See *Vistula.*

Višnja Gora (Yugosl.)	vēsh'-nyä gô'-rä	veesh'-nyah go'-rah
Višnjica (Yugosl.)	vēsh'-nyǐ-tsä	veesh'-nyi-tsah
Visočica (Yugosl., riv.)	vǐ'-sô'-chǐ-tsä	ve'-so'-chi-tsah
Visočka Ržana (Yugosl.)	vē'-sôch-kä rzhä'-nä	vee'-soch-kah rzhah'-nah
Vistula (Pol., riv.)	*Eng.* vǐs'-chŏŏ-lə	vis'-chu-luh

Polish *Wisła*, vē'-slä [vee'-slah]. Russian spelling *Visla.* German *Weichsel*, vīk'-səl [vaik'-suhl].

Vitačevo (Yugosl.)	vē'-tä'-chĕ-vô	vee'-tah'-cheh-vo
Vitanje (Yugosl.)	vē'-tä-nyĕ	vee'-tah-nyeh
Vitebsk (Rus.)	vē'-tĕpsk	vee'-tepsk
Viterbo (It.)	vē-tĕr'-bô	vee-tehr'-bo
Vitèz	vē'-tāz	vee'-tayz

Hungarian word meaning *hero* which, prefixed to a name, is an official Hungarian title roughly equivalent to *knight.* Following a name it keeps its meaning of *hero.*

Vith, St. (Belg.) See *Saint Vith.*

| Vitiaz (N.E. New Guinea, str.) | vē'-tyĕs | vee'-tyes |

The assumption is that the name is Slavic in origin.

Viti Levu (Oc., Fiji)	vē'-tē lĕ'-vŏŏ	vee'-tee leh'-voo
Vítkovice (Cz.)	vēt'-kô-vǐ-tsĕ	veet'-ko-vi-tseh
Vitolište (Yugosl.)	vē'-tô'-lǐ-shtĕ	vee'-to'-li-shteh
Vitória (Brazil)	vē-tôr'-yə	vee-tor'-yuh
Vitoševac (Yugosl.)	vē'-tô'-shĕ-väts	vee'-to'-sheh-vahts
Vitré (Fr.)	vē-trĕ'	vee-treh'
Vitry (Fr.)	vē-trē'	vee-tree'
Vittoria (Sicily)	vēt-tô'-ryä	veet-to'-ryah

Vittorio Emanuele. See *Victor Emmanuel.*

Vittorio Veneto (It.)	vēt-tô′-ryô vě′-ně-tô	veet-to′-ryo veh′-neh-to
Vi Van Dinh (Indo-Ch. polit.)	vē vän dĭn′ or dĭn′(y)	vee vahn din′ or din′(y)
Vivarit, Liqen i (Alb., lake) See Butrint.		
Vivaro (It.)	vē-vä′-rô	vee-vah′-ro
Vivis (Switz.) See Vevey.		
Vizagapatam (India)	vĭ-zăg′-ə-pə-tăm′	vai-zag′-uh-puh-tam′
Native Vaisakhapattanam.		
Vizcaya (Sp., prov.)	vēth-kä′-yä or vēs-	veeth-kah′-yah or vees-

Also called Biscaya, q.v. English Biscay, bĭs′-kā [bis′-kay].

Vize (Turk.)	vē′-zě′	vee′-zeh′
Vizeu (Port.)	vē-zě′-ŏŏ	vee-zeh′-u
Vizianagram (India)	vĭz′-ĭ-ə-nŭg′-rəm	viz′-i-uh-nuhg′-ruhm
Vizille (Fr.)	vē-zēl′	vee-zeel′
Vizzini (Sicily)	vēd-zē′-nē	veed-zee′-nee
Vkra (Pol., riv.) See Wkra.		
Vlaardingen (Neth.)	vlär′-dĭng-ən	vlahr′-ding-uhn
Vlachtwedde or Vlagtwedde (Neth.)	vläk(h)t-wěd′-ə	vlahk(h)t-wed′-uh
Vladički Han (Yugosl.)	vlä′-dĭch-kĭ hän′	vlah′-dich-ki hahn′
Vladigerov, Pantcho (Bulg. musician)	vlä-dĭ-gě′-rŏf, pän′-chŏ	vlah-di-geh′-rof, pahn′-cho
Vladimir (Rus.)	vlä-dē′-mĭr	vlah-dee′-mihr
Vladimirci (Yugosl.)	vlä′-dĭ-mĭr-tsĭ	vlah′-di-mihr-tsi
Vladimir Volinski (Pol. >Rus.)	vlä-dē′-mĭr vŏ-lēn′-skĭ	vlah-dee′-mihr vo-leen′-ski
Polish Włodzimierz, q.v.		
Vladivostok (Rus.)	vlä′-dĭ-vŏs-tôk′	vlah′-di-vos-tok′
Also Anglicized as vlăd′-ĭ-vŏs′-tŏk [vlad′-i-vos′-tok].		
Vlahčane (Yugosl.)	vläk(h)′-chä-ně	vlahk(h)′-chah-neh
Vlahov, Dimitar (Yugosl. polit.)	vlä′-hŏf, dĭ-mē′-tär	vlah′-hof, di-mee′-tahr
Vlasco Ibarra, José María (Ecuador. polit.)	vläs′-kô ē-bär′-rä, hô-sě′ mä-rē′-ä	vlahs′-ko ee-bahr′-rah, ho-seh′ mah-ree′-ah
Vlasenica (Yugosl.)	vlä′-sě-nĭ-tsä	vlah′-seh-ni-tsah
Vlašić planina (Yugosl., hills)	vlä′-shĭch plä′-nē′-nä	vlah′-shich plah′-nee′-nah
Vlasina (Yugosl., riv.)	vlä′-sĭ-nä	vlah′-si-nah
Vlasinsko Blato (Yugosl., marsh)	vlä′-sĭn-skô blä′-tô	vlah′-sin-sko blah′-to
Vlaška (Yugosl.)	vlä′-shkä	vlah′-shkah

Vlaški Do (Yugosl.)   vlä'-shkĭ dô'   vlah'-shki do'
Vlasotince (Yugosl.)   vlä'-sô-tĭn-tsĕ   vlah'-so-tin-tseh
Vlasulja (Yugosl., mt.)   vlä'-sōō-lyä   vlah'-soo-lyah
Vleuten (Neth.)   vlû'-tən   vlœ'-tuhn
Vlieland (Neth., isl.)   vlē'-länt   vlee'-lahnt
Vlijmen (Neth.)   vlĭ'-mən   vlai'-muhn
Vlissingen (Neth.)   vlĭs'-ĭng-ən   vlis'-ing-uhn
    English *Flushing*, q.v.
Vlodava (Pol.)   See *Włodawa*.
Vlona (Alb.)   See *Vlonë*.
Vlonë (Alb.)   vlô'-nə   vlo'-nuh
    Italian *Valona*, q.v. Greek *Avlon*, äv-lôn' [ahv-lon'].
Vloshchova (Pol.)   See *Włoszczowa*.
Vlotslavsk (Pol.)   See *Włocławek*.
Vltava (Cz., riv.)   vəl'-tä-vä   vuhl'-tah-vah
    German *Moldau*, môl'-dou [mol'-dau].
Vnukovo (Moscow air-   vnōō'-kŏ-vŏ   vnoo'-ko-vo
    port)
Voelkischer Beobachter   fûl'-kĭsh-ər   fœl'-kish-uhr
    (Ger. newspaper)   bĕ-ô'-bäk(h)-tər   beh-oh'-bahk(h)-
                                              tuhr
Voerendaal (Neth.)   vōō'-rən-däl   voo'-ruhn-dahl
Voeringfoss (Nor.)   vû'-rĭng-fôs   vœ'-ring-fos
Vogël, Fand i (Alb., riv.)   vô'-gəl, fänd' ē   vo'-guhl, fahnd' ee
    The smaller tributary of the *Mat*, q.v.
Vogelkop (NEI, New   fō'-gəl-kôp   foh'-guhl-kop
    Guinea)
Vogenwaarde (Neth.)   vō'-k(h)ən-wär'-də   voh'-k(h)uhn-wahr'-
                                              duh
Voghera (It.)   vô-gĕ'-rä   vo-geh'-rah
Voiron (Fr.)   vwä-rôN'   vwah-roN'
Voïussa (Alb., riv.)   See *Vijosë*.
Vojnić (Yugosl.)   voi'-nĭch   voi'-nich
Vojnik (Yugosl., mt.)   voi'-nĭk   voi'-nik
Vokeo (NEI, Schouten)   vô-kĕ'-ô   vo-keh'-o
Volcano Isls. (Oc.)   vŏl-kä'-nō   vol-kay'-noh
Volchansk (Rus.)   vŏl-chänsk'   vol-chahnsk'
Volda (Nor.)   vôl'-dä   vol'-dah
Volendam (Neth.)   vō'-lən-däm'   voh'-luhn-dahm'
Volga (Rus., riv.)   *Eng.* vŏl'-gə   vol'-guh
                          Rus. vôl'-gä   vol'-gah
Volhynia (Pol.)   *Eng.* vŏ-lĭn'-yə   vo-lin'-yuh
    Polish *Wołyń*, vô'-lĭn(y) [vo'-lin(y)]. Russian *Volyn*, vŏ-lwēn'(y)
    [vo-lween'(y)].

Volkhov (Rus., riv.)   vôl′-hŏf   vol′-hof

Volkhovstroi (Rus.)   vôl′-hŏf-stroi′   vol′-hof-stroi′

Völkischer Beobachter (Ger. newspaper) See *Voelkischer* . . . . .

Volkovisk (Pol. >Rus.)   vŏl-kŏ-vēsk′   vol-ko-veesk′
    Polish *Wolkowysk*, q.v.

Vollenhove (Neth.)   vôl′-ən-hō′-və   vol′-uhn-hoh′-vuh

Volnovakha (Rus.)   vôl′-nŏ-vä′-hä   vol′-no-vah′-hah

Volochisk (Rus.)   vŏ-lŏ-chĭsk′   vo-lo-chisk′

Vologda (Rus.)   vô′-lŏg-dä   vo′-log-dah

Volokolamsk (Rus.)   vŏ′-lŏ-kŏ-lämsk′   vo′-lo-ko-lahmsk′

Volos (Gr.)   vô′-lô(s)   vo′-lo(s)

Volosovo (Rus.)   vô′-lŏ-sŏ-vŏ   vo′-lo-so-vo

Volozhin (Pol. >Rus.)   vô-lô′-zhĭn   vo-lo′-zhin
    Polish spelling *Wołożyn*.

Volsci, Castro dei (It.)   vôl′-shē, kä′-strô dä   vol′-shee, kah′-stro
                                     day

Volscian Hills (It.)   *Eng.* vŏl′-shən   vol′-shuhn
    Italian *Monti Lepini*, môn′-tē lĕ-pē′-nē [mon′-tee leh-pee′-nee].

Volsk (Rus.)   vôl(y)sk′   vol(y)sk′

Volta Redonda   vôl′-tə rĭ-dôn′-də   vol′-tuh ri-don′-duh
    (Braz. steel plant)

Volturno (It., riv.)   vôl-tōōr′-nô   vol-toor′-no

Volujica (Yugosl., point)   vô′-lōō′-yĭ-tsä   vo′-loo′-yi-tsah

Volyn (Pol.)   See *Volhynia*.

Vomero (It., Naples)   vô′-mĕ-rô   vo′-meh-ro

Von Arnim, Jürgen   fən är′-nĭm, yür′-gən   fuhn ahr′-nim, yür′-
    (Ger. general)   guhn

Vo Nguyen-giap   vô′ nwĭ′-ən-yäp′   vo′ nwi′-uhn-yahp′
    (Vietnamese general)

Vonitsa (Gr.)   vô′-nē-tsä   vo′-nee-tsah

Vonkhotsk (Pol.)   See *Wąchock*.

Von Neurath, Konstantin   fən noi′-rät, kôn′-   fuhn noi′-raht,
    (Ger. diplomat)   stän-tēn′   kon′-stahn-teen′

Von Papen, Franz (Ger.   fən pä′-pən,   fuhn pah′-puhn,
    diplomat)   fränts′   frahnts′

Von Ribbentrop, Joa-   fən rĭb′-ən-trôp,   fuhn rib′-uhn-trop,
    chim (Ger. diplomat)   yō′-ä′-k(h)ĭm   yoh′-ah′-k(h)im

Von Rundstedt, Gerd   fən rŏont′-shtĕt, gĕrt   fuhn runt′-shtet,
    (Ger. general)   gehrt

Von Schirach, Baldur   fən shē′-räk(h), bäl′-   fuhn shee′-rahk(h),
    (Ger. polit.)   dŏŏr   bahl′-dur

Von Vietinghoff, Heinrich   fən fē′-tĭng-hôf,   fuhn fee′-ting-hohf,
    (Ger. general)   hīn′-rĭk(h)   hain′-rik(h)

Voorburg (Neth.)   vōr′-bûrk(h)   vohr′-bœrk(h)

Voorhis, Jerry	võr′-ēz	vohr′-eez
(Calif. polit.)		
Voorhout (Neth.)	võr′-hout	vohr′-haut
Voorne (Neth., isl.)	võr′-nə	vohr′-nuh
Voorschoten (Neth.)	võr′-sk(h)ō-tən	vohr′-sk(h)oh-tuhn
Voorst (Neth.)	võrst′	vohrst′
Vorde (Ger.)	vôr′-də	vor′-duh
Vordingborg (Den.)	vôr′-dĭng-bôr	vor′-ding-bor
Voreioi or Voreiai	vô′-rē-ē or vô′-rē-ĕ	vo′-ree-ee or vo′-ree-
Sporades (Gr., isls.)	spô-rä′-dĕs	eh spo-rah′-des
English the Northern Sporades, spôr′-ə-dēz [spor′-uh-deez].		
Vöringfoss (Nor.)	vû′-rĭng-fôs	vœ′-ring-fos
Vormsi (Est., isl.)	vôrm′-sĭ	vorm′-si
Russian and German Worms, q.v.		
Voronezh (Rus.)	vŏ-rô′-nĕsh	vo-ro′-nesh
Voroninski (Rus.)	vŏ-rô′-nĭn-skĭ	vo-ro′-nin-ski
Voronov, Nikolai (Rus.	vô′-rŏ-nŏf, nĭ-kŏ-lī′	vo′-ro-nof, ni-ko-lai′
general)		
Voronovo (Rus.)	vô′-rŏ-nŏ-vŏ	vo′-ro-no-vo
Voronya (Rus., riv.)	vŏ-rô′-nyä	vo-ro′-nyah
Vörös, János	vû′-rûsh, yä′-nôsh	vœ′-rœsh, yah′-nosh
(Hung. general)		
Voroshilov (Rus.) See Nikolsk Ussuriski.		
Voroshilov, Klementi E.	vŏ-rŏ-shĭ′-lŏf,	vo-ro-shi′-lof,
(Rus. general)	klĕ-mĕn′-tē	kleh-men′-tee
Voroshilovgrad (Rus.)	vŏ-rŏ-shĭ′-lŏf-grät	vo-ro-shi′-lof-graht
Voroshilovsk (Rus.)	vŏ-rŏ-shĭ′-lŏfsk	vo-ro-shi′-lofsk
Vorozhba (Rus.)	vŏ-rŏsh-bä′	vo-rosh-bah′
Vorskla (Rus., riv.)	vôrsk′-lä	vorsk′-lah
Võru (Est.)	vû′-rōō	vuh′-roo
Russian Werro, q.v.		
Vorys, John M.	võr′-əs	vohr′-uhs
(U.S. representative)		
Vosges (Fr., mts.)	vōzh′	vohzh′
Voskopoja (Alb.)	vô-skô′-pô-yä	vo-sko′-po-yah
Voskresensk (Rus.)	vŏs-krĕ-sĕnsk′	vos-kreh-sensk′
Voskresenskoe (Rus.)	vŏs-krĕ-sĕn′-skŏ-yĕ	vos-kreh-sen′-sko-yeh
Voss (Nor.)	vôs′	vos′
Vossenack (Ger.)	fôs′-ə-näk	fos′-uh-nahk
Vostok (Oc.)	vəs-tôk′	vuhs-tok′
Voukolies (Crete)	vōō-kô-lyĕs′	voo-ko-lyes′
Voulettes (Fr.)	vōō-lĕt′	voo-let′
Voulgaris, Petros (Gr.	vōōl′-gä-rēs, pĕ′-trôs	vool′-gah-rees, peh′-
polit.)		tros

Voutré (Fr.)	vōō-trĕ′	voo-treh′
Vouxa (Crete, cape)	vōō′-ksä	voo′-ksah

Also called *Bouza*, bōō′-zä [boo′-zah]; *Triton*, trĕ-tôn′ [tree-ton′]; and *Trypiti*, trĕ-pē-tē′ [tree-pee-tee′].

Vozarci (Yugosl.)	vô′-zär-tsĭ	vo′-zahr-tsi
Voznesensk (Rus.)	vŏz-nĕ-sĕnsk′	voz-neh-sensk′
Voznesensky, Nikolai (Rus. polit.)	vŏz-nĕ-sĕn′-skĭ, nĭ-kŏ-lī′	voz-neh-sen′-ski, ni-ko-lai′
Vračar (Yugosl., mt.)	vrä′-chär	vrah′-chahr
Vraćevšnica (Yugosl.)	vrä′-chĕf′-shnĭ-tsä	vrah′-chef′-shni-tsah
Vrakhori (Gr.) See *Agrinion*.		
Vranište (Yugosl.)	vrä′-nĭ-shtĕ	vrah′-ni-shteh
Vranje (Yugosl.)	vrä′-nyĕ	vrah′-nyeh

Bulgarian *Vranya*, vrä′-nyä [vrah′-nyah].

Vranjevo (Yugosl.)	vrä′-nyĕ-vô	vrah′-nyeh-vo
Vranjska Banja (Yugosl.)	vrän′(y)-skä bä′-nyä	vrahn′(y)-skah bah′-nyah
Vranovci, Gornji (Yugosl.)	vrä′-nôv-tsĭ, gôr′-nyĭ	vrah′-nov-tsi, gor′-nyi
Vrapčište (Yugosl.)	vräp′-chĭ-shtĕ	vrahp′-chi-shteh
Vratarnica (Yugosl.)	vrä′-tär′-nĭ-tsä	vrah′-tahr′-ni-tsah
Vrattsa (Bulg.)	vrät′-sä	vraht′-sah

Also spelled *Vratca*.

Vražogrnac (Yugosl.)	vrä′-zhô-gər′-näts	vrah′-zho-guhr′-nahts
Vrbas (Yugosl.)	vər′-bäs	vuhr′-bahs
Vrbaska (Yugosl.)	vər′-bä-skä	vuhr′-bah-skah
Vrbnica (Yugosl.)	vərb′-nĭ-tsä	vuhrb′-ni-tsah
Vrbnik (Yugosl.)	vərb′-nĭk	vuhrb′-nik

Italian *Verbenico*, vĕr-bĕn′-ē-kô [vehr-ben′-ee-ko].

Vrbovsko (Yugosl.)	vər′-bôv-skô	vuhr′-bov-sko
Vrčin (Yugosl.)	vər′-chĭn	vuhr′-chin
Vreeland (Neth.)	vrä′-länt	vray′-lahnt
Vreeswijk (Neth.)	vräs′-wīk	vrays-waik
Vrginmost (Yugosl.)	vər′-gĭn-môst	vuhr′-gin-most
Vrgorac (Yugosl.)	vər′-gô-räts	vuhr′-go-rahts
Vrhnika (Yugosl.)	vərk(h)′-nĭ-kä	vuhrk(h)′-ni-kah
Vrmdža (Yugosl.)	vərm′-jä	vuhrm′-jah
Vrnjačka Banja (Yugosl.)	vər′-nyäch-kä bän′-yä	vuhr′-nyahch-kah bahn′-yah
Vršac (Yugosl.)	vər′-shäts	vuhr′-shahts

Hungarian *Versec*, vĕr′-shĕts [vehr′-shets].

Vrška Čuka (Yugosl., mt.)	vərsh′-kä chōō′-kä	vuhrsh′-kah choo′-kah
Vrteška (Yugosl., mt.)	vər′-tĕ′-shkä	vuhr′-teh′-skhah

[581]

Vucht (Neth.)	vûk(h)t′	vœk(h)t′
Vučitrn (Yugosl.)	vōō′-chĭ-tərn′	voo′-chi-tuhrn′
Vught *or* Vucht (Neth.)	vûk(h)t′	vœk(h)t′
Vukovar (Yugosl.)	vōō′-kŏ-vär′	voo′-ko-vahr′
Vulcan (N.E. New Guinea)	vŭl′-kən	vuhl′-kuhn

Also called *Manam*, q.v.

Vunakanau (Oc.)	vōō′-nä-kä-nou′	voo′-nah-kah-nau′
Vuori, Eero (Fin. polit.)	vōō′-ô′-rē, ā′-rô	vu′-o′-ree, ay′-ro
Vursell, Charles (U.S. representative)	vûr-sĕl′	vuhr-sel′

Vutrint (Alb.)   See *Butrint*.

Vyartsilya (Fin. >Rus.)	vyärt′-sĭ-lyä	vyahrt′-si-lyah

Finnish *Värtsilä*, q.v.

Vyazma (Rus.)	vyäz′-mä	vyahz′-mah
Vyborg (Fin. >Rus.)	*Rus.* vwē′-bŏrk	vwee′-bork

Finnish *Viipuri*, q.v.

Vyeprj (Pol., riv.)   See *Wieprz*.

Vyg (Rus., riv.)	vwēg′	vweeg′
Vygozero (Rus.)	vwēg-ô′-zĕ-rŏ	vweeg-o′-zeh-ro
Vyshinski, Andrei Y. (Rus. diplomat)	vĭ-shĭn′-skĭ, än-drā′	vi-shin′-ski, ahn-dray′
Vyshnii Volochek (Rus.)	vĭsh′-nĭ vŏ-lŏ-chŏk′	vish′-ni vo-lo-chok′

Vysoké Tatry (Cz., Pol., Rus., mts.) See *High Tatra*.

Vysokoe (Rus.)	vĭ-sô′-kŏ-yĕ	vi-so′-ko-yeh
Vytegra (Rus.)	vwē′-tĕ-grä	vwee′-teh-grah

Waag (Cz., Hung., riv.)   See *Váh*.

Waal (Neth., riv.)	wäl′	wahl′
Waalre (Neth.)	wäl′-rə	wahl′-ruh
Waalwijk (Neth.)	wäl′-wĭk	wahl′-waik
Waardenburg (Neth.)	wär′-dən-bûrk(h)	wahr′-duhn-bœrk(h)
Waban (Mass.)	wô′-bən	waw′-buhn
Wąchock (Pol.)	vôN′-hôtsk	voN′-hotsk

Russian *Vonkhotsk*, vŏn-hôtsk′ [von-hotsk′].

Waco (Tex.)	wā′-kō	way′-koh

Cf. *Hueco Tanks*.

Wada (Jap. name)	wä-dä′	wah-dah′
Wadden Zee (Neth.)	wäd′-ən zā′	wahd′-uhn zay′
Waddingsveen (Neth.)	wäd′-ĭngs-vän′	wahd′-ings-vayn′
wadi	wä′-dĭ	wah′-di

An element, meaning *water course* or *valley*, in Arabic place names. It may be necessary to look up the other part of the name.

Wadi el Akarit (Tun.)	wä′-dĭ ĕl ä-kä-rēt′	wah′-di el ah-kah-reet′

Wadi Halfa (Sudan)	wä'-dĭ hăl'-fə	wah'-di hal'-fuh
Wadi Kebir (Tun.)	wä'-dĭ kə-bēr'	wah'-di kuh-beer'
Wadi Zigzaou (Tun.)	wä'-dĭ zĭg-zou'	wah'-di zig-zau'
Wafd (Egypt. pol. party)	wäft'	wahft'
wafdist	wäf'-dĭst	wahf'-dist

A member of the *Wafd*, wäft' [wahft'], an Egyptian political party.

| Wageningen (Neth.) | wä'-k(h)ə-nĭng'-ən | wah'-k(h)uh-ning'-uhn |
| Wagga Wagga (Austral.) | wô'-gə | waw'-guh |

When pronounced, the name is usually thus shortened from wô'-gə wô'-gə [waw'-guh waw'-guh].

Wagina (Oc., Solomons)	wä-gĭn'-ä	wah-gin'-ah
Wahlhausen (Ger.)	väl-hou'-zən	vahl-hau'-zuhn
Waigeo (NEI)	wī-gē'-ô	wai-geh'-o
Wailu (Oc., New Caledonia)	wä-ē'-lōō	wah-ee'-loo
Waingapoe *or* Waingapu (NEI, Solomons)	wīn-gä'-pōō	wain-gah'-poo
Waiseron (NEI)	wī'-sə-rôn	wai'-suh-ron

Waithayakon, Prince Wan (Siam. diplomat) See *Wan Waithayakon*.

Wakasugi, Kaname (Jap. diplomat)	wä-kä'-sōō-gē, kä-nä'-mĕ'	wah-kah'-soo-gee, kah-nah'-meh'
Wakayama (Jap.)	wä-kä'-yä-mä	wah-kah'-yah-mah
Wakde (NEI, isl.)	wäk'-də	wahk'-duh
Wakkanai (Jap.)	wäk-kä'-nī	wahk-kah'-nai
Walachia (Rum.)	*Eng.* wŏ-lā'-kyə	wo-lay'-kyuh

Rumanian *Muntenia*, mŏŏn-tĕ'-nyä [mun-teh'-nyah].

| Walbrzych (Ger. >? Pol.) | väl'-bzhĭk(h) | vahl'-bzhik(h) |

German *Waldenburg*, q.v.

Walcheren (Neth., isl.)	wäl'-k(h)ə-rən	wahl'-k(h)uh-ruhn
Walckenaer *or* Valckenaar (NEI, bay)	wäl'-kə-när'	wahl'-kuh-nahr'
Wałcz (Ger. >Pol.)	välch'	vahlch'

German *Deutsch Krone*, q.v.

| Waldenburg (Ger. > ?Pol.) | väl'-dən-bŏŏrk(h) | vahl'-duhn-burk(h) |

Polish *Walbrzych*, q.v.

| Waldniel (Ger.) | vält'-nēl | vahlt'-neel |
| Waldshut (Ger.) | välts'-hōōt | vahlts'-hoot |

Walk (Est., Latvia) See *Valk*.

Wallaroo (Austral.)	wŏl-ə-rōō'	wol-uh-roo'
Wallendorf (Ger.)	väl'-ən-dôrf	vahl'-uhn-dorf
Wallerstadten (Ger.)	väl'-ər-shtät-ən	vahl'-uhr-shtaht-uhn
Wallgren, Mon C. (U.S. senator)	wôl'-grĕn, mŏn'	wawl'-gren, mon'

| Walter, Bruno (Ger. musician) | väl'-tər, brōō'-nō | vahl'-tuhr, broo'-noh |
| Walvis Bay (S.W. Afr.) | wôl'-vĭs | wol'-vis |

Also called *Walfish Bay*, wôl'-fĭsh [wol'-fish].

| Wamel (Neth.) | wä'-məl | wah'-muhl |
| wan | wän | wahn |

An element, meaning *gulf* or *bay*, in Japanese place names.

Wan-an (Ch. Kiangsi)	wän-än	wahn-ahn
Wanawana (Oc., Solomons)	wä-nä-wä'-nä	wah-nah-wah'-nah
Wangaratta (Austral.)	wăng'-gə-răt'-ə	wang'-guh-rat'-uh
Wang Ch'ung-hui (Ch. polit.)	wäng chŏŏng-whā	wahng chung-whay
Wang-kiang (Ch., Anhwei)	wäng-jyäng	wahng-jyahng
Wang Shih-chieh (Ch. polit)	wäng shû-jyĕ	wahng shuh-jyeh
Wan-hsien (Ch., Szechwan)	wän-shyĕn	wahn-shyen
Wanne Eickel (Ger.)	vän'-ə ĭk'-əl	vahn'-uh aik'-uhl
Wan-nien (Ch., Kiangsi)	wän-nyĕn	wahn-nyen
Wan-t'ing (Ch., Yünnan)	wän-tĭng	wahn-ting
Wan-tsai (Ch., Kiangsi)	wän-dzī	wahn-dzai
Wan Waithayakon, Prince (Siam. diplomat)	wän' wī'-tə-yä-gôn'	wahn' wai'-tuh-yah-gon'
Wappingers Falls (N.Y.)	wŏp'-ĭn-jərz	wop'-in-juhrz
Warazup (Burma)	wä-rä-zŭp'	wah-rah-zuhp'
Wardha (India)	wär'-də	wahr'-duh
Waremme (Belg.)	vä-rĕm'	vah-rem'
Wareo (New Guinea)	wä-rĕ'-ô	wah-reh'-o
Warmenhuizen (Neth.)	wär'-mən-hûî'-zən	wahr'-muhn-hœi'-zuhn
warmonger	wôr'-mŭng-gər	wawr'-muhng-guhr
Warnaffe, Charles du Bus de (Belg. leader)	vär-näf', shärl' dü büs' də	vahr-nahf', shahrl' dü büs' duh
Warnambool (Austral.)	wôr'-nəm-bōōl	wor'-nuhm-bool
Warnsdorf (Cz.)	*Ger.* värns'-dôrf	vahrns'-dorf

Czech *Varnsdorf*, q.v.

Warnsveld (Neth.)	wärns'-vĕlt	wahrns'-velt
Warong (Burma)	wä-rōng'	wah-rohng'
Warren, Avra Milvin (Am. diplomat)	wär'-ən, ā'-vrə mĭl'-vĭn	wahr'-uhn, ay'-vruh mil'-vin
Warsaw (Pol.)	*Eng.* wôr'-sô	wor'-saw

Polish *Warszawa*, vär-shä'-vä [vahr-shah'-vah].

Warszawa (Pol.)   See *Warsaw.*

Warta (Pol., Ger., riv.)   vär'-tä   vahr'-tah·
  Russian spelling *Varta.* German *Warthe,* vär'-tə [vahr'-tuh].

Warthe (Ger., Pol., riv.)   vär'-tə   vahr'-tuh
  Polish *Warta,* vär'-tä [vahr'-tah].

Warwick (Eng., R.I., Va.)   wä'-rĭk *or* wôr'-ĭk   wah'-rik *or* wor'-ik
  Elsewhere usually wôr'-wĭk [wor'-wik].

Wasatch (Utah)   wô'-săch   waw'-sach

Washoe (Mont., Nev.)   wŏsh'-ō   wosh'-oh

Wasielewski, Thad F.   vä-shă-lĕf'-skĭ, thăd'   vah-sha-lef'-ski, thad'
  (U.S. representative)

Wasile (NEI)   wä-sē'-lĕ   wah-see'-leh

Wasilewska, Wanda   vä-sĭ-lĕf'-skä,   vah-si-lef'-skah,
  (Pol. Rus. novelist)   vän'-dä   vahn'-dah

Wassenaar (Neth.)   wäs'-ə-när   wahs'-uh-nahr

Watdek (Oc.)   wät'-dĕk   waht'-dek

Wateringen (Neth.)   wä'-tə-rĭng-ən   wah'-tuh-ring-uhn

Waterloo   *Eng.* wô'-tər-lōō'   wa'w-tuhr-loo'
    Flem. wä-tər-lō'   wah-tuhr-loh'

Watom (Oc., New Brit.)   wä-tôm'   wah-tom'

Wattenscheid (Ger.)   vät'-ən-shĭt   vaht'-uhn-shait

Waugh (Eng. name)   wô'   waw'

Waukegan (Ill.)   wô-kē'-gən   waw-kee'-guhn

Waukesha (Wis.)   wô'-kə-shô   waw'-kuh-shaw

Wavell, Sir Archibald   wā'-vəl   way'-vuhl
  (Br. general)

Waw (Burma)   wô'   waw'

Waxahachie (Tex.)   wŏk'-sə-hăch'-ĭ   wok'-suh-hach'-i

Waxweiler (Ger.)   väks'-vī-lər   vahks'-vai-luhr

We (NEI, Sumatra, isl.)   wä'   way'

Wedde (Neth.)   wĕd'-ə   wed'-uh

Wedemeyer, Albert   wĕd'-ə-mī'-ər,   wed'-uh-mai'-uhr,
  Coady (U.S. general)   kō'-dĭ   koh'-di

Weel (Neth.)   wāl'   wayl'

Weerd (Neth.)   wārt'   wayrt'

Weerseloo (Neth.)   wār'-sə-lō   wayr'-suh-loh

Weesp (Neth.)   wāsp'   waysp'

Weesperkarspel (Neth.)   wäs'-pər-kär'-spəl   ways'-puhr-kahr'-
    spuhl

Weeze (Ger.)   vā'-tsə   vay'-tsuh

Węgobork (Ger. >Pol.)   văN-gô'-bôrk   vaN-go'-bork
  German *Angerburg,* q.v.

Węgrów (Pol.)   văN'-grŏŏf   vaN'-gruf
  Russian *Vengrov,* vĕn'-grŏf [ven'-grof].

Wehrmacht (Ger., "army")	*Eng.* vĕr'-mäkt	vehr'-mahkt
	Ger. vär'-mäk(h)t	vayr'-mahk(h)t
Weichel, Alvin F. (U.S. representative)	wī'-kĕl	wai'-kel
Weichsel (Pol., riv.) See *Vistula*.		
Weidenau (Ger.)	vī'-də-nou	vai'-duh-nau
Wei-hai-wei (Ch., Shantung)	wä-hī-wä	way-hai-way
Weilburg (Ger.)	vīl'-bŏŏrk(h)	vail'-burk(h)
Weiler	vī'-lər	vai'-luhr

A German word, meaning *hamlet*, common in Alsatian place names and rendered in French -*viller*, -vē-lĕr' [-vee-lehr'].

Wei Li-huang (Ch. general)	wä lē-whäng	way lee-whahng
Weimar (Ger.)	vī'-mär	vai'-mahr
Wei-ning (Ch., Kweichow)	wä-nĭng	way-ning
Weir, Ernest T. (Am. businessman)	wĭr'	wir'
Weirton (Pa.)	wĭr'-tən	wir'-tuhn
Weiss, Samuel A. (U.S. representative)	wīz'	waiz'
Weissenburg (Ger.)	vīs'-ən-bŏŏrk(h)	vais'-uhn-burk(h)
Weissensee (Ger.)	vīs'-ən-zā'	vais'-uhn-zay'
Weissenstein (Est.)	*Ger.* vī'-sən-shtĭn	vai'-suhn-shtain
	Rus. vä'-sĕn-stän	vay'-sen-stayn

Estonian *Paide*, q.v.

Weisskopf, Victor F. (Am. scientist)	wīs'-kŏpf	wais'-kopf
Weisweiler (Ger.)	vīs'-vī-lər	vais'-vai-luhr
Wei Tao-ming (Ch. polit.)	wä dou-mĭng	way dau-ming
Weiterstadt (Ger.)	vī'-tər-shtät	vai'-tuhr-shtaht
Weizmann, Chaim (Zionist leader)	vīts'-män, k(h)ä'-yĭm'	vaits'-mahn, k(h)ah'-yim'
Wejherowo (Pol.)	vä-hĕ-rô'-vô	vay-heh-ro'-vo
Wels (Austria)	vĕls'	vels'
Welz (Ger.)	vĕlts'	velts'
Wemeldinge (Neth.)	wä'-məl-dĭng'-ə	way'-muhl-ding'-uh
Wenatchee (Wash.)	wə-năch'-ĭ	wuh-nach'-i
Wenau (Ger.)	vä'-nou	vay'-nau
Wên-chow (Ch., Chekiang)	*Eng.* wĕn-chou	wen-chau
	Ch. wŭn-jō	wuhn-joh

Also called *Yung-chia*, q.v.

Wenden (Latvia) Latvian *Cēsis*, q.v.	*Ger.* vĕn'-dən	ven'-duhn
Wene, Elmer H. (U.S. representative)	wēn'	ween'
Werbig (Ger.)	vĕr'-bĭk(h)	vehr'-bik(h)
Werden (Ger.)	vĕr'-dən	vehr'-duhn
Werdohl (Ger.)	vĕr-dōl'	vehr-dohl'
Werkendam (Neth.)	wĕr'-kən-däm'	wehr'-kuhn-dahm'
Werne (Ger.)	vĕr'-nə	vehr'-nuh
Werneuchen (Ger.)	vĕr'-noi-k(h)ən	vehr'-noi-k(h)uhn
Wernigerode (Ger.)	vĕr'-nĭ-gə-rō'-də	vehr'-nih-guh-roh'- duh
Werra (Ger., riv.)	vĕr'-ä	vehr'-ah
Werro (Est.) Estonian *Võru*, q.v.	*Rus.* vĕr'-rŏ	vehr'-ro
Wervershoof (Neth.)	wĕr'-vərs-hōf	wehr'-vuhrs-hohf
Wervicq (Belg.) Also spelled *Wervick*.	vĕr-vēk'	vehr-veek'
Werzhbolovo (Lith.) Lithuanian *Virbalis*, q.v.	*Rus.* vĕrzh'-bŏ-lŏ'-vŏ	vehrzh'-bo-lo'-vo
Wesel (Ger.)	vā'-zəl	vay'-zuhl
Wesenberg (Est.) Estonian *Rakvere*, q.v.	*Ger.* vā'-zən-bĕrk(h)	vay'-zuhn-behrk(h)
Weser (Ger., riv.)	vā'-zər	vay'-zuhr
Wesermuende *or* Wesermünde (Ger.)	vā'-zər-mün'-də	vay'-zuhr-mün'-duh
Weshka (Egypt)	wŭsh'-kä	wuhsh'-kah
Wessel (Austral., cape, isls.)	wĕs'-əl	wes'-uhl
West Allis (Wis.)	wĕst' ăl'-ĭs	west' al'-is
West Bromwich (Eng.)	brŭm'-ĭch *or* -ĭj *or* brŏm'-ĭch *or* -ĭj	brum'-ich *or* -ij brom'-ich *or* -ij
Westdongeradeel (Neth.)	wĕst'-dông-ə-rä-dāl'	west'-dong-uh-rah- dayl'
Westdorpe (Neth.)	wĕst-dôr'-pə	west-dor'-puh
Westerbork (Neth.)	wĕs'-tər-bôrk	wes'-tuhr-bork
Westerdam (Neth.)	wĕs'-tər-däm'	wes'-tuhr-dahm'
Westervoort (Neth.)	wĕs'-tər-vōrt	wes'-tuhr-vohrt
Westfalen (Ger.)	vĕst-fä'-lən	vest-fah'-luhn
West Indies. See *Indies*.		
Westkapelle (Neth.)	wĕst'-kä-pĕl'-ə	west'-kah-pel'-uh
West Meath (Eire)	wĕst' mēth'	west' meeth'

Westmoreland	*Eng.*, *Va.* wĕst'-mər-lənd	west'-muhr-luhnd
	N. H. wĕst'-mər-lănd'	west'-muhr-land'
	Pa. wĕst-mōr'-lənd	west-mohr'-luhnd
Weston (Borneo)	wĕs'-tən	wes'-tuhn
Westphalia (Ger.)	*Eng.* wĕst-fā'-lĭ-ə	west-fay'-li-uh
German *Westfalen*, q.v.		
Weststellingwerf (Neth.)	wĕst'-stĕl-ĭng-wĕrf'	west'-stel-ing-wehrf'
Westzaan (Neth.)	wĕst-zän'	west-zahn'
Wetar (NEI)	wĕt'-är	wet'-ahr
Wettin (Ger.)	vĕ-tēn'	veh-teen'
Wetzlar (Ger.)	vĕts'-lär	vets'-lahr
Wewak (N.E. New Guinea)	wĕ'-wäk	weh'-wahk

There is a possible English pronunciation wē'-wăk [wee'-wak].

Weyerhauser *or* Weyer-haeuser (Am. lumbermen)	wī'-ər-hou'-zər	wai'-uhr-hau'-zuhr
Weygand, Maxime (Fr. gen.)	vĕ-gäN', mäk-sēm'	veh-gahN', mahk-seem'
Whelchel (Ga. name)	wĭl'-kĭ *or* wĕl'-chĕl	wil'-ki *or* wel'-chel
Whelchel, B. Frank (U.S. representative)	wĕl'-chĕl	wel'-chel
Wherry, Kenneth S. (U.S. senator)	whĕr'-ĭ	whehr'-i

White, Margaret Bourke (Am. photographer) See *Bourke White*.
White Russia   See *Belorussia*.

Wiart, Henri Carton de (Belg. polit.)	vyär', äN-rē' kär-tôN' də	vyahr', ahN-ree' kahr-toN' duh
Wickersham, Victor (U.S. representative)	wĭk'-ər-shăm	wik'-uhr-sham
Wickham (Eng. name)	wĭk'-əm	wik'-uhm
Wicklow (Eire)	wĭk'-lō	wik'-loh
Widener (family name)	wīd'-nər	waid'-nuhr
Widuchowo (Ger. > Pol.)	vĭ-dŏŏ-hô'-vô	vi-du-ho'-vo
German *Fiddichow*, q.v.		
Wiechen (Neth.)	wē'-k(h)ən	wee'-k(h)uhn
Wied (Ger., riv.)	vēt'	veet'
Wieliczka (Pol.)	vyĕ-lēch'-kä	vyeh-leech'-kah
Wieluń (Pol.)	vyĕ'-lŏŏn(y)	vyeh'-lun(y)
Russian *Velyun*, vĕ'-lyŏŏn(y) [veh'-lyoon(y)].		
Wien (Austria)	vēn'	veen'
English *Vienna*, q.v.		
Wiencke (NEI)	wēng'-kə	weeng'-kuh

Wiener Neustadt (Austria)	vē′-nər noi′-shtät	vee′-nuhr noi′-shtaht
Wieprz (Pol., riv.)	vyĕpsh′	vyepsh′
Russian *Vepr*, vĕp′r [vep′r].		
Wierden (Neth.)	wēr′-dən	weer′-duhn
Wieringen (Neth.)	wē′-rĭng-ən	wee′-ring-uhn
Wieringermeer Polder (Neth.)	wē′-rĭng-ər-mār′ pôl′-dər	wee′-ring-uhr-mayr′ pol′-duhr
Wierzbnik (Pol.)	vyĕzh′-bnĭk	vyezh′-bnik
Russian *Virzhbnik*, vērsh′-bnĭk [veersh′-bnik].		
Wietze (Ger.)	vē′-tsə	vee′-tsuh
Wieuwerd (Neth.)	wē′-wərt	wee′-wuhrt
Wigglesworth, Richard B. (U.S. representative)	wĭg′-əlz-wûrth	wig′-uhlz-wuhrth
Wigry (Pol.)	vē′-grĭ	vee′-gri
Russian spelling *Vigri*.		
Wije (Neth.)	wī′-ə	wai′-uh
wijk	wĭk′	waik′
An element, meaning *town*, in Dutch place names.		
Wijk aan Zee (Neth.)	wĭk′ än zā′	waik′ ahn zay′
Wijk bij Duurstede (Neth.)	wĭk′ bī dür′-stā′-də	waik′ bai dür′-stay′-duh
Wijmbritseradeel (Neth.)	wĭm-brĭt′-sə-rä-dāl′	waim-brit′-suh-rah-dayl′
Wilanów (Pol.)	vē-lä′-nŏŏf	vee-lah′-nuf
Russian *Vilyanov*, vē-lyä′-nŏf [vee-lyah′-nof].		
Wilcannia (Austral.)	wĭl-kăn′-yə	wil-kan′-yuh
Wildervank (Neth.)	wĭl′-dər-vänk	wil′-duhr-vahnk
Wilejka (Pol. > Rus.)	vĭ-lä′-kä	vi-lay′-kah
Russian spelling *Vileika*.		
Wilhelmshaven (Ger.)	*Eng.* vĭl′-hĕlmz-hä′-vən	vil′-helmz-hah′-vuhn
	Ger. vĭl′-hĕlms-hä′-fən	vil′-helms-hah′-fuhn
Wilja (Pol. > Rus., riv.) See *Viliya*.		
Wilkes Barre (Pa.)	wĭlks′ băr′-ĭ	wilks′ behr′-i
Wilkomir (Lith.)	*Rus.* vēl′(y)-kŏ-mĭr	veel′(y)-ko-mihr
Lithuanian *Ukmergè*, q.v.		
Wilkowischki (Lith.)	*Rus.* vēl′(y)-kŏ-vē′-shkĭ	veel′(y)-ko-vee′-shki
Lithuanian *Vilkaviškis*, q.v.		
Willamette (Ore., riv.)	wĭ-lăm′-ĭt	wi-lam′-it
Willapa (Wash.)	wĭl′-ə-pä	wil′-uh-pah
Willaumez (Oc., New Britian)	wĭl-lou′-mĕz	wil-lau′-mez

Willemstad (Neth.; W.I.)	wĭl′-əm-stät	wil′-uhm-staht
Willey, Earle D. (U.S. representative)	wĭl′-ĭ	wil′-i
Willkie, Wendell L. (Am. polit.)	wĭl′-kĭ	wil′-ki
Wilno (Pol. >Rus.)	*Eng.* vĭl′-nə	vil′-nuh
	Pol. vēl′-nȏ	veel′-no

Russian *Vilna*, vēl′(y)-nä [veel′(y)-nah]. Lithuanian *Vilnyus*, vĭl′-nĭ-ȏȯs [vil′-ni-us].

Wiltz (Luxem.)	vĭlts′	vilts′
Wilwerwiltz (Luxem.)	vĭl′-vər-vĭlts	vil′-vuhr-vilts
Wimereux (Fr.)	vēm-rŭ′	veem-rœ′
Winant, John G. (U.S. ambassador)	wĭn′-ənt	wain′-uhnt
Windau (Latvia)	*Ger.* vĭn′-dou	vin′-dau

Latvian *Ventspils*, q.v. Russian *Vindava*, q.v.

Winder (Ga.)	wīn′-dər	wain′-duhr
Windorah (Austral.)	wĭn-dȏ′-rə	win-doh′-ruh
Winiewicz, Józef (Pol. diplomat)	vĭ-nyĕ′-vĭch, yȯȯ′-zĕf	vi-nyeh′-vich, yu′-zef
Winnebago (Wis., lake)	wĭn′-ə-bā′-gō	win′-uh-bay′-goh
Winnemucca (Nev.)	wĭn′-ə-mŭk′-ə	win′-uh-muhk′-uh
Winnepesaukee (N.H., lake)	wĭn′-ə-pə-sȏ′-kĭ	win′-uh-puh-saw′-ki
Winnweiler (Ger.)	vĭn′-vī-lər	vin′-vai-luhr
Winschoten (Neth.)	wĭn′-sk(h)ō-tən	win′-sk(h)oh-tuhn
Winterswijk (Neth.)	wĭn′-tərs-wĭk	win′-tuhrs-waik
Winterthur (Switz.)	vĭn′-tər-tȯȯr	vin′-tuhr-tur
Wisła (Pol., riv.) See *Vistula.*		
Wisłok (Pol., riv.)	vē′-slȏk	vee′-slok
Wisłoka (Pol., riv.)	vĭ-slȏ′-kä	vi-slo′-kah
Wismar (Ger.)	vĭs′-mär	vis′-mahr
Wissant (Fr.)	vē-säN′	vee-sahN′
Wissembourg (Fr.)	vē-säN-bōȯr′	vee-sahN-boor′
Wisserkerke (Neth.)	wĭs′-ə-kĕr′-kə	wis′-uh-kehr′-kuh
Wisznia (Pol., riv.)	vēsh′-nyä	veesh′-nyah
Witos, Andrzej (Pol. polit.)	vē′-tôs, än′-jä	vee′-tos, ahn′-jay
Witos, Wincenty (Pol. polit.)	vē′-tôs, vĭn-tsĕn′-tĭ	vee′-tos, vin-tsen′-tih
Wittem (Neth.)	wĭt′-əm	wit′-uhm
Witten (Ger.)	vĭt′-ən	vit′-uhn
Wittenberg (Ger.)	*Eng.* wĭt′-ən-bûrg	wit′-uhn-buhrg
	Ger. vĭt′-ən-bĕrk(h)	vit′-uhn-behrk(h)

Wittlich (Ger.)	vĭt'-lĭk(h)	vit'-lik(h)
Wkra (Pol., riv.)	fkrä'	fkrah'

Russian spelling *Vkra*. Upper reaches called *Działdówka*, q.v.

Włocławek (Pol.)	vlô-tslä'-věk	vlo-tslah'-vek

Russian *Vlotslavsk*, vlŏ-tslävsk' [vlo-tslahvsk'].

Włodawa (Pol.)	vlô-dä'-vä	vlo-dah'-vah

Russian spelling *Vlodava*.

Włodzimierz (Pol. >Rus.)	vlô-jē'-myĕzh	vlo-jee'-myezh

Russian *Vladimir Volinski*, vlä-dē'-mĭr vŏ-lēn'-skĭ [vlah-dee'-mihr vo-leen'-ski].

Włoszczowa (Pol.)	vlô-shchô'-vä	vlo-shcho'-vah

Russian spelling *Vloshchova*.

Wobbegong (Austral.)	wŏb'-ə-gŏng	wob'-uh-gong

This name, which seems native, is said to be derived from *woebegone*.

Woburn (Mass.)	wō'-bərn *or* wōō'-	woh'-buhrn *or* woo'-
Wocław (Danzig >Pol.)	vôts'-läf	vots'-lahf

German spelling *Wotzlaff*.

Woensdrecht (Neth.)	wōōns'-drĕk(h)t	woons'-drek(h)t
Woerden (Neth.)	wōōr'-dən	woor'-duhn
Woerth (Fr.)	vûrt'	vœrt'
Woerther See (Austria, lake)	vûr'-tər zä'	vœr'-tuhr zay'
Woëvre (Fr.)	vô-ĕv'r	vo-ev'r
Wognum (Neth.)	wôk(h)'-nəm	wok(h)'-nuhm
Wolbrom (Pol.)	vôl'-brôm	vol'-brom
Wolcott, Jesse P. (U.S. representative)	wôl'-kət, jĕs'-ĭ	wawl'-kuht, jes'-i
Wold, Terje (Nor. polit.)	vôl', tĕr'-yə	vol', tehr'-yuh
Woleai (Oc., Carolines)	wô-lĕ-ī'	wo-leh-ai'
Wolfaartsdijk (Neth.)	wôl'-färts-dīk'	wol'-fahrts-daik'
Wolfenden, James (U.S. representative)	wŏōl'-fən-dən	wul'-fuhn-duhn
Wolfrathausen (Ger.)	vôlf'-rät-hou'-zən	volf'-rät-hau'-zuhn
Wołkowysk (Pol. >Rus.)	vôl-kô'-vĭsk	vol-ko'-visk

Russian *Volkovisk*, vŏl-kŏ-vēsk' [vol-ko-veesk'].

Wollin (Ger. >Pol.)	vô-lēn'	vo-leen'

Polish *Wolyń*, q.v.

Wollongong (Austral.)	wŏōl'-ən-gŏng *or* wŭl'-	wul'-uhn-gong *or* wuhl'-
Wollseifen (Ger.)	vôl'-zī-fən	vol'-zai-fuhn
Wolmar (Latvia)	*Ger.* vôl'-mär	vol'-mahr
	Rus. vôl'(y)-mär	vol'(y)-mahr

Latvian *Valmiera*, q.v.

Wołomin (Pol.)	vô-lô'-mĭn	vo-lo'-min

Wołożyn (Pol. >Rus.)	vô-lô′-zhĭn	vo-lo′-zhin
Russian spelling *Volozhin*.		
Wolsztyn (Pol.)	vôl′-shtĭn	vol′-shtin
Wolvega (Neth.)	wôl′-və-k(h)ä	wol′-vuh-k(h)ah
Wolverton, Charles	wŏŏl′-vər-tən	wul′-vuhr-tuhn
(U.S. representative)		
Wołyń (Ger. >Pol.)	vô′-lĭn(y)	vo′-lin(y)
German *Wollin*, q.v.		
Wong Wên-yü (Ch. polit.)	wông wŭn-yü	wong wuhn-yü
Wonseradeel (Neth.)	wôn′-sə-rä-däl′	won′-suh-rah-dayl′
Wonthaggi (Austral.)	wŏn-thăg′-ĭ	won-thag′-i
Woodlark (Oc.) See *Murua*.		
Woodruff, Roy O.	wŏŏd′-rŭf	wud′-ruhf
(U.S. representative)		
Woodrum, Clifton A.	wŏŏd′-rəm	wud′-ruhm
(U.S. representative)		
Wooster (Ohio)	wŏŏs′-tər	wus′-tuhr
Worcester (U.S., Eng.)	wŏŏs′-tər	wus′-tuhr
Workum (Neth.)	wôr′-kəm	wor′-kuhm
Worley, Eugene	wûr′-lĭ	wuhr′-li
(U.S. representative)		
Wormerveer (Neth.)	wôr′-mər-vär′	wor′-muhr-vayr′
Worms (Est., isl.)	*Ger., Rus.* vôrms′	vorms′
Estonian *Vormsi*, q.v.		
Worms (Ger.)	*Eng.* wûrmz′	wuhrmz′
	Ger. vôrms′	vorms′
Wörther See (Austria,	vûr′-tər zā′	vœr′-tuhr zay′
lake)		
Wotho (Oc., Marshalls)	wôt′-hô	wot′-ho
Wotje (Oc., Marshalls)	wôt′-jĕ	wot′-jeh
Wotzlaff (Danzig >Pol.) See *Wocław*.		
Woubrugge (Neth.)	wou-brûk(h)′-ə	wau-brœk(h)′-uh
Woudenberg (Neth.)	wou′-dən-bĕrk(h)	wau′-duhn-behrk(h)
Wouk, Herman (Am.	wŏk′	wohk′
author)		
Wouw (Neth.)	wou′	wau′
Wrangell (Alaska, Attu)	*Eng.* răng′-gəl	rang′-guhl
	Rus. vrän′-gĕl(y)	vrahn′-gel(y)
Wriezen (Ger.)	vrē′-tsən	vree′-tsuhn
Wrocław (Ger. >? Pol.) See *Breslau*.		
Wronki (Pol.)	vrôn′-kĭ	vron′-ki
Września (Pol.)	vzhĕsh′-nyä	vzhesh′-nyah
Wrzeszcz (Danzig >Pol.)	vzhĕshch′	vzheshch′
German *Langfuhr*, läng′-fōōr [lahng′-foor].		

Wu-ch'ang (Ch., Hupeh)	wōō-chäng	woo-chahng
Wu-chin (Ch., Kiangsi)	wōō-jĭn	woo-jin
Also called *Ch'ang-chow*, q.v.		
Wu-chow (Ch.,	*Eng.* wōō-chou	woo-chau
Kwangsi)	*Ch.* wōō-jō	woo-joh
Wuelfrath (Ger.)	vülf'-rät	vülf'-raht
Wuerm (Ger.)	vürm'	vürm'
Wuerselen (Ger.)	vür'-sə-lən	vür'-suh-luhn
Wuerttemberg	*Eng.* wûr'-təm-bûrg	wuhr'-tuhm-buhrg
	Ger. vür'-təm-bĕrk(h)	vür'-tuhm-behrk(h)
Wuerzburg (Ger.)	*Eng.* wûrts'-bûrg	wuhrts'-buhrg
	Ger. vürts'-bōŏrk(h)	vürts'-burk(h)
Wu-hu (Ch., Anhwei)	wōō-hōō	woo-hoo
Wu-i (Ch.) See *Wu-yi*.		
Wu-i-shan (Ch., Che-kiang, Kiangsi, mts.)	wōō-ē-shän	woo-ee-shahn
Wu-kang (Ch., Hunan)	wōō-gäng	woo-gahng
Wülfrath (Ger.)	vülf'-rät	vülf'-raht
Wu-ning (Ch., Kiangsi)	wōō-nĭng	woo-ning
Wuntho (Burma)	wŏŏn'-*thō*'	wun'-*thoh*'
Wupper (Ger., riv.)	vŏŏp'-ər	vup'-uhr
Wuppertal (Ger.)	vŏŏp'-ər-täl	vup'-uhr-tahl
Würm (Ger.)	vürm'	vürm'
Würselen (Ger.)	vür'-sə-lən	vür'-suh-luhn
Württemberg (Ger.) See *Wuerttemberg*.		
Würzburg (Ger.) See *Wuerzburg*.		
Wurzen (Ger.)	vŏŏrts'-ən	vurts'-uhn
Wu-shan (Ch., Szechwan)	wōō-shän	woo-shahn
Wusterhausen (Ger.)	vōōs'-tər-hou'-zən	voos'-tuhr-hau'-zuhn
Wu-t'ang (Ch., Chekiang)	wōō-täng	woo-tahng
Wu-ti Ho *or* Wu-ti River (Ch., Yünnan)	wōō-dē hŭ	woo-dee huh
Wu-yi (Ch., Chekiang)	wōō-yē	woo-yee
Also spelled *Wu-i*.		
Wyalusing (Pa.)	wī'-ə-lōō'-sĭng	wai'-uh-loo'-sing
Wycech, Czesław (Pol. polit.)	vĭ'-tsĕk(h), chĕs'-läf	vi'-tsek(h), ches'-lahf
Wygmael (Belg.)	wīk(h)'-mäl	waik(h)'-mahl
Wygonowskie, Jezioro (Pol., lake)	vĭ-gô-nôf'-skyĕ, yĕ-zhô'-rô	vi-go-nof'-skyeh, yeh-zho'-ro
Russian *Vigonovskoe, Ozero*,	vē'-gŏ-nôf-skŏ-yĕ, ô'-zĕ-rŏ [vee'-go-nof-sko-yeh, o'-zeh-ro].	

Wyndham (Austral.)	wĭn′-dəm	win′-duhm
Wynyard (Austral.)	wĭn′-yərd	win′-yuhrd
Wyoming (U.S.)	wī-ō′-mĭng	wai-oh′-ming

Occasionally stressed on the first syllable.

Wysokie Mazowieckie	vĭ-sô′-kyĕ mä-zô-	vi-so′-kyeh mah-zo-
(Pol.)	vyĕ′-tskyĕ	vyeh′-tskyeh

Russian *Mazovetsk*, mä-zŏ-vĕtsk′ [mah-zo-vetsk′].

Wyszków (Pol.)	vĭsh′-kō͝of	vish′-kuf

Russian *Vishkov*, vĭsh′-kŏf [vish′-kof].

Wyszogród (Pol.)	vĭ-shô′-grō͝ot	vi-sho′-grut

Russian *Vishogrod*, vĭ-shô′-grŏt [vi-sho′-grot].

Wythe (Va.)	wĭth′	with′
Wytheville (Va.)	wĭth′-vĭl	with′-vil

Xanten (Ger.)	ksän′-tən	ksahn′-tuhn
Xavier	*Eng.* zā′-vyər	zay′-vyuhr
	or zăv′-ĭ-ər	zav′-i-uhr
Xenia (Ohio)	zē′-nyə	zee′-nyuh
Xeres (Sp.) See *Jerez*.		
Xertigny (Fr.)	sĕr-tē-nyē′	sehr-tee-nyee′
Xions (Pol.) See *Książ*.		
Xochimilco (Mex.)	sô-chē-mēl′-kô	so-chee-meel′-ko
	or shô-	*or* sho-
Xoconoxtle (Mex.)	sô-kô-nôs′-tlĕ	so-ko-nos′-tleh
Xyda (Crete)	ksē-dä′	ksee-dah′

y

In Dutch *y* is interchangeable with *ij* and *ei*. A consultant
may have to look for all three forms before he finds his word.

Yabbenohr (Oc., Kwajalein)	yäb′-bə-nōr	yahb′-buh-nohr
Yablonovy (Rus., mts.)	yä′-blŏ-nŏ-vĭ	yah′-blo-no-vi
Yablunkov (Cz.)	yä′-blō͞on-kôf	yah′-bloon-kof
Yaeju Dake (Okinawa, Japan)	yä-ĕ′-jō͞o dä′-kĕ	yah-eh′-joo dah′-keh
Yafa (Pal.) See *Jaffa*.		
Yagur (Pal.)	yä-gō͞or′	yah-goor′
Yahya Muhammad Hamid ed Din (Ruler of the Yemen)	yä-yä′ mō͞o-hăm′-məd hă-mēd′ ĕd dēn′	yah-yah′ mu-ham′- muhd ha-meed′ ed deen′
Yaila (Rus., mts.)	yī′-lä′	yai′-lah′
Yakima (Wash.)	yăk′-ə-mə	yak′-uh-muh
Yakovlev, Aleksandr S. (Rus. general)	yä′-kŏv-lĕf, ä-lĕ-ksän′-dər	yah′-kov-lef, ah-leh-ksahn′-duhr

Yakutat (Alaska)	yăk′-ə-tăt′	yak′-uh-tat′
	or yŭk′-ə-tăt′	yuhk′-uh-tat′
Yalman, Ahmed Emin	yäl′-män, äk(h)-mĕd′	yahl′-mahn, ahk(h)-
(Turk. editor)	ä-mēn′	med′ ay-meen′
Yalta (Rus.)	yäl′-tä	yahl′-tah
Yalutorovsk (Rus.)	yä-lōō-tô′-rŏfsk	yah-loo-to′-rofsk
yama	yä-mä	yah-mah

An element, meaning *mountain*, in Japanese place names.

Yamada (Jap.)	yä-mä′-dä′	yah-mah′-dah′
Yamagata (Jap.)	yä-mä′-gä-tä	yah-mah′-gah-tah
Yamaguchi (Jap.)	yä-mä′-gōō-chē	yah-mah′-goo-chee
Yamanashi (Jap.)	yä-mä′-nä-shē	yah-mah′-nah-shee
Yamazaki (Jap. name)	yä-mä′-zä-kē	yah-mah′-zah-kee
Yambol (Bulg.)	yäm′-bŏl(y)	yahm′-bol(y)
Yame (Oc., Bougainville)	yä-mĕ′	yah-meh′
Yamethin (Burma)	yə-mĕ′-*th*ĭn	yuh-meh′-*th*in
Yamna or Jamna	yäm′-nä′	yahm′-nah′
(NEI, isl.)		
Yampol (Rus.)	yäm′-pŏl(y)	yahm′-pol(y)
Yanagita (Jap.)	yä-nä′-gē′-tä′	yah-nah′-gee′-tah′
Yanam or Yanaon	yä-näm′	yah-nahm′
(Fr. India)	or yä-nä-ôN′	yah-nah-oN′
Yandoon (Burma)	yăn-dōōn′	yan-doon′
Yang-ch′ü (Ch., Shansi)	yäng-chü	yahng-chü

Also called *T'ai-yü-an*, q.v.

Yäng-lou-ssŭ (Ch.,	yäng-lō-sə	yahng-loh-suh
Hupeh)		
Yang-pi (Ch., Yünnan)	yäng-bē	yahng-bee
Yang-tz′e Kiang or	*Eng.* yăng-sē	yang-see
Yang-tz′e River (Ch.)	*Ch.* yäng-tsĕ	yahng-tseh

See *chiang or kiang* for the pronunciation if it is desired.
The use of *River* is usually preferable.

Yanina (Gr.) See *Ioanina*.

| Yanisyarvi (Fin. > Rus.) | yä′-nĭs-yär′-vĭ | yah′-nis-yahr′-vi |

Finnish *Jänisjärvi*, q.v.

Yanov (Pol.) See *Janów* and *Janów Podlaski*.

Yanovski, B. N.	yä-nôf′-skĭ	yah-nof′-ski
(Rus. scientist)		
Yantra (Bulg., riv.)	yän′-trä	yahn′-trah
Yaoundé (Fr. Cameroons)	yä-ōōn-dĕ′	yah-oon-deh′
Yap (Oc., Carolines)	yăp′ or yäp′	yap′ or yahp′
Yapen or Japen (NEI)	yä′-pən	yah′-puhn
Yarmolintsi (Rus.)	yär-mô′-lĭn-tsĭ	yahr-mo′-lin-tsi

Yaroslav (Pol.) See *Jarosław*.

Yartsevo (Rus.)	yär′-tsĕ-vŏ	yahr′-tseh-vo
Yarylgach (Rus.)	yä-rĭl-gäch′	yah-ril-gahch′
Yaselda (Pol. > Rus., riv.)	yä-sĕl′(y)-dä	yah-sel′(y)-dah

Polish *Jasiołda*, yä-shôl′-dä [yah-shol′-dah].

| Yashshera (Rus.) | yä′-shchĕ-rä | yah′-shcheh-rah |
| Yasinya (Cz. > Rus.) | yä′-sĭ-nyä | yah′-si-nyah |

Czech spelling *Jasiňa*. Hungarian *Kőrösmező*, kŭ′-rûsh-mĕ′-zû [kœ′-rœsh-meh′-zœ].

Yasuda (Jap., zaibatsu)	yä-sōō′-dä′	yah-soo′-dah′
Yasuhito, Chichibu no Miya (Jap. prince)	yä-sōō′-hē-tô, chē-chē′-bōō nô′ mē-yä	yah-soo′-hee-to, chee-chee′-boo no′ mee-yah
Yavapai (Ariz.)	yăv′-ə-pī	yav′-uh-pai
Yavino (Rus.)	yä′-vĭ-nŏ	yah′-vi-no
Yawata (Jap.)	yä-wä′-tä′	yah-wah′-tah′
Yawnghwe (Burma)	yông′-whä′	yawng′-whay′
Yazoo (Miss.)	yăz′-ōō	yaz′-oo
Yeadon (Pa.)	yā′-dən	yay′-duhn
yearling	yĭr′-lĭng *or* yûr′-	yihr′-ling *or* yuhr′-

Both pronunciations are well established in American usage.

Yeats, Wm. B. (Irish poet)	yāts′	yayts′
Yebawgyi (Burma)	yā-bô-jē′	yay-baw-jee′
Yedo (Jap.)	*Eng.* yĕd′-ō	yed′-oh
	Jap. ĕ-dô′	eh-do′

Modern *Tōkyō*, q.v.

Yefremov (Rus.)	yĕ-frĕ′-mŏf	yeh-freh′-mof
Yegorevsk (Rus.)	yĕ-gôr′-yĕfsk	yeh-gor′-yefsk
Yegorlyk (Rus.)	yĕ-gŏr-lwēk′	yeh-gor-lweek′
Yeisk (Rus.)	āsk′	aysk′
Yelansk (Rus.)	yĕ-länsk′	yeh-lahnsk′
Yelets (Rus.)	yĕ-lĕts′	yeh-lets′
Yelnya (Rus.)	yĕl′(y)-nyä	yel′(y)-nyah
Yelsk (Rus.)	yĕl(y)sk′	yel(y)sk′
Yemen (Arabia)	yĕm′-ən	yem′-uhn
Yen-an (Ch., Shensi)	yĕn-än	yen-ahn
Yenangyaung (Burma)	yä-nän-joung′	yay-nahn-jaung′
Yen-ch'ing (Ch., Sikang)	yĕn-chĭng	yen-ching
Yenikale (Rus.)	yĕ′-nĭ-kä′-lĕ	yeh′-ni-kah′-leh
Yen-ki *or* Yen-chi (Manchu.)	*Eng.* yĕn-kē	yen-kee
	Ch. yĕn-jē	yen-jee
Yenotaevsk (Rus.)	yĕ-nŏ-tä′-yĕfsk	yeh-no-tah′-yefsk
Yen-t'ai (Ch., Shantung)	yĕn-tĭ	yen-tai

Also called *Cheefoo*, q.v., and *Chih-fu*, q.v.

Yepifan (Rus.)	yĕ-pĭ-fän′(y)	yeh-pi-fahn′(y)
Yerevan (Rus.)	yĕ′-rĕ-vän′	yeh′-reh-vahn′
Also called *Erevan*, q.v.		
Yerres (Fr.)	yĕr′	yehr′
Yesagyo (Burma)	yā′-zə-jō′	yay′-zuh-joh′
Yeşilköy (Turk., Istanbul, airport)	yĕ-shēl′-kûĭ	yeh-sheel′-kœi
Ye-u (Burma)	yā-ōō′	yay-oo′
Yevpatoriya (Rus.)	yĕf-pä-tô′-rĭ-yä	yef-pah-to′-ri-yah
Yeya (Rus., riv.)	ā′-yä	ay′-yah
Also spelled *Eya*, q.v.		
Yezd (Iran)	yĕzd′	yezd′
Yi- For Chinese names beginning in *Yi-*, see *I-*.		
Yi-hwang (Ch., Kiangsi)	See *I-hwang*.	
Ying-k'ou (Manch.)	*Eng.* yĭng-kou	ying-kau
	Ch. yĭng-kō	ying-koh
Yi-wu (Ch., Chekiang)	See *I-wu*.	
Yi-yang (Ch., Kiangsi)	See *I-yang*.	
Ylín (P.I.)	ē-lēn′	ee-leen′
Yo-chow (Ch., Hunan)	*Eng.* yō-chou	yoh-chau
	Ch. yō-jō	yoh-joh
Also called *Yo-yang*, q.v.		
Yokkaichi (Jap.)	yô-kä′-ē-chē	yo-kah′-ee-chee
Yokohama (Jap.)	*Eng.* yō′-kə-hä′-mə	yoh′-kuh-hah′-muh
	Jap. yô-kô′-hä′-mä′	yo-ko′-hah′-mah
Yokosuka (Jap.)	yô-kôs′-kä	yo-kos′-kah
Yokota (Jap., Tokyo, airport)	yô-kô′-tä′	yo-ko′-tah′
Yomiuri (Jap., Tokyo, newspaper)	yô-mē′-ōō′-rē′	yo-mee′-oo′-ree′
Also called *Yomiuri Hoochi*, yô-mē′-ōō′-rē′ hô′-ô-chē [yo-mee′-oo′-ree′ ho′-o-chee].		
Yon (Fr., riv.)	yôN′	yoN′
Yonai, Mitsumasa (Jap. polit.)	yô′-nä-ē, mē-tsōō′-mä-sä	yo′-nah-ee, mee-tsoo′-mah-sah
Yonne (Fr., riv.)	yôn′	yon′
Yosemite (Calif., nat. pk.)	yō-sĕm′-ə-tĭ	yoh-sem′-uh-ti
Yoshida, Shigeru (Jap. polit.)	yô-shē′-dä′, shē-gĕ′-rōō	yo-shee′-dah′, shee-geh′-roo
Yo-yang (Ch., Hunan)	yō-yäng	yoh-yahng
Also called *Yo-chow*, q.v.		
Ypres (Belg.)	*Fr.* ē′pr	ee′pr
Flemish *Ieperen*, q.v. The name is so un-English that one must sympathize with the popular British wī′-pərz [wai′-puhrz].		

Ypseloreites (Crete, mt.) See *Ide Oros.*

Yreka (Calif.)   wī-rē'-kə   wai-ree'-kuh

Ysel (Neth.)   ī'-səl   ai'-suhl

  Also spelled *Yssel* and *IJssel,* q.v.

Yser (Fr., riv.)   ē-zĕr'   ee-zehr'

Ysleta (N.M., Tex.)   *Eng.* ĭs-lĕt'-ə   is-let'-uh

                    Sp. ēs-lĕ'-tä   ees-leh'-tah

Yssel (Neth.) See *IJssel.*

Ystad (Sw.)   ü'-städ   ü-stahd

Ystgaard, Hans (Nor.   üst'-gôr, häns'   üst'-gor, hahns'
  polit.)

Yü, O. K. (Ch. polit.)   yü *or* yē   yü *or* yee

  Also spelled *Yui* but pronounced as above. Dr. Yü's formal name is
Yü Hung-chün, yü hŏong-jün [yü hung-jün]. As a gesture of friendli-
ness to the U.S., Dr. Yü adopted the initials "O. K." as his familiar
name. Cf. *Chiang Kai-shek.*

Yüan   yüän   yü-ahn

  A principle division or department of the Chinese government.

Yüan-an (Ch., Hupeh)   yüän-än   yü-ahn-ahn

Yüan-ling (Ch., Hunan)   yüän-lĭng   yü-ahn-ling

  Also called *Ch'en-chow,* q.v.

Yuba (Calif.)   yōō'-bə   yoo'-buh

Yucatán (Mex.)   *Eng.* yōō-kə-tăn'   yoo-kuh-tan'

                   Sp. yōō-kä-tän'   yoo-kah-tahn'

Yü-chiang (Ch., Kiangsi) yü-jyäng   yü-jyahng

Yü-ch'ien (Ch.,   yü-chyĕn   yü-chyen
  Chekiang)

Yudin, P. F. (Rus.   yōō'-dĭn   yoo'-din
  educator)

Yugoslavia   *Eng.* yōō'-gô-slä'-vĭ-ə yoo'-go-slah'-vi-uh

  Serb-Croat *Jugoslavija,* yōō'-gô-slä'-vĭ-yä [yoo'-go-slah'-vi-yah].

Yü-hang (Ch., Chekiang) yü-häng   yü-hahng

Yü-hsien (Ch., Hunan)   yü-shyĕn   yü-shyen

Yü-hwan (Ch.,   yü-whän   yü-whahn
  Chekiang, isl.)

Yui, O. K. (Ch. polit.) See *Yü.*

Yü-kan (Ch., Kiangsi)   yü-gän   yü-gahn

Yukhnov (Rus.)   yōōk(h)'-nŏf   yook(h)'-nof

Yu-ki (Korea)   yōō-kē   yoo-kee

Yü-kiang (Ch., Kiangsi)   yü-jyäng   yü-jyahng

  Also spelled *Yü-chiang,* q.v.

Yü-lin (Ch., Kwangsi,   yü-lĭn   yü-lin
  Shensi)

Yung-ch'ang (Ch., Kansu) yŏong-chäng   yung-chahng

Yung-ch'ang (Ch., Yünnan)	yŏŏng-chäng	yung-chahng
Also called *Pao-shan*, q.v.		
Yung-chi (Manchu.)	yŏŏng-jē	yung-jee
Yung-chia (Ch., Chekiang)	yŏŏng-jyä	yung-jyah
Also called *Wên-chow*, q.v.		
Yung-ch'wan (Ch., Szechwan)	yŏŏng-chwän	yung-chwahn
Yung-fêng (Ch., Kiangsi)	yŏŏng-fŭng	yung-fuhng
Yung-hsin (Ch., Kiangsi)	yŏŏng-shĭn	yung-shin
Yung-hsiu (Ch., Kiangsi)	yŏŏng-shyōō	yung-shyoo
Also spelled *Yung-siu*.		
Yung-kang (Ch., Chekiang)	yŏŏng-käng	yung-kahng
Yung-p'ing (Ch., Hopeh)	yŏŏng-pĭng	yung-ping
Yung-têng (Ch., Kansu)	yŏŏng-dŭng	yung-duhng
Yün-hsien (Ch., Yünnan)	yün-shyĕn	yün-shyen
Yün-nan (Ch., prov.)	*Eng.* yŏŏ-năn	yu-nan
	Ch. yün-nän	yün-nahn
Yün-nan-fu (Ch., Yünnan)	*Eng.* yŏŏ-năn-fōō	yu-nan-foo
	Ch. yün-nän-fōō	yün-nahn-foo
Yurev (Est.) See *Jurjev*.		
Yurev Polski (Rus.)	yōōr'-yĕf pŏl'(y)-skĭ	yoor'-yef pol'(y)-ski
Yü-shan (Ch., Kiangsi)	yü-shän	yü-shahn
Yushkozero (Rus.)	yōōshk-ô'-zĕ-rŏ	yooshk-o'-zeh-ro
Yü-tu (Ch., Kiangsi)	yü-dōō	yü-doo
Yverdon (Switz.)	ē-vĕr-dôN'	ee-vehr-doN'
Also called *Yverdun*, ē-vĕr-dûN' [ee-vehr-dœN'].		
Yvetot (Fr.)	ēv-tō'	eev-toh'
Ywataung (Burma)	yŏŏä'-toung'	yu-ah'-taung'
Yzeure (Fr.)	ē-zûr'	ee-zœr'
Zaafran (Libya)	zä-fə-răn'	zah-fuh-ran'
Also called *Sidra*, q.v., and *Sirte*, q.v.		
Zaamslag (Neth.)	zäms'-läk(h)	zahms'-lahk(h)
Zaandam (Neth.)	zän-däm'	zahn-dahm'
Zaandijk (Neth.)	zän-dīk'	zahn-daik'
Žabalj (Yugosl.)	zhä'-bäl(y)	zhah'-bahl(y)
Žabari (Yugosl.)	zhä'-bä-rĭ	zhah'-bah-ri
Żabinka (Pol.)	zhä-bēn'-kä	zhah-been'-kah
Russian *Zhabinka*, zhä'-bĭn-kä [zhah'-bin-kah].		
Ząbkowice (Ger. >? Pol.)	zäNb-kô-vē'-tsĕ	zahNb-ko-vee'-tseh
German *Frankenstein*, q.v.		

Zablán (P.I.) See *Sablán*.

Žabljak (Yugosl.)	zhäb'-lyäk	zhahb'-lyahk
Zabłudów (Pol.)	zä-bloo͞'-do͞of	zah-bloo'-duf

Russian *Zabludovo*, zä-bloo͞'-dŏ-vŏ [zah-bloo'-do-vo].

Zabotin, Nicolai	zä-bŏ'-tĭn, nĭ-kŏ-lī'	zah-bo'-tin, ni-ko-lai'
(Rus. general)		
Zabrež (Yugosl.)	zä'-brĕzh	zah'-brezh
Zabrze (Ger. >Pol.)	zäb'-zhĕ	zahb'-zheh

German *Hindenburg*, q.v.

Zabul (Iran)	zä-bool'	zah-bul'
Zacatecas (Mex.)	sä-kä-tĕ'-käs	sah-kah-teh'-kahs

In the English of the Mexican border, pronounced zăk'-ə-tā'-kəs [zak'-uh-tay'-kuhs].

Zaccaria (It.)	tsäk-kä-rē'-ä	tsahk-kah-ree'-ah
Zadar (Yugosl. <It.)	zä'-där	zah'-dahr
Italian *Zara*, q.v.		
Zadonsk (Rus.)	zä-dônsk'	zah-donsk'
Zafrana (Dodec.)	*Gr.* zä'-frä-nä	zah'-frah-nah
	It. tsä-frä'-nä	tsah-frah'-nah
Zagarolo (It.)	tsä-gä-rô'-lô	tsah-gah-ro'-lo
Zagazig (Egypt)	zä-gä-zēg'	zah-gah-zeeg'
Zaghouan (Tun.)	*Ar.* zäg-wăn'	zahg-wan'
	Fr. zäg-wäN'	zahg-wahN'
Zagora, Stara (Bulg.)	zä'-gŏ-rä, stä'-rä	zah'-go-rah, stah'-rah
Zagorsk (Rus.)	zä-gôrsk'	zah-gorsk'
Zagreb (Yugosl.)	zä'-grĕb	zah'-greb

German *Agram*, äg'-räm [ahg'-rahm].

Zagrebačka (Yugosl.)	zä'-grĕ-bäch-kä	zah'-greh-bahch-kah
Žagubica (Yugosl.)	zhä'-goo͞-bĭ-tsä	zhah'-goo-bi-tsah
Zagyva (Hung., riv.)	zŏd'(y)-vŏ	zod'(y)-vo
Zahedan (Iran)	zä-hĕ-dän'	zah-heh-dahn'
zaibatsu	*Eng.* zī-băt'-soo͞	zai-bat'-soo
	Jap. zä-ē'-bä'-tsoo͞'	zah-ee'-bah'-tsoo'
	or zä-ē'-bäts'	zah-ee'-bahts'

Family industrial combines that dominate Japanese business.

Zajac (Yugosl.)	zä'-yäts	zah'-yahts
Zaječar (Yugosl.)	zä'-yĕ-chär	zah'-yeh-chahr
Zákány (Hung.)	zä'-kän(y)	zah'-kahn(y)
Zakharov, G. F.	zä-hä'-rŏf	zah-hah'-rof
(Rus. general)		
Zaklików (Pol.)	zä-klē'-ko͞of	zah-klee'-kuf

Russian *Zaklikov*, zä-klē'-kŏf [zah-klee'-kof]

Zakopane (Pol.)	zä-kŏ-pä'-nĕ	zah-ko-pah'-neh

[600]

Żakowski, Julian (Pol. polit.)	zhä-kôf'-skĭ, yōō'-lyän	zhah-kof'-skih, yoo'-lyahn
Zakynthos (Gr., isl.) Also called *Zante*, q.v.	zä'-kĕn-thô(s)	zah'-keen-tho(s)
Zalaegerszeg (Hung.)	zŏ'-lŏ-ĕ'-gĕr-sĕg	zo'-lo-eh'-gehr-seg
Zălău (Rum.) Hungarian *Zilah*, zĭ'-lŏ [zi'-lo].	zə-lû'-ŏŏ	zuh-luh'-u
Zaleshchiki (Pol. > Rus.) Polish *Zaleszczyki*, zä-lĕsh-chĭ'-kĭ [zah-lesh-chi'-ki].	zä-lĕsh'-chĭ-kĭ	zah-lesh'-chi-ki
Zalew Wiślany (Ger. > Pol., Rus., lagoon) German *Frisches Haff*, q.v. Russian *Frishes Gaf*, frē'-shĕs gäf [free'-shes gahf].	zä-lĕf vēsh-lä'-nĭ	zah'-lef veesh-lah'-ni
zaliv An element, meaning *bay*, in Yugoslav and Russian place names. It may be necessary to look up the other part of the name.	zä'-lĭf	zah'-lif
Zaliv Petra Velikogo (Rus.)	zä-lēf' pĕ-trä' vĕ-lē'-kä-vŏ	zah-leef' peh-trah' veh-lee'-kah-vo
Zaltbommel (Neth.)	zält-bôm'-əl	zahlt-bom'-uhl
Zama (Tun.)	*Eng.* zā'-mə *or* zä'-mä	zay'-muh *or* zah'-mah
Zambales (P.I.)	säm-bä'-lĕs	sahm-bah'-les
Zambezi (Afr., riv.)	*Eng.* zăm-bē'-zĭ *native* zäm-bē'-zē	zam-bee'-zi zahm-bee'-zee
Zamboanga (P.I.)	säm-bô-äng'-gä	sahm-bo-ahng'-gah
Zamora (Sp.)	thä-mô'-rä *or* sä-	thah-mo'-rah *or* sah-
Zamość (Pol.) Russian *Zamoste*, zä-môst'-yĕ [zah-most'-yeh].	zä'-môshch	zah'-moshch
zan An element, meaning *mountain*, in Japanese place names. See *san*.	zän	zahn
Zandvoort (Neth.)	zänt'-vōrt	zahnt'-vohrt
Žanjica (Yugosl.)	zhä'-nyĭ-tsä	zhah'-nyi-tsah
Zante (Gr., isl.) Greek *Zakynthos*, q.v.	zän'-tĕ	zahn'-teh
Zanzibar (Br. E. Afr.)	*Eng.* zăn-zĭ-bär' *native* zän-zē-bä'	zan-zi-bahr' zahn-zee-bah'
Zanzur (Libya)	zän-zōōr'	zahn-zoor'
Zapadna Morava (Yugosl., riv.)	zä'-päd-nä mô'-rä'-vä	zah'-pahd-nah mo'-rah'-vah
Zapadnaya Dvina (Rus.)	zä'-päd-nä-yä dvĭ-nä'	zah'-pahd-nah-yah dvi-nah'
Zapata (Cuba, Texas)	sä-pä'-tä	sah-pah'-tah
Zaplanje (Yugosl.)	zä'-plä'-nyĕ	zah'-plah'-nyeh

Zaporozhe (Rus.)	zä-pŏ-rôzh′-yĕ	zah-po-rozh′-yeh
Zapotitlán (Mex.)	sä-pô-tē-tlän′	sah-po-tee-tlahn′
Žapsko (Yugosl.)	zhäp′-skô	zhahp′-sko
Zara (It. > Yugosl.)	dzä′-rä	dzah′-rah

Serb-Croat *Zadar*, q.v.

Zaragoza (Sp.)	thä-rä-gô′-thä	thah-rah-go′-thah
	or sä-rä-gô′-sä	sah-rah-go′-sah

English *Saragossa*, săr′-ə-gŏs′-ə [sehr′-uh-gos′-uh].

Zaraisk (Rus.)	zä-rīsk′	zah-raisk′
Zarasai (Lith.)	zä-rä-sī′	zah-rah-sai′
Zarat (Tun.)	zä-răt′	zah-rat′
Zaravecchia (Yugosl.)	*It.* dzä-rä-vĕk′-kyä	dzah-rah-vek′-kyah

Serb-Croat *Biograd*, q.v.

Žarkovo (Yugosl.)	zhär′-kô-vô	zhahr′-ko-vo
Żarnowiec (Pol.)	zhär-nô′-vyĕts	zhahr-no′-vyets

German *Zarnowitz*, tsär′-nô-vĭts [tsahr′-no-vits].

Żarów (Ger. >? Pol.)	zhä′-rōōf	zhah′-ruf

German *Sorau*, q.v.

Zarzis (Tun.)	zär′-zĭs	zahr′-zis
Žatec (Cz.)	zhä′-tĕts	zhah′-tets
Zaton (Yugosl.)	zä′-tôn	zah′-ton
Zatonje (Yugosl.)	zä′-tô-nyĕ	zah′-to-nyeh
Zator (Pol.)	zä′-tôr	zah′-tor
Zatrijevač (Yugosl.)	zä′-trē′-yĕ-väch	zah′-tree′-yeh-vahch
Zauia (Libya)	zä′-wĭ-ä	zah′-wi-ah

Also called *Ez Zauia*, q.v.

Zauta en Nofilia (Libya)	zou′-tä ĕn nô-fē′-lyä	zau′-tah en no-fee′-lyah

Also called *En Nofilia*, q.v., and *Nofilia*, q.v.

Zavala, Zavalla (Tex.)	sä-vä′-lä	sah-vah′-lah
Zaverda (Gr.)	zä-vĕr′-dä	zah-vehr′-dah
Zavertse (Pol.) See *Zawiercie*.		
Zavidovo (Rus.)	zä-vē′-dŏ-vŏ	zah-vee′-do-vo
Zavikhost (Pol.) See *Zawichost*.		
Zavishin (Rus.)	zä-vē′-shĭn	zah-vee′-shin
Zavitaya (Rus.)	zä-vĭ-tä′-yä	zah-vi-tah′-yah
Zawchaung (Burma)	zô′-choung′	zaw′-chaung′
Zawichost (Pol.)	zä-vē′-hôst	zah-vee′-host

Russian *Zavikhost*, zä-vē′-hŏst [zah-vee′-host].

Zawiercie (Pol.)	zä-vyĕr′-chĕ	zah-vyehr′-cheh

Russian *Zavertse*, zä-vĕr′-tsĕ [zah-vehr′-tseh].

Zawyet Shammas (Egypt)	ză′-wyĕt shăm-măs′	za′-wyet sham-mas′
Zbąszyń (Pol.)	zbôN′-shĭn(y)	zboN′-shin(y)

Zbrucz (Pol., riv.)   zbrŏŏch'   zbruch'
    Russian spelling *Zbruch*.

Zdołbunów (Pol.)   zdôl-bōō'-nŏŏf   zdol-boo'-nuf
    Russian *Zdolbunovo*, zdŏl-bŏŏ-nô'-vŏ [zdol-bu-no'-vo].

Zduńska Wola (Pol.)   zdŏŏn'(y)-skä vô'-lä   zdun'(y)-skah vo'-lah

Zea (Gr., isl.)   zē'-ä   zee'-ah
    Also called *Keos*, q.v.

Zealand (Den., isl.)   *Eng.* zē'-lənd   zee'-luhnd
    Danish *Sjælland*, shĕl'-län [shel'-lahn].

Zebib (Tun., cape)   zə-bēb'   zuh-beeb'

Zebla (Tun.)   zĕb'-lä   zeb'-lah

Zebrzydowice (Pol.)   zĕb-zhĭ-dô-vē'-tsĕ   zeb-zhi-do-vee'-tseh
    German *Seibersdorf*, zī'-bərs-dôrf [zai'-buhrs-dorf].

Zečević, Vlado   zĕ'-chĕ-vĭch, vlä'-dô   zeh'-cheh-vich, vlah'-
    (Yugosl. polit.)   do

Žeden (Yugosl., mts.)   zhĕ'-dĕn   zheh'-den

zee   zā'   zay'
    An element, meaning *sea*, in Dutch place names.

Zeebrugge (Belg.)   *Eng.* zē'-brŏŏg-ə   zee'-brug-uh
                  Flem. zā'-brûk(h)-ə   zay'-brœk(h)-uh

Zeeland (Neth., prov.)   *Eng.* zē'-lənd   zee'-luhnd
                  Du. zā'-länt   zay'-lahnt

Zeeuwsch-Vlaanderen   zā'-ōōs vlän'-də-rən   zay'-oos vlahn'-duh-
    (Neth.)   ruhn

Zefat (Pal.) See *Safad*.

Żegań (Ger. >? Pol.)   zhĕ'-gän(y)   zheh'-gahn(y)
    German *Sagan*, q.v.

Żegiestów (Pol.)   zhĕ-gyĕ'-stŏŏf   zheh-gyeh'-stuf

Žegligovo (Yugosl.)   zhĕ'-glĭ-gô-vô   zheh'-gli-go-vo

Žegovac planina   zhĕ'-gô-väts   zheh'-go-vahts
    (Yugosl., mts.)   plä'-nē'-nä   plah'-nee'-nah

Zegrze (Pol.)   zĕg'-zhĕ   zeg'-zheh
    Russian *Zegrzhe*, zĕ'gr-zhĕ [ze'gr-zheh].

Zehden (Ger.)   tsā'-dən   tsay'-duhn

Zehsis (Latvia)   See *Cēsis*.

Zeilsheim (Ger.)   tsīls'-hīm   tsails'-haim

Zeist (Neth.)   zīst'   zaist'

Zeitz (Ger.)   tsīts'   tsaits'

Żelechów (Pol.)   zhĕ-lĕ'-hŏŏf   zheh-leh'-huf
    Russian *Zhelekhov*, zhĕ'-lĕ-hŏf [zheh'-leh-hof].

Zelenika (Yugosl.)   zĕ'-lĕ-nĭ-kä   zeh'-leh-ni-kah

Zelenikovo (Yugosl.)   zĕ-lĕ'-nĭ-kô-vô   zeh-leh'-ni-ko-vo

Železnik (Yugosl.)   zhĕ'-lĕz-nĭk   zheh'-lez-nik

Zelhem (Neth.)   zĕl'-hĕm   zel'-hem

Zeliński, Michał Rola (Pol. polit.) See *Rola Zeliński*.

Željin (Yugosl., mt.)   zhĕ′-lyĭn   zheh′-lyin

Zell am See (Ger.)   tsĕl′ äm zä′   tsel′ ahm zay′

Zellin (Ger.)   tsĕ-lēn′   tseh-leen′

Zelvinou (Alb.)   See *Delvinë*.

Zemedelsko Zname   zĕ-mĕ-dĕl′-skŏ znä′-   zeh-meh-del′-sko
    (Bulg. newspaper)   mĕ   znah′-meh

Zemgale (Latvia, prov.)   zĕm′-gä-lĕ   zem′-gah-leh

Zemun (Yugosl.)   zĕ′-mōōn   zeh′-moon

Zemzem (Libya)   zĕm′-zĕm′   zem′-zem′

Zen, Keinosuke (Jap.   zĕn′, kä′-nô-sōō-kĕ   zen′, kay′-no-soo-keh
    polit.)

Zengg (Yugosl.) See *Senj*.

Zenica (Yugosl.)   zĕ′-nĭ-tsä   zeh′-ni-tsah

Zenjan (Iran)   zĕn-jän′   zen-jahn′

Zenkov (Rus.)   zĕn(y)-kôf′   zen(y)-kof′

Zenta (Yugosl.)   See *Senta*.

Žepče (Yugosl.)   zhĕp′-chĕ   zhep′-cheh

Zephyrion (Crete, point)   zĕ-fē′-rē(-ôn)   zeh-fee′-ree(-on)
    Also called *Agios Ioannes*, q.v.

Žeravino (Yugosl.)   zhĕ′-rä-vĭ-nô   zheh′-rah-vi-no

Zergian (Alb.) See *Zerqan*.

Žernovnica (Yugosl.)   zhĕr′-nôv′-nĭ-tsä   zhehr′-nov′-ni-tsah

Zernovo (Rus.)   zĕr-nô′-vŏ   zehr-no′-vo

Zerqan (Alb.)   zĕr′-kyän   zehr′-kyahn

Zerqani (Alb.)   See *Zerqan*.

Zervas, Napoleon (Gr.   zĕr′-väs, nä-pô-lĕ′-ôn   zehr′-vahs, nah-po-
    general)   leh′-on

Zeta (Yugosl., riv.)   zĕ′-tä   zeh′-tah

Zetska (Yugosl.)   zĕt′-skä   zet′-skah

Zevenaar (Neth.)   zä-və-när′   zay-vuh-nahr′

Zevenbergen (Neth.)   zä′-vən-bĕrk(h)′-ən   zay′-vuhn-behrk(h)′-
        uhn

Zevenhuizen (Neth.)   zä′-vən-hûĭ′-zən   zay′-vuhn-hœi′-zuhn

Zeya (Rus.)   zĕ′-yä   zeh′-yah

Zgropoljci (Yugosl.)   zgrô′-pôl(y)-tsĭ   zgro′-pol(y)-tsi

Zhabinka (Pol.)   See *Żabinka*.

Zharkovski (Rus.)   zhär-kôf′-skĭ   zhahr-kof′-ski

Zhdanov, Andrei A.   zhdä′-nôf, än-drä′   zhdah′-nof, ahn-dray′
    (Rus. polit.)

Zheltov, Alexei   zhĕl′-tôf, ä-lĕk-sä′   zhel′-tof, ah-lehk-say′
    (Rus. general)

Zhirardov (Pol.)   See *Żyrardów*.

Zhitomir (Rus.)   zhĭ-tô′-mĭr   zhi-to′-mihr

Zhizdra (Rus.)	zhĭz'-drä	zhiz'-drah
Zhlobin (Rus.)	zhlô'-bĭn	zhlo'-bin
Zhmerinka (Rus.)	zhmĕ'-rĭn-kä	zhmeh'-rin-kah
Zhukov, Georgi K.	zhōō'-kŏf, gĕ-ôr'-gĭ	zhoo'-kof, geh-or'-gi
(Rus. general)		
Zhukovka (Rus.)	zhōō'-kŏf-kä	zhoo'-kof-kah
Zhulat (Alb.)	zhōō'-lät	zhoo'-laht
Zhulati (Alb.)　See *Zhulat*.		
Zia ed Din Tabatabai,	zē'-ä ĕd dēn' tä-bä-	zee'-ah ehd deen'
Säid (Iran. polit.)	tä-bī', sä-ēd'	tah-bah-tah-bai',
		sah-eed'
Žiča (Yugosl.)	zhē'-chä	zhee'-chah
Zicher (Ger.)	tsĭk(h)'-ər	tsik(h)'-uhr
Zičijevo (Yugosl.)	zē'-chē'-yĕ-vô	zee'-chee'-yeh-vo
Zidanimost (Yugosl.)	zē'-dä-nĭ-môst'	zee'-dah-ni-most'
Ziebingen (Ger.)	tsē'-bĭng-ən	tsee'-bing-uhn
Zielenzig (Ger.)	tsē'-lən-tsĭk(h)	tsee'-luhn-tsik(h)
Zielona Góra	zhĕ-lô'-nä gōō'-rä	zheh-lo'-nah gu'-rah
(Ger. >? Pol.)		
German *Gruenberg*, q.v.		
Zierikzee (Neth.)	zē'-rĭk-zā'	zee'-rik-zay'
Žijeva planina	zhē'-yĕ-vä plä'-nē'-	zhee'-yeh-vah plah'-
(Yugosl., mt.)	nä	nee'-nah
Zijpe (Neth.)	zī'-pə	zai'-puh
Zilah (Rum.)　See *Zălău*.		
Žilina (Cz.)	zhē'-lĭ-nä	zhee'-li-nah
Zilovo (Rus.)	zē'-lŏ-vŏ	zee'-lo-vo
Zilupe (Latvia)	zē'-lōō-pĕ	zee'-lu-peh
Russian *Rosenovskaya*, q.v.		
Zimmern (Ger.)	tsĭm'-ərn	tsim'-uhrn
Zimovniki (Rus.)	zĭ-môv'-nĭ-kĭ	zi-mov'-ni-ki
Zinovevsk (Rus.)	zĭ-nô'-vyĕfsk	zi-no'-vyefsk
Zinten (Ger.)	tsĭn'-tən	tsin'-tuhn
Žirije (Yugosl.)	zhē'-rĭ-yĕ	zhee'-ri-yeh
Italian *Zuri*, q.v.		
Zir'in (Pal.) See *Jezreel*.		
Zirona (Yugosl.)	*It.* tsē-rô'-nä	tsee-ro'-nah
Serb-Croat *Drvenik*, q.v.		
Žirovnica (Yugosl.)	zhē'-rôv'-nĭ-tsä	zhee'-rov'-ni-tsah
Zistersdorf (Austria)	tsĭs'-tərs-dôrf	tsis'-tuhrs-dorf
Zit (Tun.)	zēt'	zeet'
Officially *Ste. Marie du Zit*.		
Žitkovac (Yugosl.)	zhēt'-kô-väts	zheet'-ko-vahts
Žitni Potok (Yugosl.)	zhēt'-nĭ pô'-tôk	zheet'-ni po'-tok

Žitorađa (Yugosl.)	zhē'-tô-rä'-dyä	zhee'-to-rah'-dyah
Zittau (Ger.)	tsĭt'-ou	tsit'-au
Zlatar (Yugosl., mts.)	zlä'-tär	zlah'-tahr
Zlatibor (Yugosl., mts.)	zlä'-tĭ-bôr	zlah'-ti-bor
Zlatoust (Rus.)	zlä-tŏ-ōōst'	zlah-to-oost'
Žljeb (Yugosl., mts.)	zhlyĕb'	zhlyeb'
Zlochev (Pol. >Rus.)	zlô'-chĕf	zlo'-chef

Near Tarnopol. Polish *Złoczów*, zlô'-chŏŏf [zlo'-chuf].

Złoczew (Pol.)	zlô'-chĕf	zlo'-chef

Near Łódź. Russian spelling *Zlochev*.

Złoczów (Pol. >Rus.) See *Zlochev*.

zloti (Pol. currency unit)	zlô'-tĭ	zlo'-ti
Zmiev (Rus.)	zmĭ-yôf'	zmi-yof'
Znamenka (Rus.)	znä'-mĕn-kä	znah'-men-kah
Znojmo (Cz.)	znoi'-mô	znoi'-mo
Zobten (Ger. >? Pol.)	tsôb'-tən	tsob'-tuhn

Polish *Sobótka*, q.v.

zócalo (Mex., "plaza")	sô'-kä-lô	so'-kah-lo
Zoelen (Neth.)	zōō'-lən	zoo'-luhn
Zoetermeer (Neth.)	zōō-tər-mär'	zoo-tuhr-mayr'
Zoeterwoude (Neth.)	zōō-tər-wou'-də	zoo-tuhr-wau'-duh
Zolachev (Rus.)	zô'-lä-chĕf	zo'-lah-chef
Zolforata (It.)	tsôl-fô-rä'-tä	tsol-fo-rah'-ta
Zolotonosha (Rus.)	zŏ-lŏ-tŏ-nô'-shä	zo-lo-to-no'-shah

Zombkovitse (Pol.)　See *Ząbkowice*.

Žombolj (Rum.)	S.-C. zhôm'-bôl(y)	zhom'-bol(y)

Rumanian *Jimbolea*, q.v.

Zombor (Yugosl.)　See *Sombor*.

Zomeren (Neth.)	zō'-mə-rən	zoh'-muh-ruhn

Zonari (Dodec., Rh., point)　See *Cum Burnu*.

Zonguldak (Turk.)	zôn-gŏŏl'-däk	zon-gul'-dahk
Zook, George F.	zŏŏk'	zuk'
(Am. educator)		
zoological	zō'-ə-lŏj'-ĭ-kəl	zoh'-uh-loj'-i-kuhl

The temptation to say zōō- in this word and in *zoology* should be withstood.

Zoppot (Danzig >Pol.) See *Sopot*.

Zorin, Valerian A	zô'-rĭn, vä-lĕ-ryän'	zo'-rin, vah-leh-ryahn'
(Rus. diplomat)		
Zorina (Rus. name)	zô'-rĭ-nä	zo'-ri-nah
Zoschchenko, Mikhail	zô'-shchĕn-kŏ,	zo'-shchen-ko,
(Rus. author)	mĭ-hä-ēl'	mi-hah-eel'
Zossen (Ger.)	tsôs'-ən	tsos'-uhn
Zoutkamp (Neth.)	zout'-kämp	zaut'-kahmp

Zović (Yugosl.)	zô'-vĭch	zo'-vich
Zriba (Tun.)	zrē'-bä	zree'-bah
Zsombolya (Rum.) See *Jimbolea*.		
Zuara (Libya)	zōō-ä'-rä	zoo-ah'-rah
Zubtsov (Rus.)	zōōp-tsôf'	zoop-tsof'
Zuellichau, Züllichau	tsül'-ĭk(h)-ou	tsül'-ik(h)-au
(Ger. >Pol.)		
Polish *Sulechów*, q.v.		
Zuelpich (Ger.)	tsül'-pĭk(h)	tsül'-pik(h)
Zuetina (Libya) See *Ez Zuetina*.		
Zug (Switz.)	tsŏŏk(h)'	tsuk(h)'
zuid *and* zuider	zûĭt' *and* zûĭ'-dər	zœit' *and* zœi'-duhr

An element, meaning *south*, in Dutch place names. It may be necessary to look up the other part of the name.

Zuid Beveland (Neth.)	zûĭt' bā'-və-länt	zœit' bay'-vuh-lahnt
Zuidbroek (Neth.)	zûĭt-brōōk'	zœit-brook'
Zuider Zee (Neth.)	*Eng.* zī'-dər zē'	zai'-duhr zee'
	Du. zûĭ'-dər zā'	zœi'-duhr zay'
Zuid Holland (Neth., prov.)	zûĭt' hôl'-änt	zœit' hol'-ahnt
Zuidhorn (Neth.)	zûĭt-hôrn'	zœit-horn'
Zuidlaren (Neth.)	zûĭd-lä'-rən	zœid-lah'-ruhn
Zuidwolde (Neth.)	zûĭt-wôl'-də	zœit-wol'-duh
Zuilen (Neth.)	zûĭ'-lən	zœi'-luhn
Zujović, Streten (Yugosl. polit.)	zōō'-yŏ-vĭch, strĕ'-tĕn	zoo'-yo-vich, streh'-ten
Žukovac (Yugosl.)	zhōō'-kô-väts	zhoo'-ko-vahts
Zuleika Dobson	zōō-lē'-kə	zu-lee'-kuh

Mr. Max Beerbohm asks that the name of his heroine (and Byron's) "on no account [be called] Zulīka."

Zuleta Angel, Eduardo (Colom. diplomat)	sōō-lĕ'-tä än'-hĕl, ĕ-dwär'-dô	soo-leh'-tah ahn'-hehl, eh-dwahr'-do
Zülpich (Ger.)	tsül'-pĭk(h)	tsül'-pik(h)
Zundert (Neth.)	zûn'-dərt	zœn'-duhrt
Zungaria (Ch., Sinkiang) See *Dzungaria*.		
Zuñi (Am. Indian)	*Eng.* zōōn'-yĭ	zoon'-yi
	Sp. sōō'-nyē	soo'-nyee
Županja (Yugosl.)	zhōō'-pä-nyä	zhoo'-pah-nyah
Županjac (Yugosl.)	zhōō'-pä-nyäts	zhoo'-pah-nyahts
Žur (Yugosl.)	zhōōr'	zhoor'
Zuri (Yugosl.)	*It.* tsōō'-rē	tsoo'-ree
Serb-Croat *Žirije*, q.v.		
Zurich (Switz.)	*Eng.* zōōr'-ĭk	zur'-ik
German *Zürich*, tsü'-rĭk(h) [tsü'-rik(h)].		
Žut (Yugosl., isl.)	zhōōt'	zhoot'

Zutfen (Neth.)	*Eng.* zŭt'-fən	zuht'-fuhn
	Du. zût'-fən	zœt'-fuhn
Also spelled *Zutphen.*		
Žuti Kamen (Yugosl., mt.)	zhōō'-tĭ kä'-mĕn	zhoo'-ti kah'-men
Žužemberk (Yugosl.)	zhōō'-zhĕm-bĕrk	zhoo'-zhem-behrk
Zvenigorod (Rus.)	zvĕ-nē'-gŏ-rŏt	zveh-nee'-go-rot
Zverevo (Rus.)	zvĕ'-rĕ-vŏ	zveh'-reh-vo
Zvezda (Rus. magazine)	zvĕz-dä'	zvez-dah'
Zvezdan (Yugosl.)	zvĕz'-dän	zvez'-dahn
Zvižd (Yugosl.)	zvēzhd'	zveezhd'
Zvolen (Cz.)	zvô'-lĕn	zvo'-len
Zvornik (Yugosl.)	zvôr'-nĭk	zvor'-nik
Zwalmen (Neth.)	zwäl'-mən	zwahl'-muhn
Zwaluwe (Neth.)	zwä'-lü-wə	zwah'-lü-wuh
Zwammerdam (Neth.)	zwäm'-ər-däm'	zwahm'-uhr-dahm'
Zwartsluis (Neth.)	zwärt-slûĭs'	zwahrt-slœis'
Zweeloo (Neth.)	zwä'-lō	zway'-loh
Zweibrücken *or* Zweibruecken (Ger.)	tsvī-brük'-ən	tsvai-brük'-uhn
Zwicky, Fritz (Swiss Am. scientist)	tsvĭk'-ĭ	tsvik'-i
Zweig, Stefan (Austrian Am. author)	tsvīk(h)', shtĕ'-fän	tsvaik(h)' shteh'-fahn
Zwickau (Ger.)	tsvĭk'-ou	tsvik'-au
Zwijndrecht (Neth.)	zwīn'-drĕk(h)t	zwain'-drek(h)t
Zwischenahn (Ger.)	tsvĭsh'-ə-nän	tsvish'-uh-nahn
Zwoleń (Pol.)	zvô'-lĕn(y)	zvo'-len(y)
Zwolle (Neth.)	zwôl'-ə	zwol'-uh
Zwollerkerspel (Neth.)	zwôl'-ər-kĕr'-spəl	zwol'-uhr-kehr'-spuhl
Zworykin, Vladimir Kosma (Rus. Am. scientist)	zwôr'-ĭ-kĭn, vlăd'-ĭ-mĭr	zwor'-i-kin, vlad'-i-mihr

Russian zvŏ-rĭ'-kĭn, vlä-dē'-mĭr kŏz-mä' [zvo-ri'-kin, vlah-dee'-mihr koz-mah'].

Zymierski, Michał Rola (Pol. polit.) See *Rola Zymierski.*

Żyrardów (Pol.)	zhĭ-rär'-dōōf	zhi-rahr'-duf

Russian *Zhirardov,* zhĭ-rär'-dŏf [zhi-rahr'-dof].

Zyria *or* Zerea (Gr.) See *Kyllene.*

Żywiec (Pol.)	zhĭ'-vyĕts	zhi'-vyets

ø is commonly used in Norwegian orthography for *ö* or *œ*. In this book spellings with both *ö* and *œ* are listed, for each may occur in the English spelling of Norwegian names. The use of ø did not seem important enough, from our point of view, to justify the listing of a third spelling.